St Augustine

Serge Lancel

SAINT AUGUSTINE

translated by
Antonia Nevill

scm press

© Librairie Arthème Fayard 1999
Translation © SCM Press 2002

British Library Cataloguing in Publication data

A catalogue record for this book is available
from the British Library

0 334 02866 3

First published in 1999 by Librairie Arthème Fayard
English translation first published in 2002 by SCM Press
9–17 St Albans Place, London N1 0NX

SCM Press is a division of
SCM-Canterbury Press Ltd

Typeset in Palatino by MATS, Southend-on-Sea, Essex
Printed in Great Britain by
Creative Print and Design, Wales

To the memory of Henri-Irénée Marrou
and Anne-Marie La Bonnardière,
and to André Mandouze.
I am indebted to them for bringing me a little
closer to the child of Thagaste, the bishop of
Hippo and the doctor of Grace.

Contents

Illustrations

Fig. 1 – The Christian quarter of Hippo and the great basilica. Taken by E. Stawski from the vestiges unearthed by E. Marec (*Monuments chrétiens d'Hippone*, fig. 1).

Fig. 2 – The great basilica and its north-east annexes, viewed from the east. A suggested axonometric reconstruction by R. Naz (*Monuments chrétiens d'Hippone*, fig. 19).

Fig. 3 – 'Hippo's Numidia' (plan by S. Lancel).

Foreword

Serge Lancel of the University of Grenoble is an acknowledged master of the ancient history of north Africa. He has written major books on Carthage and Hannibal. We owe to him four volumes (in *Sources Chrétiennes*) of edition and exposition of the fascinating minutes of the conference at Carthage in AD 411 when the Donatist and Catholic bishops, the latter led by Augustine, confronted one another in impassioned argument by order of the western emperor. His spade has excavated important sites of Roman Carthage.

With this present volume he has directly tackled the majestic figure of Augustine, father of the essential features of both Catholic and Protestant doctrines of the Church and sacraments and a defining mind for the doctrine of grace in controversy with Pelagius, the earliest surviving British writer, and his formidable supporter Julian of Eclanum. His text is addressed to the common educated reader, and that is underpinned by numerous erudite notes to justify his verdicts and to inform the inquisitive where the evidence for his statements can be found. He has the advantage of being able to exploit the considerable number of new Augustinian documents discovered during the past 25 years, the new letters found by the Austrian scholar Johannes Divjak in two French libraries and the twenty-six new sermons found by François Dolbeau in Mainz city library. The Institute of Augustinian Studies at Paris has been the fosterer of a quantity of distinguished monographs mainly centred on Augustine. The present masterly volume makes it easier for English-speaking readers to grasp what has been going on.

The reader of this book is invited to share in the author's intimate and sympathetic knowledge of the greatest figure of Christian Antiquity.

Henry Chadwick

Introduction

The illustration on the cover of this book is held to be the oldest portrait of St Augustine. Its antiquity is in no doubt, since this fresco in the Lateran in Rome is commonly dated to the middle of the sixth century. In it we see a man in the prime of life, his hair already considerably receded, wearing a long, white, sleeved tunic ornamented with a purple band visible on the right shoulder and also on the fold that falls over the right foot; in this instance, it is the sign of priestly dignity. He is sitting on a rather clumsily depicted kind of curule chair, with a back that seems to hold him as if in a conch shell or a widely opened corolla. His left hand grasps a scroll – a *volumen* – which bears witness to his erudition and may also be interpreted as symbolizing his works; his right hand holds open and points to a large *codex*, which obviously represents 'the Good Book'. This picture is linked with the well documented series of representations of 'intellectuals', *mousikoï andrès*, to which Henri-Irénée Marrou had called attention, but also heralds another illustrative group – that of the vignettes depicting clergy and mitred bishops in medieval illuminations, thus marking the transition between the end of Late Antiquity and the early Middle Ages, in which it is truly representative of Augustine.

However, unlike either group, it is not conventional; from the former, in particular, it has not inherited the almost exclusive use of full frontal portraiture, the stiff and 'posed' look. The forward leaning movement enlivens the torso; above all, the face is astonishingly 'personal'. Once seen, there is no forgetting the intense gaze of the eyes, beneath the forehead with its two deep furrows; the rather pronounced nose; the small but well-defined and full-lipped mouth, separated by a firm line from a resolute chin clearly visible in a short stubbly beard (shaving was not a daily occurrence in Antiquity!). Nothing could be less 'run-of-the-mill' than this face. But how, with such concern for likeness, could anyone achieve the portrait of a man who had died over a century earlier, unless by reproducing a painting – on a wooden panel, on parchment? – made at Hippo during his lifetime and transported to Italy after his death, in order to illustrate in Rome a memory whose renown was already immense? The reader who perseveres to the end of this book will see, several hundred pages further on, that this question is also raised regarding the transference of the bishop's works, after his death. With Augustine, nothing is ever ordinary, or really simple, starting with his 'portrait'.

Whoever undertakes to write a book on St Augustine certainly suspects that he is embarking on a venture with every likelihood of being enthralling, but may not get the full measure of all its implications beforehand. He tells himself he is going to write a biography, and opens the *Confessions* without closing his eyes to the fact that they are something quite other than a collection of pieces of information; but the information that he first finds quite enchants him. Here he discovers an extremely gifted young boy, who professes to hate school but succeeds magnificently; next, an adolescent tormented by a puberty that reveals a temperament he will have to reckon with. Then a young man who, without any apparent complexes, gives sexual life its share yet at the same time opens himself fully to the life of the intellect, with a desire for social progress over which one can already sense that his soul's disquiet will increasingly cast its shadow. The writer understands that the Manichaeism of Augustine's twentieth year is no more than a spiritual side-tracking; the student, and then the young teacher, linger there a little too long, but he trusts them.

And with good cause. At thirty, in Milan, the master of rhetoric shows what he is made of. The discovery of the 'books of the Platonists' fulfils the aspirations conceived ten years earlier on reading Cicero's *Hortensius*; but another discovery soon follows, that of St Paul, and puts Augustine existentially on the razor's edge. He cannot stay there long, although Monica, by sending Adeodatus' mother away and negotiating the conditions of a fine marriage, has opened the path to a suitable compromise. In a perfectly reasonable way, Augustine's mother was backing both horses: she wanted success for him in this world, and salvation in the next. She would gladly have seen him as a high-ranking civil servant and Christian philosopher, as the fancy took him, and a good paterfamilias besides. But Augustine was not a man of half measures and compromise. The weight of the flesh had become burdensome to him; his soul had been too weighed down by it. Later in life, the old bishop, his senses a little dulled, would come to a more positive appreciation of the body, as we shall see. But in the ardour of his thirty years, the young man dragged it like a ball and chain. Lacking a miracle, he needed an admonition miraculous enough to heal him, God's finger being placed precisely on what was causing the wound. This is what happened in the garden in Milan, and the crisis was resolved in a quite different manner from that foreseen by Monica, who was able to grasp that her son's salvation was to be achieved by way of the radical choice of continence and renunciation of the world.

But in 'romantic' terms, the consequences were serious. The hero did not marry, and had no children. Worse, he soon lost the son he had had outside wedlock, after burying his mother and best friend, and shrouding the female companion of his youth in silence. He became a priest, then a bishop, to devote himself for a good forty years to repetitive tasks: services, preaching, the very demanding duty of helping the faithful. What could be more disappointing for a biographer? To cap it all, the latter soon realizes that once the source of information contained in the *Confessions* has dried up – and this 'drought' casts a veil over everything that follows Monica's death – there is a cruel lack of any guiding thread to continue following Augustine to Thagaste, and then to Hippo. The writer must fall back on the *Letters* – true, a prodigiously rich mine – and the *Retractations* (Reappraisals) in order to connect the chronology and accompany the unfolding of his deeds over the years and, as they roll by, the accomplishment of works which, for the bishop, take the place of the private life he has lost.

Whoever has launched rather rashly into writing such a book realizes fairly soon that the bishop's adventures are the controversies and battles which he wages with redoubtable pugnacity, and that his offspring are the works which he produces with a prolificacy that had not been known in the Latin language world since Cicero.

Aut libri, aut liberi, he too could have said, and more pertinently than others. But then he must attempt to embrace an immense number of works, which for centuries have fed theologians' commentaries and still give rise to innumerable glosses – a labour that could be regarded as impossible. Must we then be resigned to leaving St Augustine only to the specialists, who talk about him among themselves in all the great cultural languages and understand one another without having to spell it out? Of course, there are excellent books on St Augustine available at least in libraries, if not in bookshops – and they are mentioned in the bibliography at the end of this volume – but very few of them are truly accessible to a readership that is exacting but insufficiently used to the exegetic and critical subtleties of the experts on the early Fathers of the Church to be able to profit from them satisfactorily. Let me add that St Augustine is the only great author in the literature of Antiquity whose textual *corpus* is still growing. Some fifteen years ago, around thirty of the bishop's unpublished letters were found in Paris in the collections of the National Library and in the manuscript collection of Marseille's municipal library; and more recently nearly as many new sermons came to light in the collections of the Mainz city library in Germany; and what I know of the lacunae in these two groups of texts – on which it is possible to put a fairly precise figure – enables me to assert that research into the manuscript collections of old Europe has not yet finished adding to the published works of St Augustine. And even if the fundamentals of these works have been known since the humanistic era, even if the broad lines of the bishop's actions and his thinking are chiefly drawn by his great writings, these unpublished items add enough little touches to justify their being taken into account in a fresh overall look at his life and works.

St Augustine, the man and his works: thus described not so long ago – it was the title of a good book by Gustave Bardy which will soon be over sixty years old. The phrase must not be dismissed, provided the two aspects are not separated, and importance is given to showing how the bishop's works, often born of certain occasions – without being occasional works – fit in with the current of a life that was rich in meetings, actions and reactions. Such is the effort that has gone into this book,[a] which has tried carefully to show the shifts and developments, when they are perceptible, at the same time clearly marking the major turning-points that fix directions on which the bishop will not turn back: the absolute primacy of grace, on which his thinking is unvaried from 396 onward, and the dogma of original sin, acquired in all its severity at the outset of the anti-Pelagian controversy, in 412–13, whereas his attitude towards miracles, for instance, changes noticeably through the dual action of a deepened theological reflection and the factual contribution of St Stephen's relics being brought to Africa. Nor has it been forgotten – this is not so common – that this doctor of the Church was a bishop, living and working in a diocese, within the walls of basilicas and monasteries, in a town and countryside peopled with men and women whom we meet above all in his letters and sermons.

Lastly, one does not live for a while in the company of St Augustine without coming to regard him not *sub specie aeternitatis* – such as his own 'eternity' has made him – but in relation to what we ourselves are experiencing at the end of the second millennium after Jesus Christ, separated from him by over fifteen centuries that weigh heavily – especially the one that has just ended – in comparisons of behaviour and ways of thinking. It would be difficult to conceive of a St Augustine in our own times, which are so far from being normative, so strongly devoted to inessentials – with the exception, of course, of the charitable dimension, which is not wanting, luckily for those who have suffered most from the last 'century of blood and tears'; and it would be inappropriate, absolutely pointless and even absurd to try to imagine how, having by some impossible means returned to this world, he would adapt his 'message' to our culture. Let us leave him to his own culture, of which he was the honour, even more than the glory, even in the extremes of his severity. Let us turn the question around and ask ourselves rather what lesson we may draw from his life, quite apart from any strictly religious option. But that question has just been answered: because he set highly exacting standards on the honour of being a man in his own times, St Augustine may perhaps be entitled to inspire our own.

Notes

a.   I am delighted to say that my text had the benefit of a first reading by my friend and
      colleague, Aimé Gabillon, and emerged the better for it. I give him my thanks.

Notice to the reader: notes indicated in the text by figures may be found at the end of the book, grouped by chapter.

Part I

A Son of Thagaste

CHAPTER I

Thagaste

Not so long ago, Souk Ahras, a large township on the Algerio–Tunisian border, still presented the almost unchanged image of those small colonized towns which France had implanted in Algeria in the second half of the nineteenth century, laid out under the fine illusion that in this land History was resuming a course that had merely been interrupted, and that the Gallic cock was taking up the heritage of the Roman she-wolf: the heritage of the two Romes – imperial and Christian. As often occurred elsewhere, the early days were difficult and dangerous, occupation being at first mainly military. Returning to Constantine en route overland from Tunis, Flaubert had made a stop there in late May 1858: 'an atrocious, cold, muddy new town', he would comment in the journal of his voyage on his return to Croisset. A few decades later, the pacification of the Hanencha, the working of the Ouenza mines, and the opening of railway lines which restored the place to the communications junction it had been in Antiquity ensured the prosperity of Souk Ahras. During the *belle époque*, if one were not too concerned over the realities of a political and racial segregation far removed from the Roman world, in front of the bandstand in the main square one might have imagined oneself back in the golden age of Septimius Severus. Did people give much thought to the country's only offspring to achieve universal renown? At least his name had been given to a church, as well as to the little museum housed in its crypt, very modest it is true, because the building of the modern town had mostly obscured the ancient site.

When Augustine was born there, on 13 November 354,[1] the place was called Thagaste: a pre-Roman place-name, which is no surprise in this Numidian territory, where three centuries of Roman presence had not effaced the traces of an earlier dual culture. Augustine seems not to have known about the old indigenous background, made plain for us by so many Libyan inscriptions in the region; but it is he especially who informs us about the survival in that same region – and paradoxically so far from the territory of Carthage itself – of the Punic language, or what remained of it, which had to be spoken if one was to be understood in the rural areas. On the maritime border of 'Hippo's Numidia' contributions from across the sea of fairly ancient Jewish groups and of Greek-speaking communities had been added to this substratum and those survivals. Valerius, Augustine's predecessor in the episcopal chair of Hippo, was Greek, and the name of his best friend, his *alter ego*, Alypius, reveals the same origin. It was certainly not this relative cultural complexity that formed Augustine – we shall soon see that his was strictly a Latin culture – but we should bear it in mind; it was more than just the surroundings in which, first priest, then bishop, he was to develop for nearly forty years.

For the governor – the 'legate' – stationed in the regional capital, Hippo Regius (Bône, now Annaba), where he represented the proconsul of Africa, and thus imperial authority, Thagaste had been a *municipium* for about two centuries, that is to say, a self-governing community where all free men were Roman citizens, even before the edict of Caracalla in 212 extended the benefit of that citizenship to all the Empire's inhabitants. For want of good preservation, on the site of Thagaste, of those stone archives provided by honorific and dedicatory inscriptions that customarily filled the forum, it would be quite difficult even to outline what specialists call a 'municipal prosopography', an at least partial list, spread over a timespan, of its principal magistrates and priests: duumvirs, curators and flamens. It is quite exceptional to find, as at Thamugadi (Timgad) at the end of the nineteenth century, a 'photograph' assembling all the notables of a city at a precisely known period – the end of the emperor Julian's reign in 363 in the case of the 'album' of Timgad.[2] Setting aside a fragment of an inscription mentioning its first protector, Romanianus, it is to Augustine alone that we owe the rare evidence available to us about the ruling class in his city, to which his family belonged, though only of modest rank.

For the reasons given above, our archaeological knowledge of the site is reduced to very little. Plans that were drawn up early in the last century, based on very incomplete excavations carried out when the modern town was under construction, confirm the indication (*civitas parva*[3]), in an ancient text, of its relatively small size – some ten hectares. But they do not allow us to discover how it looked. This is a great pity because, contrary to what is sometimes thought, although all those towns possessed one forum, sometimes two (our main squares), a curia (our town halls), a basilica (our law courts), several temples (our churches), these buildings were arranged according to plans that were noticeably less repetitive than those of the colonizing villages which were often erected on the same sites some fifteen centuries later. One cannot therefore use neighbouring towns as a basis for picturing Thagaste, even more so because, unlike the military colonies established by Rome *ex nihilo* in central Numidia, with the strict and standardized layouts of which Timgad is the archetype, there were ancient cities like Thagaste, where Roman-style rebuilding had not erased native flights of fancy. West of Souk Ahras, the important and still well preserved ruins of Khamissa, the former Thubursicu Numidarum, near the source of the Medjerda, show how those towns might have looked, fluidly following the contours of this mountainous landscape.

Augustine died in 430 within the walls of a Hippo besieged by the Vandals, but he was fortunate enough to be born and live the larger part of his life in a country which had remained on the fringes of the great movements that had already submerged other areas of the Empire, notably the Gauls. The evil that gnawed at his Africa – a schism, Donatism, with the social disorders that it sometimes brought about – weakened it sufficiently to create a breeding-ground for rebellions – of Firmus, and then Gildo; but that evil obtained chiefly in the Mauretanias and central Numidia (the central Algerian region and the plateaux of the present-day Constantine area). Not until the late fourth century, spreading north and east, did it reach the regions near Hippo. These were very real troubles, that compelled Augustine to sustain the longest struggle of his episcopacy, but they had no profound effect on the life of the African provinces. The Moorish and Gaetulian barbarians who, on the south and west frontiers or in the isolated parts of the mountains, kept a watchful eye on the giant's weaknesses were still held in respect. Africa remained prosperous. Clearly visible in the urban finery of the towns, at that time restored and often embellished, it has been possible to discover traces of a new golden age in the second half of the fourth century; after the bad patch of the third century, there was a return to the brilliant lifestyle they had known under the Antonines and Severi.[4] And, despite one or two hitches, order reigned in that immense territory, from the present-day Algerio–Moroccan borders to the shores of the Syrtes. 'The greater part of our Empire, loyally subject to our civil administration'[5]: that is how, in the autumn of 410, the emperor Honorius described Africa, in a dated official document from Ravenna, where he was lying low while Alaric and his Goths occupied Rome before sweeping down into southern Italy.

African by birth, Roman by culture

A large part of what motivated Augustine as an adolescent and young man cannot be understood unless we are sufficiently aware of both the cultural formation of his deep-rootedness in Africa and the social milieu into which he was born. In Antiquity, one's name, and firstly that taken from one's father, the gentilitial or clan name, gave an initial indication. The use of a forename that had never been truly distinctive had fallen into disuse, and in the two-name system that tended to become the rule for anyone with no great ancestry, Augustine's family name was Aurelius.[6] This almost certainly dates the Romanization of his forebears at the latest to the era of Caracalla's edict (212). In 196, the son of Septimius Severus had received from his father the glorious name of Marcus Aurelius, who himself had it from Antoninus! Augustine's family had thus been Roman, from a legal standpoint, for at least a century and a half, and culturally no doubt even longer. Here is something that strangely limits the significance of the calculations that have been made on the statistical probability of the bishop of Hippo being of Berber blood; which, for all that, is almost a certainty, at least on his mother's side. Although his father's name, Patricius, is one of the common-or-garden Latin names of the Late Empire, his mother's, Monnica (Monica), which occurs particularly often in the region, is the diminutive of Monna, a well attested indigenous name which also belongs to a local deity whose cult is mentioned on an inscription at Thignica (Aïn Tounga, in the middle valley of the Medjerda).

Yes, but is it important? Unless to argue from this ancient anchorage in African soil an instant recognition in one of its sons of the imprint – like an 'indelible stamp', 'defying all analysis' – of a 'moral and physical climate' peculiar to that land, to which Augustine is supposed to owe his temperament, 'hot, impulsive, extreme'.[7] Indeed? Let us beware of becoming entrapped in the clichés of a 'mesological' determinism that goes back to Sallust, if not Herodotus, rejuvenated in the mid twentieth century by the supporters of 'environmentalism'. With even greater reason, regarding Monica's son, we should refuse to lapse into an anachronistic exoticism or illusory local colour. It has already been forcefully said: 'what counts is civilization, not chromosomes'.[8] Augustine's political models were Roman, and Roman all his cultural references. Yet he would never reject his origins, and even, in a letter written to the grammarian Maximus of Madauros, the town where, as a young adolescent, he had opened his mind to classical culture, he would defend the Punic names of two local martyrs (Miggin and Namphamo) against the grammarian's gibes, in terms that denote a certain 'African consciousness'.[a] Similarly, not without pride, in his *City of God* he would recall, as one does a national glory, the African *origo* of Apuleius, Madauros' great son.[b] Nevertheless, this Africa of which he boasts is an Africa incorporating Roman qualities and free from any political particularism; the only true particularism we must remember in the bishop of Hippo is his feeling of belonging to a Church that is strong enough in the witness of its own martyrs and the teaching of its first doctors to be able jealously to affirm its autonomy within the bosom of Catholicism, in the face of the see of Rome.

A poor young man?

Let us return to Augustine's family circle. The main piece of information on his father's social standing comes to us from the bishop's biographer, Possidius. Patricius belonged to the middle class of the *honestiores*, as they were then called, in other words small property owners of free and legitimate birth who were obliged by a 'cens', fundamentally a property based rating, to have 'curial' status, to be members of their city's curia, and thus subject to the financial constraints imposed by the exercise of municipal offices.[c] The state of Patricius' fortune probably did not enable him to assume the most honorific, and also most burdensome, duties – those of duumvir, curator or flamen; but like every decurion he took part in local management, permanently anxious to maintain his rank and not go to swell the mass of 'small fry' (the *humiliores*), men reduced to working other people's land, practically without any civic existence, restricted in their city to the *munera sordida*, compelled to offer their manual labour in a personal *corvée* in the service of their community.

Speaking of his father's situation, and thus his own, Augustine hesitated between two adjectives, 'modest',[d] and 'poor'.[e] Poverty is always relative, unless the threshold is defined. Patricius must have been slightly above that threshold, for he would have ceased to be of curial rank had he fallen below it; but the threshold was sometimes fairly low. One of Constantius II's laws had specified a little earlier – in 342 – that whoever possessed twenty-five *jugera* and farmed as many on the imperial estates was to be curial, and that even those who did not have this minimum could be appointed to the curia.[9] Fifty jugera were the equivalent of some dozen hectares, which was a small amount in the farming conditions of Antiquity, and even at Thagaste, where abundant rain in winter and spring, followed by a dry summer, favoured good harvests. Of Patricius' tiny estate[f] we know only the 'vineyard', near which lay the famous pear tree with its fruit of bitter repentance.[g] The family lived off this small estate, in a subsistence economy that naturally precluded not only any amassing of capital, but even any over-expenditure. Not, however, keeping servants; Augustine mentions his nurses, in the plural, and also the maidservants, still in the plural, who worked in his mother's house as in his father's.[h] In our day that is certainly a luxury, but in those days merely a few more mouths to feed frugally. There is no reason to see Patricius and his people as anything other than a family of provincial petits bourgeois, chiefly concerned to safeguard their dignity, economizing on everything to ensure the advancement of the boy with so much promise.[i] The father made sacrifices to send his son for three years to the school of the grammarian at Madauros, and we shall see that at the age of fifteen Augustine experienced the disaster of a year of total idleness at Thagaste, for want of funds to send him to pursue higher studies at Carthage.

I said earlier that poverty is relative, especially in the eyes of those who live in it. As a child, Augustine could compare the lot of his family at Thagaste with that of the lord of the city. It is fairly obvious that the opulence of Romanianus had dazzled him, and that Romanianus had been the model he had then set himself in order to escape the mediocrity of his own condition. In 386 at Milan, where he was awaiting baptism while, for his part, his former protector had gone to the imperial Court in an attempt to sort out his legal affairs, which were in a state of collapse, Augustine dedicated to him one of his dialogues of the period, the *Contra Academicos*. A brilliant page detailed the munificence of Thagaste's benefactor in the time of his splendour, the richness of the games he offered, the abundance of the feasts he held, the magnificence of his hunts, his baths, his residence.[j] A text to place alongside the famous 'mosaic of the lord Julius', which similarly depicted the life of those great landlords.[10] When he wrote this piece, Augustine had already given up the idea of making a career, and he exhorted Romanianus to pursue another kind of happiness. But at the age of fifteen, idle and awaiting his destiny, all he knew was that unless he escaped upwards, three years later at the legal age of eighteen laid down by a law of Constantine, applicable notably in Proconsular Africa,[k] he would have to enter the curia and throughout his life bear the burden that was now overwhelming his father. It was a serious incitement to get on in the world, when he could see no other possible way of succeeding. Romanianus' lifestyle must have already aroused in him the heartfelt cry that he would later attribute to his parishioners, simultaneously filled with admiration and green with envy before the splendour of the wealthy: 'Only *those* people exist, only *they* are alive.'[l]

Notes

a. *Ep.*, 17, 2.
b. *City of God*, VIII, 12; 14.
c. *Vita Aug.*, I, 1.
d. *Conf.*, II, 5: *patris, municipis admodum tenuis.*
e. Cf. *Sermon* 356, 13: *Augustinum, id est hominem pauperem de pauperibus natum.*
f. The *pauci agelluli* of *Ep.* 126, 7.
g. *Conf.*, II, 9. See p. 20.
h. *Conf.*, I, 7; IX, 17–18 and 20.
i. *Conf.*, I, 26, *in fine: bonae spei puer appellabar.*
j. Contra Acad., I, 2.
k. *C. Th.*, XII, 1, 7.
l. *Sermon* 345, 1. See also *Enarr. in Psalm.* 32, 2, *serm.* 2, 18.

CHAPTER II

Monica

Before devoting himself entirely to Mother Church, as he approached the age of forty, Augustine had had a concubine for about fifteen years, of whom he had been very fond and who had given him a son; then, at the same time as a fleeting engagement, a second short-lived liaison. But only one woman really counted in his life, and that was his natural mother, Monica.

As we may guess from reading a few pages of Book IX of the *Confessions*, Patricius had taken a wife in Thagaste from a milieu close to his own. He had married Monica, as his son would describe it in a phrase borrowed from Virgil, 'in the fullness of her nubility',[a] which means that he had not married a child, a practice that was in any case more rare then in Africa than in Rome itself.[1] The couple had three children, in what order we do not know: a girl, who remains anonymous to us, but who, once widowed, would later become the superior of a community of nuns,[b] and two boys,[2] Augustine and Navigius, whom we shall find with his brother in Italy, at Cassiciacum, then at Ostia at their dying mother's bedside. Was Navigius the elder? It is quite probable, when we know that Monica was twenty-three at Augustine's birth,[c] unless we accept that, having married young, she waited a few years before bearing her first child.

Augustine's silences regarding his father are as eloquent as what he says about him. Perhaps it should be added, for the sake of fairness and to explain those silences at least in part, that in Antiquity even more than nowadays a child's first years were chiefly women's concern, and that Augustine would lose his father in his sixteenth year, whereas afterwards he would still have seventeen years in which to maintain an often difficult, sometimes intermittent, but always exceptionally rich dialogue with his mother. True, but at the same time, reading what Augustine's words both say and omit, one cannot help getting the impression that Patricius, probably preoccupied with the concerns of his farm and his municipal duties, remained somewhat of an unknown quantity for his son. Not that he would have been an inattentive or negligent father; to fund his son's studies he had imposed sacrifices on himself out of all proportion to the state of his fortune, moved by the conviction, which he shared with Monica, that only cultural advancement would hoist his Augustine above a condition whose confines he could see only too well.[d] He was not recompensed for his efforts, as he died prematurely in the very year of his son's departure for Carthage, 370 or early 371. Remarkably, Augustine mentions his death only incidentally.[e] And subsequently that vanished father would scarcely enter his thoughts, at least those he expressed; in a letter to his friend Nebridius, in 388/9, he would refer to him once, merely as an example of somebody one remembers, and only as something that has been lost.[f]

It is equally significant that in fact, when writing his *Confessions* some ten years after his mother's death, he spoke a little of his father but only in regard to his conjugal relations with Monica. He was, says Augustine, basically a good man, but quick-tempered and violent.[g] Monica had the good sense not to oppose him; she would let the storm pass and then endeavour to reason with him. She had succeeded in as much as her hot-tempered husband never laid a finger on her, and she even managed to promote the image of a fairly harmonious couple. To her women friends, who expressed their astonishment while lamenting their own fate as beaten wives, she would laughingly reply that the contract which had been read to them on their wedding day was the charter of their bondage![3] A husband was a master whom they had to know how to disarm, without going so far as open rebellion. Similarly, she had resigned herself to Patricius' infidelities, patiently waiting until, finally reaching her husband, divine grace gave him chastity at the same time as faith. For Patricius – and this too had left him on the fringe of the duo formed by Augustine and his mother – had remained a pagan until the eve of his death.[h]

A Christian woman among others

This ultimate conversion was one of the greatest achievements of a wife whose entire conjugal conduct shows finesse and calm tenacity. I said earlier that Patricius and Monica belonged to the same milieu; at least the same social milieu, for they form one of the historically recognizable rare examples of those 'mixed' marriages, religiously speaking, which must have been quite frequent in mid-fourth-century North Africa.[4] Increasingly subject to restrictions and surveillance since the end of Constantine's reign, and even officially persecuted by his sons, notably Constantius II, paganism remained vigorous in the bosom of municipal elites, where it was a factor of social conservatism. Chronologically short-lived, the pagan reaction of Julian the Apostate (362–3) in fact had lasting consequences for the continuation of the ancient forms of worship.[5] We shall see later that, once a bishop, early in the fifth century, Augustine was not able to avoid debate with the supporters of a paganism that was still locally pugnacious, especially in his Numidia, at Calama (Guelma) and Madauros. He had retained a vivid memory of having seen in the latter town, when he was about twelve, decurions and notables going through the streets in a frenetic procession led by followers of Bellona.[i] However, coexistence with Christian followers, who were increasingly numerous among the lowly people, was generally tranquil, and must have been so at Thagaste.

So Monica had been born into a Christian family and was, as we would say today, a practising believer. The religious practices of Christians at that time, in North Africa, sometimes included aspects that would be surprising to us, such as the custom of taking offerings of food to the tombs of the martyrs, for agapes that only too often degenerated into orgies; an obvious survival of the pagan festival of the *Parentalia*.[6] Of course, Monica did not indulge in those excesses. If the baskets she brought to the cemetery contained, besides gruel and bread, a pitcher of unadulterated wine, when the time came to share libations with other faithful, she herself would take only a tiny amount, diluted with water, sipped from a goblet in front of every tomb visited. Was this sobriety a memory of some experience in her early youth? Augustine tells this story which he says he heard from the lady herself.[j] Raised in temperance by an old serving-woman who enjoyed the complete trust of Monica's parents, she had fallen into a bad habit. Well-behaved girl that she was, she was sent to the cellar to fetch wine from the cask, but before using the goblet she had brought to fill the carafe she would just wet her lips with the wine, not because she liked it, says Augustine, but out of childish mischief. But gradually she had acquired a taste for it, to the point where she was drinking entire goblets of it with great gusto. Fortunately she had cured herself of this incipient liking for drink in a burst of pride: the maidservant who accompanied her to the cellar, having fallen out one day with her young mistress, insultingly called her a 'little wine-bibber'.[7] Stung to the quick, Monica had immediately stopped her habit.

Augustine's insistence on narrating this episode, and the importance he attaches to this 'weaning away' – in which it is not surprising that he sees divine intervention behind the mocking servant – are first and foremost significant of his profound aversion to excessive drinking, which was never one of his failings, but in which he recognized one of the most shameful forms of sensual slavery. The anecdote also emphasizes one of the outstanding traits of his mother's personality, revealed here even in her adolescence: strong willpower, which she would use in maintaining her demanding moral standards, as well as in making a success of her married life, despite Patricius' weaknesses, before employing it in her sometimes rather heavy-handed efforts to ensure her son's success in this world, and his salvation in the next.

A very present mother

Let us recall here a remark by one of Augustine's most penetrating biographers: 'Few mothers can survive being presented to us exclusively in terms of what they have come to mean to their sons, much less to a son as complicated as Augustine.'[8] The reader of the *Confessions* and the *De beata vita* will find it easy to recognize that Monica who, even in her absence, was always so present in her son's first thirty years, emerges from this test fairly well in the reflection of her left to us by that son. At the very beginning of the treatise, Augustine, who was then celebrating his thirty-second birthday in November 386, at Cassiciacum, surrounded by his family and a small group of friends, first salutes the presence of his mother, 'who I believe deserves the credit for everything in my life'[k] – a subtler and more ambiguous version of his unwritten 'I owe her everything.' At Cassiciacum Augustine lived in perfect harmony with his mother, in a communion of soul and heart that would culminate a year later in the 'ecstasy of Ostia', a few days before Monica's death. The wrenching and bitterly resented wound of his separation from Adeodatus' mother, the year before, had healed over, and had then been washed away by the waters of baptism in spring 387. The new convert, at peace with himself, no longer had any dispute with his mother. In the calm autumn of the Milanese countryside, Monica was ever-present in the conversations inspired by her son; first in her housekeeping role, of course, but she also participated fully in the discussions, aided to a spiritual 'accouchement', like Alypius, Licentius and the others, by the maieutics of her son. The pertinence of her replies, inspired by plain good sense since she had no theoretical training, more than once aroused the admiration of her listeners, and primarily of her son who, to encourage her to stay on these speculative heights, did not hesitate to tell her that she had already entered the citadel of wisdom.[9]

Despite her intellectual shortcomings, Monica's ardour in this quest for the truth had truly impressed Augustine. A few days later, in another dialogue – the *De ordine* – in which maternal participation was less, he would renew his homage, recalling that on his birthday, during the exchanges of the *De beata vita*, Monica's spiritual presence had imposed itself upon him to the point where in his view nothing had seemed more fitting to the practice of true philosophy.[l]

Some dozen years later, through the pen of a son who had meanwhile become a man of the Church, Monica is presented mostly as one of the instruments of grace – if not the chief one. In the *Confessions*, the figure of his mother appears idealized, although the gaze brought to bear on her does not lose all its clearsightedness and the grievances are not entirely erased. A good Christian already while her son was still seeking his true path in life, Monica had some hard times in the early days, but she still had some way to go until her death at Ostia. She was still on the 'outskirts of Babylon' – the bishop of Hippo would thus place her with the images and words of *Jeremiah* 51[10] – when, worried about Augustine's new-found virility in his sixteenth year, she merely warned him against fornication, and mainly adultery, rather than thinking of channelling his sexuality in a youthful marriage which, together with that of a bright future, would have sounded the knell of her worldly ambitions for her son. Were the same all too human thoughts prompting her in Milan in 385, when, to ensure the fine marriage that was briefly contemplated, she had insisted upon the departure of his concubine? True, she had hoped that baptism would follow the marriage,[m] as her son says, while finding it rather difficult to forgive her for such a cruel procedure, considering her intentions. But the further we read in the *Confessions*, the more we see gratitude finally win the day, together with thankfulness for the exemplary value of her entire life.

In the course of these pages, Monica appears less as a model than as a permanent point of reference, a beacon whose light, sometimes dimmed – as when he deserted and fled from his mother on his departure for Rome in 383 – marks out an as yet uncertain route. In the spring of 385, in Milan, rediscovering an Augustine who had broken with Manichaeism but did not yet adhere to the Christian faith, she would assure him of her conviction that before she departed this life she would see him a faithful Catholic.[n] She had spared no effort to achieve this goal, neither prayers nor tears nor the hard-won courage to ban her son from her house on his return from Carthage in 373. With other early Christians, she shared the gift of those visions in which divine revelation comes, for those who know how to interpret it, to throw light on the path ahead and do away with doubt. For instance, the inspired dream she had in the depths of her despair, when Augustine was in his twentieth year.[o] She had seen herself standing on a wooden rule, and a luminous young man approached her, joyful and smiling; when he asked her the cause of her sadness and daily tears, she replied that she was weeping for the perdition of her son; then the young man – surely Christ – told her to look more closely to discover that where she was standing, there also stood her son. And Monica saw Augustine, standing by her side on the same rule.[11] That is how they would be, both close to the divine, one summer evening in 387 at Ostia.

The last few decades of our twentieth century were more distant from

Monica's mental universe and her social environment than the fifteen preceding centuries, which leaves a great deal of room for simplification and even caricature. Where Augustine saw an exemplary Christian widow, always giving alms and going to church twice daily to pray and not to gossip,[p] we would be tempted to see a visionary bigot, somewhat inflexible and totally lacking in what we call a sense of humour.[12] With a nudge from Freudianism, the worried and perhaps over-attentive mother, passionately set on 'travailing in the spirit' for the one she had travailed for in the flesh,[q] has been perceived as carnally possessive and abusive by analysts for whom the *Confessions* sometimes seem to serve up their dubious theories on a platter. For example, this phrase of Augustine,[r] recalling his Christian childhood while his father was still a pagan, and stating simply that Monica 'did her utmost to make thee, my God, my father rather than him'.[13] We are told that the feeling of guilt, which in fact is strong in Augustine – and subsequently characteristic of medieval and modern Christianity – was the result of difficult relations between a son of genius and a devout and dominating mother.[14] The doctrine of original sin, an Augustinian creation, would emerge from it. Thus, according to this interpretation, for centuries a major feature of the moral character and religious feeling of our western world would be the outcome of neuroses engendered in Augustine's psyche in his earliest childhood by his relationship with his mother.

Let us return to Thagaste, on the ides of November 354. Let us imagine Patricius, the too-quickly forgotten father, and his wife, bending over the cradle of their newborn son. Was it at that moment that they decided on the name he was to be given? In the case of a male infant, naming was the father's choice, but we can wager that Monica had her say in giving him the name Augustine, made commonplace for us by over a thousand years of countless bearers of this Christian name, but in those days so rare,[15] and above all so ambitious: literally the 'little Augustus' or the 'little emperor'. Did his parents, in the foreknowledge of a unique destiny, bestow it on one who would make it illustrious? Bearing this diminutive, a child would grow whose posthumous glory would one day eclipse that of the masters of the world.

Notes

a.   *Conf.*, IX, 19.
b.   *Ep.* 211, 4; Possidius, *Vita Aug.*, XXVI, 1.
c.   *Conf.*, IX, 28, *in fine*.
d.   *Conf.*, II, 5 and 8.
e.   *Conf.*, III, 7: 'I was then nineteen, and my father had been dead for over two years.'
f.   *Ep.* 7 (to Nebridius), I, 1.

g.   *Conf.*, IX, 19.
h.   *Conf.*, IX, 22.
i.   *Ep.* 17, 4.
j.   *Conf.*, IX, 18.
k.   *De beata vita*, I, 6: *nostra mater, cuius meriti credo esse omne quod vivo.*
l.   *De ordine*, II, 1.
m.   *Conf.*, VI, 23.
n.   *Conf.*, VI, 1.
o.   *Conf.*, III, 19.
p.   *Conf.*, V, 17.
q.   *Conf.*, V, 16.
r.   *Conf.*, I, 17.

CHAPTER III

A Numidian childhood

Antiquity never paid much heed to childhood, an unformed age that lacked social status or any true personal existence;[1] people preferred to keep quiet about it, except to lament the premature disappearances, in funerary poems carved on epitaphs which often go beyond the conventions of the genre and are little masterpieces of real pathos, with a forcefulness matching the feeling that these *aôroï*, in Greek, *immaturi*, in Latin, had been seized by death before they had begun to live. Moreover, even in the view of those most tolerant of egotism, the first years were no more indicative of the adult than the chrysalis is of the butterfly to come. It would not have crossed the mind of a Cicero, Seneca or Pliny to evoke the young boys they had been, still less the crying babes.

Augustine, however, does not keep quiet about his childhood, and that return to the earliest days of his life, seen as a continuum he has experienced, is in itself very novel. The narrator of the *Confessions* does not avoid the earliest age of all, *infantia*. Having no actual memories, he sees it through the eyes of the good women who had known him in his swaddling clothes, or quite simply reconstructs it from what he can observe of very young babies, whose eagerness for sensory perception impresses him.[a] Like them, he benefited from the milk of human kindness, that consolation for being in the world which God's goodness bestows through mothers and wet-nurses.[b] But the bishop in whom the doctrine of original sin is beginning to take shape has no sympathy for a little being whose innocence stems only from weakness, who is helpless but cannot disarm one who is able to see all its potential harmfulness.[c] Even its tears, he says, are revenge or blackmail, and its heart is not free of jealousy! Such a pessimistic view may astonish, although so 'modern' a recognition of this initial unconscious perversity should not surprise a century nourished on Freud, or a theology lucidly aware of the criminal heritage that weighs both culturally and genetically on the children of mankind.[2] But the man who is expressing himself in this way is no longer the father of Adeodatus, the son who died some ten years before; nor is he yet the theologian who will originate the canonical codification of the baptism of the newborn because of original sin,[3] but purely and simply the Christian who, in the first pages of this 'confession of praise and sin', giving an account of his past life, believes he should not miss out his earliest infancy although, as he says, he finds it hard to consider it as an integral part of his life here below.[d] He knows that this little 'innocent' body, still free from personal sin because lacking in judgement, contains a soul capable of saving itself, but also with the potential for perdition.

A schoolboy in Thagaste

Learning speech, which marks the beginning of the 'second childhood' – *pueritia* – inspired Augustine to an analysis which could be said to make him the father of child psychology. When he writes that 'words, falling into their place in various sentences, duly rendered their meaning',[e] he was already acknowledging the importance of what we term 'prosodic indications', in the very young infant's recognition of the phonology and syntax of its maternal language. But when he entered elementary school, things changed for the worse. We encounter the first big surprise: indubitably so intellectually gifted, and an overall 'good pupil', as we shall see, Augustine says that he detested the school system of his time – which however hardly differed, at that age, from what we learn about a young Roman pupil's day from a document of the early third century,[4] which shows a little boy from a social milieu not much above that of the young Augustine. True, strokes of the whip might punctuate exercises (in reading, writing or sums), if the master deemed them badly executed. And, as H.-I. Marrou reminds us, 'snatching one's hand from the rod' had become a metaphor synonymous with school life.[5] But schoolboys in our own times were still trying to snatch their fists away from the ruler of some descendant of the 'black hussars of the Republic', and yet managed to survive.

But we have to believe Augustine, so painful do the bishop's memories seem when he evokes the life lived by the schoolboy. The portrait that he pens, which we find it hard to imagine as realistic, if from the mystic, the theologian, the writer and man of the Church we extrapolate the child, is not that of one who is 'good at composition'. He did not like studying; he says so and reiterates it.[f] To be more exact, he rebelled against the constraints of education, in which he differed little from most small boys since the world began. The petulant, undisciplined, playful child, who committed petty pilferings in his home to share and swap with his playmates,[g] feared above all things being flogged at school and perhaps even more so when it was with the approval of his parents.[h] However, though those constraints and punishments may have been painful to him, he does not condemn them, whatever the supporters of the 'play activity' concept of school may think, admitting that he would have learnt nothing if he had not been obliged to.[i] At the age of seventy-two, in one of the last books of the *City of God*, the old bishop would return once more to his furthest memories and again would recall in strong terms the brutality of school training: if offered the choice between dying or starting childhood over again, he says, who would not choose death![j] But in this context we have a better understanding of the meaning behind his lament: dependent, subject to the will of adults, in a frantic quest for freedom by escaping into play, childhood is emblematic of the misery of the human condition since the Fall.

The bitter roots of Greek

It is sometimes forgotten that the Roman Empire was bilingual; or, more precisely, that besides the many local variants of everyday speech used in addition to the official language – Latin – knowledge of a second language for trade and culture, Greek, which was in fact the second official language in the eastern half of the Roman world, was essential for anyone wanting to make a career in the imperial administration, or become part of the cultured elite. Only a good grounding in Greek enabled one to be numbered among the *utraque lingua eruditi*, the passport to success. As I mentioned earlier, although there were

Greek-speaking communities in North Africa at the time, this province of the Empire was not especially remarkable for its centres of Hellenism. Nevertheless, Greek was taught as early as in elementary school, even in such a modest township as Thagaste. And Greek was specifically one of the subjects that disheartened the young Augustine.[6] There is a simple and understandable reason. For centuries it had been the Roman tradition that the two languages should be learnt in parallel, and often even that Greek should be taught first; but in those times, in well-to-do families, this was up to a governess or 'pedagogue', household servants who were themselves Greek or Greek-speaking. Augustine did not have the benefit of those facilities that were reserved for the children of aristocratic circles. As he himself remarks, while he had learnt Latin amidst the caresses of his nurses, with laughter and play and the happy activity of pre-school life,[k] it was from the _magister_ that he received the first rudiments of Greek. He thus found himself – but at a much more tender age and with his learning faculties still intact – in the situation of our modern students who discover somewhat late in the day the verbal suppleness and richness of ancient Greek: marvellous words, but graphically as prickly, with their accents and 'smooth' or 'rough' breathing, as roses with their thorns. In the _Confessions_, another metaphor suggests itself to Augustine: the sweetness of the good Homer, he says, seemed spoilt for him by the gall of the difficulties of a foreign language.[l]

What level of Greek did he attain? Put like this, rather naively, the question risks remaining unanswered. At all events we should not take as gospel what he himself said one day, claiming that he knew precious little about the Greek language, in fact almost nothing.[m] Once again, it was H.-I. Marrou who supplied the most probable solution to this oft debated problem. Knowing French or German may mean, at the very least, that one knows enough, when undertaking research for example, to be able to grasp an article published in a learned magazine, if necessary with the help of a dictionary; it may also mean – and this is quite another matter – that one enjoys reading or rereading Racine or Goethe in the original text and, better still, that those authors can fill the memory in the same way as a Shakespeare, and can be summoned up at the prompting of an emotion, as when Nero mechanically quoted a line from the _Iliad_ on hearing the horsemen sent to pursue him.[n] Although Augustine probably never ceased making progress in Greek, and was more at ease with it towards the end of his life than in his adolescence, we can assume, with Marrou, that he 'knew' Greek in the first rather than the second fashion;[7] in short, that he was not truly an _utraque lingua eruditus_, in the real meaning of the term, as Cicero had been, who was able to start a sentence in Latin and finish it in Greek, and who thought in both languages; or Pliny the Younger, who had shown similar ease in Trajan's time; or Apuleius, the champion of high culture in North Africa in the Antonine period. A good two centuries later, the position of Greek had considerably weakened in the western world, and not only on the shores of the South. Augustine was not the only one to have but a partial grasp of the legacy of Hellenism,[8] and to benefit from it chiefly by way of translations, as we shall see in the case of the _libri Platonici_. Even before the end of Antiquity and the fragile Byzantine 'renaissance', this forgetfulness of Greek in the West was the cultural prelude to the dichotomy which would dominate the history of the Mediterranean in the medieval era.

Although in this account Augustine is far from careful about exact chronology, we must assume it was in the early part of his childhood, before his tenth year, that he suffered the sudden attack of illness – the text mentions the *stomachus*, but the Ancients spoke of the stomach as Toinette, in *Le Malade Imaginaire*, speaks of the lung – which put the child in sufficiently grave danger for his baptism to be contemplated.° Alarmed, Monica was already hastening preparations for it when this childish ailment disappeared as suddenly as it had come, and the baptism was postponed for fear that, with adolescence, new blemishes might occur to taint its purification. The young Augustine therefore remained accessible to all spiritual adventures on the road of that complicated itinerary that would finally lead to baptism in Milan in the spring of 387. But we are indebted to the account of this episode for one essential piece of information in the perspective of his 'conversion'. For the bishop who is reviewing his childhood here is quite positive on one point: like his mother, the child Augustine believed in Christ, and certainly accompanied Monica to church; at birth – *ab utero matris* – he had received the sacrament of the catechumens, by the laying on of hands, the sign of the cross and being touched with salt.ᴾ As he would say later in one of his homilies on the Gospel of John (XI, 3), comparing the catechumens with those who were baptized, 'he already believed in the name of Christ, even though Christ did not yet believe in him'. In this the conversion he experienced shortly after he was thirty differs noticeably from several famous conversions of agnostics, to which it has sometimes been rather too hastily likened.

A schoolboy at Madauros

Augustine very soon exhausted the scholastic possibilities in Thagaste. We shall see that in his twentieth year, having completed his own training at Carthage, he would return for a time to his native town to teach as *grammaticus* – comparable with at least the current first cycle of French secondary education. But in his childhood, that level of studies did not exist in Thagaste, and probably in his eleventh year he would have had to go to Madauros.

Some thirty kilometres – about a day's journey at that time – separate Souk Ahras from Mdaourouch, which perpetuates the ancient name, Madauros, almost unchanged across the centuries and in local parlance. At the feet of the djebel bou-Sessou, which marks the horizon to the south, anyone venturing there today will discover at the end of a track a little group of ruins that were unearthed at the beginning of the twentieth century and now lie sleeping as they await the unlikely recommencement of the excavations. In the centre, encroaching on the forum, is the fortress – to which as elsewhere, under a brief Byzantine domination in the sixth century, an urban civilization resorted when it was reduced to being on the defensive – and this encloses as if in the hollow of its hand a charming little theatre, half swallowed by the walls of the fort, but protected by them. When Augustine arrived there, the town, which had remained modest, away from the major routes and bordering on Gaetulia and the ancient territory of the Musulamii, was still living on the memory of its great son, Apuleius. He could have seen on the forum the statue that had been dedicated by his fellow-citizens to the 'Platonic philosopher', as he had described himself, with no false modesty – a label subsequently unchallenged by Augustine, who had a good knowledge of Neoplatonism and was quite proud of the man from Madauros.[9] In the second half of the fourth century, the town seems to have subsisted mostly on its olive groves and oil presses, being fairly well-to-do, as evidenced by the considerable works of restoration attested then by inscriptions. During Augustine's stay, in 366–7, the great summer baths benefited from repairs and real embellishments.[10] And with Stéphane Gsell one may think that 'the pride of having produced Apuleius must have contributed to making Madauros a town where great literature was held in high esteem',[11] and whose schools enjoyed a reputation that exceeded the town's modest status.

Augustine is not very explicit about the course of studies he followed there; he mentions it incidentally, as one speaks of a period without much history – and therefore probably happy – just before his calamitous year of inactivity after his return to Thagaste in 369. If he does not speak of it more extensively, it is because he has already foreshadowed it in essence in Book I of the *Confessions*, where a distinction is not always clearly made between his first training at the elementary school of the *magister ludi* at Thagaste, and that of the *grammaticus*, the secondary schooling that followed at Madauros. But the phrase he uses for that brief mention – 'a first stay away from home to initiate me into literature and the art of oratory'[q] – plainly shows that he was then well beyond the first rudiments and that the grammarians of Madauros pushed the instruction of their pupils to quite some lengths.[12] They did not hesitate to encroach on the programme of the rhetors, as this exercise bears witness – the *ethopoiea* or character portrayal of someone in a given situation – in which Augustine excelled: in this instance, he had to imagine and write a prose version of the speech uttered by Juno, 'annoyed at not being able to divert the king of the Trojans from Italy'.[r] Whereas the young child had often been discouraged by his first learning attempts – although the bishop recognizes that they are fundamental and irreplaceable, for they provide the tools for an entire lifetime – the twelve-year-old loved Latin literature passionately, especially Virgil, the Virgil of the *Aeneid*, which he knew by heart, as would Racine: 'I delighted', he says, 'in those empty spectacles (this is clearly the bishop speaking) – the wooden horse full of armed soldiers, the burning of Troy, and even the shade of Creüsa herself.'[s] For Augustine, those years at Madauros were a time of a first blossoming, at that age of grace when young adolescents, as yet spared the perturbations of the flesh, enthusiastically sample their first experience of literary essays. And for him poetry would always be a treasure, probably soon buried under the layers of a complex intellectual stratigraphy, but whose beauty he would never forget. Many features reveal that constant presence of poetry in Augustine, at various levels. To one of his correspondents who had sent him a note that finished with a couplet of five hexameters, the last of which included one foot too many, the old bishop mischievously replied that if the writer had intended to catch him out on a metrical system that for him had become a distant memory, then he had not succeeded![t] And in a page of Book VIII – probably written around 405 – of one of his major works, the *De Trinitate*, in the litany of 'good things', he would place poetry above all other goods, just after God, who is good itself.[u]

At all events, Augustine remained very reserved about those three or four years spent in Madauros. The joy of opening up to the life of the spirit must have helped him to pass over a good many things. In a world in the throes of religious change, the little Numidian city had remained a bastion of paganism; but with the local saints, Miggin and Namphamo, whose martyrdom must have dated back to the persecution by Commodus in 180, the Christian community in Madauros had obtained an early place in the martyrologies.[13] But in the 360s, the fate and very survival of that community was problematic; and the three churches, one of which was for burials, attested by archaeology in the late period probably no longer existed.[14] Immersed in pagan surroundings, the young catechumen doubtless found it difficult to observe the religious practices to which his mother had accustomed him at Thagaste. Perhaps he was staying with a relative or one of his teachers; those poorly paid pedagogues supplemented their meagre income by boarding some of their pupils. We know one of them, Maximus, thanks to a letter sent by him some twenty years later to Augustine, who was then newly converted and living at Thagaste. And although it is by no means certain that the old master was addressing his former student, it is quite clear that the boy had known him at that time.[15]

In his letter, Maximus waxed ironic on the martyrs of Madauros who, in his opinion, had merely undergone the deserved punishment for their crimes. He, the *grammaticus Romanus*, made fun of their native names, and was annoyed to think that their cult should be preferred to that of the immortal gods.[v] Besides, like many 'enlightened' pagans of his time, he contrasted the God of the Christians with a supreme God, who could be invoked under various names, not excluding the traditional deities whose statues, standing in the city's forum, he regarded as salutary forms of protection. In his reply, Augustine did not attempt to get him to detail his theology; it would have been a waste of time. But he made a point – and this display of 'African awareness' would always be one of his constant traits – of defending Namphamo by name (he thought that in Punic the name meant 'the man who is fit', whose coming brought good fortune) against the sarcastic remarks of the grammarian who, a cultural parvenu, too easily forgot his origins. He also added a few memories. Yes, he well remembered having seen, as a child, two statues of Mars on the forum at Madauros, one naked and the other with a breastplate, and opposite them the statue of a man brandishing three pointed fingers at them in a gesture of magic defence. At least, that is how the little boy interpreted it – and the bishop was no fool, now making use for polemical ends of a childhood memory! – a gesture which was more likely to be the traditional one of a Roman orator.[w] Then, he also remembered those frenzied processions through the streets and squares of the city by its principal personages. It was at Madauros, in his twelfth year, without any suspicion then that the bishop would find material there for his protracted battles, that Augustine first became aware of the resistance of paganism, strong in the simplicity of its rites, the beauty of its iconographic and monumental decoration and the attraction of its festivals, which still appealed to the imagination of the populace.

The pears of idleness

Probably in the summer or autumn of 369 Augustine returned to Thagaste. He had changed. The first to notice was his father, Patricius, when he saw him one evening at the baths 'clothed in his stirring adolescence', as the author of the *Confessions* prettily puts it.[x] For him it was a matter for rejoicing; he could already picture himself surrounded by grandchildren, but Monica, like all mothers, was dismayed to see that her little boy had turned into a great pubescent lad, with appetites she knew only too well from having seen them at work in Patricius. She gave him a lecture, short and to the point: no fornicating, and above all no committing adultery with anyone's wife. For the young man this was old women's talk, and he would have blushed to pay any heed![y] As for the bishop, when he thinks back to that wretched year of kicking his heels and running riot, he blames his parents – chiefly his mother, who morally guided the household – for not having thought of containing their son's sexual inclinations within the bounds of a conjugal commitment. And with cause, he adds, conjecturing from what he remembers of the thoughts that prompted them. For the fine hopes they both nurtured for his social elevation – Patricius in a more flatly bourgeois fashion, Monica concerned over an additional benefit for her son's soul – ran a strong risk of being ruined by a premature marriage which would have put an end to his studies and halted any advancement.[z] The plan was to send Augustine to Carthage to complete his education, no matter what the moral risk. And Patricius busied himself getting together the necessary funds for his son's keep. But meanwhile studies were interrupted, and he thus spent a year in complete idleness.

And excesses. Oh! the reader of Book II of the *Confessions* seeking spicy details will have scant reward for his prurient curiosity. Everything is said, without being expressed; or rather, nothing is said, but everything must be read between the lines of an impassioned and sumptuous prose. Although in these baroque pages we take into account the bishop's exceedingly strict view when he relives the blackest year of his youth, there remains the suggestive power of a language which no one in Antiquity had yet used to evoke the carnal urges of adolescence. 'What did I delight in but to love and be loved? But I did not keep within the bounds of an exchange between souls, wherein lies the luminous path of friendship. Dark clouds arose from the murky depths of fleshly concupiscence and the seethings of puberty.'[aa] Of course, some people who have ventured to decode these sentences have attempted to uncover an improbable homosexuality, which everything subsequently in Augustine's emotional behaviour clearly rules out, and to read into another sentence that follows an admission of solitary pleasures, which in fact are not unlikely. That he had a few little passing love affairs, perhaps some with servants, and that he competed with comrades of his own age, as he says, there is no doubt. But Thagaste, the modest 'Babylon' of their frolics, where everything was common knowledge, imposed its small provincial town limitations upon them. The main things that must have been missing from their licentiousness were girls and opportunity. But in the end, these indications that are passed on to us about the tumult in the body of this sixteen-year-old adolescent are infinitely precious. We are thus warned of the reality of the obstacles which Augustine's demanding sensuality would place in the path of his conversion or, more precisely, of the difficulties his ardent nature would experience fifteen years later, in adding the conversion of his will to that of his intellect.

However, Book II of the *Confessions* does not close with the evocation of those torments and escapades, but with another kind of 'fornication', that 'of the soul' – the famous episode of stealing pears. The story takes but a few lines. In the vicinity of a vineyard belonging to Augustine's family stood a pear tree whose fruit, states the narrator, was not particularly delectable. One night when the young rascals had stayed out very late, they ransacked the pear tree, ate a few of the pears, which had no other savour than that of forbidden fruit, and threw the rest to the pigs.[bb] In our day, when the countless temptations of the consumer society, combined with the collapse of educational restraints, prompt the young unemployed to hitherto unimaginable behaviour, stealing a few pears may make us smile. When juvenile delinquency was confined to such pranks, who among us has not 'scrumped' fruit in an orchard or pinched a few grapes from a vine? In itself, the theft of the pears was a peccadillo; and we shall never know what reverberations it had in Augustine's conscience, once the 'high' of that act of fun committed in a gang had subsided. What matters is that, when he had reached maturity and become a bishop, Augustine retained more than a memory of it, a deep impression on his soul. From that disastrous year of idleness at Thagaste, this is the sole precise event that surfaces, or at least the only one on which the writer of these memoirs confers the status of *exemplum*, feeling the need to follow the eight lines of the account with seven pages of commentaries.

All this doubtless means that the memory of the theft of the pears stayed with him throughout his life, first as a cause of remorse and then, with his conversion, as the sad illustration of the damage man can suffer from free will, powerless to direct him towards the fullness of his being, but always enough to make him fall into evil, that non-being. A gratuitous act of vandalism – and not a petty theft carried out from necessity – the pillaging of the pear tree was much more serious than an adolescent sexual urge. In his *Commentary on Genesis*, around 410, Augustine would take a stand against the commonly held idea that the only sins one can commit are those that involve the sexual organs.[cc] Long before Freud, he knew that the *libido* – or 'concupiscence', as he calls it – had other vectors. But already, writing the *Confessions*, he was bitterly questioning himself: 'Wretched one! What did I find to love in you, my theft, nocturnal infamy of my sixteenth year?'[dd] Can one love evil for evil's sake? Probably, but there must have been favourable conditions for those adolescents. Gathering his memories, deepening his analysis, Augustine comes to the conclusion that on his own he would not have committed this transgression; what mattered was the involvement of the group, this downslide of friendship – a human value that was essential to him – reduced here to mere complicity, in other words to naught.[ee] In the final analysis, without straining the Augustinian text, the theft of the pears appears as a 'parable of original sin'.[16] And as often happens with Augustine, the richness of the harmonics here is such, in the pages devoted to the episode – though slightly marginal to the text – as to allow possible, if not always convincing, comparisons: the pillaged pear tree could thus symbolize the tree of the knowledge of good and evil, the fruit which Eve tasted;[17] and this tree would be matched symbolically by another, the tree of life, in other words the fig tree in the garden in Milan, beneath which Augustine would begin to undertake his own redemption . . .

The year 370 was drawing to a close, and with it would end this parenthesis, an empty time between the finish of childhood and entry into life, the life of the spirit and of the heart. Adding a generous supplement to the viaticum collected by Patricius, Romanianus allowed Augustine to leave for Carthage.

Notes

a. Especially their hunger for visual perception: cf. *De Trinitate*, XIV, 7 (text dated around 418).
b. *Conf.*, I, 7.
c. *Conf.*, I, 7: *Ita imbecillitas membrorum infantilium innocens est, non animus infantium.*
d. *Conf.*, I, 12.
e. *Conf.*, I, 13.
f. *Conf.*, I, 19: 'I hated my studies, and loathed being forced to do them' (cf. I, 14: 'If I showed myself to be lazy in learning, I was beaten').
g. *Conf.*, I, 30.
h. *Conf.*, I, 14.
i. *Conf.*, I, 19: *Et urgebar tamen, et mihi bene fiebat . . . non enim discerem nisi cogerer.*
j. *City of God*, XXI, 14.
k. He says so in one of those practically untranslatable compound sentences, with quasi-rhymes, which are one of the characteristics of his style: *inter blandimenta nutricum, et ioca arridentium, et laetitias alludentium* (*Conf.*, I, 23).
l. *Conf.*, I, 23.
m. *Contra litt. Petiliani*, II, 91: *Et ego quidem Graecae linguae perparum assecutus sum et prope nihil*: a little jest from a great bishop who wishes to show his opponent – here the Donatist Petilianus – that it is not necessary to be expert in Greek to know that 'catholic' means 'universal'.
n. Suetonius, *Nero*, 49.
o. *Conf.*, I, 17.
p. *Conf.*, I, 17, initio.
q. *Conf.*, II, 5.
r. *Conf.*, I, 27.
s. *Conf.*, I, 21.
t. *Ep.* 261, 4.
u. *De Trin.*, VIII, 3.
v. *Ep.* 16, 2.
w. *Ep.* 17, 4.
x. *Conf.*, II, 6.
y. *Conf.*, II, 7.
z. *Conf.*, II, 8.
aa. *Conf.*, II, 2.
bb. *Conf.*, II, 9.
cc. *De Gen. ad litt.*, X, 23.
dd. *Conf.*, II, 12.
ee. *Conf.*, II, 16.

CHAPTER IV

Carthage

'Do we remember happiness as one who has seen Carthage remembers it?' The city's name fleetingly appears in passing in the famous analysis of memory in Book X of the *Confessions*.[a] But we shall know nothing more of the adolescent's wonder on discovering the African capital, or of the emotions of the bishop twenty years later, returning to the city where he would so often express himself. We expect a man like Augustine to tell us everything, including things that he was not concerned to tell us. We must accept that this very modest mention is the equivalent of an evocation of the great city and its many splendours.

The traveller covering the 175 miles – around 260 kilometres – separating Thagaste and Carthage would use the last sections of the major road linking the capital with its grain stores, the *castella* of the high plains of Constantine and Setif.[1] It was several days' journey, with halts at Le Kef (the ancient Sicca), Le Krib (Musti), Aïn Tounga (Thignica) and Medjez el-Bab (Membressa). There one rejoined the winding course of the Medjerda, which one had left when departing from Thagaste. Between the Medjerda and the Wadi Miliana, the way passed through that little 'Mesopotamia', whose agricultural richness had for centuries made it one of the most fertile and urbanized areas of the ancient world.

Approaching the Gulf of Carthage, leaving Tunis and its lake on the right, one arrived in the then still narrow peduncle of the isthmus, in sight of the metropolis, at the rear of its marine facade. At first glance it was probably not very different from the view the traveller gets today when leaving the airport and seeing the site along the same axis: at Sidi Daoud, he can already see the cathedral, built by Cardinal Lavigerie at the end of the nineteenth century and occupying the exact site of the ancient Capitol, with a similar elevation. But in the late fourth century, the upper town of Roman Carthage was even more impressive. On the summit of the plateau which had been artificially constructed on the ruins of Punic Byrsa, and 'corseted' by strong retaining walls, the vast esplanade overlooked by the Capitol was bordered on one side by colonnades, on another by the library mentioned by Apuleius,[b] and on yet another by one of the most immense judiciary basilicas in the ancient world.[2] In the heart of this 'open town', Rome displayed an imperial power that had reached its apogee in the very period when the monumental centre had been completed, in the second half of the second century.

The big city

Early in the Victorian era, the young Engels would discover London, the first 'megapolis' of our modern world, and marvel at those streets where you could walk for a long time without being able to see their end. For a large town is primarily that: a structured space where even the longest saunter is always channelled, where towering facades arrest and hold the gaze, while the squares liberate it by restoring a view of the sky. Coming from his little township, where the nearby mountains confined the horizons, Augustine must have had the same kind of impression when he arrived in Carthage. On the scale of the world at that time, the 'Alexandria of the West' was a very big city, challenging Antioch for third place, but was incontestably the second town in the western Mediterranean, though far behind Rome, it is true. According to Ausonius, it still maintained that rank some years later, at the time (388) when Augustine embarked at Ostia to return to Africa. The rhetor from Bordeaux, who knew what he was talking about (he had been praetorian prefect for the Gauls, Italy and Africa in 378–9), had amused himself by writing an *Ordo urbium nobilium*, classifying the seventeen most famous towns of his time, from Rome to his native Bordeaux; and in his opinion, Carthage was always the third town in the Empire, after Rome and Constantinople.[c] Dare one suggest a figure? It might not be exaggerating a probable reality to estimate its population, all classes included, at between 200,000 and 300,000 inhabitants; laughable, when we think of the urban monsters we live in, but for Antiquity it carried considerable demographic weight.

I mentioned earlier the young Engels' surprise when he discovered London in the mid-nineteenth century. In late era Carthage, too, one could spend hours tramping the decuman and cardinal streets, in their squared layout which was as regular as that of a well kept plantation, as a text of the period says.[d] On its major lines, those of the cardinal roads – especially to the north-east, on the lowest slopes of the plateau that now leads to Sidi bou-Saïd – the town had eventually overflowed its layout in four 'centuries' drawn up by the surveyors of the Augustan era. Running parallel with the coast, from the present-day quarter of Bordj Djedid as far as the ports, the streets stretched for two kilometres. Immediately bordering the shore, where in Punic times a rampart had stood, erected against possible threats from seaward, a *lungomare* had now been developed – sadly missing in modern Carthage – a boulevard that overlooked the sea from a height of between four and five metres and presented an un-interrupted promenade along 1800 metres, from the terre-plein of the commercial docks to beyond the baths of Antoninus, which it embraced by forming a recess, a bulge on the shoreline. This increased the views over the Gulf of Carthage, bounded to the north and east by the soft lines of Cape Bon, so near given a westerly wind, to the south by the hillocks of the Bou Kornine, and behind them in the background, by the elongated silhouette of the Zaghouan, whence the water that supplied the whole town descended by aqueduct. Without a doubt, Augustine's first gaze would have fallen on this bay, and the sea that he was seeing for the first time – as a child he had had to imagine it by looking at a glass filled with water, as he says in a letter to his young friend Nebridius.[e] He was now contemplating 'the grandiose spectacle it presents, when it is mantled with different hues; many shades of green, purple, blue'.[f] Midway along this boulevard one came to the top of the *decumanus maximus*; turning there, at the end of the prospect opened out by this broad avenue descending from Byrsa to the sea, the gaze would be arrested by the triple nave of the great basilica, seen in profile, resting on the strong structures of the present-day 'apses of Beulé'. On the right, the town rose in terraces up the hills, dominated by the twin semi-circular and back-to-back bulks of the tiers of the odeon and theatre. A fascinating, and also intimidating, sight, an impact that would for ever affect the ambitious young provincial 'coming up' to the capital and there for the first time finding himself face to face with the realities of his future.

Amare amabam

But Augustine was no Rastignac. His 'Here's to the two of us, Carthage!' had nothing of the cold vow of success at any price made by Balzac's young arriviste; instead, the exclamation of a young man eager to love and be loved. The opening of Book III of the *Confessions* is famous:

> I came to Carthage, where a cauldron of shameful loves loudly seethed all around me. I was not yet in love, though I was in love with love; feeling a lack deep within me, I hated myself for not feeling it more deeply. I sought something to love, being in love with loving . . .[g]

In the whole literature of Antiquity, Greek or Latin, there is no text in which the words 'love' and 'to love' recur so often in so few lines: love as the being's craving, the desire to love vehemently revealing a need, in terms which remind us – unsurprisingly: Neoplatonism had trodden that path – that in Plato, Eros is the son of Poros, resourcefulness, but also of Penia, poverty. And Augustine in his seventeenth year, had less of Poros than of Penia. Moreover – at least, here the bishop speaks for the student – thirsting for love, he was sorry that his thirst was not even greater.[3]

With body and soul so disposed, it is hardly surprising that the young man hastened to find in Carthage what Thagaste was incapable of offering an adolescent. The big town was not merely a sumptuous environment. Writing half a century later, Salvian was probably exaggerating when he described a Carthage 'overflowing with vices and seething with iniquity, teeming with inhabitants and even more with depravities'.[4] But that pious and morose rhetoric may just have hit the mark when describing a large port open to the four winds, a rich town where there was no lack of temptation for 'university' youngsters often with too much leisure. The bishop has left a rather unflattering but probably broadly true portrait of the young student, from which it emerges chiefly that Augustine lost no time in falling into the famous 'cauldron':

> I therefore fell headlong into the love in which I longed to be ensnared. My God, my mercy, with what bitterness didst thou season that sweetness! For I was loved, and reached the joy that binds, and in my joy I was caught up in the tangles of misfortune, to be scourged with rods, with red hot irons, of jealousy, suspicion, fear, anger and quarrelling.[h]

Nearly four centuries earlier, Ovid had said that the best way to engage in amorous dalliance was to frequent the circus or the theatre. It is all the more probable that Augustine followed this advice because, in the *Confessions*, the admission of those stormy love affairs is immediately followed by that of his passion for the theatre. As a child he had thrilled at the story of Dido's woes enough to reveal even then his sensitivity to drama. And, so powerful was the mirror effect of the dramatic scene, that the young lover he had become, now gratified, now betrayed, was united from his theatre seat with the stage lovers, now sharing their joys, now distressed by the sadness of their dissension.[i] But, as the bishop notes, making a fair copy of his student memories,[5] it was above all the misery of separated lovers, the heartbreak of their separation, that fascinated Augustine the spectator. Regarding the public's support for the actor's performance, these pages contain an analysis which would not be met again until Diderot and his *Paradox on the actor*, though in greater depth and conducted mainly from the viewpoint of the actor and his craft. And another no less valuable piece of information is passed on to us: it is almost certain that as well as the mimes and pantomimes – the only shows reported by Tertullian at the beginning of the third century[6] – plays from the great tragic repertory were still being staged in Carthage, or at least theatrical adaptations of the most dramatic episodes of classical epics, fuelled by the love of Dido and Aeneas, and their reunion when the hero descended to Hades.[j]

In Carthage, shows were often presented in the street or on the forecourt of temples as well. Augustine would see those temples close, one after another, some thirty years later, but in his youth the ancient cults, though increasingly under threat, were still vigorous. We may recall that at Madauros the young boy had first encountered this still militant paganism when he was present at the procession of the followers of Bellona. In the capital, religious events had quite another dimension, and very often the *tableaux vivants* they presented had a far more erotic tone than shows given in the theatre. This was especially so in the most important festival, which took place over several days in the spring in honour of Caelestis – the Roman version of Tanit, Carthage's tutelary deity – at that time identified with Magna Mater. That assimilation was the justification for the presence in this unmasked carnival of the eunuch priests of Cybele, the *galli* who, with flabby limbs, their faces painted with white lead and their hair drenched in perfume, minced effeminately through the streets. Augustine and his comrades mingled with the public to watch them go past, keeping an eye also on the actors and actresses who, on the vast paved square in front of the goddess' temple, in the south part of the town not far from the docks, crudely represented the loves of Cybele and Attis, with lascivious postures more eloquent than words. Forty years later, putting these cults in the dock in the *City of God*, Augustine had retained a lively enough memory of those scenes to visualize himself once again on that open ground, following as best he could the unfolding of the shows amid the teeming throngs, eyes fixed in turn on the statue of the goddess and the procession of prostitutes, then on the actors whose erotic mimes, he writes, were such as to provide the young married women present, if they did not turn their eyes away, with the most persuasive sexual education.[k]

A face behind a church pillar

There is no place like the theatre, says Ovid, for chance flirtatious encounters, and he could have added temples; it was still true, but now there were churches as well! It will not be forgotten that from infancy Monica had accustomed her son to attend services with her. In Carthage, churches would increase in number at the cusp of the fourth and fifth century, but in Augustine's youth there were already several and, for want of any mention on his part, it would be useless to try to pinpoint the one he frequented. In one of those churches the author of the *Confessions*, in the Christianly encoded style he adopts when his narrative plunges into the intimacy of his past conduct, accuses himself of having 'coveted the fruits of death and arranged the means of procuring them': his way of saying that the student made sheep's eyes at some pleasant young maidens whom he did not yet think of clothing in the garments of sin.[l] A recently discovered text echoes this veiled confession and throws a cruder light on the promiscuity which, in churches, made liaisons and affairs easier. It was a sermon preached by Augustine in Carthage, at the invitation and in the presence of the bishop of the town, Aurelius, probably in the cathedral, the *basilica Restituta*, on 23 January – the day after the feast of St Vincent, in whose honour the assembly took place – in 404 or 405. Augustine recalls that in his youth, when vigils were observed, the two sexes were not separated. All entered by the same narrow passage, where women were already being exposed to gibes and taunts.[m] He also states that in those times, in the suburban church of the *Mappalia*, where the tomb of St Cyprian lay – one of the Augustinian high points of Carthage, to which I shall return – in place of hymns, saucy ditties were sung to embarrass the women present.[n] Thirty years later, such licentiousness was no more than a memory; Aurelius had imposed order.

Was it in the church of the *Mappalia* – his 'parish' – that Augustine met the one with whom he would live, remaining faithful to her, for nearly fifteen years? He tells us only that what made him find her, outside wedlock, was 'a wayward passion, devoid of prudence'.[o] But with this concubinage which would last and be sanctioned shortly afterwards by the birth of a son, he swiftly put an end to those sentimental strayings. If we note that son's age – about fifteen years[p] – when he was entered for baptism in the spring of 387 at Milan, he must have been born in either 371 or 372; which means that Augustine had met his mother barely a year, and more likely only a few months, after he arrived in Carthage. Patricius, his father, had just died and Monica, helped by the generosity of Romanianus, was from then on the only one who could subsidize him. The young man who, on arriving in the big city, had at first yearned to appear 'elegant and urbane'[q] now settled down with this unglamorous but stabilizing liaison.

It would be useless to search the *Confessions* or elsewhere for the name of the woman who, with tact and dignity, would remove herself from the scene fifteen years later. Why this silence about her name? She was probably of modest origins, from Carthage's lower classes; but even the humble have a name, the only one that the epitaphs of the time make known to us. There must be a quite different reason why we are still ignorant of hers. As far as we know, Augustine had no grievance against her; and, on a more positive note, he even seems to have had nothing but praise for the companion and mother. But we shall see that this carnal attachment, which had ended only shortly before his conversion, early in 386, had been its chief obstacle. To utter, to write the name of the one who had for so long shared his bed, was to hear again the inflection of her voice, breathe again the perfume of her body. It was to bring to life again, forever mingled, the old joys and wounds. The *damnatio nominis* – the enforced forgetfulness of her name – was the heavy lid placed on his casket of memories.[r]

Notes

a.   *Conf.*, X, 30.

b.   Apuleius, *Florides*, IV, 18, 85.

c.   Ausonius, *Ordo urbium nobilium*, 2–3: in a subtle balancing act, the poet puts the two cities almost on equal footing.

d.   *Expositio totis mundi et gentium*, 61, SC, vol. 124, p. 202.

e.   *Ep.* 7, 6.

f.   This image came to life again in a text dated 426 / 7 (*City of God*, XXII, 24, 5).

g.   *Conf.*, III, 1: *Veni Carthaginem et circumstrepebat me undique sartago flagitiosorum amorum. Nondum amabam et amare amabam et secretiore indigentia oderam me minus indigentem. Quaerebam quid amarem, amans amare* . . . As do most translators, I have not tried to render the play on words *Carthago/sartago* (the word usually meaning 'frying pan'), whether the pleasantry was Augustine's, or one common among the students.

h.   *Conf.*, III, 1.

i.   *Conf.*, III, 4.

j.   This is suggested in a sentence from *Sermon* 241, 5.

k.   See *City of God*, II, 26, 2; see also II, 4 and VII, 26.

l.   *Conf.*, III, 5. The 'fruits of death' come from Rom. 7.5, quoted from an old Latin version of the Apostle.

m.   *Sermon Dolbeau* 2 (*Mainz* 5), in F. Dolbeau, *Vingt-six Sermons au peuple d'Afrique*, Paris, Ét. aug., 1996, p. 330.

n.   *Sermon Dolbeau* 2, p. 330: *Impudicae cantiunculae.*

o.   *Conf.*, IV, 2.

p.   *Conf.*, IX, 14.

q.   *Conf.*, III, 1: *elegans et urbanus esse gestiebam.*

r.   This silence may also mean that when Augustine was writing his *Confessions*, Adeodatus' mother was still alive, probably tucked away incognito in some religious community. By respecting her anonymity, the *damnatio nominis* also protected that incognito.

CHAPTER V

From Cicero to Mani

A student's life at Carthage was not always peaceful, above all for the newcomers, who were prey to raggings, those rites of passage that are as old as all youngsters. Augustine, however, seems to have been spared the usual japes; he had enough personality to be able to impose some respect on the ringleaders – the *eversores*, as he calls them in an almost untranslatable word[a] – without taking part in their little games, which he sometimes laughed at while at the same time condemning them. And perhaps he already had some inkling that, as a teacher a few years later, he in his turn would have to put up with those bad manners, of which he would soon grow tired and whose excesses he would claim were the prime cause of his departure at that time for Rome.[b]

We would have every reason to suppose that Augustine was an earnest student, even without the testimony of one of his former fellow-students, Vincentius, bishop of Cartennae (Ténès, in Algeria), who in 407/8 reminded him that he had formerly known him when he was studying hard and leading a tranquil and sober life at Carthage.[c] It comes as no surprise when he himself tells us that he shone in his studies: he was the best in the rhetor's school.[d] As he says further, those studies led directly to the profession of lawyer, a speciality recognized as lucrative in Africa at least since Juvenal. They therefore implied the reading and commentating of that prince of Roman orators, Cicero, and particularly those speeches for the defence which had made him the greatest Latin specialist in the legal genre. But Cicero himself, in his own time, demanded a training in philosophy of the would-be orator.[e] That tradition of a minimum of philosophical culture in the baggage of the apprentice lawyer had not yet been lost, since Augustine states that by following the usual study programme he had come to the book 'of a certain Cicero, whose language is generally admired, though not so much his inspiration'.[f] This book, he adds, contains an encouragement to philosophy and is entitled the *Hortensius*.

The Hortensius

Cicero had named this work – a dialogue – after his main rival in eloquence in the Rome of that period. The book is lost, but we possess enough fragments of it (around one hundred, including fifteen in Augustine himself[1]) to recognize that it was what had been described since Aristotle as a 'protreptic', in other words a speech of 'exhortation', written with the aim of showing the importance of research and the love of wisdom in the way one conducted one's life. Augustine was nineteen when he read the *Hortensius*, and it left a deep impression on him. At the same age, Pliny the Younger, like all the young nobles of his era, was doing a stint as an officer in a legion quartered in Syria; he was to be found less often in the barracks than at Beirut, where he was following the lessons of a Greek philosopher. But nothing in those of his works that have come down to us gives any indication that this teaching had awakened his soul to ultimate goals, whereas for Augustine the discovery of Cicero's book happened at such a stage of his intellectual development that the lasting enthusiasm born of its reading immediately manifested itself, as if he had had a revelation, in a radical transformation of his fundamental plan for living. 'This book', he says, 'changed my feelings and my prayers, and entirely altered my purposes and desires.'[g] And the apprentice rhetorician adds that, for the first time, his attention was held not by the way in which things were said, but the things said themselves: *pectus, non linguam*.

True, Augustine continued his rhetorical studies for some years, before teaching them himself. However, a flame had been ignited in him and, though its brightness might sometimes fluctuate, it would never be extinguished. Right up to the calm days of the retreat at Cassiciacum, he would live torn between the desire to arrive at certainties and to make a career in the world. In the *Soliloquies*, written at the end of 386, he says that reading Cicero's book had been the start of his diminishing taste for wealth.[h] But he had to make a living and, since he was not yet spiritually in a condition to satisfy the highest intellectual demands, continue in the disappointing search for material riches. By his own admission, Augustine was still intent on doing so during his Manichaean years.[i] He still had the same aspirations at Milan, when a meeting in the street with a beggar who rejoiced in his poverty and found happiness in a glass of wine and a few coins, seemed to illustrate to him the emptiness of his own ambitions.[j] The ideal of life glimpsed at Carthage in 373 – a life completely directed by the love of wisdom – would recede before him like a mirage for some dozen years. But, recounting in Book VIII of the *Confessions* the last convulsive movements before his liberation, he would still return to the reading of the *Hortensius* and his nineteenth year as the starting-point for his quest.[k] So convinced was he of the excellence of Cicero's book as a 'protreptic', that he would place it in the hands of his two young students, Licentius, Romanianus' son, and Trygetius, as a 'propaedeutic' before the discussions at Cassiciacum.[l]

Worldly ambitions and the desire for social success were not the only obstacles placed in the way of Augustine's full and total adhesion to the project of an existence devoted to the pursuit of wisdom, which he seemed to find in Cicero. We must never forget that in his childhood he had received an initial religious immersion, a first 'preparation' that could not fail to colour in specific fashion the influences that would successively leave their mark on his soul and sensibilities. When he tells us that on reading the *Hortensius* the only thing that tempered his enthusiasm was not reading Christ's name in it, we must beware of seeing this as some sort of naivety. It is no chronological blunder or historical ignorance, nor is it, as one might suspect, an anachronism 'of memory', the bishop-author of the *Confessions* intervening in the memories of a young man and placing them, after the event, in a spiritual context which would not have been his at the time. The sentence that follows in the text properly establishes that need with an unmistakable tone of truth: 'This name (of Christ) my child's heart had imbibed with my mother's milk and kept it deep within; and without this name no book, be it ever so literary, so elegant, so truthful, could ever win me over entirely.'[m]

Thus, by way of a detour that was surprising but explicable in view of what had attracted him in the *Hortensius* – the elevation of thought turned to a philosophical salvation here below for want of salvation pure and simple – Cicero had led him back to the central figure of his childhood's religion. Augustine then resolved to apply himself to reading the Scriptures.[n] He probably knew no more of them at that time than the very incomplete amount he could have obtained from the liturgy of the services: the music of the words rather than a knowledge of the text. It was therefore his first serious contact with the Bible.[o] But while his reference to Christ gave the impression that he meant to refer to the Gospels, what he says about his first biblical experience seems to indicate that his initial encounter was with the Old Testament. It was a disappointment, for two reasons; the first is obvious, and he says so without mincing his words: 'This book seemed to me unworthy of comparison with the majesty of a Cicero.'[2] The Bible was read in those times in the old Latin versions, varying according to the provinces – the 'old Roman' differing from the 'old African' – but sharing the common feature that they had been written with no art, in a frequently clumsy and always rustic Latin. For a student trained in the art of speaking, shaped in the Ciceronian mould, it came as a shock. Had he been able to carry on regardless, had he by some unlikely chance been sensitive immediately to that poetry of words, so alien on first approach for a 'classicist', he would still have been put off by the biblical text, penetrating which the author of the *Confessions* – reliving that first failure in his mind's eye – vividly compares to entering a cavern: you must lower your head to go in, which the proud are unable to do; but then the eye becomes accustomed and the vault soars above you. Augustine had remained at the entrance; the little he had read of the 'historical books' had horrified him. We shall soon see him lend an indulgent ear to the Manichaeans, who derided the kings and prophets in the Bible. The Gospels, which he started on at that time with a critical and 'rationalist' approach, disappointed him no less. Some thirty years later, he would admit in a sermon that the discrepancies in the two genealogies of Christ in Matthew (1.1–16) and Luke (3.23–38) had disheartened him.[3] The man who sought a truth that would make sense of life, but was not yet ready humbly to undertake the internal toil demanded by the constraints of faith, was at the age of nineteen about to become easy prey for the followers of Mani.

Manichaeism

Of all the words ending in -ism, Manichaeism is probably the one that nowadays suffers the heaviest conceptual reduction. In our current usage, a Manichee is someone for whom good and evil exist, like day and night, water and fire; no transition, no blending. Perhaps at its origins Manichaeism had been given to such simplification; but if in the fourth century such a caricature of it could have been possible, it would be incomprehensible that Augustine should have allowed himself to be drawn into it, still more that he should have stayed with it for nine years, till he was nearing thirty.

When Augustine became a 'hearer' in the sect, Mani had been dead for exactly a century.[4] He had experienced a 'passion' in Susiana, in the heart of the Sassanid Persian kingdom, at that time a powerful empire stretching from Palmyra to India, from the Caspian Sea to the Indian Ocean, and frequently an even match for Rome. The emperor Valerian, taken prisoner in 260 by Shapur, had some knowledge of it. Under Shapur's reign, Mani had increased the number of his missionary journeys, travelling through the Empire in every direction, from Baluchistan in the east to the frontiers of Armenia in the north, and to Egypt in the south. At Alexandria, reached from the coasts of the Red Sea, there were many conversions in the late third century. It was probably from there that Manichaeism passed into Africa, perhaps imported by one of Mani's twelve apostles, Adimantus.[5] In 297, from Alexandria, the emperor Diocletian issued an edict to the proconsul of Africa strongly condemning the introduction into the Empire of this superstition from Persia, and sentencing the leaders of the sect to death and confiscation of their possessions.[6] In that period, the new religion had already penetrated Palestine and would reach Rome after the great persecution, in the time of Pope Miltiades (311–14), then pass into Gaul by way of Italy and from there into Spain. However, after the height of its diffusion in the fourth century, the force of the persecution to which it was subjected by both Church and State, soon led to its decline in the West. The members of the sect disappeared or melted into other sects, such as Priscillianism in Spain. At the end of the fifth century only a few isolated groups were left, notably in Vandal Africa.[7] In contrast, in the East it enjoyed a lasting survival, even after the Arab conquest, and still more in the Far East, where Manichaean communities persisted until the thirteenth century in Chinese Turkestan.

The diversity of sources relating to Manichaeism is connected with this geographic dispersal. There is no doctrinal corpus in Antiquity that is expressed in such a wide range of languages: Greek and Latin, of course, but also Coptic, Arabic, Syriac, Middle Iranian (Pahlevi), ancient Turkish and Chinese. Linguistically very varied, the texts are no less heterogeneous in their content, including direct sources (written by Mani himself, by his apostles or their successors) and indirect (chronicles, catalogues of heresies, polemical rebuttals, including those of Augustine). Moreover, the Manichaean 'Revelation' may have been altered, here and there, by local adaptations, due to the religious mindset peculiar to the regions in which it was preached; thus, in view of the importance assumed by the dramatic myth of the *Jesus patibilis* in the doctrine of which Augustine was a follower, one may suspect a 'Numidian' variation of Manichaeism.[8] For all these reasons, it is difficult to give a summary description of the chief features of the Manichaean 'Revelation'. I shall try, however, in order to assess what Augustine's commitment may have been in broad outline, while not ignoring the fact that we shall never know just how far he went in his initiation and whether he took an overall view of the doctrine – queries to which his polemical writings do not give a full answer.

Mani appeared as the successor to the great religious systems already revealed. But, unlike Zoroaster in Persia, Buddha in India and Jesus in Palestine, who had written nothing themselves and had left it to their disciples to codify a teaching which had not been fixed from the outset and could therefore be subject to deviations, Mani had passed on his 'Revelation' in his own hand and in his lifetime had sanctified the works, originally composed in Syriac, which contained it. These books were subsequently retranslated identically in several languages, and carefully copied on materials that in their beauty often yielded nothing to the most sumptuous manuscripts of our medieval Bibles. Augustine had handled one of those vellum *codices*, delicately bound and illuminated, treasures for antiquaries, he said, which he later suggested ironically that his erstwhile co-religionists should eat boiled, if they were not afraid of the black of the ink and the animal hide of which they were made!P Only fragments remain of Mani's principal works, the *Living Gospel*, the *Treasure of Life*, the *Pragmateia* (or *Treatise*), the *Book of Mysteries*, the *Book of Giants*. We must add – though here we enter the work of his epigones – a text such as the *Letter of Foundation* (*Epistula fundamenti*, largely reproduced in a refutation by Augustine) and chiefly the collections found in Egypt and the Far East: the *Kephalaia* (or 'Chapters'), brought to light at Fayoum,[9] as well as the *Book of Prayers and Psalms*,[10] invaluable for a knowledge of the Manichaean liturgy, and the documents unearthed in Central Asia, notably the oasis of Tourfan, as well as in China (the 'Chinese Compendium', known as the 'Chavannes–Pelliot Treatise', from the name of its finders).[11]

As it may be reconstructed at least on those bases, Manichaeism is a 'gnosis', knowledge to which access is gained by way of the revelation contained in a sacred discourse. A 'gnosis', or the gradually acquired knowledge by the initiate that brings him salvation by revealing his origins to him and making him aware of his own being, his present condition in the existing world and the means of freeing himself from it. This sacred discourse had taken the form of a myth whose aim was to overlay and replace all pre-existing religious myths, but it was an artificial myth, a very complex cosmogony, born in Mani's thinking of the considered experience of the gnostic which he himself was, experiencing his situation as a human creature as bad, because it was a temporary and abnormal blend of conflicting substances: Spirit and Matter, Good and Evil, Light and Darkness. The result of a fall, this mixture presupposed a primordial state where the two heterogeneous substances were separate. Salvation consisted in a return to that earlier state of radical separation. The myth elaborated on the basis of this 'intuition' thus comprised three phases: a time past, a time present – lived by man in his 'mingled' situation – and a future time, when the original separation would be re-established. These were the famous 'Three Times' (*initium, medium, finis*), for which Mani's followers glorified their Master because he had been able to distinguish between them. In particular, Felix, an 'elect' whom Augustine would eventually confound in 404, but who stoutly maintained that Mani was truly the Paraclete announced by Christ – in John 16.13 – because he had been the only one to instance the three times.q

In the beginning, therefore, the Light and the Darkness, or, if preferred, the kingdom of God (Good) and the kingdom of Evil, were separate. The kingdom of God stretched northwards: it was a land of light, peace and purity, that manifested itself in five hypostases (or 'dwellings'): Intelligence, Reason, Thought, Reflection and Will. Below, confined in the south, was the kingdom of Evil, the realm of anarchy, disorder and brute force, symmetrically formed by five 'worlds': Smoke, devouring Fire, destructive Wind, murky Water and Darkness. But the breaking of that separation – the beginning of the 'middle time' – was due to the frenzy of the Prince of Darkness, who tried to invade the kingdom of Light. God decided to oppose him by himself, by means of his own soul, which he 'evoked' through the intermediary of the 'Mother of Life': this combatant was to be 'primordial Man' (the god Ohrmizd in the Iranian versions), who would set out for battle together with his five 'sons', fire, air, water, light and ether, which were the constituent elements of his soul. On the point of succumbing to the attack, precipitated into the infernal abyss, primordial Man offered himself up, with his five sons, to the demons of Darkness: it was a voluntary sacrifice, but also a stratagem by which the divine substance became henceforward blended with the obscure substance of Matter, satisfying the rapacious Darkness for the time being, but preparing the way for future redemption.

This redemption was to be obtained at the end of a long procedure. To save primordial Man, God proceeded to a second emanation of himself: he 'evoked', one after the other, the Friend of Light, the Great Architect and the living Spirit. The latter, accompanied by his five sons, went to the frontier of the kingdom of Darkness and, by extending his right hand, managed to hoist primordial Man out of the blackness; but he had left behind him his soul – the five sons mentioned earlier. Again it would be the living Spirit who would undertake to save it, by arranging the world, after the fashion of the Greek Demiurge, distinguishing three parts in the luminous substance mingled with Matter: the one that is safe from all contact forms the two great lights, the Sun and the Moon; the part that is only slightly affected makes up the stars; there remains the Earth, whose salvation is yet to be accomplished. That would be the task of a new 'evocation', in the person of a third 'emanation' or 'envoy'[12] (sometimes identified with the god Mithras), whose twelve daughters match the signs of the zodiac. His purpose is to liberate Light buried in Darkness, to effect the reassembly of the living Soul by bringing back its scattered limbs to their original source. To do this, he puts in operation a celestial, or rather cosmic, mechanism, whose cogwheels are the three spheres of winds, fire and water. The Moon is the chief agent of this vast rescue: the first fortnight of the month, through the 'column of splendour' (the Milky Way), the particles of Light (souls) ascend to the Moon and swell it until it becomes the full Moon; then it transfers this liberated light to the Sun which, in turn, sends it on its way to its original home. All this celestial traffic must have intrigued Augustine who, in his twenties, took an interest in the sky, and we shall see that the Manichaeans would fall out with him on this subject.

In addition to this mechanism, the Third Messenger made use of a dynamic similar to human urges, in the form of an act of seduction. He appeared in the splendour of his beauty to the Archontes (or demons) of Evil, who were both male and female, provoking their desire and causing them to spread, with their seed, part of the light they had imprisoned. But their sin also spread; from the seed scattered on the moist earth was born a sea monster which Adamas-Light pierced with his spear; from that which fell on dry earth plants were born. As for the female Archontes, they gave birth to 'abortions' which, hurtled on to the land, devoured the plants' buds and thus assimilated some of the light; then, to perpetuate their demonic issue, they interbred, giving birth to animals. The portion of light gathered on the Earth, which had yet to be saved, was thus dispersed among the animal and vegetable kingdom. Even more grave, so as to imprison indefinitely the portion of light he still held, the Prince of Darkness conceived the idea of creating two beings who would forever be enslaved to his plan by sexual desire. After devouring all the diabolical offspring (the 'abortions' and their issue), two huge demons copulated, and from their coupling Adam and Eve were born. Deep in brutish ignorance because of such origins, Adam was rescued by a saviour who awakened him to self-awareness. But he succumbed to the temptations of the flesh and engendered descendants marked by the demonic stigma of lust, who continue to couple and procreate, thus prolonging the imprisonment of luminous souls in dark corporeal matter. That situation would come to an end only with the advent of the myth's third 'time', signalled at first by a period of apocalyptic disasters, then by a last judgement and a general conflagration that would last 1468 years; at the end of this *ekpurosis*, the last particles of Light which would then be saved would reascend to the sky, the visible world would be annihilated, while Matter would be buried forever in a kind of vast pit. Then only would the initial separation of Light and Darkness be re-established.

Thus set out in broad outlines, at the risk of over-simplification and reduction, the doctrine reveals its essence, a fundamental dualism, coherent in both its cosmogony and its anthropology: like the world, man is a composite, or rather a mixture of light and darkness, good and evil. And it was Manichaean belief that this dualism was experienced by man even in the geography of his body, his upper part holding the good – as light, at the beginning of the world, lay in the north – while evil resided in his lower part, as darkness reigned originally in the south. And just as the dynamic set to work at the cosmic level was directed to the full and complete liberation of light, so all man's efforts – at least if he wanted to ensure his personal salvation without waiting for the final *ekpurosis* – lay in diminishing the portion of darkness within himself, by means of asceticism and continence, at the same time trying to increase his share of light, above all taking care not to harm the light in this world which, though omnipresent, was scattered, imprisoned in matter and surrounded by darkness.

So the followers of Mani were hemmed in by codes of conduct that were in theory very restrictive. They covered every aspect, but were grouped more precisely under three headings, matching three ways of acting, themselves symbolized by three organs or parts of the body: the mouth, the hand and the 'bosom', which were 'sealed' by three 'seals' (*signacula*), and the Manichee was obliged to observe these with scrupulous respect. The 'seal of the mouth' obviously proscribed any word that might attack the divine light, but above all strictly defined a whole series of food taboos. Meat was prohibited, being looked upon as a pile of filth from which every soul must be free; and wine, too, because the fermentation and maturing had caused any divine substance to disappear from the juice of the grape. And in Christian churches, crypto-Manichees could be recognized by the fact that at the eucharist they accepted the host but refused the chalice. In this vegetarian diet certain foods were at a premium, such as melons, figs, cucumbers, olives and the oil they produced. But – and here we come to the domain covered by the 'seal of the hand' – the perfect Manichee was not allowed to gather these 'fruits of light' for himself, or to grow them or prepare any food whatsoever; these were sins given over to the aspirants or 'catechumens', even if they were afterwards absolved! And for the strictly obedient Manichee the same 'seal of the hand' proscribed the exercise of any professional activity, the enjoyment of any material possessions, and banned him from seeking any social position. Lastly, the 'seal of the bosom' embraced the area of sexuality; it stipulated continence, absolutely banned procreation, since to procreate meant perpetuating the imprisonment of luminous souls in the darkness of the body.

It is already clear that such demanding rules implied a strict hierarchization of

Manichaean society, with a variety of offices, and that they could be observed only by a minority. Under the clergy – bishops and priests – who specifically formed the Church of the sect, this minority was composed of 'elect' or 'perfect', who lived in scrupulous observance of the three 'seals'; at least, in theory, for once Augustine had been freed from their grasp, he did not spare them his sarcasm and recounts how, one day when he was with a few friends in one of Carthage's most frequented squares, he had seen and heard three of these 'elect' 'wolf-whistling' vulgarly after women going past.[r]

Below these 'elect', in some cases with aspirations to swell their number, the 'hearers' formed an indispensable rank and file, obliged to carry out the food-producing tasks forbidden to the 'elect'. They simply had to observe a kind of 'decalogue', a set of fundamental precepts, some of which in any case had from time immemorial been part of the common basis of practical social morals: do not commit murder or adultery, do not lie, shun avarice and duplicity; but also do not fall into idolatry or magic, and practise piety as understood by the Manichaean Church. Observance of these minimal rules was not enough to secure their personal salvation *hic et nunc*, but left them with the hope of being reborn one day in the body of an 'elect'. Meanwhile, they were free to devote themselves to the activities of the profane world, to till the soil, trade, build, have jobs and possess goods. The most restrictive taboos were not their affair: they could eat meat, drink wine, marry or live with a concubine and even have children. From 373 Augustine was one of these 'hearers'; he was getting on for nineteen.

Notes

a.   *Conf.*, III, 6: this is most often translated as 'rowdies'; one could risk 'raggers', but the Latin word implies more brutality.
b.   See *Conf.*, V, 14.
c.   *Ep.* 93, 51 (reproducing the beginning of the letter received from Vincentius).
d.   *Conf.*, III, 6: *Et maior iam eram in schola rhetoris.*
e.   *De oratore*, I, 56–7; 68–9; 76–83; 143; *Orator*, 11–18, 113–19.
f.   *Conf.*, III, 7.
g.   *Conf.*, III, 7.
h.   *Sol.*, I, 17.
i.   *De util. cred.*, 3: 'the beauty of a woman, the luxury of wealth, the vanity of honours'.
j.   *Conf.*, VI, 9.
k.   *Conf.*, VIII, 17; see also *De beata vita*, I, 4.
l.   *Contra Acad.*, I, 4.
m.   *Conf.*, III, 8.
n.   *Conf.*, III, 9.
o.   The bishop would say regretfully to his flock later that because he had not committed those books to his memory when he was young, he could not trust it to comment on them in his sermon: *Sermon Dolbeau 23 (Mainz 59)*, 19, in F. Dolbeau, *Vingt-six Sermons au peuple d'Afrique*, p. 610.
p.   *Contra Faustum*, XIII, 6 and 18.
q.   *Contra Felicem*, I, 2 and 9. On these three times, see the translation of the 'Pelliot Fragment' in H.-C. Puech, *Le Manichéisme son fondateur et sa doctrine*, Paris, Publications de musée Guimet, 1949, pp. 158–9.
r.   *De moribus ecclesiae catholicae et manichaeorum*, II, 68: the verb used, *adhinnire*, suggests the whinnying of a stallion at a passing mare!

CHAPTER VI

A Manichaean rhetor between Thagaste and Carthage

One does not join a sect for the facility it affords for keeping a concubine, especially when one's name is Augustine. He himself explained his reasons for following Manichaeism, and in several texts, but some of these – in the *Confessions* – fail to give us 'objective' information, because they are too highly coloured by the continuing vexation he felt at having been ensnared in a trap which had held him prisoner for too long, and others are obscured by metaphysical or allusive forms of expression that have not made the exegetists' task any easier.

One instance is the frequently examined page of the *De beata vita*, in which, just after his conversion in the autumn of 386, Augustine wrote:

> In my case, at the age of nineteen, after becoming acquainted at the rhetor's school with Cicero's book the *Hortensius*, I was inflamed with such a love of philosophy that I contemplated devoting myself to it without delay. But, on the one hand there was no lack of fog to lead me astray from the path, and on the other, I confess, I had my eyes fixed for a long while on the stars that plunged into the ocean, by which I was led into error. In fact, on the one hand childish religious fear (*superstitio quaedam puerilis*) diverted me even from planning my research and, on the other, when I had grown bolder (*factus erectior*), and driven away the mists, convincing myself that it was better to give credence to those who propose rather than impose (*docentibus potius quam iubentibus*), I came across men who held that the light we see with our eyes is a worthy object of worship equal to what is supremely divine.[1]

In these lines that sum up the first years of Augustine's intellectual journey – and make up part of what it has been proposed to call his 'first confessions'[2] – three words have tested the perceptions of commentators. There is general agreement, however, in interpreting the *superstitio quaedam puerilis* enveloping the young Augustine like a fog as the reverent awe of a Christian catechumen such as himself, hindered from taking the path of rational investigation by a faith that was all the more restrictive because it was poorly illuminated. And we should be less hesitant to understand it in this way because several years later, having become a priest, in a little treatise dedicated to his friend Honoratus who had remained a Manichaean, Augustine reminded him that at least one – if not the chief – of the reasons why he had joined the sect had been the Manichaeans' cleverness in showing him that he had been impeded in his search for the truth by this *superstitio*,[a] which had sidetracked him from his quest. After the revelation brought about by his reading of the *Hortensius*, then the disappointment caused by an unprepared immersion in the Bible, the young man now questioned an authority which the Manichaeans were able to present to him as paralysing.[3] It was all the easier for him to side with these men who boasted that they could bring their hearers to God through reason, without imposing a belief, because in their teaching he found the name of Christ, sadly missing in Cicero. On the day of his acceptance into the sect, his 'illumination' as the Manichaeans called it, the basic doctrinal text was read to him, the 'Foundation Epistle', which began with these words: 'Mani, apostle of Jesus Christ by the providence of God the Father.'[b]

The snare of Manichaean Christology

And indeed, much use was made of Christ's name in the sect. Manichaean 'Christology' combined three images of Jesus, two of which were mythical and only the third apparently having a historical dimension. The first was that of Jesus the Splendour, a transcendent and cosmic being, the initiator of the last stage of the reconquest of Light. A second image of Jesus was that of the *Iesus patibilis* nailed to the immense 'cross of Light', that was the world, of which he was the soul 'hanging from every piece of wood';[c] he was the one, diffused throughout the whole of nature, that one must be careful not to harm – this involved respect for the 'seal of the hand'. Superimposed on these two figures was the Jesus of the Gospels, but his real historicity was denied in the Manichaean definition: he was the son of God, with no earthly parentage, which did not bother the young Augustine, whom we have seen vexed by the differing genealogies of Christ! He had certainly come into this world, in the land of the Jews, but without a true body, and without having truly suffered on the cross, unless in mystical fashion.

These three figures of Christ seemed to be superimposed in the hymns that were sung in Manichaean liturgical assemblies, as they are restored to us by the texts discovered at Medinet Madi in Egypt, in which the name of Christ the Saviour was repeated from psalm to psalm:

> Come, my Saviour Jesus, do not abandon me. I have loved thee, I have given thee my soul. (Ps. 244)

and again:

> Let us worship the Spirit of the Paraclete. Let us bless our Lord Jesus, who has sent us the Spirit of Truth. He has come and delivered us from the strayings of the world. He has held a mirror before us; we have looked into it and seen the universe. When the Holy Spirit came, he revealed to us the path of Truth and taught us that there are two Natures, of Light and of Darkness, which were separate from each other in the beginning.[4] (Ps. 223)

Augustine would certainly have chanted those and other similar hymns with the sect's faithful followers. In the state of philosophical and religious un-preparedness of his nineteenth year – but with a great need for a belief – he accepted this docetic image of a transcendent Christ, as he would recognize it later:

Our Saviour himself, your only-begotten Son, I pictured as having emanated from the substance of your body of light, for our salvation; thus I could believe nothing about him except what my vain imagination suggested to me. I thought that a nature such as his could not have been born of the Virgin Mary without being mingled with the flesh; and I could not see him mingled with it without being sullied. I was therefore afraid to think of him as born of the flesh, so as not to be compelled to believe him tainted by the flesh.[d]

Lacking an adequate intellectual framework – and training in the Scriptures – the semi-clever young man, already concerned about his salvation, had let himself fall into the trap of those whose approaches he would compare to the guile of bird-catchers, 'who set their bird-lime snares at the edge of a pond to trap thirsty birds'.[e] And the lime with which these traps were smeared was a 'mishmash of words, composed of the name of God, of our Lord Jesus Christ and of the Paraclete, our comforter, the Holy Spirit.'[f] It needed only to season that mishmash with a few Pauline references to obtain the trinitarian 'credo' of Faustus of Milevis, which was also Augustine's for a while:

Of God the omnipotent Father, of Christ his Son and the Holy Spirit, we worship the one and identical divinity under this triple name. But we believe that the Father dwells in that supreme and original light which Paul calls 'inaccessible' (1 Tim. 6.16), whereas the Son lives in this light here, which stems from it and is visible; and because the Son is a dual being, as Paul acknowledges when he says that Christ is the Power of God and the Wisdom of God (1 Cor. 1.24), we believe that his power dwells in the sun and his wisdom in the moon. As for the Holy Spirit, who is the third majesty, we confess that all the air is his region and receptacle; and it is by his power and spiritual effusion that the earth conceived and engendered the suffering Christ (*Iesum patibilem*), who is the life and salvation of men, and hangs from every piece of wood . . . This is our belief.[g]

Twenty years later, reflecting on this 'hotchpotch of syllables', the author of the *Confessions* found it held the bitter taste of disappointment.

He had, however, before his twentieth birthday another reason for siding with those 'men who are delirious with pride, carnally minded and excessively garrulous'.[h] To the problem of evil, notably the evil within us, Manichaeism provided answers that were physically ascetic but morally comfortable.[5] His reading of the *Hortensius* had added its philosophical warnings against the pleasures of the flesh to those that Augustine may have retained from his childhood's religion. But the young man, subject to fleshly appetites and still prompted by worldly ambitions, kept his guilty conscience. Reliving the prodromes of his true liberation, in 386, and mentally reviewing those twelve years of internal struggle, the author of the *Confessions* would find a nice expression to evoke the reprieve which in his youth he had conceded to himself rather than asked for: 'Give me chastity, give me continence, but not just yet!'[i] Just a moment more, my God! In the nick of time, Manichaean dualism provided him – and lightly, too, for the 'hearer' was spared the pallors and mortifications of the 'elect' – with an indisputable moral comfort, exonerating him from sin and numbing his feelings of guilt, if not completely freeing him. He would admit that ten years later, when he was still in touch with 'elect' of the sect in Rome, he was still taking advantage of that facility. 'It seemed to me', he says, 'that it is not we who sin, but I know not what strange nature that sins within us . . . , and I was happy to excuse myself by accusing some unknown "other" who was within me but not myself'.[j]

Augustine varies on how much he was committed to Manichaeism; sometimes we see him playing down its significance. True, in the eyes of the Christian, the bishop, it had been a far from brilliant period; but we may also acknowledge that these varying assessments correspond to real variations, intermittences or fluctuations. Augustine did not keep a 'Manichaean diary'; had he done so we might have noted many doubts and lukewarm periods over the ten short years before his final break with it. Once the crisis was over, in 386, he said, describing a frequently 'wait and see' attitude, that 'while not approving, he had believed that under those veils the Manichaeans were concealing something of moment from him that they would later reveal to him'.[k] There are doubtless several ways of interpreting those lines; they may be seen as a way of 'putting himself in the clear' after the event – which is hardly Augustine's style; it is probably truer to recognize it as the desire to judge on the actual evidence, and the perhaps naive hope which the young 'hearer' may have held at that time of making some progress in this 'gnosis'.[6] Elsewhere he would describe himself as the travelling companion of those 'men who preferred the brightness of a fine ear of wheat to the life of the soul'; he followed them for a long time, he says, but with caution, and 'dragging his feet'.[l] Around the same period, addressing his friend Honoratus, he would give him what seems a perfectly plausible reason for the reserve he maintained in his relations with the Manichaeans, one that probably increased with the passing years. He asks:

> What prevented me from joining them completely; why did I remain in the ranks of the 'hearers' and did not abandon the hopes and affairs of this world, unless it was because I realized that they were more loquacious and eloquent in refuting others than strong and certain in demonstrating their doctrine?[m]

Which was a way of saying that a once glimpsed hope of obtaining a clearer view of the Manichaean 'revelation' had ultimately been disappointed.

One thing is sure, however: at nineteen, a certain impulse carried Augustine towards the Manichaeans: the kind one gets at an age when one is off one's guard – *incauta aetate* – and particularly receptive to friendship. He himself would recognize that he had been seduced by a sort of kindness he had felt among the 'elect' of the sect; and still more had he yielded to his youthful hotheadedness, to the intoxication – the word is not too strong – he felt when going from success to success in his arguments with 'ignorant Christians'.[n] His proselytism worked wonders, to the great joy of his new friends, who had been quick to spot the advantage to be gained from this brilliant recruit, an already formidable debater, equipped with all the armoury of classical rhetoric. It was then, and in this context, at the age of around twenty, that Augustine developed a liking for controversy, and the passion for refuting and convincing was born that would permanently impel this great intellectual. Perhaps it was his one weakness, too, because only a prodigious capacity for work would ensure that this ardour did not prevent him from finishing long-term and exacting works such as the *De Trinitate* or the *City of God*. There is no doubt that numerous Christian victims of the young proselyte remained unknown; but he also carried with him his dearest companions: Honoratus, already mentioned; the anonymous friend he was soon to lose at Thagaste; Romanianus, his protector and, last but not least, Alypius, when the latter became his student at Carthage around 380.

A teacher at Thagaste

These names bring us back to Thagaste, where Augustine returned in the year following his encounter with the Manichaeans. He was now twenty, and had reached the final stage of his studies in rhetoric. Until then, like the child Adeodatus and his mother, he had lived on allowances from his mother, supplemented by the generosity of Romanianus, and it was time he started earning his living. Since he had renounced a career as a lawyer, the only profession open to him was teaching. In his small natal town there was naturally no question of teaching rhetoric, so he taught grammar; and we may suspect that Romanianus was the benefactor, like Pliny the Younger, when early in the second century, in his small hometown of Comum, he had borne the major part of the expense of creating a chair of *grammaticus,* to save his fellow-citizens having to send their children to Milan, with all the financial drain that involved.[o] It may be recalled that, for want of this type of education on the spot, the young Augustine had had to spend three years at Madauros.

It was a difficult reunion for both mother and son. Whereas, several years earlier, Monica had done her utmost to ward off the risk of a premature marriage, she now found her son committed to a liaison with a woman of inferior status, and the father of an illegitimate son. And her dreams, which she had shared with Patricius during his lifetime, of seeing her Augustine as a prince of the forum had evaporated. It was a schoolmaster who returned to the town. She probably already knew all this, but his recent adhesion to Manichaeism was the last straw. She refused to have the heretic under her roof or at her table.[p] Augustine had to accept Romanianus' hospitality for a while.[q] He certainly did not lose by it: what we know through him of the opulence of Thagaste's 'patron' enables us to guess that his 'town house', in size and quality, must have been the equal of the beautiful Romano-African residences of that time, at least the equivalent of the 'house of Bacchus' at Djemila, with vast and sumptuous mosaic-floored reception rooms.[7]

However, Monica soon regained better feelings about her Augustine. Above all, the anguish caused by what she considered his spiritual death was lessened a little following a dream in which she had seen herself standing on a wooden rule, in the presence of a radiant young man who asked her the cause of her distress; and on her reply that the cause was her son's perdition, the young man had told her to look carefully beside her and see that where she was standing, there also stood her son; and she had seen him standing on the same rule. Recording the episode in his *Confessions,* Augustine adds that when analysing the dream with his mother, with all the conviction of his youthful certainties, he had tried to make her interpret this dream as an invitation to *her* not to despair of becoming what *he* was. But Monica had reproved him without the slightest hesitation: what the apparition – obviously divine – had said to her was that where *she* was, there *he* was also (*ubi tu, ibi et ille*). It was Augustine's turn to be impressed, if not shaken, by his mother's certainties.[r]

Shortly afterwards, Monica received another solace which contributed not a little to calm her anxieties and at the same time improve her relations with her son. She had appealed to a neighbouring bishop, whom she had implored to have a talk with Augustine in order to disprove his beliefs and bring him back on to the right road. But this bishop had himself been a Manichaean in his youth; because he had trodden that path, he knew it would be a waste of time to try to take on one of the sect's neophytes, one who in addition was puffed up with pride at having already led several others into error. And he made Monica promise to continue praying for her son, assuring her that he would eventually, through reading, discover for himself the falsity of the doctrine with which he was for the time being infatuated. And when she persisted, he rather impatiently dismissed her, leaving her as a viaticum this consolatory oracle: It was impossible, he said, that the son of tears such as hers should perish![s]

Augustine had reintegrated the family home, with his companion and the little Adeodatus, then aged barely three, whose too recent existence earned him the same relegation to the background as his mother in the brief chronicle[8] of that Numidian year. In the pages of the *Confessions* referring to it, Thagaste scarcely makes an appearance. The township offered no future to an ambitious young man, but life probably drifted on fairly pleasantly, warmed especially by friendships. In the company of Romanianus, his son Licentius – still very young, it is true – Alypius and others who remain anonymous, like the friend whose untimely disappearance we shall soon see, all linked at that time by a common attachment to Manichaeism, Augustine enjoyed the pleasures which he details so well in a page relating, if not to Thagaste, at least to those years:

> Chatting and laughing together, doing one another little kindnesses, reading pleasant books together, jesting and being serious; disagreeing sometimes but without ill-humour – as one may disagree with oneself – and using those rare differences to season our many agreements; learning and teaching, in turn, longing for those who were absent, and rejoicing when welcoming those who joined us; and thanks to those expressions emanating from the hearts of people who love one another, shown on their faces, in their voices, in their eyes and a thousand charming gestures, our souls were as though fused together and from being many we became but one.[t]

True, the man who wrote this page in 397/8 fleshed it out with memories of other happy experiences of community life: the memorable 'retreat' at Cassiciacum in the autumn of 386, the Christian *otium* of the return to Thagaste in late 388, to say nothing of the cenobitic life of the bishop. But we may already credit the young Augustine with the feelings which inspire these lines, and which are at the heart of his affective personality: a profound fondness for sharing the particulars of individual existence, that goes far beyond the ordinary interchanges of social life and concerns others in their totality, physical, intellectual, moral and spiritual. And this unrestricted sharing, this amicable agreement among people is complete only when it is accompanied by a full consensus on 'all things both divine and human', according to the fine Ciceronian definition of friendship, which Augustine had adopted as his own.[9]

The lost friend

The thunderbolt of unhappiness strikes us where we are most vulnerable. Augustine was stricken in the midst of his friendships at the end of the year spent at Thagaste. There he had rediscovered a childhood friend, schoolfellow and playmate, and now that they were both twenty the secret alchemy of friendship had changed that former comradeship into a deep communion; doubtless because 'divine matters', as Cicero said, had a hand in it. A Christian, but insecure in his faith, the young man had fallen victim to the proselytism of his former schoolmate. From then on they were very closely united in Manichaeism: 'My soul', says Augustine, 'could not do without him.'[u] Some months later this friendship – 'sweeter to me than all other sweetness in my life until then' – was shattered by death.

Augustine grieved all the more because at the last moment the 'divine matters' had parted the two friends. Laid low by fever, soon unconscious, the sick friend was baptized unbeknown to him, in the bosom of his Catholic family. Augustine was not upset by this baptism *in articulo mortis*, convinced as he was that his friend's soul would retain the imprint of what *he* had taught him rather than that of a sacrament administered to an insensible body. When there was some improvement, Augustine tried to joke with his sick friend about the baptism he had received while unconscious. To his great surprise, the latter, who now knew himself to be baptized, indicated that Augustine should avoid such talk if he wanted to preserve their friendship. A few days later a relapse carried him off.

Augustine was appalled. He had lost his friend twice over, in body and soul. The analysis of his dismay that he gives in the *Confessions*[v] is not only remarkable because it is without any other instance in the literature of Antiquity. Never subsequently have better words been found to describe the agonizing emptiness where the heart had been full of presence, the void in the soul where it had overflowed with abundance, which leads so many people to depression and death. 'I had become a huge puzzle to myself', he says. The loss of his friend had left him a stranger to himself, as if deprived of his innermost being. Augustine admits that at the time he contemplated suicide. In his *Confessions* (IV, 9) he would say that he vainly questioned his soul, and if he said 'Hope in God!' it quite rightly disobeyed him, 'because the beloved man it had lost was so much better and truer than the phantasm in which he had ordered it to hope': the material and non-transcendent god in which he believed at that time was no help to him at all. And although he overcame the ordeal, it had not been for the pointless rhetorical reason he gives, which in the evening of his life made the old bishop shudder when he reread the text for his *Retractations*.[w] But he had developed a horror of Thagaste. Only to Romanianus did he reveal his desire to get away from the place that had now become odious to him, knowing that he could overcome the reluctance of a benefactor whose main concern was the wellbeing of his town, which Augustine's departure would deprive of a very uncommon teacher.[x] Once more provided with allowances from his protector, he left again for Carthage. He was then aged twenty-two.

Notes

a.   See *De utilitate credendi*, 2, and the fine analysis by A. Solignac in *BA*, 13, p. 126, n. 1.

b.   *Contra epist. fund.*, V, 6.

c.   *Contra Faustum*, XX, 2.

d.   *Conf.*, V, 20.

e.   See *De utilitate credendi*, 2.

f.   *Conf.*, III, 10.

g.   See *Contra Faustum*, XX, 2.

h.   *Conf.*, III, 10.

i.   *Conf.*, VIII, 17.

j.   *Conf.*, V, 18.

k.   *De beata vita*, I, 4.

l.   This is the sense of the adverb *pedetentim*: cf. *De duabus animabus*, IX, 11, text probably written in 391.

m.   *De utilitate credendi*, 2.

n.   *De duabus animabus*, IX, 11.

o.   See Pliny, *Ep.* IV, 13, 3–6 (letter addressed to Tacitus).

p.   *Conf.*, III, 19.

q.   *Contra Acad.*, II, 3.

r.   *Conf.*, III, 20.

s.   *Conf.*, III, 21.

t.   *Conf.*, IV, 13.

u.   *Conf.*, IV, 7.

v.   *Conf.*, IV, 9–11.

w.   *Conf.*, IV, 11: 'And perhaps I feared to die only lest he should die wholly whom I had so greatly loved!' He comments thus on this sentence in the *Retractations* (II, 6, 2): 'This seems more a worthless declamation than a serious confession, although such foolishness is in some sort tempered by the addition of the word "perhaps".'

x.   *Contra Acad.*, II, 3.

CHAPTER VII

First achievements

What had happened to Apuleius two centuries earlier happened to Augustine, but with shorter training. He returned to the capital, where he had been a student, to become a teacher. Describing the post he occupied for ten years, first at Carthage, then at Rome and Milan, the author of the *Confessions* is not short of pejorative expressions: 'During those years I taught rhetoric, peddling the verbosity that enables you to conquer, myself conquered by my passions.'[a] Let there be no mistake, however; not just anyone could teach rhetoric in the African capital. Augustine had been appointed to a municipal chair, therefore within the structure of higher public education.[b] We know from Libanius, who in the same period and in a comparable city – Antioch – was in this situation, that it was the curiae (municipal councils) who were in charge of recruiting teachers. They appointed them by decree,[1] and similarly by decree could terminate their contracts. They also set the level of pay; in Antioch, Libanius complained of the mediocrity of his salary. Augustine, however, remained discreet on this point; true, he intimates that in Rome, where he did a quick course some years later, his salary was higher – though it was a private post – but what made him determined to leave his position in Carthage was the unbridled rowdiness, the permanent indiscipline of the student population. Was he involved personally, and was that the price of success, or quite simply the fact that these were 'public courses'? Students would force their way into classes where they had no business to be, he complained.[c] Such irruptions were made all the easier because teaching was carried out in buildings that were themselves public; in Libanius' case, it was the very hall in which the meetings of the curia of Antioch took place. As for Augustine, an incident in which Alypius was the unfortunate protagonist, and to which I shall return, leads one to think that he was lecturing in premises near the forum.

Our academics, who keep a jealous watch on the recruitment of their colleagues, accompanied by many superfluous committees and hearings, will be anxiously wondering about the methods of choice in those days. Competition to apply for these posts, the possible stepping-stones to other more prestigious careers, was sometimes very keen. There was no lack of intrigues, cabals and various other forms of intervention. Augustine's total silence on the circumstances of his own appointment prevents any guesswork, save perhaps the supposition that, here again, the influence of his friend Romanianus may have been a determining factor. For that influence went beyond the regional framework of Thagaste and the surrounding Numidia; we have good reason to think that he then enjoyed titles which made him a notable of the province of Africa, if not, by exceptional advancement, even a member of the senatorial aristocracy.[d]

We shall see that to obtain the post in Milan Augustine had to submit an essay to Symmachus, which the latter liked, recommending its author to the people of

Milan. But at Carthage, the brilliant young man was already known outside the narrow circle of his fellow-students and teachers. At the age of twenty, when still a student, he had achieved a triumph: among other books, notably manuals of liberal arts,[e] which he read in addition to the tuition he received, he had unearthed on the shelves of the library in Carthage a copy of Aristotle's *Categories*. His rhetoric teacher, and some other learned men in his circle, who could talk of nothing else, had awakened his curiosity.[2] He had read the work without any help, probably in the Latin translation by Marius Victorinus.[3] As we might expect, the author of the *Confessions* would reproach the student, at that time in the thrall of Manichaean anthromorphism, for having applied the Aristotelian categories to God. There remained his intellectual prowess, very real in a young man who had had little preparation for logical conceptualization, and his extraordinary thirst for learning – 'the art of speaking and debating, geometry, music and arithmetic'[f] – and also the swiftness to understand and penetrating judgement of which he was perfectly aware, and which made him an unequalled young intellectual in the Carthage of that time. Such mental superiority was necessary for a teacher who was barely four or five years older than his listeners. The best among them sensed an inspiration in him which went beyond that of a mere purveyor of words, and that if they would but make the effort he was capable of pushing them beyond their own limits.[4]

Alypius

It is a pity, but we lack the material to write a book on Augustine's students, as it was possible to do about those of Libanius.[5] The reason is clear. Whereas Libanius had taught for nearly half a century, about forty years of which were spent in Antioch, with great dedication as a teacher for students who sometimes remained with him for several years and became his friends, Augustine was rhetor at Carthage for a mere seven years. This explains why of the more limited number of students who flowed past him only a small group surfaced, the clan of the 'Numidians', who would also cross the sea to be found with their master in Italy. Among them was Trygetius, another native of Thagaste, who was at first a refractory student but, after a detour with the army, would show spontaneity and spirit in the dialogues at Cassiciacum. Licentius, the son of Romanianus, had made a similar journey; whereas he had initially despaired of giving him a taste for even mediocre literary studies, Augustine would later rejoice at his great keenness for philosophy.[g] But in this small group of students who were also compatriots, even then one could be singled out for the strength of the bond that linked him to Augustine, being of much the same age – Alypius.

Related to Romanianus, Alypius was born at Thagaste into a family of probably slightly superior rank to Augustine's, and had been the latter's pupil when he was teaching grammar there in 374–6. The two young men had found each other again at Carthage, though their relations were at first infrequent. For some reason unknown to us, Alypius' father was not on good terms with Augustine and had forbidden his son to follow the rhetor's classes. With nothing to do, Alypius had not fallen, like his older friend, into the 'cauldron of shameful loves' – Augustine tells us that he had little inclination towards these pleasures[h] – but he had developed a passion for circus games. This was an absorbing and far more time-consuming passion. We know how strongly the crowds were attracted to the races, at Carthage as elsewhere, the enthusiasm that surrounded the charioteers, and the social and even political weight carried by the various factions in the town.[6] A love for shows, that 'concupiscence of the eyes', had been Alypius' weakness in his earlier youth. Augustine also recounts how later, in Rome, Alypius had one day reluctantly allowed himself to be dragged off by friends to watch gladiatorial fights – a spectacle that was even more costly to the soul. In the amphitheatre he had at first kept his eyes closed, determined to hold out; but at the most dramatic moment – when one of the combatants in the arena fell – the great clamour that arose made him open his eyes, and he then let them feast at length on the bloody savagery that had first reached him via his ears and from then on was a slave to that atrocious voyeurism.[i] It seems that at Carthage Alypius contented himself with the circus and its races, and therefore frequented the lower part of the town, on its south-west edge where, in the present-day area of Yasmina, the circus stretched some 500 metres in length, a size that made it the second largest in the Roman world, after the Circus Maximus in Rome.[7]

Alypius, however, had not broken his contact with Augustine. He did not observe the paternal ban to the letter, and from time to time attended his courses as a 'free listener'. One day when he was there, Augustine – not deliberately, he says, though it is hard to believe – chose as an illustration of the theme he was developing a comparison taken from the circus games and their public, 'making several biting remarks against those who were enthralled by them'.[j] Alypius felt he was being targeted, but instead of taking umbrage, accepted the lesson and from that day onwards did not set foot in the circus.[8] He persisted with his father, and finally had the ban on his attending Augustine's lessons lifted. He began to frequent them assiduously and, Augustine adds, was ensnared with him in the nets of the Manichaeans, which suggests that the father was not altogether wrong to mistrust Augustine!

On the subject of Alypius, an anecdote clearly from that date is recorded by Augustine for edifying purposes, but it interests us also for the light it throws on the topography and living conditions in Carthage at that time. One day, around noon, to prepare the exercise he was about to perform in Augustine's class – a declamation he was going to give – Alypius was walking back and forth in the forum, holding tablets and stylus in his hand, and in front of the 'court', says Augustine specifically. Engrossed in his work, he had not noticed the arrival of a young man who, with the help of an axe that he had concealed about him, attacked the balustrades that overlooked the 'Goldsmiths' street' (the *vicus argentariorum*)[9] and started to cut out the lead. Alerted by the noise, the goldsmiths who had their shops down below hastily sent some men. The thief, however, had already disappeared at top speed, while Alypius, intrigued at seeing him running away as fast as his legs could carry him, drew near to take a look and picked up the axe that the other had abandoned when he fled. He was on the point of being arrested and marched off to be thrown into prison when an architect of the public buildings, providentially passing that way, and knowing Alypius, stood as guarantor for him and explained the misunderstanding; soon the real thief was apprehended and arrested.[k] What the author of the *Confessions* drew from this story is the lesson Alypius was able to learn from it, having emerged, as he says, 'the richer in experience', better armed, as a man destined for the magistracy – but who would in fact become a man of the Church – to beware of damning others on mere appearances. But this account also contributes a precise text's valuable confirmation of the most up-to-date archaeological evidence. The balustrades that overhung the 'Goldsmiths' street', onto which the shops opened, were those that enclosed with guard rails the forum of the upper town, in other words, the vast artificial esplanade of Byrsa, and the 'court' to which Augustine alludes must be identified with the large judicial basilica whose location recent excavations have enabled us to pinpoint accurately.[10] And it also confirms the evidence found on the site, notably on the edges of this monumental centre, of the reality of the worrying damage inflicted in the public domain, in a Carthage which was nevertheless peaceful and prosperous at that time.[11]

In the same years in Carthage, and perhaps even before he began teaching rhetoric, Augustine had made the acquaintance of a young lad a few years his junior, who by his sensitivity as well as his origins and social position, introduced a new tone into the little circle of 'Numidian' friends surrounding their master. Nebridius was one of those comfortably off Carthaginians who divided his time between the capital and the family home near Carthage where his parents lived the noble life of the great country landowners of the period. The friendship of this distinguished young man, who had no need to make a career for himself, soon became very dear to Augustine; it was among those that could enable him to forget the black days he had lived in Thagaste. He was certainly thinking of this friendship, and that of Alypius, when he included in the *Confessions* his beautiful words on the balm with which passing time soothes life's wounds if at least the solace of friendship is not lacking.[1] But the presence of Nebridius at his side was not only a consolation. Through the independence of his mind, the pertinence of his remarks and the moral strictness which his friend recognized in him,[m] he was to play an active part in Augustine's intellectual development, during those Carthaginian years which may be described as decisive, in so far as a growing scepticism with regard to Manichaeism was preparing the ground for other achievements.

The lure of astrology

We do not live permanently in a state of having to make choices. The philosophical need to incline to the perfect life, glimpsed since his reading of the *Hortensius*, remained at the back of the young rhetor's mind, but it was not his most current preoccupation. Augustine was then living from day to day as an intellectual of modest origins who aspired to become a 'cultural new arrival'.[12] There was no shortage of examples; they were before his very eyes. When he had started in his chair of rhetoric in 376, the proconsuls' palace, near which he taught, was occupied by Hesperius. The proconsul then in office was none other than the son of the rhetorician from Bordeaux, Ausonius, who after thirty years in the profession had become the private tutor of the emperor Gratian, and having reached his sixties, had begun a second career, as rapid and brilliant as it was late in the day, which would lead him to the praetorian prefectship for the Gauls, Italy and Africa in 378–9, and to crown everything, the consulship. Ausonius had taken advantage of this to set up all the members of his family, and it was his son-in-law, Thalassius, whom Augustine would see succeed Hesperius in 377! These achievements were such as to turn the head of an intelligent and ambitious young man; at the least, it was immensely encouraging. Augustine could not have been unaware of the existence and names of these two governors of eminent rank in the hierarchy of the top officials in the Late Empire, but it is uncertain whether he ever had the occasion to meet them.

That chance occurred two or three years later.[13] Augustine had taken part in a dramatic poetry competition, and had not needed the services of a 'haruspex' – magic sacrifices, rebuffed with horror – to carry off the prize; and he had the honour of receiving his crown from the hands of the proconsul, Helvius Vindicianus.[n] The governor was also a learned man, one of the most famous doctors of that era when medicine, long the province of the Greeks, was beginning to develop schools of some renown in North Africa. His notice of the laureate lasted longer than just the ceremony. He received him several times and thus learned during those conversations that among other reading matter Augustine was taken with the works of 'makers of horoscopes', in other words, astrologers. In his youth, Vindicianus too had let himself be attracted by astrology, to the point of considering making it his profession – a very lucrative one, as we know. As he had been able to understand Hippocrates, he told himself, he was quite capable of assimilating *those* works. Yet he had deserted them to devote himself to medicine, because he had discovered their falsity and did not wish to earn his living by deceiving the next man. The proconsul had quickly assessed Augustine's capabilities; he went further, paternally advising him to let an object of idle curiosity drop, since rhetoric assured him of an honest means of earning a living. And when the young man countered with the apparent accuracy of a good number of predictions made by astrologers, Vindicianus replied that this must be ascribed to chance.

The old proconsul did not manage to convince Augustine, and his friend Nebridius had no more success, at the same time, in his efforts to turn him away from astrology,[14] which would remain a strong temptation for a few years to come. Alas, Augustine gives no explanation of what he expected of it; we can hardly believe that his motives remained circumscribed by the three areas in which the expertise of horoscope-makers lies – health, money and love. Of his youthful penchant for astrology, the author of the *Confessions* gives two successive explanations, one of which, the seductive astuteness of astrologers in exonerating the individual from personal responsibility,[o] seems rather a reflection *a posteriori* by the Christian and bishop. But the other accounts more truly for Augustine's attitude in that period. As he had replied to Vindicianus, he did not believe in chance; or, rather, he did not wish to believe in it. Was it not better, especially when it was our existence that was at stake, to exorcise chance by substituting a personal determinism linked to cosmic order? Thus the following justification, which clearly reveals Augustine's state of mind in those days, shows what might be termed a rational need: 'I had not yet found any decisive proof which unambiguously made it clear to me that what the astrologers said in their consultations resulted from chance or fate, and not from a methodical observation of the stars.'[p] In this sense, his adherence to astrology was parallel to his 'reasoned' – and cautious – faith in Manichaeism.

The credence he gave at that time to divination was a secondary and connected belief, but it also had a hard time. We must read in the *Contra Academicos* the anecdotes concerning one Albicerius, a then famous soothsayer in Carthage, to whom Augustine was not unwilling to resort, for example to find a lost spoon.[9] In the same period, one of Augustine's students, a young 'clarissimus' named Flaccianus, who would become proconsul of Africa in 393, also tested Albicerius' indisputable gifts. Invited by him to say what he was thinking at that precise moment, the seer replied: 'A line of Virgil'. 'Which one?' insisted Flaccianus. And the other, who was by no means well up in the humanities, easily recited the line. Flaccianus admitted that he had done well, but ascribed the merit of such prowess to some demon that was inspiring the seer. So for him, as for his teacher, divination was not deniable, but must not be confused with knowledge, still less with wisdom.

Augustine's attachment to astrology was to outlive his break with the Manichaeans, but not by long. In Book VII of the *Confessions* he recounts how he made the definitive break, a good few years after the warnings of Vindicianus and Nebridius. He seems to have been already in Milan (therefore in late 384 at the earliest) when he had a decisive encounter with a man named Firminus, whom he describes as a friend and cultured man who, on a matter of some importance, had asked him for an astrological consultation. Augustine did not refuse him, though adding that he hardly believed in it any more. And thereupon, rather surprisingly, Firminus told him a story which, apparently without his being aware of it, went as far as it was possible to go against the credibility of horoscopes.

His father, passionately keen on astrology, had a friend who was no less besotted, to the point where both noted the position of the stars even at the birth of their family pets' offspring! It happened that when Firminus' mother became pregnant, one of this friend's servants started her pregnancy at the same moment. The two women gave birth to a son at the same instant, with such perfect simultaneity that it was impossible to pick out the least difference in the stars' position. Yet Firminus, the son of a good family, made a brilliant career in the world, whereas the servant's son, born into slavery, continued to live in it.[r] This story was a flash of inspiration for Augustine; his last hesitations yielded on the spot and, reconsidering the horoscope he had just reluctantly made for Firminus, he told him that to come anywhere near the truth he would have had to take into account his origins and upbringing, and likewise for the slave. Finally disillusioned, he had to go on the attack, confound the 'eccentrics' he had followed all too long. To do so, he would resort to an argument he deems peremptory, perhaps suggested to him by one of his readings of Cicero, if not by a sermon he might have heard then from the lips of Ambrose: that of twins, born within so short an interval that it did not allow any observable change in the stars' position.[15] And he quoted the example of Esau and Jacob (Gen. 25.24–6), the latter emerging from his mother Rebecca's womb holding his brother's heel: an astrologer should have been able to predict the same destiny for these twins whose fate would be so different.[16] A little later, in a text datable to 388/9, he would finally settle accounts with the astrologers, of whom he would mordantly say, 'They claim to enslave our actions to celestial bodies, barter us with the stars and sting us for the price at which they sell us!'[s]

The *De pulchro et apto*

Let us return to the Carthaginian period, between his twenty-fifth and twenty-ninth year. With his companion, to whom he was faithful, and the little Adeodatus, who was growing up, Augustine led an ordered and studious life, reading a great deal. Even by the end of his adolescence he had on his own assimilated the books relating to what were called the 'liberal arts' – as well as the properly literary disciplines, dialectics, arithmetic, music, geometry and astronomy – a whole range of formative disciplines which, by way of Cicero, went back to Hellenistic Greece.[17] And perhaps, as early as the years of his Carthaginian teaching post, he had it in mind to mark that *enkyklios paideia* with his personal stamp, already thinking ahead to those *Disciplinarum libri* which he would in fact sketch out in Milan, though only the *De musica* would survive.[18] To supplement his training in rhetoric, strictly speaking, he had read and was probably still reading some historians – actually, rather the 'abbreviators' – and some 'ancient' writers: Varro, Justin, Florus, Valerius Maximus. Above all, at that time he read 'numerous philosophical writings that he had retained in his memory'.[t] Assuredly, this reading was also an integral part of the 'further training' of a good rhetor, according to Ciceronian precepts, and it may be recalled that, in this kind of context, he had discovered the *Hortensius* at the age of nineteen. But we may also recall the 'initiatory' effect of that discovery: it had been strong enough to inspire the young man to broaden his philosophical horizons even before he came across the famous *libri Platonicorum* that he would not find until he went to Italy. All these books were so many milestones in a search for wisdom that had begun in the fever of the revelation of the *Hortensius*; but for Augustine – and he says so himself[u] – they were also touchstones for testing the veracity of the Manichaean doctrine. What was he reading, then? Perhaps the Latin translations, by Apuleius, of Platonic texts, but probably mainly 'doxographic' collections, in other words, anthologies of opinions, works at second hand, that were very useful for gaining initial access to the principal schools of thought in the ancient world.[19]

We would have a more accurate view of the directions taken by Augustine following his reading if his first work were available, written about 380,[v] and entitled *De pulchro et apto*, which for want of a better translation could be rendered as 'Of the beautiful and the fitting'. This treatise had already been lost when he was composing his *Confessions*, and its author was scarcely concerned.[20] At the time, however, he must have held great hopes for an undertaking intended both to serve his career by making him known and to test his dialectic capabilities. Indeed, for his reputation, he had dedicated the treatise to a prominent rhetor in Rome, where he enjoyed public remuneration.[w] For Augustine, Hierius was at that time the very symbol of the success to which he aspired: Syrian by birth – as *he* was African – Greek-speaking, but having achieved supreme freedom of expression and eloquence in Latin, and passably acquainted with philosophy into the bargain: 'This rhetor', he asserts, 'belonged to that race of men whom I loved to the point of wanting to resemble them.'[x] From him Augustine expected some sort of recognition, though he was sufficiently conscious of the worth of his own work, judging it for himself, to contemplate it already with a kind of narcissistic satisfaction.

Augustine was especially concerned with aesthetic problems at that time, and they fuelled his teaching. To be more exact, he set out these problems by comparing two concepts, that of the 'fair' or 'beautiful' (*pulchrum*), which is the result of the harmony of a whole, and that of the 'fitting' or 'suitable' (or 'appropriate': *aptum*), which results from a complete harmony with another thing. This proposition of the problem, of course, was not without precedent in the philosophical tradition of Antiquity, and in the last analysis there is no doubt that its origin lay with Plato. Trying – too hard! – to find a possible connection, we arrive at the *Hippias major*, a dialogue in which Socrates plays cat and mouse with the conceited sophist of Elis, asking him to propound various definitions of beauty, which argument wrecks, one after the other. So it goes with the one identifying the fair (*to kalon*) with the fitting (*to prepon*).[21] In Plato's dialogue, supporting the idea proposed to him by Socrates, to see whether what is 'fitting' may not be the essence of what is 'beautiful', Hippias thoughtlessly puts forward the example of a man who, otherwise ugly or ridiculous, would appear to advantage with suitable clothing or shoes. Socrates has no difficulty in showing him that the example is irrelevant, pointing out that this 'fittingness' confers on the object – or individual – a beauty that is more apparent than real. It is not in this spirit that Augustine also evokes the harmony of the shoe with the foot it suits, in the first glimpse he gives us of his work;[y] it is in any case an obvious image which, when taken out of trivial use, can find a home in various philosophical contexts.[22] For Augustine – and this emerges clearly from a second analysis that complements the first,[z] if the 'beautiful' is what is fitting (or 'pleasing': *decet*) by itself, the 'fitting' (*aptum*) is what suits (or pleases) because it is adapted to some other thing. Looked at in this perspective, far from the very briefly exposed and swiftly rejected problem in the *Hippias major*, the *pulchrum*, fittingness of everything, and the *aptum*, fittingness of the part to other things, are two forms of beauty, one involving the other.[23]

Thus Augustine defined beauty, leaving his mind, as he says, to range through the world of 'corporeal forms'. Starting from what could be reached through the senses, he attempted to attain the spiritual but as he confesses rather touchingly, the quivering thoughts he tried to fix on incorporeal things always came back to the lines, colours and bulk of matter, unable as he was then to rise above the corporeal world. This vain attempt left him a prisoner of Manichaean dualism, which he applied to the moral analysis of the soul, where he made the distinction, on the one hand, between virtue, the kingdom of peace and unity and, on the other, vice, the realm of discord and a fundamental divisiveness. In an inharmonious co-existence, which seemed to him incurable, there was a reasonable and pacific soul, the essence of truth and sovereign good and, 'in the divisions of irrational life', the substance of sovereign evil, living by itself and independently of God. Augustine appeared then to be still pledged to the doctrine of Mani; but at the same time this dualist conceptualization was expressed in terms that suggest other sources of inspiration. For he gave virtue (that is, the reasonable soul, substance of truth and sovereign good) the name of 'monad' – 'as a sexless spiritual element' – and vice (or the substance of irrational life and evil) the name of 'dyad', the principle, for example, of anger in the perpetration of crimes, or sensuality in the exercise of debauchery. It has been clearly shown that here he was using a vocabulary derived from

Neopythagorean speculations that may have reached him by way of those 'doxographic' anthologies mentioned earlier.[24] Against a background of Manichaeism, therefore, we may glimpse the varied readings and temptations of a still very eclectic Augustine.

Faustus of Milevis

The author of the *Confessions* cannot find enough scorn for the aberrations of the Manichaean 'hearer' which he had been steadfastly, if not always enthusiastically, for nine years, dragging with him in his 'extravagances' the friends 'seduced by and with him'. He would reproach himself for having brought their food to the 'elect' so that they should not break the 'seal of the hand', 'in order that they might, in the dispensary of their belly, fabricate angels and demons for our liberation'.[25] This kind of activity in the service of the 'elect' was standard practice for the 'catechumens', likened in the Tebessa manuscript to Martha waiting upon Mary at Bethany (Luke 10.38–42). Elsewhere, he admits having attended the services of the sect, listened to readings of their fundamental texts, taken part in March in the great annual festival of the *Bema*, which commemorated Mani's 'passion'. Although his early proselytism had abated, his loyalty remained, come what may, despite doubts which gradually grew, fuelled particularly by what he was reading. Among other writings – part of those *multa philosophorum* which he increasingly contrasted with the sect's fables[aa] – collections of physics and astronomy that he was able to get to know, at least at second hand, through texts by Apuleius and Varro, and perhaps also through Ciceronian extracts from the *Phenomena* of Aratos. What Augustine discovered – even though he himself had probably not acquired the technique of such computations[26] – was the existence of laws, mathematically deduced from rigorous observations, which enabled eclipses of the Sun and Moon to be calculated and predicted several years in advance, with all desirable accuracy as to the year, the month, the day and even the hour when the phenomenon would occur, together with its intensity.[bb] And he could see nothing there to correspond with the woolly metaphysics of the Manichaeans, and their extravagant theories on the eminent role of the two great luminaries in the 'recovery' of Light, the captive of Darkness, or their ridiculous explanation of the eclipses which, according to them, were due to the often-repeated gesture of primordial Man, who veiled his face to avoid seeing the fate reserved for the wretched souls battling with the Demon because they had not been able to escape from the clutches of Matter!

Other factors intervened to shake Augustine's Manichaean 'convictions'. It may be recalled that his first contact with the Bible had been rather discouraging and that even the New Testament had put him off. Nevertheless, he had not completely lost sight of those texts and, when in Rome, he would remember the controversies that a certain Helpidius had already had with members of the sect in Carthage. The latter claimed that the New Testament, as the Catholics produced it, had been falsified – they did not say exactly by whom – with the aim of steering the Christian faith in the direction of Judaic law.[cc] In these disputes, Helpidius' arguments seemed sound to Augustine, and the defence of his adversaries weak; but the Manichaeans were astute enough to say that on this point they reserved the revelation of their truth to their faithful, in a small select group! During these years, the one who most urged him to call his false certainties into question was his friend Nebridius, who followed him to Milan, and whose stringently questioning intellect he would always acknowledge.[dd]

Nebridius had been almost the only one in Augustine's circle to resist the Manichaean contagion; he had created a sensation in this small group and upset the members of the sect by attacking the heart of their doctrine with a fundamental question. We have seen that in Mani's mythical cosmogony, at the start of the 'middle time', breaking the original separation, the Prince of Darkness tried to invade the kingdom of Light; God, as we know, decided to oppose him himself, by means of 'evocations', or hypostases, in a combat whose main outcome would be the sad and enduring mingling of the divine substance with the obscure substance of Matter. But, objected Nebridius, what could the 'race of darkness' (*gens tenebrarum*[ee]) do against God, if God refused to join battle with it? And Nebridius had foreseen that he would entrap his adversaries in a dilemma with no way out: if they replied that God had joined battle because the race of darkness might harm him, they were attacking the dogma of divine inviolability and incorruptibility which they shared with Christians. If the answer was that the race of darkness could not harm him, in that case there was no longer any reason to embark on a struggle in such conditions that they would result in a part of God – or his descendants – being corrupted and debased by its mingling with evil. In Augustine's circle, it was considered that 'Nebridius' argument' had scored a bull's eye.[27] The Manichaeans were at a loss; to avoid the dilemma, one of them had been bold enough to suggest that God had not wished to avoid evil, or at least through his goodness had wanted to come to the assistance of that restless and perverse power of evil in order to control it. But by saying this, he was contradicting his sect's books, which asserted that God was on his guard against his enemies.[ff]

But soon a confrontation would decisively put paid to Augustine's hesitations. Probably upon his initial entry into the sect, he had heard from his co-religionists about the existence of a famous Manichaean 'bishop', named Faustus. Like himself, this Faustus was a Numidian, from Milevis (Mila in the present-day district of Constantine), where he had been born shortly before the middle of the century into a poor and pagan family. In his way he too was a 'cultural new arrival', but more modestly: Augustine, who quickly sized up an adversary, would not credit him with a knowledge of the 'liberal arts', but only a passing acquaintance with Cicero and Seneca and a few Latin poets;[gg] on the other hand, he would not dispute his facility for speaking in polished language, the charm of his words and the suppleness of his intellect.[hh] Faustus must have resembled those great sophists of classical Greece whose natural aptitude and ingenuity were sharpened by innumerable verbal contests and lectures, though at the cost, in Faustus' case, of serious afflictions of his vocal cords, the price of his speeches and sermons.[ii] He appears to have lived his missionary 'episcopacy' in Rome for some time, in indolent opulence,[28] which explains why Augustine, with impatient curiosity, had had to wait to meet him. For the Manichaeans in his circle, who were often unable to answer his questions, loudly boasted of this Faustus as a man who, in the twinkling of an eye, would smooth out all difficulties and resolve all his problems.

Faustus finally arrived, and Augustine's disappointment matched his long wait. At first he found him charming, relaxed and with a much more persuasive way of dealing with the usual expositions of those in his sect. That was the assessment he made, from a distance, of 'the cupbearer who so sweetly offered precious draughts'.[jj] For, surrounded as he was by a circle composed of hearers, Faustus was not easy to approach. At last the chance arose for a conversation in a small group: flanked by his friends, Augustine revealed to the 'bishop' the questions he had been asking himself. He soon realized that he was not going to obtain the hoped-for enlightenment, notably on the discrepancies he had found between the data of astronomy and Manichaean fables relating to the sky, the stars, the Sun and the Moon.[kk] With unexpected modesty and frankness, which redoubled the growing liking of his interlocutor, Faustus declined to take responsibility for his lack of knowledge. Augustine found him a good loser, but remained unsatisfied. However, it was not the end of their relationship; they shared a liking for literature, and the young rhetor went as far as adapting his lessons to the affinities and turn of mind of his new listener – but the impetus that had inspired Augustine all those years in his efforts to make progress in this 'gnosis' was henceforward shattered. Faustus, having been a 'death-trap' for so many people, had unwittingly freed one from where he had been ensnared. Without yet breaking away from the Manichaeans, from then on he was awaiting another guiding light.

Departure for Rome

Augustine was not slow to leave Carthage. In his *Confessions* he would give as his principal reason for leaving the lack of discipline among his Carthaginian students, which had finally become unbearable. But a whole bundle of motives now combined to spur him into crossing the sea. His beloved Alypius had already preceded him to Rome to practise law;[ll] Augustine had friends there (probably Manichaean) who were enthusiastically urging him to come and join them, painting in glowing colours the prospect of a higher salary and a more prominent social position; later in life, the bishop would see divine inspiration in this siren song.[mm] Besides, and chiefly, the rhetor had exhausted his resources at Carthage, both in pursuing his worldly ambitions and satisfying his intellectual needs.

Why did Monica have to be there on the day he left? Was it a mother's instinct, or had she known about the departure which her son had found it hard to keep from her? More probably, her son had told her of his decision, and Monica had hastened from Thagaste to say her goodbyes.[nn] But Augustine had not foreseen how devastating those farewells would be; although he knew his mother very well, none the less he had underestimated the physical torment that the separation would cause.[oo] And they weathered this storm, just the two of them, for neither his companion nor Adeodatus, who were not travelling with him, were present on the beach where the drama was played out. Monica insisted on accompanying her son to the shore, hoping up to the last moment to keep him with her or leave with him. To get rid of her, Augustine could do nothing else but make a pretence: he claimed he did not want to leave a friend who was waiting for a favourable wind in order to embark. 'I lied to my mother, a mother like her, and off I went', he would write later, investing this act of fundamental selfishness with the significance of a flight that was salutary in every sense of the word.

The ship about to leave was anchored not in the town's main port, but in the little bay at the outlet of the present-day 'Hamilcar's ravine', on the heights of which the ruins of the so-called St Monica's basilica can still be seen. At that time a chapel to the memory of St Cyprian stood there, and Augustine persuaded his mother to enter it to collect herself.[29] 'That night, furtively, I departed; but not she; she remained there weeping and praying.'[pp] Reliving the drama, the bishop, addressing God, used this sentence to comment on the maternal prayers: 'But you, in your profound design, fulfilling the essence of her wishes, ignored what she begged of you then to make me what she always asked of you.' The Eternal Father hears her plea, but reads her heart better than she can and rectifies the prayer himself! And he goes on: 'The wind blew and filled our sails, hiding the shore where, when morning came, she was wild with grief.' Thus, in the distant past, Dido had long wept over the flight of Aeneas, as the young Augustine had learnt on his school bench.

Notes

a.   *Conf.*, IV, 2. In the same tone, he had called his childhood schoolmasters *venditores grammaticae* (*Conf.*, I, 22). In the summer of 386, when he finally renounced this profession, he says that he had decided to 'withdraw the service of (his) tongue from the chatter market' (*Conf.*, IX, 2).

b.   *Conf.*, VI, 11: . . . *cum* . . . *rhetoricam ibi professus publica schola uterer*.

c.   *Conf.*, V, 14.

d.   Cf. *Contra Acad.*, I, 2, the eulogy in which allusion is made to 'honours going beyond the municipal setting'.

e.   *Conf.*, IV, 28.

f.   *Conf.*, IV, 30.

g.   Cf. *De ordine*, I, 16.

h.   *Conf.*, VI, 21.

i.   *Conf.*, VI, 13: one of the finest pages in the *Confessions* for its effective description, acute analysis and superb style.

j.   *Conf.*, VI, 11.

k.   *Conf.*, VI, 14–15.

l.   *Conf.*, IV, 13: 'Time takes no time off, and does not pass through our senses without effect.'

m.   *Conf.*, IV, 6: *adulescens valde bonus et valde castus* (cf. on the meaning of this phrase, G. Madec, in *Rev. des ét. aug.*, VII, 1961, pp. 245–7).

n.   *Conf.*, IV, 5 (and VII, 8 for the proconsul's name).

o.   *Conf.*, IV, 4.

p.   *Conf.*, IV, 6.

q.   *Contra Acad.*, I, 17: Augustine asked Licentius to consult Albicerius.

r.   *Conf.*, VII, 8.

s.   *De diversis quaestionibus LXXXIII*, 45, 2.

t.   *Conf.*, V, 3.

u.   *Conf.*, V, 3: 'I compared certain doctrines with the long fables of the Manichaeans.'

v.   He says that he was then twenty-six or twenty-seven: *Conf.*, IV, 27.

w.   *Conf.*, IV, 21; it seems that this Hierius performed in Trajan's forum.

x.   *Conf.*, IV, 23.

y.   *Conf.*, IV, 20.

z.   *Conf.*, IV, 24.

aa. Above, p. 51.

bb. *Conf.*, V, 4 and 6.

cc. *Conf.*, V, 21. On this claimed Jewish corruption of the Gospels, cf. *De util. cred.*, 7.

dd. Cf. *Conf.*, VI, 17: *quaestionum difficillimarum scrutator acerrimus*; in 408, in a letter to Bonifatius of Cataquas, Augustine expresses himself similarly on Nebridius' intellectual demands: *Ep.* 98, 8.

ee. *Conf.*, VII, 3.

ff. Cf. *De moribus manichaeorum*, II, 25.

gg. *Conf.*, V, 11.

hh. *Contra Faustum*, I, 1.

ii. *Contra Faustum*, XXI, 10: lesion of the vocal cords, laryngitis or tracheitis? The vague use of the word *stomachus* makes it unclear. In 386, when Augustine complains of troubles which seem to be of the same kind, he still hesitates between *pectus* and *stomachus*.

jj. *Conf.*, V, 10.

kk. *Conf.*, V, 12.

ll. *Conf.*, VI, 13 and 16.

mm. *Conf.*, V, 14.

nn. It cannot be ruled out that during the Carthaginian years Monica, who had been a widow for several years, may have come to live with her son, though nothing in the *Confessions* indicates it.

oo. It is the *carnale desiderium* that receives its just punishment from the scourge of sorrows: *Conf.*, V, 15.

pp. *Conf.*, V, 15.

CHAPTER VIII

Between Rome and Milan

In the autumn of 383, on the threshold of his thirtieth year, Augustine arrived in Rome, still the magnificent city which had made such an impression on the emperor Constantius twenty-five years earlier. Resident in the eastern capital founded by his father, Constantine, he had made his triumphal entry into the Eternal City, and had spent a long time visiting all its districts, with unflagging admiration.[a] So Rome must have looked to Augustine after he landed at Ostia, but if there was any enchantment it was short-lived. There is no trace of it in the *Confessions*, and we may look in vain through his entire works for a sign of the eye's wonderment, an almost physical nostalgia such as would inspire Rutilius Namatianus in 417 to a vibrant eulogy of the Rome he left so regretfully, although the city he hymned had suffered the ravages of Alaric's hordes a few years earlier. True, it was easier then for a pagan to be an unconditional admirer of Rome; everything there spoke of a grandeur to which the Christian Empire was but a recent heir. The pages of the *City of God* that may be cited are less a praise of Rome than an often moving invitation to her to discover in the new religion the conditions and means of a different greatness, even better than the old.[b]

As we shall see, Rome left Augustine with no happy memories. Scarcely had he arrived when he fell ill, contracting fevers that put his life in danger. Rome was indeed a splendid city, but over-populated and, despite the efforts of those in charge of maintaining the town's drains and the bed of the Tiber, the lack of hygiene was on a par with the magnificence of the monuments. In the time of Constantius, mentioned above, when a prince of the royal family of Persia who had taken refuge there was asked his opinion of the town, he replied, 'What I like about it is that one can die here just as well as anywhere else.'

Augustine, however, eventually recovered from the fevers in the home of a Manichaean 'hearer' who had given him hospitality.[c] For all that it was persecuted, their community survived without too much difficulty in the anonymity of a large city, and Augustine was immersed in a materially as well as intellectually comfortable situation. He even frequented a few 'elect', but did not align himself with them – or with his host, whose confidence in the sect he worked hard to sap[d] – nor was he easy or docile to converse with. He sometimes yearned to return to the Catholic faith of his childhood, and was glad to meet Helpidius again, whose victorious jousts with the 'elect' on the subject of the Scriptures had already impressed him at Carthage, but he remained imprisoned in Manichaean dualism. He himself said, with a kind of desperate humour, how he was at that time overwhelmed beneath the weight of those 'masses' – those 'substances' of evil and good of which he pictured physical and ponderous forms – whose almost fleshly materialness barred his access to any spirituality.[e]

The temptation of scepticism

He then took refuge in doubts. What may be termed his 'sceptical temptation' dates from the early days of his time in Rome, fuelled by his reading of the philosophers of the New Academy. We may recall – above p. 37 – that page of the *De beata vita* (I, 4) written in the autumn of 386, in which he describes his journey since his nineteenth year as a perilous crossing: the Academics, he says, at that time held the tiller of his wind-tossed vessel 'for a long period'; in other words, his year in Rome, 384, and probably all of 385, before his reading of the *libri Platonicorum* and discovery of St Paul gave his thinking a decisive reorientation. Ten years after the revelation due to his reading of the *Hortensius*, he returned to Cicero, who was still the principal intermediary in his access to the philosophies whose ultimate goal was to define the sovereign good. In 79–78, Cicero himself had been nearing thirty when, accompanied by his brother Quintus and cousin Lucius, he made the journey to Athens, where he had met his friend Atticus.[f] For those young people on the 'Grand Tour', which would also take them to the East, it was a pilgrimage to the source of the main currents of thinking in the ancient world, and Cicero would say that in the gardens of Academos he had especially meditated before the *exedra* a (semi-circular bench) where Carneadus[g] was wont to sit. He had not been able to meet him, but some years previously in Rome he had followed the lessons of Carneadus' successor and continuator, Philo of Larissa; he had also listened to Antiochus of Ascalon, and it was this man, currently principal of the Academy, whom he met in Athens during his stay.

In his *Academica*, a dialogue in two parts, very little of which is preserved, written in 45, a terrible year for him, following the death of his daughter Tullia, Cicero had set out the differences which quite clearly distinguished the two branches of the Academy in his time. With Carneadus, followed by Philo, it had taken the route of probabilism, refuting the possibility of all true or scientific knowledge. Such an attitude of mind was in reaction against the Stoic doctrine, basically that of Zeno of Citium, who two centuries earlier had held that, between the true images and false images supplied by our senses, which were the basis for intellectual perception, there was a criterion of certainty or evidence that enabled a distinction to be made between them. The Academics rejected the reality of this criterion, and thereupon the suspension of any judgement became the rule in every domain, including and foremost that of moral life. So, whereas for the Stoics a wise man was one who did not give his approval to what was not true, the Academics considered that the only wise man was one who refused to give his approval in any circumstances. Antiochus of Ascalon had subsequently followed a path that deviated from the one taken by Carneadus and Philo. Reacting against them in his turn, and anxious to return to the sources of Platonism, he pointed out that two schools had emerged which both admitted the possibility of knowledge, that of the Stoics and that of Aristotle. With the Stoics, Antiochus thought that a criterion of certainty existed without which it was useless to hope to attain any kind of truth: armed with this criterion, therefore, the wise man could take the right actions and achieve moral rectitude, enabling him to attain a happy life, no matter how afflicted he might be by all fate's blows. At the same time, with the Peripatetics he thought that in order to live a happy life possession of moral good was necessary but insufficient; more precisely, that the so-called 'good things' – the 'preferables' of the Stoics: health, wealth, renown and the like – must be added if the wise man was to attain the *vita beatissima*. Antiochus had thus reached a sort of synthesis, but at the price of a contradiction in the area of moral life that deterred Cicero. As has been shown, the teaching had certainly been useful in acquainting him with the many variants of the post-Socratic philosophies, and developments from one school to another; thus his eclecticism was born or strengthened.[h] But he preferred Philo's lessons and held firm to his probabilism: as Plato had put it, there was a truth in the world of Ideas, but we are never sure of attaining it, for without a criterion it is always perceived in the form of probable opinion. The wise man, therefore, would be he who, while refusing his approval for want of certainty, passed his life in a steadfast search for truth; he would find his happiness in the exercise of that virtue.

At the point he had reached, Augustine discovered in the *Academica* a kind of antidote to the Manichaean dogmatism from which he was still finding it difficult to detach himself, and he may have considered Cicero's eclectic scepticism as a sort of expectant position appropriate to his own case. In the *Confessions* he would write:

> Henceforward despairing of going further ahead in that false doctrine (Manichaeism), I had resolved to keep to it, for want of a better alternative, but more half-heartedly and indifferently. It even crossed my mind that the philosophers known as the Academics had been wiser than the rest when they affirmed that one should doubt everything and that man is incapable of apprehending any truth.[i]

Another text relating to this Italian period, between Rome and Milan, gives the measure of his perplexity, to which the thinkers of the New Academy suggested a temporary solution:

> Once I was settled in Italy, I began seriously to wonder not just whether I should remain in the sect, which I regretted having joined, but also what means I should adopt to attain the truth ... Sometimes it seemed impossible to find, and my thoughts turned favourably towards the Academics. By contrast, however, reflecting on the perspicacity of the human mind, I sometimes told myself that if truth eluded it, it was only because the method of seeking eluded it, and that this method must in fact be obtained from a divine authority.[j]

Naturally, it is chiefly through the *Contra Academicos*, the dialogue of autumn 386, that we are able to discover how Augustine lived through this 'sceptical temptation', and how he turned his reading to good account. Four centuries after Cicero, certainly with the help of Ciceronian texts but also apparently aided by a work by Varro, the *Liber de philosophia*,[k] lost today, he travelled the same route, struggling to comprehend, in the succession of schools, the reasons for their positions and differences. Of course, we must take account of the fact that, in those debates at Cassiciacum, he looks again at the doctrine of the *Academici* in the light he now gathers from the more recently discovered Platonic books; but his personal reflections might well have preceded that fresh enlightenment. We see him anxious to exonerate the Academics from the reproach of a too radical scepticism: this scepticism in the end appeared to him to be a kind of screen intended to shield the spiritualistic arguments of the Platonic school from the attacks of the Stoic and Epicurean materialists.[l] A sentence from the *Confessions* seems to retrace the path he followed in his perception of the New Academy's arguments: 'I believed at that time (when he first discovered them) that their doctrine was truly what it is commonly held to be; I had not then penetrated their real meaning.'[m]

He doubtless soon dissociated himself from the Academics' probabilist theories, and was not slow to surmount the radical doubt and suspension of judgement of the Sceptics. A mind such as his would have been unable to sustain so negative an attitude for long. It is not certain, however, that he immediately defined the position – in itself also probabilist, but an optimistic probabilism – he would adopt regarding the Academics in the dialogue of Cassiciacum: 'There is no difference', he would say, 'between them and me except that they think it probable that the truth cannot be found, whereas I think it probable that it *can*.'[n] But frequent reading of those texts had been an important stage in Augustine's spiritual progress between Rome and Milan, and must have been responsible for his final break with Manichaeism, which occurred at the end of 384; it must have helped him to close the parentheses on those errors he had pursued for nearly ten years. Making a self-assessment upon his arrival in Milan, he would write:

> Thus, following the example of the Academics, as they are interpreted, I had doubts about everything and wavered between all doctrines; then I decided that I should at least abandon the Manichaeans, judging that in the midst of my doubts I should not remain in a sect to which I already preferred some of the philosophers. To those philosophers, however, I absolutely refused to entrust the cure of my languishing soul, because they were unaware of the saving name of Christ. So I resolved to remain a catechumen in the Catholic church commended to me by my parents, until such time as a sure light came by which I could steer my course.[o]

Here, I hope the reader will not suffer a feeling of '*déjà lu*'. Yes, the absence of Christ's name discredited these philosophers as it had discredited the *Hortensius* some ten years earlier. But those ten years had not been pure loss. Augustine had adopted a waiting position, but he had been enriched by a new receptiveness.

Milan

Rome was no longer the centre of a government that had become bipolar and, in the West, dithered between several new capitals, Trier, Milan and even Ravenna, its refuge in days of misfortune. But Rome was still the symbolic centre of the Empire, the 'sacred' City, and the focal point of all ambitions and desires, as Constantinople would be a few centuries later. It was no longer the imperial court's place of residence, but still that of the traditionalist, old senatorial aristocracy who for the most part were touchy about their paganism, at the very time when the widows and daughters of those patricians on the Aventine were coming under the austere influence of Jerome, before his departure for Ostia en route for the East, in August 385. His and Augustine's paths had crossed at that time, but they had not met.

These aristocrats concentrated all the wealth they obtained from their immense estates in sumptuous palaces, islands of luxury in a town that was in economic decline, a prey to unemployment and famine, welcoming gladiators, mimes, dancing girls and other players with open arms, but closed to foreigners, and especially intellectuals.[1] Nevertheless, the example of the Syrian Hierius, to whom he had dedicated his *De pulchro et apto* four years earlier, encouraged Augustine to try to make a career there. He had to be satisfied, on a more modest scale, to form a student 'clientele', probably through the intervention of his Manichaean friends; as in every minority and persecuted community, they enjoyed a strong and active solidarity. Augustine's position was thus the precarious one of a *Privatdozent* or unsalaried lecturer working from home. He himself says that he had begun to gather a few pupils about him, to whom he taught rhetoric; but it was not long before he discovered the inconvenience of his situation. In Carthage, teachers had feared the bad conduct of their students, and the violence of their ragging. In Rome, more closely monitored by the authorities,[2] they were better behaved, but their dishonesty left without any resources a teacher who lacked official status and fixed remuneration. To avoid paying their tutor, they came to an agreement amongst themselves, left his courses en masse and went to one of his colleagues.[p] As there was no means of appeal, this practice was irremediable.

In Augustine's misfortune, luck assumed the aspect of the first man in Rome, the prefect of the city, Symmachus. In the summer of 384, when he held the prefectship which ended early in 385,[3] Q. Aurelius Symmachus, nicknamed Eusebius, was well into his forties. He had been proconsul of Africa in office in Carthage when Augustine, then aged nineteen, was finishing his studies in rhetoric, and it is very unlikely that the student had been able to get anywhere near this top official who was some dozen years his elder. Once again, his Manichaean friends helped him by providing him with an introduction to Symmachus.

As it happened, the town of Milan had appealed to Symmachus to find it a professor of rhetoric, and had specified that the man chosen would, for his journey, have the advantage of the services of the imperial post. The Milanese approach was nothing unusual: in the West Rome still had the best and largest body of teachers available;[4] it was also a good – and inexpensive – way for Milan to keep on good terms with Symmachus. Together with Praetextatus and Nicomachus Flavian, and more radically than they, Symmachus was then the leading light in the pagan clan in Rome's senate. In 382 the emperor Gratian had taken a highly symbolic action against this clan by having the altar of Victory removed from the senate's assembly hall, though Julian had restored it at the time of his 'pagan reaction'. Feelings had run high in the bosom of the pagan party and Symmachus had been chosen to go to Milan to demand the deferment of that decision. In vain; supported by Pope Damasus and, on the spot, by bishop Ambrose, the Christian senators, who more or less balanced their pagan colleagues in number, had persuaded the emperor not to yield, and Symmachus had not even been received in audience. The following year, Gratian, who had been assassinated in Lyon, was succeeded by a twelve-year-old boy, Valentinian II; though in reality it was his mother, Justina, a Christian of Arian faith, who from 383 had practised a subtle balancing game between the Christian side, under the patronage of Ambrose, and the pagan coterie in the Roman senate.

During the summer of 384, the senate had again asked for the abrogation of Gratian's antipagan measures, and notably the restoration of the altar of Victory to its rightful place, and the prefect of the city had been given the task of making a report to this end.[q] On the point of yielding, the Court of Milan had retreated in the face of protests from Ambrose, who threatened to excommunicate the young emperor, but relations had remained good with the pagan party, especially with Symmachus, as evidenced by texts datable to the end of that year.[r]

Nor is it surprising that Manichaean circles in Rome had been in touch with the pagan prefect of the city or that in return Symmachus was sympathetic to their approach on behalf of their protégé. Between this supporter of traditional religion, which was increasingly counterblasted by the imperial government and the 'heretics' who were violently hostile to the Catholics and persecuted by that same government, there could be objective alliances. In the autumn of 384, as has been said, Symmachus could have had 'a thousand reasons to appeal to a non-Catholic for such an important post'.[5] Nevertheless, the prefect made Augustine undergo a test: 'I submitted a trial discourse to him,' he would say; 'he found it to his liking, and sent me to Milan.'[s]

Milan, where Augustine arrived in the autumn of 384, in time for his thirtieth birthday, certainly did not share the urban brilliance of Rome, or even Carthage, but the town had the advantage of agricultural riches and the livestock breeding quality of northern Italy's plains, which were less unbalanced by great estates than central and southern Italy. And a glance at a map is enough to understand the growing importance of the town and its region in this Roman world of the West, simultaneously grappling with the barbarian world of the north and centre of Europe, and in increasing symbiosis with it. The presence of the Court at Milan, where it was nevertheless not in the front line, as at Trier or Sirmium, was of course connected with strategic reasons, and the town's location at the convergence of Alpine passes as well as on the transverse axis linking the Illyrian world to Gaul. But it also showed in concrete form the displacement of the centre of gravity of the Roman West, slipping north-westwards, even before the approaching loss of North Africa after the Vandal invasion in 430. Striking imperial coinage since the middle of the third century, the seventh town in the Empire according to the classification set out by Ausonius, Milan was also the place from which, in the spring of 313, the famous letters – wrongly known as the 'Edict of Milan' – signed by Constantine and Licinius, had been sent, giving Christians their freedom and restoring their places of worship to them. Even more clearly than in Rome, at the Milvian Bridge, the Christian Empire had taken its first steps early in the fourth century. The importance assumed by the town in the new religious order was thus connected not only with the exceptional personality of its bishop, who at that time was Ambrose. Of course, not everyone in Milan was a Christian, and the general of Frankish origin, Flavius Bauto, who was the most influential minister in the Court and would receive the new rhetor's homage when he entered the consulship, was probably pagan. But because of its cultural openness, the great northern metropolis was a particularly propitious place for making an important decision on one's inner life.

In those autumn days of 384, however, the future of his spiritual life was not what most concerned Augustine. The town's new 'master of rhetoric' must have had to start work at once: in addition to his 'back to university' classes, he made his debut as official orator. The first occasion was on 22 November, the tenth anniversary of the young Valentinian II's proclamation as 'Augustus', a celebration known as the *decennalia*.[6] To commemorate these jubilees, it was customary to utter one of those ceremonial speeches, the best example of which remains Pliny the Younger's *Panegyric to Trajan*, and of which, for the Late Empire, a range of preserved texts offers a whole panoply of sycophantic rhetoric. Especially heavily praised was prowess in war, indispensable in those times of incessant invasions, rebellions and usurpations, and also often emphasized was the ruler's wise policy for his subjects. But what could be said in the case of Valentinian II, an adolescent then aged fourteen, rather colourless and under guardianship, who would die strangled at twenty-two without having achieved anything outstanding in his short life as emperor of the West? Augustine's speech has not come down to us, but we know that on the point of declaiming it he was feeling awkward: 'My heart was full of care,' he would later recall, 'feverish with the thoughts that consumed it.'[t] On that day – a memorable one for him – accompanied by a few friends, he came across a beggar in a Milan street, whose cheerful inebriation and contentment with so little contrasted strongly with the lofty ambitions that were gnawing at him. As for the speech, he managed, he would say, 'by spouting a lot of lies intended to prompt the plaudits of listeners who were by no means fooled by them'. It was a crucial ordeal for him, as he knew, and among his other worries was anxiety about his African-Roman accent, which might raise a smile but might also provoke jeers.[7] Such had been the fate of the great African emperor of the late second century, Septimius Severus; but what in a prince could pass for another charming quirk was a handicap for a professional orator.

We must suppose that Augustine did well out of this exercise, for a few weeks later he would repeat it on another no less solemn occasion: the entry into office as ordinary consul, on 1 January 385, of Flavius Bauto, who had as his colleague in the East his future son-in-law, the young emperor Arcadius. There was no lack of material for the eulogy of this 'master of the militia', provided one was not afraid of showering praises upon a forceful soldier, who had distinguished himself against the Goths in Thessaly, next in the Balkans, then for having halted a branch of the Alemanni in Rhaetia – the centre and east of present-day Switzerland – and finally, in the last days of 384, carried off a victory over the Sarmatians, on the banks of the Danube. Moreover – and this made him an indispensable minister for Valentinian II and his regent mother – Bauto barred the Alpine passes against the attempts of Maximus, a usurper whom it was difficult to keep confined in Gaul. All this was highlighted by Augustine, who played his part much more easily because the 'master of the militia' was a friend of his protector, the prefect of the city of Rome. And it has sometimes been suggested that the test speech submitted to Symmachus, which earned Augustine the chair in Milan, may have been the draft of the panegyric to Bauto.[8]

In Milan, Augustine was a very busy man. His mornings, he tells us, were given over to his students; the remainder of the time he kept for preparing his classes,[u] but making an effort to keep some free time to visit his friends in high places (*amicos maiores*), whose support he considered necessary. Why? Not in order to keep the chair where he was having great success, but to use them as a kind of springboard to rise even higher. When receiving him in Rome in the summer of 384, Symmachus had doubtless not neglected to tell him something he had written to one of his correspondents, that literary success often opened the path to a fine career.[v] There was no need to repeat the lesson to an ambitious young man, who was mindful of the dazzling success of Ausonius and his family, and several others, such as Manlius Theodorus whom he was soon to meet. His purpose? He would reveal it in the *Confessions* (VI, 19): to make use of his influential friends, who were by now fairly numerous, to obtain some honorific post (*aliquis honor*), for example, while awaiting something better, at the least the governorship of a province.[9]

Alypius came to join him in Milan, and the example he provided at that time was not such as to turn him aside from his own ambitions. When he had finished his law studies in Rome, Alypius had at first stayed there to enter the imperial administration in the post of assessor to the 'Count of the Italian Treasury', in other words a top civil servant in charge of managing the imperial finances – comprising various revenues and taxes – in the 'diocese' (group of provinces) of Italy-Africa. In his role of assessor, Alypius placed his legal capabilities at the service of an administration where there was no shortage of lawsuits; his capabilities, but also – Augustine was keen to emphasize[w] – his incorruptible honesty. Doing battle with a very influential senator who had tried to obtain preferential treatment by the use of intimidation, Alypius had been unyielding. He had held firm in the face of attempted corruption and threats, and the magistrate to whom he was only an adviser had been glad of his resistance, placing the responsibility for refusing the favour on the stubbornness of his assistant, who said he was prepared to resign. Augustine told himself that it *was* possible, therefore, not to lose one's soul in the emperor's service. His friend had experienced only one temptation in carrying out his duties – because he was passionately fond of books, then a rare and precious commodity, he had been tempted to take advantage of the scribes in his office to have manuscripts copied; but he had resisted.

Nebridius, too, came to join his two friends. He had the advantage over them in that he was able to live off his private income; sheltered from need, he was also sheltered from temptations. Augustine, however, would never use his Carthaginian friend's enviable situation as a reason to belittle his merits. Quite the reverse: he could go on inexhaustibly about his unselfishness, intelligence and completely spontaneous ardour in the search for the truth that fascinated him. It was solely his love of wisdom and the hope of finding it at Augustine's side that had prompted Nebridius to leave his mother and father and the rich estate on the outskirts of Carthage.[x] In Milan, where he was not short of recommendations, he shunned high society, and while he could have employed his culture and intellect more advantageously, he had accepted, out of friendship, a modest post assisting Verecundus, a grammarian of Milan, who would later put his country house at Cassiciacum at Augustine's disposal, and who was at the time in need of an assistant in his school.[y]

At the beginning of 385 Augustine had thus reconstituted the little nucleus of friends he needed so much, for he would never be a solitary man. What was missing, except the tenderness that had warmed his childhood, and also the presence of that body, desire for which, just as much as his ambitions, raised a still insurmountable barrier between him and the place where he might find a spiritual life? In the spring of 395, the mother he had furtively, shamefully, abandoned two years before on the Carthaginian shore crossed the sea in her turn. She did not quite walk on the water, but very nearly![10] Reunion with her son at once erased the scars left by so many fears and tribulations, when Augustine informed her that he had covered half the road, and was no longer a Manichaean though not yet a Catholic Christian. She told him how certain she was from then on that she would see him a faithful Catholic before she departed from this life.

Monica had brought with her what her son was still lacking so that his fleeting and all too human happiness on this earth, which was nearing its end, was complete; the little Adeodatus, now an adolescent, and the unnamed companion, impalpably present, whose very existence we might doubt if our ears did not ring with Augustine's laments when the unfortunate woman was soon driven from his bed, sacrificed to the tyrannical mirage of social advancement.[11]

Notes

a. Ammianus Marcellinus, *History*, XVI, 10, 6–15.
b. *City of God*, II, 29.
c. Constantius, a rich Roman, who would a little later after Augustine's departure for Milan realize the project of a Manichaean 'monastery' that would end badly: see *De mor. manich.*, II, 74.
d. *Conf.*, V, 19. His host and friend Constantius would later become Catholic: see *Contra Faustum*, V, 5.
e. *Conf.*, V, 20.
f. See P. Grimal, *Cicéron*, Paris, Fayard, 1986, pp. 71–4.
g. *De finibus bonorum et malorum*, VII, 4.
h. P. Grimal, *Cicéron.*, p. 74.
i. *Conf.*, V, 18–19.
j. *De utilitate credendi*, 20.
k. See *City of God*, XIX, 1–3: Augustine used this book, which he must have known for a long time, to develop the replies given by the philosophers to the problem of the sovereign Good.
l. This is what clearly emerges from the final considerations of the *Contra Acad.*, III, 37–40.
m. *Conf.*, V, 19.
n. *Contra Acad.*, II, 23.
o. *Conf.*, V, 25.
p. *Conf.*, V, 22.
q. Symmachus, *Relationes*, 3.
r. Symmachus, *Relationes*, 21 and 23; *C. Th.*, I, 6, 9.
s. *Conf.*, V, 23.
t. *Conf.*, VI, 9.
u. *Conf.*, VI, 18: *Quando praeparamus quod* emant *scholastici?*, once again with that metaphor of venality (*emere*), so common when the bishop of Hippo speaks of his first occupation.
v. Symmachus, *Ep.*, I, 20, 1 (to Ausonius, letter dated 378).
w. *Conf.*, VI, 16.
x. *Conf.*, VI, 17.
y. *Conf.*, VIII, 13.

CHAPTER IX

Ambrose

'And I came to Milan, to bishop Ambrose, known throughout the world as one of the most eminent men, and as your devout servant.'[a] In the spiritual and emotional chronology of the *Confessions*, which does not always match the calendar reconstructed by historians, Ambrose was the first person to come on the scene when Augustine arrived in Milan, and it may indeed be that on the 'agenda' of the Master of Rhetoric freshly appointed to the imperial residence a visit to the bishop was among his very first engagements. A sentence that follows the text just quoted confirms that it was merely a simple presentation: 'That man of God gave me a fatherly welcome, and for the foreigner that I was he showed the kindly feelings of a bishop.' In fact, the bishop of Milan had welcomed as was fitting to his ministry this young African who had come to his fine city to occupy a prominent post, but he had no reason to fling his arms about him straight away; indeed he could not have been unaware that the appointment was due to his ideologically most determined enemy, Symmachus, even supposing he had not known that Augustine's recommendation to Symmachus had itself been through the intervention of the Manichaean community in Rome. If, when recomposing the memory of those years that were so important for him, Augustine subsequently portrayed Ambrose as a 'key figure' at the start of his stay in Milan or, perhaps, if he made him the most emblematic figure of all in that period which was in any case so full of meetings, it is quite simply because Ambrose would soon be the one who would bring ecclesiastical sanction to the 'conversion' and render it definitive by baptizing him in the spring of 387.

Bishop by surprise

Everything about Ambrose would fascinate someone like Augustine and, first and foremost, impress him. The little man he saw in his ever-open house (which one entered without being announced), with his high forehead, long face and large eyes,[1] silently reading[2] – and whom he left to his meditation without daring to disturb him – he knew to be the very man who had accomplished an extremely delicate diplomatic mission in Trier, during the winter of 383–4. This consisted in dissuading the usurper Maximus from having the young Valentinian II brought to him, under the pretext of protecting him. A few months later, this same man had won the day against Symmachus and Bauto in the affair of the altar of Victory. But was Augustine aware at the time of how Ambrose had come to occupy the episcopal see of Milan? On the death of bishop Auxentius, in 373, the situation in the town was critical; the dead prelate was of Arian faith, thus the representative of a minority that was important but in decline in the face of Catholic dominance in the city. A turbulent mob burst into the basilica where the bishops of the province held their meeting, assembled to ordain a successor to

Auxentius, and both factions put pressure on an electoral body which was itself divided and irresolute. The rising had to be put down and order re-established. Rather than bring in the troops, the governor of the province chose to intervene in person; he entered the church, obtained silence, began to speak and made the people listen when he appealed for calm. The crowd then acclaimed him and with one voice demanded this unanimously respected governor for their bishop – a governor who was none other than Ambrose.

At the time of that 'tumultuous' election, Ambrose was thirty-three or thirty-four. He was a Roman of Rome, the exact contemporary of Symmachus, to whom he was related, and was not of low birth. If Symmachus' father had ended his career as prefect of the city of Rome, Ambrose's had, while still a young man, held the praetorian prefectship in the Gauls, residing at Trier, where the future bishop of Milan was born.[3] But a premature and probably violent death had cut short a career which had promised a brilliant future, and the young Ambrose had returned to Rome with his mother, his brother Satyrus and his elder sister, Marcellina, who would take the veil, be consecrated by Pope Liberius and have a place in the correspondence of St Jerome as one of the noblest female Christians in Rome.[b]

After following the cycle of liberal studies, Ambrose had taken law and, once an advocate, had been singled out by one of the most important men of the time, Probus, a Christian, who had made him his assessor at the time of his first prefectship of the praetorium for Italy and Illyria, around 368. The young man had thus lived several years as a 'government attaché' at Sirmium, on the Danube. Soon afterwards, aged about thirty, Ambrose had been promoted *consularis Aemiliae et Liguriae*, residing in the imperial court, and with the promise of the most brilliant career of the century had the faithful of Milan not decided otherwise.

This kind of 'run-up' made the bishop a pastor far from the norm in a period, it is true, when the norm was scarcely fixed and the exception was often the rule. A thousand miles from a court abbé, but also from a rural curé – which many bishops were at that time – Ambrose numbered among the great spiritual leaders who had made, and continued to make, history in the fourth century – and not only religious history – and who sometimes wrote it as well. Enabled by his training to win over a howling mob, he was also determined through his convictions to mobilize crowds of followers, though in non-violence, when the higher interest of his Church seemed to him to be at stake. We shall soon see an example, and we know that the enduring mark he would leave was to have been the first prelate to make an emperor give way – and what an emperor, the great Theodosius! – and subject him to public penitence, thus brilliantly consecrating the primacy of the spiritual over the political and creating a precedent that would weigh heavily for many centuries on the relations between Church and State.

A simple leader of men does not become a pastor of souls overnight – while still remaining a leader of men – without great terror. Augustine, who had travelled less of a journey, would soon experience that feverish state when he was elected and ordained priest against his will at Hippo, and was obliged to ask his bishop for time to prepare himself to face the preaching obligations imposed upon him. As for Ambrose, certainly Christian from birth, but baptized after his accession to the episcopacy, and less familiar with the Scriptures than with Cicero and Virgil, he had much to learn. His biographer, Paulinus of Milan, even says that, returning home after the famous election, he had a reaction of withdrawal and wanted to 'take refuge in philosophy'.[4] He himself would say, more simply, in a text in which his first sermon may be recognized, addressed to his clergy in 374, that since he had had to teach before he had learnt, he had had to learn and teach simultaneously.[5]

The man of action, who had become studious in order to be a good pastor, had learnt a great deal by the time Augustine met him. He had the advantage over his new interlocutor of having had good training in both languages in his youth, and therefore had direct access to his colleagues, the Greek Fathers of the Church, who were very nearly his contemporaries and whose exegetic works were available to him: the 'Cappadocians' in particular, and above all Basil of Caesarea and Gregory of Nazianzius. Through them Ambrose discovered the theological tradition which followed, that of Origen, and further still, had access to the allegorical exegesis and philosophical syncretism of Philo of Alexandria, the Jewish thinker who had striven to demonstrate the perfect accord between Greek thought and the biblical revelation. Applying the allegorical method to the Old Testament, in particular the Pentateuch, without in any way ceasing to defend the literal sense, Philo had devoted himself to uncovering the deep significance concealed behind the strangeness of certain precepts of the Law. Origen had developed and perfected this 'hermeneutic' system. The Scriptures in their entirety, Old and New Testament, had a spiritual meaning for him that could be discovered only by the asceticism of contemplation. There were no stumbling blocks in the Bible, except for those who held fast to the literal sense, the 'carnal'; if one aimed further, at the 'moral sense', it was necessary to use allegorical exegesis in an anthropological perspective that was Philo's; if one sought the 'spiritual sense', by means of the same method, one could flush out in every detail from the history of the Old Testament figures significant of the history of salvation. To arrive at the meaning, one had to 'crack the nut', said Origen;[6] and Ambrose applied that method.[7]

For all that he was very busy in the first weeks of his stay in Milan, Augustine had taken the time to go and listen to several of the bishop's sermons. His motives were complex and somewhat secular. He had never burnt his boats with the Church, in which he had been a catechumen; in this instance, something quite different drew him to hear the preaching; his first contact with Ambrose had left him with a vivid memory of his somewhat distant affability, his magnetism tempered with aristocratic reserve. Curiosity also urged him on; the professional speaker was eager to experience the eloquence of that other *seminator verborum* (as the Stoic and Epicurean philosophers who surrounded him in Athens had called the Apostle, Paul).[c] At first, he seems to have been rather disappointed; certainly, the much vaunted eloquence was real, the arguments more learned than those of Faustus, the Manichaean 'bishop', but less attractive.[d] Ambrose's 'soteriological' discourse impressed him, but he still remained on the outside. In the long run, however, the content of this pleasing form finally reached him; as he would himself say: 'The things to which I had been indifferent now also penetrated my mind, together with the words I loved to hear.'[e] What shook him most, however, was to hear from Ambrose's lips interpretations in a spiritual sense of many passages from the Law and the Prophets that were in effect victorious refutations of the Manichaeans' sarcasm on the subject, of which he had long been a prisoner. Without committing himself straight away to the path of Catholic faith, and still rooted in a 'methodical' uncertainty that was largely the result of his reading the philosophers of the New Academy, he was at least indebted to these elucidations for having definitively created in his mind a *tabula rasa* of Manichaean ideas.

Monica comes to Milan

As for Monica, she made no mistake. Her son would say later:

> She loved that man (Ambrose), as if he were an angel of God, for she knew that it was he who had led me to that state of doubt and wavering through which, she had a sure intuitive feeling, I would have to pass in order to go from sickness to health, with an interval of sharper danger, which doctors term 'crisis'.[f]

She was even more zealous in her churchgoing, above all when Ambrose was to speak.

In the ordinary exercise of her devotions, bringing her African customs to Italy, Monica was nevertheless in for a surprise. Anyone who has not seen the vast funerary sites of late-period Africa, especially in the Mauretanias, and particularly at Tipasa and Cherchell, with their multitudes of agape tables – the *mensae* – sometimes open to the skies, sometimes surrounded by enclosures, their semi-circular stonework swamping the tombs of the deceased in whose honour people gathered to feast, cannot imagine the actuality and popularity of a practice whose quite early development in a specifically Christian context[8] has been revealed by archaeology. In the vicinity of these tables, around which the participants took their places, arranged like the spokes of a semi-circle with the table itself at the hollow centre, everything was arranged to ensure the comfort and tidiness of this *refrigerium* (both 'refreshment' and 'restoration'), the name given to these feasts of communion with the dead. Often their names, written on the mosaic that adorned the table, made their presence even more real for the banqueters. But on occasion these pious feasts degenerated into orgies,[g] even brawls between overheated fellow-guests, and not so long ago a mosaic inscription was brought to light at Tipasa, in Algeria, in which the participants at the banquet themselves warned against excess and exhorted one another to behave properly.[9]

Monica's practice was peaceable, 'convivial' in the best sense of the word, and discreet. The *meribibula* of Thagaste had not relapsed into her childish error;[h] she was content to send round from tomb to tomb, besides a basket of plain victuals – porridge and bread – a little goblet from which wine mixed with water was shared by the faithful who were present.[i] That, at least, was what she had done in Africa, for in Milan the cemetery-keeper would not let her enter. He was acting on the instructions of his bishop, who had forbidden such practices, not only to remove any occasion for drunkenness in those places, but also, and perhaps mainly, because the agapes were a continuation of the pagan *Parentalia*, which had originally been celebrated during nine days at the end of the winter, in February. At the height of his battle against paganism's attempts to return on the offensive, Ambrose could not allow himself to tolerate what ran the risk of appearing as a heritage or survival.

After some soul-searching, Monica had no difficulty in conforming to the orders of a bishop from whom she was prepared to accept anything, so greatly did she hope he would prove to be her son's salvation. What she had hitherto spent on provisions in honour of the dead, she now converted into alms for the poorest of the living. Perhaps the most important point for us is that, between Monica and Ambrose, this readily accepted ban had been the first opportunity for a tentative relationship between a great bishop and this 'grass-roots follower' who also happened to be Augustine's mother. Probably a little later, Ambrose's attention had again been drawn to her indirectly, this time by Augustine himself, regarding one of his mother's scruples that he does not mention in the *Confessions*. According to the custom of the African Church, Monica was in the habit of fasting on Saturdays; but she had noticed that this practice was not followed in Milan, which perplexed her. To help her out of this awkward situation, Augustine had questioned Ambrose who, pretending to believe that he was asking the question on his own account, though at that time it mattered little to him, had replied, 'When I am here, I do not fast; when I am in Rome, I fast on Saturdays; wherever you may be, respect the local custom if you wish to scandalize no one.'[j]

In fact, Ambrose had not been fooled and had understood perfectly well that in this affair the young rhetor had acted as intermediary between himself and a modest follower, but one he already knew well enough through her regular attendance to praise her good qualities and piety to her son – perhaps not without a tinge of mischievousness.[k] Just as Monica counted on the bishop to ensure her son's conversion, perhaps Ambrose was secretly banking on the mother to help him pull Augustine out of the uncertainties in which he was still bogged down. He did not know then that the crisis would be resolved a year later quite differently from what he may have hoped and Monica may have wished; she who in her heart's desires for her son always combined a Christian life and worldly success.

The perplexities of ambition

'I longed for honours, gains, marriage . . . ,'[l] Augustine had come to Milan to realize his career ambitions, and incidentally to advance along the path glimpsed since his reading of the *Hortensius* twelve years earlier. For Monica, as I have just said, the two went hand in hand. The Christian in her doubtless gave priority to ecclesiastical sanction of the spiritual progress she sensed in her son, but the mother was no less keen on his success in this life. Among the important people she noticed in Milan, from rather a distance, there was no lack on the Christian side of good examples of dignitaries who had been able to reconcile the demands of faith with those of their career, such as Ambrose himself prior to his episcopacy, or Probus and Manlius Theodorus. That double success came by way of marriage, and a 'good' marriage, of course. And the mother who, terrified by her Augustine's wildness in his sixteenth year, had nevertheless refused to channel it in too early a marriage that would dig the grave of his hopes,[m] now aspired to 'establish' him comfortably, and if possible even better. Monica was a coherent and determined woman in pursuit of the targets she had set herself.

In her mind, marriage, the social condition of Augustine's success, was to be followed by baptism, the condition of his salvation. So keen was her desire to see her son take a wife in a milieu in keeping with his ambitions that – with Augustine's consent and even, if we read him well, at his request – she actually sought a divine revelation on the matter, employing a sort of matrimonial theurgy whose failure she was the first to acknowledge:

> Every day, at my request and at her own desire, she begged you with heartfelt cries to reveal to her in a dream something concerning my future marriage. Never would you do so. She had visions of fantastic images, such as are conjured up by the lively power of the human mind when it is set upon a matter; she told me of them, but without the confidence she was wont to have when they came from you; she spoke of them disparagingly.[n]

It is therefore not surprising that, for want of divine assistance, in order to achieve her aims she urged, if not compelled, Augustine to a separation which wounded him very deeply, and whose conditions offend our modern sensibilities. To put the matter in a nutshell that is true to the way in which Augustine himself would tell it later, the companion who had shared his bed for sixteen years, in a concubinage considered by both Roman law and the Church as a 'de facto marriage', had become an obstacle to the proposed marriage; she was therefore asked to make way for an alliance with a more prominent family. Although we know that such an occurrence was commonplace at that time, it is all the more shocking when the person who benefited by it was Augustine. It may be supposed that the family of the young bride-to-be had stipulated the repudiation of his concubine as a condition of their consent.[10] That is certainly a plausible explanation, but does not exonerate Monica and her son from the blame for such an action. People have also suggested the theory of a pious conspiracy between Monica and Adeodatus' mother, who had perhaps voluntarily disappeared from the scene.[11] But we may read nothing in the *Confessions* or elsewhere in support of this consoling supposition, which in any case merely puts a halo on the companion by ascribing to her a freely granted sacrifice.

An additional heartbreak, she had been asked to make the immense sacrifice of returning without her child. 'She left for Africa', says Augustine, 'vowing (to God) to know no other man in the future, and leaving with me the natural child I had had with her, my son.'[o] If it had been a girl, she might have been able to take her back home; in this regard, across eras and cultures, there are many instances. More precisely, in this case the mother pledged to chastity would have brought up her daughter with the prospect of religious consecration, and that would have been the end of it; whereas in the context of worldly success in which Augustine continued, every possible string would have to be pulled for the young Adeodatus, a 'boy who showed promise' as much as, if not more than, his father at the same age, and this – not to mention his father's feelings – ruled out a return to Africa into the obscurity of the maternal milieu.

So painful an event is recorded here in a tone of such contained emotion, with such reserve and tact that we are surprised by it. Our own times are so fond of repentance of every kind that we cannot help being frustrated. But we must keep in mind that just before 400, when he wrote these lines, Augustine still bore the open wound of an even more painful loss, which he shared with his former companion – that of his son. Adeodatus had died prematurely, soon after the return to Africa, in 389/90. Silence does not mean forgetting, but it is sometimes the only remedy for a wounded heart. I expressed earlier my feeling about the cloak of anonymity cast over Adeodatus' mother, at best as a veil of con-secration.[p] When he was composing his *Confessions*, or slightly before, Adeodatus' father paid homage to her, still without naming her:

> Here we have a man and a woman; he is not another woman's husband, and she is not another man's wife. They have carnal relations not with the aim of procreating children, but only to satisfy their lust; nevertheless, they have made a reciprocal commitment not to have relations, he with another woman, she with another man. Can their union be called marriage? Certainly, if need be and without absurdity, if their commitment holds good until the death of one of them, and if, while not intentionally seeking issue from their relations, they do not avoid it.[q]

There could be no clearer acknowledgement of the quality of marriage in the long concubinage he had experienced with Adeodatus' mother, nor a clearer confession that responsibility for the break-up of that 'marriage' rested with Augustine.

There is no need to read between the lines of the *Confessions* to realize that the physical and emotional bond linking Augustine to his companion did not make him the most active agent in the quest for another family status. 'Tireless were the efforts to make me enter wedlock'; and he becomes more specific: 'I wooed, I became engaged, *mostly thanks to my mother's efforts*.'[r] And assuredly Monica had been the principal agent in this 'matrimonial negotiation', at the end of which Augustine found himself 'affianced' to a very young girl. 'She was still two years from marriageable age, but as she was pleasing, I waited.'[s] His fiancée was therefore a little girl of about twelve years, who was 'pleasing' probably because of her social rank and her 'expectations' – but perhaps she was 'attractive' into the bargain! The ex-fiancé, having given up every matrimonial prospect, would outline his portrait of the ideal wife in his *Soliloquies* a year later: 'Beautiful, modest, well-mannered, educated or capable of being so, with a large enough dowry to enable her husband to look forward without problems to a studious *otium*.'[t] Only the specific point of the 'studious *otium*' distinguishes this aspiration from that of all potential husbands in the context of those 'arranged' marriages which were the rule at that time, to ensure economic and social cohesion in the upper classes, and still are nowadays in the conventions of many cultures, with, let it be said in passing, a far from negligible rate of true marital success.

There was nothing for it but to wait. But in this waiting period, Augustine failed to do so! 'Less enamoured of marriage than slave to pleasure', he had meanwhile found himself another woman; but this liaison, which was short-lived, was not strong enough to close the wound left gaping by the departure of Adeodatus' mother.[u] And solely for his physical relief, without much emotional gain, but with the only result a trivialization of his sexual life, in itself degrading, he had placed himself in the adulterous situation he would later describe: 'If a man goes with a woman until such time as he finds another to wed who is commendable for her rank or her wealth, in his heart he is an adulterer, not towards the one he desires but towards the one who shares his bed.'ᵛ

Augustine's attachment to his companion was not the only restraint that had confined him to relative inertia in this marriage plan, as in every other area except the day-to-day exercise of his profession. To say that he was divided is putting it mildly: in 385 any decision-making that really involved the future seemed an impossibility. A few sentences from the *Confessions* form a superb indication of the uncertainties amid which he was then vacillating:

> I was already thirty, still wallowing in the same mire, eager to enjoy a present that was escaping and dissipating me, while I told myself 'Tomorrow I will find it, the proof will appear to me and I will grasp it. Faustus will come and make everything plain to me. O great men of the Academy, can nothing certain be attained for the conduct of life? But no, let us search more carefully and not despair. Already what seemed absurd in the books of the Church is no longer absurd; they can be otherwise interpreted, and favourably. I will place my feet on the step where, as a child, my parents placed me, until a clear light appears. But where shall I seek it? When shall I seek it? Ambrose has not the time, and I have not the time to read. And where shall I seek the books? Where and when obtain them? From whom borrow them? Let time be reserved, hours be set aside for the salvation of the soul! A great hope has arisen: the Catholic faith does not teach what I used to think, and what I wrongly accused it of teaching.'ʷ

We must accept the belief that these lines, written some fifteen years later, truthfully retrace the perplexities of the first year in Milan, even if their apparent foreshortening may astonish us. Of course, Faustus would come no more and the philosophers of the Academy were already behind him, but the irony could not efface all the surviving traces of old or recent errors. True, the first sermons he had heard from Ambrose had removed the entanglements from the Old Testament and begun to set the very fragile faith inherited from his childhood on a foundation he could accept intellectually. But he lacked the time, and perhaps the books, to make much progress along that route, and Ambrose, who was too busy, was hardly ever available. And as once Hercules had hesitated between vice and virtue, Augustine was still teetering between the Christian hope he was beginning to glimpse and the charms of secular life that were now being offered to him. 'But wait a moment! The things of this world are also pleasant. They have their sweetness, and not a little. We must not lightly abandon the impulse that drives us to them, for it would be humiliating to return to them again!'ˣ

Among the small circle of Africans in Milan who clustered around Augustine, the same mental tribulations prevailed; Alypius and Nebridius, his closest friends, were in the same boat: 'There we were, three hungry mouths, mutually inspiring hunger in one another.'ʸ But with slight differences. Alypius in particular made his plain to see: of the three he was the most attracted at the time by the idea of a community life dedicated to the quest for wisdom which was beginning to take shape among the friends, and for that reason was very hostile to the marriage planned by Augustine, endlessly telling him that there was no worse obstacle. There was no great merit in his saying so, for apparently chastity hardly bothered him. *He* would not have regretted the celibacy of Ambrose's position, whereas it seemed such a hardship to Augustine.ᶻ As an adolescent,

Alypius had experienced physical love, but had soon lost his liking for it, had no good memories of it and had since lived in celibacy.[aa] He regarded his friend, 'caught in the birdlime of sensual delights', rather as a phenomenon, to the point where Augustine had felt himself obliged to explain that there was a fair margin between the utter delights of the liaison he himself was enjoying and the few furtive pleasures whose distant memory made it easy for Alypius to be scornful. His demonstration was so persuasive, it appears, that Alypius, hearing Augustine speak so highly of the joys of wedlock, had come to want it for himself, not as a result of a sensuality in which he was decidedly lacking, but out of sheer curiosity.[bb]

Meanwhile, the small circle of Africans in Milan who were close to Augustine had expanded slightly. Navigius had rejoined his brother and their mother, if he had not already come with Monica in the spring of 385. And as his cousins, Rusticus and Lartidianus, would soon make their appearance, present at the latest at the 'retreat' of Cassiciacum,[cc] the family circle of Thagaste, in the widest sense, was rebuilt around Augustine; members hastened to join the 'local boy who had made good'. Probably still in 385, Romanianus, constant protector and provider of funds, had also come to Milan, not because of his friend and protégé's success – although this repaid him for so much of his kindness – but to sort out serious business affairs with the imperial Court.[dd] He was very likely accompanied at the time by his son Licentius, whom we shall see similarly attending the debates at Cassiciacum the following year. Helped by his wealth, which was still considerable despite the recent setbacks that were worrying him, Romanianus was an ally of some weight in the community project nurtured by Augustine and Alypius; and in fact it was thanks to him – and Verecundus – that it would be realized for a few months in the present-day Lombard countryside. Perhaps the inspiration for it had come to Augustine because he knew of a Manichaean 'monastery' recently founded in Rome by his host and friend, the 'hearer' Constantius; and an enduring attachment still connected Romanianus with Manichaeism.[12] At all events, the friends had pushed ahead with their plans to quite an extent. They had proposed that the assets available to each of the participants should be pooled to form a communal fund. The community seemed able to gather about ten members; each year two of them would be appointed as officers to manage it, the others being relieved of all material cares. But this fine project, devised by men, came to grief when its authors began to wonder whether their wives would agree – some were married and others, like Augustine, were hoping to be. Merely asking the question, apparently, was enough to provide the answer! The matter was not mentioned again.[ee]

In the midst of his perplexities, and even if for the time being the ideal of a philosophical life led communally had shown itself to be fanciful, Augustine at least had the solace of his discussions with his two soundest friends, his firmest intellectual supports, Alypius and Nebridius. For instance, he debated with them on the 'extremes of good and evil' – the title of a treatise by Cicero – and would confess that in this vast debate in which all the doctrines of the ancient world were contrasted, he would willingly have awarded the palm to Epicurus, had he not believed that a life for the soul existed after death, with the reward or punishment for one's actions, which Epicurus denied.[13] But he did not abandon Epicurus when nurturing the idea – conceived as unreal and expressed in unreal terms – that we would be happy if we were immortal and our life unfolded in a perpetual bodily sensuality, with no fear of losing it. It was contradictory, he knew, and did not conceal from himself that, despite several 'metaphysical escapades' – such as the belief, mentioned above, in the life of the soul after death – he was still the prisoner of a materialism whose tyranny was becoming burdensome and shameful now that he had, as he said, gone beyond 'adolescence'.[ff] However, he had begun to liberate himself; for instance, he had long since rid himself of an anthropomorphic conception of God,[gg] but was still seeking to form an 'idea' of him, almost necessarily closer to the image than the concept; and since he imagined God as 'an immense being who penetrated the whole mass of the universe and was possessed by all things', he had to admit that the body of an elephant contained more of God than the body of a sparrow, since the elephant was bigger and occupied more space![hh] And he was still faced with the major question, insistent as ever, to which twelve years earlier he had thought to find a ready-made answer in the Manichaean doctrine: where does evil come from?[ii] Rejecting a convenient dualism left him temporarily without a solution.

Notes

a.   *Conf.*, V, 23.
b.   Jerome, *Ep.* 45, 7.
c.   Acts, 17, 18.
d.   *Conf.*, V, 23.
e.   Translation cannot exactly render the play on assonance which is one of the charms of Augustinian prose: *Veniebant in animum meum simul cum verbis, quae* diligebam, *res etiam, quas* neglegebam (*Conf.*, V, 24).
f.   *Conf.*, VI, 1.
g.   This is one of the reasons invoked by Ambrose for putting an end to them in Milan.
h.   See above, p. 10.
i.   *Conf.*, VI, 2.
j.   *Ep.* 36, 32 (letter from Augustine to the priest Casulanus); see also *Ep.* 54, 3.
k.   *Conf.*, VI, 2: 'Often, when he noticed me, he could not refrain from praising her to me, congratulating me on having such a mother.'
l.   *Conf.*, VI, 9.
m.   See above, p. 20.
n.   *Conf.*, VI, 23.
o.   *Conf.*, VI, 25.
p.   See above, p. 27.
q.   *De bono coniugali*, V, 5.
r.   *Conf.*, VI, 23.
s.   *Conf.*, VI, 23.
t.   *Soliloquies*, I, 17 (winter 386–7).
u.   *Conf.*, VI, 25: *Procuravi aliam*, perhaps a slave concubine: it was an easy way out.
v.   *De bono coniugali*, V, 5.
w.   *Conf.*, VI, 18.
x.   *Conf.*, VI, 19.
y.   *Conf.*, VI, 17.
z.   *Conf.*, VI, 3: 'Only his celibacy seemed to me a hard thing to bear.'
aa. *Conf.*, VI, 21.
bb. *Conf.*, VI, 22.

cc. See *Beata v.*, I, 6.

dd. *Conf.*, VI, 24; *Acad.*, II, 4: this text records the lawsuits in which Romanianus was engaged.

ee. *Conf.*, VI, 24. The word Augustine uses to describe their female companions is *mulierculae*: 'weak women', incapable of rising to the level of this grand design!

ff. *Conf.*, VII, 1: *Iam mortua erat adulescentia mea mala et nefanda, et ibam in iuventutem.*

gg. *Conf.*, VII, 1.

hh. *Conf.*, VII, 2.

ii. *Conf.*, VII, 7: *Et quaerebam unde malum, et male quaerebam et in ipsa inquisitione non videbam malum.*

CHAPTER X

386: Intellectual conversion

In the autumn of 385, Augustine had been in Milan for a year. His professional success was undeniable and, with his proposed marriage, the promise of social success was no less. It was a triumphal march 'along the broad and beaten ways of the world',[a] but on the path which the *Hortensius* had pointed out to him in his twentieth year – soon to be the Way of the Lord[b] – he was still marking time. And then, in the space of a few months, everything accelerated. However much one tries to clarify a chronology that is difficult to pinpoint in detail, less than a year would pass before Augustine emerged from the impasses into which he had entered.

Augustine's spiritual state a few months prior to his 'deliverance' is probably difficult to grasp, especially for someone of our own times. Great intellectual that he was, from Carthage to Milan by way of Rome he had had access to all the currents of thought in the pre-Christian ancient world, very often through Cicero, but also through the convenient intermediary of the 'doxographies', the anthologies of philosophical opinions and positions which he seems to have consulted first and foremost during his Carthaginian years.[c] On what the great masters of the Hellenistic era had thought about sovereign good and final causes, in other words, the best way for man to conduct his life on this earth, he knew almost as much as a Seneca or a Tacitus might have known in their time.[1] After experiencing its temptation, and not without some risks,[d] he had at last overcome the scepticism of the New Academy. For a 'gentleman' of the classical era, and even the most demanding kind, one who expected philosophy to provide the definition of a way of life on this earth, it would have been broadly sufficient.

But, like many men in Late Antiquity, both pagan and Christian, Augustine was concerned about his salvation. It was this, even more than a hoped-for reply to speculative questions, which had prompted him to enter the 'Church' of Mani, a choice that had weighed heavily on his spiritual development for about a decade. He was indebted chiefly to the meeting with Ambrose, at the end of 384, for the first 'actualization' of a latent – or virtual – Christianity, faintly nourished by childhood memories[e] and practices that were not internalized. He was now not only restrained by the 'attractions of a woman and honours'[f] – worldly *impedimenta* – but led astray by the mists of a 'befouled heart'.[g] This 'mental clutter'[2] was due to his mind being filled with the images that obsessed him. At the beginning of Book VII of the *Confessions*, retrospectively analysing with great acuity his erring ways of that time, he would say that his 'heart' protested violently, though in vain, against the 'fantasies' of his imagination, and that he struggled fruitlessly to drive from his mind, as one would a swarm of mosquitoes, 'the tumultuous and swirling horde of unclean images'.[h] But in a text that dates from his Christian *otium* at Thagaste, he had already drawn a lesson from it for the use of Romanianus, to whom the text was dedicated: 'You have to understand', he wrote in 390, 'that religious error would be impossible if the soul did not honour as its God a soul, a body or its own fantasies.'[i] While his soul was still thus 'befouled', a second and strong impetus towards spiritual progress had come to him from Ambrose, following an initial phase, shortly after his arrival in Milan, when he had listened to the bishop, not unproductively but rather with a wait-and-see attitude.

We saw earlier that Monica, assiduously following Christian practice, formed a connecting link between the bishop who was patiently waiting for Augustine to find himself and her son, who was still unsure of himself, but concealing his uncertainties in the pastor's presence. Through his mother, Augustine was obviously aware of everything that was happening in Christian circles and churches in Milan. A great deal was going on, and it was of major importance.

A Milanese spring

In those years Milan was exposed to a local repercussion of the Arianism that had been condemned at the Council of Constantinople in May 381, and banned at least in the East by an imperial decree of Theodosius. The Arian bishop of Durostorum, a town in lower Maesia on the Danube (today Silistra, on the Romanian–Bulgarian frontier), had therefore gone to Milan to try his luck, with the support of the empress mother Justina, who was herself of Arian faith. The conflict which had been brewing since the coming of this rival bishop broke out in the spring of 385, doubtless on the occasion of the Eastertide baptisms, when Justina, who had meanwhile become regent, demanded of Ambrose that he should hand over to the Arian community and its bishop – who in Ambrose's eyes was a semi-Barbarian to boot – a basilica *extra muros*, the *basilica Portiana*. Ambrose's resistance, backed by a popular uprising that rumbled at the gates of the palace where he was defying Justina, caused the regent to back down temporarily. But this 'Catherine de Medici of Arianism'[3] was tenacious. On 23 January 386 she had a law promulgated under the terms of which freedom of worship was granted to those who upheld the 'homoean' faith,[j] defined by the Council of Rimini in 359 and confirmed at Constantinople in 360; moreover, whoever impeded that freedom of worship became liable to the death penalty.[k]

The latter threat smacked of intimidation, but the Court had provided itself with the legal means of making Ambrose yield. The Arian bishop, Auxentius,[4] asked for a basilica for Easter. The Court proposed to the Catholic bishop that the dispute should be settled by a special jury before the imperial consistory. Ambrose was in a strong position because of his completely legitimate accession to the episcopal chair of Milan and the solidarity of the town's Catholic community, who were well in the majority, and his refusal made confrontation inevitable. Its culmination lasted a whole week, from Friday 27 March, two days before Palm Sunday, to Good Friday, 2 April 386.[5] Ambrose recounted every detail of those days of struggle in a letter to his sister Marcellina.[l]

Since February, he had shut himself into the *basilica Portiana* (probably the present-day basilica of San Lorenzo) with the crowd of faithful, as if preparing for a siege. On 27 March, the Court attempted a diversion: they no longer wanted the *Portiana*, which was outside the walls, but the great New Basilica, *intra muros*; Ambrose refused. The next day, Saturday 28, the prefect of the praetorium in person came to the cathedral where Ambrose was officiating; he returned to the subject of the original demand, the *Portiana*, but this met with the same refusal by the bishop, to the acclamations of his flock, who were already simmering with excitement. The next day, Palm Sunday, 29 March, when the Court decided to attack the *basilica Portiana*, the entire town rose up; a mob occupied the New Basilica, while in the besieged *Portiana* Ambrose held firm, pitting Milanese nationalism against the Gothic soldiers charged with maintaining order, who were mostly Catholic themselves and quickly 'turned' when the bishop threatened them with excommunication. The crisis reached its peak on the Thursday of Holy Week, 2 April. At dawn Ambrose was in the *Portiana*, while the great basilica was occupied by a crowd of faithful to whom the bishop sent several priests so that he could remain in the threatened place of worship, which was still besieged by troops but where the pressure was lessening, with soldiers defecting and joining Ambrose's followers. The bishop spent the night in the church with them, keeping up their courage with his sermons, and singing hymns and psalms with them. The next day, Good Friday, the Court capitulated.

Augustine was well placed to know in detail what was going on, for Monica was among those faithful who opposed the regent empress' will with their passive resistance. 'While by night', he would write, 'the faithful mounted guard in the church, ready to die with their bishop, my mother was there, in the forefront of the anxiety and vigil, living in prayer.'[m] And he added that it was on this occasion, to prevent the people from languishing through sorrow and tedium, for the first time in the West hymns and psalms were sung after the fashion of the Christian East. To those who accused him of rousing the people and even bewitching them with his hymns, Ambrose replied that there was a kind of magic in a song in which each day the Trinity was proclaimed.[n] There is also no doubt that Monica was present at the great festivals which soon afterwards, from 17 to 19 June, followed the discovery of the relics of the holy martyrs Gervasius and Protasius, revealed by Ambrose just at the right moment to 'have heaven ratify his opposition to the heretic regent'.[6] And heaven was in fact on the bishop's side, because a blind man was miraculously cured during the transfer of the relics to the Ambrosian basilica.

Even if one was not seized by the fever that shook Milan in the spring of 386, it was difficult to remain completely unaffected. 'We none the less felt the city's agitation and consternation', Augustine would say. But the event did not seem to have had any further hold on him: the way in which he reports the finding of the relics clearly indicates that he was not an eye-witness, nor had he seen the healing of the blind man; and, as has been rightly pointed out, the very fact that he said nothing of it in the texts recounting the stages in his inner development is enough evidence that the entire sequence, from the people's mobilization at the end of March to the festivals in June, had little or no influence on that development.[7] Augustine must at that time have had a rather awed admiration for this bishop whose bravado in the face of secular power probably impressed him, but also worried him a little; for his own situation was that of a layman holding an official post in Milan. Later, as a bishop of great prestige, but in a diocese that was marginal in relation to the centres of government, he would not experience these high-level confrontations, which Ambrose's past as a top civil servant made it easy for him to master. At Hippo Augustine would encounter crowd disturbances, but would never himself be in the position of having to oppose public authorities, either physically or intellectually, drawing the masses alongside him, as Ambrose did, with the urgent duty to succeed without spilling any blood. He would be spared that ordeal.[o]

Would the 'conversion' of Augustine be in any way the 'conversion of an individualist intellectual, unwilling to go along with the enthusiasms and impulses of the crowd'?[8] The sentence is rather off-putting in that it suggests a quest for personal salvation conducted by a professional man who is indifferent to the upheavals in the life of the community all around him; but in relation to the events in Milan in the spring of 386 it is not basically untrue. Augustine had not been a 'participant', and could not have been even had he wanted to since, unlike his mother, he did not belong to Milan's Catholic Christian community. But between the end of 385 and the summer of 386, there had been times other than those intense weeks for him to have some contact with the bishop. And we know that on those more ordinary occasions Augustine often listened to Ambrose. 'I heard him every Sunday', he writes.[p] This was echoed in what he wrote in the *De beata vita*, in the autumn of 386, still very close to the events, when he says 'he had often noted in *the discourse* (of Ambrose) that the idea of God excludes all idea of body, as does also the nature of the soul, for of all beings the soul is the one that comes nearest to God'.[q] The word he uses here to recall the bishop's sayings – *sermones*: both 'exchange of speech' and 'sermons' – might suggest private conversations with Ambrose. And he did have some, like the one intended to clarify the question of Saturday fasting that tormented Monica. But these tête-à-têtes were certainly infrequent; initially the bishop had intimidated him, and subsequently he found him far too busy to come to his aid personally.[r] In fact, it was Ambrose preaching from his pulpit whom Augustine heard.

The ingenuity of exegetists therefore naturally turned to those of Ambrose's sermons and treatises which are attributable to this period, searching them at the same time for a content likely to have influenced Augustine and dates compatible with what is known of the chronology. Therefore they would date to the end of 385 or beginning of 386 the sermons in which Augustine 'often' heard the bishop repeat St Paul's words: 'The letter killeth, but the spirit giveth life'[9] (2 Cor. 3.6). But it seems an idle search, since the Pauline phrase, with such methodological value, must have been in almost constant use in the mouth of a preacher engaged in the spiritual exegesis of texts from the Old Testament. It is understandable that his hearer made a note of its recurrent appearances. There is probably more likelihood of truly tracking down the written traces of a commentary on Genesis (1.26 and 9.6: 'Man was created in God's image'), hearing which filled Augustine with joy:[s] only the soul, because of its spiritual nature, was the image of God, and that finally put paid to the Manichaeans' mockery of the Christian God in the image of the man he had created and like him possessing a man's body. This commentary, with an express reference to the Manichaeans, is to be found in the sermons of Ambrose's *Hexameron*, which it is agreed were preached during Holy Week in 386.[10] And one of the difficulties recorded by Augustine in the midst of the perplexities he was then suffering, concerning free will as a cause of evil, similarly refers to the sermons in that same series: 'And I directed my attention to what I *heard said*, namely that the free will's decision is the cause of our doing evil.'[t] It emerges incidentally that, even without taking part in the vigils and nocturnal occupation of the church, Monica's son ventured there all the same as a listener during that famous week.

Neoplatonism

In May or June following the Eastertide of 386 Ambrose preached a series of sermons – including the *De Isaac* and the *De bono mortis* – in which, as in the *De Iacob*, preached previously, there is a heavy use of themes that hark back to the *Enneads* of the emperor Gallienus' favourite thinker, Plotinus, who in the middle of the third century had developed in Rome, but in Greek, an original philosophy that rethought Plato's doctrine and had made him the master of what is conveniently termed Neoplatonism.[11]

As the principal author of these unchallengeable comparisons says in conclusion of a long study, the sermons quoted

> present in the context of the testaments, revised and emended according to Catholic dogmas, the fundamental doctrines of the *Enneads* on the sovereign good, the origin of evil, the ascent of the soul towards God to the point of ecstasy, the celestial fatherland, the liberation achieved by the death of the body, and the perpetual life of the Blessed.[12]

The same method of textual parallels has shown the presence of 'Plotinian themes' – or more broadly, Neoplatonic, even tending to the Platonic – in Augustine's texts dating to this period, or slightly later (the *Contra Academicos*, the *Soliloquies*), or relating to it (the *Confessions*). With these links a third phase could thus be identified, even more important than the preceding two, in the bishop of Milan's influence on the rhetor searching for his path in life. It is not absolutely sure, however, that Ambrose's sermons initiated Augustine into certain essential elements of Plotinian doctrine – or at least they may not have been the only things to fill his mind with Platonism and Neoplatonism:[13] for in those decisive spring and summer months in 386, he was keeping company with an 'intellectual' circle in which pagans and Christians mingled, and this played a role as important as Ambrose's in accelerating Augustine's progress.

Parallel with that of Ambrose, the powerful influence of the 'Milanese circle'[14] is undoubted. In the front ranks of its members was Manlius Theodorus, to whom Augustine would soon dedicate his *De beata vita*. Flavius Manlius Theodorus was the Christian counterpart of pagan dignitaries such as Symmachus and Nicomachus Flavianus – but unlike them and Ambrose, he was of modest origins – who were capable of leading an intellectual life worthy of the name at the same time as pursuing their career in high office in the imperial administration. After being prefect of the praetorium for the Gauls, he was living at that time in philosophical retirement in his *suburbanum* near Milan; he had taken advantage of it to write a history of philosophy and various other treatises whose existence is known to us through the poet Claudian, who wrote a verse panegyric for him on the occasion of his consulship in 399; for Manlius Theodorus had returned to office at Stilicho's instigation at the end of the century. We know from Augustine himself that Theodorus was a fervent disciple of Plotinus and, in the same text, Augustine credits him, like Ambrose, with edifying words on God and the nature of the soul from which he had benefited.[15]

In Ambrose's entourage in Milan, Augustine must have had a fairly early meeting with the priest Simplicianus who, although he was older,[16] would succeed his bishop, after having been his mentor. Simplicianus had written nothing but read much of the philosophers, especially Plotinus, to whom he had been introduced in his youth by Marius Victorinus, who had translated the works into Latin. We shall see a little later that the conversation Augustine had with him on the conversion of Marius Victorinus was one of those 'triggers' which hastened his own maturation. Probably in the early summer of 386 he had already had a series of conversations on the connections that could be established between the Neoplatonic system and the Prologue of St John's Gospel; these would make it easier for Augustine to weigh up the concordances and discordances between Neoplatonism and Christianity. In Milanese ecclesiastical circles, Simplicianus more directly than Ambrose was the architect of Augustine's 'conversion'.

Several other names crop up, not in the *Confessions*, but in the dialogues of autumn 386, or in Augustine's first letters dating to this period, of people who seem to have been a part of this network of intellectual relationships. For example, the enigmatic Celsinus,[17] whose name is connected with the 'Platonic books', since in the *Contra Academicos*, addressing Romanianus, Augustine recalls that Celsinus described the books as 'well filled'.[u] Two of his correspondents in that era may be added, Hermogenianus and Zenobius. The first is perhaps Clodius Hermogenianus Olybrius, a great personage, Ausonius' colleague in the consulship of 379, and son of a Christian poetess, Faltonia Proba, with whose family Augustine would later have correspondence.[v] During the winter of 386–7 Augustine wrote Hermogenianus the first of his preserved letters, asking his opinion of the way he had interpreted the New Academy's scepticism in his *Contra Academicos*. His correspondent therefore must also have been something of a philosopher; but he was not a Christian. In his social sphere, as would often be found, it was left to the women to join the new religion. As for Zenobius, the recipient of the second preserved letter from Augustine, a short note, he seems to have been in the service of the Court, which he would quit in a hasty departure, lamented in the *De ordine*, a dialogue dedicated to him, which to some extent he had prompted because he had sent Augustine a poem on 'order'.[w] He appears to be the same man (Augustine would gather from a letter from his brother Dioscurus in 410) who became *magister memoriae*, a very high office close to the emperor.[x] Zenobius was very obviously not a Christian and he too was a 'Platonist'; it was the communal immersion in Neoplatonism that brought pagans and Christians together in this small intellectual circle.

Did he belong to this circle, and if so, who was the 'man swollen with monstrous pride' who, at the end of spring 386, procured for Augustine 'certain books of the Platonists, translated from Greek to Latin'[y] which we shall find later were translated by none other than Marius Victorinus?[z] Everything possible has been done to try to penetrate the anonymity of this mysterious initiator. People have suggested Manlius Theodorus,[18] Porphyry[19] and even the enigmatic Celsinus.[20] After all, his name matters little. One thing is certain: he was not a Christian, since in Augustine's view he was part of those 'prideful' men who rejected the mystery of the incarnation.

But, and this is what counts, those books had a phenomenal effect on

Augustine at the time. Reading them, he experienced once again that firing of the imagination he had known at the age of nineteen on his discovery of the *Hortensius*. He himself recorded the impression in strong terms, and with identical images, in two texts that were chronologically very close to this 'revelation'. 'I was on fire', he would say in the *De beata vita* (I, 4); and in the *Contra Academicos* (II, 5), including Romanianus in his own enthusiasm, spinning out the metaphor a little, he would feel the need to describe this sudden conflagration, to tell how, on the tiny flame that still smouldered in them, 'those books sprinkled the perfumes of Arabia and distilled a few drops of their precious essence: and the blaze that resulted was incredible, Romanianus, incredible'. And there, as in the *De beata vita*, he would add that had it not been for the regard he still held for the example presented to him by great dignitaries, leading a virtuous life in pursuit of wisdom in secular society and in marriage, he would have dropped everything then and there and without further ado 'severed his moorings'.[aa]

Theories have proliferated about the nature of these *libri Platonicorum* which had caused such a 'liberating impact'[21] on him. In his *City of God* – thus after 412 at the earliest – Augustine listed those whom he designated 'Platonists': the Greeks, Plotinus, Iamblichus, Porphyry, and also the bilingual Apuleius.[bb] But there is no trace of the latter in the first works, and none of Iamblichus anywhere. In the *De beata vita*, he noted reading a 'small number of books by Plotinus',[cc] while the *Contra Academicos* contains a eulogy of a Plotinus so close to his master that Plato seems to live again in him,[dd] and in the *Soliloquies* we find Plotinus closely associated with Plato in what he has written about God.[ee] Which quite rightly led Paul Henry to the conclusion that 'of all the Neoplatonic philosophers, Plotinus alone is quoted in the documents that refer us to the era of Augustine's conversion'.[22] There is now fairly general agreement that Augustine first of all read Plotinian texts[23] and that if he read Porphyry it was afterwards, and not in Milan or at Cassiciacum in 386.[24]

'I withdrew completely into myself'[ff]

What Augustine says of his inner experiences in a text separated from them by only a few months reassures us that the account he gives afterwards in Book VII of the *Confessions* is not an artifical reconstruction, but the result, which we may take to be credible, of 'an intense effort of memory to reconstitute truthfully a spiritual climate of ten years before'.[25] He had not received what he had read in the 'books of the Platonists' as intellectual information, but they had created in him the conditions for a reflective withdrawal into himself, experienced with great intensity.

> Warned (by these books) to return to myself, I entered my innermost being led by your guidance . . . I entered, and saw with my soul's eye, feeble though it was, I saw above the eye of my soul, above my mind, the unchangeable light, not the ordinary light that all may see, nor a light of the same kind yet stronger, as though that light would have a more dazzling brilliance and by its power fill everything. No, it was not that, but different, far different.[gg]

So begins the account of an experience that may quite legitimately be termed mystical, put into words which evoke specifically Plotinian themes, but are freely adopted in a spiritual context that may already be said to be Christian.[26] Similarly, Plotinus is still in the background when Augustine admits that this light sharply brought home to him that he was far from God in the *regio dissimilitudinis*: 'You struck my feeble gaze with the power of your beams of light, and I trembled with love and dread, and I found myself to be far from you in the *region of unlikeness*.' Before becoming Plotinian, the latter concept harked back to Plato;[27] but in the Neoplatonic perspective, it is related to the imprisonment of the soul in perceptible realities, into which it sinks as if in a quagmire: the soul enters the 'region of unlikeness' in a movement that distances it from the divine Being.[hh] Conversely, for Augustine, it is when the soul turns towards God and enters his light that it perceives the situation, becomes aware of the abyss separating it from him as an ontological difference between the created and the Creator. Augustine continues, making the Being who sends this dazzling light say: 'I am the food of the strong: grow and you shall feed on me; and you shall not change me into yourself, like the food of your flesh, but you shall be changed into me', in other words, inserting into the account of the crisis he had experienced some twelve years earlier a eucharistic component that seems to have been added. The mystical experience culminates shortly afterwards. To the lamenting Augustine – remembering his recent inability to conceive of the incorporeal – who asks if 'truth is nothing, because it is diffused neither through finite nor infinite space', God replies 'from afar' as he had answered Moses when revealing his 'eternal name': 'Yea, verily! I am that I am (Exod. 3.14).' And Augustine receives this reply mystically: 'And I heard as one hears in one's heart, and there was absolutely no room for doubt.'

For well over half a century people have tried to show that this section of the *Confessions* – from VII, 16 to 23 – relates not to a single experience, but a series of 'spiritual anabases', reworked in the bishop's memory, that these 'empty attempts at Plotinian ecstasies' were dual if not plural.[28] The interpretation depends largely on the way the texts are read: by the 'biographer', mainly concerned with retracing the different phases of Augustine's life, or by the 'phenomenologist', intent on discovering, behind the apparent repetition of situations, the insistent resumption of the description of a state, on the one hand – the human condition, with its weaknesses, even when armed with Neoplatonic philosophy and mysticism – and on the other, an asceticism, a specific and precarious action. Noteworthy in these pages is the use of the imperfect tense to render 'continuity' – or efforts – and the perfect tense – the 'past historic' – to convey actions, and sometimes success. This play of the tenses is remarkable in chapter 23. Augustine begins by recording his attempts – usually vain – describing the unsettled situation that is often the contemplative's lot: 'This joy I had in my God was not a settled joy: I felt myself drawn to you by your beauty,[29] but soon was dragged from you by my own weight and fell groaning to the ground. That weight was my carnal custom, but the remembrance of You stayed with me . . .' It has rightly been emphasized[30] that this map of spiritual experience, combining the sweetness of the call that is heard, the momentum of the upward flight, then the bitterness of feeling the dragging weight and finally the grief of the fall, are to be found in Book X of the *Confessions*, in a passage in which the 'present tense' of the writing, matching the 'imperfect tense' of the memory, confirms that the instability of the mystic remained the bishop's fate:

> And at times you admit me to a most unaccustomed depth of feeling which attains such ineffable sweetness that, if it reached its fullness in me, something would happen that is measureless against this life here below. But I sink back into our world of wretched burdensomeness and am once again engulfed in the ordinary life that holds me fast, and I weep mightily, but mightily it holds me.[ii]

Detaching it from this background of aborted or imperfect attempts, in the same chapter 23, Augustine describes in the past historic one of those fleeting moments of successful spiritual asceticism in Milan, in the summer of 386, not necessarily the only one but an excellent example:

> Thus, I gradually passed from bodies to the soul, which perceives by means of the body, and thence to its inner power, to which the body's senses communicate external perceptions – limits that animals too can reach – and thence again to that power of reasoning which gathers what the senses grasp in order to judge it. When this power found itself variable in me, it raised itself up to its own understanding and drew my thoughts away from habit, withdrawing it from the swarms of contradictory fantasies, to discover in what light it was bathed when it unhesitatingly proclaimed that the immutable must be preferred to the mutable, and whence came its knowledge of the immutable itself. For if it had not by some means known, it would in no way have preferred it to the mutable. Then, in a flash of trembling sight it came to the Being himself . . . But I could not fix my gaze, and my frailty was forced back and reduced me to my ordinary view; and I was left with only a loving memory yearning for a dish of which I had, as it were, caught the aroma but was not yet able to eat.

In this page we again find the narrative style, in the 'perfect', already used at the beginning of the account of his first inner experience, in chapter 16;[iii] but it has its own particular quality in comparison with the first account. Initially by the use of the dialectic of degrees: the ascent is described here as gradual, raising the senses to the intelligence which judges them, thence mounting to the self-knowledge which, thinking by itself, discovers the light already at work in it causing it to prefer the immutable to the mutable. And, as O. Du Roy has written, an even more important difference, 'what Augustine uses here systematically, is this path discovered thanks to the first experience when, summoned to his innermost self, taken out of himself, God had paved the way for him . . . At the summit of this ascent, his soul glimpses God, but cannot sustain its gaze.'[31]

With the 'ecstasy of Ostia' we shall again find the same gradual rise and the same return, with its accompanying powerful longing. The psychic climate, however, will not be the same; the sighs Augustine heaves with Monica will not be the groans of the soul frustrated because of its frailty. For in the meantime his baptism will have taken place, and Augustine will have learnt that perfect bliss is not of this world. Perhaps it is above all because the Ostia experience will take place 'in a climate of withdrawal, prayer and humility which will enable him to surmount the metaphysical *dissimilitudo* by accepting it and will lay open his whole soul to the penetration of divine grace'.[32] In other words, because the conversion of his will has followed the conversion of his intellect.

The conversion of the intellect

From the Neoplatonists Augustine had received not only encouragement to spiritual exercise; through them he had gained access to a philosophy which seemed able to answer many of the questions he had been asking himself for some dozen years; to be more exact, the reflective withdrawal into himself, the first condition of an 'anagogic' ascent towards the divine, after that fleeting grasp of the Being, had enabled him, thanks to that illumination, to achieve a view of the world that was to become the basis of his metaphysics. Many of the articles of that philosophy, notably in its most strictly ontological aspects, would remain the fixed points in his thinking in the rest of his works, including his preaching as bishop.

Very naturally, in Book VII of the *Confessions*, the assessment the author makes of his new metaphysical acquisitions occurs just after his account, in chapter 16, of his spiritual apprehension of God and the soul:[33]

> And I beheld all things below you, and saw that it cannot be said absolutely that they exist or absolutely that they do not exist: they are, in truth, because they are from you, but they are not, because they are not what you are. For what truly exists, is that which endures immutably.[kk]

There is therefore between beings – the 'things' – a hierarchy of well-defined ontological density starting from the Being and dependent on him. God is the Supreme Good, and what is corruptible and mutable, very low down on the ontological scale, is also good, since created by God. As for evil, whose origin had obsessed Augustine for a long time, 'it was not a substance, because if it were a substance, it would be good'.[ll] The right question regarding evil was not, 'Where does it come from?' but, 'What is it?', as he would soon develop it in two of his early works.[mm] In this Augustine was reacting like a good disciple of Plotinus, but also as a listener to Ambrose, who had probably drawn his attention to the definition of evil as the deprival of good in his preaching in the spring of 386.[34]

Deprival of good or lack of being, in ontological terms, when it is a matter of physical evil, it is also the absence of harmony between certain elements of creation and certain others, whereas all the elements of this creation are good in themselves and we must accept nature as it is – 'our earth has its own cloudy and windy sky, which is consistent with it'[nn] – and God has also created the viper and the little worm good, matching them with the lower parts of his creation.[oo] As for moral evil – or the evil within us: *iniquitas* – it was not, as a facile Manichaeism had at first suggested to him,[pp] another nature within us which sinned. No, 'it was not a substance, but deviated from the supreme substance, yourself, O God, the perversion of the will towards baser things, casting out its inner good and swelling outwardly'.[qq] Ideas of Plotinian origin which, swiftly modified by specifically Christian additions – the Prologue to the Gospel of St John, St Paul's Epistles – complemented by them and reassimilated through them, would lastingly form the intellectual framework of the Augustinian doctrine of the universe, God and mankind.[35]

Towards the end of Book VII of the *Confessions*, just before mentioning his reading of St Paul, Augustine marked the spiritual, though not intellectual, boundaries of this 'intellectual conversion', well pleased that he had first read those *libri Platonicorum*. He would write:

> I prated as one well skilled, and if I had not sought your way in Christ, I would have ended up not *fine*, but *finished*[rr] ... Where indeed was that charity that builds on the foundation of humility, which is Christ Jesus? And when would those books teach it to me? If you wished me to become acquainted with them, before I had meditated upon your Scriptures, I believe it was in order to impress the feelings they inspired in me on my memory so that later I would be able to distinguish the difference between presumption and confession, and between those who saw whither they should go yet knew not how, and the *way* that leads not only to behold but even to dwell in the blessed *fatherland*.

He adds that if he had read those books after, and not before, the Scriptures, he would have risked being led astray by them from the 'way', that is, led to believe that they were just as capable of putting him on the 'way'. This is something even those least acquainted with Augustine would find hard to believe.

Again in the *Confessions*, recalling the Manichaean errors of his youth and his reading of the philosophers which had helped him to escape from them, and which seemed truthful to him, like the Neoplatonists dealing with the Creator and Creation, he states, 'Even when those philosophers were telling the truth, I should have passed them by, for love of you.'[ss] And perhaps that is why he himself had not become a philosopher; or rather, that after the *Dialogues* of Cassiciacum he did not remain a philosopher in the classical sense of the word.[36] But if he had remained at the stage where he was in Milan at the beginning of the summer of 386, after reading the Neoplatonists, and had continued to sigh with them for the fleetingly glimpsed 'fatherland' without being able to find the 'way' there, he would probably have become no more than a by-product, among others, of this dying Neoplatonism.[37] 'Going beyond' philosophy would lead him to salvation, but equally, without his being aware of or concerned by it, to the greatest renown among men, which too is immortal.

Notes

a. *Conf.*, VI, 24.
b. *Conf.*, VI, 26: *et constitues nos in tua via.*
c. See above, p. 51.
d. See above, pp. 60–1, and *Contra Acad.*, II, 23: 'That had made me lazy and completely indolent.'
e. To which Ambrose's words had restored credit: cf. *Conf.*, VI, 5: *Gaudebam, deus meus, quod ecclesia . . . in qua* mihi *nomen Christi* infanti *est inditum non saperet* infantiles nugas.
f. *Beata vita*, I, 4: *Ne in philosophiae gremium celeriter advolarem*, uxoris honorisque illecebra detinebar.
g. *Conf.*, VII, 2. 'Heart' is to be taken here in the biblical and almost Pascalian sense.
h. *Conf.*, VII, 1.
i. *De vera religione*, 18.
j. From the Greek *homoios*, 'similar', expressing the similarity of the 'persons' of the Holy Trinity, rather than their consubstantiality according to the Nicene creed.

k.   *C. Th.*, XVI, I, 4.
l.   Ambrose, *Ep.* 20, 25–6.
m.   *Conf.*, IX, 15.
n.   Therefore the symbol of a truly trinitarian faith as opposed to Arianism: *Contra Auxentium*, 34.
o.   Or he would be loath to do so, as in Carthage in the summer of 413, when he would say that he was powerless, after the death of Marcellinus, to save all those whom the Count Marinus had thrown into prison: see below, p. 268.
p.   *Conf.*, VI, 4.
q.   *De beata vita*, I, 4.
r.   *Conf.*, VI, 3 and 18; on the latter text, see above, p. 74.
s.   *Conf.*, VI, 4.
t.   *Conf.*, VII, 5; cf. *Hexameron*, I, 8, 31.
u.   *Contra Acad.*, II, 5.
v.   *Ep.* 130, 131, 150, the latter, around 414, commemorating Demetrias' taking the veil: cf. below, p. 332.
w.   *De ordine*, I, 20.
x.   *Ep.* 117: *Frater Zenobius magister memoriae factus est.*
y.   *Conf.*, VII, 13.
z.   *Conf.*, VIII, 3.
aa. *De beata vita*, I, 4, to contrast with *Conf.*, VI, 19, *in fine*.
bb. *City of God*, VIII, 12.
cc. *De beata vita*, I, 4, where the reading *Plotini* is to be preferred to *Platonis*, who also features in the tradition.
dd. *Contra Acad.*, II, 41.
ee. *Soliloquia*, I, 9.
ff. *Contra Acad.*, II, 5.
gg. *Conf.*, VII, 16.
hh. In this sense, the *regio egestatis* evoked by Augustine in *Conf.*, II, 18, *in fine*, to portray the spiritual desert of his adolescence, is close to the Plotinian perspective.
ii. *Conf.*, X, 65.
jj. Above, p. 84.
kk. This statement in *Conf.*, VII, 17 is to be found almost unchanged in *Enarr. in Psalm.* 134, 4.
ll. *Conf.*, VII, 18.
mm. See the *De mor. manichaeorum*, II, 2; in the same period (388), he would reply to Evodius in *De libero arbitrio*, I, 6: 'You ask how it comes about that we do evil; one must first examine what doing evil is.'
nn. *Conf.*, VII, 19.
oo. *Conf.*, VII, 22.
pp. See above, pp. 39–40.
qq. *Conf.*, VII, 22. Plotinus is clearly underlying here: *Enn.*, V, 1, 1, 4–8.
rr. *Conf.*, VII, 26: note the contrast and play on words, typical of Augustine's style: *peritus/periturus*.
ss. *Conf.*, III, 10: *Etiam vera dicentes philosophos transgredi debui, prae amore tuo.*

CHAPTER XI

386: Conversion of the will

Just as it is difficult to establish the chronology of the strictly intellectual phase of Augustine's conversion at the end of the first few months of 386, so it is to pinpoint during the summer of the same year the phase that witnessed the last of his resistance crumble. In this precipitate sequence of events we must content ourselves, not without difficulty, with a relative chronology; everything happened within the space of a few weeks to culminate in the 'August enlightenment' in the Milan garden.

He still had a few stages to go, on the road leading to it, and at that point Augustine met Simplicianus along the way. The *Confessions* report only one meeting with the old priest of Milan,[a] but there is good reason to think that Augustine did not wait to confide in him until the summer of 386 was well advanced. Much later, when he was composing Book X of the *City of God*, around 415 – and when Simplicianus, who had meanwhile become bishop of Milan, had departed this life – he revealed that he had often heard him recount the story of the 'Platonist' among his friends – thought to be Marius Victorinus, and the story would have taken place in Rome – who was wont to say that the beginning of the Prologue to John's Gospel should be written in letters of gold and placed in the most prominent places in churches.[1] It is therefore likely, although not definitely stated anywhere, that it was Simplicianus, at one of their first meetings, who acquainted Augustine with those famous verses. It cannot be ruled out, however, that he had come to know them independently of the old priest, at the time when he was reading the *libri Platonicorum*, so prevalent was it in Neoplatonist circles – a custom that had long been held[2] – to consider John's Prologue as having been inspired by Neoplatonism.

Of that assimilation – one might almost say appropriation – confirmation may be found in two pages of Book VI of the *Confessions*, in the famous passage where Augustine, taking stock of his Neoplatonic reading and simultaneously balancing the points of agreement and divergence of those texts with Christian texts,[b] sums up the former with the very terms used at the start of the Johannean Prologue – and quotes it verbatim up to John 1.10 – as expressing, if not to the letter at least faithfully in spirit, the equivalence of the Christian *Verbum* and the Platonic *Logos*.[c] 'But,' he adds, '"that he came unto his own and his own received him not, but to as many as received him he gave the power to become the sons of God, even to them that believe on his name" (John 1.11–12), *this* I did not read in those books.'[d] Similarly, he had not read 'that the Word became flesh and dwelt among us'.[e] With even more reason, he had not read about the incarnation of the Son and his crucifixion, as he says, continuing his antithetical style, and now quoting Pauline texts.[f]

When, therefore, during those tightly packed weeks, did Augustine 'seize upon'[3] St Paul? Here again, probably following one of his meetings with

Simplicianus, consequent upon the exaltation produced by reading the *libri Platonicorum*, but also by the dissatisfaction of a too fleeting vision of the 'fatherland'. We shall see that the priest would also tell him of an experience he had had that was an excellent example, the exhortatory power of which would be as effective as the reading material he would suggest. But when Augustine tells us at the beginning of Book VIII of the *Confessions* that he was going to confide 'the upheaval in his soul' to Simplicianus, one might think that Paul's Epistles were the first remedy the old pastor recommended. A careful reading of the *Confessions*, VII, 27, seems to show that it was not his first discovery of the Apostle who, on the original reading had not appeared to him to be free from internal contradictions, sometimes going as far as disagreement with the Law and the Prophets.[g] A second eager and careful reading revealed the unity of these texts, and also that they were in accord with everything he had read in the Platonic books, but 'strengthened by grace'.[h] Let me quote the conclusion of both the Pauline readings and Book VII of the *Confessions*:

> For it is one thing to perceive the land of peace from a wooded mountain peak, and not to find the way to it, striving in vain towards it through impassable regions, amid attacks and ambushes laid by fugitives and deserters, under their leader, the lion and the dragon: but a different thing to keep to the path that leads to that land, built under the protection of the heavenly Ruler, safe from the brigandry of those who have deserted the heavenly army; for they shun that way like a torture.[i]

He thus resumed the distinction already made between 'those who see where to go without knowing the way' – the Platonists – and 'the One who is the Way leading to the blessed homeland, which one must dwell in and not merely see' – who is Christ.

'A man of outstanding wisdom'

Augustine had heard about Jesus Christ since his earliest years, and it will be remembered that with those magic syllables, adapted to their own ways, the Manichaeans had concocted the birdlime to ensnare him in their trap. He had now escaped from that snare, but his 'Christology' was still fairly rudimentary; combined with the clarifications lavished upon him by Simplicianus, it was probably his reading of St Paul that helped him to dispel an error in which he would later recognize the doctrine of a heresiarch by the name of Photinus.[j]

He admits it openly: 'My opinion of Christ, my Lord, was limited to seeing him as a man of outstanding wisdom, who could have no equal.' Fifteen centuries later, Ernest Renan would startle his audience by presenting Christ as an 'incomparable man' in his inaugural lesson to the Collège de France. But even then Augustine was not so positivist. At a time when a widespread liking for *mirabilia* made their acceptance easy even for a Christian poorly educated in the faith, he had accepted without difficulty the dogma of Christ's virgin birth, which he had heard in childhood. And following the sentence just quoted, he writes that in his eyes this 'wisdom' was chiefly due to the fact that 'being marvellously born of a virgin to be the example of the contempt to be felt for temporal things in order to obtain immortality, (Christ) seemed to me, through the divine solicitude for us, to have merited very great authority in his teaching. But what mystery lay in "The Word made flesh" I could not even imagine.' On the subject of Christ and his life, Augustine accepted all that could be read in the Gospels: Jesus had eaten and drunk, slept and walked about like a man; he had gone through the gamut of human feelings, and had had a human soul and intellect. But because he could not conceive that this changeable creature was hypostatically united with the unchangeable Word, this Christ, who had combined in himself all the best of man, was in his view no more than a man of superior wisdom, a participant in the divine wisdom, but not a God made man. Did he owe this conception of Jesus to his reading of Porphyry? Some have thought so.[4] However, unlike Augustine, Porphyry probably did not believe in Christ's virgin birth.

In the same period, Alypius, whose evolution was proceeding in parallel with Augustine's and who debated these problems with his friend, had for his part constructed a false idea of the Catholic doctrine on Christ which was creating an obstacle to his adherence to the faith. Writes Augustine:

> He thought that the Catholics believed in a God clothed in flesh, so that in Christ was only God and flesh, and he thought they did not attribute the soul and mind of man to him; and as he was convinced that the deeds of Christ recorded by tradition could not have been performed except by a living and rational being, he moved only slowly towards the Christian faith.[k]

Those ideas belonged to Apollinaris of Laodicea, a Syrian theologian of the period who, prompted by a concern for theological coherence, refused to accept the existence in Christ of a soul united with a body, and thus a possibility of sin and the compromise of salvation. According to him, in the person of Jesus the Word had come in contact with man's flesh after the manner of the union of soul and body in ordinary humanity. Thus Christ was not composed of a human nature, soul and body, united with a divine nature, but was only a body animated by a divine nature. In this way any risk of dualism was avoided, but at the same time the strictly human reality of salvation was denied. These views of Apollinaris had been condemned as heretical shortly beforehand at the Council of Constantinople in 381, but their power to attract would last for a long while to come. They were part of the nebulous Christology of the period, and must have circulated in Milan as they would in the East until the Council of Chalcedon, in 451.[5]

How example is contagious: the conversion of Marius Victorinus

We must return to Simplicianus. Among the conversations Augustine had with the old priest, compressed to a unity by the spiritual dramatization in the Confessions, one in particular had a special driving force. At the time of this encounter, probably July 386, in parallel with his philosophical and theological edification, Augustine had changed greatly on the moral plane. He says so clearly: 'I had become disgusted with my worldly life; it had become burdensome, now that my former passions for honours and wealth no longer encouraged me to bear such heavy bondage.'[l] But, he adds, he still felt bound by the impossibility of giving up women. What was to be done? Among the faithful who filled the church which he now frequented with increasing diligence he saw two kinds of status coexisting, of married men and those who were celibate. He had read 1 Corinthians 7, and did not know which side to take. He also says that he had already found the precious pearl which, selling all that he had, he should have bought[m] – yet he still hesitated. For the moment he was in greater need of living references than of indoctrination.

It was Simplicianus who provided them. The old priest had taken Augustine's measure and sensed that in him humility needed to triumph over the pride of the intellectual; he therefore told him the story of Marius Victorinus, whom he had known when he was a young man. If ever there had been a great intellectual in Rome in that era, laden with all the vanities of this world, he was surely the one: many senators had been his disciples and – a signal honour – in his lifetime he had seen his statue erected on the Roman Forum. Towards the end of his life the old master, who had translated Plotinus and was one of the leading lights of Neoplatonism, had begun to read the Scriptures, and had confided in Simplicianus that he had become a Christian. To which the priest had answered that he would not believe him or number him among the faithful until he had seen him in church. Thereupon, Victorinus had said ironically, 'So is it walls that make Christians?'[n] This philosopher, who had been led towards a sort of deist faith only by an inward maturation, nurtured by both secular and Christian reading, found it hard to conceive that Christianity could also be the assembly in one place of men and women united by the same belief.[o]

One day, however, he sought out Simplicianus: 'Let us go to the church,' he said, 'I want to be a Christian!' After following an initial catechesis, Victorinus put his name down for baptism. But an ordeal awaited him; it was customary in Rome, in the baptismal liturgy, for the profession of faith to be pronounced in the presence of all the faithful from a raised dais. Showing their consideration for him, the priests suggested to Victorinus that he should recite this credo more unobtrusively and not in public, as shyer people were advised to do, said Simplicianus. But the philosopher rejected this offer and mounted the dais to declaim the words amidst the acclamations of the crowd of faithful chanting his name.

Simplicianus had hit the target. 'The moment he told me about Victorinus, I was on fire to imitate him.'[p] Augustine felt all the more involved in this precedent because he was professionally in the same situation as his Roman colleague. To round off his *exemplum*, Simplicianus did not forget to add that, shortly after his conversion, Victorinus had been placed in a difficult position by the emperor Julian's law forbidding Christians to teach oratory and great literature; the rhetor had chosen 'to abandon the school's prattle rather than the divine Word'. And Augustine envied him the good fortune of having been presented with a choice from the outside, whereas he was prey to an internal conflict.

For, although Simplicianus' lesson in humility had struck home, he remained fettered by the chains of what he calls *consuetudo* in the *Confessions*, the inveterate weight of the body's habits. He sums it up: 'There were two wills in me, one old the other new, the former carnal and the latter spiritual, contending with each other; and their conflict laid waste my soul.'[q] No one after him would better express this struggle between sluggishness and grace, the slumberer's lingering on the bed from which he would really like to tear himself, the 'I'm just coming!', the 'a moment more!', with which the flesh indefinitely puts off the soul.[r] To free himself from those final bonds, Augustine would need further admonitions.

The longest day: the tales of Ponticianus

During those days when everything was happening so quickly, Augustine was not alone in his anxieties. With him he had Alypius, who was then available and awaiting new office, having been legal assessor for the third time. Nebridius was sharing the life of his two friends. As we saw – above, p. 65 – he had taken a modest position assisting a Milanese grammarian, Verecundus, in his school.

One day when Nebridius was absent, a certain Ponticianus visited Augustine and Alypius. He, too, was African, and they were acquainted with him; at that time he held a prominent post at Court. On a little table nearby, Ponticianus noticed a book, which he picked up, opened and, to his surprise – for he had expected to find one of the rhetor Augustine's 'tools of his trade' – discovered that it contained the Epistles of St Paul. He himself was a Christian and was pleasantly surprised to find them in the hands of his compatriot.

Guided by the unexpected discovery of this spiritual association, a conversation began. Ponticianus told the two friends the story of Anthony, the Egyptian monk, father of all anchorites. There was double astonishment, both of the narrator who, realizing that his hearers did not know the story, lingered over it, and of Augustine and Alypius, who were astounded by the deeds of this athlete of God and amazed that they had only just heard about him.[6] With Ponticianus, the two friends were going to have one surprise after the other, and listen to him with increasingly passionate interest. For though Anthony's spiritual heroism held some fascination for them, a hermit's life in the desert was not likely to exert the strongest of temptations over them. What followed would prove overwhelming in quite a different way.

Ponticianus passed imperceptibly to the monastic life that was beginning to develop in the West. To the great astonishment of Augustine and Alypius, who had never heard of it, he revealed that outside the walls of Milan itself there was a monastery, its upkeep supported by Ambrose. Mainly – and it was here that the 'tales' of Ponticianus struck at the soul of his two hearers – he delved into his own memories. Some years before, when he was serving at Trier in the body known as the *agentes in rebus*,[7] one day when the emperor was spending the afternoon at the circus games, and he thus had some free time, he had taken advantage of it to go for a walk with three of his comrades in the gardens that stretched beyond the ramparts. They had split into two pairs, and while Ponticianus and his companion went their way, the other two happened to come across a hut where anchorites were living. And there, Ponticianus continued, they found the book telling the story of Anthony's life. Reading it, one of the two marvelled and was inflamed by it. What followed, Augustine puts in his *Confessions* in a direct style which makes it obvious that the emotional dialogue between the two *agentes in rebus* in Trier is the one he had with himself as his liberation drew near. Where does our work lead us? the one with the book in his hands said to his friend. What more can we hope, after many pains and dangers, than to be 'friends of the emperor', whereas to be the 'friend of God', if I so desire, can be achieved this instant?[s] They did not deliberate for long. When Ponticianus and his friend rejoined them, the two friends, one taking the other along with him, had already decided to abandon everything in this world.[8] They stayed in the hut, 'fixing their hearts upon heaven', while Ponticianus and his friend returned to the imperial palace, 'their hearts dragging in earthly things'.[t]

At the end of this account, it was Augustine's turn to have his heart in the dust; the image of that conversion, which should have been his own, was what touched him most. Once more he looked back into himself, reliving an accelerated form of the twelve years that had elapsed since he read the *Hortensius*. Twelve years during which he had made every effort to find the truth, from Mani to the New Academy, from the Academics to the Platonists. And now that he had exhausted the paths of philosophy, he was not one step further forward. He saw simple men, armed with nothing but their own humility, reach the goal. It was in this state of extreme agitation that he threw himself upon Alypius, crying, 'What is wrong with us? The unlearned rise up and take heaven by storm, and we, with our knowledge but no heart, do nothing but wallow in flesh and blood!'[u]

The longest day: the garden in Milan

Augustine's internal turmoil had taken him to the bottom of the little garden which he and Alypius used, as far as possible from the house, as if to materialize the beginnings of a hermitical life, that breaking away which he longed for but could not yet accept. Alypius had followed him, step by step and silently. 'My desire for solitude could not be disturbed by his presence,' he says, 'and yet could he for a moment have deserted me in the state I was in?' The closeness of the two friends, despite the very marked difference in their temperament, can never be adequately described.

But now alone with himself in his torment, Augustine became aware of a split in his innermost soul. True, the analysis he makes of it in the *Confessions* lies in the perspectives which were now those of the priest, then the bishop who had reflected much on free will and devoted several books to refuting Manichaean dualism. It was also written with the words and enriched with the literary memories of the former rhetor, and relies on his habit of narrative dramatization, so that these pages, like the celebrated account in the epilogue that closes them, of all the texts in Antiquity – and perhaps in all literature – are probably the ones that have been most closely scrutinized with the avowed intent of distinguishing authenticity from fiction, and isolating 'raw life' from literary rewriting. This would have greatly surprised Augustine who, here as elsewhere, was very careful to point out the distance that necessarily separates feelings which have been experienced and the words used to recount them after such a lapse of time, and had pondered enough on the mechanisms of memory to know that the reconstruction of the thing remembered has nothing in common with reading a page of the intimate diary that one has not written.

So it came about that in the garden in Milan he planned an analysis of will which retrospectively appears to be fed by ideas that would be fully developed later within the setting of the anti-Pelagian controversy. But the weaknesses of that will were the ones torturing Augustine on that August day in 386, and causing him to begin to settle accounts with the Manichaeans. If he was prey to a simultaneous dual craving that was tearing him apart, it was not because two souls within him, one good, one bad, were in conflict,[v] but because the dissociation of his soul, one part of which was drawn downwards by the weight of his bad habits, prevented him from fully exerting his will towards a truth he none the less recognized. Adam – though in the full freedom of his origin – had experienced that fall, and had dragged his sons after him.[w]

In the *Confessions*, Augustine manipulates the puppets of this internal dispute as if in a theatre. First, his soul's old mistresses: 'They enthralled me, my old friends, plucking gently at my fleshly garment, and murmuring softly, "Are you sending us away, then? And from that moment on shall we never more be with you, and never more will you be permitted to do this or that, never more?"'[x] Titillating reminders of fairly precise pleasures whispered behind his back, 'as it were plucking at me furtively to make me look back at them'. Our hero[9] resists, but hesitates, his steps are hindered, while the 'tyrannical habit' ironically whispers to him, 'Do you think you could do without them?' But on the other side, the side where 'he trembles to go', the lady Continence is there to come to his aid. Making use of an imagery that will often be found later in portraying the elect of the Last Judgement, she shows him the countless throng – men and women, young and old, virgins and aged widows – all children born to her by the Lord. Why will he not join them, she seems to ask with a faintly ironic smile. But he still hears the whisperings of his old friends, and he blushes and continues to waver.

This last struggle brought such a cloud of anguish into Augustine's heart that there arose in him 'a mighty storm, accompanied by a great outpouring of tears'.[y] To give free rein to them, he went away from Alypius and lay down under a fig tree.[10] There, in the midst of his tears, he uttered pitiful cries: 'How long, how long? Will it be tomorrow, always tomorrow?[11] Why not this very hour have an end to my iniquities?'

'Take up and read!'

Thus did I speak, and I wept in the great bitterness of my crushed heart. And lo, I heard a voice from the neighbouring house, whether of a boy or a girl I know not, chanting and repeating several times: 'Take up and read! Take up and read!' And immediately, with a changed countenance, I began most earnestly to wonder whether it was usual for children in any kind of game to sing such words, but I could not remember ever having heard the like. So, holding back my tears, I rose, seeing no other interpretation of this divine order than a command to open the book and read the first chapter I might light upon.

Indeed, I had heard it said of Anthony that, chancing to come in while the Gospel was being read, he took it as a personal admonition, as if what was being read was intended for him: 'Go, and sell that thou hast and give to the poor and thou shalt have treasure in heaven. Come and follow me,'[z] and that this oracle had converted him to you.

I therefore hastened to return to the place where Alypius was sitting, for that was where I had placed the Apostle's book when I had risen. I seized it, opened it and silently read the first chapter my eyes fell upon: 'Not in rioting and drunkenness, not in chambering and wantonness, not in strife or envying. But put ye on the Lord Jesus Christ, and make not provision for the flesh to fulfil the lusts thereof.'[aa]

I would read no further; there was no need, for instantly, as the verse ended, it was as if a soothing light spread through my heart and all the shadows of doubt melted away.[bb]

One must take this text and read it as Augustine took the book of the Apostle and read it in the light of the garden in Milan, cleared of all the glosses with which an extraordinary exegetist relentlessness has flooded it. And see those glosses as no more than the homage – almost worship – rendered by philologists to the lines which narrate with such simplicity the trembling instant when everything topples, and twelve years of torturing hesitations make way for a certainty on which to build a new life, as if on a rock. The fig tree under which Augustine was lying may well recall the one under which Nathaniel lay,[12] but is that a reason to doubt its existence? Because it is – in a certainly original place: the 'garden' – a tree that is both commonplace and symbolic, should one question its reality,[13] whereas no one has any doubts about the 'second pillar in the entrance to the choir, on the right, on the side of the sacristy', near which Claudel, in Notre-Dame de Paris, experienced the happening that would, as he said, dominate his entire life? And the voice that Augustine heard of a boy or a girl, who knows? – an 'angel voice', assuredly – did it come from the 'neighbouring house' or the 'divine house', as it is written in the oldest manuscript to preserve this text?[14] It really was the 'house next door', but it was obviously 'divine', like the admonition that emerged from it.[15]

As we know, the commonplace and well attested ancient practice of 'drawing lots' (reading your future), by delving into Homer and Virgil just as much as into the Scriptures, is thought to underlie the kind of consultation Augustine applies to the Epistles of St Paul.[16] It does not necessarily follow that he subjected himself to a whole ritual which ancient and medieval texts tell us about, or transposed it into a 'romanticized', or at least fictional, form. In any case, the scene described in the *Confessions* offers only a vague similarity to those rituals of *sortilegium*. Augustine is in doubt, not about the meaning of what he hears, but about its concrete reality: was it a nursery rhyme, or a game, during which children ordered one another, in a kind of chanted refrain, to take a book and read it, using the words – *tolle, lege* – that would naturally be spoken in Latin?[17] And that it was a sign from heaven, a divine admonition, Augustine is even more convinced when he discovers the content of the verse on which his eyes alight when he opens the book. For, contrary to what has been said and reiterated,[18] this precept of Christian morality, in itself so banal, was for him the least banal it could possibly be; of all the texts he could have lighted upon in a 'blind' consultation of the Pauline letters, this one bore the strongest message for him. Not, of course, regarding 'rioting' and 'drunkenness', nor 'strife'; but Augustine's whole life from adolescence to this hour of grace highlights that the most solid barrier to his aspiration to the perfect life was not ambition, or the pursuit of honours or wealth, but what St Paul calls 'the satisfaction of the flesh and its lusts'. And if there was a miracle, it was that this verse, precisely, of the Epistle to the Romans came just at the right moment to unlock the final bolt.[19]

Back to the garden in Milan. As soon as he had read the decisive text, Augustine closed the book, first marking the page. Then he had rejoined Alypius and told him everything that had happened. A victim of the same 'storm', Alypius had asked to see the passage; and had read the continuation: 'But him that is weak in the faith, receive him' (Rom. 14.1), and had applied to his own situation this verse, which is quite anodyne in comparison with the harsh medicine that the preceding lines had suggested to Augustine. But we know that the chaste Alypius had no need of such stern admonishments. Then the two friends went to find Monica, whose joy erupted when she saw that she had not shed so many tears in vain, that her earlier dream was coming true, and that her son was henceforward 'standing with her on the rule of the faith': that was well worth giving up grandchildren born of her flesh.^{cc} The paths to another existence were opening up before Augustine. He was nearly thirty-two.

Notes

a. *Conf.*, VIII, 1 and 3–5. Cf. above, p. 83 on the personality of Simplicianus.
b. This is the *ibi legi/ibi non legi* rhythm of *Conf.*, VII, 13–14.
c. *Conf.*, VII, 13.
d. *Conf.*, VII, 13, *in fine*. It emerges fairly clearly that the text of the Johannean Prologue which the Platonist cited by Simplicianus wanted to see written in gold letters in the churches did not go beyond John 1.5.
e. *Conf.*, VII, 14, *initio*.
f. *Conf.*, VII, 14, quoting Phil. 2.6–11, and Rom. 5.6 and 8.32.
g. *Conf.*, VII, 27. It is probable that it was the Manichaeans, at the time when he was committed to them, who pointed out these apparent contradictions; cf. J. J. O'Meara, *La Jeunesse de saint Augustin*, p. 204.
h. *Conf.*, VII, 27: *Inveni quidquid illac verum legeram hac cum* commendatione gratiae tuae *dici*.
i. *Conf.*, VII, 27.
j. *Conf.*, VII, 25.
k. *Conf.*, VII, 25.
l. *Conf.*, VIII, 2.
m. *Matt.* 13.46.
n. *Conf.*, VIII, 4: *Ille autem inridebat dicens: 'Ergo parietes faciunt christianos?'* On this saying of Victorinus, see the commentary by P. Courcelle, *Recherches*, pp. 383–91.
o. *Conf.*, VIII, 5.
p. *Conf.*, VIII, 10.
q. *Conf.*, VIII, 10.
r. *Conf.*, VIII, 12.
s. *Conf.*, VIII, 15.
t. *Conf.*, VIII, 15, *in fine*.
u. *Conf.*, VIII, 19. He would add: 'I said something of the kind'; but apart from the actual words, it must be admitted that even some dozen years later he had retained a vivid recollection of that crucial moment.
v. *Conf.*, VIII, 24.
w. *Conf.*, VIII, 22, *in fine*.
x. *Conf.*, VIII, 26.
u. *Conf.*, VIII, 28.
z. *Matt.* 19.21.
aa. *Rom.* 13.13–14.
bb. *Conf.*, VIII, 29.
cc. *Conf.*, VIII, 30, *in fine*.

CHAPTER XII

Cassiciacum

Sometimes the fortunes of the calendar – in this instance the university calendar, as we would call it – work things out well. The decisive crisis had occurred in the first few days of August 386.[a] Augustine had at once resolved to resign his post as Milan's professor of rhetoric, 'gently to withdraw the service of (his) tongue', as he puts it, 'from the chatter market'.[b] To do so he needed a socially serious reason that could be accepted by his students' fathers, who were little inclined to grant his freedom to a teacher from whom they were expecting much for their children's success. They would have waved Augustine's conversion aside. But, in that summer of 386, professional overwork – and perhaps also the psychosomatic 'spin-off' from such a spiritual stampede – had got the better of his lungs. He found it hard to breathe, complained of chest pains and could no longer manage to express himself in clear and prolonged speech[c] – a sorry misfortune for a teacher. Here, at least, he had a good excuse for resigning discreetly, and not in a blaze of glory, which he wished to avoid.[d] We must not forget that this was a quasi-official position, obtained on a political recommendation at the highest level (of Symmachus). As it happened, the long vacation at the end of the university year – the equivalent of our 'summer holidays' – began on 23 August and would not end until mid-October; these were the *feriae vindemiales*, the 'grape harvest holidays'.[1] So he had only a little over fifteen days to wait before he would be free. He had needed courage, he would say, to endure with patience, and also because he no longer had the motivation of pecuniary interest to help him bear his burden.[e]

At last the end of August arrived. Augustine could not stay idle in Milan, where he had come two years earlier to conquer the world. Above all, he needed not only physical rest but tranquillity to take stock of himself, something he had never been able to do throughout all those years when he had been chasing success. In short, he needed to make a retreat. There was a nice Latin word for this: *secessus*, a voluntary withdrawal, a break with all obligations, far from the world and its bustle, alone with himself or, preferably, with chosen companions, in a pleasant rural setting not too far away; not a profound solitude but an accessible refuge. And this refuge was at the place known as Cassiciacum, the estate of his friend Verecundus the grammarian, who offered him and his small group of friends and relatives the use of it. Verecundus was not only generous, he was a man of paradox: he also wished to become a Christian, and his wife, who already was, had shown him the way; but that was exactly what held him back, for this man who was obsessed with the absolute wanted to be a Christian in perfect continence. As Augustine says, not without a touch of mischief, 'He claimed not to want to become Christian in any other way than the one in which he could not be!' Meanwhile, his friends urged him at least to be a good husband.[f] This believer in 'all or nothing' would end by falling ill a year later and would receive baptism *in articulo mortis*, when Augustine had already left for Rome. In exchange for the country retreat he had let his friends enjoy, at the base of the first foothills of the Alps, he would inherit 'the mountain running with milk, the mountain with lush pastures (Ps. 68.16)'.[g]

Happiness at Cassiciacum

When trying to find the exact location of 'the Cassiciacum estate' – *rus Cassiciacum* – people hesitated for a long time between Casciago, near Varese, and Cassago in the Brianza, some thirty kilometres to the north-east of Milan, almost midway between Monza and Lecco. Everything connected with his beloved Lombardy was close to Alessandro Manzoni's heart, and he initially opted for the first, before rallying in support of the second, which is now generally preferred, without any firm evidence but with some good arguments in its favour, among which distance plays an important part,[2] as it is less than that from Casciago to Milan.

Augustine and his little band settled in at Cassiciacum, if not at the end of August, then probably early in September.[3] With him at first were those closest to him: his mother, Monica, and his son, Adeodatus, who was now an adolescent of fifteen, very bright and quite capable of following the discussions, if not taking an active part in them. Then there was Augustine's brother Navigius, who disappears from the scene from time to time, and the two cousins Lartidianus and Rusticus, who do little more than make up the number. Concern with his business affairs had recalled Romanianus to Africa, and he would take no part in the debates of the *Contra Academicos*, which were dedicated to him; but his son, Licentius, was there, making his presence very much known, as much as and even more than Trygetius, a young man who, like Licentius, was a native of Thagaste, less 'intellectual' than his young compatriot, but with a fighting spirit, to the point where the master said kindly of him that 'he had an answer for everything'.[h] This 'ill-assorted company'[4] has sometimes caused sneers, but without taking account of the somewhat erratic presence of Alypius, it is true.

If there was one absence to be regretted – and Augustine did so keenly – it was that of Nebridius. Not yet a Christian, he had shared with his two friends the joy of their liberation, and was then labouring to rid himself of a false idea of the nature of Christ which was akin to Docetism, an ancient and very widespread heresy according to which Jesus' fleshly body was only a semblance. It was probably one of the last vestiges, now fossilized in him, of the Manichaean ideas which, it may be remembered, he had so keenly and effectively combated. Nebridius had an alibi for not being at Cassiciacum in the autumn and winter of 386; he was kept at Milan by his teaching duties in Verecundus' school. Regretfully, he was unable to enjoy the philosophical *otium* of Cassiciacum, or take part in the dialogues that started in November. And if he was with Augustine some weeks earlier, during the 'grape harvest holidays', which must have been a free period for him too, there is no mention of it.[5] At least, by means of an exchange of letters, of which Augustine's survive,[6] Nebridius was able to follow from Milan the work of this rural 'seminar', from which his great intellectual acuity was missing.

In the green hills of the Brianza, where the Lombardian Prealps to the north and east limit the view which in fine weather extends westward as far as Monte

Rosa, Augustine did not free himself overnight from his *aestus saeculi*,[i] the equivalent of our modern 'stress'. He did not wake up one fine morning to find himself 'lighter', as Renzo, Manzoni's hero, also fleeing from Milan, would feel, and on the point of crossing the Adda taking the time to admire the sky of Lombardy, 'so beautiful when it is fine, so brilliant, so serene'.[7] So much accumulated fatigue and anguish had left their mark. Even at the end of November, when the discussions of Book III of the *Contra Academicos* took place, Augustine was still complaining of lassitude, the lasting consequence of his teaching rhetoric in Milan, and we find him very pleased that he has only to pronounce a short exordium before a small audience to launch the debate, which spared him from having to strain his voice to the detriment of his health.[j] In the same period, at the time of the *De ordine* debates, he sometimes seemed psychologically frail. He was delighted to note the progress of his students, especially Trygetius, who had had to make up a lot of ground;[k] but the next morning, he could not put up with him and Licentius bickering like children, the latter demanding loudly that a blunder by Trygetius be recorded, and he then laughing at the reprimand Licentius earned: the two young men were astounded to hear their master launch into an impassioned exhortation to them to keep themselves up to the level of the themes of their debate, a heated tirade that ended in a flood of tears.[l] Soon afterwards, they ran out of tablets to continue the records, and the continuation was postponed until later; it was just as well, for Augustine had to admit that the vehemence of his entreaties had put his voice and lungs to the test.[m]

Despite these handicaps and some remnants of his erstwhile distress, which kept him awake at night – no less than the harassment of the more precise restlessness of the flesh[n] – Augustine was happy at Cassiciacum. For the first time, and even if it was more of a 'teaching seminar' than the philosophical community planned at Milan, he was realizing a dream, and this realization was accompanied by his henceforward completely peaceable relations with Monica, who had been promoted to 'house mother', and who was not above occasionally inserting into the debates a grain of good plain common sense which her son was generous enough to find apposite, as it sometimes was.[o] Augustine would subsequently always live in exclusively masculine enclosed worlds; without being aware that he was for the last time enjoying that maternal warmth extended to all the little group, he shows in the texts he wrote at the time that he greatly appreciated it. Verecundus' estate rang with the laughter of Licentius' and Trygetius' outbursts of merriment. But Monica's smile, and that of her son in return, graced a number of pages of the *De beata vita*.[p]

Daily life at Cassiciacum was harmonious, as life can be in the countryside. Like all rural properties, the *rus Cassiciacum* consisted of a dwelling house and farm buildings, in the midst of cultivated fields, meadows and woods. Augustine and his party did not remain shut in the house. The first debate of the *Contra Academicos*, on 10 November, did not begin until sunset, nearly all the day having been spent outside directing the work in the fields in the company of Verecundus' tenant farmers.[q] Even without that necessity, the beauty of the sky was enough to bring out the little group, who settled down to their debate in the meadow next to the house.[r] They came in at the end of an already shortened day and lit lamps in order to continue their discussions indoors.[s] When the weather was gloomy, they usually foregathered in the villa's small bath-house – probably in the *tepidarium* – whose buildings formed a small annexe.ᵗ The master and his pupils slept in a vast room which served as a dormitory, accentuating even more the cenobitic nature of this 'retreat'; and it was in this dormitory, early in the morning of 20 November while it was still dark, that Augustine, Licentius and Trygetius, who had happened to wake up, began the debate whose development would form the third dialogue of Cassiciacum, the *De ordine*.

The three *Dialogues* of Cassiciacum

The *Contra Academicos, De beata vita* and *De ordine* are Augustine's first three preserved works, and the first after his conversion. They were composed on the basis of dialogues recorded by one or two stenographers – the *notarii* mentioned in the texts – or sometimes reconstructed from memory,ᵘ and subsequently rewritten by Augustine, but in a limited lapse of time – November and December 386 – which guarantees their fidelity to the debates that were actually held.[8] This is also what makes them so interesting; in texts dated a few months after the decisive phases of his intellectual and spiritual evolution, Augustine is a witness to his state of mind at the time, taking stock of his thoughts and convictions.

The *Dialogues* are also the first texts that can be contrasted with the author of the *Confessions* rediscovering the road to Cassiciacum twelve years later in his memory: Augustine versus Augustine. No one has passed up the opportunity, and no one has failed to find differences in the presentation. For example: in the *Soliloquies*, Augustine complained of a violent toothache which, he says, still enabled him to preserve his intellectual powers but not to increase them – which is easy to believe.ᵛ And he adds that if at that time the light of truth had been revealed to him, he would no longer have felt the pain or at least would have been able to bear it more easily. In the *Confessions* he writes that when his toothache had worsened to the point where it prevented him from speaking, he had the idea of asking all those present to address a prayer to God on his behalf.ʷ He wrote the text on a wax tablet and gave it to them to read; hardly had they read it, on their knees, when the pain vanished. Did the bishop 'invent' the tablet and the prayer after the event? That would be seriously to accuse him of a pious falsification *a posteriori* and without the slightest hope of producing any proof. The truth is that in the *Confessions* the memory of what happened at Cassiciacum is written into a context of thanksgiving which fills the entire book; in the *Dialogues*, the perspective is not the same. After Gaston Boissier, Prosper Alfaric was not wrong to say that in order to know the state of Augustine's soul when he wrote them, we must turn to them rather than to the *Confessions*. Yes, but they must be read with integrity. 'Both morally and intellectually', wrote Alfaric, 'it was to Neoplatonism that (Augustine) was converted, rather than to the Gospels.'[9] This famous sentence, in which all the French university 'laicism' of the late nineteenth century is expressed, rests on a questionable interpretation of the *Dialogues*.[10]

In any case, is there such a gap between the *Confessions* and the Cassiciacum writings? The bishop would write, 'What I did there in the literary field, which was doubtless already in your service, *but where, in this pause as it were, the school of pride still breathed*, these books bear witness, in which I debate with my friends and with myself, alone before you.'[x] 'A pause' – *pausatio* – a time the new convert allowed himself to get his breath back between conversion and baptism, a time of allowing the dust to settle too, when the intellectual, at first on holiday and then freed from his duties, is still the man of letters in love with that philosophy – the 'school of pride' – which still had the merit of having revealed to him where to find God, although the credit was due to the Gospels and St Paul for having shown him the way to reach and remain with him. Besides, Augustine may well have decided to resign from his chair in Milan, but at Cassiciacum he was still a teacher. Of literature, first of all; on the syllabus of Licentius and Trygetius, it was still Virgil, and more Virgil.[y] And a teacher is tempted to apply to his students – especially if he sees they are ready to profit from it – the formulas that have been beneficial to him: remembering himself at nineteen, he gave them the *Hortensius*; and as Cicero's book seemed to have the same power of awakening that he had experienced at their age, he quite naturally wanted to put their abilities to the test by advancing them along the path of philosophy.[z] It was also a means for him to clarify his own ideas. He was therefore, together with Alypius who sometimes took his place in this role, the compère in Ciceronian-type dialogues. At the same time, and for the first time in his life – if one excepts the *De pulchro et apto*, which has not been preserved, and the ceremonial speeches delivered in Milan – revising the first rough outlines and rewriting the 'stenograms', he was very consciously producing a literary work, with an evident concern for its publication and circulation. Romanianus would be the first recipient, and with some speed, of the *Contra Academicos* dedicated to him, but Hermogenianus would soon have his copy;[aa] similarly, the *De beata vita* was addressed to Manlius Theodorus and he would soon have it in his hands. Zenobius, for his part, would be quick to read the *De ordine*, which was dedicated to him. There was still something of the self-consciously 'literary' in the Augustine of that period. From that last dialogue let me quote – for the chance will not occur again! – the sentence that is remarkable for its author's false modesty:

> As for my books, if they should chance to fall into the hands of a few people who, having read my name, do not ask 'Who is he?' then put aside the volume, but whether from curiosity or a love of study, cross the threshold, unconcerned by its poor appearance . . .[bb]

Reading the first pages of the *Contra Academicos*, one is struck by the authority with which the primacy of the spiritual over the temporal is affirmed. Augustine honours Romanianus with this dialogue, but at the price of an initial admonishment of rather surprising severity: perhaps his 'patron' from Thagaste was wrong still to be bogged down in Manichaeism, but after all it was his former protégé who had led him astray. If Augustine expresses the devout wish that 'God will restore him to himself',[cc] well and good. Romanianus was rich and powerful and, at least for a provincial, *beatus* to the highest degree, in the secular sense of the word; happily, his luck had turned and he had started to clear up his affairs! We must read, or reread,[dd] the portrait of the local lord, soon to be caught up in his downfall, or in a first salutary stumble. In his time, Bossuet would warn the great no differently. This little speech of exhortation from the start gives a foretaste of the ambition of the *Contra Academicos*, but also of the two other dialogues, whose debates overlap one another throughout that fruitful fortnight in November 386.

Henceforward 'taking refuge in the lap of philosophy'[ee] Augustine too can dream about writing a 'protreptic', as Cicero had in the past. Romanianus is his first target, but he has not got him close at hand, and probably deep within himself he has scant hope for the time being of converting this man who is too engrossed in his affairs and whose commitment to the pursuit of wisdom is perhaps less eager than he is willing to admit.[ff] So Augustine will turn his efforts towards the son, Licentius, whom he holds up as an example to his father, and Trygetius, his companion. The 'protreptic' will be put into operation by means of the intellectual and moral edification of the two young men. Hence, in the three dialogues, and more clearly in the *Contra Academicos*, there is a 'little manual of initiation into philosophy' aspect, or more precisely, along the lines of the search for truth and the definition of happiness, which necessarily gives much space to the commonplaces of the thinking of Antiquity. And since the scepticism of the New Academy had at one time been his chief obstacle to progress in his search for truth, and risked being so for his young students, Augustine used the opportunity to develop his position with regard to the Academics.[gg] So, for the first dialogue,[hh] came a title which only partly renders its content. I shall return to this text in an attempt to give an overall evaluation of the *Dialogues* as a 'platform' of Augustinian thought in the autumn of 386, but note straight away what is immediately revealed by the initial discussion, begun in the afternoon of 10 November, on the fundamental question posed to all the speakers: what is to be understood by a 'happy life', and how to achieve it.[ii]

It is not surprising, therefore, that the problem central to all moral philosophy in Antiquity should be the subject – and title – of the dialogue whose debates commenced on Augustine's thirty-second birthday, 13 November, and involved all the participants for three consecutive afternoons. Of his *De beata vita* the author says, at the end of his address to Manlius Theodorus, that it is the most 'religious' of the discussions at Cassiciacum; and when the old bishop reread the text when making his reappraisal, the *Retractations*, it was the one that found most favour in his eyes. He would mainly lament the fact that the copy in his library had lacunae.[jj] There is one lacuna that the biographer is glad does not affect the dedication in which, extending somewhat lengthily the metaphor of the sea journey and its perils, Augustine retraces a shortened version of his intellectual itinerary during the twelve years he has just lived through; despite its brevity, it is an invaluable account, in which some people claim to see his 'first *Confessions*'.[kk] A lacuna also, coming nearly midway in the dialogue,[ll] does not compromise its coherence which, unlike the other two, it owes to having been developed in a consistent fashion and one more firmly centred on a major theme. Besides its coherence and unity, the main characteristic of the *De beata vita* – giving this little dialogue its charm – is that of the three it is the one in which Augustine's maieutics are used to best advantage, with only minimal resort to purely philosophical references and texts,[mm] his interlocutors being absolute novices, including his brother Navigius, his son Adeodatus and his mother Monica. It was a means for Augustine to signify that the truth can be attained even without the assistance of Platonic edification, particularly, as in Monica's case, when Christian illumination enlightens common sense.[nn]

Unlike the above, the *De ordine*, like the *Contra Academicos*, is a dialogue in which the dialectic, when it fails to advance the line of argument, very often makes way for sustained expositions, a form of expression to which Augustine resorts, notably when he realizes that his little group is wandering and there is a need to get back on course.[oo] At the same time, of the three dialogues it is the one which by its 'overture', in such a surprising, original and lively fashion, best introduces us to the 'English public school' atmosphere foreshadowed by the life at Cassiciacum. Having slept a few hours, says Augustine, he had woken as usual in the middle of the night and meditated in the dark – for, although at home in Africa oil cost nothing, to light lamps at night in Italy was a luxury from which even the rich shrank.[pp] A noise attracted his attention, the sound of running water, not the regular sound of rainfall but the intermittent noise of a sort of small flow whose course was now and then interrupted or obstructed. At the same moment, Licentius indicated that he was awake too, by hitting the wood of his bed to scare away a mouse that was annoying him; asked to give his view on the sound that had intrigued Augustine, he suggested an explanation that satisfied his master, as it did Trygetius, who had also been roused from his sleep: the sound was of dead leaves – it was mid-November – from time to time obstructing the wooden channels that brought the estate running water; then the build-up of pressure broke the 'plugs', which tended to form again before being scattered once more. Because it entered a chain of cause and effect, the noise that had intruded on their ears, at first perceived as strange, was well within the order of things, in 'order' purely and simply.

Embarked on in so lively a fashion, the debate progressed swiftly. Before day broke, hailed by a long prayer by Augustine, the master and his two students had already tackled the problem that had lain at the heart of Augustine's preoccupations for years, and especially during the first months of 386: what was to be done about disorder, in other words, evil? Must it not be admitted that it did not fall outside order?[qq] But the persistent question remained: had evil always existed, or had it one day started to exist? A provisional, and incomplete, answer would come later, at a second session of debates, from Monica's lips: God had allowed evil to exist, but he had not left it outside order.[rr] But at the end of the dialogue, the questions posed by this fundamental problem were left in the air:

> How is God not the author of any evil and, if God is omnipotent, how is so much evil committed? Had evil always existed or did it begin with time? And if it had always existed, was it subordinate to God? If so, had this world always existed in which evil was under the dominance of divine order? If, on the other hand, this world had begun to exist, how, before this beginning, had evil been sustained under the power of God? And what need was there to create the world and include in it, for the wretchedness of souls, the evil that had previously been mastered by divine power? If there had been a time when evil was not under God's dominance, what suddenly occurred that had never before happened in the earlier times of eternity? For it would be perfectly stupid, not to say impious, to suggest that God had formed a new plan.[ss]

Rereading this dialogue, the author of the *Retractations* would say that at this point, with companions who were such novices, he was not in a position to deal with such difficult material, and had contented himself with speaking of the order to be followed in their studies.[tt] The old bishop was casting a very reductive eye over a text which, though it set out the undertaking of the *Disciplinarum libri*, had a different aim and was developing a rational programme in relation to faith. In the *De ordine*, addressing Monica, Augustine had included his mother in the number of people who could be introduced 'by guiding them through the gilded and painted portals, into the sanctuary of philosophy'.[uu] He had very lofty ambitions, for himself as well as his group, since in the little concluding part of his dialogue, he unveiled the ultimate aim of the study plan he proposed to the 'retreatants' of Cassiciacum: it culminated in a metaphysical search, centred on a dual problem – of the soul, and of God.[vv] He was outlining for himself the path he would follow for many long years. And to make it crystal clear that what mattered to him was not a knowledge of the world and its laws – knowledge of the 'perceptible world' – he had insisted on making plain, still addressing his mother, that 'philosophy' meant literally 'love of wisdom', complementing that reminder by a reference, not to Plato but to St Paul (Col. 2.8) and quoting John 18.36: 'My kingdom is not of this world.'[ww]

It becomes dazzlingly apparent from reading them, that the very real discussions which gave rise to the dialogues of Cassiciacum were veritable feasts for the mind for Augustine and his entourage; and they were gratifying for the 'ringmaster', who obviously derived pleasure from watching his students' progress,[xx] and recording their positive contributions to the debates, with a very understandable paternal pride when they involved Adeodatus.[yy] However, nothing smacks less of 'intellectualism' than these pages where, in the budding Augustinian dialectic of *intelligere* and *credere*, primacy still seems awarded to the paths of intellect. The strong Plotinian echoes in these dialogues, fed by Neoplatonism, have been rightly remarked upon,[11] but their Platonic ideas are only one of the favoured means of reaching understanding of a God who would not, however, be the God of the philosophers. At the end of the *Contra Academicos*, a text of major importance must be read in order to grasp Augustine's position at Cassiciacum in autumn 386. He finished his concluding exposition by affirming that we attain truth under the double impulsion of authority and reason.[zz] And he added:

> Thus for me it is a certainty that I will absolutely not stray on any point from Christ's authority, for I find none stronger. As to what one must seek with the most subtle reasoning – for my feelings are that I ardently desire to grasp the truth not only through faith, but also through the intellect – I am confident that, *for the time being,* I can find among the Platonists doctrines that are not contrary to our mysteries.[ab]

At Cassiciacum, Augustine reread Plotinus, but he also read the Psalms;[ac] he had confidence in philosophy, endowed with the highest mission, but also assessed its limitations, and was already extolling the 'learned ignorance'[ad] which would remain one of the mainsprings of his convictions as theologian and mystic. A few lines of the *De ordine* fairly sum up Augustine's religious attitude some months after the crisis in the Milan garden:

> Philosophy promises reason, but liberates only a tiny number of men; however, it induces them not only not to scorn the Christian mysteries, but to understand them as they should be understood. True philosophy, genuine philosophy, bears no other

responsibility than to teach the supreme principle of things, the immensity of the intelligence that resides in him, everything that has flowed from him, with no loss to himself, for our salvation: this principle is the one God, omnipotent, thrice-powerful, Father, Son and Holy Ghost, as taught by venerable mysteries, sincere and unshakeable profession of whom liberates peoples . . . As for that sublime matter, that so great a God deigned to assume for our sake a body like our own, the lowlier it appears, the more it is filled with mercy and the more it is inaccessible to the pride of the clever.'ae

The *Soliloquies*

Winter had arrived at Cassiciacum. Some weeks earlier, Augustine had sent his letter of resignation to the Milanese authorities, stressing his respiratory difficulties and chest pains which, in fact, still persisted at the end of 386.[12] At the same time, he had written to Ambrose to express his repentance and desire to receive baptism very soon, asking his advice on what he should read to that end. The bishop recommended him the first book of the Prophets, Isaiah; but whereas the Psalms had touched his heart and opened a path in his soul, the prophet's vehemence deterred him. He had to defer that reading until later,[13] and likewise the discovery of the famous prophetic saying that would soon become the initial reference of his dialectic in the understanding of the faith: *Nisi credideritis, non intellegetis* (Isa. 7.9). Having in his turn become a pastor and commenting upon this same Isaiah to his faithful flock, Augustine would one day say this was one of those texts which, for want of having read them in his adolescence, he now needed to have before his eyes in a book, whereas his memory remained uselessly cluttered with secular literature.af

Were Licentius and Trygetius still with him as winter began? From the silence about them, we may assume that life had caught them up in its usual whirl. The dormitory had emptied. In a letter to his beloved Nebridius, early in 387, we find Augustine holding dialogues with himself, stretched out on his bed, in the still of the night.ag His friend had received the *Dialogues* and congratulated the master on having apparently attained wisdom; Augustine was not fooled by the compliment, which he ascribed to friendly encouragement: what would Nebridius have said if he had received the *Soliloquies*? Augustine had created this neologism, almost apologetically, to give a title to what was not a 'monologue' but the dialogued product of splitting it into two;ah as Socrates would have done with his *daimon*, he conversed with his Reason and listened to this good genius, confessing his wishes, doubts and residual inadequacies. The instrument of this introspection, his Reason bluntly informed him that his human weakness still formed the obstacle to the *fruitio Dei*: was his 'inner eye' – a Plotinian image which the bishop would always use – sufficiently purified to be able to look at the Sun? Augustine submitted to this scrutiny of his conscience. He had long ago given up a desire for wealth, and more recently for honours. He had kept his sensuality in check for a long time, too, as regards eating, drinking and the pleasures of bathing. But women?, insisted Reason, who was nobody's fool. Augustine's reply was categorical: he had definitively renounced marriage, and declared that 'To cast a man's soul down from his citadel, there was nothing to equal a woman's caresses and that bodily contact without which one cannot speak of possessing a wife.'ai And if he happened still to pursue the dream of a philosophical *otium* lived among his friends – which presupposed wealth and social standing – Reason willingly agreed that the goal in prospect, ambition to achieve wisdom, in this case justified the desired material means. In this first book of the *Soliloquies*, there is a confidential tone, fairly rare in Augustine, something like rough outlines of 'confessions', in the secular and almost Rousseau-esque sense of the word.

Useful as it is for establishing Augustine's moral state a few months after his conversion, this 'self-portrait' aspect of the *Soliloquies* is not what gives them their full value. Above all, even more clearly than the *Dialogues*, they form a first milestone on the metaphysical quest whose goal is unveiled in the last page of the *De ordine*. At the end of the long initial prayer, to which I shall return, Reason asks Augustine what he wants to know; the answer lies in a few words: *Deum et animam scire cupio.*[aj] He feels the satisfaction of such a lofty ambition to be a burning duty, which cannot allow him to expect help from others than himself, or from works written by others than himself,[14] in resolving the difficulties he foresees. In the first place, it presupposes an analysis of the process of true knowledge, and for a start, of its conditions. Augustine remembers his fleeting successes, but mainly the failures experienced during his attempts at contemplation in the early summer of 386.[ak] God will not manifest himself to the intellect unless the soul's eye is in a fit state to look upon him; that eye must be healthy, which will be guaranteed by faith, as it alone can free him from passions; faith must be joined by hope, which alone will encourage perseverance and overcoming the lack of success of the first attempts; lastly charity is needed, that is to say, the love of that light which is promised to the soul.[al] Thus Augustine renders in Christian language the commandments of an *exercitatio animi* he had found in Neoplatonism. If these conditions are filled, the soul will be able fully to benefit from God's illumination, receive his light directly, and no longer be satisfied with the merely reflected light that shines in the visible world.[am] Here again, Augustine was following Plotinus, himself an heir to Plato, but he did so because, as he will say more precisely in the *City of God*, he already considered that in this matter the Neoplatonic doctrine matched the teaching of the Gospels.[an]

The second book of the *Soliloquies* opens with a reaffirmation of the fundamental requirement. Reason invites Augustine to pray for the success of their undertaking. This second prayer is very short: 'You, God, are always the same, make me know myself, make me know you.'[ao] To know oneself, that is, to know one's soul, in order to know what is closest to it and in whose image it has been made; to make use of the Socratic precept – tacitly underlying here – for the highest knowledge, all the theological effort that will later be put to work in the second part of the *De Trinitate* is already programmed here. It needs to be based on sure foundations, on a primary certainty relating to the subject itself of this act of knowing, which is why Reason immediately reveals to Augustine a *cogito* – already outlined in the *De beata vita*[15] – which prefigures that of Descartes, though more rudimentary and without his syllogistic development. 'Do you know that you think?' asks Reason – 'I know' – 'So it is true that you think?' – 'It is true'.[ap] A little later, in the *De libero arbitrio*, and in a way that is more obviously Cartesian before the term existed, the certainty of being as a thinking creature, even if in error, will serve as a basis to begin the proof of God's existence.[aq] Here it is the solid ground on which Augustine can get a foothold to commit himself to the first of the two paths he has mapped out, that of the knowledge of the soul. Questions related to the nature and origin of that soul would occupy his mind all his life, and he would always hesitate over the manner of its creation by God. But in the winter of 386–7, he was at least freed from all doubt about its imperishable nature. Very probably by way of Plotinus' treatise *On the Immortality of the Soul*, he borrows from Plato the line of reasoning drawn from the survival of truth, of which the soul is the subject.[ar] When Augustine confesses his disquiet, Reason replies: 'Stop moaning! The human soul is immortal' – 'How do you prove that?' asks Augustine. And Reason sums up the results they have already reached:

> If all the attributes of a subject must always survive, then the subject must always survive. Now, all science has the soul as its subject. Of necessity, therefore, the subject always survives, if science itself continues to survive. But science is nothing other than truth, and truth survives forever . . . Therefore the soul always survives.[as]

We have seen that several 'prayers' intersperse the *Soliloquies*, including the ardent appeal, *noverim me, noverim te*, so significant of the essential quest. These prayers strongly express the conviction held by Augustine, unlike the philosophers who are too arrogantly confident of the powers of their reason alone, that he needs help to arrive at the truth he is seeking about himself and about God. 'May I return to myself and to you under your guidance', he implores from the depths of his 'darkness' in an invocation[at] in which we rediscover the mystical attitude of the return to oneself before conversion towards God, 'under his guidance', found in the 'spiritual anabases' of the end of the Milanese spring, as they are reported to us in the *Confessions*.[16] And then – but one should say 'first', since Augustine has placed at the beginning what we would be tempted to read as a finale – there is the great and beautiful orison of the beginning of the *Soliloquies*: an admirable text, which has been analysed and commentated many times,[17] its outpouring of inspiration lasting over five long pages. This 'philosopher's prayer', as it has been called[18] – though it is chiefly true of its fourth part (*Sol.*, I, 4) – from which the incarnation is still missing, and in which the trinitarian definition of God then only appears just beneath the surface, should be read as a hymn of repentance, faith and love.

Notes

a.   Augustine states that his decision was taken scarcely twenty days before the grape harvest holidays: *Conf.*, IX, 2: *paucissimi dies*, and IX, 4: *Nescio utrum vel viginti dies erant*.

b.   *Conf.*, IX, 2.

c.   *Conf.*, IX, 4.

d.   *Conf.*, IX, 3.

d.   *Conf.*, IX, 4: *quia recesserat* cupiditas, *quae mecum solebat ferre grave negotium*.

f.   *Conf.*, IX, 6.

g.   *Conf.*, IX, 5, *in fine*.

h.   *Contra Acad.*, I, 24.

i.   *Conf.*, IX, 5.

j.   *Contra Acad.*, III, 15.

k.   *De ord.*, I, 16.

l.   *De ord.*, I, 29–30.

m.   *De ord.*, I, 33.

n.   *Sol.*, I, 25.

o.   On Monica's activities at Cassiciacum, see above, p. 10.

p.   *De beata vita*, II, 10; II, 16; III, 21; IV, 27. In the *Confessions* (IX, 8), he would idealize his mother's presence at Cassiciacum in strong terms: 'When she joined us, my mother was there with a woman's outward appearance, a man's faith, the assurance of the elderly, maternal tenderness and Christian piety.'

q.   *Contra Acad.*, I, 15.

r.   *Contra Acad.*, I, 25.

s.   *Contra Acad.*, III, 44.

t.   *De ord.*, I, 25.

u.   Such is the case of the nocturnal dialogue held in the dormitory at Cassiciacum, recorded by the speakers when day came: 'The discussions were recent, and how could such remarkable things elude the memory of three such attentive people?' (*De ord.*, I, 26).

v.   *Sol.*, I, 21.

w.   *Conf.*, IX, 12.

x.   *Conf.*, IX, 7.

y.   *Contra Acad.*, I, 15; II, 10; *De ord.*, I, 26.

z.   *Contra Acad.*, I, 4.

aa.   *Ep.* 1.

bb.   *De ord.*, I, 31.

cc.   *Contra Acad.*, I, 1.

dd.   *Contra Acad.*, I, 2: see above, p. 7.

ee.   *Contra Acad.*, I, 3: *in philosophiae gremium.*

ff.   *Contra Acad.*, II, 4–5.

gg.   See above, pp. 60–1.

hh.   At least according to the order of publication emerging from the *Revisions*: *Retract.*, I, 1.

ii.   *Contra Acad.*, I, 5: *Defini ergo, ait Trygetius* – addressing Augustine – *quid sit* beata vita.

jj.   And consequently the text that we read (*Retract.*, I, 2).

kk.   *De beata vita*, I, 1–4; see above, p. 37.

ll.   *De beata vita*, III, 22, just before a quotation from Cicero's *Hortensius*.

mm. Here we find quoted only the *Hortensius*: II, 10; III, 22; IV, 26.

nn.   Cf. *De beata vita*, IV, 27, where Augustine admires his mother for having discovered by sheer strength of mind the philosophical maxim he was preparing to reveal.

oo.   See for example *De ord.*, II, 24 and the 'résumé' formed by Augustine's subsequent discourse: II, 24–7.

pp.   *De ord.*, I, 6.

qq.   *De ord.*, I, 17–18.

rr.   *De ord.*, II, 23.

ss.   *De ord.*, II, 46.

tt.   *Retract.*, I, 3, 1.

uu.   *De ord.*, I, 31.

vv.   *De ord.*, II, 47: . . . *philosophiae disciplina . . . cuius duplex quaestio est: una de anima, altera de Deo.*

ww. *De ord.*, I, 32.

xx.   In *De ord.*, I, 10 and 21 to greet Licentius' progress, and in I, 16, that of Trygetius.

yy.   See *De beata vita*, I, 6: II, 12; III, 17.

zz.   This will be reaffirmed in the *De ord.*, II, 16: *Duplex enim est via quam sequimur cum rerum nos obscuritas movet, aut rationem aut certe auctoritatem.*

ab.   *Contra Acad.*, III, 43. The word *sacra* (mysteries) is here translated according to customary convention.

ac.   *Conf.*, IX, 8–11.

ad.   *De ord.*, II, 44: . . . *de summo illo deo, qui scitur melius nesciendo.* See below, p. 369.

ae. *De ord.*, II, 16.

af. *Sermon Dolbeau* 23 (*Mainz* 59, complementing *Sermon* 374), 19, in F. Dolbeau, *Vingt-six sermons au peuple d'Afrique*, p. 610.

ag. *Ep.* 3, 1: *Diu mecum in lecto situs cogitavi, atque has loquelas habui, Augustinus ipse cum Augustino.*

ah. *Sol.*, II, 14.

ai. *Sol.*, I, 17. However, Reason will make him confess his nocturnal obsessions later (I, 25).

aj. *Sol.*, I, 7. Same mention in I, 20: *Ut animas nostras et deum simul concorditer inquiramus* and in I, 27: *Animam te certe dicis et deum velle cognoscere? – Hoc est totum negotium meum.*

ak. See above, pp. 84–6.

al. *Sol.*, I, 12.

am. *Sol.*, I, 23.

an. *City of God*, X, 2, comparing Plotinus, *Enn.*, V, 1, 10, 10 18, and John 1.6–10.

ao. *Sol.*, II, 1: *Deus semper idem*, noverim me, noverim te.

ap. *Sol.*, II, 1: *Cogitare te scis? – Scio – Ergo verum est cogitare te? Verum.*

aq. *De lib. arb.*, II, 7: it is accepted that book I and the beginning of book II were written in Rome in 388.

ar. Plato, *Phaedon*, 78 b–82; 84 ab; see also *Menon*, 86 b.

as. *Sol.*, II, 24.

at. *Sol.*, II, 9.

CHAPTER XIII

Ostia

Augustine and his companions made their way back to Milan in the first weeks of 387. 'When the time came for me to give in my name, we left the countryside to come back to Milan.'[a] The reason for the return also indicates its approximate date; we know from Ambrose himself that in his church one could 'give in one's name' – enrol for the baptismal catechesis – at Epiphany (6 January);[b] the list of those aspiring to baptism (the *competentes*) was drawn up, and enrolments ended, at the beginning of Lent. As Easter fell on 25 April in 387, and the first Sunday in Lent was therefore 14 March, the return from Cassiciacum took place between January and mid-March. Augustine would state that Alypius had managed to gain such mastery over his body that 'he could walk barefoot on the frozen soil of Italy' during this journey, which tends to place it in the midst of the Lombard winter, January–February.

Augustine was henceforward freed from his teaching duties, but his *otium* remained very busy. On its own, preparation for baptism was very demanding; through penitence[c] and fasting, it called for corporal as well as spiritual action; he would later recall the weeks when, with the other *competentes*, he spent his days being 'catechized, exorcized and examined'.[d] Anyone else but he would have found himself sufficiently occupied. The *Confessions* are very quiet about that Milanese spring, but thanks to the *Retractations* we know that he took advantage of this period of relative freedom not to break the metaphysical momentum he had gained at Cassiciacum. The *Soliloquies* had remained unfinished; so on his return to Milan he wrote a book, *The Immortality of the Soul*, which he would present in the *Retractations* as a *commonitorium* – something between a rough draft and an aide-mémoire – intended in his mind to provide material to complement the *Soliloquies*. He says that this writing fell into public hands without his knowledge and against his wishes, and had thus been numbered among his works – something that the old bishop would view without enthusiasm, when he reread a work whose too dense texture and excessive conciseness made it, on his own admission, tedious to read.[e]

It has recently been shown that this little book was inspired more by Porphyry than by Plotinus, used in a rather dry outline where the creative force of the *Soliloquies*[1] is not to be found. The *De immortalitate animae*, however, is a good follow-up; to establish the lasting nature of the soul, it opens by resuming the argument already formulated in the *Soliloquies*, drawn from the subsistence of truth, of which the soul is the subject.[f] There follows, at first, a series of variations on reason, notably its immutability, unlike the body, which constitutes a further proof of its immortality. The second part of the development is intent on demonstrating the soul's indestructibility. Here again, the demonstration makes the body its starting-point: a body can be divided at will, or sent towards non-existence, but will never attain nothingness.[g] With all the more reason, the same applies to the soul. Stupidity, madness or the weakening of reason can make it tend towards non-being, but cannot lead it to non-existence.[h] The soul, by definition, is life which animates whoever lives; it cannot abandon its own self, it cannot be deprived of life since it is the one that gives life.[i] Deriving its being from God, in other words, from an essence who has no opposite – that opposite would be non-being – the soul cannot lose its being and therefore cannot perish.[j] But, the objection will be raised, could it not deteriorate? Change into a body? For instance during sleep? But in sleep it is the use of the body that is diminished for the soul, not the soul's own life.[k] Nor does it risk being debased by its action in the body, where it is not housed spatially, being irreducible to space.[l] Thrown higgledy-piggledy into an over-dense material, this metaphysics is rather a deterrent; but a number of these themes on the soul would subsequently continue to inspire Augustine.[2] What one remembers from their collection in a text written during Lent in 387 is that only a few days before his baptism, Augustine was still feeling the need to 'grasp the truth not only through faith but through the intellect', as he had said in the *Contra Academicos*;[m] he was in the same frame of mind as in the preceding autumn.

In the course of his *De immortalitate animae*, Augustine made explicit reference to the 'liberal arts',[n] and the word *disciplina* – by which we understand 'intellectual' or, even better, 'scientific' education – appeared in the first words of the text as a significant element of its *incipit*. For Augustine had not lost sight of the study plan he had set out in detail in the *De ordine*: grammar, rhetoric, dialectic, music, geometry and astronomy.[o] All these liberal arts, which had complemented his first education as an adolescent at Madauros and then Carthage, he had assimilated as a gifted autodidact around his twentieth year, as he recalls in the *Confessions*, as it were reproaching himself for a knowledge which at that time had remained rather empty, because, he says, 'I had my back to the light and my face turned towards illuminated objects; so my own face, which saw they were illuminated, was not itself illuminated.'[p] But now he knew that these liberal arts were useful and, during his last year in Milan, his reading had made him see that their use, step by step, gave access to knowledge of the soul, which was thereby purified; in short, they were a propaedeutic to that study of the soul, which he had also said in the *De ordine* should be the concern of the *discentes* – those who had still to learn – whereas questions relating to God – the second path that had to be opened up – were the concern of the *iam docti*, those who were already learned.[q] Harking back to this enterprise of spring 387 in his *Retractations*, Augustine confirms the spirit in which he had approached it, without being able to bring it to its close: 'Through the intermediary of corporeal things (*per corporalia*) I myself wanted to attain, or lead others to attain, incorporeal things (*ad incorporalia*).' In other words, it was not, as has sometimes been suggested,[3] simply to take stock of the past before his baptism and the start of a new life that Augustine, with so little time ahead of him, launched himself into a programme of work that might be regarded as immoderate. It was not just the former rhetor's 'farewell to arms'.

Whatever Augustine's genius and ability to work, to finish the *Disciplinarum libri* in the space of a few months,[r] while, since his return to Milan, he had in any case been much engaged in preparing for baptism, was rather to attempt the impossible – although to do so, and at least for part of the project, he was able rapidly to marshal his professional capabilities. That was how he was able to finish the book on *Grammar* quickly, based on the notes that he possessed. Later, at Hippo, he would notice that the book had disappeared from his library; the lost work survived, probably in part, in the form of a summary which manuscript tradition ascribes to him.[4] Similarly, he had available all the necessary elements for the composition of his *De musica*, a very deceptive title for us, since it is about the music of verse, at least in the first five books written in Milan before his baptism, and is no more and no less than a treatise on metrics. To this often very technical edifice Augustine would later add a spiritual 'storey' to which I shall return.[5] As for the other 'disciplines', dialectic, rhetoric, geometry, arithmetic, philosophy,[s] the *Retractations* say 'only the beginnings (*principia*) of the books dealing with them have been preserved'.[6] And the bishop adds that he had afterwards lost them; perhaps, he reflects, they were not lost to the whole world. This is a word of hope for us, as the discoveries over the last twenty years have comforted us with the conviction that, when dealing with St Augustine, 'rummaging' in the great manuscript collections of old Europe may still hold some happy surprises.[7]

Baptismal waters

Of the monuments from the end of Antiquity that are still preserved, perhaps the baptistery is the one with the strongest emotional impact. This impression is due to its perfect structural and architectural conformity to the initiatory ritual of a liturgy that was born two thousand years ago on the banks of the Jordan. To those men and women for whom descending the two or three steps to their immersion in the ordinary baths was a customary, if not daily, 'feel-good' activity, the only true pleasure in everyday lives that were rough and comfortless, the symbolism of total immersion in the baptismal font was immediately accessible. The frequent beauty of those round or polygonal basins, sometimes four-lobed or cruciform,[8] a decorative mosaic lining them and reflecting through the film of water, further helped them to understand its sacred nature and more easily imagine that they would emerge spiritually regenerated, as they emerged physically relaxed from the swimming pool of the public baths; and that coming out, clad in a white tunic, they would have cast off the 'old man' whose sins lay on the ground with the clothing left at the edge of the baptismal font.

Thus it was for Augustine, when he received baptism from Ambrose's hands,[t] on Easter eve, the night of 24–5 April 387, being plunged into the octagonal basin of the baptistery probably erected by Ambrose himself, alongside the *basilica nova*, the future basilica of St Thecla, on the site of the present-day Duomo.[9] In the crowd of 'neophytes' surrounding them, his son Adeodatus and Alypius were alongside him. The *Confessions* are never simply 'narratives', nor would they be on this occasion, however unique. Augustine writes merely: 'And we were baptized, and the turmoil of our past life fled far from us.'[10] Of his very real emotion, such as gripped the prodigal son at a welcome he had not dared to hope for, he would recount the outpourings in the days that followed, when he sang with his new brethren the hymns which Ambrose had introduced in his church a year earlier to galvanize his flock in the struggle against the pro-Arian machinations of Justina.[u]

How I wept to hear your hymns and canticles, greatly moved by the voices whose sweetness resounded in your church! Those voices flowed into my ears, and the truth was distilled in my heart; from it issued a seething flood of feelings of piety, and my tears streamed down, and all was well with me![v]

Perhaps it was during those days of exaltation that Augustine visited the monastic community of Milan, whose head was a priest, 'the best and most learned of men', whose name we shall never know.[w] It was probably at that time, too, that the small group of Africans gathered around Augustine was joined by a new recruit in the person of Evodius. This young man, who then appeared for the first time, was also originally from Thagaste – decidedly a breeding-ground of talent. He, too, had served in the imperial political police and, like the two *agentes in rebus* in Trier whose 'turning'[x] Ponticianus had recounted, he had 'given up the secular militia to enter your (God's) own'.[y] The call to another life was doubtless keenly heard by noble-hearted men who had been induced to dirty their hands in the service of the emperor. Evodius had already been baptized when he came to know Augustine. He would always remain a close friend, and we shall find him as bishop of Uzalis, not far from Utica, the target of particular attacks on the part of Donatists, who remembered that as a youth he had been an auxiliary of the imperial government, and could not forgive him for it.

Having reached Milan in the autumn of 384, there Augustine had accomplished in two years a complete moral and spiritual revolution, ending in the baptism received from Ambrose. What more could he do? In Milan he had known everything: dazzling professional success, the promise of a brilliant social elevation, but also the grievous tribulations of a soul that was at last reconciled with itself after finding the true way. Should he not break away from this town where he had broken away from his ambitions? And after benefiting with Ambrose and the old priest Simplicianus from the influence of the faith which had helped him so much in his own conversion, it would not be a lack of gratitude – quite the contrary – to draw back in order to become a source of influence in his turn – nowhere better than at home in Africa. He probably also felt that his relationships with his Milanese friends, like Hermogenianus and Zenobius, on which he had at one point set great store, had come to a sudden end; and even with Manlius Theodorus, on whom he had placed too many hopes, and who had let him down.[11] Moreover, quite simply, he had to earn a living. Who would subsidize him? The decision to abandon the profession of rhetor was irrevocable; the hospitality of various friends, such as Verecundus, could not last indefinitely; and the eternal provider of funds, Romanianus, had crossed the sea. All these humble details, about which the *Confessions* are silent, must among other things have carried some weight in the decision to return to his homeland: 'We sought some place in which we might be most useful in your service and were returning together to Africa. We were at Ostia, on the mouth of the Tiber, when my mother died.'[z]

Ostia

Augustine and his family, accompanied by Alypius and Evodius, left Milan at the beginning of September 387, at the latest. If they had delayed any longer they would have been caught up in the turmoil which was then hurtling down from the West through the passes of the Cottian Alps – Maximus and his army, who had unwisely been summoned to the rescue against the Sarmatians by the young Valentinian II and his mother Justina. On 8 September the saviour-turned-usurper entered a Milan that had been deserted by the imperial Court. It must therefore have been during the summer that Augustine and his entourage, travelling from Milan to Rome, did the reverse of the journey he had made alone nearly three years before, and more slowly and less comfortably now, because he no longer benefited, as he had then, from the facilities of the public post. After a last stage at Rome, they arrived at Ostia, and stopped there to rest in a dwelling that overlooked an interior garden, as was the norm in houses of that era: 'It was away from all the disturbance, after the fatigue of a long journey; there we rebuilt our strength for the crossing.'[aa]

We thus know that Augustine and his family were not living in the harbour area – at Porto – on the other side of the Tiber's small arm, but some kilometres to the south, in the colony of Ostia. The extensive excavations carried out in the middle of the twentieth century have revealed the particular situation prevailing there at the end of Antiquity;[12] with the displacement of major maritime activity around the great hexagonal basin created by Trajan and continually maintained thereafter, life had ebbed away a little from the old city; the large collective dwellings – the *insulae* – were threatening to collapse but, at the same time, fine houses had continued to be built for the rich families of traders and shipowners on what was still, on the fringes of the port properly speaking, an important trading centre. Augustine, who had no lack of recommendations, was accommodated in one of these *domus*.[13] Ostia was the 'gateway to Africa'; there is no doubt that it held a welcoming African colony, long Christianized since, early in the third century, Minucius Felix, flanked by Octavius, had taken the hundred strides on the beach to convert their friend Caecilius Natalis.[14] Besides, Augustine himself says that hardly had they arrived at Ostia when Monica found herself surrounded by a little group of her son's friends, with whom she spoke freely of the death she sensed approaching.[bb]

Never had mother and son been so close to each other. Augustine fixed that proximity for us in an image of such pictorial clarity that it became inscribed, just as it was, in Augustinian iconography, from medieval miniatures right up to Ary Scheffer's famous mid-nineteenth-century canvas. He says that one day God's secret workings had placed them on their own, standing side by side, leaning on their elbows at a window overlooking the garden.[cc] All circumstances had combined so that in their profound intimacy they together experienced that exceptional moment whose narration is the crowning point of the *Confessions*. As he recalls and reconstructs it, without claiming that his memory can give it word for word, their tête-à-tête had begun from a meditation on what eternal life might be like in the beyond, that truth which 'the eye has not seen, nor the ear heard, and which has not entered the heart of man' (1 Cor. 2.9). They were both of the opinion that, as far as they could tell, the delights of our fleshly senses hardly merited comparison, or even mention. Then began an ascent like those Augustine had experienced at Milan the year before, no longer undertaken on his own, but in the communion of thought that united him with Monica.[15]

Then, rising with more ardent impetus towards the *'Selfsame being'*, we proceeded step by step through all bodily things, to the sky itself, whence the Sun, Moon and stars cast their light. And we rose still higher within ourselves (*interius*) fixing our thought, our speech and our wonder on your works. And we came to our own souls and went beyond them to attain that region of inexhaustible abundance in which you feed Israel forever on the pastures of truth, where life is Wisdom, the principle of all that is, has been and will be, without having been made, for it is as it has always been and forever shall be . . . And while we were speaking of that Wisdom, to which we aspired, we touched it for an instant[16] in a total surge of our hearts (*toto ictu cordis*). Then we sighed and left behind bound to it the 'first-fruits of the spirit'[dd] and returned to the sound of our own mouths, where our words begin and end.

As he had already experienced at Milan, Augustine knew from this 'anabasis', renewed in his mother's company, that it is impossible to elevate oneself to divine wisdom except in the brief instant of an 'ecstasy', which must itself pass through an 'instatic' phase, through the exacting experience of the inner self. And afterwards, one must return to the everyday and changing world here below, and to the human word that has a beginning and end, contrary to the creator Word, 'who remains in himself without becoming old'.[ee] But the return is no longer felt as a fall; and the sigh breathed by Augustine and Monica at Ostia is probably one of 'an incompletely assuaged desire',[17] but not an expression of hopelessness. We must read what follows, not only for the beauty of their form but also and chiefly for what they reveal of the mastery Augustine has acquired in the spiritual method of approaching God, and the hope he now draws from it, the 'stanzas' dedicated to inward silence as a condition of receiving the divine Word within ourselves without any intermediary:

If in any man the tumult of the flesh were silenced,
silenced the images of earth, water and air,
silenced even the heavens, and if the soul also were silenced
and went beyond itself, no longer thinking of itself,
and fancies and imagination also silenced;

if every tongue and every sign
and everything that exists only by passing away
were absolutely silent in a man –
for if one can hear them, all these things say:
'We did not create ourselves,
but were created by him who abideth for ever' (Ps. 99.3, 5)

that said, if they now kept silent,
since they have quickened our ears
to him who created them,
and if he alone spoke,
not through them, but by himself,

so that we heard his word
not by fleshly tongue, nor angelic voice,

nor sound of thunder, nor by the enigma of parable,
but that him, whom in all these things we love,
we should hear himself, without all these things –
as on the instant, straining our very being
and the rapture of our thought
we reached the eternal wisdom above all things –
if that were sustained, and other visions
of a far lower kind vanished,
and this one alone ravished and absorbed and enveloped
the beholder in those inward joys
and that eternal life were such as that instant
of knowledge we now sighed after . . .

would that not be the meaning of the words:
'Enter into the joy of thy Lord' (Matt. 25.21)?
And when will this be? Will it not be the day when
'we shall all rise again, but shall not be changed' (1 Cor. 15.51)?[ff]

It was formerly noted in these texts – in the account of the 'ecstasy' properly speaking as in the 'discourse on silence'[18] that follows – that Augustine resorted to a Neoplatonist language which had proved itself for a long time in the human expression of the approach to the divine, and with which he was familiar from his reading and doubtless also by his own transcription of his experiences.[19] And a recently discovered text by the bishop – an unpublished sermon dated 1 January 404 – where he refers to the spiritual experiments in which cultivated pagans of the early fifth century still indulged, strikingly confirms, by the very precise comparisons which can be made with the 'ecstasy of Ostia', that this exercise was based on a method inherited from Plotinus.[gg]

But this 'Plotinistic' fabric is also interwoven with scriptural references – mainly from the Psalms and St Paul – that one would not take to be elements of a biblical dressing added afterwards by the author of the *Confessions*. Probably in the spring of 386, listening to the sermons of Ambrose, who 'enveloped the paraphrases of Plotinus in a language inspired by Scripture',[20] Augustine had acquired the habit of rethinking Neoplatonism through scriptural forms. And in the weeks and months that had followed, his reading of the Pauline epistles, then his deep immersion in the Bible during his baptismal catechesis, had further increased that facility for marrying the symbolism of the Scriptures with the Plotinian dialectic of degrees. So one may easily accept that 'the conversation he had with his mother presented an amalgam of Plotinian thought and biblical expressions that are perceptibly identical to that which we can analyse in his written work'.[21]

Was St Augustine one of the great mystics? If there is a domain where simple mortals are badly placed for establishing classifications and awarding prizes, it must be the one where an act at the very summit of spirituality takes place. What we must at least admit, with one of the best researchers into Augustinian mysticism, is that throughout his whole life Augustine remained committed to a spiritual method of approaching God which he had tried in his Milanese period, one consecrated by that moment of grace at Ostia in Monica's company, without ever concealing from himself that 'though we need to make an effort to move towards God, it is God alone who decides on the meeting and remains in control of it'.[22] Augustine's life, as we know it, because he often leaves us to guess at more than he tells us about it, was punctuated by those encounters obtained in that ephemeral state of spiritual 'weightlessness' he described so well, when addressing his flock, in one of his sermons.[23]

Monica, who had just accompanied him to one of those peaks, was reaching the end of her struggle on this earth. She told her son what he already knew, that she had attained the goal she had set herself in this life when she saw him become a Catholic Christian.[hh] A few days later a fever confined her to bed. Augustine remembered that she had often been worried about her burial place, which she had planned to share with her husband, at Thagaste, moved at the time by feelings that were so common among Christians and pagans alike, and expressed by the author of the *Confessions* in the rather precious terms of funerary poetry.[ii] When Navigius and he were both at her bedside, they were all the more surprised to hear her say that she was not concerned about where her body should be buried, provided that she lived on in their memory and was not forgotten in their prayers. And Augustine learnt a few days later that, with the presentiment of her death as they arrived at Ostia, she had revealed this new eschatological approach: 'Nothing', she had said, 'is far for God, and I need not fear that at the end of the world he will not know where to find me to raise me up.'[jj]

After nine days' sickness, Monica died at the age of fifty-six. A dozen years later, Augustine would relive in his mind those hours of mourning which the sharpness of grief had etched in his memory. At the moment when Monica breathed her last, Adeodatus had not been able to restrain his cries; those present quietened him. And Augustine, who had closed his mother's eyes, violently restrained himself from weeping and caused himself great suffering. But in his view, and of those around him, a death such as that, neither an unhappy nor total demise, should not cause weeping or lamenting. His heart was bleeding, but his soul ordered him to keep his burning eyes dry.[kk] The day of the funeral, he continued to hold back his tears and after the burial went to the baths, in the vain hope of driving away 'the bitter sweat of sadness';[24] then, shattered, he slept. When he awoke, there came into his mind one of Ambrose's[25] hymns, in iambic verse, which he had often heard his mother sing,[ll] and which he had himself sung at his baptism. At that point he released all the tears he had been holding back and in a short storm let them flow freely, 'making a bed of them beneath his heart'.[mm]

In December 1945, in a little courtyard adjoining the church of Santa Aurea, at the exit from Ostia Antica towards Rome, some young people who were digging a hole to plant a basket-ball post discovered the fragments of an inscribed marble plaque.[26] These preserved the left part of Monica's epitaph, already known from medieval manuscripts which had transcribed its text, ascribing it to a former consul named Bassus, 'of most illustrious memory':[27] he was very probably Anicius Auchenius Bassus, consul in 408, who composed and had this epitaph carved in Augustine's lifetime, when he was then a bishop, doubtless in the first years of the fifth century and after the sack of Rome by Alaric in 410.[28] It associated mother and son in the same renown, which is conferred by virtues and far above the fame achieved through great exploits.

Notes

a.   *Conf.*, IX, 14.
b.   Ambrose, *In Luc*, IV, 76.
c.   This is the 'primordial penitence' spoken about in *Sermon* 351, 2.
d.   *De fide et operibus*, VI, 9.
e.   *Retract.*, I, 5, 1.
f.   *De immortalitate animae*, 1.
g.   *De immortalitate animae*, 12.
h.   *De immortalitate animae*, 13–14.
i.   *De immortalitate animae*, 16–17.
j.   *De immortalitate animae*, 19.
k.   *De immortalitate animae*, 23.
l.   *De immortalitate animae*, 25.
m.   See above, p. 106.
n.   *De immortalitate animae*, 6.
o.   *De ord.*, II, 35–44.
p.   *Conf.*, IV, 30, evident allusion to the Platonic myth of the cavern.
q.   *De ord.*, II, 47: *Prima* (i.e. *quaestio de anima*) *est illa discentibus, ista iam doctis.*
r.   If one supposes that he had commenced work on it in the autumn of 386 at Cassiciacum.
s.   This last treatise in place of the treatise on astronomy which normally completed the cycle: *De ord.*, II, 42.
t.   *Ep.* 36, 32: Possidius, *Vita Aug.*, I, 5–6.
u.   See above, p. 80.
v.   *Conf.*, IX, 14.
w.   *De mor. eccl. cathol.*, I, 70.
x.   See above, pp. 94–5.
y.   *Conf.*, IX, 17.
z.   *Conf.*, IX, 17.
aa. *Conf.*, IX, 23.
bb. *Conf.*, IX, 28.
cc. *Conf.*, IX, 23.
dd. Rom. 8.23. On these 'first-fruits of the spirit', read the note by A. Solignac in *BA*, 15, pp. 552–5.
ee. *Conf.*, IX, 24, *in fine.*
ff. *Conf.*, IX, 25. A French verse translation by G. Bouissou can be read in *BA*, 14.
gg. *Sermon Dolbeau* 26 (*Mainz* 62), 27 (F. Dolbeau, *Vingt-six Sermons au peuple d'Afrique*, p. 386).
hh. *Conf.*, IX, 26.
ii. *Conf.*, IX, 28: 'One might say that it had been granted to her, after a long journey overseas, that so united on earth they should both lie in the same grave.'
jj. *Conf.*, IX, 28, *in fine.*
kk. *Conf.*, IX, 29: 'My eyes, at the violent command of my mind (here *animus*) sucked back the fountain of their tears until they dried', and 30: 'My soul (here *anima*) was wounded and my life as if torn apart.'
ll. *Hymn. Ambr.*, I, 2: *Deus, creator omnium* . . . ; cf. *Beata vita*, IV, 35, and *Conf.*, IX, 15.
mm. *Conf.*, IX, 33.

CHAPTER XIV

A second season in Rome

Leaving Monica buried at Ostia, as she had wished, Augustine and his party should have embarked for Africa as they had originally planned.[a] It seems that they would still have had time to do so before the 'closure of the sea', from 11 November to 10 March, a period when sailing on the 'regular'[1] maritime routes was in theory interrupted.

But for the first time the course of Augustine's personal life, which had hitherto been merely on the fringes, was influenced by external events. If the little band of 'children of Thagaste' did not take to the sea to return home in the autumn of 387, it was very probably[2] because of the military consequences of Maximus' usurpation, his army having wasted no time in dominating Italy, while its leader was officially recognized at Rome in January 388. Africa, brought into the affair by the defection of 'Count' Gildo, a native ruler who had been promoted by Theodosius, had rallied to him. The sea routes, patrolled by the usurper's fleets, were not safe, and we know from a letter from Ambrose to Theodosius[b] that Maximus was vanquished at sea at Sicily before being beaten on land in Illyria and finally massacred at Aquileia. Augustine would have had to wait until calm was restored, after the usurper's death, in order to return to Africa.[c]

For various reasons, not the least of which was the mourning that had overwhelmed him, there was no question of his remaining at Ostia. Augustine thus withdrew to Rome, with his household, and in the company of Alypius and Evodius. There he would spend the best part of a year in conditions and with a social status which remain something of an enigma for us. During his first year in Rome, in 383–4, he had found a refuge in the bosom of the Manichaean community, in particular with a 'hearer' named Constantius, a rich Roman who had become his friend.[d] Moreover, apart from the solidarity of the sect which had obtained accommodation for him, he had at that time been a rhetor and, for all that his students paid him badly, had nevertheless been able to earn enough to live on from teaching, the more so because he had then been on his own in Rome. He now found himself without any resources that we can discern, saddled with a family – at the least his son Adeodatus and brother Navigius, not to mention his two friends – and of course having burnt his boats with his former Manichaean friends. Everything leads to the supposition that the little group of Africans, en bloc, had the benefit of friendly hospitality in Catholic circles. Was it with the same Constantius? We know only that he ended by becoming Catholic some years later.[e]

The first anti-Manichaean polemic

It may be recalled that, while in Milan, Augustine had heard of the Manichaean 'monastery' which Constantius had contemplated in Rome. A simple 'hearer', but immensely wealthy and influential, he found it hard to endure the criticisms levelled against his friends in the sect for their wanderings and dissolute customs. To put an end to it, he had planned to have live with him, at his own expense, all his Manichaean 'brethren' who were determined to follow a 'rule of life taken from the *Letter of Mani*'.[f] Reading that text had discouraged many; some, however, had accepted and stayed, the 'bishop' of the sect at their head – though more out of respect than sincere conviction, as was soon evidenced by the quarrels that erupted between people who accused one another of shortcomings, to the point of a revolt by those who eventually avowed openly that the 'rules for living' were intolerable. Constantius had thought he could settle the situation by confronting them with this dilemma: either they had to observe all those precepts, or regard as inept the one who had laid down all these rules that no one could follow. That was the end of the 'monastery'; the bishop himself fled, leaving behind him in a concealed food-safe comestibles purchased on the sly with funds that were themselves secret. Yet at first he had made quite a good impression on Augustine: 'A rustic and uncultivated man, but his very rusticity seemed a safeguard for good morals.[g]

Once back in Rome, probably first-hand from Constantius himself, Augustine made sure of the truth of all this, which he had learnt in Milan from a witness he calls irrefutable. In the Christian milieu in Rome, many rumours were circulating about the Manichaeans, such as the one accusing them of practising a very special communion among themselves involving animal and even human semen, just as they consumed the seeds of plants, in pursuit of their conviction that they could thereby prevent bits of the soul – or light – from being reimprisoned in matter.[3] For the time being, it was no more than a suspicion in Augustine's mind, and he refrained from giving it credence.[h] In any case the Manichaeans left themselves wide open to attack on the moral plane. And, according to the *Retractations*, if it was in Rome, just after his baptism, that Augustine began a polemic against them which he was to pursue for years, then the provocations of his former friends were the cause.[i]

He did this in a work in the form of a diptych: a first book, *Morals of the Catholic Church*, to be followed by *Morals of the Manichaeans*.[4]

These two small works by Augustine are not among those most frequently referred to, and with good reason, for they reveal nothing that can be taken as a fundamental or definitive experience in his anthropology or theology. For the first time, however, we see the faithful believer as such expressing himself, taking on the defence and illustration of a Church of which he has been a member for less than a year, at the same time revealing himself to be a redoubtable polemicist. We must read the portrait of the Manichaean sensualist who, in his strict observance of the 'seal of the mouth', rejects with horror the three fingers of bad wine drunk by the poor Catholic, and the morsel of rancid bacon with which he seasons his daily diet of cabbage, whereas his own table groans under a profusion of vegetarian, but refined, dishes and unfermented, but varied and exquisite, drinks.[j] Augustine could not forgive the Manichaeans for having spiritually sterilized his youthful years, and no doubt he could not forgive himself for allowing the impetus he had acquired at nineteen by reading the *Hortensius* to become bogged down in the mire of their dualism. He felt he had been duped.[k] There is a settling of scores in this anti-Manichaean polemic which gives it its bite. But it is also a rescue operation: he had saved himself; now he had to ensure the salvation of those he had carried with him when he himself was militant within the sect, and who had sometimes stayed in it,[1] before the struggle against the Manichaeans came to be felt, by the priest and then the bishop, to be quite simply a pastoral duty. When in 388, he took up his tablets and stylus in Rome, he would have been astonished to learn that some fifteen years later he would still be clashing swords with their leaders in Africa.[5]

Lovers of corrosive irony and the picturesque will find what they are looking for in the pamphlet forming the second part of the diptych, but it is mainly in the first part, which promotes the Catholic Church, that Augustine begins the reasoning which he will use tirelessly to confound the Manichaeans. He will, he says, avoid badgering them as far as possible.[m] And since his adversaries loudly proclaimed their rationalism and scorned authority – that is, that of the Scriptures – he would keep only to the means of reason,[n] at least at the beginning of this refutation. Reason tells us the goal to which man aspires: a happy life.[o] With such an exordium, Augustine seemed to be setting up another *De beata vita*, but on new foundations. In the Cassiciacum dialogue, he was still reliant on the ideas professed by the Stoics and Platonists on the distinction between soul and body and on the independence of the wise man, whose bliss is a state of the soul, in comparison with the body and the vicissitudes of existence.[p] And in the *Contra Academicos*, in the same period – autumn 386 – he still thought that the sovereign good of man consisted in reason, and that his bliss could be a life led according to reason.[q] For Augustine now, it mattered little that the starting-point of anthropological thought was the idea that man is composed of a soul and a body:[r] and even supposing that one wanted to keep a purely corporeal definition of man, it could not be denied that what constitutes the wellbeing of the body is not pleasure, or the absence of suffering, or strength or beauty: what makes the wellbeing of the body is the soul, first because it gives it life.[s] But then one must ask what makes the sovereign good of the soul: is it virtue, as the whole of classical Antiquity thought, with various nuances depending on the various schools? Yes, without a doubt, virtue perfects the soul; but unlike his predecessors, Stoics, Peripatetics or Neoplatonists, Augustine no longer thinks that virtue has a potential existence in man; to attain virtue, the soul must follow as it would a guide something that transcends it; and that something is the selfsame cause of that good, in other words, God; and to reach God is to attain beatitude.[t]

But, adds Augustine, it is precisely at this point that reason becomes powerless: 'Having reached the divine, it turns aside; it cannot fix its gaze, it trembles, is inflamed, burns with love, is dazzled by the light of truth and returns to its habitual shadows, not from choice but from faintness.'[u] When man reaches this point in his asceticism, the reason in him must be superseded by authority, in other words, the teaching of the Scriptures. Here also we find the thread of the anti-Manichaean polemic, for though the Manichaeans held the Gospels and St Paul to be acceptable, rejecting the Old Testament which they read as Augustine himself had read it for a long time, they obviously could not accept its concordance with the New Testament, of which in any case they made a 'heretical' interpretation, expurgating, as if they were mere interpolations, all references in it to the authority of the Scriptures of the Old Testament. Whether dealing with charity or the exercise of virtue, the whole continuation of the first book of *De moribus* is devoted, in opposition to the Manichaeans, to showing the fundamental agreement of the Old and New Testaments and the oneness of the God who is professed in both.[v] The work culminates in a page which especially justifies its title – *On the morals of the Catholic Church* – and which is a hymn to the Church not only as educator of its faithful, but also and chiefly as a guarantee of the family bonds, the social contract and the political bases of the earthly city.[6] Having only just entered this Church, Augustine assigns to it the most exacting of roles, and the most dangerous in a human society – that of universal mentor.

Discovering Christian Rome

He had begun to see this Church come alive in Milan, first from outside, then more intimately from the first weeks of 387; in Rome, he deepened his knowledge. To say that he saw the Eternal City with a new eye is an understatement; in fact, he was really seeing it for the first time. And what he discovered was the great Christian city, which had of course escaped him during his first stay in 383–4, when he was immersed in Manichaean circles. This time, Augustine was moving in Christian circles. During the ten months he spent there, he frequented them assiduously, at different levels, with the curiosity of a neophyte avid to learn everything. It may be said that Augustine was never 'fond' of the Eternal City; but he doubtless perceived the urban metamorphosis it was experiencing at that time, the outcome of which Jerome would encapsulate some fifteen years later in a famous and powerful sentence, *movetur urbs sedibus suis*: Rome was already no longer in Rome, in a completely concrete and material sense; good folk were deserting the Capitol and the half-ruined temples to hasten to the tombs of the martyrs.[w]

Especially in the Vatican, which Augustine also visited. There he met with some surprises, for instance when, in Alypius' company, he found that unlike Milan, where Ambrose kept a watchful eye on respect for his ban on funeral meals – as Monica had discovered – agapes on the tombs were common currency at St Peter's in Rome.[x] When the two friends expressed their astonishment, they were told that the frequently renewed papal ban could not be imposed on the crowd of pilgrims who constantly flowed in from everywhere, and all the more so because the *ager Vaticanus* was a long way from the Lateran, where Peter's successor then resided. But the Romans themselves were very fond of this custom, as is shown by the banquet offered to the poor in St Peter's, in 395, by the rich senator Pammachius, on the occasion of his wife's funeral, with the approbation of both Paulinus of Nola and Jerome. For his part, Augustine remained very critical in this regard and, addressing the Manichaeans in the final exhortation of Book I of the *De moribus*, he did not exonerate his own community from the dead weight of what in his view was too great a number who 'drank to excess over the dead, offered repasts to the corpses and ascribed their gluttony and drunkenness to religion'.[y] He also attacked those who 'worship tombs and paintings', which could be a foretaste of his later retort – we know this from one of the recently published new sermons – to the criticisms of pagans who accused Christians of 'worshipping the columns in the churches'.[z] He was again surprised – though it was not such an important matter – by the Roman custom of fasting on Saturdays,[aa] when it had been forbidden by Ambrose in Milan, as he well knew.[bb]

Augustine was especially interested in the cenobitic aspects of Christian life in Rome. Extolling to the Manichaeans those exemplary existences whose model had come from Egypt, he first recalled the Milanese monastery he had visited at the time of his baptism. He added that in Rome he had known several comparable ascetic communities, led by those brethren who were distinguished for their age (*gravitas*), wisdom (*prudentia*) and knowledge of the Scriptures (*divina scientia*); copying the monks of the East and Paul himself, they lived in self-sufficiency by the work of their own hands; and they practised prolonged fasts in which their abstinence from meat and wine was not motivated by taboos, as with the Manichaeans, but solely by the desire to subdue the concupiscence of the flesh;[cc] nevertheless, such voluntary austerities were never forced upon those who were not in a condition to endure them. These male establishments had their female counterparts, houses that assembled widows or virgins; they spun and wove to earn their living, but were quite capable of seeing that others received moral and religious education.

The *De quantitate animae*

If Augustine did not live in this fashion during his Roman year, it was because he knew himself to be in transit, and would have to defer until his return to Africa together with his friends, the realization of the plan for a communal life which he had dreamed of for some years.

But in a less formally monastic framework, the reality of his life in Rome must not have been very noticeably different. That is certain as regards his intellectual life. During the months of 387–8, when it was not devoted to his anti-Manichaean polemic, it remained fixed on the pursuit of the two main directions of spiritual search he had set for himself at the time of Cassiciacum: the knowledge of God and of the soul.[dd] With regard to the second problem, under the title *On the Greatness of the Soul* he composed a text that stemmed directly from the *Soliloquies* and the *De immortalitate animae*. But he returned to the formula of the dialogue, which had succeeded so well in the autumn of 386 in the Lombard countryside. Beside him he had Evodius, the newcomer in his entourage, but a native of the country, who joined his family; on Monica's death, this young man had been the first to grasp the psalter and intone a chant in which all the household had joined.[ee] It was Evodius whom Augustine associated with his reflection on the soul at that time, in the course of conversations whose formal reality there is no reason to doubt: around 414/15, the bishop of Hippo reminded his colleague at Uzalis of them, as well as the texts that resulted from them, as they seemed to have slipped Evodius' memory.[ff] Only Augustine could have told us what the level of Evodius' intellectual involvement really was; we can at least note that the written text is not content merely to award him the thankless role of 'foil'.[7] He credits him with having straight away given a vigorous momentum to the debate, from the outset posing the fundamental questions on the soul: Where does it come from? What is its 'quality' and what its 'quantity'? Why was it given to a body? And what becomes of it at the time of its union with that body, and also when it is separated from it?[gg]

Of course, the subsequent pages in the *De quantitate animae* meet all Evodius' expectations. At the date of this text, Augustine had not yet found definitive answers to all the questions, and some would gradually mature in him up to the years of the composition of the *De Trinitate*. As an essential basis, he already had Neoplatonic philosophical material at his disposal; but he knew very well he would have to make use of scriptural material too. That is why the reply to the first two questions is quick and cautious: the soul comes from God and was created by him, that is certain, but here dealt with in a few words;[hh] on the ways in which it had its origin and became incarnate in the body, he would have occasion to return many times, in his commentaries on Genesis and very soon in the *De libero arbitrio*.[8] As for the soul's *qualitas*, he contents himself by replying to Evodius that the soul 'resembles God', which means of course that it has neither the same power nor the same substance;[ii] and the last three questions formulated by his young friend, deferred to the end of the exchange, are skirted.[jj] In keeping with the title but contrary to its intent, the essence of the dialogue is thus devoted to saying what comprises the 'greatness' of the soul; and the larger part of that development to showing that this greatness must not be conceived in terms of space: the soul is incorporeal, lacking extent and therefore indivisible. In the course of this long demonstration, in answer to an impatient interruption by Evodius who asks what the soul really is, Augustine retorts abruptly that it is 'a substance endowed with reason, made to govern a body';[kk] this definition is important, for it lies at the base of a still dualist anthropology, still of Platonic inspiration, and already formulated in another way in the *De moribus*: 'Man, as he appears to man, is a reasonable soul using a mortal and earthly body.'[ll] It then remains to explain how this 'reasonable substance' can 'use' a body, itself another 'substance', since the hypothesis of a division of the soul and its local diffusion is rejected. Only in embryo in the *De quantitate animae*, the solution would be spelt out much later in a letter to Jerome: the soul acts in the entirety of the body it animates by means of a kind of 'vital tension'.[mm] The end of the dialogue is taken up by a sort of 'vertical section', not of the soul, but its functions or, to put it better, its accomplishments. These are the 'degrees' of the soul, a ladder with seven rungs, on which, starting from the third – the one where arts and sciences, social, political and religious institutions thrive – of all animate beings man is the only one, if he affords himself the spiritual means, to pursue an ascent that will bring him near to wisdom and the divine, and finally to the contemplation of God, acquired at the seventh and last step.[nn] Having reached that final stage, the soul no longer feels anything other than the desire to liberate itself through the death of the body from the last shackles that still prevent it from clinging entirely to truth. We shall later find this 'scalar' progression, leading from knowledge to wisdom,[oo] in the *De doctrina christiana*.

The treatise on free will

Addressing the Manichaeans, Augustine stated at the end of his text that the soul had received free will from God.[pp] Uttered for the first time, this key word announced his intention of getting to the bottom of the problem that had preoccupied him for so many years – the origin of evil. It may be recalled that for a long time Augustine had found a solution in Manichaean dualism which, without truly satisfying him, had suited him for its convenience. Twelve years later, the rejection of this handy dualism had left him without an answer when faced with the haunting question: *unde malum?*[qq] Then, reading the *libri Platonicorum*, especially Plotinus' works, had revealed to him that, far from being a 'substance', evil was the result of the 'perversity of a will that twists aside towards baser things'.[rr] He had gone more deeply into that discovery, made at Milan in the spring of 386, at Cassiciacum in the same year, as is shown by certain developments of the *De ordine*, among others, which reveal that his thoughts were still wavering as he tried to establish the relation between God and evil.[ss] Decidedly, he would have to lance the abscess, which he did, still accompanied and assisted by Evodius. This was the subject of the first book of the *De libero arbitrio*, which we know to have been written during this second year in Rome.[9]

A deliberately provocative attack was put in Evodius' mouth: was not God the author of evil? It was easy for his companion to answer that there was evil and evil: if it was a matter of the evil that we suffer as punishment for sin, yes, God was its author; but at the root of an earlier evil was the human creature. However, Augustine felt obliged to recognize a semblance of 'pertinence', beneath the apparent 'impertinence', in Evodius' initial question: 'If sins come from those souls which God has created, and if those souls proceed from God, how can those sins not be almost directly related to God?'[tt] There lay a 'chain effect'[uu] which the Manichaeans did not hesitate to exploit, and to dispel it he would put to work a dialectic that would largely go beyond the limits of Book I of this treatise. For the moment, it was necessary first to examine what is an evil act,[vv] notably adultery and homicide. The analysis of this last example led quite naturally to considerations on the limits of the punitive competence of civil law, valuable in themselves for the light they throw on Augustine's first penal and sociological reflections.[ww] The law of men, secular law, is of necessity applicable to men whose perverted will clings only to transitory and inferior good: wealth, honours, pleasures, bodily beauty and even liberty, at least as it was commonly understood, doing as one pleased.[xx]

For true freedom is 'that of happy men who abide by the eternal law'. They bring into play a 'good will' which in itself is a good thing that one has only to want in order to possess it, 'with such ease that to possess what they want is nothing other than to want it';[yy] a formula whose optimism – here justified in the framework of a completely theoretical anthropology – might later seem an embryonic Pelagianism before the term existed.[10] But if that will breaks down, genuine freedom is lost, and thus, by means of his free will, man can fall from his initial ontological status – that of Adam before the Fall – and go astray in sin. Therefore the one responsible for moral evil is not God, but the free choice of human will. If this seemed to be settled at the end of Book I of the *De libero arbitrio*, Evodius would not give up: one might wonder, he objected, whether God did the right thing in giving us this free disposal of our will for, if we were deprived of it, we would not be exposed to sin; so that indirectly God could still be held to be the cause of moral evil. Augustine admitted it: but this analysis, though satisfying from a psychological viewpoint, was not so with regard to faith. It was necessary to go beyond, leaving man aside a little, and emphasize God's all-embracing love. That would be the subject of Books II and III, which were probably not finished before 395, the date when he would send the entire work to Paulinus of Nola.[zz] 'I began it as a layman, and finished it as a priest', he says much later of the 'Treatise on Free Will',[ab] thereby underlining the importance and coherence across time of this work, which formed a bridge between the two parts of his life, and which had initiated reflections on the freedom of man, its consequences and limitations, that would accompany him up to his last years.

During that summer of 388 the state of war ended which had prevented Augustine and his group from returning home. Leaving Thessalonica in June, the emperor Theodosius had crossed the north of the Balkans by forced marches, ascending the Sava valley, and had seized Aquileia, where the usurper Maximus, who had sought refuge there, was murdered by his soldiers. That happened in late July or August 388. At the same time, the re-establishment of safety at sea, notably in Sicilian waters, once again allowed regular links with Carthage. Passing through Ostia, Augustine and Adeodatus doubtless visited Monica's grave. During September, he saw the African coast again, after an absence of five years which had changed him into quite another man.[ac] He would soon be thirty-four.

Notes

a. See above, pp. 115–16.
b. Ambrose, *Ep.* 40, 23.
c. *Contra litt. Pet.*, III, 30.
d. See above, p. 58.
e. *Contra Faust.* (text dated c. 400), V, 5.
f. *De mor. manich.*, II, 74. This is probably not the 'Foundation Letter', known by its Augustinian quotations, but rather one of the 'letters' whose Coptic manuscripts, found in Egypt around 1930, did not survive the bombing of Berlin, where they were preserved, in 1945.
g. *De mor. manich.*, II, 74.
h. *De mor. manich.*, II, 66.
i. *Retract.*, I, 7, 1: 'After my baptism, when I was in Rome, I could not bear in silence the Manichaeans' bragging about their continence or their false abstinence.'
j. *De mor. manich.*, II, 29–30.
k. This is the word he himself uses: *novem annis quibus me* ludificastis (*De mor. manich.*, II, 34).
l. For instance, his childhood friend Honoratus, for whom he would write the *De utilitate credendi* in 391/2.
m. *De mor. eccl. cathol.*, I, 2: 'I would rather heal them than fight them, if it is possible'; he had no illusions.
n. *De mor. eccl. cathol.*, I, 3.
o. Remember that these are the first words of the *De beata vita* by Seneca: *Vivere . . . omnes beate volunt.*
p. *De beata vita*, IV, 25.
q. *Contra Acad.*, I, 5, resumed in *Retract.*, I. 1, 2.
r. *De mor. eccl. cathol.*, I, 6.
s. *De mor. eccl. cathol.*, I, 7.
t. *De mor. eccl. cathol.*, I, 9: *Oportet ut aliquid aliud sequatur anima, ut ei virtus possit innasci*, and I, 10: *Si (deum) assequimur, non tantum bene, sed beate vivimus.*
u. *De mor. eccl. cathol.*, I, 11.
v. See especially *De mor. eccl. cathol.*, I, 15; 16; 26; 30; 34; 57.
w. Jerome, *Ep.* 107, 1 (to Laeta, line 401).

x.   *Ep. 29, 10* (to Alypius): *Quoniam de basilica beati apostoli Petri quotidiane* vinolentiae *proferebantur exempla.* The word *vinolentia* ('drunkenness') is typical of Augustine's usual tone on this topic.

y.   *De mor. eccl. cathol.,* I, 75.

z.   *De mor. eccl. cathol.,* and *Sermon Dolbeau 26 (Mainz 62),* 10 in F. Dolbeau, *Vingt-six Sermons au peuple d'Afrique,* p. 374.

aa.   *Ep. 36, 9, 21* (to Casulanus).

bb.   See above, p. 71.

cc.   *De mor. eccl. cathol.,* I, 70.

dd.   See above, p. 108.

ee.   It was Psalm 100.

ff.   *Ep. 162, 2.*

gg.   *De quant. an.,* 1. But it may also be said that Augustine has put in Evodius' mouth a stereotyped list of questions about the soul such as were commonly found in the 'doxographies'; they are to be found more or less in this order in the *De ordine,* II, 17.

hh.   *De quant. an.,* 2.

ii.   *De quant. an.,* 3. In the *De immortalitate animae,* 24, he had already placed the soul in a middle position between God and the body, a concept to which he would adhere (cf. *Enarr. in Psalm.* 145, 5, and *Ep.* 140, 3: *In quadam medietate* (anima rationabilis) *posita est*).

jj.   *De quant. an.,* 81.

kk.   *De quant. an.,* 22.

ll.   *De mor. eccl. cathol.,* I, 52.

mm.   *Ep. 166, 4* (dated c. 415); cf. below, p. 363.

nn.   *De quant. an.,* 70–9.

oo.   *Doctr. chr.,* II, 9–11.

pp.   *De quant. an.,* 80.

qq.   *Conf.,* VII, 7; cf. above, p. 76.

rr.   *Conf.,* VII, 22; cf. above, p. 87.

ss.   *De ordine,* II, 46.

tt.   *Lib. arb.,* I, 4. Just before, he had quoted Isaiah's words (Isa. 7.9), 'If you do not believe, you will not understand', but declaring his desire to deal with this problem of evil by reasoning.

uu.   Cf. *De duabus animabus,* VIII, 10: . . . *quasi per quamdam* catenam *ad deum mala et peccata connecti.*

vv.   *Lib. arb.,* I, 6: *Prius ergo discutiendum est quid sit male facere.*

ww.   Cf. notably in *Lib. arb.,* I, 9–10, the discussion on the case of the slave who kills his master to avoid grave cruelty on his part.

xx.   *Lib. arb.,* I, 31–2.

yy.   *Lib. arb.,* I, 29.

zz.   *Ep. 31, 7,* where he also says that he had already sent part to Romanianus. For the continuation of the *De libero arbitrio,* see below, pp. 180–2.

ab.   At the very end of his life, in 428/9, in the *De dono perseverantiae,* XII, 30.

ac.   He would say so himself addressing the Donatists who reproached him for his past: *Alii ivimus, et alii redivimus* (*Enarr. in Psalm.* 36, 3, 19).

CHAPTER XV

Otium at Thagaste

When he disembarked at Carthage in the autumn of 388, Augustine did not go immediately to Thagaste. He and Alypius received the hospitality of a Christian friend named Innocentius,[a] a former highly-placed official in the offices of the *vicarius* of Africa. The unfortunate man suffered from fistulas, and their frequent incisions, even performed by the best surgeons, were real torture; but for the last and most resistant of them he would enjoy a miraculous cure. Among those who came to his bedside was one of the deacons of Carthage, its future bishop, Aurelius, and there Augustine met for the first time the man who he little thought would be his principal colleague for thirty-five years, at the heart of the African clergy. In Innocentius' entourage was also the bishop named Saturninus, who in those years had the see of Uzalis (El Alia), not far from Utica.[1] In his friend's house, Augustine was visited by one of his former students, Eulogius, who in his turn had become a teacher of rhetoric, thus giving his master the best proof a student can give of the excellence of his teaching: he told Augustine that while he was in Milan he, Eulogius, then in some difficulty, had in a dream heard him giving the correct interpretation of a text by Cicero which was to be the subject of his lecture the next day![2]

However, the Carthaginian stay did not last long; just time enough to see his dear Nebridius, who was living not far away, having returned before them. At Carthage there were still too many and too close memories, whose almost physical reality it was hard to face. Furthermore, and perhaps mainly, after his dreams in Milan, and the successful but brief experience at Cassiciacum, a practical possibility was forming of realizing the plan for the communal life which had become inextricable from a Christian life for someone who, reflecting later upon this intermediate phase, would define himself as *nondum quidem clericus, sed iam deo serviens*.[b] In mid-October at the latest, the little band once again took to the main highway leading to Numidia and reached Thagaste. The house Augustine and Adeodatus came back to was now empty of the older generation.[3] The family possessions, including the slave domestic staff, were now the property of the offspring of Patricius and Monica, free of any obligation to forefathers who were no longer in this world. Possidius says, obviously considering only the 'hero' of his 'hagiographic' biography, that Augustine 'decided to settle in the house and lands that belonged to him, but no longer regarding them as personal property'.[c] Which means to say – how can it be taken otherwise? – that he had turned over[4] to the (Church) community of his native town the assets he had inherited from his father (though in joint ownership with his brother and sister), while keeping the use and profit to enable him to live there with those who shared his commitment, especially Alypius and Evodius, but also his 'own people' in the family sense of the term.[5]

The letters to Nebridius

A great historian of Christian Africa would say of the house at Thagaste that 'it marks a transition between the studious villa at Cassiciacum and the monasteries properly speaking that will appear at Hippo'.[6] It is important, first of all, to show the differences in comparison with the Lombard 'retreat'; externally they are barely perceptible. For Nebridius who, living in Milan, had not experienced Cassiciacum and now similarly watched the Thagaste enterprise from afar, in the Carthaginian countryside where he lived the grand life with his mother, it still appeared to be a community of philosophers. Being unable to participate in person, he did so by correspondence, as he had at the time of Cassiciacum, in autumn 386. 'It is my joy,' he wrote to Augustine, 'to treasure your letters as the apple of my eye. They are great letters, not in size, but for the subjects they deal with, and they contain great elucidations of great subjects. They will speak to me, now of Christ, now of Plato, now of Plotinus.'[d] The young man suffered from his isolation, however, and was rather impatient at seeing Augustine, whom he would have liked to invite to his country estate, near Carthage, kept at Thagaste by what he believed to be mainly the entreaties of his fellow-citizens,[e] and was counting on the help of Romanianus and Lucinianus (probably Licentius' brother) to wean him away from what Nebridius regarded as local clutches. There is no doubt that even then Augustine was held to be a sage who could be consulted on a variety of matters. But Nebridius apparently found it difficult to comprehend the great existential difference that distinguished Thagaste from Cassiciacum. To go and stay for a few weeks, even months,[f] in the country house lent by a friend, with his mother, son and two students was one thing; to liquidate his assets, keeping only the usufruct, and live as a 'servant of God' in voluntary privation was quite another – an irreversible situation, which at the same time led nowhere, or rather, had no eventual future but true monasticism, or entering the clergy. In this lay the 'transition' of which Paul Monceaux spoke, and which we find easier to perceive than Nebridius, because we know what followed. Augustine replied to his young friend in a tone of tender affection that, even had he been able to bear the fatigue of travelling the distance that separated them, he could not envisage abandoning those who needed him more than Nebridius in the place where he had decided to maintain a strong presence. As for going to and fro between Thagaste and Carthage, he would be with neither one nor the others, and would thus break the commitment he had made to a life that was both contemplative and of use to the community. He suggested that Nebridius should resort to a closed litter – a *basterna* – to take the road to Numidia in greater comfort; but, he added, how would his mother, who already found it hard to endure his absence when he was in good health, agree to let him leave when he was ill?[g] And in fact, Augustine would soon suffer the great grief of losing him.

This irremediable separation of the two friends, before their final separation, has left us a small packet of letters written by both which, in the preserved correspondence of Augustine, is the most important among documents of this kind,[7] and without doubt also the most moving. In the exchange which began in the Cassiciacum era, the most numerous, datable to the three short years at Thagaste, give us invaluable information both on the type of instruction from which Augustine's family members were benefiting at that time, and also on what he himself expected from a life which was not passively contemplative.

Nebridius was not one to be content with expeditious or merely conventional replies.[h] His own letters are short, but teeming with difficult and urgent questions. Augustine wrote to him once that, having made the time to re-read them to take stock of the replies he still owed him, he had found enough to exceed both the intellectual capacities (*ingenium*) and spare time (*otium*) of anyone at all. And, he added, the problems raised by Nebridius were so difficult that a single one was more than enough to absorb him.[i] As he had done at Cassiciacum, Augustine used the still of the night to satisfy that spiritual eagerness,[j] first by exhorting his friend – as a remedy for the solitude of which he complained – to retreat into his innermost self,[k] and find a pleasant dwelling in his own mind,[l] and, as Augustine for his part was doing with those closest to him, to practise that *exercitatio animi* which is the surest way to reach God. This led Augustine to speak of the benefit he himself expected to derive from his *otium;* he resorted to a word whose ambitious formulation has prompted many commentaries: *deificari*, an audacious term indeed, a real challenge for the translator, who hesitates between 'to deify oneself (in retreat)', or 'to be made like God (in retreat)'. It has been thought that Augustine took his inspiration for the expression and the context in which it appears from texts by Porphyry which he had studied at least indirectly during these years.[8] But besides, in a page of the *De moribus ecclesiae catholicae*, a work he had resumed then after the first draft written in Rome one or two years before, he emphasized that a contemplative life in a specifically Christian monastic setting was what could most bring him closer to God.[m] Up to a point, the *fruitio dei* was a *deificatio*. And in a page from the *De vera religione*, dating from the same period, commenting on a verse of Psalm 46, he defines the *otium* that makes possible, or at least facilitates, this *deificatio*: it is not the repose which consists in idleness (*desidia*), but 'the repose of thought (*cogitatio*), which frees it from space and time'.[9] The concept of 'deification' would remain in Augustine's thinking and vocabulary, but with a swift and radical modification of meaning from the initial Neoplatonic perspective; just a few more years, and his reflections on grace would be enough for him to ascribe to God alone the power of 'deification' for the benefit of man, through the mediation of Christ.[10]

The exchanges of letters at the time of Cassiciacum had been concerned with the distinction between the perceptible world and the intelligible world. Now the two friends were preoccupied with problems relating to knowledge. Augustine was intent upon correcting Nebridius' erroneous ideas on the workings of imagination and memory. Of the first he more or less said it was 'the mistress of error and falsity'.[n] As for memory, he was still following the Platonic line defined at Cassiciacum in the *Soliloquies;*[o] it was useful not only to cause images of our past to be reborn; it also served to raise into clear consciousness knowledge that had previously been acquired by the soul.[p] We shall see that he would soon drop that theory of 'reminiscence', in favour of 'illumination' or 'enlightenment' dispensed by the inward Master; but that doctrine was beginning to dawn in the last lines of his penultimate letter to Nebridius.[q]

Of all the questions raised by Nebridius in his short notes, not the least difficult – as his correspondent pointed out – was the one about the incarnation, by which in fact the problem of the Trinity was approached. The young man, who until a fairly recent date had remained curiously dependent on Manichaean ideas about

Christ,[r] asked why the Son, and not the Father, had become incarnate for our salvation. And Augustine was surprised that his friend had not also mentioned the Holy Ghost.[s] For him this was an opportunity to set out clearly and briefly, for the first time, a trinitarian theology whose genesis can be traced from the writings at Cassiciacum.[11] In a necessarily summary formulation, and following a schema he had derived from his Neoplatonic reading – Plotinus, then Porphyry – but reviewed in the light of his own spiritual experience, Augustine started from an ontological explanation of the Trinity. He wrote to Nebridius, 'There is no nature, and absolutely no substance, which does not possess in itself and manifest, first that it *is*, then that it *is this thing or that thing*, and thirdly that it *remains* as much as possible in the very thing that it is.'[t] Each of these three dimensions – or properties – of the substance refers to one of the persons of the Trinity: the first, existence (*esse*) makes known the Principle (or Cause) of nature and relates to its Creator, the Father; the second, Form (*species*), refers to the Son, while one must recognize in the Holy Ghost the Permanence (*manentia*) in which all things are. Augustine could then return to the special role of the Son, and explain the mystery of the incarnation, from the starting-point of his 'property' as Form (*species*):

> Form, which is attributed exclusively to the Son, is also connected with teaching (*disciplina*) and a certain type of art – if one may use that word in matters of this kind – and with the intelligence by which the soul is formed in its representation of reality. Thus, since the result of that assumption of the human condition was to inculcate in us a teaching of life and a moral example, it is not unreasonable that all this should be attributed to the Son.[u]

It is surprising enough, therefore, to find that around 390 – the date of this text – Augustine assigns an essentially pedagogic role to Christ incarnate: reading it, it would appear that the salvation brought by the Son of God is realized on the plane of knowledge, and not on that of redemption. In other words, there emerges 'the moralizing nature of Augustinian soteriology in this period'.[12] But it is only fair to add that Augustine was not proposing here to deal with the purposes of the incarnation in an exclusively and specifically soteriological perspective.[13]

In his *Letter* 14, Augustine expressed the belief that, given the intellectual capabilities he recognized in his correspondent, together they stood a good chance of clarifying the questions he was asking himself about Christ's humanity.[v] This was the last letter Nebridius received before he died, probably in the early months of 391. Some years later, the bishop remembered those last exchanges with emotion, when he recalled the friend who was now in the paradise where everything which Augustine's poor human wisdom had formerly so avidly questioned was now revealed to him:

> He now lives *in Abraham's bosom* – whatever that bosom means[14] – yes, that is where my dear Nebridius dwells, a sweet friend for me, and for you, Lord, a freed man who has become your adoptive son. It is there that he lives, for where else could such a soul be? It is there that he lives, in the place about which he asked me so many questions, me, a poor inexperienced human being. He no longer lends an ear to my lips, but puts the lips

of his spirit to your fount, and drinks his fill of your wisdom to slake his thirst, in endless bliss! And I do not believe that he will be so intoxicated by it that he will forget me, since you, O Lord, from whom he drinks, you remember us.[w]

The first Christian apologetic

Among Augustine's major qualities, pride of place must go to an indomitable pugnacity. He had already had many occasions to use that passion for refuting and convincing, first of all, in his youth, in favour of Manichaeism,[x] and then against it. The former rhetor would not be finished with the Manichaeans for quite some time. With the *De moribus*, he had successfully attacked them on the moral plane, but he remembered the mockery that those in the sect had reserved for the Scriptures: facile criticisms and jests, true, but which hit their target when addressed to men who had remained too 'carnal', as he himself had experienced during his years in Carthage. So they had to be opposed by means of another reading of the Bible, a 'spiritual' reading, clear and firm, but also accessible; for he had been reproached for the excessive difficulty of his preceding anti-Manichaean writings.[y]

This was the subject of his first work of exegesis, where he quite naturally began at the beginning: *On Genesis, against the Manichaeans*. He had kept a vivid memory of Ambrose's sermons on the *Hexameron*, which he had listened to in the spring of 386 or 387; but his own commentary was clearly distinguishable from them, following the text point by point, selecting the Manichaeans' objections point by point and giving them an immediate reply. And that was straight from the first words of Genesis: 'In the beginning, God created the heavens and the earth.' The followers of the sect were wont to say What beginning? And what was God doing before he created the heavens and the earth?[15] Referring to a passage from John's Gospel, according to the 'old Latin' text which was then current in Africa,[z] Augustine replied that *principium* was not to be understood as the beginning of time in a chronological sense, but that God had created the heavens and earth *in Christo, cum Verbum esset apud Patrem*.[16] But chiefly, sketching an analysis of time and eternity to which he would often return in order to make it more precise,[17] he told them that there was no such thing as *before* the creation of the heavens and earth; before God, who exists in a motionless eternity, made time, there *was* no time.[aa] Above all preoccupied with replying in haste to a Manichaean propaganda that seems to have been active then in that area of Numidia, here Augustine does not go more deeply into his exegesis. In his elucidation of the text, he pauses only at what is directly the object of the polemic on the part of his adversaries; so for the time being the famous *fiat lux* is left aside.[bb]

But even in this first approach to Genesis, tackling verses 26 to 31 and the creation of man on the sixth day, 'in the image and likeness of God', it was too good an opportunity to miss in settling scores with Manichaean anthropology. The sect derided this text, asking if God had a nose, teeth and a beard. In his youth, even Augustine had found it difficult to rid himself of that anthropomorphic concept of God, later to substitute an 'idea' that was still too spatial.[cc] As Ambrose had been the first to teach him, neither one nor the other was characteristic of Christians, for whom this man created by God in his own image and likeness referred to the 'inner man', endowed with reason and intellect. [dd] It was as a 'spiritual man' that he had made his appearance at the time of the Creation, and only after being driven from Paradise had he become 'animal': the 'tunics of hide' in which Adam and Eve had clothed themselves – Gen. 3.21 – signified their mortal condition, due to the sin they had committed, according to an explanation that went back as far as Origen,[18] and also the evil suggestions that came to them through their senses.[ee] It is up to us, who came into the world after sin, to make the journey in reverse, the way opened to us by Christ, and to try to reinstate the lost paradise. And that was how the rest on the seventh day was to be understood, also mocked by the Manichaeans: Did God really need rest? they asked. But in reality, that *requies Dei*, the seventh day, meant our own rest, which our good works in God's name would earn for us, if we are capable of them.[ff]

For the six days of the Creation, as presented by Genesis, are both an account of past events and a prediction of the future, and symbolize the ages of the world, or rather, of the human race. The first age extends from Adam to Noah; this is the infancy of the world, its evening the Flood; and as the earth is covered by the waters of the Flood, the memory of our childhood is obliterated by the Flood of forgetfulness. The morning of the second day begins in Noah's time, 'when the firmament was fixed between the waters and the waters': this is the childhood of humanity, in the evening of which God produces the confusion of languages among those who built the Tower of Babel.[gg] The third morning begins with Abraham and with him a third age, similar to adolescence: humanity enters an era of promise, people then honour God, receive the Scriptures and the Prophets.[hh] Then comes the fourth morning, with the reign of King David, the fourth age, the dazzling youth of the world, the first accomplishments of humanity.[ii] But with the captivity in Babylon comes a fifth morning, the dawn of the fifth age, that of man's middle life;[jj] the evening of this age is marked by the multiplication of sins among the people of Israel, so blinded by them that they will not recognize Christ's coming. With the preaching of the Gospels the sixth day glimmers, the one of the *senectus* of the old man, but also of the new man, still carnal but regenerated through Christ; and the evening of the sixth day will see the end of the centuries. Then the seventh day will dawn, that of rest in God, which will have no night.[kk]

With this initial commentary on Genesis Augustine distanced himself for the first time – but not without hope of returning – from the speculative type of work he had engaged in until then. And as would often happen subsequently, even outside the necessarily popular genre of preaching, the former rhetor and Neoplatonist philosopher here made way for a Christian believer who was a better interpreter than most of the sacred text, with no other ambition than to serve it with the utmost effectiveness; which did not prevent a certain personal lyricism from adding its inspiration to that of the biblical poetry.[ll] In this initial attempt, beginning to read the first text of the Old Testament in the figurative sense,[19] distinguishing between 'history' and 'prophecy', he observed twice that though heresy is an evil, it is a necessary one, for the duty imposed on the faithful to refute and confound it stimulates intellectual alertness and the desire for a better understanding of the Scriptures;[mm] there was therefore a good use for heresy and heretics. Saying this, Augustine was anticipating the role he would soon be playing in the Church.

A similarly apologetic work, but with quite a different scope, and at the same time a provisional synthesis of his religious thinking, was the treatise *De vera religione* (*'On true religion'*) written for Romanianus. With this book he was fulfilling a promise that went back to autumn 386. It may be recalled that during that period Augustine, regretting the absence of his former patron from the conversations at Cassiciacum, had dedicated their first results to him, the *Contra Academicos*. But, foreseeing even then that this first 'protreptic' would not succeed in dispersing all Romanianus' 'religious error' – *superstitio*, by which we understand 'Manichaean heresy' – in order to complete his conversion Augustine hinted that he would be sending another text.[nn] Now, in a letter of around 390, he announced that he would shortly be dispatching the text he had just written.[20] And in a few sentences, he reminded his correspondent of his earlier promise, assured him of his anxious concern for him and specified the things he should shun:

> Since it is several years since I promised to write to you, my very dear Romanianus, about my thoughts on the true religion, now the time seems to have come, for the affection that binds me to you can no longer bear to see you endlessly wavering in impassioned questions. Therefore, rejecting all those who are neither philosophers in their religious practice nor religious in their philosophy; likewise rejecting those who, arrogantly stubborn in their false conviction or their disagreement, have deviated from the rule of faith and Catholic communion; lastly, rejecting those who have refused the enlightenment of the Holy Scriptures and what is called the New Testament, the grace of a spiritual people – attitudes whose criticism I have just sketched as briefly as I can – we must adhere to the Christian religion.[oo]

This was a clear identification, for the benefit of Romanianus and any potential reader of this 'fine essay on the essence of Christianity',[21] of three categories of adversary: to start with, the followers of ordinary paganism and, in third place, the Manichaeans, to whom his friend still gave allegiance. Between the two, how can we fail to recognize the supporters of a certain Neoplatonism? There would thus appear to be two 'editorial layers' in the *De vera religione*, one targeting Manichaeism, the other, to some extent superimposed, being a criticism more specifically directed against Porphyry.[22]

Probably, but what lies at the heart of the book, below those two 'strata' and, more deeply, beyond the denunciation of a certain philosophical arrogance, is the expression of an accord between Platonism and Christianity. Let us remember what Augustine said at Cassiciacum in 386 about 'being confident of his ability to find among the Platonists, *for the moment*, doctrines that do not conflict with our mysteries'.[pp] That 'moment' was still lingering at Thagaste, a few years later. Nevertheless, Augustine's thinking had become noticeably more precise and at the same time had shifted; it now appeared to him more clearly that once 'Christian times' – *christiana tempora* – had arrived Platonism had fulfilled itself in Christianity. Read the part in the *De vera religione* in which Plato has a dialogue with one of his students, in whom Augustine himself can be recognized. The philosopher is portrayed teaching how, by detaching oneself from what may be observed through the senses, one may raise oneself to the level of the intelligible and the divine, something that is inaccessible to a being who has remained the slave of his senses and imagination, who can only provoke his mockery. The text continues:

Let us suppose that while the Master was preaching this doctrine, the student asked him, 'Should someone exist, a man of divine greatness, capable of persuading people at least to *believe* these truths, insofar as they cannot *understand* them, or insofar as those who can understand them, even removed from the false ideas of the masses, are smothered under the weight of common errors, if that man existed, would you deem him worthy of divine honours?' Plato, I believe, would have answered that this was an impossible task for a man, unless God's own virtue and wisdom had set him apart from the law of nature; or unless from the cradle, by other means than the moral authority of men, they had enlightened him by an inward illumination; unless they had endowed him with so great a grace, so strong an ascendancy, in short with such majesty that his scorn for all that the wicked desire, his patience in enduring all that they fear, his fulfilment of all they admire, give his love and extraordinary authority the means to convert humankind to such a saving faith.[qq]

It is the word 'saving' that best conveys the meaning, and which sums up the passage – in fact a real *leap* in the spiritual domain – which Augustine was ready to credit to Plato, supposing that he had lived in the *christiana tempora*. But what Plato had historically been unable to do four centuries before the spread of the Gospels, his disciples had sometimes done two centuries afterwards.

Augustine would often return to this fulfilment of Platonism in Christianity. Around 410, in his long 'Letter to Dioscorus',[rr] he would go further, suggesting that his correspondent should regard as two simultaneous phenomena, both due to the coming of Christ and his preaching, on the one hand the great emergence of late Platonism in the form of the Neoplatonic schools, and on the other, the conversion to Christianity of numerous adherents of Neoplatonism. 'Some of them,' he wrote, thinking more particularly of the school of Plotinus, 'recognized that Christ personified Truth itself and the wisdom they were striving to attain, and enlisted under his banner.'[ss] Along this path, Augustine rediscovered the thought processes he had followed since reading the *libri Platonicorum* at Milan in the spring of 386. In the *De vera religione*, he writes that it is essential for the man seeking his salvation to believe firmly that 'philosophy, or the love of wisdom, is not one thing and religion another'.[tt] Although there is no antinomy or otherness, there is however no equation between the two: true philosophy and true religion are not identical. Still in the 'Letter to Dioscorus', the bishop would state clearly, with all the weight of episcopal authority, that if they want to practise their philosophy religiously, 'even bishops of the Platonic family, modifying their attitude somewhat on the points that Christian doctrine does not approve, must piously bow their head before the only forever victorious king, Christ'.[uu] Twenty years earlier, with the only difference of a less 'missionary' formulation at that time, Augustine was already following this line, when he observed that all that was needed was 'a few little changes in language and thinking' for many of the pagan philosophers of his time to become Christian, thus following an evolution like that of the Neoplatonists in a recent period.[vv] But these small changes, a mere nothing, were none other than the quintessential acknowledgement of the Word Incarnate, the act of faith that made the transition from a philosophy of the next world to a religion of salvation.[23]

Augustine devoted the entire second part of his treatise to showing how 'true religion' actualizes that programme of salvation. It requires both 'the authority that demands the intervention of faith and prepares man for the intervention of reason', and 'reason, which leads to understanding and knowledge'. And if, when all is said and done, the proof of truth is the 'supreme authority', to creatures of flesh, immersed in time, resorting to faith is imperative in the first place almost as a pedagogic necessity. First a *temporalis medicina* is required: 'One must lean on the place where one has fallen in order to pick oneself up.'[ww] This education in authority concerns the individual, but has been applied to humankind throughout history. And here, with a fuller orchestration than in the *De Genesi contra Manichaeos*, Augustine resumes the 'ages of the world' which correspond analogically to the ages of man, and demonstrate on the scale of the history of humanity the existence of a divine plan, which accompanies and guides the 'old man' in his efforts to become 'the new man, the inner man, the celestial man'.[xx] And for the first time we see the image of two peoples take clear shape:

> one, formed of the crowd of the impious, which bears the image of earthly man from the beginning of time to the end; the other, made up of generations devoted to the one God, but who, from Adam to John the Baptist, led the life of earthly man with a sort of 'worldly justice': its history is called the Old Testament. In all, it is the promise of an earthly kingdom; but this history, overall, does no more than outline the image of the new people and of the New Testament, a promise of the heavenly kingdom.[yy]

This is the first appearance of a theme destined for magnificent developments; for some years later, the 'two peoples' would become 'two loves' and two cities[zz] – Babylon and Jerusalem – and their contrast the foundation of the old bishop's masterpiece, the *City of God*.

An 'intellectual' in Numidia

As the years went by, since his resignation from the chair of rhetoric in Milan in the summer of 386, Augustine had changed from teacher to 'intellectual', almost in the sense in which we understand the word, though with differences in status implied by quite another conception of public life and its 'media treatment'.[24] Life at Thagaste could not be simply 'contemplative'. In Italy, in Rome and Milan, Augustine had frequented only intellectual circles, either Christians or with Platonist leanings, where he was received and acknowledged as a university man on a sabbatical abroad might be. Now, he was home, and his sphere of influence was noticeable beyond the close circle of family and friends, such as Romanianus or Nebridius, for whom it was a kind of directing of conscience which could be exercised for their benefit, if necessary by letter.

Indeed, we now see new correspondents entering the scene, foreign to Augustine's immediate entourage, and turning to him as an intellectual guide. For example, Caelestinus, who received at his own request some anti-Manichaean texts – at this date probably the two books of the *De moribus* – and, as a free gift, a short but compact advice on the difference in nature that distinguishes the body, the soul and God.[ab] Similarly, to one Gaius with whom Augustine conversed during a stay with him,[25] a whole series of works was sent by carrier, and he was expected to read them carefully and critically, in a suitable fashion to enable him to join the ranks of a Church from which he was probably divided by a remaining vestige of Manichaeism. The warm letter sent to

Antoninus, in the same era, gives a hint of some worry that the schismatic temptation might produce a fissure in the bosom of this Christian family.[ac]

However, the exchange that most reveals the 'intellectual function' which Augustine assumed and for which he was recognized in his Numidian homeland, is the one he had at that time with a grammarian at Madauros, named Maximus, who was old enough at the date of these letters to have been one of the child's schoolmasters in 365–8. Maximus had probably got wind of his return and his youthful fame, but it seems to have been Augustine who took the initiative in the exchange by making an amicable and considerate approach. In the letter from him that is preserved, the old grammarian uses a baldly pretentious amphigory to profess a henotheistic faith: the world, he says, is full of gods, starting with the forum of his nice town of Madauros; he however believes in a single God, father of all mortals, invoked by all nations under different names, adding (a platitude of no consequence) that 'God is a name common to all religions';[ad] of course. But that does not prevent him from asking Augustine to enlighten him on this God of the Christians who is worshipped, he claims, in 'secret places',[ae] nor does he refrain from making ironic allusions to the local martyrs, whose native names – Miggin, Namphamo – seem to him unworthy of comparison with the majesty of Jupiter, Juno or Minerva.[af] He said the wrong thing, and for two reasons. First, Augustine did not accept that, as one African addressing another African – and since they were both in Africa – Maximus should deride Punic names, survivals among others of an old culture, prior to Rome, whose contributions had been nothing to be ashamed of; this was his first opportunity to parade an 'African awareness' that he would never feel to be in opposition to his fundamental Romanness. Next, if Maximus was in a mood to joke about holy nomenclature, there was enough to laugh about with the names given to the minor deities of traditional pagan religion, such as Stercutius, Cloacina and the bald Venus.[ag] With this last tirade, Augustine attacked paganism head on for the first time, mining with witty eloquence a vein he would resume much later when evoking at greater length the many *numina* of Roman religion in the *City of God*.[26]

Speaking of the Thagaste years, Possidius, his biographer, says of Augustine that 'by his conversations and books he taught both those who were present and those who were absent'.[ah] We have just looked at the latter, to whom the writers and recipients of lost letters should doubtless be added, some of whom are named by Possidius.[27] Besides the little group of faithful followers – Alypius, Evodius and perhaps Severus, Augustine's compatriot and fellow-student in their young days – those present are anonymous. But there must have been many who came to Thagaste to consult him, and of those consultations we still have – better than mere traces – actual records. This is the collection entitled *De diversis quaestionibus LXXXIII*, published some years later by gathering notes that had at first been scattered, as the bishop states in his *Retractations*: 'These questions were scattered over a large number of sheets, because, in the early days following my conversion and return to Africa, my brethren questioned me when they saw that I was available.'[ai] Taken down in shorthand by a *notarius*, then fair copied, Augustine's replies had been preserved without any order; the bishop subsequently had them collected and compiled into a book, numbering them to make them easier to read. These texts, which fall into the great ancient tradition of 'questions and answers' – illustrated among others by Plutarch's *Table talk* – do not all date from the Thagaste years; but in many of them, notably among the first, we find an echo of the topics that preoccupied Augustine in that period, especially in his anti-Manichaean polemics; for instance the replies relating to the nature of the soul, free will, the origin of evil or even the person of Christ.[aj] Among the questions in this first series, *Question 12* is remarkable, entitled 'Question of a wise man'. The *Retractations* explain:

> It is not mine, but I was the one who made it known to a few of the brethren who were then questioning me on these subjects with much curiosity. It is the question of a man called Fonteius, from Carthage, who wrote 'On the purification of the spirit to see God', while he was still a pagan; but he died a Christian after being baptized.[ak]

From which it may be seen that, on the one hand spiritual asceticism of a Neoplatonic kind still preoccupied Augustine and his entourage, and on the other, that he was in close contact with philosophical circles at Carthage.

The discussions with Adeodatus (the *De magistro*)

Augustine had definitively given up his teaching career. However, he had to become a teacher once again, to deal with the language, of the masters and the Master – and for the benefit of a chosen student, his own son.

The memory of that last teaching period had remained very vivid when he was writing the *Confessions*:

> There is a book of mine entitled *On the Teacher*, in which Adeodatus and I hold a conversation. You know that all the thoughts expressed in it as from the lips of my interlocutor are his, when he was in his sixteenth year.[28] I know many more wonderful things about him. I was awed by such intellect.

A moving tribute from a father to this 'unfulfilled son' of whom he could say with the greatest conviction that, 'in that boy he owned nothing but the sin'. And he added, 'Of course we nurtured him with your teaching, but you, and you alone, inspired us to do so.'[al] The whole essence of the *De magistro* is contained in that sentence.

When he was Adeodatus' age, Augustine had left to study his rhetoric at Carthage. Staying with his father at Thagaste, the boy pursued his studies under his tutelage. After all, he was at a good school. As early as the Milanese spring of 387, it may be recalled, Augustine had begun work on those *Disciplinarum libri* by which he was rebuilding the entire doctrinal edifice of the university teaching of his time.[am] The edifice remained incomplete, but at least with Book VI of the *De musica*, written during the Thagaste years, probably early on,[29] its author had had an idea of the crowning achievement he was ambitious for it to be. With this book, he truly passed 'from corporeal to incorporeal things'.[an] Adeodatus was to be the first user of this redefined cursus and the first to benefit from the *exercitatio animi*.

There has been much argument about the blueprint of the *De magistro*.[30] The plan is obvious, however, at least in broad bulk, with two clearly distinct parts. After some brief preliminaries, the dialogue opens with the aims of language.

Augustine and Adeodatus quickly agree that the object of language is to teach, or better, to tell, evoke or remember things,[31] by means of *words* which are the *signs of things*. Thereupon, the father quotes a line from the *Aeneid* (II, 659) to his son, who recognizes it straight away, and asks him to break it down into words. It is not a matter of grammar, however, but the philosophy of verbal communication; communication that may be gestural, for at a pinch things can be 'shown' without the use of words, as deaf-mutes and mimes do.[ao] But a 'tripartite distinction' effected by Augustine enables questions to be clarified and the discussion centred again on language. There then follow 'metalinguistic' exchanges of stunning virtuosity between father and son, notably when the two speakers come to analyse 'signs that signify the signifiable': for example the word *homo*, a noun that is phonetically broken down into two syllables, but is understood as meaning 'man' by virtue of the natural law of language which acts so that, on hearing these signs, attention is brought to bear on the things signified.[32]

Towards the end of the first part of the *De magistro*, it seems accepted that there is nothing which can be taught – or about which one can be informed – without signs, and since it is a matter of language, without the help of words.[ap] But the dialectic retort is near. To prepare the way, Augustine sows doubt in Adeodatus' mind and embarks on the dissociation he will make between the *signum* and the *res* – the word and the thing – by recalling an activity in which he himself had indulged as a child in the Thagaste countryside;[aq] to discover how the bird-catcher handles his rods, you have only to watch him do it. There are therefore things that one learns – or is informed about – without signs.[ar] Going further, Augustine breaks away from the dialogue formula and, as we saw that he sometimes did in the conversations at Cassiciacum, launches into a sustained exposition (*oratio continua*). On closer examination, he goes on, we find nothing that is learnt by its sign: for, language being made of signs, when one utters one of these signs by saying a word, either the thing of which the word is the sign is already known by the person addressed, and he is therefore not informed by the sign, or he does not know the thing of which the word is the sign, and is thus no better informed. 'So,' he says, 'it is the sign that is learnt by knowledge of the thing, rather than the thing by the utterance of the sign.'[33] In this case, words have at best merely a function of recall, if we already know the things of which they are the sign, or of information, if we do not know them.

The objection may be raised that this line of argument is valid only in the domain of the perceptible, when communication is aimed at material objects or practical behaviour. But it is equally true, says Augustine, in the world of ideas, and at this point he takes his reader into an initial formulation of his theory of knowledge, with the doctrine of the 'internal teacher'. If a student listening to his master's words understands the sense of the idea he is trying to convey, that signifies – paradoxically – that the master has taught him nothing. For, so that the teacher's language may have meaning for the student, the student must already have that meaning present in his mind, and it is the sense which he already has that informs the words he hears.[as] Thus in Plato's *Menon* Socrates was able, when posing questions on geometry, to make an ignorant slave discover intelligible realities that were to be found in his mind even before he was questioned. But now Augustine no longer thought that 'to learn is to recall', as he had been accepting not so long ago.[at] Of Platonism he retained at least what seemed to him an essential fact, that man does not make truth: he finds it. But for the innateness of knowing, the theory of reminiscence, he substituted the theory – destined for a fine future up to St Bonaventure in the thirteenth century – of the enlightenment of the inner man by the Truth which governs the soul itself, which is Christ, the immutable and eternal Wisdom of God.[34]

There was therefore no horizontal communication of knowledge, nor of consciousness, and teaching must be kept to a salutary humility.

> Who would be stupidly curious enough to send his son to school in order to learn what the teacher thinks? But when the teachers have set out in their words the disciplines they profess to teach, then those who are called their students examine within themselves whether what has been said is true, by contemplating the inner Truth, in proportion to their abilities. That is when they learn; and when they have inwardly found that they have been told the truth, they praise their teachers, unaware that they are praising the taught rather than the teachers – always provided that the latter know what they are talking about.[au]

And Augustine concludes by referring to Matt. 23.10: 'Call no one our master on earth, for the only Master of all is in heaven.'[35]

In fact, the real conclusion was drawn by Adeodatus, who spoke again at the very end: words, he acknowledged, only alert man so that he will learn. Saying this, he did not condemn language, any more than his father had done. And how could Augustine have condemned those words with which he would for such a long time feed those who listened to his sermons, the recipients of his letters, the readers of his works? But one who had acquired complete mastery of speech and, before his retirement, had made his career in the 'chatter market',[av] was in a good position to weigh up the deficiencies of language, its tricks and perversions. At the beginning of the *Confessions*, recalling the mythological hotchpotch with which his studies as an adolescent had been encumbered, he says: 'I do not blame the words, which are like choice and precious vessels, but the wine of error that drunken teachers poured from them to us.'[aw] There was a good use of words, and words had their usefulness, as he admitted at the end of the *De magistro*: it was no small usefulness, and he promised to return to the subject one day.[ax] He still had forty years of life in which to put it to the test.

Forty years during which he would have to live with the memory of the son who disappeared all too soon. For Adeodatus died at some unspecified date, shortly after these conversations, and before the beginning of 391. He was then at most eighteen or nineteen. We may remember that, at Monica's death, Augustine had violently restrained 'the remnants of childhood in him'[ay] and had finally broken down in tears after painful self-control. On the death of Adeodatus, did such strong faith save him from an all too human distress? He suggests so in the *De vera religione*, writing, probably shortly after the death: 'The man who loves God with all his heart is not afflicted by anyone's death, knowing that what does not die for God is not dead for him.'[az] Now, he could not doubt his son's salvation. In the *Confessions*, addressing God, he says: 'You swiftly removed his life from earth, and I now remember him with a greater sense of security, in that I no longer fear for his childhood, or his youth or his whole life.'[ba] Like the beloved Nebridius, in the same period, Adeodatus was now safely 'in Abraham's bosom': his baptism accomplished, he had been withdrawn from this world 'lest his mind be perverted by wickedness' (Wis. 4.11).[bc] Much later, the bishop would say that 'it is a gift from God to end one's life before passing from good to evil'.[bd] But could the father physically forget that 'unfulfilled son'? That he lived to the evening of his life with poignant regrets for that unachieved promise, with thoughts of the child he admired, grievously present in his absence, like a lost limb, is revealed by a sentence in his last book, where Cicero speaks for him: 'Do not these words of Cicero for his son come from the viscera of every father, when he says to him in a letter: "Of all people, you are the only one I would wish to surpass me in everything"?'[be]

Notes

a. *City of God*, XXII, 8, 3; the text does not breathe a word about the presence of either Adeodatus or Evodius, though they had made the crossing in their company.
b. *City of God*, XXII, 8, 3.
c. *Vita Aug.*, III, 2.
d. *Ep.* 6, 1, in Augustine's correspondence.
e. *Ep.* 5.
f. On the chronological difficulties, see above, p. 100.
g. *Ep.* 10, 1.
h. On his intellectual demands, see what Augustine says in a letter dated 408: *Ep.* 98, 8.
i. *Ep.* 11, 1. It was mainly a warning to his friend not to add to the 'pile' (*acervus*)!
j. *Ep.* 3, 1 (from Cassiciacum); 13, 1 (late one night, at Thagaste).
k. *Ep.* 9, 1: *Confer te ad tuum animum et illum in deum leva, quantum potes.*
l. *Ep.* 10, 1.
m. See above, p. 124; *Mor.*, I, 67.
n. *Ep.* 7, 5.
o. *Sol.*, II, 35.
p. *Ep.* 7, 2. Cf. *De quantitate animae*, 34: 'What is called "learning" is nothing other than recalling and remembering.'
q. *Ep.* 13, 4.
r. Cf. *Conf.*, IX, 6, and above, p. 100.
s. *Ep.* 11, 2.
t. *Ep.* 11, 3.
u. *Ep.* 11, 4.
v. *Ep.* 14, 3.
w. *Conf.*, IX, 6.
x. Cf. above, p. 40.
y. Cf. *De Genesi adversus manichaeos*, I, 1.
z. John 8.25, Jesus' reply to the Jews who asked him who he was: *Principium, quia et loquor vobis.*
aa. *Gn. adv. man.*, I, 3–4;
bb. *Gn. adv. man.*, I, 13: *Et dixit deus: fiat lux, et facta est lux. Hoc non solent reprehendere Manichaei . . .*
cc. Above, p. 76.
dd. *Gn. adv. man.*, I, 27–8.
ee. *Gn. adv. man.*, II, 41.
ff. *Gn. adv. man.*, I, 34.
gg. *Gn. adv. man.*, I, 35–6.
hh. *Gn. adv. man.*, I, 37. The theme would be widely developed in *City of God*, XVI, 12–34.
ii. *Gn. adv. man.*, I, 38, theme developed at length in *City of God*, XVII, 8–19.
jj. *Gn. adv. man.*, I, 39: *declinatio a iuventute ad senectutem, nondum senectus, sed iam non iuventus.*

kk.   *Gn. adv. man.*, I, 40–1. The first Augustinian formulation of the periodization of the history of the world.

ll.   See the imagery of *Gn. adv. man.*, I, 43, amplifying that of the biblical text: Gen. 1.20–1.

mm.   *Gn. adv. man.*, I, 2; II, 3. An echo, already, of the *oportet haereses esse* (1 Cor. 11.19), which he would quote verbatim in the *De vera religione*, 15.

nn.   *Contra Acad.*, II, 8: *aliqua disputatio de religione.*

oo.   *De vera rel.*, 12. The short critical presentation of the three attitudes rejected was made in I, 1–VI, 11.

pp.   *Contra Acad.*, III, 43.

qq.   *De vera rel.*, 3. See the commentary on this page by A. Mandouze, *Saint Augustin*, pp. 491–4.

rr.   Letter 118, a lengthy reply to a young man of Greek origin who says he is the brother of the new *magister memoriae*, Zenobius, perhaps the dedicatee of the *De ordine*: cf. above, p. 83.

ss.   *Ep.* 118, 33.

tt.   *De vera rel.*, 8.

uu.   *Ep.* 118, 21.

vv.   *De vera rel.*, 7: *paucis mutatis verbis et sententiis* Christiani fierent.

ww.   *De vera rel.*, 45.

xx.   *De vera rel.*, 48–9.

yy.   *De vera rel.*, 50.

zz.   *City of God*, XIV, 28.

ab.   *Ep.* 18, 1 and 2.

ac.   *Ep.* 20, 3.

ad.   *Ep.* 16, 1.

ae.   *Ep.* 16, 3.

af.   *Ep.* 16, 2.

ag.   *Ep.* 17, 2. Stercutius was the god of septic tanks, but Cloacina is nevertheless something other than exclusively the goddess of drains that Augustine seems to see in her.

ah.   *Vita Aug.*, III, 3.

ai.   *Retract.*, I, 26, 1.

aj.   *De div. qu.*, 1, 2, 3, 4, 6, 7, 8, 9, 10, 13, 14, 16, 18, 21, 22, 23, 24.

ak.   *Retract.*, I, 26, 2.

al.   *Conf.*, IX, 14.

am.   Cf. above, pp. 113–14.

an.   *De musica*, VI, 2: *ut a corporeis ad incorporea transeamus.*

ao.   *De magistro*, 5.

ap.   *De magistro*, 31.

aq.   *De quantitate animae*, 36.

ar.   *De magistro*, 32: *nullo significatu, sed re ipsa.*

as.   *De magistro*, 40.

at.   Cf. *Soliloquies*, II, 35; *De quantitate animae*, 34; *Ep.* 7, 2 (to Nebridius).

au.   *De magistro*, 45.

av.   *Conf.*, IX, 2: cf. above p. 99.

aw.   *Conf.*, I, 26.

ax.   *De magistro*, 46.

ay.   *Conf.*, IX, 29: *meum quiddam puerile, quod labebatur in fletus.*

az.   *De vera rel.*, XLVII, 91.

ba.   *Conf.*, IX, 14. Cf. *De correptione et gratia*, 13, on those whom an early death, after receiving baptism, removes from the dangers of this life.

bc.   Cf. *De gratia et libero arbitrio*, 45, lines 426/427, where the memory of Adeodatus seems to be underlying.

bd.   *De correptione et gratia*, 19.

be.   *Contra Iulianum opus imperfectum*, VI, 22, which quoted a lost letter of Cicero. The book, later than the *Retractations*, belongs to the period 428–30.

Part II

The Bishop of Hippo

CHAPTER XVI

Hippo Regius: Priesthood

At the end of 390 Augustine was thirty-six. In under five years he had transformed himself into a completely different man, and he now found himself at another turning-point. The death of Monica in 387, followed by that of Nebridius and, most of all, of his son – to say nothing of the brutal separation in 385 from Adeodatus' mother – had one after the other severed the emotional bonds which ordinarily stabilize most mortals. But his reactions to his mother's death had revealed an uncommon spiritual calibre; and he had found another kind of stability in the almost monastic life at Thagaste, in the company of his remaining friends, Alypius, Evodius and Severus, with whom he had a deep communion. We have just seen how this climate of amicable argument had favoured the development of several important works.

It was precisely at this time that the works written during those three years, and in addition the first Italian essays – partly revised at Thagaste – were beginning to circulate. They had the limited circulation of writings in a period when 'distribution networks' were strictly dependent on the private initiative of a few interested readers or the author himself, and when that selfsame distribution was connected with the manual reproduction of the work, less reliant on the existence of good copyists than on the supply of 'paper' (*charta*), which was often lacking.[1] Restricted though it may have been, the circulation of Augustine's first works, probably mainly along a Thagaste–Carthage line and doubtless also with a certain local diffusion in Numidia, was all the more remarkable, and remarked upon, because as far as we know it took place in a doctrinal void from which, after the death of Optat of Milevis, there emerged only the singular figure of an out-of-the-ordinary Donatist, Tyconius, the value of whose exegetical contribution Augustine would soon recognize.

The personal fame reflected upon Augustine drew people's attention to him more than he would have wished. Within a radius of one hundred kilometres around Thagaste, and more especially towards the east, in line with the valley of the Medjerda in the direction of Carthage, there were many bishoprics, as we shall see, with bishops of greater faith than culture. A pastor of Augustine's quality was the object of covetousness, and he was not unaware of the then common practice of episcopal elections carried out against the will of the interested party. He had the example of Ambrose, which was well known to him, to put him on his guard, which is why, as he went about, he was careful to avoid places where the bishop's chair was vacant.[a] Such was not the case in Hippo, the principal city and main outlet to the sea for the Numidia known as 'Proconsular' because, unlike continental Numidia, with Constantine and Lambaesis as its poles, it was attached to the old province of Africa, governed by the proconsul in residence at Carthage, from where he sent one of his 'legates' on secondment to

Hippo. The town thus added some political importance to a genuine economic influence.

During the winter of 390–1, Augustine went to Hippo. As he would say much later, he went there at the request of a friend to pay him a visit, with the idea of hastening his conversion to a monastic life.[b] Possidius adds the interesting detail that he was an *agens in rebus*, a member of the corps of imperial police among whom the violence of the government they served seems often to have induced depths of feeling, as we have seen.[c] When he met this friend, Augustine found that his ardour had somewhat cooled, and he had had to intensify his conversations and exhortations. On arriving at Hippo, however, he had another idea in mind – finding somewhere to establish a real monastery.[d] Little did he imagine the price he would have to pay to achieve his goal.

Hippo Regius

Hippo was one of those coastal settlements where the sea's rages and the rivers' floods combine their contrasting efforts, and seem to have taken malicious pleasure in spoiling what men had built without heed for natural constraints.

If the Gentlemen of Port-Royal, in the mid seventeenth century, enchanted at the thought of discovering that the name Hippo Regius had in another form been the name of their famous abbey, thus eternally pledged to house their doctrinal battle, had been able to visit the African site they believed to be eponymous with their own,[2] they would have seen nothing more than was seen by those who began to take an interest in it two centuries later. Already, early in the eighteenth century, Dr T. Shaw, chaplain of the small English colony in Algiers, had been shown at 'Bona' the 'site and debris of St Augustine's monastery':[3] in fact, vestiges of the great baths; archaeologists well know that these tall and massive piles of rubble, which are both very solid and unsuitable for re-use, everywhere form islets of resistance to the action of time and man. Even at the beginning of the twentieth century, in the ruins situated between the two wadis that enclose the site, the Seybouse to the east and the Bou Djemaa to the west, the *Knissia* was still to be seen, the 'basilica of Peace' for Europeans, then the only visible sign on the surface of a town whose disappearance, early in Islamic times, had occurred on the fringes of history.[4] In the battle between the sea and the rivers, the latter had won, covering with a thick layer of clay and silt a site from which emerged only the two hillocks that punctuate it, the hill known as St Augustine's and the 'Gharf el-Artran', which had thus reverted to the islets they had doubtless been at the dawn of time.

The reconquest of the ancient site of Hippo is relatively recent. It was decided upon by a learned society, the academy of Hippo, and was the work of a man who devoted twenty years of his life to it, Erwan Marec. There was a gradual reappearance of the area of villas on the seafront, the eastern boundary of the city on the ancient shoreline, the forum, the theatre, a market, a network of streets, two other bathing establishments adding to the great baths already known, and lastly the episcopal group, to which I shall return. The size of the great public plaza, a few fine pieces of statuary and the quality of the mosaics revealed an urban importance and prosperity argued for by the texts. As often happens, however, archaeology initially promised more than it could finally fulfil: the 'cyclopean' walls of the villas fronting the sea, with their superb bosses, were not 'Phoenician' and did not bear witness to the very great antiquity suggested by certain sources, which remained only a probability. There were the retaining walls, rebuilt on several occasions on successive shorelines between the first century BC and the second AD[5]. The first, pre-Roman Hippo has yet to be found. It rested perhaps on 'St Augustine's hill', which was unfortunately decapitated in the first years of the twentieth century, but on those terrains which have been so deeply altered on many occasions by alluvial deposits since the beginning of historical times only a large-scale campaign of prospection, both geomorphological and archaeological, would enable its extent to be redefined.

The town that Augustine discovered shortly before the end of the fourth century had benefited from many years of good fortune, linked first to its natural harbour facilities, with convenient landing places in the estuaries of the two rivers and mooring sheltered by the foothills of the Cap de Garde from westerly gales, which were the most feared in the vicinity. It was in this port that Caesar's ally, Sittius, had captured the Pompeian fleet in 46 BC.[6] In Augustus' era, the town had acquired the status of *municipium*, before receiving the honour of becoming a Roman colony, probably in the time of the Flavians. Consequently, from that period on, all citizens were by right Roman citizens. The main square bears witness to that political recognition; the esplanade of the forum, one of the most vast in Africa, is also one of the most ancient, dated as it is by the carving on its pavement of the monumental dedication of the consul C. Paccius Africanus, proconsul in AD 78.

A port gains its importance as much for its purpose as for its natural features. The riches to which Hippo's served as an outlet were mainly agricultural. With the exception of the forests of the Edough massif, which overhung the town, the lowlands of the hinterland, mainly to the south-west towards Calama (Guelma) were good for wheat. Farther still, past the small barrier of the Numidian Alps, on whose foothills vineyards and olive groves rose in terraces, lay the vast cereal crops of the Constantine area, and yet farther the cereal-growing plains of the Setif region. In Augustine's time, sending their produce by way of ports that ensured links with Ostia, the main ones being Rusicade (Philippeville, now Skikda) and Hippo, they were Rome's prime source of food supplies. At Hippo a high-ranking imperial functionary held office, with the task of purchasing wheat to supply the Eternal City.[7] That was the result of a story that had begun when Nero had decided that Africa, which was nearer, should supplant Egypt in supplying the Empire's capital with two thirds of its provisions. He had had no problem in effecting that decision, since he confiscated the vast estates of several great landowners and had them put to death.[8] In his time, therefore, these *latifundia* had become part of the imperial patrimony and used for an extensive cereal monoculture; they were situated mainly in Africa Proconsularis – broadly the territory of present-day Tunisia, augmented by a whole eastern fringe of Algeria, following a line from Annaba, in the north, to the Algerio–Tunisian borders, in the south. Then, from the end of the first century AD, the advance of Romanization westwards had gradually liberated those territories formerly acquired by Rome from their colonial status and had restored them to a balanced polyculture, often so well illustrated in mosaics.[9] The wheat necessary for Rome

– and its army since Septimius Severus' institution of a new tax in kind, the *annona* – would be increasingly provided by the exploitation of new lands, recovered in Numidia and even farther westwards from the old stamping-grounds of tribes who were now confined and settled.[10]

The agricultural world that had been born in these vast regions, formerly freely ranged by the Musulamii, Suburbures and Nicives, was typified by a complex and very inegalitarian social stratification. Small landowners, among whom was Patricius, Augustine's father, formed its middle class,[11] certainly numerous compared with an oligarchy of very wealthy property owners that had been rebuilt after Nero's confiscations, but very much in the minority in relation to a mass of small settlers who eked a living from a metayage system, with a right of use of rented land or areas recuperated from fallow land.[12] Rather more seriously, in the course of time the demographic boom had encouraged, on the margin of the needy but stable peasantry, the growth of a real agricultural proletariat, hiring out their labour according to seasons and requirements. The social instability of these agricultural workers, with their precarious living conditions, could not fail to have local consequences in the history of that period, when religious struggles often recruited their troops from the marginalized. There was no need to penetrate very far into Hippo's countryside to meet these marginals, behind the beautiful mosaics in the foreground and, once he had become a bishop, Augustine would have that experience.

Priest by surprise

Passing through Hippo to meet a friend who wanted to talk to him about his monastic vocation, Augustine had had to prolong his stay, as we have seen, because of the man's wavering. There he attended church and took part in the services without keeping on the alert, since the bishopric was duly provided with a bishop. But he, Valerius, was old; Greek by birth, he was a mediocre speaker in Latin and knew no Punic at all, though it was a good thing to know at least a few words to use with the rustic faithful, who spoke the remnants of Carthage's ancient language, very much bastardized,[13] as a kind of patois. In a text from this era, Augustine records a detail about his bishop which is very significant in this respect: in a conversation between peasants Valerius had heard the word *salus* – or at least something near it – and had asked one of them who also knew Latin what the word meant; he had answered 'three' (*tria*), and Valerius had gone into ecstasies over the remarkable meeting, between one language and the other, of 'salvation' and the Trinity![e]

Moreover, the Christian community headed by Valerius was not in a good position at this time. The Manichaeans prospered at Hippo, under the leadership of a 'priest' named Fortunatus, whom Augustine had known previously at Carthage when they had been co-religionists in the sect,[f] and whose clever proselytism had won followers among the town's citizens as well as in the little foreign colony.[g] At the same time, the community itself was divided: the Donatists there were in a strong position, and their bishop, Faustinus, was able to indulge in a gesture as serious and symbolic as forbidding bakers to cook bread for the Catholic minority.[h] Valerius clearly lacked the stature to stand up to them, even less to put the situation right. Was Augustine unaware of this state of affairs? The faithful of Hippo, for their part, were only too conscious of it, and when the old bishop declared in his sermon that he needed a priest who was capable of helping him, there was a unanimous shout from the congregation. Immediately recognized, surrounded, dragged into the apse to the bishop in his chair, Augustine was ordained priest forthwith.[i]

He had not been able physically to oppose this enforced ordination. He burst into tears and, Possidius recorded later, some of the congregation mistook the meaning of his tears, seeing them as chagrin for entering the clergy through the back door, instead of acceding directly to the episcopacy![j] Assuredly, those tears had quite a different significance; as Possidius also says, setting down what Augustine later confided to his friends, looking ahead to his almost inevitable elevation to the position of bishop, 'he had the premonition of the multiplicity and immensity of the perils that the guidance and government of a church would bring to bear on this life'.[k] Here again, even though Hippo was not Milan, the image that came to his mind, symbolic of such a heavy burden, was that of Ambrose, whom he had seen so terribly busy, faced with such important responsibilities. But there was still something else at the root of the knot of anguish which had formed in his heart; such a rude change of destiny implied a farewell to what had been his considered aspiration, since Milan and Cassiciacum in 386, of which the *deificari in otio*, of course, in his letter to Nebridius told of his strong spiritual need, a life of the spirit and of prayer in a monastic setting, which did not rule out serving others but did not put it in institutional terms. In the evening of his life, making an appraisal of it in a sermon to those people to whom he had devoted his life, the bishop says: 'I had said farewell to all worldly hopes, and what I might have been I no longer wished to be; but by no means did I seek to be what I am.'[l] On that day early in 391, with a few fine books already behind him, but with an immense work in gestation in his head, he knew that henceforward days would no longer suffice, and that night vigils would have to be added to daily work: *in die laborans et in nocte lucubrans*, as Possidius would write.[m]

Augustine already had a pretty sound theological training, and ran no risk of finding himself actually in the situation Ambrose had experienced, of having to learn while teaching, but he was aware that Valerius had appealed to him particularly for the ministry of preaching.[n] And for the first time in his life, someone who knew how to speak before the high and mighty of this world, address a cultivated public, correspond with people who were more or less his peers, now had to envisage speaking before the lowly of Hippo, before fishermen (*piscatores*) who were also sinners (*peccatores*), for whom Christ had come more than for philosophers and the erudite, and whom he had to reach with their own words. He had already been reproached for the difficulty of understanding certain of his works;[o] besides complementing his scriptural reading, he needed to learn to speak in simple terms – *ad usum populi* – of things as complicated as the soul, God or the Trinity. Only just ordained, he asked for leave, for both study and meditation.

The letter he addressed to his bishop was preserved. Nothing, he says first, is more satisfying than the office of bishop, priest and even deacon, but nothing is more wretched than to perform it for the vainglory of the social status that accompanies it. And nothing is more difficult than to do it when fully conscious of the lofty mission entrusted to a bishop, priest or deacon.[p] He continues:

> I was ordained when I was thinking of giving myself time to get to know the divine Scriptures, and I had made my arrangements so as to benefit from the *otium* necessary for this *negotium*. And, to tell the truth, I did not yet know what I lacked for this task, which now torments and crushes me . . . Perhaps your Holiness will object: 'I would like to know what is missing in your education.' My reply is that the things I don't know are so many that I could more easily enumerate those that I know than those I would like to know. I would dare to say that I know and hold with firm faith what concerns my own salvation; but how could I make use of this knowledge for the salvation of others, 'seeking not what is useful to me but what is useful to the greater number for their salvation' (cf. 1 Cor. 10.23)? And perhaps, or rather without any doubt, there are counsels written in the holy books which, by knowing and meditating upon them, the man of God may improve his service in ecclesiastical matters and even, in the hands of sinners, either live without failing his conscience, or die, but without losing the only life that is worth Christian hearts sighing for, in humility and meekness. But how could that be obtained except as the Lord Himself says: 'by asking, seeking, knocking at the door' (cf. Matt. 7.7; Luke 11.9)? That is to say, by means of prayers, reading and tears. It is with this aim that I wanted to ask my brothers to obtain from your very earnest and venerable Charity a little time, just until Easter, which I now desire and hereby request.[q]

Augustine obtained a few weeks' liberty from Valerius. Perhaps not quite until Easter, which fell that year on 6 April, for there is at least one sermon delivered by the new priest included in the series of 'quadragesimal' catechesis sermons, to bear witness that his priestly ministry began at Hippo as early as March 391.[14] Where did he go for his brief additional spell of training? Probably Thagaste, at his home, or rather in the 'monastery' he would leave to Alypius. For he would have had to settle his affairs, before organizing his life and that of his future companions at Hippo in the real monastery for which Valerius had offered him the material wherewithal. The bishop had in fact given him a house with a garden near the cathedral-church.[15] At the cost of accepting the priesthood, and having to give up a great deal, Augustine had attained the goal to which he had aspired for a good few years. We shall have occasion to return to both the concrete realities and the developments and regulatory arrangements of the monastic life he would live at Hippo for nearly forty years.

Still against the Manichaeans

That really put paid to the contemplative life. From a strictly ecclesiastical point of view, the first three years of his priesthood would culminate in the role – extraordinary for a priest in the West – played by Augustine at the general council which met at Hippo on 8 October 393; but they were very busy years,[16] still and primarily occupied by the fight against the Manichaeans. He resumed his attack, now with pastoral motives; the sect was influential in Hippo. But besides, of those whom he had previously drawn with him into error he could still try to rescue one last companion of his youth, Honoratus, who had not followed the Italian journey. For him, he wrote the *De utilitate credendi*, like a long letter.

Both form and tone give this little book its unique charm. It is a pseudo-dialogue, during which Augustine imagines his friend's objections and provides both the questions and the answers, with mock exchanges that are often insistent, with a quick rhythm, and tireless artifice.[r] To move Honoratus and urge him to the same examination of his conscience, Augustine retraces the path they had followed together during their Carthaginian years; thus, before the *Confessions* and following a small autobiographical page of the *De beata vita*, this step into the past is a first light thrown on the intellectual demands of their common youth and the consequences they brought in their wake.[s] There was nothing gratuitous here in Augustine's emphasis on the route he had taken; before putting forward his arguments, he wanted by his own example to show how faith had saved him from the snares, doubts and difficulties of using intellect alone, and setting out his own case had an educational value. Honoratus was a cultured man; Augustine would speak to him about the Old Testament as they had heard about Virgil in their adolescence. It was no good launching oneself into Virgil or Terence without a guide; initiators, and good ones at that, were required, and if the grammarian, confused by some obscure passage or finer point, chose to criticize the poet instead of admitting his confusion, he would find it hard to keep his students, even if he paid them! The same applied to the Scriptures; it was as foolish to trample on them before trying to understand them as it would be to trample on a ray of sunshine passing through the window, in order to counter the Manichaeans. The Scriptures required a commentary before any interpretation.[t]

Honoratus was also a fine intellectual, proud of the power and prestige of reason; this was where Augustine needed patience and skill. He placed little emphasis on the problem of evil, temporarily left aside as if for a continuation that did not materialize.[u] On the crucial point, the necessary primacy of belief in religious matters, Augustine advanced cautiously, avoided a head-on confrontation with his correspondent, played with the word 'reason'. 'Perhaps', he wrote, 'it is on this point that you are trying to find a reason, to persuade yourself that you must not put reason before faith in order to learn.'[v] He would chivvy this Manichaean even less than those addressed at the beginning of the *De moribus*.[w] Augustine admitted – or pretended to – that a small number of men, including his friend, were capable of reaching the divine by a rational approach.[x] But was that any excuse for giving the majority an example of foolhardiness and abandoning them to their weakness? In any case, believing and being credulous were two different attitudes of mind. Augustine was showing Honoratus that belief was a normal thought process which, for example, conditioned social relationships, primarily family ones.[y] Transposed onto the religious plane, this disposition of 'trust', a prerequisite of belief, meant for the great mass of humanity resorting to a wise man, the mediator between man and God; now, what greater wise man was there than Christ, to whose authority the Manichaeans themselves referred?[z] In the dialectic of reason and faith, such as Augustine himself had experienced and now set forth clearly, Honoratus, like Romanianus[aa] just recently, had completed only a tiny part of the journey. The exercise of his reason had no doubt prepared him for the intellectual comprehension of divine matters; now he had to complete the act of faith, before using his reason for understanding the content of that faith. For the use of simple followers, who did not have the rational – or arrogant – approach of the intellectuals, Augustine would later sum up the step to be taken in one of those synthetic expressions with which he so often studded his texts: 'If you cannot understand, believe in order to understand; faith precedes, understanding follows.'[17] His friend, thus admonished, does not appear to have taken this step immediately.

The *De utilitate credendi* was addressed to Honoratus alone and, without entering into a metaphysical critique of Manichaeism, was concerned essentially with faith. In the same period, 391/2, Augustine felt the need to express himself in a sort of circular letter addressed to all the friends of his adolescence and youth who had shared his error.[bb] This was the little book which he entitled *De duabus animabus* – 'On the two souls' – at the cost, it must be said, of an inexact interpretation of the Manichaean doctrine, which recognized not two 'souls' in man but the coexistence – and conflict – of two 'natures': soul and body, light and darkness. In tone, this text is a long *mea culpa*. At an age when one is trustful, the Manichaeans had easily exerted their persuasive seduction on a young man whose successes in his jousts with 'ignorant Christians' had also gone to his head; that was why he had too long followed 'men who preferred a good ear of corn to a living soul'.[cc] Reliving in his mind those years when he had been their travelling companion, he belatedly finds all the answers he should have made to their materialism and dualism. However, in self-defence, he states that in those days he had not yet heard about the way in which the mixture of good and evil, light and darkness, was brought about, nor what had been the cause, and therefore his ignorance of the details of the Manichaean myth of the 'middle time' robbed him of the arguments he could have used to oppose the sect's supporters.[dd] Quite naturally, this retrospective criticism was centred on the problem of evil, and the false solutions offered by Manichaeism. Augustine reiterated that one sinned by will alone, defined as 'an impulse of the soul, free from all constraint, inclined either not to lose something, or to acquire it'.[ee] There also followed, as a definition of sin – 'sin is therefore the will to keep or obtain what justice (in the sense of a morally irreproachable act) forbids and from which one can freely abstain'[ff] – a formula he would soon use word for word in his debate with Fortunatus.

This dispute with the Manichaean 'priest' of Hippo took place at the request of the town's Christian community, Catholics and Donatists for once gathered together, worried by Fortunatus' mounting success. The encounter occurred in public[18] and, following a choice that we shall see in other circumstances, was held in a place that was both 'neutral' and sufficiently roomy: baths, in this instance the 'baths of Sossius'.[19] The exchanges between the two champions were dated – 28 and 29 August 392 – and recorded like public meetings, and Augustine's publication of them in book form appears not to have detracted from their freshness.[gg] This above all gives them their interest, for Fortunatus made a lame defence and his opponent did not have to work very hard to confound him. Faced with Augustine's exceptional mastery of language, here we have a living picture of the Manichaean's clumsiness and sidestepping, duly picked up by his adversary – that way of not replying, or replying with another question, when things became awkward for him.[hh] It was agreed that the debate should bear not on the morals of either side but on the articles of their respective faiths. Fortunatus had brought with him not the Manichaeans' canonical writings, but the Gospels and St Paul; for he would not be quoting a long passage from the

Apostle from memory.[20] Augustine answered him with the same texts – which he knew better than his opponent[21] – reproaching him for playing with an anthology of quotations taken out of context which it was easy to make appear contradictory to one another.[ii] But at last the debate began, and Augustine straight away attacked Fortunatus on the status attributed to God by the sect, theoretically reputed by them to be incorruptible and inviolable, but in actual fact exposed to violence and corruption in the development of their cosmogony. This, it may be remembered, was the first part of 'Nebridius' argument', whose effectiveness Augustine had long appreciated; he soon complemented it to place his adversary in a dilemma:

> My argument will be brief and, I believe, perfectly clear to all. If God could in no way suffer from the nation of darkness, because he is inviolable, there is no reason for him to have put us down here to endure evil. If, on the other hand, he could suffer in some way, he is not inviolable and you deceive those to whom you say he is inviolable.[jj]

Fortunatus replied evasively and Augustine returned to the charge in vain; his opponent sidestepped again, asking what was the Catholic's view on the origin of the soul; he probably knew that it was a question over which Augustine hesitated, and would always hesitate.[kk] They returned to the question of evil, and Augustine resumed the definition of sin that was well to the fore in his mind as he had set it out recently in his text 'On the two souls'.[ll] The first day's debate soon drifted to the nature of Christ and ended in confusion, not least because of the uproar created by the audience, who disliked the way the Manichaean was making use of the Scriptures.

The next day, the dispute resumed on the problem of evil. Augustine reaffirmed that evil came from the deliberate sin of the soul, to whom God had given free will. Fortunatus scored a point here, however, retrieving the objection presented by Evodius at the end of Book I of the De libero arbitrio: if sin came from the voluntary action of the soul endowed with free will, God was a party to evil, since he was responsible for granting the soul free will.[mm] The Manichaean did not, however, draw any inferences from this and came back to the sect's central position on this matter, the affirmation of a fundamental dualism that he claimed to base on Pauline texts which, read rapidly and out of context, seemed to argue for the coexistence of two natures in man.[nn] This was manna for Augustine, who had no difficulty in showing him that the Pauline anthropological description applied not to the first man, the original sinner by the choice of his free will, but to his descendants, living after the flesh and according to 'the wisdom of the flesh, the enemy of God' (Rom. 8.7) and subject to necessity – he would also say 'habit'.[oo] Fortunatus' feeble defences fell one after the other. In the end he admitted – this was at the heart of the myth of Mani's 'three times' – that to defend himself God had been constrained to send the soul, therefore that he was ruled by necessity. He retracted, however, and to confound him his adversary had to have the 'shorthand notes' of the debate read out.[pp] One last time, Augustine challenged him with 'Nebridius' argument', and Fortunatus was nonplussed; his silence echoed other silences, already encountered by Nebridius and his friends in debates of this kind. Personally, Fortunatus admitted that he was beaten, if not convinced; he confined himself to reporting his adversary's line of reasoning to his superiors. We know from the *Retractations* that he did not become a Catholic; but he left Hippo.[qq]

With this public debate the 'intellectual' had entered the arena for the first time, the kind of joust where the rout of the adversary, recorded by the 'notaries', was sanctioned by the frequently noisy assent of the audience. The former rhetor, now a priest, and soon to be a bishop, was not fooled by this 'media attention'. He was well aware that among the people who crowded to these events, many had come for the 'show', as if it were the theatre. Some years later, he would thus describe the attitude of the crowd who had flocked to his encounter with Fortunius, the Donatist bishop of a neighbouring town, Thubursicu Numidarum (Khamissa): most had come not to hear a cause debated with the wise desire to understand more clearly, but to enjoy the performance of two actors.[rr] Augustine knew, without empty complacency, that in future in these jousts he would have to turn to good account a talent recognized by everyone and of which he himself was very conscious. From now on he would be on a stage from which he would not exit until his death.

Disciplina

On his return to Italy in the autumn of 388, in Carthage Augustine had met one of that great city's deacons, Aurelius.[22] Without going through the priesthood, he had become bishop of Carthage, and thus primate of Africa, probably during 392.[23] Shortly after his ordination, he wrote Augustine a letter, now lost but its tenor is partly revealed by the reply he received. We know that the new spiritual leader of the Church of Africa had commended himself to the prayers of his correspondent, that he had agreed to Alypius' remaining at Thagaste as a living example of the ascetic ideal he had experienced with his friend – which suggests that Alypius might have been called upon by other churches to enter either the priesthood or the episcopacy – and that he had even made a gift of land to the *fratres* at Thagaste.[24] In his letter, did he raise the problem of the agapes in the cemeteries? At all events, this was the almost exclusive topic of Augustine's reply. To stigmatize the collective scandal they represented in his view he spontaneously recalled St Paul's text, reading which, as the result of a 'divine' inspiration in the garden in Milan, had dispersed the last clouds in his mind.[ss] There was nothing of greater urgency for the new priest than to extirpate from the mass of the faithful in his Africa practices which made them 'carnal' men, and more than just symbolically. For 'chambering' and 'wantonness', it went without saying. But 'rioting' and 'drunkenness' in honour of the blessed martyrs, not only on their anniversaries but virtually every day? Augustine emphasized in his letter that, either because they had never existed or because they had been suppressed, these customs were unknown in the Churches overseas and in Italy,[25] with whom the communities in the African provinces were in unfortunate contrast in this regard. And, in fact, archaeology bears witness in abundance to the presence of the 'agape tables' – the *mensae* – in the palaeo-Christian sites of North Africa.[26]

On this subject Augustine knew that he had an ally in Aurelius, someone who shared his mental outlook and had the same will to see it prevail. To put an end to these practices, he could count on a primate who, as a simple deacon in his church, had already condemned them.ᵘᵘ It was up to the metropolitan church to set the example, and it did so. But the evil was so widespread and deep-rooted that the authority of a councilᵛᵛ was necessary to get rid of it. That is what Augustine suggested in his letter, with a surprising freedom on the part of a priest, moreover one recently ordained, which gives clear evidence of the personal prestige he already enjoyed in the ecclesiastical circles to which he was still a newcomer. On the basis of this text alone it is impossible to affirm that the general council which actually met at Hippo on 8 October 393 was decided then and there between Aurelius and Augustine; nevertheless it is noteworthy that in the series of African general councils this was the first to be held outside Carthage; and holding a general council away from the mother-city would always be an exception. Under the primacy of Aurelius, only the meeting in Numidia at Milevis (Mila) in 402, then again at Augustine's town in 427,ʷʷ can be cited subsequently. The choice of Hippo in 393 was more than a simple coincidence with Augustine's recent ordination to the priesthood.

At the council of Hippo which, as we shall see later, was largely devoted to restoring discipline, especially among the clerics, a rule was in fact decreed prohibiting banquets in places of worship and their surroundings, and that canon was afterwards reissued.²⁷ But, in this matter as in others, the reissue of a conciliar decision mainly reveals the difficulty of putting a law into practice. Even in Carthage, Aurelius' efforts were not immediately crowned with success. As time passed, festivals in honour of St Cyprian, around his tomb, on 13 and 14 September, at the *Mappalia*,²⁸ had become the occasion for gorging and dancing, against a background of saucy ditties.²⁹ In 401, the banning of those dances had provoked a riot. At Hippo, Augustine was still a priest when he had to take a firm stand to put an end to the excesses that were the local equivalent of the Carthaginian deviations from the cult of St Cyprian. They took place in honour of the city's patron saint, St Leontius, at a festival held in the basilica founded by him early in the fourth century, the *basilica Leontiana*.³⁰ Each year, 2, 3 and 4 May were three days of rejoicings, with the significant name *Laetitia*, 'Jubilation'.

In 395, Augustine undertook to put things in good order. That year the three days of the *Laetitia* coincided with the Ascension; for him they were three taxing days whose vicissitudes he recounts in a letter to Alypius, who had shortly before become bishop of Thagaste and had just passed through Hippo.ˣˣ Augustine had made no mystery of the fact, some days beforehand, that this time he intended to challenge the customary excesses, but he knew that there was unrest among the faithful and that some had decided to carry on regardless. His sermon of 2 May, Ascension Eve, for which he had notably chosen as his text a particularly apt verse from Matthew's Gospel,ʸʸ was delivered to only a small congregation. The next day, Ascension Day, there was a large audience for his sermon; Augustine had a reading given from Matt: 21.12, on Jesus driving the dealers from the Temple, then he reread the verse and commented on it: with how much fiercer indignation would the Lord have driven the drunkards from his church.ᶻᶻ That was the introduction to a sermon which alternated readings and commentaries on an anthology of carefully chosen texts, closing with a few lines from the Epistle to the Galatians: 'Now the works of the flesh are manifest: fornication, uncleanness, idolatry, witchcraft, hatred, rivalries, strife, heresies, hatred, drunkenness, revellings and such like; I say to you now as I have said before, that those who do such things shall not inherit the kingdom of God.' The reading was interrupted for a moment so that the preacher could ask his hearers how Christians could be recognized 'by the fruits of their drunkenness', since the Lord had commanded that they should be known by their fruits, then resumed: 'For the fruits of the spirit are love, joy, peace, longsuffering, gentleness, goodness, self-control.'[ab] The day ended in a dramatic climax, reached when Augustine reduced his congregation to tears by reading and commenting upon two verses from Psalm 89, stating that God punishes those who break his commandments, but does not withdraw his forgiveness.[ac] At the end of his sermon the preacher himself was in tears, but could believe he had emerged the victor.

However, the night had not brought counsel in the way he had hoped. The next day, Friday 4 May, was the anniversary of the 'deposition' – interment – of St Leontius, and it was for that day that 'gullets and bellies were making ready', as Augustine crudely put it.[ad] He was informed that some of his yesterday's congregation were jibbing and contrasting him with previous pastors; were they not Christians too, those who in the past had not raised these prohibitions? For the rebels, this priest with his demanding spirituality could be nothing but a gloomy killjoy. Momentarily bewildered, he contemplated resignation after denying his responsibility by freely quoting Ezek. 33.9: 'The watchman is absolved if he warns against danger, even if those he warns refuse to guard against it.' But when he went to take his place in the chancel, the very people whose reluctance he had heard about came to him and allowed themselves to be won over to nobler feelings. Then, instead of the text from Ezekiel, Augustine launched into a sermon that included a historical retrospective. When Christianity had burgeoned, after the persecutions, concessions had had to be granted to the recently converted gentiles; holding festivities in honour of the martyrs was a way of compensating for the sacrifice they were making by abandoning their pagan festivals.[31] Then Augustine urged the faithful rather to imitate the churches overseas, which did not follow these practices; and he paused for an instant over the case of St Peter's in Rome, and explained why it was excepted.[ae] Thereupon the faithful were invited to gather in the afternoon to alternate sacred readings and the singing of psalms instead of the customary rejoicings. It would therefore be easy, he added, to see 'who was following his spirit and who his belly.'[af]

And so the afternoon turned out, in the presence of the bishop and his priest. Augustine was viewing with some relief the approaching end of a day that had been so perilous for him, when Valerius asked him to speak again – something he could gladly have done without. However, far from weakening, he seized the opportunity in this last and short sermon to contrast the *spiritalis celebratio* of the Catholics with the drunken revellings of the Donatists, echoes of which could be heard from their basilica.[32] Then he added two Pauline quotations – Phil. 3.19 and 1 Cor. 6.13 – to his panoply of texts from the Scriptures, his only weapons apart from his personal faith and strength of conviction, in the face of many 'semi-Christians' who had joined the new religion often clad in the tatters of the old, going from paganism to Christianity without having inwardly completed their cultural transition. 'It is a hard task', he would say later, 'to destroy the idols in one's heart.'[ag] In the night beginning to darken over the Christian quarter of Hippo, hymn-singing continued to rise from the mingled crowd of men and women.[ah] If he had ever had any doubts, Valerius now knew that he had a true successor.

The council of Hippo (8 October 393)

Two years before the memorable episode of the *Laetitia* in May 395, when Augustine had asserted the pastoral qualities which made him the perfect successor for Valerius, an event had taken place at Hippo which had attracted the entire African episcopate's attention to him, this time on a theological plane. On 8 October 393, presided over by Aurelius of Carthage, the general council of the Church of Africa had assembled, the first since the origin of this Church to hold its sessions away from Carthage. The bishops gathered in the *secretarium* of the basilica of Peace, the Catholic cathedral church.[33] The *secretarium* was a multi-purpose hall: 'sacristy', premises intended for reception of the faithful by the clergy, probably also the place where the bishop exercised his ecclesiastical jurisdiction, and which may have housed the library.[34] It has been supposed that it must have been of considerable size to be capable of accommodating a plenary council;[35] but in fact the bishops assembled at that time at Hippo must not have been very numerous. In that period, the western ecclesiastical provinces – the Sitifian and Caesarian Mauretanias – which were still linked with Numidia, had no statutory or primatal existence and therefore sent no delegates to the council.[36] Tripolitania, which had only five bishoprics, was represented at best by one bishop and, statutorily, the provinces which were regularly constituted from an ecclesiastical standpoint – as well as Proconsular Africa, Numidia and Byzacenia – had a voice at the general council through three delegates. Considering that Numidia, the host province in that year, must have had a larger representation, one might allow that some twenty bishops, probably not more – though we must add the secretaries who recorded the debates – occupied the *secretarium* of the basilica of Peace on 8 October 393.

They did first-class work. The discussions and canons properly speaking of this general council have been only partly preserved,[37] but the essential, that is, the measures that were taken, was preserved in an abridged version, known as the breviary of Hippo, some forty of whose articles subsequently formed the basis of the Church of Africa's conciliar legislation, notably in matters of ecclesiastical discipline, and as such was often reproduced, or at least quoted, at later councils.[38] A concern to regain control of clerics of all kinds, from readers to bishops, can be clearly seen, as well as care to redefine their attitude vis-à-vis the pagans, on one hand, and Donatists, on the other. There was also a concern to avoid anarchic situations and long drawn out disputes, arising in particular from encroachments by either side. The Church of Africa was now a large body whose cohesion must be ensured against schismatics; that is why one of the council of Hippo's first decisions was to institute an annual general council, to which the various regularly constituted provinces, under the authority of their primates, must send three legates selected from their own provincial councils. Of course, for various reasons, it happened that in a fair number of years no plenary council was held; but most certainly, through the impetus of the primate of Carthage, with this measure the African Church had forged itself an institutional tool which Aurelius would use efficiently – notably to maintain his position vis-à-vis the see of Rome – ably seconded by a few great bishops, with Alypius and Augustine in the forefront.

For the time being, in October 393 at Hippo, there is absolutely no doubt that the latter, in his role of priest, was not allowed to take part in the work of the council. But he made his presence felt, however, for the signal honour – unprecedented as far as we know – fell to him, after the recital of the symbol of Nicaea, of delivering a speech on the dogma in the presence of the bishops. On their part it was the acknowledgement of an eminent intellectual superiority being humbly placed at the service of the Christian pastorate. On Aurelius' part, it was probably also the opportunity to make Valerius' innovation official, as it might have caused some offence. Augustine himself would say that he published this doctrinal exposition at the urging of several bishops who were present,[ai] in a book he entitled *De fide et symbolo* – 'On faith and the symbol'. It was a rapid synthesis of the Catholic doctrine, set out according to the articles of the *Credo*. Hesitations and weaknesses have been picked out in this text, notably on the characterization of the Holy Ghost within the Trinity.[39] I would prefer to emphasize here the personal note on which Augustine ended by taking up the last words of his discourse, summing up his own credo, to which his experience and long meditation on that experience had led him, words that must be quoted as he uttered them in order to taste their magnificence: *Quae pauca verba nota sunt ut* credendo *subjugentur Deo, subjugati recte vivant, recte vivendo cor mundent, corde mundato* quod credunt intelligant.[aj] The bishops listening to Augustine that day could make no mistake; henceforward a genius in the manipulation of words, the like of whom Africa had not known for two centuries, since Apuleius and Tertullian, would be a part of their Church.

Notes

a.   *Sermon* 355, 2; *Vita Aug.*, IV.
b.   *Sermon* 355, 2.
c.   *Vita Aug.*, III, 2; cf. above, p. 115.
d.   *Sermon* 355, 2: *Quaerebam ubi constituerem monasterium et viverem cum fratribus meis.*
e.   *Ep. ad Rom. inchoata expositio*, 13. But the conjunction was not false like that between 'Hippo Regius' and 'Port-Royal'; in Hebrew, *shalosh* means 'three'.
f.   Possidius, *Vita Aug.*, VI, 4.
g.   *Vita Aug.*, VI, 1.
h.   *Contra litt. Pet.*, II, 184.
i.   *Serm.* 355, 2: *Apprehensus, presbyter factus sum.*
j.   *Vita Aug.*, IV, 2. Above, p. 68, such had been Ambrose's ordination, when he was elevated to the episcopacy when still a layman, and not even baptized.
k.   *Vita Aug.*, IV, 3.
l.   *Sermon* 355, 1.
m.   *Vita Aug.*, XXIV, 11.
n.   By doing so, Valerius was introducing something new; it was not customary in the western Church and he was criticized for it (cf. *Vita Aug.*, V, 3); but it gained acceptance and soon afterwards Aurelius of Carthage allowed priests to preach in his presence (*Ep.* 41, 1).
o.   Above, p. 134.
p.   *Ep.* 21 (to Valerius), 1.
q.   *Ep.* 21 (to Valerius), 3 and 4.

r. As 'But, you will say' or 'You will doubtless say to me': cf. *De util. cred.*, 16, 17, 21, 23, etc.

s. *De util. cred.*, 2, 3, and 20.

t. *De util. cred.*, 13; cf. also 17.

u. *De util. cred.*, 36; for the envisaged continuation, cf. also *Retract.*, I, 13, 8.

v. *De util. cred.*, 22.

w. Cf. above, pp. 122–3

x. *De util. cred.*, 24.

y. *De util. cred.*, 26.

z. *De util. cred.*, 28–33.

aa. With various nuances relating to personal differences, the line of reasoning in the *De utilitate credendi* naturally rejoins that of the *De vera religione*: cf. above, p. 136.

bb. *De duabus animabus*, 24.

cc. *Duab. an.*, 11.

dd. *Duab. an.*, 16: 'To tell the truth, I had not yet heard an explanation of what mixture this was about.'

ee. *Duab. an.*, 14.

ff. *Duab. an.*, 15, a definition approved by the *Retractations*, I, 15, 4, which incidentally are often critiques for this book.

gg. *Retract.*, I, 16, 1.

hh. *Contra Fort.*, 10–11; 25.

ii. This appears to have been the common method of the Manichaeans: cf. *Contra Adimantum*, III, 3, and XIV, 1–2.

jj. *Contra Fort.*, 7.

kk. *Contra Fort.*, 9–10; on Augustine's hesitations over the origin of the soul, cf. above, p. 126.

ll. *Contra Fort.*, 17 = *Duab. an.*, 15.

mm. *Contra Fort.*, 20; cf. *Lib. arb.*, I, 35, and above, pp. 127–8.

nn. *Contra Fort.*, 21, quoting Rom. 8.7, Gal. 5.17 and Rom. 7.23–5.

oo. *Contra Fort.*, 22.

pp. *Contra Fort.*, 27–8.

qq. *Retract.*, I, 16, 1.

rr. *Ep.* 44, 1.

ss. *Ep.* 22, 2, quoting Rom. 13.13–14; cf. above, pp. 96–7.

tt. *Ep.* 22, 3, *initio*.

uu. *Ep.* 22, 4, *in fine*.

vv. *Ep.* 22, 4.

ww. Cf. below, p. 473.

xx. *Ep.* 29, 2.

yy. Matt. 7.6; 'Give not that which is holy to the dogs, and cast not your pearls before swine.'

zz. *Ep.* 29, 3.

ab. Gal. 5.19–21 and 22–3, quoted in *Ep.* 29, 6.

ac. Ps. 88.31–4; *Ep.* 29, 7.

ad. *Ep.* 29, 8, *initio*.

ae. *Ep.* 29, 10; cf. above, pp. 24–5.

af. *Ep.* 29, 10, *in fine: qui mentem, et qui ventrem sequeretur*.

ag. *Enarr. in Psalm.* 80, 14: *Magnum opus est intus haec idola frangere*.

ah. *Ep.* 29, 11, *in fine*.

ai. *Retract.*, I, 17.

aj. *De fide et symbolo*, 25: 'These few words are made known to the faithful so that, by believing them they submit themselves to God, that by submitting themselves they lead a righteous life, that by leading a righteous life they purify their hearts and that, with hearts thus purified, they may understand what they believe.'

CHAPTER XVII

Donatism

The word is modern, but the realities it conceals, both religious and social, and sometimes even political, were some of the most burdensome in North Africa throughout the fourth and into the fifth century, before the Vandal invasion. Over such a vast territory – present-day Algeria and Tunisia, and the western coastal fringe of Libya – its manifestations were naturally not all of the same kind. At the end of the fourth century, an average Christian of Tacape (Gabes) might almost have been unaware of, or at least only have known from hearsay, what was an obsessive matter for an inhabitant of, say, Thamugadi (Timgad) or Caesarea (Cherchell).

So scattered geographically, the situations also varied in time; for instance, in the case of Augustine's native town, Thagaste. In June 411, Alypius, who was its bishop, would proudly exclaim that his city 'had long enjoyed unity' – within the Catholic Church, of course – and prayed that it would be the same everywhere.[a] But it had not always been so. In a letter written around 407/8, Augustine acknowledges that his native town had once been entirely Donatist, and ascribed to fear of imperial laws a reversal of the situation so complete that he had no hesitation in saying that the memory of the schism had been lost.[b] This turning-point may probably be dated to the great repression of the *tempora Macariana* in the mid fourth century.[1] Augustine's youth had thus been spent in ignorance of a religious movement which he must at most have heard talked about, at least during his Numidian or Carthaginian years, as his departure for Italy had then removed him from what was happening in Africa. Basically, he had discovered Donatism and its realities only when he arrived at Hippo and became a man of the Church himself. Manichaeism, which he had fought so hard because it had infected his youthful years, and would continue to fight because of the dangers it still presented for others, was a matter external to that Church. Now, however, he discovered an old family quarrel – the worst kind, as we know – and found himself confronted by a hotchpotch of hackneyed resentments and rehashed hatreds. He urgently needed to get to grips with this affair, which was quite new to him, and did so with the extraordinary aptitude, which he displayed in everything, for rapidly assimilating the many facts about a complex problem. So that we can follow him in the debates and polemics which would occupy him, to 411 and beyond, we must retrace the road with him, under the guidance – more or less – of those to whom he himself resorted.

Prehistory of a schism

Historically, it all began in the great upheaval of the persecution by Diocletian and Maximian, in 303, which had presented Christians, in Africa and elsewhere, with dramatic choices. But many historical events would not reach their full development without favourable 'breeding-grounds', on various levels – economic, social, cultural. So Donatism could be said to have had a 'prehistory', marked by the unclear activities of a substratum, both social and religious, and also a 'foregoing history', whose budding cracks subsequently opened into wide fractures.

A substratum is by definition hard to pin down. Economically and socially, I briefly mentioned earlier the one detectable as underlying Donatism,[c] in its crudest manifestations which were on its fringes. As we saw, the prevailing method of rural economy, chiefly in Numidia and Sitifian Mauretania, since at least the end of the second century AD, had brought in its wake the emergence of a sub-proletariat composed of seasonal and nomadic farm workers, alongside a class of peasants who were poor but rooted to the land. The 'circumcellions', to whom I shall return, would form a manoeuvrable mass for the toughest splinter of the schismatic Church, and in the middle of the fourth century the time would come for them to play their own game in veritable 'Jacqueries'. Even harder to assess is the incidence of what is called 'the religious background'[2] of Donatism, the fact that to a large extent, and above all in the rural areas, the pagans of North Africa came to Christianity by way of the cult of Saturn, inherited from that of a Punic Baal-Hammon.[3] Texts show that until well into the fourth century people worshipped a cosmic god, under the name of Saturn, master of heaven and earth and the infernal realm, who continued to have influence in popular religion at a time when Christianity was increasingly gaining ground. Animal victims – lambs and kids – were still being sacrificed, following a substitution rite, to this pre-eminent if not unique god. But the human sacrifice practised earlier as an offering to the great Punic god and his partner Tanit lay just below the surface; and that sacrificial tradition might partly account for the rash of quasi-ritual suicides observed among the circumcellions in the middle of the fourth century, notably in Numidia.[4]

More directly and precisely, for they were in the area of Christian practice, echoes of the arguments born half a century before under the episcopacy of St Cyprian still resounded in people's consciousness.[5] The persecution by Decius, in 250, had been a foretaste of what would happen in Africa two generations later. Bidden to sacrifice to the gods of the empire, many adherents and even clergy, including bishops, had killed themselves, or had bought 'certificates' – *libelli* – testifying to the sacrifice. Once the torment of the persecution was over, in the spring of 251, Cyprian, who had temporarily left his episcopal see of Carthage to give the persecution less of a hold and maintain a leader for his Church, found himself faced with the serious problem raised by the mass of those who had lapsed. Caught between the frequent brazenness of those *lapsi* and the arrogance of the 'confessors' who wanted to impose on the bishop the authority conferred upon them by their resistance, Cyprian referred the solution of these difficulties to the councils held in 251, then 252: A broad pardon was granted to the renegades, who were banned only from entering the priesthood.

This was not the end of the bishop's troubles. Stirred up by five priests who had already opposed his ordination, a schism was born out of the persecution and its sequel, incidentally parallel to the one in Rome, setting Novatian against Pope Cornelius, and not without links. Cyprian triumphed over his Novatianist opponents but, just as the persecution had given rise to the affair of the *lapsi* and the problem of their reconciliation, from the resorption of the schism emerged a controversy that was pregnant with consequences: should repentant heretics or schismatics be rebaptized? Whereas in Rome people were satisfied with penitence and the laying on of hands, the already inveterate African practice was rebaptism. In a long letter[d] Cyprian had stated his position: heretics, who had left the Church, had *ipso facto* lost the grace of baptism and from then on could not confer it upon others; it was therefore necessary to repeat the baptism they had given. This doctrine was confirmed, in 255 and 256, by two councils who thus consecrated a formal disagreement with Rome and Pope Stephen. Two years later Valerian's persecution erupted and in September 258, Cyprian suffered a martyrdom in Carthage which would retrospectively set a glorious seal on all his deeds.

The great persecution

The great persecution that shook the whole Empire early in the fourth century thus found in Africa a terrain to some extent undermined by these antecedents. Paradoxically, of the various edicts that formed the counts for prosecution, this time it was not the last, published in the spring of 304, imposing the obligation to sacrifice on all Christians, which had the heaviest consequences for the African communities.[6] It was the first edict, which reached Africa in the spring of 303; this ordered the handing over of the holy Scriptures and liturgical objects, at the requisition of the local authorities who, in the case of refusal, would pass the matter on to the governors. This text opened the black period to be known later as the *dies traditionis* – 'the days of handing over', but also of 'treason', because of an implicit and inevitable play on words.[e]

Reactions were varied, probably revealing local particularisms as much as differences in personal temperaments. In Carthage, bishop Mensurius replaced the Scriptures with heretical books which he allowed to be taken away, an astute but inglorious attitude for which he was soon blamed. At Cirta (Constantine), in Numidia, bishop Paulus made no difficulties about handing over the liturgical objects; but at Thibiuca, in Proconsular Africa, on the banks of the Medjerda, where the edict had been proclaimed on 5 June 303, bishop Felix refused to hand over the holy books to the 'curator' of the city; he was thrown into prison in Carthage and, since he persisted in his refusal, was beheaded by order of the proconsul. The latter, the famous Anullinus, was probably not the sinister executioner endowed with the gift of ubiquity which hagiographic writings have made of him, but was more likely a highly placed civil servant who carried out orders from higher up without any particular feelings of malice. But it is true that in 303–4 we find him cropping up all over the place in Proconsular Africa.

In the library of the episcopal seminary of Gorizia, on the Italo–Slovene border, originating from the capitular archives of Aquileia and preserved in a thirteenth-century manuscript, some fortunate hand recently lighted upon a new testimony to the exploits of Anullinus.[7] The proconsul had taken himself off to T(h)imidia Regia, the little town very near Carthage, in the lower valley of the Miliana; there a good twenty or so faithful had been summoned to appear, denounced by the inhabitants of the place for having celebrated Mass together. Their spokesman was one Gallonius, and the governor had a dialogue with him that forms the essence of these 'Records'. When Anullinus asked him to hand over the

Scriptures, Gallonius replied that he had hidden them in a place known only to him,[8] and he stuck to his guns even when, on the rack, his flesh was torn with iron claws. The proconsul lost his patience; these Christians with their wretched little mysteries were wasting his time.[9] When asked where he came from, Gallonius proudly replied, 'from Nazareth', which his companions chorused. In fact, they were not originally from T(h)imidia Regia, but various rural places one of which was named exactly;[10] their presence in the little town was thus only transitory or mere happenstance.

The epilogue to this trial was the death sentence for the little group, which included six women, for holding an illicit meeting. Two of its members, who had aggravated their case by saying sacrilegious things about the emperors, Diocletian and Maximian, were sentenced to be burnt at the stake, the punishment for lèse-majesté. As for Gallonius, in his capacity of ringleader – though nothing in the text indicates that he was a cleric, or even a simple lector, which he must have been – he was taken to the neighbouring town, Uthina (Oudna), where other faithful, an equal mixture of men and women, were waiting to hear their fate. In front of Anullinus, who had joined them, Gallionus underwent new tortures, without weakening; and while his co-religionists were condemned to beheading, he also suffered his 'passion' on the pyre to which the proconsul had dispatched him without any penal motive, thus earning the reputation for cruelty which posterity ascribed to him, often with less justification. As it was made public, that 'passion' was dated to 31 December 303; but in the Carthage calendar, the *Timidenses* martyrs are mentioned on the date of 31 May,[11] and this is probably the date that should be re-established for these Records, early in summer, which is more appropriate to the presence of these rural, perhaps seasonal, workers – of the circumcellion kind? – in this small town in Proconsular Africa.[12]

The birth of the schism

The storm of persecution raged in Africa for another whole year, and came to an end early in 305, leaving deep scars. The confessors, when they had survived – which in itself was suspect – in other words the 'pure', or those who claimed to be, rejected the *traditores* – 'handers-over' and 'traitors' – real or supposed: among the latter, falsely accused, Felix the bishop of a Proconsular township south of Carthage, Abthugni (Henchir es-Souar) which owes its emergence from obscurity only because of the ceaseless implication of its pastor throughout the century that followed the event. The divisions had begun to come to light in the bowels of the prisons where the 'confessors', real or false, were already casting anathema on the 'traitors'. When the time came for scores to be settled, it sometimes appeared that the situations were far from being clear-cut. For instance, at Cirta (Constantine), in the spring of 307, a meeting prior to the election of a successor to bishop Paulus, who had died, revealed behaviour on the part of the Numidian bishops that was to say the least uneasy, as they gathered around their primate, Secundus of Tigisis, for an examination of conscience.[13] This 'confessors'/'traitors' divide, often ambiguous and fallacious, was coupled with a marked and doubtless longstanding opposition between Numidians and Carthaginians, which had notably had the opportunity of showing itself at the time of the election of a successor to bishop Mensurius.[14] One of the dead bishop's deacons, Caecilianus, had been elected to the see of Carthage and promptly ordained by three neighbouring bishops, including Felix of Abthugni. Challenges began, variously motivated. Caecilianus was not very popular locally; he was accused of harshness towards the 'confessors' imprisoned at the time of the persecution;[f] moreover, by thwarting her suspect piety, he had made an enemy of an influential and scheming lady, Lucilla. Caecilianus was also immediately exposed to the machinations of two people, apparently priests, whose ambition had been to be elected in his place and who made common cause against him with some notables, the disloyal guardians – and unmasked in their disloyalty – of the church's treasures in Carthage, entrusted to them by the deceased Mensurius.[g] Giving this clique impetus was the action of a Numidian prelate who had initially remained in the shadows, 'Donatus of Casae Nigrae', who must doubtless be identified with the eponymous bishop of the sect, despite Augustine's hesitation on this point. Indeed, the Numidians held the custom that the bishop of the African mother-city should be consecrated by their primate. Secundus of Tigisis rounded up seventy bishops of his province at Carthage; declaring the ordination of Caecilianus null and void because one of his consecrators, Felix of Abthugni, had himself been a 'traitor', this council elected and consecrated in his stead a former lector of bishop Mensurius. This lector, Maiorinus, was a very good friend of the wealthy Lucilla, who was said to have paid for his election! This schism was thus a reality in 308/9, just at the time when, for historians, the imperial usurpation of Domitius Alexander opened a kind of 'void in factual history' in Africa.

The nascent schismatic Church enters history more clearly at the commencement of Constantine's reign. Early in 313, the emperor sided with Caecilianus, and ordered him to share out the grants he was sending 'among the servants of the holy Catholic religion'.[15] Shortly afterwards, the proconsul Anullinus – of the same name and probably related to the persecutor – received a letter from Constantine specifying that the clerics who benefited from the exemptions from *munera civilia* – valuable dispensations from heavy municipal burdens – were to be those under Caecilianus' authority.[h] Thus unrecognized and swept aside, the schismatics reacted swiftly; on 15 April 313, they handed to the proconsul, to be passed on to the emperor, a 'letter from the Catholic Church on the crimes of Caecilianus, addressed by the supporters of Maiorinus'.[i] So those who were soon to be known as the Donatists went on the offensive, with the first challenge that inaugurated the immense development of the 'Caecilianus affair' – the *causa Caeciliani*. They asked for judges: an ecclesiastical tribunal that was held in Rome at the Lateran on 2 October 313 witnessed the clash of Caecilianus and Donatus, the latter appearing this time in the limelight as head of the sect. Caecilianus was exonerated, but the Donatists did not regard themselves as defeated, and from then on there would be appeal after appeal. At Arles, on 1 August 314, there was an important council which had the result, among others, of making the Africans abandon their tradition of rebaptizing of heretics.[16] Felix of Abthugni was soon absolved at Carthage on 15 February, 315.[17] The schismatics, however, appealed to the emperor in Rome, Brescia and finally, Milan, in the autumn of 316. On 10 November 316, Constantine notified the vicarius of Africa, Eumalius,[j] of his definitive verdict and the absolution of Caecilianus.

The Constantinian period and the *'tempora Macariana'*

Repression of the schism followed at once. Early in 317, at the latest, came a law ordering the dissolution of Donatist communities and the confiscation of their basilicas to the benefit of the Catholics, on pain of exile for the recalcitrant. Carried out remorselessly this law brought about brutal evictions, notably in Carthage at the place known as Avioccala, where the bishop was slain in front of his altar, together with several of his flock. The Donatists had their first martyrs. They again appealed to the emperor, who replied with a gesture of appeasement; to the rescript freeing the Donatist bishops from their exile, which he sent on 5 May 321 to the vicarius of Africa, Verinus, he added a circular letter to the Catholic bishops of Africa which was in fact a real edict of tolerance. Constantine vacillated between firmness and leniency. In 330, his letter to a group of Catholic bishops from Numidia was a long admission of impotence in the face of the schismatics, who at Constantine – the former Cirta, rechristened with the emperor's name – had seized a church which had been built on his orders. Constantine let them have the church and promised the Catholics that he would have another basilica built as compensation, at the expense of the internal revenue.[18] As the years went by, during this period, the schismatic Church had swollen to the extent that it was able to assemble in Carthage, probably in 336, a general council numbering 270 bishops.[k]

As we have just seen, the Donatists were the most solidly entrenched and most active in Numidia; it was also in this province that disturbances began to arise, and a movement appeared, rural in both origins and development. Around 340, bands of 'circumcellions' were to be seen for the first time, roving the countryside.[19] They acted under the command of two ringleaders, Axido and Fasir, whom their troops called the 'leaders of the saints', a title revealing an inspiration intended theoretically to be religious – but in many historical contexts outlaws have liked, and still do, to adorn themselves with an aura of holiness – and their action took the form of a peasant revolt directed against the landowners, forcing creditors to destroy their IOUs and the *domini* to free their slaves; those who refused were given a thrashing or even put to death. Others paid the price of this scenario of social inversion; their carriages were attacked, their servants installed in them and the owners forced to run in front of the vehicles like grooms. Augustine knew about these deeds, as we do, from reading Optat of Milevis (III, 4), and added several details in the same key, describing some of these owners tied to a millstone like beasts of burden, and forced to turn it, against a backdrop of burnt-out farms.[l] These peasant revolts reached a point where the Donatist bishops of the region, overwhelmed by a movement they could not control, had to make up their minds to call upon the secular arm – of the 'Count' of Africa, Taurinus – against these rebels who claimed them as their authority. A clash with the Count's troops at a place called Octava, caused many victims among the circumcellions, who were afterwards regarded as martyrs, but at the same time the Donatists rather inconsistently included Taurinus in the ranks of the persecutors.[20]

Soon afterwards, between 343 and 345/8, Constantine's successor, his younger son Constans, sent two commissioners, Paulus and Macarius, to Africa. They were to prepare for the re-establishment of religious unity by offering help to communities. This 'soft' handling was given a bad reception by the Donatists, first by the sect's leader, Donatus, who flatly spelled out his doctrine of non-interference by a persecuting government in the affairs of his Church,[m] and sent all his communities a circular urging them to accept nothing. In Numidia, hostility to the rounds of the two imperial commissioners turned to armed confrontation when another Donatus, the schismatic bishop of Bagaï (Ksar Baghai), a veritable fortress of religious opposition in the heart of the province, called upon the circumcellions, who invaded the markets and neighbouring areas and transformed the local basilica into a fortified camp. In the same region, and soon afterwards, ten Donatist bishops mandated by a council of the sect sought to meet Macarius at Vegesela (Ksar el-Kelb). They had cause to rue the day; the commissioner had them arrested and flogged, and kept one of them prisoner, Marculus, who was executed after four days' detention in the place called Nova Petra, not far from Diana Veteranorum (Aïn Zana). He was said to have been thrown from the top of a rock. Catholics, including Augustine later, saw it rather as a ritual suicide, which was not without examples at that period.[n] What is certain is that this 'martyrdom', celebrated by a 'Passion' dated 29 November 347, earned 'domnus Marculus' long veneration.[21] Shortly before, during the same year, the emperor Constans had published an 'edict of unity', and in August the proconsul of Africa had an order for the enforcement of that edict proclaimed in Carthage. By publicly tearing up the notice, a loyal Donatist, Maximianus, achieved a martyrdom shared by one of his companions, Isaac, who abetted him in this deed. The episode is known through a 'Passion'[22] written by a certain Macrobius, who must be identified with the fourth incumbent of the episcopal see of the Donatists in Rome. The Donatist community in Rome probably owed its development in this period to the exile then inflicted upon a number of schismatic bishops and clergy. Others rallied to the cause of unity – which is what happened, as we saw earlier, in Augustine's home town – and sometimes negotiated with their Catholic colleagues in their dioceses to share 'parishes' – *plebes* – which foreshadowed the solutions that were often laboriously put into operation to heal the schism in the early years of the fifth century.[23] Catholic communities then seem to have jogged along peaceably until the accession of the emperor Julian, and during those years Donatus exited from history, rather obscurely, just as he had entered it.[24]

The thirty years of the Donatist primacy of Parmenianus

The two brief years of Julian's reign were a godsend for the Donatists; the pagan reaction suited them perfectly. Scarcely had he been enthroned, early in 362, when the new emperor received a petition from their bishops asking for their exile to be ended and their places of worship restored to them. An imperial rescript gave them satisfaction.[o] Their returned liberty resulted in excesses and massacres, notably at Tipasa in Caesarian Mauretania, where two Donatist bishops from Numidia, Felix of Idicra and Urbanus of Forma, were the instigators of violence, with the passive complicity of the province's governor.[p] Proconsular and Sitifian Mauretania were not spared the unrest but, soon afterwards, it was once again in Caesarian Mauretania that the situation was most worrying. After Julian the Apostate's death, in June 363, 'Count' Romanus, head of the army of Africa until 372, by his brutal policies provoked the armed rebellion of a Moorish prince, Firmus, who seized Icosium (Algiers) and Caesarea (Cherchell); but he was unable to enter Tipasa, which was protected by its local patron saint, St Salsa, whose help he invoked in vain.

Firmus was hand in glove with the Donatists, as was seen at Rusiccade (Skikda, formerly Philippeville), in Numidia, where he took advantage of the complicity of the town's schismatic bishop to have the gates opened.[q] Donatists allied to Firmus – known as Firmiani – persecuted the followers of a rather scant splinter group of the Donatist Church, geographically confined to the westernmost coastal fringe of Caesarean Mauretania: the 'Rogatists', from the name of their leader, Rogatus, bishop of Cartennae (Ténès) between 371 and 372 and 407 and 408. On several occasions Augustine would affirm the reality of the persecution of those dissidents, but the form it took remains unclear;[r] similarly, the characteristics of 'Rogatism' – the rejection of violence, the demand for an almost immaterial Church – are somewhat vague. Augustine acknowledged their difference, while deriding their small number.[s]

Immediately after Firmus' death, defeated by 'Count' Theodosius, father of the future emperor, the imperial attitude hardened against the schismatics. Edicts and laws followed one another regularly: a text addressed on 20 February 373 to the proconsul of Africa, banning the repetition of baptism and ordering the deposing of any bishop who contravened the ban;[25] Gratian's constitution dated 22 April 376, confiscating the meeting places of the 'heretics';[26] an edict by the same emperor, dated 17 October 377, confirming the preceding; but it was addressed to Nicomachus Flavian, then 'vicarius' of Africa – that is, governor general of all its territories – and the Catholics suspected this great pagan lord of leniency with regard to the Donatists.[27] With the accession of Theodosius, in 379, the repression was strengthened. For a dozen or so years, a whole series of laws were promulgated, targeting the 'heretics', the last in date being the one which, on 15 June 392, inflicted a fine of ten *librae* of gold – a considerable sum – on 'heretical' clergy.[28] But, addressing Parmenianus, the sect's leader in 372–3, some time around 390, Optat, the Catholic bishop of Milevis, made a clear distinction between the Donatists, who in his view were schismatics, and real heretics.[t] So until the schism became a heresy, this whole arsenal of laws could not become operational.

The first anti-Donatist initiatives of Augustine as priest

Upon being elected successor to Parmenianus, around 390–1, the new Donatist bishop of Carthage, Primianus, created the conditions for a split in the bosom of his Church by excommunicating one of its deacons, Maximianus, for reasons that have remained obscure but were perhaps connected with the rivalry between the two men for the succession of the dead bishop. Augustine seized upon this episode with all the more keenness, almost relish, because in his view it was the very history of the origins of the schism repeating itself, with this very similar detail – a kind of 'déjà-vu' – that as Lucilla had in the past done for Maiorinus, a pious wealthy woman was backing Maximianus in Carthage.[u] Having roughly dismissed some forty bishops who had come to hold enquiries in the neighbouring regions, particularly Byzacenia, in the south of Proconsular Africa, Primianus was sentenced on 24 June 393 by a council which at Cebarsussi, in

Byzacenia, assembled more than one hundred bishops from that province, who chose Maximianus as bishop of Carthage.²⁹ Although the condemnation of Primianus had been mainly Byzacenian, the reaction took place in Numidia. On 24 April 394, at Bagaï, 310 bishops who had come from all the African provinces, but mostly from Numidia and the Mauretanias, condemned Maximianus and the twelve who had consecrated him.ᵛ On the basis of this condemnation, Maximianist bishops were deposed, and the Primianists turned to the magistrates and courts to obtain the devolution to their benefit of the basilicas held by their adversaries. This was a boon for Catholics and Augustine, who did not hesitate to use this example as a pretext for appealing to the secular arm against the Donatists.³⁰

As we have just seen, the Primianist reaction had been strongest in Numidia, the cradle of the most radical elements of the sect since its origin. Militant Donatism now had its main base at Thamugadi (Timad), and from there, in 388, a bishop named Optatus spread a reign of terror, in alliance with the circumcellions. But his strength came most of all from the support he received from a Moorish prince, Gildo, Firmus' younger brother, who, initially 'Count' of Africa for some ten years and thus leader of its armies, ended by rising against Rome, as his brother had done a quarter of a century earlier.³¹ Gildo's death in 398 brought in its wake the downfall of Optatus of Timgad, who died in prison having symbolized for those ten years what Augustine would call the 'groaning of Africa'.ʷ And we shall see that similarly in 'Hippo's Numidia', where the situation is particularly well known thanks to Augustine, the last years of the fourth century and the beginning of the fifth resounded with the outbursts and aggression of the circumcellions and Donatist clergy.

Augustine had been quick to assess the dangers of this deep-rooted division, a fracture that was difficult to reduce because it brought into play not theological subtleties – which could have enticed only a handful of adherents – but simplifying outlines which found a broad response in the popular mentality; first of all that Manichaean – in the modern sense of the word! – contrast between the 'pure' and those who had lapsed, and their spiritual descendants, marked for ever by a second original sin even graver than the first. Before undertaking the rebuttal of the 'leading lights' of Donatism, both the early ones – Donatus himself and then Parmenianus – and also contemporaries – Petilianus of Constantine, Emeritus of Caesarea and the grammarian Cresconius – the most pressing matter was to address those whose emotional attachment gave the schism its greatest strength. Augustine's genius in this affair was to have had from the outset the intuition that it was necessary to break the spell which had placed a large number of simple folk on the side of the Donatists. Composing his *Retractations* thirty-five years later, the old bishop still had in the forefront of his mind the apt inspiration he had had in 393 for his first work against the schismatics. He wrote:

> I wanted the cause of the Donatists to come to the knowledge of the humblest people, ignorant and unlettered, and be engraved in their memory as much as was in my power. I therefore composed a psalm for them to sing in the order of Latin letters, the kind called 'alphabetic'; but I went no further than the letter V. I left aside the last three letters and in their place added an epilogue at the very end, as if their mother church was speaking to them. Similarly, the refrain that is taken up again and the prologue, which

is also to be sung, are not in letter order . . . I wanted this psalm to be written not in the manner of a classical poem, so as not to be constrained by metrical requirements to use words that are seldom used by the people.[x]

There could be no better way of both setting out his intentions and describing the process used in this astonishing piece of work of just under 300 lines of 'blank verse'. There were probably precedents: indeed, shortly before him, Parmenianus seems to have composed some psalms like this in verses which, if not rhyming, were at least more or less assonant;[y] and the memory of the hymns invented by Ambrose to keep his flock's courage up during the battles of the Milanese spring of 386[32] still sounded in Augustine's ears. Nevertheless, he appeared to be the real inventor, if not of a genre, at least of a form of versification that marked a complete break with classical Latin metrics and must be regarded as the origin of Romance poetry; and, literary expert that he was, it must have cost him dear when, in the same period, he was receiving and commenting upon the impeccable hexameters of his young friend Licentius, expressing the hope that his life was as well ordered as his verses![z] But for Augustine it was out of the question to propose to the good people of Hippo and elsewhere that they should get into their heads a scholarly poem structured in metred lines, all the more so because he was the first to notice that his compatriots' ears had difficulty in perceiving the comparative length or brevity of vowel sounds.[33] Conversely, the prevalence in spoken language, already old in that period, of a marked accent – as in Italian for example – gave every chance, in a popular audience, to verse with a strong beat in its rhythm, of syllabic and no longer metric structure. To simplify memorization still further, each line of sixteen syllables, divided by a strong caesura into two hemistichs of eight syllables, rhymed or rather 'assonated' with the next line, with which it formed a unit of meaning.[aa] Conceived in this way, the *Psalm against the Donatists' side* was composed, besides an epilogue of thirty lines, of twenty stanzas, each of twelve lines, the first line beginning with a letter of the alphabet, from A to V, and between each stanza, like a *ritornello*, came a *hypopsalma* that all the people would chorus: 'All ye who love peace, now judge the truth.'[34] From parallelisms to antitheses and plays on words to chiasmus, Augustine had placed his stunning verbal dexterity[35] at the service of a very simple aim: to show that the Donatists based their false conception of the Church on a history that was itself distorted. Their aberrant ecclesiology was the intent to include only the pure in the Church and to exclude sinners; their historical error was to blame others exclusively for the misdeeds they themselves had committed during the persecution. In addition, there was an even graver sin, the split for which the entire responsibility lay at the schismatics' door. To demonstrate this, Augustine followed and summed up what was still at that time his only source, Optat of Milevis and his *Treatise against the Donatists*.[36]

The 'alphabet psalm' was a little work *ad usum populi*, above all for the use of the Catholic community, invited to chant it in the church; in principle it was oral literature, but it may be imagined that copies of it circulated among the Donatist followers, too. At the same time, the intellectual who was well versed in the techniques of refutation through his anti-Manichaean controversies began to attack the schismatic positions on a doctrinal plane. He therefore composed a *Contra epistulam Donati*, at the end of 393 or beginning of 394. By doing so he was acting in orderly fashion, and doubly so: for an initial attack on the founder of the sect was a good method, and it also meant taking things in chronological order at the start of a campaign that he could foresee would be lengthy. For the 'Letter on baptism' whose criticism he was undertaking was a text written by Donatus probably soon after the council in 396 which had brought together 270 schismatic bishops.[bb] At the time of that meeting, the sect's leader had suffered a setback, in that he had had to bow to a majority inspired by bishops from the Mauretanias, who were hostile to rebaptism.[cc] The Donatist primate had felt the need to justify his position, and that was the intent of the 'Letter', which is unfortunately lost, in the same way that we have not preserved Augustine's refutation! But the attention given to it in the *Retractations* enables us both to restore the tenor of Donatus' text in broad outline and to note that when he obtained it the priest of Hippo still had some way to go in his knowledge of all the facts. Notably where the repetition of baptism was concerned; he admits in the *Retractations* that he had wrongly ascribed its innovation to Donatus.[dd] Actually, the Donatists had remained faithful to the doctrine of St Cyprian in this matter, whereas the rest of the African Church had renounced it following the council of Arles in 314. They had doubtless aggravated St Cyprian's error by claiming that not only dissidents – heretics – but also sinners administered a worthless baptism. It had to be honestly admitted, however, that the foundations of the Donatists' baptismal theology were already to be found in the writings of the martyr bishop. In elaborating the controversy that Augustine would wage at length with the schismatics, this would not be his easiest task.[ee]

Also in this period, Augustine committed himself to a path that he would follow tirelessly for a quarter of a century, until the memorable encounter with Emeritus at Caesarea (Cherchell), in the summer of 418.[ff] The former professor, the man who had once confounded the Manichaean Fortunatus and had caused him to leave town, must quite naturally have sought direct dialogue with these other opponents. Indeed, the occasion presented itself, linked precisely with a very recent case of repeated baptism. It was said that a Catholic deacon had just been rebaptized by a bishop named Maximinus, the Donatist incumbent of a bishopric bordering on that of Hippo. This deacon was in office in a distant rural sector, the *villa Mutugenna*.[gg] Augustine went there at once; he was not able to meet the deacon in person, but had learnt from his relatives that he was now well and truly a deacon in the Donatist church. In the absence of Valerius, he therefore approached Maximinus, so that a lapse of time could not let the affair, which he considered serious, 'grow cold', as he wrote. However, he took great care not to sound aggressive to his correspondent; he invited him to a discussion which, on both sides, would be free of polemical argumentation: let us leave aside, he proposed, the *tempora Macariana* on your part, and on mine the cruelties of the circumcellions; it was the cause of the Church that he intended to debate with Maximinus. We do not know what success this initiative had immediately, but it received its reward later; Maximinus was subsequently won over and became the Catholic bishop of the *castellum Sinitense*.[37] Let us note also that in this affair Augustine was already acting like a bishop: 'I cannot let the rebaptism of our deacon pass in silence,' he wrote, 'indeed I know how wrong that silence would be for me. For I have no intention of spending time of pure emptiness in ecclesiastical honours, but rather to render an account to the Prince of all shepherds of the flocks who may be entrusted to me.'hh Expressing himself thus, he was merely anticipating the actual event by a short time.

Notes

a. *Gesta conl. Carth.*, I, 136, *SC*, 195, Paris, Éd. du Cerf, 1972, pp. 784–5.
b. *Ep.* 93, 17.
c. Cf. above, p. 150.
d. *Ep.* 69 (to Magnus).
e. Augustine would often call it the *persecutio codicum tradendorum*, the 'persecution tending to make the (sacred) books be handed over'.
f. Cf. *Acta Saturnini*, 30; Augustine, *Brev. coll.*, III, 26.
g. Optat, I, 18; Augustine, *Ep.* 43, 17.
h. Eusebius, *Hist. eccl.*, X, 7, 2; *Gesta conl. Carth.*, III, 216, *SC*, 224, p. 1158
i. *Gesta conl. Carth.*, III, 220, *SC*, 224, pp. 1160–62; cf. Augustine, *Ep.* 88, 2.
j. *Contra Cresc.*, III, 82.
k. *Ep.* 93, 43.
l. *Ep.* 185 (to Bonifatius), 15.
m. Optat, III, 3: 'What has the emperor to do with the Church?'
n. *C. litt. Pet.*, II, 32, 46; *C. Cresc.*, III, 54.
o. *C. litt. Pet.*, II, 24; *Ep.* 105, 9.
p. Optat, II, 18.
q. *Ep.* 87, 10.
r. *C. ep. Parm.*, I, 16, 17; *C. litt. Pet.*, II, 184.
s. *Ep.* 93, 49: *vestrum gregiculum*.
t. Optat I, 12.
u. *Ep.* 43, 26; *C. Cresc.*, IV, 8–9; *Gesta cum Emer.*, 9.
v. *C. ep. Parm.*, II, 7; *C. Cresc.*, III, 59; *Gesta cum Emer.*, 10–11.
w. *C. ep. Parm.*, II, 4: *Optatum Gildonianum decennalem totius Africae gemitum.*
x. *Retract.*, I, 20.
y. *Ep.* 55, 34; *Praedestinatus, De haeresibus*, 43.
z. *Ep.* 26, 4 (dated 394).
aa. The assonance is uniformly in -e, which represents a tour de force over nearly 300 lines. The unit of meaning (or sentence) is confined to a line, rarely to a hemistich of eight syllables.
bb. Cf. above, p. 167.
cc. *Ep.* 93, 43. These particular features of the schismatic communities of the western provinces will live again later among the 'Rogatists': see above, p. 169.
dd. *Retract.*, I, 20, 3.
ee. In the *De baptismo*, in particular, written in 400–401, Augustine would examine at length the problem of St Cyprian's authority in the baptismal controversy; cf. below, p. 282.
ff. Cf. below, pp. 351–3.
gg. *Ep.* 23, 2.
hh. *Ep.* 23, 6.

CHAPTER XVIII

Elevation to the episcopacy

Possidius, who would himself soon be leaving to take up the duties of his bishopric at Calama (Guelma), around 397, but who was then living in the lay brothers' monastery at Hippo, testifies to the real reversal in the situation for which the Church was beginning to be indebted to Augustine. The Church which had only recently been laid low, crushed by the triumphant Donatist majority, was now raising its head again.[a] This was true, first in Hippo itself; but the reports of Augustine's vigorous action and his renown gradually spread in 'Hippo's Numidia', which corresponded to the territories of the area north-east of present-day Constantine, and along a line from Hippo to Carthage. However, although for the man of the Church the battle against the Donatists had become an obligation and even a priority, for the Christian the chief adversary was still Manichaeism, perhaps even more than paganism, something that we may find surprising. At the same time – though this concern went hand in hand with the anti-Manichaean struggle – Augustine felt a pressing need to be clearer about the Bible, the Old Testament as well as the New. He had had to return to Genesis to be able to rebut Mani's disciples, but first of all to settle his own doctrine about the Creation in comparison with the Neoplatonic ideas that had filled his youth. He also needed to delve more profoundly into St Paul, doubtless for his pastoral requirements, but mostly for his own account, to deepen his understanding of his faith.

Genesis and the Psalms

All specialists on St Augustine have reached this finding: he constantly meditated on the biblical account of the Creation, upon which he commented on five occasions.[1] He had approached it for the first time in the context of the anti-Manichaean controversy, to protect the sacred text from their sarcasm;[b] he would return to it in the last books of the *Confessions* and in Book XI of the *City of God* and, chiefly, from 400–401, he would devote the twelve books of his treatise *The Literal Interpretation of Genesis*. But he was already hatching this major work in his mind during his priesthood. He even began to dictate it, and of this first attempt there survives the 'unfinished book' which he explains in the *Retractations*. There he recalls that at first, opposing the Manichaeans, he had treated the account in Genesis in the allegorical sense; this had not been completely satisfactory for although the text supported, even invited, this interpretation, confining himself to it might seem as if he wanted to evade certain difficulties. He wished to explain it *ad litteram*, 'according to the letter': not, of course, literally, but understanding the account not as a parable or explanatory myth, but as the 'story' of a genesis. However, he adds, 'my inexperience in explaining the Scriptures made me give way beneath the burden'.[c] Coming to the creation of man on the sixth day

(Gen.1.28) he had left his commentary unfinished, unpublished and destined for destruction, after he had subsequently brought this task to a successful conclusion in twelve books. However, when he reviewed these pages in 427, he made a point of adding a few lines – paragraphs 61 and 62 – though without going to the end of the commentary on that 'sixth day', in order to make his early attempt more acceptable. And while recommending that people should preferably read the *opus* in twelve books on the subject, he had wanted the *liber imperfectus* to be preserved as testimony to his first efforts; as if he were thinking of his future exegetists, who were often so careful – perhaps too much so – in retracing the 'genesis' of his work in its various aspects!

In fact, this short but admirably condensed text[2] clearly shows how he had developed since 389, the date of the *De Genesi adversus manichaeos*. Unexpectedly – although its author was now a priest and had just declaimed the dogmatic discourse before the assembly of bishops at Hippo – it opens with a profession of faith: which was a clear statement that what was to follow was contained strictly within the framework of that faith. Augustine approached the sacred text with infinite precautions, defined the human limitations of his intelligence,[d] let it be understood that beyond the allegorical meaning, already explained by him in his essay of 389, the first chapter of Genesis, with its six days, mornings and evenings, had been conceived for the needs of our feeble imagination.[e] In fact, as another text says, without contradicting the 'historical' account, 'He who dwells in eternity had created everything at the same time' (Sir. 18.1). The Creation had taken place in a 'lightning flash' – the *ictus condendi*,[f] which prefigures our theoretical 'big bang' and is its metaphysical expression – in a boundless time, since time itself was born with that creation. The first words of Genesis, the famous *in principio*, thus had a double, even a triple, meaning: it was 'the first sun on the first morning', as Péguy would say, the affirmation of a cohesive order in the Creation – a priority, in some sort, that he would analyse later in the *Confessions* (XII, 40) – and also that source of divine wisdom, the prime cause, the Word from which everything issued. It is the third meaning, though without excluding the other two, which has the greater importance in the *De Genesi ad litteram*. Augustine accepted the ambiguous richness of this many-faceted theme and wondered where to place the creation of the angels, in the fulfilment in time of a Word that lay outside time.[g]

He registered some definitive facts, however. God was not, as the Platonists had recently still believed, a 'demiurge' doing his best to fashion a formless matter, like something placed at his disposal. There it was necessary to challenge a text of the Book of Wisdom,[h] the distant echo of the *Timaeus*, and to affirm, following a path which Porphyry, commenting upon Plato's *Timaeus*, had already pointed out, that God had created matter. But what was to be understood by 'the heaven and the earth'? Was 'the earth' formless and unorganized matter, but rich in potential development, whereas the 'the heaven' was spiritual matter already 'formed' at the moment of its creation?[3] These exegeses would become clearer later, in Book XII of the *Confessions*, and in the great commentary that would be elaborated during some fifteen years; but in 393 Augustine was still wavering. He still did not feel that he knew enough about the Scriptures; was still not sure enough of himself. One should never, he said, state anything without giving it serious thought.[i]

But a verse of Genesis inspired him then to develop a theme which he would not take up later in any other commentary, and which by itself is sufficient justification for the old bishop not to have thrown this little unfinished book on the fire. They are the few pages commenting upon Gen. 1.26: 'And God said, Let us make man in our image, after our likeness.' The link connecting creation to its Creator is a bond of resemblance. But are the two words, image and likeness, merely a redundancy? One must therefore question what is the image and what the likeness. The images that compose the universe created by God express a Likeness in themselves, by virtue of which everything that exists can have something of the nature of God.[j] But how could the Likeness – the *similitudo dei*, by which everything had been made – give things their form? There, said Augustine, was a problem that by far exceeded human understanding.[k] However, one could get some idea by considering that in the Creation the likeness was an image of oneness, which belonged only to God. It was true of things or living beings, where there was oneness in species only by the resemblance of individuals among themselves. The same applied to the soul, which was not one and not happy except insofar as the constant similitude of its actions and virtues conferred on it an appearance of oneness. And that meditation finished with the fleeting gleam of an aesthetic discourse; beauty in nature, Augustine concluded provisionally, lay above all in the harmony and proportion of parts with one another, the expression of their resemblance and relationship with God's creative oneness;[l] it was the same for human art, whose beauty lay in the affinity of the elements of the same composition, and in which symmetry was notably the guarantee of a harmonious unity.[m]

With the exception of the account of the Creation, to which he paid specific attention, initially connected with his efforts to refute Manichaeism, if there was one collection of texts in the Old Testament which very early on had awakened, even more than Augustine's interest, his complete heart-and-soul attachment, it was the Psalms, which he was reading at Cassiciacum. He writes in the *Confessions*: 'What cries I uttered up to you, my God, when I read the Psalms of David, songs of faith, accents of devotion, which exclude the boastful mind!'[n] He had brought back to Africa the psalter which he had probably acquired at Milan, from among Ambrose's entourage, and which had never left his side since then; the one which was at Monica's bedside at Ostia and was grasped by Evodius to sing Psalm 101,[o] and it was on the basis of this copy that, in the early days of his priesthood, he had conceived the idea of making a continuous commentary on them. Between 391 and 392, and 394 and 395, Augustine steadily composed commentaries on the first thirty-two Psalms, taken in order. They were not explanations freely improvised before the faithful as the lector gradually went through the text, but 'dictated' commentaries, mostly fairly short, and clearly distinguishable from the great *enarrationes*, in which the preacher would often seem to be almost physically present, to a point where his face-to-face contact with his audience is perceptible in the text. Because they were not spoken before the congregation they have a more elaborate style, sometimes even an erudite tone, with references to the Greek text;[p] but one can spot the real concerns of the new pastor, his permanent anxiety to counter the Manichaeans, but now mostly the Donatists and their allies, the circumcellions. In one of these dictated commentaries, attacking the latter, he evokes their terrible cudgels, these 'israels' – as the circumcellions themselves called them – also mentioned in the same period in the 'alphabetical Psalm'.[4]

Rereading those songs which had moved him so greatly in the months following his conversion, Augustine was now in a position to develop their main themes. He places significant emphasis on the humility necessary for a Christian, in the image of Christ's,[q] and significant also – already perhaps the forerunner of a development that would delay no longer – is his insistence on the texts which state or suggest that we cannot move towards God by ourselves, or be converted without his help,[r] that our merits have little weight in the eyes of divine mercy.[s] Glory is due to God alone, for it is he who acts. And Augustine quotes for the first time – but without drawing all its inferences – the verse from St Paul that he would soon regard as conclusive: 'What hast thou that thou didst not receive? Now, if thou didst receive it, why dost thou glory as if thou hadst not received it?'[t]

The Sermon on the Mount and St Paul

Augustine would soon feel the need to go more deeply into reading the Pauline epistles but, if we follow the order indicated in the *Retractations*, he first wanted to comment on the Sermon on the Mount, not as we read it in Luke, where the beatitudes appear abruptly contrasted in an eschatological discourse, but rather in Matthew, where they outline a programme of virtuous life crowned by the promise of a heavenly reward. There one could find, he said, 'the perfected model of Christian life'.[u] In the first pages of this text we doubtless also find some unexpected arithmetical considerations, centred on the number of the beatitudes in Matt. 5.3–10. There are eight; but, remarks Augustine, the eighth – blessing those who are persecuted for righteousness' sake – only carries the first – which blesses the poor in spirit – to its highest perfection.[5] We quickly see the aim of this little manipulation: the seven beatitudes remaining represent the seven degrees of the soul's ascent to God, and here we find the 'scalar plan' already used in Rome, in 388, in the *De quantitate animae*,[v] before finding it resumed soon in the *De doctrina christiana*. Augustine continues: these seven degrees are matched by the seven gifts of the Holy Spirit, freely interpreted on the basis of Isa. 11.2–3.[w] Here, similarly, the attitude of humility has the limelight: is it not the way of access to the first of the beatitudes? And this commentary on the Sermon on the Mount sees the first appearance of a quotation that would soon become a key text: 'God scorneth the proud, but he giveth grace unto the lowly.'[6] At the same time, the increasing affirmation of the need for divine grace, if not yet its primacy, is accompanied by the bitter realization that, with the *consuetudo peccati*, the man in search of spiritual progress is condemned to drag a chain whose pull and weight increase almost automatically with time. There is never any end to casting off the old man; Augustine knows that better than anyone: he has only to remember the past years of not so long ago. But he had found his salvation in St Paul, and he still recommends the Apostle to anyone who feels 'an untamed violence holding him in slavery' rebelling within himself.

Let anyone who feels within himself, against his proper will, the lure of carnal voluptuous pleasure due to the habit of sin . . . remember as far as he is able, what peace he has lost by his sin, and let him cry out, 'Wretched man that I am! Who will deliver me from this body of death? The grace of God, through Our Lord Jesus Christ!'[7]

He had to read and reread St Paul, and now venture to comment on him, especially the Epistle to the Romans, forever connected in Augustine's memory with the decisive hours of the summer of 386, in the garden in Milan. The first opportunity was a series of conversations he had with Christians in Carthage, where he had gone for the council that met on 26 June 394.[8] They urged him to let his words be recorded,[x] and the outcome was a little book entitled *Commentary on some propositions on the Apostle's Epistle to the Romans*. Forging ahead, back in Hippo, Augustine composed a *Commentary on the Epistle to the Galatians*, and even undertook an overall commentary on the entire text of the *Epistle to the Romans*; but he would say in his *Retractations* how, having launched into a long digression on the very difficult question of sinning against the Holy Ghost (Matt. 12.32), he had given up, deterred in advance by the length that the commentary promised to attain, and had contented himself with explaining the first lines of the text (Rom. 1.1–7). But with this first little 'corpus' of exegeses, to which were added some of the last replies of the *De diversis quaestionibus*, he was already placing himself in what it has been suggested to call 'the generation of St Paul'.[9]

Truth to tell, although he would soon become, and remain for posterity, its most striking representative, he had at first been in the rearguard. The first Latin commentator on St Paul, at the beginning of the second half of the fourth century, had been Marius Victorinus, and we may recall how stirred Augustine had been to hear the account from Simplicianus' lips of the great Roman rhetor's[10] conversion only a few weeks before his own. In Italy, in the time of Pope Damasus, in the years 366–84, an anonymous person whom scholars, in the wake of Erasmus, have named Ambrosiaster, had commented on all the Pauline letters. Jerome, too, had to be taken into account; in his early days in Bethlehem, some years before, he had given an explanation of the Epistle to the Galatians, which had reached Hippo in 394. Augustine did not agree with the 'soothing' interpretation proposed by Jerome of the incident between Peter and Paul at Antioch (Gal. 2.11–14) and asked him to take note of his criticism.[y] But that first letter never reached its destination and a second letter, written towards the end of 397, resuming his complaints and rather tactlessly suggesting that Jerome might 'sing a palinode'[z] on this point, had gone astray in Rome, and then done the rounds passing from hand to hand before eventually reaching its addressee in Palestine. It is hardly surprising that, with such beginnings, it took some twenty years for correspondence between the two men to settle down. And when it had barely begun, their dialogue on St Paul had come to a sudden end. He would carry on however, as we know, despite setbacks and, faced with Jerome's touchy readiness to take offence, the bishop would slightly temper his initial inflexibility,[aa] but basically without making any concessions. Augustine held fast to his refutation of Jerome's interpretation of Gal. 2.11–14; we see it still in a previously unpublished sermon, recently published, delivered at Carthage in 397, in which he attacked those – including Jerome, though he was not named – who thought that the dispute between Peter and Paul was simulated and for appearance's sake.[bb]

Augustine was unable to hold this dialogue on St Paul in Africa itself with

Tyconius, for it seems that in the last years of the fourth century the erudite and subtle Donatist theologian was no longer in this world. Tyconius considered absurd and utterly contrary to the divine promises of universality made to the Church the claim of those in his sect, confined to this little corner of Africa, to represent it by themselves alone; and he worsened his case, in the eyes of his hierarchy, by challenging moreover that there were none but the 'pure' in its ranks. This independent spirit had earned him a letter of reprimand from the Donatist primate at that time, Parmenianus, the contents of which are known to us in broad outline from the refutation that Augustine issued later.[cc] He hailed Tyconius' lively intellect,[dd] and although he waited till the end of his life to indulge in a complete examination of the Donatist theologian's *Liber regularum*,[ee] more than thirty years earlier he had read enough of it to have some idea of Tyconius' penetrating intellect and to be helped by it in his own elucidation of the Pauline texts.

In particular, by the 'rule' which Tyconius had entitled *De promissis et lege*. This third rule was a long meditation on the Pauline theology of justification by faith and not by works; Tyconius pondered especially over the function of the Law, evoking the story of Abraham (Gen. 12 and 15). The patriarch had received the Promise and had been justified by faith. One therefore had to wonder 'why, after the promise of faith, which can in no way be destroyed, had the Law been given, which does not proceed from faith and by whose works no one is justified'.[11] The answer was given by St Paul: the Law, until Christ's coming, had played a teaching role (Gal. 3.24). It was to reveal sin, and in fact had made it abound; but it had been imposed with a view to grace, which only faith obtains and which alone delivers from sin. Tyconius set out his commentary in beautiful and strong imagery.

> We have borne imprisonment, like the Law which threatened us with death and surrounded us on all sides with an insurmountable wall whose enclosure had but one gateway, grace. And Faith was the guardian of that gate, so that no one could flee that prison unless faith opened it for him. Whoever did not knock at the gate died within the Law's enclosure.

And he ended with these words: 'We have borne the Law like a *teacher*, who urged us to seek faith and impelled us towards Christ.'

Although Augustine was severe towards this 'third rule' as he presented it in the evening of his life, saying that it seemed to him more of 'a great question posed than a rule to be used to resolve questions',[ff] there is no doubt that it was helpful to him in the period of his first Pauline exegeses. But it is true that his thinking is firmer. Taking his inspiration from St Paul, but assisted by Tyconius' commentaries, Augustine divides human history into three phases: before the Law (*ante legem*), under the Law (*sub lege*), under grace (*sub gratia*) – to which eschatological time is added: *in pace* – and develops the idea that in none of these eras was man able – or is able – to glory in himself or by himself. Before the Law, he was given over entirely to concupiscence and sin; under the Law, he has knowledge of sin and transgresses the prohibition (Rom. 7.7–11); under grace, he receives the gift of good actions, and cannot therefore boast of it.[12]

Of course, Augustine had known from experience, since the summer of 386, how heavily God's action could weigh in man's spiritual evolution. These initial meditations on St Paul, with Tyconius as his guide, were now steering him towards the formation of his own theology of grace. But doubts remained, and so did questions. If one read some of St Paul's texts, was not God holding human liberty cheap? Augustine thus found himself faced with Rom. 9.11–13, resuming Gen. 25.23, and Mal. 1.2–3: 'I loved Jacob, and hated Esau.' What was the meaning of the choice of Jacob and reproof of Esau even before their birth? 'Some people', commented Augustine, 'are disturbed, thinking that here the Apostle has trampled on the free choice of the will.'[gg] His reply, for the time being, consisted of bringing divine foreknowledge into play: God had chosen Jacob because he knew that Jacob would believe, and reproved Esau because he knew he would refuse to believe; and this even before man's free will could be manifested in them, which responds or does not respond to the call God sends him.[hh] In another commentary, however, datable to the same period, and also inspired by a verse from the Epistle to the Romans (9.20), Augustine went further by spontaneously citing – and for the first time – what would later (but with quite a different orchestration) become one of the key texts in the Pelagian controversy: 'And since we cannot even have the will unless we are warned or summoned, either in our innermost heart, where no man can see, or externally, by an audible word or some visible sign, it follows that this "will itself is God who worketh in us"' (Phil. 2.13).[ii]

Etiam peccata

Mirages of the 'intertext'! Tacked on by Claudel as an epigraph to his *Soulier de satin*, these two notes escaped from an immense symphony have acquired, out of context, a strange and above all such an uncertain autonomy of meaning: sins too? Really? The worst thing would be to follow them with three suspension points, to leave them in the very un-Augustinian vagueness of a potential discourse.

In Book III of the Treatise on Free Will we meet this *etiam peccata*, which therefore dates from the very last days of Augustine's priesthood.[13] And the paradox[14] is that these two words which, by the grace of Claudel, appear so 'Augustinian', are contained in a sentence in which, before refuting it, Augustine formulates an objection which might be put to him:

> If our sorrows themselves complete the perfection of the universe, something would have been lacking in that perfection if we had always been happy. Thus, if the soul falls into sorrows only through sin, then *our sins themselves* are necessary to the perfection of the universe that God has created.[jj]

The answer was easy: sin being only a defect, a non-being, neither sins themselves nor sorrows as such were necessary to the perfection of the universe, but only souls as souls. And he added, 'Provided that souls themselves are not lacking which, if they sin, fall into misfortune and, if they sin not, obtain happiness, the universe always has its fullness and perfection.'[kk] A little later, in 397/8, this *etiam peccata* would come back to him, in relation to great men whose misdeeds are recalled to serve as an example,[ll] and in a theological context connected with that of the *De libero arbitrio*: our sins are not transformed into graces; but our sins may be the opportunity which God uses to ensure the salvation of those whom he has chosen. And this is doubtless what Claudel rightly intuited, even had the certainty if his eyes had fallen on *De libero arbitrio*, III, 46:

> I declare that one can find no way of attributing our sins to God our Creator, when I find him worthy of praise even concerning those very sins, not only because he punishes them, but also because one commits them only by straying away from his truth.

It will be remembered that in the early months of 388, in Rome, in the form of a dialogue in which Evodius was his interlocutor, Augustine had undertaken to analyse the free choice of human will, with the initial purpose of countering the Manichaeans' allegations about evil and its origin.[mm] Having become a priest at Hippo, and in the final days of his priesthood, he had resumed that interrupted work.[15] His perspectives had changed, as had his state of mind. If the word were not so baldly secular, one might speak of disenchantment; but the fine optimism of the new convert in the 380s had become a little gloomy, upon contact with creatures rather than Scriptures.[16] How could he stay the same, when onerous concern for the salvation of others overtook the quest for his own salvation?

Before becoming bishop of Uzalis (El Alia), not far from Utica, Evodius was living those years in the monastery of Hippo,[nn] and had naturally remained as Augustine's partner in the continuation of the *De libero arbitrio*. At the start of Book II, he got the discussion going again by asking his friend to explain why God had given man free will: did that gift not lie at the origin of sin? Begun by this question, the discussion took them a long way, for God's very existence, Augustine thought, was gradually being involved, and first needed to be established. Nearly all this section of the work is devoted to seeking intellectual proof, both of God and of the 'superior good' that comes from him. Then, *in fine*, they could come back to free will: man's free will is also a good thing, but a 'medium'[oo] as opposed to 'superior' good. It can aspire to both the best and the worst, turn towards the base and then die to God: 'Thus man, having become arrogant, inquisitive, sensual, is seized by another life which, in comparison with the superior life, is a death.'[pp] But where does it come from, this 'movement of perversion, which we recognize as constituting sin'?[qq] What, then, is the origin of sin?

Augustine would spend a large part of the remainder of his life answering this question, but the reply already occupies the last section of the dialogue. The soul does not fall into sin as an apple falls from the tree; its movement is therefore not 'natural', or necessary, and so is deliberate and thus blameworthy. On this point, Evodius expresses his quandary: God, who has foreknowledge of every future event, knows in advance about any sin that is to come; is not this foreknowledge in itself a necessity that is incompatible with a free will?[rr] Augustine gets rid of this objection. A closely argued line of reasoning – in a small marvel of dialogue that is truly 'Platonic' in its form[ss] – makes Evodius admit that, God having created everything once and for all – and nothing by repeated creations – he knows in advance what a future will may be potentially, but not necessarily written into the order of things. His indisputable prescience does not therefore interfere with our will.[tt] The very long development that follows, on the good of the Creation, succeeded in making the *De libero arbitrio* as a whole into a 'theodicy', as it has been called.[17] Evodius had listened in silence to Augustine's sustained exposition, and said he was finally convinced that there was indeed no foundation for our imputing our sins to God. But he has one last objection: the cause of sin is man's evil will, but what is the cause of the will? From Augustine, now in haste to have done with this long discussion and move on to another aspect of his theme, man's unhappy condition, he receives a rather ironic reply: if, says his friend, I can find this cause for you, will you not then go looking for the cause of this cause?[uu]

Of all the works written in this period, the *Treatise on free will*, together with *On the two souls*, is the one which the old bishop would take up later in the *Retractations* with the greatest attention. Pelagius, in support of his doctrine, had treated himself to the luxury of calling Augustine himself, among others, as witness, by quoting a passage from Book III in his *De natura*.[vv] He could just as well have picked out this or that piece from the *Two souls*, like the one in which it was stated that sin could be found in will alone.[ww] Considerably overdoing the connection, to the point of paradox, it has been said that 'at this time, indeed Augustine was, on paper, more Pelagian than Pelagius'.[18] It would have been better, in any case, to say 'Pelagian before the term was invented'. We know how he defended himself against it. In the *Retractations* he writes: 'In all these words, the grace of God is not mentioned, because it was not the subject at that moment.'[xx] Perhaps he might more correctly have said that at the moment – uncertain, unfortunately for us – when he was finishing Book III of the *Free will* he had not yet meditated deeply enough on grace. Or rather, by starting his study of the Pauline texts, he had merely begun the gestation of a doctrine whose definition would appear clearly only in his replies to Simplicianus some time later. Nevertheless, even in Book III of the *De libero arbitrio*, where Pelagius had believed he could find arguments in favour of his ideas, the features were already taking shape of a line that would soon be distinctly mapped out. Freedom of choice stayed on, but the 'merit' of the creature facing the Creator was challenged; it already owed him its existence, and must not make a merit of its conversion: 'What merit is there in turning to him from whom you have your existence, so that he shall make you better after giving you your being?'[yy] Conversion was already appearing as a dutiful response to the summons of grace.

Ordained a bishop

Valerius, the old bishop of Hippo, was fully aware that in Augustine he had a pearl, inviting attention and covetous looks, especially from communities with a vacancy for a bishop. According to Possidius, it even happened during these years that Valerius, warned of a concerted attempt to take his priest away from him, concealed him in a secret hiding-place.[zz] That was not the solution, however, so prompted by his advanced years and deteriorating health, Valerius decided to take the only action possible if he wished, in his lifetime, to keep Augustine in Hippo's church. He wrote a confidential letter[ab] to Aurelius of Carthage, in which, on the grounds of his age and health, he begged that Augustine should be ordained bishop at Hippo, with the rank of 'co-bishop', while waiting to succeed him. By doing this, Valerius was addressing the highest authority of the Church of Africa, but he unwisely neglected the local hierarchy, the provincial primacy, to whom he was responsible. Let Possidius tell us what happened:

> His wish and entreaties received a favourable reply. Then, in the presence of Megalius, bishop of Calama, then primate of Numidia, whom he had invited to Hippo, he unexpectedly announced his intention to the bishops who chanced to be there, to all the clergy of Hippo and to all the faithful. When all had listened to him, congratulated him and, with loud cries, expressed their wish that this should be done, the priest refused to accept the episcopacy in the lifetime of his bishop, as it was counter to the Church's custom. But, as everyone assured him that it *was* the custom, citing examples from churches overseas and in Africa itself, he yielded and received ordination to the higher rank.[ac]

Much can be said about the good Possidius' curious account. It is hard to believe that the bishops – whose presence was indispensable at Augustine's ordination[19] – 'chanced' (*forte*) to be there, to be confronted without warning with Valerius' secret plans, at the same time as a primate of Numidia, invited under a false pretext; while the protagonist, apparently also taken by surprise, at first refused – for good reasons, which we shall see – only to end by giving way to pressure and accepting his promotion under constraint.[ad] It is obvious that Possidius, more or less consciously, has narrated the scene to conform to the typology of the 'tumultuous' and forced election, following an outline that recalls what had happened some years before. Just as his hero had been ordained priest against his will, he now found himself with the episcopacy thrust upon him. Possidius therefore stressed the surprise angle, and an apparent improvisation.

There can be no doubt, however, about Augustine's resistance; not to his clerical promotion – he had been preparing himself for that since joining the priesthood and we have seen that in many respects he was already *de facto* Valerius' 'coadjutor'. But he found fault with the conditions in which this promotion had come about. And rightly so. It was all very well to tell him, in order to mollify him, that there were precedents,[ae] elsewhere and even in Africa; albeit not well versed in canon law, he had serious misgivings that this ordination, in a see which already had an incumbent, was highly irregular. In fact, soon after his ordination, he learned that in 325 the council of Nicaea had prohibited the ordination of two bishops in the same see.[20] Possidius scrupulously tells us about it, and Augustine himself would confirm it when, in 426, appointing the priest Eraclius to succeed him after his death, he would refrain from ordaining him bishop, so that his episcopacy should not be tarnished by the same error that had been committed in his own case, without his knowledge and, he would add, also without Valerius' knowledge.[af]

There remains Megalius, the primate – in other words, the 'doyen'[21] (*senex*) – of Numidia, and the role he played in this affair. The good Possidius, who succeeded him in the see of Calama, did not want to attack his memory. We know, however, that the Numidian primate took a lot of persuading and that Augustine's ordination, dealt with briskly in the fine account of the *Vita Augustini* and represented as having immediately followed his election, in fact happened over a series of episodes. Megalius had initially opposed the ordination of Valerius' priest and had set out his complaints and reasons in a letter which, many years later, was still circulating in Donatist circles.[ag] Megalius had flown into a rage, Augustine would say, and acted in a moment of anger.[ah] But what lay behind that anger? The letter is lost and we are reduced to hypotheses. Not everyone liked Augustine, and his enemies were not all on the side of the Donatists or Manichaeans. But in fact, one complaint was that he had been a Manichaean, and it was easy for his former friends to pour oil on these flames. The *Confessions* had not yet provided Augustine's adversaries with an object for their scorn and derision, but the priest of Hippo's past was known to many; moreover, his genius put others in the shade and aroused jealousies in his own camp. Whoever was the first to spread the ridiculous story of the love philtre that Augustine was said to have given a woman, with her husband's knowledge, and even complicity, was not necessarily a Donatist or a Manichaean! If one adds that the touchy Numidian prelate might have taken umbrage at an arrangement which seemingly had been arrived at directly between Valerius and Aurelius of Carthage, going over his head, we can better understand Megalius' opposition. Nevertheless, the primate of Numidia had had second thoughts about his position; at a council he had made amends for his hostile attitude towards Augustine,[22] and finally proceeded to his ordination.

One last, and not least, point of uncertainty remains: the date of this major event in Augustine's life. It must have taken place between May 395, the date on – or soon after – which, while still a priest, he gave details in a letter to Alypius, who was already a bishop, of the way he had regained the upper hand with the faithful of Hippo on the occasion of the *Laetitia*, and 28 August 397, the date of the general council that met at Carthage, where he was present as a bishop. Within this timespan, one text alone indicates at least a year, if not an exact date, mentioned in relation to the eponymous consuls: 395. But this text, the *Chronicle* of Prosper of Aquitaine,[23] is often blamed for its inexactitudes, so that in order to put a date on Augustine's ordination, we are reduced to scrutinizing the related chronology that emerges from the exchanges of letters in this period between Augustine, on the one hand, and on the other Paulinus of Nola, the great lord from Bordeaux, a disciple of Ausonius and himself a poet, ordained priest in 393–4 and settled soon after in Campania, at Nola, where he lived a monastic life and became bishop in 409. Careful examination of this correspondence, notably the letter addressed by Paulinus and Therasia to Alypius, then bishop of Thagaste, before the end of a year which can hardly be other than 394,[ai] and the one in which Augustine himself informs his friends in Nola of his new status,[aj] has led many exegetists to place this episcopal ordination in Hippo in the summer of 395.[24] The last word on this thorny question of dates has probably not been uttered, and other calculations give 396 a chance.[25] But, apart from the fact that dating Augustine's episcopacy to the summer of 396 would necessitate placing the first works registered at the beginning of the second section of the *Retractations* – including the fundamentals of the *De doctrina christiana* – in the space of a few months, the sequence of names that can be read in another letter from Paulinus of Nola, addressed to Romanianus this time, is a strong invitation to situate Augustine's promotion at Hippo less than a year after that of Alypius at Thagaste.[26] Now, this dear companion, this *alter ego*, became bishop in his home town at the beginning of the winter of 394–5, at the latest.

When Augustine acceded to the episcopacy, he had just turned forty: the middle of his life, the age when, in Antiquity, having reached the last years of *juventus*, man, in the fullness of his faculties, remained for a fairly long time at a stage – *gravitas*, the ripe age – before starting down the slope of *senectus*. Augustine needed all his strength. His major works had yet to be written, while a thousand tasks awaited him, and he would soon have to bear on his own the burden – the *sarcina episcopatus* – that Valerius had placed on his shoulders.

Notes

a. *Vita Aug.*, VIII, 2.
b. This is the *De Genesi adversus manichaeos*: cf. above, pp. 134–5.
c. *Retract.*, I. 18.
d. *De Gen. ad litt. lib. imp.*, 8: *res enim secretissima est et humanis coniecturis impenetrabilis*.
e. *Gn. litt. imp.*, 28, *in fine*.
f. The words will be used in the *De Genesi ad litteram*, IV, 51, but the concept is already implied here.
g. *Gn. litt. imp.*, 7. The final commentary will keep this 'aporetic' aspect of open interrogation.
h. *Wis.*, XI, 18 (cf. *Timaeus*, 51a) quoted and contradicted by *Gn. litt. imp.*, 10.
i. *Gn. litt. imp.*, 10, *in fine* and 29.
j. *Gn. litt. imp.*, 57, *in fine*.
k. *Gn. litt. imp.*, 59, *initio*.
l. *Gn. litt. imp.* 59, *in fine*.
m. Cf. *De vera rel.*, 59, on the symmetry of the two arcs.
n. *Conf.*, IX, 8. Psalm 4 in particular had transported him.
o. *Conf.*, IX, 31.
p. For example in *Enarr. in Psalm.* 3, 5; 4, 6; 9, 7.
q. *Enarr. in Psalm.*, 7, 5–7; 13, 7; 15, 10; 21, 7 and 30.
r. *Enarr. in Psalm.*, 1, 1; 4, 5; 18, 15.
s. *Enarr. in Psalm.*, 6, 5.
t. *Enarr. in Psalm.*, 3, 3, quoting 1 Cor. 4.7.
u. *De sermone Domini in monte*, I, 1: *Inveniet in eo . . . perfectum vitae christianae modum*.
v. *Serm. Dom. in monte*, I, 3, 10.
w. *Serm. Dom. in monte*, I, 4, 11.
x. *Retract.*, I, 23, 1.
y. *Ep.* 28, 3–4 (dated 394/5).
z. *Ep.* 40, 7.
aa. See the protestations of friendship in *Ep.* 82, 28–33 (dated 404).
bb. *Sermon Dolbeau* 10 (Mainz 27), 4, in F. Dolbeau, *Vingt-six Sermons au peuple d'Afrique*, p. 47.
cc. This is the *Contra epistulam Parmeniani*, datable to between 400 and 404–5.
dd. *C. ep. Parm.*, I. 1.
ee. At the start of the part of the *De doctrina christiana* contemporary with the *Revisions*: III, 42–56.
ff. *Doctr. chr.*, III, 46. He pays him homage, however, in this other sentence: 'The third rule bears on "the Promises and the Law"; it could be given another title, "The Spirit and the Letter", as I did when I wrote a book on this subject.'
gg. *Exp. qu. prop. ex epist. ad Rom.*, 60, *initio*.
hh. *Exp. qu. prop. ex epist. ad Rom.*, 61 and 62.
ii. *De div. quaest. LXXXIII*, 68, 5.
jj. *De libero. arb.*, III, 26.

kk. *De libero arb.*, III, 26.

ll. *Doct. chr.*, III, 33.

mm. Above, p. 127.

nn. *Ep.* 158, 9.

oo. *De libero arb.*, II, 52.

pp. *De libero arb.*, II, 53.

qq. *De libero arb.*, II, 54.

rr. *De libero arb.*, III, 4.

ss. *De libero arb.*, III, 6–8.

tt. In the same period, or shortly after, Augustine was already going further by commenting on Rom. 9.11–13, and God's prescience about Jacob and Esau: cf. above, p. 180.

uu. *De libero arb.*, III, 47–8.

vv. *De libero arb.*, III, 50.

ww. *De duab. an.*, 12. Julian of Eclanum, a little later, would not hesitate to do so: cf. below, pp. 420–1.

xx. *Retract.*, I, 9, 4.

yy. *De libero arb.*, III, 45.

zz. *Vita Aug.*, VIII, 1.

ab. *Vita Aug.*, VIII, 2.

ac. *Vita Aug.*, VIII. 3–4.

ad. *Vita Aug.*, VIII, 4: *compulsus atque coactus succubuit.*

ae. He would recall in a letter to Paulinus of Nola that this was how they had allayed his scruples: *Ep.* 31, 4.

af. *Vita Aug.*, VIII, 5; *Ep.* 213, 4 (26 September 426).

ag. *Contra Cresc.*, III, 92.

ah. *Contra litt. Pet.*, III, 19.

ai. *Ep.* 24 = Paulinus, *Ep.* 3.

aj. *Ep.* 31, 4.

CHAPTER XIX

396–397

Even in the fullest lives there are specially favoured periods, when months and perhaps years seem to count for double, in an expansion of time which opens up ample space for deeds and works. In Augustine's life, which could hardly be called leisurely, the first two years of his episcopacy are among those in which even the most airy chronology – for, as we have seen, there are sometimes uncertainties and therefore choices to be made – is able to record the richest results, in both the pastoral field and his development of fundamental texts.

Augustine grasped with determination an episcopal office that he does not appear to have shared for very long with the incumbent. We do not know the exact date of Valerius' death, which must of course have preceded his successor's official appearance in the Records of the Church of Africa, in August 397. There is usually agreement in placing the old bishop's death during 396;[1] but it may be seen that real responsibilities had fallen on his 'coadjutor' when he was ordained. It is quite certain that Valerius had complete confidence in his co-bishop, and delegated wide powers to him, especially in an area where his health and age no longer allowed him to assume them himself, namely, representation.

So it was that Augustine, just ordained bishop, had the opportunity for the first time of taking part in an episcopal consecration. This was for his friend Profuturus, probably a few years his junior, who had lived alongside him in the Hippo monastery. Profuturus was the 'brother' he had chosen, when he himself was still a priest, to take to Jerome in Bethlehem the famous letter in which, among other things, he indicated his disagreement on the sense of Gal. 2.11–14.[a] Jerome's renown was already considerable, and the trip to Palestine had other motives than simply bearing letters. Alypius had made the journey before his accession to the episcopacy in 393–4, and, commending Profuturus to Jerome, Augustine had no hesitation in saying how much he hoped Jerome would be able to teach his friend. Making a play on his name, he added that Profuturus could only become more 'profitable'[b] thereby. He did not know then that the 'future' of Profuturus would last only a few short years. And when, early in 397, in a letter written from Hippo he spoke freely to him, as one can to one's 'alter ego',[c] about his health, which was poor even then, he little thought that he would not see him again.

Profuturus did not make the trip to Palestine, because he had been appointed to the see of Cirta (Constantine), most probably during the summer of 395; and at the end of that summer or in the autumn of the same year, Augustine went to Cirta, in company with Alypius, to proceed with his consecration. On their way, the two friends stopped at Thubursicu Numidarum (Khamissa), some forty kilometres west of Thagaste, to stay with the Donatist bishop there, Fortunius.[2] A small group of Donatist followers who lived at Thiava, and were part of Fortunius' diocese, had arranged for them to meet him. The Donatist bishop was easy to deal with and disapproved of his sect's violence. The long debate

Augustine had with him was very open and was mainly a basic discussion on the *causa ecclesiae*, although on occasion the historical grievances surfaced.[3] Because it was in principle the fundamental arrangement of a confrontation that the bishop of Hippo would seek for another fifteen years before obtaining it, the main thing to remember about this meeting is that his interlocutor accepted the idea of a debate assembling ten bishops from each side;[d] but Fortunius committed only himself and the dialogue stopped there.

During these years Augustine learned to his cost how difficult it was to maintain that dialogue. The reserve shown to him by the Donatist hierarchy, to put it mildly, was connected with his success among the followers of the sect, at Hippo and its neighbouring areas. Possidius says that, having listened to the Catholic bishop, they reported his words to their own pastors who, when they wanted to re-establish their truth, found themselves refuted by their flock, who carried their replies back to Augustine.[e] An untenable situation! In these conditions, it is understandable that the overtures made to Proculeianus, the Donatist bishop of Hippo, suddenly came to an end. Evodius had undertaken to make the approaches; at a meeting on neutral ground – a friend's house – Proculeianus had declared himself quite willing to hold a debate with Augustine in the presence of several well-disposed persons.[f] Valerius was absent from Hippo at the time, but his 'coadjutor' was confident in advance of his agreement. By letter, he put forward several methods to the Donatists: a debate between several participants, duly recorded, or else a simple dialogue for two, or perhaps an exchange of letters.[g] But he had to come down a peg or two; Proculeianus soon increased his excuses. At first he said he would in theory accept a meeting setting ten bishops from each side against one another, but then suggested to Augustine that they should go to Constantine for that, where the Donatist could count on reliable friends – perhaps already including the famous Petilianus – or at least to Milevis (Mila) where, he said, a council of his Church was being prepared. But in the meantime, Valerius died; from then on Augustine had to shoulder the responsibilities of the bishopric of Hippo on his own, and it was there, on the spot – without leaving the territorial boundaries assigned to his charge – that he must hold the debate with Proculeianus.[h] If the latter was afraid to be put at a disadvantage by the former rhetor's cultural superiority, Augustine was willing to cede his place to his colleague from Turres, a neighbour who was then visiting Hippo:[4] Samsucius had no secular culture, but was sound in matters of faith.[i]

The matter had started off badly, and only one incident was required to put paid to it for good. At that juncture, Augustine had had to reprimand a young man of the Catholic faith who was, in fact, a nasty tearaway who beat up his mother and who, out of spite and a desire to provoke, threatened to join the schismatic church: 'I'll go over to the Donatist side, and I'll drink your blood!'[j] He had put his threat into effect – at least the first part – and had just been rebaptized. Augustine had made a formal complaint about him to the municipal authorities, at the same time by letter calling as witness one of Hippo's dignitaries, Eusebius, who was asked to act as intermediary. But Eusebius, probably the pagan curator of the city, who gained by having sympathies in both camps, was not anxious to set himself up as a judge between the two bishops, and as for Proculeianus, he refused to receive any of his adversary's letters in the future. Not answering the bishop of Hippo's letters would subsequently be the consistent attitude of the Donatist leaders, as Possidius confirms.[k] In this same period, when passing through a rural community in his diocese, Augustine had to put up with abuse from one of their priests, who was however officiating on the estate of a noble Catholic lady. It was becoming very clear that the struggle against the schismatic Church would be long-running and certainly no picnic.

The *Ad Simplicianum* and the primacy of grace

We must not forget Simplicianus and the decisive role he played in the summer of 386, during those weeks when Augustine was still wavering, on the brink of conversion.[l] Ten years later, the old Milanese priest who had revealed St Paul to him remembered himself to the bishop of Hippo. Ten years later: we have to base this on the date of these new epistolary contacts; we have no choice, because the chronology is often so uncertain. In the *Retractations*, the replies to Simplicianus' questions are presented as the first work following his episcopal ordination, which has been placed during the summer of 395. Moreover, from the address of Augustine's letter accompanying his dispatch, we cannot infer that the addressee now held the rank of bishop of Milan, which would be after Ambrose's death, in April 397. What is expressed in the body of the letter, quite apart from any hierarchical relationship, is the deference and even affectionate reverence that might be felt towards a spiritual father.[m] We may thus, without being more precise, date the *De diversis quaestionibus ad Simplicianum* to the first months of 396. [5]

Probably by way of Paulinus of Nola, Simplicianus had been informed of Augustine's recent writings, in particular the first little corpus of Pauline exegeses.[n] The questions he put related, on the one hand, to various texts of the Book of Kings and, on the other, to certain difficult passages from the Epistle to the Romans, and the bishop of Hippo gave his answers first on the texts from St Paul. The priest of Milan's questions on verses 7.7–25 and 9.10–29 of this epistle tallied with the dissatisfaction that Augustine had felt following his first commentary. In the preface, he wrote: 'Not satisfied with my study and the preceding explanation, I have perused the apostolic words and the content of these sentences with greater care and attention.'[o]

Of Augustine's new meditations on the passages from St Paul, those most fraught with consequences are assuredly the ones he elaborates regarding the second question put to him, on Rom. 9.10–29. But taking the letter in order, he first tackles Rom. 7.7–25 at some length. Simplicianus seems to have asked his correspondent to clarify the following difficulty for him: how is it that the Apostle, who is personally 'given grace' – and expresses himself so at the end of his letter: Rom. 12.3 – speaks in this passage as if he were 'under the Law'? It was easy for Augustine to reply that, in saying this, St Paul had put himself in the place of the man who lives 'under the Law'[p] and would wish to accomplish the good which the Law commands, but is powerless to do so without the help of grace. He quoted the Apostle: 'For the will is present with me; but how to perform that which is good I find not' (Rom. 7–18), and commented:

For those who may not fully understand then, those words of the Apostle would seem to eliminate free will. But how can he eliminate it, when he says 'the will is present'? It is certain, indeed, that the will itself is within our power; but powerlessness to accomplish good is the result of the fault due to original sin.[q]

And he added,

> This powerlessness does not come from man's first nature, but is the punishment of sin, the punishment from which our mortal condition emerges, like a second nature from which the Creator's grace delivers us when we have been subjected to him by faith.

Note that these texts[r] are the first by Augustine in which we meet the *peccatum originale*: the 'sin of origin', or 'original sin'. The two translations are possible[6] and, not without oversubtlety, can be used for two different interpretations, between which theologians are still divided.[7]

It would seem, however, that in this period Augustine laid more stress on the 'penalty' (*poena*) that weighs on the human creature because of his 'sin of origin' than on an original guilt (*reatus*), and that his conception of sin, *hic et nunc*, was one of personal sin. There will be occasion to return to the theology of original sin in relation to the vast elaborations in the anti-Pelagian debate. Meanwhile, Augustine salvaged free will. But what was left of it? Let us read what he says a little further on in his commentary on Rom. 7.24–5:

> For the man who is vanquished, condemned, chained, no longer a victor, despite the Law, but rather a transgressor, there is nothing else to do than cry humbly: 'Wretched man that I am! Who shall deliver me from the body of this death? The grace of God through our Lord Jesus Christ.' What remains of free will in this mortal life, in fact, is not that man can achieve justice when he wishes, but that with humble piety he turns to him by whose gift he may achieve that justice.[s]

But could everyone receive that gift?

The response to this vital question came with the one Augustine kept for Simplicianus' queries on Rom. 9.10–29. In the '83 various questions', around 393–4, commenting on Rom 9.16 – 'So then it (salvation) is not of him that willeth, nor of him that runneth, but of God that sheweth mercy' – he emphasized, also quoting Phil. 2.13, on the prior action of God, by calling (*vocatio*) on human will.[t] No one could pride himself, he added, on having been called; but he admitted that one could pride oneself on having answered the call.[u] It was still attributing too much to merit. He was now rereading the Apostle with the avowed intention of following his major line of thinking (*intentio*), which was that no one should glory in the merit of his works.[v] And thus faith, that is to say, the response to the call, should also be ascribed to God. Augustine took up 1 Cor. 4.7, but now drew the full inference from it:

> If anyone boasts of having deserved mercy by believing, let him understand that he who gave him the gift of belief is he who grants mercy by inspiring faith; and that he took pity on him, making him hear his call while he was still an unbeliever. This, indeed, is when the faithful is distinguished from the impious. In fact, the Apostle says, 'What hast thou that thou hast not received? And if thou hast received it, why glory as if thou hadst received nothing?'[w]

But then, if faith itself was a gift from God, would God be unfair in making this gift to one and not another? It came back to the problem of the choice of Jacob and reprobation of Esau. Remember the solution proposed by Augustine in his first commentary on the Epistle to the Romans;[x] that consisted in taking account of divine foreknowledge. God had chosen Jacob because he knew that Jacob would believe, and had condemned Esau because he knew he would refuse to believe, before any evidence in either of a free will that responds, or not, to the call it receives.

Resuming this problem, Augustine pondered at length on the Pauline text. There is nothing less drily dogmatic than the pages of his answer to Simplicianus' second question. There is much anxiety, not to say anguish, in the gropings of the commentary.[y] It is even quite distressing to see the commentator, in his attempts to safeguard free will as much as possible, envisaging differing methods of 'call' – that is distinct types of grace. For instance, if, according to the Gospel words, 'many are called but few chosen' (Matt. 22.14), Augustine says it is because only those are chosen who have received a call appropriate to their nature. And from Simeon to Nathaniel, there is no lack of examples of those who answered the call after they had been affected by various admonitions. 'Who would dare to claim', adds Augustine, 'that God lacked a means of calling Esau's spirit, with the help of his will, to the faith by which Jacob was justified?'[z] As the answer is in the negative, and the suggestion of God's injustice to be ruled out completely, Augustine in desperation is compelled to admit that if all are not called equally to have the will, it is because some are left to their damnation. Here arises the sombre image[aa] of that 'lump of mire' (massa luti), 'mass of sin' (massa peccati) formed by humanity since Adam; from that mass, like a potter manipulating his clay (Rom. 9.20–1), God makes either fine vessels, or vessels for common, if not base, use. And as the vessel cannot blame the potter for the use for which it has been made, so the creature cannot dispute the work of the Lord, who sometimes damns one, sometimes justifies the other, having taken both from the same clay.[bb]

Once again, Augustine wished to declare the value of free will. But between the answer to Simplicianus' first question and this answer to the second, his thinking on the subject had irrevocably moved on. The only aim of free will, he had said previously, was for man in this life to turn to God to ask for grace.[cc] At the end of his meditation on Rom. 9.10–29, free will no longer had other than a virtual existence: 'Free will', he still maintained, 'has great importance; it exists, certainly, but what can it do for men who have sold themselves to sin?' Where, then, could this free will be implemented? For in the same page Augustine continued: 'When we are drawn to what must carry us to God, it is by his grace that it is inspired in and granted to us; it is not obtained by our will, or actions or by our merits.'[dd] Rereading these pages thirty years later, the old bishop would write these words which, as well as the result achieved, sums up the ordeal that his spiritual wrestle with St Paul had been: 'In resolving this question, I did my utmost in favour of the human will's free choice, but the grace of God prevailed.'[ee]

It is evident that these pages of the Ad Simplicianum mark a turning-point in the Augustinian debate about grace and free will; and it is unarguable that this reorientation, subsequently further emphasized and sometimes misunderstood, lies at the root of the hardenings in post-Augustinian Augustinism. What matters here is to try to explain it by replacing it in the context of the situations experienced by Augustine at that time and, if possible, to understand it without over-dramatization. I think people such as Gustave Bardy are not wrong to emphasize the impact on Augustine's line of thinking of the experience he had recently been having, as a pastor in Hippo, of a community of faithful where the effects of sin were more often in evidence than those of grace.[8] His direct and favoured perception of them served only to strengthen his own memories. Until the garden in Milan, he himself had been 'carnal', eternally repentant, then 'lapsed', a slave to concupiscence, which he now knew was the punishment due to the 'sin of origin'. And his second reading of St Paul had painfully revealed, or confirmed, what he had known in his flesh since the torments of his pre-conversion: our free will – that is to say, our human will – which he had been right to affirm indefatigably against the Manichaeans, sufficed to do evil, to turn aside from God; but to do good, to turn to God, we needed grace, which lay only in God's hands.

But is that any reason to think that Augustine lived through this stage as a personal drama, that this very real pessimism, on the doctrinal plane, was accompanied by deep disillusion?[9] That would be to leave the area of exegesis and enter the realm of divination, for the author of the *Ad Simplicianum* gives no grounds for such a hypothesis. Is it even right to regard it as a break, not only in Augustine's psychological and moral equilibrium, but even more fundamentally in his system of thinking? It has been said that in 396 the philosopher had changed into a theologian,[10] or that, breaking with the philosophical tradition he had hitherto followed, Augustine had replaced speculative research with a regression into myth.[11] In fact, though he had preserved his Neoplatonist intellectual framework, he had stopped hoping to find salvation in Neoplatonism ten years earlier, in 386. The future author of the *City of God*, or quite simply the man who, describing himself, suggested at the end of his Pauline exegesis of 396 that 'every man with a penetrating mind and well versed in liberal studies may seem eligible for grace',[ff] could not easily be said, in his reflections on man and his history, to have agreed to a deficit of rationality. The *exercitatio animi* so often advocated could not harm – quite the reverse. But he quickly added that the most estimable people saw themselves daily outstripped, when it came to faith, hope and charity, by courtesans and ham actors who had been suddenly converted. Salvation was something else. He had known that since, in the Milan garden, he had bitterly noted that the ignorant reached heaven, whereas with their 'heartless science' he and Alypius 'were still wallowing in flesh and blood'.[gg] The true debate, to which he would return thirty years later,[hh] as we shall see, was not between free will and grace, it was between liberty and grace. Liberty, he said in the *De libero arbitrio* was the affair of happy men who adhere to the eternal law.[ii] But he would no longer say that it was enough to want a will for good in order to possess it. He had recently learnt that access to such a true freedom was not granted to all and from then on his anthropology would feel the effects of that theological need which it was only too easy to feel, on the moral plane, as an irreducible pessimism.

At Carthage in 397

The year 397 was one of mourning for western Christianity. Martin died on 8 November, at Candes, on the Poitou and Touraine borders, and his body was brought back to Tours for burial on 11 November. Throughout the ages, St Martin would give his name to millions of men and thousands of places in what would soon be France, and for fifteen hundred years the anniversary of his burial would be one of the most popular feast-days of the Church's eldest Daughter, until in the twentieth century that celebration would be obliterated under the layers of other memories. The demise of Martin, a prestigious monk-bishop, could have been affecting for Augustine, but it probably passed unnoticed by him. On the other hand, he was surely not unaware of Ambrose's death, which occurred on 4 April. At the moment when two of the most outstanding bishops of the preceding generation left this world, Augustine attained an official existence in the Church.

The year had started badly for him. Towards the end of the winter, he wrote to his friend Profuturus that he was confined to bed with an attack of haemorrhoids – one of his rare misfortunes – which would not let him walk, stand or sit.[jj] We know almost everything about Augustine's soul, but we have to imagine his body. Is it really necessary? he would probably have protested. And it is true that in this regard, unlike a Montaigne or a Rousseau, who leave little to the imagination about their woes, Augustine feeds our curiosity very meagrely; in this he is the worthy heir to a long ancient tradition which found physical self-portraits most distasteful. At least we know from him about the apparently pulmonary illness which had given him a good excuse for resigning from his professorial chair in Milan,[kk] his one clearly identifiable weakness,[12] already revealed in his childhood by the attack of breathlessness which had momentarily caused his parents to envisage a baptism *in extremis*,[ll] and perhaps also by the fever which had attacked him in Rome.[mm] Apart from that, the 'patient' Augustine was able to put his overall good health to the service of a capacity for work and a moral and psychological strength that were exceptional. But this soul of steel was not housed in a body of the same calibre, and we sometimes see a regret escape him, as in the letter written from Thagaste to Nebridius, where he more or less says to his friend – who, for his part, would have been well content with such a corporeal shell – that his *able to* does not match his *want to*.[nn]

Stendhal said of Mr Leuwen senior that he feared only two things in this world: boring people and damp air. Augustine hated journeys and cold weather. Of the first, he had more than enough; he was so often on the road that his travels have been the subject of a large book.[13] At least he managed to avoid travelling in the winter cold. If you have not seen the stony skeleton of Djemila or Timgad in January, emerging from a shroud of snow, you cannot know what winter is on these high wind-lashed plains. And on the coast there is then a penetrating damp that the braziers of old did as little to dispel as the present-day 'kanouns' (a sort of terracotta brazier).

Quite naturally, his difficulty in enduring the harshness of the bad season increased with age; in one of the recently published new letters he says that, at the beginning of March – this was in 420 – he had had to refrain from attending a council in his province, in central Numidia.[oo] And a few months before his death – he was then seventy-five – he excused himself to his colleague, bishop Nobilius, for not being able to go to him, in mid-winter, for the dedication of a church. He did so with bravura, in a delightful madrigal of which it is difficult to translate the play and the music of the words: 'I could come, were it not winter; I could snap my fingers at the winter, were I young: for either the heat of youth would bear the weather's rigours, or the cold of age would be tempered by summer's heat.'[pp]

To return to the early days of 397, Augustine was able to recover from his physical sufferings by not budging from Hippo during Lent and the Easter celebration that followed. To be in the midst of his faithful for Easter was always his unexceptionable rule. That year, the festival fell on 5 April, the day after Ambrose's death, and it was not until the second fortnight of the month that he took the road for Carthage; there he would stay for five months, until the end of September. What was he going to do there? Until a fairly recent date, his only known motive for this journey was to take part in the general council which met at the end of August. But what about the rest of the time? We are indebted to the perspicacity of two scholarly Benedictines in the 1930s for showing us that a series of some thirty sermons should be dated to 397; Possidius' catalogue – known as the *Indiculum* – which files them in liturgical order, says that they were preached at Carthage between Ascension Day and the end of August.[14] A good number of these sermons had been identified, notably coming from a manuscript of the Grande-Chartreuse, now lost. But a dozen were still missing; among others, they were retrieved from a collection of sermons of the Carthusians of Mainz, in Germany, where a fifteenth-century manuscript presents them, reproduced by medieval copyists, without many intermediaries, from the manuscript preserved at Hippo.[15]

This splendid discovery thus confirms what prompted Augustine's long stay at Carthage – preaching. He could not have done so without Aurelius' express invitation, but there is no trace of this for 397, either in the sermons already identified by the Benedictine scholars or in the 'Dolbeau sermons'. Nevertheless, to persuade the bishop of Hippo to desert his flock for five months, there must have been a very strong summons, an approach whose urgent nature may be imagined in the light of what we are told by another Dolbeau sermon – this one belonging to the 'Mainz-Lorsch' collection – datable to a few years later. In this sermon, preached on a 23 January, in the presence of Aurelius and doubtless in his cathedral-church, the *basilica Restituta*, we learn from the lips of Augustine himself[qq] that he had received from his primate, Xanthippus, a summons to take part in the sessions of a provincial council set for 28 January, at Constantine. And he recalls that, besides this invitation, he had good reasons for going to Constantine, which he had been insistently urged to visit by Fortunatus, the bishop of the town, ordained to the see after being a priest at Thagaste, and who had been one of the first of his circle of students and friends. Yet, Augustine continues, 'such a forceful and weighty letter reached me from brother Aurelius, your bishop, that it swept aside all my earlier arrangements'.[rr] He added that he was complying with God's will by yielding to Aurelius' entreaties, although he should really have been at the council of Numidia, with his primate, Xanthippus.[16]

We can only guess at the urgent matter that had provoked Aurelius' pressing invitation that winter, probably 403–4, and convinced Augustine, despite the dislikes we have just seen, to undertake in bad weather a much longer journey than the one which would have taken him to Constantine. It was perhaps due to the necessity for a dialogue at a crucial phase of the anti-Donatist struggle. In the spring of 397, the primate of Carthage quite simply wanted his communities and churches to receive the benefit of a talent he had known since the council of Hippo in October 393. He had all the more reason for inviting a brilliant preacher to preach in his town because he himself had authorized his priests to speak in his presence;[ss] what better teaching could they have than the example which Augustine would be able to give them?

Thus it was that all summer long in 397 the bishop of Hippo, followed by his secretaries who took notes of his words, visited Carthage's ecclesiastical areas, preaching in urban and suburban churches according to a double calendar, both liturgical and martyrological. He began this preaching campaign on 6 May, the anniversary of the suffering of the martyrs of Lambaesis, James and Marien, victims of Valerian's persecution in 259.[tt] He spoke again on Ascension Day, 14 May, preached twice for Pentecost, 23 May,[uu] and several times in June.[vv] Aurelius assembled a synod which seems to have been provincial, on 26 June; but although he had nothing to do with the Numidian bishops, it is very likely that Augustine was present. The only surviving deliberation is the repeat of the previous ban on bishops travelling overseas – basically to appeal to the Pope, in Rome, or to go to the imperial Court – without their primate's permission. If the bishop of Hippo's advice was asked, he could only have agreed, as he would always counter appeals to Rome and would never again cross the sea, leaving the responsibility for diplomatic missions to Italy to his friends, most often Alypius and Evodius. The synod at the end of June perhaps also had as its aim the preparation of the general council two months later, 28 August, in which Augustine would take part for the first time as the delegate bishop of his province. In the meantime, he had preached some fifteen sermons, half of which were found in the Mainz collection.[17] He stayed on in Carthage after the date of the council, because it is known that on 13 and 14 September, the eve and anniversary of St Cyprian's suffering, he preached on two occasions,[ww] in one of the 'Cyprian basilicas', although it is not clear whether it was at the place of the martyrdom – thus on the *mensa Cypriani*, at the place called *ager Sexti* – in the large suburb north of the town, not far from the present-day built-up area of La Marsa, or in the *memoria*, the funeral basilica of the *Mappalia*, which itself was away from the centre, on the northern edge of the city, if, as it seems, it is to be identified with the monument now known as St Monica's basilica.[18]

It is not surprising to find in these sermons a trace of the directions taken shortly before in the *Ad Simplicianum*. For instance, regarding the acquisition of faith, whose initial – or perhaps better, 'initiatory' – nature, prior to any merit of which one could boast, is clearly formulated in one of these sermons, delivered in the second fortnight of July 397. Before its subsequent disappearance, this sermon was known to the Venerable Bede in his time – early eighth century – and the learned English monk had extracted the most striking sentence from it to enrich his commentaries on the Gospel: 'It is not the merit of your good works which has led you to faith, but faith shows you the way so that your good works may follow.'[xx] The text of 1 Cor. 4.7, forcefully commented upon in the reply to Simplicianus' second question,[yy] occurs as a frequent reference in the preachings of summer 397; for example, in the sermon given on 21 August in honour of the festival of a martyr of Utica, St Quadratus, whose name (the 'Square' or the 'Squared') lent itself to some quaint variations. But it is another image in this text which suggests the idea of the free gift of grace. To be in the dark, says Augustine, we have only to close our eyes; but to see clearly, it is not enough to open them, we must have light, which is given to us: 'What hast thou that thou didst not receive?'[zz] he concludes. In *Sermon* 160, dated early in the summer of 397,[19] the Pauline text benefited from a broader orchestration and this sermon seems very close to the inspiration that moved Augustine in the first lines of his second reply to Simplicianus.[ab] Addressing Carthage's faithful, he developed the theme, as he had done for the old priest of Milan, that the error of Judaism was to be avoided, entrenched in its claim to establish its own justice in strict observance of the Law and thus remaining irremediably attached to the 'old man' and cut off from salvation. Even more than 1 Cor. 4.7, the keystone of this sermon was 1 Cor. 1.31: 'He that glorieth, let him glory in the Lord', together with Wis. 8.21: 'No one can attain continence unless by God's gift.'[20]

But of course, in these words uttered before simple believers, when speaking of faith and grace, he was not able, as he had been when addressing an elderly churchman (and a saintly person, to boot), to get to the bottom of matters that were too likely to drive to despair folk who were already over-inclined to yield to it. And, it must be said in passing, the people of Carthage often appear in the discourse of this exceptional preacher. Those men and women with whom Augustine had rubbed shoulders without giving them much thought in his youthful student days, and whom he had seen again from a different, and rather more distant, viewpoint from his professorial chair, he now had before him, of course differing from one another but, in the eyes of the pastor he had become, overall a dangerously vulnerable *massa peccati* whom he had to lead to their salvation. Carthage was there with its many big-city temptations, which he had experienced for himself without succumbing too much. But how could he not remember their shared youth and think of Alypius, when he evoked for Aurelius' flock the devotees of the circus, who confused love with their devouring passion, and wanted to make others share it, with insults on their lips for those whom it left cold?[ac] Life went on as he had known it: charioteers still drew the crowds, as did the 'hunters' in the amphitheatre, when the great hunts – *venationes* – were held in the arena, starting early in the morning, but never too early, as he mischievously remarks,[ad] to prevent the true fans from dragging themselves awake. Among these, fascinated by the sight of blood as Alypius had formerly been in Rome, there were also Christians, who had by no means cast off the old man. But at the same time Augustine also experienced in Carthage men and women who were joined in marriage and sometimes, like his friends Paulinus and Therasia in Italy, tried to live chastely within that union; but unless both partners equally sought that sublimation it could prove the enemy of good. This was the occasion and subject of a sermon in which his ideas on 'The Good of Marriage' were tested out before being more fully developed shortly afterwards.[21]

Augustine knew that life was hard for the lowly, so he had to give them a dream, as a bishop can do, without promising anything, but painting the essentials in glowing colours. In those times a premature death – far short of our modern life expectancy – ended an existence of hard toil. Augustine used the example of the soldier who at least had the advantage of a meagre pension when he became a veteran after twenty years' service; but even if he managed to make old bones, rarely would he spend as much time in leisure as he had in hard work.[ae] And if he died in combat, the soldier in this world thereby lost his hoped-for reward, which the soldier of Christ won by that same death. And what a reward! Not a time of rest equal to – or at the best, double – the time of toil and woe, but an everlasting reward: 'Indeed, we shall not rest where time will be long, but in a place where there will no longer be any time at all.' The preacher was speaking here, of course, of the martyr's crown, but he let his hearers glimpse what would follow the modest martyrdom of their often difficult lives, if their charity got them to heaven.

The measure of loving God is to love without measure

This charity / love was precisely the theme of one of the finest sermons of the summer of 397. The reading for that day, at the end of June or beginning of July, had been the reply Jesus gave to the Pharisee who had asked him what was the greatest commandment: 'Thou shalt love the Lord thy God with all thy heart, with all thy soul and with all thy might', answered Jesus, taking up the words of Moses,[af] and this was the first and greatest commandment. But he had added a second: 'Thou shalt love thy neighbour as thyself'; and on these two commandments hung all the Law and the Prophets.[ag] As for the Apostle, from whose Epistle to the Romans this passage had also been read, he said that the precept forbidding adultery, murder, theft and covetousness were summed up – like every other precept – in these words: 'Thou shalt love thy neighbour as thyself.'[ah] Instead of complementing each other, was there not a risk that the two commandments might seem incompatible? And did not St Paul's insistence on the second come down to emptying the first of its substance? To resolve this difficulty, Augustine's demonstration was to give prominence to the fact that we must first love God in order truly to love ourselves, to love not our body or our feelings, but our soul; only then are we in a position really to love our neighbour, and to draw him towards purposes of which we are not ashamed.[ai] Therein lay charity: both in the love of God and the love of one's neighbour; there could not be one without the other.[aj] But still more must we have this double love, because it is not a human attribute but a divine gift. 'Weep, believe, implore, obtain', says the bishop to the believer who lacks this love; and adds, 'What the law commands, faith gives'; and once more quotes 1 Cor. 4.7: 'What hast thou that thou didst not receive?' but without emphasizing the disinterested nature of a gift that might leave some people outside the divine choice.

As for God's love, if faith gives it to us it can know no bounds; or more exactly, no measure. Of the necessary boundlessness of love when it concerns God, the declaration had been read much earlier in someone close to Augustine, his fellow-citizen and friend Severus, in a letter he had written to him from Milevis, where he had been ordained bishop shortly after Augustine's ordination at Hippo. 'In this love', said Severus, 'no measure is imposed on us, since the measure of that love is to love without measure.'[ak] It has long been suspected that this very Augustinian sentence, of which an echo, or perhaps a meeting point, can be found in St Bernard, might have had Augustine himself as its author. And in fact, in the sermon briefly analysed above the original formulation[al] is to be found of what, in Severus' letter, is a quotation – one can easily be sure from rereading the letter – made after reading this sermon, which had been received by him (and probably by others as well) at the same time as the rest of the sermons of the preaching campaign in the summer of 397, circulated thanks to Aurelius rather than Augustine. Such teaching by example must not be allowed to benefit only the Carthaginian clergy.

Anyone visiting the site of Tipasa today, reaching the western boundary of the ancient town, on a level with the great Christian basilica, crosses the rampart through a postern on the cliff edge. Before him, closing the horizon, the Chenoua stretches into the sea. The funeral basilica of bishop Alexander is not far away. The visitor now makes his way amid pines and mastic trees in the domain of the dead, who are present everywhere, but 'back in the picture', and here so barely credible as dead people. It is there, in this ground that is so physically fascinating for the living, that at a turn in the path he sees rising from the artemisias a simple stone stele bearing a few carved words: 'Here I understand what is called glory: the right to love without measure.'[am] Shortly after his death, the friends of Albert Camus had wanted in this way to perpetuate the testimony of a man who, when young, had read St Augustine,[22] but at Tipasa came to recognize the perfume of the gods in the scent of the artemisias, and like Sisyphus to enjoy 'the water and the sunshine, hot stones and the sea'. Naturally, the author of *Noces* could not have read the *Dolbeau Sermon* 11, for obvious reasons. And there is little likelihood that he chanced to see Severus' letter.[23] 'The right to love without measure' which he affirmed at Tipasa was absolutely worldly. May we, however, be permitted to identify it as the distant echo, weakened and deflected in a deliberately agnostic conscience,[24] as the impoverished avatar of a magnificent expression whose reduction to strictly human dimensions has made it lose its dazzling brilliance?

Christian culture

Also in this period of such effervescent activity, probably in the autumn of 396 and the following winter, Augustine buckled down to a task which he himself recognized as 'great and arduous',[25] without being aware yet that he would not immediately complete it. It is certain that in the spring of 397 he had reached the end of his *De doctrina christiana* because, citing in it those who, from Cyprian to Hilary of Poitiers, had known how to extract the best of paganism, but passing over the living in silence,[an] he omits Ambrose of Milan, who would die on 4 April, and about whose death he would learn some weeks later when he arrived in Carthage.

Augustine had started on the work at Aurelius' instigation. Although the work's title is not mentioned, it is almost certain that, in the letter which the bishop of Hippo – in association with Alypius – sent to the bishop of Carthage in 396, he is talking about the *De doctrina christiana*: 'I am not unmindful of what you have commanded me to do and, on the subject of the seven Rules or Keys of Tyconius, I am waiting to hear your thoughts, as I have often written in my letters.'[ao] We know how much Augustine was indebted to Tyconius, whom he had discovered when still a priest.[ap] Although his independent mind had earned him the condemnation of his own sect, Tyconius had a whiff of sulphur about him, all the same. In the context of the anti-Donatist battle that was mobilizing the Catholic Church and would require a strong discipline from it in relation to the sect's members until at least 411, Augustine had to show caution, and Aurelius even more so. We have no trace of the latter's reply to the bishop of Hippo's repeated questions regarding Tyconius' 'Rules'. And Augustine would wait until 427 and the complement he would then give his work to indulge in a long critical analysis of the Donatist theologian's *Liber regularum*. But in the meantime, that would not prevent him from quoting from it and sometimes recommending its reading.[26]

After making several attempts, with varying success, at the exegesis of the Old and New Testaments, and after a dazzling debut as a practitioner of Christian preaching, as we have just seen, with this book Augustine became a professor again. But this time the title of the chair had changed. The texts on the syllabus were no longer those of Cicero or Virgil, or even the Neoplatonists; it was the Bible, and the theme Christian hermeneutics. But though the author to be explained was no longer Virgil, a good guide was still needed, perhaps more than ever, to gain entry. Four or five years earlier, Augustine had insisted to his friend Honoratus on the necessity for a masterly introduction to the Scriptures.[aq] One may suppose that among the new bishop's entourage this magisterial approach was sometimes resented, or at least that its usefulness was not always appreciated. This would explain the occasionally surprising tone of the 'foreword'; the author declares his intention of offering the rules of interpretation to those who might be 'desirous and capable' of learning them.[ar] Which meant, although it was immediately made plain, that reluctance and criticism were expected. Among the detractors he could foresee, Augustine particularly challenged, with as much obvious irony as declared reverence, those who, secure in their divine inspiration, claimed to read the holy texts without the help of any rules. Those 'charismatics' had nevertheless learnt their mother tongue by hearing it, and Greek and Hebrew, if they knew them, by having studied them. They were free not to teach their children these languages, in the hope that, as had happened to the apostles when they were filled with the Holy Spirit who had descended upon them, it would come to pass that they too would effortlessly be able to speak the languages of all nations![27]

Once past the 'foreword', the work's opening lines show the overall plan. To deal with the Scriptures, said the author, one must first decipher what they imply, then envisage the manner of expressing what one has understood. First, then, discovery; next expression.[as] He would not, however, tackle the methods for the latter until the end of his life when, coming upon his incomplete work as he was right in the midst of the *Retractations*, he forthwith finished the third book, which he had left dangling, and in the same impulse wrote an additional book to conclude a project devised thirty years earlier. 'I made a final addition,' he wrote, 'and thus completed the work in four books: the first three help in understanding the Scriptures, the fourth in setting out what one has understood.'[at] A very remarkable loyalty to his commitments on the part of a worn out old man – he was then seventy-three – who had in the interim responded practically, in a whole lifetime of pastoral activities and preaching, to the questions he had posed theoretically at the start of his episcopacy. Book IV of the *De doctrina christiana* is thus presented to us with all the richness contained in long years of experience.[au]

Staying for the time being with what was written in 396–7, there are many interpretations to be made from the first two books and the beginning of the third.[28] Its original scope had undoubtedly been that of a 'manual', more particularly intended for the training of clergy, and it was in this spirit that Aurelius could have 'given an order' to its author. But it is true that the expansion which takes shape in Book II soon after its commencement and which, becoming more pronounced later, leads Augustine to bring secular sciences and disciplines into his 'Christian Institution', strongly suggests that the 'studious and gifted young people, fearing God and seeking the happy life' whom the author was addressing at that time[av] extended beyond the narrow confines of a 'seminary' in the ecclesiastical sense. H.-I. Marrou was not wrong to take the broader view and see it as a programme of Christian culture or rather, perhaps, a programme of 'traditional classical culture *in usum christianum conversa*'.[29] That presupposed an adequate familiarity with the cultural heritage of paganism. Augustine illustrated this theme vividly, taking up the exegesis of the texts from Exodus which had already caught his attention some years earlier. On their departure from Egypt, profiting from Moses' advice, the Children of Israel had carried off the gold and silver jewellery that the Egyptians had unwisely entrusted to them (Exod. 3.22 and 12.35–6). He had first given a literal explanation, saying that God had allowed them to be rewarded in this way for their labour and the miseries they had endured in Egypt.[aw] But now, the justification of the act recorded in Exodus was more profound; the Egyptians had put their wealth to bad use, and it was right that it should pass into the hands of better owners. The same went for the liberal arts, and it was licit and justified to 'salvage' them.[ax] Soon after, recalling in the *Confessions* how he had 'converted' for his own use the contribution of the *libri Platonicorum* which he had just read, Augustine would re-use this metaphor of the Egyptian gold, which in the last resort belonged to God, no matter where it was found.[ay]

Even leaving aside the complementary material added by Augustine in the period of the *Retractations*, the abundant richness of the *De doctrina christiana* allows very varied angles of approach. However, it is essential to realize the conceptual framework which gives the structure its solid build. From the first chapters, two pairs, one distinguishing, the other normative, interacting with each other, give an overall shape to the first two books. The first is the contrast *res/signa*, things and signs: in the forefront among the things are the realities which are the subject of Christian teaching, the content and the articles of faith, developed at length and detailed in the first book. As for the signs, of which Augustine gives a theoretical definition at the beginning of Book II that enables him to be presented sometimes as the 'father of semiotics',[30] they are formed by scriptural language, which one must know how to interpret – initially to the first degree – and often decipher, in order to attain the realities of Christianity. But the second pair at once comes in, the essential difference between the *frui* (enjoyment) and the *uti* (use). Things, said Augustine, a combination of spiritual and material realities, offer themselves to man. But it is up to him, with the help of grace, to make the distinction between those he can enjoy and those he must only use, and only the spiritual realities, which are in the order of the divine, are also of the order of the *frui*.[az] From the first pages of the work, there is a strong interweaving of dogma and morality. The dogmatic truths relating to God – one and three, timeless and changeless – are matched by the moral truths which man puts into practice in his life if, instead of using it for itself, he uses it with a view to the only enjoyment that is worth anything.[ba] But – need it be added? – the enjoyment of this supreme good is not of this world. The ultimate goals, for which the biblical texts of course supply the keys, will only be attained in the 'fatherland'. Augustine resumed the metaphor of the journey, which he had often used, as had others, to illustrate his own path in life,[bc] but now influenced by his reading of St Paul (2 Cor. 5.6). Above all, it was important not to confuse the exile and the kingdom, but prepare oneself by a judicious 'use' of this terrestrial exile for a return to the 'fatherland', and joys of which the perceptible world, created by God, could offer only imperfect images.[bd] Decidedly, he was a long way from his nineteenth year, when reading the *Hortensius* had launched the student in pursuit of a *summum bonum* to be enjoyed, with the help of reason, in this world.

From the outset of this undertaking, within the strongly constructed 'teleological' and theological framework, Augustine had placed an 'educational' content whose success would sound the knell of the most questionable practices of ordinary paganism,[31] and whose spread would eventually either render traditional classical culture commonplace,[32] or at least 'secularize' it, or sometimes give it a Christian interpretation, and ultimately feed the western Middle Ages for centuries.[33] But what happened then and there? By Augustine's own admission, during the inventory of his library in 426, he found the copy of this work not only unfinished but halted in the middle of an elaboration, after a quotation from Luke 13.21.[be] The book was assuredly unfit for publication in this state. We find it quoted once, however, in the *Contra Faustum*, an anti-Manichaean pamphlet dated to 398–9: so it must have had a minimum circulation. Study of the manuscript tradition of the *De doctrina christiana* confirms that there was an edition originally limited to the first two books, which appear in a manuscript of St Petersburg – written at Carthage around the middle of the fifth century – following the first three works written by Augustine after his episcopal ordination.[34] One is thus led to think that in the spring of 397, when leaving for Carthage, he had taken with him, transcribed onto a *codex* by the efforts of Hippo's ecclesiastical *scriptorium*, his entire output since his elevation to bishop, notably what he had managed to complete of his latest work,[bf] by that date, the development of which had at least been suggested to him by Aurelius. Then his brilliant preaching campaign had begun, and continued throughout the summer.

Although the bishop of Carthage had been the instigator of the theoretical treatise, did he want to give preference to the circulation of the sermons, choosing the preacher's dazzling demonstrations rather than the lessons of the teacher, whose 'manual' had remained incomplete and, moreover, seemed to be weighed down by the rather tactless severity of the 'foreword'? It is a possible hypothesis.[35]

Although it remained fairly confidential, the 'short version' of the *De doctrina christiana* was not lost. In the middle of the fifth century, a cleric found it again in the episcopal library of a Carthage that had meanwhile become Vandal, and had a copy made. And it was this copy – albeit rather inaccurate – that another cleric, escaping the Arian persecutions by going into exile, brought into Europe (late fifth or early sixth century?), where it lay for a long time in the collections of the abbey of Corbie, before ending up in St Petersburg. But around the same period, shortly after Augustine's death in 430, the entire episcopal library of Hippo was transported to Rome and, among the books thus saved, was the original copy in four books of the *De doctrina christiana,* completed by its author in 426–7, and which had hardly had the time to circulate far in Africa itself. I shall have occasion to return to this marvellous transfer, so fraught with consequences for the intellectual education of the medieval world.

Notes

a.   Cf. above, p. 178.
b.   *Ep.* 28, 1: *fratrem Profuturum quem nostris conatibus, deinde adiutorio tuo vere profuturum speramus.*
c.   *Ep.* 38, 1: quia mihi es alter ego, *quid libentius tecum loquerer, nisi quod mecum loquor?*
d.   *Ep.* 44, 12.
e.   *Vita Aug.,* IX, 4.
f.   *Ep.* 33, 2.
g.   *Ep.* 33, 4.
h.   *Ep.* 34, 5.
i.   *Ep.* 34, 6.
j.   *Ep.* 34, 3.
k.   *Ep.* 35, 1. *Vita Aug.,* IX, 3–4.
l.   Cf. above, p. 90.
m.   *Ep.* 37, *initio*: addressing a respected elder, Augustine does not remark upon his own episcopal rank.
n.   Above, p. 178.
o.   *Ad Simplicianum,* I, *praefatio.*
q.   *Ad Simpl.,* I, qu. 1, 1 and 9.
r.   Cf. also *Ad Simpl.,* I, qu. 1, 10.
s.   *Ad Simpl.,* I, qu. 1, 14.
t.   Cf. above, p. 180.
u.   *De div. quaest. LXXXIII,* 68, 5.
v.   *Ad Simpl.,* I, qu. 2, 2.
w.   *Ad Simpl.,* I, qu. 2, 9.
x.   Above, p. 180.
y.   For example, in the repetitions and incessant questionings of the *Ad Simpl.,* I, qu. 2, 8–11.
z.   *Ad Simpl.,* I, qu. 2, 14.
aa.   Already outlined in *De div. quaest. LXXXIII,* 68, 3.
bb.   *Ad Simpl.,* I, qu. 2, 21.
cc.   *Ad Simpl.,* I, qu. 1, 14; cf. above, p. 190.
dd.   *Ad Simpl.,* I, qu. 2, 21.
ee.   *Retract.,* II, 1, 1.
ff.   *Ad Simpl.,* I, qu. 2, 22.
gg.   *Conf.,* VIII, 19.
hh.   Cf. below, pp. 425 ff.
ii.   *De lib. arb.,* I, 32.
jj.   *Ep.* 38, 1: *Ego in lecto sum, nec ambulare enim, nec stare, nec sedere possum,* rhagadis *vel* exochadis *dolore et tumore.* Medicine was Greek, as were the words for the illnesses; the first of the two terms used suggests a fistula, and the second clearly describes external haemorrhoids.
kk.   *Conf.,* IX, 4; above, p. 99.
ll.   *Conf.,* I, 17; above, p. 17.
mm.   *Conf.,* V, 16; above, p. 58.
nn.   *Ep.* 10, 1, with a play on words that is hard to convey: *Huc accedit infirmitas corporis, qua ego quoque, ut nosti,* non valeo quod volo, *nisi omnino desinam quidquam* plus velle quam valeo.

oo. *Ep.* 22*, 1, *BA*, 46 B, p. 346.

pp. *Ep.* 269: *Possem venire si hiems non esset; possem hiemem contemnere si iuvenis essem: aut enim ferret rigorem temporis* fervor aetatis, *aut temperaret frigus aetatis* fervor aestatis.

qq. Among others: this text, even apart from its homiletic content, is prodigiously rich.

rr. *Sermon Dolbeau* 2 (= *Mainz* 5), 2, in F. Dolbeau, *Vingt-six Sermons au peuple d'Afrique*, pp. 328–9.

ss. *Ep.* 41, 1.

tt. *Sermon* 284, *in natali martyrum Mariani et Iacobi.* On these martyrs, see Y. Duval, *Loca sanctorum Africae*, II, p. 702.

uu. *Sermon* 266 and *Sermon Dolbeau* 8 (*Mainz* 21).

vv. *Sermon Dolbeau*, 9, 10 and 11.

ww. The *Denis* sermons 11 and 22.

xx. *Sermon Dolbeau* 14 (= *Mainz* 44), 2, in *Vingt-six Sermons au peuple d'Afrique*, p. 108. Bede's extract in any case gave a more satisfactory text than the Mainz manuscript (*fidem* in Bede, instead of *finem*).

yy. above, pp. 190–1.

zz. *Sermon Dolbeau* 18 (= *Mainz* 50), quoting 1 Cor. 4.7, in *Vingt-six Sermons au peuple d'Afrique*, p. 214.

ab. *Ad Simpl.*, I, qu. 2, 2.

ac. *Sermon Dolbeau* 11 (*Mainz* 40), 8 and 9, in *Vingt-six Sermons au peuple d'Afrique*, pp. 63–4. Cf. above, p. 47, on Alypius and his circle.

ad. *Sermon Dolbeau* 11 (*Mainz* 40), 11.

ae. *Sermon Dolbeau* 15 (*Mainz* 45), 4. Length of service – twenty years – had not changed for centuries.

af. Deut. 6.5.

ag. Matt. 22.37–40.

ah. Rom. 13.9.

ai. *Sermon Dolbeau* 11 (*Mainz* 40), 11; *Vingt-six Sermons au peuple d'Afrique*, p. 65.

aj. *Sermon Dolbeau* 11 (*Mainz* 40), 13, p. 66.

ak. *Ep.* 109, 2: *In quo iam nullus nobis amandi modus imponitur, quando ipse modus est sine modo amare.*

al. *Sermon Dolbeau* 11, 9 (*Vingt-six Sermons au peuple d'Afrique*, p. 64): *Amandi deum modus est sine modo <amare>. Ama ergo* . . . We have to restore *amare*, which the copyist skipped before *ama ergo*.

am. A. Camus, *Noces*, Gallimard, 1950, p. 19.

an. *Doctr. chr.*, II, 61.

ao. *Ep.* 41, 2.

ap. Above, p. 179.

aq. *De utilitate credendi*, 13; above, p. 152.

ar. *Doctr. chr.*, prologus, 1: *Haec tradere institui volentibus et valentibus discere.*

as. *Doctr. chr.*, I, 1.

at. *Retract.*, II, 4, 1.

au. Cf. below, pp. 461–3.

av. *Doctr. chr.*, II, 58.

aw. *De div. quaest. LXXXIII*, qu. 53, 2.

ax. *Doctr. chr.*, II, 60–1.

ay. *Conf.*, VII, 15.

az. *Doctr. chr.*, I, 2–4 and 20.

ba. *Doctr. chr.*, I, 20, 37, 39.

bc. Cf. above, pp. 37 and 104.

bd. *Doctr. chr.*, I, 4.

be. *Retract.*, II, 4, 1. The work then stopped at III, 35.

bf. With a transcription deliberately interrupted at the end of Book II for obvious reasons of presentation.

CHAPTER XX

The *Confessions*

Great books appear when their time is ripe, above all when they are the repositories of irreplaceably personal words which achieve their deepest meaning in the setting of a closely circumscribed area of someone's life. This is certainly true of the *Confessions*. If we had nothing to put a date on them but the *Retractations*, and the rather imprecise chronological slot these assign to them, one would not imagine placing them much later in the years lived as a bishop by a man whose life was no longer his own and who, once past the striking revelations that contained no vain self-complacency, would forever renounce taking his *ego* as the subject of a discourse in the first person, except in his letters, and the part that all correspondence gives to personal secrecy and introspection. For us now, and for a wide range of readers over the centuries, from those who skim through them hastily looking for the thread of an existence and hoping to come upon the confidences of a 'bared heart', to those who marvel at the heroic fulfilment of an exceptional soul in its dialogue with God, the *Confessions* are St Augustine's major work. And with good reason, and that is without even mentioning the spellbinding dimension of this long poem. But what was the view of the author himself, who despite everything had remained a man of letters, though so little the 'literary lion', and considered his personal *historiola* if not worthless, at least outmoded and empty as soon as he had witnessed it? A few months before his death, he observed that of all his works this was the one which had reached the widest and most favourable readership;[a] but to learn how the old bishop regarded his *Confessions* when he reread them, it is best to open the *Retractations* at the brief page which is devoted to them – it is one of the shortest notes. Looking back over thirty years, he certainly did not disown them but no longer felt the need – obvious in the case of many other works – to return to them at length, either to justify or find fault with them.[b]

He retained what had always seemed to him to be their essence, a praise of God likely to turn men's hearts and minds to him: that was what had prompted him to write them, and that was the effect he felt upon rereading them. He was indifferent to what 'others', as he said, that is, unbelievers, thought of them; what was important to him was that the thirteen books of the *Confessions* had pleased, and continued to please, numerous 'brothers'.[c] But, in the evening of his life, the bishop would certainly not have written this testimony which, in his middle years, he had felt an imperative need to set down. Right in the middle of the *Retractations*, as we have seen, he paused to complete his unfinished *De doctrina christiana*. And resuming his book with the analysis of Tyconius' *Rules*, he came to the evangelical commentary – in Luke 17.28–33 – on the sin committed by Lot's wife when she turned back. And this was the gloss he put on the ban she had transgressed, to her undoing: not looking back means not subjecting the life one has renounced[d] to scrutiny. For the septuagenarian bishop, a retrospective look over his personal journey through life, which in this world was approaching its end, was no longer fitting. Rather than engage in an undertaking which would by then have been akin to 'Memoirs', he had better things to do, now that his works were complete or very nearly so: to look back over them, embrace the whole of the monument he was preparing to bequeath, make his own criticism of them, also to defend and sometimes justify them. As has been rightly said, 'the *Retractations* are the *Confessions* of Augustine's old age'.[1] The paradox is that he dealt so rapidly and reservedly about the work of his mature years which ensures him a unique place in universal literature, leaving it up to his readers to find in it the reasons why, at the beginning of his episcopacy, he should have felt such a burning obligation to write it.

The date and genesis of the *Confessions*

There is broad agreement in dating the *Confessions* between the end of 397 and 401.[2] The first premise in this 'margin' is the death of Ambrose, who is mentioned as deceased when Augustine, at the beginning of Book VII, recalls the role played by Simplicianus in his conversion.[e] Now, we know that the bishop of Milan died on 4 April 397, and the months immediately following are ruled out, since Augustine, busy with his preaching at Carthage until the early autumn of that year, could not have launched himself into such an absorbing enterprise before his return to Hippo. It is therefore easy to accept that the 'autobiographical' part, in other words, the first nine books which compose a homogeneous 'narrative' whole, could have been written in the space of a few months, starting from the end of 397. Did he then mark time for a while? At the beginning of Book X, he makes a clear allusion to the beneficial effect of his *Confessions* on those who read or listen to them: they stir hearts, prevent them from sinking into despair and saying 'I cannot'; as for the 'good', they take pleasure in hearing about the misdeeds committed in the past by those who are henceforward liberated from them.[f] It is for the former that he agrees to reveal himself as he is now,[g] leaving aside other readers, 'a race curious to know about others' lives, but slow to mend their own!'[h] By this, he lets it be known that the work, up to its present point, had come to the knowledge of a public with two countenances, which presupposes that it had begun to be spread, by the circulation of a fair copy, accessible to several categories of reader, and probably also of a limited number of copies. But that does not in any way mean that the author stopped for long in his work of composition.

Certain clues even lead one to think that Book X, in which he reveals himself as he is at present, and Books XI to XIII, devoted to the Scriptures, were not long in following. We must return to the exchange of letters between Augustine and his friend Severus, the bishop of Milevis (Mila), which, as we saw, followed the Carthaginian preaching campaign of summer 397, but not as long after as has been thought. Of a quite different calibre from Alypius, the gentle Severus was no less dear to Augustine. Receiving a letter from him that was both rhetorical and touching, Augustine replied in terms well suited to shedding a little balm in Severus' heart, who found it hard to bear the distance that separated him from his 'sun': their souls, he said, were one;[i] and we must believe that Augustine's morale-boosting way of addressing his friend was known, as one of Augustine's correspondents, whose name is unknown, writing in this period to express his regret at not having been able to meet him, consoled himself by adding that having at least found Severus, he had found 'half his soul'.ʲ Besides its emotional content, the expression was eminently literary; Horace had used it about his friend Virgil, in the anxious presentiment of a death which in fact had smitten the poet on his return from Greece, and it is the same one that Augustine wittingly employs in the *Confessions* when in Book IV he laments the death at Thagaste of a friend who had been dear to him.ᵏ But there are other points of contact in the *Confessions* with that exchange of letters 109 and 110, which it seems permissible to date to 398 at the latest.³ Particularly remarkable, in Augustine's reply to his friend, are the sentences that echo, very exactly, his preoccupations at the beginning of Book XI, and the way in which he expresses them. Thus we see him regretting the lack of time to give thanks to God for having made him fit to preach his word: '*The drops of time*', he says, 'cost me dearly', and a little further on, he says that he does not want the hours when he finds himself freed from the *service* he owes to men,ˡ to be used for anything other than meditation and expounding the divine word. Using almost the selfsame terms, he excuses himself to his friend Severus for not being able to write a longer letter: 'You know', he writes, 'that because of the *necessities of my service*, only too few are *the drops that time distils* for me.'ᵐ For want of precise and irrefutable indications, there is therefore the strong assumption that the work begun at the end of 397 was finished well before 401.

Although it escapes nobody that such a work, more than any other, must have been dictated by an inner need, there have sometimes been attempts to retrace its genesis and thus to uncover the closest causes, if not, rather more riskily, the circumstances of his motives. Here chronology resumes its rights, and everything in Augustine's life that might have acted as a spur or a starting-point must be replaced in it; among others, and chiefly, his relations with Paulinus of Nola. For the last few decades, thanks notably to the work of Pierre Fabre and Pierre Courcelle,⁴ we have had a better knowledge of the birth of that friendship, the postal vagaries and slowness which, between Nola in Campania and Hippo, via Carthage, frustrated it, and the probable reasons for Paulinus' long silence – upsetting for Augustine – which must have played a part in an initial circulation of the long first part of the *Confessions*.

It was Alypius, apparently first contacted by a letter from Paulinus, who laid the foundations of this relationship by sending him five of Augustine's anti-Manichaean writings, in 394; in exchange, he asked Paulinus to let him have a copy of the *Chronicles* by Eusebius of Caesarea, which he knew were accessible to his correspondent. Paulinus willingly agreed and asked if, in return, Alypius would write the history of his life according to the customary rules of biographies; giving details of his local and family origins, the stages of his education, how and by what routes he had been converted and entered the priesthood.ⁿ There was not the slightest risk that the one who was thus entreated would see it as an incongruous lack of tact, or the result of a simple 'mundane' curiosity; those men seeking the 'perfect life' felt a sincere need to exchange among themselves 'edifying' accounts of their respective paths in life and their religious experiences. Thereupon, despite a few contretemps due to the inevitable delays in transmission and the to-ings and fro-ings they entailed, direct contact by letter had been established between Paulinus and Augustine, shortly before the latter's accession to the episcopacy. The long letter received by Paulinus towards the end of spring 395 is not only a superb piece of epistolary literature, but also a fine example of that communication of minds which can be established with words, when attention is paid to another person whom one has not met, but knows to be spiritually very close. Augustine commended to his correspondent his dear Licentius, of whom he rather despaired;[o] and as Alypius, from modesty, had not dared to write the autobiography requested, he assured Paulinus that, at the entreaty of the interested party, he himself would take on the task.[p] But then the episcopal ordination at Hippo intervened, followed by a long silence from Campania. In a letter addressed to Romanianus, Paulinus greeted, as he puts it, not a 'succession', but an 'accession' to the episcopacy during the incumbent's lifetime, using a sentence – 'who would have believed it before it actually took place?'[q] – which perhaps reveals real disapproval rather than surprise. Some have thought so, on rather fragile foundations, and it has also been supposed that the stir caused by the ordination had made itself felt as far afield as Nola, together with the ill will shown by Megalius and the unpleasant comments from Donatist circles at the time of the event.[5] What is certain is that Augustine disliked this silence to the point of becoming impatient, as a short note carried by Severus to Campania around the end of summer 397 reveals: was it possible to leave him and his circle in such 'thirst', for two summers, and two *African* summers, into the bargain.[r]

Whatever the reasons for this hiatus, it seems to have ended fairly quickly. There is no doubt that, as early as 398, Paulinus was one of the recipients of the limited edition that Augustine made of the first 'autobiographical' part of his *Confessions*, as we have seen. He was evidently one of those ascetics who, in their youth, had been spared the excesses of which the author accuses himself, and who, he says, will often laugh at him – indulgently and affectionately, he hopes – when they read his text.[s] And indeed, as he read the *Confessions*, Paulinus discovered more or less what he had asked of Alypius a few years previously: a 'biographical note' on the bishop of Thagaste, inserted of course into Augustine's own biographical plot, but as an excursus, a text containing its own justification, at least for the part about their shared youth where the elder could look at the younger from a viewpoint that was still external;[t] for afterwards, whether still in Italy or after the return to Africa, their paths were so interwoven that Augustine could no longer speak of his friend without also mentioning himself. In the implementation of that synergy between grace and free will, conversion, then the choice of the 'perfect life', Alypius had been closely associated with him, and could not be treated separately.

In the person of Paulinus of Nola, and because of his wishes, the Italian ascetic milieu may thus be regarded as the origin of the *Confessions*, in one of the motives provided by circumstance. But in the history of every great work such triggering or prompting factors may be discovered, and taking them into account may throw light on its genesis, but leaves the problem of its significance untouched. More fundamentally, it may probably be said that Augustine would not have conceived this book in the same way before the major turning-point in his life of the *Ad Simplicianum* and the revelation of the primacy of grace, which the *Confessions* so magnificently illustrate. Conversely, we must resolutely resist the suggestions of those who have sought to see it as a plea *pro domo*: Augustine supposedly defending himself against those who challenged the reality of his baptism, then the validity of his episcopal ordination, and vilified him for his Manichaean past. It would be a singular apology for oneself, coming from a man who is always accusing, rather than excusing, himself![6] Actually, it was the account in the *Confessions* which provided weapons for Augustine's detractors in Africa, particularly the Donatists; and the author was perfectly well aware of it.

The structure and intent of the *Confessions*

In his *Retractations*, Augustine indicated his view of the work in its ensemble: 'From the first to the tenth book,' he said, 'it is about me; in the other three books, it is about the holy Scriptures, starting from these words: "In the beginning God made the heaven and the earth", up to the rest day on the sabbath.'[u] Today's reader,[7] in agreement with the author for setting apart Books XI to XIII, legitimately introduces a distinction between Books I to IX, which form a retrospective, 'autobiographical' section, encompassing a clearly demarcated period of life – from the first to the thirty-third year – and Book X, which is 'introspective', and notes in the present tense Augustine's state of mind when he is writing the *Confessions*. In a work that presents an undeniable unity of fact, he thus discerns three parts that are unequal in volume and importance. In terms of a 'plan', the reader is presented with an ensemble that he may consider unbalanced, or at least outside the norm, if he approaches it from the outside, so to speak, and according to classical rules.

Much effort has therefore been expended on the 'plan' of the *Confessions*, by looking at them as a 'literary object' among many others in the vast field of the literature of Antiquity. First, looking at them overall: why thirteen books, arranged in 9+1+3? Related to the arithmological preoccupations that were still widely current at the time and had also engaged Augustine's mind,[8] this distribution seems strange and irreducible to the customary binary, ternary, decimal or duodecimal schemas. Thoughts then turn to the *Metamorphoses* of Apuleius, the son of Madauros who was well known to Thagaste's son, and their no less 'abnormal' composition in 10 + 1 books. The connection is made easier by what the two books have in common. Each in its own manner, they are both an account of 'conversion', and in both can be found similar driving forces behind the downfall of the respective heroes, Lucius being turned into a donkey, and Augustine falling into the 'region of dissimilarity': on both sides, the same emphasis is placed on those prime causes of perdition, *concupiscentia* and above all, *curiositas*.[v] At first glance, it may therefore come to mind that, with regard to those that precede them, the last three books of the *Confessions* have the same relationship – the divine plan compared with the human plan – as Book XI of the *Metamorphoses*, in which the grace of Isis gives Lucius rebirth, after ten books in which his wanderings and tribulations are recounted. But, apart from the fact that, in the 'narrative' books the rhythms and contents are totally unalike, the differences in theological perspective are such that it is hard to see a relevant comparison.[9]

Or again, and here the exercise at first seems more justified, the philologist's subtlety has been trained on the really unified 'sub-ensemble' formed by the first nine books of the *Confessions*. Then we have to take stock of this 'ennead', either to see it as an 'Aeneid',[10] or to try to find the principle of its composition in another famous 'ennead', certainly well known to Augustine, Virgil's *Bucolics*, where there is general agreement in reading the eclogues as matching, two by two, on either side of a symmetrical axis formed by the fifth Bucolic. And, following this construction, the axis of the work would be Book V, in which we see Augustine go from Carthage to Milan by way of Rome, and this 'Roman book' would be 'the pivot of the work, just as the city of Rome is itself the geographical pivot of the route that takes Augustine from Carthage to Milan'.[11] But by its author's own admission, this ingenious system is unsound and presents glaring dissymmetries that break an order conceived according to a contrived line that is itself questionable. The error of this 'architectural' view (or any other similar inspiration) lies in striving at all costs to recognize in the *Confessions* a literary unity which they do not possess – and which Augustine did not try to impose on them – favouring a too strictly 'autobiographical' approach to the first nine books. That this book, which is unique in the literature of Antiquity, is a work of art is patently obvious, but it is a work of art in its own right. The great unity of the *Confessions* is of the psychological and theological kind, and their beauty owes nothing to a harmony of composition that was consciously imposed following rules inspired by strictly aesthetic canons.

> *You are great, O Lord, and greatly to be praised: great is your power and your wisdom without end.* And man, being a simple part of your creation, desires to praise you; man who bears everywhere with him his mortality, who bears everywhere with him the witness of his sin and the witness *that you resist the proud*: yet man, this part of your creation, desires to praise you. You make us delight in praising you, because you have made us inclined towards you, and our heart is restless until it begins to find rest in you (*et inquietum est cor nostrum, donec requiescat in te*).[w]

From the first words of this introductory invocation the reader knows that the *Confessions* – this plural title was Augustine's own,[x] and signifies no more than the multiplicity of the experiences he is confessing and the praises he pours out[12] – will take the first apparent form of a dialogue with God, who will be addressed often in inspired if not 'divine' language – with the poetically and liturgically consecrated words of the Psalms[13] – by one of his creatures who is particularly conscious of his finitude and even non-being – mortality, sin – and filled with the conviction that the fullness of being will not be his until his ultimate end, and by the grace of a 'conversion' which is its condition in this life.

The speech to God will thus be a long discourse of gratitude, first a confession of praise; but the man who, in the text, is on 'first name terms' with God does not shut himself up with him in an exclusive tête-à-tête.[14] '*Our* heart is restless', says Augustine, bearing witness on behalf of all mankind in fraternal humility and using to express the seat of this existential unrest the word 'heart' which, taken from the Psalms, so often bursts into his text to designate the moral centre of the human being, simultaneously body and soul, in a sense that is Pascalian before the term was invented.[15] And from the outset we may note that the expression of this fundamental disquiet, which comes like a cry, is matched at the very end of the book by the prayer in which Augustine asks God for 'the peace of repose, the peace of the sabbath, the peace that has no evening'. He adds, 'If God rested on the seventh day, it was to tell us in advance through the voice of his book that when our work is done we too, in the sabbath of eternal life, shall find our rest in him.'ʸ Thus, in the opening lines of the *Confessions*, as the writing dynamic of the entire work, a fundamental tension is put in place which will be resolved at the end of Book XIII by an eschatological reading of the first chapter of Genesis. Perhaps the former rhetor did not have a 'plan' when he began his work, but the *servus Dei* did not undertake this confession of praise without having in his mind the theological coherence that gave it its entire direction.

The confession of praise is also the confession of a mortal and sinful man, therefore an act of contrition and penitence, from which one may possibly expect the beneficial effects of a 'psychotherapy'.[16] Augustine 'makes a confession', he talks about himself in a way that was quite unheard of for his contemporaries. Of course, Late Antiquity had not completely overlooked the retrospective look at oneself; but whether it was Philo of Alexandria or Dion of Prusa, or, closer to Augustine, St Cyprian – in the *Ad Donatum* – or Hilary of Poitiers – in the first pages of his *De Trinitate* – these writings solely described the intellectual or spiritual paths taken, the quest for truth or God. And Augustine had already cast brief glances at his still recent past.ᶻ But for the first time, without complacency or any attempt at justification, a man who was intellectually one of the greatest in his time – and who knew it – a bishop who in a few years had become the focal point for a part of Christianity, was taking the risk of throwing his life to the lions. Not to God, who knew all about it in any case, and knew what was to come,ᵃᵃ and to whom only the act of contrition, the profession of faith and confession of praise were directed, but to men, to all the book's potential readers or listeners, even if it meant providing weapons to those among them who might use it for polemical ends or to denigrate him. It was in full consciousness of the risk, weighed in Book X as if in a sort of 'postface',ᵇᵇ that the choice was made to 'recount' his life.

Augustine's reflections on the course he took did not stop with the *Confessions*. In a commentary on the Psalms, which dates from some dozen years later, he returned to throw more light on what he calls the *enuntiatio vitae*. It was necessary, he said, 'to recount one's life' (*enuntiare vitam suam*), not for self-satisfaction or self-use, but to be useful to others 'in such a way as to invite others to receive the life one has received oneself'.ᶜᶜ To narrate one's life is thus a 'service', which as such accompanies the confession of faith and praise to be the second, if not the first, motive for the book. At the opening of Book X, the moment when he declares the present state of his soul, Augustine writes: 'I wish to "tell the truth" in my heart, before you in confession, but also in my book, before many witnesses.'ᵈᵈ If those witnesses are not malicious, Augustine's intention is that they shall benefit. Not that he considers his life to be 'edifying'; he does not unveil it like something precious and a model to be followed, as Seneca had done when, sentenced by Nero, at the moment of taking his life he said to the friends surrounding him that, for want of anything else, he bequeathed them at least the essential, 'the image of his life'.ᵉᵉ In his own view it was edifying only insofar as it showed how, with the help of grace, and on condition of an active receptivity to his call, man can emerge from the 'region of dissimilarity' and turn to God. There was nothing exemplary in Augustine's life but the path of his conversion, and thus the *Confessions* are a Christian protreptic based, not on a discourse of philosophical or spiritual edification, but on autobiographical facts.

However, if we refer to a recent definition of autobiography that may be deemed acceptable – 'a retrospective account in prose which a real person makes of his own existence when it emphasizes his individual life'[17] – it is not easy to say that Augustine's work is primarily autobiographical.[18] Though it is true that the *Confessions* are irreplaceable for the information they give us about their author's early life as far as his thirty-third year, whoever skims through them to seize upon the anecdotal aspects, skipping the rest, will soon have finished.[19] And in the strictly autobiographical element of the text there are often omissions or silences, infinitely more numerous than the blanks which almost inevitably strew every text that purports to be predominantly autobiographical. Of Augustine's family, the only figure to emerge – but in what high relief! – is his mother's, not to mention here the evasion in his memory of Adeodatus' mother, explained earlier;[ff] or the son himself, tenderly cherished and grievously lost, whose name alone we would know – belatedly and parsimoniously uttered – if the *De beata vita* and, chiefly, the *De magistro* had not sketched the intellectual portrait of his marvellous precocity. Moreover, chronology does not observe a straight line in the narration, and we can pick out various anachronisms, which are however minor and unsurprising in an arrangement of memories whose prime aim is not to feed a consistent and homogeneous narrative of a rethought life.[20]

In a famous page of Book X, Augustine tells in imagery how he mobilized those recollections, preserved and classified in the vast 'palaces' of his memory.

When I am in this palace, I summon up all the memories that I desire. Some come forth immediately; others need to be sought after for longer and as if dragged from some more secret stores; some rush forth in crowds and, while another is asked for and sought, they leap into the midst as if to say 'Are we not the ones, perhaps?' And my heart's hand waves them away from the face of my remembrance, until the one I desire extricates itself from obscurity and emerges from its hiding-place before my eyes. Other memories come forth without effort, in orderly and continuous file; those that appear first give way to the ones that follow, and hold themselves in reserve, ready to reappear at my wish. This is exactly what happens when I retell something from memory.'[21]

Set out like this, Augustine's mastery of remembrance is impressive; it assuredly included some flaws, which the author of the *Confessions* occasionally recognizes; it does happen, he admits, that his memory betrays him. Thus he no longer knows (*Conf.*, IV, 20) whether his *De pulchro et apto* comprised two or three books; he now wonders (V, 11) whether Faustus' intellectual personality really had the charm he attributed to it; he no longer remembers (VIII, 14) why Nebridius was absent when Ponticianus visited them in Milan, and he has forgotten (IX, 27) the answers given to Monica during their last conversation in the garden at Ostia.

But most frequently that memory has been deliberately selective, leaving aside memories that are least significant in the perspective of 'confession'. Thus, after recalling Monica's dream when she despaired of ever seeing him break free from the Manichaeans, he writes, 'I pass over many things, in my haste to come to those which drive me to confess them to you.'[hh] And, as if to excuse his remarkable silence about the months spent at Cassiciacum, which with hindsight appear to him to be still too stamped with 'the school of pride', he mentions his haste to move on to more important episodes.[ii] It was that same sense of haste, due to the feeling that time was strictly meted out to him, which had prevented him from extending this scrutiny of his past life until the time of his accession to the episcopacy, as he acknowledges only at the beginning of Book XI.[jj] Henceforward, caught up as he was in his duties, 'each drop of time cost him dear' and he preferred to use these limited hours in meditating on the Scriptures to complete his *Confessions*, by doing so following an overall plan whose theological coherence we saw earlier. He will therefore not speak of the 'exhortations, consolations and acts of guidance' by which God led him to preach his word and dispense his sacraments to the people.[22] Pressing time is the only reason given for the stance he has adopted in keeping silent about the years passed in the priesthood from 391, and also the years of *otium* at Thagaste after returning from Italy, and even the short year spent in Rome after Monica's death at the end of summer 387. However, Augustine's introspective gaze did not stop at his rebirth, in spring 387, by the baptism received from Ambrose's hands, an end which might have been expected both from the point of view of testimony and the confession of praise. The last of his memories which are brought out are those of the tears shed at Ostia on the tomb of his dead mother, this last human weakness before his entry into the heroic world of the *servi Dei*. And even, *in fine*, Patricius, the father who is elsewhere so little present, is linked with Monica in the appeal to prayer for 'those by whose flesh you brought me into this life, I know not how.[kk] The *Confessions* are always so much more than the mere demonstration of a theologian!

So there are several ways of reading them, and if some are more reductive than others, there are no really bad ones. But the best, or more precisely, the one that answers the author's wish, is to read them as the testimony of a man who passionately desired to place his experience at the service of 'educating in the transmission of faith'.[23] That desire to make the narrative serve protreptic ends is constantly there in the text.[24] At the beginning of Book II, reliving his black sixteenth year at Thagaste, Augustine says in parenthesis,

> I am recounting this, but to whom? Not to you, my God; but before you I recount it to my race, the human race, however small may be the number of those who happen upon this writing. And why? Obviously so that I and my possible reader may consider from what depths we must cry to you.[ll]

And when, reaching the end of his account, after the initial publication of the first nine books, he knew from the reactions of the first readers that his *Confessions*, 'when they are read and heard, move the heart and prevent it from falling into despair',[mm] and that there was a likelihood that his goal might be achieved, he went further in affirming the purpose he had set himself by writing them: 'Let my brothers' soul love that in me which you teach should be loved, and lament that which you teach should be lamented . . . let them rejoice at the sight of my good deeds, and sigh over my delinquencies.'[nn] The richest reading of the *Confessions* is without doubt a reading of 'imitation' and spiritual communion. Petrarch would read them so, keeping always within reach the copy that a friend had given him, and would say that the book had made as much impression on him as Cicero's *Hortensius* had on Augustine himself.[25]

Does this mean the exclusion from this reading of those whom Augustine, using the Psalmist's words, calls the 'strange children',[oo] in other words, those who are on the fringes of the faith to which he had adhered? At least self-excluded from a full interpretation of the *Confessions* is 'the race that are eager to know another's life, but slothful to correct their own':[pp] the label applied in the author's lifetime to a narrow fringe of malicious readers, chiefly from among the Donatist or Manichaean circles. Today it would cover a much vaster potential readership, enticed by the hoped-for singularity of an uncommon life or, worse still, by some wrongly-scented whiff of scandal; in both instances a readership who would be poorly satisfied and swiftly disappointed, and equally rejected by Augustine.[qq] But beyond those for whom Augustine wrote more especially, his future fellow-citizens in the 'City of God', the book will always find a wide audience among those who will marvel at the route accomplished by the son of Thagaste, even if, with all due respect to Augustine, in this 'adventure of reason and grace', they sometimes remain more impressed by the effort of the first than the action of the second. They will always be grateful to him for having placed the honour of being a man at its highest level in the field of the intellect.

The writing of the *Confessions*

In the abundant Augustinian iconography so admirably collected and commented upon by Jeanne and Pierre Courcelle, from the windows, miniatures and paintings of the fourteenth and fifteenth centuries to the great compositions of the eighteenth,[26] three major series can be perceived: the sometimes piously naive imagery of the conversion, the deeds of the preacher and polemicist, scourge of the Manichaeans and Donatists, and lastly, the author of the most voluminous work – and also the best preserved – bequeathed to us by Antiquity. St Augustine the writer, thus St Augustine 'writing', depicted, in medieval and postmedieval imagery, a writing instrument in his hand, in front of a table or desk. This representation is a metaphor, such as those that come to us spontaneously and often anachronistically, when we imagine him 'tossing' his ideas 'onto paper', with a ready 'pen'. And on occasion Augustine himself fell in with this metaphorical use of the writing instrument.[rr] But the metaphor is vastly distant from reality, as a few words in the 'prologue' of his *Retractations* clearly reveal: for the bishop, 'writing' (*scribere*) meant dictating.[ss]

For us, far removed from the torments once caused by nib pens, with their spluttering and scratching, and their pernicious propensity for discharging their load of ink without warning in untimely splotches, writing is no longer anything but effortlessly gliding over the smooth surfaces of paper whose quality equals its superabundance, using graphic instruments that are totally devoid of their 'sacred aura', but wonderfully practical. Or again, it is fingering the keyboard of a machine which makes second thoughts easier and visually converts the act of typing onto a screen. Because writing in itself is no longer a labour, we find it hard to imagine the sheer physical effort that writing required at the end of Antiquity. Still in use for the initial tasks – stenographic records and the longhand composition of short texts, notably for correspondence – was a base material that was heavy and not easy to handle, despite its reduced size:[27] tablets coated with a thin layer of wax on which the dry point of a stylus traced its groove. At a later stage of development, the text was put down by means of a calamus,[tt] or reed pen, dipped in ink on the less rustic, but rare and costly, material of a prepared leaf of papyrus – the *charta*, ancestor of our paper – or a piece of parchment – the *membrana* – which had the advantage, because of its thickness, of being re-usable after washing or scraping. The price of these materials, and the frequent difficulty of procuring them, which ruled out any clumsy botching, as well as the difficulty of achieving a standardized writing with only rudimentary graphic tools, was a good reason for leaving their use to professionals for the most part, scribes or secretaries – the *notarii* – or to real book craftsmen, the *librarii*. The great of that world have left the act of writing to these practitioners; their own handwritings were a rarity, pointed out as such, and the emperor Titus was regarded as a phenomenon in his time because he amused himself by rivalling the speed of his stenographers and imitating others' handwriting.[uu] A generation later, Pliny the Younger told of his own practice: one summer, in his Tuscan villa, having awoken early, in the shuttered silence and darkness of his bedroom, he mentally composed, sentence by sentence, the text he had in his mind, then called his secretary, who let in the daylight and took notes of the sentence he had worked on, this ploy being repeated as many times as necessary. During the course of the day, secretaries would thus accompany their master, with the necessary writing equipment, in his outings on foot or by carriage.[vv] It was the whim of a great lord who, by these devices, made up for a lack of inspiration, and took his tablets with him to the hunt to kill time if no boar was forthcoming.

Between Pliny the Younger, one of the richest men of his time, and Augustine, who possessed nothing of his own except his genius, there was this point in common: that the bishop of Hippo was no shorter of good secretaries than the former consul and friend of the emperor Trajan. For that he was indebted to the ecclesiastical organization which either trained its secretariat itself, or recruited it from the imperial administration. Then bishop of Uzalis, Evodius had with him the son of a priest in a neighbouring township, a good shorthand writer – *strenuus in notis* – and conscientious copyist – *scribendo bene laboriosus* – whom he had noticed when the young man was a clerk in the proconsul's offices at Carthage.[ww] The incumbent of an important diocese, residing in one of Africa's major towns where, as we shall see, the tasks of the *episcopalis audientia* were specially heavy, Augustine was permanently assisted by a little squad of secretaries, not attached to him personally but to the church of Hippo, of which they were lay staff,[xx] but some were assigned for his personal service for editorial needs which for the most part were scarcely separable from the episcopal function properly speaking. Like Caesar before him and Napoleon much later on, Augustine was certainly capable of keeping several secretaries at a time fully occupied. Once the calm of night had descended, by lamplight, the *notarii* came in relays to seize in mid-air and take down whatever was on their bishop's mind, and first the most urgent items, answers to be provided. For those men whose availability was unlimited and who undertook immense tasks, the long winter nights represented precious working-time. They had not invented the *lucubratio* – the studious vigil by the 'small light' (*lucubrum*) of a lamp – but it was at the end of Antiquity that, for the men of the Church, this working by lamplight became one of the essential components of their heroic lives and the condition *sine qua non* of the development of their works.[yy] St Jerome joked about it: having to reply to one of his opponents – named Vigilantius, one may imagine the puns! – he declared that all he needed was a single 'tiny little vigil' (*una lucubratiuncula*) in order to refute the man's 'inanities'.[28] We joke about them, too, when we speak pejoratively of 'elucubrations', without giving a thought to the great works which were born of those hours snatched from sleep, taken down from dictation by the smoky light of oil lamps.

Augustine lived like this for thirty-five years, 'working by day and waking by night', as Possidius says.[zz] At the very end of his life, after 426, when he had unloaded the heaviest of his *sarcina episcopalis* onto Eraclius, he in no way ceased to *lucubrare*; quite simply, day was added to night for carrying out his 'literary' operations! In a letter to Quodvultdeus – the deacon who succeeded Aurelius to the see of Carthage after the brief interregnum of Capreolus – who was asking him to start work on a *De haeresibus*, he replied that when he had finished with Julian of Eclanum,[ab] he would devote his days to that treatise; his nights, he added, were sufficiently occupied by his *Retractations*.[ac] But throughout his entire 'active' episcopacy, once he had dealt with the liturgical service, his obligations as ecclesiastical judge, receiving visitors, pastoral rounds and Saturday and Sunday preaching, there were few available hours left in the day. Once evening had fallen, however, long stretches of tranquillity opened up and, accompanied by his secretaries, he put them to good advantage.

If one wanted to make an anthology of texts, taken from his letters, in which he speaks of both his excessive workload and the necessity for using his nights to keep abreast of urgent tasks, there would be an overabundance of choice. For instance, the letter he wrote early in 412 to the tribune and notary Marcellinus, who had become his friend after the great confrontation between Catholics and Donatists over which he had arbitrated in the preceding spring at Carthage, and who pursued him with queries on fundamental questions:

> If I could give you an account of all my days and wakeful nights expended on other indispensable tasks, you would be much saddened and astonished at the number of matters that bother me and simply cannot be deferred, and prevent my doing what you ask of me . . . I have no lack of work to *dictate* as a priority, matters which present themselves in circumstances that brook no delay. For instance, the summary of our conference Proceedings, a pretty tedious task which I have had to carry out, because I saw that no one else wanted to read that pile of papers, and also the letter I have addressed to the Donatist laymen about this same conference, which I have just finished at a cost of several nights' toil.[ad]

In the same period there were, in addition, several long letters, one of which, addressed to Honoratus, was the size of a book.[ae] A few years later, in a letter written to Possidius in December 419, and recently rediscovered, he listed all that he had dictated in a few weeks since his return from Carthage, where he had preached all summer and up to the beginning of autumn, after taking part in the general council at the end of May. He had in particular dedicated his Saturday and Sunday nights to his sermons on John's Gospel, he said, and concluded: 'In all, since my arrival, that is to say, between 11 September and 1 December, I have dictated about six thousand lines.'[29] It was most often a matter of work to be given priority, which prevented him 'from devoting himself to dictating material which he would prefer', as he said in a letter to Marcellinus.[af]

He meant the composition of the great works which were in his head and for which only time was lacking. That is why the dictation of one of his major works, the *De Trinitate*, was done in bits and pieces, staggered over many years – about a quarter of a century, between 399–400 and 420–6.[ag] Of course, the extreme difficulty of the subject, and the keen awareness of the responsibility he was shouldering in giving expression to such a delicate theological matter would, on their own, have suggested that he should avoid any undue haste. In one of his letters to Marcellinus, dated spring 412, under pressure from his friend, but also from others such as Florentius, bishop of Hippo Diarrhytus (Bizerta), to publish his *De Trinitate* straight away – as well as his great commentary on Genesis – he gave his reasons for not rushing without due consideration,[ah] and quoted Horace's words, which pierced his heart like a warning: 'No word once uttered can ever be put back.'[30] That was literally true of this literature which was spoken before it was written; but it was precisely this method of working and the discontinuity which his duties and busy life forced him to introduce into the composition of a lengthy opus which could nearly have caused it never to see the light of day. Did Augustine know stenographic signs – *notae*? In his *De doctrina christiana*, he had spoken of their usefulness and recommended the study of them,[ai] and we know that schools existed in those times where the technique was taught.[31] But even if he had some knowledge of this coded system, the inevitable personal variations from one *notarius* to another would have made it difficult for him to 'reread' directly from the tablet. In any case, we know from Possidius what his practice was: first, reflection or meditation on the material to be dealt with, then dictation, then the work of correction – *emendatio* – on a text duly transcribed into longhand, and legible.[aj] Legible at least for the author,[32] but certainly full of errors, whatever the quality of Augustine's secretaries. In the same period, Jerome, who was scathing in his comments, came straight out with his criticisms of one of his Spanish friends' copyists, whose errors in copying Jerome's own works had made him shudder, especially when the errors were patently due to a desire to correct supposed mistakes.[33] Augustine had therefore made corrections on at least one copy of the first books of his *De Trinitate*; but because he was so busy, and anxious not to hurry anything, he had not been able to spare the time to review the whole work, proceed with revising it and eliminating the inevitable disparities or discordances in a composition that had been spread over so many years, when, around 415, he noticed that the part of the treatise that had already been edited – Books I to XI and part of Book XII – had been removed, probably (he does not pinpoint the culprits) by the clergy of Hippo who knew from his *scriptorium* about the existence of the text and had not been able to resist a desire to become acquainted with it. Very much upset – he says so in a letter to Aurelius of Carthage[ak] – he had been tempted to denounce this theft in a circular letter, to let it be known that a possible edition of the text not revised by himself was nothing to do with him, and that he might even give up continuing its development. But yielding to many entreaties, and obeying his primate's orders, he had finally decided to add to and complete his work, which he would publish a few years later.

The reader may perhaps be surprised at this long detour in reaching the writing of the *Confessions*. It was not without its uses, however, in making more understandable what an intellectual feat it must have been to 'speak' a long work in this way, keep it in one's mind as a living unity over long periods, before seeing it in black on white through two transcriptions. Soon, perhaps tomorrow, a technology in which various forms of progress elbow one another out of the way will place at our disposal voice-recognition machines which will transcribe a 'first draft' onto the screen by itself, without the need for the slightest graphic operation. Then, if some redoubtable traps such as homophony can be avoided, we might believe ourselves back in the working conditions of a St Augustine; but – although at the cost of a great loss of 'conviviality' in a world increasingly dehumanized by technology – with an ease and rapidity of use that Augustine would have found most enviable. For although his workers were totally devoted to him, they did not have the permanent availability or, above all, the passivity and objectivity of a machine. St Jerome says somewhere that it is difficult to pause and reflect faced with a secretary 'shouldering arms', his 'stylus' poised, waiting for the words to be uttered. And Augustine, who commented upon Psalm 45, without taking himself for God, must have been haunted by the Psalmist's words: '*Lingua mea calamus scribae velociter scribentis.*'[al]

The *Confessions* happily show the effects of having stemmed from that flow of words. Augustine had no need, as Flaubert would have later on, to 'process' his sentences; the words had passed his lips before being fixed in the wax of the tablets, they had been music before becoming the score. The text derives much of its charm from his native skill in self-expression, which is certainly more perceptible in the original than in any translation, however successful.[34] Let me be precise: there is oracy and oracy. Although all Augustine's texts – with the exception of short handwritten notes[35] – were dictated and thus first 'spoken', in their first draft, that of the *Confessions* stands out from the rest in that it is a discourse with God, whom one does not address with ordinary words but, if not always with ones that are his own – those from the Bible, and notably the Psalms – at least, in the invocation, praise and thanksgiving, have the ever-present sense of the distance which, like the two poles of an electric arc, simultaneously separates and unites that transcendent God and his humble creature. The result is pages of sustained lyricism – with strong dramatic intensity in the evocation of human tribulations – frequently expressed in little poems made up of a rhythmic, sometimes assonant, prose which may justifiably be presented typographically in the form of 'verses',[36] even when the translator most often fails to render their verbal music.

What the reader notices immediately in many pages of the *Confessions*, what first entices and holds him, is their power to enchant, which asserts itself from the moment of the introductory invocation.[am] Even without being a specialist in the literature of Antiquity, the reader is not slow to realize that part of the book's richness consists in the diversity of tone, and the writer's astonishing aptitude for varying his 'writing' according to the differing aspects of his work. The *Confessions* do not have a 'style', but a whole range of ways of putting things – in particular the development of sentences – depending on whether the author becomes narrator, analyst of himself or others, metaphysician or exegetist of the divine word.[37] The unifying principle in the first nine books – but also in the tenth – is this constant and very lucid introspection, always conducted under the gaze of God – oh! that *tu scis* ('Thou knowest'), which so often gives emphasis to the text – which guarantees the consistency of a work that is powerfully original and forever impossible to categorize.

It may be that the literary approaches and realizations of the *Confessions* affect us in their diversity because we have the confused feeling that they are 'modern', in the sense that Baudelaire would give the word in the mid-nineteenth century. It is not anachronistic to use it, in that Augustine was situated at the junction of two worlds, and fully aware of that situation, as many pages of the *De doctrina christiana* make evident. 'Modernity' is still the conscious expression of a departure towards a cultural elsewhere, with an impetus which gathers speed from being based on realities from which one distances oneself without completely repudiating them. Augustine's 'modernity' in the *Confessions* is not a tabula rasa. The threads of a triple heritage intertwine and unite in him: of classical culture, which still surfaces;[38] of the Bible, especially the poetic books and books of wisdom as well as the Pauline texts; and an added, more recent tradition, of the first Latin-speaking Fathers of the Church, Tertullian, Cyprian, Hilary of Poitiers and, lastly, Ambrose who, after Cicero, was his true master. All of them had begun before him to 'convert the ancient culture'. When in Book X he cries, 'Too late have I loved you, O Beauty, so ancient yet so new, too late have I loved you!' in a wonderful invocation taken up so often down the centuries and eventually turned round,[an] he was certainly not greeting the discovery of a new canon of aesthetics, regretting that he had made it so tardily; he was speaking of his too belated meeting with God. But without excessive subtlety it has been possible to show that here the inspiration of the Song of Songs, on the love of Beauty versus beauties, conceals the Neoplatonistic leanings of an Augustine still aspiring to baptism, at Cassiciacum.[39] On both the spiritual and artistic planes, his new gains were made without loss, his conversion intervening without a break, in an enriching combination of successive cultural contributions.

One final word on the *Confessions*: they remain Augustine's work for the 'general public', easily accessible to all readers, at least all those who have a liking for great human ventures.[40] And I repeat, not everyone will read them at the same level. But it is the fate of all the finest works of art – and this is equally valid for works of the intellect – to attract even where they remain a little short of the goal pursued by those who have conceived them. Certain of Raphael's or Poussin's paintings draw us to them by secondary attractions that leave the eye on the fringe of the painter's intentions, which are often hardly guessed at. The property of genius is to be able to please the majority while reserving for the few the privilege of enjoying it to its finest point.

Notes

a.   *De dono perseverantiae*, 53.
b.   Unless to take up the expression, which now seems to him 'inappropriate and mannered', of his sorrow at the loss of a childhood friend (*Conf.*, IV, 11) and to return to the definition he then gave of the 'firmament' in the divine Creation (*Conf.*, XIII, 47): cf. *Retract.*, II, 6, 2.
c.   *Retract.*, II, 6, 1.
d.   *Doctr. chr.*, III, 54. Same idea on this theme in *City of God*, X, 8.

e.   *Conf.*, VIII, 3.
f.   *Conf.*, X, 4.
g.   *Indicabo me talibus*, repeated three times in *Conf.*, X, 5–6.
h.   *Conf.*, X, 3.
i.   *Ep.*, 100, 4: *cum sis altera anima mea, immo una sit anima tua et mea.*
j.   *Ep.* 270.
k.   *Conf.*, IV, 11.
l.   *Conf.*, XI, 2.
m.   *Ep.*, 110, 5.
n.   Paulinus, in Augustine, *Ep.* 24, 4.
o.   *Ep.* 27, 6.
p.   *Ep.* 27, 5.
q.   Paulinus, in Augustine., *Ep.* 32, 2.
r.   *Ep.* 42.
s.   *Conf.*, V, 20, *in fine*. Cf. also II, 15, where a sort of portrait of the *spiritalis* Paulinus was may be seen.
t.   *Conf.*, VI, 11–16.
u.   *Retract.*, II, 6, 1.
v.   Augustine adds only *superbia*. On the sin of curiosity in Apuleius, see P. Courcelle, *Les Confessions de Saint Augustin*, pp. 101–9.
w.   *Conf.*, I, 1; in quotation marks, scriptural quotations or references: Pss. 48.1; 96.3; 145.3 and 1 Pet. 5.5.
x.   Apart from *Retract.*, II, 5, 1, see the testimony of *C. Faustum*, I, 1 and *C. litt. Pet.*, III, 20.
y.   *Conf.*, XIII, 50 and 51.
z.   In the *De beata vita*, I, 1–4, in the autumn of 386 and in 391–2 in the *De utilitate credendi*, 2, 3 and 20: see above, pp. 37 and 153.
aa.   *Conf.*, X, 2: 'What thing within me could be hidden from you even if I would not confess it it you?'
bb.   *Conf.*, X, 3; see above, p. 205.
cc.   *Enarr. in Psalm.* 55, 14: *ut alios etiam invites ad accipiendam vitam quam et tu accepisti.*
dd.   *Conf.*, X, 1.
ee.   Tacitus, *Ann.*, XV, 62: *imaginem vitae suae relinquere testatur.*
ff.   See above, p. 27.
gg.   When recalling his baptism at Milan in spring 387 and his premature death, probably at Thagaste, a few years later: cf. *Conf.*, IX, 14 and above, pp. 114 and 142.
hh.   *Conf.*, III, 21.
ii.   *Conf.*, IX, 7.
jj.   *Conf.* XI, 2.
kk.   *Conf.*, IX, 37.
ll.   *Conf.*, II, 5.
mm.   *Conf.*, X, 4.
nn.   *Conf.*, X, 5.
oo.   Ps. 144.7, cf. *Conf.*, X, 5, and *Enarr. in Ps.*, 55, 16 and 20.
pp.   *Conf.*, X, 3.
qq.   These Augustine warns in advance, saying: '(This Confession), I make not with bodily words and sounds, but with words uttered by the soul and the cries of meditation, which your ear knows' (*Conf.*, X, 2).
rr.   For example when he says, at the beginning of Book X, *in stilo meo* – the *stilus* is the style for writing on tablets – to mean 'in my book' (*Conf.*, X, 1).
ss.   *Retract.*, prol., 2, where the texts resulting from speeches jotted down are distinguished from those he has dictated: only the latter are 'written' texts.
tt.   More rarely with a brush: as for pens, they come in only at the end of Antiquity.
uu.   Suetonius, *Titus*, III, 3.
vv.   Pliny the Younger, *Letters*, IX, 36, 2–3.
ww.   *Ep.* 158, 1 (line 414); Evodius had the sadness of losing him at the age of 22, which suggests

that the young *notarius* must have started his career in the administration when he was still an adolescent.

xx. They are mentioned as such – *notarii ecclesiae* – in the *Acta ecclesiastica* recording the minutes of his succession in 426 (*Ep.* 213, 2).

yy. Pliny the Elder, a prodigious worker, went to bed early but started work just after midnight: Pliny the Younger, *Letters*, III, 5, 8.

zz. *Vita Aug.*, XXIV, 11.

ab. The last champion of Pelagianism: this is the famous *Opus imperfectum*, which Augustine's death would leave uncompleted: cf. below, p. 417.

ac. *Ep.* 224, 2.

ad. *Ep.* 139, 3. On this letter, and the whole of the exchanges between Augustine and Marcellinus, read M. Moreau, *Le 'Dossier Marcellinus' dans la Correspondance de Saint Augustin*, Paris, Ét. aug., 1973.

ae. *Ep.* 140 = *De gratia novi Testamenti*.

af. *Ep.* 139, 3.

ag. Cf. below, pp. 368–9.

ah. *Ep.* 143, 4.

ai. *Doctr. chr.*, II, 40.

aj. *Vita Aug.*, XXIV, 11: *Vel de inveniendis divinis rebus cogitaret, vel de iam inventis aliquid dictaret, aut certe ex iam dictis atque* transcriptis *aliquid emendaret.*

ak. *Ep.* 174.

al. *Enarr. in Psalm.* 44, 6: 'My tongue is the reed of a nimble scribe.'

am. *Conf.*, I, 1; cf. above, p. 209.

an. *Conf.*, X, 38. The 'reversal' was by Renan, whose route had been the opposite of Augustine's, in the famous *Prayer on the Acropolis*.

CHAPTER XXI

A monk in his monasteries

During the summer of 399, Augustine took the road back to Hippo once more, coming from Carthage where he had stayed nearly as long as he had two years earlier. At the end of April, he had taken part in the proceedings of a general council which had decided, among other things, to send a delegation to Honorius charged with obtaining from the young emperor a law guaranteeing respect for asylum in the churches.[a] This privilege already existed *de facto*, but still without official recognition, at least in the West, and was analogous to that traditionally enjoyed by the temples of pagan cults. But in fact, something new had quite recently happened in that area; after a long resistance lasting nearly a century, the days of paganism were now numbered. On 8 November 392, Theodosius had signed its death warrant, banning attendance at temples throughout the Empire and sacrifices, even within private homes.[b] Nevertheless, decreed in the East, it had not been immediately applied in Italy, and in Africa the broadly independent policies of Gildo, the all-powerful master of the militia since 386, and in open rebellion since the summer of 397, had let it go unheeded. But Gildo had succumbed a year later and, succeeding in the West his father Theodosius, who had died in 395, the young Honorius was now able to pursue his religious policy under the regency of Stilicho. On 1 January 399, Flavius Manlius Theodorus had taken office as sole consul for the West; he was the great Christian dignitary with whom Augustine had rubbed shoulders at Milan in 386, and to whom he had dedicated his *De beata vita*.[c] On 29 January, a new law was promulgated at Ravenna,[d] banning pagan cults, and a few weeks later, on 19 March, the Counts of Africa Gaudentius and Jovius, acting on the emperor's orders, dismantled temples and destroyed 'idols'.[e] Moreover, it was probably in that year, rather than some years later, that for the Easter festival – which fell on 10 April in 399 – the Catholic faithful in Carthage, headed by their bishop Aurelius, seized the temple of Juno Caelestis, the pagan patroness of the town where twenty-five years earlier the student Augustine had watched their annual festivities with curiosity.[1] It was evidently time for Epigonius and Vincentius, the two ambassador bishops, to go and demand from the emperor, on behalf of the churches of Africa, full recognition of the right of asylum which was no longer available to the temples, henceforward abolished. And we shall see that Augustine was always punctilious in the defence of this right, which was often held up to ridicule. Let it be said in passing, though I will return to it, that the political death of paganism left it socially and culturally very much alive: for Hippo's bishop a new, multi-faceted problem was beginning, a new personal involvement, which would sometimes be more than a battle of ideas.

In the spring of 399, Augustine had as usual preached on several occasions in Carthage. It is not surprising to find echoes of the imperial anti-pagan offensive in his sermons, notably in one which specifically alludes to the destruction of idols: they must first be broken in the hearts of pagans. Christians, he added, refrained from making inquiries outside the public domain in order to seek them out. 'Many pagans', he said, 'keep these abominations on their property; do we go there to smash them?'[f] In fact, the pagan property-owners in question had often taken precautions; they had put their cult statues in a safe place, sometimes adding those they had rescued from temples doomed to destruction.[g] Sixteen centuries later, Paul Gauckler, Director of Antiquities in Tunisia, had the good fortune to come across one of these deep and carefully walled-in hiding-places in Carthage itself, and to unearth from it a race of gods and goddesses, their marble figures now forming part of the Bardo Museum collections.[2]

On the return route, ascending the Medjerda valley, Augustine had halted at Bulla Regia (Hammam Darradji), where Epigonius, who had probably already returned from his mission to Italy,[3] had his episcopal chair. He was there on 1 August, and the fierce heat[4] had not prevented him from giving a sermon in honour of the Maccabees. We see him lecturing the faithful, who in his view were still too inclined to enjoy pagan spectacles,[h] which shows that in the towns of the interior, to say nothing of the countryside, paganism's cultural entrenchment was still strong. But it was not just the scorching heat that urged him to return to Hippo, where the sea breeze helped to pass the month of August. He had to finish his *Confessions*, start putting the *De Trinitate* on the stocks, and all this without prejudice to the episcopal duties which were ordinarily his daily bread.

Continentia

In this period of writing Book X of the *Confessions*, Augustine placed himself humbly and entirely under the influence of grace. The meditation in which he engaged, without any complacency, was often marked by doubt. Following his lyrical outpouring on the 'Beauty so ancient and so new', too belatedly loved, he notes:

> There is contention between my joys, for which I should sorrow, and my sorrows for which I should be joyful; and on which side victory may lie, I know not . . . My evil sorrows contend with my virtuous joys; and on which side victory may lie, I know not.[i]

And having evoked what human life is, using Job's words, he shows his wholehearted submission in terms that would soon startle Pelagius: 'All my hope lies only in the immense greatness of your mercy. Give what you command and command what you will' (*Da quod iubes et iube quod vis*).[j] In more concrete terms, the bishop who is aware of his fallibility awaits more specific help from God. 'You command our continence,' he goes on. *Continentia* in the text; the word goes far beyond the English translation in its comprehensiveness; this *continentia*, Augustine himself comments, still using a Plotinian vocabulary, 'is what binds us together and brings us to the One, from whom we have deviated by slipping into many things'; in other words, losing our way in love of creation and creatures, which distances us from God's love, the love whose exclusive demands we must accept for our salvation. 'For he loves you too little who loves anything, even together with you, that he loves not for your sake.'[k]

Augustine uses the words of 1 John 2.16 to sum up the three concupiscences against which he must still and always guard: 'Assuredly you command me to be continent against *the concupiscence of the flesh, the concupiscence of the eyes and worldly ambition.*[l] He is not equally weak in the face of these three temptations. It was a good while ago, he says, some dozen years, that he renounced all consciously pursued carnal satisfaction. But in 'the vast halls of his memory' there remain images that have been fixed there by long previous habit (*consuetudo*); weakened by his long vigils, he is assailed by these images in his sleep, he says, to the point where they bring him not only to a pitch of pleasure, but even to consenting to that pleasure in an exact replica of the act itself. These liberties taken by what would much later be called the 'unconscious' trouble him; even if he does not see them as a misdeed, he cannot come to terms with these nocturnal lapses of reason. Could not God, by some superabundance of grace, quell the lascivious movements of his slumbers, completely disengage him from 'the bird-lime of concupiscence'? Or will he have to await the hour when 'death will be swallowed up in victory'?[m]

Satisfying physical desires also means eating and drinking. Augustine learned to treat food as medicine; but satisfaction is itself a form of enjoyment, and that bothers him; the soul is only too apt to 'veil a matter of sensual delight under the pretext of concern for health'![n] He even admits to yielding occasionally to gluttony.[o] As for drink, that had never been a weakness of his fundamentally sensual nature; and we know how much he detested the 'pious' drunkards who held their sessions on the tombs. What Monica had told him of her youthful exploits as a *meribibula* had probably also served as an early warning to him. As for scents, the author of the *Confessions* says he does not care about them or seek them out, and is quite prepared to be without them, for ever if necessary. However, on this subject he notes that he is not absolutely sure of his deter-mination.[p] When it comes to sounds, his predicament is plainer; the bishop still vividly remembered the strong emotions he had experienced in Ambrose's church in Milan at the time of his conversion. Even today, he says, music by itself can enchant him, and he feels sinful for being affected by it more than by the words.[q] He is then divided: he would tend to approve of Athanasius, who had the Psalms chanted in Alexandria with such slight inflections of the voice that it was more like recitation than singing; however, while not wishing to lay down the law on this matter, all in all the emotional force of melody seems to him a benefit to religion.[r] The Donatists, he notes around the same period, criticized the Catholics for excessive soberness in their church singing.[s]

'There remain the delights of these fleshly eyes of mine.'[t] This is where Augustine finishes with 'the temptations of fleshly desire', as he says. But they are perhaps the most difficult to have done with! How to prevent what delights the eyes from ensnaring the soul as well? Augustine contrasts the inner light that guided Tobias, Isaac and Jacob with the light that floods the world, sculpts shapes, gives things their colour and emphasizes men's art, that 'corporeal light which, with its tempting and dangerous sweetness, seasons the life of the world for its blind lovers'.[u] Try as he may, he cannot 'prevent his feet from becoming entangled in these beauties'. At least he has long ago conquered vulgar curiosity; the theatre itself no longer attracts him, and if he reproaches himself for idle distractions, such as in the countryside, following with his eyes a dog chasing a hare, or, in his cell, a lizard catching flies, he tries to turn these things into praise for his Creator, who has willed and ordained them.[v]

Lastly, *ambitio saeculi*, the position one holds in this world in the eyes and minds of men. Augustine had renounced a career one August day in Milan, thirteen years before. But, like it or not, in Hippo, in Carthage, virtually everywhere in his Africa, and soon overseas as well, he has become a prominent personage, what we would call a 'star'. And just as surely as if he were a celebrated rhetor, a court poet or a high-ranking imperial official, he is admired, and subjected to the temptation of deriving joy and pride 'from being feared or loved by men'.[w] Now, in that vanity lies the gravest sin, and perhaps the most difficult to avoid. Augustine is perfectly aware of this: 'Our daily furnace is the human tongue.'[x] But how to escape it? To remove ourselves from praise, must we abandon a virtuous life and good works, which invite it? On the other hand – and he recognizes his susceptibility[y] – how is one not to fall into vainglory, which feeds on it? In this regard, more than any other, Augustine knows that to stay in *continentia* he is in need of grace: he aspires above all to that end, and it is in this domain of special vulnerability that God must 'give what he commands, command what he wills'.[z]

A monk first and foremost: the lay brothers' monastery at Hippo

Augustine would probably not have written these pages of Book X as we have just read them if, in keeping with his initial desire, he had remained a simple *servus Dei*, whether at Thagaste or at Hippo, where he went not in search of priestly fortune but the means to found a monastery. With rare foresight, writing his *De moribus ecclesiae catholicae* in Rome in 387, he ended his diptych on monks, who are out of the world, and clergy, who are exposed to it, with this lucid note:

> It is very difficult here (in the situation of clergy) to observe the way of perfect life and keep one's soul calm and tranquil. In a word, the latter (the clergy) are where they learn to live, and the others (the monks) are where life is lived.[aa]

In 391 at Hippo, accepting the priesthood had been the price he had had to pay for the foundation of the monastery. And Augustine had entered a situation that would evolve: first, 'monk-priest', he had become 'monk-bishop' as Valerius' coadjutor and then, on the latter's death, had entered the life of a 'bishop-monk'.[5] With sole responsibility for a large diocese around an important town and a big port, he could no longer continue without some adjustments to live a strictly monastic life, above all with his demanding conception of what the episcopacy entailed – limitless service and duties.[6] At the close of his life, in 425, he gave his explanation in a touching text – both assessment and testament – to which I shall have occasion to return:

> I attained the episcopacy. I saw that a bishop must constantly show himself to be full of humanity towards those who came or passed through . . . But this kind of hospitality could not be tolerated in a monastery, where it would not be fitting. That is why I wanted to have a monastery of clerics with me in the episcopal residence.[bb]

To say nothing here of the nuns' convent, whose establishment seems to have come later and whose location remains uncertain,[7] from 397 two institutions coexisted around Augustine at Hippo: the *episcopium*, the monastery of clergy, gathered in the bishop's house and its outbuildings, and the lay brothers' monastery, established at the outset in a garden, the property of the church of Hippo, which Valerius had granted to Augustine.^{cc} Did this congregation, which in 391 had succeeded the quasi-monastery of Thagaste,^{dd} have some difference in status? As at Thagaste, people lived together there on a basis of communal resolutions rather than 'vows'. Possidius, who had been one of the first members, stresses the continuity between Thagaste and Hippo in the observance of a 'rule' which rested mainly on community of possessions:

> At the very first, when he returned to the country from overseas,^{ee} he had ordered that no one in the society should possess anything of his own, that everything should be held in common and distributed to each according to his needs.

Augustine, priest and then Valerius' coadjutor, lived in this way for several years in the company, amongst others, of a few close friends who were themselves exceptional and left him one after another to accede directly to the episcopacy. Before the departure for Calama (Guelma) of Possidius himself in 397–8, and of Evodius for Uzalis in roughly the same period, Profuturus left for Cirta (Constantine), and Severus for the see of Milevis (Mila) between 395 and 397. Possidius put at around ten the number of these bishops who, like Augustine, remained monks, and had emerged from Hippo's *monasterium* as if from a seminary.^{ff}

When he left this community because of the new constraints of being a titular bishop, Augustine may have wished – as some maintain – 'to compensate for his own physical absence by the presence of his Rule in the first monastery at Hippo'.[8] And with certain margins of uncertainty, chiefly relating to dates, the origins of this Rule have been reconstructed. There is agreement in thinking that its first outlines were probably due to Alypius who, himself bishop-monk at Thagaste in 395, and taking his inspiration from a few principles he had acquired during a visit to Jerome at Bethlehem not long before, had drawn up an *Ordo monasterii*, in whose style his own stamp is noticeable.[9] Passed on to Augustine and approved by him, the text was adopted and applied at Thagaste, while at the same time or shortly afterwards the bishop of Hippo, following his friend's example, put into writing an oral teaching he had begun to give some years earlier to the lay brothers of his monastery. This is the *Praeceptum*, which Alypius in his turn would come to know, have copied and combine with the *Ordo monasterii* to turn into a first *Codex regularum*: the first nucleus of the 'rule of St Augustine' which, initially through Paulinus of Nola, would spread in Italy and then through all the Christian West.[10]

Paulinus of Nola was behind the original circulation of the Rule. Conversely, as we have been able to show, he had first contributed to setting the spiritual climate of the first Augustinian congregation, referring in one of his letters to Augustine, in 395–6, to the spirit that moved the one he himself had instituted in Campania with Therasia.[11] Of the founding text provided by Acts 4.32–5, he cited verse 32a in particular: in the multitude of believers there 'was but one heart and one soul'.^{gg} In the *Praeceptum* – and the recognition that he had received it is as good as a chronological indicator – we find this passage 32a, which comes at the front, just after the introductory sentence, to establish the monastery's charter spiritually: 'The first point – which is the reason you are assembled here – is to live in unanimity to the house, and to have within you a single soul and a single heart reaching out to God.'[hh] At once the fundamental obligation to have 'everything in common', reaffirmed, takes on another sense:

> Call nothing your 'own property', but let all things be common to you, to each of you your superior will give board and lodging, not equally for all because you are not all equal in health, but rather to each according to his needs. Indeed, you read in the Acts of the Apostles[ii] that they had all things in common and that each received according to his needs.

Not inappropriately, the term 'spiritual communism' has been ventured to describe the cenobitic lifestyle conceived and put into effect by Augustine.[12] In that sort of communism, the thing that benefited everyone without limitations and without consideration of individual needs was the community of heart and soul.

Augustine's fundamental and indestructible personal love for the monastic life did not prevent him from clearsightedly evaluating its demands, which were sometimes incompatible with the personal weaknesses of some novices or the constraints exerted by their surroundings. One instance was that of Laetus, who had created a problem in the very first years of the lay brothers' monastery.[13] He seems to have had a sincere vocation; but he had left the monastery to settle family matters and the letter addressed to him by his superior in reply to the one – not preserved – which in his helpless confusion he had written to the brothers in his community, clearly shows that if the young novice had sacrificed the attractions of the perfect life to the protection of material interests, it was because he was under his mother's thumb. With a remarkable 'spiritual bluntness', Augustine explained that, above and beyond voluntary privation, to live in a community it was necessary to agree to a more radical, emotional, relinquishment, carrying renunciation to the point of severing family ties. To begin, he quoted Luke 14.26: 'If anyone comes to me and hates not his father, mother, wife, children, brothers and sisters, and even his own soul, he cannot be my disciple.'[jj] And he added this comment:

> All one's own belongings are in fact hindrances which prevent one from obtaining, not possessions that pass away with time, but communal possessions that last for eternity. Because a woman is your mother, that does not make her my mother. These are things which are temporal and pass, as you can see that the fact that she conceived you, carried you in her womb, gave birth to you and fed you with her milk already belongs in the past. But a sister in Christ, this she is for you and me and all those who are promised the one celestial heritage, and God for a father and Christ for a brother, in the same company of love . . . You can observe this very easily in your mother's case. Indeed how does it come about that she twists you round her little finger now that she has got you in her net,[kk] and having slowed down your impetus she is deflecting you and leading you astray, unless it is because she is your own mother? For inasmuch as she is the sister of all those for whom God is father and the Church their mother, she is no hindrance to you, or me or all our brothers who hold her, not in private affection, as you do in your home, but in public affection in God's house . . . What I have just said about your mother must be understood in regard to all kinship of this kind. Let each

man question himself regarding his soul, to hate in it a private feeling which without a doubt is worldly, and to love in it that communion and society of which it is said: 'They had but one soul and one heart outstretched to God' (Acts 4.32a). So, indeed, is your soul not your own; it is also that of all your brothers, whose souls are yours, or rather, whose souls combined with yours are no longer souls, but one single soul, the one soul of Christ . . .[14]

We do not know how Laetus interpreted these lines, or what became of him; but, rereading them, one cannot help thinking back to the relationship Augustine had with his mother, a *mater propria* if ever there was one. But Monica was not Laetus' mother; even before her death at Ostia, some ten years earlier, had left only her essence, a sublimated image, she had known how to accompany her son on his path, while she still lived strip off the outer layer of corporeal mother to become a sister in Jesus Christ for her son and, as he wrote at the end of Book IX of the *Confessions*, 'a fellow-citizen in Jerusalem the eternal'.[ll] The memory of Monica's last months of earthly life permeates this objurgation to Laetus.

Augustine's monks sometimes caused him even graver disappointments, most often due to their instability or ruthless ambition. The latter seems to have been behind the desertion of two brothers who, at the time I am speaking of, had left the Hippo monastery to seek their fortunes in the clergy at Carthage. Rather hastily, and without taking the time to find out about them, Aurelius had ordained one of them, named Donatus; but feeling some scruples, he had written to Hippo before making a decision on the second. Regretfully, Augustine had taken formal note of Donatus' ordination, suggesting to his primate both clearly and discreetly that he should not repeat his error with the second brother.[mm] Without lecturing Aurelius, he put forward his arguments about the error: it was doing a grave injustice to the clergy, he said, to admit deserters from monasteries, therefore bad monks, whereas it was customary to admit only the best of them to holy orders. And was there not a risk that ordinary folk would say, 'Bad monk, good priest!' rather as they said, 'Bad flautist, good conductor!'? We must suppose that his protest was heard, as the general council of 13 September 401 took a decision banning this practice.[nn] But, like many others, this canon was made to be overturned, and Augustine learned of it again, to his cost, some time later when, after a fairly brief spell in his monastery, another of his monks, one Donantius, managed to get himself ordained deacon by the primate of Numidia, who at that time was Xanthippus of Thagura. Being informed of the situation, the latter sent Donantius back to Hippo and Augustine, no longer knowing what to do with him, made him the doorkeeper of St Theogenes'; but he was not even worthy of this modest enough post and the priests in charge of the chapel sent him away.[oo] Eventually, many years later, Donantius managed to get himself put forward as deacon by the faithful in his little native town, not far from Thagaste, which was answerable to a new episcopal department created by Augustine at Thiava, on the southern borders of his own diocese. The bishop of Hippo wrote to his colleague Honoratus, putting him on his guard against the dubious character of this Donantius, who had claimed his unwilling attention for some fifteen years![15]

Augustine was anything but naive and had no illusions about human nature. He knew full well that there were false monks, as there were false priests and false believers.[pp] It was in the monasteries that the finest souls were to be found, and the best spiritual successes, but there also were the hardest downfalls.[qq] They matched expectations. Pascal would say, 'He who wants to play the angel is playing the beast.' The bishop of Hippo was particularly mistrustful of those whom St Benedict would later call 'gyrovagues', those individuals who 'in the outer trappings of monks wander through the provinces, sent nowhere, appointed nowhere, staying nowhere, domiciled nowhere, peddling phylacteries and dubious relics, living by begging'.[rr] He knew from experience that the difference between them and the circumcellions, if it existed, was only that they were slightly less harmful. And, deploring the wrong they did to the *congregati* by the fact of their common denomination of *monachi*, he lumped together all the *vagantes*, to whichever Church they belonged.[ss] Some of these vagabonds of God were marked out by their long hair, which they let grow 'for fear that a shaven holiness had less effect than a hirsute holiness';[tt] they harked back to the tradition of the Old Testament patriarchs, Samuel and Samson, and when they claimed to explain their reluctance to do any kind of work by the Gospel phrase of 'the fowls of the air, which sow not neither do they reap' (Matt. 6.26), Augustine made fun of these black birds who put barbers out of work for fear of being plucked and no longer able to fly!

On the cusp of the fourth and fifth centuries, these wandering monks who were resistant to any kind of occupation apparently teemed in Africa as they did in the East, where they attracted the sarcasm of St Jerome.[uu] And in the monasteries themselves, there were far too many who expected to live on nothing but the offerings they considered to be owed to their piety. This situation decided Aurelius to ask Augustine to write something on the subject, and in 400–401 this appeared as the little book entitled *The Work of Monks*. The bishop of Hippo based it on the Pauline precept: 'If any would not work, neither should he eat' (2 Thes. 3.10); but in a remarkable sociological approach to recruitment to monasteries, he took account of social differences and economic realities. There was no question of forcing into a manual labour exceeding their strength – and not compatible with their condition and upbringing – nobles who had brought sometimes considerable wealth to the community where they would finish their lives; other tasks could usefully be assigned to them.[vv] But the monks who came from the elite of contemporary society – big landowners, senators, high-ranking dignitaries of the Empire – were in a very small minority. Augustine noted that the mass of the *servi Dei* were of very modest origins, sometimes even slaves: freedmen or slaves to whom their masters granted freedom so that they could enter the monastery. The largest numbers had come from the humble peasantry,[ww] or from the ranks of lowly craftsmen from the towns. The latter were used to physical labour; they had no grounds for withdrawing from it or finding it an obstacle to meditation and prayer.

A monk despite all: the monastery of the clergy

Once he had become a bishop, as we have seen, Augustine had had to give up living a truly monastic, cloistered or at the very least withdrawn, existence.[xx] But he was not a man to renounce his ideal of community life; the alternative solution consisted in throwing open the 'episcopal palace' to all the clergy of Hippo, whom he forbade to have separate premises. The *monasterium clericorum* was born, certainly a 'first' in the Africa of that time.[16] That implied for married clergy – there could well have been some among the older men, as the rules about celibacy were then fairly recent[17] – an obligation to be physically separated from their wives, with whom they lived chastely in any case. They were also, and chiefly, obliged to surrender all their possessions, to the benefit of the church of Hippo or another church, or in favour of their own families if the situation demanded it, to have bed and board with their bishop, and be fed and clothed at the community's expense.[yy]

Possidius, the master's occasional table companion after his episcopal ordination at Calama, and a witness of this daily life at least until 397, has left us a picture drawn after Augustine's death in simple words which it is best to quote.

> His table was frugal and modest; sometimes meat was added to the fresh or dried vegetables;[18] but there was always wine, for he knew and taught that, as the Apostle says, 'all that God has created is good, and no food is to be prohibited if it is received with thanksgiving: for it is sanctified by the word of God and prayer' (1 Tim. 4.4)[zz] . . . As for wine, we know the Apostle's words when writing to Timothy: 'Drink no longer only water, but use a little wine for thy stomach's sake and thine often infirmities' (1 Tim. 5.23).

Possidius adds further on that the consumption of wine was regulated, with a number of cups strictly allocated for each person, and the rule stipulated that every swearword which inadvertently slipped out was to be punished by the loss of a glassful. They probably had to be very careful not to let rip, for in the bishop's entourage these human soft touches were a rarity. He continues his description of those communal meals:

> At his table, only the spoons were silver; receptacles were of terracotta, wood or marble, not out of poverty but by a voluntary rule. But Augustine was always hospitable.[19] At his table he preferred reading and discussion to eating and drinking, and against the scourge that is so widespread among men, he had had written up in the refectory:

> > *Whoever enjoys attacking the life of those who are absent*
> > *by his scandalmongering*
> > *Let him know that his own life is not worthy of this table.*[20]

> He thus warned all his guests that they must refrain from extreme and spiteful stories. One day when a few of his circle, colleagues in the episcopacy, had forgotten the inscription and were contravening it in their speech, with a depth of feeling he reproved them harshly, to the point of telling them that he could do nothing more than have the lines obliterated or get up from the table and withdraw to his room. I was a witness to the scene since I, with others, took part in this meal.[ab]

Naturally, we would like to know more, leave the dining room with Possidius and visit the rest of the *episcopium*. He would not let us into the bishop's chamber, or the clerics' cells, and being more concerned with establishing Augustine's moral image than detailing his physical appearance, he contents himself by underlining the honest simplicity of his attire and bed:

Regarding his clothing, footwear and bed, he remained within the bounds of moderation and suitability, without excessive elegance or an affectation of carelessness: for usually, in this respect, when men display too much concern for outer appearance, or conversely show negligence, in both instances 'they are seeking their own interest, not that of Jesus Christ' (Phil. 2.21). But he kept to the happy medium, 'turning neither to right nor left' (Num. 20.17).[ac]

There is nothing to be gleaned from Augustine himself to illuminate or clarify this edifying text. What he says about his garments in texts that date from his last years confirm Possidius' comments, for example, when he declines to accept a *byrrhus* – a hooded winter cloak – because it is too costly (fine for a bishop, he adds, but not when that bishop is called Augustine!), or to receive in a private capacity the gift of a linen tunic; but he would wear it like any other brother to whom it could just as well be given.[ad] And in the same spirit he thanks Palatinus, a faithful follower who had offered him a whole batch of cilices, those goat-hair shirts which could be used without distinction by all members of the Hippo community.[ae]

As we have seen, the renunciation of all personal belongings and the sharing of a communal life, in a freely accepted privation, were the material basis of the clerics' monastery as they were of the lay brothers' congregation. They were also its spiritual foundation: 'Whoever wishes to live with me will possess God,'[af] said Augustine. In relation to the whole of the Catholic community in Hippo, loyalty to this commitment was also the fundamental article of a moral charter. Overburdened in any case by his pastoral and civic responsibilities, Augustine was reluctant to have anything to do with the management of accounts. Possidius says that, for the administration of the Church's possessions, he trusted the most capable clerics, to whom he delegated the work. No one ever saw him, keys in hand or the seal ring on his finger;[ag] which means that he never dreamt of personally checking whether the members of his clergy had completely liquidated their assets when they entered holy orders.

At the close of 425, when Augustine had just turned seventy-one, an unpleasant truth came to light. The bishop happened to notice that, unbeknown to him, one of his priests had kept control of his personal assets. This came as a great shock. Januarius (the name of the priest) was looking after a small fortune for and on behalf of his daughter, who was still a minor, living in a nearby convent, until the time when she could make use of it. At a pinch, it was admissible, but approaching death had made him change his arrangements and, as if he regarded the money as his own, he had just willed it to the church of Hippo. This placed the old bishop in an impossible situation. First, by acting in this way Januarius had openly mocked the rule of poverty; then, by disinheriting his daughter to the benefit of the Church, he was causing that Church to have the dubious reputation of getting rich by questionable procedures.

Augustine's reaction was on a par with the scandal that was looming. On 18 December 425, from the pulpit, before a large assembly comprising, as well as his clergy and the *seniores*, a large section of Hippo's Christian community, he dealt with the matter in all its details and made his decisions known. Of course, he refused to accept this inheritance.[ah] And he made his practice clear: yes, he did accept legacies; for instance, he had accepted that of Julianus, because he had died childless; but he had refused that of Bonifatius, a big shipowner, first because Bonifatius had disinherited his son, but also for reasons of ecclesiastical 'deontology', because in this case acceptance would have transformed 'the Church of Christ into a marine transport company', with profits but also the risks inherent in that kind of enterprise, which the community could not shoulder in the event of setbacks. And he reminded his listeners that there were no reserves, everything being given to the poor.[21] Then he came to the basic question which, in his view, was presented by Januarius' attitude. It was a matter of knowing whether the vow of poverty should be an absolute rule for the members of the *episcopium*, or whether it might include adjustments. For himself Augustine did not want that. But whatever it might cost him, because thirty years earlier he had conceived the idea of the episcopal monastery in question, it seemed to him better to re-examine the decision he had taken than to pretend to keep to it; he wanted no hypocrites about him.[ai] He therefore accepted that, in future, one could remain a cleric in his church while still maintaining free use of one's possessions and the availability of a private residence. But there was no question of leaving this option open indefinitely. Augustine gave his clergy a few days' grace in which to choose between simple membership of the clergy and the communal 'perfect life'. It was nearly Christmas; the date fixed for each member to make his own decision was Epiphany.

At the beginning of January 426, the people were gathered for Epiphany in Hippo's cathedral. Soon after entering the pulpit, Augustine asked the congregation for their special attention, and had the deacon Lazarus read the founding text, the ideal outlined in Acts 4.31–5. And when, after the reading, the deacon handed the book to his bishop, Augustine himself reread the verses, adding, 'You have just heard our ideal: pray to God to make us capable of attaining it.'[aj] Then he announced the good news: 'Here is a great cause for joy; I find that all my brother clergy who live with me, priests, deacons and sub-deacons, including my nephew Patricius, are as I would want them to be.'[ak] They had all renewed their vows of poverty and commitment to the communal life that the bishop had hoped to hear them solemnly confirm. There followed a long report which he considered indispensable, taking as his witnesses the whole of a community who he knew were sometimes critical, setting out the arrangements which everyone was obliged to observe in order to fall completely in line. Augustine began with the deacons, the traditional managers of ecclesiastical possessions. Valens still had some assets in joint ownership with his brother, himself a sub-deacon of Severus at Milevis; once the succession was settled, he would free his slaves and give his lands to the Church. Patricius, the nephew, who had just lost his mother, was in the process of dividing the inheritance with his brother and sisters; he would give up his share, which would come to the church at Hippo. Faustinus, a former soldier, rightly and duly gave up half his possessions to the benefit of his brothers and made a gift of the rest to the church in his native township. The deacon Severus, who was blind, still had a few plots of land in his own area; he would give them to his local church, which was poor. As for Eraclius, said Augustine, he was a model cleric, whose foundations were well known: at his own expense, he had had the chapel of St Stephen built at Hippo; he had just presented to the Church the small house he had had built beside the cathedral, which had originally been intended for his mother, and he was making arrangements forthwith to free his slaves who were living in the monastery.[al] Of the sub-deacons, Augustine continued, there was little to be said; they were all poor. That left the priests. Augustine was swift to dispel any malicious talk about them, starting with Leporius, who had made a gift of all his possessions even before entering the clergy. They were indebted to him, he added, for the construction, thanks to the gifts of the faithful, of the basilica of the Eight Martyrs and a hostel (*xenodochium*); he had bought a house, counting on using its materials for the achievement of the basilica,[22] but as he had not needed them, the house was now rented to the benefit of the Church; and, driving the nail home, Augustine added, 'It is incorrect to say, as you do, "towards the priest's house" or "in front of or behind the priest's house", for it does not belong to him.'[am] As for Barnabas, it is wrong to say that he bought a house and land from a certain Eleusinus; he accepted it as a gift and himself presented it to the monastery which was built there; and the running of that monastery, which he has carried out for a year, has brought him only debts.[an] In short, Barnabas was irreproachable.

Augustine had no illusions. He finished this long account of mandates by predicting that it would probably not put an end to the lies and stories; but he promised to return to it if the need arose. Meanwhile, he forcefully reaffirmed an episcopal authority which complete absence of personal compromise had left intact: any failing in that reaffirmed vow would bring irrevocable expulsion. He concluded:

> If there should be one of my clerics keeping a personal possession in order to bequeath it, I will strike his name from the list of members of my clergy. He can appeal against me before a thousand councils, go wherever he pleases to lay complaints against me,[23] with the Lord's help he will never again be a cleric where I am bishop.[ao]

All the same, that memorable Epiphany of 426 had the twilight tones of the end of a reign. Some months later, in September 426, repeating the process from which he himself had 'benefited' thirty years before – but avoiding the error committed by Valerius by elevating him to the episcopacy while he (Valerius) was still alive – Augustine had Eraclius acclaimed, the perfect deacon who had meanwhile become a priest, on whose shoulders he would place a share of his tasks, and whom he would appoint to succeed him when he died.[ap]

Notes

a.   *Concilia Africae*, CCL 149, pp. 193–4.
b.   *C. Th.*, XVI, 10, 12.
c.   Above, p. 104.
d.   *C. Th.*, XVI, 10, 15.
e.   *City of God*, XVIII, 54.
f.   *Sermon* 62, 17.
g.   These buryings are mentioned in one of the new recently-published sermons, datable to shortly after 400: *Sermon Dolbeau* 4 (*Mainz* 9), 8, in F. Dolbeau, *Vingt-six Sermons au peuple d'Afrique*, p. 519, 1. 207.

h.   *Sermon Denis* 17, 7.

i.   *Conf.*, X, 39.

j.   *Conf.*, X, 40. The word was prefigured in the initial prayer of the *Soliloquies* (I, 5): Iube *quaeso, atque impera quiquid vis, sed sana et aperi aures meas, quibus voces tuas audiam.*

k.   *Conf.*, X, 40.

l.   *Conf.*, X, 41.

m.   *Conf.*, X, 42, *in fine* (1 Cor. 15.54).

n.   *Conf.*, X, 44: *ut obtentu salutis obumbret negotium voluptatis.*

o.   *Conf.*, X, 45. Differentiating between *ebrietas*, he uses the word *crapula*, which here means over-repletion, regarding eating rather than drinking.

p.   *Conf.*, X, 48.

q.   *Conf.*, X, 49.

r.   *Conf.*, X, 50.

s.   *Ep.* 55, 34.

t.   *Conf.*, X, 51.

u.   *Conf.*, X, 52.

v.   *Conf.*, X, 57.

w.   *Conf.*, X, 59.

x.   *Conf.*, X, 60: *Cotidiana fornax nostra est humana lingua.*

y.   *Conf.*, X, 61, *initio.*

z.   *Conf.*, X, 60.

aa.   *De mor. eccl. cathol.*, I, 69.

bb.   *Sermon* 355, 2.

cc.   Above, p. 152.

dd.   Above, p. 131.

ee.   *Vita Aug.*, V, 1.

ff.   *Vita Aug.*, XI, 3.

gg.   Paulinus of Nola, in Augustine, *Ep.* 30, 3.

hh.   *Praeceptum*, 2, ed. L. Verheijen, *La Règle de saint Augustin*, I, Paris, Ét. Aug., 1967, p. 417.

ii.   Acts 4.35.

jj.   *Ep.* 243, 2. Let me add, however, for the reader who is less familiar with these texts, that in Luke 14.26, 'hate' (*odisse*, in Latin) is a bad, but unfortunately traditional, translation of a Hebrew term meaning 'to detach' or 'distance oneself'.

kk.   *Ep.* 243, 4.

ll.   *Conf.*, IX, 37, *in fine.*

mm.   *Ep.* 60, 2.

nn.   *Concilia Africae, CCL*, 149, p. 204.

oo.   *Ep.* 26*, 1, *BA*, 46 B, p. 390.

pp.   Cf. *Enarr. in Ps.* 132, 4, 1.

qq.   Cf. *Ep.* 78, 9.

rr.   *De opere monachorum*, 36.

ss.   *Enarr. in Ps.* 132, 3, 10.

tt.   *De opere monach.*, 39.

uu.   Jerome, *Ep.* 22, 28.

vv.   *De opere monach.*, 33

ww.   *Ex vita rusticana: De opere monach.*, 25: we must believe Augustine, although we know how difficult it was for most of them to escape the hereditary obligations of a rural condition.

xx.   Cf. above, pp. 224–5.

yy.   *Vita Aug.*, XXV, 1.

zz.   *Vita Aug.*, XXII, 2.

ab.   *Vita Aug.*, XXII, 7.

ac.   *Vita Aug.*, XXII, 1.

ad.   *Sermon* 356, 13. He would, however, make an exception for the tunic which the nun Sapida had made for her brother Timothy, deacon at Carthage, who died before being able to wear it; he accepted this personal gift, and sent Sapida an exquisitely delicate letter: *Ep.* 263.

ae. *Ep.* 218, 4.
af. *Sermon* 355, 6.
ag. *Vita Aug.,* XXIV, 1.
ah. *Sermon* 355, 3.
ai. *Sermon* 355, 6.
aj. *Sermon* 356, 1–2.
ak. *Sermon* 356, 3: *tales inveni quales desideravi.*
al. *Sermon* 356, 7.
am. *Sermon* 356, 10.
an. *Sermon* 356, 15. Like the passage relating to Leporius, the development concerning
     Barnabas is taken up again in the *Proceedings* of the council of Carthage of 5 and 6 February
     525: *Concilia Africae, CCL,* 149, pp. 280–1.
ao. *Sermon* 356, 14.
ap. *Ep.* 213, 5.

CHAPTER XXII

A bishop in his churches, at Hippo

Sermon 356 is a moving and invaluable text on more than one count, but especially because, only a few years from his death, it is an appraisal of the buildings or alterations achieved or desired by the bishop throughout his episcopacy. Augustine's building activities while he was bishop are known to us only from his indications, and in any event they were fairly modest and can easily be summed up in chronological order.

Augustine's acquisitions during his priesthood

We already know that, prior to his episcopacy, his first initiative was the foundation of the lay brothers' monastery, necessarily followed by the construction of buildings, on a plot of land – a 'garden' – granted by bishop Valerius. Let me quote the words with which, at the end of 425, Augustine recalled his predecessor's gesture of thirty-five years earlier: 'Having learnt of my project and desire, the old Valerius, of holy memory, gave me a garden in which the monastery stands at present.'[a] And Possidius adds a topographical hint that is far from negligible, despite its ambiguity: *Monasterium* intra ecclesiam *mox instituit.*[b] Obviously, Possidius did not mean that the monastery had been established 'in the church'; his *intra ecclesiam* means that the 'garden' donated by Valerius was not only an ecclesiastical domain, which goes without saying, but more exactly a property very probably situated within the perimeter enclosing the basilica and its annexes.[1] Of course, no 'record', if one ever existed as such, of the numbers in this monastery has come down to us; but we may suppose that he was able to gather many people about him, at least in certain periods. For, apart from the monks properly speaking, he would take in the homeless poor, like the little Antoninus, the future unlucky bishop of Fussala, who lived there for several years with his stepfather,[2] while his mother, who had been separated from her lover, was taken into a hospice for the poor – *matricula pauperum* – another foundation that a new recently-published letter of Augustine has made known,[c] adding its material reality, which one would like to locate on the plot, to that of the lay brothers' monastery.

The number in the clergy's monastery is easy to assess in real terms, at least for a given period: in 425–6, it gathered some fifteen people around Augustine, priests, deacons, subdeacons and lectors; a modest band, who individually took up little space, and could have been housed without too much difficulty in the annexes to the bishop's house. As for the nuns' convent, the date of its foundation is unknown to us, but the bishop's own sister was its superior for a time,[d] and it was certainly physically separate from the other congregations; we are not even sure that it was at Hippo. At some date, between 411 and Augustine's death in 430,[3] this convent was shaken by a rebellion of the nuns against their superior,

Felicitas, who had succeeded Augustine's sister, a revolt that was apparently due to the then novelty of the arrival of a male superior, called Rusticus. The bishop responded to this small insurrection with a sharp reprimand, the famous *obiurgatio*, as a preamble to the detailed statement – *informatio* – of the nuns' own rules, which form one of the components of the *Regula Augustini*.[4]

We saw earlier that Augustine attributed the building of a *memoria* – or 'chapel' – to St Stephen to his future successor to the see of Hippo, Eraclius, who at that time was still a deacon. Surprisingly, hardly had the body of the protomartyr been 'discovered' near Jerusalem, in 415, when his relics reached North Africa, to be immediately circulated – one might almost say 'diluted' – arousing everywhere an even greater fervour than in the East. They had reached the shores of the present-day Maghreb, at first in the East, and around 420 Evodius had housed them in a *memoria* at Uzalis, not far from Utica, which had swiftly become an active centre of pilgrimage and the scene of many miracles, thus immediately receiving a double publicity.[5] In Hippo's Numidia itself, we find an astonishing dissemination of the protomartyr's relics: at Calama, with Possidius, where they worked wonders; at Aquae Thibilitanae (Hammam Meskoutine), Castellum Sinitense and several rural churches in the dependency of the diocese of Hippo, which had their chapel dedicated to St Stephen or, failing that, at least a reliquary.[e] Hippo also had to have its *memoria*, to house a few remains of the venerated saint: 'a little dust', the bishop would say, 'to gather many people.'[f] This was one of Eraclius' good works, when he had it built at his expense and apparently dedicated it early in the summer of 425.[6] It was still new when, on Easter Day 426, Paulus, a pilgrim from Caesarea in Cappadocia, who had come there after visiting several other sanctuaries in vain, was cured of his illness – uncontrollable trembling – as was his sister Palladia, two days later, on 13 April 426.[7]

We must pause a moment over the exact circumstances of these two miraculous cures, as Augustine related them, for they are not without some topographical information. The brother and sister had arrived at Hippo about a fortnight before Easter; they went to the church every day 'and were especially assiduous in attending the chapel of the most glorious Stephen':[g] Augustine's words set out plainly an inner view of the *memoria* in comparison with the *ecclesia*, which makes one wonder if it is metaphorical or really spatial. The continuation may help us. On Easter Sunday morning, 'the young man', says Augustine, 'was at prayer, clinging to the balustrade of the holy place where the martyr's relic lies';[h] he suddenly collapsed to the ground, as if asleep, but no longer shaking – then got to his feet unaided, cured. In the church, there were immediate cries of joy and songs of thanksgiving. People rushed, says Augustine, 'to the place where I was sitting, just as I was preparing to go and see',[i] meaning where he was liturgically to celebrate the Easter service, in his episcopal chair, in the raised apse of the cathedral-church – for he could not celebrate the Easter office elsewhere – the *basilica Pacis*, also known as the *basilica maior*, as we shall soon see.[8] Even before he had had time to rise from his chair to go and see what had happened in the chapel, the young man who had received the miracle came up to him, fell at his knees and stood up again to receive the bishop's kiss. Then they both took a few steps towards the congregation, whom the bishop greeted, amidst acclamations. When silence was restored, the customary scriptural texts for the

Easter festival were read; afterwards, Augustine, who had returned to his chair, would say only a few words: the facts spoke for themselves.[j]

The account of the miraculous happening that took place for Palladia the next day but one confirms in detail the topographical hints contained in the first one. On Easter Sunday, Augustine had kept Paulus at his table and made him tell his story, which was duly recorded by the bishop's secretaries. On the Monday, he had spoken very briefly,[k] to announce to the faithful that the next day, Tuesday, the *libellus* would be read out, containing the account given by Paulus both of his preceding tribulations and his miraculous cure.[9] While Augustine was reading it, on the Tuesday morning, brother and sister stood together on the steps of the apse so that they could be clearly seen, the young man upright and still, the unfortunate young woman still shaken by her spasms of trembling. Once the reading was over, the two young people had left the apse and the bishop had begun to speak of their story, when he was interrupted in mid-flow by shouts.[l] After descending the steps of the apse, Palladia had gone to pray at the *memoria* of St Stephen; scarcely had she touched the balustrade when, like her brother, she had fallen in a state of catalepsy before, like him, picking herself up again, cured. Relating the facts in the *City of God* shortly after they had taken place, Augustine says that, having heard the cries arising from St Stephen's chapel, he had seen the faithful returning to the basilica with the young woman, coming from the martyr's *memoria*.[m] That compels a redefinition of the spatial relationship of chapel and basilica: St Stephen's *memoria* was not, strictly speaking, situated within the church, as a note preceding this chapter of the *City of God* suggested; but it was contiguous, adjacent, with easy and rapid means of communication with the basilica proper, one of whose aisles it overlooked. This must be borne in mind when trying to compare the textual data with those of archaeology on the site.

Eraclius had seen to the building of St Stephen's chapel, at his own expense. The priest Leporius, although born into a wealthy family, could not do the same because he had stripped himself of all his possessions when he entered the clergy. So, on his bishop's orders, he had taken on fund-raising in order to fulfil his building projects. First, to construct a hostel – *xenodochium* – perhaps made necessary by the influx of pilgrims to St Stephen's *memoria*. This hostel had just been completed in early January 426.[n] With the money collected for the requirements of this enterprise, he had bought a house – in the place known as Carraria, probably a suburb of Hippo – counting on re-using the materials for another building ordered by the bishop, the basilica of the Eight Martyrs; but this re-use had not been necessary. The basilica, too, was brand new in the early days of 426; we have the building before our eyes, said Augustine.[o] Perhaps this basilica was the enlarged rebuilding of a more modest chapel; in a sermon dated around 410, delivered on a 10 December for the anniversary of St Eulalia, the Spanish martyr, Augustine celebrated their worship, associating them with the Twenty Martyrs, together with Crispina of Theveste (Tebessa) and Cyprian of Carthage.[p] And one may suppose that the building of the *xenodochium* had been made necessary not only by the arrival of St Stephen's relics, but also by the increase in local martyrological cults, following a process that was to be found at that time almost everywhere in North Africa.[10] These cults, like that of St Salsa at Tipasa, exerted a huge attraction, feeding the flow of pilgrimages which went far beyond local or strictly North African circuits.[11]

If one takes into account the long duration of his episcopacy – nearly thirty-five years – Augustine's building achievements seem modest and it is noticeable that, apart from the lay monastery, which was an initial necessity, Augustinian developments date to the end of his priesthood. But he had received quite a fine monumental heritage from Valerius and, from 405 at the earliest to 412 at the latest, the basilica of the Donatists and possible annexes had been added.

The church of Hippo's property heritage on Augustine's arrival

When Augustine became a priest at Hippo in 391, the Catholic community there comprised two principal churches, which were urban.[q] Without a doubt the 'basilica of Peace', to which I shall return, had this status, and so, very probably, did the Leontian basilica, which was the older of the two.

In May 395, it was in the *basilica Leontiana* that Augustine had undergone the crucial hours which had been decisive for his life in the clergy. It may be recalled that at that point he had found himself on a knife edge, ready 'to shake the dust off his garments' and leave, faced with the obstinacy of the faithful who did not want to give up their customary orgies on the occasion of the feast of St Leontius.[r] The church from which his determination and charisma had then removed such practices had been erected in honour of the bishop who had given it his name, but there was no certainty that this eponym signified the consecration of a martyr who remains poorly attested.[12] Subsequently, Augustine preached there on several occasions in different periods,[s] and on 24 September 427, he welcomed Aurelius there, who had come in his capacity of primate of Africa to preside over a general council.[13] It is therefore certain that, without being the cathedral-church, the Leontian basilica continued to be used throughout Augustine's episcopacy. From the relevant texts few details emerge of a kind to make us 'see' the edifice and locate it in the city. We know that it was spacious, but only from a sentence that is more rhetorical than deliberately descriptive,[t] and a few words from Augustine enable us to state that access to its apse was by climbing a few steps,[u] but that difference in level from the nave was a commonplace arrangement. And with regard to its situation in the relative topography, we have very little to go on; nothing could enable us to say, as has sometimes been suggested, that it was near the bishop's house;[14] on the other hand, it is quite true that it was close enough to the church which, at the end of the fourth century was still in the hands of the Donatists, for the noisy drunkenness of the rival sect's followers to be heard from within its walls.[v] But the limits of such considerations are soon evident, since we know absolutely nothing of the Donatist basilica's location.[w]

A further word on the Leontian basilica, in connection with one of Augustine's letters which gives a perfect verbal picture of the enclosing and interpenetration of public and private, Church and private possessions, which characterize Hippo's ecclesiastical topography and of which the map record of the excavations in the 'Christian quarter' gives us a similar graphic image. At the end of 408 or beginning of 409, the bishop took advantage of the presence in Hippo of its intendant to send a letter to Italica, a Roman noblewoman and rich landowner in Africa. The keen alarm felt at that time in the Eternal City[x] failed to prevent the lady Italica from placing her good offices – and perhaps her financial aid as well – at the service of a transaction which was then current between the bishop and a young man of senatorial rank, named Julianus. He owned a house in Hippo which the bishop said was 'adjacent to his walls',[y] in other words, to the walls of the cathedral-church. Augustine certainly had his eye on this house; but it seems that he was not in a position to obtain it from its owner – or rather, his legal representatives – except by making an exchange. The bishop says a little further on,

> For the house we can offer (in exchange), they do not want; and the one they want, we cannot give them. Indeed, it was not left to the Church by my predecessor, as they have wrongly heard, but forms a private enclave in his former estate and adjoins one of our two churches, the old one, just as the house in question adjoins the other church.[z]

This impasse would not be resolved until the end of the bishop's life if, as is generally agreed, Julianus is to be identified with a man of the same name of whom Augustine would say, late in 425, that he had accepted his legacy – the famous house? – because he had left no descendants.[aa] So we may recognize the Leontian basilica in this *antiqua ecclesia* onto which the private house abutted that could obviously not be a fair exchange for the acquisition of Julianus' house. And for its part, no less obviously, this coveted house belonging to Julianus juxtaposed the main church, the *nova* compared with the *antiqua*, in other words, the *basilica Pacis*.

The basilica of Peace had been the scene of two events which, separated by thirty years, had been the setting for the whole of Augustine's priestly life. In September 393, it was in the *secretarium* of the basilica of Peace that, very exceptionally for a priest speaking before bishops gathered in a council, he had delivered his dogmatic exposition, *De fide et symbolo*.[bb] And on 26 September 426, it was in the church itself, in the presence of all his clergy and two neighbouring bishops, Martinianus and Religianus, that the bishop, returning from Milevis where he had settled the succession of his beloved Severus, would have his priest Eraclius acclaimed as his future successor[cc] by all the assembled faithful. Meanwhile, in December 404, he had debated for two days in this same church with the Manichaean Felix,[dd] finally confounding him. The fairly rare mention – only three occurrences – of this official (and enigmatic[15]) name, 'basilica of Peace', must not conceal the fact that, even more than the 'old' church – the Leontian – the 'new' church was the principal place of worship for Hippo's Catholic community. It evidently covers the frequently attested and apparently more popular designation of 'Major basilica,'[16] and was the town's cathedral-church. Augustine, who preached there so many times and was so familiar with its premises, did not bother to leave us a precise description. He says somewhere[ee] that its length was double its width, but if one wants to use as argument a comparison with the monument found in the excavations, one must remember that this virtually 2:1 ratio between length and breadth was fairly commonplace in the palaeo-Christian churches of North Africa. We also know, from the account of the miraculous cures of Paulus and Palladia, that access to the apse was by way of several steps.[ff] Moreover, the introductory sentence of the final prayer observed in a number of sermons, known quite certainly to have been delivered in the basilica of Peace, or Major basilica, could well give a valuable hint as to the building's orientation. The words *conversi ad dominum* ('turned towards the

Lord') give these texts rather an abrupt close, for want of a transcription by the copyists of the short prayer that followed.[gg] 'Turned towards the Lord', that is, turned towards the east. But should this injunction be taken literally? Did it really involve a movement of the body? It has often been thought that this movement was entirely spiritual, the congregation being associated in thought with the celebrant who, in fact, speaking from an apse on an east-west line, was facing the altar and, beyond, the church's facade, therefore east.[17] The final passage of a new, recently-published sermon by Augustine puts an end to these waverings. Just before the invitation to the last prayer, before the departure of the catechumens, the bishop addresses the entire congregation, playing on the dual sense of the word 'conversion'. It is not only a matter, he says, of looking towards the east, when a moment before one was facing west; that is an easy matter. But the movement must be made within oneself: 'You turn your body from one cardinal point to the other; turn your heart and your love towards another love.'[hh] So we have confirmation of the reality of a physical 'conversion' of 180 degrees, and at the same time the 'orientation' – that is, the east-facing situation – of the church's facade where the faithful heard this exhortation at the end of the sermon. This was the case of the basilica of Peace, or *basilica maior*, and we must bear it in mind when comparing the textual data with those of the actual terrain.

In addition to this urban cultic heritage were several burial chapels, situated outside the walls. We have already noticed St Theogenes', where the bishop had found a job as doorkeeper for one of his former monks, who was unreliable and a bad lot.[ii] Bishop of Hippo in the mid third century, Theogenes, like Cyprian himself, had succumbed to Valerian's persecutions.[18] His *memoria* does not figure very largely in Augustine's preaching, and his cult does not appear to have been very popular. Much better attested in the texts is the chapel of the Twenty Martyrs. The vaguer the history and personality of these martyrs remain, the more their *memoria* seems to have been the object of an assiduous worship, as Augustine himself says;[jj] notably, in the *City of God*, he reports that it was the scene of a miracle, in an account which suggests that this chapel, where the bishop preached many times, must have been situated not far from the shore.

Archaeological facts

Let me say it straight away: even more than at Carthage, where it is already difficult to match up the two parallel series of documentation – the texts and the monuments – relating to the town in Christian times, which are both abundant, at Hippo there are immense difficulties in linking the data from the ground, which are sparser, with almost a plethora of textual testimonies. For the bishop's works, from which all these clues have emerged, have survived in plenty, whereas the city's survival was accompanied by its deterioration during the few centuries it lasted: actually, it suffered a long drawn out death. Even if the vestiges of Hippo Regius were completely exhumed – for the ancient town in its entirety is far from being brought to light – it would be harder to interpret them in the full coherence of the urban fabric they would reveal than those of other comparable sites, Timgad or Djemila, for instance. These were towns abandoned after their violent and sudden death, protected by the shroud of their own ruins, and when they were excavated their monumental ornamentation appeared to be largely preserved, the network of streets intact, with houses that had kept not only the shell of their structures but also, in many instances, the original mosaic decoration which an often flourishing Late Antiquity had added as a final touch. Everywhere archaeology proves that there is nothing more disastrous for towns than a slow demise.

That is what happened at Hippo where, after Augustine's death and the fall of the town, which the Vandals seized in 431, human habitation continued for centuries; certainly in good conditions for the few years during which the victorious Barbarian king Genseric made it his capital, before installing himself at Carthage in 439. But only tombs remain of the Hippo during the century of Vandal presence, and the arrival of Belisarius at the head of the Byzantine army does not seem to have halted an inexorable decline, although the town remained a bishopric, at least nominally. Still later, the town which had stayed outside the lines of Arab penetration, at the beginning of the eighth century, did not have to suffer the invasion battles, and it seems that the Christian community of Hippo survived the Moslem conquest, as happened in several centres of Ifriqiya, and even at Bougie, up to the early eleventh century. But it existed under the surface, and on the fringes of a history which touched the town only when Buna al-Hadita ('New Bône'), was moved farther northwards, to the site of present-day Annaba; but not without its founders carrying off everything remaining in the dying town that could still be used in the new buildings. Threadbare, probably already half-covered by the floods of its two rivers, the old town had had its day.

In the Hippo excavations, many alterations and patchings-up tell of those five centuries of vegetative life; especially in the 'Christian quarter', where the walls have partly disappeared,[kk] and the floors are pitted with clumsily fashioned burial places. In all fairness and to restore the full dimensions of a complex archaeological reality, I must add that the difficulties in interpreting these meagre vestiges are not all due to 'post-Augustine' damage and deterioration. Unlike what happened elsewhere – for example, at Tipasa or Djemila, to keep to the same region of the ancient world – where the main church found its place on available ground on the fringe of an urban centre that was too built-up to house it, at Hippo the basilica discovered thanks to Erwan Marec's excavations was after a fashion inserted among pre-existing buildings in an 'island' shaped like an irregular polygon, and here also in a peripheral area, not far from the seashore. Analysis of the structures brought to light has revealed that at a date which must have been after the Peace of the Church (312)[19] the Christian community must have acquired on this 'island', if they did not already own it, a house with a porticoed courtyard at its centre, whose surface area represented the front half of the future basilica; annexes extended it north and eastward and notably, in the latter direction, a group of rooms where the complex of the baptistery would be installed.[20] On the site of the razed house – though they kept its mosaics, which were re-used to decorate the new edifice, and added others, not without some clumsy joins[21] – a triple-naved basilica was built, on a north-west/south-east axis – (the apse to the north-west, in the heart of the island) – imposed by the neighbouring buildings.[ll] In this way the architects obtained a structure which, with its 37 metres' length (excluding the apse) against 18.50 metres' width,[mm] belongs to the category of large basilicas, without in any way being able to rival the vaster churches in this region of the Christian world.[22] But archaeologists are unanimous in noting the somewhat 'do-it-yourself' aspect of the construction, the modesty, not to say poverty, of the decoration and even the unfinished impression it leaves. When H.-I. Marrou visited the site he recalled the beginning of a sermon preached in Carthage on the theme of Psalm 26.8: 'Lord, I have loved the beauty of thy house.' In the church where he was speaking, Augustine had only to raise his eyes to admire 'the splendour of the marble and gilded panelling',[nn] but he warned his listeners to seek rather the beauty of God's house among his faithful and his saints. At Hippo, in this triple-naved basilica Christians ran no risk of being led astray by such empty glamour.

But was that basilica with its three naves the town's cathedral-church, the 'basilica of Peace', or 'Major basilica'? Careful analysis of the chronological indications enables us to say that the building was constructed and laid out around the middle of the fourth century, and as its lifespan went well beyond the date of Hippo's capture by the Vandals (431), it was therefore in use throughout the whole of Augustine's episcopacy. It by no means follows that it was his cathedral-church during those thirty-odd years: to be exact, one can say only that this building belonged to the Catholic community from the moment – at the beginning of 412, at the latest – when the churches that had been in the hands of the Donatists were passed over to them. There was nothing in the typology of these buildings or their liturgical arrangements to differentiate between one basilica and another. Judging by internal criteria alone, it cannot be ruled out that the church with three naves was built by the schismatic community during the fair number of years in the second half of the fourth century when the religious policies of the emperors and their representatives in Africa allowed a relative freedom of action.[oo] Well then, Donatist basilica – transferred to the Catholics after 412 – or Catholic cathedral-church? To make a decision, it is not enough to observe that the religious building in question is in an enclosed situation matching the terms used by Augustine in his *Letter* 99 to describe the environment of the two Catholic basilicas: the conditions of the developing town could very well have led the sect to modify its places of worship with the same constraints. Nor can one plead the existence of the baptistery to conclude its identification with the Catholic cathedral-church: the Donatists, who also baptized – and re-baptized, as the Catholics complained so often! – of necessity had their own baptistery. There is plainly a very narrow margin for forming an opinion. More than the building's 2:1 ratio of length to width mentioned by Augustine when speaking of his church in one of his texts,[pp] there is one element which might tip the scales: the axis of the triple-naved basilica, with its facade to the east – or more precisely, east-south-east – thus with an orientation, in the strict sense, that obliged the congregation, at the moment of exhortation to prayer which rounded off the sermon (*conversi ad dominum*), to make a half-turn so that they, like their bishop, were facing east.[qq] Without closing my eyes to its flimsiness,[rr] I will keep to this theory, which therefore places me, with the traces unearthed by E. Marec, in the presence of the 'basilica of Peace'.

If the reader is willing to accept it, in my company, he will reap the consequences, for now we have to try to pin down the connection with this 'basilica of Peace', located on the ground and mapped (Fig. 1), of the various premises which the texts examined earlier relate to it, explicitly (St Stephen's chapel, house of Julianus) or implicitly (the communal house of the bishop and

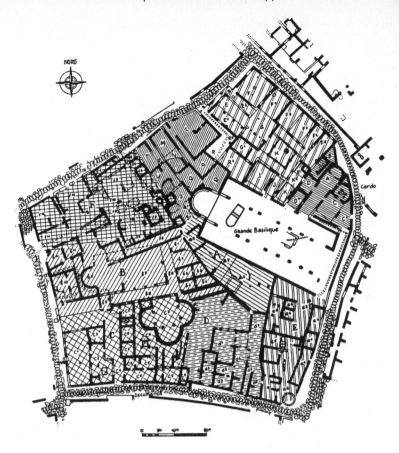

Fig. 1 – The 'Christian Quarter' of Hippo. Taken by E. Stawski from the vestiges unearthed by E. Marec. (*Monuments chrétiens d'Hippone*, fig. 1).

his clergy, or 'monastery of the clerics'). E. Marec thought that the *memoria sancti Stephani* should be sited in the small three-lobed building – marked c7 on Fig. 1 – which opens on to a double portico, in the western annexes.[23] Even more than improbable, for typological reasons,[24] it is impossible if one takes into account the very precise spatial data in the account of the miraculous cure of Paulus and Palladia.[ss] From this we gather that St Stephen's *memoria* communicated directly with the basilica and was not far from its apse: a little chapel opening onto the right side-wall of the church could have housed the venerated relics.[tt] The 'house of Julianus' raises another problem: the excavator would have to recognize it among the ensemble of buildings, including a small porticoed courtyard, flanking the basilica to the north.[25] Augustine did not gain possession of this dwelling until around 425; it could not, therefore, have been the *domus episcopi* prior to that date, a use for which it seems so well adapted, judging only by the plan. And a careful scrutiny of the plan persuades me, with H.-I. Marrou, that this ensemble of rooms communicated from the outset with the right side-aisle of

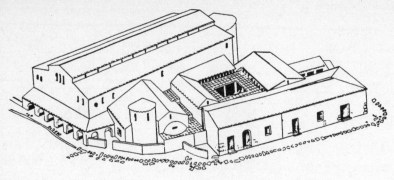

Fig. 2 – The great basilica and its north-east annexes, viewed from the east. In the foreground, the baptistery. A suggested axonometric reconstruction by R. Naz (*Monuments chrétiens d'Hippone*, fig. 19).

the triple-naved basilica, and could very well have housed the bishop and his clergy at the beginning of Augustine's episcopacy.[26] So the label *domus Iuliani* would have to be applied to another block of dwellings: why not the complex of rooms which seems to communicate with the basilica, which abuts onto them on the south?[27] Many queries, as we see, and few certainties. One thing, however, is for sure: contrary to my belief, if it is not the basilica of Peace, attested as early as 393, if the worst comes to the worst, as in all the cultic ensembles in Hippo from 412 onwards, Augustine must have officiated and preached in this triple-naved basilica, which became the religious edifice of Catholic worship; his feet trod the mosaics and he spent long hours there with his people.

The most inventive – and here the most fervent – archaeology cannot restore more than men have left. In the apse of the triple-naved basilica, the *synthronos* or semi-circular masonry bench edging the back wall has a gap in the middle, leaving a gaping space for the episcopal chair.[uu] All we can do, in front of this negative, is dream of the blissful impression that must have been produced in the hearts of this black-robed man's flock; when he was seated there, he talked to them about themselves, the world and God as no one had ever before spoken in this Latin-tongued West.

Notes

a. *Sermon* 355, 2. If there were any need, this formulation proves that this monastery still coexisted at the time with the monastery of the clerics.
b. *Vita Aug.*, V, 1.
c. *Ep.* 20*, 2, p. 294, lines 27–8.
d. *Vita Aug.*, XXVI, 1.
e. *City of God*, XXII, 8, 11–17.
f. Cf. *Sermon* 317, 1: *Exiguus pulvis tantum populum congregavit: cinis latet, beneficia patent.*
g. *City of God*, XXII, 8, 22: *Ecclesiam quotidie et* in ea *memoriam gloriosissimi Stephani frequentabant.*

h.   *City of God*, XXII, 8, 22: *cum . . . loci sancti cancellos ubi* martyrium *erat idem iuvenis orans teneret.*

i.   *City of God*, XXII, 8, 22: *Inde ad me curritur, ubi sedebam iam processurus.*

j.   These would be the few lines of *Sermon* 320 in which Augustine apologizes for his tiredness; remember, he was over seventy.

k.   This is the very short *Sermon* 321.

l.   *Sermon 323, 4: Et, cum haec diceret Augustinus, populus de memoria sancti Stephani clamare coepit.*

m.   *City of God*, XXII, 8, 22: *Ingressi sunt cum illa in basilicam in qua eramus, adducentes eam sanam de martyris loco.*

n.   *Sermon 356, 10: Habebat xenodochium aedificandum, quod modo videtis aedificatum.*

o.   *Sermon 356, 10: Opus ante oculos habemus;* which does not necessarily mean that there was a view over this basilica of the Eight Martyrs from the cathedral-church.

p.   *Sermon Morin* 2.

q.   They are thus distinct from the cemetery basilicas, which I will refer to later.

r.   Above, p. 158.

t.   *Ep. 29, 6: totum tam magnae basilicae spatium.*

u.   *Ep. 29, 8: namque ante horam qua* exedram ascenderemus *ingressi sunt . . .*

v.   *Ep.* 29, 11: cf. above, p. 158.

w.   Unless, of course, we identify it with the basilica discovered by E. Marec. I shall return to this.

x.   Alaric had brought the seige to Rome and the Senate had to pay him to depart, at immense cost.

y.   *Ep. 99, 1: de domo clarissimi et egregii iuvenis Iuliani, quae nostris adhaeret parietibus.*

z.   *Ep.* 99, 3.

aa. *Sermon* 355, 4; cf. above, p. 231.

bb. Above, p. 160.

cc. *Ep.* 213, 1, *initio.*

dd. *Contra Felicem*, II, 1, *initio.*

ee. *Tract. in Epist. Ioh.*, IV, 9.

ff. Cf. above, p. 237.

gg. It is sometimes kept, however; for instance in *sermon* 34.

hh. *Sermon Dolbeau* 19 *(Mainz* 51), 12, in F. Dolbeau, *Vingt-six Sermons au peuple d'Afrique,* p. 164; text commentated, pp. 171–5.

ii. Donantius: above, p. 227.

jj. *City of God*, XXII, 8, 10: *Ad viginti martyres quorum memoria est apud nos celeberrima;* there follows the story of the miracle which helped the poor tailor, Florentius.

kk. Notably this is the case of the facade wall of the triple-naved basilica.

ll. However, there is a slight difference of angle in relation to the initial house, as is still shown by a curiously preserved front wall in the south-east corner: cf. Fig. 1, p. 243.

mm. Or a 2:1 ratio, let me emphasize (cf. above, pp. 239–40).

nn. *Sermon* 15, 1.

oo. Cf. above, pp. 168–9.

pp. Above, pp 239–40.

qq. Above, p. 240.

rr. It is not certain that the *Sermon Dolbeau* 19 is anterior to the period – 412 at the latest – when all these places of worship became strictly catholic.

ss. Above, pp. 236–7.

tt. I would put it in the $D1$ premises adjoining the baptistery complex and opening on to the right side-aisle: Fig. 1.

uu. It was doubtless made of marble, and its material was the reason for its disappearance.

CHAPTER XXIII

A bishop in his diocese

When Augustine became Valerius' 'coadjutor' in 395, was he aware that he would soon inherit one of the largest dioceses, if not *the* largest, in the African Church at that time? Yes, without a doubt, for being a citizen of the city whose territory began at the southern limit of Hippo's he was well placed to know its size. And he could not have been unaware of what we historians have finally learnt, that the domain assigned to a bishop most frequently corresponded in area with the civil frontiers of its episcopal city and sometimes even exceeded them. He therefore knew that his duties would be all the heavier.

In the spring of 411, Carthage was invaded by hundreds of bishops, evenly divided between Catholics and Donatists, who had come from all the regions of North Africa to attend the great conference which, as we shall see, was intended to settle the dispute between the two Churches. Despite this influx, not all were present, and if the number of chairs which were vacant at that time are added to the number of absentees, we arrive at the impressive total for the whole of the African provinces of some six hundred bishops at the beginning of the fifth century.[1] The great personal diversity of the incumbents was matched by the no less great disparity between the bishoprics: a disparity in the true numbers of faithful, who were numerous in the large towns like Carthage, Cirta or Setif, but sometimes reduced to small flocks, even, in extreme cases, to one single 'sheep' facing the bishop![2] A disparity, too, in the status of these episcopal districts, which in their own way reflected the varied political, economic and social history of these vast territories. There was a big contrast between extreme west and extreme east, between the Mauretanias and Carthage's hinterland in the broadest sense, the 'little Mesopotamia' which developed south-westward from the mother-city, between the Medjerda and the Wadi Miliana, where small and medium-sized towns followed on from one another often at five kilometre intervals. There, urban density was such that several dozens of these towns were never episcopal sees, the bishoprics of the region sometimes grouping together the populations and territories of two or three towns.[3] This density was hardly less on the coastal fringe of Byzacena, the present-day Tunisian Sahel. Conversely, with the double exception of central Numidia, where the episcopal institution had profited by the urban development created by former military colonization, and the high plains around Setif, where it had the benefit of their agricultural richness, the bishoprics, often rural or semi-rural, seem to have been scattered, on the one hand, in the interior of Byzacena (now the Tunisian steppe), and on the other, and chiefly, in the vast stretches of Caesarean Mauretania (the Algiers and Oran regions).[4] It was in these regions, and notably along the entire coastal frontage of present-day Algeria, that the dioceses with the largest areas were situated.

A wealthy but over-large diocese

Hippo's bishopric was part of the episcopal districts which were largely open to the Mediterranean coast, with a fine, deep hinterland, bounded on the south-west, towards Calama (Guelma), by the Numidian Alps, and to the south and south-east, in the direction of Thubursicu Numidarum (Khamissa) and Thagaste (Souk-Ahras), by the heights where the source and upper reaches of the Medjerda lie. Its contours can be mapped out a little more exactly by studying the documents which pinpoint, to the west, south-west and east, the boundaries of Hippo Regius' civil territory and thus determine from those points the corresponding bishopric's minimum coverage. To the west, this *ager publicus* had its frontier marked by a boundary stone situated some thirty kilometres from Hippo as the crow flies (point 1 on Fig. 3). Past this boundary, one entered the

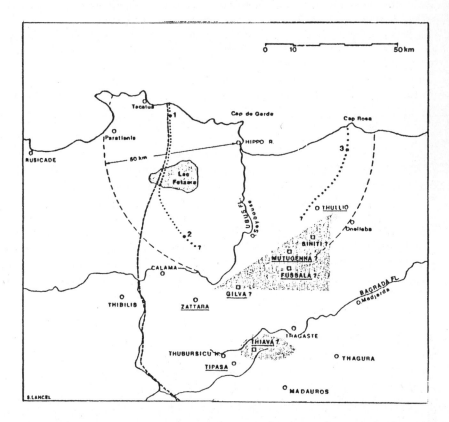

Fig. 3 'Hippo's Numidia', the hinterland of Augustine's episcopal see. The dotted line shows the probable extent of the diocese, marked out by boundary stones (points 1, 2 and 3), confining the *ager publicus* of Hippo Regius. Sites marked by circles have been identified and are accurately located; squares denote hypothetical localities. The names of bishoprics are in capitals, and these are underscored where the localities were not yet bishoprics at the end of the IVth century. The shaded areas (around *Fussala* and *Thiava*) indicate margins of uncertainty for the suggested sitings. (Plan by S. Lancel)

territory of the former Cirtian Confederation, of which Rusicade, the nearest town, on the coast, was a colony; and crossing that boundary meant also leaving the province of Proconsular Africa and entering the province of Numidia.[a] To the south-west, two epigraphic documents enable us approximately to situate the boundary separating Hippo's territory from that of Calama (point 2 on Fig. 3). Lastly, to the east, some forty kilometres from Hippo as the crow flies, a boundary-marker has enabled us to fix a point of the frontier which separated Hippo's municipal territory from that of Thabraca (Tabarka) (point 3 on Fig. 3).[5] On that side, the line that can be traced from Cap Rosa southward must have passed west of the territory of Thullio (Kef Beni Feredj), described by Augustine[b] as a *municipium* (thus as a self-governing community with full rights). So the civil boundaries of Hippo Regius can be put on a map – shaded on Fig. 3 – with a fairly good probability eastward as well as westward, but leaving the outline of the southern part blank, on either side of the middle course of the Seybouse.

There are a few immediately usable data on the situation of the ecclesiastical boundaries in relation to these civil frontiers. For instance, the context of Augustine's passage regarding the *municipium* of Thullio clearly establishes that at the date of the text (around 420) the bishop of Hippo had a priest in that town, which was not yet an episcopal see.[c] In Augustine's lifetime, and probably throughout the fifth century, the bishopric of Hippo went beyond the boundaries of the civil territory. On the other hand, to the south-west, there is nothing to suggest that the ecclesiastical boundaries were not superimposed on the civil frontiers at the confines of Hippo's territory and that of Calama. It is very obvious from the map that the small basin of the upper reach of the Seybouse, on an east–west line, which forms the territory of the latter town, is demarcated to the north by the watershed of the Numidian Alps. As there was no other episcopal district between Possidius' bishopric and Augustine's, this natural frontier must have been an ecclesiastical as well as a civil boundary. To the west, we saw above that the frontier between Proconsular Africa and Numidia, which coincides in part of its outline with the civil limit of Hippo's territory, can be represented graphically with a relatively satisfactory approximation; but from the ecclesiastical viewpoint, we are still in the province of Numidia on either side of this line, and there is nothing *a priori* to prevent the bishopric of Hippo from extending beyond it to the west. The nearest known bishopric on this side is that of Rusicade (Skikda, ex-Philippeville): the ancient localities of the peninsula of Takouch (ex-Herbillon) which can be sited precisely, like Tacatua and Paratianis (Fig. 3), are not shown on any episcopal list; the strongest likelihood is that they were answerable to the see of Rusicade. Our greatest uncertainties are towards the south, in the two great lines that opened on to the heartland of Numidia, by Thagaste (Souk-Ahras) and Thubursicu Numidarum (Khamissa). Our documents suggest that this mountainous region was a problem from a pastoral point of view, as we shall see, and here the situation appears more unsettled, even in Augustine's lifetime, with new bishoprics being created in order to give a better response to the difficulties that arose there.

With the exception of the succession of escarpments immediately to the west of the town, stretching from Cap de Garde into the turbulent peninsula of Herbillon, the main part of the diocese thus marked out occupied the alluvial plains created by the deposits from two very active rivers, the Wadi el-Kebir to the west and the Seybouse to the east. Mostly in these fertile basins lay the domains (*villae, fundi, possessiones*), numbering around twenty, which are mentioned in the various Augustinian texts that throw a little light on the real contents of this bishopric, and on a rural landscape which has left no epigraphic traces and therefore nearly always manages to avoid identification on the ground. For the social body of cultivators (*coloni*), governed by a big landowner (*dominus* or *domina*) or a farmer (*conductor*), did not form a political body likely to have some form of public expression preserved for us by inscriptions which would reveal the names and denominations of these places; which is why the possibility of pinpointing and transposing these large rural estates onto a map is very rare. For this reason, setting aside Hippo Regius (Annaba, ex-Bone), Hippo's great plain, on either side of the course of the Wadi Seybouse and, to the south, the foothills of the Numidian Alps, appear as a blank on the map (Fig. 3). But this blank must not be interpreted as empty space; it is simply that archaeological traces, which have remained anonymous and also less dense and less obvious than in an urban context, have for the most part slipped through a net of prospection that was formerly too slack and little suited to its purpose.

We shall have occasion to see further on that during his pastoral visits to the farthest corners of this vast diocese, Augustine was sometimes liable to perilous encounters with the lay auxiliaries of the Donatist clergy, the circumcellions, who were recruited from the fringes of the agricultural proletariat. There were probably a good many rural spots where the population included followers of both sides without, however, possessing a single place of worship, like the *villa Titiana*, a modest estate near Thubursicu Numidarum, where in 395 Augustine had suggested to his colleague Fortunius to hold a conference.[d] But many of these farming centres did have their church, or at the least a chapel,[e] where deacons and priests officiated. Augustine did more than just keep an eye on the rural clergy, who must not be left to their own devices, the more so because members often proved to be unreliable or unmanageable. On the first count, in 401–2 the bishop of Hippo had to settle the complicated affair of Timotheus, who had not long been sub-deacon of the place known as Subsana – which we cannot locate – after being lector successively in four communities: Subsana itself, then three other places in Hippo's diocese. After that, he had gone to Milevis (Mila), to Severus, to be taken on in his diocese; but Severus had prudently sent Timotheus back to Subsana.[f] The affair had set a precedent for, soon afterwards, the general council which met at Milevis on 27 August 402 had issued a ban for the future on anyone who had been a lector – even if only once – in a church from being able to be retained for the clergy in another church.[6]

Unreliability or indiscipline, it was all one. Augustine was mistrustful of those countryside clerics, the 'rustic and illiterate troop',[g] as he called them in a letter of 420. In his correspondence we see a procession of many sub-deacons, deacons or priests, exercising their ministry in rural areas, and whose conduct attracts the bishop's attention. For instance, the aptly-named Rusticianus, whose priest had decided to excommunicate him because of his bad habits. To cap it all, Rusticianus had run up debts, and to escape both his creditors and ecclesiastical authority had taken refuge with the Donatist bishop of Hippo, Macrobius, begging him for a new baptism.[h] That took place in 410, in a period, shortly prior to the decisive conference at Carthage, when the Donatists, encouraged by a recent liberal measure, were openly acting quite freely. But these practices of desertion by rural clerics caught transgressing went back a long way. In the earliest days of his episcopacy, Augustine had been faced with this kind of situation:[7] in 395, when still 'coadjutor', he had had to deal with the case of Primus, another sub-deacon in office in a domain – the *ecclesia Spaniensis*[i] – who had a taste for nuns; he had had to expel him from the ranks of the Catholic clergy. Primus went over to the other side, taking with him two nuns who worked in the same estate, and all three joined a group of circumcellions, in whose company they indulged in every sort of excess.[j] Not all these delinquent clerics went over to the rival Church, however. Abundantius, for example, was quite a bad lot; priest of a rural 'parish' – the *fundus Strabonianensis* – in the diocese of Hippo, he had begun by embezzling some money, to the detriment of one of his faithful flock, then he had aggravated his crime by lunching and dining, on Christmas Eve 401, with a loose woman with whom he had spent the night. Augustine had suspended him *a divinis*, subject to an appeal before an ecclesiastical court, and had written to the primate of Numidia to notify him that he could not risk leaving in the care of such a priest a community that was particularly exposed, 'amid the baying of the mad dogs'[k] of Donatism.

From these texts, to which can be added those of the new, recently discovered letters, we see that the moral matters which kept the bishop of Hippo busy occurred in the rural contexts of his diocese. Not that we should necessarily conclude that country areas had the monopoly; it was simply that there they were made easier and were more prominent. Although nuns were often the victims, not only clergy were involved; at the *saltus Hispaniensis*, an intendant (a *procurator*, and Augustine would say that he should be 'degraded' as a cleric would be in the same circumstances) assaulted a nun who had come from another villa to spin some wool.[l] Elsewhere, one midsummer night, another nun and a priest were out on a terrace, the protagonists in a prettily portrayed 'nocturne' from which not even the providential storm was lacking (saving the virtue of both); and Augustine notes on this occasion that clerics must avoid roaming alone in the countryside when doing their rounds, so as to escape temptation.[m]

The inevitable division of the diocese of Hippo

In 395, Augustine had assumed the duties of the diocese of Hippo with the energy and drive of his early forties intact. Ten years later, without having become *senex*, he was already physically less capable. In the same period Donatist pressure, which was strong in nearly all his diocese, had been further strengthened, reaching a 'peak' in the years 404–5, which called for appropriate responses on an increased number of fronts. At the same time, the bishop of Hippo was more and more in demand outside his see, whether to preach – notably at Carthage – or to put in an appearance in various places, especially conciliar meetings.[8] A pretty rapid appraisal of the different elements of this situation led Augustine, with the blessing of Numidia's provincial primateship, to re-balance his diocese by the promotion to bishoprics of small rural centres situated in the most distant and least accessible sectors of its south and south-east confines.

Of the ten or so episcopal sees shown on the map (Fig. 3) at the south and south-east boundaries of the diocese of Hippo, half were not yet bishoprics at the end of the fourth century. Unfortunately, their locations are not all precisely fixed, and a graphic representation has some uncertainties. However, the site of one of them is well known: the municipium of Zattara (Kef ben-Zioune) not far south-east of Calama. It did not lie on one of the more frequented routes, those used by Augustine as he went about Numidia, and this may well explain why it does not figure in the Augustinian documents that have reached us. Nevertheless, the silence of the texts remains astonishing; for Zattara was an episcopal see by the date of the conference in Carthage in 411, where its bishop had his seat, and the bishopric is well attested subsequently, in both the Vandal and the Byzantine eras. It may thus seem surprising that the bishop of Zattara never appears among the interested parties or participants in litigation or debates, on the occasion of which we see Augustine accompanied by his closest colleagues, geographically speaking: Alypius of Thagaste (especially at the debates – in 395 – with the Donatist, Fortunius of Thubursicu Numidarum, then in 402, at the time of the thorny affair of the legacy of Honoratus, priest of Thiava), and Samsucius of Turres, Augustine's usual 'consultant' in the years 395–407;[n] Possidius of Calama and Xanthippus of Thagura (Taoura), primate of Numidia from 401; and opposite him, on the Donatist side, Fortunius of Thubursicu Numidarum and Crispinus of Calama. The silence on the bishop of Zattara with regard to affairs that often concerned the region at whose centre the locality lay, and in files which take their chronological place between the end of the fourth century and earliest years of the fifth, may be explained by a belated episcopal creation. At the Carthage conference in June 411, the incumbent of the see of Zattara, Licentius, had no Donatist competitor; he was in 105th position on the Catholic list, therefore probably with a seniority of seven or eight years, which would put his ordination around 403 or 404.[9] One might theorize that Licentius had been the first bishop of Zattara, and the creation of a bishopric in that mountainous area south-east of Calama – which could not have been done without the agreement of Possidius – would thus have been one of the first realizations of new episcopal divisions which would spread in this region as the years passed, most often to reinforce the pastoral presence in districts far from Hippo, which were difficult of access and canvassed by the schismatic Church, into the bargain.

One of these new creations, the *ecclesia Mutugennensis*, was a little prior to the Carthage conference. While still a priest, in 394 or 395, Augustine had reacted without delay to the news of the rebaptism of a Catholic deacon in office in a rural community of the diocese of Hippo, the *villa Mutugenna*.[o] Responsible for this rebaptism was a bishop named Maximinus, then a Donatist, but who rallied round several years later and brought with him into the bosom of the Catholic Church his bishopric of the *castellum Sinitense*. We know from Augustine himself that this *castellum* – 'country town' – was situated on the marches of Hippo's civil territory,[p] and from a nearby passage in the same text[q] it can be inferred that Siniti must not have been very far from Fussala, which would soon be the subject of concern, and thus situated like Fussala in the mountainous vicinity of the south-east borders of Hippo's territory.[10] The first Catholic incumbent of this new see sited at the *villa Mutugenna*, Antonius, signed his Church's mandate in 166th place at the 411 conference, a rank which enables us to estimate his seniority in the episcopacy at that date at about three years.[r] His rival, bishop Splendonius, was 257th on the list of Donatist bishops, which means that at the date of the conference the reaction of the schismatic Church to the creation of the new bishopric in the heart of the Catholic Church was very recent. Clearly, the Donatists were not willing to yield without a fight a terrain over which they had been in a strong position for a long time.

The disastrous affair of Antoninus of Fussala

In the autumn of 411, Augustine came back from Carthage where he had spent several months. He had preached a great deal during the summer, ending his cycle of sermons as usual at the celebration of St Cyprian's feast-day, 13 and 14 September. But the main event of the year had been the conference in June, which had concluded with the defeat of the Donatists. Certainly, not all of them had been disarmed and there was continued anger at the quite severe residual outbreaks of violence on the part of the circumcellions,[s] but the unambiguous condemnation of the schismatic Church and the civil authorities' rediscovered firmness towards it brought about numerous conversions within its ranks. In the space of a few months, the religious face of many townships in the country and mountainous areas changed spectacularly; for example, the *castellum* of Fussala, in a region which, says Augustine, had long been taken over by the Donatist Church, to the point where the township itself did not have a single Catholic.[t] The change of heart, he adds, in a letter written some dozen years later to Pope Celestine, did not come about without hardship, or great suffering endured by the Catholic priests who had been established there to assist in and consolidate the return to unity. At the end of 411, it was becoming urgent to ordain a bishop to take charge of these regained lands – where religious peace was still fragile – which were too distant to command the bishop of Hippo's full pastoral attention.

Where was Fussala? The *castellum*, says Augustine, had a common boundary with the territory of Hippo Regius, to which it was external but at the same time, from the ecclesiastical point of view, was a part of the diocese of Hippo.[u] He adds only that it was forty miles, or slightly under sixty kilometres, away from his episcopal town.[v] This figure, which Augustine specifies in his letter to Celestine to show him that such a distance made it necessary to appoint a bishop there, is unfortunately unaccompanied by any hint as to direction; it was obviously an actual distance, by road; converted into kilometres as the crow flies, the figure should be reduced to forty-five or fifty, at the maximum. If, with the aid of compasses, we mark on a map a fifty-kilometre line from Hippo, we see that to the west/north-west it makes a perceptible inroad into the territories of the coastal places on the Herbillon peninsula, such as Paratianis (Fig. 3). These localities were clearly outside Hippo's territory, so there is little likelihood of finding Fussala in this direction, the more so because in this vicinity the stagnant waters of Lake Fetzara must have limited settlements in Antiquity as much as they do today. To the south-west, the fifty-kilometre radius goes considerably beyond the frontier separating Hippo's territory from that of Calama, so we cannot look for Fussala on that side either. Lastly, towards the east, the fifty-kilometre radius passes well beyond the line, known at one point (point 3 of Fig. 3), and probable on either side of this point, of the territorial border of Hippo

Regius. It would therefore appear that our investigation needs to centre on the south and south-east confines of Hippo's territory, in the vast triangle formed by Calama in the west, Thullio in the north and Thagaste in the south. And, in the broad zone thus demarcated, various clues, the most significant of which emerge from the topographical data of the episcopal enquiry held in the spring of 421 into the misappropriations by Antoninus of Fussala,[11] lead to the probable localization of the episcopal see of which he was the first incumbent in the mountainous region of the Reguegma, east of the middle course of the Seybouse (Fig. 3).[12]

In his clerics' monastery, it is known that Augustine had at his disposal a veritable breeding-ground of future bishops. For this new bishopric which urgently needed to be provided for, he had set his heart on a priest who had the advantage of sufficient acquaintance with the Punic language, then a kind of patois, a bastardized version of Carthage's language, whose use was necessary in many places, especially the wide rural zones of Hippo's Numidia.[13] A date had been set for his ordination, and the primate of Numidia, who had come a long distance, was present on the appointed day to preside at Fussala,[w] when at the last minute the prospective priest 'stood them up'. What was to be done? Could Augustine let his primate, who was an old man, leave again after so long and arduous a journey, all for nothing? Above all, could he disappoint the expectations of the local faithful, who had been brought back into the Catholic fold not long before and whose need of pastoral supervision he knew. He had with him, on his journey, a young lector named Antoninus, who was almost a son to him. He had arrived at Hippo while still a child with his mother and the man she had married; in the destitution of displaced persons, probably of peasant origin, they had sought material aid from the Church, which had taken them under its wing. But Augustine, knowing that the woman had remarried while the child's father was still living, had separated the couple; she had been taken in at the hospice for the poor aided by the Church,[14] while the child and his stepfather had found refuge in the monastery. The years had passed, gravely summed up by the bishop in a nutshell: 'He died, she became old, the child grew.' [x] Antoninus had become a young man who gave every satisfaction in his office of lector, to the extent that the superior of the clerics' monastery, the priest Urbanus, future bishop of Sicca Veneria (Le Kef), acting on the orders of the absent Augustine, had considered nominating him for the priesthood in a large domain in the diocese of Hippo. But, as if moved by foreknowledge of a higher destiny, Antoninus had refused. At Fussala, on that day, he was still a lector, and in that capacity was part of his bishop's entourage; moreover, he was available. And he too knew Punic, a master card in a place like Fussala. Did Augustine hesitate? Later, blaming himself, he would insist on the exceptional nature of such a promotion, which made a bishop of a lector aged twenty without the slightest experience of the clericate. But, caught unawares, he imposed this pastor on the faithful of Fussala, who trusted him. In the sermon he gave on the occasion of this ordination,[y] he concluded by considering the possibility that a bishop might behave badly while at the same time preaching the truth. Such an instance, he said, had been foreseen in the Gospel, and quoted Matt. 23.3: 'Do as they tell you, but do not as they do.' Highly prophetic words, as shown by what followed.

At first somewhat panic-stricken by the magnitude of his responsibility, the young man soon got the measure of the authority entrusted to him and the material gains he could derive from it. A *castellum* was a township without municipal status,[15] and with no institutions other than, at best, a council of elders (*seniores*), modelled on the *djemaa* in Berber country. If he had the nous to surround himself with a team of loyal and efficient auxiliaries, a bishop could be virtually in command. Antoninus wasted no time. To start with, he ordained as priest to work alongside him an ex-secretary from Augustine's entourage who had been expelled from the monastery after a whipping for having associated with some nuns; and, in such an environment, a deacon who had been assigned to him following normal procedure soon revealed his capacity for creating a nuisance.[z] However, the worst was the third acolyte he chose, a former soldier, probably a deserter, who, decorated with the title 'defender of the Church' (*defensor ecclesiae*) headed a surveillance militia he had personally recruited. In a very short time, Antoninus had imposed his features on the figure of *episcopus* or *clericus tyrannicus* that we find outlined in the Church of Africa's conciliar deliberations,[16] also in the image of a bishop/gang-leader, equally present in African tradition and illustrated a few years earlier by the Donatist bishop Optat of Timgad.

Defensores ecclesiae as a permanent post had been instituted by a law of emperor Honorius dated 15 November 407;[17] as their name indicates, their duties were to defend the interests of the churches to which they were appointed. Antoninus perverted the institution to his own profit and used the services of the *defensor ecclesiae* and his henchmen to 'shake down' his flock. In his letter of autumn 422 to Pope Celestine, Augustine discreetly summed up his former protégé's misdeeds, though setting them out at greater length in the enclosure accompanying the letter.[aa] But he went into the details in the one that he sent at roughly the same time to the lady Fabiola, the pious, wealthy and influential Roman aristocrat with whom Antoninus had taken refuge, seeking her support. The young bishop had been fairly easily absolved of four ill-founded accusations of rape; apparently debauchery appealed to him less than lucre. But in that area all was grist to his mill: 'Money, furniture, clothing, cattle, crops, wood and stone for building, all was lost for whoever fell into his hands.'[18] Antoninus was chiefly motivated by the acquisition of property – sheer plundering: one of the vendors had been illegally confined to force him to yield his property at a low price. As often happened in Antiquity, when materials were hard to obtain, an old building was bought so that the stones could be used to build a new one.[bb] In this way, by reusing materials from demolitions, he had had a fine house (*domus*) built in the township of Fussala, of which Augustine said that 'it had nothing in it that could not be shown to have come from another's property by pointing at the place whence it came'![cc] Over and above the genuine need he, as first bishop of Fussala, had to be housed, Antoninus had realized the dream of the poor lowly peasant who had been transplanted to a town while still a child. It was obviously to save this 'bourgeois' house, the symbol of his power and monument to his worldly success, that he clung so tenaciously to his episcopal see.

For, despite a probably severely imposed law of silence, Antoninus' misdeeds were finally made known; but his extortions and depredations had been going on for nearly ten years. Early in 421, the complaints of the faithful at Fussala provoked the meeting of an episcopal court of first instance at Hippo, presided over by Augustine and Alypius, accompanied in theory by some ten bishops, probably from neighbouring sees.[dd] Even for what we would call common law crimes, Antoninus was lucky enough to have the benefit of 'court privilege'[19] (trial by an episcopal court). His peers judged him with great leniency: he kept his episcopal rank, escaped excommunication by partly recompensing his victims, but lost his authority over the township of Fussala itself, where soon afterwards the provincial council of Numidia proceeded with the ordination of another bishop. The solution, dictated by respect for the rule banning transfers,[ee] consisted in dividing the communities between the two incumbents of the see which had been thus dismembered. Antoninus kept eight *plebes* which appeared to be less hostile to him; but he wanted another to be added, near to the town, in a rural estate where he wished to establish his episcopal residence.[ff] The peasants on this estate had suffered a lot from Antoninus; they wrote to their mistress – their *domina* – that if she allowed this to happen, they would all leave her immediately.[20]

In fact, it was Antoninus' intention to be fully reinstated in his episcopal office, so there was nothing for it but to cross the sea to appeal to Pope Boniface, which he did before the latter's death on 4 September 422. We have to believe that, even in his little mountainous corner of Hippo's Numidia, Antoninus had got wind of the arrangements decreed by the general council which had met at Carthage in May 419 in regard to another outstanding affair – of the priest Apiarius, of the diocese of Sicca. They had provisionally authorized right of appeal to the apostolic see.[21] Antoninus had astutely, and deceitfully, obtained from his primate, Aurelius of Macomades, a letter of recommendation to Boniface, to whom he presented his own version of what had occurred. Whatever Augustine's feelings about this appeal to Rome, he could not disregard it, for his initial personal responsibility was very much involved; he accepted the intervention of the Roman see the more willingly because Boniface had entrusted authority for the second phase of proceedings to African bishops and not papal legates.

Among some thirty of the bishop of Hippo's letters, discovered twenty or so years ago by a Viennese scholar in the Bibliothèque nationale in Paris, and in the manuscript collection of the Bibliothèque municipale in Marseille, letter 20*, to Fabiola, is the most unexpected, and most exciting, document. In it we can follow, step by step, the peregrinations of the episcopal commission which, probably in the summer or autumn of 422, held its first sessions in the small Numidian town called Tegulata – merely a name for us. Naturally, Alypius and Augustine took part. The latter, in his very complete account, does not hide his feelings, horrified by the conduct and cunning of Antoninus, yet ready to argue for leniency provided that the interested party shows the desire to make amends and accepts the solution of conciliation proposed in the first instance. But the young bishop of Fussala was an underhand character. When, at the hearing, a priest of Fussala acting as the spokesman for a determined opposition to his person on the part of the clergy and followers in the little town spoke out, Antoninus challenged him and claimed the letters the priest had with him were forgeries.[gg] It was therefore decided to go to Fussala to get the matter clear in their minds; if it turned out that the inhabitants no longer wanted their bishop, Antoninus was to receive the eight communities already proposed to him, plus five others which Augustine had unofficially promised him; the matter of Thogonoetum, the domain that had so vigorously made its hostility known, was still suspended. At Fussala, some days later, the commission which met together round the provincial primate no longer included Alypius, who had returned to Thagaste, or Augustine, who was painfully aware that he was not *persona grata* in that place where the villagers regarded him as the source of all their woes.[hh] The on-the-spot inquiry revealed the terrorism exerted by the bishop over his followers in all its reality; confronted with him, they persisted in their rejection, expressed in shouts and boos.

But the episcopal commission had not seen the last of its troubles and surprises; Antoninus was determined to cloud the issue. He had said he wanted to obtain the rural community of Thogonoetum, while knowing perfectly well that the *domina* of this property considered him undesirable, and he himself had advised the lady not to agree. This was therefore a manoeuvre on his part, as a letter from the aristocratic lady soon confirmed, backed up by her oral testimony.[ii] Augustine no longer knew which way to turn. To try to influence Antoninus, he was ready to propose granting him two more communities, but the other commissioners opposed this. And because nothing had been settled, the faithful in Thogonoetum, who had roughly heckled the primate of Numidia, had been excommunicated by him. Augustine feared that they would be cast into 'peasant despair' – their *tristitia rusticana*, as he describes it[jj] – and that the spiritual disarray of these uncultivated people, left to their own devices when they had only just been weaned from schism, might lead to their downfall. He had been able to measure the scope of the damage caused in that little community. In order to get to Fussala, where it had been decided to proceed with a new hearing of Antoninus' former followers, but this time not in the presence of his successor, it was necessary to go through Thogonoetum. Having arrived in the evening, the next morning the commission saw all the faithful assembled in the church. Harangued in Punic by the primate, Aurelius of Macomades, and enjoined by him to set out their complaints against Antoninus by individual depositions recorded in the minutes, they stubbornly refused. They were afraid, they said, that by doing so they would be providing weapons to be used against them in fresh persecutions by their former bishop. And when he insisted, they left the church in a body, nuns included, dumping the members of the commission. They would not return for the church service until the primate promised to do nothing against their wishes when giving them a bishop.

From there, the commissioners went on to Fussala. It had been planned to re-interview the inhabitants, virtually all of whom were peasants, taking separately the *coloni* of each estate, in the presence of their stewards (*actores*) and their 'overseers' (*procuratores*), who were slaves, but not in the presence of their farmers (*conductores*), who were free men.[kk] A farmer was a *quasi dominus* – one of them had been in a position to ask the primate and bishops to come to him[ll] – and there was suspicion of the pressure he, like a *dominus* or *domina*, might be able to exert on his peasants. Quite the reverse: the testimony given to the tribunal by these 'supervisors' or stewards, who were in daily contact with the peasants, whether on a private estate or imperial lands, showed no reluctance. They were there less as witnesses of Antoninus' extortions or as guarantors of the rights of tenure of the despoiled *coloni* (for not all these *coloni* had individual grievances to put forward), than to 'supervise' their peasants, and ensure their appearance before the episcopal tribunal.[22] The precaution was not unnecessary; in fact, as at Thogonoetum, the faithful proved more than reluctant at the idea of having to make an individual deposition, and it was no easy matter to overcome their opposition. They made up for what they felt to be a dangerous constraint on them by frequently accusing Augustine, who was going through the most painful ordeal of his pastoral life.[mm]

The denouement was played out in a township near Fussala (Fig. 3, p. 247), the *castellum Gilvense*, where an urgent ecclesiastical matter had summoned the primate.[23] The episcopal tribunal's report was damning for Antoninus, all the more so because bishops chosen by himself had also had a hand in it. His reaction was surprising: when it was suggested to him that if he wanted to remain a bishop the only possibility open to him was to accept, without any more fuss, control of the communities that had been designated for him, he replied that he wanted none of them and 'had the firm intention of settling in à distant retreat, far from the world, away from envy, as God's servitor'.[nn] Did he hope to disarm his judges with this attitude of humility, obtain their pardon, return to the *statu quo ante*? His contrition was feigned. Pressed by Augustine to prove his sincerity by recording his wish for peace in the minutes, or at least in some form of written document, he refused point blank and, finally unmasking himself, he shouted 'in a terrible tone of voice and manner' that nothing could make him give up returning to his church in Fussala. And rising angrily to his feet, he announced that he was leaving for Rome to appeal once more to the apostolic see.[oo]

There was nothing more to be done than to inform the said see by assembling all the minutes and sending them, together with a report from the primate of Numidia; which was done, said Augustine, with all possible speed. Probably in the autumn of 422, at the same time as a letter to Boniface's successor, Celestine, in which he concealed nothing of the responsibility he had assumed when making that over-hasty ordination, he wrote to the lady Fabiola, with whom he knew that Antoninus would once again seek refuge,[pp] providing a more detailed account of the affair to give her a better understanding of her protégé's moral character and help her alter the direction of her conscience, which he asked her to exercise in his regard.[qq] What became of him, of his second appeal to Rome, and the epilogue to the whole affair, we do not know. Nor do we know anything about Antoninus' successor to his see, and whether this bishop, ordained with no less haste than the one he was replacing, was able to hold on to it. A sentence in a letter from Augustine, between 421 and 427, to Quodvultdeus, deacon and future bishop of Carthage, leads one to think that the bishop of Hippo had again taken on the *cura pastoralis* of Fussala, at least temporarily, as an *interventor*.[rr] The undertaking of dividing a too vast diocese had for the time being reached its limits. But the bishopric created for and by Antoninus had not ceased to exist. In the late fifth century, a bishop of Fussala figured on the registers of the province of Numidia.[24] With a documentary irony, if not an irony of history, his name was Melior!

Notes

a.   This emerges clearly from a letter from Augustine (*Ep.* 115) regarding a certain Faventius, steward on a large estate, who had taken refuge at Hippo to escape the authority of the consular governor of Numidia; this estate was the *saltus Paratianensis* (cf. *Paratianis* on the map Fig. 3).

b. *De cura pro mortuis gerenda*, 15: municipii Tulliensis, *quod Hipponi proximum est.*

c. *De cura pro mortuis gerenda*, 15.

d. *Ep.* 44, 14: the absence of any church made it a neutral and apparently relatively calm place.

e. A *memoria* of the Milanese martyrs Gervasius and Protasius is indicated by Augustine at the *villa Victoriana*, less than 30 miles from Hippo: *City of God*, XXII, 8, 8.

f. *Ep.* 62 and 63.

g. *Ep.* 202, 7: *Rustica et minus instructa clericorum turba*; this was around the time when Augustine was living through the painful experience of Fussala: cf. below, p. 252.

h. *Ep.* 108, 19; cf. also 106, 1.

i. Very probably the *saltus Hispaniensis* which we shall see further on in a similar affair.

j. *Ep.* 35, 2.

k. *Ep.* 65, 1

l. *Ep.* 15*, 3 and 4, *BA*, 46 B, pp. 266–9 and 497 for the commentary.

m. *Ep.* 13*, 1 and 3, *BA*, 46 B, pp. 256–61.

n. Augustine liked to say of this bishop, to show his trust in his judgement, that he was not well-read on the secular level but was well-educated in matters of faith.

o. Cf. above, p. 172.

p. *City of God*, XXII, 8, 11: *in castello Sinitensi quod Hipponiensi coloniae vicinum est.*

q. *City of God*, XXII, 8, 7.

r. *Actes de la conference de Carthage en 411*, I, 133, SC, 195, p. 756.

s. Cf. below pp. 301–2.

t. *Ep.* 209, 2, to Pope Celestine.

u. *Ep.* 209, 2; *Ep.* 20*, 3: *in quodam Fussalensi castello quod Hipponiensi cathedrae subiacebat.*

v. *Ep.* 209, 2: *Ab Hippone memoratum castellum milibus quadraginta seiungitur.*

w. This primate was Silvanus at that time, bishop of Summa, very probably in central Numidia.

x. *Ep.* 20*, 2: *Ille obiit, illa senuit, puer crevit.*

y. *Sermo Guelferbytanus* 32, 9, in *Miscellanea Agostiniana*, I, Rome, 1930, p. 571.

z. *Ep.* 20*, 5.

aa. *Ep.* 209, 4 and 6. We do not have this enclosure, the contents of which are resumed in the letter to Fabiola.

bb. We saw above (p. 232) that this was the measure initially planned by Leporius for building a basilica at Hippo.

cc. *Ep.* 20*, 31.

dd. The number of twelve bishops was statutorily required to judge one of their peers.

ee. This ban on transfers from one see to another was peculiar to the Church of Africa.

ff. That is to say, to make it his *matrix* or *principalis ecclesia*: *Ep.* 20*, 8–9.

gg. *Ep.* 20*, 13.

hh. *Ep.* 20*, 15.

ii. *Ep.* 20*, 17–19. The *domina* was of 'clarissimus' rank, therefore of the senatorial nobility.

jj. *Ep.* 20*, 20.

kk. *Ep.* 20*, 20; read *cum actoribus vel procuratoribus sine* (and not: *sive*) *conductoribus suis.*

ll. Cf. *Ep.* 20*, 19.

mm. *Ep.* 20*, 23.

nn. *Ep.* 20*, 24.

oo. *Ep.* 20*, 25.

pp. Her lands in Africa were probably near Fussala, and the bishop could have had occasion to meet her.

qq. *Ep.* 20*, 27.

rr. *Ep.* 224, 3. Augustine was recommending a priest from Fussala to Quodvultdeus, asking him to help him in his dealings in Carthage because, he said, it was a matter of affairs concerning men *qui . . . ad curam pertinent nostram.*

CHAPTER XXIV

A bishop in the world of his time

The story of Antoninus of Fussala is certainly an extreme case, with special conditions. It none the less illustrates, even to the point of caricature, the place a bishop could occupy in the secular world at that time, and the importance of the role he could play, for better or worse. Augustine by no means shied away from this secular function, which for him soon became one of the most engrossing. In 400/401, exhorting the monks to manual work in the little book that Aurelius of Carthage had urged him to write, he sighed:

> When it comes to my own creature comforts, I would much prefer to do some manual work at set times, as is laid down in well regulated monasteries, and take advantage of the other moments to read, pray or study the holy Scriptures, than be exposed to the stormy complexities (*perplexitates*) of other people's squabbles in secular affairs that have to be settled by a judgement or concluded by an intervention.[a]

But, he added, such tasks were not to be avoided by a bishop, since the Apostle – 1 Cor. 6.4–6 – had stipulated that Christians should judge Christians rather than see their cases referred to pagan courts.

Moreover, the public authorities must admit episcopal jurisdiction, and the latter must enter the legal domain. This had been accepted since the emperor Constantine had in principle legalized it in 318 by obliging secular judges to recognize it.[b] Subsequently, however, the *episcopalis audientia* had seen its area of competence restricted as the years went by.[1] At the very end of the fourth century, Arcadius' law for the East, and a similar constitution by his brother Honorius for the West, had limited the scope of this episcopal jurisdiction, which was excluded from handling criminal cases. A little later, in 408, the same Honorius laid down that in civil matters a bishop's judgement could be only a procedure of arbitration, valid if both parties agreed to resort to it.[c] In the period when Augustine was bishop, the *episcopalis audientia* was a sovereign jurisdiction exclusive of any other only in the domain where the 'court privilege' was fully exercised, in other words, in cases involving a cleric, as we have just seen in the Antoninus affair.[2] But in civil cases, the vast field of applying arbitration and, in criminal ones, his power to intercede, made the bishop a leading actor in the social theatre.

The bishop in civil society: pursuing injustice and defending the weak

Possidius tells how, day in day out, the bishop of Hippo, surrounded by his secretaries, was obliged to hold morning sessions in the *secretarium* of his church until lunchtime, often skipping lunch.[d] It was not only Christians who besieged him.[e] And because he did not have at his disposal the armour of all the intimidating apparatus of a court of justice, or the defence of the secular arm, he knew that in many cases his arbitration would earn him the lasting resentment of one of the parties. Every plaintiff likes the judge before he judges, he observed; and he had no illusions about the way the judgement would be received. Had the richer of the two been satisfied? Then the bishop-judge must have received a present, or he was afraid to offend him. Did the poorer win the case? The judge acted thus because he did not want to seem hostile to the poor, he had sacrificed justice to public opinion: in short, he had practised a sort of inverse class distinction, as we might say.[f] In fact, Augustine certainly inclined towards the latter aspect of judiciary practice, and he made no excuses for it. In this regard, he made a significant distinction between rich and poor concerning the same misdeed, for example a theft, the poor alone benefiting from extenuating, if not absolutory, circumstances: 'It is one thing to sin in need, another to sin in plenty. If a poor beggar commits a theft, his crime is the result of his hunger. Why should a rich man who is overflowing with so much steal another's property?'[g]

Although in Augustine's work the *Sermons* give us most information about the spirit of his judicial practices, it is the *Letters* which give us concrete examples of his interventions. And in the voluminous corpus of that correspondence, the collection of some thirty unpublished letters discovered some decades ago is particularly valuable for the light that some of them throw on the worried eye with which the bishop surveyed some alarming aspects of his contemporary society, in the last ten years of his life and episcopacy, where the published dossier is placed chronologically.[h] One, dated in the spring of 420 and written to Alypius who was on a mission in Italy at the time, gives us an insight into the heart of Augustine's social concerns. In the first part of 'Letter 22*', he remarked on two things. First, an increasingly noticeable ossification of that society, which in the first instance was harming the body he represented, the Church. A council that had just been held in Numidia, which the cold season had prevented him from attending – it was the beginning of March – had passed on their grievances: it was more and more difficult to recruit clerics, because of legislation that fixed everyone by heredity in his social category.[3] In his time, Augustine, the son of a curial,[i] had been able to escape this. But, while economic difficulties were growing there had been a hardening of attitude among those – first and foremost the 'curators' of the towns – who watched to see that no one shirked his duties or financial responsibilities. To exempt local clergy from these impediments, which threatened them with ultimate extinction, the bishop proposed the setting up in each community of a quota of individuals who would have the benefit of immunity from charges and could thus gain entry to the clerical orders.[j]

But above all, it was the economic aspects of this social situation, especially the heavy taxation and the injustices committed in levying it, which provoked Augustine's second reaction in this text. The Church, he said, was bombarded with complaints from poor citizens who turned to it in an attempt to escape the tyranny of dishonest enforcers of the municipal authorities, who put pressure on them.[k] To his great regret, here Augustine reached the limits of his judiciary powers, or rather of his capacity to protect (*tuitio episcopalis*): abusive tax-collectors, who had a tendency to reduce the tax burden on notables and the wealthy to the detriment of the powerless, laughed in his face, for they knew very well that the bishop was not empowered to take action against them,[1] and had plenty of opportunity to complain to a higher authority (of provincial governors) about the bishop's interference, claiming that he was hindering the requirements of the public service.

It was a stroke of luck when these bureaucrats, even at the local level, did not raise too many difficulties about seeing him. They were hardly in any hurry, and Augustine's feelings were piqued as well as his perfectly legitimate concern to have respect shown to his episcopal dignity. In a sermon preached at Hippo during the summer of 409, he openly expressed the humiliations to which he was exposed on behalf of his faithful flock. He had to wait in the antechamber, see others less worthy than he to be received without a wait take precedence; and once he was admitted, more often than not he had to endure rebuffs rather than obtain satisfaction for his request.[m] The most mortifying thing, he continued, was that if he failed, the faithful who had entreated him were not at all grateful for the steps he had taken and even doubted whether he had done anything! The text without doubt reveals one of Augustine's weaknesses – he was over-sensitive – but even more, as has been rightly observed, the limits of Christianization in an African city at the beginning of the fifth century,[4] or more exactly, the limits of a bishop's actual power in the face of a completely 'lay' administration, in the sense we give the word, whose representatives, even when they themselves were Christians, were jealous of their autonomy relative to another hierarchy.

In his letter of spring 420, Augustine could see only one way of succeeding in giving this protection, where he himself failed, and that was to have a *defensor civitas* appointed at Hippo. We saw earlier that *defensores ecclesiae* existed, and how someone like Antoninus had been able to pervert this office in the service of his own misdeeds.[n] As the name indicates, the 'defender of the State' had a civil role and when the function was originally instituted he embodied an 'opposition force', installed by the emperors, especially the great Theodosius,[5] to protect ordinary people from those with power abusing their authority. But, diverted from its initial objective, this 'defence' had become – where it still existed – a simple mechanism for local institutions,[6] to the point where the general council that met at Carthage on 13 September 401 had asked the imperial government for the appointment of 'defenders' whose functions were to be redefined.[7] We must suppose that this request had produced no result, or that not all towns had benefited, since twenty years later Augustine was repeating the request. So that the 'defender' should be able to command respect, he must have a suitable social rank and be assured of the confidence of his mandators, the citizens of the town. Augustine had his candidates ready: an imperial official named Ursus, and two faithful Catholics of Hippo, should consent to this duty be refused to an official, a point over which there was some doubt.[o] Unfortunately, we do not know what happened.

As a citizen of the terrestrial city, Augustine was a man of the establishment.[p] Though it may shock our conscience (forgetting that our own societies were slavers up to the mid-nineteenth century and sometimes beyond, and that before any abolition the Church, through the voice of Gregory XVI, merely condemned the traffic), Augustine was not an abolitionist. All around him, everyone had slaves, including some of his own clerics, although he urged them to set these free.[8] And by the device of one of those economic and social 'boxes within boxes' which we find hard to imagine, there were even 'slaves of slaves' – they were called *servi vicarii* – whose reality at that time is confirmed by one of the bishop of Hippo's recently rediscovered sermons.[q] For Augustine, slavery was an evil – in his view one of the social consequences of original sin[9] – that was an economic necessity according to the equilibrium of the production systems then in force which he would not have dreamt of challenging. But he could not accept that this evil whose principle he admitted should undergo in his time and with his knowledge, around him, any extension or upsurge in a diversity of forms, some of which were on the boundaries of legality. And sometimes Augustine, who had not studied law and had only the empirical knowledge of it gleaned from his practice as episcopal judge, felt the need for consultation. This is revealed in one of the new letters, addressed to a jurisconsult named Eustochius. The questions he put concerned the different ways in which a free person could find himself reduced to slavery, often in an insidious manner. He had to be informed of these delicate problems of civil law for, he said, 'if we can, following the apostolic doctrine, order slaves to be subject to their masters, we cannot impose the yoke of slavery on free men'.[r] Certain of these cases were contentious, such as knowing what was the status of a child born of a slave and a free woman, and the complexity of a jurisprudence which, in the case in point, went back as far as the emperor Claudius, was enough to disconcert the bishop. But, by the sole fact that it was asked, another question bore witness to the harshness of that society, aggravated by the difficulties of the period. It was to know what was to become of children whose parents – themselves probably victims of poverty – sold their labour for a fixed number of years: did the death of the parents who had 'hired' them out put an end to the contract, and restore their legal freedom? Or were they compelled to fulfil the number of years anticipated?[s] There was a great risk because, when the children concerned reached their majority at the age of twenty-five, if their parents had died in the meantime and they themselves were not aware of their state, they could remain forever in a *de facto* state of slavery.[10] The complicated legislation and the weight of custom rather blurred the boundary between slavery by birth and temporary slavery, which was theoretically redeemable, as well as between statutory slavery and *de facto* slavery. Augustine was a little lost, as, in the same letter, we see from his curious questioning of Eustochius as to whether it was permissible for a landowner to reduce his peasants (*coloni*) or his peasants' children to slavery: these *coloni* enjoyed an inalienable personal freedom, but their obligation to work the land was a real alienation, which might lead to confusions.[11]

In those years, close to the Vandal invasion of Africa, to the accelerated disintegration of the empire of the West, of which the bishop of Hippo was a privileged witness, there was something worse and even more brutal to threaten personal liberty. Of the newly published letters, *Ep.* 10*, to Alypius, who was once again on a mission in Italy, is the most alarming document. The letter is dated 422/3, and we can perceive in its almost septuagenarian author a noticeable weariness in the face of the events which were overwhelming him, all the more so because Christians in his diocese were involved, not only as victims but also as executioners. At a time when the public authorities were increasingly failing to lend support, the whole of Africa, said the bishop, had become prey to slave traders, the *mangones*.[t] Working for them, hired men rigged out as soldiers or Barbarians went in howling bands through the country areas, which they terrorized, choosing isolated places. They would burst in during the night, killing the men and carrying off women and children to sell. The continuation of the letter throws light on this terrifying situation and explains how it began. These slave traders, Galatians from Asia Minor, who specialized in the traffic,ᵘ had been ready for a long time to get down to the job with their gangs of 'beaters' in Africa. Ordinarily they operated – with the blessing of the authorities – along the boundaries of the territories controlled by Rome, making incursions beyond the *limes* into the heart of the non-Romanized populations and as far as the Saharan tribes; the Mauretanias, with their long penetrable frontier extending from the mountains of the Hodna as far as present-day Morocco, were specially the purveyors of slaves.¹² Augustine knew of these practices and, in so far as they affected only Barbarians and infidels, it must be said that he was hardly moved by them.ᵛ But with the gradual foundering of the imperial rule and growing insecurity not only in the territories of the West but even in Numidia, the traders' greed could now be indulged with fewer risks than in Roman land. And on top of everything – and for Augustine as for every Roman, the world seemed turned upside down – it sometimes happened that it was the Barbarians' turn to obtain cheap slaves for themselves in this way!ʷ The victims of these raids were most often assembled and 'parked' on the coast before being shipped like cattle and deported overseas. It was all the more heartrending that in those distant exiles they lost all ability to summon witnesses to prove their identity, and thus any hope of recovering their freedom some day.

At the same time as sending his friend Alypius a copy of Honorius' law suppressing such crimes,ˣ the bishop of Hippo gave a few examples of the Galatians' activities. The most striking instance, which chiefly prompted Augustine to take steps, related to a few months earlier. Informed of the detention, somewhere along the coast near Hippo, of a group of captives from several regions of Africa but mostly Numidia, the faithful of the town had mounted a veritable commando action to release them: some one hundred and twenty people had thus been freed, among whom only five or six – but nevertheless! – had been sold by their parents.ʸ The bishop is careful to make it clear that he was absent at the time: though happy with the outcome, he does not uphold the method; the Church has no business to resort to fisticuffs. But he is worried about what may happen next, for the *mangones* have not given up. They know influential people in Hippo who are in league with them,ᶻ in defiance of the proconsular authority who is on the side of the law. And Augustine is worried about his protégés, for they have not all been able to take refuge in the church, whose right of asylum is inviolable and where they are in safety; those who are lodged in the town with members of his flock remain in danger. This explains why he is sending the letter, enclosing Honorius' law, to Alypius: the bishop is counting on his friend to find support at Court against the machinations of the *mangones* and their local accomplices.

While blaming them for the means they had used, the bishop could derive some pride from his followers' achievement, but he had equal reason to feel mortified – there were also some black sheep within his flock. A peasant (*colonus*) who worked on the church of Hippo's lands, and who was by no means needy, had sold his own wife to the Galatians! And a middle-class townswoman was enticing poor women from a nearby mountainous area, under the pretext of buying wood from them, then confining them, not without some mistreatment, to sell them on as slaves. Who would have believed it? commented the bishop.[aa] Such audacity, in the city where the proconsul of Africa's legate resided, was indeed most worrying. It spoke volumes about the setback to one of the major attainments of every urban civilization – personal safety – just a few years before the coming of the Vandals.

From punishment to intercession

Augustine detested violence, but he was not laxist. He could not be so in a dangerous civil society, nor could he when faced with a schismatic Church using really warlike means. That war would have to be countered with the weapons of a legal war, and in a letter to the *vicarius* of Africa, Macedonius (to which I will return), the bishop set out an initial theoretical acceptance of punishment, legitimized in his view by its preventive function: fear of laws and the secular arm that applies them is the beginning of wisdom. He writes:

> The power of the king, the judge's right to the sword (of justice), the torturer's iron pincers, the soldier's weapons, the rules of authority, even the severity of a good father, were not instituted idly. All these things have their norms, their causes, their reasons, their usefulness. When they inspire fear, the wicked are kept at bay and the good live more tranquilly among them.[bb]

Regarding the conduct to follow towards slaves, Augustine noted that this preventive function was coupled with a curative action:

> The duty of one who is without fault must therefore be not only to do no ill to anyone, but also to prevent or punish misdeeds, in order to correct by punishment the one who is chastised or frighten the rest by this example.[cc]

The punished culprit would improve because of his punishment and a social betterment would result. More fundamentally for Augustine, punishment imposed by men's justice, if correctly rendered and applied, was also a work of divine justice; for punishment restored not only social order, but also divine order, which sin tended to overturn. Punishment was therefore just and constituted a good, whatever the person chastised might think about it, and what mattered most was that it should prompt repentance, so that the punishment achieved its main purpose, which was moral even more than social. In one of his last texts, the old bishop condenses this basic idea in the form of a rough syllogism: 'Punishment is the penalty for sin, and assuredly the penalty for sin is just; consequently punishment is just, and as everything that is just is a good thing, so punishment is a good thing.' [dd]

But the inhuman harshness of the law was the answer to the violence of men. The bishop was caught between a rock and a hard place: charity, or love, implied the correction of the sinner, but not his excessive suffering, and must rule out his death. On the first point, Augustine is very explicit in the commentary he makes on Honorius' law, a copy of which he had sent to Alypius together with his letter about the *mangones'* activities. It was necessary to remind people of the law's existence, if necessary obtaining an official republication, and brandish the threat of punishment it contained in the faces of the traffickers and their accomplices. But he asked that they should not have to undergo strict application of the penalty, for the one envisaged, as well as exile and confiscation of property, was flogging with a lead-tipped lash – more or less the equivalent of a Russian knout – which often led to the death of the culprit in terrible agony.[ee] Similarly, he had nothing but aversion for the 'torturer's iron pincers', which he mentioned in the passage quoted above from his letter to Macedonius, because they were the sinister emblem of an inquisitorial torture which Christians had suffered so much during the persecutions. He had already urged the tribune and notary Marcellinus to hold firm to his resolution to ban all this paraphernalia – the rack and use of fire, too – for obtaining confessions: the birch should be enough.[ff] At that time, it was a matter of bringing down the criminal circumcellions; but his position was unchanged when, in 408 at Calama, the uprising of the pagans against the church and clergy had unleashed a legal action. Augustine had been alerted by Nectarius, one of those local notables who supported an 'enlightened' paganism whom we shall meet further on. Nectarius informed him of the fate of his fellow-citizens, who risked carrying the marks of the 'question' on their flesh forever, returning home 'free, but having undergone torture'.[gg] In his reply, the bishop resumed the quoted passage and tried to calm his correspondent: 'Far be it from me to inflict or have inflicted any such thing on any of our enemies.'[hh] And he urged him to let him know at once of any possible threat of such judicial cruelty, so that he might intervene. Towards the end of his life, in the *City of God* Augustine returned to this problem that tormented him: besides the fact that it implied brutal denial of the concept of the presumption of innocence, the most serious thing about inquisitorial torture was that its violence could extort false confessions and lead the innocent to suffer capital punishment.[ii]

For the bishop, the latter was another torment. In principle, he admitted that the need for maintaining social equilibrium and preserving public order forced the judge, as a last resort, to give the ultimate sentence.[jj] But it repelled him, and we often find him making efforts to dissuade the judge from resorting to it, in order to avoid the irreparable, or more exactly, to avoid the culprit's total perdition, by ruling out any possibility of repentance on his part. For, although the culprit must be punished, the man must be saved: 'Let the man not be killed, in order that someone may repent; let the man not be killed, in order that someone may mend his ways.'[kk] In the letter to Marcellinus already quoted, the bishop urges the imperial judge, in punishing the crime that he has discovered, not to call upon an executioner who was not required in order to discover it.[ll]

Augustine and the right of asylum

Augustine maintained that his duty as a bishop was to intervene in favour of the guilty, and that he experienced a feeling of failure, even offence, when he did not succeed – language that a high-ranking official such as Macedonius, although a Christian, found it hard to understand.[mm] This duty of intervention found a special application in asylum, the right to which the bishop vigorously defended. The safeguarding of the innocent who might seek refuge extended to the unwavering protection of the guilty who might find asylum there. 'It is better', he said, 'to protect even the guilty in the church than to see the innocent taken from it by force.'ⁿⁿ On this subject, the bishop of Hippo was inflexible; he showed it notably in the Faventius affair. This was a farmer (*conductor*) who worked lands on a great estate situated on the western borders of Augustine's diocese.[13] Having got into dispute with the property-owner, a rich and powerful man, he had taken refuge in the church at Hippo while awaiting the outcome of the bishop's intercession. After several days, he had ventured to go out and, on his way back from dining with a friend in the town, he had been arrested by a squad commanded by one of the Count of Africa's officers, Florentinus, after which he could not be found. However, Augustine had managed to trace Faventius' whereabouts, but the priest he had sent to where the man was being held prisoner had not been able to communicate with him. But on the following day, through another priest, the bishop informed Florentinus of the law which, in this type of affair, granted accused persons the right to be interrogated by the local authorities, giving them thirty days in which to prepare their defence while released on probation.ᵒᵒ It was a wasted effort; Faventius had been transferred to Cirta.[14] The bishop of Hippo could do nothing other than alert his colleague in the episcopacy of the Numidian capital, Fortunatus, about the case; this he did, at the same time sending a request to the governor of the province, Generosus.ᵖᵖ

What finally became of Faventius is not known. Another affair of asylum, in a different context, illustrates the bishop's tenacity and sometimes ill-rewarded generosity. A certain Fascius had run up debts, to the considerable total of seventeen gold *solidi*, and to escape his creditors and physical duress had taken refuge in the church; but the town's Christian community found itself obliged to pay in his stead. Out of human respect, Fascius claimed, he was against that solution. Augustine therefore decided to borrow the amount from a rich Christian follower in Hippo, Fascius pledging that he would repay him in due course. But he disappeared, and the bishop had to make a collection among his flock and make up the shortfall by drawing on the church's funds.�q�q In this particular instance, the right of asylum had ended in abuse and disillusion, but for the bishop that was no reason not to maintain the strictness of his principles. It was not a rare sight, he noted around 404, for an officer of the law who had been sent to apprehend a delinquent in a church to stop on the threshold, though it was the fear of God rather than respect for the law that prevented him from entering.ʳʳ It was therefore necessary to have official confirmation of a law that was too often held up to ridicule. An apparently fiscal affair which, around the end of 419, led the faithful to seek asylum in the church in Carthage was the chance for Aurelius, Augustine and Alypius to call upon the Court for this legislation to be brought back. A ruling by Honorius responded in a very liberal sense, granting all those who took refuge in churches a free zone of fifty paces all around, and declaring sacrilegious anyone who did not observe this; under this law, moreover, the bishop had permission to visit the prisons to take care of the sick, feed the poor and be informed of prisoners' cases so that he could intervene with the relevant jurisdiction.[15]

Many years later, an incident occurred outside Hippo to which Augustine's attention was drawn and which revealed the bounds to be set in the exercise of this right. A bishop named Auxilius, of an unknown see, an inexperienced novice,[ss] had collectively excommunicated the Count Classicianus and his family, because this high-ranking personage had entered the church with a small escort to extract some individuals who had taken refuge there. Everyone in this affair was in the wrong: Classicianus, for having violated the church's asylum with armed men; Auxilius for having rashly extended the anathema to the noble's entourage, who really had no choice, and having granted asylum to people who did not deserve it; and the men themselves, perjurers who had taken refuge in the church to avoid their commitments.[16] Augustine intended to infer a double lesson from this: the problem of collective excommunications must be referred to the next African council and, if need be, to the apostolic see, but also whether or not dishonest men should be excluded from the benefits of the right of asylum. But by then Augustine was *senex*,[17] in the last years of his episcopacy and the last good days of the Church of Africa, and as far as we know this project was not followed up.

The limits of intercession: the drama of summer 413

The story of Classicianus shows that Augustine's intercession could be of advantage to important people. In this particular case, however, the bishop's intervention had stayed within the ecclesiastical sphere and, whatever the outcome, the bishop's moral credit was likely to remain intact and his soul untroubled. But it was quite another matter if he risked interfering with the heavy machinery of political power; and in 413 Augustine had that bitter experience.

Two years earlier, at the conference in Carthage at which the two rival Churches had met for a decisive confrontation, the bishop of Hippo had struck up a friendship with the tribune and notary Flavius Marcellinus, whom the emperor Honorius had appointed to arbitrate. Augustine had found him to be a Christian of exacting faith, eager to learn about theology and philosophy,[tt] with an intellectual disquiet persuasive enough to have at least stimulated, if not given rise to, the groundwork of the *City of God*, whose first three books would be dedicated to him.[uu] The bishop's friendship had extended to the brother of the imperial commissioner, Apringius, whose proconsulate in that same year, 411, had fortunately coincided with Marcellinus' mission. In those troublous years, however, the main power did not lie with the proconsul, in any case geographically confined to Proconsular Africa, or even with the governor, whose authority extended to all African provinces, the *vicarius* of the Praetorian prefect, but with the head of the army of Africa.[18] Since 408, that role had been occupied by the Count Heraclianus, who had received it as a reward for the murder of Stilicho; and we shall see that the general, at the time of the greatest danger in 410, had kept Africa clear of disaster – probably less from loyalty to his emperor than to preserve and consolidate his own opportunities. The fragility of Honorius' government excited covetousness; that of Heraclianus came to light in 413, the year of his consulship. Late in spring, he mobilized all the vessels in the fleet that kept Rome supplied with wheat, and with this armada made for Italy. But his march on Ravenna was halted in Sabina, at Otricoli, and Heraclianus returned to Africa with the remnants of his army. The usurper was now a public enemy, and an order of 5 July 413 put a price on his head, inviting both civilians and soldiers to hand him over, together with his accomplices.[vv]

That summer, as often happened, Augustine was in Carthage, where he was preaching at Aurelius' invitation, more particularly emphasizing the 'orthodox' doctrine relating to the baptism of infants and original sin.[ww] When it came to politics, the bishop of Hippo was a legitimist and had no time for usurpers; but he had even less liking for hunting men down. In a sermon preached on 17 July for the feast-day of the Scillitan martyrs, Augustine launched into the theme of the need for friendship, developing it in a way that would not have disgraced Seneca: every man, he said, was the next man's neighbour.[19] But suddenly the most burning current topic arose; the bishop questioned his hearers, still with the urgent tones of a diatribe: 'Ask yourselves. Is he an unknown creature? He is a man. Is he a personal enemy? He is a man. Is he a public enemy? He is a man.'[xx] All those in the *basilica Novarum* where the sermon was delivered, had got the message and were holding their breath; but the fate of Heraclianus was sealed.

And that of his accomplices, real or presumed. Carthage's prisons were filling.[yy] Among others, Marcellinus and his brother Apringius were there. Why? Augustine, who visited and helped them, does not make the reasons for their incarceration clear: a settling of scores is probable and there is a hint at the Donatists' revenge.[20] Their fate was in the hands of the Count Marinus, the victor over Heraclianus at Otricoli who immediately replaced him in his office in Africa. Marinus played a cruel double game; he authorized and even encouraged an episcopal approach at Court, and let it be known that nothing would be done until the result was known. But at the same time, he took an irreparable step. He had the two brothers brought out of prison on the eve of St Cyprian, 13 September, as if to let them think they were being pardoned; but it was for a summary sentence, followed immediately by execution. Their two heads rolled on 14 September. Augustine had been powerless. He would describe at length his devastation and grievous impotence, hardly content to be assured that at least all those threatened by repression who had found refuge in the churches were physically safe there. He had to leave Carthage secretly, to distance himself from appeals for help to which he was unable to respond.[zz] His departure was a flight, and he was well aware of it. He would wait nearly three years before he returned. And in a letter written some months after this drama, in the spring of 414, to Caecilianus, the emperor's envoy extraordinary, whom he suspected of complicity with Count Marinus in the death of Marcellinus, he thought himself obliged to give the reasons for his absence from Carthage: no, it was not in order to avoid meeting him; the bishop pleaded his tiredness, which increased with age; and above all he declared his desire to devote such time as running his diocese would allow to going more deeply into some important theological questions on which he hoped to leave something useful for future generations.[ab] This patent return to 'cherished studies' which he had never abandoned, could not fail, in such circumstances, to have the significance of a retreat.

Augustine, the committed protagonist in a compassionless civil society which was affected by the disintegration of political government and increasingly stressed by the economic crisis afflicting the whole of the moribund ancient world, may appear to us to be in a perilous situation. Ten years before his accession to the episcopacy, in his retreat at Cassiciacum in the autumn of 386, he had already got the measure of the social body's fragile balance, and the evil in it that must be accepted as inevitable. The executioner (a terrible word in Latin: *carnifex*) was its emblematic figure:

> What can be more frightful? What more cruel, more hard? But he occupies a necessary place within the framework of the law, he is part of the order of a well-governed state and though he is in himself culpable (*nocens*), for others he is the scourge of the wicked.[ac]

Later the bishop would make efforts to cheat the executioner of his victims, but would not dream of rendering him definitively unemployed. Nor was there any question of retiring to an Aventine of other-worldliness. By his active presence in the city, even more than a simple follower, the pastor was certainly involved in a more or less equitable distribution of justice; but to distance oneself from a world that could be deemed perverted was to deprive oneself of the means of improving it. He did not have too many illusions about his effectiveness, as witnessed by the dramatic inability of the Church to save the most devoted of its sons in the person of Marcellinus. The company of saints was not on this earth, or even in the Church of the present time, as the Donatists wished to believe.

Notes

a. *De opere monachorum*, 37. Cf. also *Enarr. in Psalm.* 118, *Sermon* 24, 3, where he admits, not without some regret, that a bishop cannot be, like Christ, above the crowd (cf. Luke 12.14).
b. *C. Th.*, I, 27, 1.
c. *C. Th.*, I, 27, 2.
d. *Vita Aug.*, XIX, 3.
e. *Enarr. in Psalm.* 46, 5.
f. *Enarr. in Psalm.* 46, 25, *Sermon* 2, 13.
g. *Enarr. in Psalm.* 72, 12.
h. Quoted in the translated and commentated edition: *BA*, 46 B, Paris, Ét. aug., 1987.
i. See above, p. 7.
j. *Ep.* 22*, 2, *BA*, 46 B, p. 348.
k. *Ep.* 22*, 2, *BA.*, 46 B, p. 348.
l. *Ep.* 22*, 3, p. 350.
m. *Sermon* 302, 17.
n. Above, p. 254.
o. *Ep.* 22*, 4.
p. Cf. below, p. 370.
q. *Sermon Dolbeau* 21 (= *Mainz* 43), 5, in F. Dolbeau, *Vingt-six Sermons au peuple d'Afrique*, p. 275.
r. *Ep.* 24*, 1, *BA*, 46 B, p. 382 (on the 'apostolic doctrine', cf. Tit. 2.9).
s. *Ep.* 24*, 1, *BA*, 46 B, p. 384.
t. *Ep.* 10*, 2, *BA*, 46 B, p. 168.
u. Cf. *Ep.* 10*, 7 and Ammianus Marcellinus, XXII, 7, 8 (for the era of Julian the Apostate).
v. In his letter to Hesychius of Salonae (*De fine saeculi*), c. 420, he reported the abduction of non-Christian Barbarian captives who had increased the Romans' slave domestic staff: *Ep.* 199, 46.
w. *Ep.* 10*, 5.
x. *Ep.* 10*: 3–4, a law that was part of a plentiful arsenal of suppression, but has not come down to us; see the note by C. Lepelley in *BA*, 46 B, pp. 472–4.
y. *Ep.* 10*, 7.

z.   *Ep.* 10*, 8: *Non enim desunt* patroni *Galatis*; Augustine prudently does not give exact names
      or titles. We should not think of officials, but rather of rich and powerful landed property-
      owners, in league with the Galatians to eliminate smallholders in order to seize their land.
aa.   *Ep.* 10*, 6.
bb.   *Ep.* 153, 16.
cc.   *City of God*, XIX, 16.
dd.   *Contra Iulianum opus imp.*, V, 26.
ee.   *Ep.* 10*, 4. A 'novella' of Valentinian III, dated 451, making provision for the punishment
      of such misdeeds by very heavy fines, seems to respond to Augustine's concern for a
      softening of the legislation: cf. C. Lepelley, in *CRAI*, 1981, p. 460.
ff.   *Ep.* 133, 2.
gg.   *Ep.* 103, 4.
hh.   *Ep.* 104, 1.
ii.   *City of God*, XIX, 6.
jj.   *Sermon* 302, 16.
kk.   *Sermon* 13, 8: *Homo non necetur, ut sit quem paeniteat; homo non necetur, ut sit qui emendetur.*
ll.   *Ep.* 133, 2, *in fine*.
mm.   *Ep.* 153, 1: *Quaeris a me cur officii sacerdotii nostri esse dicamus intervenire pro reis et nisi
      obtineamus offendi quasi quod erat officii nostri minime reportemus.*
nn.   *Sermo Guelferbytanus* 25, in *Miscellanae Agostiniana*, I, Rome, 1930, p. 258.
oo.   *Ep.* 115, to Fortunatus, bishop of Cirta, c. 410.
pp.   *Ep.* 116.
qq.   *Ep.* 268, 3.
rr.   *Sermon Denis* 19, 2, in *Miscellanea Agostiniana*, I, p. 99.
ss.   Cf. *Ep.* 250, 2: *collega necdum anniculus*: he had less than a year in the episcopacy.
tt.   For example, he had read the *De peccatorum meritis,* and this had raised a question in his
      mind that he had submitted to Augustine: that had been the origin of the *De spiritu et littera*,
      written in 412, and dedicated to him (*Retract.*, II, 37).
uu.   Cf. below, p. 395.
vv.   C. *Th.*, IX, 40, 21.
ww.   Main themes of the *Sermons* 293 and 294, dated 24 and 27 June 413: cf. below, p. 332.
xx.   *Sermon Denis* 16, 1: *Inimicus est? Homo est. Hostis est? Homo est.*
yy.   It was enough, said Augustine, to have just one informer, from whom no proof was asked:
      Ep. 151, 4.
zz.   *Ep.* 151, 3: *Fateor: cum tantum malum nullo pectoris robore potuissem tolerare, discessi.* In this
      affair, he was cruelly lacking in both the political sense and also the firmness of a man like
      Ambrose.
ab.   *Ep.* 151, 13.
ac.   *De ordine*, II, 12.

CHAPTER XXV

The unity of the Church

In Late Antiquity the major disputes were religious. In a rigidly-structured society – often given State aid and kept under close surveillance, where any kind of protest was ruled out, the interaction allowed by economic mechanisms weak or non-existent, politics reserved for the exclusive benefit of an absolute centralized government, which had not long since become openly theocratic, and for that of all-powerful local lords – free expression of individuals and social groups, and even the urban masses, was confined to the sphere of religious belief and relations with the deity. At the age of thirty, witnessing the impassioned clashes between Catholics and Arians, under Ambrose, Augustine had realized that the lever enabling the crowds to be stirred up was at that time an appeal to their religious conscience. Having become a priest, then a bishop, he had learnt enough of Arianism's turbulent history over the preceding decades to know that in these weaponless battles, in which the subtleties of dogma were a special kind of dynamite in the hands of the astute, the enemy could be brought down only if made to acknowledge its defeat publicly. In that way it was not in a position to start fires and unleash violence. That had been the lesson of so many confrontations and councils throughout the fourth century.

Now, at the start of the fifth century, bishop Augustine's adversaries were the pagans and the Donatists. From now on, paganism was condemned by the imperial government; nevertheless, it could not be regarded as defunct as long as a few great intellectuals, who were often also powerful lords, continued to sing its praises and vaunt its ideological merits in the face of the new popular religion. Augustine could not avoid a debate with them. But the battle that had taken pride of place with him, ever since he had spoken 'with the voice of the Church',[a] was the one he had to wage against the Donatists. We saw earlier that he had re-established the position in Hippo itself in a very short time;[b] but in the rural areas of his diocese schism was well and truly present, and often in the majority. On a broader scale, almost everywhere in Africa, in the late fourth century, Donatism was at the pinnacle of its power. It prospered in the breeding-ground of peasant poverty, which the schismatic priests had every opportunity to attract with an ecclesiology that highly extolled a rejection of the 'impure', freely interpreted as compromise with worldly things and temporal power. On the cusp of the fifth century, there was a great danger that schism might derive vigour from the gradual weakening of the Empire and its divisions in Africa itself, as Gildo's venture had shown during a decade.[c] In the end, the tares ('discord') might invade the whole field. Here again, to fight meant to try to convince the Donatists of their error – and to have all African Christianity witness their rout – on the dual basis of a history that they had falsified and a conception of the Church that had emerged from those falsifications of history. However, around 400, Augustine was not aware that he would finish with Donatism only through legal coercion, and that he would pay for his triumph with a defeat.

The last anti-Manichaean crusade

But for the time being – let us not mince words – he had a few scores to settle with the Manichaeans; in fact, he had not lost sight of them since entering the priesthood. Even when still only a newcomer, we may recall how magisterially he had dismissed Fortunatus, the Manichaean 'priest' of Hippo, who had never been seen again: that had been his first duel in the arena.[d] Also prior to his accession to the episcopacy in 394, he had set about, not a flesh-and-blood Manichaean this time, but a more fearsome phantom, a direct disciple of Mani, Adimantus.[1] This 'apostle' of the Master's doctrine had resided in Egypt in the middle of the third century, founding monasteries and writing several works. During Augustine's priesthood, some of Adimantus' texts, doubtless from Alexandria, had reached Carthage; they had been sent on to Hippo, and Augustine had been swift to refute them. He would say in his *Retractations* that he had replied to some of the Manichaean's *disputationes* in sermons delivered in the church, which clearly shows that, to his way of thinking, controversy was part of his pastoral duties; and indeed these direct refutations, *coram populo*, were probably the best medicine he could advocate. Occupied with urgent tasks, he had also had to leave some answers pending and forgetfulness, he said, had eventually concealed them.[e]

The *Contra Adimantum* shows, however, that it was not merely a matter of pouring contempt on the Manichaean's commentaries on the Scriptures. Augustine was well placed to know what confusion could arise in the minds of Christians who were not enlightened in the faith, from the way in which Adimantus compared the Old and New Testament by contrasting the texts. It was not the first time that Augustine would amend the 'fleshly' interpretation of the Manichaeans by a 'spiritual' reading: he had already tried twice concerning the account of the Creation,[f] and would return to it in the *De Genesi ad litteram*. But he had not yet applied himself to refuting a work at least as pernicious as Marcion's *Antitheses* in the second century. The demonstration given in 394 to re-establish the unity of the Scriptures would seem a little too systematic to the old bishop when he reread it. The priest had written:

> (Among the people who had received the Old Testament) there were so many signs and such preparation for the New Testament that we can find in the Gospel and the apostles' preaching no precept, no promise, however difficult and divine they may be, that is missing from those ancient books.[g]

The author of the *Retractations* would amend: 'I should have added "almost" and say "almost no precept", "almost no promise".'[h] Like Marcion, Adimantus had contrasted Yahweh and Jesus, the Old Testament's God of vengeance and the Gospels' God of forgiveness, the law of fear and the law of love. Using other parallels – and sometimes using those of Adimantus – Augustine showed that 'the words they hated to see ascribed to God in the Old Testament were righteous enough to be found in the New, and those they praised and celebrated in the New

Testament were also to be found in the Old'.[i] He thus compared Ps. 55.23 with Matt. 6.26 and 34 on the 'fowls of the air which sow not neither do they reap'. Of course, at the least there was a difference in tone, in spiritual atmosphere, between the two groups of texts, but – and Augustine insisted on this – above all there was a transition from darkness to light. He took the example of God's rest on the seventh day and the sabbath. The old texts had been elucidated in a spiritual sense, 'the Lord had not abolished the sabbath to destroy what it represented, he had unveiled it in order to bring to light what it hid'.[j] Jesus, and the Apostle after him, had 'opened up' the Scriptures.

Some years later – he was now bishop and had written the *Confessions* – Augustus rediscovered Faustus of Milevis. Not the speaker (now dead) whom, while judging him, he had appreciated in his youth, but one of his works which had come into his hands after some of the 'brothers' at Hippo had read it, and had naturally asked their bishop to respond.[k] When speaking of Faustus in his *Confessions*, Augustine was looking at him through the somewhat indulgent spectacles of his memories.[l] His view changes in the *Contra Faustum*; here, the Manichaean doctor is no longer anything but a laborious wordsmith, a 'wretched prattler'.[m] If he has fallen lower than low, it is because Augustine has read his *Capitula*, a collection of short controversies in which the Manichaean cheaply comes off best by putting in the mouth of a Catholic opponent a feeble or clumsily presented objection which he then has every opportunity of sweeping quickly aside, ridiculing his supposed interlocutor; all on the basis of scriptural texts interpreted by Faustus in his own way.[2] His mockery was chiefly directed at the Old Testament, and he strove to prove that Christians shared its rejection with Manichaeans.[n] But he also attacked the Gospel, the major dogma of the incarnation, and tried in particular to cause confusion by showing the discordances relating to Christ's genealogy,[o] which in fact had puzzled Augustine in his youth. Using the form of an imaginary dialogue – *Faustus dixit: Augustinus respondit* – the bishop of Hippo made a vigorous reply, modulating the tone and volume of his answer according to the gravity of the question raised by Faustus. As in the *Contra Adimantum*, he gave special importance to proving the coherence of the Scriptures, insisting on the fulfilment of one by the other. He concluded one of his more elaborate replies in this way:

> The entire organization of the ancient archives (*veteris instrumenti*) concerning generations, facts, sayings, sacrifices, instructions, all the proclamations of the prophecies, and the histories and figures, that was all a gestation for the coming of the King who was going to reign and the Priest who was going to sanctify his faithful followers, the One who, full of grace and truth (John 1.14), with his grace helping in the execution of his precepts and by his truth seeing to the accomplishment of his promises, came not to destroy the Law, but to fulfil it (cf. Matt. 5.17).[p]

The dogmatic value of this series of refutations made the *Contra Faustum* a book to which Augustine accorded a special importance, as is shown by the cross-references to it which he made subsequently.[q] However, the confrontations and debates with the Manichaeans, that had greatly occupied him since his conversion, were coming to an end. On 7 and 12 December 404, he had one last heated exchange with an 'elect' of the sect.[3] This man, named Felix, had come to

Hippo with Manichaean texts in order to spread the good word. But the municipal authorities had seized his books and Felix, who called himself 'Christian' at the same time as a follower of the law of Mani, had asked for Augustine's intercession, probably through the intermediary of some of the bishop's followers. Augustine stipulated that a debate should take place, in right and due form.[4] The two men met in the 'church of Peace', which we saw earlier was Hippo's principal church, the 'Major basilica'.[r] Augustine was not slow to realize that his interlocutor, though lacking culture, was a tougher debater than Fortunatus had been some years before. He found him 'wily';[s] and in fact Felix had the art, summary but effective at least in its delaying tactics, of replying to one question with another. At the outset, he complained that he could not defend his ideas if deprived of his books, and Augustine offered him, so that he could read it himself, the letter from Mani known as the Founding Epistle,[5] which began with these words: 'Mani, apostle of Jesus Christ by the providence of God the Father'. And as the bishop asked him to give proof that Mani really was an apostle of Christ, the other retaliated by challenging him to prove that Christ had really sent the Holy Spirit, the Paraclete, as related in John 16.7–13: this set the tone for the debate. For Felix, Mani was the Paraclete, but his declaration was in vain in the face of Augustine's powerful demonstrations, supported by massive readings from the Gospel and St Paul. The Manichaean said he was impressed by his opponent's episcopal rank, and terrified by the fear of imperial laws; he felt very isolated, looking around him for any who might judge in his favour, and finding none.[t] Pressed by the bishop's formidable dialectic, Felix asked for some time in which to furbish his replies; Augustine gave him until the following Monday, on the guarantee of a follower chosen from among those in the front row leaning on the chancel rail.[u]

On Monday, 12 December, the debate resumed in the church. Augustine immediately reminded his adversary of the key question that had left him speechless on the preceding Wednesday. It was still the famous 'Nebridius' argument': if God could not be harmed, why would he enter into a war against the race of darkness, as the Manichaeans declared? And if he could be harmed, he was not the incorruptible God professed by Christianity and whom the Manichaeans also claimed to worship.[v] Felix replied by demanding his book! Then, following an affirmation by the Manichaean of the existence of two natures, one good the other evil, the dispute went on to the nature of evil and free will.[w] But with 'Nebridius' argument', Augustine maintained the pressure on Felix. Sticking to his tactics, the latter replied with another question; he was wavering, however, and in the end admitted that whoever said God was corruptible deserved anathema.[x] Lastly, after a long digression on the nature of the soul, and numerous exchanges partly summarized in the minutes, Felix confessed himself vanquished and signed a form of anathema against Mani and his doctrine modelled on one presented to him by Augustine. If we are to believe Possidius – at least, this is the conclusion the biographer drew from those *Proceedings* – the Manichaean became a Catholic.[y]

Having got under way with this last physical confrontation, was that why Augustine composed his *De natura boni*, about the same period, a doctrinal exposition on the nature of God, the Supreme Good, followed by a refutation of Manichaean dualism? It was a kind of brief manual for the use of all, clergy or simple followers, who might have to cross swords with Manichaeans. He also wrote a *Contra Secundinum,* as its title indicates, a reply to one of the sect's 'hearers' who, from Rome, had sent him a long, convoluted letter, in which he dared to exhort the bishop to join the ranks of Mani's followers! Apparently, he well knew his correspondent's past as a rhetor and his youthful errors.[z] He was obviously wasting his time. Rereading his text, the old bishop reckoned that it was the best of all those in that vein;[aa] in any case it was the last in date. For some time, the need to give a reply to the upholders of Donatism, on the plane of ecclesiology as well as on the count of falsifying history, had been foremost in Augustine's concerns.[6] And at ground level itself, the battle against the schismatics was a matter of urgency.

Augustinian diplomacy in the face of Donatism

At the end of the fourth century, the Donatists were under threat from a whole arsenal of repressive measures, notably due to Theodosius the Great.[bb] Although formally condemned by the imperial government, they were not doing too badly. Some years later, when this legislation, which had increased, was finally applied, Augustine gave a passing explanation of this paradox: 'There was no lack of laws, but there might just as well have been: they were dormant in our hands.'[cc] Targeting heretics, they were inoperative as long as schism was not identified with heresy, and we shall see that this identification would be the major turning-point in the anti-Donatist struggle. But that was not the only explanation: had these laws been applicable, judges would have been needed to have them enforced; but at the very end of the fourth century, the highest local authorities in Africa were not in the least inclined to do so. For ten years or so, chiefly in Numidia, the Donatist leaders had been able to rely on the connivance, if not the support, of the Count of Africa, the all-powerful Gildo, and his dissidence towards the imperial government had shielded them from any action against them. During those years – apparently in 395 – the Catholics had turned in vain to the *vicarius* of Africa, Seranus, to have the notorius Optat of Timgad – who was under Gildo's protection – condemned according to the term of the law of 15 June 392, which inflicted a fine of ten gold *librae* on heretics.[dd] Becoming proconsul of Africa soon after, Seranus, in the case of the episcopal see of Membressa (Medjez el-Bab), had made a judgement in favour of the hard wing of the schismatic Church when there was a settling of scores between 'Primianists' and 'Maximianists'. The bishop Salvius, an old man, had been driven from his chair and forced to parade in shame in the streets of his town, amid dancing and shouting, with the corpses of dogs hung around his neck.[7]

It is noteworthy that in the last decade of the fourth century, in Africa, the machinery of State was no less favourable to the Donatists than in the brief reign of Julian the Apostate;[8] and local authorities, even if not actively in connivance, were often very reluctant to become involved in this religious struggle and choose a particular side. Remember Eusebius' evasiveness at Hippo, when he was implored by Valerius' coadjutor to intervene but in the event did nothing.[ee] That wait-and-see attitude would persist, even when, on several occasions, the imperial government clearly indicated its wish to have done with the schism: the edict of 12 February 405 threatened a fine of twenty gold *librae* not only for governors of provinces who failed to apply the sanctions but also, for the same reason, for 'defenders of the cities' and notables in general.[ff] In 407 and 409, that threat was reiterated against provincial and municipal authorities who persisted in closing their eyes to the Donatists' machinations.[9]

Locally, the *de facto* authorities formed by the great landed property-owners had also to be taken into account. Many of them were 'Donatists', probably less from conviction than from a concern to be in tune with their peasant grass-roots, from whose heart the schismatic Church recruited not only the majority of its followers but also its strongarm men, the circumcellions. A typical instance is of one Celer, and the story of his progress. Augustine was set on winning over to his Church this personage of senatorial rank, who owned land in his diocese, first in order to snatch him away from his 'old liaison' (*consuetudo*) with the Donatists,[gg] but also to persuade him that through the intermediary of men in his service, Paternus and Maurusius, he should act in the cause of 'Catholic unity' in the region of Hippo.[hh] Augustine would win the case, and Donatism would recede from Celer's properties; but the situation was delicate. In 412, when his steward, named Spondeus, absented himself to go to Carthage, that was all it took for the schism to become reactivated on Celer's estates, and for Donatist churches there to re-open.[ii] The bishop of Hippo's personal diplomacy with regard to these men, who were locally influential but often themselves engaged in difficult matters, was an essential piece in the game he played during these years. To Pancarius, a newcomer to one of the diocese's rural areas – a place known as Germaniciana – who was spreading hostile talk emanating from the Donatists against the local Catholic priest, Augustine wrote to warn him and ask him to make sure that there were no schismatics where there had been none before his arrival.[jj] The bishop also had some trusty friends among these great landowners, but this did not imply that *ipso facto* all the men in their service were good Catholics; but it was easier for him to urge them to throw all their weight in the right direction. In this way he persuaded Pammachius, the Roman senator who was a friend of Jerome, to bring back to the fold all his peasants who had been won over to Donatism on the immense estates he owned in the high plains of central Numidia.[kk] And he suggested that Pammachius should have the letter of thanks he had received from the bishop of Hippo read by those around him in the Senate in Rome, to encourage other senators to follow his example on the lands they owned in Africa.[ll]

On the cusp of the fourth and fifth century, Augustine's vigilant firmness regarding the schismatics was still following diplomatic paths, and that was not simply a suitable attitude on his part. He had *a priori* every reason to believe in the virtues of a dialogue which had not turned out so badly with the Manichaeans; the only problem was to manage to engage in one. We may recall the excuses of Procleianus in 395/6; but in the same period, the semi-success of the encounter with Fortunius of Thubursicu Numidarum had been an encouragement, all in all. A little later, taking advantage of what an intermediary had told him of his desire to correspond, Augustine wrote to one of his Donatist colleagues in a diocese near Hippo, Honoratus, asking him to reply on a fundamental point of their ecclesiological difference: how was it possible that the Church of Christ, destined to spread among all nations, was, according to them, no longer represented except by some Africans?[mm] Datable to the same years is an exchange of correspondence – only the bishop's letter remains – between Augustine and one of his relatives, Severinus, who was keenly exhorted not to dwell as a brother apart, especially as he was a blood brother.[nn]

Every opportunity had to be grasped. Probably in the spring of 399, the bishop of Hippo had had occasion to meet in Carthage his Donatist colleague from Calama, Crispinus, who had seemed open to debate and ready to pursue it, according to public rumour.[oo] Augustine did not propose a new meeting and hoped to keep it to an exchange of letters. Did he suspect Crispinus' good faith, despite the latter's earlier approaches?[10] In this instance, events proved him right, for soon afterwards Crispinus acted contrary to his declared good intentions by forcibly rebaptizing the peasants of a former imperial estate, the *fundus Mappaliensis*, which he had just acquired by an emphyteutic lease. If he was to be prosecuted under the terms of the law of 15 June 392, which had not yet been applied in Africa, he risked the penalty it prescribed, the payment of a fine of ten gold *librae*. Augustine offered him an alternative solution, a debate in front of the peasants concerned, translated into Punic so that they could be the judges and say to which communion their free will directed them.[pp] Crispinus refused, but that was not the end of the story, and we shall meet this person again.

The genesis of the great anti-Donatist treatises

Every time we take a close look at the rather precisely dated traces of Augustine's life, we are seized with dizziness. Like 397, the year 400 is one of those crammed years that, in case of chronological doubt, one is tempted to lighten the Augustinian calendar rather than make it heavier. Yet the bishop of Hippo did not go to Carthage that year, as no council was held there. We know that before the council, if it was held at the end of the summer, or after, if it met at the end of May or early June, Augustine would yield to Aurelius' entreaties for a series of sermons which would keep him in the mother-city for several weeks, if not months. Perhaps he took advantage, that year, of his availability during the summer to make one of those long tours through the numerous churches in his diocese, like the one he mentions in a letter to Celer, already quoted.[qq]

Besides his habitual pastoral obligations, Augustine was at the time very busy with his literary work. He had just completed his *Confessions*,[rr] and was working on two long and exacting works, the *De Trinitate* and the *De Genesi ad litteram*. As we have just seen, his polemical activity was divided between his desire to have done with the Manichaeans and his more recent concern to reduce the Donatist schism, and he had a growing feeling of the urgency of this latter task. Bringing it to a successful conclusion meant that he would not content himself with simple exchanges of letters, but would achieve his aims by writing full refutations, comparable with those he had used – and was still using – against the Manichaeans. As so often occurred in Augustine's life, going from thought to deed was fortuitous.

For some unknown reason, probably in the spring of 400, he went to Cirta. Shortly beforehand, a Catholic in that town, Generosus, had received a strange letter in which a Donatist priest of the same town claimed to have received from an angel the mission to convert him.[ss] He revealed the matter to his bishop, Fortunatus, the successor to Profuturus, who had died prematurely, and as

Augustine and Alypius were both with Fortunatus at the time, Generosus – for his edification – received a letter, signed by the three bishops, in which the bishop of Hippo's hand is clearly visible.[tt] And as they were at Cirta, a centre of anti-Catholic protest from the outset, but also one of surrender at the time of the great persecution, this letter written as a rapid aide-mémoire for Generosus' use took good care not to omit the records of the seizures made in the town church on 19 May 303, from which it emerged that Silvanus, then sub-deacon and consecrated bishop a few years later, was well and truly a 'traitor'.[11] With this, if need be, he could put Petilianus in his place; he was the current Donatist bishop of the town and, like all his colleagues, champion of a Church 'without spot or blemish'. Petilianus had at first been its victim: a young lawyer, still a catechumen in the faith of his Catholic parents, he had been veritably abducted by the schismatics, who had forcefully rebaptized and subsequently ordained him against his will.[uu] Twenty years later, Petilianus had become one of the leaders of his Church. He was not a great thinker, but wily and pugnacious; we shall see how ready he was to fight in the debates of 411 at the conference in Carthage.

In his bizarre letter to Generosus, the Donatist priest had mentioned a pastoral letter written by Petilianus to his clergy in polemical terms against the Catholic Church. That letter was also circulating in the town among the Catholic followers; it was shown to Augustine who forthwith undertook to refute it.[12] He did so in the form of a letter addressed to his own faithful in Hippo, and the initial refutation constitutes the first book of the *Contra litteras Petiliani*, and there is every reason to suppose that the bishop wrote it immediately on his return home. But originally only the first part of the document had been passed on to him; afterwards, he was sent the complete text and, although in Augustine's opinion the supplement added little, he felt obliged to resume his criticism within the rules, doing so as he had for his *Contra Faustum*, in the style of a debate, Petilianus' quoted text being immediately followed by a developed refutation: this was the subject of the very long second book of the treatise.[vv] However, the schismatic bishop of Constantine knew of Augustine's text and, in his turn, trotted out an *Epistula* which was not lacking in personal attacks. Meanwhile, the *Confessions* had been published and provided much food for slander, above all about their author's Manichaean past. Petilianus also defended his theology of the sacraments and argued, quite feebly, over the history of the schism. A reply was called for; this would be the third book of the *Contra litteras Petiliani*, which Augustine was unable to complete before the end of 402 or 403.

Even at the time of his early episcopacy, Augustine was in possession of a solid dossier on the origins of the schism and its historical developments throughout the fourth century, as is revealed, after the 'alphabetic Psalm', by the long letters 43 and 44, which summed up the situation following the meetings with Fortunius of Thubursicu Numidarum.[ww] Building the dossier of what he often called the *causa ecclesiae*, the definition and defence of the true Church, with its doctrinal implications, took him a little longer. There, too, he took advantage of circumstance.

We may recall the strong impression made on him by the writings of Tyconius, which he had discovered during his priesthood, when he had found the Donatist theologian a good guide in his approach to St Paul. We know that Tyconius was a free thinker who did not accept the restricted views of his hierarchy on a

'Church of the pure', confined to Africa, which had caused him to have his knuckles rapped by Parmenianus. In 394, Augustine was unaware of the Donatist primate's letter of reprimand. When he set about refuting this letter, in the *Contra epistulam Parmeniani*, the document had just come into his hands. It was the chance he had dreamt of – the more so because its starting-point had been provided by a doctrinal dissension in the very heart of the schismatic Church! – to undertake a profound debate for which the bishop felt himself to be filled with a pastoral mission.[xx] Can a date be put on the start of this enterprise? Book I alludes to the 'recent laws' on the smashing of idols and banning of pagan sacrifices, laws issued by Honorius in the early months of 399.[yy] It can therefore be accepted that Augustine began the work in 400 or 401 at the latest.[13]

He composed this treatise in parallel with the text he was writing against Petilianus. The two works were not superfluous: although the fairly brief first book against Parmenianus' letter was still centred on the historical wrongs committed by the Donatists, Augustine was evidently in haste to tackle the scriptural dossier,[zz] which he had not neglected in his replies to Petilianus, but to which the very form of open debate had imparted a 'splintered' presentation. The aim of Books II and III was a sustained dispute about the *testimonia* on which Parmenianus relied. Rereading his treatise after twenty-five years, the bishop remembered what with hindsight seemed to him to be the essential; in this book, he wrote in the *Retractations*, 'a new question is posed and resolved: do the wicked corrupt the good in the unity and communion of the same sacraments?'[ab] This, formulated after the event in a few words, was the central question, in which the main ecclesiological debate could be summed up. But it could be resolved only by dealing with 'additional' questions as important as those relating to the validity of baptism, whoever the minister might be. Augustine knew that he still had to define his stance on this problem and first to clarify for himself that of St Cyprian, with whose authority his opponents covered themselves.[14] In Book II of the *Against Parmenianus*, he postponed that study till later.[ac] In fact, he hardly waited at all: the seven books of the *De baptismo* are generally agreed to date to the first two or three years of the fifth century.

Composed in 405–6, Augustine's last, and also most voluminous, great anti-Donatist treatise is, curiously, an unexpected sequel to the controversies against Petilianus, begun in 400. The genesis of this *Contra Cresconium* is a good illustration of how difficult it was to circulate written works in that period – the slowness, the restrictions and the risks. The first answer given by Augustine to the schismatic bishop of Constantine's pastoral letter – the first book of the *Contra litteras Petiliani* – had fallen into the hands of a lay Donatist, a grammarian by profession. Was Cresconius making a point of replying *proprio motu* or had it been suggested to him by the prelates of the sect?[ad] At all events, probably because Augustine was working on his second refutation of the bishop of Constantine, Cresconius became embroiled in this duel and wrote a pamphlet of his own devising, addressed to the bishop of Hippo.[15] It took such a long time to reach its destination that in the initial sentence of his reply, which was itself much delayed, Augustine wondered when his text would get to Cresconius.[ae] As he would state in his *Retractations*, the emperor Honorius had already published his 'laws against the Donatists' when he wrote his four books.[af] These laws, components in their ensemble of the famous 'edict of union', which I shall mention later, date to the beginning of 405; and in any case it took Augustine many months to dictate the 500 big pages of the *Contra Cresconium*, quite apart from all his other tasks.

He tirelessly carried on his demonstrations of the inconsistency of the schismatics, who reproached their adversaries for crimes of *traditio* of which they themselves had been guilty, and for having sought arbitration from the secular government for which they too had appealed. There followed repetitions of the facts themselves; but those were inevitable, seeing that Augustine, as a good advocate and responsible pastor, thought it his duty to reply to each and every attack. Supposing that a wider circulation of the texts could have given him the material opportunity, he would have considered it shirking that duty if he referred Cresconius to his earlier writings. Despite the repetitions, the long reply to the grammarian has its own features. Its special tone has partly to do with the opponent's personality: Cresconius, any more than Petilianus, did not spare Augustine his personal attacks, but he had neither the cunning nor the guile of the Donatist bishop. There was some jubilation on the bishop of Hippo's part when he saw Cresconius sometimes rashly leave himself open to attack. For instance, when the grammarian risked giving his definition of heresy and schism: 'Heresy is the sect of people who follow different doctrines, schism a division between upholders of the same doctrines.'[ag] Cresconius evidently considered that he, and those of his Church, were not in heresy – condemned by the imperial laws – but in schism. Then why rebaptize? retorted Augustine, who pictured himself emerging from a mousehole and bursting unexpectedly into the midst of an assembly of Donatists practising second baptism, and brandishing Cresconius' letter which demonstrated its pointlessness and absurdity.[ah] Augustine soon revealed the essence of his thinking on heresy: it was an 'inveterate schism'.[16] That may be regarded as rather too convenient a definition. But let us not forget that the year was 405, the excesses of the circumcellions and radical wing of Donatism were at their height, Honorius' laws placing schism and heresy in the same category because of rebaptism had just been published, and we must admit that the events he was experiencing could have influenced the bishop of Hippo's stance.

In any case, could Donatism still be looked upon as a simple schism when it had recently split itself into two fiercely opposing factions? One last originality in the *Contra Cresconium*, by comparison with the preceding anti-Donatist texts, was precisely that it systematically exploited the dissensions in the bosom of the rival Church – the whole of Book IV was devoted to it. Early in the last decade of the fourth century, partisans of Primianus, primate of the schismatic Church, and those of Maximianus, a Carthaginian deacon who had been excommunicated by the primate, had clashed fiercely. In this affair alone, there was enough for Augustine to confound the Donatists. First, the very history of the Maximianist schism's origins mirrored those of the Donatist schism: the 'déjà-vu' impression was striking.[ai] Then, the appeal to the secular arm: the Primianists, dominant Donatists, who had shamelessly called down the repressive resources of imperial legislation against their own schismatics, were in no position to blame the Catholics for resorting to it against the Donatists.[aj] The same went for rebaptism: by not practising a repeat baptism with regard to Maximianists who had rallied round, the Donatists had thereby condemned their practice with regard to

Catholics.[ak] Lastly, if Maximianus' 'crime' had not corrupted his followers, who were subsequently received into the Donatist communion and had their honours restored, how could the 'crime' of Caecilianus, always supposing it could be proved, have been able to corrupt the Catholic Church?[al] The entire history of this dispute thus proved that, for the sake of unity, a mixture of the 'wicked' and the 'good' must be tolerated in the Church of the present time.

Developing a theology of the Church

Between 400 and 406, Augustine had accumulated thousands of pages against the Donatists, and we must further add dozens of letters and sermons,[17] not forgetting the lost books, indicated as such in the *Retractations*.[am] This 'bombardment' may seem excessive to us, the expenditure of energy out of all proportion, and it is a fact that it was due only to the bishop of Hippo's fabulous capacity for work that he was not completely engulfed in this polemic. It is hard for us to imagine what was at stake in terms of the defence and protection of an institution – the Church – of which it might be said that it was one of the main pillars of the society of that time; but we shall see in the following pages that Donatism exposed that society to a real and serious risk. Against the danger of subversion, Augustine's writings by themselves were ineffective; but they had another, fundamental function to the advantage of the Church, which was indebted to the bishop of Hippo for a first attempt – pursued thanks to the Pelagian controversy and subsequently achieved in the *City of God* – to define its spiritual reality, above and beyond its terrestrial and temporal body.

It has been jestingly said of Augustine that when he was listening to the Donatists he was thinking of something else.[18] We must hope so, for his sake, for their arguments were dismally repetitive, sombre and lacking in perspective. When they were not raking over, for the nth time, the crimes of *traditio* committed by those who had consecrated Caecilianus early in the fourth century, and chiefly one of them, Felix, an obscure bishop of a township in Proconsular Africa (Abthugni, Henchir es-Souar, in Tunisia) whom they had managed to make famous,[an] they shut themselves away in a Church that resembled a besieged hideout. They had a predilection for spatial imagery that expressed the idea of enclosure, especially for what they read in the Song of Songs (4.12): the Church was 'the garden enclosed, the fountain sealed'.[ao] The Ark in which Noah had taken refuge lent itself to the same symbolic use: a symbol that was assuredly universally admitted by Christians in the wake of the apostle Peter (1 Pet. 3.20–1) – and thus by Augustine himself[ap] – but whose meaning the Donatists had distorted by insisting on the watertightness of this abode. One of their bishops, Augustine recounted, told his flock that these wooden structures had been caulked with pitch on the inside as well as the outside. True – cf. Gen. 6.14 – but the interesting thing was the exegesis given by the Donatist: on the inside, to prevent the leakage of the salutary waters of baptism, and externally to prevent the sullied waters getting in from outside.[19]

Listening to the Donatists, Augustine's idea was to counter their ecclesiology with a different conception of the Church. The difficulty he encountered was that this vocabulary of interiority and exteriority, inclusion and exclusion, had already been used a century and a half earlier – it is true, in the quite different context of a persecuted and cruelly assailed Church – by the great African martyr, Cyprian. The commentary made by the bishop of Carthage in the mid-third century on the above-quoted text from the Song of Songs was remarkable.

> If the bride of Christ, the Church, is an enclosed garden, a closed thing cannot be opened to strangers, to the profane; if it is a sealed fountain, anyone who is outside, with no access to the fountain, cannot drink from it or receive the mark of the seal. And if a well of living water is unique and within, the one who is outside cannot be given life and sanctified by that water which only those who are within may use and drink.[aq]

Augustine could subscribe to the famous saying of the bishop of Carthage, *extra ecclesiam nulla salus*, but not to the theology of the sacraments that accompanied it. For he knew now what he had not known when, as a priest, he had written against Donatus' letter:[ar] that Cyprian had protected with his authority the rebaptism of heretics,[20] and that the foundation of the Donatists' baptismal theology was to be found in his writings, whose authenticity he did not for a moment dream of challenging, unlike some Catholics of his time.[as]

What was to be done? A *Contra donatistas* could be written, but there was no question of writing a *Contra Cyprianum;* as both African and martyr, Cyprian was doubly untouchable. In the *De baptismo,* Augustine's efforts would go into disassociating the bishop of Carthage from the Donatists, robbing the latter of the prestigious patronage of which they boasted. It was not so easy: he had to show that, despite his error,[21] Cyprian was still a master whose spirit had been betrayed by schismatics. Between the bishop of Carthage and the Donatists, Augustine could first drive a wedge on the moral plane. Cyprian had considered baptism of heretics as useless, but he had not by any means wanted to break communion with those who thought otherwise, judging that divergences on this point should not be the occasion for schism.[22] Added to that, relative to the Donatists, was a difference on the doctrinal plane since, although like them he rejected the baptism of heretics, Cyprian had accepted the validity of a baptism administered by sinners. Augustine could therefore have the support of his authority against the schismatics when he stated that communion with sinners did not destroy membership of the Church.

Depriving the Donatists of their Cyprianic backing in their sacramentary theology was a necessary operation, but it was not enough. Based on a criticism of their ecclesiology, another needed to be constructed, retaining earlier contributions, such as those of Optat of Milevis, but going beyond them. Donatus' Church had lived for nearly a century on ideas that were simple but strong, like all slogans: it was the Church of the martyrs and the Church of the pure. The mystique of martyrdom was at the heart of the Donatists' popular religion; it had naturally reached its peaks of demonstration during the high points of confrontation with the secular authority in the mid-fourth century, notably when the presence of soldiers made it easier to provoke martyrdom by getting oneself killed, if one did not commit suicide, singly or in a group.[at] In the same period, one of their pamphleteers, Vitellius Afer, had written a little book whose title alone spoke volumes: 'Of the hatred inspired in the world by the servants of God'. The Donatists always presented their eponymous leader, Donatus, as a true hero, 'haloed with the glory of the martyr'[23] and still considered themselves honoured, a century after the peace of the Church, to be 'the Church that suffers persecution': that was how they would describe themselves 'officially', before the imperial judge, at Carthage in June 411.[au] Invoking the discourse on the Beatitudes, Augustine of course replied that it was not enough to be persecuted in order to be saved, always supposing that were true; one must be persecuted for justice.[av] This Church of martyrs also proclaimed itself as the Church of the pure, the pinnacle of irreproachable men, doubtless in the area of ethical life, but chiefly in that of religious life. The Church had to be like the Bride of Christ in St Paul, 'without spot or wrinkle' (Eph. 5.27), and here and now, without distinction between its terrestrial, historical state and its celestial, eschatological future. For them the field in the parable was not the world, but Africa, their Africa,[aw] and they did not want to wait until harvest time to see the good grain separated from the tares, whose existence among them they denied because they claimed to have already done the work of the reaping angels.[ax] One may imagine the formidable effectiveness of such discourse on simple souls.

The Catholics, however, had not waited until the very end of the fourth century and the bishop of Hippo in order to react. In 366/7, Optat, bishop of Milevis (Mila), the episcopal see now occupied by the beloved Severus, had been the first to undertake a written refutation of a collection of the works of Parmenianus, then leader of the sect, because he had not been able to hold a verbal debate with him.[24] And, some twenty years later, to the six books of his *Treatise against the Donatists* he had added a seventh, to reply to the objections raised by his adversaries against the books already published.[ay] The bishop of Milevis had also had the great merit of assembling as a supplement to his work a collection of official documents and pieces from the archives, chiefly relating to the origins of the schism, which he used in his historical refutation of the Donatists' accusations, and which Augustine himself frequently quoted.[25] If we are initially indebted to Optat, and often to him alone, for the portrayal of the serious disturbances against the backdrop of Numidia in the middle of the fourth century with the emergence of the circumcellions' movement,[az] he was also the first to have countered the schismatics' arguments with a coherent ecclesiological position. In the face of Donatist pretensions that they alone represented the *catholica* when they were confined in their African retreat,[26] Optat had demanded for his followers the title of 'Catholics' in the only acceptable sense of the word, which referred – from the Greek *katholou* – to the universality of communion, whereas the schismatics wanted to interpret it in the sense of the fullness of the sacraments. And they wrapped their geographical illusion in a forced and approximate interpretation of the Song of Songs, where the Bride asks her Beloved: 'Tell me, O thou whom my soul loveth, where thou makest thy flock to feed, where thou takest thy rest at noon.'[27] They understood from this that Christ had taken his flock to Africa! It was easy for the bishop of Milevis to challenge these claims with texts, notably drawn from the Psalms, which let it be clearly understood that in its capacity of the Betrothed, the Church must extend throughout the entire universe.[ba] In this regard, Augustine only complemented the scriptual dossier compiled by Optat.

In many other respects, too, the bishop of Hippo appears as the heir to a theology of the Church already more than outlined by the bishop of Milevis several decades previously;[28] but the heritage is refined and enriched. Optat had

defined the Church as a *corpus mixtum*, a mixture of the good and the wicked,
righteous and sinners. Augustine enlarged this theme, using a whole apparatus
of texts to work on it – mainly drawn from the Gospel according to St Matthew –
not all of which had been quoted by the bishop of Milevis: the imagery of the
winnowing and separation of the chaff from the grain on the last day (Matt. 3.12),
the parable of the net brought to the shore where the good and bad fish are sorted
(Matt. 13.47–50). Thus the Donatist slogan of the Church's purity, *hic et nunc* –
which the schismatics were confident of attaining by winnowing here below![bc] –
was challenged by Augustine's distinction between the two states of the Church,
by re-establishing a tension between its historical present – *ecclesia quae nunc est* –
and its eschatological future – *ecclesia qualis futura est*.[bd] He added – and this
above all was his personal mark – a second distinction regarding the Church in
present time, which for him was not a monolith, or a place in which one settled
entirely once and for all, or from which one was excluded once and for all.
Everyone could see that there were sinners within the Church, and righteous
people outside it. Through simplism, the Donatists had made a sect out of a
complex ecclesiastic reality. They set out in principle a perfectly homogeneous
Church, composed of the pure, *integri*, which, carefully separated from the other
one that had been sullied by the progeny of the *traditores*, was the single, perfect
Bride of the Song of Songs, the sealed Fountain that alone dispensed the saving
waters of baptism. Augustine answered them by fixing two levels of ecclesiastic
reality, one of which was of course the sacramental institution, with participation
in the sacraments on the part of the faithful; this he called the *communio
sacramentorum*.[29] This level, of the communion of the sacraments, where the
Donatists were situated by virtue of a perfectly valid baptism,[30] just like Catholics
who could possibly be wicked, was a level of external, or corporeal, adherence,
or yet a level of appearance compared with a true situation. 'Many sinners', said
the bishop, 'are in communion with the Church's sacraments, without in any way
being within the Church.'[be] Or, in other words, if they were in the Church,
physically, carnally, they were not 'of' the Church, on a level of spiritual truth.
They were not placed on the other level of ecclesiastic reality that Augustine had
distinguished, calling it *societas* (or *congregatio*) *sanctorum*,[bf] composed of the
faithful 'saints', united in love by God's active presence within them. As a shrewd
exegetist of Augustinian ecclesiology has written, Augustine

> pushed the necessity for purity farther than the Donatists: for they clung only to
> ecclesiological purity, of a Church of *integri* from which in fact only those who defaulted
> with regard to the Church were excluded: *lapsi, traditores*, persecutors, the
> excommunicated. Augustine stuck to *theological* purity.[31]

At the time of this reflection on the Church to which his controversies with the
Donatists had led him, the theme of the two cities began to take shape in
Augustine's mind.[bg] There was nothing better than the argument about sinners
within the Church for proving that until Judgement Day Babylon and Jerusalem
were intermingled and that, 'in the course of its pilgrimage in the world, the city
of God numbered in its bosom men that were united with it through participation
in the sacraments, but who did not share with it the eternal destiny of the saints.'[bh]
The Church itself, the Church of present times, of the terrestrial city, a temporary

country between Babylon and Jerusalem,[32] was part of these 'perishable machines' destined to disappear once the edifice destined to remain was built: *Architectus aedificat per machinas transitorias domum mansuram.*[bi] The bishop who uttered these words at the end of his life, showing the faithful of Hippo the walls of the basilica where he was preaching, resorted to this image when thinking of the incarnation of Jesus, his death and resurrection.[bj] But it was also valid for the Church of the *civitas terrena*, the transitory instrument of men's salvation.

Notes

a.   *Sermon* 129, 4: *Voce ecclesiae loquor*, in a mainly anti-Donatist text.
b.   Above, p. 174.
c.   Cf. above, p. 170.
d.   Above, pp. 154–5.
e.   *Retract.*, I, 22, 1.
f.   Cf. in particular above, pp. 134–5.
g.   *C. Adim.*, III, 4.
h.   *Retract.*, I, 22, 2.
i.   *C. Adim.*, IV.
j.   *C. Adim.*, II, 2.
k.   *Contra Faustum*, I, 1.
l.   Above, p. 55.
m.   *C. Faust.*, XXIII, 6.
n.   See notably *C. Faust.*, IV, 1 and VI, 1, on the material aspects of the ancient Law.
o.   *C. Faust.*, II, 1; III, 1; VI, 1. He would return to it again in XXIII, 1.
p.   *C. Faust.*, XIX, 31, quoted in the lightly reworked translation by G. Madec in *Introduction aux 'Revisions' et à la lecture de saint Augustin*, p. 86.
q.   Notably in the *City of God*, XV, 7, 2; XV, 26, 2; XVI, 41.
r.   *Contra Felicem*, II, 1. On this basilica, cf. above, p. 239.
s.   This is the sense of the word *versutior*: *Retract.*, II, 8.
t.   *C. Felicem*, I, 15.
u.   *C. Felicem*, I, 20.
v.   *C. Felicem*, II, 1.
w.   *C. Felicem*, II, 2–8. In the *Retractations*, the bishop excuses himself for not having tackled the problem of grace at that time: it was not, he says, his intention.
x.   *C. Felicem*, II, 14.
y.   *Vita Aug.*, XVI, 4.
z.   *Contra Secundinum*, XXIV.
aa.   *Retract.* II, 10.
bb.   Above, p. 169.
cc.   *Contra Cresconium*, III, 51.
dd.   *Contra litt. Pet.*, II, 184.
ee.   Above, p. 188.
ff.   *C. Th.*, XVI, 6, 4, S 4.
gg.   *Ep.* 56, 2.
hh.   *Ep.* 57, 2.
ii.   *Ep.* 139, 2.
jj.   *Ep.* 251.
kk.   *Ep.* 58, 1.
ll.   *Ep.* 58, 3.
mm.   *Ep.* 49, 3. This undated letter is later than 396.

nn.   *Ep.* 52, 1.
oo.   *Ep.* 51, 1.
pp.   *Ep.* 66, 2.
qq.   *Ep.* 56, 1; the date of 400 for this letter is not certain.
rr.   On the date when the *Confessions* were completed, see above, p. 206.
ss.   *Ep.* 53, 1.
tt.   This is letter 53, datable to between 27 November 399 and 19 December 401 from the mention of the latest pope then in office, Anastasius (*Ep.* 53, 2).
uu.   Cf. *Contra litt. Pet.*, II, 239 and *Sermo ad Caesar. eccl. plebem*, 8.
vv.   Cf. *C. litt. Pet.*, II, 1; *Retract.*, II, 25.
ww. Above, p. 187.
xx.   *Contra epist. Parm.*, I, 1.
yy.   Cf. above, p. 221.
zz.   Cf. *Contra epist. Parm.*, I, 21, *in fine*.
ab.   *Retract.*, II, 17.
ac.   *Contra epist. Parm.*, II, 32.
ad.   Augustine shrewdly says that should Cresconius, a layman, fail, the bishops of his sect could always disown him: 'His victory would be ours, his defeat his own' (*Contra Cresc.*, II, 7).
ae.   *Contra Cresc.*, I, 1.
af.   *Retract.*, II, 26.
ag.   *Contra Cresc.*, II, 6.
ah.   *Contra Cresc.*, II, 7.
ai.   *Contra Cresc.*, IV, 63–7.
aj.   *Contra Cresc.*, IV, 56–62.
ak.   *Contra Cresc.*, IV, 13–32.
al.   *Contra Cresc.*, IV, 33–50.
am.   *Retract.*, II, 19, 27, 28, 29.
an.   This is the famous 'Felix of Aptonge' of Lenain de Tillemont and subsequent ecclesiastical literature, the name of his see having been scratched in the manuscript tradition.
ao.   Cf. Parmenianus in Optat, II, 13, and Cresconius in *C. Cresc.*, I, 40 and IV, 77.
ap.   *Enarr. in Psalm.* 103, 3, 2; *In Ioh. evang.*, IX, 11 and 14.
aq.   Cyprian, *Ep.* 69, 2, 1.
ar.   *Retract.*, I, 21, 3.
as.   *Ep.* 93, 39.
at.   Cf. above, pp. 167–8, the story of 'domnus Marculus' and the long reputation for sanctity of this person.
au.   *Actes de la Conférence de Carthage en 411*, III, 258, SC, 244, p. 1195.
av.   See, among other texts, *Ep.* 185, 9, quoting Matt. 5.10.
aw.   *Contra epist. Parm.*, II, 5.
ax.   Cf. Matt. 13.38 and *Contra epist. Parm.*, I, 21 and II, 5.
ay.   Optat, VII, 1.
az.   Optat, III, 3–4.
ba.   Optat, II, 1–13.
bc.   Since Parmenianus thus took himself to be God the Father, Augustine called him 'the Winnower' (*ventilator*): *Contra epist. Parm.*, III, 18.
bd.   Cf. *Enarr. in Psalm.* 9, 12; the phrase will reappear similarly in *City of God*, XX, 9, 1.
be.   *Epist. ad cath.*, 74.
bf.   *Societas sanctorum*: *In Ioh. evang.*, 26, 17; *congregatio sanctorum*: *De baptismo*, I, 26.
bg.   Cf. *Contra epist. Parm.*, II, 9, and the first appearance in this test of the contrast between Jerusalem and Babylon.
bh.   *City of God*, I, 35. At the time of writing of this text, c. 412, the anti-Donatist struggle was still very recent.
bi.   *Sermon* 362, 7.
bj.   The resurrection is the subject of this great and beautiful sermon.

CHAPTER XXVI

The Carthage conference of 411

The Catholic episcopacy had not been slow to adopt the bishop of Hippo's personal approach in his attempts to have meetings with the Donatist bishops. In 401, the general council which had gathered on 13 September decided to hold discussions with the rival episcopacy 'in a spirit of peace'.[1] Armed with a mandate setting out the limits of a possible negotiation, and in the formulations of which Augustine's hand was noticeable, a delegation of bishops was to go from one diocese to another preaching peace and unity and trying to persuade Donatist clergy and faithful of the futility of the differences that set them against the Catholic Church. It was also planned to use the schismatics' own dissensions against them, by having the governors of provinces draw up and make public records of the quarrels between Primianists and Maximianists. This project for an itinerant embassy certainly failed; at least nothing further is known about it. Two years later, it was not resumed but replaced by far more precise and exacting measures devised by the council that met at Carthage on 25 August 403.

The 403 plan for a meeting and the aftermath

It was like a dress rehearsal for the procedures which would effectively emerge eight years later, in 411, but with this substantial difference: that it was the Catholic Church, and not the imperial government, which took the initiative for the encounter, and no arbitration was planned. However, a government presence had been requested, as necessary: on 13 September, mandated by the council, Aurelius of Carthage asked the proconsul Septiminus to order the local magistrates in each city to place themselves at the disposal of the Catholic bishop. Septiminus immediately issued an edict which satisfied the Catholics, with partisan preambles that were not of a kind to encourage the Donatists to respond positively to these invitations.[2] Similar arrangements emanating from the *vicarius* of Africa gave the Catholics like facilities in provinces other than Proconsularis.[3] With the backing of this order, the Catholic bishop in every town or locality was thus able to have his Donatist counterpart notified of the form of convocation drawn up by the council of 25 August 403; the schismatic bishop's response had to be registered by the municipal magistrates in the official records which, supplemented by the edicts of the various governors and the text of the Catholic *mandatum*, throughout all Africa formed as many *gesta municipalia* as there were localities where Catholics and Donatists were face to face.[4]

The tone of the opposing Church's reply was set by Primianus. The Donatist primate had a deacon read a declaration which tersely expressed a categorical blunt refusal, absolutely in keeping with the schismatics' ecclesiology: it would be shameful for the sons of martyrs to meet with the mob of 'traitors'.[a] At the same time, the seething primate also denounced the collusion between the Catholics and the imperial government. Shortly afterwards, to establish a common stance with his colleagues, Primianus convened a council, which officially rejected the confrontation.[b] Augustine was then no luckier with Proculeianus than he had been eight years earlier. The Donatist bishop of Hippo, summoned thanks to Augustine before the municipal magistrates, made the excuse of the council that his Church was to hold in order to postpone his reply; on his return, summoned again, he rejected the conference.[c] Crispinus, bishop of Calama, played the same game; appearing for the second time before the magistrates in the presence of Possidius, he distinguished himself by expressing his refusal in the form of a rather incoherent and risible collection of biblical verses.[d]

The clearest result of the Catholic initiative, backed by the authorities, was to exacerbate the other side's feelings. The Donatists felt they were in a stranglehold, and their reactions were often very angry. The first to pay the price was Possidius: at Calama and in the diocese, the schismatics resented the ridicule which their old bishop's convoluted reply had earned. One of his priests, of the same name and also a relative, sought to avenge him soon after by setting an ambush for Possidius, who was then on a perilous tour in a sector where the schismatics were very much in the majority.[e] Alerted in time, the bishop altered his route and took refuge on a property where he thought he would be safe; but the other Crispinus' vengeance pursued him there. Augustine has given us a vivid, emotional and detailed account of how, in that house,[5] surrounded by the fires lit by the priest's henchmen, Possidius, who had been reached by his assailants, and subjected to insults and blows, owed his survival only to Crispinus' fear of committing the irreparable in front of so many witnesses. At Calama, it was expected that the schismatic bishop would have his priest up before the ecclesiastical court to punish him; but he took no action. Summoned to Carthage by the proconsul, he denied everything, but was confounded by Possidius, who nevertheless interceded for him so that he should not have to pay the fine of ten gold *librae*. Matters could have stopped there, with his colleagues' approval; but no, he thought it his duty to appeal against the proconsul's sentence to the emperor – Honorius at that time – who nonsuited him by a rescript of 8 December 405.[6] If Crispinus thought he could buy himself a martyr's halo for ten gold *librae* – a good round sum, it is true – he obtained no satisfaction: the Catholic bishops managed to have it returned to him. In any case, added Augustine, 'it was not the penalty that made the martyr, it was the cause'.[f] And Crispinus' cause was loathsome.

Matters between the two Churches had reached the point where such leniency could not be worth while. Shortly before, the misadventure of Restitutus had shown that, when subjected to pressure from the Catholics, the Donatists were not disposed to give in. Restitutus was a priest with the schismatics at the place known as Victoriana, a rural parish in the diocese of Hippo.[g] Shaken by the demonstration of truth, Augustine says, he had gone over very willingly to the Catholic Church; sadly, he rued the day. His former co-religionists, abetted by a band of circumcellions, had forcibly seized him, beaten him black and blue in front of all the assembled villagers, then rolled him in a pool of mud before derisively draping him in some rush matting and exhibiting him in this attire from one public square to the next.[h] In vain had Augustine complained to Proculeianus. In the diocese of Hippo these gentle conversions, due to the bishop's powers of persuasion, were increasing at that time, but converts were risking their lives: one, named Marcus, also a rural cleric, at Casphaliana, had only just escaped death. Another priest owed his safety only to flight, and his adversaries had taken their revenge on his sub-deacon by stoning him.[i]

If the new converts – renegades in the Donatists' eyes – were especially targeted, Catholic bishops were not safe either, as we saw in the case of Possidius. Augustine himself, who in this period was often travelling through the farthest-flung rural areas in his diocese, was very exposed. We already know from two texts, one by Possidius,[j] that one day during one of these tours, only a mistake on the part of his guide saved him from falling into an ambush laid by a band of circumcellions; but those two texts lacked any chronology. The very clear allusion that he makes in one of his recently published sermons, which can be dated almost certainly to 1 January 404, shows that it was within this period – probably the summer or autumn of 403 – that he had almost miraculously escaped that danger.[7] Some were less fortunate, even in Proconsularis. At Thubursicu Bure (Teboursouk), in the heart of the formerly urbanized sanctuary of the middle Medjerda, the bishop of the place, Servus Dei, accompanied by his father, an old Catholic priest, had been set upon in the middle of town while, flanked by his lawyers, he was awaiting the decision of the proconsul on church property wrongfully appropriated by the schismatics. The old priest had died as a result, but Servus Dei had survived his wounds; he had crossed the sea, as much to place himself in safety as to bear personal witness in high places to the circumcellions' violence.[k] Other seriously molested bishops had done the same.

The best example was that of Maximianus of Bagaï; it must be said that this Maximianus had accumulated plenty of reasons for deserving the wrath of the Donatists and circumcellions. He could hardly have done better: he had betrayed his own side by going over to the Catholics, and in Bagaï (Ksar Baghai), which for decades had been one of the fortresses of schism in deepest Numidia.[8] And now he was militating in favour of his new community, for example, obtaining by legal decision the restitution of a basilica established in a rural domain, the *fundus Calvianensis*.[9] That was just too much for his former friends to swallow. Augustine left an extraordinary narration – in two concordant versions written with an interval of over ten years[l] – of the attacks to which they subjected him, and which he survived by a miracle. Caught by surprise in the said basilica, Maximianus had thought he could find a more spiritual than material refuge beneath the altar; as often at that time, the altar was of wood. The attackers smashed this supposedly sacred shelter, dragged him out and beat him savagely with the debris, as well as with bludgeons and swords. The bishop was losing blood copiously, chiefly from a large wound in the groin, but did not die from it because his assailants, dragging him half-dead across the church floor, caused the dust to stanch his haemorrhage. Catholic clergy came to the aid of their bishop and carried him away; but soon afterwards Maximianus again fell into the hands of his aggressors, who once more maltreated him and finally, when night had fallen, threw him from the top of a tower. But providence was watching over him: at the foot of the tower, a pile of manure broke his fall; a peasant passing by stepped aside to answer a call of nature, noticed a body lying there, called his wife who was carrying a lantern, recognized the bishop and carried him to his home, moved by compassion, but perhaps also by the hope of some reward.[10] 'In short', concluded Augustine, 'Maximianus got better as if by a miracle; he lives, and on his body you can count more scars than he has limbs.'

At the imperial Court, where the escapee had joined Servus Dei, the sight of his badly sealed wounds made a great impression. There is no evidence that these victims of the Donatists and circumcellions crossed the sea on official assignment, but the fact is that these living exhibits[m] were far more eloquent than a long report. Did they get to the emperor before the delegation sent by the general council of 16 June 404, which could have arrived in Italy only during the summer? It seems so, by reading Augustine: when the two legates of the African Catholic Church, Evodius of Uzalis and Theasius, bishop of Memblone, not far from Utica, arrived at the Court, which had transferred to Rome, the ground was already prepared.[11] There was no longer any need for them to argue at length that the very firm instructions of which they were the bearers should be given consideration by an emperor who already knew what had to be done. The African Catholics were demanding that Theodosian legislation should be brought back into force against heretics, and notably the application to the Donatists of the famous fine of ten gold *librae* as punishment for violence or infractions committed for religious reasons;[12] they also asked that schismatics should come under a law of 381 banning heretics from making or receiving donations or legacies.[13] In the end, it meant condemning the rival Church to extinction by economic asphyxia. This 'gentle' demise suited the Catholic episcopacy very well, Augustine first and foremost.

The 'edict of union' of 405 and Donatist reaction

But the imperial chancellery went further; it prepared a batch of rulings that arrived in Africa in the spring of 405. A very brief *edictum de unitate* addressed on 5 March to the proconsul Diotimus[14] was in fact an order to make public the decrees issued in the preceding weeks, divided among several constitutions, all bearing the date 12 February in the same year. In reality, this 'edict of union' contained the intention, clearly displayed in the introduction to one of these laws, purely and simply to proscribe Donatism.[15] Because of rebaptism, schism was likened to heresy, and found itself retrospectively hit by all the legislation that had suppressed it since the time of Constantine and his sons. The re-establishment of religious unity in favour of the Catholics thus entailed the confiscation to their advantage of the rival Church's places of worship but, in Hippo at least, two years would elapse before the measures were applied. Sentences of exile could even be pronounced against schismatic bishops and clergy: the bill relating to this measure has not come down to us, but Augustine's testimony is definite on this point.[n] Honorius had really and truly signed the legal death warrant of Donatism.

Donatism had no future, but the Donatists had decided to sell their present dear. Times had changed, of course, but an already long history had taught them that there was a gap between the promulgation of a law and its application in all places and in all circumstances. In fact, there were various outcomes to the 'edict of union'. In Carthage, unity had been re-established in the early summer and, when it met on 23 August 405, the general council rejoiced over and made note of it, deciding in particular to send two Carthaginian clerics to the Court bearing a letter of thanks. But because it was aware that only in Cathage had unity been realized, the council at the same time sent missives to all the governors urging them to set about this task throughout the provinces and in all the towns.[16] In Augustine's see, the situation was in contrast and overall unfavourable to the Catholics; in Hippo itself, where the presence of the proconsul's legate ensured that the law had some force, the schismatic bishop Proculeianus, had had to yield, without however immediately abandoning his church. In the diocese's rural areas, it was another story. In a short letter addressed in 405/6 to the *vicarius* of Africa, Caecilianus, while congratulating him (in a rather overdone fashion that smacked of *captatio benevolentiae*) on his actions in favour of unity almost everywhere in the African provinces, Augustine let it be clearly understood that around Hippo and in the neighbouring regions, bordering on consular Numidia, there was still much to be done.[17] The bishop knew from experience that one must not rely only on imperial officials to obtain satisfaction; that is why he also addressed a large property-owner, Festus, so that he would lean heavily on his own men, over whom he had a hold.[o] The Donatists, said Augustine in this letter, were resisting in two ways: maltreating people or shamming dead.[p] All in all, he preferred the latter; for the circumcellions' maltreatments were cruel. One of their favourite practices was to blind Catholic clerics with a mixture of lime and vinegar;[q] on the estates, they set fire to houses and ripe crops, and smashed the big jars to waste their contents of oil or wine.

At the head of the schismatic Church, they were well aware of the new determination of the emperor and imperial government, and that the attitude of haughty disdain traditionally displayed by the sect with regard to secular authority was no longer appropriate. Realism demanded that its leaders should become a little more flexible[18] and, by talking with the wielders of that authority, try to influence their policies. Thus at the beginning of 406 a delegation of Donatist bishops went to Italy; they were led by their primate, Primianus, and in their ranks, so it seems, was a bishop named Maximinus, whom we have already met[r] and shall see again. On 30 January, at Ravenna, the delegation was received by the praetorian prefect for Italy and Africa. The exact and complete tenor of the conversations held on either side at this audience eludes us because, in the debates of the 411 conference, when a reading of the minutes was called for by the Catholics, the Donatist spokesmen opposed it so stubbornly that they managed to prevent their being produced.[19] But Augustine's allusions give a fairly accurate picture. The schismatic bishops present in Ravenna had asked the prefect to organize a meeting with their adversaries; indeed, they said, a Catholic bishop named Valentinus was there at the same time as they.[20] But he was not at the Court for that purpose and had received no mandate from his peers; and for his part, the prefect replied that the emperor alone had the authority to decide on such a confrontation: he (the prefect) had authority only to have the laws applied under the terms of which the complainants said they were persecuted.[s] Dictated by a real and therefore in principle understandable confusion, but ill prepared and unsuited to its purpose, the approach in Ravenna ended for the time being in a failure for the schismatic Church and soon revealed itself as tactically unwise. It had involved itself in something that would swallow it up entirely; for when the debate was at last officially arranged, the Catholics would make great play of the fact that their adversaries, at least this time, had been in the position of 'petitioners'. In the pettifogging disputes of 8 June 411, that would be a decisive turning-point.

Dilige et quod vis fac[21]

Although they were often accompanied by brutal reactions, the number of conversions increased. When a cleric was involved, *a fortiori* a bishop, they implied a fairly massive rallying of the community of which he was the pastor. By the same token, the Catholic Church began to be faced with problems of 'welcoming' and integrating these communities within the framework of existing bishoprics. In 407, the general council that met on 13 June had to tackle the question. A distinction was drawn between the 'before' and 'after' of the 405 edict of union, by a decision to grant a kind of 'premium' to the Donatist bishops who, before any compulsion, had been able to convert their communities solely by virtue of their personal commitment: in such cases they could retain their pastoral guidance and places of worship.[22] Conversely, subsequent to the edict of union, those communities and their Church possessions were to come under the leadership of the Catholic bishop of that diocese or, if one did not exist, to be attached to a neighbouring Catholic bishopric.[23]

That must have been the case of Maximinus of Siniti, with whom Augustine had had a brush in the period of his priesthood,[t] and who accompanied Primianus to Ravenna early in 406. Maximinus had rallied to the Catholics after his return from Italy. Though belated, his rallying was not without merit, for the pressure exerted by the circumcellions remained strong in the mountainous confines of the south-east of the diocese of Hippo.[24] The Donatists had sent a 'town crier' (*praeco*) there to warn the populace: 'Whoever enters into communion with Maximinus will have his house burnt!'[u] One of Augustine's recently published sermons enables us to put a closer date on this courageous step, which was also a success for the bishop of Hippo. In it we find Maximinus accompanying him on the tour during which this sermon was delivered. Augustine is pleased to present him to the congregation[v] and makes tactful mention of the difficulties in which his (recent) conversion has placed Maximinus, during which he has supported him by being present in Siniti. The two bishops travelled together to the town where this sermon was delivered.[25] Better still, Maximinus in person – an eleventh-hour labourer and proud of it[26] – briefly took the floor to make an official declaration of his conversion to the Catholic side. Augustine, for his part, was overjoyed that unity had at last been achieved in his episcopal city, not without troubles,[w] and still a little behindhand in the depths of his diocese because of the slow-wittedness (*rusticitas*) of the rural inhabitants.[x] If one were to hazard a date for this sermon, and at the same time for Maximinus' conversion and his own speech, the mention of the re-establishment of unity in Hippo would allow it. For Augustine there would be no unity as long as the Donatists possessed and used a place of worship there. He says so in a commentary on the First Epistle of John which we know to have been preached in the episcopal town during Easter Week 407: 'If we are in a state of unity, why are there two altars in this town?'[y] In order to obtain the devolution of Donatist churches to the Catholics everywhere, and notably in Hippo, there was still a need to fight, make representations to the central government – as we see the Carthaginian council do in June 407 – and for the emperor, duly approached, to issue an order to his praetorian prefect, on 15 November of the same year, jointly targeting the possessions of the pagans and the vast nebulous swarm of heretics, including the Donatists.[27] So rather than in the autumn of 406,[28] one would therefore date to the following year Maximinus' conversion and the somewhat 'promotional' celebration of it in Augustine's rediscovered sermon.

But, whether this conversion took place in 406 or autumn 407, it was at all events later than the edict of union: according to the arrangements of the council in June 407, Maximinus could not expect to benefit from preferential treatment. He received it thanks to Augustine's desire for reconciliation, strongly expressed in words and demonstrated in actions. What had to be eliminated, as the letter to the schismatic primate of Numidia said, was 'the error, not the men in whom it was made manifest'.[z] With even greater reason, the men who had rejected it, even if belatedly, must be kept.

The commentary on St John's first Epistle that Augustine had undertaken during Eastertide of 407 had brought him past Easter, to the end of that spring. The famous *Dilige et quod vis fac* ('Love and do as you will'), found in one of the sermons in this series,[aa] potentially misleading and even alarming if it is taken out of its context – above all if the second part is emphasized! – rediscovers the meaning imparted to it by Augustine if it is replaced in the setting of that act of reconciliation to which he had completely committed himself following the 'edict of union'. There was a loftier way of justifying recourse to the secular arm than by saying – even if it was equally true – that it was not persecution but legitimate defence, as he did in the same period when writing to Emeritus (someone we shall meet again).[bb] If, in every human act, what mattered was the 'charitable' intent – in the strong sense of *caritas* or *dilectio* – the greatest proof of love that could be given to brethren who were set apart was not to leave them in their perdition: thus punishment and even coercion could be justified. Augustine would soon say that there was a bad, 'unjust' persecution, and a 'just' persecution, in which one could persecute out of love.[cc] The vast intermingling of people and ideas caused by the Carthage conference and the reactions it provoked would help him to define his attitude.

The Carthage conference of June 411

On 23 August 408, Stilicho died a violent death in Ravenna, the victim of the machinations of an antigermanic clique – he was of Vandal origin on his father's side – at a moment when the Empire in the West was weakened by a usurpation which, having started in Britain – England – had cost it Gaul and Spain, while the Danubian Barbarians were storming the Rhine frontier and the heavy threat posed by Alaric, for his part, was growing increasingly acute. It was the end of a *de facto* regency that had lasted since, on his death in 395, Theodosius had entrusted the young Honorius, then an eleven-year-old, to the care of the man who had been his generalissimo. Some years later, the marriage of Honorius and Stilicho's daughter had further increased the regent's power at the head of a divided and weak government.

Stilicho was supposed to have been the inspiration behind the young emperor's religious policies. In the summer news travelled fast. When his death was announced, the Donatists were eager to believe that the measures taken against them had been invalidated, as contrary to the imperial will; it seems that they even went as far as circulating a forged edict of tolerance.[dd] Fresh violence immediately erupted, localized particularly in the north of Pronconsularis, two Catholic clerics, Macarius and Severus, notably falling victim, whereas the two plenipotentiaries of the summer of 404, Evodius of Uzalis and Theasius of Memblone, paid with their wounds for that embassy so despised by the Donatists; their neighbour in Utica, bishop Victor, was himself seriously manhandled. At the general council which met in Carthage on 13 October 408, the second in that year, after the meeting on 16 June, it was decided to send a legation to the Court, led by Restitutus of Thagora and Florentius of Hippo Dhiarrytus (Bizerte), with the mandate of intervening on the two fronts then mobilized by the Catholic episcopacy, against the pagans and against the Donatists.[ee] In Augustine's circles, there was a sense of reliving the nightmare of 404: following the example of Maximinus of Bagaï, Catholic clergy went overseas to take refuge from the circumcellions.[ff]

Luckily for the bishop of Hippo and his friends, the new 'strong man' of Ravenna, the master of offices, Olympius, was determined to follow the same line as his predecessor. Early in the winter of 408–9, Augustine sent him an appeal for help, in the form of a little letter written in the elaborate style he used with the great of this world. This personal approach duplicated the official one of the bishops sent by the council, and had the same aim:[gg] to obtain confirmation of the earlier legislation. But Olympius had already taken action before his correspondent could be notified of it at Hippo: an order of 24 November laid down the death penalty for Donatists who were caught disturbing the ceremonies of Catholic worship.[29] Early in the following year, 15 January 409, a text addressed to the prefect of the praetorium threatened heavy punishment for any governors or magistrates who were not zealous enough in repressing heresy, particularly Donatism.[30] That did not happen in the case of the recipient of the ruling of late November 408, the proconsul Donatus, and Augustine, who had known him as a young man,[hh] had enough influence over him to be able to implore him not to apply the law in all its harshness: sins must be put down, but at the same time leaving sinners the possibility of repentance.[ii] It may be remembered that the bishop of Hippo had always adopted this position on the death penalty.

Regarding the Donatists, throughout 409 the same line was followed, again affirmed in June by a new text in the same strain;[31] but a few months later this religious policy was subjected to the vicissitudes of a central government which was badly destabilized by growing external threats. Olympius, a supporter of armed resistance to Alaric, but who had failed to contain him, was dismissed. At the Court of Ravenna, the Germani were once more in favour and found themselves being granted high offices and, to take account of their religious particularities – they were Arians and sometimes even pagans – Honorius had to repeal the law he had made on 14 November 408 at Olympius' instigation, reserving service in the Palace for Catholics only.[jj] At the same time – spring 410 – the emperor sent the leader of the army of Africa, Heraclianus, an edict of tolerance, under the terms of which freedom of worship was guaranteed to both heretics and pagans.[32] Perhaps, as has been suggested, this measure was simply dictated by circumstance, to calm minds and strengthen solidarities in the African provinces at a time when Alaric was hoping to seize them in order to sever Rome from its wheat supply. But with regard to the Donatists, it meant a return to the situation of legal shortcomings prior to the 'edict of union' of 405. The disarray of the Catholic Church may be imagined. In Hippo, Augustine saw the new, recently ordained schismatic bishop, Macrobius, make his triumphal entry into the town, escorted, amid the singing crowds, by bands of circumcellions supervised by their leaders. He had to hand back the basilica that had been confiscated in 407, and Macrobius' clerics washed its ornamental tiling with a great deal of salt water to cleanse it of its stains.[kk]

The Donatist bishops wasted no time in taking advantage of this retrieved freedom of action, a 'freedom for perdition', as Augustine would later call it.[ll] Hardly was Macrobius reinstalled in his basilica when he rebaptized a Catholic sub-deacon, Rusticianus; he was no loss, being a black sheep,[mm] but the effect was lamentable. The Donatist bishop left unanswered a long letter from Augustine, which calmly examined the overall cause of dispute setting the two Churches against each other, but was not short of *captatio benevolentiae*.[nn] It was high time to react. Meeting on 14 June 410 in Carthage, the general council resolved to send to the Court the most important delegation ever dispatched by the African Church in that period: four bishops crossed the sea, including Possidius of Calama, whose appointment (certainly due to Augustine, who was present at the council) met the need to have the particularly worrying situation in Hippo's Numidia aired in high places. The Catholic ambassadors obtained an audience the more easily because Honorius had been freed from all worries concerning Africa when, thanks to the loyalty of Heraclianus, Count of Africa, Flavius Attalus' fairly timid attempt to gain control of it had failed. He had been the prefect of Rome in 409, whose usurpation of the Empire had been imposed on the Roman Senate by Alaric and upheld by it for a few months until the summer of 410. On 25 August, the chancellery of Ravenna sent Heraclianus a ruling repealing the previous text, and issued an edict of proscription and even capital punishment against heretics convicted of the crime of assembly.[33]

But it was not the Catholic embassy's sole mission to have the edict of tolerance revoked; it also had a mandate to ask the emperor to convene a conference between the two Churches, and on this point, too, it received satisfaction. A document dated Ravenna, 14 October 410, charged Flavius Marcellinus, a high-ranking official of the body of 'tribunes and notaries' with the task of organizing without delay the confrontation between the two episcopacies as asked for by the Catholics.[34] To this end Marcellinus received from Honorius the delegation of judiciary powers, together with an assurance of the active assistance of the administrative services in Africa. The preamble of the text, however, left no doubt as to the expectations of the emperor and his councillors. The 'vain error and sterile schism' of the Donatists was denounced in advance, their heresy (*superstitio*) condemned, whereas 'the complete truth of the Catholic religion' was already considered to be established, in Honorius' opinion. The purpose assigned to the imperial commissioner was clearly defined, in terms that ruled out any possibility of real arbitration: it was necessary for 'manifest reasons to confound heresy at the conclusion of the debates'.[35] So the Donatists were declared heretics in advance!

The state of Italy after Alaric's capture of Rome in late summer of 410 somewhat delayed Marcellinus' mission. The imperial commissioner was unable to get his edict of convocation made public in Carthage and spread throughout Africa until 19 January 411. His text referred to the imperial order, but was obviously concerned with softening its brutal partiality. He commended the merits of open discussion and was shrewd enough to stress that the demand for a conference had not emanated from the Catholics alone.[36] He set the date of 1 June 411 for the opening of the debates; in the meantime, municipal magistrates and, in every place, the *de facto* authorities such as intendants, procurators and notables were required to notify all bishops of both parties of the convocation, and to send a report to the commissioner informing him of the replies. In exchange for their acceptance, Marcellinus promised that confiscated basilicas and ecclesiastical property would be restored to the Donatists, and suspended from the date of notification of his edict the execution of all repressive laws previously brought against the schismatics.[37]

It was therefore in an atmosphere of truce that the imperial commissioner's envoys launched out in all directions over the African roads. Even though the partisan tone of Honorius' text, duly brought to their notice,[38] was scarcely of a kind to leave them many illusions about their chances of prolonging the division of the African Church, the Donatist bishops, at the instigation of Primianus of Carthage, made a mass movement. Their idea was to make up their numbers, and in any case the recovery – albeit temporary – of their basilicas and Church possessions was a very tempting bait. There was obviously no question about the participation of the Catholics. At the end of a hard winter, when illness and then convalescence had forced him to stand back a little and stay at least a few weeks in the countryside,[39] Augustine had gone to Carthage after Eastertide. He was there in May and was able to be present, on 18 May, at the Donatist bishops' ostentatious procession. His Catholic colleagues would soon be arriving and he was concerned for their lodgings[oo] in the town, which was usually populous but at this time further encumbered by the wave of refugees who, in the preceding autumn, had deserted Rome and also fled from southern Italy, which was ravaged by Alaric's Goths. Among them was Felix, the Donatist bishop of Rome, who does not appear to have been a person of much substance, and the British monk Pelagius, whom Augustine glimpsed once or twice, though he was too preoccupied with preparations for the conference to pay him much attention.[PP] These bishops, who were scattered around the large town, had their meeting points in their respective cathedrals. For the Donatists, it was the *Theoprepia*, the church 'of the Divine Majesty';[40] the Catholics met in the *Restituta* basilica, which one is tempted to identify with the vestiges of the very ruined monument unearthed recently in the heart of the ancient town, a little north of the ports area.[41]

Informed of the arrival of the protagonists, Marcellinus was then able to start the final phase of his mission. By a second edict, published between 18 and 25 May, he laid down in precise detail the procedure for the conference. No more than seven bishops from either side, acting as spokesmen and appointed beforehand, could take part in the debates; they could be assisted by seven counsellor bishops, while each party could also select a certain number of bishops whose duty would be to oversee the work of the secretaries and shorthand-writers in drawing up the minutes. If not taking part in the debates, the mandators were to ratify in advance, by means of a synodal letter bearing their signatures, all the proceedings of the bishops mandated by them.[42] The two parties reacted differently to this text. While giving a mandate to their spokesmen, the Donatists immediately asked the imperial judge if they could all have access to the meeting-hall: it was clear – they said so expressly[43] – that they wanted to make a display of their numbers; at the same time, the Catholic episcopacy agreed without reservation to the procedure set out by Marcellinus. But more important than this agreement, which was not suspect, were the advances made to the Donatists with the aim of disarming their resistance by letting them understand that there would be neither victor nor vanquished in the event of the most probable outcome – the acknowledgement of the rights and theological rectitude of the Catholic Church. It was not a matter of triumph but of reconciliation, and the Catholic episcopacy were thinking ahead to the practical details of that reconciliation. They had a double proposition: if the Donatists were to win the cause, the Catholic bishops would remove themselves at once to the advantage of those who had made them see the truth.[44] If things should go the other way, they would welcome the Donatists who rallied to the cause of unity by sharing episcopal responsibilities with them, so that they would not lose their dignity or authority; if the faithful refused to accept this co-existence, the two bishops would step down to leave room for a new pastor.[45] In this way the Catholics left their adversaries an honourable way out. The sincerity of these proposals, in which Augustine's hand is recognizable, could not be doubted; but they were formulated in a peaceable perspective that might appear unreal in the true climate of confrontation.

This became evident at the opening of the conference, on 1 June. Whereas on the Catholic side only spokesmen, counsellors and officials concerned with the minutes – eighteen bishops in all – were present, all the Donatist bishops crowded into the *secretarium* of Gargilius' baths,[46] determined to impose their physical presence. And, as they suspected the Catholics of fraud in their signatures to the mandate, they demanded that their adversaries also be present. Becoming tired of it all, the imperial judge granted this demand and allowed all the Catholic bishops to enter.[47] Thus in a sometimes stormy atmosphere there was a procession of hundreds of bishops, during which the Donatists twice had occasion to make their presence felt: first to recognize their Catholic rivals who replied to the roll-call of their names after the reading of their mandate. After this confrontation, the bishops having withdrawn two by two, Marcellinus might have hoped at last, after reading the Donatist procuration, to proceed with the debate proper. But then it was the Catholics' turn to call for the individual appearance of their adversaries.[48] The imperial judge had to resign himself, and there then began the long procession of Donatist bishops, peppered with various incidents and challenges, which sometimes led the schismatics into difficulties, but fully realized their desire to drag out proceedings in time-consuming skirmishes. The evening was well on when the meeting broke up, having achieved nothing. But the Donatists' obstinacy rewarded us with the unique document comprising the minutes of that first day: an overall picture of the African episcopacy of those times plus, thanks to schism, the members of a dual hierarchy, all gathered together, with the exception of a tiny minority who had been kept away from this meeting by age or illness, but also by distance, which in itself explains the slackening of administrative ties, increasingly noticeable the farther west one goes from Carthage. In western Caesarean Mauretania (present-day Orania), the convocation might not even have reached some bishops. There, the length of the journey was in itself a hindrance: between Pomaria (Tlemcen) and the African capital was a road of some 1200 kilometres, and the minutes indicate that some bishops died en route! To go from Tusuros (Tozeur) to Carthage, it would have taken the local bishop about a fortnight.

However incomplete it may be, historians can draw a great deal from a 'group photograph', which is far more eloquent than a 'report'; it throws light on the numerical importance of the two Churches at that date – quantitatively, they are fairly well balanced, with a slight advantage to the Catholics – and on their geographical distribution.[49] But to these objective data can be added what is often revealed by the clashes and altercations among these men for the majority of whom the experience of that 1 June 411 was the most important in their lives, and who were not always content merely to answer the roll-call and authenticate their signature. The particular appearance and the history of many bishops come under a spotlight that was often unique. We learn little about the individuals themselves; but in the vast majority of cases there was little to learn. The prevailing impression is of a 'rank and file' manoeuvred by a few 'generals', among both the Donatists and the Catholics,[50] in other words, headquarters staff formed on either side for the proceedings of the conference, and in the front rank the spokesmen who would carry the whole weight of the debate.

On that first day of standing about and hubbub, the sound of Augustine's voice was barely heard unless to support his primate, Aurelius, who was opposed to the introduction of all the Donatist bishops, and to reply when his name was called among the Catholic representatives; he and his rival, Macrobius, acknowledged each other without incident or comment. When the debate resumed, on 3 June, only the spokesmen were in the lists, with Augustine in the front ranks on the Catholic side. But again that day the procedural wiliness of Petilianus of Constantine – seconded by Emeritus of Caesarea (Cherchell) – prevented their getting down to a fundamental discussion. Petilianus began by refusing to sit alongside the Catholics, thereby obliging the imperial judge to rise: eventually everyone was standing! Luckily, the sitting – if it can be called that – did not last long, because the Donatists objected that they had not yet been supplied with fair copies of the minutes of the first session.[51] For this reason they asked for an adjournment; Augustine intervened to ask the judge to grant their request, although it escaped neither him nor Marcellinus that the opposing side was merely trying to gain time.[52]

Some days later, the Donatists had their backs to the wall. But, to the great impatience of the judge and the Catholics, who were anxious to get down to the crux of the matter (*principale negotium*), on the morning of 8 June Emeritus calmly challenged the need to establish 'the parties' qualifications'[53] beforehand. In the Donatists' view, there was no doubt that their adversary was the petitioner; and in fact, by their request of summer 410, the Catholics had undoubtedly assumed that role; the indictment and burden of proof fell to them. But the unfortunate approach by the Donatists to the praetorian prefect in January 406[54] enabled Marcellinus to acknowledge that the conference had been sought by both parties.

If that were the case, the petitioner was the one who was indicting the other.[55] This was a major turning-point in the dispute: the controversy on a point of law was in fact followed by recourse to archive documents. The Donatists succeeded in preventing the reading of the prefectural records of 406, but at the cost of a proposal that proved disastrous for them, which consisted in having all the documents relating to the schism read in chronological order. Diverted from its strictly juridical framework, the dispute *de persona* opened out, by way of a search for historical responsibility, onto what lay at the very heart of the debate.[56]

On the Catholic side, backed by the other spokesmen for his Church, chiefly Alypius, but often Fortunatianus of Sicca as well, Augustine had now taken charge of operations. He presented the opposing side with a clear alternative: they must choose between the cause of the Church and the 'Caecilianus affair'; the two cases called for different, mutually exclusive, procedures. The Catholics asked only to base the debate on the Scriptures, but the opposing side must not drag them into the area of history.[57] As it was making no progress, the debate became increasingly impassioned: Petilianus accused the bishop of Hippo of being a 'son of Caecilianus', and Augustine responded by disassociating the cause of Caecilianus, whatever it might be, from that of the Church. In the midst of interruptions, tumult and shouting, he thus gained the opportunity, in a roundabout way, of resuming the ecclesiological debate on the basis of scriptural texts.[58] Then the most dramatic moment of this confrontation occurred, the attack *ad hominem*: Petilianus rudely interrupted Augustine to demand the name of his consecrator. Augustine at first ignored him, but then gave the name of Megalius, being careful not to link his cause with that of the Church.[59]

Next the Donatists produced the synodal letter committing their spokesmen, and Augustine immediately undertook to refute its arguments on the Church, which according to them should include only the good and pure: the schismatics acknowledged the relevance of the parable of the nets (Matt. 13.47–50), but maintained that the 'bad fish' meant the hidden guilty, of whom priests were unaware, unknown to the good and as such not in a position to do them any harm.[60] At this stage of the debate, the lacuna in the only manuscript to pass on these *Proceedings* to us deprives us of the living words of the bishop of Hippo, but the résumés that survive enable us to follow the unfolding of the arguments to the end.[61] Augustine developed the major themes of the Catholic *mandatum*: the distinctions between the two times of the Church, tolerance of the wicked among the good in the prophetic texts, spiritual rather than material and sociological interpretation of the discrimination between pure and impure in the Scriptures.[62] The Donatists, clinging to their static conception of a historical Church 'without spot or wrinkle', did not understand – or pretended not to – the distinction between the two states, and even less the distinction between two levels of reality in the visible Church, *hic et nunc*, accusing the Catholics of conceiving of two Churches, one of which would be mortal.

The debate on the Church's cause was coming to an end. Instead of having been conclusive and reconciliatory, as Augustine had hoped, it had been no more than a disappointing interlude. The two parties again threw their mutual persecutions in each other's faces[63] and fought on, to the accompaniment of more and more items from the archives deposited with the clerk, one after the other. The Donatists could not be other than losers in this game, for it could end only in proving the falsity of the accusations brought against Caecilianus early in the fourth century, and his justification, and also showing that there had been pure and impure on both sides in the time of the persecution.[64] As the hours passed, the Donatists' disarray became a rout. Petilianus soon gave up arguing, over-come by hoarseness – a diplomatic hoarseness, the other side insinuated.[65] To those of their spokesmen who were still in the lists, Marcellinus offered a last chance to give foundation to their grievances against Caecilianus, by opening the dossier of his consecrator, bishop Felix of Abthugni; but a reading of those minutes similarly led to their embarrassment.[66]

The match had been played and lost for the Donatists. One last time the judge urged them to produce some supporting evidence for their arguments; then he invited both sides to retire while he drew up his judgement. It was pitch dark when Marcellinus read this judgement which 'decided in favour of Catholic unity'.[67] On 26 June, the imperial commissioner brought his mission to an end. An edict signed by him assured the Donatists, who could return home with nothing to fear, that it was up to them to enjoy the sweetness of unity, accompanied by the promise – made by the Catholics – of a generous shareout; but it also listed the measures to be taken against those who refused to submit: the banning of all religious meetings, the immediate restitution of the basilicas and Church possessions, the confiscation of estates on which circumcellions continued to be tolerated. Augustine's victory was complete; but it was too crushing not to have a rather bitter taste.

Cogite intrare

The appointment of Marcellinus to act as arbiter at the conference had proved a wise one. The imperial commissioner was a man of his word and noble hearted; a true gentleman. Before and during the confrontation, his attitude towards the Donatists had been irreproachable, and at the time the interested parties had been glad to acknowledge it.[68] He had even made the elegant gesture, before the debates opened, of proposing that an assessor of the Donatists' choosing, of equal or superior rank to his own, should join him to direct proceedings.[69] They refused, following the logic of their procedural behaviour, as they did not wish to appear in the role of petitioners.[70] Subsequently, however, their public condemnation pursued the tribune and notary. They accused him, after the event, of having been bribed by the Catholics.[qq] In their eyes, there was no doubt about the connivance between the high-ranking official and the bishop of Hippo – an opinion shared by certain modern historians.[71] We saw earlier (p. 268) that the unfortunate Marcellinus paid with his life, in September 413, for the judgement he had given in June 411.

What is certain is that the Donatists, though hard hit, had not yet resigned themselves to considering it a definitive sentence. They were very conscious of their numbers, only slightly reduced by the rallyings of 405 and 406, which prompted them to further daring, such as appealing to the Court against Marcellinus' ruling.[72] But in their African isolation they did not fully realize that in Ravenna the government could no longer allow the continuance, for religious reasons, of a sometimes rebellious climate in the only provincial bloc which, for just under twenty years, had been spared the great movements throughout the western Empire which had already reduced it almost everywhere to situations of dividing with the Barbarians. In his text of autumn 410, Honorius had denounced the subversion caused by the schism in Africa, 'that is to say, for the greater part of the Empire, loyally subject to the civil government'.[73] After Alaric's capture of Rome and the unleashing of his hordes through Italy, this expression was no more than a standard fomula. The reply to the Donatists' appeal could be no different from that expressed in the order sent on 30 January 412 to the praetorian prefect for Africa. For the first time, the imperial chancellery no longer threatened the death penalty, but laid down extremely heavy financial sanctions[74] against lay followers of the schismatic Church, painstakingly itemized from top to bottom of the social scale, not forgetting the circumcellions, in last place; in unprecedented fashion, they were accounted one group amongst others[75] and as such obliged to pay penalty fines, which the insolvency of its members could not help but render illusory. As for those whom the edict did not consider to be free and responsible, the slaves – but also, curiously enough, peasants who were tied to the land (the *coloni*) – it relied on the constraints exerted by the masters (*domini*) to bring them to heel. Lastly, bishops and clergy were not forgotten; their refusal to submit would cost them exile, into which they would be taken *manu militari* after handing over their places of worship and church possessions to the Catholics.[76]

The eradication of a schism that had endured for over a century was not so easy. On 17 June 414, a charter intended for the proconsul of Africa reminded him of these financial sanctions and extended them to all those, imperial or private farmers, or administrative staff who in one way or another were guilty of complicity with the Donatists, notably in concealing insubordinate clerics destined for deportation.[77] Confiscation of possessions could be ordered against recalcitrant Donatist followers, who were moreover deprived of the possibility of making a will or being party to a contract, thus spelling civil death for them. In the years 415–17, islands of resistance still survived here and there among the Donatist communities. To those years belongs a recently published letter from the bishop of Hippo to his colleague Novatus, bishop of Sitifis (Setif),[rr] in which he rejoices to learn that in a nearby locality all the basilicas had been handed back to the Catholics and that the schismatics had been converted en masse, with the exception, however, of a group of municipal notables who had managed to escape the governor's vigilance – a *vicarius* of Africa whose name remains unknown – by obtaining from him an 'interlocutory sentence' that had allowed them to avoid prosecution.

In the months, and even years, following the conference, the capacity for doing harm of the circumcellions and Donatist clergy had remained almost intact in many places, despite the reaffirmation of sanctions that were often difficult to apply. Augustine experienced this in his diocese, where Macrobius, prohibited from staying in Hippo itself, roamed the country areas at the head of a band of fanatics of both sexes, and had confiscated chapels opened for him by force.[ss] It was a stroke of luck if these fanatics were content to turn their violence against themselves, like Donatus, a schismatic priest of Mutugenna, who had chosen to throw himself down a well.[tt] The main targets were Catholic clergy, such as a priest named Restitutus, in Augustine's personal entourage, who was killed in an ambush, or another named Innocentius, who was blinded in one eye and mutilated.ᵘᵘ But like all terrorism, that of the Donatist outlaws aimed at fighting fear of the law with an even more terrible fear, and for preference struck at converts for victims, to provide an example: such was the fate of the wretched Rogatus, bishop of Assuras, whose tongue and one hand the circumcellions cut off.ᵛᵛ

There could be no other response to such crimes than repression. True to himself, however, Augustine ruled out 'an eye for an eye' and, as he had done in 408 to the proconsul Donatus, he wrote to Marcellinus during the winter of 411–12 asking him not to apply the talionic law to the torturers of his clerics, Restitutus and Innocentius.ʷʷ Two years later, he similarly interceded with the *vicarius* of Africa, Macedonius, and the 'governor general' of the African provinces, a very Christian man but one who was conscious of his position as secular judge,ˣˣ countered the bishop's leniency with the need not to let crime go unpunished. But this correspondence in the years 413–14 also showed how far the bishop had gone in his acceptance of the force of the law, excluding the death penalty.ʸʸ Already, in a letter dated 407/8, addressed to one of those who had seen him as a young man in Carthage, Vincentius, bishop of Cartennae (today Ténès), a moderate Donatist, Augustine had revealed very frankly the road he had travelled in this respect. He had at first considered, he wrote, that no one should be forced into religious unity, but influenced by word alone, won over by reason alone; otherwise, there was a great risk of having nothing but false Catholics in the place of former declared heretics.ᶻᶻ He was still thinking along those lines around 400, when he stepped up his attempts at meetings and engaged in writing his great treatises in refutation of the sect.

A few years later, enforced conversions might still be false, but the bishop of Hippo had resigned himself; his experience as a pastor had got the better of his theoretical position. Reality had shown him that in his own town fear of the law had been stronger than reasoned argument to 'turn' a majority who only recently had still been schismatic, and that its spur was often needed in order to triumph, not over true religious convictions, but rather over real sociological sluggishness. How many men and women, in Hippo as elsewhere, remained in Donatism for the simple reason and motive that they had been born into it, if no one came to shake them out of their inertia!ᵃᵇ They had to be jostled (*coacti*) a little, on condition that some meaning was attached to the action by adding doctrinal explanation to legal compulsion;ᵃᶜ this was the definition of fraternal correction with regard to the schismatics. It must be added that the Catholic Church had adopted pastoral means of welcoming and absorbing the newcomers; we have seen that, in the earliest years of the fifth century Augustine, at the expense of his own territorial domain, had set the example of reducing his provisions for reception and granting of benefits by creating new episcopal departments on the fringes of his diocese. Next, and perhaps chiefly, his growing affirmation of the primacy of grace helped him to pay no heed to the fear that these enforced rallyings were nothing but false conversions. A little later, he wrote to Gaudentius of Thamugadi, who rejected every constraint and threatened to perish in his burning church, that recalcitrants such as he were mistaken, 'for want of a knowledge of the Scriptures and the power of God who gives men the will even when they are being pushed in spite of themselves'.[78]

Augustine felt no need to elaborate a theory of coercion in religious matters, but he wanted at least to clarify his ideas on its legitimacy. This he did belatedly, in 417, because the interminable aftermath of the schism did not allow him to turn over a new leaf any sooner, and still obliged him to justify his attitude. Datable to that year is the long letter he addressed to a young captain then starting out on an exceptional career, and whose destiny was to run alongside his own for a long time, until the siege of Hippo in 430.[79] Bonifatius was at that time posted, as a military tribune, to the Numido-Mauretanian *limes*, one of the most sensitive in Roman Africa. There he successfully contained the Moorish tribes who were testing its penetrability, but his office also brought him into contact with Donatists who came under his jurisdiction, and about whom he was trying to form an opinion. Somewhat naively, he had written to Augustine to learn from him what difference there was between them and the Arian heretics[ad] – a good opportunity for the bishop of Hippo to enlighten the officer on the reasons for and consequences of, not a heresy, but a schism. To start with, he recommended him to read his shortened version of the Records of the conference, which could be obtained for him, he said, by the bishop of Vescera (Biskra), his colleague Optatus, or his friend Novatus of Sitifis,[ae] so we know that Bonifatius was then on patrol between the southern foothills of the Aurès and the chott el-Hodna; it was there that Augustine, accompanied by Alypius, was soon to visit him, at Thubunae (Tobna).

But the letter was mainly intended to justify the legislation that Bonifatius could apply, and its author took advantage of it to sum up the situation regarding his own conduct, as he had done on other occasions, notably in an 'address to the Donatists' (*Ep.* 105), datable to 409/10, and in the letter to Vincentius, already quoted. In it we find, complemented and assembled in a final dissertation, the articles of a personal credo worked out over twelve years of observations and struggles which had doubtless led him towards a fundamentally pessimistic realism in his reflections on the chances of the faithful in general, and schismatics in particular, finding their salvation by themselves. He thus wrote to the young officer that teaching was without any doubt worth more than the fear or the pain of punishment in order to lead men to the love of God, but that experience had shown him, and was still showing him, that like fugitive slaves, most of them needed the whip of secular penalties![af] The wise had to be given an opportunity to progress,[ag] and the weak a strength they could not find within themselves, but which they could internalize, turning necessity into, if not a virtue, at least their own will.[ah] The parable in Luke 14.23 on the lord who, to make up for the shortfall in his invited guests, sends his servants out into the highways and byways to compel passers-by to enter his house, was a good illustration: *Quoscumque inveneritis, cogite intrare.*[ai]

It was, as we would say nowadays to signify the intolerable, wanting to make someone happy in spite of himself; and that is what the Donatists said, too, declaring that one should not be forced into good.[aj] And they, whose slogan was that they were the Church 'which suffers persecution, not the one which inflicts it', considered both wicked and unjust the legal persecution of which they were victims, at the instigation of the Catholics. It was not the Donatists' happiness that Augustine desired, however, but their salvation, which was quite another matter; the salvation from which, according to his theology of the Church, these separated Christians were excluded, no matter how valid their sacraments. In this eschatological perspective, the purpose of the coercion justified it: it was good if its purpose was good. We see again the spirit of the *Dilige et quod vis fac*, which had already inspired the letter to Emeritus around 407/8: the Catholic Church persecuted 'for love's sake'.[ak] This deliberately provocative combination of words probably shocks us today even more than it grated on the Donatists, because over the centuries it has acquired sometimes sinister resonances. Must we dwell on it? Only to say that these texts must be read while keeping in mind the strict demands that dictated them, but in their time never caused, either directly or indirectly, any physical attack, still less any death.[80] Augustine was not the father of Augustinianisms, nor was he responsible for Torquemada.

Notes

a. *Actes de la conférence de Carthage*, III, 116, SC, 224, p. 1075; cf. also *Brev. conl.*, III, 4 and *Ad don. post conl.*, XVI, 20.
b. Allusions to the council, date unknown to us, in *Contra Cresc.*, III, 49 and 50; *Ep.* 76, 4.
c. *Ep.* 88, 7.
d. *Contra Cresc.*, III, 50.
e. He was going to the *fundus Figulinensis* (the 'Potters' farm'): *Ep.* 105, 4.
f. *Contra Cresc.*, III, 51. The phrase occurs in the same period in the same context in *Ep.* 89, 2 and a little later in *Ep.* 108, 14.
g. *Ep.* 105, 3.
h. *Contra Cresc.*, III, 53; *Ep.* 88, 6.
i. *Ep.* 105, 3.
j. *Vita Aug.*, XII, 1–2. The other text is by Augustine himself: *Enchiridion*, 17.
k. *Contra Cresc.*, III, 47.
l. *Contra Cresc.*, III, 47 (in 405/6) and *Ep.* 185, 27 (in 417).
m. Barely; Maximianus did not survive his wounds for long.
n. *Contra Cresc.*, III, 51; *Ep.* 185, 26: *in episcopos vel ministros eorum exsilio constituto.*
o. *Ep.* 89, 8.
p. *Ep.* 89, 6: *Resistunt autem duobus modis: aut saeviendo, aut pigrescendo.*
q. *Ep.* 88, 8; cf. also *Ep.* 111, 1: the Barbarians who were invading the Roman world at that time were no worse.
r. Above, p. 172.
s. *Ep.* 88, 10.
t. Cf. above, p. 172.
u. *Ep.* 105, 4.
v. *Sermon Dolbeau 27 (Mainz 63)*, 2, in F. Dolbeau, *Vingt-six Sermons au peuple d'Afrique*, p. 312.
w. *Sermon Dolbeau 27*, 2, p. 311: *In Hipponiensi civitate . . . diu parturivimus, tandem vidimus unitatem.*
x. *Sermon Dolbeau 27*, 2, p. 312. Augustine would experience this peasant slow-wittedness later at Fussala: cf. above, p. 256.
y. *In epist. Ioh.*, III, 7.
z. *Ep.* 88 (to Januarianus), 10: *ut, in quibus fuerit inventus, non homines sed error ipse tollatur.*
aa. *In epist. Ioh.*, VII, 8: 'Love and do what you will: if you keep silent, do so from love, if you speak, speak from love; if you correct, do so from love; if you pardon, do so from love; have in yourself the root of love: from that root can come nothing but good.'
bb. *Ep.* 87, 8. Cf. below, p. 351.
cc. *Ep.* 185, 11.
dd. *Ep.* 105, 6.

ee.   *Concilia Africae, CCL*, 149, p. 219.

ff.   *Ep.* 97, 2.

gg.   *Ep.* 97. Augustine enclosed with his letter an aide-mémoire (*commonitorium*) intended for the legates sent by their council, which he had not attended, and asked Olympius to pass it to them on their arrival: *Ep.* 97, 4.

hh.   *Ep.* 112, 1 and 3.

ii.   *Ep.* 100, 1: *Sic igitur eorum peccata compesce ut sint quos poeniteat peccasse.*

jj.   *C. Th.*, XVI, 5, 42.

kk.   *Ep.* 108, 14.

ll.   *Ep.* 108, 18: *Contra Gaudentium* (419), XXIV, 27.

mm.   Cf. above, p. 249.

nn.   *Ep.* 108, 2: Augustine had heard it said, he wrote, that Macrobius was 'a young man who was upright by nature'.

oo.   *Sermon* 357, 5: Augustine was calling upon the hospitality of the faithful.

pp.   *De gestis Pelagii*, XXII, 46; cf. below, p. 325–6.

qq.   *Ad donatistas post conlationem*, I, 1; cf. also *Ep.* 141, 1 and 12.

rr.   *Ep.* 28*, 1, *BA*, 46 B, p. 402.

ss.   *Ep.* 139, 2.

tt.   He had pulled through, thanks to the Catholics, and it had earned him a long letter from Augustine: *Ep.* 173.

uu.   *Ep.* 133, 1; 134, 2.

vv.   *Gesta cum Emerito*, 9.; cf. also the new letter 28*, 7, *BA*, 46 B, p. 412.

ww.   *Ep.* 133, 1.

xx.   *Ep.* 155, 17: *in terreni iudicis cingulo.*

yy.   Cf. above, p. 264.

zz.   *Ep.* 93, 17.

ab.   *Ep.* 93, 17, *in fine*: *ideo permanebant in parte Donati quia ibi nati erant.*

ac.   Thus he wrote in 408 to the proconsul Donatus: 'to force (*cogere*) without teaching (*docere*) was the result of a zeal that was more harmful than advantageous' (*Ep.* 100, 2, *in fine*).

ad.   *Ep.* 185, 1.

ae.   *Ep.* 185, 6. In the new letter 28*, 2 (*BA*, 46 B, p. 406), Augustine, one or two years before, had drawn Novatus' attention to the interest for his church of acquiring his *Résumé* of the *Proceedings* of 411.

af.   *Ep.* 185, 21, in which Augustine also invoked the testimony of Terence in *The Adelphi*.

ag.   Augustine quoted the Book of Proverbs (9.9) in his letter to Vincentius to justify the turnarounds at Hippo and elsewhere.

ah.   *Sermon* 112, 8: *Foris inveniatur necessitas, nascitur intus voluntas.*

ai.   *Ep.* 93, 5; 173 (to the Donatist priest who had thrown himself into a well), 10; 185, 24; *Contra Gaud.*, I, 28.

aj.   *Ep.* 185, 23: *nec ad bonum se cogi oportere contendunt.*

ak.   *Ep.* 185, 11: *Proinde ista (ecclesia) persequitur diligendo.*

CHAPTER XXVII

Dialogue with the pagans

Indefatigable Augustine! We think of him completely occupied in arguing with the Donatists, having demolished the Manichaeans, and at the same time we see him doing battle with the pagans. His multifarious activities do not fit easily into compartments, which I resort to only for clarity's sake. Present on all fronts, Augustine is in other places just as much as where you would expect him to be.

In the space of a quarter of a century, the religious components of the world he inhabited had radically changed. The very active and sometimes even provocative paganism he had witnessed as an adolescent at Madauros, and as a young man at Carthage, was a mere shadow of its former self at the time of his accession to the episcopacy. Five years later, in 400, in a work written to refute those who accused the Evangelists of contradicting one another – the *De consensu evangelistarum* – Augustine was glad to portray a paganism thrown back onto the defensive at every level. First, in a concrete and material fashion, because by virtue of the legislation enacted in 399 the practice of pagan forms of worship was prohibited,[a] and the 'idols' themselves were in danger of being destroyed: he said that the last sect members, by now a small number,[b] were reduced to hiding themselves and their gods if they wanted to continue with their sacrifices. But he claimed that they were also smitten by a sort of intellectual timidity in the face of the Christians; they hardly dared to mutter their anti-Christian slanders among themselves,[c] forced to nibble like rats on their little 'tremulous and warmed-over' objections, with a greater fear of being heard than a desire to be believed.[d] We must obviously make allowances, in these words, for his concern to exorcise a real ideological resistance.

Nevertheless, what was universally true was the inversion in relative strength. Augustine was obliged to rein in the iconoclastic ardour of the faithful; especially in Carthage and its environs, where lowly people were only too inclined to let themselves be carried away by a dynamic of antipagan persecution and to invade private properties to destroy altars and sack sacred woods. Those were the ways of bandits or circumcellions, Augustine said in reproof. The bishops found it hard to restrain their flocks. On 16 June 401, the Carthaginian plebs, who knew that the general council was convened in their town that day, surged through the streets shouting out their impatience to see the idols fall as in Rome.[e] The same day, the council which had met in the *secretarium* of the *basilica Restituta* noted this demand and, to avoid having to mask illegal actions, the bishops called for the suppression of every vestige of idolatry everywhere in Africa, emphasizing that it still existed in coastal localities and private properties; the law needed to order their destruction, at least unless they had any ornamental value.[1] This restriction was important, and took account of both the known imperial desire to preserve towns' monumental adornment and municipalities' attachment to their cultural heritage. On several occasions, and in the very texts banning the ancient cults, the imperial chancellery had ordered care to be taken to preserve buildings; and the authorities were to be responsible for taking down the religious statues.[2] A law would soon order that disused temples were to be put to secular public use,[3] and their transformation into Christian basilicas, at least in that period, was rare and exceptional. To counter a 'cultural revolution' which could have swept everything away, both central and local political government were generally wise enough to stress that the outdated and firmly condemned cultic function of pagan monuments must be disassociated from their heritage value and ornamental status for the towns.[4] They were thus able to ensure the preservation of a patrimony which, in Africa, most frequently dated back to the golden age of Septimius Severus, and which had benefited in many instances from the renovations of the Valentinian period, in the second half of the fourth century. But that cultural resistance also testified to the difficulty of changing mindsets in their local environments.

Paganism's local resistance

In that same summer of 401, the proconsul in office in Carthage had allowed the golden beard to be shaved from a statue of Hercules which was famous in the town, and which Augustine had seen in his youth. In terms of an assault on art, it was not too bad, and was just as much an attack on the god's dignity, as the bishop sardonically remarked when, commenting on this act, he noted that all in all it was more ignominious for Hercules to lose his beard than to see his head fall.[f] But what was possible in the capital, with the complicity of the governor, did not go down well in the provinces. Two years before, the same Hercules had caused blood to run in Sufes, a small town in Byzacena, nowadays Sbiba, in the high plains of central Tunisia. Christians had destroyed the god's statue, and immediately a manhunt had begun which had ended with sixty dead among the community responsible. On top of that, the municipal authorities had lodged a complaint for destruction of public property and demanded that the statue be replaced! We still have the short letter, burning with indignation and scathing irony, that Augustine[g] addressed to those in charge in the town: he had enough marble and sculptors at his disposal to restore their lost statue; but would *they* give him back the sixty Christians who had died at Sufes? Moreover, it was clear that the pagans had the upper hand in that small town: notables had been at the head of the revolt, and those who had been at the forefront of the slaughter held leading positions in the municipal council.[h] It came as no surprise to Augustine, who already knew that pagan reaction still had solid foundations at local levels, and would have confirmation of it at the expense of other Christian communities.

The most powerful illustration of this situation, as well as the most para-doxical, since it came to light in the bishop of Hippo's almost direct sphere of influence, was set a few years later in the small town of Calama (Guelma), where Possidius was bishop. On 14 November 407, the imperial chancellery had sent the prefect of the praetorium a text indicating a firm wish to have done with all the last external signs of paganism, and this was to be put into effect in all provinces: cult statues still in place were to be taken down; temples in the public domain or situated on imperial estates were to be assigned to secular community uses, while property-owners would be obliged to destroy their private sanctuaries; lastly every public demonstration of pagan nature – feast, festival or procession – was strictly forbidden and, in cases of failure to comply, bishops received authority to call on public forces.[i] In the large towns, especially Carthage, police surveillance had begun to be exerted against the pagans even before the promulgation of this edict. In one of the recently published new sermons, Augustine almost involuntarily reflected that repression: he said there was no official antipagan persecution, but that the police had eyes and ears, and anyone who swore by Mercury retracted pretty quickly at the sight of a plain-clothes orderly's cape.[j]

We know that the law of autumn 407 was public almost everywhere in Africa by early summer of 408. But scorning the law, on 1 June 408, an ostentatious procession, full of noise and accompanied by dancing, went through the streets of Calama, provocatively making a detour in front of the church doors, with an audacity (says Augustine, who probably recalled the excesses he had witnessed as a child at Madauros) which outstripped that shown by the pagans in the time of Julian the Apostate. Clergy who protested were subjected to a hail of stones in reply. And when, a few days later, bishop Possidius went to the curia to notify the municipal council of the imperial law and demand that it be respected, the church was stoned again. In the following days, fanatics even set fire to it and killed a cleric; the rest of the clergy and Possidius saved themselves only by fleeing. Trembling in his hiding-place, the latter heard his pursuers egging one another on and saying that if they could not get their hands on the bishop they would have had all that trouble for nothing.[k]

This last uprising had lasted from five in the afternoon to a very late hour on that summer night. The municipal authorities, magistrates in office at their head, had done nothing to re-establish order; the only one to bring help, Augustine notes, had been a stranger – a *peregrinus* – passing through the town, to whom several clergy owed their lives. It was obvious, the bishop commented, that besides the culprits themselves, the non-intervention of the other citizens was due to their fear of those who brought rain and fine weather to the town, and whom they knew to be enemies of the Church.[l]

The bishop of Hippo was intent on dealing with this matter himself, as it had taken place at the gates of his diocese and placed one of his dearest disciples in danger. In response to a notable of the town, Nectarius, a moderate pagan, he agreed to intervene to ensure that reparation for the harm done excluded the tortures and executions provided for by the law. Several months later, in the spring of 409, to his great surprise he received a second letter from his correspondent who implored him to do everything possible to alleviate the monetary penalties inflicted on those responsible for the events of the preceding year. In his first letter to Nectarius, the bishop had indicated to him that, even when their possessions were affected, the culprits could still have enough to live on, 'to live on badly', which he meant in the moral sense as he had no illusions about their contrition. But the other pretended to have understood it in the material sense, and returning to the attack, suggested that it was more painful 'to live badly than to finish with one's misfortunes by death'![m] In other words, death was preferable to a wretched life, the result of the confiscation of one's property, which reduced those who were thus punished to penury – *inopia*: the word used in the texts of laws to designate this penalty; an additional proof that the humble folk of Calama were nothing but the tool of the local wealthy aristocracy in this anti-Christian revolt.

Owing to his advanced age, Nectarius was no longer in office in any responsible post in his town, as he says in his first letter; he was therefore exempt from any personal involvement in the affair; and he was indebted to his classical culture for having been chosen by his peers to intercede with the bishop of Hippo. Of his two interventions, the second is more interesting, as it throws light on the other sort of adversary, besides the fanatical upholders of the ancient rites and old festivities, who on ideological grounds still opposed the in-depth Christianization of municipal life. Nectarius sang the praises of the civic love one must have for one's town, and it was clear that for him municipal patriotism went hand in hand with the moderate and courteous exercise of an enlightened paganism, nurtured on literature: it would not have taken much questioning to make him confess that he had little in common with the yelling mobs who had attacked the church. But on the other hand, his devotion to his little home-town implied his loyalty to an entire religious tradition, to the calendar that had marked the rhythms of local life for centuries; all that prevented him from seeing himself in the new religion, which was far too universalist. Nectarius believed in heaven, in his own way, which was pretty well that of Cicero in his famous text, the *Dream of Scipio*, which was read by all intellectuals in the Late Empire. He did not make too much effort to attract Augustine's good graces – for himself and his fellow-citizens – when he told him that he had heard his call to the worship of the most high God (*deus exsuperantissimus*) and contemplation of the celestial city, but he stated precisely by which route he hoped to arrive there – that of civic merits. He wrote:

> After the death of the body, there is a kind of advancement to the city on high for those men who have deserved well of their birthplace; and those who have ensured the safety of their homeland by their counsel or by their works will dwell with God.[n]

He could thus easily believe that he belonged to the same world as his correspondent, on whom at the close of his letter he called down the blessing of the 'supreme God', in astute terms that were ambiguous enough to let its recipient believe he had won a new recruit.[o] In passing, however, he let slip his true colours by invoking the opinion of those philosophers – he did not name them, but Augustine could easily recognize the Stoics – according to whom all misdeeds were equally important and therefore called for equal forgiveness.[5] It was easy for the bishop to reply that on this score one would inevitably be led to pardon none of them.[p]

Nectarius and his ilk, at the heart of the cultivated municipal elites in moribund Roman Africa, could feel some pride in corresponding with someone like Augustine and receiving long letters from him; but they distanced themselves from the piety of humble Christians and their cult of martyrs, especially local ones: remember the sarcastic remarks of Maximus, the grammarian of Madauros, about Miggin and Namphamo, and the followers of their sect. But they were similarly detached from the followers of the old popular pagan religion, who in their view were assuredly 'half-wits'. Sociologically, they had no roots, and their refined paganism had no future. It could even happen, in towns where the civic majority were pro-Christian, that they adjured their ideas for the sake of a career: a good post in the community was well worth a Mass!

This was surely the case in Hippo, where in the spring of 401 the good folk suspected a certain Faustinus of wanting to be converted solely in order to obtain the post of municipal tax-collector more readily. Augustine himself was none too sure of the sincerity of this aspirant for baptism.[q] Meanwhile, they most frequently held firm in the face of the church, in their *curiae* which were bastions of a kind of vaguely spiritualistic 'laicity' in which for many their civic pride did duty as religious feeling. Of course, the Empire was officially Christian, but in the provinces, at town level, a real status of 'separation of Church and State' placed the municipal authorities, vis-à-vis the bishop, in a kind of confrontation that French townships experienced not so very long ago, when there was still a curé in every village: from open warfare to armed peace, and more rarely *entente cordiale*.

Harking back to a few ready-made ideas that were still current among historians less than a century ago,[6] it was not difficult to show clearly that not only had the clerical institution failed to dethrone the municipal institution in order to take its place, but that the curia and the clergy had formed parallel hierarchies without any hold over each other.[7] Taking the analysis further, it has been shown that, in a way that is paradoxical only in appearance, St Augustine lived less 'in Christianity' in his times than we do today in our largely 'dechristianized' societies.[8] Let me make myself clear: in the community which he headed, and the one he visited so often in Carthage, and in many others, to which he also bears witness, Christianity was generally lived very intensely, with an involvement in the liturgy that has become an exception these days. But, on emerging from the church, one re-entered a world where the new religion left no evident mark or sign of its influence anywhere. 'We cannot even find the equivalent in St Augustine's Africa', writes Claude Lepelley, 'of the ceremonies that endure in today's officially secular France, such as Masses for the dead on the field of honour, ordered by communes, or the blessing of ships.'[9] Even when the last feverish surges of pagan reaction had died down – there was hardly a trace of them beyond the first decade of the fifth century – public life in the towns and villages of Roman Africa was not Christianized for all that. Augustine had difficulty in imposing on the majority of the faithful the liturgical calendar that marked out the rhythm of their lives throughout the year, as it was effectively rivalled by a traditional calendar that had remained very attractive. In 399 Honorius had abolished 'sacrilegious rites', but there was no question of suppressing occasions of popular 'rejoicing':[10] the people still and always needed feast days. And what they enjoyed most, at the end of December, was not the birth of Christ, but the great spectacular shows – the *munera* – which were held in the amphitheatre during this period, and which emptied the churches, much to Augustine's displeasure.[11] It was above all during those days that he experienced with the greatest sorrow his situation of exile and captivity in the heart of the earthly city.[r]

Dialogue with the Roman aristocracy

I shall again have occasion to say that the end of 410 and the year that followed were a real turning-point in Augustine's life. We have seen that 411 was the year of Donatism's liquidation, by judicial decision and also very largely in actual fact.

Moreover, for Augustine it was a season of outstanding meetings. The Rome whose surface he had no more than brushed, as a young unknown in 385 and even 388, now came to him in the form of a frequently ancient and always wealthy nobility, who were arriving to seek in their Carthaginian palaces and manors in the interior, in the midst of their estates, the comfort which the sack of the Eternal City and the devastation of Italy had caused them to lose on the other side of the sea. Beyond the African shores, the bishop of Hippo's renown did not yet go beyond a few ascetic circles, like that of Paulinus at Nola, but on his home ground he was famous, and the dazzling role he had played in those days of June 411 at Carthage could not have passed unnoticed. The refugees, who were sometimes Christian, included some great names, and they were full of curiosity about this bishop, from reading whose *Confessions* they had already learnt a great deal.

Sometimes they had properties in Augustine's own area, in Hippo's Numidia, so neither he nor they had to travel very far to meet. During the winter of 411–12, the ailing Augustine had absented himself from Hippo for a while and, on his return, he had been too concerned by the situation of his community, which had deteriorated during his absence, to be able personally to welcome outstanding guests. That is what he wrote in the spring of 411 in a letter addressed jointly to Albina, Pinianus and his wife Melania the Younger.[s]

These persons were among the most illustrious and rich that the Rome of those times could produce. Albina was a descendant of the Caeonii – her father was Caeonius Rufius Albinus, prefect of the city in 389–91 – and her brother was Volusianus, whom we shall meet further on. She had married Valerius Publicola, who was descended on his father's side from the ancient family of the Valerii Maximi – he had the signal honour of bearing the same name as the co-consul with Brutus, the founder of the Republic in Rome – and her mother was Melania the Elder, who had just died in Palestine, where she had founded a monastery.[12] The couple's only surviving child, Publicola, had inherited a sizeable fortune, constituted in particular by vast properties in Africa, notably in the land of the 'Arzuges', on the Saharan borders of present-day South Tunisia. Because of this he, or rather his farmers, were in more or less direct contact with Barbarian nomads, and the fears that such 'contagion' inspired in this high-principled nobleman had caused him to get in touch with Augustine to inform him about it. We still have a long letter from him – in fact a whole series of questions – and the bishop's reply, the exchange dating to around 398.[t]

Two children were born to Albina and Publicola, one being Melania the Younger, who was thus the granddaughter of Melania the Elder. At the age of thirteen, this second Melania had married Valerius Pinianus, who was then seventeen. It was not a mismatch: the young man's father was Valerius Severus, prefect of the city for 382. This very young couple had had two children, both of whom died at a very early age. Soon afterwards, Pinianus yielded to Melania's wish – she being then twenty and he twenty-four – to live an ascetic life as servants of God. As early as 408, Melania had left Rome, accompanied by her husband, her mother Albina, and Rufinus of Aquilaea, the learned translator of Origen, whom she had taken under her wing. All these people, including the consecrated virgins she had recruited chiefly from among her domestic slaves, had settled in the luxurious palace which Melania had kept near Messina, on the

Sicilian coast. It was there, at the end of the summer of 410, that they had learnt of Alaric's sack of Rome, and that the Barbarians were now sweeping southwards intent on invading Sicily. Thereupon, Rufinus died and had no further part in what happened to the company; they were cast up on an island – probably Lipari – by a storm while they were trying to reach the African coast, and had to pay a ransom to the Goths who had captured them, before eventually finding a safe refuge.

In the winter of 410–11 they were staying at Thagaste, where the presence of Alypius, a great friend of their mutual friend Paulinus, doubtless attracted them just as much as concern for the material interests they still had in the region.[13] At her birth, Melania possessed a fortune that made her 'the richest heiress in the Roman world' – her annual income alone was estimated at 120,000 gold *solidi*, before the liquidation of her immense estates.[14] Scarcely had she and Pinianus arrived in Africa when they sold the lands they owned there, in Mauretania (present-day western and central Algeria), in Numidia (eastern Algeria) and Proconsularis (Tunisia and the Algerio-Tunisian borders). To avoid the rapid squandering of the sums obtained by those sales, Augustine and Alypius, as well as Aurelius of Carthage, had advised them to invest in pious foundations, having premises built and giving endowments for their upkeep.[15] Thagaste, as their first port of call, was naturally the first to benefit from this manna, and in particular Alypius' church, which was soon adorned with precious hangings and provided with some beautiful liturgical equipment, very costly objects, but which also aroused great envy all around, as the *Vita Melaniae* does not fail to tell us. For this sumptuous enrichment probably caused more stir in the environs than the two monasteries, also set up at Thagaste by Melania and Pinianus, one of which housed one hundred and thirty nuns and the other eighty monks,[16] both constituted with sufficient revenues for their maintenance. There is no doubt that the news soon reached Hippo, and had obviously preceded Melania and Pinianus when, in the spring of 411, accompanied by Alypius, they went to visit Augustine in his cathedral.

The Pinianus affair

While the *Life of Melania* breathes not a word, we are indebted to Augustine for a detailed account[u] of the effervescence, even the tumult, which filled his church on that day and which involved him in one of the most serious difficulties of his episcopal life. For during the service, just before the dismissal of the catechumens, the crowd of faithful suddenly began to shout that they wanted Pinianus as priest. The bishop saw a replay of the scene in which he had been the victim, some twenty years earlier, but with the great difference that this time the one they wanted to impose as a priest had not been chosen on his merits, as he had before Valerius, but rather because of his wealth. He had probably foreseen this eventuality, and promised his guest that he would resist the demand, for at the first shouts he left his chair in the apse and advanced towards the crowd in the nave, to declare that he would not ordain Pinianus against his will and that, if they insisted on having him for priest, they would no longer have him, Augustine, for bishop.[v] No matter, replied the crowd, after a moment's wavering – 'like a flame', he would say, 'that a draught makes flicker for an instant' – let another bishop proceed with his ordination! Augustine declared to the notables who had joined him in the apse that he would never consent, and that to ordain Pinianus against his will would ensure without fail that the young man would quit the town immediately he had been ordained. But a little later, he would confess in his letter to Albina that the shouts of the crowd massed before the apse were such that he no longer knew what to do and feared the worst for Alypius, whom the mob held responsible for this impediment and were showering with insults. He even said that, although he had considered it, he had to give up the idea of leaving the church together with Alypius, as he feared that the dense crowd through which they would have to make a path might do Alypius some harm.ʷ

Then Pinianus himself intervened to effect a delicate negotiation. He let it be known that if he were ordained in spite of himself he would leave Africa, whereas he would stay in Hippo if nothing was forced upon him, words that were like a cooling breeze to Augustine before he heard Alypius, whom he wanted to include in any decision, say drily: 'Let no one ask *my* opinion on the matter!'ˣ As for the crowd massed in the church, though disappointed at first, they accepted this solution on condition that Pinianus pledged never to accept a clerical position outside the church of Hippo. Meanwhile, to one side, Pinianus and Melania were weighing up the consequences of such a commitment and wanted to add resolutive clauses: for example, an enemy invasion, or some Barbarian incursion that might force them to leave the town. Melania wanted to add the risks of an unhealthy climate or an epidemic, but her husband made her keep quiet. Between them they agreed on a restrictive formula – yes to this commitment, 'except in case of necessity' – but merely reading it out caused tumult to break out again. Pinianus had to renounce it, to the immense joy of those present.ʸ

The denouement of this crisis was approaching but, as we shall see, it was a singular denouement. Augustine was weary of a session in which the sudden new developments, the tremendous tension and the sharp attacks on Alypius had put him through a tough ordeal. Nevertheless, he kept at Pinianus' side when he presented himself to the people to repeat the terms of his pledge. But the faithful, who were mistrustful, demanded the signature of a text. Pinianus yielded; but the bishops – Augustine and Alypius – were then asked to countersign it. There was no question but that the bishop of Thagaste would comply; but Augustine was beginning to do so when, very oddly, Melania intervened and interposed herself; and the bishop of Hippo remained, calamus in air, with his signature incomplete.ᶻ Even more bizarrely, no one insisted any longer that the protocol be finished in right and due form, and after so many emotions the assembly dispersed at an end that was not really an end. And in fact, the horrified Pinianus and Melania quickly left Hippo and never set foot there again. We know that they lived another seven years at Thagaste before departing for the Holy Land. Did they share Albina's anger towards Augustine, when she wrote an irritated letter to him from Thagaste blaming him for his passivity and, rather unfairly, his quasi-connivance with a manifestly moneygrubbing community?[17] If so, their reaction softened with time: in 418, from Jerusalem where they had just settled, they wrote to Augustine to tell him of their encounter with Pelagius, and the bishop immediately replied with his text *The Grace of Christ and Original Sin,* which he dedicated to them.

Augustine's texts recording this scene with such care for accuracy in the transcription of its vicissitudes, even if strictly physical and ambulatory,[18] speak volumes about the difficulties of governing the Christian community in Hippo. The lowly folk of the diocese's country areas were not the only ones to reveal that *rusticitas* which their pastor sometimes bitterly noted.[aa] In the town, too, the faithful could show themselves to be hot-tempered, morally coarse and easily moved to violence. Of course, they respected their bishop, but Alypius had only just escaped bearing the brunt of their anger and disappointment. It was not the first time that the material interests of their respective dioceses set the two bishops at loggerheads. In 402, a priest named Honoratus had died in his community of Thiava, which was then still dependent on the diocese of Hippo.[bb] But earlier, Honoratus had been a monk at Thagaste, and had kept his own possessions throughout both callings, so that on his demise his legacy had created a dispute between the monastic community under Alypius and the ecclesiastic community headed by Augustine.[cc] This time, however, what was at stake was an immense fortune, which had begun to affect Alypius. Augustine had been deeply sickened by the extreme animosity he had seen and heard expressed in his church against his friend, but at the same time he could not remain insensitive to the material aspirations of those men who were so poor, unhealthy, ill-clad, ill-housed in their smoky and smoke-ridden 'slums'.[dd] This explains why, while clearly stating his theoretical position of hostility to the forcible ordination of Pinianus, he found it easy to support a solution – which was nevertheless rather extorted from him – that gave a glimpse of the possibility that this ultra rich man, who had not given everything to Thagaste, might one day be ordained at Hippo and, on his death, let his community have the benefit of part of his inheritance.[19] The precedent of Honoratus of Thiava must necessarily have been in his mind.

Exchanges with Volusianus

Augustine, too, might well have said what has been attributed to several others: 'God preserve me from my friends, I will take care of my enemies myself.' For we shall see that in the end he had less trouble with the pagan Volusanius than with his very Christian sister, Albina.

It is highly probable that Rufius Antonius Agrypnius Volusianus arrived with the wave of refugees at the end of summer 410. He belonged to the noble family of the Caeonii, where the prefecture of the city of Rome had been handed down from father to son since the Constantinian era, and his father had even had the signal honour of repeating this office in 390/1. That father was pagan – one of the most cultivated in his time, according to Macrobius[20] – but his mother was Christian, and the couple thus illustrated the situation of religious division of which we have seen other examples.[21] In those families, even if only recently, Christianity had come down from mother to daughter. Volusianus, in the midst of his mother, sister and niece (who was none other than Melania the Younger) was for the time being clinging to a well-bred, broad-minded paganism, which was firmer in its doubts relating to the major dogmas of the new religion, rather than positively entrenched in traditional philosophical convictions.

He was one of the most brilliant representatives of what, some thirty years earlier, Symmachus had called in all seriousness 'the best part of the human race'ee – the Roman senate and its related families. Many of the members of that elite were descendants of the first *gentes* of Rome and, as well-read men, cultivated a nostalgia for those far-off times when their ancestors had exerted real power on a par with their personal virtues, culture and eloquence. As has been said, the choice of their models, poets or philosophers, their taste for sterile celebrations, revealed their resignation to a gilded impotence.[22] The offices with which the Empire continued to entrust them, outside a Rome which had become the museum of that ancient history, enjoyed an intact prestige, but no longer had anything but the appearance of an authority shared with others, and supervised by others who held the true power – that which was conferred by the command of armies. For instance, the proconsulship of Africa, which Volusianus seems to have occupied as a young man, prior to 410, but of which no trace remains.[23]

In those months of 411/12, at Carthage, where he kept up a correspondence with the bishop of Hippo, Volusianus was apparently completely at leisure, although Augustine, out of deference for this great lord, alludes in his first letter to their respective occupations, which were certainly more burdensome in his own case.ff Together with a few other fine minds of his rank, he had created an informal 'circle' at Carthage, where each could hold his own in the field of rhetoric and, principally, poetry.gg The letter from Volusianus to the bishop – a small monument of elegant and hollow epistolary literature – gives us some idea of those 'Carthaginian nights': the art of eloquence and its secrets always took first place, followed by poetical activity; and the author of the letter did not refrain from reminding the recipient that he had excelled in both fields, probably less to flatter him than to intimate that, apart from their differences in status – and even though the bishop had regrettably taken the wrong direction! – they were both in essence part of the same world.hh He knew that even philosophy was a subject familiar to his correspondent – another topic for this literary coterie's learned conversations – Volusianus went on, quoting the Lyceum, the Academy, the Painted Porch, Epicurus and his followers, to confess in the end that none of these doctrines was truly intellectually satisfying.ii

Then he donned a mask: amid these uncertainties, he continued, one of us bluntly raised the question of whether there was anyone sufficiently well versed in Christian wisdom to encourage him in his hesitant steps towards joining the Church, by means of true or convincing argument: success guaranteed, an amazed silence fell on all those present. Augustine, however, would have had no problem in decoding this scholastic process and recognizing Volusianus beneath the anonymity. And he could not be mistaken: indeed, in his own entourage this personage was too immersed in Christianity not to be a little won over by it. But he was quibbling about the fundamental articles of that faith, the eternal stumbling-blocks of the positivist: how could they accept the incarnation, an affront to reason that was further aggravated by a virgin birth?jj And how could divine transcendence come to terms with the very ordinarily human life of Christ? His miracles were taken into account, but the healing of the possessed and even Lazarus' resurrection did not impress Volusianus.[24] In short, the great nobleman was putting the bishop with his back to the wall: his reputation depended on his providing a satisfactory answer; and as Nectarius had done before, as a way of showing his religious receptiveness, at the end of the letter he invoked the protection of the supreme Deity on his correspondent.[kk] But Augustine had learnt to distrust these final, or initial, courtesy phrases, and the misleading pleasure they could bring him, such as he had felt, for instance, when reading this salutation, 'To our father Augustine, eternal salvation in the Lord', at the head of a letter which from that point on showed that its authors were undoubtedly infidels.[ll]

It was not the first time that Augustine had held a dialogue with one of the many enlightened pagans of the Roman senatorial aristocracy. At a date that is uncertain but prior to 408, the year of this person's death – he was massacred at the same time as Stilicho, of whom he had been a supporter – he had had an exchange of letters about the divine nature of Christ with one Longinianus, who has been positively identified with Flavius Macrobius Longinianus, prefect of the city in 401/2, who practised a Neoplatonist type of deism; and the bishop had encouraged him to persevere in his search for moral perfection, doing without purification rituals – those of Orphism and the revelation of Hermes Trismegistus – which his correspondent cited, calmly confessing himself to be a 'pagan' (*paganus*), evidence that the label was no longer regarded as pejorative by those who wore it.[25] And it was assuredly easier for Augustine than for us to recognize, in the way that a Longinianus or a Volusianus saw Christ, the arguments of Porphyry as expressed in his *Philosophy of Oracles* or in a pamphlet entitled *Against the Christians*.[26] In the first decade of the fifth century, he had not avoided epistolary debate with these followers of Neoplatonist theologies, not least because his long familiarity with those texts, during his youth, made it easier for him. Around 408, for instance, through the intermediary of a Carthaginian priest named Deogratias, he sent a reply to six questions inspired by Porphyry's anti-Christian arguments and, he would say in his *Retractations*, posed by a 'friend' whom he wished to see become a Christian.[mm] And we may recall how astutely Augustine had used Platonism for his own ends, in his letter to the young Dioscorus in 410, by showing how, in his opinion, it had been fulfilled in Christianity.[nn]

Confronted with these powerful and influential great aristocrats, assembled in their literary coterie in Carthage, the game to be played was more important and the stakes were higher; all the more so because the bishop was aware that quite a few of them did not share Volusianus' family reasons for showing at least a little indulgence towards Christians. The look they cast at Christianity, a religion of the people, generally combined social haughtiness and intellectual pride. Augustine is probably not overdoing it when in one of his recently discovered unpublished sermons, dated 1 January 404, he makes one of these notables say, 'Me! Become a Christian, be what *my doorkeeper* is and not what Plato was, or what Pythagoras was!'[oo] And to describe the arrogance that their Neoplatonist intellectual exercises earn them, he resumes in this text the metaphor of the 'homeland' and the 'way' to it that had come to his mind in the final page of Book VII of the *Confessions*.[pp] As he himself had been until the decisive days of the Milanese summer in 386, they were encamped on the 'mountain peak of their philosophical vanity', from where they could see the 'homeland' in the distance, but were unable to reach it, because first of all they had to descend and take the path that began with the humility of faith, in order to be able to ascend to it.[qq]

Augustinians never cease to detail the richness of this very fine text, one of the bishop's most carefully elaborated, but in which he did not put all pagans in the same basket. Among these 'prideful' people, he distinguished two kinds: the one which irritated him most felt the need to resort to a 'mediator' to achieve his mystical aims. In the bishop's view, anyone who proposed himself as such to these candidates for the divine vision, seeking purification, could be none other than the devil.[rr] It was the devil who suggested that they should find this mediation by practising theurgic rites, compelling the deity, or by initiations into various mysteries, which some people 'collected', as had quite recently been done by the famous Agorius Praetextatus – who had died in 384 – a *mystes* of Eleusis, but also an initiate into the mysteries of Hecate, Cybele and Mithras.[27] Of course, the bishop adds, as those cults were now prohibited, the rites or initiations continued to be performed in secret. This clandestinity involving a far from negligible number of those whom Roman society considered the most prominent still appeared to him as a threat, the possibility that this hidden yeast might once again make the dough rise. Such a fear seems astonishing to us, who find it *a posteriori* ill-founded, because we know what was going to happen. But after all, a text such as Macrobius' *Saturnalia*, celebrating pagan reaction in aristocratic circles and reviving 'Symmachus' circle', was written and circulated in the last years of Augustine's life.

Augustine did not confuse those people whom he considered lost, and whose contagious effect on others he still feared, with the pagans who declared the emptiness of sacrificial rites: Pythagoras[ss] had been one such, so it was said. And as Christ's redemptive action had been able to be exerted even before his incarnation,[tt] certain wise men of pre-Christian Antiquity could have found salvation in their practices that were free from all mediation, despite their reprehensible arrogance. In a letter written a little later to Evodius, Augustine told his friend that he did not willingly exclude the great souls of paganism, poets and philosophers,[uu] from eternal happiness. But since Christ's birth there has been a true mediator, and for Augustine it was a matter of winning for him at least those who had turned away from the false mediator. Volusianus seemed to belong to this category, and the disquiet he displayed could be understood as a sincere appeal, requiring a special apologetic action, *ad hominem*. At the same time, Marcellinus, the loyal and devoted imperial judge of the conference, was pressing Augustine to give his pagan friend an answer, and at the end of his letter did not fail to inform him that a very rich landowner in the region of Hippo, who was a member of their circle, had lavished a stream of ironic compliments on the bishop and implied that his conversations with him had left him unsatisfied.[vv] It was a way of suggesting an additional objective to Augustine, reminding him of the rule *cuius fundus, eius cultus* ('where the property is, there the religion is'), a variation for estates of the adage *cuius regio, eius religio*, true when it referred to splits between Donatists and Catholics, but just as valid in the relationship between Christianity and paganism. Converting one of these fine gentlemen would bring several hundred of his yokels into the Church. The reward was not to be despised, and as he did for Donatists who had more or less repented, the bishop could tell himself that grace would come just when needed to give substance to these somewhat expeditious conversions.

Thus, in the spring of 412 Volusianus received a fine, long letter, whose author well knew that it would go the rounds of Carthage's salons, like the one he wrote at the same time to Marcellinus.[28] Augustine evaded none of the questions raised by either of them, and his reply to Volusianus, notably, went well beyond the solution of material – and materialist – objections which may have brought a smile to his lips, for he rediscovered in them some conceptual difficulties that he himself had experienced in Milan before the spring of 386. For instance, on the mystery of the incarnation, about which he suggested to his correspondent, by way of explanation, the formula of 'hypostatic union' of the two natures, divine and human, in the unity of the 'person' of Christ, which prefigures what would be maintained later at the time of the debates of Chalcedon.[ww] The result was a brilliant little essay, certain pages of which are a foretaste of the developments to come in the *City of God*, the great book which the bishop was working on in that same period, its main themes already taking shape in his mind. In particular, it contains a magnificent summary of sacred history, its lyrical inspiration being one of the splendid triumphs of those dictated texts, whose movement, verbal abundance, rhythm and play of assonance, placed at the service of a heartfelt desire to persuade, contained everything likely to attract a cultivated nobleman such as Volusianus. However, the bishop took the precaution of warning his reader: what he was going to read about the economy of salvation predicted by the Scriptures had in itself its own driving force, a capacity for persuasion; but it confirmed the primacy of faith in the dialectic between intellect and belief: it was the latter that opened up an access closed by unbelief.[xx]

Unfortunately, we know nothing of Volusianus' reaction. He had a long and outstanding career, which led him to the prefectship of the praetorium in 428–9. In 436 he went to Constantinople, where the young emperor of the West, Valentinian III, sent him on an embassy to arrange his marriage with Eudoxia, daughter of Theodosius II. There, leaving Jerusalem and her monasteries, his niece Melania the Younger came to join him, to help him in his mission. Early in 437, she found her uncle dying, and converted him on his death-bed. Shortly before, Volusianus had received a visit from the patriarch Proclus, bishop of Constantinople, and the story goes that he said to Melania, 'If we had three men like the lord Proclus in Rome, you would not find a single pagan!'[yy] Augustine was far from his thoughts then, but his words had worked their way into his soul.

In a sermon dated 417 – the year in which Volusianus had become prefect of the city of Rome, like his father and grandfather before him – the bishop said that from henceforth the nobility as well were nearly all caught up in the nets of the fishers of men, Christ's followers.[zz] We have seen that on the approaching extinction of paganism in the bosom of the upper classes Augustine swung alternately between confidence and anxiety. On that day he was in an optimistic phase.

Destroy the idols in your heart[ab]

If it were only a matter of converting pagans! There were often more than mere nuances between the spiritual requirements of the bishop and the realities of the Christianity lived by many of his flock. But Augustine could also remark this discrepancy and the remnants of paganism among the faithful when he preached at Carthage or when he was visiting other communities outside his diocese.

It was exceptional for him to preach to pagans. The recently published sermons give an instance, however, of when he preached early in 404 at Boseth – a small town in Pronconsularis that is difficult to localize but was perhaps near Tignica (Ain Tounga).[29] There appears to have been a mixture of Christians and pagans in the congregation, before the latter had to exit during the celebration of the religious office. Just before they left the church, Augustine once again urged them not to put off their conversion any longer, not to say 'Tomorrow I shall become a Christian',[30] and not to go to the astrologer to ask which would be the best day to become one! And, turning to the believers, he made them understand that it was not just words – his own or others' – but their own behaviour, that is, the example they themselves set, which would be the best encouragement for those who were still hesitating.[31]

Now, that example was not always of a kind to impart the image of a true change *in intimo cordis* to those pagans who were watching the Christian community. Truth to tell, in its bosom too, astrologers were continuing to enjoy their takings, something that the bishop deplored but could understand, since he had been loyal to them for some years during his youth. But he could not accept that catechumens or, even worse, baptized Christians who were unfaithful to their baptism, were still resorting to astrologers to guide their lives, just like ordinary pagans.[ac] Such things were unfortunately very commonplace, and he had remarked on it even in the times of his priesthood at Hippo, when he saw believers avoid the day after the calends – the second day of the month – for embarking on a journey, and take no decision without consulting the almanacs in which unlucky days were marked according to the 'Egyptian' tradition.[ad] Around 400, in his book *The First Catechesis*, the insistence with which the bishop put aspirants to baptism on their guard against astrologers shows how widespread the evil had become.[ae] Christians, he would say still later, were going to consult them secretly,[af] which is why, when one of them came to be converted, the bishop drew special attention to his case; he was pointed out to the community and, as happened to the magicians' books burnt in front of St Paul at Ephesus, his were made into a joyful auto-da-fé.[ag] Augustine would have liked to see even the names of the planets disappear, as they were the charlatans' stock-in-trade, and he suggested that his parishioners should abandon the traditional names of weekdays in favour of sabbatical denominations:[32] 'Mercury's day' – the French 'mercredi', would thus have become 'the fourth day after the sabbath' (*quarta sabbati dies*) and the 'Moon's day', the 'second'.[ah] But they rejected this cultural revolution, beside which the adoption of the Republican calendar in France at the very end of the eighteenth century would be a mere amiable masquerade. And, with all due respect to the great soul of their illustrious bishop, they were quite right!

On the other hand, among a good number of his flock Augustine could justly deplore the persistent strength of the old underlying magic and superstition, which had always been paganism's not-so-secret drawer, and in Africa was particularly well stocked.[33] The practice of combating headaches with the help of magic strips of cloth was still in use – the devil's bands, said the bishop;[ai] weary of it all, Augustine recommended applying the Gospels to their forehead, not forgetting to remind them that they were not intended for that, but meant rather to cure the ills of the soul than those of the body.[aj] And what could he say about placing the host on the eyes of a child whose lids were stuck together?[ak] Augustine noted that when their children's health, if not life, was at stake, parents lapsed into their old habits. Around 408, he had occasion to reply to questions raised by his episcopal colleague, Bonifatius of Cataquas, who reflected the anxieties of fathers and mothers of baptized infants (*parvuli*): was there a risk of harming them – and if so, what risk – should sacrificing to demons be resorted to in the case of physical danger? It was easy for Augustine to reassure them: nothing could diminish the salvific efficacy of a sacrament which, in this instance, had not been contrary to the recipient's will.[al] It did not escape him that small infants were presented for baptism first to preserve their health or help them to recover. But its spiritual value was not compromised because of that intention – which in any case was not the infants'.[am] And if baptism could have a curative effect on the adults as well, who could complain, provided, of course, that it had not been undertaken like a simple thermal cure?[34]

Nor was the bishop unaware of the secular stench released by the bonfires on St John's day, a truly pagan festival of the summer solstice disguised as a celebration of the Baptist, although he defended his followers against the sardonic accusations of the Manichaean Faustus of Milevis.[an] The battle against those who strayed was endless. Many were the recent Christians who, like Lot's wife, were tempted to look back, and whose perdition must be avoided. We may recall the future bishop's dramatic engagement in the *Laetitia* affair, in the spring of 395. Augustine had won the fight, but in this regard the Christian populace was still in need of continued teaching. The cult of saints and martyrs was the permanent area for such instruction. How many times had the bishop spoken out either on the tomb (*memoria*) of St Cyprian, or the place where he was tortured (his *mensa*)! On the latter spot an altar had been erected, not as if to a god, the preacher felt obliged to specify – it was Cyprian himself who was an altar to the true God.[ao]

Lastly, concerning miracles, in those years around 410 – and of course in preceding years – Augustine had perceptibly distanced himself in comparison with many of his followers. He had given his explanation, as early as the time of his retreat at Thagaste,[ap] and then in his early priesthood, in the *De utilitate credendi*. Miracles, he wrote then, had been useful in the Church's early times, even indispensable to substantiate Christian preaching: Christ, he would say in a sermon, had not performed miracles for miracles' sake[aq] – even such an astonishing one as the resurrection of the widow's son (Luke 7.11–17). Faced with the pagan world's prodigies, this supernatural Christian had performed his task. But they must not be overdone. 'These miracles would affect no one were they not astonishing; and they would cease to astonish if they were usual.'[ar] That was his thinking around 390/1. And in *The First Catechesis*, some dozen years later, he advised a pastor approached by any neophyte who had been attracted to religion by a miracle or some dream not to delay in committing him 'to the sounder path of the Scriptures'.[as] The bishop would move on considerably on this subject, and I will return to it. He had not experienced a miracle, except perhaps one August day in the garden in Milan;[35] but he admits in the *Confessions* that he sometimes felt a need – which he regarded as well-nigh diabolical! – to ask God to send him a sign. And what clearer sign could God give him than a miracle? But he rejected the temptation and was content with what God might be pleased to grant him – grace.[at]

Notes

a. Cf. above, p. 221.
b. *De consensu evang.*, I, 21: *pauci pagani qui remanserunt.* Cf. also I, 29 and 39. In a recently published sermon, dated early 404, Augustine still insists on this small residue: *Sermon Dolbeau 25 (Mainz 61), 25: Iam pauci foris remanserunt,* in F. Dolbeau, *Vingt-six Sermons au peuple d'Afrique,* p. 266.
c. *De cons. evang.*, I, 10.
d. *De cons. evang.*, I, 13.
e. *Sermon 24, 6: Utique hoc clamastis: 'Quomodo Roma, sic et Carthago'.*
f. *Sermon 24, 6: Fratres, puto ignominiosius fuisse Herculi barbam radi quam caput praecidi.*
g. Why him? We do not know: Sufes, which was not even in his province, was in no way under his episcopal jurisdiction.
h. *Ep.* 50, dated 399. The affair certainly had legal consequences, but they are unknown.
i. *C. Th.*, XVI, 10, 19.
j. *Sermon Dolbeau 4 (Mainz 9), 8 (F. Dolbeau, Vingt-six Sermons au peuple d'Afrique,* pp. 519–20): *Confiteatur aliquis Mercurium . . . quando unum vel birratum stationarium viderit: 'Non feci, non interfui, non sacrificavi'.* The *birratus stationarius* is an orderly in a *birrus* (or *byrrhus*), a civilian garment.
k. *Ep.* 91, 8.
l. *Ep.* 91, 9.
m. Nectarius, in *Ep.* 103, 3: *Gravius est enim male vivere quam mala morte finire.*
n. Nectarius, in *Ep.* 103, 2, a text directly inspired by Cicero, *De Republica,* VI, 13.
o. In *Ep.* 103, 4: *Deus summus te custodiat et legis suae te conservet praesidium atque ornamentum nostrum.* It is more flattering than truly Christian! But Nectarius' father was converted at the end of his life: *Ep.* 91, 2.
p. *Ep.* 104, 17.
q. *Sermon Morin 1,* in *Miscellanea Agostiniana,* I, pp. 589–93. He says, in *Enarr. in Psalm.* 7, 9, that only God, 'who looks deeply into hearts and minds', can in this instance distinguish the true from the false.
r. *City of God,* XIX, 17: *dum apud terrenam civitatem velut captivam vitam suae peregrinationis agit.*
s. *Ep.* 124.
t. *Ep.* 46 and 47. The identification of this Publicola, Augustine's correspondent, with Valerius Publicola has sometimes been challenged. After careful analysis of the texts, it was reaffirmed by M. Moreau, in *Rev. des ét. aug.,* 28, 1982, pp. 225–38.
u. In the form of two letters, one to Alypius, whom the people of Hippo accused of having an interest in wishing to keep Pinianus in his diocese (*Ep.* 125), and the other to Albina, who suspected the people of Hippo, and Augustine himself, of wanting, for the same reasons, to attach her son-in-law to their church (*Ep.* 126).
v. *Ep.* 126, 1.
w. *Ep.* 126, 2.
x. *Ep.* 126, 3. The bishop of Thagaste obviously wanted to clear himself of any responsibility in this affair.
y. *Ep.* 126, 4.
z. *Ep.* 126, 5: *tamen obtemperavi, ac sic remansit mea non plena subscriptio.*
aa. Cf. above, p. 256.
bb. Cf. above, p. 251.
cc. See the developments of this dispute in *Ep.* 83, especially 83, 4.
dd. *Sermon 170,* 4. Augustine contrasted the *domus fumosae, fumigatae,* inhabited by the *boni* (his people), with the *domus marmoratae, laqueatae,* owned by the *iniqui.*
ee. *Pars melior humani generis:* Symmachus, *Letters,* I, 52, letter to Agorius Praetextatus, one of the 'caciques' of this senatorial class, and the 'pope' of paganism at the close of the fourth century.
ff. *Ep.* 132: *propter occupationes varias et meas et tuas.*
gg. *Ep.* 135, 1.

hh. See the objection, reported by Augustine, made by cultured pagans to cultured Christians: *Magnus vir, bonus vir, litteratus, doctus: sed quare christianus? (Enarr. in Psalm.* 39, 26).

ii. *Ep.* 135, 1.

jj. *Ep.* 135, 2. It was one of the most common objections. P. Courcelle has listed a catalogue of these criticisms: 'Propos antichrétiens rapportés par saint Augustin', in *Recherches augustiniennes*, 1, 1958, pp. 149–86.

kk. *Ep.* 135, 2, *in fine.*

ll. *Ep.* 232, 2.

mm. The *Sex Quaestiones contra paganos expositae* are the subject of letter 102. Cf. *Retract.*, II, 31.

nn. *Ep.* 118. Cf. above, p. 137.

oo. *Sermon Dolbeau* 26 *(Mainz* 62), 59 (F. Dolbeau, *Vingt-six Sermons au peuple d'Afrique,* p. 413): *Et hoc futurus sum quod est* ostiaria mea, *ac non potius quod fuit Plato, quod Pythagoras?*

pp. *Conf.,* VII, 27: cf. above, p. 91.

qq. *Sermon Dolbeau* 26 *(Mainz* 62), 59: *Quid enim prodest illis quod de longinquo patriam vident superbientes? Non inveniunt viam, quoniam ad illam altitudinem patriae ab humilitate incipit via.*

rr. *Sermon Dolbeau* 26, 28, p. 387: *Cum ergo viderent et quaererent purgationem,* diabolus ille superbus superbe quaerentes et superbe se iactantes praeoccupavit *et* pro mediatore *se opposuit, per quem videretur eis animas suas posse purgari.*

ss. *Sermon Dolbeau* 26 *(Mainz* 62), 36, p. 394.

tt. *Sermon Dolbeau* 26 *(Mainz* 62), 38, p. 395.

uu. *Ep.* 164, 4.

vv. *Ep.* 136, 3.

ww. *Ep.* 137, 9–11. On the christological aspects of letter 137, cf. G. Madec, *La Patrie et la Voie,* Paris, Desclée, 1989, pp. 228–34.

xx. *Ep.* 137, 15: *intellectui fides aditum aperit, infidelitas claudit.* There follows, on two pages (chap. 15 and 16) a dazzling demonstration of the fulfilment of the Old Testament by the New.

yy. *Vita s. Melaniae*, Greek version, 53, *SC*, 90, p. 232.

zz. *Sermon* 51, 4: *Intus est iam pene tota nobilitas.*

ab. *Enarr. in Psalm.* 80, 14: *Magnum opus est intus haec idola frangere.*

ac. He is fulminating against this in the *Sermon Dolbeau* 14 *(Mainz* 44), 7 (F. Dolbeau, *Vingt-six Sermons au peuple d'Afrique,* pp. 112–13), preached at Carthage in the summer of 397. Here we find the famous *cras, cras,* theme, as in *Sermon Dolbeau* 25, 27, quoted earlier.

ad. *Exp. in Ep. ad Galat.,* 35.

ae. *De catechizandis rudibus,* 11; 48; 55.

af. *Tract. in Ioh. evang.,* VI, 17.

ag. *Enarr. in Psalm.* 61, 23 (Acts 19.19): cf. also *Tract. in Ioh. evang.,* VIII, 8.

ah. French *lundi* (Italian *lunedì,* but also English Monday or German *Montag*), the first day of the week being Sunday *(dies dominica),* the day following the sabbath.

ai. *Sermon* 4, 36: *ligamenta diabolica;* cf. also *Enarr. in Psalm.* 70, 1, 17, on the mothers who swathe their children's foreheads with these 'sacrilegious ribbons'.

aj. *Tract. in Ioh. evang.,* VII, 12.

ak. *Contra Iulianum op. imp.,* III, 162: the story of the little Acatius, who was then five.

al. *Ep.* 98, 1.

am. *Ep.* 98, 5.

an. *Sermon* 196, 4; *Sermon Morin* 1, 4; *Sermon Frangip.* 8, 5; *c. Faustum,* 20, 4, for the Manichaean's criticisms.

ao. *Sermon Denis* 14 (preached in 401), 5.

ap. In the *De vera religione,* 47.

aq. *Sermon* 98, 3.

ar. *De utilitate credendi,* 34.

as. *De cath. rud.,* 10.

at. *Conf.,* X, 56: 'A sign from thee, O Lord, . . . by how many machinations does the *enemy* work on me to suggest that I should seek it of thee!' It makes one think of Bernanos. And further on: 'Do what thou wilt, if thou grantest, and continuest to grant, that I may freely follow thee.'

Part III

The Doctor of Grace

CHAPTER XXVIII

Pelagius

It's a small world. In Augustine's time it was even smaller and, of all the roads leading to and from Rome, some were used more than others in the autumn of 410, after Alaric's capture of the city, especially those that channelled the exodus of fugitives in search of hospitable lands, southwards towards Sicily and, principally, Africa. The shortest route to safety was the *via Ostiensis*; at Ostia, which was more overflowing than ever, one could embark for Carthage, but also for Hippo Diarrhytus (Bizerte), Thabraca (Tabarka) and Hippo. And it was at Hippo that one of these refugees landed – Pelagius. He probably did not choose this destination deliberately; like all the rest who were there, in haste to shake Italian soil from their feet, he doubtless boarded the first boat that was leaving, which happened to be going to Augustine's town.[1] The ancient world was small; yet at the end of autumn 410, the paths of Pelagius and Augustine failed to cross. Not that the bishop shrank from a meeting that curiosity alone would have made him seek. At the time, he was simply unaware of Pelagius' arrival at Hippo, and we know why: he was either ill or convalescent during those weeks, and absent from his episcopal town.[a] In any case, the refugee did not linger there and, as Augustine says, he had neither the time nor the opportunity to cause much stir.[b] Pelagius would take away from his stay in Hippo only the short, prudent note – though attentive and more than courteous – in which the bishop had welcomed him to the town, and of which Pelagius would later say that it expressed Augustine's great desire to see his unexpected visitor and converse with him.[2]

There is something frustrating, if not paradoxical, about this failed rendezvous – arranged by the larger frame of History yet denied by the smaller incident – if one reflects that in the remaining twenty years of the bishop's life he would spend the best part of his energy and intellectual resources in the debate against Pelagius and his disciples that, in terms of renown, would take him far beyond Africa; it would give rise to the most outstanding Augustinian contribution to come down through the centuries and, for posterity, often eclipse other aspects of his great works and other facets of his remarkable person. These two men, whose spiritual confrontation was so strong, barely noticed each other, while fate had at first done everything possible to bring them face to face; for Pelagius had hastened on to Carthage, where he knew he would be able to find some of the nobility to whose homes he had been admitted in Rome, like Jerome before his departure for Palestine. And for his part, Augustine had left Hippo for the metropolis in the spring, to prepare with Aurelius and his colleagues for the grand confrontation with the Donatists. We know that he was there in May 411, and he himself tells us that he had one or two glimpses of the British monk who, even physically, would scarcely pass unnoticed;[3] but in those days of late May and early June, he was far too busy with the preparations for the conference to pay him much heed.[c] Someone who was not usually bothered by having several irons in the fire was too much in demand for this enterprise of major importance to be able to spread his attentions. On the evening of 8 June, the bishop had some free time once more, but Pelagius had already taken to the sea again to go to Palestine, where John of Jerusalem would extend him the warmest of welcomes.

There is no doubt that Augustine regretted not having been able to profit from that untimely and too hasty visit to arrange a meeting, as he had for some dozen years known by reputation the man who he had reason to think would become his main adversary in the future. Although he had not been able to follow Pelagius' progress step by step in the palaces of the Roman aristocracy, especially in the bosom of the powerful Anicii family, and under the patronage of a priest who would later become Pope Sixtus III,[4] Augustine had been kept informed about him, notably thanks to Paulinus of Nola, who had connections with the monk, without sharing his ideas, although he was somewhat curious about them. There is still speculation about the identity of the 'brother and colleague in the episcopacy' who, one day in Rome around 404/5, had occasion to quote the famous sentence from Book X of the *Confessions* in front of Pelagius, 'Give what you command, and command what you will',[d] which was so significant of its author's submission to divine grace. Pelagius had leapt up and immediately launched into an impassioned refutation.[e] It could have been Evodius, bishop of Uzalis, Augustine's old companion, who spent several weeks on a mission to Rome during the summer of 404;[5] it could also have been Paulinus of Nola himself,[6] to whom Pelagius had subsequently sent a long letter, defining his own doctrine regarding grace, and this had finished up in the bishop's hands. On reading it, Augustine would feel that he had really reduced grace to the absolute minimum.[f] In roughly the same period, Pelagius wrote and published his *Commentary on St Paul's Thirteen Epistles*, including an explanation of the Epistle to the Romans which affirmed that, by virtue of baptism, man had the possibility of not sinning and of living like the Son of God: the author clearly knew the Augustinian texts on the Apostle dating from his priesthood, and was replying to them, as well as to the commentaries addressed to Simplicianus at the beginning of Augustine's episcopacy.[7] Thus in 411 the bishop of Hippo knew in theory what he had to deal with in Pelagius' system of setting human freedom in man's relationship with God, even if he had not yet seen the British monk's text, the *De natura* (now suggested to have been written also in the years 405/6[8], to which we shall soon see him give particular attention. The bishop's tactful consideration is all the more remarkable with regard to someone whose name he quotes for the first time in his first anti-Pelagian text, early in 412, praising him as a Christian of eminent virtue;[g] it was doubtless because he foresaw the prospect of a long struggle ahead of him, in which respect for an adversary whose spiritual quality he acknowledged was a necessary preliminary.

The first developments in the anti-Pelagian controversy

Pelagius had left Africa, but it was in Africa that the first scene in the fate of what was to be Pelagianism was enacted; for when he departed, Pelagius had left a few disciples behind, and they were not slow to propagate ideas which, even before challenging those of the bishop of Hippo, went counter to opinions that were commonly held in local Christian communities. One was a man who, during these years, would appear to be his chief lieutenant, a Roman of aristocratic origins named Caelestius: a man 'with a very sharp intellect', Augustine would say later,[h] but lacking his master's prudence and moderation.[9] It was probably he who, in the summer of 411, circulated in Carthage making speeches about the baptism of infants who, according to him, were baptized 'not for the remission of sins, but to be sanctified in Christ'; speeches that had come to the bishop of Hippo's ears.[i] He had considered them shocking, but as they emanated, he said, from men without much authority, he had not thought it right to refute them other than by allusions in sermons or conversations.[j] Caelestius had already attracted notice; moreover, he committed the imprudence of putting himself forward as a candidate for the priesthood in the heart of the Carthaginian clergy. But orthodoxy was keeping watch in the person of another of those refugees who, in 411, were turning the African mother-city into the temporary second capital of the western Empire. He was the Milanese deacon, Paulinus, a friend of Augustine – at whose request he would shortly afterwards write a *Life of St Ambrose*[10] – and took it upon himself to summon Caelestius to appear before an episcopal tribunal.

The hearing took place in the autumn, October or November,[11] and Augustine, having returned to Hippo after an absence of several months, did not take part; but naturally he was informed of the proceedings, and what he would quote from them seven years later in his treatise *On Original Sin* passes on to us the words exchanged in the tense atmosphere of the session.[k] Caelestius had summed up his thinking in a short text, which was read out to the audience, and for his part Paulinus of Milan, his prosecutor, had gathered together in six propositions that he wanted to hear the accused condemn, the essentials of the arguments that had been attributed to him. Caelestius was said to have taught that Adam had been created mortal and, sinner or not, was doomed to death; that his sin had wronged only himself, and not humankind; that infants at birth are in the situation of Adam before the Fall; that humankind in its totality does not die because of Adam's sin, or have the benefit of resurrection by virtue of Christ's resurrection; that the Law gives access to heaven in the same way as the Gospel; lastly, that even before Christ's coming there were men who were free from sin.[12] These texts clearly bore witness that the fundamentals of Pelagianism had already taken shape by that date.

Aurelius, bishop of Carthage, presided over the hearing, setting out the matters at issue and attempting to relax the atmosphere a little; but Paulinus of Milan did not deal gently with Caelestius. Pressed with questions, notably on the second proposition, relating to original sin, the accused hummed and hawed, and admitted only that he was not sure about the transmission of Adam's sin to the rest of the human race because, he said, he had heard various opinions on this subject upheld by Catholic priests. 'Names!' Paulinus brusquely interrupted him. Caelestius came out with the 'holy priest Rufinus', in whom, among the various bearers of a name that was so common then, and made illustrious by several people, modern historians have thought it possible to recognize Rufinus the Syrian, author of a *Book on Faith*, and there is fairly general agreement on identifying him with a priest of the same name, a monk of Bethlehem and friend of St Jerome.[13] Put in a tight spot, Pelagius' friend thought he could get out of it by professing that infants needed to be baptized,[1] but the tribunal was not disposed to be satisfied with this concession which, any more than the diplomatic affirmation of his doubt about original sin, did not save him from condemnation and excommunication. He would appeal against the finding to the see of Rome. Meanwhile, without even supporting this appeal, he embarked for Ephesus, where he managed to obtain a place in the priesthood.

In the winter of 411–12, Augustine was absorbed in tasks that would brook no delay, because they were the results of the conference with the Donatists in the preceding June, and he could not shirk them. The *Minutes* had been made public in Carthage at the end of June, and sent to the cathedral church of various dioceses, including Hippo, but the bishop was the first to acknowledge that no one wanted to get down to reading such a pile of papers.[14] So, at the beginning of the winter of 411–12, he made a 'summary' – the *Breviculus conlationis* – coupled shortly afterwards with a substantial circular letter addressed to the Donatist followers, with the aim of dissociating the sect's 'grass roots' from the hierarchy, making their bishops, and especially their representatives at the conference, look like bad shepherds and men of bad faith, incapable of admitting their downfall.[15] Augustine's mind was also occupied by the problems raised by Volusianus and the solutions to give for them.[m] He yielded, however, to the entreaties of the tribune and notary Marcellinus, who was worried by the progress, which he perceived in Carthage, of the ideas sown by Caelestius concerning original sin. He seems to have given in during the autumn of 411, if not the summer, sending his friend what he calls in a letter the *libri de baptismo parvulorum* – 'On the baptism of infants' – which are a reply to various questions raised by Marcellinus, to whom the texts are dedicated. After receiving them, the recipient sent them back to him, and in the midst of all his preoccupations the bishop could no longer remember the reason.[n] But when he reread them, he had found them wanting and had waited until he could find the time to resume and complete them. Such was the genesis, between autumn 411 and spring 412, of Augustine's first anti-Pelagian work, the *De peccatorum meritis et remissione*.[o]

Of all the bishop of Hippo's works, this is perhaps the least unexpected, since the author scarcely needed any prompting on these topics: 'He had refuted Pelagius', it has been said, 'even before he knew him.'[16] Without too much of a paradox, one might add that it is also the least original, at least in its theological and ecclesiological motives, in that it embraces ideas on the need to baptize infants that were current in the Church at the end of the fourth century;[17] and also – though this is where it is less Augustinian – in that it anticipated a desire, widespread among the mass of the faithful, for a sort of 'automatic' guarantee of the remission of sins: that is how a very average Christian might understand grace. But what gives the *De peccatorum meritis* its powerful originality is that, already in this first work, when he had as yet only an incomplete knowledge of Pelagius' writings, Augustine had a clear awareness of the theological issues at stake in the debate that was commencing, and all its implications. It is hardly surprising that Book I, after gathering texts relating to redemption in the Old and New Testaments, dwells at length on the problem of the baptism of young children. Augustine had already turned it over in his mind on several occasions. In the *De baptismo*, some ten years earlier, he had questioned himself on its opportuneness, or rather, its justification: an infant was in a different situation from that of the good thief who had made an act of faith and received grace without baptism, and of adults who were baptized but sinners, who often took the sacrament without faith.[p] He had returned to it in 408, in his long letter to Bonifatius of Cataquas: it was the faith of those who presented the infant for baptism that was added to the sacrament to make it effective.[q] Going further, in the present book, he ascribed to the collective faith of the communion of followers, in the Church, the effectual virtue of the sacrament to the benefit of an infant who is too young to express its own will.[r] With a sort of pragmatism that would grow in him with the passing years, instead of seeing the institution of baptism of infants as the ecclesiological consequence of the doctrine of original sin, he saw it conversely as the proof of that doctrine's truth; and if the Pelagians conceded that they should be baptized, they had also to acknowledge that children, too, needed the mediation of Christ through the sacrament.[s] On the *post mortem* fate of children who died unbaptized, the Pelagians held a 'generous' but ambiguous view: they denied them access to the Kingdom (of heaven), as for all non-baptized, but granted them the benefit of an uncertain eternal life. When Pelagius was questioned about their fate, and pressed to say where they would go after death, he is reputed to have said, 'Where they are *not* going, I know; but where they *are* going, I know not.'[t] Which was his way of saying that they were not going to the kingdom in the skies, nor to eternal death, but suggesting without actually affirming a 'third place', that could prefigure the *limbus puerorum* of medieval theology.[u] Faithful to his own ideas, Augustine did not exclude them from that eternal death, even if he envisaged the gentlest possible form of damnation for them.[18]

The anti-Pelagian direction of the work becomes clear in Book II, a long dissertation on *impeccantia*, given in four points. First, the question of whether one could be without sin in this life: the reply, rapidly delivered, is yes, man has that possibility, if he has the will, with the help of God's grace.[v] But – second point – has it happened, does it happen, on earth that however great, just, courageous, wise, pious or merciful a man may be, he can be absolutely without sin? Duly reasoned on the basis of scriptural texts, the answer is no.[w] Then – third point – given that man has the possibility of being without sin, if the divine will comes to the aid of his own will, how comes it that he is *not*? The reason is that men do not want to accomplish what is just, either because it eludes them, or because they do not like to.[x] In any case – fourth point – supposing that someone is without personal sin, he cannot be in 'sinlessness', because of the original sin transmitted to all Adam's physical descendants, the only one who is exempt being our unique mediator, Christ, who for our salvation assumed the appearance of our sinful flesh.[y]

The composite structure of the work is given prominence by the beginning of Book III, whose epistolary title reflects its origin, a long letter sent by the bishop to Marcellinus, as a supplement to the first two books. Augustine told him that he had just discovered some 'writings of Pelagius': these were commentaries on St Paul by the British monk. He interpreted them as a plain and clear-cut negation of original sin, which he had not refuted in the two preceding volumes, he wrote, because it had not crossed his mind that anyone could think or say such things![z] Naturally he would attack this refutation in the pages that followed, but without attaching blame to Pelagius, admitting – or feigning to do so – that the latter was passing on the arguments of a third party.[aa] As I said earlier, on a personal basis he would deal tactfully with Pelagius for a long time.

At the end of the winter of 411–12, only just freed from his concerns and pastoral obligations in the anti-Donatist battle, Augustine seems to have been totally caught up in the defence of grace. In the letter to Marcellinus, already quoted – Ep. 139, 6 – among other works on the stocks, he notes a 'book' intended for 'our dear Honoratus', the friend of his youth who was already the dedicatee of the De utilitate credendi, who had asked him to answer five questions on evangelical or Pauline texts. The bishop did so in the form of an extended letter – Ep. 140 – which figures among his works under the significant title of the Book on grace in the New Testament. And, as he would emphasize in his Retractations, without evading a precise answer to Honoratus on the points he had raised, he added his handling of a sixth question on the grace of the New Covenant, 'with an eye to the new heresy that is inimical to the grace of God'.[bb] At the close of this long letter, to describe the 'adversaries of grace', Augustine used words that qualified them as respectable adversaries; there was nothing despicable about them, they lived in chastity and deserved praise for their works; they had nothing in common with the Manichaeans and several other heretics, and the Christ they revered was the true Christ, equal and co-eternal with the Father. They had only one shortcoming, but it was gross! They ignored the justice of God, which they replaced with their own.[cc] And Augustine compared them to the foolish virgins, who had forgotten to provide themselves with oil, and in whose faces the door was shut . . .

But in the person of Marcellinus, Augustine had an intellectually demanding correspondent, in whom we may suspect that a certain sensibility to Pelagian argument still kindled a spiritual uneasiness. On reading the De peccatorum meritis et remissione, particularly Book II, Marcellinus had been deeply troubled by Augustine's statements relating, on the one hand, to man's potential 'impeccability', if his own will did not run counter to divine assistance and, on the other, the negation of his historical 'impeccancy'. It seemed absurd to him 'that something could be said to exist of which there was no example',[dd] whereas he did not doubt, added the bishop, that a camel had never happened to pass through the eye of a needle, although Christ had said that for God it was possible. Augustine replied to these new questions from his friend in the spring of 412, in the De spiritu et littera ('Of the Spirit and the Letter').

The title was borrowed from a key Pauline saying: 'The letter killeth, but the Spirit giveth life' (2 Cor. 3.6), on which the book set out a profound commentary, keeping not so much its obvious sense for allegorical exegesis as the relationship it expresses between the two covenants, between the 'Law of works' (the Judaism of the Old Testament) and the 'Law of faith' (the Christianity of the New).[ee] Here Augustine was probably remembering the third rule of Tyconius, De promissis et lege, which he had discovered shortly before his episcopal ordination, and which could have been called De spiritu et littera, as he would say in Book III, 46, of The Christian Doctrine. He resorted to powerful imagery and words to differentiate one from the other. What the Law of works commanded with threats, the Law of faith obtained by belief; the excerpt from the Confessions which had become famous since Pelagius had latched on to it in Rome returned here to illustrate the attitude of the faithful seeking grace in the New Covenant: in the Old, God said,

'Do what I command', whereas in the Law of faith one addresses God, saying, 'Give what you command.'[19] Augustine stressed the distance that separates the two Testaments, one imposing a completely external Law, like the stone tablets bearing the commandments, the other a completely internal Law, written within the heart, causing delight and arousing love through the spirit that gives life, whereas the other, the ancient Law, brought fear and provoked transgression through the letter that kills.[20] At the end of his book, the bishop returned to his initial theme, or rather to Marcellinus' anxious remark, which had rekindled his reflections – that contradiction which worried him between the affirmation of a potential 'impeccability' and the negation of a true 'impeccancy'. There was no contradiction; for God everything was possible. As for man, in order not to fall into sin, his will, supported by grace, needed to be so strong and enlightened that nothing concerning justice remained hidden from him or escaped his yearning.[ff] Christ alone had achieved that perfection.

Did this last text satisfy the demanding faith of its dedicatee? The subsequent exchanges between the two men are silent on the subject, but Augustine had not yet finished with his friend's intellectual probings, which during 411 and 412 were such that Marcellinus could be portrayed as an instigator, if not inspirer, and speak of his spiritual 'companionship' with the bishop.[21] In a letter which he sent to him in the spring or summer of 412, Augustine answered him on a question bearing on considerations relating to the origin of the soul in Book III of the *Treatise on free will*, a text that was already old, dating from an era when the author could have been taken for a Pelagian before his time.[gg] The bishop defended himself for having written something definitive on such a subject at that time,[hh] but said he must chiefly be grateful to his correspondent for giving him the opportunity to reveal his feelings regarding his works: a lasting critical gaze. He said, 'I confess that I strive to be among those who write as they progress and progress as they write.'[ii] He preferred to correct himself rather than drag 'companions in error' with him. And – something that will assuredly surprise us – some fifteen years in advance, he already had in mind a clearly outlined plan for the critical work he was to undertake in 426/7, in the form of the *Retractationes*: 'To gather together and expose, in an *ad hoc* work, everything that rightly displeases me in my books.' And he added that people would then see that he was not showing himself any benevolent partiality.

When he received this letter, Marcellinus had barely a year to live before his dramatic end, described earlier.[jj] Augustine, who wept over that death because he had not been able to prevent it, would never forget the impetus he had received from his friend in the development of his thinking on these difficult problems. In 415, in the *De natura et gratia* and, a little later, the *De gestis Pelagii*, he would refer to his exchanges with Marcellinus 'of happy memory', thus associating him with that part of his works which places him foremost in the history of theology in the West.

The confrontation with Pelagius

In his *Retractations*, which he was already planning in 412, regarding the *De spiritu et littera* Augustine states explicitly that he had 'fiercely combated the adversaries of God's grace'.[kk] In his first writings against the 'adversaries of grace' – again, less directly against Pelagius than those, including Caelestius, whose words he wanted to believe were merely being reported by the British monk – he had straight away grasped the importance of the issue. It seemed to him that by this effort to base 'justice' – in other words, a life free of sin – on the strength of human conscience alone,^{ll} there was a great risk that the asceticism advocated by these people, who were estimable in themselves, thus all the more dangerous, no longer left anything to the action of grace, as he conceived it: a supernatural aid personally granted to the Christian through the essential and exclusive mediation of Christ. And he feared too that even if Christ's divine status was not called into question, he would himself be no more than a model for living; and in his eyes that was the negation of Christianity.

The publication and circulation of these first anti-Pelagian texts resulted, at least locally in Africa, in convincing some of those 'adversaries of grace', and causing others to be a little more discreet: the remainder, notably in Carthage, henceforth 'muttered' in their corner.^{mm} Augustine had not dropped his guard. At Aurelius' request, he had made infant baptism and original sin the principal theme of a sermon preached on 27 June 413 in the *basilica Maiorum*.ⁿⁿ In 414, he sent Anicia Juliana a little treatise entitled *De bono viduitatis* ('On the good of widowhood'). Juliana was one of those great Roman ladies whom the misfortunes of the times had brought to Africa with their families – at least, in her case, those who were left, for shortly before she had lost her husband prematurely; he was the noble Anicius Hermogenianus Olybrius, consul for the year 395. But she had her mother-in-law with her, Anicia Faltonia Proba, as well as her daughter, Demetrias who, like Melania the Younger, was one of the richest heiresses in the Roman world. In 413 the young girl had decided to take the veil. In such a prominent milieu, the event could hardly pass unnoticed, and the greatest names in Latin-speaking Christianity – including Pope Innocent and Jerome^{oo} – had taken steps to help this prestigious nun with their advice. Augustine had greeted this *velatio* with a little letter of congratulations sent to her mother and grandmother, recommending that Demetrias should read his *De sancta virginitate*, which he had written around 400.^{pp} At the repeated request of Juliana, he had written the long letter on widowhood, which was also addressed to the entourage of these pious women, and in the text he had been careful to put his correspondents on their guard against those who, in their exaltation of the free choice of human will, by doing so came to abolish recourse to prayer.^{qq} Who knows if it was precaution or foreboding? For that same year, 414, from the East where he was then living, Pelagius sent Demetrias (who had returned to Rome with Juliana and Proba) a famous letter – one of the rare preserved texts by him,[22] which he acknowledged – in which he explicitly stated his thoughts. Augustine would not know of it until two or three years later.

Meanwhile, Pelagian ideas had started to burgeon. Still in 414, Augustine received from Syracuse, in Sicily, a short note in which a man named Hilarius informed him of the ideas circulating around him on 'impeccancy' and the absence of sin in children.^{rr} In reply, the bishop sent him a long letter (*Ep.* 157) which he regarded as a sequel or fourth Book to the *De peccatorum meritis* and which, as such, would form part of the dossier of his anti-Pelagian treatises, in the same way as the book *On the perfection of man's justice*, sent to two Spanish bishops, Eutropius and Paulus. Augustine had received a sort of 'tract' (*chartula*) in which, under the title 'Definitions', he had recognized the style of Caelestius.[23]

But by then – one should say at last! – and above all, perhaps in the autumn of 414 Augustine had received Pelagius' *De natura* from the hands of two *servi Dei*, Jacobus and Timasius.[ss] Both were indebted to the British monk for having abandoned their hopes in this world and for living as servants of God.[tt] One, Timasius, seems to have been part of Pinianus' entourage and, failing an always possible but here unlikely homonym, to have played a role in the celebrated scene in the church at Hippo, which I related earlier.[uu] If one follows the hypothesis that dates Pelagius' writing of his *De natura* to well before his departure for Palestine, one could also easily agree that Jacobus and Timasius did not send it to the bishop of Hippo from the Holy Land, but that they gave it to him in Africa, where they had remained with Pinianus and Melania themselves, probably on the outskirts of Thagaste.[24] The only cause for surprise would be that the two young people who, by this hypothesis, had known Augustine at least since the winter of 410–11, had waited four years to let him have a work which had long been in their possession.

As may be imagined, Augustine did not wait as long to refute it. However, his reply, the *De natura et gratia*, would not be ready before the late spring of 415. We can deduce this date from the chronology attributable to the comings and goings between Hippo and Palestine – those two poles of the anti-Pelagian battle in 415 – of a young Spanish priest named Paulus Orosius. Drawn by Augustine's renown, Orosius had visited him to submit a few theological problems.[25] He seems to have been mainly concerned about the fact that he had noted some survivals of Priscillianism in his own area, and the bishop of Hippo would write a little book for him, *Against the Priscillianists and the Origenists*.[vv] But he was then writing his reply to Pelagius, and was far more worried about the advances of what he took to be a new and formidable heresy. He sent the young priest to Jerome, entrusting him with a long letter intended for the hermit of Bethlehem, in which, regarding the origin of souls, he was particularly anxious to know if 'creationism' – the creation of souls by God 'one for every human being born' – was truly compatible with the doctrine of original sin.[ww] Orosius left for Palestine, taking with him for Jerome, in addition to the file on the sentencing of Caelestius at Carthage in the autumn of 411, a whole range of Augustine's works: the three books of the *De peccatorum meritis et remissione* and the letter to Hilarius of Syracuse, but not the *De natura et gratia*, on which the bishop was still working and about which Orosius could announce only that it was 'under way' when he reached Jerome early in the summer of 415.[26]

Augustine had seized with anxious haste upon the book he had received from Jacobus and Timasius, and had read it with extreme attentiveness.[xx] Until then, with the exception of a few commentaries on the Pauline epistles, theoretically properly 'Pelagian' but which he preferred to see as recorded by the author from arguments that were not his own, he had had in his hands texts emanating from disciples who spread the master's doctrine while protecting his person. Now, before his eyes he had Pelagius' own words; and in them he discovered, to use his own terms, 'a man inflamed with a very ardent zeal against those who, instead of imputing their sins to human will, would rather incriminate human nature'.[yy] In other words, Pelagius was positively a 'naturalist'; he thought that God had created in man a good nature, free from sin, endowed with a free will that allowed the human creature to choose between good and evil. If it was a matter of Adam before the Fall, Augustine could agree.[zz] But now, when he spoke of nature, it was of a debased nature, corrupted by sin. For Pelagius, nature had not been weakened by sin, which was not, he said, a 'substance', but simply one act among others.[ab] It was only an accident, which could not by itself be the generator of other sins, or lastingly affect the exertion of a will that preserved intact the capability of choosing good. Pelagius refused to contemplate a moral weakness resulting from an original sin, and was therefore resolutely opposed to the idea of the transmission of Adam's sin. At the most he admitted that sin could be transmitted from one generation to the next by imitation,[ac] by virtue – if one may use the word! – of example, which also meant that, insofar as men were sinners like Adam, they were mortal like him.[27] Such a system of thinking resulted in diminishing, if not denying, the supernatural power of redemption, and reducing the contribution of Christ to a re-establishment of original justice. Augustine reacted forcefully, even indignantly, to such remarks. To Pelagius' nature and free will, he applied what the Apostle had said of the Law: if man could be justified by natural law and the free choice of his will, then 'Christ is dead in vain' (Gal. 2.21); then the cross is torn down, held to be non-existent.[ad]

However, the forcefulness of the reaction did not rule out a measured and prudent approach to an interlocutor whom he still refused to name. The following year, in the *De gestis Pelagii*, Augustine said that he had not mentioned the author's name in the refutation of his book, 'judging that he would succeed better if, by safeguarding their friendship, he dealt tactfully with the honour of the man for whose writings he no longer had to have consideration'.[ae] It even happened that, the better to avoid an attack *ad hominem*, the bishop ascribed the theories he was quoting to a number of persons;[af] but we also see him address this unnamed adversary, take him to task in a fraternal manner,[ag] and note points of agreement with him to which the subsequent discourse unfortunately gives the lie immediately afterwards.[ah] That was not simple tactical cleverness on Augustine's part, or pure literary convention. The sincerity of his intentions has been confirmed by the recent publication of a hitherto unpublished letter which he sent to Jerome in the summer of 416. In it he certainly regretted the little ruses effected by Pelagius in his defence but, returning to his refutation of the preceding year, he still justified his omission of his adversary's name in the text. 'I would wish', he said, 'to correct him as a friend, something I still desire, I confess, and I do not doubt that your Holiness also wishes it.'[ai] These last words were an attempt to exorcise the hermit of Bethlehem's jealous aggressiveness, which was well known to Augustine. Did he really hope to lead Pelagius to a change of heart? At least he knew that there were no more possible compromises between them than there are between water and fire.

Events in Palestine

Meanwhile, in Jerome's circles, many things had been happening in Palestine. At Jerusalem, where he had been established for two or three years, Pelagius had at first received a warm welcome from the bishop, John. But not everyone there was a friend; his ideas were disturbing, and Jerome had not been slow to take a dislike to a man who had formerly been his friend. His letter to Ctesiphon, one of

Pelagius' rich protectors and his firmest support on the spot, was a manifesto,[aj] and he did not conceal the fact that he had started work on an indictment of Pelagians, in the form of 'Dialogues'. The arrival of Orosius, bearing a whole dossier of information – even if it involved Caelestius rather than Pelagius himself – crystallized all these hostilities. The Spanish priest managed to get the bishop of Jerusalem's agreement to a meeting of an ecclesiastical assembly, on 28 July 415, where he recounted the events that had led up to the condemnation of Caelestius at Carthage in 411, and produced the relevant documents. Jerome was absent, but everyone could sense his presence in the corridors. Introduced at his own request, Pelagius got off lightly by acknowledging man's need for divine grace in order to achieve perfection;[28] it was rather short, but no more was asked of him. In this eastern environment, where Greek was the language used, the Latin-speaking Orosius was at a disadvantage. The assembly, growing weary of it all, ended by declaring that it was a matter of a Latin heresy, to be brought before Latin courts, and it was therefore agreed to submit a report to Pope Innocent.[ak]

They took their leave with words of peace, but in a fairly gloomy atmosphere. The late July session had left its scars, and Jerome's work, his *Dialogues against the Pelagians*, which was beginning to circulate, was not such as to heal them. In the autumn, Orosius, who had come to pay his respects to John of Jerusalem on the occasion of the Feast of Dedication, found himself rebuffed by the bishop in no uncertain terms. He was blamed for having had too much to say and for having blasphemed by declaring that, even with God's grace, man could not abstain from sin. The accuser was put in the position of the accused! He replied in the *Liber apologeticus*, which was simultaneously a report of the July assembly, a plea *pro domo* and a pamphlet against Pelagius and John of Jerusalem. Meanwhile, duly apprised of the affair, Pope Innocent had entrusted the indictment to two Provençal bishops, Heros, former bishop of Arles, and Lazarus, former bishop of Aix. It happened that both were in exile in the Holy Land, after being deposed for their involvement in the activities of the usurper Constantine, who had set up his short-lived residence at Arles in 408. This questionable choice[29] effectively gave, if not 'Latin judges', at least Latin prosecutors for a 'Latin heresy' but, as Pelagius lived in Palestine, Heros and Lazarus addressed the formal charge to the Metropolitan of the province, Eulogius of Caesarea. And the court with the duty of examining it met at the end of December 415 near Caesarea, at Diospolis (now Lydda); as well as the Metropolitan himself and John of Jerusalem, it comprised a dozen bishops, most of whom were eastern.[al] Before this synod, Pelagius had to answer to a heterogeneous range of accusations, hastily compiled by Orosius and Jerome, made up of isolated sentences or extracts from texts, whose origin was in any case attributable more to Caelestius than to himself.[30] He was not too hard put to it to defend himself, dissociating his position from his disciple's, giving finely-shaded replies to the most important points raised and with evident concern to lighten the doctrinal weight of his propositions. Thus, on the point of whether man can, if he wishes, be without sin and follow the commandments of God, he astutely pointed out that no one achieved this 'impeccability' throughout life and definitively, and that it was the result of the simultaneous interaction of personal effort and divine grace.[am] But Pelagius could not escape ambiguity, or rather, something strongly resembling a retraction, if he wished to emerge unscathed from this trial. He managed to do so by dissociating himself from

Caelestius on a fundamental subject, when he cast anathema on 'those who said' – it was to do with his disciple, but he challenged the attribution of these words – that 'the grace and succour of God are not granted to us for each of our deeds, but dwell in free will or yet in the Law and doctrine'.[an] The British monk had done more than 'hide behind clever screens of words', as Augustine later wrote.[ao] In fact, by agreeing to a denial of an essential principle of Pelagianism, Pelagius had obtained from the Diospolis synod a judgement absolving him from the charge of heresy, and proclaiming his adherence to the communion of the Church.[ap] Jerome was no angel of mercy, but he had seen through Pelagius' game when, at the time of this 'lamentable synod',[31] he wrote to Augustine that 'this very pernicious heresy still feigns repentance to retain its freedom to teach in the churches, for fear, if it appeared in the broad light of day, that it would die once it was thrown out'.[aq]

Between Carthage and Rome

Pelagius had not been slow to exploit the dividends of his questionable success by sending Augustine, in the winter of 415–16, his own version of the Diospolis *Records*, from which he had carefully expunged all the anathemas pronounced by him against his own supporters' arguments, so that he appeared to have been cleared by the synod without making any concessions.[32] But even before he had received this text and, chiefly, a copy of the original documents from Diospolis, Augustine already knew what he had to deal with. In the spring of 416, three messages from Jerome had reached him, one by way of Lazarus, one of Pelagius' prosecutors in Palestine;[ar] he had also been visited by Orosius, who had not completely wasted his time in the East, since he had brought back some relics of St Stephen, which had been discovered rather miraculously just when the assembly was sitting at Diospolis.[33] Augustine would write to Jerome that he had 'learnt much'[34] from Orosius. The latter had first stopped at Carthage, where his arrival had coincided with the meeting of the ordinary council of the province of Proconsularis, probably in May. He had passed on to the assembled African bishops an informative letter, signed by Heros and Lazarus, of which he had been the bearer.[as] Brought up to date by this, Aurelius and his colleagues had reacted sharply against a judgement that seemed to them to have annulled, without proper consideration, the one which had been brought against Caelestius by the ecclesiastical assembly in Carthage in the autumn of 411, and appeared to restore every opportunity for the propagation of the budding heresy.

Meanwhile at Hippo, around mid-May, Augustine received from the hands of Palatinus, a citizen of Hippo who served as a deacon in the East, a short written justification – the *Chartula defensionis*, that the bishop could later compare with the genuine *Records* from Diospolis – which Pelagius had sent him, but without the slightest accompanying letter. It was an offhand procedure, commented Augustine, and permitted any later denial.[at] The bishop reported this to his flock, adding that he would wait until he received the genuine *Records* before replying. He also informed his hearers of an alarming piece of news that Palatinus had just imparted, or confirmed, about two monasteries at Bethlehem which had been set on fire during uprisings that had notably targeted the establishment where Eustochium, the daughter of Paula, and Jerome himself lived. These disturbances among the populace probably had a more xenophobic, particularly 'anti-Latin', motivation than one that was specifically Pelagian, but their occurrence shortly after the debates at Diospolis might suggest a correlation. We must remember that the bishop's speech from his chair marked a turning-point in his attitude, not regarding the heresy – he had immediately identified it as such and opposed it – but regarding its initiator and author, Pelagius, now named and denounced as such.[au] Nevertheless, there was still the faint hope of fraternal correction expressed in letter 19* to Jerome.

A few weeks later, early in the summer of 416, the bishops of the province of Numidia gathered in Severus' episcopal town, Milevis, and their synodal letter to Pope Innocent supported that of their colleagues of Proconsularis, resuming their arguments and, in addition, raising the question of original sin,[av] in an allusion clarified by the very Augustinian quotation from Rom. 5.12 and 1 Cor. 15.22. For good measure, the pope was favoured at the same time with a long missive, co-signed by Aurelius, Alypius, Evodius and Possidius, and of course Augustine himself, whose personal stamp was easily recognizable in both form and detail of the reasoned argument. A series of documents was also enclosed for Innocent's edification: the *Records* of Caelestius' sentence at Carthage in 411, Pelagius' *De natura* and Augustine's refutation, the text of the very tendentious account Pelagius had given of the session at Diospolis and a first Augustinian response which the pope was asked to transmit to the addressee.[aw]

For his part, Jerome was not to be left out. He had finished his *Dialogues against the Pelagians* and sent them to Africa, of course, but also to the Court at Ravenna, and Augustine assured him, in his letter of summer 416, that he knew from hearsay that these texts, circulated in the corridors of power, had produced their intimidatory effect: the number of Pelagius' supporters there had dwindled by the minute.[ax] To the deployment of all this artillery, the bishop of Hippo made ready to add his own cannonade. In order to obtain more accurate information, in a letter datable to these months in mid-416, he had asked John of Jerusalem to send him a genuine copy of the Diospolis *Records*.[ay] His answer came, not from John, who died a few months later, but – as we have discovered from a recently retrieved document[35] – from Cyril of Alexandria, the future 'hero' of the council of Ephesus (431), at the end of the winter of 416–17 at the latest. Pinianus and Melania could have known of it before their departure from Africa in the spring of 417.[az] As soon as he received it, Augustine set to work. Early in 417,[36] the result was the *De gestis Pelagii*, where the mechanism behind which Pelagius had taken cover at Diospolis is meticulously dismantled. He had been personally exonerated, but behind the smokescreen with which he had surrounded it, Pelagianism itself had not been condemned and, despite some carefully chosen wording, had preserved its virulence. And the tone henceforth is harsher: Pelagius' clever little moves, which were unworthy of a great figure, had got the better of Augustine's initial tactful handling.

The *De gestis Pelagii* had been written for Aurelius, for his guidance.[ba] Naturally, it would be communicated to Innocent, but the pope's religion was already decided and he had not waited for either the genuine *Records* from Diospolis or Augustine's demonstration in order to make up his mind. Three letters, dated 27 January 417, reached Africa in early spring, in reply to the two synodal letters of the preceding year and the letter signed by Aurelius, Augustine

and their three colleagues: while strongly affirming the rights of the see of Rome,
they approved the African bishops' action, refused to ratify the *Records* of
Diospolis and, by virtue of apostolic authority, declared Pelagius and Caelestius
excluded from communion until their repentance.[37] Innocent had not thought it
of any use to publish a sentence of excommunication on the interested parties, or
to convene a synod to confirm the see of Rome's assent to the position stated by
the African episcopacy; and he himself made his exit on 12 March 417, leaving his
successor, Zosimus, with the task of exploring possible avenues which papal
procedure had left open. Innocent's death was evidently soon known in Carthage
and Hippo. But for Augustine, the question had been settled by the apostolic see,
as was right and proper,[bc] and he did not envisage a return to it. At the end of
summer 417, he was preaching in Carthage, and on 23 September gave voice to
his famous *Causa finita est*. In his eyes, the pope's rescripts had put a final full stop
to the affair; all that remained was to hope the same would happen to the error.[bd]

   Obviously, he could not have known, on that day, that two days previously, 21
September, the new pope had dictated and despatched to the African episcopacy
a letter announcing that the Roman synod had granted absolution first to
Caelestius and then Pelagius. The first of the two to appeal, Caelestius, had got
off the hook, before Zosimus, regarding the baptism of children and free will, by
agreeing with all the opinions expressed on these subjects by Innocent himself.[be]
His successor could do no other than be satisfied. As for Pelagius, true to a tactic
that had not served him badly at Diospolis, he had presented a profession of faith
– *libellus fidei* – which, on the whole, was reassuring, if one was content with what
he said without pushing him into a corner. Thus he affirmed the existence of free
will, but added that 'we always need divine aid'.[bf] He must have shown himself
to be as equivocal and cautious as he was during the summer of 417 in his
conversations with Pinianus and Melania, as they had reported them to
Augustine, particularly on the subject of grace, when he declared that he cast
anathema 'on those who admitted that grace was not necessary, not only at every
hour and every instant, but even for each of our actions'.[bg] At the sight of such
declarations, it was difficult for Zosimus not to conclude that the British monk
had been slandered – notably by the Provençal bishops Heros and Lazarus,
whom the new pope held in the lowest esteem – when his orthodoxy was not
suspect. Zosimus ended his letter by picturing the African bishops' joy upon
learning that Caelestius and Pelagius had never strayed from the communion
and truth of the Catholic Church![38]

   Carried by a Roman deacon, Zosimus' letter had reached Carthage early in the
autumn and came as a bombshell. Paulinus of Milan, Caelestius' prosecutor six
years before, was still living there; he was invited by the pope to come to Rome
to uphold his initial accusation. He refused; the affair, he said, now went beyond
him personally and was henceforth a matter for the Church as a whole. He added
that Caelestius had no good grounds for a new appeal, as he had not supported
the one he had lodged after his sentence in autumn 411.[39] The African
episcopacy's own reply was organized in haste. It was now October–November
and time pressed. There were apparently intensive exchanges of letters and
messages between the Roman curia and the see of Carthage before the winter
break in sea communication, and probably even when the sea was in theory
closed, from 11 November.[40] In view of the urgency, Aurelius had not been able

to assemble a council, only a simple 'crisis team' with which Augustine was doubtless involved by means of intermediary couriers. The texts resulting from this dialogue which were sent to Rome were a firm opposition of legal nature – an *obtestatio* – to the procedure adopted by Zosimus in this matter. The pope took his time in responding; the period of *mare clausum* left him the whole winter but, once that was over, on 21 March he sent the African episcopacy a letter in which the very rigid declarations about the see of Rome's jurisdictional authority poorly concealed his changes of mind. He now accepted what he had denied in the preceding autumn, that the Church of Africa should be fully associated in settling the Pelagian affair.[41] Although there is still argument over this point,[42] it is probable that the side taken by the imperial government carried some weight in the papal scales. Honorius' intervention in the dispute materialized on 30 April 418, with the publication of an edict condemning Pelagius' arguments and sending Caelestius into exile with his supporters.[bh] By doing so, he was doubtless responding to the Africans who had asked for his backing, but with less concern for theology than for preserving public order, which he judged to be threatened by the continuation of the quarrel. On 29 April, the eve of this publication, the pope's letter arrived at Carthage at a time when the bishops summoned by Aurelius for the general council were assembling. The more relaxed attitude it revealed opened the way to the decisions that the council would take on 1 May.

On that day, in the *secretarium* of the *basilica Fausti*,[43] over 200 bishops gathered, from all the African provinces excepting Caesarian Mauretania, to whose situation I will return. The council's agenda was laden, for it also had to resolve delicate problems of discipline and pastoral and territorial areas of competence, the material aftermath of the regained unity following the conference of 411, and the solution could no longer be deferred. But the assembled bishops first tackled the doctrinal questions that had originally prompted their meeting and, in a few ecclesiastical canons, unequivocally defined the positions that would earn excommunication for those who upheld them: the 'mortal' nature of Adam, the non-necessity for the baptism of infants, and a minimal or reductive conception of grace.[bi] These texts were sent without delay to the see of Rome, accompanied by a synodal letter recalling the excommunication pronounced by Innocent, which was to continue until Caelestius and Pelagius had made clear professions of faith on the necessity for and true role of divine grace. The African episcopacy remained at the ready, but to avoid keeping all the bishops present away from their sees, it was decided to elect a small interprovincial commission, to pursue this affair, among others, and remain in contact with Rome. For Numidia, Augustine was a member, as well as Alypius and a bishop named Restitutus, chosen for his great seniority.[44] But this time the affair seemed to be really over, from an ecclesiastical point of view, and as far as Caelestius and Pelagius were concerned. At the end of June, Zosimus sent a long circular letter (*tractoria*) to all the Churches, for them to undersign and circulate, which definitively sanctioned the sentence of Caelestius and Pelagius.[45]

Grace and original sin

While Caelestius, driven out of Rome and soon banished from Italy, handed on the torch of Pelagianism to Julian of Eclanum in the West, and rejoined Pelagius in an East that was still in dispute, in 418 Augustine had acquired a 'global' dimension at a time when the enclosed world he lived in was still confined to the Mediterranean shores. He corresponded with Cyril of Alexandria, and we have recently learnt that he was in contact with Atticus of Constantinople.[46] In the Roman curia, it was now taken for granted that he was a force to be reckoned with, like the solid trio he formed with Aurelius and Alypius. The priest Sixtus, future pope, who had for a while been susceptible to the Pelagian heresy, had thought it a good idea to couple his own letters to Aurelius and Augustine himself with the papal rescript bearing the condemnation. And the bishop of Hippo, who spared no effort in a good cause, would reply to his short note with a missive of a good twenty pages in modern size.[bj] But the real crowning triumph had come from Jerome, who wrote to him that the entire universe was singing his praises, that Catholics venerated and respected him as the restorer of the old faith, and that the hatred all heretics bore towards him was henceforth the clearest sign of his renown.[bk]

To bring this first phase of the anti-Pelagian battle to a close, Augustine had a very long last word. At Carthage, where we know he had remained after the general council of 1 May, he had received a letter, probably around the end of July, from Albina, Pinanius and Melania, written from Jerusalem where they had arrived in the preceding year. They were happy to let him know without delay that they had met Pelagius and made what they considered not unsuccessful efforts to bring him back to the true faith. They were obviously unaware of the latest developments in the affair and Zosimus' *tractoria*, which took quite a time to reach the East in the summer of 418. In Carthage, Augustine was even busier than at home in Hippo, but he did not want to postpone his reply and, as the messenger was in a hurry to leave again, he dictated without stopping the good hundred pages that make up the two books of the *De gratia Christi et de peccato originali*.

To disabuse his friends and refute Pelagius, Augustine now had at his disposal better than hearsay, words or writings emanating from his disciples or texts challenged by their author.[47] As Jerome had elegantly prophesied, 'the rat had betrayed himself by his own tracks'.[bl] In the last three years before his sentence, the British monk had in fact increased the defences or doctrinal texts of which he claimed authorship; chiefly the 'profession of faith' – *libellus fidei* – and accompanying letter sent to Pope Innocent – and read by Zosimus after the latter's death – the letter to Demetrias and a treatise, the *Pro libero arbitrio*, dated 416.[48] Augustine now kept scrupulously to these texts and his refutation thereby gained in accuracy and soundness.

On the Augustinian concept of grace, the work dictated at Carthage in the summer of 418 added little to a doctrine that had seen the light of day as early as the writing of the *Ad Simplicianum* in 396,[bm] and seemed firmly in place at the start of the anti-Pelagian controversy, notably with the *De peccatorum meritis*, early in 412.[49] But the emphasis given at the time of the controversy to the need for baptizing babies, the discussions on *impeccantia*, and the insistence on original sin had somewhat overshadowed the bishop of Hippo's major grievance against Pelagius and his disciples, which was that he saw them as the enemies of grace. Here the doctrine was reaffirmed with strong wording, Pauline in inspiration, but specifically Augustinian in form, such as this sentence on the gift of grace: 'The grace of God would in no way be grace if it were not in every way purely a gift.'[bn] This free gift is for Augustine the very foundation of grace: the spirit breathes where it wills, without being preceded, or summoned, by merit. Grace is given to man inwardly, and not 'by the Law and doctrine', as Pelagius would have it.[bo] Augustine also forcefully took issue with the tripartition used by the monk in his analysis of human capabilities in the fulfilment of the 'divine commandments' – we would say moral acts – by which he made the distinction between the 'ability to be righteous', the 'will to be righteous' and 'righteous action' itself. For Pelagius, the first part alone, potential ability, was an ontological fact, granted to our nature by the Creator, who could strengthen it within us by an 'adjuvant' grace.[bp] The two other components, the will and the act itself, belonged to man, and were the existential developments of his freedom.[bq] It was easy for Augustine to reply that such an attitude was contrary to the Apostle's, who had written to the Philippians that it was God who worked both will and action within them (cf. Phil. 2.13). Pelagius was not unaware of St Paul's statement, but saw 'God's working' as no more than an encouragement.[br] He did not totally throw out grace, but confined it within a restrictive definition, where it consisted only in the remission of sins;[bs] or according it only a teaching role, at best an enlightening function or the value of a sign;[bt] or seeing it as no more than an aid 'so that men can more easily accomplish what their free will orders them to do'.[bu] Nothing repelled Augustine more than the spiritual pride of the ascetic who, in the innermost recesses of his heart substitutes his own 'justice' for that of God; what he calls a *superba impietas* seemed to him to be ingratitude towards God.[bv] Using simpler words, the pastor said the same thing as the theologian; in a sermon preached in 416, the bishop exclaimed, 'If God has made you man, and if you make yourself righteous, then you are doing better than God has done!'[bw] This is echoed by one of the final sentences of Book I of the *De gratia Christi* on grace 'in which (God) makes us righteous not through our own righteousness, but through his, so that our true righteousness is that which comes to us from him'.[bx]

In 418 the question of grace and of original sin were linked in Augustine's mind, as they are in the work's title. He says so positively:

> That is why whoever claims that human nature has no need of the doctor, the second Adam, on the pretext that it was not contaminated in the first Adam, is guilty of enmity towards divine grace, not in a question where doubt or error are allowed without harming faith, but within the very rule of the faith that makes us Christians.[by]

And in this page of his book – the last before the exposition of the properly sacramental corollaries (on baptism and marriage) to his demonstrations – he ended by quoting once more St Paul's decisive text:

> And therefore, since 'by one man sin entered into the world and, by sin, death, and so death passed upon all men, for that all by him have sinned',[50] as a result all the 'masses doomed to perdition' became the prey of him who would destroy them. So no one, absolutely no one, has been, is or will be freed from that except by the Redeemer's grace.[bz]

As has been well demonstrated,[51] on this crucial question here we have the outcome – reaffirmed many times in subsequent years – of a progression in which the *Ad Simplicianum* had marked the first stage, as it had in his conception of grace. At that time, 396 (cf. above, p. 190), in the texts in which the expression *peccatum originale* appeared for the first time, Augustine stressed the punishment (*poena*) that weighs on man because of his 'sin of origin' rather than on an original guilt (*reatus*): in that period, even though he accepted the Apostle's words that every man has been handed down from Adam a flesh condemned to death which weighs down his soul, for him sin remained strictly personal. But in the same texts, the sombre image of the 'mass of sin' – *massa peccati* – that had been piling up since Adam through a carnal concupiscence common to all men initiated a turning-point in Augustine's thinking.

Reflection on the situation of the infant in relation to sin played a major role in the development of Augustinian doctrine. We may recall the pessimistic look which the bishop cast retrospectively on his own childhood in a text from Book I of the *Confessions*, just a little after the *Ad Simplicianum*.[ca] A few years later, around 408, the questions raised by Bonifatius of Cataquas on the baptism of infants provided an opportunity for Augustine, in a reply I have already quoted,[cb] to go into detail about the status of the earliest age in the *massa peccati*: born of sinful flesh, the infant is said to be a sinner, *peccator ex peccatore*, but the sin that dwells within it, the *libido* of which and with which it is born, as yet exists in it only presumptively, in embryo, before producing in the adult its 'fruits of death'. I have already said, and will return to it, that on the origin of the soul Augustine inclined more to a 'Traducianism' – transmission by generation – which had been fairly traditional in Africa since Tertullian, and favoured the expression of a rigorous doctrine on original sin. However, precipitating a development whose progress certain people have sometimes perceived in his pastoral experience,[52] it had taken the intrusion of the Pelagians into this spiritual scene to cause him to formulate the idea itself for the first time in the *De peccatorum meritis*, and to recognize the sin contracted at birth in infants as a sin in the full sense, with the irremediable consequences this entails unless it is redeemed by baptism. On this point, the text of 418 stabilized a position without adding anything new. But for the bishop, the most difficult part probably still remained – to define the conditions in which original sin is transmitted and, always affirming the need for divine grace, to safeguard what might remain of human freedom after accepting that most serious of determinisms, the determinism of predestination. He would be led to this – and his own approach to the frontiers of heresy – by the repercussions of the controversy with Julian of Eclanum.

One last word on Pelagius: there was more to him than the ambiguities and rather inglorious disavowals behind which he took cover at Diospolis because he well knew that a heresiarch, recognized and condemned as such, was in his time not only excluded from the Church, but practically doomed to a civil death. And our non-religious era may have a leaning towards Pelagius that would match Augustine's aversion, not as a person but because of his ideas, and for the same reasons! But we would be very unwise, not discerning beneath the attractive exterior of a 'Promethean' attitude the very real rigours of an implacable asceticism. For the British monk, the denial of original sin was not to allow or excuse any other, it was a declaration of war on all the others. We have only to read the 'Letter to Demetrias' to be convinced; its exaltation of the strengths of human nature[cd] and affirmation of the ability of human freedom always to choose the best[ce] serve only to extol striving and privation, of which Job, 'the most illustrious of God's athletes' was for him the symbolic figure.[cf] Pelagius advocated a robust religious 'meritocracy',[cg] compared with which the more modest and conventional exhortations of Jerome could be taken for those of a Court priest[ch]. Pelagius criticized Augustine for a doctrine of inhuman grace, but only in order to preach a superhuman morality.[53]

Superhuman or not, the bishop of Hippo could see it as nothing other than a moralism which tended to sap the very foundations of Christianity, the incarnation and redemption. Reading Pelagius, he could imagine himself some thirty years earlier, in the time when philosophy was offering him asceticism and wisdom without divine revelation or aid. In a letter written during the summer of 417 to Paulinus of Nola, who was himself rather suspected of sympathy for Pelagianism, he stated bluntly that the Pelagians – of fine intelligence, certainly[ci] – had the same effect on him as the philosophers 'of this world' who tried to persuade themselves and others that one could arrive at the 'happy life' – in the lofty sense of the word: *beata vita* – by the strength of one's own will alone.[cj] And the attraction that in their time they were able to exert over the souls of their contemporaries, if they too disregarded a stern asceticism, was comparable to that with which Pelagius is still haloed in the eyes of modern theologians (not, however, suspected of heresy), by the device of bringing back into perspective his *intellectus fidei* and his ideas on grace.[54] But in that case, it would be like Augustine taking up the Apostle's cry, 'Christ is dead in vain' (Gal. 2.21).

Moreover, and perhaps above all, a serious matter for one who had just emerged from a twenty-year fight against schism, the bishop had sensed another schism in the wind. In all likelihood, this was the deeper meaning of the words written to him by Jerome – who liked to express himself in often sibylline parables – who saw him as another Lot, preferring to escape alone from the ruins of Sodom than to stay with those who would have to perish there. And he added that Augustine would understand what he meant by that.[ck] In fact, it was merely imagery; Augustine was not alone, having at least all Africa behind him. But to remain true to ideas which had first been his own before becoming those of the African episcopacy as well, he had taken the risk of a confrontation with the see of Rome. And on his side, Zosimus had risked a split with a great province of Christianity. Pelagianism had also jeopardized the unity of the Church.

Notes

a. Above, p. 296. In the same period, Consentius, who had come specially from the Balearics to see Augustine, would have to give up the chance of meeting him: *Ep.* 119, 1.
b. *De gestis Pelagii*, XXII, 46.
c. *De gestis Pelagii*, 46.
d. *Conf.*, X, 40; cf. above, p. 222.
e. *De dono perseverantiae*, 53.
f. *De gratia Christi*, I, 38, which chronologically places the letter (around 405/6) and names Paulinus of Nola.

g.   *De peccatorum meritis et remissione*, III, 1.

h.   *Contra duas epist. pelag.*, II, 5.

i.   *De peccat. meritis et remissione*, III, 12.

j.   *De peccat. meritis et remissione*, III, 12, and *Retract.*, II, 33, *initio*.

k.   *De gratia Christi et de peccato originali*, II, 2–4.

l.   *De gratia Christi et de pecc. orig.*, II, 3.

m.   Cf. above, p. 316.

n.   *Ep.* 139, 3, *initio*.

o.   That is, *On the punishments deserved by sins and their remission, and on the baptism of infants*, to use the full title that appears in the *Retractations* (II, 33).

p.   *De baptismo*, IV, 31.

q.   *Ep.* 98, 7.

r.   *De pecc. mer.*, I, 38.

s.   *De pecc. mer.*, I, 39.

t.   *De gratia Christi et de pecc. orig.*, II, 23.

u.   Augustine would return to this *locus medius* of the Pelagians in the *De natura et origine animae*, I, 11. On these problems, cf. below, pp. 448–9.

v.   *De pecc. mer.*, II, 7.

w.   *De pecc. mer.*, II, 8–25.

x.   *De pecc. mer.*, II, 26–33.

y.   *De pecc. mer.*, II, 34–59.

z.   *De pecc. mer.*, III, 1.

aa.   See, for example, a sentence such as *quae Pelagius insinuat* eos *dicere*, qui contra originale peccatum disputant' (*De pecc. mer.*, III, 4).

bb.   *Retract.*, II, 36.

cc.   *Ep.* 140, 83.

dd.   *De spiritu et littera*, 1; cf. also *Retract.*, II, 37.

ee.   *De spiritu et littera*, 21.

ff.   *De spiritu et littera*, 61–4.

gg.   Cf. above, p. 182.

hh.   *Ep.* 143, 5.

ii.   *Ep.* 143, 2: *Fateor me ex numero eorum esse conari qui proficiendo scribunt et scribendo proficiunt.*

jj.   Cf. above, p. 268.

kk.   *Retract.*, II, 37: *In quo libro, quantum deus adiuvit, acriter disputavi contra inimicos gratiae dei.*

ll.   Cf. *De pecc. mer.*, II, 6.

mm.   *Ep.* 157 (dated end of 414), 22: *iam* occulte mussitant, *timentes ecclesiae fundatissimam fidem.*

nn.   *Sermon* 294, notably 19; cf. *De gestis Pelagii*, XI, 25.

oo.   The latter would send him his long letter 130, a veritable treatise on virginity.

pp.   *Ep.* 150, written in 'fine style': *Haec est uberior fecundiorque felicitas non ventre gravescere, sed mente grandescere, non lactescere pectore, sed corde candescere.*

qq.   *De bono viduitatis*, 21–2.

rr.   *Ep.* 156.

ss.   *De gestis Pelagii*, 47.

tt.   *Ep.* 177, 6. Letter 19* confirms that they had been very dear pupils of his: *Ep.* 19*, 3, *BA*, 46 B, p. 291.

uu.   *Ep.* 126, 6; cf. above, pp. 312–13.

vv.   *Retract.*, II, 44.

ww.   *Ep.* 166, 7–10. Jerome had sent Marcellinus an opinion in this sense: *Ep.* 169, 13.

xx.   *De nat. et gratia*, 1.

yy.   *De nat. et gratia*, 1, and farther on, 7.

zz.   Cf. *De libero arbitrio*, III, 52. Augustine referred Pelagius to this text: *De nat. et gratia*, 81.

ab.   *De nat. et gratia*, 21.

ac.   *De nat. et gratia*, 10.

ad.   *De nat. et gratia*, 1; 2.

ae.   *De gestis Pelagii*, 47.

Pelagius

345

af. *De nat. et gratia*, 10: *Non damnatur*, inquiunt, *quia . . . .*

ag. *De nat. et gratia*, 22: *O frater! Bonum est ut memineris te esse christianum.*

ah. *De nat. et gratia*, 52.

ai. *Ep.* 19*, 3, in *BA*, 46 B, p. 290.

aj. Jerome, *Ep.* 133, notably 5–13.

ak. Orosius, *Liber apologeticus*, 6.

al. Augustine would give their names in his *Contra Iulianum*, I, 31. Heros and Lazarus were absent, because of the illness of one of them: *De gestis Pelagii*, 2.

am. Cf. *De gestis Pelagii*, 16. A good exposition of the debates in G. de Plinval, *Pélage*, pp. 286–92.

an. *De gestis Pelagii*, 30.

ao. *Ep.* 4*, 2 (to Cyril of Alexandria)*, BA*, 46 B, p. 108: *cum sese callidis verborum latibulis occultasset.*

ap. *De gestis Pelagii*, 44.

aq. Jerome, *Ep.* 134, 1 (= Augustine, *Ep.* 172, 1).

ar. *Ep.* 19*, *BA*, 46 B, p. 286.

as. *Ep.* 175, 1 (synodal letter from the bishops of Proconsularis to Pope Innocent).

at. *Sermon* 348 A, 7, according to the whole text for which we were recently indebted to the acuity of F. Dolbeau, 'Le sermon 348A de Saint Augustin contre Pélage', in *Rech. aug.* 28, 1995, pp. 37–63 (p. 57 for this passage).

au. *Sermon* 348 A, 6, *Rech. aug.* 28, 1995, p. 56.

av. *Ep.* 176 (synodal letter from the bishops of Numidia: § 2 for the quotation from Rom. 5.12 and 1. Cor. 15.22).

aw. *Ep.* 177 (§ 15 on the last point).

ax. *Ep.* 19*, 2. For the date of the letter, cf. M.-F. Berrouard, in *Rev. des ét. aug.*, 27, 1981, pp. 265–7.

ay. *Ep.* 179, 7.

az. Cf. *De gratia Christi et de pecc. orig.*, II, 11, and the note by A. C. De Veer, in *BA*, 22, p. 684.

ba. *De gestis Pelagii*, 1.

bc. He spoke of this in a letter to Paulinus of Nola during the summer of 417: *Ep.* 186, 2, *in fine*.

bd. *Sermon* 131, 10.

be. Cf. *Contra duas ep. pelag.*, II, 6. See also, on Caelestius' answers to Rome, *De gratia Christi et de pecc. orig.*, II, 5–6.

bf. Pelagius, *Libellus fidei*, 13 (*PL*, 45, 1718).

bg. Cf. *De gratia Christi et de pecc. orig.*, I, 2.

bh. Edict of Honorius of 30 April 418: *Collect. Quesnelliana*, 14, *PL*, 56, col. 490–3.

bi. *Concilia Africae*, *CCL*, 149, pp. 69–77 and 220–3. These texts form the most important doctrinal contribution to the voluminous African canonical corpus.

bj. *Ep.* 194, a digest of Augustinian doctrine on unmerited grace, whose unforeseen circulation in Africa itself would sow discord in the monastic community of Hadrumetum: cf. below, p. 426.

bk. Jerome, who always found it hard not to speak about himself, adds that he had a part in this renown by sharing Augustine's hatred of the heretics: *Ep.* 141 (= *Ep.* 195 of Augustine).

bl. Jerome, *Ep.* 133 (*ad Ctesiphontem*), 11, *in fine*.

bm. Cf. above, pp. 189–92.

bn. *De gratia Christi et de pecc. orig.*, II, 28, *in fine*.

bo. *De gratia Christi*, I, 33; 45.

bp. *De gratia Christi*, I, 15, *in fine*: (*gratia*) *qua ipsa possibilitas adiuvatur.*

bq. *De gratia Christi*, I, 4, 5 and 7.

br. Cf. *De gratia Christi et de pecc. orig.*, I, 11, quoting Pelagius' *Pro libero arbitrio.*

bs. *De gratia Christi*, 1, 2.

bt. *De gratia Christi*, I, 8, quoting sentences from Pelagius' *Pro libero arbitrio.*

bu. *De gratia Christi*, I, 30, quoting verbatim a sentence from *Pro libero arbitrio*; cf. also I, 23 and 28, quoting the *Letter to Demetrias*, 25 (*PL*, 30, col. 40) and rebelling against the *facilius* which minimizes the role of grace.

bv. *De pecc. mer.*, II, 28.

bw. *Sermon* 169, 13.

bx. *De gratia Christi et de pecc. orig.*, I, 52, where, as in all these texts, 'righteous' and 'righteousness' must be understood in the sense of a morally irreproachable, even saintly, life.

by. *De gratia Christi et de pecc. orig.*, II, 34.

bz. *De gratia Christi et de pecc. orig.*, II, 34.

ca. Cf. above, p. 15. For the date of the *Confessions*, cf. above, p. 205.

cb. *Ep.* 98; cf. above, pp. 320 and 329.

cd. *Ad Dem.*, 2, *initio*: *Quoties mihi de institutione morum et sanctae vitae conversatione dicendum est, soleo primo humanae naturae vim qualitatemque monstrare et quid efficere possit ostendere.*

ce. *Ad Dem.*, 3 and 8, *initio*.

cf. *Ad Dem.*, 6.

cg. *Ad Dem.*, 17: *Dispares sunt in regno caelorum per singula merita mansiones. Diversitas enim operum diversitatem facit praemorium.*

ch. Compare the *Letter to Demetrias*, and Jerome, *Ep.* 130 to the same recipient.

ci. *Magna et acuta ingenia*: the tone is obviously slightly ironic (*Ep.* 186, 13).

cj. *Ep.* 186, 37.

ck. *Ep.* 195 = Jerome, *Ep.* 141.

CHAPTER XXIX

418–419

When he left Hippo during the last fortnight of April 418, Augustine was unaware that it would be for an absence of several months, extended by the longest journey he had made during his episcopacy, taking him to the other extremity of his Africa. Even less did he suspect that ahead of him lay a *biennium* – a two-year period – crammed with various events and travels that would find him more often away from home than in his episcopal city. With his customary immediate reaction to the stimuli of circumstance, Augustine would seize the opportunity of epistolary contacts and meetings with people far from Hippo to indulge in clarifications – which he would cautiously regard as not definitive – about the soul, its origin and nature. During that winter of 386 at Cassiciacum, when Reason had asked him what he wanted to know, the young man then awaiting baptism had ambitiously replied that his aims were God and the soul.[a] The bishop now knew that the second was no easier to attain than the first.

He was still very busy in Carthage, as we know, and especially in the summer of 418, to the point of leaving letters unanswered, contrary to his usual practice. When he finally returned home around the end of October, he wrote to Marius Mercator, from whom he had received correspondence three or four months earlier in the metropolis, that if he had not replied it was not the carrier's fault, but due to urgent and absorbing duties[b] – and he was not the sort of man to hide behind pretexts. We already know of some of these engrossing affairs, besides the customary campaign of urban and suburban preaching: the follow-ups to the steps taken by the council in May, and the long dictation of the *De gratia Christi et de peccato originali*. In addition there was his participation in the episcopal commission that had been given the task of dealing with Leporius, receiving his retraction and countersigning it. Leporius was a monk from south Gaul who, currently subject to an excommunication order against him by Proculus, bishop of Marseille, had taken refuge with Augustine, together with two companions, Domninus and Bonus. It is likely that, having arrived at Hippo in the spring, the trio had accompanied the bishop who was going to Carthage for the 1 May council, and that the arguments which had provoked the excommunication had been examined and amended in the weeks that followed.[1] Leporius had a lofty idea of divine transcendence and majesty, and was loth to admit the existential realities of the incarnation, suffering, passion and death of God born as man. This seemed to him to be a religious impropriety, and he feared that the Word becoming flesh implied a corruption of the divine substance. He saw Christ as a *perfectus cum deo homo*, in a hard-to-translate and somewhat sibylline formula that gave an inkling of the idea of a 'perfect man' whose human nature was juxtaposed to the divine nature rather than truly united with and assumed by it.[2] The theological mists created by the fear of violating the divine transcendence were in any case heavy with other related potential deviations, such as the one that would come to light with Nestorius in the East, some ten years later.

Leporius and his two companions had appeared before the commission formed by Aurelius of Carthage, Augustine, Florentius of Hippo Diarrhytus (Bizerte),[c] and a fourth bishop, named Secundus. They made no difficulties about mending their ways, and Leporius drew up a retraction, the *Libellus emendationis*, in which the bishop of Hippo's influence has been recognized.[3] Its text was sent to Proculus of Marseille and one of his colleagues in south Gaul, accompanied by a letter attesting that the excommunicated men had repented of their error.[d] As for Leporius, he probably stayed with the man whose welcome had enabled him to escape the state of outcast suffered by heretics; it is quite likely that he entered Hippo's clerical community, and may be recognized in the homonymous priest whose unselfishness and efficiency as a builder the bishop praised, at the beginning of January 426.[e]

The long journey to Caesarea (Cherchell) in the summer of 418

In his belated reply to Marius Mercator, Augustine gave his correspondent another reason for the delay in answering him: on leaving Carthage he had set out to visit the far distant areas of Caesarean Mauretania (the present-day Algerian and Oranian regions), and during his journey, when his attention was required here and there, he had found no opportunity for having a letter carried.[f] He remained discreet about the reasons for his journey: 'Church matters', he said (*ecclesiastica necessitas*).

Other texts relating to the episode give us a little more information. First, he was not alone, but travelled with Alypius and Possidius, joining both on the highway leading westwards. We also know that the three bishops were on a mission as papal legates, duly furnished with letters from the apostolic see.[g] It is a great pity that Augustine did not keep a diary of his journey, but on 18 September he was at Caesarea, the provincial capital and main staging-post – but not necessarily terminus – of a peregrination that seems to have included a few meanders.[h] By that date at the latest, since leaving Carthage he had completed a carriage journey of over 1000 kilometres, in small stages punctuated by halts, and in the worst of the summer heat.[4]

He had probably started out towards the end of July, after receiving Zosimus' instructions in Carthage. Some days afterwards, flanked by Alypius and Possidius, who had joined him, he was still travelling in familiar, Numidian territory, where his stops were tantamount to reunions with 'brothers' who were also old friends: at Constantine, where Fortunatus had been bishop since the untimely death of Profuturus;[5] at Milevis, the episcopal see of his dear Severus; at Sitifis, where Novatus, a bishop for fifteen years and now primate, kept a firm hand on his little Numidian border province. Once past the last *castella* of the Sitifian high plains, where bishoprics were almost as thickly distributed as in Carthage's hinterland, one approached the vast expanses of Caesarean Mauretania, where ecclesiastical establishments were more widely scattered. Here, too, our uncertainties begin about the route taken by Augustine and his companions, first regarding the way they tackled the crossing of the great Kabylia. They probably avoided the magnificent but not very negotiable coast road, but after crossing the Saua (the Wadi Soummam) at Tubusuptu (Tiklat) rejoined the coast using the track opened up in the massif by the Wadi Sebaou, once the forested contours between Adekar and Azazga had been passed. Beyond Rusuccuru (Dellys), the coastal bishoprics punctuated this vast maritime front with the same equidistant regularity as the Punic 'ports of call' that had been established on these shores since the sixth century BC. And Augustine and his friends now rediscovered an institutional Christianity – with bishops and their clergy – living in isolation, cut off from the distant African metropolis, with a cultural horizon that was more western than eastern, and with a clear inclination to turn to Rome rather than Carthage to have its ecclesiastical differences settled. We shall see that the effects of this relative autonomy and tendency to look 'overseas' were behind the mission entrusted by the pope to the bishop of Hippo.

In his *Life of Augustine*, Possidius lifts a tiny corner of the veil. Without describing it exactly, the words he uses fix his objective: it was a matter of 'bringing ecclesiastical matters to their conclusion';[i] the jurisdiction delegated by the pope to Augustine and his two colleagues was therefore a jurisdiction of appeal, in affairs that certainly concerned the Church of Africa, but at a stage of development that had gone beyond the courts of first instance, which were specifically African, or had perhaps short-circuited them, since they had already been referred to the see of Rome. Augustine himself was not interested in satisfying his correspondents' curiosity – and therefore ours, since his letters are our main source of information on this affair as on many others – regarding the details of a mission for which he was accountable only to his principal, Pope Zosimus; and that account is missing. But it is in a letter, not to Zosimus, who died at the end of 418, or his immediate successor, Boniface, but to the occupant of the apostolic see in their wake, Celestine, that we find at least allusions to the affair of summer 418. In the autumn of 422, Augustine was striving to counter the manoeuvres of Antoninus of Fussala, who had left to appeal to Rome for the second time.[j] In his letter to Pope Celestine, the bishop of Hippo emphasized that the sanction about which Antoninus was complaining – the loss of his chair, if not his episcopal status – had sometimes been taken by the apostolic see judging in a lower court or confirming judgements made in other proceedings. And he recalled recent examples concerning bishops of Caesarean Mauretania. Laurentius, bishop of Icosium (Algiers), had found himself in the same situation as Antoninus, dispossessed of his see without losing his episcopal dignity. Two other prelates had suffered different ecclesiastical sanctions, similar to a sort of 'quarantining' outside their diocese: for example, Priscus, the incumbent of a distant bishopric at Quiza, at the mouth of the Wadi Chelif, and a bishop named Victor, probably the incumbent of the see of Malliana (Khemis Miliana, formerly Affreville), some fifty kilometres south of Caesarea.[k] Priscus, in particular, complained in 418 of the situation that prevented him from acceding to the primacy of his province, as he should have been able to do given his seniority.

The misdeeds for which Laurentius had been punished elude us. But in the other two cases it may be seen that the sanction taken – the penalty of a communion reduced to the limits of the interested party's bishopric – is precisely the one that the council of 1 May 418, which had just been held, had envisaged for bishops who either proved negligent about the conversion and integration of

Donatists in their dioceses, or refused to submit to the arbitration necessitated by the disputes which frequently resulted from the conversion of Donatist communities.[6] It was chiefly a question of territorial allocations: delicate to resolve everywhere, they were particularly so in a province where the bishoprics were vast and often geographically badly defined. Did such cases of indiscipline provoke the sanction? There is room for query, for in 418 the bishops of Caesarean Mauretania had accumulated quite a number of misdemeanours: we saw that they were conspicuous for their total absence from the general council of 1 May 418;[1] now this same penalty of being deprived of communion outside the limits of the bishopric was also the one envisaged for bishops who, mandated by their primate to represent their province at the council, failed to appear without offering a valid excuse.[7] In this instance, for the meeting of 1 May 418, which was as important on the doctrinal level as within the disciplinary setting, the absence of the Caesarean representatives had, if not an excuse, at least an explanation: the deficiency in the primatal institution itself.

However that may be, the sanctioned bishops had appealed to Rome, and that is how Augustine, Alypius and Possidius came to be mandated to make enquiries on the spot and judge the appeal by delegation of papal jurisdiction. On Zosimus' part, that was a courtesy to a Church of Africa whose sensibilities his recent experiences had taught him to handle tactfully. The investigation on the spot was by no means a sinecure; it involved hearings, of which the procedures followed in the Antoninus of Fussala affair may give us some idea,[m] and travel within a broad radius around the provincial metropolis, Caesarea, probably as far as Quiza (Sidi bel-Atar, formerly Pont-du-Chélif), some 150 kilometres farther west. It must certainly have taken the three legates several weeks to bring matters to a conclusion. On his way, Augustine took advantage of the opportunity to root out some weeds: on the return journey, at Malliana, he drove out of the town a sub-deacon whom he had convicted of Manichaeism.[8] As for the bishop of the town, Victor, he does not appear to have done well out of the legates' enquiry.[n] Conversely, both Laurentius and Priscus were re-admitted to the communion from which they had been excluded. The former would take part in the general council that met at Carthage in late May 419 as the legate of his province, in the company of two other 'coastal' bishops close to his see, of Rusguniae (Cap-Matifou) and Rusuccuru (Dellys).[9] As for Priscus, thanks to tallying mentions in two new letters from Augustine, we have recently learnt that in the autumn of 419 he returned from Rome, where his cause had triumphed – probably because of a favourable report from the three African bishops – landing at Carthage and going on from there to stop at Hippo before returning to his distant see of Quiza.[10] But Augustine, Alypius and Possidius had not yet finished with Caesarean Mauretania, as we shall see.

Summer's end at Caesarea (Cherchell)

The provincial capital was the headquarters of the episcopal commission that had met at the summons of the three papal legates and the metropolitan bishop, Deuterius, and assembled a group of Mauretanian bishops, including two from the nearby sees of Caesarea, Rusticus of Cartennae (Ténès) on the coast towards the west, and Palladius of Tigava (El Kherba) in the Chelif valley.[o]

In this town where, from the outset, life had revolved around the port which was sheltered by the islet that had given it its name in Punic times,[11] Augustine was doubtless glad to find residential conditions similar to those at his home in Hippo. The two towns were of comparable size, though Hippo enjoyed the advantage of a larger economic role and greater port activities. Another feature which must have struck him, as a traveller, from whichever side he approached the town (probably from the east, coming from Tipasa), was the way the provincial metropolis was enclosed, surmounted by steep mountainsides and without any real hinterland. Looking south and east from the islet that sheltered the port, one could see the defence wall which Juba II had provided for the town early in the first century AD, creating in Hellenistic style a vast territorial envelope which he could never have expected to be filled, and which never was. And although the event dated back to the days of Augustine's adolescence, he knew the history of Donatism and was aware that those ramparts had not protected the city from Firmus' activities; in 372 the latter had by trickery managed to have the gates opened for him, probably thanks to the complicity of the town's Donatist bishop, as had occurred elsewhere.[12] He also knew that a moderate dissident splinter group, the Rogatists, had opposed the toughest schismatics – Firmus' allies; these clashes of a mere generation ago had necessarily left an aftermath which, in the view of Augustine and his companions, could at least partly explain local difficulties in putting paid to the schism, and consequently the disciplinary problems that were the reason for their mission.

Besides these stormy periods, which were always liable to be fuelled and aggravated by the movements of the barely Romanized tribes camped at the town's gates,[13] the city had a tradition of violence that was apparently its very own. Augustine knew this, and put an end to it. In Book IV of the *De doctrina christiana*, written several years later, he recounts how, during his stay at Caesarea, he had learnt of the existence of a 'savage custom' which seemed to him to go back to the mists of Antiquity, and in which the inhabitants, at set days in the year, divided into two groups to stone one another to death. This fratricidal combat, he said, was known as the *caterva*, or 'free-for-all'.[p] In a sermon he delivered at the time, the bishop of Hippo attacked Deuterius' parishioners head-on about this practice; he overwhelmed them, moved them to tears and, by the power of his words, achieved what no urban policing had ever managed – the eradication of this barbaric custom, to the extent that several years later it had not reappeared. In the *De doctrina christiana*, his victorious preaching is presented as an exemplary success for the 'sublime style'. What a pity it is lost or, taking the optimistic view, that it has not yet been rediscovered.

The encounter with Emeritus

On the other hand, the texts of two more oratorical performances by Augustine at Caesarea are preserved. These were delivered in singular circumstances, being addressed, as well as to the crowds of faithful who were listening to him, to the mute shadow of an old adversary, a rather pathetic picture of a Donatism reduced to silence, if not clandestinity. The day after 8 June 411, at the end of the conference where he, together with Petilius of Constantine, had been the stoutest champion of his Church, Emeritus had returned home to Caesarea, vanquished but not convinced. Unlike one such as Gaudentius who, at Timgad, would choose an attitude of 'heroic' confrontation, Emeritus had of his own accord calmly secluded himself in an internal exile.

One will always wonder what impulse made him emerge from his retreat and go to town, on 18 September 418, when he could have been in no doubt that Augustine, whom he knew to be present, would seek to meet him. Emeritus was standing in the main square,[14] and it was there that Augustine spotted him when, with his two friends, he was on his way to the church where he was preparing to speak.[q] He hurried over to him and invited him to accompany them. News of this meeting had travelled like lightning round the town, and the *Ecclesia maior* was packed,[15] the congregation having been won over to Augustine in advance, Catholics of the old school and repentant Donatists mingled together. Emeritus followed Augustine and his companions without hesitation, but hardly had he set foot in the church when he turned towards them and uttered these words, which were sibylline only in appearance: 'I cannot not wish what you want me to wish, but I can wish what I want.' Augustine made no mistake: the more he was surprised by a curiosity on Emeritus' part, concealed beneath a feigned submission, tinged with pride, the more he could foresee his obstinacy; but the bishop of Hippo chose to interpret his attitude as a simple little delay (*morula*) before the final surrender of this stubborn man.[r] And a silent Emeritus was subjected to a long homily punctuated by the shouts of the congregation, who urged him to make up his mind without further ado.

It must be imagined that Emeritus made it a point of honour not to avoid the visiting bishop of Hippo, lest he might seem to have come under his spell, for the next day but one, 20 September, he was back in the *Ecclesia maior*, alone before the row of bishops and clergy adorning the apse. It was an unequal match, but there was really no match at all. Augustine was clear-sighted; when he saw the church half-filled by former Donatists, he cherished no illusions as to the value of their presence: many of them, men or women, were physically present, but their mind was elsewhere.[s] The silence of Emeritus eloquently expressed the innermost reluctance of these unwilling converts. To persuade their erstwhile bishop, lead him to repentance and obtain a dazzling conversion before their very eyes, was a formidable risk to take. Augustine overlooked nothing to reach an outcome which he would have hoped to be as broadly peacemaking as his victorious battle against the *caterva*. At the start of the session, in an initial dialogue which came to a sudden end, he had reminded the Donatist of his and his Church's failure in the debates at the Carthage conference; to which Emeritus replied that he had only to refer to the *Records* to know whether he had emerged as vanquished or victor, whether truth had prevailed against him or whether he had been crushed by force.[t]

Augustine really wanted to take him at his word, but there was no question of reading those interminable minutes, then and there, but he advised Deuterius to have them read out in future during Lent.[u] He could at least have the texts read that showed most plainly the Catholic episcopacy's desire for reconciliation. Alypius shouldered the task, reading the fundamentals of the synodal letter in which, on 25 May 411, responding to the edict organizing the conference published by Flavius Marcellinus, the Catholics had promised to adhere to it. In this text, it may be remembered,[v] Aurelius and his colleagues pledged to remove themselves, should their adversaries' views triumph, and, in the opposite case, would afford them a generous welcome. Augustine interrupted this reading with several comments. He continued by emphasizing everything in the recent history of the schism that most typically illustrated the Donatists' inconsistency in their refusal to return to Catholic unity; for instance, the episodes of the Primianists' condemnation of the Maximianists, during which Emeritus had distinguished himself by casting anathemas in a flamboyant and nonsensical style, and the bishop of Hippo took mischievous pleasure in quoting long extracts from these fine chunks of prose.[w] Of those who had been condemned, labelled asps and vipers, among other choice epithets, by Emeritus, at least two had been unconditionally reintegrated, including Felicianus of Mustis. Regarding the latter, it was easy for Augustine to speak sharply to the caster of anathemas: since in the end he had embraced his brother Felicianus whom 'the thunder of his mouth had condemned', why could he not do the same with his brother Deuterius, to whom he was further bound by family links?[x] The Donatist must have been in torment; but he kept silence, true to the line of conduct he had adopted at the outset of the session when, urged by Augustine to say why he had come, he had turned to the stenographer awaiting his reply and said simply, *Fac*,[y] thus terminating a career as a prolific orator with the shortest word he could utter.

In the evening of 20 September 418, he withdrew once more into the shadows from which he had emerged purely as a loser during three days. But the failure was Augustine's because, by wanting to prove too much, he had succeeded only in hardening the Donatist in his shell of wounded pride. There was no doubting the bishop of Hippo's noble and charitable intentions, but his pedantry sometimes had the weight of the steamroller. Certainly, Emeritus was not an easy customer, but this way of trying to obtain his salvation had been the surest means of casting him into outer darkness.

The origin of the soul

As happens in every life, and frequently did in Augustine's, it was not the scheduled event, the one behind the mission – the *ecclesiastica necessitas* – which was to be of the greatest consequence to the bishop, but rather the results of meetings which occurred during that mission. For it led him to discover the existence in that 'Far West' of a clerical and monastic milieu which was very much alive and curious about theology.

During his stay in Caesarea, at a date we cannot fix precisely, a monk of the region, Renatus, was presented to him. This monk was the bearer of a letter written by a bishop named Optatus who, knowing that some of the Caesarean episcopacy were assembled in the metropolitan see at that time, liaising with the mission ordered by Pope Zosimus, had addressed a letter to them asking for these bishops' counsel on a thorny question which was dividing his own community – the origin of the soul.[z] The bishop of Hippo was not the addressee, but Optatus, who had learnt of his presence on this occasion, asked him also to enlighten him, through the intermediary of Renatus. A few days later, Augustine was visited by a certain Muresis, related to Optatus, who presented himself on his behalf, with a request duplicating that of Renatus. Much time has been spent in conjecture on where

Optatus lived and from where he wrote. One of the letters that have recently come
to swell the Augustinian epistolary *corpus* has lifted a corner of the veil. Optatus
was a 'Spanish bishop',[aa] which need not be taken literally; rather than in the
Iberian peninsula, his bishopric may have been situated in Tingitan Mauretania,
which in the Late Empire was part of the 'diocese' – in the 'regional' and
administrative sense – of Spain, from both the ecclesiastical and civil points of
view. In this sense, even with his African-sounding name, Augustine could have
regarded Optatus as 'Spanish'; if he resided in Tingitana, somewhere[bb] the other
side of the Mulucha (Moulouya), which formed the frontier, he could have been in
regular contact with his Caesarean brothers, despite a probably considerable
distance. The absence of a secure and permanent cross-frontier road link on an
east–west line – unless perhaps along a hypothetical coastal trail[16] – was no obstacle
to the circulation of ideas, or to the men who passed them on.[17] It cannot be ruled
out, however, that Optatus was the incumbent of a Spanish bishopric, situated in
Baetica. Occupied since 412 by Siling Vandals, in 417–28 the south of Spain had
been ravaged by a war of reconquest waged by the Visigoths to the advantage of
the Empire;[18] the shores of western Caesarean Mauretania were close by and
offered to those coming from Andalusia or the Levant the same refuge that
Carthage and the eastern provinces had offered in 410 to those arriving from Italy,
fleeing Alaric's Goths. Landing on the present-day Oranian coasts, the Spanish
refugees remained in the western sphere of influence, following a geographical and
cultural division which we no longer have, but which still obtained in Augustine's
day, as in his letter to Vincentius of Cartennae (Tenes) – *Ep.* 93, 24 – he noted with
some chagrin that Caesarean Mauretania felt itself to be 'closer to western than
southern regions, and did not even like to be known as Africa'.[19]

With that capacity we have seen so often for not postponing a reply when he
deemed it urgent, even in the midst of the most engrossing occupations,
Augustine answered Optatus immediately. He had carriers at his fingertips, and
to wait until his return to Hippo would have been to defer the reply by several
months. It was a delicate question, however; a recently ordained bishop, his
correspondent had entered into conflict on his home ground with older clergy
who held to 'traducianism', the doctrine which maintained that the human soul
is propagated from one generation to the next beginning with Adam. Optatus
was of the opinion – shared, he said, in his province by a number of priests and
followers – that God, Creator of all things, was also the Creator of every soul,
past, present or yet to come; this was the 'creationist' theory on this thorny
problem. He had asked for the small Mauretanian synod's arbitration, and
declared himself ready to bow before the judgement of a little group of lay
'experts', and was now asking for that of the bishop of Hippo.

In his letter the bishop showed the greatest caution. This was a subject that had
occupied his mind for nearly thirty years,[cc] and its theological implications made
it difficult to adopt clear-cut and definitive positions on the matter. First of all, he
had to tell his young colleague: 'I want you to know that in none of my many
works have I ever hazarded a firm reply to this problem.'[dd] Augustine continued
by declaring that in the end it mattered little if the origin of our soul eluded us,
provided that we were quite clear about the way in which it is saved,[ee] and he
would really have liked to leave it there. Outlining first the dilemma between the
creation of each individual soul *ex nihilo* and parental transmission, and noting

that no scriptural text made any distinctions on this point,[20] he reaffirmed, in a manner clearly indicating his theological priorities, that the essential thing was the safeguarding of the faith 'by which we believe that no man, no matter how old or young and tender his age, is delivered of the old death and bonds of sin contracted by his first birth, except by the only mediator between God and men, the man Jesus Christ'.[ff] Having said that again forcefully, he still had to put Optatus on his guard against the consequences of his 'creationist' persuasions. If, by defending this argument, he meant to insinuate that these souls, drawing their innocence from their newness, could not be damned before using their free will to sin, he was falling into heresy; if he admitted that these new souls did not escape perdition when they left the body without baptism, he was not a heretic, but he then had to explain how they could have deserved their condemnation, obviously avoiding making God responsible – as the Manichaeans did – for their sin or their condemnation.[gg] But if, disheartened by these difficulties, Optatus embraced the argument of those who would have it that all souls come from Adam's, by propagation, he would fall into other difficulties. First, how to conceive of this transmission, which certainly agreed best with the doctrine of original sin? And Augustine touched on its mysteries, with undeniably poetic imagery, but which showed him still to be reliant in this area on Platonist dualism, that made it so hard to explain the transmission of a soul of spiritual nature by way of a bodily conception.[hh]

Patently disturbed by Optatus' over-hasty certainties, Augustine wanted to know more about them; he therefore asked his correspondent to send him a *libellus fidei* which he had written. Meanwhile, he listed the most recent of his own writings; in reply to his dear Marcellinus who, curious about these problems, had turned to him on Jerome's advice,[21] it may be recalled that the bishop had written him a letter a few years earlier which had doubtless disappointed the high-ranking imperial official. For he had referred him to the *De libero arbitrio* which then concluded on a *non liquet*[ii] and – just as he was now doing to Optatus – he had not disguised from him that this question of the soul's origin, which was certainly intellectually exciting, seemed secondary to him in the perspective of the search for salvation. Wherever the soul originated, the chief concern must be to save it.[22] And he had finished his letter with a promise to himself to seek aid and assistance in the state of ignorance in which he found himself.[jj] This he did by resorting to picking Jerome's brains, in a long message to which the *Retractations* give the status of a book.[kk] At the end of summer 418, he was still awaiting a reply from the hermit of Bethlehem, and now had to confess to Optatus that while waiting he was not permitted to communicate his own letter to anyone, and it could be read only at his home in Hippo.[ll] To conclude, he firmly put the young bishop on his guard against falling into Pelagianism.

Towards mid-October, Augustine, Alypius and Possidius at last returned to their Numidia. After six months' absence from his community, the bishop of Hippo found a huge backlog of work and couriers who were being held up. Besides the letter he had received in Carthage during the summer, a second from Marius Mercator awaited him at Hippo; he also owed an answer to the priest Sextus and the deacon Caelestinus, the future pope, in Rome. A Roman cleric, Albinus, was on the spot, ready to embark for Ostia before the closure of the sea. Augustine hastily dictated his replies and gave them to him.[mm]

With the start of winter, a long period of tranquillity opened out before him, until the Eastertide of the following spring, and he was able to devote it to his diocese and his personal work. During these years, Augustine used his free time as much as possible on two of his major works, his *Treatise on the Trinity* and *City of God*. But correspondence in Africa itself knew no winter respite. We possess at least one of those letters, dated early winter 418–19, which he sent to his colleague Asellicus – a rare and charming name, 'the little donkey'! – incumbent of a see in a distant oasis on the fringe of the desert, Tusuros (Tozeur). At that time it was the land of the 'Arzuges', a semi-barbarian border district, astride the *limes*, distinguished in this area amongst other things by linear constructions, walls, whose state of preservation is still impressive, but which served more to filter traffic than to bar its way, despite their name (*clausurae*). A great lord like Publicola had immense estates there.[nn] In May 411, Asellicus and his Donatist rival, Aptus, had made the journey to take part in the conference at Gargilius' Baths in Carthage, a praiseworthy undertaking for, as Asellicus had occasion to remark, it had taken them nearly a fortnight to cross the 350-odd kilometres, as the crow flies, to the metropolis.[23] Augustine had heard him say so but, as he spent so much time on the road, it needed more than that to impress him. Seven years later, Asellicus sent him his kind regards. There was a Jewish colony at Tusuros, as in many other cities in that ancient eastern Africa,[24] and the bishop complained that one Aptus – who seems to have a fraternal likeness to Asellicus' aforementioned Donatist competitor[25] – 'was teaching Christians to turn to Judaism'.[oo] Asellicus had been upset by this and had informed his provincial primate of Byzacena, Donatianus, bishop of Thelepte, who had passed on to Augustine the task of replying to him.

The bishop of Hippo wrote *Adversus Iudaeos*, a small treatise which is usually, though without any proof, dated to the last years of his life solely because it is not taken into account in the *Retractations*. Despite the literal title ('Against the Jews'), this is not an anti-Semitic pamphlet; one would look in vain through all Augustine's works for a trace of anti-Semitism based on cultural 'findings' or inspired by racial prejudices, such as may be found in contemporary pagan writers, for instance in the venomous poem by Rutilius Namatianus.[26] Augustine does not attack the Jews as a people, or even a community, but their religious attitude.[27] On several occasions, in his sermons, this traveller accustomed to the main roads, had the notion of comparing the Jews, bound to the Law, testifying to God, but remaining on the margin of Christian salvation, to the milestones along the roadsides 'which show the way without making any progress themselves'.[28] As might be expected, the letter to Asellicus was a long reflection on the Law, clarified by constant references to St Paul, more precisely Romans 2, 4, 6 and 7. At the end of his letter, Augustine came to the grievances against Aptus: the latter recommended abstinence from certain meats, according to Mosaic law, and prescribed the observance of ancient practices – including circumcision, no doubt, although it is not mentioned in the text – which were rejected by Christians 'because they are merely the shadow of things to come', as the Apostle says (Col. 2.17).[pp] The New Covenant, continued the bishop, had rendered the majority of those rules obsolete; as for the other precepts, those of universal scope and for all time, and which are summed up in the greatest commandment (Luke 10.27) if we observe them, he emphasized, it is not through our human will, as is claimed by those who want to establish their own justice, but through the grace of God. Did Augustine mean that, in his eyes, this signified that the slight tendency to Judaism piloted by Aptus at Tusuros was an unexpected incarnation of Pelagianism on the fringe of the desert? If so, the text would betray what might be taken for a rather obsessional projection.

419: from a busy spring to a heavily-laden autumn

Pope Zosimus was a stubborn man. His setback in the spring of 418 in his confrontation with the Africans over the Pelagian affair had not finally deflected him from wishing to impose the pre-eminence of the Roman see over that of Carthage. In the autumn of that year, a complaint was referred to the Roman curia from a bishop in the Byzacenian province, who had been tried on a matter apparently involving fiscal problems by a synod on which laymen had sat, which was an irregularity. Zosimus did not follow up his advantage, however, and contented himself with a sarcastic letter about those ecclesiastical judges who were themselves violating the Church's canons.[29] But at the same time[30] another affair erupted that was destined for wider repercussions. In the diocese of Sicca Veneria (Le Kef), if not in the episcopal town itself, a priest named Apiarius had been ordained. For misdeeds that are unknown to us,[31] this priest had been excommunicated by his bishop, Urbanus, who had the special prestige of having lived in close association with Augustine and, notably, had for several years been the superior of the clerical monastery at Hippo.[qq] That did not stop Apiarius appealing to Rome against the sanction imposed on him. This time, the pope took the matter seriously, and despatched a delegation to Carthage, under the leadership of an Italian prelate, bishop Faustinus, whose see was in the Picenum, and who was armed with a papal *commonitorium* setting out the terms of his mandate: Urbanus in person was threatened with excommunication if he did not withdraw a sanction which the appeal proceedings might reveal to be ill founded. What the pope obviously desired was to impose the appeal jurisdiction of the see of Rome on the African episcopacy, based on the decisions taken at the council of Serdica in 343.

But on 26 December 418, Zosimus died. A laborious election replaced him in the spring of 419 with a much more conciliatory successor, Pope Boniface. Before his installation, however, the long weeks of uncertainty had been heavy enough with threats of a schism in Rome to make Honorius consider calling a council in Spoleto at the end of March, in order to stabilize the situation. Alongside Aurelius,[32] Augustine was to represent Africa, together with Alypius. In the end the journey was not necessary, but Augustine left his episcopal town very early: Easter fell on 30 March that year, and the day after the following Sunday he started off for Carthage, but this time by the coastal route, which passed through Thabraca (Tabarka). He took this road in order to be present at the last moments of his friend Florentius, the bishop of Hippo Diarrhytus (Bizerte) in whose company he had examined Leporius[rr] the year before. On 17 April, he was in the *basilica Florentia* in the town, where he had delivered the dedicatory speech a few years earlier,[ss] but now it was to preside over the funeral of the dead bishop,[tt] and it is probable that he stayed in the town for a time to arrange, with some colleagues, for the election and ordination of Florentius' successor.[33]

On 25 May at the latest, he was in Carthage for the opening of the general council, and had certainly been there several days beforehand to make preparations for it with Aurelius. In the *secretarium* of the *basilica Fausti*, the bishops were as numerous as the year before, and this time the delegates from Caesarean Mauretania were present. Meanwhile, the Apiarius affair had been temporarily settled: the priest had made amends, the excommunication had been lifted and he had been authorized to exercise his ministry again, but somewhere other than Sicca. It would later become known that he had ended up at Thabraca, where his conduct would earn him a new excommunication some years later![34] There remained the fundamental questions that this affair had raised, on the relations between Rome and Africa and the right of appeal to the apostolic see. On 25 May the Roman legate, Faustinus, insisted that the *commonitorium* which he had had from Pope Zosimus be read before the council; in support of the papal position in favour of appeals to Rome, the text quoted 'canons of the council of Nicaea'. With Alypius as spokesman, the African episcopacy replied that they were willing to respect the decisions of Nicaea, but that in the Greek version of the canons of Nicaea there was nothing similar to Pope Zosimus' quotations, nor in the copies preserved in Carthage. And Alypius proposed that they should write to the great churches of the East, at Constantinople, Alexandria and Antioch, to have the matter clarified. However, now that the dispute between Apiarius and his bishop Urbanus was settled without harm to the latter, the tone in Aurelius' entourage was conciliatory. The council decided to follow up Alypius' proposal but also, in the meantime, to accept the 'canons of Nicaea' as they appeared in the text of the late Zosimus, with their favourable implications for the position of the see of Rome. It fell to Augustine to formulate this acceptance, which for the time being put an end to the debate between Rome and Carthage.[35] We have seen that Antoninus of Fussala would make use of it,[uu] and it would take the scandal of Apiarius' subsequent offence at Thabraca and his second appeal to Rome to make the African Church decide resolutely to free itself of Rome's 'supervision' in disciplinary matters. This would be the famous canon of the twentieth council of Carthage, in 424/5: 'Let no one dare to appeal to the Roman Church' (*Ut nullus ad ecclesiam Romanam audeat appellare*),[36] a stark ending to a progress at the outset of which Tertullian, and above all Cyprian, had begun by declaring most rigidly Africa's autonomy and the legitimacy, in certain instances, of opposition to Rome. That position had softened slightly with Optat of Milevis, at the end of the fourth century, but in the eyes of the Africans, who believed that episcopal powers came directly from Christ, who had not acted through Peter to confer them on the apostles, though the bishop of Rome was the link of episcopal intercommunion and personified the unity of the Catholic Church, he did not have the legal delegation of the community.[37] And although they accepted the pope's authority in doctrinal matters, it was for 'charismatic' and not jurisdictional reasons, as the confrontation with Zosimus in 417–18 over Pelagius and Caelestius had plainly shown.

As it had done in the preceding year, the council did not break up until it had internally appointed a commission charged with the task of continuing its work on a restricted scale. For Numidia, Augustine, Alypius and Possidius were to sit; we may note that this was the trio entrusted a year before by the Roman curia with settling the affairs of Caesarean Mauretania; we shall see that this was not mere chance. It met on 30 May in the *secretarium* of the *basilica Restituta*, smaller but more central premises,[38] and finalized a few disciplinary decrees concerning cases of accusation brought against clergy; two gave a reminder of the responsibility of the bishop – and notably the danger that lay in his being the sole judge – and lead one to think that the action of Urbanus of Sicca in the recent affair of Apiarius was behind this legislation.[39] This last word is apposite, because in essence the compilation of the *Register of Carthage* dates to this summer of 419; it is an invaluable collection of texts put together as a foundation for the Church of Africa's disciplinary practice. It was mainly the work of Aurelius and his Carthaginian clergy, but very probably with the help of Alypius and perhaps of Augustine, who remained at Carthage until the early days of September.

While Alypius set sail from the African metropolis for a long mission to Italy,[40] the bishop of Hippo and the faithful Possidius went home to Numidia together. Augustine was back by 11 September, as was recently revealed to us by a newly published letter that allows us to enter his study in the autumn of 419. In this letter addressed to Possidius,[vv] he brings him up to date on his writing activities since his return from Carthage, setting them between two precise dates – he who is always so stingy with details about his calendar! – the one of his arrival in Hippo and that of the letter itself, 1 December 419.[ww] We therefore know his output during those ten weeks, interrupted as it was by various requests to which he had to respond without delay, to the detriment of his long-drawn-out works such as the *City of God*; he says he had to postpone his plans for returning to it after completing it as far as Book XIV.[xx] In this letter to Possidius, a confidant to whom he could express himself unrestrainedly and openly, he speaks bluntly of his weariness and irritation at these spokes put in the wheels of his greatest ambitions: 'I find it hard to bear that the stuff I am obliged to dictate, from all quarters, prevents me from working on what I have in preparation, without rest or respite.'[yy]

Among these 'special occasion works', the final full stop he gave to his lengthy dispute with the Donatists was the completion of his *Contra Gaudentium*. Gaudentius, one of the sect's spokesmen at the time of the Carthage conference, was bishop of Thamugadi (Timgad), the principal stronghold of the schism since its origins. In theory it had not been so since the summer of 411, but several years after the conference, central Numidia was still a mission land for the Catholics. Dissidents still held more or less clandestine gatherings there, like the 'council' probably held in 418 at which even Petilianus of Constantine was present.[zz] What is more, Gaudentius had managed to preserve his church at Thamugadi, and in 418, when a high-ranking imperial official, the tribune Dulcitius, at last prepared to apply the religious legislation in this region, his answer was to shut himself up in it, threatening to burn himself and his people alive. Dulcitius was in no way brutal, and there was no question of giving the Donatist the satisfaction of making him a martyr. The tribune tried persuasion, trying to edge Gaudentius gently towards the solution of an 'internal exile' without fuss, which had been that of Emeritus at Caesarea. But nothing did the trick; cooped up in his church, the recalcitrant bishop wrote letter after letter, and was unshakable. Weary of it all, Dulcitius passed the dossier to Augustine.

Written in the winter of 418–19, at the latest in the following spring, since an allusion is made to the encounter with Emeritus in the preceding summer, Book I of the *Contra Gaudentium* was a reply to those famous letters which had come from the hands of Dulcitius. Even more than the fate of the Church's possessions, it was the human consequences of the Carthage conference that fuelled the debate. False rumours of Emeritus' conversion had reached Gaudentius' ears. Augustine was compelled to admit his failure, but rightly stressed that if the bishop of Caesarea had 'passed into the Catholic peace' at that time, his former friends would not have failed to say that he had yielded to force rather than to the truth.[ab] He had more luck with Gabinius, who in 411 represented the schismatic Church at Vegesela (Ksar el-Kelb); for if Thamugadi was its stronghold in Numidia, Vegesela was par excellence its capital, where since the middle of the fourth century the *memoria* of 'domnus Marculus', martyr to State persecution of the Donatists,[ac] had been venerated on a par with a holy tomb. An annoying example for an intransigent Donatist, Gabinius' conversion was manna from heaven for Augustine, even though Gaudentius was swift to insinuate that in this instance his Numidian colleague had yielded to threats. In other times, the penitent would have paid dearly for this volteface, but in 418 the terrorism of the circumcellions seemed at last to have been eradicated.

The text of this first book reached Timgad and provoked the recipient to a reply that was really no reply: 'he could neither answer nor keep quiet', the author of the *Retractations* would say,[ad] but the bishop of Hippo had come to that conclusion immediately, in his letter of 1 December to Possidius.[ae] He was not going to leave him with the last word! During November, therefore, he dictated a much shorter second book, but of more clearly ecclesiological inspiration, since the Donatist had thought it a good idea to call upon Cyprian to witness in his favour, and had resumed the customary arguments of those in his sect on the *hic et nunc* division of the pure from the impure. Augustine had no difficulty in showing his adversary that the Cyprianic interpretation of the parable of the good seed and the tares ran counter to his own.[af] He concluded on a variant of the famous *Causa finita est*, uttered by him at Carthage two years before concerning the Pelagians;[ag] Gaudentius' empty words had by themselves put an end to the affair, and all that remained for him to do was to return to the straight and narrow.[ah] That was asking a great deal. We do not know the epilogue to this return of the flame of Donatism in Numidia, but it is unlikely that Gaudentius resorted to the last extremes; with his blustering and bragging, he gives the impression that he was the kind of person who makes a great deal of noise so that people will restrain him from doing himself an injury.

The genesis of the *De natura et origine animae*

Among the many requests that had cut across Augustine's great editorial projects in the autumn of 419, there were also, and chiefly, the results of his journey and stay in Caesarean Mauretania in the preceding year. Optatus, the 'Spanish bishop', had received the bishop of Hippo's first and long letter – *Letter* 190 – which had not budged him an inch, either in his hasty 'creationist' convictions or in the desire, which he reiterated, to receive for his guidance both Augustine's letter to Jerome and the latter's response. This is what he told him in a message brought to Hippo by a priest named Saturninus, whom the bishop must have found on his return from Carthage.[ai] In reply, Augustine confirmed that he was still awaiting an answer from Bethlehem, and once more put his young colleague on his guard against the dangers of an insufficiently considered opinion. He concluded:

> This is what I deemed right to reply to your Holiness, as you are almost certain that the propagation of souls is to be condemned; in any case, if I had to answer those who affirm it, I would perhaps show how they are ignorant of what they believe they know, and how much they should fear daring to affirm it.[aj]

It was partly to reveal to him beforehand the outline of what would constitute the *De natura et origine animae*, once its various components had been assembled. But what Augustine did not tell Optatus was that he had already begun writing the book.

It owed its genesis to a combination of circumstances, whose protagonists were the members of that spiritual milieu which we began to glimpse so unexpectedly in the distant western Caesarean Mauretania, and it was their actions that contributed to its step-by-step composition. The long warning letter which Augustine had written to Optatus,[ak] when he was still in Caesarea in the summer of 418, must have circulated pretty quickly, travelling the circuits of restricted diffusion imposed at that time by copying techniques. But a copy of the letter had come into the hands of a 'Spanish priest' named Petrus,[al] whose 'Spanishness', like that attributed to bishop Optatus, offers us the alternative: African from Tingitana or Spaniard from Baetica? But we are told that Petrus lived in the Caesarean region,[am] and this piece of information makes one incline rather to the second option, suggesting that Petrus (and probably Optatus, too), fleeing from the disturbances of that time in the south of Spain,[an] had found a temporary refuge there.

It was with Petrus that 'a certain Vincentius Victor'[ao] found the text of *Letter* 190 to Optatus. This person was a young layman, still a 'Rogatist' not long before, but recently won over to the Catholic community, who had added to his name, Victor, that of Vincentius, as a testimony to his admiration for the moderate Donatist, incumbent of the see of Cartennae, who had died a short time before. Augustine had learnt this while making his own discreet enquiries, and as he had some esteem for Vincentius, one of his former fellow students at Carthage, his initial consideration for Victor was favourable.[ap] But we glean an interesting detail, for it thus becomes very likely that it was Cartennae, about a hundred kilometres west of Caesarea, which was the heart of this small community of 'spiritual men', who were passionately interested in problems pertaining, amongst others, to the nature and origin of the soul. Vincentius Victor shared Optatus' 'creationist' opinions, and the caution displayed by Augustine in the letter addressed to the 'Spanish bishop' surprised and even shocked him. In his turn he produced a work in two books, which was much to Petrus' liking, and was circulated by him. That was how the monk Renatus, the first intermediary between Optatus and Augustine, came to know about it. He took umbrage at the somewhat cavalier treatment of the bishop of Hippo, to whom he hastened to transmit the text from Caesarea where he was staying or passing through. When Augustine wrote to Possidius *Letter* 23*, which is so invaluable to us, he had recently received Vincentius Victor's *libellus*, and considered that it teemed with errors and absurdities; he also found it agreeably written and thus all the more dangerous. That is why, at the end of autumn 419, he had written a first book of refutation to the monk Renatus, while proposing to reply as soon as possible to the author himself.[aq] That reply would form Books III and IV of the treatise *On the nature and origin of the soul*; but to make Book II, he would insert a long letter addressed to Petrus: the dedicatee of Vincentius Victor's text, this priest must not be neglected, dazzled as he was by the young layman's eloquence and agog to serve as a sounding box for his ideas.

Augustine had finished building the various layers of this composite treatise in the spring of 420.[41] With such an elaborate development, it would be idle to see an overall plan in it, and unfair to complain about its inevitable repetitions. The refutation of Victor was dispersed through the four books, but gathered together and resumed in a more coherent fashion in the last two. It emerges that, from his reading of *Letter* 190 to Optatus, Augustine's correspondent had at least gleaned the problem set out by the bishop of Hippo, and that he shared it: he did not deny the existence of original sin, or the need to baptize the newborn, or Christ's indispensable mediation for their salvation. Rather than simple intellectual curiosity, however, it was a material problem for Christian pastorship, raised by the fate of children who died unbaptized, which prompted the queries of Vincentius Victor and the little group for whom he was spokesman on the origin of the soul.[42] It was to save them from eternal damnation that, repudiating a traducianism which condemned them *ipso facto*, he had turned towards a radical creationism.

But Augustine found it easy to show him that, by doing so, he was sinking into a series of contradictions and errors. The first was to affirm that the soul conceived directly by God, in the same way as that of Adam, had not been created by him from nothing (*ex nihilo*), but of his own nature.[ar] Which was to say that this soul, born of the breath of God, could only be a part of God; Victor defended himself by maintaining that the soul is corporeal, while God is spirit, in which he parted ways with Tertullian (whom he had obviously read), who upheld the corporeality of both; but Augustine could justly find these metaphysics rather comic.[as] In any case, the young man expressed himself in terms which suggested that he did not rule out the existence of the soul before it was united with the body, which, remarked Augustine, made him fall into the Priscillianists' error.[at] The bishop listed an inexorable catalogue of all these errors; but it must be noted in Victor's defence, so to speak, that some of them were inspired by a spirit of fundamental mercy: thus, by misinterpreting John 14.2: 'In my Father's house there are many mansions', which he wanted to understand as 'outside the kingdom of God', a place of welcome for the non-baptized,[au] he was joining the Pelagians, on whom the council of Carthage of 1 May 418 had cast anathema for precisely that reason.[43] There was also the reference to the story of the young Dinocrates in the *Passion of Perpetua and Felicitas*: the little boy (aged seven) was suffering at the edge of a large fountain whose coping was too high for him to be able to drink from it – plainly the image of a *refrigerium* from which he was excluded for want of baptism, it was commonly thought, and Victor shared that view – and the ceaseless prayers of his sister Perpetua ensured his salvation;[44] but, retorted Augustine, if he achieved salvation – although the text did not say so – it was probably because he had received baptism.[av] The last error highlighted by the bishop of Hippo was in his view the most serious, for Victor was unafraid to profess that 'some people, who had departed this life without Christ's baptism, went for a time (*interim*) not directly to the kingdom of heaven, but to Paradise; but at the resurrection they would finally come to the beatitude of the kingdom of heaven'.[aw] Augustine was indignant – even the Pelagians had not dared to say that! The young layman from Caesarean Mauretania, with the blissful unawareness of simple generosity of spirit, was heading directly towards what we might hold to be an agreeable heresy.[45]

And how about Augustine? Where did he stand, on the soul and its origin, in that winter of 419–20, thirty-three years after the ambitious declaration made to Reason at Cassiciacum?[ax] On the nature of the soul, he clung tenaciously to a number of certainties, already acquired in part at the time of the remarks exchanged with Evodius in the second year in Rome, 388, which had supplied the material for the *De quantitate animae*,[ay] enriched and defended against the materialist philosophers in a few superb pages of Book X of the *De Trinitate*,[az] and finally confirmed in 415 in the long letter to Jerome, in which he had taken stock of the matter.[ba] The soul is immortal, in a certain way, which is not God's, whose creation it is without being a part of him. Would he still say, in as clearly dualist a fashion as in the discourse with Evodius, that the soul is 'a substance endowed with reason, made to govern a body'?[bc] At least he was still forcefully affirming, on the basis of the same analyses, that the incorporeal soul animated the body indivisibly and, as he put it with a dynamic image, by virtue of a 'sort of vital tension'.[bd]

On the soul's origin, his almost unique certainty was a negative one; he had written it to Optatus and repeated it to the monk Renatus: he vigorously rebutted the Origenist idea whereby the soul might end up in a body as if in a prison, 'constrained by the faults of a sinful life led earlier in the celestial spheres or some other part of the world'.[be] He was still dependent on the problematics of Platonism when he failed to rule out one of the four hypotheses already formulated in the *De libero arbitrio*, that of a pre-existent soul possibly created by God in the first day of the world, and his description of the incarnation of the soul, its coming into the body, often still remained reliant on a dualist vocabulary: for instance, when he evoked that 'intervening period (*medium*) which goes from the instant when the soul has been sent into the flesh until its separation from the flesh'.[bf] But a concept was dawning in him that tended to diminish the ontological reality of a possibly pre-existent soul by denying it any conscious personal life before its union with the body.[bg]

Loyal in this to the western and notably African tradition, Augustine was the more tempted by traducianism because the doctrine of the propagation of souls through generation was, at first sight, the one that seemed to him most easily compatible with the doctrine of original sin. But only at first sight, and he did not disguise the inextricable difficulties which could be escaped only at the price of a corporeal conception of the soul; that had been Tertullian's choice, but it was not *his*.[bh] In the autumn of 419, in his second letter to Optatus, he still hesitated to rid himself of that option: 'I confess', he said, 'that I have not yet discovered how on the one hand the soul draws its sin from Adam – which cannot be doubted – and on the other, is not itself drawn from Adam.'[bi] However, he was increasingly inclined towards creationism, provided that the transmission of Adam's sin to each newly created soul could be explained. At the very end of his life, in the

Contra Iulianum, reflecting on 'the soul' and 'the flesh', he would still pose the alternative: 'Either the composite of the two, tainted, is drawn from man, or one of the two (the soul) is corrupted in the other (the flesh) as in a tainted vessel.'[bj] Even supposing that the soul is created immediately by God, it is immediately infected by this corrupt vessel of the body. But he would refuse to make a choice and added: 'Whichever of the two solutions is correct, I am more inclined to learn about it than to say anything, so that I do not have the audacity to teach something of which I am ignorant.'

The bishop of Hippo's exchanges with the little spiritual milieu of the African extreme west had nevertheless helped him to get a clearer view of his own anthropology and, in pastoral terms, he had not wasted his time. In the *Retractations* he would say that he had received a letter from Vincentius Victor in which the young man amended his arguments.[bk] At the end of 419, however, the affairs of Caesarean Mauretania were still keeping him busy, on a different level. In November, Priscus of Quiza[bl] arrived, coming from Rome via Carthage, where he had first seen Aurelius. It may be recalled – above, p. 349 – that Priscus was among those bishops from Caesarean Mauretania whose cases had prompted the joint mission of Augustine, Alypius and Possidius during the summer of 418. Regaining his chair and being restored to his rank following favourable appeal proceedings, he had *ipso facto* acceded to the provincial primacy and if, on the long road that led to his bishopric, he had halted at Hippo – he would also do so at Calama with Possidius – it was less out of deference to Augustine than to discover how to settle, with his accord, a thorny matter which now concerned him above all else.

Deuterius, bishop of Caesarea, whose guests Augustine and his friends had been in the preceding year, had just died, leaving the metropolitan see vacant. It was an awkward problem. The town's population – or at least pressure groups that were demographically in the majority, and restless – were demanding a certain Honorius, a 'bishop of the province'. Canon law proved an obstacle for, though the see of Caesarea was vacant, the bishop desired by the faithful was not eligible, and the best established disciplinary practice according to African tradition was opposed to his 'transfer'.[bm] The story, which we see becoming clearer through the letters – all recently rediscovered – which Augustine wrote during the winter of 419–20, was scarcely banal; it was almost incredible. A long time before,[46] Honorius' father, who was himself a bishop in a see situated within the geographical boundaries of the bishopric of Cartennae – but not in the episcopal town itself – had been transferred to Caesarea. Everything had stemmed from this first illicit 'transfer'.[bn] For when the father departed, he had ordained his own son to the see he was quitting.[bo] On the father's death, Deuterius had succeeded him to the metropolitan see but, in the autumn of 419, his own death opened up the possibility for the son, Honorius, to follow in his father's footsteps and, like him, install himself in the chair that had become free once again. A bishop, certainly, but a marginal bishop – one too many, so to speak – Honorius probably did not appear on the official list, the *matricula*, of the province's bishops. Everything combined to attract him to Caesarea: to the precedent created by his father – the beginning of a 'line'! – was added the personal interest of the incumbent of the see of Cartennae, Rusticus, who could envisage, when this movement took place, that communities which had long been usurped would return to his see. In short, some astute propaganda had conquered the declared opposition of a small group of 'religious' men – including the monk Renatus with whom the bishop of Hippo had remained in touch, and a revolt had forced a local episcopal commission, urgently summoned and assembled in the town, to accept Honorius' temporary installation in the see of Caesarea.[bp]

It remained for Honorius to consolidate his position; to this end, he had not hesitated to make the journey to Hippo in the depths of winter. Early in 420, he was with Augustine, busily soothing his alarm and promising to act in accordance with his wishes 'for the peace of the Church and in keeping with ecclesiastical discipline' – 'May the Lord make him speak the truth!' the bishop wrote to Renatus, giving him little credence.[bq] He knew very well that Honorius was an intriguer, who was preparing to cross the sea, not only to lodge an appeal with the apostolic see, but also to plead his cause at the Court. And it was chiefly there that Augustine feared the results of Honorius' tortuous machinations, whereas he had a certain trust in the judgement of pope Boniface.[br] In fact, it was in Rome that the affair of bishop Honorius – like that of Antoninus of Fussala two years later (above, p. 257) – would find its epilogue; and similarly it remains unknown to us. Meanwhile, Augustine must have thought, there was a lot going on in Caesarean Mauretania, peculiar happenings, and not always very Catholic.

Notes

a. *Soliloquies*, I, 7; cf. above, p. 108.
b. *Ep.* 193, 1.
c. It is Florentius' participation in this commission that enables us to date it; he would die the following spring.
d. Augustine's *Ep.* 219.
e. Cf. above, p. 232.
f. *Ep.* 193, 1.
g. *Ep.* 190, 1, mention confirmed by Possidius, *Vita Aug.*, XIV, 3.
h. According to the terms used in the letter to Mercator: *Ep.* 193, 1.
i. *Vita Aug.*, XIV, 3: *ob terminandas . . . ecclesiasticas necessitates.*
j. Above, p. 257.
k. *Ep.* 209, 8.
l. Above, p. 339.
m. Above, pp. 255–7.
n. At the date of letter 209 to Pope Celestine (Autumn 422), he was still under the sanction.
o. *Gesta cum Emerito*, 1. It was not, however, a real synod of bishops of the province, as a sentence from the *Retractations*, II, 51, might lead one to think.
p. *De doctrina Christ.*, IV, 53. The word *caterva* means 'band' and, by derivation, 'fighting in bands'. The French word 'mêlée' is proposed by P. Monceaux, *Hist. litt. de l'Afrique chrét.*, VI, p. 174.
q. *Gesta cum Emerito*, 1.
r. *Sermo ad Caes. eccl. plebem*, 1: *Non vos ergo permoveat, fratres*, aliqua morula, *dum vult quod vult*.
s. He says this with the ecclesiological contrast *intus/foris*: *adhuc corde positi in parte Donati praesentiam nobis exhibent corporalem sive viri sive feminae, carne intus, spiritu foris (Gesta cum Emerito, 2).*
t. *Gesta cum Emerito*, 3.

u.   *Gesta cum Emerito*, 4. Augustine expressed himself on this subject in the same terms as in letter 28* addressed to Novatus of Sitifis one or two years earlier: *Ep.* 28*, 2, in *BA*, 46 B, p. 404.

v.   Cf. above, p. 297. Augustine's *Ep.* 128 = *Gesta conl. Carth.*, I, 16.

w.   Cf. *Gesta cum Emerito*, 10 and 11. He quoted from the council of Bagaï in 394, which had been among his dossier of archives for years. But the fact that he had them with him at Caesarea in September 418 leads one to think that he had been hoping for this final confrontation, and had been prepared for it.

x.   *Gesta cum Emerito*, 10, *in fine*.

y.   'Do (your work)', i.e. record what will be said without bothering about me (*Gesta cum Emerito*, 3, *in fine*). Possidius, who was present, reported the scene in the same terms: *Vita Aug.*, XIV, 7.

z.   *Ep.* 190. 1.

aa. *Ep.* 23A*, 3, *BA*, 46 B, p. 372.

bb. It would be unwise to be specific, in our present state of ignorance of the Tingitana ecclesiastical map.

cc. Since the *De libero arbitrio*, III, 55–9, around 391.

dd. *Ep.* 190, 2.

ee. *Ep.* 190, 3.

ff. *Ep.* 190, 5, based on 1 Tim. 2.5.

gg. *Ep.* 190, 13.

hh. *Ep.* 190, 15.

ii. *Ep.* 143, 7, referring to *De libero arbitrio*, III, 59. Cf. above, p. 331.

jj. *Ep.* 143, 11.

kk. *Ep.* 166; it is the *De origine animae*: *Retract.*, II, 45. On this letter entrusted to Orosius in the spring of 415, see above, p. 333.

ll. *Ep.* 190, 21.

mm. *Ep.* 193, 1, *in fine*.

nn. Above, p. 311.

oo. *Ep.* 196, 16.

pp. *Ep.* 196, 16.

qq. Above, p. 253.

rr. Above, pp. 347–8.

ss. In the autumn of 411: *Sermon* 359.

tt. *Sermon* 396.

uu. Above, p. 255.

vv. The beginning of this letter is missing, and thus the address; but its content clearly identifies Possidius as its addressee: cf. M.-F. Berrouard, in *BA*, 46 B, pp. 532–4.

ww. *Ep.* 23*A, 3, *in fine*, *BA*, 46 B, pp. 376–8: *Itaque dictavi ex quo veni, id est a tertio idus Septembres usque ad kalendas Decembres, versuum ferme sex milia.* On these 'dictations', see above, pp. 215–16.

xx. *Ep.* 23*A, 3, *BA*, 46 B, p. 374.

yy. *Ep.* 23*A, 4, *BA*, 46 B, p. 378.

zz. *Contra Gaudentium*, I, 47–8.

ab. *Contra Gaudentium*, I, 15.

ac. Cf. above, p. 168.

ad. *Retract.*, II, 59.

ae. *Ep.* 23*A, 3: 'I have written again to Gaudentius, who thought he had replied to what I had originally answered.'

af. *Contra Gaudentium*, II, 5 and 10, quoting notably *Letter* 54 of St Cyprian.

ag. Above, p. 338.

ah. *Contra Gaudentium*, II, 14.

ai. *Ep.* 202 A, 1.

aj. *Ep.* 202 A, 19.

ak. *Ep.* 190: above, p. 355.

al.   *Retract.*, II, 56.

am. *Retract.*, II, 56, *initio.*

an.   Cf. above, p. 354. Perhaps Orosius, in 415, had first taken this route before carrying on to Augustine.

ao.   *Retract.*, II, 56; *De nat. et orig. animae*, II, 18.

ap.   *De nat. et orig. animae*, III, 1 and 2.

aq.   *Ep.* 23*A, 3; cf. also *Ep.* 23*, 1, addressed to Renatus and announcing the despatch of the book at the end of 419.

ar.   *De nat. et orig. animae*, III, 7, *in fine.*

as.   *De nat. et orig. animae*, II, 9.

at.   *De nat. et orig. animae*, III, 9: we shall see farther on that Augustine himself accepted the idea of a certain pre-existence.

au.   *De nat. et orig. animae*, III, 15–17.

av.   *De nat. et orig. animae*, I, 12; II, 14.

aw. *De nat. et orig. animae*, II, 16; III, 19.

ax.   *Soliloquies*, I, 7, cf. above, pp. 107–8.

ay.   Above, p. 126.

az.   *De Trinitate*, X, 9–16. Cf. below, p. 382.

ba.   *Ep.* 166, 3: *Nam quid de anima firmissime teneam non tacebo.*

bc.   *De quantitate animae*, 22.

bd.   *Ep.* 166, 4: *corpus, quod animat, non locali diffusione, sed* quadam vitali intentione porrigitur.

be.   *Ep.* 190, 4; cf. *De nat. et orig. animae*, I, 15.

bf.   *De nat. et orig. animae*, I, 16, *initio.*

bg.   *De nat. et orig. animae*, III, 11.

bh.   Cf. *Ep.* 190, 15.

bi.   *Ep.* 202 A, 6.

bj.   *Contra Iulianum*, V, 17.

bk.   *Retract.*, II, 56.

bl.   *Ep.* 23*A, 6.

bm. Cf. above, pp. 254–5 regarding Antoninus of Fussala.

bn.   But his 'inserted' presence in the episcopal jurisdiction of Cartennae was already illicit.

bo.   *Ep.* 22*, 8, *initio.*

bp.   *Ep.* 22*, 5.

bq.   *Ep.* 23*, 2.

br.   *Ep.* 22*, 7 and 11.

CHAPTER XXX

'Seek his face evermore':[a]
the *De Trinitate*

A medieval legend has it that, as Augustine was walking along the seashore, he met a young boy busily decanting water from a shell into a hole dug in the sand. The child – an angel, of course – is supposed to have told the wondering bishop that he would find it easier to fill the hole with sea than for him to explain the least iota of the mystery of the Trinity. In the classical era this scene was a favourite subject for religious paintings – to the extent of becoming a *must* in Augustinian iconography – for instance for Rubens, in a composition in which the bishop, heavily encased in his stole and surplice, complete with mitre and crozier, emphasizes the sweet smile and smooth body of the child, in whose portrayal the Antwerp artist has spared us his usual over-chubby curves.[b] The story would perhaps have amused Augustine, but it annoyed Henri-Irénée Marrou, who denounced it as a misrepresentation of the spirit that inspired the author of the *De Trinitate* in his theological quest.[1]

Very possibly, but at least it contained this much truth that, like the child with his shell, Augustine must have made a thousand attempts to complete a work that was constantly being interrupted and dictated in snatches, because his presence was required elsewhere, but also because he felt very strongly – as in the case of *De Genesi ad litteram* – that when dealing with such difficult matters the worst thing to do would be to rush it. That is why he had resisted the entreaties of those like his friend Marcellinus and bishop Florentius,[c] who in 412 were urging him to finish it. He even came to doubt, not the validity of the undertaking, but its appropriateness and fitness for the spiritual needs of the people for whom these books were intended. In a letter written in 414/15 to Evodius of Uzalis, who at the time was pressing him with questions about what knowledge one can have of God and his triune nature, he complained of the work they involved, but chiefly feared that they would be understood by only a few; and he added that in relation to them, priority must be given to those he hoped would be useful to the greatest number:[d] in other words, the homilies on the Psalms and his sermons. We shall see that his preaching was often a 'test bed' for more speculative texts.

At last, in 419, replying to Carthaginian clergy who were asking for enlightenment on the Holy Ghost, Augustine referred them to his treatise, which he was preparing to edit.[e] And shortly afterwards he sent Aurelius a dedicatory letter giving a succinct review of his long effort. 'I started these books in my youth,' he said, 'and I am publishing them in my old age.'[f] In fact, he had commenced work on them at the time when he was finishing his *Confessions*, around 400, and some fifteen years later, had been the victim of some of his followers' impatience, when they had spirited away an incomplete text. He had been very shocked by the theft, and had nearly given up on the task; but yielding to many entreaties, including those of his primate, he had finished the fifteen books and had sent them to Aurelius, granting full permission for them to be heard, read and also copied: for those times it was the equivalent of our 'passed for press'.[8] He did not, however, conceal the consequences of the theft from the bishop of Carthage. He had gone over and amended the first twelve books, but less fully than he would have wished, in order to avoid a disparity with those which, stolen when they were in rough outline, were already in circulation. If he could have kept to his first inclinations, he lamented, the work would have been much clearer and smoother.[2]

From 'learned ignorance' to the intellectual approach to God

Between 'simple faith' and the arrogant assurance of the Neoplatonist philosophers confident in their certainty of having come to know God through gnosis and intellectual asceticism, the way was narrow. The difficulty of the path chosen by Augustine, that of the 'understanding of faith' – *intellectus fidei* – held that there was a conceptual contradiction between the two terms that could be resolved only by a dialectical approach. The latter, which he had pursued throughout his life, was doubtless easier for him than others, because the experience of his conversion had instilled in him the need for that methodology; it had been a double conversion, we may recall, first of the intellect and then the will, in other words, the soul's adherence to what is at the heart of Christian faith.[h] From 'learned ignorance' to the intellectual quest for God, from the *crede ut intellegas* to the *intellege ut credas*, Augustine moved constantly between the two complementary poles of his faith.

Expressed many times, for him reverent agnosticism was not an attitude, but an article of that faith, strongly affirmed as early as the period immediately following his conversion: let us remember the words of the *De ordine*, provocative in their paradox, on the God 'whom one knows better by not knowing him', a formula of 'negative theology', doubtless suggested to the new convert by Porphyry.[3] In that period, Augustine had no illusions about the scope of our knowledge of the divine nature, fixing its limitations in the same text in a phrase imitated from Socrates: the soul, he said, knew God only by knowing how it did not know him.[i] Some years later, he would affirm no less forcefully the fundamental 'impertinence' of any discourse about God. In his *Contra Adimantum*, in 394, he ridiculed the Manichaeans who virtuously criticized the anthropomorphic ways of speaking of God in the Old Testament, 'as if it were to speak fittingly of him by not speaking of him thus'; they were, he added, way off the mark; only silence would be more respectful of his majesty than any human words.[j] Replying to Simplicianus, two years later, he made a remark in the same vein, saying that, in relation to God, he too could find some ways of speaking unworthy, if a single one that was fitting could be found when he was the subject.[4]

Augustine tackled the trinitarian expression of this Christian God only with infinite precaution and a gradual approach.[k] At Rome in 388, he was still evading the subject when he wrote: 'We must love God, the triune unity, Father, Son and Holy Ghost, of whom I will say nothing except that he is the Supreme Being.'[l] Ten or twelve years later in the final book of the *Confessions*, he came back to it with a kind of 'holy dread', in a realization of helplessness which nevertheless opened up a prospect:

> Who understands the omnipotent Trinity? Yet who among us does not speak of it, if it be indeed the Trinity he speaks of? Rare is the soul that knows whereof it speaks, whatever it may say concerning the Trinity. They dispute, they quarrel, but for want of peace no one sees that vision.[m]

Augustine had in mind the long commotion and the passions aroused by Arianism; and although the echoes of the quarrel had died down, twenty years after the council held in Constantinople in 381, debates on the nature of Christ would soon reawaken it. But he could see the time would come for him to undertake calmly an attempt to explain the mystery of the Trinity by showing that the human soul had similar structures which were themselves trinitarian; and the one that came to his mind called on our being, knowing and willing, a triad he would resume in other forms in the second part of his *De Trinitate*. But, although he could see the outline of future developments, he could also perceive all its difficulties. He concluded his provisional theories on the Trinity with a clear awareness of what was at issue: '(That), who could easily conceive of it? Who could find words to express it? Who would dare to give a verdict lightly one way or the other?'[n]

Faced with a question of this magnitude, as with others, the first reaction of a wide-ranging mind like Augustine's was one of intellectual humility that must not be seen as a pose. After a gap of thirty years, the old bishop had retained, if not the 'nervousness' and feeling of inadequacy recorded by the novice priest in 391 in his letter to Valerius,[o] at least an attitude of receptivity and constant searching. At the end of a series of answers given to questions posed by Dulcitius – the high-ranking official who had handed him the 'Gaudentius dossier'[p] – Augustine asked the tribune to inform him of possible solutions that differed from his own, and concluded with these words: 'I prefer to learn rather than teach.'[5] Addressed to a layman, this might be seen as mere courtesy, or feigned modesty; but the bishop of Hippo expressed himself no differently in a letter to Hesychius, bishop of Salonae, who had consulted him about the end of the world: a difficult question, he replied, on which he would rather 'confess a sure ignorance than a false knowledge'.[q]

In front of the faithful, the preacher was faced with a delicate exercise. He was there to teach them, and reverent agnosticism was no longer acceptable. Although his intellectual position of constant quest was unaltered, on these occasions 'learned ignorance' had its pedagogical limitations. They resulted in situations that were sometimes hard to handle, like the one reported in one of the new sermons recently brought to light. Augustine had approached the problems of the Trinity and, in particular, that of the incarnation of the Word, which is so difficult to imagine. He could see that his congregation was finding this rather a stumbling-block, and put himself in their place: 'And how shall I understand it? I do not know, I am incapable. (The Word) is both with the Father and in the Virgin's womb. Who could understand that?' This was posing the problem, continued the bishop, with the habits and words of 'carnal thinking'.[r] 'Do not cut

God into pieces', he told his flock, carefully weighing his words; they must stop thinking of him – and thus the Word – in a physical way. Yes, but a few moments before, again seized by the supreme ineffability of God, as if in parenthesis, he had in a way excused himself for inadequate expressions, which God could accept about himself only because they emanated from his wretched creatures (*parvuli*). 'If we wanted to say something worthy (of him), we would say nothing at all!'[s] This was somewhat disconcerting for his audience, who in any event reacted by relaxing their attention and chatting amongst themselves. The bishop finally brought them to order.[t]

In the trinitarian triad, the Word was decidedly the stumbling-block for the bishop's faithful. In a sermon dated 418, Augustine had chosen as his theme the superb – but not immediately understandable – text from the Prologue to St John's Gospel: 'And the Word was God'. Did the bishop realize his hearers' difficulties as he was speaking? He commented, 'I am speaking of God, so it is not surprising that you do not understand. For if you understand, it is not God!'[u] Our ignorance, he said, was more pious than a presumptuous knowledge. And he continued: to understand God, totally comprehend him (*comprehendere*) was impossible; but to touch him with one's mind (*attingere*), however slightly, was a great joy. God was 'incomprehensible' but he was not 'unthinkable'. The effort made to think of him comprises the entire undertaking of the *De Trinitate*, approached by a mind still burning to 'seek his face' (Ps. 105.4), but clear-sighted enough to declare in the middle of the work, 'When it comes to God, thought is truer than speech, and reality truer than thought.'[v]

The mystery of God

Early in the fifth century, the word *deus*, in the singular – 'God', with the capital letter that for us confers uniqueness upon him, the graphic sign of his majesty – had become of everyday use. According to Augustine, the polytheists were on their way out and atheists henceforth rare.[w] That was true, but the apparent universal monotheism, like a facade, concealed various divine contents. Without mentioning here the disparate cohorts of deists and other henotheists whose theology was woolly, if not non-existent,[x] Augustine had enough to do if, for the Latin-speaking faithful, he wanted to establish the doctrinal foundations of a genuine Christian monotheism, before bringing his intellect to bear on them by a sustained reflection on the Trinitarian structure of the human soul, made in God's image.

In a prologue to Book I which we know to be a later addition,[6] Augustine says that Holy Scripture, in its effort to place itself within the reach of human frailty, uses in its 'story' of God a metaphorical language which derives its imagery from the attributes of his creatures and the objects of his creation; but Scripture remains mute when it comes to characterizing God, or simply speaking of him apart from any reference to his creatures, a silence brought to its summit by the divine tautology of the 'eternal name': 'I am that I am' (Exod. 3.14).[y] Hence the extreme difficulty of speaking about God and, more precisely, for a Christian, about the 'persons' who make up this 'one and triune' God. The Judaic Bible had already offered an initial trinitarian configuration, with God, Creator of heaven and earth, the Word of God (his *Logos*, his *Verbum*), the divine instrument of this creation, and the Spirit of God, who revealed himself to the prophets to inspire them. But with Jesus the Gospels had enriched this scheme and made it more complex by introducing an element that disturbed its transcendental equilibrium. Already, for the first Christian generations, the divine Trinity had appeared to be formed as it was for Augustine. It comprised God, Creator of heaven and earth, revealed in the Old Testament; Jesus, united with a God whom he called his Father[z] by virtue of a unique filial relationship that must be understood by analogy – the language of creatures, as Augustine said; lastly, the Holy Ghost, who had already manifested itself by inspiring the prophets, who at Pentecost had descended upon the apostles,[aa] and who, according to the Christian faith, continued to breathe on the Church and communities of the faithful.

As such, this so to speak 'raw' content of the Trinity was imposed on all Christians. The problems began with the perception of the relationships between its various components, particularly regarding the Father and the Son. Even if it were understood analogically and not biologically, the difficulty of qualifying the 'persons' in their relationship to one another meant that theological thinking had to steer between several pitfalls. If divine unity was to be preserved at all costs and without risk, there was a temptation to consider the ensemble of the Trinity in a purely nominalist, or modalist, fashion: nothing really differentiated between the Father, Son and Holy Ghost, who were but three aspects of a single God. That had been the interpretation by a certain Sabellius, in third-century Rome, justly condemned as a heretic because this modalist view, with its lack of distinction between the 'persons', involved the inadmissible consequence that God himself had died on the Cross. Orthodoxy – and Augustine insisted on this point – not only maintained the true distinction between Father and Son, but also perceived a dual nature in Christ: in him man, and not God, had suffered the Passion.[bb] Divine transcendence was thus saved.

To escape the accusation of 'tritheism' – the notion of three gods in one – which the pagans did not spare in their caricature of Christianity, there was a great temptation to accentuate more clearly the real distinction between the persons. That is what a priest from Alexandria, named Arius, had done at the beginning of the fourth century. To his way of thinking, the Son was a creation of the Father, and had come into existence by the act of the Father; and as that creation had been conceived by him as timeless, happening before time and before the world, Arius had not introduced a historical event into a theogony, but rather a principle of hierarchic subordination: proceeding from the Father, the Son, God's *logos*, was both posterior and inferior to him. It was a philosophical explanation of the mystery of the incarnation, in a conceptual framework that belonged to Neoplatonist speculation, a descending type of triad being superimposed on the Judaeo-Christian triad, in which the 'hypostases' are distinct but not hierarchized.[7]

We know about the impassioned debate that followed, a long crisis of more than sixty years, marked by interventions from the imperial government, constantly complicated by the linguistic incompatibilities of Greek East and Latin West, and characterized by the massive invasion of the categories of Aristotelian logic into theological discourse.[8] The intrusion of philosophical analysis in the comprehension of a God conceived as a plurality of 'persons' in a divine unity was inevitable, but its first consequence was necessarily that the (Greek) terms used as discriminants to describe the nature of the 'persons' in relation to one another were not 'scriptural'. In the Scriptures one could find neither the idea of *homoousios* – consubstantiality – affirmed at Nicaea in 325 and confirmed at Constantinople in 381, nor that of *homoiousios* – of a more external than truly substantial likeness, adopted at Rimini and Seleucia in 359, that 'homeism' which was to become the basis of the belatedly Christianized Germanic peoples' credo, before they invaded all the West and disseminated this watered-down Arianism. In the controversies, people hurled these key words at one another's heads, while rejecting those of their adversaries on the grounds that they were not 'scriptural' – but that was true of both sides! Augustine could not fail to remember his exchanges, around 405–10, with Pascentius, an Arian high-ranking civil servant in the fiscal administration. Pascentius had challenged Alypius and Augustine to show him the word *hom(o)ousion* in the Scriptures, and they had had to agree that in fact it was not there.[cc] But, retorted Augustine, the same could be said for *ingenitus* ('not begotten') to which Pascentius clung with regard to God the Father: it was no reason for not admitting the idea, commented the bishop, who adhered to it no less than did the Arian notable.[dd] The lesson to be learnt was that the Scriptures should be read with the aim of finding in them, by inductive reasoning, what almost age-old ideological sparring had frozen in a militant vocabulary.

This was the target Augustine set himself when he approached his lengthy undertaking; that is, in his own words, 'the justification of this statement: the Trinity is the one true God, and it is correct to say, believe and think that the Father, Son and Holy Ghost are one and the same substance or essence'.[ee] And it was by seeking answers in the Scriptures that one must look for the way that leads to him of whom it was said, 'Seek his face evermore!'[ff] (Ps. 105.4). But to Augustine, on the threshold of a treatise whose importance he knew and whose difficulties he foresaw, it seemed that he must first fix the terms clearly, explaining his own credo in the wake of his orthodox predecessors:

> All the Catholic interpreters of the Old and New Testament have proposed to show, in keeping with the Scriptures, that the Father, Son and Holy Ghost, in their indivisible equality[9] of one and the same substance, testify to their divine oneness; thus that they are not three gods, but a single God, although the Father begot the Son, and therefore the Son is not identical to the Father, and the Son was begotten by the Father, and therefore the Father is not identical to the Son, and although the Holy Ghost is neither the Father nor the Son, but only the Spirit of the Father and the Son, equal to the Father and the Son by belonging to the unity of the Trinity.

He continued with an initial affirmation of the distinction between their personal manifestations:

> It is not, however, the Trinity itself which was born of the Virgin Mary, was crucified and buried under Pontius Pilate, and on the third day rose again and ascended into heaven: that was the Son only. Nor was it the Trinity which, in the form of a dove, descended on Jesus on the day of his baptism (Matt. 3.16); nor on the day of Pentecost, after the Lord's Ascension, in the midst of a celestial roaring like that of a violent storm,

did it descend in separate tongues of flame on each of the apostles (Acts 2.1–4): that was the Holy Ghost alone. It was not the Trinity that said to Christ from the heights of heaven, 'Thou art my beloved son' (Mark 1.11), while John was baptizing him or on the mountain when the three disciples were with him (Matt. 17.5), or when the voice resounded from heaven saying, 'I have glorified it, and will glorify it again' (John 12.28): that was only the voice of the Father speaking to the Son. And yet the Father, Son and Holy Ghost, in the same way that they are inseparable, act inseparably.

'That is my faith,' Augustine concluded, 'because that is the Catholic faith.'[gg]

He knew, however, that it was not enough to detail the symbol of faith, as he had just done, to smooth out all the difficulties on behalf of those trying to understand how this Trinity could act indivisibly. As he would explain further on, it was a matter of getting them to accept, by means of carefully chosen examples from the Scriptures, 'how, in this Trinity, what pertains to all the "persons" is attributed to each, by virtue of the inseparable action of their single and identical substance'.[hh] In this demonstration, the bishop was careful not to omit the Holy Ghost, regarding which, in his dogmatic speech delivered before the council at Hippo in 393, the priest had regretted that this subject had not exercised the exegetists' skill as much as the Father and the Son.[ii] He will not fail to state its perfect divine equality with the other two persons,[jj] although he postpones to the end of his treatise, in Book XV, the detailed exposition of its own nature, its 'specific property', so to speak – which is to be love, and the inspiration of love – in the bosom of the divine Trinity.[kk] But in this section of the work he gave greater attention to the relationship of the Son with the Father, noting the presence in the Scriptures of texts which 'suggest or even openly declare' that because of the incarnation the Son is inferior to the Father; for instance, the affirmation of Christ himself in John (14.28): 'My Father is greater than I', a line that the Arians did not fail to exploit in a 'subordinationist' sense.[10] That was an opportune moment for Augustine to bring in the 'rule of discernment' which he drew from St Paul: 'He who, being of divine nature, would not take advantage of being equal with God, but made himself of no reputation and took upon himself the form of a servant (*formam servi*) and was made in the likeness of men' (Phil. 2.6–7).[11] All the rest of the first book is devoted to making the distinction in Christ between what pertains to his humanity (*forma servi*) and what to his divinity (*forma dei*).

The theme is resumed at the start of the following book for, Augustine notes, one may read ambiguous expressions in the New Testament and not know which way to interpret them: either about the 'inferiority' of the Son for having assumed the state of a creature, or about the origin he derives from the Father, despite his equal status with him. In the second respect, the bishop distinguishes another rule: yes, the Son proceeds from the Father, comes from him, but this *nativitas* does not mean *inaequalitas*; and this rule applies also to the Holy Ghost.[ll] But Augustine was well aware that the 'subordinationists' did not consider themselves defeated, and they returned to the attack at sight of another verse from John: 'Whom the Father will send in my name' (John 14.26), relating to the Holy Ghost, sent like Christ himself. Now, they objected, the sender is superior to the one sent.[12] The reply consisted in saying, on the basis of other texts from the Fourth Gospel – John 1.10–11; 16.28 – that the Son, like the Holy Ghost, had been sent to where they already were, by virtue of an eternal immanence. The problem remained, however, that nowhere in the Scriptures do we read of the Father alone having been sent.[mm] The 'missions' of the two other 'persons' were clearly identified in the texts, for those who knew how to interpret them. That of the Son was his incarnation, to which I will return at length; those of the Holy Ghost had to be recognized in its interventions in visible form – the dove over Christ and the tongues of flame over the apostles.[nn] But why was there no mention of 'mission' relating to the Father, with regard to those material and perceptible phenomena through which his presence was revealed in the Old Testament, for example the burning bush?[oo] How should one account for this difference in treatment which seemed to introduce a distinction between the three 'persons' of the divine Trinity?

This was to pose the difficult problem of theophanies and the question of knowing how to distinguish them from 'missions'. There were, in fact, three questions. First, to ascertain who, in the Old Testament, had manifested himself to the Patriarchs – Father, Son or Holy Ghost, or the Trinity itself, without any distinction of 'persons'? It also must be asked whether these appearances were produced through the intermediary of creatures formed for that purpose, or by angels. Lastly, before the incarnation, had there been 'missions' of the Son and the Holy Ghost, and if so, what differences were there between those and the ones recorded in the Gospels? Books II, III and IV of the work successively answer all those questions. The first chapters of Genesis at once served Augustine as a test-bed for the method he could employ in his replies. For he could not avoid the first of these theophanies, the most famous and also the one with the heaviest consequences for humankind, the reproof of Adam in the Garden of Eden.[pp] Was it purely auditory, and did it rule out a visible manifestation of God? The bishop was hesitant: 'it cannot be said that there was only the sound of a voice, when it is written that God was walking; nor can one say that the one who was walking in that place was invisible, because Adam himself says that he had hidden from God'.[qq] And whatever form it had taken, who had instigated that theophany? Who was that walker in the first garden? Biblical syntax, Augustine recognized, did not distinguish 'persons'. It would seem to have been God the Father himself, he who in the introductory account of the Creation says *Fiat lux*; but it cannot be ruled out that, as later to Abraham beneath the oak of Mamre (Gen. 18.1), he manifested himself first to Adam, 'through the meek intermediary of a changeable and visible creature, yet remaining immutable and invisible in himself and in his substance'.[13] Augustine preferred not to conclude for the time being, and left open the possibility that the first theophany might have involved the indivisible Trinity.[rr] This initial encounter with the Scriptures immediately revealed all the difficulties of the undertaking.

At the end of Book III, with the help of further reflection, the bishop returns not to Adam but to the story of Abraham, and states firmly that, as to Noah before him and Jacob and Moses after him, God did not appear directly, but through the intermediary of angels.[ss] It remained to be shown how the 'mission' of the Son – and of the Holy Ghost – was distinct from these Judaic theophanies. This 'mission' was the incarnation, clearly defined for Christian thinking from St Paul: 'When the fullness of the time was come, God sent forth his Son, made of a woman' (Gal. 4.4). It is the subject of the next book, and the incantatory and mystical tone of its opening at once gives the sense of the importance Augustine ascribes to this exegesis, and what existential echoes it awakens in him.[tt] Two texts immediately spring to his mind: first, the one from the Epistle to the Romans which says so superbly that God proved his love for humankind by sending his Son for this 'mission' of salvation (Rom. 5.8–10). Next, the Prologue to John's Gospel, which had been one of the founding texts of his Christology ever since the decisive days at the end of the Milanese spring in 386. And how could he not relive in his mind those feverish weeks he had subsequently experienced, when commenting on this verse: 'But the light shineth in the darkness, and the darkness comprehended it not' (John 1.5), which he interpreted as, 'this darkness is the demented souls of men, blinded by the depravity of cupidity and lack of faith'?[uu] The Lord, he continues, has doubly redeemed us, in that double 'reality' which we are, in body and soul.[vv] To pay for our double death, the Saviour gave his own and only death.

One and two make three, Augustine notes, and the total of these three figures is six, the first of the 'perfect numbers', equal to the sum of its divisors.[ww] This is the start of what a modern reader, rather pressed for time, will identify with some astonishment as an arithmological digression to the glory of the number six, such a frequent symbol of perfection in the Scriptures, as the bishop shows, from the six days of the Creation to the thirty-six (square of six) hours that elapsed from the evening of Christ's entombment until the morning of his resurrection.[xx] And if modern readers remain sceptical about this numerical symbolism, they will not be altogether wrong, the more so because Augustine, who nevertheless would have liked to see some mystical meaning in it, acknowledges, as the good Pythagorean which in some respects he had remained, that his readers may themselves find other, equally likely, perhaps even preferable, reasons behind it.[yy] But it would be somewhat naïve on our part to express surprise at finding this cultural heritage weighing so persistently on the old bishop. Regarding the number six, he can be even more surprising, for instance when, in his treatise on Genesis, he declares without turning a hair that if God completed the Creation of the world in six days, the number is not perfect because God kept to it: if he kept to it, it was because the number six is perfect![zz]

At times disconcerting, the *De Trinitate*, like the subject itself, is always a difficult book, constantly abandoned and resumed by its author over some twenty years. It is frequently stitched together by associations of ideas: unless it was guided by the preceding numerical considerations, assuredly eloquent images of the 'many', how else could we understand the evocation of the coming of Christ, the sole mediator, who brings together the many in one? This 'hymn to the One and Only', in the middle of the great first part of the treatise, is the culminating point of Book IV:

> It was fitting that at the will and command of a compassionate God, the many should themselves acclaim the coming of the One; and that amid the cries of the many the One should come, and that the many should testify together that the One had come; and that, freed from the burden of the many, we should come to him, the One; and that being dead in spirit through many sins, doomed to die in the flesh because of sin, we should love him who, without sin, died in the flesh for us, the One and Only; and that we, having faith in his resurrection and rising ourselves with him in spirit through faith, we

should be made one in the one just One; and that we should not despair of ourselves rising in the flesh when we observed that we, the many members, had been preceded by the one head: may we in him, purified now by faith and later made whole again by sight, thus fully reconciled to God by the Mediator, cling to the One, enjoy the One and dwell forever in the One.[ab]

The theme of Christ's mediation is thus the central theme of these pages devoted to the 'mission' of the Son; and it is constructed in the form of a diptych in which the opponents are humility and pride, the mediation for life and the mediation for death, Jesus and the devil. I said earlier that the bishop's sermons often served as a test-bed for large sections of the theologian's treatises. That seems to have been the case in this instance, if we return to the newly-published great sermon to which I have already referred for the details it gives on the lines followed by Augustine in his debate with the pagans.[ac] In both texts he paints the same portrait of the devil, who had taken good care not to go where he was leading man, 'for though in his ungodliness he is spiritually dead, he has not suffered the death of the flesh, since he was never clad in it'.[ad] He had therefore retained great prestige in the eyes of the common herd, who were seduced by the magicians' sleight-of-hand, but also for loftier and more intellectually demanding souls, to whom he suggests purification rites in the temples – 'sacrilegious rites': *sacra sacrilega* – by means of real theurgic performances.[ae] In Book X of the *City of God*, Augustine would manage to settle scores with the diabolical feats of paganism's magi, by contrasting the visible miracles of the invisible God.[af] But here this figure of the devil, the antithesis of Christ, the only true mediator, seems to be at least approximately dated by parallel approaches in the sermon preached at Hippo or Carthage on 1 January 404.[14]

One 'Being', three 'Persons'

Having reached this stage in his work, Augustine could not escape debate with the Arians, on their own ground, with their 'so guileful argumentation' (*versutissima argumenta*),[ag] that of a philosophical discourse perceptibly distanced from scriptural realities, in which the categories of Aristotelian logic occurred.

Of all the adversaries he had had to confront, on the ideological, doctrinal or even ecclesiological plane, from the Manichaeans to the Pelagians, by way of the Donatists – and the pagans – the upholders of Arianism were the only ones with whom he had at first had only an indirect and 'bookish' acquaintance. Of course, he had gained his first experience of the heretical Church long before, back in the Milanese spring of 386. But it may be recalled – above, pp. 80–1 – that he had been present as an outsider, without being personally involved, except through Monica, in Ambrose's disputes with that community. Then he had returned to his Africa which at that time was virtually free of the Arian heresy. Arianism had not been a problem for the bishop at Hippo until the end of the first decade of the fifth century. The Donatists were quite enough, as he said in a sermon prior to 411, in which he rejoiced that at least he did not have to have a brush with the 'Eunomians', as in the East: each has his own cross to bear.[ah]

But the waves of Italian refugees in the autumn of 410 had carried some of this scum with them: the bishop could now see a few of these heretics before him in the church, mingled with his flock.[ai] Between the frequently lasting consequences of this migration and the growing penetration of Arians into higher government posts and the armed forces, Augustine's opportunities for contact with the heresy's followers had multiplied. In common with Alypius, he had had exchanges with Pascentius. Around the same period, the two bishops, once more working together, had successfully undertaken the conversion from Arianism of a certain Maximus, who practised medicine at Thaenae in Byzacena (Henchir Thina, on the south side of the Tunisian Sahel).[aj] In the autumn of 419, in the midst of all that was awaiting him on his return from Carthage, Augustine had found an Arian *libellus* sent to him by Dionysius, one of his friends, who lived in a township, Vicus Iuliani, on the southern confines of the diocese of Hippo;[ak] a sign that at that time there were henceforth enough Arians in the region for their texts to be in circulation. In this instance, it was a sort of 'catechism' in thirty-four very short articles, excepting the last. In the *Retractations*, the bishop would say that his correspondent had urged him to answer it,[al] insisting quite un-necessarily, for Augustine was now well aware that the 'Eunomian' gangrene had reached his Africa and was not the sort of ill to be treated with disdain; in any case, that was not his way, and the *Contra sermonem arianorum* that he dictated forthwith was a point-by-point refutation of this catalogue of heretical propositions. Indeed, it was no longer a question of ignoring the 'Eunomians': two years later, he rejoiced before his flock over the conversion of one of them, while deploring three others' persistence in the heresy, in Hippo itself.[am] Arianism had scarcely been one of Augustine's worries at the start of his episcopacy, but in the end it had caught up with him: one of the last controversies he would have to engage in, less than three years before his death, was with Maximinus, an Arian bishop from Illyria. He had landed with the entourage of the new Count of Africa, the Goth Sigisvult, dispatched against Bonifatius, who had entered on a rebellion against the Court of Ravenna: Maximinus versus Augustine was in some way the spiritual version of that confrontation. Despite the Arian's boastfulness, the bishop of Hippo emerged with the advantage.[an]

In terms of pastoral duties, the anti-Arian struggle came last in the long list of battles waged by Augustine, and there is no doubt that it gave him the opportunity to enrich and hone his knowledge of certain points in the heresy as it was then being spread through the western Empire; but he had not needed the *Sermo arianorum* to fall into his hands in the autumn of 419 in order to know what he had to deal with on the essentials of its theology.

In Books V, VI and VII of the *De Trinitate*, Augustine attempts to refute it fundamentally, in long developments that smack of a composition which has been spread over too long a period of time, and is not free of resumptions, if not repetitions. To start with, we can see this Latin-speaker quite obviously hindered by the translation into his language of concepts elaborated in Greek by eastern theology. In the first place, not to tackle the conceptual problematics of the three components of the Trinity straight away, it was a matter of settling the most appropriate Latin term for saying what they had in common in the divine unity. The Greeks used *ousia*, which is the 'Being' in Platonic language; but in that of the eastern theologians the word wavered between two meanings: 'substance', but also the universal 'essence'. In their confusion, the Latin-speaking Fathers had transcribed the Greek word without translating it. The first among them,

Tertullian, had chosen to translate, and had rejected *essentia* in favour of *substantia* to express that one and the same spiritual material formed the being of the three divine realities.[15] At first, Augustine was hard put to it to decide between the two, although he can be seen to lean towards *essentia*.[ao] He would later recognize that by doing so he was going against custom, which favoured the word *substantia*.[ap] But matters became complicated when arguing about the formula for the Trinity. The Greeks said *mia ousia, tres hypostaseis*, one 'being' (or 'essence', or 'substance'), three 'hypostases'. In a letter addressed to Pope Damasus, Jerome had already rebelled against this vocabulary which, translated into Latin, ended up as a sacrilegious absurdity, for *hypo-stasis* could only be rendered by the word which is the copy of its components, *sub-stantia*; thus the Greek formula for the Trinity became in Latin: one 'essence' (or 'substance'), three substances![aq] In his treatise, Augustine picks out what ends up in Latin as an absurd tautology: 'The Greeks,' he says, 'also use the word "hypostasis", but I do not know what difference they make between *ousia* and *hypostasis*.'[ar] He would have known had he read Basil of Caesarea, especially one of his later letters, addressed to bishop Amphilocus, in which the Cappadocian attempted to distinguish what was common to the three components of the Trinity (*ousia*) from what was peculiar to each of them (*hypostasis*).[as] A little later, another Cappadocian, Gregory of Nazianzen, returning to the trinitarian formula in his famous eulogy of Athanasius of Alexandria, justified the use of the word 'hypostasis' in the same sense. 'The substance (*ousia*)', he said, 'designates the nature of the deity, whereas the "hypostasis" designates the properties of the three.' And, mocking the Latins, 'The Italians think the same but, because of the narrowness of their language and paucity of their vocabulary, are incapable of distinguishing between substance (*ousia*) and hypostasis. That is why they have introduced the "persons" in their place (in Greek: *ta prosopa*).'[at]

The introduction had taken place long ago in the West, as the actual distinction between the three 'persons' had made its appearance at the very beginning of the third century in Tertullian's *Adversus Praxean*.[16] But the Carthaginian's formula, *una substantia, tres personae*, became in the East: *mia ousia, tria prosopa*, where the last word seemed to Greek theologians to add dangerous fuel to Sabellius' modalist heresy. They therefore preferred to keep to 'hypostases' – bad luck for the Latins! Augustine remained faithful to the 'persons', but without much enthusiasm, with his constant mistrust for the human language that claims to express the inexpressible. 'One says "three persons", but less to say it than to be reduced to silence!'[au] But the problem, which was not only philological, bothered him; he returned to it at length in Book VII. He admits that God's transcendence is beyond the resources of our vocabulary, and once again sieves through the words used: for instance, 'person' – unknown in the Scriptures, though they do not contradict it; he discusses its aptness, in the place of the Greek 'substance' (*hypostasis*), to accept finally that the term matters little, provided that theological thinking strongly affirms the individuality of the three components of the Trinity in their sovereign equality and indivisible unity.[av] And to speak of that divine unity, the *ousia* of the Greeks, he calls into question Tertullian's *substantia*, but for the wrong reason, which astounds us and would have surprised his childhood's grammar teachers, by erroneously connecting it with *subsistere* (instead of *substare*). Indeed, it cannot be said of God that he 'subsists'.[aw] He definitively prefers *essentia* to *substantia*, for the right reason, for *essentia* comes from *esse*, 'to be' in the absolute and transcendent sense of the word in the 'eternal name' revealed to Moses (Exod. 3.14). In the last analysis, the Augustinian formula would be *una essentia, tres personae*.[ax]

If there is one lesson to be learnt from these pages, as Augustine wanted, it is that one should not cling too much to the 'straw of words'. We have seen with what caution the bishop refrained as far as possible in his sermons (in other words in what he said in front of his ordinary faithful), from using terms which were hallowed by theologians' use, but ambiguous or dangerous for hearers who did not possess the key; the word 'persons' was a case in point.[17] In speculative reflection on the Trinity, it could be used only as a tool, handling it with the 'tweezers' conveniently furnished by quotation marks in our translations, and making use of it, with all due precautions, to refute Arian propositions. The heretics,[18] referring to Aristotelian categories, claimed that all that was said of God was so not from the point of view of 'accident', but of 'substance'. In their view, to be 'not begotten', for the Father, concerned his substance, as 'begotten' did for the Son. From that they drew the conclusion – unanswerable in their view – that the Father and the Son could not be of the same substance.[ay] The first answer, retorted Augustine, was scriptural: the Son himself had said 'I and my Father are one' (John 10.30). But he did not neglect logical argument, and demonstrated that 'not begotten' and 'begotten', just like the terms 'Father' and 'Son', far from having to be understood in the substantial sense, designated 'relationships' in the heart of the single divine 'substance' (or 'essence').[az] In Book VI, which was very short, Augustine came up against the argument of non-consubstantiality which the Arians derived from the Apostle's words, 'Christ is the power of God, and the wisdom of God' (1 Cor. 1.24). He returned to it in the next book and, at the price of a close-knit and condensed argumentation, arrived at dogmatic positions which would subsequently remain anchoring points for all theological contemplation: the 'essential' attributes are not the 'personal' properties; they are only appropriate to the 'persons' making up the divine Trinity. The Father is not wise with the wisdom he has begotten, as if the Son alone were wisdom and the Father, considered as apart from the Son, had no part in it. If St Paul calls the Son the wisdom of the Father, it is because he is wisdom that has proceeded from the Father's wisdom: each in himself is wise, and the two together make one and the same wisdom in their unity.[ba]

Images of God

If Augustine had been content to split hairs over the 'persons' and confined himself to a dry refutation of Arianism, the *De Trinitate* would have been no more than a fundamental text of the theology of Christianity – though that in itself would have been quite a feat! In this vast diptych, the seven books devoted to seeking and setting out the dogmatic truths are matched by eight other books centred on a quest undertaken *modo interiore*, as the author says,[bc] in other words, dedicated by way of a long contemplative analysis to capturing the images of God – themselves Trinitarian – in his creation. This second and very beautiful part of the *De Trinitate* thus combines psychology and metaphysics, anthropology and theology. In these pages, for the first time the bishop pursues in a dual approach the twofold aim he had set himself just after his conversion: to know the soul and to know God, striving to attain God through his reflections in the human soul and, more broadly, to reascend to the Creator by starting from the traces of himself that he has left in his creation. And throughout this meditation, which is so Augustinian in inspiration and progress, he constantly provides food for the theologians.

Book VIII serves as an introduction to this very personal inquiry, in the form of a 'discourse on method'. The images of the triune God which Augustine hopes to discover in the soul lie at its finest point, in the *animus* (or in the *mens*), and not in the *anima*, the vital principle that we share with animals.[bd] The soul was created good, but is kept at its peak only by its voluntary conversion to the supreme good.[be] It must cleave to God through love. But how can it love what it does not know? Theological virtues will come to its aid, 'but how can faith enable us to love that Trinity whom we know not?'[bf] Augustine shows that the path of rational knowledge is a dead end, that our intellectual knowledge of the 'good' and 'just' does not by itself bring about our adherence, it is through love that we attach ourselves to the ideal which thinking allows us to glimpse.[bg] Love is in itself the principle of the knowledge of God, which answers the questions posed earlier, true love – *vera dilectio*, which is quite different from 'desire' – which comes from God and relates back to him.[bh] Whoever is filled with this love is filled with God, says Augustine, paraphrasing 1 John 4.16.[bi] Even in carnal and profane love, there is no love without an object: 'What, then, is love, if not a certain life that unites two beings or tends to unite them, the one who loves and the one who is loved?' Which suggests to the bishop the recognition in the soul of a first triadic 'graft' of the Trinity: the subject who loves, the object loved and love itself.[bj]

This is only an initial approach, immediately deemed unsatisfying.[bk] Hardly has it taken shape, when it is demolished in the next book. Augustine bids farewell to the loved object and brings the soul and its love for itself face to face. It cannot love itself if it does not know itself. Thus one reaches another triad: the soul itself, the love it has for itself and its knowledge of itself.[bl] More stable, this triad is also substantially homogeneous: the love the soul has for itself is equal to it, as is the knowledge it has of itself; what it loves is on its own level, neither above it, like God, nor beneath, like the body. The three 'persons' in this triad are equal among themselves and consubstantial, and they form a unity. Says Augustine, concluding this book:

> And there is an image of the Trinity: the soul (*mens*), its knowledge, which is its progeny and its word begotten by itself, and in the third place, love; and these three are one and the same substance. Its progeny is not smaller, since the soul knows itself just as it is, nor is love smaller, since the soul loves itself as much as it knows itself and as much as it is.[bm]

Of the three concepts of the triad over which Augustine pauses, it is the second, knowledge, which is taken up to be examined more deeply in the following book. Here the dialectical progression is remarkable. There can be no possible knowledge without the longing for it. Was the bishop remembering here his conversations of some twenty years before with his prematurely dead son, Adeodatus?[bn] His reflections began from the 'sign' which the word is, if it is perceived as such, curiously taking as his example an obsolete old Latin word which meant 'unadulterated wine', *temetum*. He who does not know it will desire to know its meaning by virtue of an ideal of intelligibility peculiar to the human mind, and which is akin to an amorous quest.[bo] The same applies to the soul vis-à-vis itself. 'It knows what knowing is, and as it loves what it knows, it also desires to know itself.'[bp] In fact, continues Augustine, in a Plotinian sort of approach,[19] the soul already knows itself as a seeking subject, 'completely present to itself': what is missing is the object of the quest, not the subject which is seeking.[bq] While the intuitive or implicit knowledge (*notitia*) it has of itself is good, through the action of a kind of Platonic recollection – though here it is a matter of traces of God in itself – the meditative knowledge (*cogitatio*) it develops risks dragging it to its downfall: drawn out of itself (and diverted from God) by its attraction to external things, the soul, retiring into itself to think about itself, returns laden with corporeal images and tends to think of itself in their likeness: 'It is assimilated to these images, not by its being but by its thinking.'[br] And the bishop again berates the error of the materialist philosophers, who conceive of the soul in corporeal terms, and explains by applying a Socratic 'know thyself' to the soul in a sort of exhortation: 'Let it not try to know itself as if it were unaware of itself, but let it recognize itself as distinct from what it knows is not itself!'[bs] At this stage of his meditation, the analysis of a sort of *cogito* enables a distinction to be made between the components of a new triad, composed of the three acts or faculties peculiar to the soul alone: memory, intellect and will.[bt] In the letter to Evodius, already quoted, around 414/15, Augustine took the example of this triad to get his colleague and old companion to understand by analogy the indivisible action of the divine Trinity: these three faculties, he said, are in the soul, but the soul cannot be summed up in any one of the three.[bu] And in a probably contemporary great sermon, the bishop gained much success among his faithful by showing them that, though to varying degrees, they all enjoyed these three faculties, which were clearly distinct from one another but operated together in their mind, in the same way that the three 'persons' of the Trinity operated inseparably in God.[bv] But in that sermon, the preacher had mentioned memory, intellect and will only by way of comparison, with the aim of teaching. To rediscover in man vestiges of God that were sufficiently demonstrative of a truly trinitarian imprint, it was necessary to pursue the *exercitatio animi*.

Readers who are unfamiliar with Augustinian dialectic may perhaps feel they are regressing when tackling the next book, in which we see Augustine undertake to seek an image of the Trinity that is easier to grasp in the 'outward man' (2 Cor. 4.16), involved in the physical world. The perception, notably visual, that he has is easily divisible into three components: the object seen, its 'retinal'[bw] image, as we might call it, and our will to perceive, which Augustine calls *intentio*. The recollection of the physical thing perceived, which is also the concern of the 'outward man', supplies a second triad: the memory of the perception, the mental image of it that remains,[bx] and the will that unites one to the other in the elaboration of this mental image. These analyses of the act of perceiving and the processes of recollection and imaginative reproduction are exercises of great virtuosity, but the bishop has to admit that the two triads are all too reliant on the perceptible to be taken for traces of God in the 'outward man'. Book XII therefore returns to the 'inward man', who vocation is to contemplate the intelligible and immutable truths, leaving it to the 'outward man' to grapple with the world and take action with temporal things.[by] Of course, it is in his unity that man has been made in God's image, but the traces of the Trinity are to be found in the 'inward man'.

In order to make himself more clearly understood, the bishop resumes the allegorical exegesis of the beginning of Genesis, firmly repulsing the ideas of those – notably the gnostics – who sought to see the image of the divine Trinity in the human family. The words 'Let us make man in our image' (Gen. 1.26) already challenged that sufficiently. Augustine adds that if it had to be admitted that the image of the Trinity was the father, mother and child, one would also have to say that man was not in God's image before a woman was made for him and a child born of them.[bz] He similarly refuses to share the opinion of some exegetists who, noting in the unity of the human creature (*homo*) the marriage of contemplative reason and active reason, tried to attribute the spirit to the man (*vir*) and bodily sense to the woman (*mulier*).[ca] But he comes up against this famous text from St Paul: 'A man ought not to cover his head, forasmuch as he is the image and glory of God; but the woman is the glory of the man' (1 Cor. 11.7). How could this be reconciled with the one in Genesis (1.27–8), which he read with a punctuation intended to emphasize the idea that every human creature is made in God's image: 'He created them male and female'?[20]

Here one cannot escape a brief digression on what is known as Augustine's 'antifeminism', if only to reduce it to its true proportions, or even to discover that it is really non-existent, at least according to the criteria of the period. As a good disciple of St Paul, the bishop publicly advocated the equality of wife and husband in their sexual life. To quote just one text, this equality is proclaimed in one of the recently published sermons, belonging to the series preached in the summer of 397, at the beginning of his episcopacy: in this matter, says Augustine, echoing 1 Cor. 7.4, the condition of both is equal.[cb] And, in another sermon, addressing the women present – wives, of course – he had no hesitation in saying: 'In matters of this kind, claim your rights!'[cd] But things were not the same in the others. The two texts quoted make no mystery of the woman's subordination to her husband;[ce] the wife was her husband's servant,[cf] as Monica had been to Patricius, though happy not to have been his slave or 'whipping-boy', we may recall. Our conscience is entitled to be offended, provided we do not forget that, until quite recently, this feminine status of subservience was still the rule in our societies and that it persists, scarcely toned down, in many cultures across the world. It must be added that working conditions in those days, in the area of economic production as well as in day-to-day living, rested largely on physical capabilities: here women's inferiority was obvious, and their social status naturally reflected this. But Augustine was a million miles from thinking that the image of God lay in the body. For him, men and women had equal potential in matters of spirituality and faith. In Book XII of *De Trinitate*, he says so expressly: the image of God dwells only in that part of the human soul which clings to eternal things to contemplate them or draw inspiration from them, and women as much as men are clearly endowed with that part.[cg] What, then, of the veil placed by St Paul on the head of woman alone? Augustine no longer thought as he had done some years before in his first interpretation of 1 Cor. 11.7 that 'women, by the very fact of being women, represent that part of the soul that is concupiscence';[ch] but in the couple who in conjunction were the male and female *homo* created by God, woman always symbolized for him the part which applied to lower realities, action in the world: the veil on her head was the religious emblem of a constraint that needed to be exerted over her, a sort of spiritual guard-rail.[ci] However, it could happen that woman could represent the 'inward man' to the highest degree: in the Gospel, it was Mary contrasted with Martha,[21] and also, in the bishop's own experience, Therasia beside Paulinus of Nola, Anapsychia beside the beloved Marcellinus and Melania beside Pinianus, but also the virgin Demetrias in Rome, the virgin Sapida in Carthage, the *famulae dei* who, rich or poor, by sublimating sex had retained and developed the best part of the soul in themselves. The paradox then was that these women who had taken the veil were the ones who least needed to . . .

The functional dichotomy of the soul, divided between dealing with the temporal and contemplating the eternal, finds means to blossom in man's two loftiest activities, knowledge and wisdom.[cj] The distinction between the two, but also the relation between them, are the subject of a transitional discussion between Books XII and XIII. The exposition is powerful, the thinking firm. For anyone who settles on knowledge (*scientia*) to make it an end in itself, there is a risk that wisdom (*sapientia*) will remain inaccessible. Augustine is not content to say, as we might these days be tempted to do in order to escape lightly from the problem, that wisdom does not rest on any scientific certainty, and that a scientific certainty could not lead to any wisdom. He admits that, to illuminate its path, wisdom needs a knowledge situated somewhere between perception of the physical world and intuition of the divine: it is not a question of sacrificing one for the other. But if a hierarchy is to be established between wisdom, the intellectual knowledge of eternal realities, and science, the rational knowledge of temporal realities, 'no one would doubt that the first should be preferred to the second'.[ck]

At the beginning of Book XIII, a long quotation from the Prologue to John's Gospel extends the distinction previously made between knowledge and wisdom. In this text, the evocation of the coming of the divine – the one and only God – into our history is related to this sort of 'knowledge', which is attained principally through faith. A subtle dialectical shift takes Augustine from the uniqueness of faith to the universality of the desire for happiness that impels humankind.[cl] Then the *Hortensius*, the book that initiated his spiritual life in his youth, comes to his mind: 'Without a doubt,' wrote Cicero, 'we all want to be happy.' In the autumn of 386, in the *De beata vita*, Augustine was already stating that he who possessed God was happy.[cm] The same conclusion would be reached by way of a new definition of the sovereign good, access to immortality, 'for, without immortality, there is no happiness'.[cn] Here we have the transition from a philosophical reflection to a theological meditation: this happy life which philosophy can procure for us in this world, but which death makes us lose, faith can assure us of it for ever, if we believe what John has written in his Prologue: 'The Word was made flesh and dwelt among us' (John 1.14). 'How much more believable it is,' comments the bishop, 'that those who by nature are the sons of men become sons of God, by the grace of God, and dwell in God, in whom and by whom alone they can be happy by sharing his immortality! It is to convince us of it that the Son of God chose to share our mortal condition.'[co] This is followed by pages on the incarnation and redemption which extend and complement the christological exposition of Book IV. By his mediation, Augustine concludes, Christ had combined in himself knowledge and wisdom: 'Our knowledge is Christ; our wisdom is also Christ. It is he who implants in us the faith that bears on temporal realities, he who reveals to us the truth that bears on eternal realities.'[22]

The *De Trinitate* is a mighty river which sweeps powerful ideas along on a course that is rich in meanders and swelled by unexpected tributaries. In Book XIV, Augustine, the *homo viator* in his apparently uncertain advance at last approaches his goal: the image of God is in the human soul, and though by sin man may well be distanced from God in the 'region of dissimilarity', this image is 'unlosable', it cannot ever be totally lost.[cp] In this soul, the bishop rediscovers the trinitarian image that he had already established in Book X, memory, intellect and will, but reinterpreting it, or rather, separating its strands.[23] An organic relationship still needed to be established between this trinitarian structure of the soul and the divine Trinity. 'If the trinity of the soul is the image of God, it is not because it remembers itself, understands and loves itself; it is because it can also remember, understand and love him by whom it was created.'[cq] In these difficult pages, where the mind flounders in its 'anagogic' approach, Augustine's entire effort is directed towards tightening the link uniting the image and its model. By externalizing itself, losing itself in the perceptible and in baser passions, the image is 'distorted', but cannot, however, itself be lost as an image of God.[cr] And 'this presence in it of the image of God has so great a power that it is enabled to cling to him whose image it is'.[cs] It is in this movement of conversion that the distorted image 'begins to be reshaped by the One who formed it. For, although it was able to distort itself, it cannot re-form itself.'[ct] But this renewal is gradual and the correspondence of the image to its model – the passage from the *imago* to the *similitude dei* – will not be perfect until the vision of God is perfect.[cu]

Having arrived at the end of such a laborious effort, Augustine looks back. He sees the long road he has travelled not only in his mind's eye: the exact references made to the preceding books show that the bishop carefully revised the notebooks (*codices*) into which his secretaries had transcribed the texts taken from dictation during all those years. Book XV of the *De Trinitate* is at first a recapitulation.[cv] The 'praise' of God that follows multiplies the images of divine perfection until in the end one is retained – wisdom.[cw] But how can this divine simplicity be reconciled intellectually with its trinitarian structure, an article of faith? At the start of Book XV, Augustine is bitterly clear-sighted. He thinks back to the mystical élan that had transported him, at the end of Book VIII when, justified by John's words, 'God is love' (1 John 4.16), he had risen to glimpsing the Trinity in the triad of the lover, the loved and love itself. But his mind, incapable of staying on those dazzling heights, had chosen to return to the creature in order to reascend to the Creator: that was the entire progress of Books IX to XIV. But, he goes on, 'now, having exerted our intellect on baser things, as much as and perhaps more than was necessary, we want to rise to the contemplation of the supreme Trinity that is God: and we cannot'.[cx]

All is not lost, of course; as said at the beginning of the book, this plunge into the 'incomprehensible' at least has the result of purifying the gaze, and making the believer understand that the fine point of religious life lies in this indefinitely extended dialectic of the fruitless quest and the disappointing 'find'; 'Faith seeks, intelligence finds . . . On the other hand, intelligence continues to seek what it has found.'[cy] Pascal would say, 'You would not look for me if you had not found me.' That does not prevent the rest of the book, at least as far as 'results' are concerned, from being the record of a failure and the analysis of the reasons for it. Augustine weighs up the trinitarian analogies used in the course of this long meditation, first emphasizing the distance that separates the human trinities from the divine Trinity.[cz] He shows the gap between the image and the divine model. Our words are inadequate. It is not enough to say, as he will later, 'every time that I have tried to discover, in the creature that we are, some analogy with the mystery (of God), my formulations have not been capable of rendering such understanding as I could have of it';[da] more fundamentally, human language, whatever personal or linguistic form it takes, the 'mental word', as Augustine says, that we use in our approach to God *in aenigma* is radically different from the word of God.[db] As for the distortion of the image in us and divine reality, it is patent if one returns to the analogous triad – nevertheless given greater importance – of the memory, intellect and will: these three faculties are mine, to varying degrees; I who possess them am one person, whereas in the Trinity whose image I can say I am, these three faculties do not belong to one God; but *are one God*; and at the same time they are three 'persons' and not one only. The image is inadequate and is finally disowned.[dc]

At this stage of his reflection, the bishop ponders, in a truly theological excursus, on the 'proceeding' of the Holy Ghost. He had already affirmed, rather hastily, that the Spirit 'also proceeded' from the Son, although it proceeded from the Father 'as from its first principle' (*principaliter*).[de] He returns to it *in fine*: as the Son is begotten timelessly by the Father, so the Holy Ghost 'proceeds' timelessly from the Father and the Son (*de utroque*). We understand that 'the Father, who in himself has the property of being the principle from which the Spirit proceeds, has similarly given the Son the property of being the principle from which the Spirit proceeds'.[24] The Spirit proceeds from the Father and the Son, but from one principle alone, which is God: this was to insist, in reaction against Arianism, on the consubstantiality of the 'persons', not conceding a lessening of that of the Son, and safeguarding the unicity of the divine principle. But, conceived like this, the 'proceeding' of the Spirit clearly differed from the *ekporeusis* of the Greek eastern theologians who, agreeing in this with the symbol of faith of the council of Constantinople (381), thought it proceeded from the Father alone, the unique principle of the Trinity. With the Augustinian formulas, stiffened by the scholasticism of the medieval West, fixed in dogma by the council of Lyon in 1274, the *filioque* dispute was born, which was to encumber Christian theology for centuries.

On several occasions in the *De Trinitate*, Augustine quotes 1 Cor. 13.12: 'For now we see through a glass, darkly'. The glass is defective and the vision clouded, but it is not in man's power to go beyond the mirror. The inevitable conclusion is that understanding of the trinitarian mystery will be granted to the faithful in the beatific vision, in the eschatological 'face-to-face' that is the reward of faith and the gift of grace. To state this at the end of several hundred pages is not, however, an admission of failure, in ascetical terms. Such spiritual exercises are not in vain. There is a virtue in the quest itself, and the work's key word in this respect is uttered not at its conclusion, but at the start of Book IX, as if defining the charter of a tireless intellectual availability applied to the realm of faith: 'Thus let us search as if we must find, and let us find as if we must search still more.'[df] At the close of a sermon which is not dated but probably earlier, the bishop says to the believer: 'To have faith, try hard to understand my words; to understand, have faith in the word of God.'[dg] The last words of the *De Trinitate* keep only the second part of this exhortation. At the end of the final prayer, the bishop steps aside: 'Lord, one and only God, God the Trinity, all that I have said in these books that comes from you, may your people recognize it; what I have said that comes from myself, pardon me for it, and may your people do likewise.'[dh] This is the Christian's true humility, rather than the author's modesty; but for the author who was already concerned with the transmission of his work and wanted to be forearmed against the appropriations of his ideas that he could foresee, it was also a way of challenging all Augustinianisms in advance.

Notes

a.   Ps. 105.4: *Quaerite faciem eius semper.*
b.   The work is preserved in the church of St Thomas, Prague.
c.   Cf. above, pp. 215–16.
d.   *Ep.* 169, 1: *a paucis eos intellegi posse arbitror; unde magis urgent quae pluribus utilia fore speramus.*
e.   *Ep.* 173A, *in fine.*
f.   *Ep.* 174, *initio.*
g.   *Ep.* 174: *eos (libros) . . . cuicumque audiendos, legendos describendosque permisi.*
h.   Cf. above, p. 87 ff.
i.   *De ordine*, II, 47, *in fine.*
j.   *Contra Adimantum*, XI.
k.   Cf. above, pp. 132–3, his exchanges of 389/90 with Nebridius.
l.   *De moribus eccl. cathol.*, I, 24.
m.   *Conf.*, XIII, 12.
n.   *Conf.*, XIII, 12, *in fine.*
o.   Cf. above, pp. 151–2.
p.   Cf. above, pp. 359–60.
q.   *Ep.* 197, 5. Hesychius however would insist, and receive the long *Letter* 199 from Augustine, 'on the end of the world'.
r.   *Sermon Dolbeau* 22 (Mainz 55), 8, in F. Dolbeau, *Vingt-six Sermons au peuple d'Afrique*, p. 561.
s.   *Sermon Dolbeau* 22 (Mainz 55), 7, *Vingt-six Sermons au peuple d'Afrique*, p. 560: *Si aliquid dignum dicere vellemus, nihil omnino diceremus.* Cf., in a slightly earlier text, *omnia possunt dici de deo, et nihil digne dicitur de deo* (*In Ioh. evang. tract.* 13, 5).
t.   *Sermon Dolbeau* 22 (Mainz 55), 9, *Vingt-six Sermons au peuple d'Afrique*, p. 561.
u.   *Sermon* 117, 5: *Si comprehendis, non est deus.*
v.   *De Trin.*, VII, 7.
w.   *Enarr. in Psalm.* 52, 2: *Rarum hominum genus est qui dicant in corde suo: non est deus.*
x.   Cf. above, pp. 19 and 308.
y.   *De Trin.*, I, 2.
z.   Cf. Matt. 12.50; 16.16; 18.19 and *passim.*
aa.   Acts 2.1–4.
bb.   From Book I, Augustine says that 'it is right to speak of "crucified God", but not by virtue

of his Divine power, rather by virtue of his fleshly weakness': *De Trin.*, I, 28 (cf. 2 Cor. 13.4).

cc. *Ep.* 238, 4.

dd. *Ep.* 238, 5.

ee. *De Trin.*, I, 4. I will return to the hesitation between *substantia* and *essentia*.

ff. *De Trin.*, I, 5.

gg. *De Trin.*, I, 7.

hh. *De Trin.*, I, 25.

ii. *De fide et symbolo*, 19.

jj. *De Trin.*, I, 13.

kk. *De Trin.*, XV, 25–38.

ll. *De Trin.*, II, 3–5.

mm. *De Trin.*, II, 8, *initio: Pater solus nusquam legitur missus.*

nn. *De Trin.*, II, 8–11.

oo. *De Trin.*, II, 12.

pp. Gen. 3.8–10.

qq. *De Trin.*, II, 17.

rr. *De Trin.*, II, 18, *in fine.*

ss. *De Trin.*, III, 25–7.

tt. *De Trin.*, IV, 1–2.

uu. *De Trin.*, IV, 4.

vv. *De Trin.*, IV, 5: *Utrique autem rei nostrae, id est et animae et corpori medicina et resurrectione opus erat.*

ww. *De Trin.*, IV, 7.

xx. *De Trin.*, IV, 10. But 36 (6^2) is also the number of months (3 years) of the fig-tree in Luke 13.6 (*De Trin.*, IV, 7)!

yy. *De Trin.*, IV, 10, *in fine.*

zz. *De Gen. ad litt.*, IV, 14.

ab. *De Trin.*, IV, 11.

ac. Cf. above, pp. 316–17.

ad. *De Trin.*, IV, 13: '*Mortem carnis non subierat, quia nec indumentum susceperat*; to compare with *Sermon Dolbeau* 26 (Mainz 62), 39: *Non enim solvitur corpore, quia non carne indutus est* (*Vingt-six Sermons au peuple d'Afrique*, p. 396).

ae. *Sermon Dolbeau* 26 (Mainz 62), 39: *pollicens etiam purgationem animae, per eas quas* teletas *appellant*; same utterances in *Sermon Dolbeau* 26, 28, 32 and 41 (pp. 387, 390 and 397), the only difference being the Greek word, which does not figure in it.

af. *City of God*, X, 7–11.

ag. *De Trin.*, IV, 32.

ah. *Sermon* 46, 18.

ai. *Tract in Ioh. evang.*, 40, 7.

aj. *Ep.* 170 and 171, the latter addressed to Peregrinus, bishop of the place, former deacon to Augustine at Hippo, who had served as intermediary.

ak. *Ep.* 23*A, 3.

al. *Retract.*, II, 52.

am. *Sermo Guelferbytanus* 17, 4, in *Miscellanea Agostiniana*, I, p. 498.

an. This was the *Conlatio cum Maximino*, followed by the *Contra Maximinum*, in two short books; on the unfolding of the controversy, see Possidius, *Vita Aug.*, XVII.

ao. *De Trin.*, V, 3. He hesitated similarly in his letter of 410 to Consentius: *Ep.* 120, 17.

ap. *De Trin.*, V, 9, *in fine*: Essentiam *dico quae* ousia *graece dicitur, quam usitatius* substantiam *vocamus.*

aq. Jerome, *Ep.* 15.

ar. *De Trin.*, V, 10.

as. Basil of Caesarea, *Ep.* 236, 6.

at. Gregory of Nazianzen, *Oratio* 21, 35.

au. *De Trin.*, V, 10.

av. *De Trin.*, VII, 7–9.

aw. *De Trin.*, VII, 10.

ax. *De Trin.*, VII, 10. He returns to the word *essentia* in the *City of God* (XII, 2) to render the Greek *ousia*, apologizing for the neologism: in fact the word had already been used in Seneca and Quintilian in the mid first century.

ay. *De Trin.*, V, 4.

az. *De Trin.*, V, 5–7.

ba. *De Trin.*, VII, 2–6.

bc. *De Trin.*, VIII, 1.

bd. On the *anima/animus* distinction, cf. here *De Trin.*, VIII, 9; the image of God is situated in the *mens* or in the *animus*: *De Trin.*, XV, 1.

be. *De Trin.*, VIII, 5.

bf. *De Trin.*, VIII, 8.

bg. *De Trin.*, VIII, 9.

bh. *De Trin.*, VIII, 10.

bi. *De Trin.*, VIII, 12.

bj. *De Trin.*, VIII, 14.

bk. Chiefly because of this triad's instability: both lover and loved may part from one another: *De Trin.*, IX, 6.

bl. *De Trin.*, IX, 3–4.

bm. *De Trin.*, IX, 18.

bn. Cf. above, pp. 140–2.

bo. *De Trin.*, X, 2–4.

bp. *De Trin.*, X, 5.

bq. *De Trin.*, X, 6.

br. *De Trin.*, X, 8.

bs. *De Trin.*, X, 12: *Nec se quasi non norit cognoscat, sed ab eo quod alterum novit dignoscat.*

bt. *De Trin.*, X, 13.

bu. *Ep.* 169, 6.

bv. *Sermon* 52, 19–20.

bw. See the brilliant analysis of this 'retinal image' in *De Trin.*, XI, 3.

bx. Read in *De Trin.*, XI, 6 how Augustine makes a fine distinction between them.

by. *De Trin.*, XII, 1–3.

bz. *De Trin.*, XII, 8, *initio.*

ca. *De Trin.*, XII, 19–20.

cb. *Sermon Dolbeau* 12 (*Mainz* 41) 4, in *Vingt-six Sermons au peuple d'Afrique*, p. 79: *aequa condicio.*

cd. *Sermon* 392, 4: *Sed ubi ventum fuerit ad illud negotium . . . clamate pro re vestra.*

ce. *Sermon Dolbeau* 12, 4: *Mulier enim subdita est viro, et in viro arbitrium, in femina obsequium.*

cf. *Sermon* 392, 4: *In ceteris omnibus ancillae estote virorum vestrorum.*

cg. *De Trin.*, XII, 12, *in fine.*

ch. *De opere monach.*, 40, text dating to 400/401: cf. above, p. 228.

ci. *De Trin.*, XII, 10.

cj. *De Trin.*, XII, 22.

ck. *De Trin.*, XII, 25.

cl. *De Trin.*, XIII, 5–7.

cm. *De beata vita*, II, 11. He repeats it shortly afterwards in the *De moribus*, I, 10; cf. above, p. 123.

cn. *De Trin.*, XIII, 10, *in fine.*

co. *De Trin.*, XIII, 12.

cp. *De Trin.*, XIV, 6.

cq. *De Trin.*, XIV, 15, *initio.*

cr. *De Trin.*, XIV, 19, *initio.*

cs. *De Trin.*, XIV, 20.

ct. *De Trin.*, XIV, 22.

cu. *De Trin.*, XIV, 23: *In hac quippe imagine tunc perfecta erit dei similitudo quando dei perfecta erit visio.*

cv. *De Trin.*, XIV, 4–5.

cw. *De Trin.*, XV, 9.

cx. *De Trin.*, XV, 10.

cy. *De Trin.*, XV, 2.

cz. *De Trin.*, XV, 11–12.

da. *De Trin.*, XV, 45.

db. *De Trin.*, XV, 17–26.

dc. *De Trin.*, XV, 43.

de. *De Trin.*, XV, 29.

df. *De Trin.*, IX, 1: *Sic ergo quaeramus tamquam inventuri et sic inveniamus tamquam quaesituri.*

dg. *Sermon* 43, 9.

dh. *De Trin.*, XV, 51, *in fine.*

CHAPTER XXXI

The *City of God*

Alaric's capture of Rome in the late summer of 410 was not exactly a bolt from the blue. There had been no lack of warnings and signs as precursors to the disaster. Even in 378, the Goths' defeat of the emperor Valens at Andrinopolis and his death at the outcome of the battle had signalled the beginning of the end for the Empire, sensed as such by a contemporary like Ambrose. Twenty years later, the echoes of that first collapse, as they may be seen in a letter from Jerome, had not yet died away: 'The Roman world is crumbling', he recorded.[a] Hardly had the fifth century begun when events moved faster. In 401–2, Alaric and his Goths crossed the Alps and burst upon Venetia; but in 405 it was not he, but another Barbarian, Radagaisus, who at the head of his Ostrogoths put Rome in danger, before being defeated by Stilicho near Florence. News of it had reached Carthage, where the pagans, Augustine would say later, were already blaming the Christians, claiming that it was their fault that Radagaisus had been able to take advantage of the weakening cult of the tutelary gods of a city that could no longer be believed eternal.[b] The twelve vultures seen by Romulus when it was founded had guaranteed it twelve centuries of life; now the end was approaching. Fearing the answer of the Sibylline Books, which had been consulted, Stilicho had chosen to have them burnt, to the indignation of traditionalist pagans such as Rutilius Namatianus, for whom those books were the guarantee of Rome's good fortune.[c] But banning the production of oracles did not prevent the manifestation of prodigies. The most worrying, reported by Claudian, had occurred under the very eyes of Honorius, when the emperor was in the midst of equitation exercises: two wolves had attacked his escort; they had been killed by spear thrusts, but from their pierced flanks and entrails two human hands had sprung forth, very much alive and grasping.[d] These two wolves were destroyers, overturning the beneficent image of the suckling she-wolf of the city's origins, and it did not take a great mind to see that they represented the two Barbarians who were threatening it, Radagaisus and Alaric.

As we know, it was the latter who perpetrated the sacrilege, eight centuries after Brennus' Gauls. On 24 August 410, he entered Rome by the Salarian Gate, approaching the city very nearly at the spot where in 211 BC Hannibal had set up camp, on the banks of the Anio, without completing his mission. But times had changed, and treachery handed the Barbarian leader his prey without his having to fight. Three days of looting, destruction, burning, rape and massacre ensued,[1] although the churches of the apostles Peter and Paul were spared, as Alaric, a Christian, acknowledged their right of asylum, and thousands of Romans, Christians and pagans alike, had taken refuge there.[e] Jerome would lament the disappearance during those tragic days of his noble friends Pammachius and Marcella amid so many anonymous dead,[2] while a vast exodus emptied the town and Galla Placidia, daughter of the great Theodosius, remained there as a hostage of the Goths.

The shock wave of Rome's capture

It was all very well to have foreseen the likelihood of the event, envisaged it as a possibility, the shock of its actual happening was no less. The writer remembers having been aware, the moment he learned about it, that the declaration of war on 3 September 1939 meant the end of his hitherto carefree childhood. Small boy that he was, he was not ignorant of the threats that had been looming at least since the preceding year. In September 410, at Hippo, Carthage, or Hippo Diarrhytus (Bizerte) where Augustine happened to be in late September on his return route home, hardly had the cause been learnt when the effects were to be seen – those thousands of refugees flooding the African coasts throughout the autumn.

The news reached the bishop at a time when the worst infamies of the circumcellions and Donatists were a closer and more urgent source of worry for him: at the time, those barbarians seemed no less fearsome.[f] But he clearly saw that what was happening in Italy was on quite another scale; and he could not completely escape a pessimism fuelled so much by recent history, renewing by its actuality the old Stoic *topos* – broadly endorsed by the vulgate of Christian theology – of the mortality common to cities and men. For the first time since empires had been built, the attacks on this one, which had absorbed them all, at least in the universe known to Augustine's contemporaries, might well mean the end of a world, if not *the* world. All around him the bishop heard laments and fears, and was conscious of a decline: 'The world is dying, the world is growing old, the world is overcome with weakness, it has the gasping breath of old age'; but he acknowledged that realization only to contrast it with the Psalmist's words: 'Have no fear: *thy youth is renewed like the eagle's* (Ps. 103.5).'[g]

Augustine had several reasons for not giving in to the surrounding catastrophism which inspired Jerome, for example, when in his letter to Ageruchia, he ended his lamentation over the misfortunes of the times, after Stilicho's death, with this cry: 'Where is salvation if Rome perishes?',[h] a cry redoubled in the rhetorical dramatization of his account of the sack of Rome, in which Virgil and the Bible are associated in an apocalyptic vision.[i] Perhaps it should be said first that the hermit of Bethlehem, a graft that had taken badly in Palestine, had remained in heart and mind a citizen of the town linked to his youth and the dazzling beginnings of his intellectual life. As we know, that was not so for Augustine, without going as far as saying that 'Rome had always left him perfectly cold'.[3] But it is true that the town had made little impression on him, he had not been at one with it and, when he twice repeated that its ruin was the crumbling of stone and wood buildings, he did not do so with a feeling of emotional or aesthetic regret.[j] He was not mourning for Roman monuments.

A man who, more than many others, was sensitive to symbols refused to let himself be moved by this one, and here is the key to his apparent indifference to Rome's misfortunes. The myth of its 'eternity', accepted by a contemporary Christian like Prudentius, at least 'by way of poetic ornament',[4] did not find favour in his eyes. In a sermon dating to the summer of 411, he attacks Virgil who, while knowing full well that kingdoms are perishable, through pure adulation had made Jupiter say he had given the Romans 'an empire without end'; and he contrasts the words from the Gospel: 'Heaven and earth shall pass away' (Matt. 24.35; Luke 21.33).[k] In any case, why be astonished that there could be an end to a city behind whose stones were men? 'What is Rome,' said the bishop, 'if not the Romans?' Man is the adornment and inhabitant of the city, but also its director (*rector*) and steersman (*gubernator*); now, the man who is all these things in the city is born to die.[l] And the city with him.

In the same spirit, in his preaching during this period, Augustine rebelled against a concept that to him seemed false and dangerous, 'the misfortunes of the times', which were to be endured as a natural cataclysm. 'Times are bad, times are difficult: this is what men say. Let us live well and times will be good: we are the times; as we are, so are the times.' And further on he insists, 'Wicked men are what makes the world wicked.'[m] The bishop's reflections here rejoin those of the critical analyst of free will, who, as a twenty-year-old at Carthage, had engraved in his memory words from the *Hortensius* that had become one of the foundations of his moral philosophy. In it Cicero challenged those who maintain that we are happy if we live as we please: it was the depravity of the will that was the cause of unhappiness.[n] It was very fitting that this theme and text were recalled in the long letter Augustine sent in 411 to Anicia Faltonia Proba, Demetrias' grandmother, who had recently returned to Rome with her household: the greater man's facility to fulfil his evil will, the more he is unhappy.[5]

Yes, but then the bishop had to confront the distress and confusion among his own faithful, who could not understand how 'in Christian times' Rome could have been defeated, sacked and burnt, and who feared the opprobrium of the pagans; the latter were only too inclined to hold these *tempora christiana* responsible for the disaster. For it was not the believers, but rather the infidels or men of little faith who asked reproachfully why God had let Rome perish as he had destroyed Sodom and all that was in it, except Lot and his family, despite Abraham's intercession (Gen. 18.23–19.26).

> One question is put to me forcefully and passionately, chiefly by men who impiously attack our Scriptures instead of piously searching them. Especially concerning the recent destruction of Rome, they say, 'Were there not fifty just men in Rome? Among so great a number of faithful, of holy and chaste men, of both male and female servants of God, could there not be found fifty, forty, thirty, twenty, ten just men? If that is incredible, then why did not God spare this city for the sake of fifty, or even ten?'[6]

Augustine was not short of answers. First, the comparison did not stand up: nothing had remained of Sodom, Rome had merely received a thrashing;[o] it was an ordeal, not a damnation. And for his flock, who were suffering pagan criticisms, the bishop supplied other arguments. It was not the first time he had had to defend the *tempora christiana* against attack. On those occasions, with a detachment that marked the new boundaries of his cultural Romanness, he had referred the attackers to 'their literature', 'their history', so rich in wars, ravages of all kinds, famines and epidemics.[7] In the present instance, he noted that 'this Rome which has just burnt amid Christian sacrifices had already been devoured by the flames amid pagan sacrifices', and on two occasions: formerly because of the Gauls, who had left only the Capitol surviving, and more recently, following the crime of Nero, who had burnt it for amusement. The misfortune of a town where burning had become a habit,[8] concluded the bishop, could hardly be laid at God's door.

The most difficult task was to reply to the questions and doubts of the faithful whose own faith had been shaken. In a sermon delivered in Carthage on 29 June 411, for the feast of the apostles Peter and Paul, Augustine had before him refugees whom the sack of Rome had caused to lose sometimes loved ones, and often at the least their possessions. The bishop could only show his compassion to this congregation, but from those shattered lives arose a murmur of bitterness, sometimes even of rebellion: 'If he would just keep quiet about Rome!' Augustine had once heard during one of his Carthaginian sermons in the summer of 411.[p] On the day of the feast of Roman martyrs, he listened to the complaints of those who reckoned that divine protection had let them down. 'The body of Peter', they hurled at him, 'lay in Rome; also the body of Paul lay in Rome, and the body of Laurence rested there with those of the other martyr saints; and Rome was wretched, devastated, smitten, crushed, burnt: where then were the tombs (*memoriae*) of the apostles?'[q] It was taking the monuments, almost physically, for ramparts. They were truly in Rome, replied the bishop, but not, alas, in the hearts of those who were saying these things and who had a far too 'carnal' conception of the cult of the apostles. To them he quoted Paul's words – in 2 Cor. 4.18 – on the things which are seen and are temporal, and the things which are not seen, but eternal: in Peter, the flesh had had but a short time, and they would not accept that his 'rock' which was in Rome also had its time![r] At the same time Plotinus' words came to his mind (*Enn.*, I, 4, 7) on human weakness in lamenting over 'the ruins of wood and stone and the death of mortals'. Let me say straight away, the words of the philosopher rather than the Apostle would come to his lips during the ordeal – the siege of Hippo – that preceded his death.[s]

The bishop tried to urge his listeners to pull themselves together, to encourage them to repentance,[t] and also to the idea that, however cruel the ordeals they had undergone, they must accept them as the holy man Job had endured his sufferings, his soul turned to whatever the future held in store for him.[u] In Hippo, surrounded by olive trees, the image familiar to Augustine was the biblical one of the olive-press, whose Latin name, *torcular*, vividly evoked the inexorable action at work to make a pure oil flow from a raw product of nature. The fruit, he would say in several of his sermons, cannot hang indefinitely on the tree, swayed by the wind as if tossed about by its desires: at the end of the year it irrevocably goes to the press.[9] And like the olive tree beneath the harvester's pole, the world is devastated before being crushed in the press.[v]

The genesis of the *City of God*

On the reflections that the event itself might have inspired, the 'theme' of the first books of the *City of God* was already outlined in the 'on-the-spot' reactions of the years 410–11. But the plan of the book in its fullness goes far beyond those first responses and we shall see that they chiefly served to hasten, in Augustine's mind, the development of a vast symphony whose major chords he already had in his head.

As for every great work, the genesis of this one was a complex process, spread over a long period. Whatever stimulus might have been given to it by the event in the autumn of 410, Augustine could not have started on it before 412. The whole of 411, as we have seen, was basically devoted to preparing for the conference in Carthage, its occurrence in June, then its aftermath: drawing up a 'Summary' (*Breviculus*), and a long circular letter (the *Ad donatistas*), which kept him busy until the beginning of 412.[w] It was then that an exchange of correspondence took place between the bishop, on one hand, and Marcellinus and Volusianus on the other, in which they eagerly plied him with questions and he gave signs that he was gestating his ideas. Volusianus was curious about Christianity, but statesman that he was, he could not see how to reconcile evangelical precepts with Roman laws, how to turn the other cheek, or give one's cloak to someone who had already taken one's coat (Matt. 5.39–40).[x] At the end of a very long reply, the bishop told him that only in a future life did a Christian expect the eternal reward that he would receive 'in the celestial and divine city';[y] but, placing himself as his correspondent on the plan of the earthly city, he affirmed that there was nothing like *fides* and *concordia* to ensure its sureness and stability, in other words, the loyal search for the common good, which on earth merges with the quest for God.[z] Nevertheless, it is in a letter to Marcellinus, a Christian and therefore deemed more receptive, and who could act as his interpreter in the midst of the Carthaginian coterie which he frequented with Volusianus, that Augustine gives the most precise replies to the alleged incompatibilities of evangelical virtues and *raison d'État*. He called Cicero and Sallust to the rescue to show that pardoning offences had been practised in ancient Rome, and that *benevolentia* and *patientia* had been part of the Republic's values.[aa] Sallust again – reporting Jugurtha's famous witticism on Rome: 'Town for sale, will perish quickly if it finds a buyer' – and Juvenal, who hymns ancient virtues in his *Satire VI*, were also quoted as witnesses of a decline that had begun at the end of the Republican era, well before the start of 'Christian times'.[10] There followed immediately a rough outline of what would be a major theme in the book to come, the idea, here so strongly and eloquently developed, that the Christian is the most loyal and reliable observer of the State's laws because he does not regard them as a goal, and adheres to them only for higher ends than those of the State; the Christian practises civic virtues to the benefit of the earthly city, but in doing so he has in view the divine city, to which he aspires.[11]

Thus some of the central ideas began to take shape for a work whose achievement would keep a 'promise' made to Marcellinus,[bb] duly recognized as such by the bishop at the date of the exchange,[cc] and presented as its fulfilment in the dedication made by the author to the one he quite rightly looked upon as its instigator.[dd] Busy as he was, however, during this period with the composition of his first anti-Pelagian texts – also undertaken, it may be recalled, at the instigation of his friend Marcellinus: cf. above, p. 328 – Augustine quickly got down to work. The first three books of the *City of God* were published as soon as they were finished.[ee] We know that Marcellinus, the dedicatee – his name still figures at the beginning of Book II – had been executed on 13 September 413: had Augustine already completed them? But if their completion followed this death, it may be accepted that the dedication had been retained as posthumous homage to Marcellinus. What is certain is that these three books had begun to circulate in

413/14: that is the rather imprecise date of an exchange of letters in which the *vicarius* of Africa, Macedonius, said with how much interest, even eagerness, he had read them.[ff]

The rapid publication of the first three books, when the last echoes of the Roman catastrophe had not yet died down, seems to have provoked a reaction. Augustine himself tells us: he was threatened with a riposte, apparently already written and awaiting the right moment to appear, but which never saw the light of day. He does not specify its author,[12] or rather authors,[13] who did not reveal themselves. He was therefore able to continue his undertaking without being delayed by controversy. Books IV and V were written in 415, in the space of a few months, between the approach to Easter and beginning of the winter, at the same time as a few commentaries on the Psalms and some developments of the *De Trinitate*.[gg] We know from Orosius that in 417 Books VI to X had been completed and that the eleventh was on the stocks.[14] Then the chronological milestones become more rare and uncertain: in 418 Book XIV was being written,[hh] while Books XV and XVI seem to date to 419/20[15] and Book XVIII may have been written in 424 or 425. At the date of the *Retractations* (426), the twenty-two books were finally completed: this long effort had continued over some fifteen years, a duration surpassed only by the elaboration of the *De Trinitate*.

The structure of the work[16]

Augustine was well aware that he was undertaking a work of great size and particular difficulty: *magnum opus et arduum*, he says in the preamble, with words that echo Cicero,[17] and already used by him at the opening of the *De doctrina christiana* (I, 1), but which here assumed their strongest resonance. In 412 he probably did not yet have an idea of the length of the task he had set himself, but from the opening lines – which we know for sure were not a later addition – he set out its principal links with such clarity that it is obvious from reading them that the work's major aims were perfectly fixed in his mind. Let me venture a translation of that comprehensive opening:

> The most glorious City of God (Ps. 87.3), as it exists both in this world of time, 'living by faith' (Hab. 2.4), in exile[ii] among the ungodly; and as it stands in the security of its everlasting dwelling 'which it now awaits in steadfast patience' (Rom. 8.25) 'until the day when judgement shall return unto righteousness' (Ps. 94.15); and will attain it hereafter by virtue of its ascendancy over its enemies, when the final victory is won and perfect peace reigns. This is the City which, by this work, undertaken in fulfilment of my promise to you, my very dear son Marcellinus, I intend to defend against those who prefer their own gods to its Founder. The task is long and arduous, but 'God is our helper' (Ps. 62.8).[jj]

The essential points have been stated or announced. First – because it is the positive part of the project – the subject of what is to be the second part of the work (Books XI to XIII): the 'city of God' in the two forms it adopts, on pilgrimage here below, then in the glory of its perfect fulfilment hereafter; next, the theme of the first ten books, the long refutation of the pagans. One of the best inspirations of the *Retractatio* to which Henri Marrou applied himself was his insistence on picking out all the intentions contained in these few concentrated lines,[18] emphasizing with what art and true feeling for the spiritual effectiveness of 'suspense' Augustine only gradually unveiled the biblical texts in their entirety – first Ps. 87.3, then Ps. 48.2–3 and 8, Ps. 46.5–6, Ps. 50.1 – which testify to the 'city of God' and are the divine sureties of the bishop's work: the opening note is sounded simply, before being taken up and expanded into a symphonic orchestration.[kk] And for a better appreciation of the artist's genius, let us remember that years elapsed between that first sumptuous flow of words and the great 'reprise' of the theme at the beginning of Book XI.

At the close of the first book, Augustine details his plan and again announces the aims of the work's second part. He says:

> The two cities are intertwined and mingled with each other in this world, until the Last Judgement separates them. Therefore, with the aid of divine grace, I will set out what I believe I must say about their origin (Books XI to XIV), their development (Books XV to XVIII) and the end that awaits them (Books XIX to XXII).[ll]

He thus defines a tripartite division for this section – justified enough by the realities of the work to allow us to resist the temptation to see it as a simple rhetorical tripartition[19] – which he still has in mind in the last lines of Book X, and will resume, in the same terms, at the beginning of Book XI and, to finish, in the *Retractations*, when he gives an overall look at the work he has just completed.[mm]

At the very end of Book I, however, before continuing, Augustine had felt the need to give a detailed view of what would form the first part of the work, with indications that are sufficiently precise to make it evident that the nine books to come were mapped out in his mind according to a very clear-cut configuration. In the first book, having got into his stride with the sermons on the fall of Rome analysed above, he had replied to the polemics and laments born directly of the event, strongly emphasizing the fact that for the first time in the history of the world Barbarians had seized a city – and what a city! – yet spared all those, believers and non-believers, who had taken refuge in the churches.[nn] This first reflection on Rome's history was also remarkable, when, in the face of the appetite for domination embodied by the old Cato, Augustine made use of the lesson in wisdom given by Scipio Nasica who, before the attack on Carthage, had understood – but without being followed – the eminent moral virtue for peoples of what in other times has been called 'the balance of terror'.[oo] Augustine had thus begun to settle matters with pagan Rome. 'But there was more to be said':[pp] first, and still, against those who blamed triumphant Christianity – especially because of the banning of pagan sacrifices – for the Roman disasters; this refutation is mainly the subject of Books II and III. Then three connected subjects are announced, which must be treated on a historical basis. It will be shown by what virtues the Romans expanded their empire over the world and why God chose to help them; then how much their false gods, far from assisting them, harmed them by their deceptions and lies. That is the subject of Book IV, at the start of which[qq] Augustine resumes his indication in I, 36, adding however that he has already expressed himself sufficiently on the topic of the deceits of the demons worshipped by the pagans. Apparently, after the separate publication of the first three books the bishop slightly altered his plan: Book V, contrasting God

with *fatum* (destiny) and ending with a panegyric of Theodosius, had probably
not been planned in this fashion in the initial project. In contrast, Books VI to X
are clearly prefigured in the last lines of I, 36: 'Finally,' he says, 'I will address
those men who, refuted and confounded by the clearest proof, try to assert that
the gods must be worshipped, not with a view to advantage in this life, but for
the sake of the life after death';[rr] and he foresees that this section will occupy him
at length. Indeed, it comprises the refutation of the Platonists and, by way of
Volusianus and his peers, targets the dangerous attractions of a philosophy of
salvation.

To help his readers find their way round the text, Augustine increases the
'milestones'. At the beginning of Book VI, he recapitulates the results achieved
throughout the preceding books, rightly presented as a coherent whole, before
again announcing the material contained in the five books to come.[ss] Similarly,
having reached the end of Book X, the author looks back and contemplates the
two blocks, each of five books, which form the great first part, before mentioning
what follows, in other words, the parallel and overlapping development of the
two cities, with the terms – *exortus, procursus, debiti fines* – already used at the very
start of the work.[tt] In a letter addressed to two monks Peter and Abraham, in 418,
he takes stock. He tells them:

> I have completed ten not very slim volumes, the first five of which refute those who
> claim that to obtain or preserve the happiness of this time and world in human affairs
> one must worship, not the one supreme and true God, but a whole host of gods. The next
> five target those who, rebelling with arrogance and presumptuousness against the
> doctrine of salvation, think they can attain the hoped-for blessedness after life here
> below by practising the worship of demons and a multitude of gods. Their famous
> philosophers are refuted in the last three of these five books.

Augustine continues by mentioning the state of progress of his work at that date:
'As for the other books, whatever the number may be after the eleventh, I have
already completed three of them, and have the fourth in hand: these books will
contain what I think and believe about the City of God.'[uu] It emerges very clearly
that the bishop knew where he was going, but that he was as yet uncertain how
long a road he had to tread; in 418, he was still unaware that this *opus magnum*
would ultimately total twenty-two books; that should impose some restraint on
speculations about the number of books making up the work.[20]

The author continues to throw light on this progress throughout the second
great part of his work, and from the outset, as we have seen, in the first lines of
Book XI. Holding his reader firmly by the hand, he warns him, at the start of Book
XV, that he is on the point of beginning the development – here called *excursus*,
no longer *procursus*[vv] of the two cities, in other words the second phase of his
tripartite plan for the second great section of his book and, having reached the
end of this section, he also indicates that he has finished with it and is preparing
to tackle the third and last, the one with the eschatological perspectives.
Augustine gives his explanation in the last three books (XIX to XXII), but in their
case, too, he has taken care to prepare his reader: at the beginning of Book XV, he
gives a glimpse of the respective ends of the two cities, 'one is predestined to
share an eternal reign with God, the other to suffer an eternal torment with the

devil'.ʷʷ And, just when he is developing this theme, he feels he must announce it in a few lines that form a transition:

> Up to now I have demonstrated the development (*excursus*) in this mortal life of the two cities, celestial and earthly, which are intermingled from their origin to their end. The earthly city has made for itself as many false gods as it pleased, taken from everywhere, even from among men, to worship them with sacrifices; the heavenly city, in exile on earth, does not make false gods for itself, but was itself made by the true God to be itself his true sacrifice. Nevertheless, both cities alike enjoy the good things of this world, or suffer its afflictions, but without the same faith, the same hope or the same love, until they are separated by the Last Judgement and each obtains its own end, which is never-ending.ˣˣ

Despite these precautions, reading the *City of God* cannot be to sail down a long tranquil river. Augustine was conscious of it, and probably these announcements and reminders were partly another way for him – so often and sometimes lengthily distracted from his work by many urgent occupations – to resettle himself and pick up the thread again. We can thus understand the long preamble to Book XVIII, which once more summarizes the first ten books, recalls the tripartite plan of the second part being edited, but also goes a little into the detail of what has already been done: following Book X, says the bishop, four books set out the origin of the two cities; then the fifteenth book tackles the history of their development, until the Flood. He continues:

> From there, up to Abraham the two cities followed their course in parallel, in history as in the Scriptures. But from our father Abraham to the times of the kings of Israel – where the sixteenth book takes us – and from then until the coming in the flesh of our Saviour himself – where the seventeenth book takes us – it seems from my account that only the city of God continues its advance.ʸʸ

Augustine acknowledges, however, that in the history of humankind it has not been the only one to develop, the two cities never having ceased to progress together, intermingled since their origins, and confesses that he has taken this route so that 'without interference by contrast with the other city, that of the city of God may appear more distinctly in its development'. He will therefore resume the account of the other city's progress since the times of Abraham, the better to establish for his readers a comparison between the two.

The subject of Book XVIII is thus to be the history of the earthly city since the time of the Patriarchs, but it may be difficult to be equally clear-cut about what follows. Augustine has fallen behind with his programme and must catch up, and he is well aware that this is a heavy burden. In Book XVII, he has to admit, 'I have to pass over many things in silence because of my concern to reach the end of this work.'ᶻᶻ At the time, he was occupied with Jewish prophecies relating to the coming of Christ. He would return to them in Book XVIII,ᵃᵇ after skimming over the history of the great 'empires' – in fact, chiefly Assyria, 'the first Babylon' – and approach the beginnings of Rome, 'second Babylon', to fulfil his promise of additional material on those prophecies, made at the end of the preceding book. Book XVIII, the longest in the whole work, is thus a 'catching-up' book, rather a 'rag-bag', cluttered with digressions – for instance on the canonical books, with an unexpected excursus on the Septuagint.[ac] This is also the book which reveals most clearly the difficulties of the gigantic undertaking to which Augustine had harnessed himself. The two cities, earthly and heavenly, are understood in the allegorical sense; yet – I will return to this later – they are simultaneously rational beings, mystical realities and historical realities. Here it is not a question of reproaching the author for not having been the historian of the ancient world that had preceded him, which he did not claim to be; he had left that role to Orosius.[21] But at the same time he could not avoid illustrating allegory with history, which could not fail to distort it. Despite some spiritual heterogeneity – manifested for instance by the quarrels of Hagar and Sara (Gen. 16.1–7), as we shall see further on[ad] – admittedly the history of the heavenly city in exile on this earth is portrayed by that of the people of Israel, or rather God's people, prefiguring the Church of Christ. But how to represent the history of the earthly city, progressing, as has been said, at the same time as the other, and closely intertwined with it? The allegorical simplification of the historical proliferation could not avoid some omissions. Here the history of the earthly city has been said to be reduced 'to a working diagram'.[22] To avoid a multiplicity of coexistences and safeguard the conceptual unity of his earthly city, Augustine in fact sums up the history of the world in the succession of two empires, Rome following the Assyrio-Babylonians.

We know from one of the recently published new letters that, after hearing it read on three consecutive afternoons in the bishop's company, it was nonetheless Book XVIII, the longest and least mastered of all, which had aroused the enthusiasm of one of his friends, Firmus, and prompted the latter's insistence on receiving all of them.[ae] A first letter from Augustine to this person was already known, expressing his sadness on learning that he was still a catechumen.[23] The text, which may be taken to be pretty well contemporaneous with the *Retractations*, and naturally later than the *City of God*, shows what importance Augustine attached to the major divisions of the plan he had followed being materialized in the publishing of the work. The twenty-two books (or 'notebooks': *quaterniones*) composing the work could not be presented, he said, in a single volume. If absolutely necessary, they could be in two, one grouping the first ten books, and the other the twelve of the second part. But although the bishop apparently left the decision to Firmus, it was obvious that his own choice favoured five volumes: two of five books and three other of four books each, giving concrete form to the famous tripartite division, recalled so many times, of the birth, concomitant development and end of the two cities.[af] But he had arrived at this material equality of treatment of the three parts only at the cost of difficult choices in the elaboration of his subject matter, and Book XVIII in particular bears the traces of this.

Jerusalem and Babylon

At the close of Book XIV, written in 418, and very marked, on the subject of original sin, by reorientations born of the anti-Pelagian controversy, Augustine ends the long developments devoted to the general theme of this book: living according to the flesh and living according to the spirit, which in the last analysis are the two highly discriminating ways whereby man can lead his life here below. Opening this conclusion, we find the celebrated sentence, the true living heart of the whole work: 'Two cities were thus created by two kinds of love: the earthly city, created by self-love, carried to the point of contempt for God; and the heavenly city, created by the love of God, carried to the point of self-contempt.'[ag] Tell me what people love and I will tell you who those people are.

This was the outcome, expressed magnificently in its compactness and the powerfulness of the two antitheses, of reflections that had been going on in Augustine's mind for over a quarter of a century.[24] He had not yet taken orders when in 390, at Thagaste, stressing for Romanianus the theme of the 'old man', living after the flesh, which the dedicatee of the *De vera religione* was still doing, he sketched the first outlines[ah] of the as yet incomplete image of the 'two peoples', on one side 'the crowd of the ungodly' and on the other 'the generations pledged to the one and only God'.[ai] Some ten years later, the image would be much more precise and enriched, around 400, in the book *The First Catechism*. The bishop wrote:

> Thus there are two cities, that of the ungodly and that of the saints, which have been going on since the origin of the human race and will continue until the end of the world, today mingled physically but separate in their wills, and doomed to be separated in the body also at the Day of Judgement.[aj]

The citizens of these two cities are already characterized: on the one hand the 'ungodly', in other words, 'all men who are enamoured of pride and worldly domination, with its puffed-up vanity and the pomp of arrogance'; on the other, 'the saints', or 'all men, all minds, who humbly seek the glory of God and not their own'. At the time of this text,[25] Jerusalem – whose name, says Augustine, means 'vision of peace' – is the allegorical figure of the heavenly city, just as Babylon, whose name means 'confusion', is emblematic of the earthly city. The two towns would soon illustrate the two cities, in the bishop's sermons, simultaneously antagonistic and yet intermingled. One of the previously unknown sermons recently published probably bears witness to their first use; in this text, datable to 404, the two cities are named and contrasted in a clearly allegorical fashion:

> Babylon receives the fruits of what it has done. There is in fact an ungodly city that extends over all the earth and, so to speak, represents the consensus of human ungodliness: in the Scriptures it is called, spiritually (*mystice*), Babylon. In contrast, there exists a city in pilgrimage on this earth which represents for all nations the consensus of piety: it is called Jerusalem. Now the two cities are intermingled, but at the end they will be separated.[ak]

Some years later, in the commentary on Psalm 65, the two cities are evoked with the very words used at the end of Book XIV of the *City of God*: 'Two cities were created by two kinds of love: the love of God created Jerusalem; love of the world created Babylon.' Shortly before, the bishop had said to his faithful: '(These two cities), mingled since the beginning of the human race, continue their path to the end of the world. Jerusalem began with Abel, Babylon with Cain.' Did he see before him his listeners disconcerted by this timeless myth? To re-establish the concrete realities of the historical view beside the allegory, he at once added, 'Only later did the buildings of these two towns rise.'[al]

This commentary on Psalm 65 is probably datable to 412, precisely the period when we see Augustine, in the *De Genesi ad litteram*, define the 'two loves'[am] by contrasting them. Also contemporaneous is the one given by Augustine not long after on Psalm 137 – that superb poem on the captivity in Babylon: 'If I forget thee, O Jerusalem, let my right hand forget her cunning!'[an] – in which we best see the central theme of the second part of the *City of God* begin to take shape. But from another series of slightly later sermons, the commentary on Psalm 62 must also be quoted, where this theme is further enriched and, to complement and render more concrete the overlapping situation of the two cities, the bishop introduces the argument that 'sometimes the worldly mix makes some who belong to the city of Babylon administer the affairs of Jerusalem, and conversely, some who belong to Jerusalem administer the affairs of Babylon'.[ao] Here again, he must have read astonishment on his listeners' faces, for he adds, 'I seem to have said something difficult for you.' Have patience, he tells them, and as proof of these intricacies in biblical times mentions, alongside certain evil kings of Jerusalem, ungodly citizens of Babylon, the three young Hebrews to whom Nebuchadnezzar entrusted the affairs of Babylon, who were confirmed in their office upon their miraculous escape from the furnace (Dan. 3.27). Then he passes to the present time, mentioning, with regard to the 'citizens of the wicked city who have a part in the government of the good city', 'the faithful and righteous who, in the towns of the earthly city, are magistrates, judges, officers, "counts" and even kings . . . performing an obligatory chore, so to speak, in a city doomed to perish'. The name of Rome is not uttered, but may be glimpsed beneath the surface of that of Babylon.

In this great work, the fundamental ambiguity persists, consciously and deliberately maintained by Augustine and with intentions that could also be called pedagogical. The Rome whose political reality his listeners and readers experienced was an obvious image of the earthly city; an 'imperfect' image, because of its complexity and the mixture of good and evil to be observed in it;[ap] but at least it conveyed some idea of the earthly city. For Augustine Rome was the true Babylon of the West; it came afterwards historically,[aq] but he was in no haste to identify it with the mythical Babylon. The myth was useful to him, however. As in the beginning of the world there had been a fratricide, by Cain, the murderer of Abel, so in the origins of Rome there lay the murder of Remus by his brother Romulus: this, said the bishop, was the reproduction of an 'archetype'.[ar] It came as no surprise that Rome had produced a Nero.[as] As for the heavenly city, similar images were even more 'imperfect' and harder to find. As Cain belongs to the city of men, Abel, said Augustine, belongs to the city of God.[at] Yes, but Abel, the shepherd, in exile (*peregrinus*) on this earth, died before the fulfilment of the promise augured by God's acceptance of his offering, unlike his brother's. Abel is only virtually representative of the heavenly city. The Israel of the Old Testament, which derives from Cain's initial act, is an earthly city, but one in which prophetic announcements of the heavenly city are manifested, as in the episode of Hagar and Sara in whom Augustine, resuming the allegorical exegesis of the biblical account in St Paul (Gal. 4.21–31), sees the example of the *civitas caelestis* and the New Covenant to come.[au] But in the tumultuous history that follows, the 'appearances' of the city of God in the earthly city of Israel are revealed with proof to the reader of the Bible: they are called Noah, Abraham, Lot and will also be called Isaac and Jacob, the latter above all being a clear prefiguration of Christ.[av]

What idea could Augustine's contemporaries, in their time, have formed of the heavenly city according to his texts? Whether or not they were Christians, by the very fact of their historical existence they held the reality of that mixture in which the two cities coexisted to the end of time – and the bishop strove to make them become aware of it. They were, as we would say today, the 'interface' between Jerusalem and Babylon. Among them, the Christians who were vastly in the majority as listeners to the sermons or readers of the book, might be tempted, as Christians, to consider themselves in anticipation as citizens of the city of God. Had not Augustine said that in the Babylon of their time there were righteous men who performed statute labour in its service, like the three Hebrews in the time of Nebuchadnezzar?[aw] Some, and not always the lesser mortals, dared to take him at his word, for instance Dardanus, the bishop's correspondent and friend, praetorian prefect for the Gauls and a great estate owner in the region of Sisteron: with his wife and brother, he had founded a Christian community, a little 'retreat' in the Alpine setting of Haute Provence, to which, in simple homage to the author of the *City of God*, he had given the name *Theopolis*.[26] Augustine, however, did not encourage his followers to react and think in this way: he had battled too much against the ecclesial conceptions of the Donatists to be inclined to do so.[ax] The Church to which his flocks belonged, the visible and hierarchical Church, *hic et nunc*, was the only one called to become the heavenly city; it was at least the part on pilgrimage here on earth, representing it impurely and imperfectly, both by excess and by default: in its ranks were men who would not be numbered among the elect and, conversely, sometimes other men who were destined to take their place in the kingdom, did not appear there.[ay] Selection would be the business of the reaping angels.

A Christian society?

In the meantime, life had to be lived, as well as possible, on this earth, adapting to the inevitable and irreducible disparity resulting from the simultaneously parallel and interwoven existence of the two cities. Here is a political and social problem that Augustine does not evade. He gives its solution in a magnificent page of his great work:

> All the time the heavenly city lives in exile (*peregrinatur*) on this earth, it recruits citizens from every nation, gathering a society of aliens (*peregrinam societatem*) speaking all languages, but taking no account of the differences in their customs, laws and institutions, by which earthly peace is established or maintained; it suppresses none of them, destroys none; but rather, it maintains and observes everything which, though different in the different nations, tends to one and the same end, earthly peace, at least provided nothing impedes the religion which teaches us to worship the one true and sovereign God. Thus the heavenly city in its pilgrimage makes use of earthly peace, and in all that concerns the mortal nature of men, it defends and seeks the compromise of human wills, so far as may be permitted without detriment to true religion and piety. In

fact, that city relates this earthly peace to the heavenly peace, which is so truly peaceful that it should be looked upon as the only peace deserving the name, at least as regards rational creatures; it is the perfectly ordered and completely harmonious fellowship in the enjoyment of God, and of one another in God. When we arrive at that state of peace, life will no longer end in death, but will be a life in sure and sober truth; and there will be no animal body to weigh down the soul in its corruption, but a spiritual body free of cravings and in every part subdued to the will. The heavenly city, while on pilgrimage in faith, possesses this peace, and by virtue of that faith lives a life of righteousness, with the attainment of that peace in view in every good action performed in relation to God and to a neighbour, since the life of a city is inevitably a social life.[az]

The quotation of this long text may be forgiven, bearing in mind that it could not be shortened, for it is no exaggeration to see it as a 'platform' summarizing the main lines of Augustine's political thinking. The bishop expresses himself as pastor, charged, with others, with the duty of guaranteeing the heavenly city in exile on this earth the best possible conditions for its 'pilgrimage'. His kingdom, also, is not of this world, so one should not expect the outline of a *De re publica* or a *Peri politeias*, even though, like Aristotle, he believes man to be a 'political animal' and concurs with the Stoics and Cicero in professing that 'a wise man's life is a social life'.[ba] But he does not believe that the wise man can find happiness in the city, and is sure that the Christian could not find his goal therein, and therefore the organization of the State is in itself not his affair. The gathering of the 'fellowship of aliens' (*peregrina societas*) is, if not a 'spiritual communism', at least the universalism of a spiritual citizenship based on the famous address of St Paul to the Galatians: 'There is neither Jew nor Greek, slave nor free man, male nor female' (Gal. 3.28). This is on the plane of faith, where Augustine stood like St Paul.[bc] The corollary was that on the political plane he accepted just as they were – with a concern possibly to alter their application, but without dreaming of reforming them in principle – the institutions current here and there in the earthly city, and first and foremost in the Roman city. The condition stipulated for this acquiescence was that the laws and ordinances of the earthly city should not go counter to Christianity and its worship. Augustine had already made himself very clear on this point: 'As for this mortal life, which ends after but a few days' course, what does it matter under what political regime a man lives, when he is doomed to die, provided that the rulers do not force him to commit ungodly and wicked acts?'[bd] And, if the worst came to the worst, the servant of God should meekly endure the most hateful of States, 'to win for himself, by his endurance, a place of glory in the heavenly republic'.[be]

But that heroic forbearance was now out of season. Apart from a brief interval, in the time of Julian the Apostate, people had been living since Constantine in a Christian empire and, in the preceding decades, far from opposing the new religion, the rulers – especially the great Theodosius – had consolidated it and hastened the decline of paganism. They had contributed much to stabilizing it by involving themselves forcefully in the battle against sects and deviancies of all kinds. Even though the bishop did not feel indebted to Honorius, who in his view had merely done his duty as a Christian ruler by bringing Donatism to a decisive halt, he nonetheless benefited from his religious policy. Reciprocity involved strict observance of imperial laws, provided those laws worked towards the establishment and preservation of social peace. At the beginning of Book XIX of the *City of God*, we read a vibrant hymn to peace, taken to the point of paradox: even wars, says Augustine, are waged with peace in mind – the peace that it is desired to impose, of course – and even robbers want peace, at least among themselves, for their own safety. Of course, there is peace and peace, and the supreme peace is that of the heavenly city. But while we wait to enjoy it, we must aim for peace among men. To define it, the bishop uses words loaded with meaning, significantly repeated: 'the peace of men, is their well ordered agreement (*ordinata concordia*)'; and the peace of the city 'is the well ordered agreement of citizens in giving and obeying orders'.[bf]

The key word can be picked out obviously: it is 'order' even more than agreement (in the Latin sense of *ordo*, which is not command). We have seen, in the *De vera religione*, how revealing is the slip by which Augustine, quoting from memory, made St Paul say 'All order (*ordo*) comes from God', when the Apostle had really said 'All authority (*potestas*) comes from God' in a text which, as one knows, is the charter of Christian obedience to the political powers (Rom. 13.1).[27] In 426, rereading his sentence of 390 for the *Retractations*, the old bishop would recognize that it was not exactly St Paul's word, but nevertheless persisted in his significant misreading, continuing to put the Apostle on his side by interpreting in his own fashion the rest of the verse: 'All that is,' he would write, 'has been ordered (i.e., "put in order") by God.'[bg] For the young Augustine, order was 'that whose observance in life led to God'.[bh] Some forty years later, a few echoes still remained of the Neoplatonist inspiration of the *De ordine* in the transcendent function which the bishop attributed to order: 'The peace of the whole universe is the tranquillity of order. Order is the arrangement of things equal and unequal in a pattern which assigns to each its allotted position.'[bi] But he no longer believed that this order, observance of which could lead to God, was to be found 'in this life', in other words in the city here below: for that, he wrote shortly after 400, 'the empire and government of human affairs need to be in the hands of wise men, religiously and truly subject to God'; and we are not there yet, he sighed.[bj] Theodosius himself, the great Theodosius, whose long reign had been the 'Indian summer' of the declining Empire and whom 'pious humility' had allowed to 'experience more joy in being a member of the Church than in dominating the universe',[28] was assuredly a model for Christian rulers, but was not regarded by the bishop as an agent sent by God to shoulder the government of men. The notion of monarchy by divine right would have been the last idea to enter Augustine's mind, which was very far from the theology of the Empire – the distant ancestor of what would much later be called 'caesaropapism', a word more convenient than well-chosen – developed a century earlier by Eusebius of Caesarea, who had had no hesitation in seeing Constantine as not only the instrument of divine power but also the image of the divine Logos.

We can realize that the surprising 'error' in the reading of Rom. 13.1, committed again at the time of the *Retractations*,[bk] that is to say, when the *City of God* was completed, was by no means a blunder. Concurring with the Apostle in imposing on Christians the imperative of obedience to the constituted authorities, the bishop no longer did so when it came to holding that these authorities (*potestates*) had been constituted by God. That would only be the case if those powers of man over man had been in the natural order of things, before the Fall. But, says Augustine, 'by nature, in the condition in which God first created man, no man is the slave either of man or of sin'.[bl] For the bishop, the natural order in relationships between humans is to be found in the setting of the family 'cell', broadly understood, as it was in Antiquity: 'Those who have concern for others are those who give orders, such as the husband to the wife, parents to children, masters to servants . . . This is what natural order lays down, and thus God created man.'[bm] Anyway, commenting on Gen. 1.26, Augustine stresses that the Creator wanted the rational being, made in his image, to have dominion only over irrational beings: 'not man over man, but man over beasts'.[29] That is why, he continues, the first righteous men – whose prototype was the short-lived Abel – were shepherds and not kings. But Abel's successors were not alone with their flocks and, being social by nature, they gathered together in human fellowship, outside any 'contract'. But, the bishop adds, though 'there is no race so social by nature, there is none so quarrelsome by perversion'.[bn] By 'perversion' we must understand the sin of origin and its inevitable consequences which, to Augustine's way of thinking, soon led to the delegation of power, granted in primitive times to the wisest, who exercised it according to the natural order like a good paterfamilias, being supplanted by ambition for power which introduced into the harmonious coherence of human communities instability, rivalry, rebellion and their results, repression, punishment and torture. Like slavery, whose origin was connected with a 'sin',[bo] the birth of States and development of Empires were the consequence – if not immediate, at least arising swiftly in man's becoming – of original sin.

Now we understand more clearly, in this perspective, the sense of the phrase quoted earlier on the peace of the city being 'the well-ordered agreement of citizens in the giving and obeying of orders'. Although some political regimes are better than others and more desirable for Christians, order, even if in the debased definition that it has in the earthly city, is so important that even a bad emperor must be obeyed, provided he has some legitimacy, according to the criteria of that city. A strong government, firm laws that the public authority enforces are indispensable for containing all the possibilities for disorder that lie in human hearts. Augustine thus appears to be a 'law and order man', in all the irreducible ambiguity that the expression comprises in our language. He was, however, the first to want magistrates and Christian governors to be involved in maintaining that order, combining leniency with firmness, tempering severity with clemency; and his own attitudes in many material situations[bp] were constructive contributions to the building of an 'actual' Christian society about which he did not dream of theorizing. At the big international Augustinian congress, held several decades ago to commemorate the sixteenth centenary of Augustine's birth, in order to define the bishop's historico-political ideal, it was thought a good idea to propose the notion of *civitas terrena spiritualis*: Henri-Irénée Marrou was not wrong in seeing this as a 'verbal monster' which shot Augustinian categories to pieces. A completely empirical Christian society, largely the result of antagonistic forces, was not only desirable but assuredly possible for Augustine. Yet never did he make a working drawing of a Christian State, or more exactly, a theocratic Christian State. He would not have been able to do so without denying – as medieval and modern Augustinians have blithely done –

the very principle of the city of God, which can come to pass only outside History.

The end of History

In his youth, Augustine's beloved Virgil had taught him how the Ancients, his predecessors, had tried to banish the anguish caused to them by Cronus, busily devouring his own children. To remedy the pessimistic myth portraying the inexorable degradation of beings and things the farther they grew from their origins – from the golden age to the iron age – was added the reassuring myth of the cyclical return, the *renovatio temporum*; nothing was irremediably lost, clement gods made the wheel turn, Hesiod's old golden age could come back, enriched with new prospects.[30] Throughout long centuries in Antiquity, that belief in a periodic renewal of the world's youth took the place of the idea of progress. At first, perhaps, if we want to search for its roots in collective psychology, it was for lack of sufficiently frequent and outstanding technical evolutions to confirm qualitatively the span of time and enable a 'before' and 'after' to be materially identified. The technological whirlwind in which we are caught up, giving us the illusion of spiralling ever faster upwards in time, makes us ill at ease when imagining the quasi-permanence – at least on the scale of a man's life – of the material cultures which served as a backdrop to the generations of that era. Surrounding Augustine, life in Africa was not noticeably very different from that in Apuleius' time, a good two centuries earlier. And it was the same everywhere in the ancient world.

Nevertheless, beneath that faith in an eternal return lay a deeper, philosophical reason. The Roman world, in the heart of which Christianity had been developing for three centuries, was still intellectually beholden to Greek thinking which, while asserting the principle of the world's eternity, that is to say, a time span with no beginning, was repelled by the idea of an indefinitely prolonged and homogeneous time-span, and replaced the idea of indefinite uninterrupted advance with that of a cyclical return, dividing the span of History into mythical 'ages'. The Stoic school, notably, conceived of a single and eternal universe, but one which passed through innumerable alternatives of births and deaths at fixed intervals.[bq] This notion, which was deeply foreign to Judaism, whose Old Testamentary writings revealed a universal and continuous History, advancing by the interplay of the singular destinies of its protagonists, was radically irreconcilable with Christian witness of the historical incarnation of a Saviour who had acted once and for all for humanity as a whole, as well as with a religious thinking which, in the flow of irreversible time, envisaged a definite eschatological horizon without any precise temporal limit. We can understand why Augustine, as he says, rebelled against 'the wise men of this world (who) thought they had to postulate periodic cycles of time in order to renew nature'.[br] With the intellectual honesty he brought to every dispute, he did not evade the apparently strongest arguments put forward by supporters of these 'cycles'. Infinite things, they said, were beyond the comprehension of any knowledge: therefore God himself could have only finite reasons for his finite works.[bs] And also questioning Christian cosmology, they added the criticism that Augustine knew all too well from having heard it in another form from the lips of the

Manichaeans:^{bt} it was unbelievable that, his goodness having at first been inactive, he had made up for his earlier inaction by suddenly starting work on his Creation. To avoid these difficulties, it was therefore better to conceive of an uncreated world permanent in its finitude, but constantly renewed cyclically as in a closed circuit – or like a mechanism that returns to its starting-point after exhausting its successive series of movements.

Augustine had long reflected on the problem of the Creation and meditated enough on time to be at ease in his replies. Many years before, he had said the essentials in the *Confessions*. Unless one admitted that there could have been an 'empty time' created by God, in the heart of which at a given moment the Creator gave life to his Creation – but that hypothesis cannot be entertained, for time, which implies movement and change,^{bu} cannot be 'empty' – it would be impossible to conceive of a time before the divine Creation, for time is itself a divine creation, and 'there was no "then" where there was no time'.^{bv} In the very heart of Creation, objections that might be raised in noting the belated appearance of 'historical man' did not perturb him. The possible computations according to the Bible reckoned man's antiquity at less than six thousand years; but, the bishop went on, as if moved by an intuition of the slow movements of prehistory, if that lapse of time since man's appearance were sixty or six hundred thousand years, even sixty or six hundred million years, or even a multiple of that, inexpressible in figures, one could still wonder why God did not make man any sooner. And whatever duration was ascribed to the period before man's appearance, those two time-spans, however great one imagined them, were like two drops of water in the infinity of an ocean.^{bw} For everything that is finite, everything that has a term, is short relative to the eternity of God, whose transcendence, as regards time – and therefore as regards creatures – is not concerned with anteriority but with being in relation to non-being. There can be no doubt: 'No creature is co-eternal with the Creator.'^{bx} The author of the *Confessions* expressed himself no differently; he said that the idea of a creature co-eternal with God was inconceivable, for it was to presuppose the attribution of a homogeneous mode of duration to heterogeneous ways of being. 'No times are co-eternal with you, because you are permanent; whereas if they were permanent, they would not be times.'^{by}

The metaphysically arguable principle of an uncreated world, both eternal and periodic, was incompatible with the Judaeo-Christian concept, born of revelation, of a progressive and finite human history. In the same way that each person's life on this earth was played out only once and that all flesh came to an end, human times also were fulfilled and reached their term. The history of humankind unfolded like a vast triptych, whose central panel was the incarnation of God made man – the 'kenosis' – his passion, followed by his glorious resurrection: a few short years in that immense expanse of time, but which gave the whole its entire meaning, of being the history of salvation.³¹ On either side of that axis were two long sequences of time, only the first of which was complete and could be envisaged historically in its entirety. The bishop separated it into 'ages', but they were historical and no longer mythical ages which, in the simultaneously parallel and 'interwoven' progress of the two cities, led from Adam to the birth of Christ.^{bz} The second – the third panel of the triptych – was the time when Augustine was living, when we ourselves live and when the indeterminate but not infinite sequence of our descendants will live. History will stop when the world has achieved its spiritual growth which, far from merging with its demographic growth, can only be held back by the latter. Of course, the Creator had said, 'Increase and multiply';[32] but to those who objected that the chastity Augustine advocated ran the risk of resulting in the extinction of the human species, far from being alarmed, he replied that 'worldly time' had been extended solely in order to complete the number of the saints: if the number were attained more quickly – and it was clear that in the bishop's mind this had nothing to do with the number of births – the end of this 'worldly time', in other words, the end of the world here below, would not be 'postponed', as he put it.[ca] Some years earlier, in the same sense, he had declared that if men abstained from marrying – and thus from procreation, which was its purpose – 'the city of God' would arrive all the sooner.[cb] The bishop's thinking on this subject had been set very early, seemingly finding its first expression in his fine sermon *On the good of marriage* which, in the recently published new sermons, apparently dates back to his preaching campaign in Carthage in the summer of 397.[cd] Quoting Eccles. 3.5 he was already saying that there was a time to embrace – that of the Patriarchs and Prophets – but that they were now in the time – of the Gospels – to refrain from embracing.[ce] Up to the resumption of this theme in 419, in the first part of the book *On marriage and concupiscence*,[cf] we may observe an unfailing Augustinian consistency on this subject.

For Augustine, with his own images and myths, the faithful interpreter of a Christian tradition as old as the texts of the New Testament, the duration of the *civitas terrena* equalled the time necessary for the recruitment of the fellowship of saints, who would people the *civitas caelestis*, celestial Jerusalem. In a letter sent in 417 to Paulinus of Nola, and co-signed by Alypius, he wrote: 'God, in his foreknowledge, has thus determined the number that will be reached by the multitude of saints.'[cg] He was echoing what can be read in the Apocalypse, when on the opening of the fifth seal we see the souls of the martyrs for the faith, calling for justice: 'Then,' says the text, 'white robes were given unto every one of them; and it was said unto them that they should rest yet for a little season until the number of their fellow-servants should be fulfilled' (Rev. 6.9–11). At the end of this time would come the Parousia, which is the end of History. Like all Christians, Augustine read Matt. 24.36 (Mark. 13.32), where Christ himself, speaking *sub forma servi*, 'in human form' said no man knew 'either the day or the hour', and it was known only to the Father. Like all Christians, he knew that the Son of Man would come unexpectedly, as in the days of Noah, or like a thief in the night (Matt. 24.37–43): a potential imminence which, in the immeasurable flow of time that has yet to elapse, put every generation at an equal distance from eternity. Any prognostication of the moment of the *adventus Christi* was useless, as he had explained at length to his colleague Hesychius of Salonae;[33] the only thing to be done was to prepare oneself for it, cultivate in oneself the spiritual first-fruits from which the yearning for Jerusalem[34] was born in the depths of the soul. At the time of the *Confessions*, Augustine had broken away from the prospect – inspired by the images from the Jewish Apocalypse and resumed in John's Revelation (20.6), of the happiness of the righteous with the Messiah in his temporal reign of one thousand years – of an earthly reign of Christ with his saints between the time of the end of the world and the time of the resurrection.[35]

The end of History would introduce the living and the dead, without any transition, into a kind of reality, or better, into a way of being, truly 'unheard of' (cf. 1 Cor. 2.9), fear of which must be dispelled for the righteous. The bishop strove to take the drama out of the Apocalypse for them, to tone down the disquieting visions, replace the idea of annihilation with one of a metamorphosis of the world they knew: what would pass and change – he repeated again using St Paul's words – 'was the outward form of the world, not its substance'.[ch] Out of the universal conflagration, by a marvellous transformation there would emerge 'a world renewed for the better, fitting for men who are renewed for the better, even in their flesh'.[ci] Hope has the last word.

Notes

a. Jerome, *Ep.* 60, 16.
b. *City of God*, V, 23.
c. *On his return*, II, 41–66.
d. *De bello Gothico*, 249–64.
e. *City of God*, I, 1.
f. *Ep.* 111, 1, dated 409/10.
g. *Sermon* 81, 8, *in fine*, delivered at Hippo in the autumn of 410.
h. Jerome, *Ep.* 123, 16.
i. *Ep.* 127 (to Principia), 12–13.
j. *Sermon* 81, 9; *City of God*, II, 2.
k. *Sermon* 105, 10, quoting the *Aeneid*, I, 279.
l. *Sermon* 81, 9.
m. *Sermon* 80, 8.
n. The text of the *Hortensius* appears in the *De beata vita*, 10, and will be quoted again in *De Trin.*, XIII, 8.
o. *Sermon* 81, 9.
p. *Sermon* 105, 12: *O si taceat de Roma!*
q. *Sermon* 296, 6.
r. *Sermon* 296, 7: *In ipse Petro temporalis fuit caro, et non vis ut temporalis sit* lapis Romae!
s. *Sermon* 296, 7; Possidius, *Vita Aug.*, XXVIII, 11.
t. *Sermon* 296, 12.
u. *De excidio urbis*, 4. The example of Job will be taken up again at the beginning of the *City of God*: I, 10, 2.
v. *Sermon* 81, 7.
w. Above, p. 328.
x. *Ep.* 136, 2.
y. *Ep.* 137, 20.
z. *Ep.* 137, 17.
aa. *Ep.* 138, 9–10.
bb. *Ep.* 136, 3.
cc. *Ep.* 138, 20.
dd. *City of God*, I, 1: *hoc opere . . . mea ad te promissione debito.*
ee. *City of God*, V, 26, 2.
ff. *Ep.* 154, 2; cf. *Ep.* 155, 2: *in primo libro trium illorum quos benignissime et studiosissime perlegisti.*
gg. *Ep.* 169, 1 (to Evodius).
hh. *Ep.* 184 A, 5.
ii. *Peregrinatur*, in the text, which is rendered insipid when translated by 'on pilgrimage'.
jj. *City of God*, I, *pref.*

kk.   First evoked allusively, the verse of Ps. 87.7: *Gloriosa dicta sunt de te, civitas die* is not quoted in its entirety until the end of II, 21, 4, to reappear, with other texts of the Psalmist in which the 'city of God' figures, at the beginning of Book XI.

ll.   *City of God*, I, 35, *in fine*. The good Possidius (*Vita Aug., praef.*, 3) will take up these three terms (*exortus, procursus, debitus finis*) to apply them to the phases in the life of his 'hero'.

mm.   *City of God*, X, 32, 4 and XI, 1, *in fine: Retract.*, II, 43, 2.

nn.   *City of God*, I, 1–7.

oo.   *City of God*, I, 30–2.

pp.   *City of God*, I, 36, *initio: Sed adhuc mihi quaedam dicenda sunt.*

qq.   *City of God*, IV, 2.

rr.   For the reader's convenience, this announcement will be resumed in the same terms in V, 26, 2, *initio*.

ss.   *City of God*, VI, 1, 1.

tt.   *City of God*, X, 32, 4. This tripartite division will be taken up again *verbatim* in XI, 1, *in fine*.

uu.   *Ep.* 184 A, 5.

vv.   *City of God*, XV, 1, 1.

ww.   *City of God*, XV, 1, 1: *quarum est una quae praedestinata est in aeternum regnare cum deo, altera aeternum supplicium subire cum diabolo.*

xx.   *City of God*, XVIII, 54, 2.

yy.   *City of God*, XVIII, 1.

zz.   *City of God*, XVII, 20, 2, *in fine*.

ab.   *City of God*, XVIII, 27–36.

ac.   *City of God*, XVIII, 42–4.

ad.   Above, p. 402.

ae.   *Ep.* 2*, 3, BA, 46 B, p. 62.

af.   *Ep.* 1*A, 1, BA, 46 B, p. 56.

ag.   *City of God*, XIV, 28, *initio*.

ah.   Above, p. 138.

ai.   *De vera religione*, 50.

aj.   *De catechizandis rudibus*, 31, in BA, 11/1, 1991, p. 157.

ak.   *Sermon Dolbeau* 4 (*Mainz* 9), 7–8, in F. Dolbeau, *Vingt-six Sermons au peuple d'Afrique*, p. 519. This is taken from the translation published by the editor in *CRAI*, 1993, p. 165.

al.   *Enarr. in Psalm.* 64, 2.

am.   *De Genesi ad litteram*, XI, 20.

an.   Ps. 137.5.

ao.   *Enarr. in Psalm.* 61, 8.

ap.   Cf. *City of God*, V, 12–18 on the Roman virtues which enabled Rome to develop its earthly city.

aq.   This will be said clearly in *City of God*, XVIII, 22, *initio*.

ar.   *City of God*, XV, 5.

as.   *City of God*, V, 19.

at.   *City of God*, XV, 1, 2, *initio*.

au.   *City of God*, XV, 2.

av.   See all of Book XVI, especially chap. 18–39.

aw.   Cf. above, the *Enarr. in Psalm.* 61, 8.

ax.   Cf. above, pp. 280–1.

ay.   Cf. *City of God*, I, 35.

az.   *City of God*, XIX, 17.

ba.   *City of God*, XIX, 5, *initio*.

bc.   Cf. his commentary in *Expositio ep. ad. Gal.*, 28.

bd.   *City of God*, V, 17, 1.

be.   *City of God*, II, 19, *in fine*.

bf.   *City of God*, XIX, 13.

bg.   *Retract.*, I, 13, 8, *initio: Quae autem sunt a deo ordinatae sunt;* which is St Paul's text, but in him *quae* refers to *potestates*, the political authorities!

bh.   *De ordine*, I, 27.
bi.   *City of God*, XIX, 13, 1.
bj.   *De Trinitate*, III, 9, *initio*.
bk.   *Retract.*, I, 13, 8, *initio*.
bl.   *City of God*, XIX, 15.
bm.   *City of God*, XIX, 14, *in fine* and 15, *initio*.
bn.   *City of God*, XII, 28, 1: *Nihil enim est quam hoc genus tam discordiosum vitio, tam sociale natura*.
bo.   Augustine notes significantly (*City of God*, XIX, 15) that the word 'slave' is not found in the Bible until Noah uses it to reprove his son Shem's misdeed (Gen. 9.25–6).
bp.   Cf. notably above, pp. 259–60.
bq.   Augustine alludes to it in *City of God*, XII, 12.
br.   *City of God*, XII, 14, 1.
bs.   *City of God*, XII, 18, 1.
bt.   Cf. above, p. 134.
bu.   Cf. *City of God*, XI, 6, resuming the Aristotelian argument.
bv.   *Conf.*, XI, 15: *Non enim erat tunc, ubi non erat tempus*; see also *City of God*, XI, 6.
bw.   *City of God*, XII, 13.
bx.   *City of God*, XII, 17.
by.   *Conf.*, XI, 17, and the commentary by E. Gilson, *Introduction à l'étude de saint Augustin*, p. 247.
bz.   Cf. notably *City of God*, XXII, 30, 5 and *passim*.
ca.   *De bono viduitatis* (text dated 414), 28.
cb.   *De bono coniugali*, 10, a remarkable text, taking into account its early date, c. 400.
cd.   Cf. above, pp. 194–7.
ce.   *Sermon Dolbeau* 12 (*Mainz* 41), 11, in F. Dolbeau, *Vingt-six Sermons au peuple d'Afrique*, pp. 82–3.
cf.   *De nuptiis et concupiscentia*, I, 14.
cg.   *Ep.* 186, 25, *initio*.
ch.   *City of God*, XX, 14; cf. 1 Cor. 7.31.
ci.   *City of God*, XX, 16.

CHAPTER XXXII

Julian of Eclanum

Probably around summer's end in 408, Augustine received a letter from an Italian colleague, Memorius;[1] this Campanian bishop asked him to send him the six books of the *De musica*, for his son's instruction. He was rather unlucky. It had been a good while since Augustine had detached himself from those *Disciplinarum libri*, written twenty years before, between Cassiciacum and Milan:[a] those delights, he said, had slipped from his hands when he had taken on the burden of the episcopacy.[b] But one has only to read the charge against great literature – history alone is spared – that fills a good page of his reply,[c] to understand that he no longer believed in the good use of these liberal arts, or in the virtue of *exercitatio animi* that he had ascribed to them at the time of Cassiciacum, even though, among the arts, those concerned with number and rhythm were still the most fitting to elevate the soul above the realities of the senses. Then, as further cause for not sending the whole of the treatise to Memorius, Augustine added a technical reason, so to speak: he had not revised and amended the first five books, which were virtually illegible because there was no clear and explicit distinction between the interlocutors – it was a dialogue – and almost unusable, he said, for want of aural recognition (which only reading the text aloud could obtain) of the length of syllables and the quality of the rhythmical music in the examples given.[d] But Memorius' son might profitably read the sixth book, a duly revised and corrected copy of which Augustine had found in his library, and which moreover contained the 'fruit' of the first five.[2] Possidius, who was on a mission to the Court that summer to complain of the snubs to which the pagans were subjecting him in his fine town of Calama, would have the task of taking the *codex* and the letter with him.

Though Augustine was not yet able to gauge the personality of the recipient, he knew enough about his status to take some precautions. Julian, Memorius' son, was a deacon, after starting out as a lector in the church of his father, the bishop. In Campania, where Greek literature had continued to be held in honour, he had received the classical education of an adolescent *utraque lingua eruditus*,[e] very probably complemented by a training period with the rhetors of Rome. Doubtless also in Rome, he had had the benefit of a philosophical training which is thought to have been strongly tinged with Aristotelianism.[3] On his return, he had married the daughter of a neighbouring bishop, Aemilius of Benevento. There had been no shortage of blessings on the young couple, even less as Paulinus of Nola, a friend of both families, had come up with an epithalamium setting forth the example of Adam and Eve's chaste simplicity before the Fall and, by its insistence on the model provided by Mary's marriage, suggested that the young people should live their union in the chastity that Paulinus himself observed with Therasia; at worst, if they knew each other physically, the future bishop of Nola could envisage their producing, in chastity, a third generation of priests!ᶠ We do not know if this theory was realized and if Julian's marriage proved fruitful, but it is certain that the blessings from on high which surrounded him had strengthened the future bishop's trust in the excellence of a sacrament that was strong enough to exorcize the evil of concupiscence.ᵍ At the time of his controversies with the bishop of Hippo, we know that he lived in a state of continence, probably adopted when he became a deacon. There is noticeably a vast difference between his experience and that of Augustine who, at the same age or even younger, had lived a relationship with Adeodatus' mother which was certainly lasting, certainly faithfully entered into, but openly motivated solely by the satisfaction of his sexual needs. And, in comparison with the son of the Campanian bishop, to give a better idea of the dual 'marginality' of the student and then teacher at Carthage, we must not forget that during those years he lived that relationship outside wedlock – sanctioned by a birth, but with no social validation – in a fragile freedom, equally deprived of an unequivocal blessing from the hypocritically chaste Manichaean milieu in which he was then half immersed.⁴

By the evidence, at the time of this exchange of letters with Memorius, Augustine had no direct knowledge of the young Julian, and he expressed his keen desire and hope that he would come to visit him while no major duty as yet required him.ʰ In fact, the young man came to Africa and stayed at Carthage, where he would later say that he had met Honoratus, the bishop of Hippo's friend and dedicatee of the *De utilitate credendi*, while still a Manichaean.ⁱ Was it in 410–11, when all Rome and part of southern Italy, including Pelagius, had flowed across to the opposite shore?⁵ If that was so, then history had maliciously repeated itself, for Augustine had apparently not had – and would not have – the opportunity of meeting this Julian with whom he was to hold written dialogues for over ten years.

Soon afterwards, around 416, Pope Innocent consecrated Memorius' son bishop of Eclanum, in Campania, not far from Paulinus' estates. Early in 417, when Pelagius was first condemned by Innocent, who was then only a few weeks away from death, the new bishop did not show himself. Was he among those targeted by Alypius and Augustine in their letter addressed the same year to Paulinus, whose former intellectual sympathy for Pelagius they knew? They had heard it said that there were people around the bishop of Nola, at least in his town, who were determined to spurn Pelagius and abandon him if he submitted, rather than follow him in his capitulation.ʲ The reinstatement of Caelestius and Pelagius by Zosimus, Innocent's successor, could only calm these potential stirrings without abating the vigilance of the sect's adherents. But one year later, the triple condemnation of the emperor (30 April 418), the general council of Carthage (1 May), and lastly of the pope himself (June–July),ᵏ unleashed a wave of resistance headed by Julian. During the summer of 418, Pope Zosimus had addressed a circular letter (*tractoria*), to be circulated and undersigned, definitively sanctioning the condemnation of Caelestius and Pelagius. In the West, the matter caused no difficulties, nor did it in Africa, obviously, nor Gaul nor Spain. But in Italy a group of eighteen bishops, led by Julian and with two centres, one in Campania, the other around Aquileia, on the Illyrian borders, refused to subscribe to the papal text. The young bishop of Eclanum had not been content with a passive refusal; shortly after the imperial rescript of 30 April, he had taken part in a Roman assembly which rejected the transmission of Adam's sin and had sent two letters of protest to the see of Rome; in company with the eighteen recalcitrant Italian bishops, he had also signed a text addressed to bishop Rufus of Thessalonica indicting the Roman clergy.[1] Above all, Julian had not been afraid to address Count Valerius, at Ravenna. This high-ranking soldier, very influential at Court, had probably been in contact since the spring of 418 with Aurelius of Carthage and Augustine, for whom he had been one of the relay points in their efforts to bring some weight to bear on the emperor's religious policies.[6] Julian said that he was writing to him to appeal for some competent judges; but at the same time he went on the attack, accusing Augustine of denigrating marriage and making it out to be the devil's work.[m] At the end of the long absence caused by the distant journey he had made as far as Caesarea in Mauretania (Cherchell),[n] Augustine had been informed of the young bishop of Eclanum's manoeuvres by three letters from Count Valerius, one brought by a non-African bishop, Vindemialis, and the others by the priest Firmus, which he found all together on his return to Hippo in October 418.[7] He replied without delay to these slanders, during the winter of 418–19, by the first book of the *De nuptiis et concupiscentia*. It was the start of a lengthy duel, which would not end until Augustine's death.

The long duel between Augustine and Julian of Eclanum

Apart from their budding difference on dogma, many things separated Augustine and the young bishop of Eclanum, the spoilt child of that southern Italy where, for many, the Africans were merely descendants of Hannibal, no matter what they did. The words *falsitas Punica*[o] would crop up again, and Julian would refer to the bishop of Hippo as the 'Punic quibbler' (*poenus disputator*). Augustine, who denied nothing of his African origins, would not see it as an insult, but would ironically pick out the word: 'You who are so proud of your earthly race, do not despise this Punic man who admonishes you: just because you were born in Puglia do not imagine that you can win a victory by birth over those Carthaginians whom you are incapable of conquering by intellect!'[p] It did not help matters that the dialogue they were to carry on for years by way of interposed books would be a to-and-fro dialogue, one of those perpetually out-of-step exchanges, when letters crossed and one side was always one reply behind the other.

Learning from his previous setbacks, due to his hesitant and muddled dealing with the Pelagius affair, this time Zosimus reacted without procrastination or weakness. Julian and his Pelagian colleagues were condemned and threatened with removal from office, unless they made an act of submission. The threat of deposition was accompanied by one of exile, and an edict by Flavius Constantius, patrician and future emperor, addressed to Volusianus, who in that year was pursuing his brilliant career as prefect of the City, at least prohibited Julian from staying in Rome. But the pope's death at the end of 418, and the difficulties surrounding his succession, which was disputed between Eulalius and Boniface until April 419, gave him several months' respite.

Probably quite early, in the spring of 419, in Ravenna, Book I of the *De nuptiis* came into the hands of Count Valerius, to whom it was dedicated, at the same time as the letter announcing its despatch. But although the powerful count was its first and main recipient,[q] by all evidence copies soon reached Rome and were quickly circulated in Italy; so it was not long before Julian knew about it and replied in the form of four books addressed to one of his friends, named Turbantius. Julian's books circulated as Augustine's book had done earlier. In the autumn of 419, Alypius was in Italy on a lengthy mission that would last until the spring of 420.[8] At Ravenna, where he stayed for quite a while, he had been able, if not to read Julian's texts, at least to hear Valerius talk about them. Before returning to Africa, he would pass through Rome, where Boniface would give him 'two letters from the Pelagians'[r] to hand on to Augustine. Meanwhile, Count Valerius had had a hybrid text hastily composed, a sort of collage containing texts by Augustine – taken from the first book of the *De nuptiis* – and their refutation in the form of quoted or summarized passages from Julian's *Ad Turbantium*.[9] Alypius was still in Rome, during the winter of 419–20, when Valerius sent it to him from Ravenna. It would be in Augustine's hands on the bishop of Thagaste's return in April, or perhaps not until May 420,[s] and without waiting to avail himself of Julian's complete text, he replied by the second book of the *De nuptiis*, dedicated to Valerius, like the first. The year 420 would seem to have been one of those rare periods of tranquillity when nothing forced him to absent himself from his diocese,[10] and throughout which he could work as he pleased; so there should be little hesitation in dating to this year – which may have run into the one following – his writing of the long refutation in four books of the 'two letters from the Pelagians', intended for Pope Boniface. Julian would mockingly describe Alypius – 'the little lackey for Augustine's sins'[t] – as the bearer of both the book destined for Valerius and those addressed to the see of Rome.[u] Doubt has recently been cast on a second journey at that date[11] by the bishop of Thagaste, for the reason that Augustine could not call upon his colleague and friend, himself a high-ranking prelate, as on a simple courier, and Julian's allegations have been seen as 'the invention of a polemicist'.[12] But the recent publication of new documents relating to these years in the correspondence of the bishop of Hippo has proved that the frequent trips by Alypius – and some others – to Italy in those times which were difficult in many respects, in fact had various motives whose details are still only partly known to us, just as the diplomatic activity which was the bishop of Thagaste's speciality still largely eludes us.[13] The Church of Africa was then engaged in battles that aimed not only at ensuring the triumph of its position in doctrinal matters, but also at supporting a society that was sapped by economic difficulties, crushed by pressure of taxation and dangerously threatened by a decline in public order, alarming signs of which were on the increase.[v] And as men like Count Valerius were rather the exception within the top-ranking imperial government, where the highest probity and impartiality were not the most widespread virtues, it may be imagined that, to achieve aims of which they were not ashamed, the African bishops charged with intendancy – which was not Augustine's field – may have resorted to those practices which roused Julian's indignation: the eighty horses fattened on Numidia's plains before travelling – with Alypius' luggage! – to the stables of the imperial Court were perhaps not entirely a figment of the bishop of Eclanum's imagination.[w] But he did not hesitate to 'pile it on', mentioning the inheritances of rich African dowagers wasted in the flames of such corruption, even suggesting – a serious and unlikely slander – that the money for the poor helped by the Church might have been used for the upkeep of the famous horses.[x]

At more or less the time when, according to Julian, Alypius was conveying his Numidian thoroughbreds to Ravenna, Augustine received the four books of the *Ad Turbantium* from one of his colleagues – a bishop, probably Italian, named Claudius – before being presented some months later with a second copy thanks to Alypius, who was then in Italy on a third mission.[y] He must have regretted the impulse that had made him write the refutation contained in Book II of his *De nuptiis* so hastily, when he realized the important differences between the original text and the extracts collected in the dossier put together by Count Valerius. Everything had to be redone, and furthermore Julian and his fellow sectarians could quite rightly complain that it was a caricature of their ideas.[z] Without wasting a moment, Augustine set to work. We may believe that despite the size of this new reply, the *Contra Iulianum* followed fairly closely on the arrival of Julian's complete text and that during the winter months of 421–22 the six books were dictated, their plan being clearly set forth in the first page.[aa] In Book I, Augustine first shows that his doctrine is that of the Church, based on an earlier tradition, before retorting to his young adversary that it is he who, with his ideas, is backing the Manichaeism for which he reproaches the bishop of Hippo. Book II, supporting the arguments of the first pages, is a collection of texts by the Fathers, eastern and western, that challenge Julian's errors.[14] In it, Augustine evokes the memory of Jerome, who had died in Palestine the year before, in the autumn of 420, and who, having passed, as he said, from West to East, had formed the link between the two Churches.[bb] Books III to VI form a detailed, book by book refutation of the four books of the *Ad Turbantium*.

This dialogue of the deaf continued, however. On receiving Book II of the *De nuptiis*, Julian launched into a reply – the eight books of the *Ad Florum*, the name of another of his companions who had remained loyal to the resistance; for Turbantius soon made amends and was reintegrated into the church fellowship by Pope Celestine.[cc] But Julian, probably in 420–21, in the time of Pope Boniface, had left for exile in Cilicia where, in company with several bishops who, like himself, were resistant to Zosimus' *Tractoria*, he had taken refuge with Theodorus of Mopsuestia, who was then still free of suspicion of heresy. This distant banishment explains why he did not know of the first *Contra Iulianum*, and similarly accounts for the long delay with which the *Ad Florum* reached Augustine, though it was composed at the start of Julian's exile, but so far away. In a letter that must be dated to the spring of 428, the bishop of Hippo wrote in reply to the Carthaginian deacon, Quodvultdeus, Aurelius' future successor,[dd] who had asked him to write a brief treatise on heresies, that he was very busy with his refutation of 'the eight books which Julian has published', after the four which he had already answered. Alypius, he says, found them in Rome – on the occasion of a fourth mission (in 427): he had had the first five copied and sent to Hippo, promising to send on the other three as quickly as possible. At the time Augustine was very occupied with a task which he deemed most urgent, writing his *Retractations*. He was now seventy-three years old; but valiantly set to work, sacrificing his nights to continuing the *Retractations* – he had finished with the books, but had to revise his letters and sermons – and devoting his days to answering Julian of Eclanum. At the date of his letter to Quodvultdeus, he was beginning his replies to the fourth book and, if the other books had not arrived, courageously intended to tackle both the expansion of his *Retractations* and the composition of the *De haeresibus* requested by the deacon.[15] The last three books of the *Ad Florum* did reach him, but death, which on 28 August 430 carried him away from a Hippo besieged by Vandals, left his second great reply to Julian unfinished in the middle of the sixth book.

Julian of Eclanum survived Augustine, but the hard-and-fast Pelagianism of which he was the ultimate champion did not outlive that final combat into which the old bishop had thrown his last efforts. On Augustine's death, Julian and his companions, including Florus, were again condemned by Pope Celestine, despite a request in their favour from the patriarch of Constantinople, Nestorius, with whom they had taken refuge on their departure from Cilicia, where they had fairly quickly been declared undesirable. The following year, the council of Ephesus (July 431) confirmed their deposition. Going from exile to exile, Julian finished his life some dozen years later, in an obscure retreat, perhaps as a schoolmaster in Sicily.

The short history of this joust between the two men writing in parallel, spread over some ten years, with lulls, intervals and many imbroglios, reveals that neither could avoid repetitions, more noticeable in Augustine, whose texts are preserved in their entirety,[16] sometimes with curious 'interlocking' effects.[ee] It also emerges that the bishop of Hippo, placed on the defensive in the face of a pugnacious opponent who had the initiative of attack, was *ipso facto* obliged to fight on the ground chosen by that opponent, to enter at length into ever more meticulous explanations and, in the end, to be led almost ineluctably to harden his position[17] – all the more so because Julian did not handle him tactfully and drove him to the edge of the patience he had at first tried to employ towards this hotheaded youngster who could have been his son. Not burdening himself with the slightest deference towards his elder – an 'asthmatic old man',[ff] he would call him – the young bishop expressed himself in a rather unusual outspokenness, which might appear refreshing had it not strayed into bad language that even shocked Augustine, who was not much in favour of ecclesiastical 'cant'. The tour de force achieved in the composition of the second reply, which had consisted in cutting into short sequences the text of the books *Ad Florum* written by the distant exile, and following them with precise answers, had given the successful illusion of a true dialogue between the two adversaries; on both sides it gave a sharper edge to the mordant drive of their prose. Julian, who had read Augustine fairly closely, used everything that came to hand and respected nothing. Picked out from the *Confessions*, the little lapse in Monica's youth, when she had been caught having a drink from the barrel in the family house, was turned into the stigma of a shameful malady of which her son had had to bear the bodily consequences.[gg] Augustine was 'more stupid than a pestle',[hh] and because he had held that in animals the *libido* was not an evil because in them the flesh did not lust against the spirit, he found himself given the title 'patron of donkeys'.[ii] Julian did not accept that naturalism was confined to animals.

Even at the height of his battle with the Donatists, Augustine had not received such blows below the belt. But something more exacerbated this antagonism; Julian went one better on Pelagius' elitism. He claimed to base his convictions on 'the writings of philosophers',[jj] and saw – or pretended to see – Augustine as the apostle of a 'blind faith' ready to take advantage of 'crowd reactions' to make his ideas prevail and, if need be, to call upon the 'populace', 'peasants' and even 'theatricals'.[kk] In his opinion, the Church had been deliberately dispossessed of its theological leadership, by Augustine and the African bishops, to the advantage of popular opinion.[ll] This was of course merely a polemical argument, the only true point being that, where infant baptism was concerned, his adversary was in perfect agreement with popular feeling. He had an additional related grievance; as we know, the bishop of Eclanum had intervened vigorously with both the Court and the see of Rome in an attempt to obtain a conciliar review of the condemnation of Pelagius and Caelestius. Not without some reason, he considered that the objection that had been carried against him had been a success for the very influential 'lobby' which in 418 the Church of Africa had represented with the imperial government. The still recent history of Arianism had shown how much weight was carried by the secular in spiritual matters: a general council could be convened if such was the emperor's will. Julian knew that Count Valerius had seen to it that this mechanism was not set in motion.[mm] Replying to him several years later, Augustine acknowledged with disarming frankness that for him there was no question of the enemies of the faith he defended being able to obtain from the powerful of this world 'a time and place to argue about it'.[nn] And the old bishop recalled the grievous experience of the troubles caused by Donatism in his Africa; only too real and sincere was his fear that the public debate desired by Julian would rekindle religious war, and with an even fiercer blaze.

Concupiscence and original sin

To defend his camp, Julian had taken the offensive. The bishop of Eclanum knew about Augustine's Manichaean past and had not been slow to grasp the polemical advantage he could gain from it.[oo] He was too intelligent and too skilled a theologian really to believe that the bishop of Hippo's anthropology could stem from the Manichaeism of his youth, but from a tactical viewpoint the angle of attack was well chosen; the accusation was not one that could be dealt with by contempt. And if Augustine reacted so quickly and devoted himself so lastingly to its refutation, it was because he had immediately perceived the danger of the campaign which Julian was centring on such a sensitive subject. His young adversary wanted to have it believed – first of all by the powerful personages whom Alypius met at Court and who were the staunch supporters of the Church of Africa in its crusade against the Pelagians – that the bishop of Hippo, still tainted by the doctrine of Mani, had a grudge against marriage, the cornerstone of a society that was not in a hurry to disappear in order to make way for the heavenly city.

Julian himself had no need to make an effort to hymn the constant goodness of nature created by God. He had had a happy youth, crowned by his conjugal bliss with Titia, daughter of Aemilius, bishop of Benevento. He had embraced abstinence when he took orders, but that short period of carnal happiness had not left him with mixed memories. Unlike Augustine, he had lived through it unperturbed. The excitement that makes the whole body tremble, then settles and concentrates itself to allow the sexual act – he called it the 'power of sensual delight' (*vis voluptatis*), that 'heat which makes itself felt before and during the work of the flesh'[pp] – was in his view the agent willed by God to make procreation possible; the union of the sexes accompanied by pleasure had been instituted and blessed by him.[qq] The *libido* was his work, and in both men and animals it was he who lit the flame of generation.ʳʳ This heat (*calor genitalis*) was quite simply the servant of husband and wife; it was good in itself, only its excesses needed to be controlled.ˢˢ For Julian, Christ himself had not been free of concupiscence; of course, he had not yielded, but it was in him as a part of human nature and his virtue had been to overcome the *libido* without whose existence there would have been only a false incarnation. In his eyes, Augustine, who exempted Jesus from concupiscence, was just an 'Apollinarist', and for good measure, the bishop of Eclanum who, in the heat of argument did not hesitate to misinterpret, went as far as accusing his adversary of having made Christ a eunuch.ᵗᵗ For all that, Julian was coherent enough in his not very demanding Christology: since Christ, he said, was born of Mary, whose flesh, like that of other men, came from Adam by propagation,[18] it would have to be said that Christ's flesh was no different from sinful flesh; but he refused to say so, not because by the fact of the virginal conception of Jesus Mary had not transmitted concupiscence to her Son's body – thus born only in the likeness of sinful flesh, as Augustine insisted, following St Paul (Rom. 8.3)ᵘᵘ – but because for him there was no such thing as sinful flesh, for the simple reason that there was no original sin.ᵛᵛ

In the same way that he outdid the elitism of Pelagius, his follower also went one better in his naturalism. For better and for worse. The pains of childbirth suffered by women were an effect of nature not of sin; for Julian, the punishment due to eating the forbidden fruit had not been inflicted on human nature, but on the person of Eve alone;ʷʷ which was contradictory and confused, to say the least, and resulted from a skewed interpretation of Gen. 3.16, as Augustine observed. And if Adam had to return to the dust from which he had come, according to Gen. 3.19, for Julian his death was natural – we would say 'biological' – and not the consequence of his sin.ˣˣ And for the bishop of Eclanum, the curse God had put on the ground and the need for man, after the Fall, henceforth to earn his bread by the sweat of his brow (Gen. 3.17–19), were not penalties for failing to respect the divine prohibition. In the same line of thinking, he used Gen. 2.15 – 'God placed the man in the garden of Eden to cultivate and keep it' – in an attempt to demonstrate that before the Fall Adam was not already leading the life of a spiritual creature in Paradise, without a care, if not idyllic. As Augustine pointed out to him, despite Julian's conventional words about this 'pleasant countryside' where Adam was 'the innocent cultivator',[19] the Garden of Eden seemed to be sad, full of hard work and a very human heaviness as soon as the Pelagian tried to minimize the initial sin and its punishment, to erase as far as possible the difference between the 'before' and the 'after'.ʸʸ For Julian, sensual delight and concupiscence had been present in Paradise before sin.ᶻᶻ

The logic of this attitude would have it that, conversely, human nature, following Adam's very watered-down sin,ᵃᵇ was not Augustine's *natura vitiata*, but 'a nature created good by a good God, which had remained so healthy in babies that at their birth they had no need of Christ's medicine'.ᵃᶜ Julian no longer had anything to lose; freed from the small doses of caution which had long hampered Pelagius, he clearly nailed his certainties to the mast. He had a unique definition of sin, applied to the only kind he knew, one's own or personal sin. Sin, he declared, was nothing other than 'a wicked will, free to abstain from the evil towards which its desires carried it'.ᵃᵈ He had not invented this definition; not without some spite he had taken up the one – and he did not fail to point it out –

that Augustine had proposed in 391/2 in his text *On the two souls* (§ 14).[af] Not without spite or bad faith, for he knew very well – a truth that his interlocutor in this reconstructed dialogue re-established at once – that this famous definition was valid in the bishop of Hippo's mind only for the 'sin of the first kind', in other words, the one that Adam had committed in the fullness of a still intact freedom.[ag] But Julian cared little for his adversary's perspectives. For him this axiom which was valid without any distinction for all sins exonerated children, 'since there was no sin without will, no will without absolute freedom, no freedom without the faculty of making a rational choice'.[ah] And naturally, Julian was a 'creationist'; we have seen that they were more numerous in the eastern than the western Churches, and he was among those who thought that souls were created one by one, on the occasion of each birth, and that every new human arrival in the world was born with the original absolute purity.[ai] It will be recalled that, at the time of this controversy, Augustine was still wavering between a modified 'creationism' and 'traducianism' pure and simple.[aj] And he confessed to Julian that he did not know.[ak] But now he found himself faced with an opponent who used the latter term not to describe those who favoured a transmission of souls through generation, as he himself had long done, but, by a shift in sense, to stigmatize, by identifying them with Manichaeans, those who firmly believed, as he did, that the original sin had been transmitted by propagation since Adam.[al]

The Augustinian doctrine of original sin was formed in a slow maturation that had begun in 396 with the Pauline exegeses of the *Ad Simplicianum*, but it was the first jousts with the Pelagians that had resulted in fixing its definitive conception.[am] From this period date the first quotations, subsequently increased by Augustine, from the text (Rom. 5.12) which for him was the scriptural basis.[20] It was, however, a source of embarrassment for him, as he quoted it[an] from the old Latin translation he had available, in which the original Greek was fairly distorted: *Per unum hominem peccatum in hunc mundum intravit, et per peccatum mors, et ita in omnes homines pertransiit, in quo omnes peccaverunt.* Julian read it in exactly the same terms,[ao] but understood it very differently. He must have referred to the Greek version, where *thanatos* (*mors*) was the subject of *pertransiit*, as it would also be later in the Latin Vulgate, and he used it to affirm, not without reason – it was the text to the letter – that it was death, and not sin, which was transmitted to all men, a death which he took to be spiritual since, for him, Adam had been doomed to a biological death even before the Fall. On this last point, Augustine had had some difficulty in ordering his ideas; when he wrote Book XIII of the *City of God*, around 418, he understood that the threat of Gen. 2.17 referred to all deaths, including the 'second death, which no other follows',[ap] and he was still following that line of thought at the time of his controversies with Julian. Anyway, he said in conclusion of this passage of arms, it mattered little whether *mors* or *peccatum* was the grammatical subject of *pertransiit*, since both had been transmitted to Adam's descendants.[aq] In this ambiguous Latin sentence, there remained the *in quo*, a relative whose antecedent was problematical. The most surprising thing was that Julian, who had already referred to the Greek text, did not do so in this instance; the explanation of the text with which he had favoured his readers in the *Ad Florum*[ar] had not gone as far as amending this incongruous relative pronoun which, in the Latin version, had wrongly replaced the Greek conjunctive, *eph'hô*, which however contained a clear and acceptable temporal or consecutive sense, and especially one more favourable to the Pelagian thesis.[21] As heedless of philology as Augustine, Julian had preserved this *in quo*, in which however, suspecting an error in the Latin translation, he was tempted to recognize a causal conjunctive phrase – 'because of which'.[as] Elsewhere he seemed to admit the relative, whose antecedent could hardly be other than Adam – he 'in whom all have sinned';[at] but that did not trouble him because, like Pelagius before him,[au] the bishop of Eclanum held that Adam's descendants had sinned not by transmission but by imitation, under the impulsion of the example given by the first man.[av] As for Augustine, he had originally considered that *quo* referred to *peccatum*, and thus understood: 'in which (sin) all have sinned'.[aw] Then a glance over the Greek text, which he too seems to have given, and above all his reading of the commentary of the Epistle to the Romans in the Ambrosiaster[ax] – which he curiously ascribes to St Hilarius – determined him to refer this relative pronoun definitely to Adam: 'in whom (Adam) all have sinned'.[ay] In 418, when he had the famous verse of Rom. 5.12 inserted in the Records of the Council of Carthage, he no longer had any doubt about the interpretation.

But Augustine was not an 'egghead' theologian, poring over texts. Against Julian's naturalism and optimism he mainly set the daily findings of his experience as a man and pastor. He had only to look around him to fuel a pessimism whose anthropological foundations his meditations on St Paul had begun to give him some thirty years earlier, but in which he found no pleasure. Anyone who has read in the last book of the *City of God* the magnificent development which occupies a central position in it will have noted the bishop's desire to take account of what he calls the 'original good', the opportunities the Creator has given man here below and his care that human intellect should know how to make use of them, despite the serious handicaps resulting from the Fall.[az] What one usually recalls, however, of this famous picture is the other panel of the diptych, doubtless painted in first in order to place more emphasis by contrast on what man owes to God's goodness, but whose sombre colours impinge more on the gaze, perhaps because one intuitively senses that they are in accord with Augustine's deepest feelings about the misery of the human condition: 'This life of ours, if it can be called a life, testifies by all the great ills with which it is filled, that all mortal descendants (of Adam) come under condemnation.'[ba] A few years later, the lament for unhappy, disgraced and suffering humanity would fill many pages of the books written against Julian. There is no complacency, no pleasure but, if not an obsession, at least the constant concern to demonstrate to the eulogist of a humanity born in innocence and free in its spiritual destiny that humankind was in reality marked by the stigma of a hereditary ill whose cure did not lie within its power alone. For Augustine, that was especially obvious in the case of childhood, which seemed to him to bear the principal, as well as the most 'undeserved', burden of that damnation.[bc] As yet blameless of any personal sin, the infant was the most shocking victim of the concupiscence of which it was born.

It was on this point that the discord between the bishop of Eclanum and the bishop of Hippo erupted most acrimoniously. For polemical ends, the former caricatured the latter's stance on marriage which, he said, as a good Manichaean he continued to present as the damnable work of the devil.[bd] When their debate had begun, it had been a good while since Augustine's reflections on the subject had matured. As often occurred in his intellectual life, an incident had cropped up to make him clarify his thinking. This had been at the beginning of his episcopacy, with the still recent fall-out from a pamphlet published in 393 by Jerome against a Roman monk named Jovinian. The latter, rebelling against what he judged to be the excessive advances of asceticism, had thereby championed the chances of marriage against abstinence, even in clerical circles. From Bethlehem, Jerome entered the lists on the opposite side, in his usual impassioned and violently polemical fashion. In the *Retractations*, Augustine says that he felt obliged to intervene to re-establish the balance by writing his book *On the good things of marriage*,[22] probably just before 400. Although the work did not argue vibrantly in favour of marriage, in order to extol abstinence compared with the matrimonial state, the bishop had thought it a good idea to write in the same year a book *On the sanctity of virginity*: people were waiting for him to do so, he said![be] In this way, on the social and religious aspects of sexuality, nothing was sacrificed of the two facets of Pauline thinking – see 1 Cor. 7 and Eph. 5 – to which the bishop was loyal as far as the conditions of his times would allow. The first of the two books had laid down the basis for a theology of marriage which adhered to three words to define its good qualities: *fides*, the fidelity of the couple to the pledge they had sworn; *proles*, the procreation that was to be the only purpose of the sexual act that marriage implied; *sacramentum*, the indissoluble bond which had consecrated the union before God. Of these three constituent elements of the 'good of marriage', the author made no secret of the pre-eminence he gave to the third.

There was similarly no need to read between the lines to become aware that the carnal effects of marriage, even when limited to their procreative end, the only one admissible – and in these conditions, regarded as licit and honourable – were merely a last resort, as far as the bishop was concerned. Failing a virginal life, preferable in his view as it was for St Paul, the perfect Christian union in his eyes was one lived in abstinence,[bf] a chastity that, if possible, was not to be confined to old couples, weakened by their years. At the height of the controversy with Julian, when he was writing his *Retractations*, in the note devoted to the book on marriage, he had quoted two sentences from among those which looked least unfavourably on the *libido*: 'what food is for man's physical health, bodily union is for the physical health of the human race. Neither is without a bodily pleasure which, measured and reduced by temperance to its natural use, could not be a passion (*libido*).'[bg] Yes, but the pastor who, in his great preaching campaign of the summer of 397, had laid great stress on Eccles. 3.5, a time for embracing and a time for refraining from embracing, had not been overly concerned with the physical health of the human race.[bh] And the little conciliatory commentary which followed the quotation from the book on marriage, in the text of 426 – 'the good and right use of passion is not passion' – could not erase from memory the terrible analysis of the *libido* that runs through the two books of 419–20, *On marriage and concupiscence* and the refutations of Julian that followed.

Because he had lived nearly fifteen years with Adeodatus' mother in a sexual relationship outside *sacramentum*, but in *fides*, Augustine knew what he was talking about when he attacked sexuality. Fuelled by memories, his description of desire and pleasure was as accurate as his bishop's Latin would allow, and could not defy honesty. If he feigned ignorance of female sensual pleasure,[bi] and the power of desire in the opposite sex, when it came to his own he had only to delve into his memory. There he rediscovered that feeling of dying to oneself, which he would now no longer describe as delectable, if he ever had, because what survived was the conclusion that the sexual act submerged the soul and obliterated everything, and that one emerged from it as from an abyss.[bj] 'The act absorbs all the functions of the soul', just like sneezing, Pascal would say, having read Montaigne who, for his part, compared it with sleep and was less offended by it. Before reaching this 'ecstasy', the body took action in a way that was completely independent of the will, at the whim of impulses which the soul was unable to control.[bk] Of all human passions, the *libido* was the only one which could annihilate the vigilance of thought; its untamed force was such that it sometimes was divided against itself, 'shaking the soul without shaking the body'.[23] Therein lay the evil of concupiscence, which made man lose his power over his own limbs. Thus, Adam and Eve, transgressing the divine prohibition, had let themselves be invaded by another law contrary to their spirit. In reprisal – *poena reciproca* – for their disobedience, their flesh, disobedient in its turn, had risen with a life of its own;[bl] contempt for God had first had this immediate sexual consequence. Only then were they ashamed of their nakedness, which they hurriedly concealed. Since then nudity had been banned in public, only tolerated by Greek naturalism in the gymnasium and wrestling school, and the Cynics had failed in their attempt to restore its honour.[bm] Hence the universal modesty which from time immemorial had caused even the most licit sexual act, duly sanctioned by marriage, to be performed everywhere in secret intimacy, sheltered from all eyes.

The flesh had lusted against the spirit, Augustine often repeated, using St Paul's words (Gal. 5.17) and had thereby given rise to the worst disorder in man, of which ill controlled sexuality was but one manifestation among many, but the most loaded with consequences since it was at the source of all life. The bishop pondered over Gen. 1.28: 'Increase and multiply.' How to understand this invitation to procreation addressed to the first man before sin? Augustine had hesitated much over the answer to give to this awkward question. Around 418, precisely in the period when his joust with Julian began, he confirmed in the *City of God* what he had started to envisage in his treatise *De Genesi ad litteram*,[bn] namely that the first couple might have had children before the Fall: 'Without sin, marriage worthy of the felicity of Paradise would have given birth to pleasant descendants without the shame of concupiscence.'[bo] But how? Augustine did not fall for some 'angel' theory, for it did not escape him that Adam lived in the Garden of Eden in an 'animal' body.[24] But if he conceded that he and his companion had sexual organs, they must have operated similarly to the other members of the body, obeying the commands of the will,[bp] without passion on either side in conception, and without pain for the woman in childbirth.[bq] Or else there was no concupiscence, and in the carnal act our first parents would have used their genital organs as 'labourers use their hands', or concupiscence must have been so subject to the will that it could never have imposed its urges independently.[25] The bishop admitted that these speculations led into another order of reality; our experience did not allow us to validate them, and they belonged to the realm of faith.[br]

We are free to look upon this vision of a sexuality without *libido* as a daydream. However, its object was not solely to try to answer a real theological question; by contrasting a sexuality subject to the spirit with the carnal act prompted by concupiscence – the concupiscence which Julian, it had been said, shamefully advocated[bs] – the bishop wanted to prove the gulf which separated the descendants of Adam and Eve after their sin from the spiritually intact descendants they could have had if, in their display of pride and rebellion, they had not so quickly transgressed the divine prohibition. The prime mover of carnal generation, concupiscence was for ever the agent of transmission of their sin. 'Because his sin had been so grave that it had brought about a serious deterioration in his nature', Adam had been transformed from the 'pure olive tree' he had been into the 'wild olive tree', and after him had transformed the whole human race into a wild olive tree.[bt] In the same way that the oleaster must be grafted to make it into a good olive tree, for the baptized the graft of baptism redeemed the error of original sin, but without radically suppressing the malign potentialities of lust in his tainted nature.[26] And just as a cultivar naturally produces only a wild stock, like the wild olive, the baptized Christian, because of the lust which continues to dwell in him and is manifested in the act of generation, naturally engenders only a creature who is always burdened by original sin.[bu] In the child, the grace of baptism removed the guilt and afterwards helped him not to add personal sins, whose occurrence would always be rendered possible till the end of his earthly life by the persistence in him of concupiscence – the sexual interpretation was only one of its aspects. Even the saintliness of ascetics was not exempt from this risk. Apart from a life of virtue and abstinence,[bv] Augustine could see no other way of limiting, if not eliminating, it than a tireless quest for, and practice of, the love of others and the love of God: 'The more the love of God establishes its reign over man, the less he is the slave of sin.'[bw]

Freedom and grace

If it mattered so much to Augustine to proclaim the disastrous power of lust – both the consequence and the agent of transmission of original sin – broadly understood as the disorder in us which inclines us towards evil and diverts us from good, it was because this debate itself lay at the heart of a still more fundamental debate – the one concerning free will and its relationship with grace.

Confronted with Julian, the bishop of Hippo must have felt rather like those teachers who, upon the arrival of a new class, heave a sigh at having to repeat once again the things they had duly dealt with in the preceding sessions; it was out of the question simply to refer the newcomer to them. And yet, he would have found satisfactory replies, spared Augustine tiresome repetitions and, in the end, would have avoided Hippo's bishop placing himself on the frontiers of heresy through his later developments on the need for grace and predestination.

Nearly everything had been said as early as 396, with the Pauline exegeses of the *Ad Simplicianum* which, on the subject of free will, had broadly corrected the analyses – 'Pelagian' before the event – of the *De libero arbitrio*, particularly in the first texts of that treatise.[bx] Rereading for the *Retractations* the first of the two books addressed to Simplicianus, the old bishop had summed up what he considered to be the essentials of his propositions, not without a certain ambiguity: 'In the solution to this question I strove greatly in favour of the freedom of the human will, but the grace of God won the day.'[by] What would have happened if he had not striven? Julian would probably have said, if he could have read this last commentary. But basically that is almost what he himself had understood, when he vehemently castigated Augustine for having totally eliminated free will from his anthropology.[bz] In reality – and to be convinced one has only to reread many pages of the texts of 396[ca] – Augustine upheld free will among the inalienable blessings of man in the definition he had always maintained, of a free decision of the will, the choice of a free will, or at least free from any external constraint.[cb] This faculty, theoretical as soon as one entered the moral domain, the bishop reaffirmed in his reply to the two letters from the Pelagians which he addressed to Pope Boniface in 420; 'Who among us would dare to affirm that through the sin of the first man free will disappeared from the human race?'[cd] But the major contribution of the texts of that period was a more clearly stated distinction between free will and freedom. In the pages written in dialogue with Evodius in Rome in 388, Augustine had given a glimpse of his greatest intellectual demand when these last words were uttered: the only true freedom was 'that of happy men bound to the eternal law'.[ce] That freedom was the one which the elect would share in heaven. It was also the one enjoyed by Adam in Paradise, the freedom, as is said in a text of 420, 'to possess, with immortality, the fullness of justice':[cf] in other words, to live without end a morally blameless life in the sight of God and following his rules. But while the elect in heaven are protected from all risk of losing that freedom by cleaving completely to God, by his sin Adam has been deprived of it as he has of immortality. Of that initial freedom of the first man before the Fall we retain only a free will whose possibilities of choice, burdened by the constraints of a corrupted nature, are henceforth part of the short span of mortal life.[cg]

Contrary to what Julian and Pelagians in general said, Augustine was always extremely careful to preserve that free will without which grace would lose its application. He would strongly affirm this when the argument raised by the Pelagians rebounded into Africa itself and, in 426, the bishop had to calm the disturbances that had arisen in a monastic community in Hadrumetum (Sousse). Florus, a member of the community, on the occasion of a return visit to his home town of Uzalis, had discovered in Evodius' library the text of the *Epistula* 194, sent by Augustine in 418 to the future Sixtus III to put him on his guard against the Pelagians. He had had a copy made of the letter, which was a veritable condensed version of the Augustinian doctrine of grace,[ch] and its unwise circulation had caused unrest in the monastery at Hadrumetum. Augustine had to intervene, write to the superior, the abbot Valentinus, unknown to whom this upset had first developed, and compose a long text to explain his stance to the brethren at Hadrumetum.[ci] In it he stressed the texts from the Scriptures which implied, even demonstrated, the existence of free will in man, before God.[cj] Still alive in the bishop's mind was the memory of the young Manichaean of his Carthaginian years, only too ready to be able to say that it was not he who sinned, but some alien nature within him.[ck] He energetically rejected any determinism, even if it were divine. He wrote to the monks of Hadrumetum:

> Let no one accuse God in his heart, but when he sins let him lay the sin at his own door; and conversely, when he acts in God's ways, let him not deprive his own will of it.

Indeed, it is when the will guides the act that one should say it is a good work and must hope, through that good work, to be rewarded by him of whom it is said that he 'shall reward every man according to his works' (Matt. 16.27; Rom. 2.6).[d]

Up to this point there was nothing that Pelagius and Caelestius, and now even Julian of Eclanum, could not have written themselves. But Augustine went further. In the second section of this long homily preached from afar, he gave the monks to understand, by referring precisely to the vows of chastity they had taken, that their acceptance of the Gospel words – 'all men cannot receive this saying, save they to whom it is given' (Matt. 19.11) – was both a gift from God and the result of free will.[cm] Nevertheless distancing himself somewhat from the radical statements of the *Ad Simplicianum* – as he had also done in the sermons of that already far-off period[cn] – the bishop, addressing the *servi Dei* and taking into account the harshness of their monastic vows, initially modified his discourse on free will and grace in the direction of the balanced phrases already put to work in a series of texts dating to the first controversies with the Pelagians: grace came to assist free will, it did not suppress it.[co] Once again free will was saved, but purely as the receptacle of grace or the simple human instrument of divine transcendence. Augustine replied in advance to the objection he foresaw from the recipients of his book: if eternal life is the reward for good works (Matt. 16.27; Rom. 2.6), how can it be said to be the gift of grace, which is freely granted independently of good works? His answer was ready, supported by John 15.5 ('for without me ye can do nothing') and by Eph. 2.8–10: our good works themselves, which earn us eternal life, are a gift of grace.[cp] Far from grace being given to us according to our merits, our merits begin the moment grace is given to us. Augustine could have taken his own example, refer to his *Confessions*, repeat the already famous *Da quod iubes et iube quod vis*; but he preferred to illustrate his argument by referring to the Apostle, commenting on the well known verse from 2 Tim. 4.7: 'I have fought a good fight, I have finished my course, I have kept my faith', which seemed to him to sum up magnificently the assumption of grace throughout a Christian life, from the *initium fidei* to perseverance in faith.[cq] And again quoting 1 Cor. 4.7: 'What hast thou that thou didst not receive?' he did not hesitate to say: 'If therefore your merits are gifts from God, God does not crown your merits as your own merits, but as his own gifts.'[cr]

Freedom for the Christian was free will informed and inspired by grace, which granted human will the ability to desire and accomplish good. When it was mainly a matter of access to faith, the *initium fidei*, Augustine's insistence on a verse of Proverbs which he frequently quoted and commented upon[27] – *Praeparatur voluntas a Domino*: Prov. 8.3, according to the Septuagint text – testified to his desire to maintain the difficult reconciliation of freedom and grace.[28] Or rather, because that reconciliation seemed to him to be theologically impossible, he sought 'to harmonize the unconditional salvific will of God with human will, in such a way that the divine omnipotence operates in the elect without harming freedom'.[29] Perhaps in regard to the conversion of St Paul, in his reply to Julian of Eclanum's two letters, in 420, the bishop had the happiest choice of words to describe the working of grace 'without harming liberty'. He quoted John 6.44: 'No man can come to me unless my Father, which hath sent me, draw him', and commented:

For he did not say 'lead him', so that we might in some way see an anterior will. Who would be drawn if he already willed it? Yet no one comes unless he wills it. One is therefore drawn to will in wonderful ways by him who can act within the very heart of men, not so that men should believe without wishing to, which is impossible, but that their not-wishing-to is changed into wishing-to.[cs]

But in the text addressed to the monks of Byzacena, the evocation of this divine magic had sometimes given place to more rigid formulas which simple souls, daily confronted with the tough demands of physical and moral asceticism, might find unfair to their efforts, and a disincentive, as when the bishop wrote that 'it was the Almighty who activated in men's hearts the very movement of their will in order to carry out through them what he had himself resolved to effect through them'.[ct] Assuredly St Paul said no differently in Phil. 2.13: 'God worketh in you both to will and to do of his good pleasure', so often quoted and commented upon by Augustine since 396.[cu]

Among other things, the interest of this unequal exchange with the *servi Dei* of Hadrumetum is that it shows how Augustine's theological writings could be received in circles that were *a priori* 'orthodox', but little versed in theology and apparently not conversant with the details of the battle waged in the preceding years by the Church of Africa against Pelagianism at Augustine's instigation, and who were also fairly representative of the 'grass roots' of Christians in Africa, regardless of the particular aspects of monastic life. The abbot Valentius thanked the bishop effusively and declared himself, like brother Florus whom he was sending on a mission to Hippo, greatly edified by the texts he had received.[30] But there was at least one monk who held that 'a person should not be reprimanded if he did not keep God's commandments: it was enough to pray for him so that he should keep them'.[cv] And this monk was clearly the spokesman for a group of brethren who were not persuaded by the Augustinian doctrine of grace, which seemed to them to imply the loss of their responsibility as sinners, for worse or for better, for the assurance of salvation which they believed they could receive by virtue of the merits of their ascetic life. Why, they asked, were they ordered to shun evil and do good if it was not they who were doing so, if it was God working in them both to will and to do?[cw] They too quoted 1 Cor. 4.7, but this time to affirm that they could not be held blameworthy for failing a gift that they had not received,[cx] or punishable for possible backslidings, if God's other gift of perseverance had not fallen to their lot.[cy] In short, they rejected St Paul's teaching in the doctrinal severity it assumed with Augustine.

Faced with this version of Pelagianism whose rise he had come upon in a Byzacena that was too open to winds from the East, the bishop reacted quickly. Florus came back to Hadrumetum bearing a new clarifying statement which had been hastily dictated. As might be expected, the author removed nothing from his theology of grace; when it came to perseverance, he very deliberately went into detail about its expression. In his very last work, a few months before his death, he would return to the importance, in this regard, of the second text addressed to the brethren at Hadrumetum:

In my book entitled *On punishment and grace*, I think I established that perseverance to the end is also a gift from God, in such a way, if my memory does not deceive me, that nowhere or almost nowhere else before did I express myself on this subject as explicitly and clearly.[cz]

A few lines further on in the same text, in a manner signifying his desire to show the continuity and coherence of his reflections on grace during at least thirty years, Augustine pointed out to his opponents – in this instance, as we shall see, monks in Provence – that the line he had followed on the independence of the gift of faith in relation to meritorious acts was already set in the second part of the book addressed to Simplicianus in 396. And it was true, as he said, that he had at the time established that even the *initium fidei* was a divine gift, and in those pages it was clearly written 'that perseverance to the end is also a gift from him who has predestined us for his kingdom and his glory'. But what could then be merely deduced was now revealed in full light.

Usually so concerned with monastic discipline, Augustine did not overlook the grave danger let loose in Valentinus' monastery by the idea of non-responsibility which the monks of Hadrumetum claimed to derive from his writings: if their will depended on God, they said, their superior ought to give up reprimanding them and simply pray for them. But that would have meant the end of all communal life. The *De correptione et gratia*, therefore, did not fail to emphasize first of all the need for fraternal correction, especially for those who, having received grace through baptism, had lost it as a result of a will that had remained free to choose evil.[da] Nor did the bishop make any concession to the monks on his doctrine. Like the grace of regeneration, the grace of perseverance was a divine gift; one had to pray to receive it but, if one did not obtain it one relapsed, in company with those who had not received the call, and also in company with children who died unbaptized, into the *massa perditionis* resulting from Adam's sin:[db] all those whom 'the foreknowledge and predestination of God had not selected from that mass of sin'.[dc] The conjunction in the same sentence of those two words, which was to become commonplace in the texts of that period, depicted quite strikingly the road he had travelled since, in 394, when commenting for the first time on key texts in St Paul, Augustine's answer to the problem of the choice of Jacob and reproof of Esau even before their birth (Rom. 9.11–13) had consisted in bringing divine foreknowledge into play.[de] A feeble reply, he said ironically in 418 in his letter to Sixtus, noting that the Pelagians had halted at that point,[df] whereas he himself, in the *Ad Simplicianum* in 396, had begun to work out his doctrine of predestination though without yet uttering the word. Now reading these lines written in the spring of 427, the monks of Hadrumetum, like those of Provence, who would read them a little later, could make no mistake: predestination, still positive, was the disinterested and limited choice of the 'elect', decided for all eternity by God, whose 'judgements are unsearchable and his ways past finding out' (Rom. 11.33), in his secret designs.[dg]

Faced with Augustine, the monks of Hadrumetum were not entirely lacking in theological resources. What must be thought of Adam's case, they asked him? From all the evidence, he had not held fast to perseverance, because he had sinned. Had he not received its grace? But if he had not, by sinning he was not, in their eyes, guilty of not having persevered. And in his case, it could not be said that, if he had not received perseverance, it was because he had not been 'distinguished' from the 'mass of perdition' by being chosen through grace, since that 'mass of perdition' was the result of his own sin.[dh] This gave the bishop the opportunity to elaborate on the distinction between two types of grace, which would have a long future. Adam, replied Augustine, enjoyed a grace that differed from our own, a blessed grace, 'by which he would never have been wicked if he had chosen to remain in it . . . If by his free will the first man had not abandoned this help (*adiutorium*), he would have remained good; but he did abandon it and in his turn was abandoned.'[di] The grace that the 'saints' receive now, less happy, is more powerful, for it is a sharing in the grace which God gave his Son, Christ, to keep him in unfailing righteousness. Through the grace which he enjoyed, the first man had been enabled not to sin, not to abandon good and not to die. He was endowed with a succour without which he could not persevere by his free will alone (this was the *adiutorium sine quo non*, from which starting-point Jansenism would develop the idea of 'sufficient grace'), whereas those who are now chosen receive succour by which perseverance is granted to them ('the *adiutorium quo*, which for Jansenius and his disciples would be 'effective grace'). The reason for this powerful positive aid was that, whereas in Paradise, for Adam established in light and peace, no temptations or stresses existed, in this world, on the contrary, in order to triumph over temptations, passions, errors – in a word, evil – a greater 'freedom' was necessary (and Augustine used the word *libertas* in the sense in which he understood it in his Christian anthropology: free will supported, if not 'inhabited', by grace).[dj]

The victorious effectiveness of this second type of grace was then celebrated by the bishop in terms that would transport the Jansenists beyond the rational, that is to say, a true assessment of the context[31] in which Augustine was speaking.

> The frailty of the human will was given assistance so that this will was activated (*ageretur*) indeclinably and insuperably (*indeclinabiliter et insuperabiliter*) by divine grace; thus, despite its weakness, the will does not falter and is not overcome by any adversity. So, through the power of God, the feeble and weak will of man perseveres in a good that is still paltry, where the strong and healthy will of the first man did not persevere in a much greater good through the power of free will . . . God allowed the one with the greater strength to do as he pleased; through his own gift, he has destined the weak invincibly (*invictissime*) to will what is good, and invincibly not to will to abandon that good.[dk]

Since this invincibility is a gift of grace, man cannot glory in it, and Augustine concludes by quoting 1 Cor. 1.31 ('He that glorieth, let him glory in the Lord'), thus declaring once again his complete adherence to the Apostle's doctrine by emphasizing the verse which, in 396, seemed to him to reveal St Paul's key thought (*intentio*).[dl] But the bishop added, in regard to the limited number of the predestined, the point of doctrine that was specifically his and would startle the monks in Provence as it was already upsetting those at Hadrumetum: 'I say this of those who are predestined for the kingdom of God, whose number is so fixed that not one person will be added or taken away.'[dm]

Does God want all to be saved?

This teaching was too inflexible, the demand for humility before God too lofty, not to put off even the most robust faith. And as Augustine's anti-Pelagian works over the last dozen years had made his theology known throughout the Mediterranean West, it could be feared that the monks of Hadrumetum were not the only ones to start muttering. Resistance sprang up on the opposite shore. In the monasteries of southern Gaul, more precisely on the shores of Provence, the intellectual leader was not the bishop of Hippo but John Cassian, a monk of both Greek and Latin culture (Scythian in origin, or Romanian as we would say nowadays), who owed his particular prestige to an uncommon 'career' – he had been a monk in Bethlehem, like Jerome, then in Egypt, before being a deacon in Constantinople – as well as a sound experience of monastic life. He had eventually settled in Marseille, around 415, where he had founded two monasteries, one of which would become the abbey of St Victor.[32] At the time when Augustine was writing his two books to the monks of Hadrumetum, Cassian for his part had written a practical manual of monastic community life, his *Institutions*, and again for monks, a theoretical treatise on the religious and ascetic life, the *Lectures*: the thirteenth – 'On God's protection' – took exactly the opposite positions to those of the bishop of Hippo, laying far less emphasis on the all-powerfulness of grace than on man's free co-operation in his salvation. Like Augustine more than thirty years before, he believed that in the gaining of faith the initiative belonged to man, God being content to make an external summons. Like the Pelagians, he reduced predestination to foreknowledge and accentuated the universality of the divine will for human salvation. Such ideas had found an easy route into people's souls, in Marseille and also in the monastic foundations on the isles of Hyères and Lérins. And the monks dwelling there were not always the first-comers. Prosper of Aquitaine, a layman completely won over to Augustine – he said he belonged to the restricted circle of the 'intrepid friends of perfect grace' – wrote that it was not easy to contradict men of a higher rank than his own. To be more exact, he was alluding to their priestly dignity.[dn] In fact, like the clerical monastery at Hippo in the good years at the turn of the fourth and fifth century, the Provençal monasteries in that period had become 'seedbeds' for bishops; men left Lérins to take office in prestigious sees: Hilarius at Arles, where he would succeed Honoratus, the superior of Lérins, Lupus (St Loup) at Troyes, Eucherius at Lyon. There was a great risk that they would act like 'drive belts'[do] for what has been called, for convenience rather than accuracy, semipelagianism.[33] In his letter, Prosper tried to make the old bishop understand that he must once more arm himself against such a cohort.[dp]

At the end of 428 or early in 429, at the same time as Prosper's letter, Augustine had been able to read one sent to him,[dq] probably also from Marseille, by a certain Hilarius – not be confused with the future bishop of Arles – similarly a layman who, in the exile in which he felt himself far from the master on the other side of the sea, recalled with emotion the teaching he had received from him at Hippo.[dr] Without any apparent collusion between the two correspondents, their letters, of equal theological depth, agreed in essence on the catalogue they drew up of the divergences they had noted regarding the Augustinian doctrine of grace.[34] It appeared from both that resistance to or, at best, mistrust of Augustinianism, had not been born yesterday in the south of Gaul; the recent publication of the *De correptione et gratia*, which had soon reached Marseille, had merely aggravated them.[ds] Differences with the doctor of Hippo began with the granting of the first grace. The most radical of the semipelagians, very close to Pelagius in this, 'forced to confess the grace of Christ and its priority in relation to all human merit', wished to recognize only an initial grace naturally given in the creative act, allowing the creature, through the action of a perfectly enlightened free will, to choose between good and evil and to attain salvation by his own strengths, in other words, his meritorious actions.[dt] For others, the initiative of entering the faith (the *initium fidei*) would seem to have been left to man, who would receive additional faith from God in return, or rather an 'increase of faith' (*augmentum fidei*), to use Hilarius' words.[du] As for the Augustinian conception of predestination, it was the subject of a massive and unanimous rejection. The Provençal semipelagians, like the Pelagians themselves, had stopped short at the point where Augustine himself, in 394, in his first attempts at explaining the Epistle to the Romans, had solved the problem posed by the divine attitude in the case of Rebecca's twins.[dv] They thus ruled out thirty years of theological reflection. For them, God's foreknowledge remained the solution to the problem: those who had been known beforehand (and not predestined) had been so because of their future faith.[dw] They even resorted to it to resolve the maddening difficulty presented by the fate of young children who died unbaptized: they were not all damned, 'they were lost or saved according to the foreknowledge which the divine wisdom had of what they would have become when they reached adulthood';[dx] the semipelagians thus conjured up what French theologians, in their jargon, call 'futuribles'.

But what the Provençal monks rejected most vehemently was the *numerus clausus* of the salvific election. They would not accept that the number of the elect was fixed in advance, without a limit and, chiefly, without the possibility of increase;[dy] nothing, they maintained, was more spiritually deflating, more likely to put an end to any desire to improve, in some, or to induce more half-heartedness, in others. They wanted to take St Paul's text literally: 'God will have all men to be saved' (1 Tim. 2.4). And it has to be added that, despite their protestations of adherence to Augustine's ideas, on this particular point the shoe pinched even disciples like Prosper of Aquitaine. At the end of his letter, when he was urging the bishop to answer the Provençal monks, we can see his anxiety about the psychological and moral consequences, for the faithful, of the doctrine of predestination: 'The idea they might have of despairing of their own predestination should not be an opportunity for them to let themselves grow slack.'[dz] There could be no better way of facing the pastor with the problem that was raised by his theology.

To the urgent questions of Prosper and Hilarius, Augustine replied in a long treatise addressed to them, divided into two books for a mainly practical reason which he himself admitted – the desire to mark a break to spare the reader the trouble of too long a reading.[ea] In any case, the central themes dealt with in each book justified in advance the separate titles that would be given to them in the Middle Ages.[eb] Against the Marseillais who acknowledged the need for grace, like it or not, but jibbed against its disinterested nature, the *De praedestinatione sanctorum* once again established that gratuitousness, in both its genesis and development. The *De dono perseverantiae*, for its part, intended to demonstrate that perseverance, and more exactly, final perseverance, was also a gratuitous gift of grace.

If Prosper was fully convinced – though in him the bishop was preaching to the converted[35] – we shall never know what the monks of Provence, apart from Hilarius, thought about it: Augustine's death, some months later, stifled those last echoes. Regarding these two works, which are often repetitive and at the least recapitulative, we must beware of yielding to the temptation to say what is sometimes regretfully said about the last productions of an old, long-admired master – two books too many! Despite his age – he was now seventy-five – and his growing weariness, the old bishop had once more allowed himself to be caught up in what cannot be called a game, unless it is the game of an eternal spiritual youth, the passion to persuade, exercising which was for him one of the forms of charity. And these books brought to the theology of grace and predestination additional touches which their author doubtless felt would be definitive – it can be sensed from certain touches in the *De dono perseverantiae*.

Had he, however, replied to the pressing questions which, through Prosper of Aquitaine, had been launched at him from overseas on the restricted dispensation of saving grace? Yes, first of all in a certain manner and a certain measure, by way of little considerations that the pastor in him whispered to the theologian. In a passage from one of their letters, which has not come down to us but which the bishop quotes, Augustine's correspondents in Marseille had reported to him the caricatural manner in which the local monks presented his teaching on predestination. To hear them speak, it was a school of despair.[ec] In the last section of the *De dono perseverantiae*, Augustine nevertheless took into account a criticism justified in spite of its being outré. In preaching, he said, the teaching of predestination must try to tone down the harshness of the doctrine,[ed] at least in form. These manipulations of pure form sometimes cause a smile: what kind of hearers could the preacher put off the scent by addressing them impersonally in the third person plural?[ef] The condemnation that would strike some and not others by a limited dispensation of the grace of access or the grace of perseverance would not appear any less irrevocable.

In his last two books, Augustine's silence on 1 Tim. 2.4: 'God will have all men to be saved', is in contrast with the insistence with which the monks of Marseille recalled the Pauline verse, according to the reports of Prosper and Hilarius. It was quoted just once,[eg] by allusion, in a development that chiefly underlined the end of the verse – God wills that all should come to knowledge of the truth – and its conclusion must be given. Inchoative or perfect faith, repeated the bishop, is a gift of God

> and we cannot doubt that this gift is granted to some, refused to others, unless we wish to contradict the very clear testimony of the Scriptures. As for knowing why it is not granted to all, this is a question that must not trouble the faithful, who believes that the sin of one man alone has brought in its wake a condemnation that is without doubt so perfectly just that he would have no reason to reproach God even if no one were delivered from it![eh]

And as for the reason why this one rather than that one should be delivered, it was not for us to try to explain a plan which God had wished to keep hidden. With the Apostle (Rom. 9.20), the bishop repeated, 'O man, who art thou that thou repliest against God?'

The way in which Augustine, chiefly in the last decade of his life, concentrated on skirting round 1 Tim. 2.4, and restricting its universal scope by various exegeses,[ei] is usually considered to be the greatest weakness – or furthest extreme[36] – of his *intellectus fidei*. No one would dream, however, of drawing the conclusion that he complacently felt some morose pleasure by leaving a good proportion of his fellow men abandoned by God. If we forget the context of doctrinal struggle in which the bishop acted and wrote, if we sever his texts from their historical setting, from their very motives, we risk distorting their sense, misunderstanding their intent, which was primarily a product of the situation at the time. Throughout his last twelve years, Augustine was a prisoner of his anti-Pelagian polemic. There is no doubt that he constantly bore in mind, with increased vigilance at the end of his life, at the time of his disputes with Julian of Eclanum, the effects that his slightest changes of position could have on such theologically sensitive subjects; he had to avoid giving the adversary any foothold: 'There was a danger of Pelagianism in over-insistence, at that time, on the universal salvific will.'[37]

All the same, it would be greatly to disparage the doctor of grace to see him as no more than a strategist subservient to the circumstances of a doctrinal combat. There is another way of interpreting the countless texts in which Augustine tirelessly repeats that all initiative belongs to God, that he grants the grace he has planned to give, as he wishes and to whom he wishes. The preaching of predestination, the predisposal of his gifts made by God for all eternity, which especially fills the bishop's last two books, can and should be taken as a pedagogy of faith.[38] 'Supposing that your doctrine of predestination of God's gifts is true, it must not be preached to the crowd', said the monks of Provence, who were afraid of disheartening the faithful.[ej] Quite the contrary, retorted Augustine, recalling the essence of his theology of grace, in a catechetic perspective, which was to be a safety-rail against pride: 'They must understand', he wrote, 'that the teaching of predestination hampers and ruins only one thing: the pernicious error which would have it that the gift of grace depends on our merits.'[ek] Furthermore, and chiefly, though for him it is theologically certain that not all shall be saved – including small infants who died unbaptized[el] – all can hope to be. If the dice are already cast in God's secret plans, we do not know for whom, or which way they will fall. There is still room for hope:

> Perseverance in obedience, you must hope for that too from the 'Father of lights from whom cometh down every good gift and every perfect gift' (James 1.17), and ask for it every day in your prayers, and by doing so be confident that you are not strangers to those predestined ones of whom God forms his people; for that you should do so is already one of his gifts.[em]

Far from thwarting the pastor's efforts, this well-explained theology was useful to him in his pastoral office. That was the bishop's testament.

As at the end of the *De Trinitate*, he added a codicil which, coming from anyone else, would be remarkably surprising in its modesty, lucidity and capacity for hope:

> Nevertheless, I would not want people to adopt all my views, but only those where it can be clearly seen that I have not been mistaken. For I am at the moment engaged in writing texts in which I have undertaken to revise my works,[en] to show that I have not followed my own line in everything. I think I have made progress in my writings, with God's help, after far from perfect beginnings. Even now, moreover, I would speak with

more arrogance than truth if I said that at my age I have reached the perfect stage of writing without being mistaken . . . There is hope for a man if the last day of his life finds him so far progressed that what is still missing from his progress may be added, and that he should require not amending but perfecting.^{eo}

Notes

a.   Cf. above, pp. 113–14.
b.   *Ep.* 101, 3.
c.   *Ep.* 101, 2.
d.   *Ep.* 101, 3, *in fine.* To understand what Augustine means, see the discussion on the first line of the *Aeneid* in *De musica*, II, 2.
e.   Gennadius, *De viris illustribus*, 45.
f.   Paulinus of Nola, *Carmina*, 25, 1. 99–102, 153–68 and 231–8.
g.   Julian of Eclanum in the *Ad Florum*, quoted in *Contra Iul. opus imp.*, I, 70.
h.   *Ep.* 101, 4.
i.   *Contra Iulianum opus imp.*, V, 26.
j.   *Ep.* 186, 29.
k.   Cf. above, pp. 339–40.
l.   Cf. *Contra duas ep. pelag.*, I, 3 and II, 5; *Contra Iul. opus imp.*, II, 178.
m.   On this letter to Count Valerius, cf. *De nuptiis et conc.*, I, 1.
n.   Cf. above, pp. 348 f.
o.   *Contra Iul. opus imp.*, III, 78; cf. also III, 199, where Julian addresses the 'Aristotle of the Carthaginians', and V, 11.
p.   *Contra Iul. opus imp.*, VI, 18.
q.   Cf. the closure of *Ep.* 200, 3.
r.   These are the two letters (one 'to the Romans', the other the missive of the 18 to Rufus of Thessalonica), which would prompt Augustine's reply, entitled *Contra duas epistulas pelagianorum*.
s.   We know from the new letter 22*, addressed to Alypius, that the latter was still in Italy at the date of the letter, March 420: cf. *BA*, 46 B, p. 346 and p. 523 for the commentary.
t.   Cf. *Contra Iul. opus imp.*, I, 7: *vernula peccatorum eius.*
u.   *Contra Iul. opus imp.*, I, 52 and 85.
v.   Cf. above, pp. 262–4.
w.   *Contra Iul. opus imp.*, I, 42 (cf. also 74).
x.   *Contra Iul. opus imp.*, III, 35.
y.   Cf. *Ep.* 207, to bishop Claudius and, for the second copy, brought by deacon Commilito, *Ep.* 10*, 1.
z.   See *Ep.* 207, and chiefly Julian's reproaches, recorded by Augustine in his *Contra Iul. opus imp.*, I, 16, 17, 19.
aa.   *Contra Iulianum* I, 3, plan recalled in the *Retractations*, II, 62.
bb.   *Contra Iulianum* I, 34 and II, 33.
cc.   Cf. *Ep.* 10*, 1 and *Contra Iulianum* IV, 30.
dd.   After the brief intervening episcopacy of Capreolus.
ee.   Cf. for example *Contra Iul. opus imp.*, I, 73, in which Augustine quotes the *Ad Florum*, which itself quotes Book II of the *De nuptiis*, replying to the *Ad Turbantium*!
ff.   *Contra Iul. opus imp.*, V, 23. This impertinence is a memory of Virgil: *Georgics*, II, 135.
gg.   *Contra Iul. opus imp.*, I, 68; cf. above, p. 10 for details.
hh.   *Contra Iul. opus imp.*, II, 117 and 159.
ii.   *Contra Iul. opus imp.*, IV, 56: *patronus asinorum*
jj.   *Contra Iul. opus imp.*, I 41.
kk.   *Contra Iul. opus imp.*, I, 33: *plebecularum catervae*; I, 41: *vulgus*; II, 14: *rurales, theatrales.*

ll.   *Contra Iul. opus imp.*, II, 2: *dogma populare;* cf. also II, 3: everything is permitted to the common herd and the seditious.

mm.   *Contra Iul. opus imp.*, I, 10; cf. also *De nuptiis*, I, 2, in which Augustine acknowledges the role played by the count.

nn.   *Contra Iul. opus imp.*, I, 10.

oo.   Julian here also made use of the accounts in the *Confessions*, notably what Augustine had said about Faustus (*Conf.*, V, 10–12): cf. *Contra Iul. opus imp.*, I, 25 and II, 147.

pp.   *Contra Iul. opus imp.*, V, 11; cf. also *De nuptiis*, II, 25.

qq.   *Contra Iul. opus imp.*, II, 39.

rr.   *Contra Iul. opus imp.*, IV, 38.

ss.   *Contra Iulianum* (the first reply to Julian), IV, 7.

tt.   *Contra Iul. opus imp.*, IV, 47–52.

uu.   *Contra Iul. opus imp.*, VI, 22.

vv.   *Contra Iulianum*, V, 52.

ww.   *Contra Iul. opus imp.*, VI, 26.

xx.   *Contra Iul. opus imp.*, VI, 27.

yy.   *Contra Iul. opus imp.*, VI, 27 and 41.

zz.   *Contra Iul. opus imp.*, I, 71.

ab.   Adam's sin, he would say, is 'one sin among others': *Contra Iul. opus imp.*, VI, 23.

ac.   *Contra Iul. opus imp.*, III, 138.

ad.   *Contra Iul. opus imp.*, II, 17.

ae.   *Contra Iul. opus imp.*, I, 44.

af.   Cf. above, p. 154.

ag.   *Contra Iul. opus imp.*, I, 47; cf. also Augustine's explanations in *Retract.*, I, 15, 4.

ah.   *Contra Iul. opus imp.*, I, 48 and 60.

ai.   *Contra Iul. opus imp.*, I, 24 and 25.

aj.   Cf. above, p. 363 and *Contra Iulianum*, V, 17.

ak.   *Contra Iul. opus imp.*, II, 178.

al.   *Contra Iul. opus imp.*, I, 6 and 66.

am.   Cf. above, p. 191 and pp. 340 f.

an.   Cf. for example *De nuptiis*, II, 45; *Contra duas ep. pelag.*, IV, 7.

ao.   Cf. *Contra Iul. opus imp.*, II, 35, 47, 57.

ap.   *City of God*, XIII, 12.

aq.   *Contra Iul. opus imp.*, II, 50, 63, 181. Cf. also II, 98: simultaneous transmission and remission of death and sin through Christ.

ar.   *Contra Iul. opus imp.*, II, 63.

as.   *Contra Iulianum* (first reply to Julian), VI, 75: Augustine saw in it a manipulation of the text.

at.   *Contra Iul. opus imp.*, II, 63.

au.   Cf. above, p. 341.

av.   Cf. *Contra Iul. opus imp.*, II, 47.

aw.   It was still his interpretation in the *De pecc. mer. et remissione*, I, 11. But in the same book he wrote shortly afterwards: . . . *In Adam, in quo omnes peccaverunt* (I, 55).

ax.   Ambrosiaster, *Ad Rom.*, 5, 12: *In quo* – id est in Adam – *omnes peccaverunt.* On the Ambrosiaster, see above, p. 178.

ay.   *Contra duas ep. pelag.*, IV, 7. Cf. also *De correptione et gratia*, 9.

az.   *City of God*, XXII, 24.

ba.   *City of God*, XXII, 22, 1.

bc.   *Contra Iul. opus imp.*, II, 116: 'Little children bear witness by their tears that they are born in wretchedness.'

bd.   Cf. *De nuptiis*, II, 53.

be.   *Retract.*, II, 23.

bf.   *De bono coniugali*, 15.

bg.   *Retract.*, II, 22, 2, quoting *De bono coniugali*, 18.

bh.   Cf. *Sermon Dolbeau* 12 (*Mainz* 41), 11 (F. Dolbeau, *Vingt-six Sermons au peuple d'Afrique*, p. 82), and above, pp. 408–9.

bi.   *De nuptiis*, II, 26: 'It is up to women to see what they feel in the secrecy of their entrails.'

bj.   *Contra Iulianum*, IV, 71. See *City of God*, XIV, 16, on the annihilation of thought during the act.

bk.   *De nuptiis*, I, 7. The theme appears in 412 in the *De peccatorum meritis*, I, 57.

bl.   *City of God*, XIII, 13; *Contra duas ep. pelag.*, I, 32.

bm.   *De nuptiis*, I, 24, and *City of God*, XIV, 20, on the Cynics.

bn.   *De Genesi ad litt.*, IX, 8–9: Adam and Eve had not had time to get down to it before the Fall!

bo.   *City of God*, XIV, 23, 2, and XIV, 26. See already, c. 410, *De Genesi ad litt.*, IX, 18.

bp.   *Contra Iulianum*, IV, 62: it is the will that gets the male member going, not the flesh lusting against the spirit.

bq.   *De gratia Christi et de pecc. orig.*, II, 40.

br.   *De gratia Christi et de pecc. orig.*, II, 40–1.

bs.   Lust was his 'beautiful client' (*pulchra suscepta*): *Contra Iul. opus imp.*, II, 59, 218 and 226.

bt.   *De nuptiis*, I, 37.

bu.   The theme appears around 419 in *Ep.* 194, 44 (to Sixtus); in 420 in *C. duas ep. pelag.*, I, 11; cf. again in *Contra Iulianum*, VI, 15.

bv.   *De nuptiis*, I, 28.

bw.   *Enarr. in Psalm.* 118, s. 27. 6: *Quanto magis regnat in quocumque dei caritas, tanto minus ei dominatur iniquitas.*

bx.   Above, p. 191.

by.   *Retract.*, II, 1, 1.

bz.   *Contra Iul. opus imp.*, I, 85 (allusion to *C. duas ep. pelag.*, I, 4) and VI, 7.

ca.   Cf. above, pp. 189–90.

cb.   It was the definition in *De libero arbitrio*, III, 8.

cd.   *Contra duas ep. pelag.*, I, 5.

ce.   *De libero arbitrio*, I, 32.

cf.   *Contra duas ep. pelag.*, I, 5.

cg.   Augustine had arrived at this definitive analysis of the limits of free will following original sin at the time – c. 390/1 – of Book III of the 'Treatise on free will': cf. *De libero arbitrio*, III, 52.

ch.   See especially *Ep.* 194, 9 on the absolute gratuitousness of grace.

ci.   Letters 214 and 215 to Valentinus and the *De gratia et libero arbitrio*.

cj.   *De gratia et libero arbitrio*, 2, 4, 5, 6.

ck.   *Conf.*, V, 18; cf. above, p. 39.

cl.   *De gratia et libero arbitrio*, 4.

cm.   *De gratia et libero arbitrio*, 7 and 8, *in fine*.

cn.   Cf. above, p. 196.

co.   *De gratia et libero arbitrio*, 9. Cf. *De spiritu et littera* (spring 412), 5; *Ep.* 157 (to Hilarius, dated 414), 5 and 10; *Sermon* 26 (18 October 418), *passim*. See also *Enarr. in Psalm.* 78, 12: 'He who is aided acts also by himself.'

cp.   *De gratia et libero arbitrio*, 19–20.

cq.   *De gratia et libero arbitrio*, 16–17.

cr.   *De gratia et libero arbitrio*, 15, *in fine*.

cs.   *Contra duas ep. pelag.*, I, 37.

ct.   *Contra duas ep. pelag.*, 42.

cu.   For the present text, *Contra duas ep. pelag.*, 33.

cv.   *Retract.*, II, 67.

cw.   *De correptione et gratia*, 4.

cx.   *De correptione et gratia*, 9. This was taking term for term a Pelagian objection which the monks of Hadrumetum could have read in *Ep.* 194, 22, as recorded by Augustine.

cy.   *De correptione et gratia*, 10.

cz.   *De dono perseverantiae*, 55.

da.   *De correptione et gratia*, 9.

db.   *De correptione et gratia*, 12–13.

dc.   *De correptione et gratia*, 16.

de. Above, p. 180.

df. *Ep.* 194, 35.

dg. *De correptione et gratia*, 17–25.

dh. *De correptione et gratia*, 26.

di. *De correptione et gratia*, 31. In *City of God*, XIV, 27, Augustine had already sketched out this theme of the *adiutorium sine quo non*.

dj. *De correptione et gratia*, 35, *initio*.

dk. *De correptione et gratia*, 38. On the exegeses of this text – which continued to be made after the Jansenist movement – read the note by J. Chéné in *BA*, 24, pp. 787–97.

dl. *Ad Simplicianum*, I, qu. 2. 2; cf. above, p. 190.

dm. *De correptione et gratia*, 39. The sentence is understandable in that Augustine conceives the *adiutorium quo* as specially ordained for final perseverance, which acts so that the Christian dies 'in a state of grace'.

dn. *Ep.* 225, 7.

do. This fear is expressed by Prosper in his letter: *Ep.* 225, 2, *in fine*.

dp. Hilarius, in his letter, confirms the social status and ecclesiastical rank of many Provençal monks, and the urgent need to react: *Ep.* 226, 9.

dq. Hilarius had written earlier (cf. *Ep.* 226, 9) and Augustine mentions in his *De praedestinatione sanctorum*, 7, the *scripta prolixiora* received by him from his correspondents. Only these two letters remain.

dr. *Ep.* 226, 10.

ds. *Ep.* 225, 2.

dt. *Ep.* 225, 4.

du. *Ep.* 226, 2; Augustine alludes to it in his *De praed. sanct.*, 3.

dv. *Ep.* 226, 3.

dw. *Ep.* 226, 4.

dx. *Ep.* 225, 5. Augustine would refute this consideration of the 'futuribles': *De praed sanct.*, 24, and would return to it again as an absurdity in the *De dono perseverantiae*, 22 and 31.

dy. *Ep.* 225, 3 and 6; 226, 5.

dz. *Ep.* 225, 8.

ea. *De praedestinatione sanctorum*, 43, *in fine*.

eb. Cf. the mentions on this in *BA*, 24, p. 437. The title that Prosper of Aquitaine gave to the whole work was *De praedestinatione sanctorum*.

ec. Cf. *De dono pers.*, 38, *initio*.

ed. *De dono pers.*, 57–62.

ef. *De dono pers.*, 61.

eg. *De praed. sanct.*, 14. On this 'last encounter of Augustine with 1 Tim. 2.4', see A. Sage, 'The universal salvific will of God in St Augustine's thinking', in *Rech. aug.*, 3, 1965, p. 117.

eh. *De praed. sanct.*, 16.

ei. Especially in the *Enchiridion* (the 'Manual'), in 421/2: cf. *Ench.*, 95, 97, 103; see also *Contra Iulianum*, IV, 42–4.

ej. *De dono pers.*, 51, where Augustine formulates in his own way the remarks in *Ep.* 225, 3 and 226, 2.

ek. *De dono pers.*, 42.

el. But it was a rarer occurrence in this period when, at Augustine's instigation, the practice of baptizing *infantuli* had become general.

em. *De dono pers.*, 62.

en. The *Retractations*, started in 426, but unfinished in 429, were never completed. I shall return to these.

eo. *De dono pers.*, 55.

CHAPTER XXXIII

Death and the hereafter

At the beginning of Book XIV of the *City of God*, Augustine daydreams aloud: if neither Adam, in the first instance, nor any of his descendants thereafter had sinned, 'human society' would have lived in a seamless happiness, and this felicity in the Garden of Eden would have continued until as a result of the divine blessing 'Increase and multiply' (Gen. 1.28), the number of predestined saints would have been complete.[a] Of course, in this unreal world, the bishop sees no need to detail the ways in which these generations would co-exist, conceived in 'animal' bodies but, thanks to the fruits of the 'Tree of Life', all equally immortal, and he continues:

> Then, they would have received a greater benediction – the one given to the blessed angels – by virtue of which each would have full assurance that he would never sin and never die; the life of the saints, who would not previously have undergone the ordeal of travail, pain and death, would have been the one which, after all those trials and tribulations, will be ours when our bodies are restored to incorruption on resurrection day.[b]

One would thus have passed from one paradise to another, or rather, with no painful transition, from a state of felicity that was full but endlessly threatened by the possibilities of Adamic freedom, to the eternally secure and firm beatitude of the kingdom of God. Humankind would therefore have been spared the vast disorder which began with the sin of the first man and his Fall and would end with the ending of time and the disappearance of the last humans subject to the mortal condition because of a nature tainted by the original sin. Death was absent from this beautiful short-cut dreamed of by the bishop. Of course, the imagined evasion of physical death occurred to the detriment of millennia of life on earth outside the Garden of Eden; but what did that matter, since life on earth had never been other than the life of an 'expatriate'?

The mortal condition

Augustine had had an early experience of death. First, when he was still a child and had felt its shadow spreading over him to the point where he himself had asked for a baptism that was finally postponed.[c] Then the death of his father, Patricius, which had little affected him in the distance of a bond that was far less than the one linking him with Monica. Above all, the death of the anonymous friend lost at Thagaste when he was nearly twenty-two: then, in the confused mixture of feelings that submerged him, the fear of his own death had rubbed shoulders with disgust at living a life which he was still loth to lose, but without yet having within his grasp the spiritual instruments to change it.[d] That was assuredly his most brutal encounter with physical death, because when Monica died he had acquired the means of healing such a serious wound; then he was compensated for the loss of his son, and of Nebridius at the same time, by the certainty he now had that they were 'in Abraham's bosom'. To the experiences he had lived through as a man, as son, father, friend, were now added forty years of life as a pastor, which were much more important in feeding his reflections on physical death.[1]

The young Augustine was probably still thinking of his lost friend and his distress at that time when he confessed to Reason, some years later, 'Now there are only three things that can move me: the fear of losing those I love, the fear of pain, the fear of death.'[e] This fear of physical death for his nearest and dearest and for himself would no longer be exactly that of the bishop for whom immortality was henceforward a state which he must help his flock to attain, but enough of it would remain to keep him very sensitive to the anguish of dying. His pastoral experience obviously underlies the ponderings of the theologian meditating on the *punctum temporis* which turns the living into the dead. His description of the torments that precede it is accurate and disturbed. He wonders about the mysterious power that comes at life's end, which, 'dissociating what was, in the living, united and closely joined, produces in him, as long as its action lasts, feelings that are painful and against nature';[2] these are the 'heavy and painful sensations' which are the evil of death.[f] Putting it bluntly, death is just that, the last struggle – the 'agony' – waged by the dying person, the passing which sometimes a single physical blow (*unus ictus corporis*) or the precipitate flight of the soul (*animae raptus*) cuts short and prevents feeling. No one is 'in death', that non-being of fleshly man, which cannot be a state. In Bossuet's famous words, between 'Madame is dying' and 'Madame is dead' lies the whole space of nothingness and eternity.

A theology of the mortal condition, however, is not elaborated on the basis of an existential fear of one's demise. The anti-Manichaean polemic provided Augustine with his first opportunity. At the time of the Cassiciacum dialogues, in the autumn of 386, he was still halted at the Aristotelian definition of the human being, which he had from Cicero: 'Man is a mortal rational animal.'[g] He had yet to extract the origin of the *mortalitas* in a Christian perspective. The dispute with his former Manichaean friends, keenly pursued from 388, prompted the emergence of this concept in Augustine's texts, in the sense of the fundamental corruption that afflicts the human body, which is frail and destined for death because of the sin which has divested it of the perfection in which God had originally created it in his image, and for which it bears the punishment.[3] Death does not come from God, said Augustine in the *De vera religione*, quoting for the first time Wis. 1.13.[4] Nevertheless, a little later, in the final pages of the *De libero arbitrio*, he was still hesitating over the question of knowing by what means 'because of our first parents we are born into a state of ignorance, difficulty and mortality since they themselves, having sinned, had been thrown into error, misery and death'.[h] At the roots of this uncertainty lay another, the one in which he found himself over the origin of souls; for he had not at that time rejected the 'creationist' hypothesis, which put him in a better position to refute the Manichaeans, and in this hypothesis he could not totally set aside the possibility that the 'unhappy – and mortal – condition' was a state of nature and not a form of punishment.[5] He would explain himself on this hesitation in the *Retractations*, ascribing it to the context, as well as in his very last book.[i]

As early as 394, a short sentence in the *Contra Adimantum* indicates the direction of Augustine's thinking on the eve of his becoming bishop, regarding 'the old life that we have received from Adam in such conditions that what was for him an act of will is natural in us'.[j] By 'natural' we must of course understand the 'corrupted nature' on which the bishop would expatiate so often during the controversy against the Pelagians. Augustine's texts could not be more clear: physical death – the first death – a punishment of sin for Adam, has become nature for his descendants;[k] the penalty had been transmitted by being changed into a biological fact, 'mortality' had entered the genetic heritage of humankind, just like the other unfortunate elements of the human condition, in a manner which the bishop found it hard to account for unless he could stop firmly at the traducianist theory of the origin of souls, to which he was inclined, while perceiving its difficulties.[l]

But for Augustine, the fact that death was a punishment for an original sin which had engendered the deterioration of our nature was a psychological obviousness just as much as a theological reflection. The Pelagians – first and foremost Caelestius, condemned for this count at Carthage in 411[m] – held that Adam had been created mortal and would have died whether or not he sinned. If that were so, men, his descendants, had no reason to fear the death that was part of their God-created nature. Now, the slightest experience of life showed that our nature, wounded by the penalty for sin, shrieked its horror of death as one might at a punishment. The pastor had only to look and listen round about him. Non-acceptance of death was not confined to the instinctive flight from it that could be observed in animals, which also display their fondness for life; man felt the additional regret for an immortality that was irremediably lost: 'If animals, which have been created to die each in its own time, flee death and cling to life, how much more so does man, who was created to live without end, if he had chosen to live without sin.'[6] 'O voice of nature, admission of punishment!' he exclaimed in a sermon in the summer of 418.[n]

Duly observable in the common run of mortals, the human fear of death was also in evidence in the New Testament texts relating to the apostles, and even Christ when he was acting and speaking *sub forma servi*, when he assumed the mortal condition. That gave the fear legitimacy. On several occasions in his preaching Augustine mentioned Peter's attitude; after the resurrection, reappearing to his disciples on the shores of the sea of Tiberias, Christ had predicted, together with his martyrdom, what Peter's state of mind would be: 'When thou shalt be old, another shall gird thee and carry thee whither thou wouldst not';[o] this, commented the bishop, showed a very human will when confronted with the fear of death. But Christ himself had experienced this anguish in the face of death, on the Mount of Olives, when he had confessed his sorrow to his disciples, and prayed that the cup should pass from him (Matt. 26.38–9), and when on the cross he had cried out his short moment of despair into which, as death approached, his Father's abandonment had cast him (Matt. 27.46). Taking on the human condition, admitting his inner turmoil, Christ was speaking then, commented Augustine, in the name of the men whose weaknesses he 'transfigured'.[7] The martyrs, who shared in Christ's glory, were indebted to his example and his help – they who loved life so much – for having been able to overcome their fear of death: *amatores vitae, mortis toleratores.*[p] And the bishop exclaimed, 'If death is nothing, what great thing did the martyrs scorn?'[q]

Here Augustine emphasized the attachment that every man can – and even must, as we shall see further on – have for this 'hideous and poverty-stricken, but sweet, yes, sweet' life. He liked to quote and comment upon St Paul's words: 'No man ever yet hated his own flesh' (Eph. 5.29). Elsewhere, in a sermon preached for the feast of Sts Perpetua and Felicitas, he said:

> So great is the strange charm of this life, which is yet so full of wretchedness, and so strong the natural horror of death in all the living, that even those who, through death, go to that life where one can never die, do not want to die.[r]

The martyrs, though so highly motivated by their faith in eternal life, had not braved death in order to escape this life. With even greater reason, what typified the common run of mortals, even the most wretched of men, was the tenacious desire to continue existing, though they knew they were doomed to death. 'Rather suffer than die', La Fontaine would say, among others. Augustine, whom the fabulist had probably read, had gone further on the subject. In 417, he wrote in the *City of God*:

> By natural inclination, mere existence is so sweet a thing that for this alone even the most wretched are unwilling to die . . . Why do they fear death and prefer to live in such distress than to end it by dying, unless because they see clearly how nature abhors non-existence? So, when they feel close to dying, they would be overjoyed if they were mercifully allowed to prolong their wretched life a little and have their death delayed.[s]

Nature abhors nothingness (*natura refugit non esse*): at a distance of nearly thirty years, this reflection – but in another perspective, which was now concerned with pastoral work and no longer purely ontological speculation – extended the one he had brought to bear on the behaviour of the suicidally inclined in Book III of the *De libero arbitrio*. The man stricken with misfortune or a prey to grief and distress wavers about the course to take. The instinct for self-preservation holds him in this life by obedience to a desire for existence which sometimes seems illusory.[t] But he may be tempted to proceed to the act with uncertain motives. Augustine exhorts him to persevere in his being, even if it is unhappy: 'If you want to escape misery, love that very will-to-live in yourself.'[u] The would-be suicide is deceiving himself if, wishing to kill himself, he believes he is choosing nothingness, whereas in fact what his nature desires is rest, that is to say, actually a growth of being. Let him therefore stoically content himself with the being that he has, giving thanks to God for it. 'As it is absolutely impossible that one should enjoy not existing, so the existence one has must absolutely not be a reason for ingratitude towards the Creator's goodness.'[8] There lies the root, of very long standing, of Augustine's condemnation of suicide: whoever makes an attempt on his own life is attacking being, thus creation. Doubtless, if we are to remain strictly on the plane of human morality, there had been several shining examples of greatness of soul in pagan Antiquity, but we must 'more rightly call great a soul who has more strength to endure a wretched life than to flee it'.[v] To the stance of the much vaunted Cato of Utica he preferred that of Regulus, who was also very highly thought of but with better cause, whose action was, in his view, that of a sort of pre-Christian martyr to his word of honour, and he had no hesitation in comparing him with the saintly Job.[w] Returning to the religious level, the bishop, for want of justification, could see only one purpose for the suicidal act – to kill oneself immediately after baptism, taking advantage of the brief state of grace accorded by the water of regeneration[x] in order to gain one's salvation. This was a demonstration, by an abhorrent absurdity, of its utter inappropriateness.

Throughout long years Augustine had been faced with a special type of suicide – a suicide of witness and protest – that of Donatist fanatics.[9] Those who indulged in it likened their deed to martyrdom, whether they had positively incurred death or whether it had struck them because of deliberate provocation, which for Augustine amounted to the same thing. He had two reasons for refusing them the glory of martyrdom. The first was ecclesiological, and the bishop had formulated it in one of his blunt maxims in the early days of his anti-Donatist struggle: 'What makes Christ a martyr is not the punishment but the cause';[y] and the obstinacy of Gaudentius who, to avoid reconciliation threatened to burn himself and his family alive in the schismatic basilica of Thamugadi (Timgad), had given him a last opportunity to reformulate it in 418/19.[z] The second reason was his repugnance at this very desire for death which appeared to him to be a sinister aping of the attitude of the true martyrs; it would never have crossed their mind to make their life the stake in blackmail and, far from embracing death, they merely endured it.[aa]

Aspects of the hereafter

We must come back to it. What always torments the mortal, above all if, as a Christian, he is not certain of his salvation – and how could he be?[10] – is taking that leap into the unknown. However imperfect it may be, we still cling to our living fleshly garment – we know where we are with it. Augustine commented on several occasions on the strong imagery of St Paul's words: 'We would not be unclothed, but clothed upon with a second garment, that mortality might be swallowed up of life' (2 Cor. 5.4).[11] Every Christian first experienced this dramaturgy in the liturgy of baptism, but this time it was his life that must be left in the changing-room. The bishop knew how much the anxiety gnawed at his faithful. He said so particularly in a sermon preached shortly before his own death: 'You would like to pass from this life to the next without having to die to live again, but remaining alive to be transformed to a better state . . . You do not want to be unclothed, and yet you must.'[bb] We could always clutch at the precedent of Enoch and Elijah, snatched up to heaven in their 'animal' and mortal body, but we should not count on it too much. In any case – and this the bishop preferred not to say in his sermons – 'this experience of the separation of soul from body remains after the removal of the bonds of sin (after baptism) because faith would be weakened if the immortality of the body followed immediately upon the sacrament of regeneration'.[cc] On this point he had to be categorical; if not, 'surely everyone would rush to the grace of Christ, with the little children to be baptized, with the principal aim of sparing the destruction of his body?' Faith could only exist on the horizon of hope (cf. Rom. 8.24). In 426/7, when for his *Retractations* Augustine reread the text addressed to Marcellinus in 412 on the remission of sins, he reacted on seeing this sentence: 'At the end of the world, it will be granted to some not to feel death as the effect of a sudden change';[dd] he would have to take a closer look at this. It had to be one thing or the other, in fact: either these men were not to die, or one must understand, with St Paul (1 Cor. 15.52), that by passing from this life to eternal life 'in the twinkling of an eye' they would not feel death.[ee] He obviously was more inclined to this solution of a happy arrival in the Kingdom, speeded up.[ff] But only the good thief was known to have made the trip in one day.[gg]

It does not take long to do the rounds of the canonical scriptural material available in Augustine's times – and in fact in the second Christian generation – to fix in a theologically irreproachable way the various 'scenarios' of the hereafter and imagine the setting in which the variants and phases of this eschatology were enacted.[12] The most important, if not the only, texts were to be found in the Gospels, and the basic one was the parable of the wicked rich man and poor Lazarus, in Luke 16.19–31. Death had reversed their situations: in the home of the dead, in torment, the rich man raised his eyes and afar off saw Abraham with Lazarus 'in his bosom', and from a distance called to Abraham asking him to send Lazarus so that, dipping his fingertip in water, he could cool his tongue to assuage the thirst with which he burned in the flames; but in vain, for a great gulf separated them, replied Abraham to compound his refusal, and prevented any passage in either direction. These few lines, in their relative topographical exactness, were of capital importance in nurturing the strictly Christian imagination of the hereafter. The hell in which the rich man was consumed by flames was 'down there', although within sight of the heavenly place which was the home of the righteous while awaiting resurrection and judgement. And that place was 'Abraham's bosom', whither Augustine was convinced his dear Nebridius had gone straight away, whatever doubts he had about the nature of the place at that time.[hh] Subsequently, the bishop had always refused to have what he called a 'carnal' perception of it.[ii] He would make mild fun of the young Vincentius Victor, who seemed to take this 'bosom' in the literal and purely bodily sense.[jj] The only thing about which he was certain was that 'Abraham's bosom', distinct from hell, was a 'paradisial' place, the place of felicity to which the good thief found himself transported on the very evening of his death.[kk] In short, a comfortable antechamber in which to await future events, and Jesus' companion on Golgotha would certainly find himself in good company with the Patriarchs and the Prophets.[ll] And Christ who, *sub forma dei*, is everywhere – he had even descended into hell – would make the waiting period sweeter until the 'face to face' vision they would all have together after the resurrection, already giving them the benefit of his beatific presence in this place.[mm] It was in this sense that Jesus had been able to tell the good thief that on the same day he would be with him in Paradise.

As I have just said, Augustine refused to imagine this transitory paradise;[13] but he was not unaware that others had tried to do so two centuries before, even in his Africa, without going so far as to try to endow Christian imagination with a repertoire capable of rivalling the rich pagan imagery which in Canto VI of Virgil's *Aeneid* was still familiar to the well-read. In the very years when the Carthaginian Tertullian was defining 'Abraham's bosom' quite clearly, emphasizing the interim refreshment (*refrigerium interim*) to be enjoyed there[nn] – a clear allusion to Lazarus' finger dipped in water which had not managed to reach the parched lips of the wicked rich man – one of the finest passions of martyrs in those difficult times for Christianity provided a kind of illustration of it. The *Passion of Perpetua and Felicitas*, which was read at Mass on the anniversary of their martyrdom, 7 March, was listened to by the faithful as if it were a *chanson de geste*: a compassionate tale, surprisingly fresh in its inspiration, punctuated by the heroine's visions. In one of the visions she had in prison, Perpetua had seen and made visible her little brother Dinocrates. In two phases: first the unhappy little boy – he had been carried off at the age of seven by a cancer that had eaten away his face – had appeared in 'a place of shadows', dirty and in rags, his face scarred by the disease that had caused his death; he was burning with fever and thirst, and was trying to stand on tiptoe to drink from a basin of water, but the coping was too high.[oo] Perpetua then prayed day and night, with tears and groans, that salvation should be granted to her little brother, and some days later another vision showed Dinocrates to her, in the same place, but now clean and well clad, 'refreshed' (*refrigerantem*), the wound on his face healed; the coping of the basin had been lowered and the child was joyfully using a gold cup that had been placed there to drink his fill of a constantly replenished water. Waking, Perpetua realized that 'he had been mercifully reprieved from his punishment'.[pp]

Of course there are ambiguities in this account: what was the 'punishment'? Perhaps for a sin – symbolized by the cancer on his face – and in this case the basin would be a baptismal font from which the previously unbaptized child eventually obtained his salvation.[qq] But this refreshing water was also enjoyed in 'Abraham's bosom'; it was the water one could have seen flowing, cool and real, on the *mensae* of the palaeo-Christian tombs of North Africa, at Tipasa and elsewhere, of which so many inscriptions celebrated the beneficial *refrigerium*, a material realization on this earth, close to the dead, of the happiness that was desired for them.[14] It expressed the flexibility and richness in meanings of a text that contained the latent, barely sketched, theme which would slowly become a clearly affirmed statement, that of 'limbo' when children were involved, and one which also showed how intense, in the popular Christian mind, was the feeling of the effectiveness of the intercession of the living for the dead, provided the living – as in the instance of Perpetua – possessed the grace which was their necessary charisma. In this regard Augustine thought no differently, having prayed, on Monica's death, for her salvation and who, in the *City of God*, stressed the virtue of the Church's prayers on behalf of the deceased whose life here below had not been wicked.[rr]

Above all, it is these images of a shadowy place where one suffers an ill-being and a thirst which, in the case of little Dinocrates, seem not to be definitive punishments, which make this page of the *Passion of Perpetua and Felicitas* one where the 'imagined vision of purgatory is outlined'.[15] They illustrate, in anticipation, the evocation in Augustinian texts of a temporary situation – one hesitates between 'place' and 'state' – far less favourable than the one where Jesus' compassion had installed the good thief. Augustine's reflections on those punishments whose transitory nature, in the best instances, placed them between physical death and possible resurrection, in parallel with the pleasures of 'Abraham's bosom', had begun well before his entry into pastoral life. He was mentioning them in 388/9 in his text *On Genesis against the Manichaeans,* with words that differentiated them clearly from eternal punishment; this penalty, or ordeal, threatened the one who in earthly life had neglected to provide himself with spiritual food: he 'would have to suffer after death either the fire of purification (*ignem purgationis*), or eternal punishment'.[16] Some thirty-five years later, first in the *Manual* then in the *City of God,* the bishop would try to proffer a reply to his faithful to what he called an *obscura quaestio.* In one of his sermons, Augustine quoted St Paul and, as was his wont, made his commentary on the text in the form of questions and answers. Explain to us, he was asked, how it is that they who, on the 'foundation' that is Christ, build not with gold, silver and precious stones, but with wood, hay and straw, will not perish, will be saved, but 'so as by fire' (1 Cor. 3.15)? He replied that he knew two categories of Christians. There were those who were not attached to the world, 'who made use of it as if they were not using it'; those, the abstinent, the impartial, the righteous, built on Christ's foundation with gold: their buildings were proof against any fire. More numerous were those who, basically faithful to Christ, were however attached to the possessions of this earth, their interests, carnal love of their wives more than was demanded by the conjugal pact.[ss] These would be saved 'as by fire', when the fire would have consumed the buildings of wood, hay and straw erected by their love of worldly things.[tt] And in another text, the pastor had already warned his flock: because it is said that through this fire we shall be saved, we tend to make little of it; let us beware of doing so, for that fire will be more terrible than anything a man may endure in this life.[17] But obviously the Apostle had ruled out from the likelihood of this terrible but temporary fire those who, on the foundation of Christ they had received, had built adulteries, sacrileges, perjuries and other crimes: there were not even words to describe these kinds of constructions, and it was eternal fire that awaited their builders.

However, between the apologues of the preacher commenting upon the Pauline epistle and the firm establishment of a theological line of thinking, a margin of doubt remained. In a letter to Cyril of Alexandria, dated 417, the bishop did not rule out that the Apostle's words were directed just as much at what happens in this life as at the particular judgement which precedes the Last Judgement.[uu] Around 421, the *Manual,* often so remarkably peremptory in its synthetic statements, appears to be retreating on this point. In it we see Augustine making a more allegorical, even metaphorical, exegesis of St Paul's text, admitting more plainly still that the fire of 1 Cor. 3.15 might chiefly designate the trials of this life,[vv] on the 'cathartic' function of which he would express himself more clearly elsewhere, when he says that 'in this life, this fire of tribulation is connected with family bereavements and calamities of every kind' which deprive us of earthly possessions and loves.[ww] And in the next chapter of the *Manual* he continues:

> It is not unbelievable that something similar should happen *after* this life . . . Some faithful (in that case) could, by a kind of purifying fire,[xx] be saved more or less rapidly or belatedly, according to how much they loved perishable possessions.

Some years later, Augustine resumed his reflections on the whole of these eschatological problems in the last books of the *City of God*. He found it difficult to make up his mind. Quoting Mal. 3.3, on the Lord who 'shall purify the sons of Levi and purge them as gold and silver', he comments: from these words it seems to emerge that for some there will be 'purificatory punishments' (the Latin says, *poenas purgatorias*). But he does not yet feel capable of deciding: 'This question of the "purificatory punishments" must be deferred until later, so that it can be dealt with more carefully.'[yy] He would in fact return to it in the following book of the *City of God*, but again for a remarkable admission of cautious uncertainty:

> Thus, after the death of the body, until we reach that supreme day of condemnation and reward which will follow the resurrection of the body, it may be alleged that in this interval of time this sort of fire is undergone not by those whose ways of living and loving here below have not been such that their wood, hay and straw are consumed; but others feel it, those who, having brought with them 'buildings' of similar materials, experience the fire of transitory tribulation that will consume them, either only in this life, or in this life and hereafter, or even hereafter and not in this life – and without entailing their damnation – I would not refute it, for it may well be true.[zz]

We thus find that nothing is less dogmatic than Augustine's last words on the possibility of a transitory situation of amendment or 'purification' that may be experienced by good Christians who, without being great sinners, have had some weaknesses for worldly things. Not only is the bishop a thousand miles from imagining a 'purgatory' in spatial terms, but the very idea of a temporary 'state' of 'being purged', between death and the Last Judgement, leaves him hesitating. We have seen that his inclination would urge him rather to spare these minor sinners, lovers of the good life, the ordeal of a transitory but terrible fire, bearing in mind that they had often already undergone their 'purgatory' with their earthly 'tribulation'; but only on condition that such human weakness did not remain impenitent. At bottom, Augustine doubtless had the hope that, conditional upon penitence, divine mercy would allow this category of faithful to be spared a 'purging' fire in the hereafter.[18] The bishop was at least sure that God's mercy would be exercised, without any need for penitence, for those children who were baptized at a tender age, whose life might happen to be cut short before their adolescence: these prematurely dead, who had had neither the time nor the opportunity to add personal sins to the one redeemed by the grace of baptism, not only escaped eternal torment – the 'second death'[ab] – but were even exempt from the slightest purificatory torment.[ac]

This 'second death' is the one promised to the wicked rich man in the sad waiting-room, kingdom of thirst, from which, raising his eyes, he sees with envy the still temporary bliss of Lazarus in 'Abraham's bosom'. The particular judgement that has sent him to this antechamber of hell – when 'his soul left his body'[19] – has definitively differentiated, before any confirmation by the Last Judgement, between his fate and that of the virtuous pauper: theoretically with no appeal, without any redemptive passage through a temporal penalty, as in the case of good Christians who are a little too fond of this world. Does Augustine unfeelingly leave these ungodly infidels, hardened and impenitent sinners, to their damnation? There was an ever-increasing number of those whom the bishop, with a trace of irony and irritation, calls 'our compassionate Christians',[ad] who were repelled by the idea of the eternal punishment of which scriptural texts relating to the 'Gehenna of fire' painted such a terrifying picture. Lacking the metaphysical capacity of Origen and his dynamic vision of a salvation which, in the end, did not exclude the prince of darkness and his angels, the compassionate of Augustine's time did not go quite as far as their leader. But their chances of reprieve were very wide-ranging. In the *City of God*, there is a catalogue of remissions of infernal punishment and even exemptions, in which a plea is made in favour of this or that category of sinner.[ae] For his part, Augustine stuck to the dogma, which was clear enough on this subject in the Scriptures. Eternity was not a relative thing, nor capable of being shortened. He wanted to take literally Jesus' last words in the eschatological speech just prior to the passover that would witness his own passion: 'And these shall go away into everlasting punishment: but the righteous into life eternal' (Matt. 25.46). The two groups had been placed by Christ on an 'equal footing' which, he thought, could not be assailed without absurdity: if life was to be eternal for the saints, this symmetry required that damnation was eternal for the rest.[af] Inflexible on the eternity of punishment, Augustine however accepted that the latter was modulated according to the behaviour of both groups in this life, objectively – it was then the 'force and heat' of the fire which varied – or subjectively, if in Gehenna it might be granted to the suffering that not all should feel the fire with the same ferocity.[ag] It was probably that modulation of the penalty that the bishop had in mind when in the *Manual* he evoked in rather sibylline fashion 'a more tolerable form of damnation' (*damnatio tolerabilior*).[ah] And although he rejected the idea of remission of punishment, he did not refuse to envisage that it could be modified and alleviated; God's mercy could grant the damned the grace of suffering lighter and gentler penalties than they had deserved.[ai] In one of his homilies, the bishop daringly asked the question: could one conceive of 'pauses' in their sufferings, at intervals? The question remained unanswered: on such a subject, he concluded, it was better to reflect in a more leisurely moment.[aj]

Another, really insistent, question was left in abeyance: the fate of children who died unbaptized. In this regard, Augustine was painfully imprisoned in the doctrine of original sin;[ak] having sinned in Adam, humankind had been saved by the redemption obtained from the new Adam. If that redemption was declared in vain in the case of children who died unbaptized, the whole edifice of his faith in the action of divine Providence crumbled. He could not admit such a flaw. We saw it in his controversy with the Pelagians, for whom there was no problem since they denied original sin. But he could not regard as tenable the attitude of a Vincentius Victor, whose kind heart, in this instance, had driven him to Pelagianism; a 'true Catholic' when upholding the doctrine of original sin against Pelagius, the correspondent of 420 had changed into a 'new heretic' when he undermined the teaching relating to baptism![al] In support of his 'compassionate' theories, he drew his argument from the fate meted out to Dinocrates in the *Passion of Perpetua and Felicitas*, and likewise from the elevation to Paradise of the good thief. But who knew, retorted the bishop, rather incautiously handling the argument *ex silentio*, if either had not been baptized?[20] Victor was even more audacious and more precise than the Pelagians on the *post mortem* destination of unbaptized children.[am] He was not going against what he read in John's Gospel:

'Except a man be born of water and the spirit, he cannot enter into the kingdom of God' (3.5), but not unreasonably he made a distinction between the Kingdom and Paradise, in which he saw 'the many mansions in the Father's house' (John 14.2); and recognizing in these 'mansions' almost spatial realities, he applied himself to finding a little place for the unbaptized.[an] Regarding the good thief, Augustine could only agree: how could the promise made by Christ be denied? But whatever it cost him in human terms, he could not accept it when it came to children, the less so because Victor did not stop there on his path of compassion, but went further than the Pelagians by forgetting John 3.5 and foreseeing that, at the resurrection, after a time in the 'mansions' of Paradise, the gates of the Kingdom would be opened up before them.[ao] Besides, the anti-Pelagian council that had met at Carthage in the spring of 418 had already bluntly put an end to this theological dispute by declaring anathema on anyone who used John 14.2 ('In my Father's house are many mansions') to claim that in the heavenly realm there was 'some medial place' where infants who had died unbaptized would live in bliss.[ap] Truth to tell, neither the Pelagians nor Victor after them had expressed themselves exactly in these words, but the game was finished.

The theologian had not weakened, but the question of little children who had died without baptism was a thorn in the pastor's soul. In 412, because he could not exonerate them from damnation, he at least affirmed that they would experience the 'gentlest damnation of all';[aq] which would be echoed some ten years later in a sentence in the *Manual* which, without actually naming children, could only be directed at them: 'The gentlest of all will be the punishment of those who have added no sin at all to the one they received from their origin.'[ar] This penalty, said another text, would be more bearable than that experienced by those who commit personal sins.[as] What else? those who find it hard to be satisfied by these soothing words will exclaim. And what answer is there except that, by these words, in spite of the rigidity of a theology which, for our taste, is doubtless over-concerned with anticipating all sidestepping and barring the way to any laxity, the bishop signified his wish to leave the ways to divine mercy open?

Life eternal in the Kingdom

For the dead, before they entered the eternity of infernal punishment or celestial bliss, time continued to elapse. What for the living is the very material time of History, the span remaining for generations to come while awaiting the Parousia, is for the dead the 'meta-physical' time which, after the 'first death' – the dissolution of human components, the soul's abandonment of that body which it had carried at arm's length and subjected to its good or wicked will – opens up until the real eschatological term: the 'second death' or eternal life, according to what the Last Judgement decides. The first death has sent the soul to a particular judgement which gives some augur of the final judgement, and even anticipates it, but it has left its mortal remains, in some form or other, on this earth. These remains are 'resting' there, as the epitaphs say in profusion, and sometimes one of them, like a martyrological inscription at Tipasa,[21] will add 'while waiting' (*interim*): waiting, of course, for the Parousia, and the resurrection that will restore the human form, either to cast it into the 'second death' or assure its eternal life.

Among his theological heritage, Augustine had found the vast dossier of the debate on the resurrection, and he did not neglect this aspect; in any case it would have been quite impossible to do so, for herein lay the weightiest part of the ideological dispute between pagans and Christians. Intellectuals on both sides were able to agree on the immortality of the soul – even there not without ambiguities – but when it came to the resurrection of the flesh, the divorce was total. And it went back a long way: we know that, on coming to the point in his discourse when he mentioned the resurrection of the dead, and firstly that of Christ, which guaranteed all the rest, St Paul had to leave the Areopagus in Athens, under the gibes of those who were listening to him, Epicurean and Stoic philosophers in the forefront.[at] The mockery would continue, from Celsius to Porphyry, and Augustine must have been in an optimistic mood to believe and affirm that this scepticism had been completely swept away; that uneducated men, a handful of fishermen, had managed to catch in the nets cast by Christ 'the rarest fish, the philosophers themselves'; that Christ's resurrection, and ascension to heaven in the same flesh in which he had returned to life, were henceforth preached in the whole world 'and that the world believed it'.[au] In fact, the ancient world contemporary with Augustine – including some of his own flock – still had difficulty in believing in the resurrection of the body, and although the bishop must have been sorely tempted to sweep such weakness away with the back of his hand, from his pulpit he had endlessly to refute even the most naïve and comical objections. I will not give the catalogue here, though it has often been drawn up.[22] But it was not for pleasure that Augustine compelled himself to have an answer for everything in his sermons, and would continue in his most carefully worked out texts to resolve the difficulties presented to him, from the most 'serious' – for example, the arguments that philosophers drew from a body's natural weight to deny the physical possibility of its resurrection![av] – to the apparently preposterous, when he pondered over the eschatological consequences of anthropophagy: the flesh of a man eaten by another would be restored to him, and God would see to the restoration of flesh to the one whom dire necessity had driven to this act.[aw]

The concern to defend the dogma of the resurrection against pagan sarcasm or to support it in the face of the doubts of certain believers was not simply a liking for apologetics on the bishop's part. The reversal of perspectives that ended in altering the hierarchic soul/body relationship of Platonic dualism, breaking with the concept of the body as the 'soul's prison' – sometimes a prison to be ashamed of[23] – had not been rapidly acquired by Christian anthropology. Ambrose continued often copiously to develop the metaphor of the body as prison.[24] Augustine must have done much work on this during his own progress, starting from his conversion. The revaluation of the body, and chiefly breaking away from discrediting it, was a relatively belated victory for him, connected with the weakening of his Neoplatonism, above all following his rereading of and meditation on St Paul. In a text dating to 387/8, in which his first mention of the resurrection appears, he was still writing: 'This resurrection of the flesh, half-heartedly believed by some, denied by others, I hold to be as certain as the fact that the sun rises after it has set'; but only to add just afterwards that what the soul wished for as its supreme reward was death, 'that is to say, flight and escape from this body here below'.[ax] Still in this period, he was admitting his loyalty to the *soma/sema* of Plato. His ideas on the incarnation had doubtless needed to mature for him to get the full measure of the dogma of the resurrection of the flesh, a component of the symbol of faith which he, like all the other aspirants to baptism in the spring of 387, had recited, and also for him to come to a real rehabilitation of the body.[25] But it must be said, too, that his doctrine of original sin resulted, among other things, in restoring the equilibrium between soul and body.[26] The soul, not the body, commits the sin. In Book XIV of the *City of God*, he writes: 'To assert that the flesh is the cause of every kind of moral vice because the soul clothed in flesh lives thus would be to take a poor view of human nature in its entirety.' And a little further in the same text: 'The corruption of the body, which weighs down the soul, is not the cause of the first sin, but its punishment; it was not corruptible flesh that made the soul sinful, but the sinful soul that made the flesh corruptible.[ay] Assuredly, the corruptible body is a weight for the soul, and Augustine recognizes the consequences of that fleshly corruption in moral life, but for him it is no longer as a body that our envelope of flesh weighs upon the soul, but insofar as it is mortal in our condition here below. In a sermon dated 5 May 418, thus more or less contemporary with the text just quoted, the bishop attacked the 'spiritualists' for whom bliss after death still consisted in liberation from the imprisoning body.[az] Some years earlier, in a great sermon on the resurrection of the body, preached for the feast of St Vincent, Augustine had already attacked those philosophers whose contempt for bodies – receptacles for sinful souls, according to them – mainly accounted for their refusal to believe in the resurrection.[ba]

Like Jerome for his part, Augustine vigorously attacked the idea, inherited from Neoplatonism and tenacious in a certain Christian tradition in the West up to Prudentius and St Ambrose, that the body is a jail assigned to the soul to punish it for a sin prior to its incorporation. In which, when all is said and done, the hermit of Bethlehem and the bishop of Hippo were merely good readers of the first chapters of Genesis. Adam's sin had not resulted in the human soul falling in the body, but in debilitating that body, rendering it mortal and passing this weakness and mortality on to his descendants. In itself, as God had created it, the body was not evil, and the elect would find it again in heaven in its original integrity. From his meditation on Genesis – and St Paul – Augustine was able to extract all the anthropological consequences, in such a way as to place the resurrection of the flesh at the heart of his theological discourse on the hereafter.[27] And he did so despite the conceptual difficulties that still came to him from a language whose dualist terminology was a not yet truly 'fossilized' residue of the philosophical training of his youth.[bc] It had certainly been easier for St Paul, who of course wrote in Greek, but came from Judaism and thought in Semitic, to imagine and to relate – in 1 Cor. 15.35–53 – the ascent to heaven of the 'complete man', sown as a 'psychic body' (the Latin uses, less happily, 'animal') and raised as a 'pneumatic body'.

Like all the Latins, Augustine speaks of 'spiritual bodies' to designate what, on the Day of Judgement, will be the resuscitated bodies of those whom the Son of Man will place at his right hand to usher them into his Father's kingdom (Matt. 25.33–4). He was perfectly well aware of the apparent contradiction in terms: 'Far be it from me, however, to believe that they will be spirits!' They will be real bodies, he insists, with a fleshly substance, but 'thanks to the lifegiving spirit' – *spiritu vivificante*: we recognize here the principle of strength, light, in a word, 'holiness' of the Pauline *pneuma* – without feeling the least heaviness or corruption of the flesh.[bd] Augustine increased the variations on this fundamental but difficult theme throughout forty years – as early as 388/9 in his explanation of Genesis, against the Manichaeans.[28] How could he convey that in eternal life even the flesh would be spiritual? It was not enough to invert the terms, to say that it was not absurd since it had happened that in this life, among 'carnal' men, even the spirit becomes carnal.[be] The flesh, said the bishop, would be spiritual, not because it would be transformed into spirit, but because it would submit to the spirit 'with a sovereign and wonderful obedience, to the point where it obtained the perfect joy of an indissoluble immortality, no longer feeling pain or corruption or the slightest reluctance'.[bf] In order to be better understood, he tried to make a comparison, referring to the first man, whose status was known and whose lot might appear enviable. Yet Adam had been created not as a 'lifegiving spirit', but as a 'living soul' (Gen. 2.7); to speak like St Paul, he was not 'pneumatic', but simply 'psychic', 'animal': and although thanks to God's protection he was sheltered from external attack, and even internal, such as illness,[bg] he needed food and drink, which the Tree of Life gave him at the same time as preserving him in the flower of youth.[bh] Whereas, given life by the spirit, the spiritual body would no longer need material support, therefore food, preserving the substance of its flesh without corporeal loss or corruption.[bi]

These subtleties on the body come to glory must have seemed very abstract, and thereby somewhat disturbing, to average Christians, who had to be given something concrete, even in such matters. In the fine sermon delivered in January 413 for St Vincent's day, we must admire the preacher's ingenuity in trying to persuade his flock in Hippo of the perfection of the resurrected bodies. The bishop achieved his effects by constantly going to the extreme. For example, physical health: to be healthy was not to be conscious of one's body, but to live in it while forgetting about it; but however light our body might seem to us, or if we were as blissfully unaware of it as a stone, it could not come anywhere near what we shall enjoy, so to speak, in Paradise. Birds may appear to us to be extremely swift, the stars move with a rapidity that defies the imagination, but it would be as nothing compared with the agility of those glorious bodies.[bj] Nor would Augustine, in the *City of God*, be loth to give comforting details for all and sundry that were not mere responses to the detractors of the resurrection. In the celestial Paradise, the skinny would acquire the embonpoint they would have liked to have in this life and, conversely, the obese would lose weight: and that is the least of it! The martyrs would retrieve the limbs they had lost – 'But there shall not an hair of your head perish', Jesus had said (Luke 21.18)[bk] – but would keep their scars, the glorious vestiges of the ordeals they had suffered for their faith. And how old would these resuscitated bodies be in the Kingdom? Would we see old men and little children together? And what about babies who died in their mother's womb? There was no reason, said the bishop after some hesitation, that they should be deprived of resurrection,[bl] and the same solution would have to be applied as for children already born, by virtue of the 'causal reason' which endowed them with the potential seeds of their development. Thus the bishop aligned everyone, in the celestial kingdom, at the age Jesus had reached at the time of his preaching and passion; because it was the age when Christ, himself re-arisen from the dead, had shown everyone the Way, and also – a wonderful coincidence only for non-believers – because it was around one's early thirties that one entered that fullest bloom of youth which Latins called *juventus*, after which the decline began into maturity and old age.[bm] And as in this company women remained women, they too in the dazzling flower of a youth that no longer roused any lustful desire, a vast crowd of both sexes in their prime pushed against heaven's gates. Augustine emphasized this beauty; nothing must mar the Kingdom where 'the children of the resurrection and the promise will be equal to the angels', at least in happiness.[bn]

In the final book of the *City of God*, the bishop tirelessly returns to the subject of the bliss of Paradise. How to represent it, make it perceivable? The comparison with Adam and Eve's experience in the Garden of Eden had shown its limitations. One way presented itself – an analogy with the best of what man had known here below: a hymn to the human spirit, the grateful enumeration of earthly goods – these are among the most beautiful pages – also had the advantage of being a hymn of praise for the work of creation. There, too, the bishop went to the limits: 'What gifts would he give to men he had predestined for life, he who had given so much to the men he had predestined for death!'[bo] And this happiness culminated in the vision of God: but then one must no longer speak of happiness, but beatitude. Commenting on St Paul's words, so often repeated by him: 'For now we see through a glass, darkly; but then face to face' (1 Cor. 13.12), Augustine meditated at length. How many times had he turned this question over and over to try to answer worried, pressing, sometimes naively expressed, questions, as when the noble lady Italica had asked him if God could be seen with the body's eyes![bp] A little later, around 413, he had written a long letter on this theme to a certain Paulina – it would appear in the *Retractations* as a treatise in one book[bq] – and the final sentence left a hope, regarding the 'spiritual body', of the reflections that he would not tackle until a dozen years later.[br] At the same time, and still on the same theme, Fortunatianus, bishop of Sicca Veneria, was favoured with a shorter letter, whose thrust spoke volumes about the real harassment to which the bishop of Hippo was subjected by these aspirants to the vision of God in this world below: Augustine begged his friend to ask pardon of one of their colleagues, to whom he had written a little too abruptly that the eyes of his body could not see God and would never see him; he was not at all repentant, however, for having written this cruel truth.[bs]

But what, then, would be the reality of the *face to face* vision of the divine?[29] Nothing could better represent the activity of this 'spiritual body' – in truth, its only one – than its contemplation of God, and therefore there was nothing more important to establish. It was easy to imagine that, like the prophet Elijah, who had been able to see his servant while being absent from his body, the elect would see God in Paradise even with their eyes shut, as the result of an inner vision. But the real question was: would they see him with the open eyes of their 'spiritual body'? Of course it was not a matter of good eyesight and one must beware, as well, of taking too literally the Apostle's 'face to face'. How could a 'spiritual body' approach God? On the point of giving up, and falling back on the wisdom of Solomon – 'The thoughts of mortals are timid and their foresight uncertain' (Wis. 9.14) – Augustine made an energetic dialectic effort. If it was true that the intelligible was perceived by the spirit and the perceptible by the body, so that their respective perceptions could not intersect, God could not be seen by the eyes of a body, even a 'spiritual' one. But it was equally true that God, himself bodiless, knew corporeal beings, and could see them. Since it had been established that bodies are seen by the spirit, why not allow that the power of the 'spiritual body' could be such that the spirit itself may be seen by the body? Now, God is spirit.[bt]

In that case, despite a lesser corporeality and an increased spirituality of the 'spiritual bodies', it would be possible to see God 'in the most transparent clarity', directly, and no longer as our understanding allows us to see him through his works, 'as in a glass, darkly' and only partially. But the bishop has one last uncertainty: either we shall see God with spiritual eyes which in their perfection will have something similar to the spirit – but the Scriptures, he admitted, offered no support in that – or, more easy to understand,

> God will be known to us and visible in such a way that he will be seen in spirit by each of us, that he will be seen by one in another, that he will be seen in himself, that he will be seen in the new heaven and the new earth.[bu]

In the universal transparency of the celestial kingdom, God, from being transcendent as he was for men on earth, will become immanent for the elect. Directly visible everywhere, he will be everywhere the object of eternal praise.

Like every city, however, the celestial city had its differences and inequalities. We are not rereading here the verse from John 14.2, on the many mansions in the Father's house, but we know this is how Augustine interpreted this text, as he had said to Vincentius Victor: the mansions meant 'the many and various merits of those who were to dwell in them'.[bv] In the final pages of the *City of God*, the image was transposed into terms of rank. In the glory and beatitude, 'there will be degrees' without a doubt.[bw] But the wonder will be that 'the blessed city will find in itself a great blessing', there will be no envy between those of varying degrees, in the serene acceptance of an organic difference and the rewarding awareness which each will have of his complementary part in the whole harmonious structure, as Augustine said in terms once again fed by St Paul's metaphors (1 Cor. 12.14–26). He was able to close his masterpiece on the luminous vision of the eternal harmony uniting the elect in bliss, as well as in praise and love of God: 'There we shall be still and see; we shall see and we shall love; we shall love and we shall praise; behold what will be in the end, and without end. And what other end have we except to reach that Kingdom which has no end?'[bx]

Notes

a. The bishop would explain later (*City of God*, XIV, 23) the methods of this procreation in Eden, without *libido*; cf. above, p. 424–5.
b. *City of God*, XIV, 10. The idea had already been sketched out in the *De peccatorum meritis*, I, 3, and illustrated by Elijah's ascent into heaven.
c. *Conf.*, I, 17; cf. above, p. 17.
d. *Conf.*, IV, 11.
e. *Soliloquies*, I, 16. This affirmation of the fear of death is not so banal coming from a thirty-two-year-old man.

f. *City of God*, XIII, 9.
g. *De Ordine*, II, 31; cf. Cicero, *Acad.*, II, 21.
h. *De libero arb.*, III, 55.
i. *Retract.*, I, 9, 6 and *De dono pers.*, 29, *in fine*.
j. *Contra Adimantum*, XXI.
k. *City of God*, XIII, 3.
l. Cf. above, pp. 354–5 and 363–4.
m. Cf. above, p. 327.
n. *Sermon* 299, 9.
o. It is in this abbreviated form that John 21.18 appears in *Sermon* 296 (= *Casin.*, I, 133), 8, preached at Carthage for the feast of the apostles on 29 June 411: cf. above, p. 394.
p. *Sermon* 335 B, 4 (= *Sermon Guelf* 31, 4).
q. *Sermon* 335 B, 3; cf. also *Sermons* 31, 3; 173, 2; 299, 8; 344, 3.
r. *Sermon* 280, 3.
s. *City of God*, XI, 27, 1.
t. *De libero arbitrio*, III, 20.
u. *De libero arbitrio*, III, 21.
v. *City of God*, I, 22, 1.
w. *City of God*, I, 24.
x. *City of God*, I, 27.
y. *Contra Cresconium*, III, 51; cf. also *Enarr. in Psalm.* 34, 2, 13.
z. Cf. above, pp. 359–60.
aa. Cf. *Sermon* 299, 8: *Amari mors non potest, tolerari potest*, referring to the apostles Peter and Paul.
bb. *Sermon* 344, 4, dated to the beginning of 428.
cc. *City of God*, XIII, 4. An initial expression in *De pecc. mer. et remissione*, II, 50, *initio*.
dd. *De pecc. mer. et remissione*, II, 50.
ee. *Retract*, II, 33.
ff. As the *City of God*, XX, 20, 2 shows in the same period, when the problem is resolved in this way.
gg. We shall see further on, however, that he had not yet reached the terminus.
hh. *Conf.*, IX, 6.
ii. *Sermon* 14 (preached on a non-datable Sunday), 4: *Nolite enim* carnaliter *intellegere quod velut in sinum tunicae Abrahae levatus sit pauper. Sinus erat quia secretus erat.* Cf. also *Contra Faustum*, XXXIII, 6.
jj. *De natura et origine animae*, IV, 24.
kk. Cf. *Ep.* 164, 8 (to Evodius), and 187, 6, to Dardanus.
ll. *Ep.* 164, 7.
mm. *Ep.* 187, 7.
nn. *Adversus Marcionem*, IV, 34. Here it is a 'temporary receptacle of faithful souls'.
oo. *Passion of Perpetua and Felicitas*, VII, 4–8, ed. J. Amat, *SC*, 417, Éd. du Cerf, 1996, pp. 128–30.
pp. *Passion of Perpetua and Felicitas*, VIII, 1–4.
qq. With the Pelagians, so thought the young layman from Caesarean Mauretania, Vincentius Victor, with whom Augustine disagreed on this point: cf. above, p. 362.
rr. *Conf.*, IX, 34–7: *City of God*, XXI, 24, 2.
ss. The bishop has in mind 1 Cor. 7.33 which he would quote when expressing himself on the same theme in *Ench.* 68.
tt. *Enarr. in Psalm.* 80, 21.
uu. *Ep.* 4*, in *BA*, 46 B, p. 114 (see commentary by Y.-M. Duval, pp. 430–42).
vv. *Ench.*, 68.
ww. *City of God*, XXI, 26, 2.
xx. *Ench.*, 69: *per ignem quemdam purgatorium . . .*
yy. *City of God*, XX, 25.
zz. *City of God*, XXI, 26, 4.
ab. *City of God*, XIII, 3.

ac. *City of God*, XXI, 16.
ad. *City of God*, XXI, 17, *initio*.
ae. *City of God*, XXI, 17–22.
af. *City of God*, XXI, 23; a similar formulation in *Ench.*, 112.
ag. *City of God*, XXI, 16, *in fine*.
ah. *Ench.*, 110, *in fine*.
ai. *City of God*, XXI, 24, 3.
aj. *Enarr. in Psalm.* 105, 2, *in fine: Sed de hac tanta re diligentius ex otio disserendum est.*
ak. See *Ep.* 166, 16, where in 415 Augustine confesses to Jerome his anguish (*angustiae*) at not being able to find humanly satisfying answers to this theological problem.
al. *De natura et origin animae*, III, 19.
am. Cf. above, p. 329, the precautions and ambiguities of Pelagius on this subject.
an. *De nat. et orig. animae*, III, 19.
ao. *De nat. et orig. animae*, III, 19 (cf. above p. 362).
ap. *Concilia Africae, CCL*, 149, p. 70.
aq. *De pecc. mer. et remissione*, I, 21.
ar. *Ench.*, 93. Cf. also *Ep.* 184 A, 2: *Minima poena, non tamen nulla.*
as. *Ep.* 186, 29 (letter addressed by Augustine and Alypius to Paulinus of Nola in 417).
at. Acts 17.30–2.
au. *City of God*, XXII, 5; cf. also XXII, 25, *initio*.
av. *City of God*, XIII, 18.
aw. *City of God*, XXII, 20, 2: this very difficult instance, commented the bishop, was unfortunately not a 'textbook case'; recent events had testified to that: probably episodes in the siege of Rome by Alaric.
ax. *De quantitate animae*, 76.
ay. *City of God*, XIV, 3, 1 and 2.
az. *Sermon* 256, 2.
ba. *Sermon* 277, 3, dated 22 January 413.
bc. An example of this conceptual confusion as a result of using a dualist vocabulary in *City of God*, XXII, 4 to describe the union of soul and body.
bd. *City of God*, XIII, 23, 1.
be. *Contra duas ep. pelag.*, I, 17.
bf. *City of God*, XIII, 20.
bg. Cf. *Retract.*, I, 11, 3.
bh. *City of God*, XIII, 23, 1.
bi. *City of God*, XXII, 24, 5, *in fine*.
bj. *Sermon* 277, 4–9.
bk. The bishop wondered nevertheless, with more amusement than concern, if all that had fallen to the barber's scissors was to be restored. His aesthetic sense made him answer in the negative.
bl. *City of God*, XXII, 13: by all the evidence, however, they could not have been baptized, and their presence in heaven raised a problem; Augustine did not bring it up here, or in *Ench.*, 85.
bm. *City of God*, XXII, 15.
bn. *City of God*, XXII, 20.
bo. *City of God*, XXII, 24, 5.
bp. *Ep.* 92, 3–4.
bq. *Retract.*, II, 41.
br. *Ep.* 147, 54, *in fine*.
bs. *Ep.* 148, 1.
bt. *City of God*, XXII, 29, 5.
bu. *City of God*, XXII, 29, 6.
bv. *De natura et origine animae*, II, 14.
bw. *City of God*, XXII, 30, 2.
bx. *City of God*, XXII, 30, 5.

CHAPTER XXXIV

Epilogue

The year 426 marked the last great turning-point in Augustine's life. Everywhere clouds were beginning to build up, and first nearest to him, in his little universe. I have already spoken of the storm that had descended on the clerical monastery at Hippo at the end of 425.[a] We know how the bishop had put the situation right, and to us it may seem a slight matter. The attitude of the priest Januarius, who had continued to look after his patrimony with the intention of passing it on to his daughter, before changing his mind and bequeathing it to the Church, was after all a mere breach of the rule of poverty. Because of the suspicions it had provoked,[b] however, this 'money business', not scandalous in itself, could have shaken the trust of the faithful in their pastor, whose episcopal credibility had been marred four years earlier by the consequences of another far graver betrayal, although it had not touched the see itself – that of Antoninus of Fussala.[c]

Some months later, Augustine's spirit was again shaken, for the man with whom, in his own words, he had formed one single soul,[d] had just died. The beloved, sweet Severus, had passed away at Milevis (Mila), where he had been bishop for a little over thirty years. Of the close circle of his oldest friends, with whom the ties went back to their shared childhood in Thagaste, Augustine had only Alypius and Evodius left. Following a rather wise practice which was starting to become a tradition, Severus had appointed his successor while he was still alive in order to avoid any wavering in his Church when he disappeared from the scene; but he had informed only his clergy, without consulting his people. On his death, it was to be feared that this appointment by a small committee might be badly received; some of the faithful had taken umbrage. At the special request of the local monastic community, Augustine went to settle the succession.[e] His presence enabled the bishop designate to be appointed without trouble,[1] probably in the basilica whose well preserved building, succeeded by a mosque which was itself old, was identified some thirty years ago in the deep levels of the western part of the old town, still 'corseted' at the time in its Byzantine defence wall.[2] On his return journey, Augustine certainly stopped at Constantine, where Fortunatus, whom he had established in that bishopric a quarter of a century earlier,[f] seems to have been still alive; and at Calama with Possidius – it was on his route. This was his last journey; having returned to Hippo, he did not leave it again for the remaining four years of his life. He would soon be seventy-two.

He had doubtless already reflected on it, but the death of his old companion and the part he had played in settling the episcopal succession made him decide to lose no time in attending to the details of his own. One Saturday in late September, he summoned his clergy and flock to attend the next morning, Sunday 26. In the apse of the basilica of Peace,[g] the bishop of Hippo was flanked by two bishops, probably neighbouring ones, Martinianus and Religianus, from unknown sees; his priests, Saturninus, Leporius, Barnabas, Fortunatianus, Rusticus, Lazarus and Eraclius were also at his side. Augustine saw that the large congregation was impatient to know the reason for this summons and quickly got down to the nub of the matter. After reminding them of his great age, the reason for his recent trip to Milevis, which he swiftly explained, was enough of an introduction; he declared his wish to have the priest Eraclius as his successor to the see. The ecclesiastical secretaries who were recording these *Acta*, faithfully noted the acclamations that punctuated his declaration and the number of times they made the basilica's walls resound: 'Thanks be to God! Praise be to Christ!' was repeated twenty-seven times; 'Grant our prayers, O Christ! Long live Augustine!' sixteen times; 'Be our father, be our bishop!' eight times.[h] A little later during the session, when the faithful had toned down their acclamations somewhat, indicating six times their desire for Augustine to remain their father and that Eraclius should be their bishop, the one who was to remain the incumbent of the see until he died had to make one thing clear: the error committed thirty years before, in the lifetime of Valerius, must not be repeated, so that what had been criticized in his own succession could not be held against Eraclius.[i] The priest would therefore wait until the episcopal chair was vacant.

Augustine remained bishop of Hippo, without a 'coadjutor'. It was not 'pre-retirement', but he handed over the part he had always regarded as the most overwhelming aspect of the burden, by transferring it to Eraclius. After bearing it for the best part of thirty years, he could allow himself to speak his mind, denounce the breaking of the contract which had been drawn between his community and himself, under the terms of which – the bishop recalled the existence of a written record of that agreement[j] – it had even been agreed that Augustine could devote himself to his studies of the Scriptures for five days a week, without being importuned. But those paper walls had soon crumbled. Very late in life, the bishop once more became the full-time intellectual he would so much have liked not to cease being. It was almost a return to *otium* but, to be accurate, the man who had at last regained a little freedom fired this last shot at his flock: 'Let no one envy me this leisure time, for it is well and truly occupied.'[k] His faithful flock would have liked to reply, twenty-five times, that he had well and truly deserved it!

A long critical look at himself

After his master's death, Possidius would write, 'So numerous are the works that he has dictated and published . . . that a studious man could scarcely read them in their entirety'.[l] It was to the critical rereading of this immense output – still not complete – that Augustine henceforward devoted the best part of the 'free time' which the appointment of Eraclius had earned him,[m] but which he still had to protect against the encroachments of his flock, if we are to believe a few words in a letter to Quodvultdeus, dated 428.[n] As was the case in many other enterprises, the intention had been in his mind for quite a long time. We may recall the famous letter to Marcellinus in the spring of 412 when, without claiming the right to make an error, he was aware of the risk of making one, rejected any self-complacency and proclaimed his duty to correct himself: to collect and reveal, in a book deliberately composed with this aim, everything in his works which rightly displeased him. That was the target he had set himself then, in the wider perspective of an 'intellectual salvation' through 'writing', seen as the instrument par excellence of a process of constant perfecting, in a quest that was above all spiritual. Remember his major statement: 'I admit that I strive to be among those who write as they progress and progress as they write.'° But when he wrote that sentence, the bishop was fifty-seven, and was just starting his major theological battle with Pelagius and his friends; his great *opus*, which would gather a lifetime's reflection on many fundamental subjects – the *City of God* – had yet to be written. There was every likelihood that, undertaken fifteen years later by an old man who was still ardently on the attack against the same adversaries, the *Retractations* would no longer exclusively match that initial inspiration, defence should overtake self-criticism, and the defence itself should smack somewhat of the theological extremes of the polemics still continuing. When a writer 'examines his conscience'[3] at the age of seventy-three, and at the same time is more than ever engaged in a fifteen-year-old doctrinal combat, can he still take a completely fair view of himself?

Before attempting to answer this question, I must stress the absolute originality of the step he was taking; it had no precedent in the literature of Antiquity and, in its amplitude – and even its principle – would have no successor. Even supposing that Augustine had been moved by the arrogant navel-contemplation which inspired Jean-Jacques Rousseau, he could have exclaimed far more deservedly that he was undertaking something which had never had a model and would not have any imitator.[p] I must also emphasize the amount of work it involved, and not just intellectually. No one before him had had,[q] and no one after him would have, the courage to blow the accumulated dust – in every sense of the word – from nearly forty years of intensive 'literary' production. Under modern publishing conditions, such an operation would present no material difficulties; in Antiquity it was, in very material fashion, a real feat. But the bishop, who possessed nothing of his own, had an appreciable advantage over many others before and around him when it came to the handling of tens of thousands of parchment sheets – a marvellously resistant material, but cumbersome and heavy! – the sum total of which comprised the 232 'books', or *codices*,[4] among which were divided the ninety-three works inventoried by the author himself. This precious, virtually indispensable, material aid was provided by the squad of secretaries who were kept permanently busy around the bishop; not only their hands, or the intimate knowledge they had of this library, but also their eyes: was Augustine still up to rereading with ease his own texts and those of others?[r] He would probably not have been able to complete all those rereadings without the help of his *notarii*.

There remained the essential part, which they could not do in his place, unless by faithfully taking his dictation, as usual.[5] In his 'prologue', which people have sometimes tried to present as being added after the event, as a kind of postface, the bishop continued to follow the line he had already fixed in 412 in his letter to Marcellinus: to review his works, 'with the severity of a judge, and make notes, as with a censor's pen' on whatever might offend him.'[s] No longer for inner use, as the *Confessions* had been, this other book in the first person was written under the gaze of God: it was important to Augustine to judge himself so that he could escape his judgement. But it was also very clear that his intention was, by a 'retractation' – we must keep the word in its actual meaning – to cut the ground from under potential censors, or simply malicious readers. They would have to be very unwise, he said, to take him to task, since he was doing so himself! In a natural movement to defend and explain his thinking, the self-criticism was thus, almost of necessity, coupled with an apologia. In any case, there was no mistaking it; Augustine, while making headway, had warned the future successor to Aurelius in Carthage, in the letter of spring 428 which I have already quoted: he was 'retouching' his work, sometimes 'correcting' – in other words, criticizing – whatever now displeased him and could displease others, and sometimes 'defending' the meaning that should and could be found in it.[t] There has been no lack of attempts to enumerate the manifestations of self-criticism – *reprehensiones* – and annotations inspired by a desire to make an apologia – *defensiones*. No easy task; the bishop was subtle and it is sometimes difficult to disentangle the one from the other. However, there is agreement more or less on two series of remarks. On the one hand, overall, Augustine came down less heavily on works that followed his becoming a bishop – they are dealt with in Book II of the *Retractations* – than on earlier texts; on the other, on his first texts, he is more frequently inclined to defend than find fault.[6]

There are at least two ways of interpreting these findings. First one may say, as Gustave Bardy did with much psychological probability, that the old bishop who, to start with, had thrown himself into the work enthusiastically, was especially attached to his youthful writings, which he was rediscovering, but later, lacking time and also strength, somewhat hastened the rhythm of his rereadings.[7] However, on the substance he had more to say – to correct, but also and mainly to defend, against those who wanted to play the 'young Augustine' against the bishop – on the first works, whose philosophical standpoints smacked much of the Neoplatonism of his formative years – on the sovereign good, which lay not in reasoning but in God,[u] on the soul, regarding which he had formerly expressed himself in terms that implied a belief in its pre-existence, although he denied it[v] – or laid himself open, for instance in the *Treatise on free will*, to interpretations which he had to foil. As has been clearly seen,[8] the anxiety 'not to leave the Pelagians any pretext' for making a Pelagian interpretation of his work underlies many points relating to texts prior to 396, in other words, the year marked by his new reflection on grace in the Pauline commentaries of the *Ad Simplicianum*. Afterwards, in the whole of Book II of the *Retractations*, when rereading what he had written, he corrects himself chiefly on points of exegesis or details of a historical nature. Does this mean that on his own admission his thinking had not advanced once that great turning-point was passed? How then are we to understand what the author announced at the end of his 'prologue': 'Whoever reads my works in the order in which they were written will perhaps find how I progressed by writing'?[w] In fact – and if we consider only this aspect of Augustinian doctrine – there was, if not 'progress', at least a perceptible development between the texts of 396 and the last text listed in the *Retractations*, the book of 426 dealing with 'punishment and grace'. On this fundamental subject, thirty years had not elapsed in vain. But what this long review clearly showed was that at the very beginning of his episcopacy Augustine, starting from his reading of St Paul, had laid down the foundations on which he would firmly build his *intellectus fidei*.

In 429, in the last pages of the *De dono perseverantiae*, Augustine said that he was still busy with those 'books whose purpose was the review of his works'.[x] Indeed, we learn from the letter to Quodvultdeus, dating from the preceding year, that the two books which we know had been completed.[y] However, he said, there remained the letters and sermons; and he added that he had reread the majority of the letters, but without having been able to dictate anything about them yet.[z] It was therefore very probable that the bishop was alluding to the annotation of the letters in the text of 429 quoted above. This annotation remained incomplete and has not come down to us. As for the sermons, even if it was his intention to revise and annotate them, one may well wonder whether it was really within his capabilities, at least for those homiletic works in their entirety. For, of those texts which resulted from a stenographic 'take' – often done outside Hippo – a certain number could well have come down to us independently of the rest of his 'written' work, without ever having been part of the bishop's library.

Book IV of the *Christian teaching*

Among the various tasks hindering Augustine's desire to have done with the chore of the *Retractations* as quickly as possible was the 'discovery' he made, as he worked, of the incomplete state in which he had left his *De doctrina christiana* in 397.[aa] With an astounding mental alertness, and with no trace of a 'join', the bishop carried on as if time had been suspended between the interruption of his text – in III, 35, right in the middle of a development on the interpretation of the Scriptures – and the resumption of his writing thirty years later. It is from an event like this that we can grasp, as if in real life, Augustine's quite exceptional intellectual capability, that aptitude for mobilizing his ideas, immediately and effortlessly summoning from his memory texts that would support his demonstration to illustrate it – in this text it was a matter of the hermeneutics of the holy texts – for placing at the service of his discourse a conceptual richness which itself drew on a *copia verborum* that was never found wanting. As if nothing had happened, the bishop continued his exposition on the plurality of scriptural interpretations, before coming to an examination of the rules of Tyconius, the postponement of which, in 397, for reasons of inappropriateness in the context of the anti-Donatist struggle, had doubtless prompted the suspension of the work.[bb]

Augustine subsequently added a fourth book in which he at last tackled the second phase of the undertaking announced as early as 397: once the keys to the meaning of the Scriptures had been acquired by whoever had to explain them to the faithful, he now had to find the best way of communicating that meaning. The ambition of the last book was therefore not only to define the ideal of the Christian orator, but to give the apprentice orator the means of putting it into practice.[cc] More than from his training in rhetoric, and even his years of teaching,[dd] Augustine was in a strong position to develop this *orationis ratio* of Christian homiletics because of the experience he had accumulated in thirty-five years of preaching and pastoral work. It comes as no surprise, therefore, that his approach tends to be pragmatic. He is well aware that many priests, and even bishops, who have not attended any school of rhetoric, will find themselves in front of an audience; so he states that reading or listening to eloquent men is the best kind of school,[ee] provided that eloquence is accompanied by wisdom. He hastens to say exactly what, in his view, the ideal of the Christian orator now is: 'a wisdom that does not aim at eloquence alone, an eloquence that does not stray from wisdom';[ff] an ideal that had already been realized in the great prophetic texts – in particular he quotes Amos, the 'peasant prophet' – but also employed in the vehement apologia which St Paul had made of himself before the Corinthians (2 Cor. 11.16–30). It was as if, in these texts, one saw wisdom emerge from her house (cf. Prov. 9.1), the heart of the wise man, followed by eloquence, her inseparable servant. That eloquence became effective when aiming at 'clearness' (*evidentia*): to attain it, one must not be afraid, should the need arise, to speak in the language of the populace to make oneself understood. When speaking of 'bones', Augustine advised the use of the word *ossum* and not *os*, as African ears, he said, could easily confuse the long syllable with the short syllable of *os*, the 'face':[gg] here speaks his experience as a preacher. He had already explained this in a homily on the Psalms, adding that it was better to be reproved by grammarians than not understood by the faithful.[hh] In another sermon, he had simplified a verbal form to make it clearer, and justified his action with one of the plays on words of which he was fond, but which in its elegance must have left his listeners somewhat flabbergasted: 'It is better that you should understand me with my barbarism, than that you should be *flooded* by my *fluency*.'[ii] With the same concern for oratorical effectiveness, he advised an 'interactive' preaching practice: to be understood, the speaker must be 'tuned in' to listeners who keep quiet; it is up to him to interpret their slightest signs, to be on the alert for their reactions.[jj] One has only to read a few of the bishop's sermons to realize that this was how he himself maintained contact with his audience.

It was all very well for Augustine to deny that he wanted to send those who were destined for sacred eloquence to a school of rhetoric, in this didactic exposition he remains reliant on the principles of secular eloquence, as Cicero had laid them down.[kk] The triple aim, 'to instruct, to please and to move', was always appropriate. The first spoke for itself and must be pursued without any special adaptation. 'To please' was obviously a trump card which anyone who wanted to instruct could ill do without. The bishop had insisted on this, many years before, in the prologue to his text *On the first catechism*.[ll] But stylistic elegance is condemned as 'verbal froth' if it is gratuitous and not put to the service of right and true speech: Augustine regretted that, in the prologue of his *Ad donatum*, Cyprian, whom he admired so much, had still indulged in the baroque way of writing – by its arabesques the passage quoted calls to mind the curves and loops of the foliage in the mosaics of that time[mm] – which typified the artistic prose of an Apuleius. But he recognized that the former rhetor had subsequently ceased to follow that path. When it came to 'moving', this was of capital importance; the lawyer used this weapon to win judges over to his cause, the preacher to win souls for God: the emotion that it aroused was the instrument of his victory.[nn]

The fulfilment of these three duties of every orator was obtained by putting the three styles into operation, like so many specific tools, which Augustine placed at the service of the three aims mentioned above more directly than Cicero had done: the 'simple' style, the 'tempered' style and the 'sublime' or 'grand style'.[9] In Cicero's view, a man was eloquent if he could deal with minor subjects in a simple style, average subjects in a tempered style and lofty topics in the grand style. Augustine combined styles and aims: 'He will be eloquent who is capable, in order to instruct, of speaking of minor subjects in the simple style; to please, of dealing with average subjects in the tempered style, and to move, of treating lofty subjects in the grand style.'ᵒᵒ But the major difference between forum and pulpit was that from the latter only great subjects were tackled, for the treatment of which the three styles could be called upon depending on the orator's purpose: the simple style for teaching, whereas injunction, rebuke or praise called for a tempered style and the sublime style was reserved for celebrating divine greatness or for influencing hearts and minds. With regard to the latter, the bishop quotes as an example of an irresistible act of oratory the personal success of his victorious preaching at Caesarea (Cherchell) at the end of the summer of 418.ᵖᵖ

The principles are Ciceronian, but the authorities invoked to illustrate them are of course those of Christian orators. It is regrettable that Augustine let slip the opportunity of developing 'stylistics drawn from the Scriptures and the Fathers of the Church',¹⁰ in some way 'theorizing' the practice of aesthetics tried out by those of his predecessors whom he most admired, St Cyprian first of all, St Ambrose next, but also by himself in so many strictly oratorical works as well as in the *Confessions*. It was probably too soon, and Cicero too close, although two centuries earlier someone like Tertullian would more markedly have kept his distance.¹¹ The result is that we see Augustine apply himself to showing that St Paul had made use of the processes of rhetoric,�q�q even if he did not consciously follow them. But he read the Apostle in the Latin translation and regretted that in their rendering the translators had been so inattentive to the play of resonances and to the *clausulae*, those variously rhythmical ends of sentences which came so naturally to him. For example, the half-verse from Rom. 13.14 which in August 386 had been the instrument of Providence for him in the Milan garden: 'And make not provision for the flesh, to fulfil the lusts thereof'; the cadence, he observed, would have been far better if, in the Latin text, the verbal form of the injunction had been placed at the end of the sentence!¹² At least he had no difficulty in showing that St Paul's natural eloquence triumphed in the sublime style, where strong imagery alternated with the movement, the impulses, one might almost say the breathlessness of inspired discourse.ʳʳ Cicero would have deplored the Apostle's lack of elegance but, like Augustine, he would have awarded him the palm for vehemence and passion.

The bishop added sincerity. The appropriateness of the life lived to the speech uttered was the best guarantee of its effectiveness. What the Christian orator must chiefly avoid was to be capable of having the finger pointed at him like the scribes and Pharisees of whom Jesus said, 'Do as they say, but do not as they do; for they say, and do not' (Matt. 23.3). If eloquence was lacking, the silent virtue of example was the pastor's supreme weapon. In thirty years of episcopacy, in the rural areas of his Africa where classical culture was rare and training in fine speaking virtually non-existent, Augustine had seen many of those priests and bishops whose strength lay mostly in their commitment to serving the faithful, successfully applying some words from the end of his book, *Quasi copia dicendi forma vivendi*.ˢˢ

A belated acceptance of miracles

Around 421, Augustine decided to reply to a letter from Paulinus of Nola which had been waiting to be dealt with for some time. For once, the delay was explained not so much by the accumulation of tasks to be undertaken[13] as by the predicament of the addressee. The bishop of Nola had acceded to the wish of a noble African lady whose son, Cynegius, had died in Italy, or to be more precise, within the boundaries of his diocese. Flora – the lady's name[14] – had begged that his remains should be allowed the privilege of reposing *ad sanctum*, near the relics of St Felix, in the funeral basilica of Cimitila neighbouring on Nola's urban centre. At the same time as telling Flora that she would be given satisfaction, Paulinus addressed Augustine to inform him of the motives that had guided his decision: was it not the Church's custom to pray for the deceased? Could one not also conclude that it was useful for the dead to be placed under the visible protection of the saints? Paulinus had arrived at this conclusion long before when burying the remains of his newborn son at Complutum (Alcalá de Henares), in Spain, near the tomb of the martyr saints Justus and Pastor.[tt] But he wanted to know the bishop of Hippo's opinion on the matter.

What had become of the mortal remains of Adeodatus? He had probably been interred among his family, at Thagaste, but his father, who had shrouded him in silence, leaves us in ignorance. Nevertheless, Augustine had kept a vivid memory of Monica's last wishes, when she had been overtaken by death in a foreign land, at Ostia, where her body had remained.[uu] He could not forget the truly Christian detachment which had caused her to renounce burial in her native country, close to living family members and beside a dead man, Patricius, with whom she had shared her life. She had been able to draw from within herself that strong spirituality which sometimes also inspired certain pagans, though minus the hope of resurrection: 'Nothing is far for God,' she had said to Augustine and Navigius, together at her bedside, 'and I need not fear that he will not know where to find me to raise me up at the end of the world.'[vv] All Monica had asked of her children was that they remember her at the Lord's altar, imploring only the intercession of their prayers. And Augustine prayed for his mother's repose, and asked his brothers in the Church to unite with him in that prayer.[ww] It was this attitude of the living in regard to the dead that Paulinus had at first recalled. But did one owe their bodies anything more than a proper burial? Did those bodies even lose anything, if the chance of the first death deprived them of burial?

These were the questions which Paulinus had invited his friend to answer, and Augustine did so by means of a small book, *On the care to be taken of the dead*, which was the last item known to us to be sent to the bishop of Nola. When he received it, Paulinus must have felt distinctly out of step. Quoting Luke 12.4 on the executioners who, having killed their victims, can do no more against them, Augustine replied very clearly that it mattered little to a Christian believer whether his body was left without a burial place. He had already expressed his views on the matter with regard to events of this kind that had occurred during the sack of Rome in 410;[xx] he now recalled the martyrs of Lyon, whose bodies had been torn to pieces by dogs before being reduced to ashes and scattered in the Rhône: their souls were none the worse for it.[yy] Tending the burial place, which was imposed on the living as a pious duty towards the dead, was none the less a consolation for them; it was their souls which benefited. The essential thing, Augustine continued, was that the link of prayer be preserved between the living and the dead, comforting for the former, useful for the latter if during their life they had deserved to benefit by it after their death. The physical presence at the place of burial was not indispensable – he knew that when he prayed for his mother; he could only concede to Flora and Paulinus that, on its own, the exceptional quality of a place sanctified by a martyr's relics was conducive to prayer and encouraged piety.[zz]

But Augustine remained intractable:

> Wherever the flesh of the deceased does or does not lie, what matters is that rest be found by the soul which, on leaving the body, carries away with it the consciousness of what makes the difference between the fate of the good and the outcast. And it does not expect help for its future life from that flesh, to which it gave the life that it has now taken away by departing and will restore on returning, for it is not the flesh that wins the privilege of resurrection for the soul, but the soul for the flesh, which it revives to be punished or glorified.[ab]

In this 'return of the soul' at the moment of resurrection there were a few whiffs of a Neoplatonism which one might have believed well and truly expired at that date – but this 'return' was here only an image summoned up mechanically by the evocation of an unchallengeable 'departure'; what mattered was that the bishop was firmly encamped on positions that ruled out any assistance given by the body to the soul which had once animated it, even if that soul was in perdition. The first, biological, death had established an uncrossable frontier between them until the end of time. Even supposing there to be some miraculous power in the relics of the holy martyr near which one wished to be buried, there was no possibility that this power could have any influence on the soul of the deceased – wherever it lay in waiting for the Last Judgement – by passing through the remains of the body deserted by life.

Augustine knew perfectly well that, by saying this, he was going against a strong trend of popular religion which, at least in his Africa – it was here that the two phenomena were most closely linked – went hand in hand with those practices of funeral meals which Aurelius in Carthage and himself in Hippo had successfully opposed.[ac] The trend was very old since at its origins lay the feeling, old as the world and variously affirmed according to differing cultures, that the dead person under the ground is not totally insensible, and reacts to whatever reaches it from the land of the living, both good – libations, agapes on the tomb, in which he participates – and bad, violations of the burial places, the fear of which is revealed in so many epitaphs, even in a Christian context.[ad] Of course, the body over whose remains feasts were held, and on whom the protection of the saints was called down, was without life, but there was the confused belief – sometimes expressed quite explicitly[ae] – that it retained the traces left upon it by the soul which had departed from it. Two centuries before Augustine, Tertullian had made fun of those who thought that 'after death, souls remained attached to their respective bodies',[af] and it has been shown that this idea of at least a temporary lingering of the soul in the body had been taken up by certain Stoic trends, according to Servius, a late commentator on Virgil.[ag]

Following the logic of such a belief, through the effect of, if not a 'contact' – 'body to body' – at least of close proximity, the dead who were buried *ad sanctos* were held to enjoy an almost physical protection of their tombs and a presence that was beneficial to them.[15] The facts spoke for themselves; the waves of tombs that pressed up against the holy places for want of being able to invade them completely were very eloquent. The phenomenon was remarkable above all in the western provinces of Africa and, when he went to Caesarea in the summer of 418, Augustine could not have failed to break his journey, either going or returning, at Tipasa. There, on either side of the town, outside the walls, to both west and east the spectacle before his eyes – which we still have on this extra-urban site that has remained as it was at the end of Antiquity – was instructive, especially to the east, around the funeral basilica dedicated to the local saint, Salsa. It was one of burial places – sarcophagi swamped by the structure of agape tables (*mensae*) or left bare and accessible to facilitate reburials and the relocation of bodies – squeezed against one another, sometimes encroaching on one another to get as near as possible to the relics of a martyr.[16] This landscape of a Christian necropolis so characteristic of the build-up, during several decades, around a primitive *martyrium*, was the solid demonstration, in stone and concrete, of the extreme difficulty of running counter to popular feeling, in its two ways of expressing itself – 'deviant' in Augustine's view, on which he held forth at length – the agapes on the tombs and, obviously connected, burials *ad sanctum*. The difficulty was all the greater because these practices were far from being unanimously considered as 'superstitious', and rebuked as such by the leaders of the churches. At grass roots level, there was often at least a tacit agreement between the rank and file of the faithful and their pastors, without whose consent nothing could be done. The bishops of Tipasa, who wanted to rest near the holy remains of their predecessors, acted no differently from their flocks in this matter, nor had Ambrose of Milan or Pope Damasus in Rome. We shall never know how Augustine had planned his own burial; when he died in his town besieged by the Vandals, this problem doubtless receded into the background. If his friends, Possidius foremost, saw to it that his body rested in a holy place – perhaps the chapel of St Stephen[ah] – they would do so in no other spirit than the one which they knew moved the bishop in this regard: the only help he could expect from it, if need be, was that the memory of the martyr alone, materialized by his relics, would arouse the piety of those who would go there and pray, and prompt their prayers on behalf of the one who would be associated with this memory. Augustine's disciples knew that this was the subtle nuance of his text *On the care to be taken of the dead*.[ai]

In this little book, however, there were other aspects that showed a shift in the bishop's thinking on the relations between the living and the dead, and more precisely on the mysterious ways in which those privileged dead, the martyrs, intervened in human affairs. The dead could do nothing for the dead, that was understood; the living could only pray for them, but it could happen that the dead might take an interest in the living. But not just *any* dead, and not in a commonplace and direct fashion; otherwise, said Augustine, his loving and worried mother, Monica, would not for a single night have deserted in his sleep the son whom she had followed over land and sea to live with him.[aj] The souls of the dead, it must be repeated, were in a place where they had no knowledge of earthly events; they were thus equally unable to share the sorrows of the living or protect the burial places of the dead. Yet, admitted the bishop, the holy martyrs, through the blessings they bestow in answer to our prayers, give proof of their intervention in human affairs.[ak] As he was addressing Paulinus, Augustine reminded him of the recognized intercession of St Felix in protecting the town, at the time when Nola had been besieged by Alaric's Goths. As to how the martyr had acted, and also those who healed or relieved suffering, he confessed that this went beyond the powers of his intellect.[al] What he was certain of, however, was that St Felix and the other martyrs who intervened in men's affairs did so because they knew about them in heaven and as the result of divine power: maybe – although the bishop hesitated a little over this – through the mediation of angels. Here one entered the realm of the miraculous.[am]

The development of Augustine's attitude towards miracles is undeniable and runs parallel with the evolution of his thinking about miraculous events. We may recall the somewhat expeditious way in which he treated the problem in the text addressed to Romanianus around 390: miracles that had been necessary, even indispensable, in the Church's early days were no longer necessary, and God himself had put an end to them, for fear that, if over-used, this supernatural edge could become blunted.[an] The idea was resumed and developed slightly one or two years later in the pages dedicated to Honoratus, also a former Manichaean, whose conversion had not been achieved: miracles must not become a habit.[ao] But the definition of a miracle still remained summary: it was an unusual event which went beyond the intellectual expectations or capacities of whoever witnessed it; at best, a distinction was made between a prodigy that aroused astonishment (water changed into wine, walking on water) from the healing and beneficent miracle which aroused gratitude in addition. Having become a bishop, Augustine, in a sermon preached around 400, replied to his faithful flock who, like himself, noted the drying up of the miraculous cures of evangelical times and seemed to regret it. Then, they had been an invitation to believe, but now the Lord showed believers even more miraculous healings: today corpses were no longer restored to life, but one could see souls live again which had formerly lain in a living corpse.[ap] All the same, the bishop's listeners must have thought that, as far as spectacle was concerned, they were missing out.

Augustine needed to complement his analysis of the miracle. He had first of all defined it principally in relation to the perception of one who had witnessed it and the shock he had received, without placing it in the order of nature or creation. It was a subjective definition. Full acceptance of the miraculous was arrived at by reflection on its ontological status. In the space of a few years, between 405 and 411/12, elaborating his great theological works gave him the opportunity to go deeper into this major problem of faith. In Book III of the *De Trinitate*, he started from the prodigies of the Old Testament: when God changed Moses' rod into a snake that became a rod again when Moses took it in his hand, to be retransformed into a snake at Pharaoh's feet (Exod. 4.4 and 7.10), that was assuredly a miracle. But it was only a transformation of matter – we would say of molecular combinations – commonplace in itself, such as nature constantly lavishes upon us; what was marvellous in this instance was that the matter revealed its plasticity with unusual rapidity and flexibility, and in unaccustomed forms. The miraculous does not abandon the order of things, but introduces itself by such an unusual process that it is acclaimed as a miracle.[aq] The 'supernatural' is nothing other than this short-cut which is so eminently remarkable because of its exceptional rarity; this hides the perpetual, daily renewed miracle of creation, which familiarity eventually makes us lose from sight.[ar]

It is not surprising to discover that the bishop set out his view of miracles chiefly in the context of his reflection on the Creation. In his *Treatise on the literal interpretation of Genesis* he takes up the problem, first of all at the point where he had left it in the text just quoted. According to what we term biological laws, it takes time and a combination of many processes for the water drawn up by the vine's roots to swell the grapes, for their juice to make wine, and for the wine to age to become the drink we like. But, as in the case of the rod that became a serpent, at the wedding at Cana a 'marvellous short-cut' enabled Jesus by one specific action to concentrate the slow mechanisms of nature.[as] Does the Creator of time need time? Augustine ponders. Yes, in the ordinary course of events, following the usual chain of causality. But we have to admit that when God created the world, he established 'causal reasons' – *causales rationes* – that work according to a double potential: some becoming and developing gradually – this is the natural order, the only one that men know – others eluding time and depending on the sovereign mastery which the Creator continues to exert over natural causality.

He returns to this later, in the same text, to develop further the idea that in this universe created by him and filled with the causes of beings yet to come, God reserves to himself the power not only to speed up the natural course of things according to his will, but also, above and beyond this 'customary nature', to be able to draw from his creation effects other than those included in what the bishop here calls 'seminal reasons' – *seminales rationes*.[at] If Balaam's ass began to talk (Num. 22.28), it was not from a natural causality, but a supernatural or transcendental causality coupled with the former.

> Thus God has, hidden within himself, the causes of certain elements that he has not placed in created things, and he actualizes these causes not through that providence by which he has made natures exist, but through the action by virtue of which he governs, as he wishes, those natures which he created, according to his will.

Therein lay the divine mechanism of the miracle, and Augustine would not surprise his readers when he added that 'this kind of action also had to do with grace, which saves sinners'.[au]

So a miracle was not an erratic phenomenon that eluded all rationality. For Augustine it had a firm theological foundation. But its impact on men's hearts was still as strong, for by this emergence from the natural order which was the only one they knew, God burst in upon them. In the *City of God*, the bishop says: 'God is always present everywhere in his entirety, but is said to "come down" when he performs an action on earth which is miraculous in being contrary to the normal course of nature, and in some way reveals his presence.'[av] When he dictated these lines, shortly before 420, Augustine had experienced – or was about to experience – the shock (the word is not too strong) of the first wave of miracles which had happened in Africa following the spread of St Stephen's relics; his long reflection on miraculous happenings had prepared him to incorporate them in his pastoral practice, to welcome in his own church, in a specially provided chapel, a small part of the remains that had proved their marvellous power,[aw] first of all with Evodius at Uzalis. The old companion of his youth – the only one now remaining, with Alypius – his partner in the *Treatise on the choice of free will*, the tireless and rather muddle-headed questioner who pestered the bishop of Hippo with his somewhat naïve letters, had found the right track – malicious tongues might have said 'struck it rich' – with the pious exploitation of this Palestinian import. Even more than Paulinus of Nola he deserved the title of *impresario* in this affair – a title recently bestowed on the bishops of that time who had 'dabbled' the most in this 'trade', based on a sociological analysis which, at least as regards Africa, rather lacks substance.[17]

In this way it is easier to explain the catalogue of miraculous events included, at first glance rather abruptly, in the final book of the *City of God*, in which it in fact cuts across a long demonstration centred on defending the dogma of the resurrection of the flesh. But we are not off the subject:[18] when Palladia rose to her feet healed, after praying while leaning on the railing separating the crowd from St Stephen's reliquary,[ax] she affirmed that God's finger had touched her, exerting his transcendent causality for her benefit, which was the most dazzling testimony on behalf of faith. The relic in itself – a little powdered bone – was merely the medium which by its presence excited the fervour of the faithful, whose prayer favoured, if not sparked, the unleashing of a supernatural causality. But it was God who had given the relic, and he who had performed the miracle.

What remains true is that it had taken many long years of theological reflection to lead Augustine to incorporate miracles in his apologetics. Perhaps, as has been said, he had also been prompted to it by the increased pressure in this direction brought to bear in Catholic communities, at Hippo as elsewhere, after 411, by the many who had come from Donatism, among whom the cult of martyrs had always had a stronger following and a greater diffusion.[19] What is certain is that comparison of two texts gives some measure of the change in his perspective over some thirty years. Addressing his *Catechism for beginners*, around 400,[20] to a young deacon of Carthage, Deogratias, Augustine came to the psychological and moral conditions in which candidates for baptism approached initiation to the faith. If the candidate did so under the influence of a divine admonition and, more exactly, driven by fear, there was nothing more favourable, he said, provided there was no delay in 'turning his attention from miracles or dreams of this kind to the sounder path of the Scriptures and their more reliable oracles'.[ay] In 428/9, Augustine wrote the last letter known to us to Alypius; to his friend who by virtue of seniority – he had preceded him into the episcopacy by at least a few months – had become primate of the province of Numidia,[21] he announced good tidings: three conversions, and by no means insignificant; besides Gavinianus, 'Count' Peregrinus and a 'leading doctor' (*archiater*) named Dioscorus, had been baptized at Easter. It was chiefly the last of these who held the bishop's attention: finally to overcome the resistance of this strong-minded individual, a veritable shower of miracles and divine coercions had been necessary. Dioscorus had vowed to become a Christian if his sick daughter was saved. She was, but forgetting his vow, the father had been struck blind. With a new promise he committed himself to fulfil the first vow if he recovered his sight. This happened and he carried out his promise, but only by half: from either carelessness or unwillingness, he had not learnt the symbol of faith and had therefore been unable to recite it; his punishment was an attack of almost general paralysis. Dioscorus had to repent, acknowledge his fault and declare in writing that he now knew it by heart; he recovered the use of his limbs but not his tongue which, giving the lie to the natural goodness of his heart, had caused him so often sacrilegiously to mock Christians. In his old age, the bishop relied increasingly on God's supernatural causality to garner conversions; and his God sometimes resembled the terrible Yahweh of the Old Testament.

The death of the bishop and the survival of his works

Among the many memories which Augustine shared with Alypius were those of the journeys undertaken in his company, and among others the one that had taken them both to Thubunae (Tobna) in 420/21.[22] It was not the longest they had made together, but the only one that had led them to what had always been in Antiquity one of the boundaries of 'useful Africa'. I remember seeing, some decades ago, that landscape which has hardly altered since it lay before the eyes of the two bishops: it was not yet desert, but the mineral world of the high plains; a little farther to the west there were only the mirages rising from the salt marshes of the chott el-Hodna; to the south-east, bordering the Aurés on their western flank and barring the way to Moorish incursions, a succession of small forts and intermittent defence walls was strung out. It was there that someone we have already met, Bonifatius, kept watch at the head of his frontier guards. The bishop of Hippo had sent him a long letter in 417 for his guidance in his relations with the Donatists.[az]

Bonifatius was a man of personal worth,[ba] but with an uneasy soul; we have seen that in those times perhaps more than in any other, the one often went hand in hand with the other. He asked himself questions and made them known to the bishop: could the life of a military man like himself be pleasing to God? Augustine hastened to send a messenger to Thubunae to reassure the tribune. Yes, a soldier could please God – even though one could be closer to him than as a member of the military – like the centurion whose faith Jesus had admired.[bc] All that was necessary was for the officer to be merciful in his battles with the Barbarians, frugal and sober in his private life and irreproachable in his married life.[bd] Alas! Bonifatius actually soon lost his wife and it greatly affected his morale; he now spoke of leaving the army and retiring to a monastery.[be] There was no longer any question of admonishing him by letter. Augustine and Alypius set out forthwith; the two bishops pointed out to him that he was far more useful in a soldier's tunic than in a monk's garb; all he had to do was live as a Christian, in chastity and without concern for the grandeurs of this world.

But a warrior of his calibre could not stay for long scanning the horizons of the south and west on that other 'shore of the Syrtes'. The end of Honorius' long reign, the uncertainties that were coming to light, and the opportunities it provided, everything combined to reawaken ambitions. The death of Constantius III in September 421, after an 'emperorship' of only a few months, hastened the course of events. When still only the general-in-chief of Honorius' armies, Flavius Constantius had been Bonifatius' patron. His demise left two people who had no liking for each other in confrontation: his widow, the beautiful Galla Placidia, daughter of the great Theodosius, whom he had married in 417 after snatching her from the hands of the Barbarians who had been keeping her prisoner since the sack of Rome, and Placidia's half-brother, the emperor Honorius. Recalled to the Court in 422, Bonifatius probably was indebted to Placidia for his promotion as Count of Africa and his appointment as assistant to the new general-in-chief, Flavius Castinus, who was to head a campaign against the Vandals in the south of Spain. But because of a disagreement, the association of the two generals broke off from the start, and Bonifatius left Ravenna to return to Africa. He was there, loyally doing his duty as a soldier – one of the recently published letters to him from Augustine[bf] seems to date to this period – when in 423 a major event occurred: the death of Honorius, who on 15 August in that year departed this world without leaving an heir to the western throne, unless it was his young nephew, Valentinianus, the son of Constantius and Placidia, who was then four. For the first time in many years – also the last time in history – the emperor of the East, Theodosius II, was able to entertain the hope of keeping the Mediterranean and all its shores under his sole sovereignty; to attain this he came to an arrangement with Castinus, who was quite prepared to administer the West on behalf of Constantinople.

But Bonifatius, too, had chosen his side. When Placidia had been exiled to Rome by Honorius early in 423, before fleeing to the East with little Valentinianus, he had made his choice and helped her with allowances; he now threatened to starve Italy by blocking grain shipments if her rights were not acknowledged – a weapon that had proved itself in the past. Meanwhile, in the western Court, all those who were not resigned to seeing it disappear, together with all their posts and emoluments, had at the end of the year proclaimed as emperor at Rome the *primericius notariorum* Iohannes. The usurper could rely on Castinus, the master of the militia, and on a young general named Aetius. The former was despatched to Africa against Bonifatius, who does not seem to have had much difficulty in getting rid of him; the second had experience of the Huns – he had been their hostage for a long while – which made him useful for recruiting troops among them destined to confront the army that Theodosius II was sending through the Balkans against Iohannes, while at the same time acting unenthusiastically to preserve the West for the Theodosian dynasty – born of the second marriage of the great Theodosius, her grandfather, Placidia was his aunt! The little Valentinianus would soon be proclaimed Caesar, before acceding to the title of 'Augustus' in 425, at the age of six. Starting in autumn 424, everything happened very quickly. Iohannes, who had not had time to receive the reinforcements which Aetius was to send him, had been betrayed by his own side, captured and beheaded on Placidia's orders. Aetius had been asked to go and display his talents in Gaul against the Visigoths, and Castinus had left for exile. The post of master of the militia was thus vacant. Bonifatius, so loyal and devoted to Placidia and the young Valentinianus, could hope to aspire to it; in his stead he saw another general chosen, Flavius Constantius Felix. As a consolation prize, he was elevated to the dignity of *comes domesticorum*,[bg] but remained in Africa, retaining all his very real full military powers. In terms of promotion, the vast hurly-burly that had followed Constantius' death had for him been a 'mug's game'.

At the end of this series of events, the Count of Africa had been summoned to

Ravenna. He had made the journey under orders from above, but had profited by it to end his widowhood by marrying Pelagia, a lady of noble Barbarian origins, probably Visigothic, extremely rich and of Arian faith. Of course, he had first of all seen to it that she was converted to the Catholic faith; but when a little girl was born in 423 from this remarriage, she had been baptized according to Arian rites. This had brought Augustine down with a bump: it was a blow on the part of a man in whom he had placed such high hopes; but moreover he had learnt that Bonifatius, 'for whom his wife was not enough', had been seen romping with concubines.[bh] The soldier-monk he had met on the battlements of Thubunae, 'girt about with the baldric of the most chaste continence',[bi] had become in a short space of time a pleasure- and power-seeking man, disappointed in his ambitions but more than ever determined to pursue them, and henceforward more concerned with ensuring his personal success than with being a rampart of Roman-ness and the Church. The Count of Africa spent his time in intrigues instead of defending Numidia's south-west flank against the ever-bolder and ever-deeper Moorish incursions. The 'devastation of Africa' in those years, which so moved Augustine,[bj] was due to the 'African' Barbarians who were no longer contained and now fought on the walls of Setif, the ancestors of those who, still not Christianized two generations later, would martyrize the mass of Catholics sent into exile by the Vandal king Huneric. Before being soon overrun, almost without a blow being struck, by Geiseric's troops, this mid-region of Roman Africa was already split. Augustine, who had never considered it his duty as a Christian and man of the Church to evangelize populations, whoever they were, living outside the world which he accepted as the temporal powers had settled it, was distressed to see it being demolished and even undermined from within.

The bishop of Hippo was still far from suspecting that he would end his days in Bonifatius' company in his episcopal town, besieged by the Vandals because of the Count of Africa's incompetence or the complicated workings of his intrigues, but this double denouement was now very close. In 427, the general was summoned to the Court to give an account of himself. His refusal to obey was regarded as rebellion by Felix, the master of the militia, but an initial expedition sent against him failed. In disgrace, deprived of his command, Bonifatius next saw the appearance of the new Count of Africa, Sigisvult, together with an army, and it was in the train of this Arian soldier that Augustine, for his part, saw the arrival of the heretic prelate, Maximinus, with whom he had entered into a dispute.[bk] During those months of 427/8, Bonifatius' personal fate becomes a little vague for us, and his attitudes confused. It was often said, even in Antiquity, that the general in difficulties had appealed to the Vandals to set them against Sigisvult's Visigoths and save his own position. The temptation might well have occurred to him: after all, the masters of the western world in that era often played Barbarian armies off against one another. But we are almost certain that on the eve of the Vandal invasion the rebel had effected a reconciliation with the imperial government; and thanks to Augustine, we have some idea of how that came about.

During the winter of 428–9, the bishop of Hippo learned of the presence on African soil of a high-ranking plenipotentiary[23] sent by the Court to negotiate a peaceful outcome to the confrontation between Bonifatius and his adversaries. Two of his colleagues, old friends, had met him. One, Urbanus of Sicca Veneria, not far from Carthage, the other, Novatus, whose home was Setif, which the at least partial collapse of the defences of the *limes* of Sitifian and Numidia now placed almost at the outposts of still-protected Africa; and both had painted such a picture of Darius – the name of the dignitary – that Augustine, who no longer went out, was very sorry not to be able to make his acquaintance. From their correspondence – on this occasion the old bishop dictated one of his last dated letters, wonderful for its alertness, charm and wit[bl] – it emerges at least that Darius' mission was to avoid any bloodshed among 'Romans', and that mission had not failed. The imperial envoy would say modestly that 'if he had not extinguished the war, he had at least set it aside'.[bm] In any case, he did not leave empty-handed: the bishop had enclosed with his letter a copy of the *Confessions*, which Darius had requested, and for good measure had added several other books.[bn]

But the die was cast. The Vandals, who had been marking time in the south of Spain for some twenty years, had not needed Bonifatius to realize that Africa was a desirable land and that its poorly-guarded fruit was ripe for whoever wished to pluck it. In May 429, their army, enlarged by Alani and Goths,[bo] crossed the Straits of Gibraltar. They hastened towards the fine provinces, Numidia and Proconsularis – the Algerian east and areas to the north and centre of today's Tunisia – and, apart from some local resistance, which was probably the exception in these regions which were already largely cut off from central government and infiltrated by rebellious tribes, only the slowness of pace of a troop of 80,000 men, women, and children, who had to be fed at the expense of the inhabitants, held up their advance along the roads of Tingitanian, Caesarean and Sitifian Mauretania.[24] In the spring of 430, they had entered Numidia without encountering any strong opposition; according to Possidius,[bp] who will easily be believed by those who know the town's natural defences, which had often been put to the test, only Cirta (Constantine) had held out as they passed. When they neared the neighbourhood of Hippo's Numidia, which was part of the province of Africa Proconsularis, the former nucleus of the Roman presence which had to be safeguarded if possible, Bonifatius tried to make a rampart of the forces still available to him: inadequate forces, chiefly the contingents of Gothic auxiliaries,[bq] for the army of the frontiers in the south – those *limitanei* whom he knew well from having commanded them some years before – were essentially faced with another and permanent threat. Defeated in open country, probably a little north of the Numidian Alps – between Thibilis (Announa) and the coast – the Count of Africa retreated with the tatters of his troops to the walls of Hippo, to which he had undoubtedly planned to fall back.

It was the end of May or beginning of June 430. A long siege was starting, without any possible escape, as the Vandals were also blocking the town on the sea side. Naturally, Augustine had remained at his post. Less than three years before, on 24 September 427, a general council, the second to assemble at Hippo after that memorable one held during his priesthood in 393, had gathered around him and Aurelius of Carthage representatives of the entire African episcopate. Alypius, still on a mission in Italy,[br] was missing from this assembly, which dealt with disciplinary matters, as if nothing had happened.[bs] But for the last time Augustine had been able to meet many bishops from his Numidia, often trained in the seminary at Hippo. In the days of misfortune that had now arrived, several were in doubt and fear; and with good cause – the Vandals came to the region preceded by a terrible reputation.[25] In the spring, Augustine had received a very alarmist letter from the bishop he had ordained some fifteen years earlier in the newly established see at Thiava, not far to the south-west of Thagaste.[bt] Honoratus was not satisfied with a copy of a letter sent previously to another bishop named Quodvultdeus to calm his fears and tell him what attitude to adopt on the arrival of the enemy; and he confessed to Augustine that he intended to flee: 'What good did it do pastors or their faithful flock', he asked, 'to see men massacred, women raped and churches set alight?'[bu] It was a very difficult problem; not everyone had urban ramparts defended by troops to whom people owed, if not the certainty of safety, at least hope and a feeling of protection. But must priests and bishops set the example of desertion, leaving the faithful, who were not all capable of fleeing, without spiritual guidance? In a long reply, doubtless the last letter he was able to dictate and hand to a courier before the town gates were closed, Augustine did not avoid any aspect of the grievous questions put by Honoratus. He at least laid down one formal rule:

> When the danger is the same for bishops, clerics and congregations, those who have need of others must not be abandoned by those whom they need. Let everyone withdraw to fortified places, but those who are forced to stay must not be abandoned by those who owe them the succour of the Church.[bv]

He did not avoid examining a suggestion probably made by Honoratus, one that was eternally linked to every persecution: should it not be arranged that some clerics are preserved by flight or in some hiding-place so that after the storm has passed the clerical community in many places should not be totally wiped out? In that case, said the bishop quoting Prov. 18.8 – 'Fate calms contentions and decides between the mighty' – the best thing was by drawing lots to leave it to God to designate those who would be doomed to possible martyrdom for the sake of their community.[bw] Possidius thought it right to reproduce this final message added to the penultimate chapter of his *Life of Augustine*, so it has doubly come down to us. The bishop of Calama (Guelma) and his people were part of the communities who had taken shelter within those nearby walls;[bx] all together or with that heroic division left to chance we shall never know. Alypius was not in Hippo; the primate of his province, perhaps he was travelling through town and countryside to keep up people's courage. Had he already succumbed? The last traces of him disappear in this catastrophe.

In the third month of the siege Augustine fell ill. He would have been seventy-six in the autumn, and privations and difficulties of all kinds undoubtedly hastened his end. Attacked by fever he retired to his room and did not move from it again. One day a person in a bad state, accompanied by a relative, arrived at his bedside begging him to lay his hands on the sufferer to heal him; at first Augustine replied that if he possessed such a power he would be the first to take advantage of it, but as the visitor said he had been told in a dream to go and see the bishop to obtain a cure in this way, he did so; and Possidius adds that the sick man went away cured. In the eyes of the faithful disciple the saint was already outlined behind the dying bishop.[26] At the start of the siege he had philo-sophically consoled himself by repeating these words of Plotinus which had already come to his lips at the time of the sack of Rome:[by] 'No great man would be greatly affected by the fact that stone and wood are collapsing and mortals dying.'[bz] But at the hour of death philosophy no longer sufficed. He asked for copies to be made of a few Psalms dealing with penitence, so that when they were placed against the walls of his room he could read them from his bed.[27] At last, on 28 August 430, Augustine rejoined Monica, Adeodatus, Nebridius, Severus and several others in 'Abraham's bosom'.

He was carried to his burial by the town's clergy, led by his appointed successor, Eraclius. Possidius was present, and we are indebted to him for knowing that the eucharistic sacrifice was performed near his remains before he was interred, as he had done for Monica at Ostia forty-three years earlier. As the 'poor man of God' that he was, he had made no will; but he left behind him a treasure and, while he was still alive, he had not failed to draw his clerics' attention to the duty they had to safeguard it for future generations:[ca] the church of Hippo's library, in other words, besides his own works, all the books by classical, and above all ecclesiastical, authors which he had accumulated thanks to the long labours of a studio of copyists – a *scriptorium* – who were both competent and devoted. It could not have escaped Possidius that the situation was extremely threatening for the preservation of this treasure, notably for its most precious part, the works of the master, which he was aware would forever fix the image of Augustine and establish his place in the Church.[cb] It was doubtless this feeling, as much as piety towards the deceased, that led him, during the long months that followed the bishop's death in the besieged town, to make a kind of catalogue of Augustine's works, sermons and letters, which were preserved in the church's library.

Possidius, however, had not given up all hope that, once peace was restored, the task he was undertaking would in the end create something other than a memorial, a useful working tool which could be employed to ask the ecclesiastical library of Hippo for the duly amended fair copy of this or that work, not only to get to know about and read it, but also to have it copied and possibly, without keeping the copy jealously for oneself, to pass it on so that other copies could be made.[cd] It was the bishop of Calama's dream that Hippo's library should continue to be what it already was, the intellectual centre from which Augustinian thinking radiated, thanks to those chains of transcripts which were the most frequent, if not the only, way of 'publishing' in that period,[28] but with the additional convenience of a well-made catalogue. This is the aim that explains the practical aspect of Possidius' *Elenchus*;[29] the disciple had taken care to perfect the *Indiculum* already established by his master,[ce] without whose existence the latter would have had great difficulty in finding his way through his prolific output, if only to write his *Retractations* in 426/7. He describes Augustine's works as 'literary objects', in their material reality: thus he tells us that the *Homilies on John's Gospel* are contained in six *codices*; these books that he could see on the church library shelves must have been fairly large – something the author generally tried to avoid – for there are 124 sermons, and they are often developed. He pinpoints a rarity: a 'notebook' whose beginning is written in Augustine's hand, but whose title is missing and whose contents we can only try to guess.[30] But the main originality of the bibliographical tool created by Possidius in relation to the existing list is that he conceived it as a catalogue by 'subjects':

against the Manichaeans, against the Donatists, against the Pelagians, and so on, in each section having the 'treatises' followed by letters which he thinks are germane to these headings. One last 'general' section collects those works, as he says, that are 'useful to all studious men'. Here one would expect to find the *De Trinitate* listed, but no! This ancestor of our librarians has anticipated the common errors of their 'subject files'; this major work was classified among the anti-Arian treatises. But let us be fair to the bishop of Calama; he may not have had a great mind, but he was conscientious and his devotion to Augustine's works was boundless. We may recall that the bishop had not had the time to finish the revision of his letters and sermons; the catalogue gives a list – albeit incomplete – of both groups, sometimes with useful chronological indications.

The outcome of the siege of Hippo remains a mystery, and the safekeeping of the bishop's works perhaps smacks of the miraculous, if at least we follow Possidius, according to whom after fourteen months of siege the town, abandoned by its inhabitants, was burnt.[cf] But in such a dramatic end, how could the fate of Augustine's library have been other than that of Alexandria's? In that case the miracle would have been that the Vandals rescued from the fire the books of a man who had fought against all heretics, and they were among that number. Should we perhaps believe another source, according to which the besiegers had lifted the siege from sheer weariness, or more exactly because famine was raging in their ranks, which may leave us rather sceptical? What is certain is that Bonifatius was able to leave the town, to resume battle a little later, probably farther east, assisted by help from the Orient, and be defeated again. Hippo thus fell to the Vandals, without too much damage in either material or human terms.[31] In any case, we know that, before seizing Carthage in 439, Geiseric took up his quarters there, and that it was to Augustine's episcopal town that an envoy of Valentinian III came early in 435 to sign an initial treaty with the Vandal king confirming the conquest – which could not have taken place amid the ruins of a destroyed town. It was probably thanks to this outcome, which was free from excessive brutality, that the bishop's library was able to be preserved. It would be nice to ascribe this rescue to Possidius; we know that the bishop of Calama – like Novatus, his colleague from Sitifis – was not banished by Geiseric until 437.[ch] Liaising with Eraclius – and there is nothing to suggest that he did not succeed Augustine – he must until that date have watched over the maintenance of a collection on which he had worked so hard to give it coherence.

In 442, a second treaty fixed the boundaries of the Vandal state for nearly a century. Alas! Hippo remained within those boundaries, which fairly broadly covered eastern Numidia,[ci] and stayed cut off from its communications with Italy. Yet there is no lack of indications that allow us to propose – without proof, but with strong probability[32] – that the very complete knowledge of Augustine's works to be found in Italy in the second half of the fifth century did not come from copies of these writings that had been circulated overseas only partially before the bishop's death, but was due to their transportation to Rome in their entirety and their inclusion in the collection of the apostolic library in the middle of the fifth century, under conditions and by means which, it is true, remain mysterious, if not miraculous. But here we must leave the famous *codices*, content in the knowledge that they have reached safe harbour. Here the history of Augustine of Hippo and his works comes to an end; and there begins that of his extensive influence; the history, which began very early, of what is called Augustinianism – but that is another story altogether.

Notes

a.   Above, pp. 230–1.
b.   The best analysis of the 'psychological' repercussions of the priest Januarius' act of indiscipline may be read in A. Mandouze, *Saint Augustin*, pp. 225–8.
c.   Above, pp. 254–7.
d.   *Ep.* 110, 4; cf. above, p. 206.
e.   *Ep.* 213, 1.
f.   Cf. above, p. 348.
g.   Cf. above, p. 239.
h.   *Ep.* 213, 1.
i.   *Ep.* 213, 3 and 4; cf. above, p. 183.
j.   *Ep.* 213, 5.
k.   *Ep.* 213, 6.
l.   *Vita Aug.*, XVIII, 9. Augustine himself had said as much of Varro (*City of God*, VI, 2). But in the sixteenth century Michel de Bay (Baius) would boast of having read them all nine times! (H.-I. Marrou, *Saint Augustin et l'augustinisme*, p. 173).
m.   At least nights; the day was reserved for his refutations of Julian of Eclanum: cf. *Ep.* 224, 2, *in fine*.
n.   *Ep.* 224, 2: 'As much as the affairs which ceaselessly assail me from all sides will allow.'
o.   *Ep.* 143, 2; cf. above, p. 331.
p.   This is the opening sentence of J.-J. Rousseau's *Confessions*.
q.   Except for Galen, in the technical fields, who in the second century AD had compiled a complete and elaborate catalogue of all his medical writings.
r.   It is not, however, totally impossible, if we believe Possidius, who states that on the eve of his death the old bishop still had his sight and hearing unimpaired: *Vita Aug.*, XXXI, 5.
s.   *Retract., prol.,* 1.
t.   *Ep.* 224, 2.
u.   Criticism of the *Contra Academicos*: *Retract.*, I, 1, 4.
v.   *Retract.*, I, 1, 3.
w.   *Retract., prol.,* 3, *in fine*.
x.   *De dono pers.*, 55.
y.   But they were not yet circulated, to the great regret of Hilarius who, from Marseille, had asked for them in 428: *Ep.* 224, 2.
z.   *Ep.* 224, 2.
aa.   Cf. above, pp. 199–200.
bb.   Cf. above, p. 198 and chiefly the note by I. Bochet and G. Madec in *BA*, 11, 2 (1997), pp. 562–81.
cc.   A good overall presentation of Book IV in M. Moreau, 'Lecture du *De doctrina christiana*', in *Saint Augustin et la Bible*, Paris, 1986, pp. 274–83.
dd.   He warned: that the reader should not expect him to dish up again what he himself had learnt and taught: *Doctr. chr.*, IV, 2 and 14.
ee.   *Doctr. chr.* IV, 5 and 8.
ff.   *Doctr. chr.* IV, 21.
gg.   *Doctr. chr.* IV, 24.
hh.   *Enarr. in Psalm.* 138, 20.
ii.   *Enarr. in Psalm.* 36, 3, 6: *quam in nostra* disertitudine *vos* deserti *eritis*, an echo of the same play on words in the *Confessions*, II, 5: *dummodo essem* disertus *vel* desertus *potius*.
jj.   *Doctr. chr.* IV, 25.

kk. *Doctr. chr.* IV, 27.

ll. *De catechizandis rudibus*, 4.

mm. *Doctr. chr.* IV, 31, quoting *Ad Donatum*, 1.

nn. Cicero had already used the word: *The Orator*, 69.

oo. *Doctr. chr.* IV, 34.

pp. *Doctr. chr.* IV, 53; cf. above, p. 351.

qq. *Doctr. chr.* IV, 11–13.

rr. *Doctr. chr.* IV, 43, quoting Rom. 8.28–39.

ss. *Doctr. chr.* IV, 61: 'Let the way of life take the place of oratorical abundance.'

tt. *Carmen* 31, 1. 607–10 (*CSEL*, 30, 2, p. 329).

uu. I must add that in Antiquity transference of the bodies of ordinary private individuals was rather an exception.

vv. *Conf.*, IX, 28; cf. above, p. 119.

ww. *Conf.*, IX, 36–7.

xx. He had chapters 12 and 13 of Book I of the *City of God* re-transcribed: *De cura pro mortuis gerenda*, 3–5.

yy. *De cura pro mortuis gerenda*, 8.

zz. *De cura pro mortuis gerenda*, 7, with some interesting notations on the body language which, in prayer, obeys the impulse of the soul but by its movements increases the soul's intention.

ab. *De cura pro mortuis gerenda*, 7.

ac. Cf. above, pp. 156–8.

ad. Cf. Y. Duval, *Auprès des saints, corps et âme. L'inhumation 'ad sanctos' dans la chrétienté d'Orient et d'Occident du IIIe au VIIe siècle*, Paris, Ét. aug., 1988, pp. 36–40 and 179–80.

ae. See the Roman epitaph (*ICUR*, VII, 18994) commentated by Y. Duval in *Auprès des saints, corps et âme*, pp. 219–22.

af. *De anima*, 51, 1 and 4.

ag. Cf. R. Turcan, 'Origines et sens de' inhumation à l'époque impériale', in *Rev. des ét. anc.*, 60, 1958, pp. 323–47, and especially pp. 340–7.

ah. Cf. above, pp. 236–7. Nothing has been found at Hippo to suggest the presence of Augustine's burial place. Possidius was present when he was interred but gives no exact indication of the location: *Vita Aug.*, XXXI, 5; see p. 476.

ai. *De cura pro mortuis gerenda*, 22, *in fine*.

aj. *De cura pro mortuis gerenda*, 16.

ak. *De cura pro mortuis gerenda*, 19.

al. *De cura pro mortuis gerenda*, 20.

am. *De cura pro mortuis gerenda*, 19.

an. *De vera religione*, 47.

ao. *De utilitate credendi*, 34.

ap. *Sermon* 88, 2 and 3.

aq. *De Trin.*, III, 11.

ar. An idea often expressed by the bishop; cf. notably *Sermon* 247, 2 (in 400) and the famous letter to Volusianus, in 412: *Ep.* 137, 10, *initio*.

as. *De Genesi ad litt.*, VI, 24: *cum aquam* miro compendio *convertit in vinum* (John 2.9).

at. *De Genesi ad litt.*, IX, 32.

au. *De Genesi ad litt.*, IX, 33.

av. *City of God*, XVI, 5.

aw. Cf. above, pp. 236–7.

ax. *City of God*, XXII, 8, 22.

ay. *De catechizandis rudibus*, 10.

az. Cf. above, p. 303.

ba. He had distinguished himself in 413, beneath the walls of Marseille, where with his own hand he had wounded the Visigoth king Athaulf.

bc. Matt. 8.5–10: *Ep.* 189, 4; this letter comes soon after letter 185.

bd. *Ep.* 189, 6 and 7.

be. *Ep. 220, 3.*

bf. *Ep. 17*,* in *BA,* 46 B, p. 276; in this the bishop says he is completely satisfied with both the soldier and the Christian. In another also recently published letter, he records Bonifatius' generous financial gifts to the Church: *Ep. 7*,* 1, *BA,* 46 B, p. 146.

bg. Augustine would give him his title in the very bitter letter he sends him: *Ep. 220, 7.*

bh. *Ep. 220, 4.*

bi. *Ep. 220, 3.*

bj. *Ep. 220, 7.*

bk. Cf. above, p. 378.

bl. *Ep. 231.*

bm. *Ep. 230, 3.*

bn. *Ep. 231, 7:* among others the *Enchiridion;* Darius was asked to let him know his feelings about these books.

bo. Possidius, *Vita Aug.,* XXVIII, 4.

bp. *Vita Aug,* XXVIII, 10.

bq. *Vita Aug,* XXVIII, 12.

br. Cf. above, p. 417.

bs. *Concilia Africae, CCL,* 149, pp. 250–3.

bt. Cf. above, p. 227.

bu. *Ep. 228, 5.*

bv. *Ep. 228, 2.* Augustine developed at length the exposition of these spiritual aids: *Ep. 228, 8* and 9.

bw. *Ep. 228, 12.*

bx. *Vita Aug.,* XXVIII, 13.

by. Cf. above, p. 394.

bz. *Vita Aug.,* XXVIII, 11 (*Enn.,* I, 4, 7).

ca. *Vita Aug.,* XXXI, 6.

cb. *Vita Aug.,* XXXI, 8.

cd. *Vita Aug.,* XVIII, 10.

ce. Augustine makes precise reference to this *indiculum* in his *Retractations,* noting that one of his writings (letter 148) has not been listed: *Retract.,* II, 41.

cf. *Vita Aug.,* XXVIII, 10.

cg. Procopius, *De bello Vandalico,* I, 3, 34.

ch. Prosper, *Epitome chronicon,* a. 437 (ed. T. Mommsen, *MGH, aa,* 9, 1, p. 475).

ci. Cf. C. Courtois, *Les Vandales et l'Afrique,* pp. 171–85 and maps.

Additional notes

PART I : A Son of Thagaste

CHAPTER I : Thagaste

1. We are indebted to him for his date of birth, on the ides of November (*De beata vita*); the exact year comes from a double mention of his lifespan (76 years) by Possidius (*Vita Aug.*, I, 1), and the date of his death on 28 August 430, by Prosper of Aquitaine.

2. Cf. A. Chastagnol, *L'Album municipal de Timgad*, Bonn, 1978.

3. *Vita s. Melaniae Iunioris*, vers. lat., I, 21, *Anal. Bolland.*, 8, 1889, p. 35. The Greek version of this *Vie* (§ 21, ed. D. Gorce, *Sources chrétiennes*, 90, 1962, p. 170) adds 'and very poor'; but this assessment must be related to the person of Melania the Younger, who stayed there in 410 with her husband Pinianus, and who was one of the wealthiest people of her time (cf. above, p. 312).

4. Cf. C. Lepelley, *Les Cités de l'Afrique romaine au Bas-Empire*, vol. I, Paris, 1979, pp. 82–108. By the same author, see a recent restatement of these positive evaluations: 'Augustin dans l'Afrique romaine de son temps: les continuités avec la cité classique', in *Internationales Symposion über den Stand der Augustinus-Forschung*, Würzburg, 1989, pp. 169–88, especially pp. 170–5.

5. *Actes de la conférence de Carthage en 411*, I, 4, ed. S. Lancel ('Sources chrétiennes', 195), Paris, 1972, p. 565. The reader must not imagine that the north of present-day Morocco is forgotten: for the Late Empire administration, it was linked with Spain, and similarly from the ecclesiastical point of view.

6. If however this name Aurelius, applied to Augustine, does not come – as has sometimes been suspected – from the placing of his usual name, Augustinus (frequent on conciliar lists of that time), immediately after that of Aurelius, primate of Africa: cf. A.-M. La Bonnardière, ' "Aurelius Augustinus" or "Aurelius, Augustinus"?', in *Revue bénéd.*, 91, 1981, pp. 231–7. Lastly, M. Gorman, 'Aurelius Augustinus: the Testimony of the oldest Manuscripts of Saint Augustine's Works', in *Journal of Theol. Studies*, n. s., 35, 1984, pp. 475–80, which concludes that Aurelius is the gentilitial name.

7. These quotations, which are somewhat surprising coming from this writer, are from A. Mandouze, *Saint Augustin. L'aventure de la raison et de la grâce*, Paris, 1968, pp. 74–5.

8. H.-I. Marrou, *Saint Augustin et l'augustinisme*, Paris, Le Seuil, 'Les maîtres spirituels', 1955, p. 11. In this contrast between nature and nurture, we would now talk about 'genetic fingerprints'.

9. Theodosian Code (hereafter called *C.Th.*), II, 1, 33, quoted by Lepelley, *Les cités de l'Afrique romaine*, p. 198.

10. This mosaic is one of the jewels of the Bardo Museum in Tunis. It is commented on by G. Charles-Picard, *La Carthage de saint Augustin*, Paris, Fayard, 1965, pp. 148–54. Cf. also K. Dunbabin, *The Mosaics of Roman North Africa*, Oxford, 1978, pp. 119–21 and fig. 109.

CHAPTER II : Monica

1. Virgil had used the expression (*plenis annis nubilis*) for the young Lavinia, daughter of King Latinus, promised to Aeneas (*Aeneid*, VII, 53). Theoretically set at twelve years, in practice nubility was around fourteen to fifteen years in Rome and on average between fifteen and seventeen years in Africa: cf. J.-M. Lassère, *Ubique populus*, Paris, 1977, pp. 487–90; lastly, P. Morizot, 'L'âge au mariage des jeunes Romaines à Rome et en Afrique', in *CRAI*, 1989, pp. 656–9.

2. It has sometimes been thought that there were several children, on the basis of *Conf.*, IX, 22: '*Nutrierat filios*'; but two are enough to justify the plural. Augustine also mentions a nephew, called Patricius, like his own father, who lived with him in the clerical community of Hippo at the date (426) of the text naming him (*s.* 356, 3); he seems to have been the son of Navigius: cf. G. Madec, 'Le neveu d'Augustin', in *Revue des ét. aug.*, 39, 1993, pp. 149–53.

3. *Conf.*, I. 19. Addressing his faithful later, Augustine would give his episcopal backing to this definition of matrimonial relations, but gently, and favouring mutual respect: cf. *sermon* 51, 22; 293; 332, 4 and the commentaries of B. D. Shaw, 'The Family in Late Antiquity: the Experience of Augustine', in *Past and Present*, 115, 1987, pp. 32–5.

4. Cf. W. H. C. Frend, 'The Family of Augustine. A Microcosm of Religious Change in North Africa', in *Atti del Congr. Intern. su S. Agostino nel XVI centenario della conversione, Roma, 15–20 settembre 1986*, Rome, 1987, vol. I, pp. 135–51.

5. Cf. P. Monceaux, *Histoire littéraire de l'Afrique chrétienne*, III, Paris, 1905 (repr. Brussels, 1966), pp. 47–53; lastly, C. Lepelley, *Les Cités de l'Afrique romaine au Bas-Empire*, vol. I, p. 344.

6. As Augustine himself notes (*Conf.*, VI, 2), who would prohibit these practices in his episcopacy and, as early as 392, while still a priest, wrote to the primate Aurelius of Carthage expressing his wish to see them banned (*Ep.* 22). Cf. above, p. 156.

7. *Meribibula*: if the word Augustine attributes to the servant girl is really hers, she was certainly verbally inventive; no other example of it is known. Its composition recalls the old vocabulary of Plautus, who was then back in favour, and the diminutive is a descendant of the verbal creations of an Apuleius.

8. P. Brown, *Augustine of Hippo. A Biography*, Faber, London, 1967, p. 29.

9. *De beata vita*, II, 10; cf. also II, 11; II, 16; III, 19; III, 21; IV, 23; IV, 27; IV, 36. For a balanced and positive assessment of Monica's contributions at Cassiciacum, read E. Lamirande, 'Quand Monique, la mère d'Augustin, prend la parole', in *Signum pietatis. Festgabe für C. P. Mayer O.S.A. zum 60. Geburtstag*, Würzburg, 1989, pp. 3–19. See also in the charming book by G. Camps, *L'Afrique du Nord au féminin*, Paris, Perrin, 1992 (pp. 92–108) the pages devoted to Monica, which are so right in tone.

10. *Conf.*, II, 8. This period of the writing of the *Confessions* is also the one when Augustine begins to develop, notably in his pastoral texts, the rich symbolism centred on the two cities of Jerusalem and Babylon, taken in the allegorical sense: cf. above, pp. 400ff.

11. On Monica's dream, see M. Dulaey, *Le Rêve dans la vie et dans la pensée de saint Augustin*, Paris, Ét. aug., 1973, pp. 158–65.

12. In fact, it was not a good idea to banter about religious matters in front of her. At Cassiciacum, young Licentius had experience of this when he found himself reproved for impropriety because he had, quite innocently, begun to sing a verse of Psalm 79 while in the privy (*De ordine*, I, 22).

13. It is hard not to recognize a nice Oedipus-style trio here. But Goulven Madec (*La Patrie et la Voie. Le Christ dans la pensée et la vie de saint Augustin*, Paris, Desclée, 1989, pp. 24–5) wants to rescue this text from the psychoanalysts, making Monica put into practice the evangelical precept: 'And call no man your father upon the earth: for one is your Father, which is in heaven' (Matt. 23.9).

14. Cf. J. Chomarat, 'Les "Confessions" de saint Augustin', in *Revue française de psychanalyse*, 52, 1988, pp. 153–74.

15. Besides Augustine, the only Augustinus we know of in Africa at that time was an obscure Donatist bishop, the only one to bear this name among the 2565 people listed in the *Prosopographie chrétienne du Bas-Empire*, vol. I, *Afrique* (303–533), Paris, CNRS, 1982. Outside Africa, the only person with this name, in that period, was the bishop of Aquileia, in North Italy; and even his existence is uncertain: cf. C. Pietri, *Roma christiana*, vol. II, Rome, 1976, p. 943, note 2.

CHAPTER III : A Numidian childhood

1. Our times are all for reinstatement, but to be persuaded of the meagreness of the topic one has only to read the few pages devoted to childhood in Roman Antiquity by J.-P. Neraudau in the voluminous *Histoire de l'enfance en Occident*, vol. I, Paris, Le Seuil, 1998, pp. 69–97.

2. Cf. C. Tresmontant, *Introduction à la théologie chrétienne*, Paris, Le Seuil, 1974, pp. 579–81.

3. Cf. the second canon of the council of Carthage of 1 May 418, in *Concilia Africae, a. 345–525*, ed. C. Munter, *CCL*, vol. 149, p. 221.

4. The *Hermeneumata pseudodositheana*, in *Corpus glossariorum latinorum*, III, 645, commented on by H.-I. Marrou, *Histoire de l'Éducation dans l'Antiquité*, Paris, Le Seuil, 1965, pp. 393–9.

5. Juvenal, I, 15: '*Manum ferulae subducere*', translated by H.-I. Marrou, *Histoire de l'Éducation*, p. 397, with a small slip over his perception of the action.

6. *Conf.*, I, 20. On this first bad memory of his youth (the second, on a quite different level, being

the theft of the pears), see J.-C. Fredouille, 'Deux mauvais souvenirs d'Augustin', in *Philanthropia kai Eusebeia, Festshcrift für A. Dihle*, Göttingen, 1993, pp. 74–9.

7. H.-I. Marrou, *Saint Augustin et la fin de la culture antique*, Paris, De Boccard, 1958, pp. 29–30.

8. Greek references, both patristic and secular, have been put under the microscope: cf. H.-I. Marrou, *Saint Augustin et la fin de la culture antique*, pp. 31–7, and P. Courcelle, *Les Lettres grecques en Occident de Macrobe à Cassiodore*, Paris, De Boccard, 1948, pp. 137–209.

9. For the dedication of the statue by the *Madaurenses cives*, cf. *Inscriptions latines d'Afrique*, I, 2115; on this title of 'Platonic philosopher', cf. Apuleius, *Apologia*, 10, 6; Augustine, *City of God*, VIII, 12 and 14.

10. *Inscriptions latines de l'Algérie*, I, 2012; cf. Lepelley, *Les Cités de l'Afrique romaine*, vol. II, p. 130.

11. S. Gsell, *Khamissa, Mdaourouch, Announa*, vol. II: *Mdaourouch*, Algiers-Paris, 1922, p. 32.

12. K. Vössing, 'Augustin's Schullaufbahn und das sogennante dreistufige Bildungssystem', in *L'Africa romana*, 9, 2, Sassari, 1992, pp. 881–99, tends to play down the advantages of Madauros.

13. Cf. Y. Duval, *Loca sanctorum Africae*, II, Coll. École fr. de Rome, 58, Rome, 1982, pp. 707–8.

14. Cf. N. Duval, *Les églises africaines à deux absides*, vol. II (BEFAR, 218 bis), Paris, De Boccard, 1973, pp. 29–34. Lastly, I. Gui, N. Duval and J.-P. Caillet, *Basiliques chrétiennes d'Afrique du Nord. I. Inventaire de l'Algérie*, Paris, Ét. aug., 1992, pp. 327–32, and fig. under no. 117.

15. Maximus' remark to Augustine: '*Vir eximie, qui a mea secta deviasti*' (*Ep.* 16, 4), is not absolutely conclusive: rather than teaching or school, *secta* means 'philosophical school' and, more broadly, 'trend of thinking'. Maximus pretended to be unaware of Augustine's childhood religious situation.

16. This is the title of a recent 'theological' exegesis of this episode: H. Derycke, 'Le vol des poires, parabole du péché originel' in *Bulletin de litt. eccl.*, 88, 3–4, 1987, pp. 337–48. Read also a subtle commentary on the rhetorical composition of the whole, as well as a reflection on Book II of the *Confessions* suggesting it to be a 'book of a hurt memory': P. Cambronne, 'Le "vol des poires" ', in *Revue des études latines*, 71, 1993, pp. 228–38. As an example of the ingenuity which exegetes put to work to 'decode' what appear to be the most flatly 'real' episodes of Augustine's account, see D. Shanzer, 'Pears before Swine: Augustine, *Confessions* 2.4.9', in *Revue des ét aug.*, 42, 1996, pp. 45–55.

17. Cf. L. C. Ferrari, 'The Pear-Theft in Augustine's *Confessions* in *Revue des ét. aug.*, 16, 1970, pp. 233–42; similarly, 'The Arboreal Polarisation in Augustine's *Confessions*', *Revue des ét. aug.*, 25, 1979, pp. 35–46.

CHAPTER IV : Carthage

1. Cf. O. Perler and J.-L. Maier, *Les Voyages de saint Augustin*, Paris, Ét. aug., 1969, p. 131.

2. Cf. P. Gros, *Byrsa III*, Coll. École fr. de Rome, 41, Rome, 1985, pp. 63–112.

3. Was Augustine thinking back to that thirst for love as a seventeen-year-old, when some twenty years later he wrote 'question 35' of the *De diversis quaestionibus*, 'If we must love love, we must nevertheless not love no matter what; for there is an ugly kind, by which the soul clings to what is inferior to it, which is passion'?

4. Salvian, *De gubernatione Dei*, VIII, 70 (*CSEL*, 8, p. 178).

5. For this page is like many others: it is the story of the adolescent or young man, but narrated by the mature man, former teacher, who was converted and became a bishop. A. Mandouze writes amusingly on this subject: 'To say the least, this 'literary confession' gives us a portrait of Augustine in Carthage which enables one to predict for him a very different career from that of pear-stealer or womanizer' (*Saint Augustin. L'aventure de la raison et de la grâce*, p. 80). Of course, but one must keep in mind that it is the bishop editing the copy.

6. Cf. J.-C. Fredouille, *Tertullien et la conversion de la culture antique*, Paris, 1972, pp. 146–7.

CHAPTER V : From Cicero to Mani

1. These fragments are collected in Cicero, *Opera*, ed. Müller, vol. IV, 3, coll. Teubner, pp. 312–27; those that appear in Augustine have been analysed by M. Testard, *Saint Augustin et Cicéron*, Paris, Ét. aug., 1958, notably pp. 19–48, and by E. Feldmann, *Der Einfluss des Hortensius und des Manichäismus auf das Denken des jungen Augustinus von 373*, Münster, 1975, pp. 77–100.

2. As a contemporary example of the reluctance to be overcome for a well-read person brought up on the classics, one could name Jerome, who in his youth went off on pilgrimage to Jerusalem

from Rome, taking his library with him as he could not do without it; when, emerging from Plautus or Cicero, he read a 'prophet', he was horrified by the 'uncultivated language' (*Ep.* 22, 30).

3. *Sermon* 51, 4–6, probably datable to the first years of the fifth century, rather than later than 417, as was previously thought (cf. F. Dolbeau, 'Le sermonnaire augustinien de Mayence [Mainz, Stadtbibliothek I 9]: analyse et histoire', in *Revue bénéd.*, 106, 1–2, 1996, p. 39).

4. The discovery of a Greek papyrus (the 'Mani-Codex') in the Cologne collections some thirty years ago contributed details on the Judaeo-Christian community of baptizers where Mani had his youth, in Babylon: cf. J. Ries, in *Mélanges T. J. Van Bavel*, vol. II, Louvain, 1990, p. 761.

5. Cf. *Contra Faustum*, I, 2, and F. Decret, *Aspects du manichéisme dans l'Afrique romaine*, Paris, Ét. aug., 1970, p. 13.

6. Cf. Decret, *Aspects du manichéisme*, p. 331, note 4. The date of this edict – or rescript – may be 297 or 302.

7. A Latin manuscript of 13 leaves discovered in 1918 in a cave south-west of Tebessa (Algeria) has been recognized as a Manichaean text, at first dated to the end of the sixth or seventh century: cf. P. Alfaric, 'Un manuscrit manichéen', in *Revue d'hist. et de litt. relig.*, n. s., 6, 1920, pp. 62–98. These days it is dated rather to the fifth century, stressing the community religion aspect of this residual Manichaeism: F. Decret, 'Aspects de l'Église manichéenne. Remarques sur le manuscrit de Tébessa', in *Cassiciacum*, XL, 1989, pp. 123–51.

8. Cf. L. H. Grondijs, 'Analyse du manichéisme numidien au IVᵉ siècle' in *Augustinus Magister*, vol. III, Paris, 1954, pp. 408–10. However, it is not certain that the symbol of the *Jesus patibilis* belongs to African Manichaeism alone: cf. F. Decret, *Aspects du manichéisme*, pp. 12–13 and 284, note 2, and W. Geerlings, 'Der manichäische "Jesus patibilis" in der Theologie Augustins', in *Theologische Quartalschrift*, 152, 1972, p. 125, n. 10.

9. Cf. C. Schmidt, *Manichäische Handschriften des staatlichen Museen Berlins*, vol. I: *Kephalaia*, Stuttgart, 1935.

10. Cf. C. R. C. Allberry and H. Ibscher, *A Manichean Psalm-Book*, Stuttgart, 1938; C. R. C. Allberry, *A Manichean Psalm-Book, Part II*, Stuttgart, 1958.

11. E. Chavannes and P. Pelliot, 'Un traité manichéen retrouvé en Chine', in *Journal asiatique*, 1911, pp. 499–617, and 1913, pp. 99–199 and 261–394. One of the best overall expositions of Manichaeism, or in any case the most accessible, is that of H.-C. Puech, *Le Manichéisme, son fondateur et sa doctrine*, Paris, Publications du musée Guimet, 1949, to which these pages owe much; read also: J. Ries, 'Introduction aux études manichéennes. Quatre siècles de recherches', in *Ephemerides Theologicae Lovanienses* (Louvain), 1957, pp. 453–82, and 1959, pp. 362–409, and an excellent little illustrated manual: F. Decret, *Mani et la tradition manichéenne*, coll. 'Les maîtres spirituels', 40, Paris, Le Seuil, 1974. Lastly, the little synthesis by M. Tardieu, *Le Manichéisme*, coll. 'Que sais-je?', Paris, PUF, 1981, re-edited in 1997. There is much to be awaited from the current study of the thousands of fragments of papyrus, wooden tablets and *ostraka* unearthed from 1982 onwards on the site of Ismant el-Kharab, 800 kilometres south-west of Cairo; cf. a first synthesis from I. Gardner and S. N. C. Lieu, 'From Narmouthis (Medinet Madi) to Kellis (Ismant el-Kharab). Manichaean Documents from Roman Egypt', in *Journal of Roman Studies*, 85, 1996, pp. 146–69.

12. Augustine himself makes no reference to this *tertius legatus*, mentioned by his friend Evodius in the *De fide contra Manicheos*, 17. One can read a good presentation of this kind of anti-Manichaean 'manual' by Evodius, from F. Decret, 'Le traité d'Evodius "Contre les manichéens": un compendium à l'usage du parfait controversiste' in *Augustinianum*, 31, 2, 1991, pp. 387–409.

CHAPTER VI : A Manichaean rhetor between Thagaste and Carthage

1. *De beata vita*, I. 4. It will not be overlooked that, in this initial address to Manlius Theodorus, Augustine uses the metaphor, which was very common at that time, of the spiritual and intellectual journey compared to a sea voyage, with its hazards. Of the three quotations, the last two say the same thing, the second expressing clearly and explicitly what the first says metaphorically. It follows that the mists of the first are matched by the *superstitio puerilis* of the second (where the word 'fog' takes it up), and that in the same way the 'stars that plunged into the ocean' are explained by 'the men who': it is they, the deceiving stars on which his eyes were fixed for so long, the bad guides who in the end left him alone with himself. Although Augustine was 'into' astrology for a while, the *astra* here do not refer to it.

2. Cf. P. Courcelle, 'Les premières "Confessions" de saint Augustin', in *Revue des études latines*,

XXI–XXII, 1943–4, pp. 155–74 (reprinted in *Recherches sur les 'Confessions' de saint Augustin*, Paris, De Boccard, 1968, pp. 269–90).

3. The *terribilis auctoritas* (authority which leads astray by intimidating) appears in the text quoted from the *De utilitate credendi*, I, 2; to become bolder (cf. *De beata vita*, I, 4: '*factus erectior*'), was to reject that authority; I do not accept the suggestion by J. Doignon, '*Factus erectior*' (*B. vita*, I, 4). Une étape dans l'évolution du jeune Augustin à Carthage', in *Vetera Christianorum*, 27, 1990, pp. 77–83, for whom it would appear to be a sudden move against the influence of divination and taking control of himself again after the 'depressing extravagances of "astrology"'.

4. I quote the texts published by C. R. C. Allberry, *A Manichaean Psalm-Book*, Stuttgart, 1938, in the French adaptation by Madec, *La Patrie et la Voie*, pp. 28–9.

5. In 387, in dialogue with Evodius, replying to the question asked by his friend about the origin of evil in us, Augustine replied: 'You raise the problem which, when I was very young, greatly perturbed me and, through weariness, pushed and drove me into heresy' (*De libero arbitrio*, I, 4).

6. On this text, see particularly F. Decret, *Aspects du manichéisme dans l'Afrique romaine*, p. 33, and, chiefly, 'Saint Augustin témoin du manichéisme dans l'Afrique romaine', in *Cassiciacum* XXXIX, 1, 1989, pp. 94–5; Mandouze, *Saint Augustin*, p. 254, note 5, seems to minimize its impact.

7. Cf. M. Blanchard-Lemée, 'La "maison de Bacchus" à Djemila. Architecture et décor d'une grande demeure provinciale à la fin de l'Antiquité', in *BAC*, n. s. 17 B, 1981, pp. 131–43.

8. In fact, the word 'chronicle' is inappropriate and should not be taken literally. The reader of Book IV of the *Confessions* soon realizes that Augustine was not concerned with chronological continuity. For example: he reports his conversations with Vindicianus, the doctor proconsul, at Carthage before speaking of his friendship at Thagaste with that former fellow-student, from whom death would separate him in 375/76. We know for sure that Vindicianus' proconsulship was in 379/81: cf. p. 49.

9. Cicero, *De amicitia*, 20, and Augustine, *Contra Acad.*, III, 13. Read the small Augustinian *De amicitia* in the *City of God*, XIX, 8. On the role of friendship in the genesis of the Augustinian cenobitic idea, cf. Mandouze, *Saint Augustin*, pp. 186–7, and Brown, *Augustine of Hippo*, pp. 61–4.

CHAPTER VII : First achievements

1. Since Julian (362–3), this municipal decree had to be ratified by the emperor's authority (*C.Th.*, XIII, 3, 5). Cf. H.-I. Marrou, *Histoire de l'éducation dans l'Antiquité*, Paris, Le Seuil, 1965, p. 442: 'This decision was linked with a whole religious policy but, with its anti-Christian edge blunted, it preserved its force under Julian's successors, as its insertion in the Theodosian Code bears witness.'

2. This *magister* and these *docti*, 'puffed up with noisy pomposity' (*buccis tyfo crepantibus*), are obviously caricatured by Augustine (*Conf.*, IV, 28). But the caricature is by the author of the *Confessions*, not by the student, who at that time was intellectually extremely docile towards his teachers.

3. Unless it was the translation, by Vettius Agorius Praetextatus, Symmachus' friend, of a paraphrase of Aristotle's work, made by Themistius: cf. P. Hadot, *Marius Victorinus. Recherches sur sa vie et ses oeuvres*, Paris, Ét. aug., 1971, pp. 193–8.

4. To understand the passion and great intellectual demands that Augustine put into his teaching, one has only to read the page of the *De ordine*, I, 29–30, where, during the conversations at Cassiciacum, he admonished Trygetius and Licentius who, trying to rival each other in the argument, had indulged themselves in empty vainglory.

5. P. Petit, *Les Étudiants de Libanius*, Paris, 1957.

6. Cf. especially G. Picard, *La Carthage de saint Augustin*, Paris, Fayard, 1965, pp. 83–6, and A.-G. Hamman, *La Vie quotidienne en Afrique du Nord au temps de saint Augustin*, Paris, Hachette, 1979, pp. 158–60.

7. Excavations of the meagre remains of Carthage's circus, pillaged in the Vandal period (second half of the fifth century) have recently been carried out very commendably by an American team: cf. J. Humphrey, *The Circus and a Byzantine Cemetery at Carthage*, Ann Arbor, The Univ. of Michigan Press, 1988.

8. Even if one does not doubt its veracity, the episode is one which makes one suspect Augustine of having sometimes 'arranged' the account in line with the famous *exempla* of moral conversions; cf. Courcelle, *Recherches*, p. 59.

9. One of Carthage's most remarkable urban achievements, according to a text of that period (around 360): *Expositio totius mundi et gentium*, 61, ed. J. Rougé, *Sources chrétiennes*, vol. 124, p. 202.

10. Cf. P. Gros, 'Le forum de la ville haute dans la Carthage romaine, d'après les textes et l'archéologie', in *Comptes rendus de l'Acad. des inscriptions et belles-lettres*, 1982, pp. 636–58, which resumes and makes more specific one of A. Lézine's old intuitions. It is not certain, however, that the damage took place in the basilica, as he suggests, and still less that the statement made by Alypius was uttered in this building. But the context at least clearly indicates that the premises where Augustine worked were situated in the neighbourhood.

11. Cf. *Conf.*, VI, 15: the architect who saves Alypius' skin had already noted damage on the forum. The young man who is finally convicted of theft is not a professional thief, but rather 'a young man of good family', and the anecdote says a great deal about the loss of civic sense.

12. The expression is Marrou's, in *Saint Augustin et l'augustinisme*, p. 13. He was not the only one of his kind in the Roman Africa of his time: cf. C. Lepelley, 'Quelques parvenus de la culture de l'Afrique romaine tardive', in *De Tertullien aux Mozarabes. Mélanges offerts à Jacques Fontaine*, vol. I, Paris, Ét. aug., 1992, pp. 583–94.

13. For the year of Helvius Vindicianus' proconsulship (379–80 or 380–81), see A. Beschaouch, *Mustitana* I, Paris, Klincksieck, 1968, p. 135.

14. I repeat that in my interpretation the purely metaphorical *astra* of the *De beata vita*, I, 4 do not refer to astrology: see above, note 1 of Chapter VI.

15. *Conf.*, VII, 10. On the Ciceronian antecedents of the matter of the twins, cf. Testard, *Saint Augustin et Cicéron*, I, p. 102: on a possible source in St Ambrose, see Courcelle, *Recherches*, p. 77, note 6.

16. Augustine will frequently return to this biblical *exemplum*: for instance, in the *Ad Simplicianum*, I, qu. 2, 3, in the *De doctrina christ.*, II, 33, and later in the *City of God*, V, 4–7, which will draw up a formal indictment against astrology.

17. See Marrou, *Saint Augustin et la fin de la culture antique*, pp. 108–9; also, *Histoire de l'éducation dans l'Antiquité*, pp. 265–79.

18. Cf. The *Retractations*, I, 6. To end this small notice, Augustine said that he had lost these rough drafts, but added that perhaps they were not lost to everyone. On what may remain of them, see Marrou, *Saint Augustin et la fin de la culture antique*, pp. 570–9.

19. Some insights into these readings, thanks to A. Solignac, are in the *Introduction* (pp. 92–3) of the edition of the *Confessions* in the *BA*, 13, Paris, Ét. aug., 1992.

20. *Conf.*, IV, 20: 'Two or three (books), I believe: *You* know, O God, because it escapes my mind. I do not have them any more; somehow or other they have gone astray.' In Augustine's eyes, they counted no more than everything else prior to his conversion, and naturally they are missing from the *Retractations*.

21. Plato, *Hippias major*, 293 d–294 e; the comparison is rightly made, but without any critical discussion, by A. Rigobello, 'Lettura del IV libro delle Confessioni di Agostino d'Ippona', in *Le 'Confessioni' di Agostino d'Ippona*, libri III–V, Palermo, 1984, p. 35.

22. For example in a Stoic text, to illustrate the idea of *opportunitas*, in the *De finibus*, III, 46, by Cicero.

23. On this subject, read J.-M. Fontanier, 'Sur le traité d'Augustin *De pulchro et apto*. Convenance, beauté et adaptation', in *Revue des sc. philos. et théol.*, 73, 1989, pp. 413–21, as a complement to the remarks by A. Solignac, in *Les Confessions*, *BA*, 13, pp. 660–72. In a letter addressed in 412 to his friend Marcellinus, the bishop will still use the distinction between the pulchrum and the aptum to take account of the 'adaptations' of the relations between God and humanity through biblical times: *Ep.* 138, 5.

24. See Solignac in *Les Confessions*, *BA*, 13, p. 673; see also, by the same author, 'Doxographies et manuels dans la formation philosophique de saint Augustin', in *Recherches aug.*, I, 1958, pp. 113–48, especially pp. 129–37. It is possible to detect in the pages relating to the *De pulchro et apto* reminiscences of Plotinus' treatise *On Beauty* (*Enn.*, I, VI), which Augustine seems to have read later, in the period of his conversion; so here it is a matter of an echo of Plotinian phrases, intervening in retrospect: cf. J. J. O'Meara, *The Young Augustine*, London, Longman, 1980.

25. *Conf.*, IV, 1. Augustine concentrates his sarcasm on the belly (*aqualiculus*, a rare and picturesque word) of the Manichaean elect: cf. also *Conf.*, III, 18, on the divine transmutation of the fig in the stomach of the Manichaean 'saint', and the texts collected by Decret, *Aspects du manichéisme dans l'Afrique romaine*, p. 308.

26. On this subject, cf. the reservations of Marrou, *Saint Augustin et la fin de la culture antique*, p. 250.

27. In his controversies with the Manichaeans, Augustine makes great use of 'Nebridius' argument'; he has recourse to it in his letter 79 addressed to a Manichaean who remains anonymous, and it would be one of his key arguments in his debates with Felix and Fortunatus (references in Decret, *Aspects du manichéisme dans l'Afrique romaine*, pp. 75 and 85).

28. *Contra Faustum*, V, 5 and 7. Unlike the puritanical Manichaeans, who slept on mats, Felix slept on feather cushions and under goatskin blankets. His return to Carthage from Rome, around 382, has been attributed to the laws of Theodosius who, in 381 and the spring of 382, depriving the Manichaeans of their citizens' rights before threatening them with capital punishment (*C.Th.*, XVI, 5, 7 and 9). But the application of these penalties was not restricted to Rome.

29. On the locality of this chapel and the point of embarkation, see S. Lancel, 'Victor de Vita et la Carthage vandale', in *L'Africa romana*, VI, Sassari, 1989, pp. 658–9.

CHAPTER VIII : Between Rome and Milan

1. Cf. Ammianus Marcellinus, *Historia*, XIV, 6, 18 and 19. On the favourite clientèles of this Roman aristocracy, see R. Macmullen, *Corruption and the Decline of Rome*, Yale Univ. Press, 1988, pp. 58–121.

2. In 370, a decree by the emperor Valentinian placed them under the authority of the prefect of the City (*C.Th.*, XIV, 9, 1), who was to quell possible disturbances, and each year send the emperor a list of the better elements so that the administration could choose from among them to supply its staff requirements.

3. Cf. A. Chastagnol, *Les Fastes de la préfecture de Rome au Bas-Empire*, Paris, 1962, pp. 218–29.

4. Cf. Marrou, *Histoire de l'éducation dans l'Antiquité*, pp. 428–30.

5. Brown, *Augustine of Hippo*, pp. 70–1, who rightly considers that Augustine left for Milan as Symmachus' 'protégé' (contra: T. D. Barnes, 'Augustine, Symmachus and Ambrose', in *Augustine. From Rhetor to Theologian*, Waterloo, Ontario, W. Laurier Univ. Press, 1992, pp. 7–13).

6. The young boy's accession to the Empire was bàck in 375, on 22 November; with the Roman way of calculating past time, his *decennalia* fell not on 22 November 385, but a year before: cf. A. Chastagnol, 'Les jubilés impériaux de 260 à 387', in *Crise et Redressement dans les provinces européennes de l'Empire*, Strasbourg, 1983, pp. 11–25.

7. Cf. *De ordine*, II, 45. Augustine says that he himself pulled the Italians up on their pronunciation; but his problem was one of tonic stress; on these questions, see S. Lancel, 'La fin et la survie de la latinité en Afrique du Nord', in *Revue des ét. lat.*, 59, 1981, pp. 276–7.

8. Courcelle, *Recherches sur les 'Confessions' de saint Augustin*, p. 82.

9. On this type of post, see the commentaries by C. Lepelley, 'Un aspect de la conversion d'Augustin: la rupture avec ses ambitions sociales et politiques', in *Bulletin de litt. eccl.*, 88, 3–4, 1987, pp. 229–46, especially pp. 239–41.

10. *Conf.*, VI, 1: 'Now my mother had come to join me; strong in her piety, she had followed me over land and sea, kept safe by you through all dangers. In times of crisis at sea, she reassured even the sailors themselves, by whom inexperienced travellers on the deep are wont to be comforted in their distress: she promised them that they would reach port and safety; for you had promised this to her in a vision.' Beyond the 'hagiography' (tinged with a faint irony), there is a hint: the rough crossing suggests a date in spring, early in the opening of maritime traffic in the Mediterranean, theoretically from 10 March.

11. The arrival of Adeodatus' mother, with her son, may be deduced from the mention of her being sent back a little later. It cannot be completely ruled out that both may have joined Augustine before Monica, but it is unlikely.

CHAPTER IX : Ambrose

1. This is the portrait to be seen in the mosaic of the chapel of St Saturus, dated early in the fifth century, and thus almost contemporary with Ambrose's old age.

2. In Antiquity it was customary to read aloud, even when reading alone and for oneself. Augustine (*Conf.*, VI, 3) suggests in this particular instance either that Ambrose avoided reading aloud to prevent being bothered by possible questions, or that he was doing so to conserve his voice.

3. It is indirectly through Augustine that we know the main things about Ambrose's life, as it was he who later suggested to Paulinus of Milan that he should write his biography, our principal

source. On Ambrose: J.-R. Palanque, *Saint Ambroise et l'Empire romain*, Paris, De Boccard, 1933; F. H. Dudden, *The Life and Times of St Ambrose*, 2 vol., Oxford 1935; G. Madec, *Saint Ambroise et la philosophie*, Paris, Ét. aug., 1974. Recently we have been able to read the new synthesis by H. Savon, *Ambroise de Milan (340–397)*, Paris, Desclée, 1997.

4. Paulinus of Milan, *Vita beati Ambrosii*, 7, ed. Pellegrino, Rome, 1961, p. 60: commentary on this ambiguous text in Madec, *Saint Ambroise et la philosophie*, pp. 23–5.

5. *De officiis*, I, 4, ed. Les Belles Lettres, Paris, 1984. On this text, see the commentary by the editor, M. Testard, in his *Introduction*, pp. 17–21.

6. Augustine himself takes up the imagery of the nut – which one must weigh in one's hand to see if it is full, then crack it – in a previously unpublished text, complementing sermon 341, recently published: *Sermon Dolbeau* 22 (*Mainz* 55), 22–3, in Dolbeau, *Vingt-Six Sermons*, pp. 574–5 (place and date: Carthage, 12 Dec. 403) see also p. 640.

7. There is agreement in thinking that Ambrose was, if not the only, at least the principal intermediary between Augustine and Origen, of whom Augustine was unable to have direct knowledge: cf. R. J. Teske, 'Origen and St Augustine's First Commentaries on Genesis', in *Origeniana Quinta*, Louvain, 1992, pp. 179–85.

8. On the first developments of this funerary architecture and arrangements, as early as the third century, see the paper by P.-A. Février, 'Le culte des morts dans les communautés chrétiennes durant le IIIe siècle', in *Atti del IX Congr, intern, di archeologia crist., Roma 21–27 se tt. 1975*, Rome, 1978, pp. 211–74.

9. *Pax et concordia sit convivio nostro*: a find by M. Bouchenaki in the necropolis of Matarès at Tipasa, reproduced in S. Lancel and M. Bouchenaki, *Tipasa de Maurétanie*, 3rd ed., Algiers, 1990, fig. 37, p. 64, and commented upon by H.-I. Marrou, 'Une inscription chrétienne de Tipasa et le refrigerium', in *Antiquités africaines*, 14, 1979, pp. 261–9.

10. This is suggested by A. Pincherle, *Vita di sant'Agostino*, Rome-Bari, Laterza, 1980, p. 51.

11. Cf. V. Arminjon, *Monique de Thagaste*, Montmélian, 1989, p. 17.

12. Cf. the *De moribus manichaeorum*, II, 74, on this Manichaean 'monastery', about which it is known from the *Contra Faustum* that it rapidly became a scandal. On the episode and the theory that Augustine might have been inspired by it, see Courcelle, *Recherches sur les 'Confessions' de saint Augustin*, pp. 178–9.

13. *Conf.*, VI, 26. For A. Solignac (note *ad locum*, in *BA*, 13, pp. 572–3), strictly speaking, this opinion of Epicurus does not appear in Cicero's *De finibus*, which is true. But M. Testard has pointed out that Augustine expresses just afterwards the epicurean theory of the height of sensual pleasure in the same terms as Cicero in the *De finibus*, on several occasions (*Saint Augustin et Cicéron*, pp. 99–100).

CHAPTER X : 386: Intellectual conversion

1. We saw him earlier refer to Epicurus (p. 75). He also had a good knowledge of stoicism (see for example *Contra Acad.*, III, 38), even though it seems exaggerated to speak of a 'stoic period'.

2. The expression is from G. Madec, in *Le Confessioni d'Agostino d'Ippona, libri VI–IX*, Palermo, 1985, p. 49.

3. The term is used by Palanque, *Saint Ambroise*, p. 140.

4. He was in fact called Mercurinus, but had taken the name of Ambrose's predecessor to gain acceptance by the Milanese: cf. G. Nauroy, 'Le fouet et le miel. Le combat d'Ambroise en 386 contre l'arianisme milanis', in *Recherches aug.*, 23, 1988, pp. 4–86, especially p. 11.

5. On the dates, see M. Meslin, *Les Ariens d'Occident (335–430)*, Paris, Le Seuil, 1967, p. 50, specifying Palanque, *Saint Ambroise*, pp. 160–1, and lastly Nauroy, 'Le fouet et le miel', notably pp. 66–8.

6. The expression is by Meslin, *Les Ariens d'Occident*, p. 53.

7. Courcelle, *Recherches sur les 'Confessions' de saint Augustin*, pp. 148–51.

8. *Recherches*, p. 151.

9. *Conf.*, VI, 6. A trace of the Pauline words in Ambrose's *De Iacob*, dated early 386: cf. Courcelle, *Recherches*, p. 98 and, for the date, Palanque, *Saint Ambroise*, pp. 444 and 515.

10. *Hexameron*, III, 7, 32; for the date, Courcelle, *Recherches*, p. 101.

11. On the relations between Plotinus and Ambrose, see P. Courcelle, 'Plotin et saint Ambroise' in *Revue de philologie*, 76, 1950, pp, 29–56; P. Hadot, 'Platon et Plotin dans trois sermons de saint

Ambroise', in *Revue des études latines*, 34, 1956, pp. 202–20; Courcelle, *Recherches*, pp. 93–138.

12. Courcelle, *Recherches*, pp. 251–2.

13. See an overall view of these concomitant permeations in Mandouze, *Saint Augustin*, p. 478.

14. The expression was initially used by Aimé Solignac, 'le cercle milanais', add. note 1 to the *Confessions*, *BA*, 14, pp. 526–35; it was recently taken up again with a variation by G. Madec, 'Le milieu milanais. Philosophie et christianisme', in *Bulletin de litt. eccl.*, 88, 3–4, 1987, pp. 194–205. See also A. Paredi, 'Agostino e i Milanesi', in *Agostino a Milano*, Palermo, Edizioni Augustinus, 1988, pp. 57–62.

15. *De beata vita*, I, 4. On the neoplatonism of Manlius Theodorus, cf. Courcelle, *Les Lettres grecques en Occident*, pp. 123–6.

16. Not far from where Ambrose lay dying, in 397, several of his deacons were quite frankly discussing who would succeed him; Simplicianus' name came up: 'Too old!' said one – '*Senex, sed bonus!*' retorted Ambrose, who had been following the conversation (Paulinus of Milan, *Vita Ambrosii*, 46).

17. Courcelle saw this Celsinus as Kelsinos of Castabala, mentioned in the *Souda* as the author of doxographies (*Les Lettres grecques en Occident*, pp. 179–81). For A. Solignac (*Les Confessions, BA*, 14, p. 535) he was Symmachus' own brother, Celsinus Titianus (and not Tatianus); but that is impossible, as Celsinus Titianus died in 380, or shortly afterwards: cf. *The Prosopography of the Later Roman Empire*, vol. I, pp. 917–18. The same chronological impossibility applies for Clodius Celsinus: *Les Lettres grecques en Occident*, p. 192.

18. Courcelle, *Les Lettres grecques en Occident*, pp. 126–8; *Recherches*, pp. 153–5.

19. J. J. O'Meara, *The Young Augustine*: the man who 'procured' for him was not necessarily a contemporary, and Porphyry had been translated into Latin by Marius Victorinus.

20. Solignac, in *Les Confessions, BA*, 13, p. 103, and Hadot, *Marius Victorinus*, p. 204.

21. The expression is Paul Henry's, 'Plotin et l'Occident', p. 78.

22. Henry, 'Plotin et l'Occident', p. 94.

23. The point was made by Solignac in *BA*, 13, pp. 682–9. A precise account was put forward by O. Du Roy, *L'Intelligence de la foi en la Trinité selon saint Augustin*, Paris, Ét. aug., 1966, pp. 69–70.

24. Du Roy, *L'Intelligence de la foi*, p. 71. After P. Courcelle, *Les 'Confessions' de saint Augustin dans la tradition littéraire*, Paris, Ét. aug., 1963, pp. 27–42, G. Madec discovered Porphyrian traces in Book VII of the *Confessions* ('La délivrance de l'esprit [Confessions, VII]', in *Le Confessioni' di Agostino d'Ippona*, Palermo, 1985, pp. 60–2). This seems indisputable, without proving an early reading of Porphyry. An excellent example of going too far with identification is given by P. F. Beatrice, '*Quosdam platonicorum libros*. The Platonic Readings of Augustine in Milan', in *Vigiliae Christianae*, 43, 1989, pp. 248–81.

25. Mandouze, *Saint Augustin*, p. 674.

26. This text from *Conf.* VII, 16, may in fact be compared notably with *Enneads*, I, 6 and V, 1 (see Solignac, *Les Confessions, BA*, 13, p. 687). But at the beginning of Augustine's text, the 'under Your guidance' [= God's guidance]' – already found in *Sol.*, II, 9 – introduces a fundamental difference in relation to Plotinus, *Enn.*, I, 6, 9, 24, which affirms in the same context: 'You no longer need a guide.'

27. Plato, *Politics*, 273 d; Plotinus, *Enn.*, I, VIII, 13, 16–17. The extraordinary subsequent fortunes of the expression in ascetic literature has been retraced by Courcelle; see notably his list of texts in *Les Confessions de saint Augustin dans la tradition littéraire*, pp. 623–40. Cf. also E. TeSelle, '*Regio dissimilitudinis* in the Christian Tradition and its Context in Late Greek Philosophy', in *Augustinian Studies*, 6, 1975, pp. 153–79.

28. Courcelle, *Recherches*, pp. 157–67; *Les 'Confessions' de saint Augustin dans la tradition littéraire*, pp. 43–58.

29. A reminiscence of Plotinus, I, VI (*On Beauty*) and VI, IX (*On the Good and the One*).

30. Mandouze, *Saint Augustin*, pp. 674–5; see also Solignac's commentary on this text in *Les Confessions, BA*, vol. 13, pp. 198–200.

31. Du Roy, *L'Intelligence de la foi*, p. 87.

32. Solignac, in *Les Confessions, BA*, 13, p. 702.

33. Even if one may think, with Du Roy (*L'Intelligence de la foi*, pp. 82 and 185–6), that in actual fact this metaphysical development dates from a year later, under the influence of Porphyry.

34. *De Isaac*, 7, 61; Augustine had kept this text among his papers; in 421, he would dish it up again to Julian of Eclanum, in the anti-Pelagian controversy: *Contra Iulianum*, I, 9, 44: *Ambrosius, in eo libro quem De Isaac et anima scripsit: 'quid est ergo, inquit, malitia, nisi boni indigentia?'*

35. Augustine *makes claims* on philosophy for Christian use; cf. *De doct. christ.*, II, 60: 'If those who are called philosophers are found to have said things that are true and correspond with our faith – particularly the case with the Platonists – not only must we not fear those things, but we must demand them, as from wrongful possessors, for our own use.'

36. On this subject, read the remarks by G. Madec, *Saint Augustin et la philosophie. Notes critiques*, Paris, Ét aug., 1996 (revised and augmented edition of a study first published in 1977), pp. 5–16; the sentence from *Conf.*, III, 10, quoted above appears as an epigraph to this book. See Mandouze, *Saint Augustin*, pp. 493–505.

37. On this subject, read – but cautiously – the evocative and attractive comments by Brown, *Augustine of Hippo*, p. 104: 'Augustine, however, would never be another Plotinus; perhaps he lacked the massive tranquillity of the great pagan. Just as the Manichaean "Wisdom" did not come to him only as an "inner" knowledge, but also as an elaborate moral regime, which enabled him for many years to master his sense of guilt and involvement in the flesh, so he now turned to find a discipline to complement the lucid spirituality of the Platonists.'

CHAPTER XI : 386: Conversion of the will

1. *City of God*, X, 29, 2: *Quod initium ... quidam Platonicus, sicut a sancto sene Simpliciano ... solebamus audire, aureis litteris conscribendum et per omnes ecclesias in locis eminentissimis propoinendum esse dicebat.* The demonstrative value of this *solebamus*, as indicating a number of meetings between Simplicianus and Augustine, on the latter's initiative, has however been challenged: see R. J. O'Connell, in *Revue des ét. aug.*, 19, 1973, pp. 87–90.

2. Already at the end of the third century, a direct student of Plotinus, Amelius, had wanted to see it as proof that the dogma of the Incarnation was derived from the Platonic doctrine of the descent of souls: cf. Eusebius, *Prep. evang.*, XI, 19, 1.

3. *Conf.*, VII, 27: *Itaque avidissime* arripui *venerabilem stilum spiritus tui et prae ceteris apostolum Paulum....* The same verb (*arripio*) is used in *Contra Acad.*, II, 5 and, despite the accompanying *titubans, properans and haesitans*, refers to the simultaneously intensive and extensive reading of the Apostle's letters, and not to the feverish seizing of St Paul's text in the garden in Milan, as Mandouze would have it, *Saint Augustin*, p. 261.

4. P. Courcelle (*Les 'Confessions' de saint Augustin dans la tradition littéraire*, pp. 36–42) saw in it a consequence of Augustine's reading of Porphyry's *Philosophy of oracles*; he was followed by Madec, who recognized an 'adoptionist' rather than Photinian deviation (cf. 'Une lecture de *Confessions*, VII, 13–27', in *Revue des ét. aug.*, 16, 1–2, 1970, pp. 106–7 and 117–19; also his *La Patrie et la Voie*, pp. 39–47).

5. On the 'Apollinarist crisis', see Tresmontant, *Introduction à la théologie chrétienne*, pp. 159–71.

6. In fact the *Life of Anthony*, written by Athanasius of Alexandria, some twenty years earlier, around 366/67, had been translated some years later by Evagrus of Antioch. The book was not yet known except in cenobitic circles, as we shall see a little further on.

7. At that time, with untranslatable words that express a function rather than a title, what would now be called, in similarly vague government jargon, 'representatives' were in fact, according to what we know about them, members of an imperial secret police, fairly well up in the hierarchy.

8. Attempts have been made to identify the two converts of Trier, and for Courcelle they are none other than Jerome himself and his friend Bonosius, *Recherches*, pp. 181–7.

9. For here, as has been seen (in particular Courcelle, *Recherches*, p. 192), it is Hercules hesitating between vice and virtue who is the prototype of this scenario.

10. For Courcelle (*Recherches*, p. 193), and subsequent upholders of its symbolic sense, this fig tree can be none other than the one beneath which Nathaniel was lying when Jesus spoke to him (John 1.48), and it is emphasized that in the customary exegesis of this text in St Augustine, Nathaniel's fig tree represents the mortal shadow of the sins of the human race, prey to concupiscence; we may also remember that, after tasting the forbidden fruit, Adam and Eve hid their nakedness with fig leaves (Gen. 3.7). But neither is there a lack of good arguments for seeing it as a real tree that had grown in the garden in Milan (cf. notably F. Bolgiani, *La Conversione di S. Agostino e l'VIII° libro delle Confessioni*, Turin, 1956, p. 110.

11. '*Quamdiu, quamdiu*, cras et cras!' Here there is probably a reminiscence of Persius, *Satires*, V, 66, in which the repeated word 'tomorrow' appears in a similar context. It is perhaps more interesting to note that St Augustine would remember it in his preaching, and the sinners who always put off

the moment of repentance till 'tomorrow' he would reproach for that *'cras, cras'*, so like the cawing of rooks when it would be preferable to hear the cooing of doves: *Sermon* 82, 14; 224, 4; *sermon Dolbeau* 25 (*Mainz* 61), 27 (Dolbeau, *Vingt-Six Sermons au peuple d'Afrique*, 1996, p. 267).

12. See above, note 10. Also L. C. Ferrari, 'The Arboreal Polarisation in Augustine's *Confessions*', in *Revue des ét. aug.*, 25, 1979, p. 43, for whom – in opposition to other exegetes – the mystical meaning of the fig tree in the Milan garden is to symbolize the rectitude of the will.

13. C. Mohrmann, 'The *Confessions* as a literary work of art', in *Études sur le latin des chrétiens*, vol. I, Rome, 1958, pp. 378–81, notes that in Augustine the symbol is usually superimposed on the reality, and especially in the case of the fig tree in the Milan garden.

14. *De divina domo* (instead of *vicina*), in the *Sessorianus*, a sixth-century manuscript; but F. Bolgiani (*Intorno al più antico codice delle Confessioni di S. Agostino*, Turin, 1954) tracked down a copyist's error which is found again elsewhere.

15. The mystical sense of this page was underlined by L. C. Ferrari, *'Ecce audio vocem de vicina domo: Conf.* 8, 12, 29', in *Augustiniana*, 33, 1983, pp. 232–45.

16. It is certain that he knew the practice, as in a letter (*Ep.* 55, 37) dated to the period of the *Confessions* he would reprove the practice of 'drawing lots' in the Gospels, when material interests were at stake.

17. *Tollere* and *legere* can have symbolic meanings, but first and foremost the usual and practical sense of taking a book in one's hands to consult it. To the numerous examples gathered by Courcelle, in *Les 'Confessions' de saint Augustin*, pp. 155–63, may be added one which escaped his staggering erudition: in an anonymous third-century text, *l'Histoire du roi Apollonius de Tyr*, chap. XXI (translated by É. Wolff, Paris, Anatolia Editions, 1996, p. 55).

18. P. Alfaric, *L'Évolution intellectuelle de saint Augustin*, pp. 393–4; P. Courcelle, 'Source chrétienne et allusions païennes de l'épisode du *"Tolle, lege"* ', in *Revue d'hist. et de philos. relig.*, 1952, p. 193; *Les 'Confessions' de saint Augustin*, pp. 190–4.

19. Courcelle, who does not wish to ascribe anything to miracles, has his own explanation on this subject: 'The *codex* of the *Epistles* was open at this page neither by chance nor by *sortilegium*, (but) simply because Augustine had reached that point in his reading when Ponticianus' visit interrupted him' (*Les 'Confessions'*, p. 194). Others, more radical, consider that the insertion of Rom. 13.13 in this account is purely fictitious and due only to the purpose of spiritual edification which moved Augustine when he was writing it around 400: L. C. Ferrari, 'Saint Augustine on the Road to Damascus', in *Augustinian Studies*, 13, 1982, pp. 151–70. In reaction to these criticisms, we may read a recent contribution by I. Bochet, 'Le livre VIII des *Confessions*: récit de conversion et réflexion théologique', in *Nouv. Revue théol.*, 118, 1996, pp. 363–84, which shows that the theological elaboration of the account does not imply that it is a fictional reconstruction of the event experienced, but reveals a fundamental interaction between spiritual experience and theological reflection.

CHAPTER XII : Cassiciacum

1. *C.Th.*, II, 8, 19: these *feriae vindemiales* followed the 'harvest holidays' in July, which did not interrupt university activities.

2. There is a very thorough discussion in Perler and Maier, *Les Voyages de saint Augustin*, pp. 179–80 and 192–6; lastly, L. Casiraghi, *Brianza Romana*, Cassago, Prov. di Como (Assoc. S. Agostino), 1992.

3. The uncertainty on this subject arises because in the *Contra Academicos*, whose debates we know began on 10 November, Augustine would say that at the time only a few days had elapsed since their settling into the countryside: *Pauculis igitur diebus transactis, posteaquam in agro vivere coepimus* (*Contra Acad.*, I, I, 4). But the inaccuracy of Augustine's chronological notes is frequently noticeable.

4. P. Brown, *Augustine of Hippo*, p. 119: 'A pious old woman, two uneducated cousins, and two private pupils, aged about 16'. Which scarcely applies to Trygetius, who was returning from a spell in the army (*Contra Acad.*, I, 4; *De ord.*, I, 5) and was certainly several years older.

5. This total absence of reference to Nebridius continues to be disturbing. A query remains over the Augustinian chronology of this summer's end in 386.

6. *Ep.* 3 and 4. On this correspondence, cf. G. Folliet, 'La correspondance entre Augustin et Nebridius', in *L'opera letteraria di Agostino tra Cassiciacum e Milano. Agostino nelle terre di Ambrogio (1–4 ottobre 1986)*, Palermo, 1987, pp. 191–215.

7. A. Manzoni, *The Betrothed*, chap. 17.

8. Their authenticity has sometimes been doubted; attempts have been made to show that the dialogues were fictitious: J. J. O'Meara, 'The Historicity of the Early Dialogues of Saint Augustine', in *Vigiliae Christianae*, 5, 1951, pp. 150–78. A refutation of these doubts may be read in G. Madec, 'L'historicité des *Dialogues* de Cassiciacum', in *Revue des ét. aug.*, 32, 1986, pp. 207–31.

9. P. Alfaric, *L'Évolution intellectuelle de saint Augustin*, p. 399.

10. On this question which was so very keenly disputed at the end of the nineteenth century, and even until quite recently, see the vigorous synthesis by G. Madec, 'Le néoplatonisme dans la conversion d'Augustin. État d'une question centénnaire (depuis Harnack et Boissier, 1883)', in *Internationales Symposium über den Stand der Augustinus-Forschung*, Würzburg, 1989, pp. 9–25 (resumed on a lighter note under the title: 'Le "jeune Augustin" ', in *Introduction aux 'Révisions' et à la lecture des oeuvres de saint Augustin*, Paris, Ét. aug., 1996, pp. 127–35.

11. Cf. for example H. Chadwick, *Augustine*.

12. He mentions this again in the *Soliloquies* (I, 26), datable at the earliest to December 386.

13. *Conf.*, IX, 13. Why did Ambrose recommend this particular reading? It might have been to test the reactions of the recently converted Manichaean, and what still remained of Manichaeism in Augustine could explain those reactions, which at that time were negative, according to L. C. Ferrari, 'Isaiah and the early Augustine', in *Mélanges T. J. Van Bavel*, vol. II, Louvain, 1990, pp. 739–56.

14. *Sol.*, II, 26: 'Am I to abandon my undertaking, expect from books written by others some argument that will help me resolve the problem?' Rather than to Ambrose of Milan, allusion is made to the philosophical researches of Manlius Theodorus, according to Courcelle (*Recherches*, pp. 203–10). As for the 'other' (*alius*, unnamed), with whom Augustine regrets he cannot communicate, he is probably Zenobius, the dedicatee of the *De ordine*.

15. *De beata vita*, II, 7: Augustine is addressing his brother Navigius: 'Do you at least know that you live? – I know it.' On the Augustinian antecedents of the Cartesian *cogito*, see G. Lewis, 'Augustinisme et cartésianisme', in *Augustinus Magister*, vol. II, Paris, Ét. aug., 1954, pp. 1087–104; and recently, M.-A. Vannier, 'Les anticipations du "cogito" chez saint Augustin', in *Revista agustiniana*, XXXVIII, 115–16, 1997, p. 665–79.

16. *Conf.*, VII, 16 (cf. above, pp. 127–30). These comparisons are made by Mandouze, *Saint Augustin*, p. 705, emphasizing also the link between this prayer in *Sol.*, II, 9 and the final prayer in the *De Trinitate*, XV, 51.

17. The various interpretations of this text are presented and discussed by D. Doucet, 'Recherche de Dieu, Incarnation et philosophie: *Sol.*, I, 2–6', in *Revue des ét. aug.*, 36, 1990, pp. 91–119.

18. The 'title' is given by Marrou, *Saint Augustin et l'augustinisme*, p. 98, but this is still the very recent interpretation of J. Doignon, 'La prière liminaire des *Soliloquia*, dans la ligne philosophique des *Dialogues* des Cassiciacum', in *Augustiniana Traiectina*, Paris, Ét. aug., 1987, pp. 85–105. But O. Du Roy (*L'Intelligence de la foi*, p. 200) saw 'in this admirable hymn a growing infusion of Christian themes into the Neoplatonic schema'.

CHAPTER XIII : Ostia

1. See J. Pépin, *Ex Platonicorum persona. Études sur les lectures philosophiques de saint Augustin*, Amsterdam, 1977, pp. 213–67. Cf. also I. Hadot, *Arts libéraux et philosophie dans la pensée antique*, Paris, Ét. aug., 1984, pp. 132–6: Porphyry's *Zètèmata* are used by Augustine quite freely.

2. See G. Madec, 'Le spiritualisme d'Augustin à la lumière du *De immortalitate animae*', in *Petites Études augustiniennes*, Paris, Ét. aug., 1994, pp. 113–19. A good commentary on the role played by this 'muddle' in the elaboration of Augustinian ontology, especially where the state of the soul is concerned: E. Zum Brunn, 'Le dilemme de l'être et du néant chez saint Augustin', in *Recherches aug.*, 6, 1969, pp. 3–102, more precisely, pp. 34–41.

3. G. Bardy, in an additional note to *Retract.*, I, 6: *BA*, 12, p. 565.

4. On the fate of the *De grammatica*, see Marrou, *Saint Augustin et la fin de la culture antique*, pp. 571–2; lastly, V. A. Law, 'St Augustine's "*De Grammatica*": Lost or Found?' in *Recherches aug.*, 19, 1984, pp. 155–83.

5. See above, pp. 140 and 413. On the *De musica*, cf. Marrou, *Saint Augustine*, pp. 266–73 and 580–3.

6. *Retract.*, I, 6. The authenticity of a treatise on dialectics handed down under Augustine's name is not accepted, however: Augustine, *De dialectica*, translated with Introduction and Notes by B. D.

Jackson, from the text newly edited by J. Pinborg, Dordrecht-Boston, 1975. French translation in M. Baratin and F. Esbordes, *L'Analyse linguistique dans l'Antiquité classique. I. Les Théories*, Paris, 1981, pp. 211–31.

7. Thanks to the 'flair' and knowledge of two learned philologists, two important batches of previously unpublished texts recently came to light: the letters retrieved by Johannes Divjak in the depths of the Bibliothèque nationale in Paris and the Bibliothéque municipale in Marseille (ed. princeps: *CSEL*, vol. 88, Vienna, 1981), and the new sermons identified by François Dolbeau in the collections of the Stadtbibliothek of Mainz and published by him (*Vingt-Six Sermons au peuple d'Afrique*, 1996).

8. Although the monuments of North Africa are not included in it, read the chapter devoted to baptisteries by Jean Guyon in *Naissance des arts chrétiens. Atlas des monuments paléochrétiens de la France*, Paris, Imprimerie nationale, 1991, pp. 70–87. Lastly, with regard to a recent book on baptismal liturgy, see a clarification of the structural development of baptisteries and its liturgical consequences: N. Duval, 'Architecture et liturgie', in *Revue des ét. aug.*, 42, 1, 1996, pp. 121–7.

9. It cannot be ruled out, however, that he was baptized in the old baptistery in Milan: cf. Perler and Maier, *Les Voyages de saint Augustin*, pp. 143–4. Lastly, M. Mirabella Roberti, 'I battisteri di Sant'Ambrogio', in *Agostino a Milano. Il battesimo. Agostino nelle terre di Ambrogio*, Palermo, 1988, pp. 77–83.

10. *Conf.*, IX, 14. Augustine's extreme discretion about his baptism continues to intrigue. The theory, advanced by H. Chadwick ('Donatism and the Confessions of Augustine', in *Philanthropia kai Eusebia. Festschrift für A. Dihle*, Göttingen, 1993, pp. 23–35), that it might be explained by his desire not to lay himself open to the criticisms of the Donatists is not really convincing.

11. On Zenobius, see above, p. 85. Courcelle, *Recherches*, pp. 208–10 has made a good analysis of the complex relations between Augustine and Theodorus.

12. Cf. P.-A. Février, 'Ostie et Porto à la fin de l'Antiquité', in *Mel. de l'École française de Rome*, 70, 1958, pp. 323–30.

13. R. Meiggs, *Roman Ostia*, Oxford, 1960, pp. 211–13, enumerates the great senatorial families who owned residences at Ostia; among others the Anicii, with whom P. Brown, *Augustine of Hippo*, p. 128, seems tempted to place Augustine's stay.

14. See the *Octavius* of Minucius Felix, where the scene takes place on a late summer's morning, during the 'grape-harvesting holidays', which were also the period of Augustine's stay at Ostia.

15. People have sometimes refused to give the 'ecstasy at Ostia' a mystical 'label', objecting that mystical experience is an individual thing: cf. J. A. Mourant, 'Ostia Reexamined: A Study in the Concept of Mystical Experience', in *Philosophy of Religion*, I, 1970, pp. 42–3. But that is to forget the communal ecstasy of St John of the Cross and St Theresa of Avila.

16. In *Conf.*, IX, 24, the reading *attigimus* is to be preferred to *attingimus*, adopted in the Skutella edition followed in *BA*, 14, p. 118. *Attigimus* had already been chosen by A. Mandouze, 'L'''extase d'Ostie''. Possibilités et limites de la méthode des parallèles textuels', in *Augustinus Magister*, I, Paris, Ét. aug., 1954, p. 73 and note 1, p. 78.

17. Courcelle, *Recherches*, p. 224.

18. The choice of words is Solignac's: 'negative discourse in which the language of creatures and the language of the spirit vigorously renounce each other to proclaim that God alone must speak, and alone speaks fitly of Himself' (*BA*, 13, p. 194).

19. See the 'pioneering' book by P. Henry, *La Vision d'Ostie. Sa place dans la vie et l'oeuvre de saint Augustin*, Paris, Vrin, 1938, notably pp. 15–36; and chiefly the 'critical edition' of these texts by Mandouze, 'L'''extase d'Ostie'' ', pp. 67–84.

20. Solignac, in *BA*, 13, p. 147 (cf. on this subject Courcelle, *Recherches*, pp. 109–22).

21. Henry, *L'Extase d'Ostie*, pp. 42–3. Rather paradoxically, Courcelle, *Recherches*, p. 226, thought that because of the presence and participation of Monica, a 'rank and file' Christian woman, the experience at Ostia was doubtless less specifically Plotinian in reality than in the account in the *Confessions*.

22. Mandouze, *Saint Augustin*, p. 701, n. 4.

23. *Sermon* 52, 16 (dated around 410/11), to be read in the translation by G. Humeau, *Les Plus Beaux Sermons de saint Augustin* (new ed. by J.-P. Bouhot), Paris, Ét. aug., 1986, pp. 218–19.

24. He would write that he had heard that the 'baths' got their name from the Greek word *balaneion* and thus, by virtue of an approximate etymology, that 'they drive anxiety from the mind' (*Conf.*, IX, 32). An architrave in the baths in the forum at Ostia bore the inscription, in Greek, *loutron alexiponon*, the 'bath that chases sorrow away': R. Meiggs, *Roman Ostia*, p. 475 and pl. XXXVIII, c.

25. On the gender of the word 'hymne', which without any reason people have wanted to feminize when speaking of Christian singing, cf. J. Fontaine, in his introduction to *Ambroise de Milan, Hymnes*, Paris, Éd. du Cerf, 1992, p. 12, note 2.

26. Meiggs, *Roman Ostia*, p. 400; for the text of the fragments: E. Diehl, *Inscr. lat. christ. veteres*, vol. IV (*suppl.*), ed. J. Moreau and H.-I. Marrou, 1967, no. 91, p. 2.

27. G. B. de Rossi, *Inscr. christ. urbis Romae*, II, p. 252, XXII.

28. On this person: *The Prosopography of the Later Roman Empire*, vol. II, pp. 219–20. Perhaps Anicius Bassus had Monica's tomb restored in the period following Alaric's destructions: W. Wischmeyer, 'Zum Epitaph der Monica', in *Römische Quartalschrift*, 70, 1975, pp. 32–41.

CHAPTER XIV : A second season in Rome

1. Cf. J.-M. André and M.-F. Baslez, *Voyager dans l'Antiquité*, Paris, Fayard, 1993, p. 438. Monica died while her son was still in his thirty-third year, therefore before 13 November 387 (*Conf.*, IX, 28).

2. The 'narrative' part of the *Confessions* stops at the death of Monica. After this, the strictly 'biographical' elements are rare, scattered and often uncertain; hence the increasing incursions of a vocabulary of hypothesis in the 'factual' account.

3. *De natura boni*, 47 (written around 405). The 'confessions' mentioned in this text might be the admissions extorted from Priscillian and his faithful followers (held to be Manichaeans) at the trial in Trier in January 385.

4. Begun in Rome in 387–8, the whole was completed or at least revised at Thagaste one or two years later, as indicated by the reference made in the *incipit* of the *De moribus* (I, 1) to the *De Genesi contra Manicheos*, which dates to 388/89.

5. The *Contra Felicem manichaeum* and the *Contra Faustum* must still be dated to 404; on these chronological problems, cf. G. Madec's clarification, *Introduction aux 'Revisions' et à la lecture des oeuvres de saint Augustin*, Paris, Ét. aug., 1996, pp. 150–3.

6. *De mor. eccl. cathol.*, I, 63: 'you teach slaves to adhere to their masters not so much by the necessity of their condition as by the attraction of duty ... you teach kings to watch over their peoples, you instruct peoples to submit themselves to their kings.' To gain some measure of the road travelled by Augustine since the autumn of 386, we must read the role – important but still 'secular' judged by our modern criteria – which he assigned to Christian wisdom for the upbringing and intellectual and moral training of the young in the *De ordine*, II, 25.

7. Contrary to what H.-I. Marrou says about it: 'The Evodius of the *De quantitate animae* has no other characteristic than to be exaggeratedly stupid and fall into all the traps laid for him by Augustine. Like the detective's 'sidekick' in our crime novels, he is there only to provide the 'master' with the opportunity to display all his knowledge' (*Saint Augustin et la fin de la culture antique*, p. 309).

8. *Lib. arb.*, III, 56–8, where four theories are examined, between which Augustine does not choose, and would always find it hard to make up his mind; cf. G. Madec's excellent note, in *BA*, 6 (1976), pp. 578–83.

9. The *Retractations* (I, 9, 1) formally substantiate this. As for the starting-point, it could have provided the title, as is suggested by the title found in Possidius' *Elenchus*, IV, 3: *Unde malum, et de libero arbitrio libri tres*; but the *Retractations* explain the definitive choice of the title. G. Madec has shown that the overall plan of the treatise, its general economy and main themes were already sketched out at the time of the discussions in Rome in 388: '*Unde malum?* Book I of the *De libero arbitrio*', in *Petites Études augustiniennes*, Paris, 1994, pp. 123–4.

10. See P. Brown, *Augustine of Hippo*, p. 148, but also the remarks of G. Madec, '*Unde malum?*' in *Petites Études augustiniennes*, p. 133.

CHAPTER XV : *Otium* at Thagaste

1. Evodius would succeed him in this see some years later, and it may be thought that his election had been prepared by contacts made in the autumn of 388.

2. *De cura pro mortuis gerenda*, XI, 13. Commentator on the *Dream of Scipio*, Eulogius would be one of the – minor – figures of Latin Neoplatonism in the late fourth century: cf. J. Flamant, *Macrobe et le néoplatonisme latin à la fin du IVe siècle*, Leiden, 1977, p. 720.

3. Patricius, his father, had departed prematurely, as we know (cf. above, p. 8) and, in a text shortly after his return to Thagaste, Augustine would say that he had never known his grandfather (*De musica*, VI, 32: *Aliter enim cogito patrem quem saepe vidi, aliter avum quem numquam vidi*).

4. The references he would later make to this act are allusive or symbolic and juridically imprecise, whether in the '*pauci agelluli paterni contempti*' mentioned in letter 126, 7 (to Albina) in 411, or the pretty sentence in sermon 355, 1 (delivered in 425): *Ego tenuem paupertatulam meam vendidi*. But they seem to imply joint ownership of family possessions. This seems more likely than a parcelling out and sharing, to the advantage of Navigius, as has sometimes been thought (P. Brown, *Augustine of Hippo*, p. 132; A. Pincherle, *Vita di sant'Agostino*, p. 98).

5. First, his son Adeodatus, who would soon vanish, but also his brother Navigius, of whom we know nothing afterwards, but who had offspring, and his sister, who would later become a nun.

6. P. Monceaux, 'Saint Augustin et saint Antoine. Contribution à l'histoire du monachisme', in *Miscellanea Agostiniana*, II, Rome, 1931, pp. 74–5. Complement with G. Lawless' 'Augustine's first monastery: Thagaste or Hippo?' in *Augustinianum*, 25, 1985, pp. 65–78, recognizing in the cenobitic life led at Thagaste all the characteristics of a lay monastery before the event.

7. Cf. the detailed accounts by Mandouze, *Saint Augustine*, pp. 554–6, and G. Folliet's analysis, 'La correspondance entre Augustin et Nebridius', pp. 191–215.

8. G. Folliet, ' "*Deificare in otio*". Aug., *Ep*. X, 2', in *Recherches aug.*, 2, 1962, pp. 225–36.

9. *De vera rel.*, XXXV, 65; cf. R. J. Teske, 'Augustine's Epistula X: Another Look at *deificare in otio*', in *Augustinianum*, 32, 1992, pp. 288–99.

10. Cf. *sermon Dolbeau 6* (*Mainz 13*), 1 and 2 (Dolbeau, *Vingt-Six Sermons au peuple d'Afrique*, pp. 459–60), text inaccurately dated to the early fifth century, where Augustine uses the epithet *deificator* for God and affirms: *Vult enim deus non solum vivificare, sed etiam deificare nos*. On the development of Augustine's thinking on this concept, see G. Bonner, 'Augustine's Conception of Deification', in *Journal of Theol. Studies*, 37, 1986, pp. 369–86.

11. This is the whole object of Du Roy's thesis, *L'Intelligence de la foi*.

12. Du Roy, *L'Intelligence de la foi*, p. 398.

13. Cf. Madec, *La Patrie et la Voie*, p. 77.

14. Over the years and in his texts, Augustine would become more specific about his thoughts on 'Abraham's bosom': cf. the note by A. C. De Veer, in *BA*, 22, pp. 845–6, and above, pp. 443ff.

15. In the *Confessions* (XI, 14), Augustine would again mention this objection and quote the pleasantry with which he was sometimes answered: 'God prepared Gehenna for those who pry into these deep subjects.' But he would add that it was too serious a matter to be settled by a jocular reply.

16. He would return to it in *Conf.*, XI, 11: *In hoc principio, deus, fecisti caelum et terram in verbo tuo, in filio tuo, in virtute tua, in sapientia tua, in veritate tua* . . . . And, in *Conf.*, XII, 29, he would pick out five meanings of the *In principio*, when Origen saw six. Cf. A. Solignac, 'Exégèse et métaphysique. Genèse 1, 1–3 chez saint Augustin', in *In principio. Interprétations des premiers versets de la Genèse*, Paris, 1973, pp. 153–71; lastly, M.-A. Vannier, 'Origène et Augustin interprètes de la création', in *Origeniana Sexta, Actes du coll. de Chantilly, 30 août–3 septembre 1993*, Louvain, 1995, pp. 729–32.

17. On Augustine's progress regarding the first chapters of Genesis, read the fine study by G. Pelland, 'Augustin rencontre le livre de la Genèse', in *Lectio Augustini*, VIII, Palermo, 1992, pp. 15–53; and the analyses by E. Gilson, *Introduction à l'étude de saint Augustin*, Paris, Vrin, 1929, pp. 242–52.

18. *Gn. adv. man.*, II, 32. Cf. J. Pépin, 'Saint Augustin et le symbolisme néoplatonicien de la vêture', in *Augustinus Magister*, I, 1954, pp. 293–306, more precisely, pp. 301–5.

19. Frequently referring to the Alexandrian exegetic tradition (Philo): see the exegesis of Gen. 3.14, in *Gn. adv. man.*, II, 26 and the commentary by Du Roy, *L'Intelligence de la foi*, p. 347.

20. *Ep*. 15, 1: *Scripsi quiddam de catholica religione* . . . *quod tibi volo ante adventum meum mittere*. The phrase *ante adventum meum* seems to signify that Augustine was absent from Thagaste for the time – necessarily quite long – of the composition of the *De vera religione*: cf. Perler and Maier, *Les Voyages de saint Augustin*, pp. 150–1.

21. The expression is by F. Van Der Meer, *Saint Augustin, pasteur d'âmes*, vol. I, Paris, 1955, p. 32.

22. Cf. Du Roy, *L'Intelligence de la foi*, pp. 309–16, in reaction against W. Theiler, *Porphyrios und Augustin*, 1933, which gave greater weight to Porphyrian influence; lastly, a qualified appreciation by F. Van Fleteren, 'Background and commentary on Augustine's *De vera religione*', in *Lectio Augustini*, X, Rome, 1994, pp. 33–49.

23. On this subject, besides the analyses by Mandouze, *Saint Augustin*, pp. 495–508, read the note by A. C. De Veer, 'Néoplatonisme et christianisme', in *BA*, 8, nouv. édit., 1982, pp. 471–83.

24. For us, an 'intellectual' is a learned or literary personage who appears in public life and thus who 'gets involved'; which implies a democracy – or at least a liberal regime – and wide-ranging and free information. In France, the 'intellectual' had a difficult birth in the eighteenth century with the 'Enlightenment', was affirmed in the following century in the person of Victor Hugo and finally triumphed with Zola; but there is no 'J'accuse' without the headline on the front page of '*L'Aurore*'.

25. *Ep.* 19; in 388–90, Augustine thus absented himself from Thagaste at least a second time: cf. Perler and Maier, *Les Voyages de saint Augustin*, p. 151.

26. *City of God*, IV, 8. Cf. Mandouze, 'Saint Augustin et la religion romaine', in *Recherches aug.*, I, 1958, pp. 187–223, especially pp. 196–9.

27. *Operum s. Augustini elenchus*, X⁵, ed. Wilmart, *Miscellanea Agostiniana*, II, Rome, 1931, pp. 182–3; cf. G. Folliet, 'La correspondance d'Augustin a Thagaste', in *Lectio Augustini*, 9, Palermo, 1993, p. 86.

28. It seems that Adeodatus was born in 372 (cf. above, p. 27); so the discussions that gave rise to the *De magistro* would have been in 388/89.

29. Cf. Marrou, *Saint Augustin et la fin de la culture antique*, pp. 580–3, however, on the probability of a revision of Book VI of the *De musica* some years later.

30. Cf. Madec's 'Introduction', in *BA*, 6 (3ʳᵈ ed., 1976), pp. 16–21 (and also by him, 'Analyse du *De magistro*', in *Revue des ét. aug.*, 20, 1975, pp. 63–71); lastly, F. J. Crosson, 'The structure of the *De magistro*', in *Revue des ét. aug.*, 35, 1989, pp. 120–7, which picks out three parts.

31. Augustine uses the word *docere*; but, with A. Mandouze, one must admit that 'one is doomed to understand nothing of the *De magistro* if one insists on translating *docere* by a word of invariably prescriptive type such as "to teach"' ('Quelques principes de "linguistique augustinienne" dans le *De magistro*', in *Forma futuri*, Turin, 1975, p. 793).

32. *De magistro*, 24. On these aspects of 'metalanguage' in the *De magistro*, cf. M. Baratin and F. Desbordes, 'Semiologie et metalinguistique chez saint Augustin', in *Langages*, 1982, fasc. 65, pp. 75–89.

33. *De magistro*, 33. This line of argument was already that of the sceptics and certain stoics: cf. M. Baratin, 'Les origines stoïciennes de la théorie augustinienne du signe', in *REL*, 59, 1981, pp. 260–8.

34. *De magistro*, 38. G. Madec, 'Saint Augustin et la maître intérieur', *Connaissance des Pères de l'Église*, 48, Dec. 1992, pp. 16ff. clearly show that here it is a matter of a Christian transformation of the Platonic theory of knowing.

35. *De magistro*, 46. We are thus all fellow-students, 'which is, to the letter, a commonplace of Augustinian preaching', as Madec puts it, who has collected a fair number of references on the theme '*Unus est magister vester Christus*', in his sermons and letters: cf. additional note in *BA*, 6 (3ʳᵈ ed.), 1976, pp. 545–7.

PART II : The Bishop of Hippo

CHAPTER XVI : Hippo Regius: Priesthood

1. *Ep.* 15, 1: Augustine would send his *De vera religione* to Romanianus, at least if writing material is not lacking (*si charta non desit*); by *charta* must be understood leaves of prepared papyrus, which were both costly and fragile; he warns him that he must be content with the quality of copy that the studio of a certain Maiorinus could offer.

2. The beginnings of the monastery of the Chevreuse valley go back as far as the early thirteenth century, the date when the first establishment was set up in a marshy dale called 'Porrois', Latinized as 'Port-Royal'. As for the pre-Roman place name *Hippo* (also represented in the ancient name for Bizerte: Hippo Diarrhytus), hypothetically linked to a semitic root, it could mean 'gulf', 'bay', and not 'port'. The coincidence about which the Jansenists of Port-Royal enthused was thus imaginary.

3. T. Shaw, *Voyage dans la régence d'Alger*, trans. J. MacCarthy (reissued Tunis, 1980). Cf. also E. Marec, *Hippone-la-Royale, antique Hippo Regius*, 2ⁿᵈ ed., Algiers, 1956, p. 89.

4. Cf. S. Dahmani, *Hippo Regius*, Algiers, Ministry of Information and Culture, 1973, p. 20, who thinks that the site of ancient Hippo was occupied until the tenth century, in other words, to the

end of the Fatimid period. That was when the town was moved nearly 3 kilometres to the north, on the site of Bône, now Annaba.

5. Cf. J.-P. Morel, 'Recherches stratigraphiques à Hippone', in *Bulletin d'arch. alg.*, III, 1968, pp. 51–2.

6. *Bellum Africum*, 96. Had this port, originally an estuarine or river-mouth port, very probably (on the Seybouse or the Bou Djemaa), subsequently been rearranged as the port of Lepcis Magna in the Severan period, or moved northwards on to the site of the present-day Bône/Annaba port? Nothing definite has been brought to light; cf. lastly the discussions of S. Dahmani, 'Le port de Bûna au Moyen Âge', in *Afrique du Nord antique et mediévale. Spectacles, vie portuaire, religion*, Paris, Éd. du CTHS, 1992, pp. 361–77.

7. *CIL*, VIII, 5351: '*Curator frumenti comparandi in annonam Urbis.*'

8. Cf. G. Picard, *La Civilisation de l'Afrique romaine*, 2nd ed., Paris, Ét. aug., 1990, pp. 69–70.

9. See the pictures collected and commented upon by K. Dunbabin, *The Mosaics of Roman North Africa. Studies in Iconography and Patronage*, Oxford, Clarendon Press, 1978, notably pp. 109–23 and figs. 95–113.

10. On this process, read Picard, *La Civilisation de l'Afrique romaine*, pp. 71–3.

11. With medium-sized properties, like those analysed by T. Kotula, '*Modicam terram habes, id est villam*. Sur une notion de *villa* chez saint Augustin', in *L'Africa romana*, 5, Sassari, 1988, pp. 339–44.

12. See the account of these kinds of status in Picard, *La Civilisation de l'Afrique romaine*, pp. 63–8. Some still survived in Vandal Africa at the end of the fifth century, as has been shown by 'tablets' found near Tebessa: C. Courtois, L. Leschi, C. Perrat and C. Saumagne, *Tablettes Albertini, actes privés d'époque vandale*, Paris, 1952.

13. On this use of Punic and the evidence we have of it thanks to Augustine, cf. S. Lancel, 'La fin et la survie de la latinité, pp. 270–3.

14. Cf. Madec, *Introduction aux 'Revisions'*, p. 40, taking up a former suggestion by S. Lenain de Tillemont, *Mémoires*, vol. XIII, p. 151.

15. For the garden (*hortus*), cf. sermon 355, 2; on the material implications of Possidius' words (*monasterium intra ecclesiam mox instituit: Vita Aug.*, V, 1) and notably on the sense of *intra ecclesiam*, cf. Mandouze, *Saint Augustin*, p. 214, note 2: it is naturally a matter of the whole of the perimeter of the Christian *insula* at Hippo, and not of the church in the strict sense of building.

16. A good overall assessment of Augustine's priesthood comes from G. Madec, 'Augustin prêtre', in *De Tertullien aux Mozarabes. Mélanges offerts à J. Fontaine*, vol. I, Paris, 1992, pp. 185–99.

17. *Sermon* 118, 1: *Si non potes intellegere, crede ut intellegas; praecedit fides, sequitur intellectus.* Cf. also In *Ioh. evang. tract.* 29, 6: *Ergo noli quaerere intellegere ut credas, sed crede ut intellegas.* The basic scriptural text, often quoted by Augustine, notably in his sermons, is as we know from Isaiah 7.9: 'If ye will not believe, surely ye shall not be established.' This dialectic would end with the developments of the *De Trinitate*: cf. above, pp. 368–9.

18. The Manichaeans too were looking for a debate, if only for publicity purposes, cf. R. Lim, 'Manichaeans and public disputation in Late Antiquity', in *Recherches aug.*, 26, 1992, pp. 233–72, notably p. 252.

19. E. Marec, *Monuments chrétiens d'Hippone, ville épiscopale de saint Augustin*, Paris, AMG, 1958, p. 224, note 6, was tempted to identify them with the private baths of the sea-front quarter, which had a vast covered gallery.

20. *Contra Fort.*, 16, reading *Ep.* 2, 1–18. F. Decret rightly insisted on the authority which the Manichaeans ascribed to St Paul: 'L'utilisation des épitres de Paul chez les manichéens d'Afrique', in *Sussidi patristici*, V, Rome, Augustinianum, 1989, pp. 29–83.

21. But cf. above, p. 107, on the need he sometimes had to read them, for want of having committed them to memory in his youth.

22. Cf. above, p. 130. We have now learned from a hitherto unpublished letter from Jerome, recently published, that Aurelius had been 'archdeacon' of Carthage – Jerome's word – at least since 382, the date when he had taken part in a legation to Pope Damasus in Rome, alongside his bishop, Cyrus, which also relocates the latter's episcopacy in the time scale: *Ep.* 27*, 1, *BA*, 46 B, 1987, p. 394.

23. Cf. A.-M. La Bonnardière, s. v. *Aurelius episcopus*, in *Augustinus-Lexikon*, vol. 1, 1994, col. 553.

24. I am following the interpretation of this letter by A. Mandouze in *Prosopographie de l'Afrique chrét.*, I. *Afrique (303–533)*, Paris, CNRS, 1982, s. v. *Aurelius 1*, p. 105, which supposes that one should read, in letter 22, 1, *fratrum coetus qui* apud eos *coepit coalescere* (and not *apud nos*).

25. In fact he was recalling the bans by Ambrose in Milan, which Monica had experienced, but

forgetting the 'tolerance' he had witnessed at St Peter's in Rome, in Alypius' company: above, p. 181.

26. More especially in the western provinces (Sitifian and Caesarean Mauretania), where they seem to have carried on despite the conciliar bans of the late fourth century.

27. 'Bréviaire d'Hippone', c. 29, re-issued at the time of the council of Carthage on 28 August 397: cf. *Concilia Africae*, a. 345–a. 525, ed. C. Munier, *CCL*, 149, 1974, pp. 41 and 185.

28. It is the basilica now generally designated as the 'basilica of St Monica', on the heights of the quarter known as 'Hamilcar's', in Carthage.

29. Cf. *sermon* 311, 5 (dated between 403 and 405); *Enarr. in Psalm.* 32, 2, 1 (September 403), and lastly *sermon Dolbeau* 2 (= *Mainz* 5), 5 (January 404 or 405): cf. Dolbeau, *Vingt-Six Sermons au peuple d'Afrique*, p. 330.

30. For E. Marec, this would be the 'basilica with five naves', but it is very doubtful; this brings one back to the delicate problems of Hippo's religious topography: above, pp. 242–4.

31. *Ep.* 29, 9. This had not escaped the Manichaeans, who used it as an argument against the Christians; Augustine would record Faustus' words thus: 'Your idols are your martyrs ... And you appease the shades of the dead as well, with wine and meats' (*Contra Faustum*, XX, 21).

32. *Ep.* 29, 11: *Et quoniam in haereticorum basilica audiebamus ab eis solita convivia celebrata.* With Mandouze (*Saint Augustin*, p. 650, note 6), in opposition to O. Perler ('L'église principale et les autres sanctuaires chrétiens d'Hippone-la-Royale', in *Revue des ét. aug.*, I, 1955, p. 305), I think it is more in keeping with the parallel drawn by Augustine – and also with the structure of the sentence – to understand *audiebamus* as meaning 'we heard' rather than 'we heard about'; which is not without consequences for theories relating to the whereabouts of the Donatist basilica.

33. For the date and place, cf. *Concilia Africae, a. 345–a. 525*, ed. C. Munier, *CCL*, 149, 1974, p. 182; for the description of the council, cf. *Retract.*, I, 17, *initio: plenarium totius Africae concilium.*

34. Marec, in *Monuments chrétiens d'Hippone*, pp. 152–6 (followed by H.-I. Marrou, 'La basilique chrétienne d'Hippone d'après le résultat des dernières fouilles', in *Revue des ét. aug.*, 6, 1960, p. 152), proposed locating this secretarium in the vast ensemble B of the western annexes of the great three-naved basilica. This is very arguable for typological reasons: cf. lastly N. Duval, 'Hippo Regius', in *Reallexikon für Antike und Christentum*, XV, 1989, col. 451.

35. Cf. for instance O. Perler, in *Revue des ét. aug.*, 1, 1955, p. 307.

36. There would however be three Sitifian bishops (Caecilianus, Honoratus and Theodorus) at Hippo in 393, who came with the precise purpose of asking for their territory to be made into an ecclesiastical province, with the creation of a primacy, which they were granted.

37. Two canons were read at the council of Carthage in 525 and five others were found by C. Munier, 'Cinq canons inédits du concile d'Hippone du 8 octobre 393', in *Revue de droit canonique*, 12, 1968, pp. 16–29; cf. also *Concilia Africae a. 345–a. 525*, pp. 20–1 and 269.

38. See an analysis by C. Munier of this canonical legislation in *Augustinus-Lexikon*, vol. 1. col. 1092–3.

39. Cf. for example the remarks by A. Trapé, *Saint Augustin, l'homme, le pasteur, le mystique* (trans. from the Italian by V. Arminjon), Paris, Fayard, 1988, p. 123.

CHAPTER XVII : Donatism

1. This, for example, is the analysis of W. H. C. Frend, *The Donatist Church. A Movement of Protest in North Africa*, Oxford, 1952, p. 184.

2. Frend, *The Donatist Church*, pp. 76–86.

3. On the details and limits of this heritage, cf. S. Lancel, *Carthage* (English trans.), Oxford, Basil Blackwell, 1995, pp. 435–6.

4. Cf. C. Lepelley, 'Juvenes et circoncellions: les derniers sacrifices humains de l'Afrique antique', in *Antiquités africaines*, 15, 1980, pp. 261–71.

5. On the facts, cf. the account by P. Monceaux, *Histoire littéraire de l'Afrique chrétienne*, vol. II, pp. 209–32; lastly, P. Mattei, 'Cyprien de Carthage', in *Histoire des saints et de la sainteté chrétienne*, vol. II, Paris, Hachette, 1987, pp. 122–6.

6. This fourth edict inaugurated the period which Christians at that time called the *dies thurificationis*, the 'days of sacrifice', refusal of which ended in the martyrdom of a heroic minority. The 'Passions' which were preserved were recently conveniently collected, translated and commentated by J.-L. Maier, *Le Dossier du donatisme*, vol. I: *Des origines à la mort de Constance II (303–361)*, Berlin,

1987, pp. 39–111. The general account of the facts by P. Monceaux remains valid (*Histoire littéraire de l'Afrique chrétienne*, vol. III, pp. 21–40).

7. P. Chiesa, 'Un testo agiografico africano ad Aquileia: gli *Acta* di Gallonio e dei martiri di Timida Regia', in *Analecta Bollandiana*, 114, 1996, pp. 241–68: no translation but with an introductory commentary.

8. 'In the heavens!' he would finally say: *Acta s. Gallonii*, 28 and 31.

9. In the face of Gallonius' obstinacy, Anullinus would exclaim (§ 32): 'So much time wasted!' (in Latin *Tantum temporis consumptum*, a very classical exclamatory accusative which misled the text's editor).

10. Some replied: *in cella Sabaratias*, which would perhaps be better read as *in Cellas Abaratias* (§ 23).

11. Cf. Y. Duval, *Loca sanctorum Africae*, vol. II, p. 725.

12. The edition of the *Acta s. Gallonii* gives 'pridie Kalendas Ianuarii', which in the abbreviated form is: *II Kal. Ian.*, to be compared with: *II Kal. Iun.*, the abbreviated form of the date 31 May.

13. *Contra Cresc.*, III, 29–30: on the date, S. Lancel, 'Les débuts du donatisme: la date du "Protocole de Cirta" et de l'élection épiscopale de Silvanus', in *Revue des ét. aug.*, 25, 1979, pp. 217–29; the date was postponed by a year, after 20 April 308, by B. Kriegbaum, *Kirche der Traditoren oder Kirche der Martyrer. Die Vorgeschichte des Donatismus*, Innsbruck-Vienna, 1986, p. 149.

14. Probably in 308; for the details, cf. S. Lancel, 'Donatisme', in *Augustinus-Lexikon*, vol. 2, 1999.

15. Eusebius, *Ecclesiastical History*, X, 6 (*Sources chrétiennes*, vol. 55), pp. 110–11.

16. For details, cf. S. Lancel, 'Donatistae', in *Augustinus-Lexikon*, vol. 2, 1999.

17. *Acta purg. Felicis*, in *App. d'Optat*, 2 = J.-L. Maier, *Le Dossier du donatisme*, vol. I, pp. 171–87.

18. *App. d'Optat*, 10 = J.-L. Maier, *Dossier*, vol. I, pp. 246–52.

19. On the circumcellions and the different aspects assumed by their movement, see C. Lepelley, 'Circumcelliones', in *Augustinus-Lexikon*, vol. 1, 1994, col. 930–5.

20. Optat, III, 4; *Gesta conl. Carth.*, III, 258, *SC*, 224, pp. 1218–19.

21. Well attested by the reminder of his martyrdom made by the Donatist bishop Dativus of Nova Petra at the Carthage conference in June 411 (*Gesta conl. Carth.*, I, 187, 75, *SC*, 195, p. 834) and by the discovery of the *memoria domni Marchuli* at Ksar el-Kelb (P. Cayrel, in *Mél. de l'École française de Rome*, 1934, pp. 114–42). Lastly, Y. Duval, *Loca sanctorum Africae*, vol. I, no. 75, p. 160.

22. *Passio martyrum Isaac et Maximiani*: Maier, *Dossier*, vol. I, pp. 259–75.

23. See S. Lancel, 'Le sort des évêques et des communautés donatistes après la conférence de Carthage en 411', in *Internationales Symposion uber den Stand der Augustinus-Forschung*, Würzburg, 1989, pp. 149–67.

24. There is no more mention of him after 355, the date when Jerome (*Chronicon*, a. 355) indicates him as 'driven from Carthage'.

25. *C.Th.*, XVI, 6, 11.

26. *C.Th.*, XVI, 5, 4.

27. *C.Th.*, XVI, 6, 2; cf. Maier, *Dossier*, vol. II, Berlin, 1989, pp. 50–2; Augustine, *Ep.* 87, 8.

28. *C.Th.*, XVI, 5, 21; Maier, *Dossier*, vol. II, pp. 69–70.

29. *Enarr. in Psalm.* 36, 2, 20, reproducing the text of the synodal letter of Cebarsussi (Maier, *Dossier*, vol. II, pp. 74–82). On the Byzacenian nature of the Maximianist schism, cf. S. Lancel, 'Originalité de la province ecclésiastique de Byzacène', in *Cahiers de Tunisie*, 45–6, 1964, pp. 139–52.

30. Cf. A. C. De Veer, 'L'exploitation du schisme maximianiste par saint Augustin dans sa lutte contre le donatisme', in *Recherches aug.*, vol. 3, 1965, pp. 219–37, especially, pp. 223–30.

31. Gildo's motives have recently been reconsidered, in the light of Orosius (VII, 36), and the idea that this rebel had a coherent African policy refuted: Y. Modéran, 'Gildon, les Maures et l'Afrique', in *Mélanges de l'École fr. de Rome, Antiquité*, 101, 2, 1989, pp. 821–72. He was probably originally motivated, in fact, by personal ambition, but that did not prevent him from being an objective ally of the Donatists.

32. Could he have known Commodian, whose poetry, in hexametric form, still wavered between classical metrics (based on quantity) and accentual rhythmics (cf. J. Fontaine, *Naissance de la poésie dans l'Occident chrétien*, Paris, 1981, pp. 39ff.)? But this poses the question of the date, which strays between the third century and the end of the fifth, of this poet, whose 'African-ness' is itself disputed (cf. lastly J.-M. Poinsotte, 'Commodien dit de Gaza', in *Revue des ét. lat.*, 74, 1996, pp. 270–81).

33. *Doct. christ.*, IV, 24: *Afrae aures de correptione vocalium vel productione non iudicant*; it followed

that one must say *ossum* (the 'bone') instead of *os, ossis*, to avoid confusion with *os, oris* (the 'mouth' or 'face'). But did this apply only to Africans?

34. I follow the text of the manuscripts (and of Augustine himself in *Retract.*, I, 20): *Omnes qui gaudetis de pace, modo verum iudicate*; but it is true that it is hard to find eight syllables in the first stich.

35. Read the *Psalmus contra partem Donati* in the good translation by G. Finaert in *BA*, 28, 1963. However, here is an example of the clever plays on words in the original (1. 36–7):

> *Maledictum cor lupinum*
> *contegunt ovina pelle.*
> *Nomen iust(i) ovina pellis,*
> *schism(a) est in lupino corde.*

36. This text is now available, translated and commentated, in the edition by M. Labrousse: *Traité contre les donatistes*, vol. I, books I and II, *SC*, 412, 1995; vol. II, books III to VII, *SC*, 413, 1996.

37. *Ep.* 105, 4: *City of God*, XXII, 8, 7. On the rallying of Maximinus, see above, p. 292. The *villa Mutugenna* itself would become a see around 408; on the men and places and their situation in relation to Hippo, see S. Lancel, 'Études sur la Numidie d'Hippone au temps de saint Augustin', in *Mélanges de l'École fr. de Rome, Antiquité*, 96, 1984, pp. 1103–4 and fig. 3.

CHAPTER XVIII : Elevation to the episcopacy

1. H. Chadwick, *Augustine*; G. Madec, *Saint Augustin et la philosophie. Notes critiques*, p. 81.

2. The edition by J. Zycha in the *Corpus* of Vienna (*CSEL*, 28, 1, pp. 459–503) is perfectible: cf. M. M. Gorman, 'The text of Saint Augustine's *De Genesi ad litteram imperfectus liber'*, in *Recherches aug.*, 20, 1985, pp. 65–86.

3. On these hesitations, notably the *caeli*, cf. E. Teselle, 'Nature and Grace in Augustine's Exposition of Genesis I, 1–5', in *Recherches aug.*, 5, 1968, pp. 99–100.

4. *Enarr. in Psalm.*, 10, 5; *Ps. c. Don.*, 171. People have tried to see these cudgels as the pole (*pertica*) used by olive-gatherers (E. Tengström, *Donatisten und Katholiken*, Göteborg, 1964, pp. 51–2). Assuredly, the circumcellions were rural and, in socioeconomic terms, seasonal agricultural workers; but they must not be over-categorized.

5. *De sermone domini in monte*, I, 4, 12. Nowadays this numerical symbolism seems to us rather gratuitous; on the same page, $7 \times 7 = 49$, to which figure one has only to add the eighth day (the day of circumcision in Gen. 17.12) to obtain 50, in other words, Pentecost! The same arithmetical gymnastics appear in letter 55, 28, datable to around 400.

6. *De sermone domini in monte*, I, 11, 32, quoting Prov. 3.34. Cf. A.-M. La Bonnardière, *Biblia Augustiniana. Le livre des Proverbes*, Paris, Ét. aug., 1975, p. 202.

7. *De sermone domini in monte*, I, 12, 36, quoting Rom. 7.24–5, making *gratia dei* the grammatical subject of *liberabit*. Thus quoted, Rom. 7.24–5 is the scriptural text that appears most often in Augustine's works, as H.-I. Marrou noted, *Saint Augustin et l'augustinisme*, p. 86. Its first appearance in Augustine dates to 389, in the *De musica*, VI, 14.

8. Whatever O. Perler and J.-L. Maier may say (*Les Voyages de saint Augustin*, p. 162), Augustine's presence at this council is an enigma: it was apparently a provincial synod of Proconsularis, where he had no business to be, even as his bishop's representative. The fact that by some means or another he took part just shows what status the priest of Hippo already held in the Church of Africa.

9. P. Brown, *Augustine of Hippo*, p. 151.

10. Cf. above, p. 93. Cf. P. Hadot, *Marius Victorinus*.

11. *De promissis et lege*, 5, 1. I quote from the edition recently made available by J.-M. Vercruysse (thesis of the University of Artois, 1997), and in his lightly retouched translation.

12. See notably, *Exp. qu. prop. ex epist. ad Rom*, 12; *Exp. epist. ad Gal.*, 24 and 46; *De div. quaest.*, 61, 7; 66, 3–7. Here I am following the recently published analyses by P.-M. Hombert, *Gloria gratiae. Se glorifier en Dieu, principe et fin de la théologie augustinienne de la grâce*, Paris, Ét. aug., 1996, pp. 85–90.

13. Augustine sends the three finally completed books to Paulinus of Nola (*Ep.* 31, 7), at the same time as he tells him of his recent episcopal ordination (*Ep.* 31, 4): therefore in 395 or 396, according to the date accepted for that ordination.

14. Which naturally did not escape either. Marrou, *Saint Augustin et l'augustinisme*, pp. 142–3, or E. Dutoit, *Tout saint Augustin*, Fribourg, 1988, pp. 173–4, or, before them, F. Châtillon, in *Revue du Moyen Âge latin*, 9, 1953, pp. 281–8.

15. Efforts have been made to pinpoint the 'join', just before II, 16, 44 (Du Roy, *L'Intelligence de la foi*, but see remarks of G. Madec, in *BA*, 6 (3ʳᵈ ed., 1976), pp. 159–62.

16. On these changes of mind between Rome and Hippo, read P. Brown's brilliant pages, *Augustine of Hippo*, pp. 146–57 ('The Lost Future'); but the portrait is broadly hypothetical and 'impressionistic'.

17. G. Madec, in *Introduction aux 'Révisions'*, p. 44.

18. Brown, *Augustine of Hippo*, p. 148.

19. The presence of at least three bishops, armed with the instructions of their primate, was required for an episcopal ordination: cf. the council of Carthage of 390, c. 12 (*Concilia Africae*, CCL, 149, p. 180.

20. Council of Nicaea, c. 8; but transgressions of the rule were fairly frequent: cf. J. Gaudemet, *L'Église dans l'Empire romain (IVᵉ–Vᵉ siècle)*, Paris, Sirey, 1958, p. 364.

21. Unlike the primate of Proconsular Africa, who was bishop of Carthage, the head of the African Church, the primates of other provinces were 'doyens', appointed to the primacy by virtue of their senority in the episcopacy. Provincial primacies were therefore not linked to a fixed see.

22. *Contra litt. Pet.*, III, 19: *a sancto concilio de hoc, quod in nos ita peccavit, veniam petivit et meruit.* One obviously thinks of the council of Hippo on 8 October 393, at which Megalius was present: cf. *Concilia Africae*, CCL, 149, p. 270. But it is a little early, even if the ordination is placed in 395, and not 396.

23. *Epitoma chronicon*, in T. Mommsen, *Chronica Minora*, vol. I, M.G.H., a.a., 9, p. 463.

24. Notably O. Perler, in Perler and Maier, *Les Voyages de saint Augustin*, pp. 164–75; J. Desmulliez, 'Paulin de Nole. Études chronologiques', in *Recherches aug.*, 20, 1985, pp. 45–50.

25. Cf. D. E. Trout, 'The dates of the ordination of Paulinus of Bordeaux and of his departure for Nola', in *Revue des ét. aug.*, 37, 1991, pp. 239–47.

26. Paulinus of Nola, *Ep.* 7, 1: . . . *epistulas receperamus, id est Aurelii, Alypii, Augustini, Profuturi, Severi*, iam *omnium* pariter *episcoporum*. On this sequence of names, see the accurate comments by Mandouze, *Saint Augustin*, p. 142, and his no less pertinent observation that Alypius' ordination at Thagaste must have hastened Augustine's consecration at Hippo.

CHAPTER XIX : 396–397

1. Perler and Maier, *Les Voyages de saint Augustin*, p. 213.

2. The community of these Thiavenses can be situated between Thagaste and Thubursicu Numidarum: cf. S. Lancel, 'Études sur la Numidie d'Hippone', pp. 1104–5. It would be promoted to the status of bishopric a few years later.

3. For example, Fortunius claimed that at the root of the schism, before the election of Maiorinus over Caecilianus to the see of Carthage, an interim bishop (*interventor*) had been killed by the Catholics: *Ep.* 44, 8.

4. The proximity of Turres to Hippo is certain; but the localities known as Turres (who owed this name to defence works which most often ensured the protection of a great estate) swarmed in African toponymy, and this one cannot be identified: see S. Lancel, in *SC*, 194, p. 137.

5. Let me add, however, that an uncertainty remains, born of the finding that subsequently Augustine, when alluding to his text, always designates it as addressed to 'the bishop of Milan, Simplicianus': cf. for example, *De praedestinatione sanctorum*, 8, and *De dono perseverantiae*, 55. On this chronological point, no one has argued with more strictness and perceptiveness than S. Lenain de Tillemont, in his *Mémoires*, vol. XIII, pp. 978–9.

6. The old Latin custom, which Augustine follows, was to prefer an adjective taken from the noun to the use of the noun's genitive: *peccatum originale* rather than *peccatum originis*. But the intrinsic meaning is the same and interpretation depends on the context.

7. For G. Bardy, who translated by 'original sin', Augustine was, as on grace, in full possession of his doctrine on original sin as early as the *Ad Simplicianum*. For A. Solignac ('La condition de l'homme pécheur d'après saint Augustin', in *Nouv. Revue théol.*, 88, 1956, p. 382), who translated by 'sin of origin', just as for A. Sage ('Péché originel. Naissance d'un dogme', in *Revue des ét. aug.*, 13, 1967, pp. 218–20), the 'sin of origin', perceived as punishment, was not yet perceived by

Augustine at that time as guilt. This is not the (recent) opinion of P.-M. Hombert, *Gloria gratiae*, p. 95, note 248.

8. G. Bardy, in the Introduction to *Ad Simplicianum*, *BA*, 10, pp. 396–7.

9. Thus Brown, *Augustine of Hippo*, p. 153: 'Even the circumstances of Augustine's final step are dramatic.'

10. F. Masai, 'Les conversions d'Augustin et les débuts du spiritualisme en Occident', in *Le Moyen Âge*, 1–2, 1961, p. 37.

11. This is how this 'crisis' is presented in the book by K. Flasch, *Augustin. Einführung in sein Denken*, Stuttgart, 1980, pp. 172–200. The author later went further, denouncing in the theology of grace developed as from 396 a 'logic of terror', the title of the work published in 1990: *Logik des Schrekens. Augustinus von Hippo. Die Gnadenlehre von 397*, Mainz, 1990 (cf. the account by G. Madec, in *Revue des ét. aug.*, 37, 1991, pp. 387–90).

12. Cf. B. Legewie, 'Die körperliche Konstitution und die Krankheiten Augustins', in *Miscellanea Agostiniana*, II, 1931, pp. 5–21.

13. And a very good book, often quoted already: O. Perler and J.-L. Maier, *Les Voyages de saint Augustin*.

14. D. De Bruyne, 'La chronologie de quelques sermons de saint Augustin', *Revue bénéd.*, 43, 1931, pp. 185–93, first proved that Possidius' *Indiculum*, based on manuscripts inventoried by him after Augustine's death, described in his section X⁶, 101–31 a volume that gathered together four months of preaching in Carthage. Then C. Lambot, 'Un *jejunium quinquagesimae* en Afrique et date de quelques sermons de s. Augustin', *Rev. bénéd.*, 47, 1935, pp. 114–24, showed that there was every likelihood of this series having been preached between May and August of 397.

15. The collection known as 'Mayence-Grande-Chartreuse', in Dolbeau, *Vingt-Six Sermons au peuple d'Afrique*, pp. 19–224. Let me make it clear, however, that in the foreword to this volume, which assembles the texts first published in the *Revue bénéd.*, the finder, François Dolbeau, wisely makes some reservations about a uniform dating of all these sermons to 397.

16. This freedom of movement – participation in the councils of his province was a formal duty for a bishop – and his favoured relations with the primate of Carthage show to what extent Augustine, without being a 'free electron', enjoyed an exceptional personal status in the bosom of the Church of Africa.

17. One of them, *Dolbeau* 15 (= *Mainz* 45), dated 22 July, does not appear on Possidius' *Elenchus*; sermon 283 gave a shortened version of it that was already known.

18. On these 'Cyprian basilicas', see a discussion in the *Augustinus-Lexikon*, vol. I, fasc. 5/6, Basel, 1992, art. 'Carthago' (S. Lancel). Lastly, L. Ennabli, *Carthage. Une métropole chrétienne du IVᵉ siècle à la fin du VIIᵉ siècle*, Paris, CNRS, 1997, pp. 21–6.

19. Its resonances, considered to be anti-Pelagian, caused it formerly to be given a later date: A. Kunzelman, 'Die Chronologie des Sermones des Hl. Augustinus', in *Miscellanea Agostiniana*, II, 1931, p. 465.

20. The same association of texts, with, as A.-M. La Bonnardière says (*Biblia Augustiniana. A.T.: Le Livre de la Sagesse*, Paris, Ét. aug., 1970, p. 105), 'the same anti-Pelagian flavour before the event', in Tyconius, *Rule III*, 13, 1–2 (according to J.-M. Vercruysse's subdivisions). Augustine's dependency with regard to this Donatist theologian here appears to be very strong.

21. *S. Dolbeau* 12 (*Mainz* 41) (*Vingt-Six Sermons*, pp. 69–84.) The *De bono coniugali* has been dated to 401, on the basis of its place in the *Retractations*, II, 22. M.-F. Berrouard suggests, with good arguments, to put back the date to around 397/98: cf. *Augustinus-Lexikon*, vol. 1, 1994, col. 659.

22. Fairly closely, since in the same year (1936) that he was writing *Noces à Tipasa* he submitted a 'diploma in higher studies' to the Algiers Faculty of Humanities, entitled 'Neoplatonism and Christian thought: Plotinus and St Augustine' (on this student work – which can be read in A. Camus, *Essais*, 'Bibl. de la Pleiade', Paris, Gallimard, 1965, pp. 1224–313 – cf. P. Archambault, 'Augustin et Camus', in *Recherches aug.*, 6, 1969, pp. 195–221).

23. But he had read Étienne Gilson, who quoted the words of Severinus (sic), as summing up Augustine's thinking (*Introduction à l'étude de saint Augustin*, p. 172). By way of Gilson, Severus' words hovered in his memory.

24. And at the same time, not rationalist: cf. this statement by him, dated 20 December 1945: 'What interests me is knowing how one can behave when one believes neither in God nor in reason . . . I wonder about it, and I would be very bothered if I were forced to choose absolutely between St Augustine and Hegel. It is my impression that there must be a bearable truth somewhere between the two . . .' (A. Camus, *Essais*, p. 1427).

25. *De doctrina christiana* (hereafter abbreviated to *Doctr. chr.*), I, 1: *'opus magnum et arduum'*; the expression would be re-used subsequently, even more truthfully, to describe the *City of God: Civ. Dei, I, praef.* The *De doctrina christiana* has recently become available in a new edition, translated by M. Moreau, commentated by I. Bochet and G. Madec: *BA*, 11/2, 1997.

26. On Augustine's perception of Tyconius, read notably A. Mandouze, *Prosopographie de l'Afrique chrétienne*, s. v. Tyconius, pp. 1122–7.

27. *Doctr. chr. prol.*, 4 and 5. There has been much speculation about these 'charismatics' targeted by Augustine: Tyconius has been recognized, or the semi-Pelagian monastic circle gathered around Jean Cassien, which would date the Prologue to the resumption of the book in 426/27: cf. these theories and their just criticism in a complementary note (by I. Bochet) to the new edition of the *De doctrina christiana*, *BA*, 11/2, 1997, pp. 429–32. But it is forgotten that this ill-temper against those who claimed to speak of the Scriptures without prior teaching was not peculiar to Augustine alone: cf. letter 53, 7 from Jerome to Paulinus of Nola.

28. On the perception of them which moderns have had for a century, see E. Kevane, 'Augustine's *De doctrina christiana*: a Treatise on Christian Education', in *Recherches aug.*, 4, 1966, pp. 97–133.

29. This last expression is by L. Verheljen, 'Le *De doctrina christiana* de saint Augustin. Un manuel d'herméneutique et d'expression chrétienne avec, en II, 19 (29)–42 (63), "une charte fondamentale pour une culture chretienne"', in *Augustiniana*, 24, 1974, p. 13. The analyses of H.-I. Marrou are developed in *Saint Augustin et la fin de la culture antique*, pp. 387–413.

30. Thus T. Todorov, *Théories du symbole*, Paris, Le Seuil, 1977, p. 56, wanted to attribute to 'Augustine's inaugural deed' 'the institution of semiotics'. In fact, these general comments are merely an introduction to what really interests Augustine – biblical hermeneutics. For an exhaustive study of 'signs' in Augustine's theological context, see C. P. Mayer, *Die Zeichen in der geistigen Entwicklung und in der Theologie Augustins*, vol. II. Würzburg, Augustinus-Verlag, 1974.

31. Including astrology, to which Augustine had sacrificed in his youth, and the use of amulets, including earrings (with all due respect to P. Brown, *Augustine of Hippo*, p. 266), wearing of which was condemned: *Doctr. chr.*, II, 30 and *Ep.* 245, 2 (to Possidius).

32. Augustine is obviously not solely responsible for this dissociation which made writers of Christian faith able to develop a secular inspiration in literature, which did not signify any adherence to religious values that pagan mythology no longer promoted.

33. Cf. M. Banniard, *Genèse culturelle de l'Europe, Vᵉ–VIIIᵉ siècle*, Paris, Le Seuil, 1989, pp. 57–64.

34. That is, after the *Ad Simplicianum, Contra epistulam fundamenti* and the *De agone christiano*. The St Petersburg manuscript has been described by A. Mutzenbecher, 'Codex Leningrad Q. v. I. 3 (Corbie). Ein Betrag zu seiner Beschreibung', in *Sacris Eruditi*, 18, 1967–1968, pp. 406–50.

35. Cf. J.-P. Bouhot, 'Augustin prédicateur d'après le *De doctrina christiana*', in *Augustin prédicateur (345–411). Actes du colloque int. de Chantilly (5–7 Sept. 1996)*, Paris, Ét. aug., 1998, pp. 49–61.

CHAPTER XX : The *Confessions*

1. G. Bardy, in his Introduction to *Révisions*, *BA*, 12, p. 217.

2. Cf. *BA*, 13, pp. 45–54, and E. Feldmann, 'Confessiones', in *Augustinus-Lexikon*, vol. 1, 1994, col. 1184–5.

3. Comparisons have been made by A. Gabillon, 'Redatation de la lettre 109 de Severus de Milev', in *Augustin prédicateur (345–411). Actes du Colloque int. de Chantilly (5–7 Sept. 1996)*, Paris, Ét. aug., 1998, pp. 431–7.

4. P. Fabre, *Saint Paulin de Nole et l'amitié chrétienne* (BEFAR, vol. 167), Paris, 1949, pp. 236–41; P. Courcelle, *Les 'Confessions' de saint Augustin dans la tradition littéraire*, pp. 559–73. But the chronology held by both must be corrected with J. Desmulliez, 'Paulin de Nole. Études chronologiques (393–397)', in *Recherches aug.*, XX, 1985, pp. 35–64.

5. Courcelle, *Les 'Confessions'*, p. 567; Pincherle, *Vita di sant'Agostino*, pp. 175–6.

6. The hypothesis of the *pro domo* plea is however still sometimes taken up, but prudently: cf. recently J.-Y. Tilliette, 'Saint Augustin entre Moïse et Jean-Jacques? L'aveu dans les *Confessions*', in *L'Aveu. Antiquité, Moyen Âge*, Coll. École fr. de Rome, 88, Rome, 1986, p. 152.

7. Since Petrarch, who was the first, in the fourteenth century, to make clear this tripartite division: *Ep. ad Donatum Apennigenam* (Sen. VIII, 6), p. 928; cf. Courcelle, *Les 'Confessions'*, p. 334.

8. Notably in the *De ordine* and the *De musica*; on these speculations, see Marrou, *Saint Augustin et la fin de la culture antique*, pp. 259–62.

9. See this comparison in a recent essay: R. Martin, in *Revue des ét. lat.*, 68, 1990, pp. 139–41; in this article the arithmological 'credo' appears very strongly maintained.

10. Beyond the play on words (risked by R. Martin, *Revue des ét. lat.*, p. 141), it is true to say that echoes of Virgil abound in the *Confessions*; but comparisons with Virgil's epic, already made by J. J. O'Meara, 'Augustine the artist and the Aeneid', in *Mélanges C. Mohrmann*, Utrecht, 1963, pp. 252–61, seem forced.

11. R. Martin, *Revue des ét. lat.*, p. 145.

12. On the specifically biblical sense of the word, present in the use Augustine makes of it, see M. Verheijen, *Eloquentia pedisequa. Observations sur le style des 'Confessions' de saint Augustin*, Nijmegen, 1949, pp. 69–70. Lastly, E. Valgiglio, *Confessio nella Bibbia e nella letteratura cristiana antica*, Turin, 1980, pp. 173–238 (on St Augustine).

13. It has been shown that the quotations from the Psalms in the *Confessions* often have a 'unifying' or 'joining' function: cf. N. G. Knauer, *Psalmenzitate in Augustins Konfessionen*, Göttingen, 1955, especially pp. 133–61, where the author analyses more precisely the role of these quotations in Augustine's text.

14. The expression 'letter to God', sometimes ventured to characterize the *Confessions* (cf. for example A. Trapé, *Saint Augustin*, p. 237), is therefore too reductive.

15. On Augustine's use of the word *cor*, see A. Maxsein, '*Philosophia cordis* bei Augustin', in *Augustinus Magister*, vol. I, 1954, pp. 357–71.

16. P. Brown uses the word 'therapy' (*Augustine of Hippo*, pp. 165 and note 2, 166 and 181), taking up a suggestion by E. R. Dodds. In fact, all confession has a liberating power and acts as a catharsis.

17. P. Lejeune, *Le Pacte autobiographique*, Paris, Le Seuil, 1975, p. 14.

18. Despite their nuances, there is no longer agreement with the views expressed by G. Misch in the chapter devoted to the *Confessions* in his monumental *Geschichte der Autobiographie*, I, 2 (3rd ed.), Frankfurt, 1950, pp. 637–78.

19. As A. Mandouze notes, adding that this 'rest' is the essential part, in his introduction to the *Confessions* in the translation by L. de Mondadon, Paris, Le Seuil, Coll. Points-Sagesse, 31, 1982, p. 16.

20. On these liberties taken with the chronology, see Courcelle, *Recherches*, pp. 44–5 and the recent observations by J.-C. Fredouille, 'Les *Confessions* d'Augustin, autobiographie au présent', in *L'invention de l'autobiographie d'Hésiode à saint Augustin*, Paris, Presses de l'ENS, 1993, pp. 169–70.

21. *Conf.*, X, 12. Behind this brilliant description lies a whole technique of memorizing which Augustine had learnt in his youth, like all apprentice rhetors: see D. Doucet, 'L'*Ars memoriae* dans les *Confessions*', in *Revue des ét. aug.*, 33, 1987, pp. 49–69.

22. *Conf.*, XI, 2. Shortly before in his text (*Conf.*, X, 70), Augustine admits that he has felt tempted to withdraw from all service and 'contemplated a plan to flee into solitude'. The time of this temptation has been placed in various periods: following his conversion, or after his accession to the episcopacy. It could just as well be at the time of the *otium* at Thagaste; but Augustine gives no hint of a solution.

23. A phrase used by J.-P. Pierron in *Revue des ét. aug.*, 41, 1995, p. 265.

24. This fundamental aim is brought out well by E. Feldmann, 'Confessiones', in *Augustinus-Lexikon*, vol. 1, Basel, 1994, col. 1134–93, especially col. 1157–64.

25. Petrarch, *Seniles*, VIII, 6, *Ad Donatum Apennigenam*, p. 928. Text commentated by E. Luciani, *Les 'Confessions' de saint Augustin dans les Lettres de Pétrarque*, Paris, Ét. aug., 1982, p. 156.

26. Five volumes – all published between 1965 and 1991 in the series of *Études augustiniennes* – have been devoted to the iconography of St Augustine by P. Courcelle and J. Ladmirant-Courcelle.

27. One may imagine the tablets – *pugillares* – on the slightly reduced model of the wooden-framed slates still used by pupils some few decades ago. Augustine had ivory tablets, which he used for his letters; having none available, he would write to Romanianus on a little sheet of parchment, apologizing for this unusual material for a letter: *Ep.* 15, 1.

28. Jerome, *Contra Vigilantium*, 3, 356 c. In the letter he sends him (*Ep.* 61, 4), Jerome tells Vigilantius he must have been named in irony because, mentally, he's a sleeper!

29. *Ep.* 23 A*, 3; read in *BA*, 46 B (1987), pp. 532–47, the commentary by M.-F. Berrouard, and notably the calculation (p. 545) made from the edition of Latin Patrology, which shows that a line of Augustine's *notarii* is the equivalent of three-quarters of a line of the Migne edition: the 6000 lines dictated in six weeks, chiefly at night, represent 4572 lines of Latin patrology.

30. Horace, *Ars poetica*, 390: *Nescit vox missa reverti.*

31. See Prudentius, *Peristephanon*, IX, 21–30, on the school of *notarii* founded at Imola by St Cassian.

32. For the text was transcribed in *scriptura continua*, the words not being separated from one another, with rudimentary or non-existent punctuation. Before being punctuated, and becoming a codex distinctus, the text was virtually illegible (Jerome, *Ep.* 80, 3, *in fine*).

33. Jerome, *Ep.* 71 (*Ad Lucinum Baeticum*), 5 '. . . the carelessness of the copyists, who write not what they find in the texts but what they think they understand of them and who, wanting to correct the errors of others, reveal their own'.

34. If not reading the *Confessions* in Latin, one should refer as often as possible to the original text, preferably a bilingual edition. The French reader has good recent translations available: by P. de Labriolle, in the Collections des universités de France (or 'collection G. Budé'); by E. Tréhorel and G. Bouissou, in the *Bibliothèque augustinienne* (vols. 13 and 14); also by P. de Mondadon (Éd. P. Horay-Le Seuil, with presentation by A. Mandouze); perhaps the keenest, most evocative, and assuredly the most freely translated from the original, too. The latest translation into French is by P. Cambronne in Saint Augustin, *Oeuvres*, vol. I ('Bibl. de la Pléiade'), Paris, Gallimard, 1998, pp. 781–1124. English readers may refer to H. Chadwick's translation, Oxford, Oxford University Press, 1998.

35. It is a rarity to *see* Augustine in the act of writing: an instance, when at the end of the *Contra Felicem* he takes a scrap of *charta* to write in a few lines the model of anathema he is proposing that his Manichaean adversary, who admits that he is defeated, should recopy: *Contra Felicem*, II, 22.

36. This is the case in the edition of the *Bibliothèque augustinienne* (vols. 13 and 14). Jacques Fontaine rightly says that these texts from the *Confessions* should be read aloud ('Une révolution littéraire dans l'Occident latin: les *Confessions* de saint Augustin', in *Bulletin de litt. eccl.*, 88, 3–4, 1987, p. 176): yes, but it is the *Latin* text that should be read aloud.

37. The best analysis of the 'style' of the *Confessions* remains, after more than fifty years, that of M. Verheijen, *Eloquentia pedisequa. Observations sur le style des 'Confessions' de saint Augustin*, Nijmegen, 1949. Cf. also the remarks of C. Mohrmann, 'Saint Augustin écrivain', in *Recherches aug.*, I, 1958, pp. 53–7, and those of G. Bouissou, in *BA*, 13, pp. 207–32. Lastly, J. Fontaine's synthesis, 'Genres et styles dans les *Confessions* de saint Augustin', in *L'Information littéraire*, 42, 1, 1990, pp. 13–20.

38. Cf. the book by H. Hagendahl, *Augustine and the Latin Classics*, Göteborg, 1967.

39. Cf. P. Courcelle, 'Le thème du regret: "*Sero te amavi, Pulchritudo*" . . .', in *Revue des ét. lat.*, 38, 1960, pp. 277–83.

40. If one had to add another, rather than the *City of God*, despite its importance, I would say the *Letters*; but the French reader will have to wait until a good translated and commentated edition to appear in the *Bibliothèque augustinienne*, modelled on what was done in vol. 46 B, devoted in 1987 to the new letters discovered by J. Divjak. English readers may refer to the fairly complete translation of the *Letters* by Sister W. Parsons SND, Washington, Catholic University of America Press, 1951–6.

CHAPTER XXI : A monk in his monasteries

1. Quodvultdeus, *Liber promissionum et praedictorum Dei*, III, 44. The most recent editor of the text, R. Braun, would like to put off the devolution of the temple of Caelestis to the Church until 407 (cf. *SC*, 101, 1964, p. 72). But there are good arguments for keeping the date to 399: cf. Perler and Maier, *Les Voyages de saint Augustin*, pp. 391–5; lastly, L. Ennabli, *Carthage*, pp. 35–6.

2. Cf. G. Charles-Picard, *La Carthage de saint Augustin*, Paris, Fayard, 1965, pp. 100–3.

3. After winning his case, as is suggested by the terms of the imperial rescript addressed on 25 June 399 to Sapidianus, *vicarius* of Africa: *C.Th.*, XVI, 2, 34.

4. Bulla Regia is one of the places in Tunisia where the summer heat is greatest; it is the only site in the ancient western world where the ground floor of houses was extended by a subterranean floor, of the same layout, to give a refuge in the summer.

5. These words in inverted commas, significant of this development, are by Mandouze, *Saint Augustin*, p. 219.

6. Cf. *City of God*, XIX, 19, where he proposes translating *episkopein* by *superintendere*, and adds that anyone who enjoys giving orders and not making himself useful could not be a bishop.

7. Cf. L. Verheijen, *La Règle de saint Augustin. II. Recherches historiques*, Paris, Ét. aug., 1967, p. 202.

8. L. Verheijen, 'Spiritualité et vie monastique chez saint Augustin. L'utilisation monastique des Actes des apôtres 4, 31, 32–5 dans son oeuvre', in *Jean Chrysostome et Augustin. Actes du colloque de Chantilly, 22–4 Sept. 1974*, Paris, Beauchesne, 1975 (pp. 94–123), p. 106.

9. Verheijen, *La Règle de saint Augustin. II*, pp. 164–72.

10. Here I take up the summary by Verheijen on completion of a long study: *La Règle de saint Augustin. II*, p. 216. Researchers are, however, not completely unanimous on this process, particularly on Alypius' share in it; for G. Lawless, *Augustine of Hippo and His Monastic Rule*, Oxford, Clarendon Press, 1990, pp. 168–70, the *Ordo monasterii* was drawn up by Augustine.

11. Cf. Verheijen, 'Spiritualité et vie monastique', pp. 99–102.

12. G. Madec, 'Le communisme spirituel', in *Petites Études augustiniennes*, Paris, 1994, p. 215.

13. The chronology of this affair has been clarified recently by an analysis of *Ep.* 243: A. Gabillon, 'Pour une datation de la lettre 243 d'Augustin à Laetus', in *Revue des ét. aug.*, 40, 1, 1994, pp. 127–42.

14. Verheijen has underlined the importance of this text in understanding Augustine's thinking on monastic life: 'Spiritualité et vie monastique', pp. 118–20.

15. *Ep.* 26*, 2, *BA*, 46 B, p. 392: at a pinch, suggested Augustine, he might serve as a lector, if that! On places and chronology, cf. *BA*, 46 B, pp. 520–2 and 557–9 (commentaries by A. Gabillon and S. Lancel).

16. But before him, Martin had done the same at Tours, Victrix at Rouen and Eusebius at Vercelli in Italy.

17. Cf. J. Gaudemet, *L'Église dans l'Empire romain*, pp. 156–63.

18. On the distinction between green vegetables (*holera*) and dried (*legumina*) in the diet of Christians, the text to read is the letter written in that period by Jerome to Furia, a young widowed Roman noblewoman; he warns her against *legumina* because of the flatulence and feeling of heaviness they cause (*Ep.* 54, 10).

19. This was customary, in order to allow travelling clergy to avoid the lack of privacy in inns.

20. This moralizing or normative elegiac couplet was probably not written by Augustine. It has been found with a variation on a Dalmatian inscription: *Revue arch.*, 18, 1941, p. 315, note 53.

21. *Sermon* 355, 4–5. A good commentary on this text is given by L. De Salvo, '*Navicularium nolui esse ecclesiam Christi*. A proposito di Aug. *Sermo* 355, 4', in *Latomus*, 46, 1987, pp. 146–60.

22. We may find this practice of re-using stone surprising, but it is found in the case of the constructions carried out by bishop Antoninus of Fussala: above, p. 254.

23. Augustine was obviously thinking of appeals to Rome, regarding which, like the whole African Church, he showed a supercilious independence.

CHAPTER XXII : A bishop in his churches, at Hippo

1. Or *one* of the basilicas: cf. E. Marec, *Monuments chrétiens d'Hippone*, p. 230: 'The preposition *intra* seems to be good confirmation that Valerius' garden and the monastery are to be sought within the boundaries of the Christian *insula*.' For the originator of these excavations, there is only one Christian *insula*, which he brought to light; but it is not certain that there is enough room in it for the 'garden' (and the monastery).

2. *Ep.* 20*, 2, *BA*, 46 B, p. 294, L. Verheijen ('Les lettres nouvelles et la vie monastique autour de saint Augustin', in *Les Lettres de saint Augustin découvertes par Johannes Divjak*, Paris, 1983, p. 125) favoured the clerical monastery for Antoninus and his stepfather.

3. For the date, see Verheijen, *La Règle de saint Augustin. II*, p. 203.

4. *Ep.* 211. The *obiurgatio* has been given a critical edition by Verheijen, *La Règle de saint Augustin*, vol. I, pp. 105–7; cf. also G. Lawless, *Augustine of Hippo and His Monastic Rule*, pp. 104–18, with an English translation. Little is known about this convent; the old article by P. Monceaux is still valid, 'Un couvent de femmes à Hippone', in *CRAI*, 1913, pp. 570–95.

5. By way of what Augustine would call the *libelli miraculorum*: for Uzalis, see the texts published at the instigation of Evodius himself, the *De miraculis sancti Stephani*: Augustine would shortly afterwards make a strong allusion to it in his *City of God*, XXII, 8, 22.

6. Cf. O. Perler, 'L'église principale et les autres sanctuaires chrétiens d'Hippone-la-Royale d'après les textes de saint Augustin', in *Revue des ét. aug.*, 1, 1955, p. 321, based on indications in the *City of God*, XXII, 8, 21 and *Sermon* 318, 1. Augustine's personal contribution was the four lines he composed and had inscribed in the cella, perhaps on the vault of the apse: *sermon* 319, 7.

7. Augustine would say (*serm.* 322, PL, 38, col. 1444) that they had enjoyed visions which told

them to go to Hippo. The date could be either 425 or 426; Lenain de Tillemont (*Mémoires*, vol. XIII, col. 1003–4) holds out for 425; the following year would seem more likely.

8. O. Perler ('L'église principale', p. 322 and note 182, and p. 323) curiously was wrong about this sentence in which he was unable to recognize the position where Augustine, quite normally, would be when he was told of Paulus' miraculous healing.

9. There Paulus told in his own words what we find taken up in the text of the *City of God*: *Orabam ego quotidie cum magnis lacrimis in loco ubi est memoria gloriosissimi martyris Stephani. Die autem dominico Paschae, sicut alii qui presentes erant viderunt, dum orans cum magno fletu cancellos teneo, subito cecidi* (*sermon* 322 = *City of God*, XXII, 8, 2).

10. On these phenomena, see Y. Duval, *Loca sanctorum Africae*, II, notably pp. 697–726.

11. The large traffic of pilgrims and the need to build places to receive them are one of the characteristics of those times; at the very end of the fourth century, Pammachius, Jerome's friend and honorary proconsul, would build a xenodochium at Porto, near Ostia (Jerome, *Ep.* 66, 11; 77, 10).

12. It is true that the Donatists honoured him on his *dies natalis* like the Catholics (*Ep.* 29, 11), which inclined P. Monceaux to place his hypothetical martyrdom during Diocletian's persecution, before the start of the African schism (*Histoire littéraire de l'Afrique chrétienne*, III, pp. 152–3.

13. *Concilia Africae*, *CCL*, 149, p. 250.

14. Perler ('L'église principale', in *Revue des ét. aug.*, 1, 1955, p. 304) in order to affirm it, relies on the reply given by Augustine to those who, to justify the imbibings of the *Laetitia*, invoked the example of what happened in Rome: the Vatican, he retorted, was a long way from the papal palace. The implication was that the distance was not the same in Hippo, which did not mean a real proximity.

15. Rare and enigmatic: to relate this name 'of Peace' to the 'peace of the Church' would mean dating the monument to the Constantinian era, which seems difficult; relating it to periods of 'entente' (enforced!) with the Donatists would not make dating it to the second half of the fourth century any easier. Moreover, the concept that was being put forward at the time was of 'unity' rather than peace.

16. Discussion in Perler, 'L'église principale', pp. 313–18.

17. It is the interpretation of a liturgist such as A. Olivar, *La Predicación cristiana antigua*, Barcelona, 1991, pp. 521–2. Cf. also the commentaries of an archaeologist like N. Duval, *Les églises africaines à deux absides*, II, p. 303, who is thinking also of a 'moral conversion', or that the injunction exhorted the faithful to turn towards the altar, which was often situated forward in the central nave.

18. In 256 he had attended the council gathered in Carthage by Cyprian (*Sent. episc.* 14) and Augustine commented on his advice on baptism in his *De baptismo*, VI, 36–7.

19. Before this date, the faithful assembled in private houses: it cannot be ruled out that the house on the site where the basilica had been built had already housed these meetings. Jean Lassus thought so: 'Les edifices du culte autour de la basilique', in *Atti VI Congr. int. di Arch. crist.*, Ravenna, 1962, p. 589.

20. For details read the publication of the excavations: E. Marec, *Monuments chrétiens d'Hippone*, pp. 23–130, complemented and corrected by the important critical article by H.-I. Marrou, 'La basilique chrétienne d'Hippone', pp. 109–54.

21. Cf. H.-I. Marrou's remarks in *Revue des ét. aug.*, 6, 1960, pp. 128–30.

22. Not to mention the basilicas of Carthage, there are many larger, for example at Tebessa and Tipasa: cf. J.-P. Caillet, N. Duval and I. Gui, *Basiliques chrétiennes d'Afrique du Nord. I. Inventaire de l'Algérie*, vol. I (Text), vol. II (illustr.), Paris, Ét. aug., 1992.

23. Marec, *Monuments chrétiens d'Hippone*, pp. 167–8 and 23–4: this three-lobed hall is noted *c7* on the plan. Marrou, 'La basilique chrétienne d'Hippone', p. 153, professed to be sceptical but proposed nothing.

24. The plan suggests rather the triclinium of a private house: cf. lastly the remarks of N. Duval, 'Hippo Regius', col. 451–2.

25. Marec, *Monuments chrétiens d'Hippone*, pp. 112–28: group of rooms centred around peristyle *H* (cf. fig. 1).

26. Marrou, 'La basilique chrétienne d'Hippone', p. 152; communication with the church was by the small room *J*.

27. This would be the block *E*, where Marec, *Monuments chrétiens d'Hippone*, pp. 230–1, would place the *domus episcopi*, from the start. The author relies on *sermon* 61, 13 to affirm that Augustine used the street to go from his house to the church; but the text does not support such a conclusion.

CHAPTER XXIII : A bishop in his diocese

1. On these data, see S. Lancel, 'Africa, organisation ecclésiastique', in *Augustinus-Lexikon*, vol. 1, 1994 col. 206–16.

2. The polemic, on both sides, must also be taken into account; on the cruel realities, see *Actes de la conférence de Carthage en 411*, vol. 1, *Sources chrétiennes*, 194, Paris, 1972, p. 122.

3. On these facts in the period under consideration (fourth–fifth century), see S. Lancel, 'Évêchés et cités dans les provinces africaines', in *L'Afrique dans l'Occident romain (1er s. av. J.-C.–IVe siècle après J.-C.)*, Rome, 1990, pp. 276–80.

4. See the map of ecclesiastical provinces and African bishoprics in the time of St Augustine, between cols. 216 and 217 of the *Augustinus-Lexikon*, vol. 1, 1994.

5. References in S. Lancel, 'Études sur la Numidie d'Hippone au temps de saint Augustin. Recherches de topographie ecclésiastique', in *Mél. de l'école française de Rome, Antiquité*, 96, 1984, pp. 1088–9.

6. *Concilia Africae*, *CCL*, 149, p. 208.

7. Cf. above, p. 172 the affair of the anonymous deacon of the *villa Mutugenna*.

8. To note the alteration of rhythm in his movements, one has only to consult the tables of 'Augustinian chronology and topology' published by Perler and Maier, *Les Voyages de saint Augustin*, pp. 395ff.

9. Cf. *Actes de la conf. de Carthage en 411*, I, 128, *Sources chrétiennes*, vol. 195, p. 732. For both Donatists and Catholics, the order governing the lists is that of seniority of ordination.

10. For a fuller discussion of the data, cf. Lancel, 'Études sur Numidie d'Hippone', p. 1103.

11. See the analysis of the episcopal tribunal's peregrinations in Lancel, 'Études sur la Numidie d'Hippone' au temps de saint Augustin', in MEFRA, 96, 1984, pp. 1099–103.

12. In the south-east corner of page 9 of the *Atlas archéologique de l'Algérie*. Over several hundred square kilometres, these folds on a north-north-east/south-south-west line, with an altitude of around 900m on their crests, are devoid of any archaeological landmarks.

13. On the use of the *lingua Punica* in Africa in the Late period, cf. Lancel, in *Revue des études latines*, 59 (1981), 1982, pp. 270–2.

14. The *matricula pauperum* (*Ep.* 20*, 2), the first and interesting occurrence of the word *matricula* in this sense. On the institution and its historical development, cf. M. Rouche, 'La matricule des pauvres. Évolution d'une institution de charité du Bas-Empire jusqu'à la fin du haut Moyen Âge', in *Études sur l'histoire de la pauvreté (Moyen Age-XVIe siècle)*, Paris, 1974, pp. 83–110.

15. Cf. C. Lepelley, *Les Cités de l'Afrique romaine au Bas-Empire*, vol. I, 1979, pp. 132–3.

16. Cf. the portrait presented at the council of Carthage in 397 by Epigonius of Bulla Regia, of those who '*quasi quadam in arce tyrannica sibi dominatum vindicant*': *Concilia Africae*, *CCL*, 149, p. 189.

17. C.Th., XVI, 2, 38, a law addressed to the proconsul of Africa, in reply to a request expressed by the council of Carthage of 13 June 407: *Concilia Africae*, *CCL*, 149, p. 215.

18. *Ep.* 20*, 6. On the addressee, Fabiola, see S. Lancel, 'L'affaire d'Antoninus de Fussala', in *Les Lettres de saint Augustin découvertes par J. Divjak*, Paris, Ét. aug., 1983, pp. 278–9. Like many Roman nobles, Fabiola had lands in Africa, where she had taken refuge after the capture of Rome, at the end of 410.

19. On its application early in the fifth century, see J. Gaudemet, *L'Église dans l'Empire romain*, pp. 242–3.

20. *Ep.* 20*, 10, where one simultaneously notes the ability of the *domina* to intervene positively or negatively in a religious matter, and the freedom of action of those *coloni* who were theoretically bound to the land (cf. C.Th., V, 17, 1, law of Constantine dated 332), but whose real mobility is shown in this text, in addition to others.

21. On these problems and the attitude of the African Church, see C. Munier, 'La question des appels à Rome d'après la lettre 20* d'Augustin', in *Les Lettres de saint Augustin découvertes par J. Divjak*, Paris, Ét. aug., 1983, pp. 287–99, in particular pp. 290–4, for this affair.

22. The agrarian structure thus appears omnipresent in the small world in which the enquiry related by Augustine takes place. In addition, the rural background in this instance made up for the lack of available clergy to assist the faithful: Antoninus had only a priest and a deacon with him, removed from office at the same time as he, and his newly ordained successor had scarcely had the time to recruit to replace them.

23. On the siting of Gilva, cf. J. Desanges and S. Lancel, in *Les Lettres de saint Augustin découvertes par J. Divjak*, pp. 97–8.

24. Cf. *Notitia de 484*, Num. 21, *CSEL*, 7, p. 120.

CHAPTER XXIV : A bishop in the world of his time

1. On this development, cf. J. Gaudemet, *L'Église dans l'Empire romain*, pp. 233–6.

2. A privilege re-issued by Honorius in a law of late 412 (*C.Th.*, XVI, 2, 41): *Clericos non nisi apud episcopos accusari convenit* . . . the reservation that follows, *si quidem alibi non oportet*, has caused much ink to flow. But it is no longer a reservation if one understands it as J. Rougé did, 'since that is not fitting elsewhere' (in *Les Lettres de saint Augustin découvertes par J. Divjak*, p. 181).

3. On this body of legislation, see Gaudemet, *L'Église dans l'Empire romain*, pp. 144–9.

4. C. Lepelley, *Les Cités de l'Afrique romaine au Bas-Empire*, vol. I, p. 396.

5. Who, in a law of 385, said that the *defensor civitatis* should have the 'bowels (of compassion) of a father' towards the lowly: *CJ*, I, 55, 4.

6. On this point, see F. Jacques, 'Le défenseur de cité d'après la lettre 22* de saint Augustin', in *Revue des ét. aug.*, 32, 1986, pp. 56–73, notably p. 61.

7. *Concilia Africae, CCL*, 149, p. 202: despite the canon's title, this does not concern *defensores ecclesiae*, but many people appointed to relieve the *afflictio pauperum* and defend them against the rich.

8. Cf. above, p. 232. Read the procedure for freeing slaves in the church in *sermon* 21, 6. More broadly, on the bishop's attitude in this area, read F. Decret, 'Augustin d'Hippone et l'esclavage', in *Dialogues d'histoire ancienne*, 11, 1985, pp. 675–85.

9. Cf. *City of God*, XIX, 15. There we find an etymology, which might be called optimistic in its falseness, of the word *servus*, of the slave as a product of war: *A victoribus cum servabantur servi fiebant, a servando appellati; quod etiam ipsum sine peccati merito non est.*

10. Following a still valid law of Constantine (*C.Th.*, IV, 8, 6) to which Augustine himself alludes in another of these letters: *Ep.* 10*, 2. On the risk connected with the sale of the work force, read the learned commentary by M. Humbert, 'Enfants à louer ou à vendre: Augustin et l'autorité parentale (*Ep.* 10* et 24*)', in *Les Lettres de saint Augustin découvertes par J. Divjak*, pp. 189–203.

11. A law of Theodosius (*CJ*, XI, 52, 1, of 393) said that they must be regarded as 'slaves of the ground itself for which they are born'. But see earlier the possibility of *migrare* which the *coloni* of Thogonoetum threatened (above, p. 255).

12. Cf. the *Expositio totius mundi et gentium*, 60, *Sources chrétiennes*, vol. 124, p. 200, and the commentary by J. Rougé, p. 319.

13. In the *saltus Paratianensis*: cf. above, p. 246.

14. The estate of Paratianis, where he was a farmer, came under the jurisdiction of the 'consularis' (governor) of Numidia: cf. above, p. 248.

15. *Constitutio Sirmondiana* 13: cf. M.-F. Berrouard, in *Revue des ét. aug.*, 31, 1985, p. 56.

16. Cf. *Ep.* 250 and *Ep.* 1* (*BA*, 46 B, pp. 42–50): this new letter is the complete text of Augustine's letter to Classicianus, of which only the last paragraph was known (= *Ep.* 250A). On these letters, see G. Folliet, 'Le dossier de l'affaire Classicianus', in *Les Lettres de saint Augustin découvertes par J. Divjak*, pp. 129–46.

17. *Ep.* 250, 2: *senex . . . et episcopus tot annorum*; he was therefore at least sixty, since he made *senectus* begin at that age: cf. *De div. quaest. LXXXIII, qu.* 58, 2: *cum a sexagesimo anno senectus dicatur incipere.*

18. It has been shown that from the end of the fourth century (around 388), the Count of Africa had lost military control of Tripolitania to the east and Caesariensis to the west, to the advantage of *duces*: cf. Y. Modéran, 'Gildon, les Maures d'Afrique', pp. 868–72. But he was left with Proconsularis, Byzacena, Numidia and Sitifiensis, or the whole of present-day Tunisia and the eastern half of Algeria.

19. *Sermon Denis* 16, 1, in *Miscellanea Agostiniana*, I, Rome, 1930, p. 75: *Omni homini proximus est omnis homo.* S. Ploque has the honour of having firmly dated this sermon to the summer of 413, by linking it, along with some others, to these events: 'L'écho des événements de l'été de 413 à Carthage dans la prédication de saint Augustin', in *Homo spiritalis. Festgabe für L. Verheijen*, Würzburg, 1987, pp. 391–9.

20. *Ep.* 151, 10. It is useful to read the analysis of this letter and its context by M. Moreau, *Le Dossier Marcellinus dans la correspondance de saint Augustin*, Paris, Ét. aug., 1973, pp. 131–5.

CHAPTER XXV : The unity of the Church

1. On Adimantus, cf. F. Decret, s. v., in *Augustinus-Lexikon*, vol. 1, col. 94–5.
2. On these *Capitula*, their real order of succession – which is not Augustine's – and their scriptural content, see P. Monceaux, *Le Manichéen Faustus de Milev. Restitution de ses Capitula*, Paris, 1933. Lastly, F. Decret, *Aspects du manichéisme dans l'Afrique romaine*, pp. 66–70.
3. The day and year (sixth consulship of Honorius) appear at the head of the *Contra Felicem manichaeum*. This date, which seems belated in the order of Augustine's concerns, has been disputed; on these debates, cf. Decret, *Aspects du manichéisme dans l'Afrique romaine*, pp. 77–8, and lastly Madec, *Introduction aux 'Révisions' et à la lecture de saint Augustin*, pp. 150–3.
4. The indications in Augustine's letter 79, together with those in *Retract.*, II, 8, and of the text of the *Contra Felicem* enable us to reconstruct the origins of the meeting.
5. Augustine had refuted it around 396/97: this is the *Contra epistulam fundamenti*, *BA*, 17, pp. 381–507.
6. It may be added that at the beginning of the fifth century the decline of Manichaean communities in Africa as elsewhere in the west deprived Augustine's fight of its pastoral motives: cf. the analyses of P. Brown, 'The Diffusion of Manichaeism in the Roman Empire', in *Journal of Roman Studies*, 1969, pp. 92–103, in particular pp. 101–2.
7. *Contra Cresconium*, IV, 58–9. Augustine had taken the trouble – probably during the summer of 404, on his return from taking part in the council of Carthage – to go and make enquiries himself at Membressa, as well as Assuras, Abitinae and Musti, all places marked by conflict between Primianists and Maximianists.
8. W. H. C. Frend, *The Donatist Church*, p. 22.
9. The text of 15 November 407 states that 'the obstinacy of the Donatists – but also the madness of the pagans – is fuelled by the deplorable inactivity of the judges, the complicity of the officials and the disdain of local councils': *C.Th.*, XVI, 5, 43; in 409, similar views were expressed: *C.Th.*, XVI, 5, 46.
10. A theory of Monceaux, *Histoire littéraire de l'Afrique chrétienne*, vol. IV, p. 275.
11. *Ep.* 53, 4, which includes the first literal quotation from this document, which Augustine would quote at greater length and analyse in his *Contra Cresconium*, III, 33 and IV, 66, in 405/06. Which proves that his dossier was already completely made up in 400 (cf. also *Contra litt. Pet.*, I, 23, and III, 69).
12. *C. litt. Pet.*, I, 1: *Cum essem in ecclesia Constantiniensi Absentio praesente et collega meo Fortunato eius episcopo*, in which Absentius is one of the little enigmas in the Augustinian manuscript tradition: it was obviously about Alypius.
13. This is the date customarily accepted: cf. G. Bonner, 'Augustinus (vita)', in *Augustinus-Lexikon*, vol. 1, col. 539. However, A. Schindler ('Die Unterscheidung von Schisma und Häresie in Gesetzgeburg und Polemik gegen den Donatismus', in *Pietas. Festschrift für B. Kötting*, 1980, pp. 228–36) suggested deferring this text to 404–5, on signs of a hardening of Augustine's position with regard to the Donatists. Moreover, one of the recently published new sermons (Dolbeau 26 (*Mainz* 62), datable to 1 January 404, offers such points of contact with *C. epist. Parm.*, II, 14–16 that it is difficult not to date these texts to the same period (cf. Dolbeau, *Vingt-Six Sermons au peuple d'Afrique*, pp. 353–8).
14. See above, p. 172, his historical waverings on the problem of repeated baptism in his *Contra epistulam Donati*.
15. On the genesis of the *Contra Cresconium*, see the introduction by A. C. De Veer, in *BA*, 31, pp. 9ff.
16. *Contra Cresc.*, II, 9. On the shifts in Augustine's thinking in applying the 'heretic' label to Donatists, see Schindler, 'Die Unterscheidung von Schisma und Häresie', pp. 228–36.
17. P. Monceaux has drawn up a list of them in *Histoire littéraire de l'Afrique chrétienne*, vol. VII, pp. 129–77, and chronological tables, pp. 279–92. For the sermons, add the new *sermons Dolbeau* 24 (*Mainz* 60), 21 (*Mainz* 54) and chiefly 27 (*Mainz* 63), to which we shall return: Dolbeau, *Vingt-Six Sermons au peuple d'Afrique*, pp. 227–42, 271–96 and 304–14.
18. R. F. Evans, *One and Holy: The Church in Latin Patristic Thought*, London, 1972, p. 65: 'The impression is inescapable that while Augustine listened to what the Donatists said, he had his mind on something else.'

19. *Epist. ad cath.*, 9. On this text of Augustine dated 400/1, whose authenticity has sometimes been challenged, see M. Moreau, in *Augustinus-Lexikon*, vol. 1, 1994, col. 808–15.

20. Cyprian wrote to Jubaianus, informing him of the council's decision of 256: 'We do not rebaptize, but we baptize those who, coming from an adulterous and profane water, must be washed again and sanctified by the true water of salvation' (*Ep.* 73, 1); it was quite clearly a repetition of baptism.

21. With potentially serious consequences: Cyprian's attitude tended to a break with the see of Rome; cf. his letter 74 condemning Pope Stephen's baptismal theology.

22. Cf. Cyprian, *Ep.* 73 (to Jubaianus), 26, 2; *De baptismo*, I, 28; II, 6 and 7; III, 5; IV, 11; V, 23; cf. also *C. Cresc.*, II, 48–9, quoting Cyprian, *Ep.* 54, 3, 1: 'even if we see chaff within the Church, our faith or our charity must not be impeded by it to the extent that it makes us leave the Church because we see that there is chaff there.'

23. *Actes de la conférence de Carthage en 411*, II, 10, *SC*, 195, p. 929: *martyrialis gloriae virum*.

24. For the date and a rapid analysis of the work, cf. *Prosopographie chrétienne du Bas-Empire. I. Afrique (303–533)*, s. v. Optatus 1, pp. 795–801. Ever useful are the developments by Monceaux, *Histoire littéraire de l'Afrique chrétienne*, vol. V, pp. 241–306. Lastly, read the Introduction of the edition translated and commentated by M. Labrousse, vol. I (books I and II), *SC*, 412 (1995) and vol. II (books III–VII), *SC*, 413 (1996).

25. On these texts, read the edition by M. Labrousse, vol. I, *SC*, 412 (1995), pp. 57–72, where we find collected the voluminous bibliography prompted by them for over a century.

26. Starting from the mid-fourth century, there had been a small Donatist community in Rome – known to the Catholics as *Montenses* (Optat, II, 4; Augustine, *C. litt. Pet.*, II, 247) or, derisively, *Cutzupitae* (*Ep.* 53, 2) – and in 411, they were represented at the Carthage conference by their bishop, Felix.

27. *Ct.*, 1, 7: *'in meridie'*, taken geographically, instead of timewise, 'at midday'. What is most surprising is that Augustine, who with a word could have corrected this blunder, agreed to this wrong interpretation and argued at length on that basis: *sermon* 138, 9–10.

28. On Augustine's debt to Optat, above all in the *De baptismo*, cf. M. Labrousse, 'Le baptême des hérétiques d'après Cyprien, Optat et Augustin: influences et divergences', in *Revue des ét. aug.*, 42, 2, 1996, pp. 223–42, notably pp. 232–42.

29. The occurrences of the expression in its various contexts have been collected by Y. M.-J. Congar, in his general Introduction to *Traités antidonatistes*, *BA*, 28, p. 98.

30. For Augustine, unlike the schismatics, it was neither the bishop, nor the college of bishops, nor even the Church in its capacity as the sum of the faithful, who performed the sacraments, but Christ, the Word Incarnate.

31. Congar, in Introduction to *Traités antidonatistes*, *BA*, 28, p. 123. May I add that these pages owe much to his analyses.

32. This is the *tertium quid* of a distinction first made by H.-I. Marrou ('Civitas Dei, civitas terrena. Num tertium quid?' in *Studia patristica*, 2, 1957, pp. 342–50), taken up and developed by P. Borgomeo, *L'Église de ce temps dans la prédication de saint Augustin*, Paris, Ét. aug., 1972, pp. 300–24.

CHAPTER XXVI : The Carthage conference of 411

1. *Concilia Africae*, *CCL*, 149, p. 199.

2. The text of the proconsular edict was quoted at the debates of the Carthage conference: *Actes*, III, 174, *SC*, 224, p. 1123. There the proconsul condemned in advance the 'heresy' (*superstitio*) of the 'leaders of a community that has gone astray' (*magistri deviae plebis*). This partiality was a sign of the imminent direct intervention by the secular authorities in the conduct of religious affairs in Africa.

3. The document has not been preserved, but was produced by the Donatists at the conference of 411: cf. *Brev. conl.*, III, 6: '*Obtulerunt ergo donatistae gesta proconsularia et vicariae praefecturae, ubi catholici petierant eos actis municipalibus conveniri.*'

4. In other words, hundreds. The procedure was not applicable where the schismatic Church had an episcopal monopoly. For details of the procedure, see the *forma conventionis* in *Concilia Africae*, p. 210.

5. The *fundus Olivetensis* (the 'farm of the olive-trees'): *Ep.* 105, 4; in the *C. Cresc.*, III, 50, Augustine gives interesting details (which he evidently had from Possidius himself: cf. *Vita Aug.*, XII, 4) on

the reactions of the witnesses, the majority of whom were Donatists, but frightened at the thought of the consequences and visibly terrorized by Crispinus and his henchmen.

6. *C.Th.*, XVI, 5, 39, to the proconsul Diotimus.

7. *Sermon Dolbeau* 26 (*Mainz* 62), 45: ... *propter hoc oderunt nos et, si facultas detur, occidunt manu circumcellionum. Sed quia dominus adiuvit,* evasimus, *gratias agentes misericordiae domini* (cf. Dolbeau, *Vingt-Six Sermons au peuple d'Afrique*, p. 401 and 353–5 for the commentary). Another quick allusion is in *Sermon Dolbeau* 4 (*Mainz* 9), 3, *Vingt-Six Sermons*, pp. 513–14.

8. During the *tempora Macariana*, in the mid-fourth century, its bishop had been the Donatus who had organized resistance in Numidia against the agents of the imperial government; his violent death had made him a martyr, in the same way as Marculus of Nova Petra (*C. litt. Pet.*, II, 32).

9. Archaeological prospecting has revealed the number and often the quality of the rural basilicas and oratories in Numidia: cf. A. Berthier, M. Martin and F. Logeart, *Les Vestiges du christianisme antique en Numidie centrale*, Algiers, 1942.

10. *C. Cresc.*, III, 47, a more detailed account than in the later letter, and richer in picturesque points (the tower, the soft bed of manure, the poor peasant's wife who at first stayed a little apart while her husband relieved himself), of which it is worthwhile to make a typological study. Augustine had read Apuleius, and that author of the picaresque tales in the *Metamorphoses* seems to be just below the surface. Which does not mean to say that the event itself was not real.

11. *Ep.* 88, 7: *Sed cum legati* Roman *venerunt, iam cicatrices episcopi catholici Bagaitani horrendae et recentissimae imperatorem commoverant ut leges tales mitterentur quales et missae sunt.* Not at Ravenna, but at Rome, where Honorius had begun his sixth consulship on 1 January 404, and where he would reside with his Court until the end of the summer. That was known in Africa: cf. *sermon Dolbeau* 25 (*Mainz* 61), 25 and 26.

12. See the text of this *commonitorium* in *Concilia Africae*, pp. 211–13.

13. *Concilia Africae*, p. 213, 1. 1049–62; *C.Th.*, XVI, 5, 7.

14. *C.Th.*, XVI, 11, 2.

15. *C.Th.*, XVI, 6, 4: ... *adversarios catholicae fidei* extirpare *huius decreti auctoritate prospeximus.*

16. *Concilia Africae, CCL,* 149, p. 214: ... *quia apud Carthaginem tantum unitas facta est* ... The compiler to whom we are indebted for these records of the council abridged them in a few lines because, he says, he reckoned the debates to be too circumstantial! It is the lack of a sense of history among the compilers of Late Antiquity and the Middle Ages that has often deprived us of great sections of Augustine's detailed writings, notably in his letters and sermons.

17. *Ep.* 86. It could be that this letter – and the administrative responsibilities it implies for Caecilianus – is datable rather to around 414 and is therefore more concerned with the repressive outcome of the 411 conference: cf. A. Mandouze, *Prosopographie chrétienne du Bas-Empire. I*, p. 179, and S. Lancel, in *Augustinus-Lexikon*, vol. 1, 1994, p. 690.

18. For ever illustrated by Donatus' famous reply: 'What has the emperor to do with the Church?' (Optat, III, 3).

19. *Actes de la conf. de Carthage en 411*, III, 110–41, *SC*, 224, pp. 1070–96. On this phase of the debates of 411, see above, p. 298.

20. Very probably Valentinus of Vaiana, who would be primate of Numidia some dozen years later.

21. This famous aphorism came to Augustine in the context of the anti-Donatist struggle, but because it declares the primacy of charitable love it obviously has far wider resonances: cf. J. Gallais, in *Recherches de sc. relig.*, 43, 1955, pp. 545–55; Trapé, *Saint Augustin*, pp. 264–7; Dutoit, *Tout saint Augustin*, pp. 119–21.

22. Thus, where the Donatist bishop and his own clergy coexisted with a Catholic clerical hierarchy was born *ipso facto* a double clerical hierarchy with the resultant problems. These problems would be even more numerous and delicate after 411. On the solutions that would be found, cf. Lancel, 'Le sort des évêques et des communautés donatistes', pp. 149–65.

23. Council of 13 June 407, c. 5, *Concilia Africae*, p. 216 (Maier, *Le Dossier du donatisme*, II, p. 150).

24. On the localization of Siniti, see above, p. 251.

25. We are in a city milieu, as evidenced by the preacher's allusions to *rusticitas*, and as also suggested by the ample dimensions of the church where he is preaching (1). Dolbeau (*Vingt-Six Sermons au peuple d'Afrique*, p. 309) thinks it might be Thagaste, with Alypius; it could also be Calama, with Possidius.

26. *Sermon* 360. The merit of having attributed this text to Maximinus of Siniti is again due to

Dolbeau, who was able to find its original title: cf. *Revue bénéd.*, 105, 1995, pp. 293–308, and *Vingt-Six Sermons au peuple d'Afrique*, p. 630.

27. *C.Th.*, XVI, 5, 43; Maier, *Le Dossier du donatisme*, II, pp. 153–7. M.-F. Berrouard made no mistake in dating the confiscation of the Donatists' church at Hippo to after this order: *Recherches aug.*, VII, 1971, p. 118.

28. As the editor of the sermon, Dolbeau, suggests, in *Vingt-Six Sermons au peuple d'Afrique*, p. 308.

29. *C.Th.*, XVI, 5, 44 (Maier, *Le Dossier du donatisme*, II, pp. 159–60).

30. *C.Th.*, XVI, 5, 46 (*Le Dossier du donatisme*, II, pp. 162–8).

31. *C.Th.*, XVI, 5, 47 (*Le Dossier du donatisme*, II, pp. 168–9).

32. The text has not come down to us, but its content is evoked in the minutes of the council of Carthage of 14 June 410 (*Concilia Africae*, p. 220) and in the edict of 25 August, abrogating it (*C.Th.*, VI, 5, 51). Cf. A. De Veer, 'Une mesure de tolérance de l'empereur Honorius', in *Revue des études byzantines*, 24, 1966, pp. 189–95.

33. *C.Th.*, XVI, 5, 51 (Maier, *Le Dossier du donatisme*, II, p. 172).

34. The date is indicated in the short extract published in the Theodosian Code: *C.Th.*, XVI, 11, 3; text in the *Actes de la conférence de Carthage en 411*, I, 4 and III, 29, *SC*, 195, pp. 564–8, and 224, pp. 998–1004.

35. *Actes*, I, 4, *SC*, 195, p. 564.

36. *Actes*, I, 5, p. 570.

37. *Actes*, I, 5, pp. 572–4.

38. On the diffusion of this text and, more broadly, on the methods of organization of the conference, see S. Lancel, in *Actes de la conférence de Carthage en 411*, general Introduction, *SC*, 194, pp. 25–34.

39. He had profited from this enforced leisure to write to Dioscorus, the brother of the *magister memoriae* Zenobius (cf. above, p. 83), a long letter (*Ep.* 118) to which I shall return; he also wrote to his clergy and his flock, feeling worried about the situation of his church in his absence (*Ep.* 122).

40. On this church and its site, cf. lastly L. Ennabli, *Carthage*, pp. 31–2.

41. Ennabli, *Carthage*, pp. 69–70.

42. Edict published in the *Actes*, I, 10, *SC*, 195, pp. 576–86.

43. *Actes*, I, 14, *SC*, 195, p. 590: . . . *ut quamprimum de numero nostro constet*.

44. Saying this, the Catholics were risking little! Augustine recounted later that the idea was unanimously accepted by those present, with the exception of an old bishop who refused and another who abstained, but who were persuaded to rethink their positions: *Gesta cum Emerito*, 6.

45. *Actes*, I, 16, pp. 594–8.

46. It was not a place of worship and therefore chosen by Marcellinus for its neutrality. We know that it was situated in the middle of the town, and was spacious, light and cool. See S. Lancel, in *Actes*, I, *SC*, 194, pp. 50–2.

47. *Actes*, I, 97, *SC*, 195, p. 698.

48. *Actes*, I, 150 (Possidius); 152; 154; 156 (Aurelius).

49. One may read of the use of these data in the general Introduction to *Actes de la conférence*, *SC*, 194, pp. 108–67.

50. Analysis of this episcopacy in S. Lancel, 'Le recrutement de l'Église d'Afrique au début du Ve siècle: aspects qualitatifs et quantitatifs', in *De Tertullien aux Mozarabes. Mélanges offerts à J. Fontaine*, vol. I, pp. 325–38.

51. *Actes*, II, 20, 23, 25, *SC*, 224, p. 934. Taken down in shorthand by several teams of *exceptores*, the voluminous minutes of 1 June were only partly transcribed in fair copy two days later (cf. *Actes*, II, 53, p. 956). The Donatists stressed their inability to have sight of the minutes in their rough state (on these technical aspects, cf. *Actes*, I, *SC*, 194, pp. 342–51.

52. *Actes*, II, 56, *SC*, 224, p. 958: 'We ask your Eminence to grant them this adjournment. It is only natural: they want to examine, discuss and come well prepared.' It will be noted that Augustine used the same words that he had used with regard to the Manichaean Felix in December 404: *C. Felicem*, I. 20. In the operation of this litigious wiliness it is difficult to come out in favour of either Catholics or Donatists: see M. A. Tilley, 'Dilatory Donatists or procrastinating Catholics: the trial at the Conference of Carthage', in *Church History*, 60, 1991, pp. 7–19.

53. *Actes*, III, 15, p. 992.

54. Cf. above, p. 291.

55. *Actes*, III, 120, pp. 1076–8.

56. See the bitter view of Petilianus: *Sensim in causam inducimur!* (*Actes*, III, 151, p. 1102).

57. *Actes*, III, 155, 187, 197, 199, 201, 214, pp. 1104, 1132, 1144, 1156. The very sound distinction Augustine made between the two cases was also one of the cleverest. In principle, the Donatists had laid down, at the start of the conference (*Actes*, I, 20), that the debate must be 'ecclesiastical'; but at the same time, knowing full well that if the matter remained on the scriptural plane it would soon be over, they could not go back on their prior objections, including the one relating to the legal standing of the petitioner, which was at the root of the production of the archive documents. They were thus condemned not to choose, without in any way being able to prevent the two cases from being tackled in succession.

58. *Actes*, III, 222, 226, 228, 230, 232, 235, 237, 242, pp. 1162–78. Regarding Caecilianus (*frater, non pater*: *Actes*, III, 233), Augustine was taking up the Gospel parables on the mixture of good and bad in the Church of this world. As for the origin of the Church to which he belonged, as Caecilianus had, he based his arguments on the texts quoted in the synodal letter produced as *mandatum* (*Actes*, I, 55) essentially on Luke, 24.46–7, and Matt., 23.9. The discussion over 1 Cor. 4.15 had been imposed upon him by Montanus of Zama, whose interpretation he corrected by quoting 1 Cor. 3.6–7.

59. *Actes*, III, 265, p. 1184: on Augustine's episcopal ordination, see above, pp. 182ff.

60. *Actes*, III, 265, p. 1224 (cf. III, 258, p. 1202 for the Donatists' text).

61. Marcellus' *Capitula* (here abbreviated to *Capit.*) and the *Breviculus conlationis* (*Brev. conl.*) by Augustine.

62. *Brev. conl.*, III, 16–18.

63. *Capit.*, 296–303, *SC*, 195, pp. 502–4: *Brev. conl.*, III, 21–2.

64. The discussions on these documents from the archives were very long. Refer to the analysis in *Actes*, I, *SC*, 194, pp. 91–102.

65. *Capit.*, 540 and 541, *SC*, 195, p. 548. The imperial judge pointed out that the defection of one of the advocates could give grounds for a petition (*Capit.*, III, 542); but the Donatists failed to seize the opportunity.

66. *Capit.*, III, 564–73, pp. 552–4. These are the *Acta purgationis Felicis* of 5 February 315, to be read in Maier, *Le Dossier du donatisme*, I, 1987, pp. 171–87.

67. *Capit.*, III, 485, p. 556; *Brev. conl.*, III, 43. Remember that it was the beginning of June: the bishops and the judge had thus remained in the session, apparently without interruption, for some dozen hours.

68. On the quality of Marcellinus' arbitration, cf. *Actes*, I, *SC*, 194, pp. 66–73, cf. also M. Moreau, *Le Dossier Marcellinus dans la correspondance de saint Augustin*, Paris, Ét. aug., 1973, pp. 112 and 142–3, and A. Mandouze, *Prosopographie de l'Afrique chrét. I. Afrique (303–533)*, sv. Marcellinus 2, pp. 671–88.

69. *Actes*, I, 5, *SC*, 195, p. 574.

70. *Actes*, I, 7, p. 576.

71. For instance, Frend, *The Donatist Church*, p. 275.

72. Their spokesmen had authenticated all their speeches in the conference with the qualification 'reserving the right to appeal', and in fact they did appeal: *Brev. conl.*, III, 16.

73. *Actes*, I, 4, lines 10–13, *SC*, 195, p. 564.

74. The fines went as far as the payment of 50 gold *librae* for the *illustres*, very lofty persons whom there was little chance of meeting among the ranks of the Donatists.

75. This unusual assimilation of circumcellions to an *ordo* is still argued about: cf. J. E. Atkinson, 'Out of order; the Circumcellion and Codex Theodosianus, 16, 5, 52', in *Historia*, 41, 1992, pp. 488–99.

76. *C.Th.*, XVI, 5, 52 (Maier, *Le Dossier du donatisme*, II, pp. 175–8).

77. *C.Th.*, XVI, 5, 54 (*Le Dossier du donatisme*, pp. 179–283).

78. *Contra Gaudentium*, I, 28. Cf. the fine analyses by P. Brown, 'St Augustine's Attitude to Religious Coercion', in *Religion and Society in the Age of Saint Augustine*, London, Faber 1972, pp. 260–78.

79. This is letter 185, one of the longest written by Augustine, to which in the *Retractations* he gave the status of a book: *De correctione donatistorum* (*Retract.*, II, 48). The bishop of Hippo would not have written at such length to the young captain if he had not had an inkling of a merit that subsequent events would reveal.

80. At Milan, in 386, Augustine, who was still outside the Church though close to Ambrose, had certainly been aware of the fate of Priscillian, pursued with hatred by his Spanish colleagues; and

he knew that it was to the Church's honour that his execution had been condemned by Pope Siricius, and also by St Martin of Tours and Ambrose himself.

CHAPTER XXVII : Dialogue with the pagans

1. *Concilia Africae*, CCL, 149, p. 196. The embassy sent to Italy was moreover duly given a mandate in this direction: *Concilia Africae*, CCL, p. 194. It doubtless obtained no satisfaction, since a second general council which met in the same year, 401, repeated its demand for the suppression of paganism, notably in rural areas: *Concilia Africae*, CCL, p. 205.

2. *C.Th.*, XVI, 10, 15; 18.

3. *C.Th.*, XVI, 10, 19 (Nov. 407).

4. This political will has been commented upon by C. Lepelley, 'Le musée des statues divines', in *Cahiers archéologiques*, 42, 1994, pp. 5–15. See also, by the same author, for both Italy and Africa, 'Permanence de la cité classique et archaïsmes municipaux en Italie au Bas-Empire', in *Institutions, société et vie politique dans l'Empire romain au IVe siecle apr. J.-C.*, Coll. École fr. de Rome, 159, Rome 1992, pp. 364–6.

5. Nectarius, in *Ep.* 103, 3: *Et si, ut quibusdam philosophis placet, omnia peccata paria sunt, indulgentia omnibus debet esse communis.* This Stoic type of anthropology was widespread in this period among the municipal élites, especially in Africa: cf. R. Hanoune, 'Le paganisme philosophique de l'aristocratie municipale', in *L'Afrique dans l'Occident romain, 1er siècle av. J.-C.–IVe siècle apr. J.-C.*, Coll. École fr. de Rome, 134, Paris-Rome, 1990, pp. 63–75.

6. For example, in Fustel de Coulanges, *L'Invasion germanique et la Fin de l'Empire*, Paris, 1890, p. 64.

7. The first architect of this review was a specialist in Late Roman law, J. Declareuil, notably in an article entitled 'Les curies municipales et le clergé au Bas-Empire', in *Revue hist. de droit français et étranger*, 1935, pp. 26–53.

8. Cf. the analyses of Lepelley, *Les Cités de l'Afrique romaine au Bas-Empire*, I, pp. 372–6.

9. *Les Cités de l'Afrique romaine*, p. 374. The author wrote this in 1979; things developed very swiftly at the end of the second millennium, and the 'parareligious' situation he was describing in France was no longer the same twenty years later. All the same, the last but one (datewise) of the presidents of the French Republic, an agnostic but 'spiritualist' – 'I believe in the powers of the spirit', he said earnestly – thought it a good idea to have a mass said in Notre-Dame de Paris for his mortal remains.

10. *C.Th.*, XVI, 10, 17: *Ut profanos ritus iam salubri lege submovimus, ita festos conventus civium et communem omnium laetitiam non patimur submoveri . . .*

11. Cf. A.-M. La Bonnardière, 'Les *Ennarationes in Psalmos* prêchées par saint Augustin à Carthage en décembre 409', in *Recherches aug.*, 11, 1976, pp. 52–90; for instance, *Enarr. in Psalm.* 147, 7: *. . . sunt qui propterea hodie non venerunt quia* munus *est.* Cf. also S. *Dolbeau* 5 (Mainz 12), 7, announcing the preaching of the *Enarr. in Psalm.* 147: *Vingt-Six Sermons au peuple d'Afrique*, pp. 427 and 440.

12. On the two Melanias, particularly the Elder, read the critical remarks by N. Moine, 'Melaniana', in *Recherches aug.*, 15, 1980, pp. 3–79.

13. It is expressly stated in the *Life of St Melania*, Greek version, § 20, ed. D. Gorce, *Sources chrétiennes*, 90, 1962, p. 170.

14. *Vita Melaniae*, Latin version, I, 15.

15. *Life of St Melania*, Greek version, SC, 90, p. 170.

16. *Vita Melaniae*, I, 22, SC, 90. p. 172. The Latin version (*Anal. Bolland.*, 8, 1889, p. 35) specifies that the members comprised contingents of both sexes from the couple's domestic slaves.

17. Albina's letter has not been preserved, but its content and tone may be inferred from Augustine's reply (*Ep.* 126), in a letter in which he tries somewhat laboriously to exonerate his parishioners from the accusation of cupidity; on this letter, see L. J. Swift, 'On the Oath of Pinianus', in *Congresso int. su S. Agostino nel XVI centenario della conversione*, Atti, vol. I, Rome, 1987, pp. 371–9.

18. See the 'scenic' analysis by Mandouze, *Saint Augustin*, pp. 631–4.

19. Augustine's attitude on this occasion is notably analysed by G. A. Cecconi, 'Un evergete mancato. Piniano a Ippona', in *Athenaeum*, 66, 1988, pp. 371–89.

20. *Saturnalia*, VI, 1, 1. On the intellectual personality of Ceionius Rufius Albinus, see J. Flamant, *Macrobe et le néoplatonisme latin à la fin du IVe siècle*, Leiden, Brill, 1977, pp. 59–62.

21. Above, p. 83. Ceionius Rufius Albinus' brother, Caecina Albinus, had also married a Christian woman. On this infiltration into Christianity by the women of this aristocratic milieu, see A. Chastagnol, 'Le sénateur Volusien et la conversion d'une famille de l'aristocratie romaine au Bas-Empire', in *Revue des ét. anc.*, 58, 1956, pp. 250–1. On the 'mixed marriages', read also P. Brown, 'Aspects of the Christianization of the Roman Aristocracy', in *Journal of Roman Studies*, 51, 1961, pp. 6–7.

22. 'It was not Accius and Virgil, Augustus or even Antoninus who had to be taken as a model, but rather Scipio and Marius. It was by giving up the command of the armies that this aristocracy condemned itself, and that explains the archaistic and outmoded nature of its powerless propaganda': A. Piganiol, commenting in the *Journal des savants*, 1945, p. 28, on the book by A. Alföldi, *Die Kontorniaten*, Budapest and Leipzig, 1943.

23. Except for the mention made of this proconsulship by his friend Rutilius Namatianus, *De reditu suo*, I, 173–4.

24. In matters of magic, others had done better! On 'Christ the magician', see G. Madec, 'Le Christ des païens d'après le *De consensu evangelistarum* de saint Augustin', in *Recherches aug.*, 26, 1992, pp. 40–7.

25. *Ep.* 233, 234 (cf. 234, 1: *per meae opinionis sententiam, ide est a pagano homine*) and 235. On these texts, cf. P. Mastandrea, 'Il "dossier Longiniano" nell'epistolario di Sant-Agostino (epist. 233–235)' in *Studia Patavina*, 25, 1978, pp. 523–40.

26. Cf. P. Courcelle, 'Date, source et genese des *Consultationes Zacchaei et Apollonii*', in *Revue de l'hist. des relig.*, 146, 1954, p. 185; lastly, Madec, 'Le Christ des païens', p. 66.

27. *CIL*, VI, 1779. On aristocratic paganism in the Christian Rome of Popes Damasus and Siricius, cf. C. Pietri, *Roma christiana*, I, pp. 427–60, and L. Cracco Ruggini, *Il paganesimo romano tra religione e politica (384–394 d. C.)*, Rome, 1979.

28. These are letters 137 and 138. They have been the subject of excellent analyses by Moreau, *Le Dossier Marcellinus*, pp. 59–77.

29. Cf. S. Lancel, in *Actes de la conférence de Carthage en 411*, vol. IV, *SC*, 373, pp. 1333–4; lastly, Dolbeau, *Vingt-Six Sermons au peuple d'Afrique*, pp. 244–5.

30. *Sermon Dolbeau* 25 (Mainz 61), 27 (*Vingt-Six Sermons au peuple d'Afrique*, p. 267): *Cras ero christianus*; *cras, cras* was the cry of the crow that did not return to the ark, and also the cry uttered by Augustine himself in the depths of his distress in the garden in Milan just before the impetus that liberated him: cf. above, p. 96.

31. *Serm. Dolbeau*, 25, 27, *Vingt-Six Sermons*, p. 266. Augustine often returns to his injunction to the faithful to set a good example, a factor in the conversion of the pagans; see H. Chadwick, 'Augustine on pagans and Christians: reflections on religious and social change', in *History, Society and the Churches. Essays in Honour of Owen Chadwick*, Cambridge, Cambridge Univ. Press, 1985, pp. 17–18.

32. *Enarr. in Psalm.* 93, 3. On these problems of naming the days and maintaining tradition despite ecclesiastical objurgations, see C. Pietri, 'Le temps de la semaine à Rome et dans l'Italie chrétienne (IVᵉ–VIᵉ s.)', in *Le Temps chrétien de la fin de l'Antiquité au Moyen Âge (IIIᵉ–XIIIᵉ siècle)*, Paris, CNRS, 1984, pp. 63–97.

33. On the whole of these practices, see the development by F. Van der Meer, *Saint Augustin pasteur d'âmes*, vol. I, pp. 108–14.

34. Augustine would mention the healing, on emerging from the baptismal waters, of an old, gouty doctor at Carthage, and a paralysed former stage-player at Curubis (Kourba): *City of God*, XXII, 8, 5 and 6.

35. A theologian would probably call it an 'internal miracle', such as that experienced by St Paul at the time of his conversion.

PART III : The Doctor of Grace

CHAPTER XXVIII : Pelagius

1. It has sometimes been supposed that Pelagius stayed two or three years in Sicily, where he would have composed his *De natura: Dict. de theol. cath.*, 12, art. 'Pelagianisme', col. 680, § 2, b, resuming a very old suggestion (1673) by a great Jesuit, Jean Garnier. But why would he have deliberately gone from Sicily to Africa, where he had no business to be? It is far more likely that his crossing to Africa was caused by events.

2. *Ep.* 146, which Augustine quotes *in extenso* in the *De gestis Pelagii*, 52, and which its recipient would keep preciously in his possession against all eventualities, and would produce later in his defence. To authenticate his message, Augustine had added the final salutation in his own hand.

3. Jerome commented upon his imposing physique, which was due, he joked, to over-indulgence in Scottish 'porridge' (*In Ieremiam, Prol.*, 4: *'Scottorum pultibus praegravatus'* – as he saw him in Palestine in 414/15), a feature confirmed by Orosius, *Liber apologeticus*, 2, 5.

4. On the Roman milieu in which Pelagius developed, besides the fundamental book by G. de Plinval, now overtaken on many points, *Pélage, ses écrits, sa vie et sa réforme*, Lausanne, 1943, pp. 47–71, read P. Brown, 'Pelagius and his supporters: aims and environment', in *Journal of Theol. Studies*, 19, 1968, pp. 93–112 and, by the same author, 'The patrons of Pelagius: the Roman aristocracy between East and West', in *Journal of Theol. Studies*, 21, 1970, pp. 56–72 (reprinted in *Religion and Society in the Age of Saint Augustine*).

5. Cf. above, p. 290. In 416 Evodius, with Aurelius, Alypius and Possidius, cosigned the letter addressed to Pope Innocent (*Ep.* 177) by Augustine against Pelagius. On this theory, see Y.-M. Duval, 'La date du "De natura" de Pélage', in *Revue des ét. aug.*, 36, 1990, p. 283, note 178.

6. According to Courcelle, *Les 'Confessions' de saint Augustin dans la tradition littéraire*, p. 580.

7. On these texts, cf. above, pp. 178–80 and 189–92. On the first texts of Pelagius, see G. Martinetto, 'Les premières réactions antiaugustiniennes de Pélage', in *Revue des ét. aug.*, 17, 1971, pp. 83–117, and also the invaluable notes by A. C. De Veer in *BA*, 22, pp. 680–94.

8. Pelagius' *De natura* is customarily dated to around 414. At the conclusion of a close examination (in 'La date du "De natura" de Pélage', pp. 257–83, especially pp. 272–8) Y.-M. Duval proposed the date 405/6.

9. Cf. on Caelestius the recent information by G. Bonner in *Augustinus-Lexikon*, vol. 1, 1994, col. 693–8.

10. Rather than 422, E. Lamirande dates it to 412/13, 'La datation de la "Vita Ambrosii" by Paulinus of Milan', in *Revue des ét. aug.*, 27, 1981, pp. 44–55 (cf. in this direction, Y.-M. Duval, 'L'éloge de Théodose dans la *Cité de Dieu* (V, 26, 1). Sa place, son sens et ses sources' in *Recherches aug.*, 4, 1996, p. 179).

11. See F. Refoulé, 'Datation du premier concile de Carthage contre les pélagiens et du "Libellus fidei" de Rufin', in *Revue des ét. aug.*, 9, 1963, pp. 41–9.

12. These propositions were passed on by Marius Mercator, but Augustine himself also quoted them in his *De gestis Pelagii*, 23. On this episode, see O. Wermelinger, *Rom und Pelagius*, Stuttgart, 1975, pp. 9–11.

13. This identification, already put forward by Jean Garnier in the seventeenth century, was not accepted by H.-I. Marrou, 'Les attaches orientales du pélagianisme', in *CRAI*, 1968, pp. 464–5 (reprinted in *Patristique et Humanisme*, Paris, Le Seuil, 1976, pp. 331–44). It is, however, more than likely: cf. the focus on it by A. C. De Veer, 'Le prêtre Rufinus', in *BA*, 22, pp. 704–11.

14. *Ep.* 193, 3: *Cum viderem neminem se velle tanto aggeri litterarum legendo committere.* On the edition of the *Actes* of 411, cf. S. Lancel, in *SC*, 194, pp. 353–63, and in *Augustinus-Lexikon*, 1, 1994, col. 681.

15. This would be the *Contra donatistas, liber unus*: on this text, cf. *Augustinus-Lexikon*, 2, 1999.

16. E. Gilson, *Introduction à l'étude de saint Augustin*, p. 200, who adds: '. . . Pelagianism was the radical negation of Augustine's personal experience or, if you will, Augustine's personal experience was . . . the very negation of Pelagianism'.

17. And even earlier: cf. G. Bonner, art. 'Baptismus parvulorum', in *Augustinus-Lexikon*, vol. 1, 1994, col. 593–4.

18. *De pecc. mer.*, I, 21: *Potest proinde recte dici parvulos sine baptismo de corpore exeuntes* in damnatione *omnium* mitissima *futuros*. He would confirm this viewpoint in the 'Manual' (*Enchiridion*, 93) with the same term (*mitissima poena*), although, for want of more precise detail, it is not known what he meant by this.

19. *De spiritu et littera*, 22: *Da quod iubes*; the phrase in *Conf.*, X, 40, already thrice repeated in *De pecc. mer.*, II, 5, as if echoing the injunctions of the *Psalms*. On the phrase and its implications, cf. C. Mayer, 'Da quod iubes et iube quod vis', in *Augustine-Lexikon*, vol. 2, fasc. 1–2, 1996, col. 211–13.

20. *De spiritu et littera*, 42. On the theological implications of these texts beyond the issues of the anti-Pelagian struggle, see I. Bochet, ' "La lettre tue, l'esprit vivifie". L'exégèse augustinienne de *II Cor.*, 3, 6' in *Nouv. Revue théol.*, 114, 1992, pp. 341–70.

21. Cf. M. Moreau, *Le Dossier Marcellinus dans la correspondance de saint Augustin*, pp. 172–3.

22. The letter to Demetrias is found in two places in the *Patrologie latine*, as an appendix to

Jerome's letters (*PL*, 33, 1099–120). In French trans. in Péronne, Écalle and Vincent, *Oeuvres de saint Augustin*, Paris, Vivès, 1873, vol. 6, pp. 339–79.

23. On this episode, see Wermelinger, *Rom und Pelagius*, pp. 29–34.

24. Cf. the article by Y.-M. Duval already quoted, 'La date du "De Natura" de Pélage', pp. 264–8 and earlier, Wermelinger, *Rom und Pelagius*, pp. 39–40. Let me make clear that the *opinio communis* is that Pelagius composed his *De Natura* in Palestine in 414, and that Iacobus and Timasius sent it from there to Augustine (cf. e.g. M.-F. Berrouard, 'L'exégèse augustinienne de Rom. 7, 7–25 entre 396 et 418, avec des remarques sur les deux périodes de la crise pélagienne', in *Recherches aug.*, 16, 1981, pp. 149–50).

25. *Ep.* 166, 2: *Ecce venit ad me religiosus iuvenis, catholica pace frater, aetate filius, honore compresbyter noster Orosius, vigil ingenio, promptus eloquio, flagrans studio.* There was a sort of warning about Orosius' religious 'activism' in this rapid portrait addressed to Jerome.

26. Orosius, *Liber apologeticus*, 3, 5: Jerome, *Dialogue against the Pelagians*, 3, 19.

27. Already declared by Pelagius in his *Commentaries on the 13 epistles of the apostle Paul*, ed. A. Souter, in Texts and Studies, 1926, p. 45.

28. Orosius, *Liber apologeticus*, 3, 6. Pelagius is supposed to have declared, following a clarification on grace made by bishop John of Jerusalem: 'That is what I too believe. Anathema on anyone who claims that without God's help man can attain the development of all his virtues' (*De gestis Pelagii*, XIV, 37).

29. He would be condemned by Innocent's successor, Zosimus: cf. Wermelinger, *Rom und Pelagius*, p. 68.

30. This dossier has conveniently been assembled by Wermelinger, *Rom und Pelagius*, pp. 71–5 (German text), pp. 295–9 (Latin text) essentially on the basis of *De gestis Pelagii*.

31. The expression is Jerome's in a letter addressed to Augustine a little later: *Ep.* 143, 2.

32. It is the *Chartula defensionis suae* (cf. *De gestis Pelagii*, XXXII, 57–XXXIII, 58) which Augustine received not by way of a certain 'Charus', whose name appears erroneously in the *De gestis*, but through Palatinus, a citizen of Hippo and deacon in Palestine.

33. On the 'utilization' of these relics in Africa, especially at Hippo, cf. above, pp. 236–7.

34. In the new letter 19*, 1, which on this phase of the anti-Pelagian controversy contains many items of information, carefully 'decoded' and clarified by the commentaries of Y.-M. Duval in *BA*, 46 B, 1987, pp. 507–15.

35. Read letter 4* (*BA*, 46 B, pp. 108–16), with the clarifications of Y.-M. Duval, *BA*, 46 B, pp. 430–42, and also of J.-P. Bouhot, 'Une lettre d'Augustin d'Hippone à Cyrille d'Alexandrie (*Ep.* 4*)', in *Les Lettres de saint Augustin découvertes par J. Divjak*, 1983, pp. 147–53.

36. The chronology ('around July 416') still maintained by G. De Plinval in *BA*, 21, p. 423 was outdated following the discovery of the new letters of Augustine.

37. *Ep.* 181, 182 and 183 in Augustine's correspondence. They were analysed with great perceptiveness by C. Pietri in *Roma christiana*, vol. II, pp. 1196–211; he also highlighted (pp. 1186–95) the skilfulness of the two African synodal letters.

38. On the convictions and aims of Zosimus, read Pietri, *Roma Christiana*, vol. II, pp. 1219–26.

39. Paulinus of Milan, *Ep.* 8, in *Collectio Avellana*, 50, *CSEL*, 35, 1, 115–17.

40. Cf. what Augustine says of these exchanges: *Tot enim et tantis inter apostolicam sedem et Afros episcopos currentibus et recurrentibus scriptis ecclesiasticis* (*Contra duas ep. pelag.*, II, 5).

41. Zosimus, *Ep.* 12 ('*Quamvis patrum*'), in *Collect. Avellana*, 50, *CSEL*, 35, 1, 115–17.

42. For Wermelinger, *Rom und Pelagius*, pp. 196–205, and Pietri, *Roma Christiana*, II, pp. 933–4 and 1230–3, there is no doubting the reality of imperial pressure on the pope. A. Pincherle, *Vita di sant'Agostino*, p. 404, has no doubt that Aurelius and Augustine inspired Honorius. Y.-M. Duval, 'Julien d'Éclane et Rudin d'Aquilée', in *Revue des ét. aug.*, 24, 1978, p. 245, has some reservations and does not want to eliminate the theory of the imperial government's backing for Zosimus' volte-face.

43. We know from the texts that this *Basilica Fausti*, which had a baptistery adjoining, was outside the walls and was vast. There is sometimes a tendency to identify it with the ensemble of Damous el-Karita: cf. lastly L. Ennabli, *Carthage. Une métropole chrétienne*, pp. 27–8 and 127.

44. Cf. 'Restitutus 4', bishop of Nova Sinna, in *Prosop. chrét. du Bas-Empire. I. Afrique (303–533)*, p. 971.

45. There is a very full analysis of this text in Wermelinger, *Rom und Pelagius*, pp. 209–14.

46. *Ep.* 6*, to be read with the clarifications by Y.-M. Duval in *BA*, 46 B, pp. 444–56; cf. also M.-F. Berrouard, 'Les lettres 6* et 19* de Saint Augustin', in *Revue des ét. aug.*, 27, 1981, pp. 269–75.

47. As has been the case for the *De natura*: cf. A. C. De Veer, 'Pélage et la paternité de ses écrits', in *BA*, 22, p. 678.

48. The letter to Demetrias is preserved (cf. above, note 22). The *Pro libero arbitrio* survives only in the quotations from it made by Augustine: they are collected in *PL*, 48, 611–13.

49. On the date of the treatise, cf. lastly B. Delaroche, 'La datation du *De peccatorum meritis et remissione*', in *Revue des ét. aug.*, 41, 1995, pp. 35–57: winter 411–412.

50. Rom. 5.12. Reliant on an old Latin translation, Augustine read; '... *in quo omnes peccaverunt*' (literally: 'in whom all have sinned'), a mistaken translation from the Greek '*eph'hô pantes hèmarton*', where the relative must be understood not as a masculine (referring to Adam) but as a neuter, and where the best interpretation of *epi* would doubtless be to understand, either in a purely temporal sense: 'after which all have sinned' (cf. on this subject J. A. Fitzmyer, 'The Consecutive Meaning of *eph'hô* in Romans, 5, 12', in *New Testament Studies*, 39, 3, 1993, pp. 321–39, whose analyses and interpretations seem preferable to those of S. Lyonnet, 'Le péché originel et l'exégèse de *Rm.*, 5, 12–14', in *Recherches de science religieuse*, 44, 1956, pp. 63–84, who holds to a sense that is more explanatory or causal – 'due to the fact that' – of the *eph'hô* so curiously rendered as *in quo* [with the ambiguity of the relative] in the old Latin translation). It does not necessarily follow, however, that this error in the Latin text read by Augustine writes off all his theological developments, which do not rest on this one verse but on the whole of section 5, 12–20 on the *Epistle to the Romans* (clearly seen by, among others, P.-M. Hombert, *Gloria gratiae*, p. 292, note 131). We return to Augustine's use of Rom. 5.12 against the background of the controversy with Julian of Eclanum (above, pp. 421–2).

51. In particular a lucid article by A. Sage, 'Péché originel. Naissance d'un dogme', in *Revue des ét. aug.*, 13, 1967, pp. 211–48.

52. Cf. Sage, 'Péché originel', p. 234.

53. This last characterization is by De Plinval, *Pélage*, p. 200 and the comparison of the two expressions by Mandouze, *Saint Augustin*, p. 415.

54. Cf. G. Greshake, *Gnade als konkrete Freiheit* ('Grace as positive freedom'), Mainz, 1972.

CHAPTER XXIX : 418–419

1. Cf. J.-L. Maier, 'La date de la rétractation de Leporius et celle du "sermon 396" de saint Augustin', in *Revue des ét. aug.*, 11, 1965, pp. 39–42.

2. See the subtle and balanced analyses of Leporius' position in F. De Beer, 'Une tessère d'orthodoxie. Le "Libellus emendationis" de Leporius (vers 418–421)', in *Revue des ét. aug.*, 10, 1964, pp. 145–85.

3. See the small note by G. Madec, 'Leporius à l'école d'Augustin', in *La Patrie et la Voie*, p. 244.

4. In the summer of 418, Augustine was in his sixty-fourth year, and certainly did not travel on horseback, but by the relatively comfortable means of the official post (*evectio publica*), which enabled him to dictate as he went. On the distances and travelling conditions, see Perler and Maier, *Les Voyages de saint Augustin*, pp. 31 and 346–7.

5. It was suspected, but has now recently been confirmed thanks to the *Sermon Dolbeau 2* (*Mainz 5*), 2 (*Vingt-Six Sermons*, p. 238), that Fortunatus was close to Augustine, having been trained in his monastery and ordained priest at Thagaste before acceding to the bishopric of Constantine.

6. Cf. *Concilia Africae*, *CCL*, 149, p. 226. On these disputes, see S. Lancel, 'Le sort des évêques et des communautés donatistes', pp. 149–65, in particular pp. 159–63.

7. Canon of the council of Carthage of 13 September 401: *Concilia Africae*, pp. 202–3.

8. *Ep.* 236, 1, letter addressed from Hippo to Deuterius, 'Metropolitan' bishop of Caesarea; that Deuterius was informed is a sign that the bishop Victor who appears among the sanctioned was actually Victor of Malliana, at the time absent from his town, probably because he was in Rome to uphold his appeal.

9. *Concilia Africae*, *CCL*, 149, pp. 230 and 234.

10. *Ep.* 16*, 3, *BA*, 46 B, p. 272, and *Ep.* 23A*, 6, p. 380. On the whole matter, cf. S. Lancel, 'Saint Augustin et la Maurétanie Césarienne', pp. 48–9.

11. Iol, before Juba II gave his capital the name Caesarea, in honour of Augustus. A good monograph on the town and its environment has recently become available: P. Leveau, *Caesarea de Maurétanie, une ville romaine et ses campagnes*, Coll. École fr. de Rome, 70, Rome, 1984.

12. On these episodes, see above, pp. 168–9. The sacking of Caesarea by the 'Barbarians' who

had infiltrated the town in Firmus' wake had remained notorious. Symmachus would say that all the gold and silver in the province had disappeared: *Ep.* I, 64, ed. J.-P. Callu, *Les Belles Lettres*, 1972, pp. 121–2 and 228.

13. The ancestors of the Beni Menacer, who gave the French army such a hard time in the insurrection of 1871: cf. P. Salama, 'Vulnérabilité d'une capitale: Caesarea de Maurétanie', in *L'Africa romana*, 5, 1988, pp. 253–69, especially pp. 267–8.

14. The *'platea'* of *Gesta cum Emerito*, 1, is perhaps the forum which random excavations recently partially brought to light at Cherchell: cf. Leveau, *Caesarea de Maurétanie*, pp. 40–2, on the forum unearthed in 1977 by N. Benseddik and T. W. Potter.

15. *Contra Gaudentium*, I, 15: *Ad ecclesiam catholicam pariter venimus; adfuit maxima multitudo*. This *ecclesia* is qualified by *maior* in *Gesta cum Emerito*, 1, *initio*. It cannot be identified with the small basilica unearthed on the forum, although it has been dated to the early fifth century: cf. N. Duval, in *Revue des ét. aug.*, 34, 1988, pp. 254–5.

16. On this absence of a permanent road link, cf. M. Euzennat, 'Les ruines antiques du Bou Hellou (Maroc)', in *Actes du 101ᵉ Congr. nat. des soc. sav., Lille, 1976, Arch.*, Paris, 1978, pp. 295–7 and 312–29. P. Salama, in his map of the road network of Roman Africa, maintains the possibility of a coastal path between Siga (Takembrit) in Caesariensis and Rusaddir (Melilla) in Tingitana.

17. Note was taken quite some time ago of the similarities in form – indications in the late period of continued relations – between the Christian epigraphic texts of Volubilis, on the one hand, in Tingitana, and of Altava, Pomaris (Tlemcen) and Numerus Syorum (Marnia), on the other hand, in Caesariensis: texts commentated lastly by G. Camps, 'De Masuna à Koçeila. Les destinées de la Maurétanie aux VIᵉ et VIIᵉ siècles', in *BAC*, n. s., 19 B, 1985, pp. 307–24, notably p. 320, an article that rightly stresses the cultural unity cemented by Christianity between ancient Caesariensis and ancient Tingitana. It is known, moreover, that in the sixth century, after their fleeting reconquest, the Byzantines gave up reorganizing Tingitana and joined Septem (Ceuta) to Caesarea in the framework of Caesarean Mauretania.

18. Cf. C. Courtois, *Les Vandales et l'Afrique*, Paris, AMG, 1955, pp. 53–4.

19. *Ep.* 93, 24: *Mauretania tamen Caesariensis, occidentali quam meridianae parti vicinior, quando* nec Africam *se vult dici, quomodo de meridie gloriabitur?* The remark was inserted in a criticism of Donatist ecclesiology, which would have it (on the basis of *Ct.* 1, 6) that the true Church was 'in the south'.

20. And with good reason: from the point of view of biblical anthropology, the problem of the origin of the soul is a false one. Cf. the lucid pages by C. Tresmontant, *La Métaphysique du christianisme et la Naissance de la philosophie chrétienne*, Paris, Le Seuil, 1961, pp. 577–612. A little further on (*Ep.* 190, 17–19), Augustine quoted several scriptural texts in one or other sense, but it was only to admit that they were not relevant.

21. Jerome (*Ep.* 165 in the Augustinian *corpus*) had been content to tell Marcellinus that the western, and more especially African, tradition inclined towards 'traducianism', whereas he himself was more 'creationist'; but he had wisely advised Marcellinus to approach Augustine.

22. On this letter, read the fair commentaries by M. Moreau, *Le Dossier Marcellinus dans la correspondance de saint Augustin*, pp. 88–9.

23. *Actes de la conf. de Carthage en 41*, II, *SC*, 195, pp. 896–7.

24. There was one at Hippo, notably, as well as at Uzalis, Evodius' see, at Simitthu (Chemtou), Oea (Tripoli), and in many other places, where these Jewish colonies were of long standing. On these settlements, see J.-M. Lassère, *Ubique Populus*, Paris, CNRS, 1977, pp. 413–26.

25. Despite the scepticism of A. Mandouze, in *Prosop. chrét. du Bas-Empire. I. Afrique (303–533)*, s. v. Aptus 2, p. 88.

26. Cf. *On his return*, I, 1. 383–99, where the clichés of the avaricious and profiteering Jew seem fixed *ne varietur*.

27. See T. Raveaux, 'Adversus Iudeos. Antisemitismus bei Augustinus?', in *Signum Pietatis. Festgabe für C. P. Mayer, Cassiciacum*, XL, 1989, pp. 37–51.

28. *Sermon* 351, 11. These texts have been commentated by P. Salama, 'La parabole des milliaires chez saint Augustin', in *L'Africa romana*, 6, 2, Sassari, 1989, pp. 697–707.

29. Cf. C. Pietri, *Roma christiana*, vol. II, pp. 1249–50. The pope's letter (*Ep.* 16: *Miror vos*) is dated 16 November 418.

30. If not in early summer 418: cf. my work in *Revue des ét. aug.*, 30, 1984, pp. 51–3.

31. Pietri, *Roma christiana*, vol. II, p. 1251, speaks of 'doubtful ordination'; in fact, we know nothing of them; the synodal letter of 26 May 419 to Pope Boniface merely reports his *omnia errata*:

Concilia Africae, CCL, 149, p. 157, line 24. Apiarius was removed from office, but kept his priestly rank: *Concilia Africae, CCL*, 149, lines 30–1.

32. *Collectio Avellana, Ep.* 26–8 in *CSEL*, 35, pp. 72–4.

33. We know from Possidus' *Elenchus* (X[6], 144, in *Miscellanea Agostiniana*, 2, p. 203) that Augustine delivered a sermon on the occasion of the election and ordination of Florentius' successor.

34. *Concilia Africae, CCL*, 149, p. 169.

35. *Concilia Africae, CCL*, 149, p. 93.

36. *Concilia Africae, CCL*, 149, p. 266. Cf. C. Munier, 'Un canon inédit du XXe concile de Carthage', in *Revue des sc. relig.*, 40, 1966, pp. 113–26.

37. Much light has been thrown on the collegial conception of the Africans by P. Zmire, 'Recherches sur la collégialité épiscopale dans l'Église d'Afrique', in *Recherches aug.*, 7, 1971, pp. 3–72.

38. Probably the cathedral-church of Aurelius. Perhaps the edifice brought to light in the locality known as 'Carthagenna', in the ports district: cf. L. Ennabli, *Carthage*, p. 70; but see the sceptical remarks by N. Duval in *Antiquité tardive*, 5, 1997, p. 321.

39. *Concilia Africae, CCL*, 149, pp. 231 and 232.

40. See F.-M. Berrouard, 'Un tournant dans la vie de l'Église d'Afrique: les deux missions d'Alypius en Italie à la lumière des Lettres 10*, 15*, 16*, 22* and 23*A de saint Augustin', in *Revue des ét. aug.*, 31, 1985, pp. 46–70, notably pp. 49–63 for the years 419–420.

41. One must admire the strict analysis that enabled A. C. De Veer (in *BA*, 22, p. 290) to arrive at this chronological approach without yet having the information in *Ep.* 23*A at his disposal.

42. For, like De Veer (*BA*, 22, p. 312), I am of the opinion that Vincentius Victor was not writing on his own account, but for that of a group of clergy who had been appreciative of his rhetorical abilities: perhaps those whom in his *Ep.* 23*A (4, initio) to Possidius, Augustine curiously calls the *Hispani episcopi*, resorting to a plural which seems an extrapolation from the single *episcopus Hispanus* named, Optatus: or could Petrus, *presbyter Hispanus*, be included in this plural?

43. *Concilia Africae*, c. 3, *CCL*, 149, p. 70.

44. *Passion de Perpétue et de Félicité*, VII, 4–10, and VIII, 1–4, to be read in the fine recent edition by J. Amat, *SC*, 417, Paris, Éd. du Cerf, 1996, pp. 128–32.

45. On the possibility that Victor might have been influenced, through the 'Spanish priest' Petrus, by the Origenist and Priscillianist ideas that were widespread in Spain at the time, as witnessed by Orosius, see A. C. De Veer, 'Aux origines du *De natura et origine animae* de saint Augustin', in *Revue des ét. aug.*, 19, 1973, p. 156.

46. For the chronology and details of the whole affair, see S. Lancel, 'Saint Augustin et la Maurétanie Césarienne (2)', in *Revue des ét. aug.*, 30, 1984, pp. 251–62, especially pp. 257–9.

CHAPTER XXX : 'Seek his face evermore': the *De Trinitate*

1. Marrou, *Saint Augustin et l'augustinisme*, p. 145. Read also, by the same author, 'Saint Augustin et l'ange. Une légende mediévale', in *L'Homme devant Dieu. Mélanges de Lubac*, vol. II, Paris, 1964, pp. 137–49, reprinted in *Christiana tempora* (coll. EFR, 35), Rome, 1978, pp. 401–13.

2. *Ep.* 174. We know that Augustine added the prologues of Books I, II, III, IV and V, the second part of Book XII, Books XIII, XIV and XV: cf. A.-M. La Bonnardière, *Recherches de chronologie augustinienne*, pp. 165–77.

3. *De ord.*, II, 44; cf. above, p. 106. On this Porphyrian influence, A. Solignac, 'Réminiscences plotiniennes et porphyriennes dans le début du *De ordine* de saint Augustin', in *Archives de philosophie*, 20, 1957, p. 461.

4. *De div. quaest. ad Simpl*, II, qu. 2. On the indescribability of God, cf. G. Madec, art. 'Deus', in *Augustinus-Lexikon*, vol. 2, fasc. 3/4, 1999.

5. *De octo Dulcitii quaestionibus*, 5, 4: *Ego enim, quod et supra de me commemoravi, magis amo discere quam docere*. The date of this text is difficult to fix: perhaps 424 (cf. G. Madec, *Introduction aux 'Revisions'*, p. 157.

6. Cf. La Bonnardière, *Recherches de chronologie*, p. 176: later than 420. The validity of these 'stratigraphic analyses' of the *De Trinitate* is sometimes challenged: cf. A. Pincherle, *Vita di sant'Agostino*, p. 255.

7. Cf. C. Tresmontant, *Introduction à la théologie chrétienne*, pp. 352–4.

8. On the more strictly western aspects of the dispute, see M. Meslin, *Les Ariens d'Occident (335–430)*, particularly pp. 353–424.

9. B. Studer has clearly shown, by gathering and commenting upon numerous texts, drawn notably from the bishop's preaching, that the concept of *aequalitas* (between the Father and the Son, but also between the three persons of the Trinity) is often put forward by Augustine to convey the Nicaean consubstantiality: cf. B. Studer, 'Augustin et la foi de Nicée', in *Recherches aug.*, 19, 1984, pp. 133–54, particularly pp. 141–54.

10. For example in the 'Declaration of Sirmium' in 357: cf. Meslin, *Les Ariens d'Occident*, p. 277. On details of the Arian use of the Johannean verse, cf. M. Simonetti, 'Giovanni 14, 28 nella controversia ariana', in *Kyriakon. Festschrift Johannes Quasten*, Münster, 1970, pp. 151–61.

11. The founding text – as the Johannine prologue is, in another sense – of his Christology, frequently quoted by Augustine in his early works before becoming as here a *regula fidei*: cf. A. Verwilghen, *Christologie et spiritualité selon saint Augustin*, Paris, Beauchesne, 1985, pp. 344–400.

12. *De Trin.*, II, 7. The Arians are not designated by name as the objectors; but must one think (with M.-F. Berrouard, in *BA*, 73 A, p. 471) that Augustine had to wait for the *Sermo Arianorum* to come into his hands in the autumn of 419 (cf. *Ep.* 23*A, 3, *BA*, 46 B, p. 372) to be able to put a name to the objection?

13. *De Trin.*, II, 17. Not that Augustine was detaching himself from a tradition (still present in Hilary of Poitiers, *De Trin.*, 4, 25) which attributed the vision of Mamre to the Son alone.

14. People have believed it possible to discern, not only in the prologue to Book IV of the *De Trinitate*, but also in the body of the book, traces of the anti-Pelagian controversy that would date it to after 411. La Bonnardière (*Recherches de chronologie*, p. 173) even wanted to see in the *phantasmata* of *De Trin.*, IV, 14 an echo of the debate against the Arians as shaped by Augustine in the *Sermo Arianorum*, thus later than 419; but this great lady of Augustinian studies may well have been mistaken here.

15. Cf. R. Braun, *Deus Christianorum. Recherches sur le vocabulaire doctrinal de Tertullien*, Paris, PUF, 1962, pp. 167–70. Generalizing *substantia* to translate *ousia*, Tertullian was in agreement with Apuleius in rejecting *essentia*.

16. Cf. Braun, *Deus Christianorum*, p. 227.

17. Cf. M.-F. Berrouard, 'La défiance d'Augustin à l'égard du mot *persona* en théologie trinitaire', in *BA*, 73 A, 1988 (regarding the *Tract. in Ioh. evang.*, 39, 3).

18. There is general agreement in thinking that Augustine is targeting the 'Eunomians' (who insisted on the '*agennesia*', the aseity of God, in contrast with the '*genitus*' Son who was therefore not of the same substance): cf. A. Schindler, *Wort und Analogie in Augustins Trinitätslehre*, Tübingen, 1965, pp. 151–3: O. Du Roy, *L'Intelligence de la foi*, p. 458. Recently the preference has been to recognize them rather as 'homeans': M. R. Barnes, in *Journal of Theol. Studies*, 44, 1, 1993, pp. 185–95.

19. References in Du Roy, *L'Intelligence de la foi*, p. 438.

20. *De Trin.*, XII, 10. See T. J. Van Bavel, 'Woman as Image of God in Augustine's *De Trinitate* XII, in *Signum pietatis. Festgabe für C. P. Mayer O.S.A. zum 60. Geburtstag*, Würzburg, 1989, pp. 267–88.

21. Cf. A.-M. La Bonnardière, 'Les deux vies. Marthe et Marie', in *Saint Augustin et la Bible*, Paris, Beauchesne, 1986, pp. 411–25.

22. *De Trin.*, XIII, 24. On this theme, cf. G. Madec, 'Christus, scientia et sapientia nostra. Le principe de cohérence de la doctrine augustinienne', in *Recherches aug.*, 10, 1975, pp. 77–85.

23. Cf. the analyses of J. Moingt in *BA*, 16, pp. 632–4.

24. *De Trin.*, XV, 47. To make it understood that this 'proceeding' is not generation, Augustine would then quote (XV, 48) a long passage from one of his sermons on John's Gospel, specifying that in this sermon he was addressing believers and not non-believers: the latter word may provide the key to this rather unexpected excursus. Note that the beginning of XV, 49 is also addressed to non-believers.

CHAPTER XXXI : The *City of God*

1. On the ravages suffered by this town, see P. Courcelle, *Histoire littéraire des grandes invasions germaniques*, 3rd ed., Paris, Ét. aug., 1964, pp. 51–5.

2. *In Ezech.*, 1, prol. In fact, Marcella would succumb some months later as a result of the ill treatment endured during those three days: Jerome, *Ep.* 127, 13–14.

3. F. Paschoud, *Roma aeterna. Études sur le patriotisme romain dans l'Occident latin à l'époque des grandes invasions*, Rome, Institut suisse de Rome, 1967, p. 236. See the more balanced analyses by H. Inglebert, *Les Romains chrétiens face à l'histoire de Rome*, Paris, Ét. aug., 1996, pp. 421–4, on Augustine's first reactions.

4. The phrase is by A. Mandouze, *Saint Augustin*, p. 322. See Prudentius, *Peristephanon*, II, 553–60.

5. *Ep.* 130, 10; comparisons made by J. Doignon, 'Oracles, prophéties, "on-dit" sur la chute de Rome', in *Revue des ét. aug.*, 36, 1990, p. 135.

6. *De excidio urbis*, 2. Datable to the last months of 411 – if not early 412 – the *De excidio urbis* appears as the outcome and conclusion of the series of sermons directly inspired by the fall of Rome; on the whole series, cf. lastly J.-C. Fredouille, 'Les sermons sur la chute de Rome', in *Augustin predicateur (395–411). Actes du colloque int. de Chantilly (5–7 Sept. 1966)*, Paris, Ét. aug., 1998, pp. 439–48.

7. Already, in a text datable probably to the winter of 403–4: *sermon Dolbeau 6 (Mainz 13)*, 13 (Dolbeau, *Vingt-Six Sermons*, p. 466): *Legant priorum saeculorum mala in suis litteris*, echoed by the *historia eorum* of sermon 296, 7 of 411. On the theme of the *tempora christiana* in Augustine, cf. G. Madec, ' "*Tempora christiana*". Expression du triomphalisme chrétien ou récrimination païenne?' in *Petites Études augustiniennes*, pp. 233–59.

8. *Sermo Casinensis*, I, 133, 9 (*Miscellanea Agostiniana*, I, p. 407) = sermon 296, 7, quoted and commentated by Madec, 'Le *De Civitate Dei* comme *De vera religione*', in *Petites Études augustiniennes*, pp. 189–213 (here p. 132), taken up from a lecture given in Perugia in 1990.

9. *Enarr. in Psalm.* 83, 1 and 136, 9. The theme appears with a remarkable orchestration in one of the recently published new sermons, perhaps delivered in Carthage in the winter of 403–4: *sermon Dolbeau 6 (Mainz 13)*, 15 (*Vingt-Six Sermons*, pp. 467–8). The symbolism of the press has been studied by S. Poque, *Le Langage symbolique dans la prédication de Saint Augustin*, vol. I, Paris, Ét. aug., 1984, pp. 157–70.

10. *Ep.* 138, 16. On Augustine's polemical use of the Latin historians, see A. Schindler, 'Augustin und die römischen Historiker', in *Augustiniana Traiectina*, Paris, 1987, pp. 153–68. Cf. also, by the same author, 'Augustine and the History of the Roman Empire', in *Studia Patristica*, XXXII, Louvain, 1989, pp. 326–36.

11. *Ep.* 138, 17. On this theme of Christian *pietas* as an agent of preservation of the earthly city, see C. P. Mayer, '*Pietas* and *vera pietas quae caritas est*', in *Augustiniana Traiectina*, 1987, pp. 119–36, especially p. 125.

12. Rutilius Namatianus has sometimes been suggested, but both the dates and the intentions of his poem make the theory rather implausible: cf. G. Bardy, in general Introduction to the *City of God*, *BA*, 33, pp. 23–4.

13. *City of God*, V, 26, 2: *audivi* quosdam *nescio quam adversus eos (libros) responsionem scribendo praeparare*.

14. Orosius, *Histories*, I, *prol.* 11. 417 is the completion date of this Spanish priest's book.

15. See Bardy, in *BA*, 33, p. 29.

16. This presentation of the main structure of the *City of God* owes much to the sober and clear exposition made of it by G. J. P. O'Daly, 'Civitate dei (De-)', in *Augustinus-Lexikon*, vol. 1, 1994, col. 979–82. Besides the Introduction by Bardy in *BA*, 33, pp. 35–52, the book by J.-C. Guy is always useful, *Unité et structure logique de la 'Cité de Dieu' de saint Augustin*, Paris, Ét. aug., 1961, to be complemented by B. Studer, 'Zum Aufbau von Augustins *De civitate dei*', in *Mélanges T. J. Van Bavel*, vol. II, Louvain, 1990, pp. 937–51.

17. The *Orator*, XXIII, 75, where Cicero uses the word before tackling genres and styles: it was not the same level of difficulty!

18. H.-I. Marrou, *Saint Augustin et la fin de la culture antique*, pp. 668–70.

19. In this sense, Studer, 'Zum Aufbau von Augustins *De civitate dei*', p. 947. But it must be added that for Basil Studer the culminating point of the *City of God* is reached at the end of Book X, with the great movement marked by strong anaphoric resumptions which is a solemn proclamation of the Christian religion as the universal way of salvation: *Haec est igitur universalis animae liberandae via* ... (X, 32, 2). In this perspective, the great second part of the work is no more than a *confirmatio*, in the almost rhetorical sense of the Latin word.

20. It is enough to read lastly – for the time being! – the pages devoted to the subject by J. Van Oort, *Jerusalem and Babylon. A study into Augustine's City of God and the Sources of His Doctrine of the Two Cities*, Leiden, Brill, 1991, pp. 77–86, to discover how pointless these speculations are. The least absurd is the remark that in the 'Alphabetic Psalm' against the Donatists – cf. above, p. 171 – the refrain (*hypopsalma*) boils down to twenty-two reprises. But one cannot see how the reason for this number, that of the letters in the alphabet, can apply in the case of the *City of God*.

21. His *History against the pagans*, in seven books dedicated to Augustine, had totally different perspectives: cf. P. Brown, *Augustine of Hippo*, p. 296, and, in a different sense, A. Mandouze, *Saint Augustin*, pp. 326–8.

22. J.-C. Guy, *Unité et Structure logique de la 'Cité de Dieu'*, p. 125.

23. This is *Ep. 1*A, BA*, 46 B, pp. 54–8 (first publication by C. Lambot in *Revue bénéd.*, 51, 1939). At the end of this letter, Augustine refers to a summary (*breviculus*) which is an elaborate table of contents; H.-I. Marrou has shown it to be the work of Augustine himself: 'La division en chapitres des livres de la *Cité de Dieu'*, in *Mélanges J. de Ghellinck*, 1951 (reprinted in *Patristique et Humanisme*, 1976, pp. 253–65).

24. On the genesis of the theme of the 'two cities' and 'two loves', see chiefly A. Lauras and H. Rondet, 'Le thème des deux cités dans l'oeuvre de saint Augustin', in *Ét. aug.*, Paris, Aubier, 1953, pp. 99–160; lastly, J. Van Oort, *Jerusalem and Babylon*, pp. 108–23.

25. And doubtless under the influence of Tyconius, among other predecessors, as there is agreement in recognizing: see G. Bardy, *Saint Augustin. L'homme et l'oeuvre*, pp. 334–5 and Van Oort, *Jerusalem and Babylon*, p. 122.

26. The dedicatory inscription carved in the rock (*CIL*, XII, 1524: cf. A. Blanchet, *Carte archéologique de la Gaule romaine*, fasc. VI, Basses-Alpes, n° 70, pp. 22–3) is still visible in the locality known as Pierre-Écrite, a few kilometres north-east of Sisteron. See H.-I. Marrou, 'Un lieu dit "Cité de Dieu" ', in *Augustinus Magister*, vol. I, Paris, Ét. aug., 1954, pp. 101–10.

27. *De vera relig.*, 77. Cf. R. A. Markus, in *Saeculum. History and Society in the Theology of St Augustine*, Cambridge, 1970, pp. 75–6, taking up the essentials of an article published in *Journal of Theol. Studies*, 16, 1965, pp. 69–82.

28. *City of God*, V, 26, 1. On this eulogy of Theodosius – 'a theological document': p. 175 – cf. Y.-M. Duval, in *Recherches aug.*, IV, 1966, pp. 135–79.

29. *City of God*, XIX, 15: *non hominem homini, sed hominem pecori*. These texts by Augustine have been subtly analysed by R. A. Markus in *Saeculum. History and Society in the Theology of St Augustine*, pp. 197–210, summarizing the essentials of an article published in *Journal of Theol. Studies*, 16, 1965, pp. 69–82.

30. See the fine pages recently devoted to this theme – notably the meaning Virgil gave to the return of the Golden Age in his IVth *Bucolic* – in the book by A. Novara, *Les idées romaines sur le progrès*, vol. II, Paris, Les Belles Lettres, 1983, pp. 682–708.

31. On this image of the triptych, see the fine pages by H.-I. Marrou, *Théologie de l'histoire*, Paris, Le Seuil, 1968, pp. 31–5, all fuelled, like the whole of this great book, by the *City of God*. An analysis and faithful reflection of it are to be found in a text by A. Mandouze, 'Une théologie de l'histoire inspirée par saint Augustin', in *De Renan a Marrou. L'histoire du christianisme et le progrès de la méthode historique*, Lille, Éd. du Septentrion, 1999.

32. Gen. 1.28; but the bishop stresses that this encouragement to procreate given to the first human couple was before the sin, and that if the man and woman had persisted in obedience to God and had procreated without concupiscence and in felicity, 'that felicity would have continued until thanks to the divine blessing the number of predestined saints had been made up' (*City of God*, XIV, 10). At the time of composing The Good of Marriage (*De bono coniugali*, 2) Augustine was still wondering whether this increase before sin must not have been purely spiritual; but now he no longer doubts that it is a matter of physical increase, obtained by bodily means: cf. *City of God*, XIV, 20–4 and already in *De Genesi ad litteram*, IX, 9.

33. *Ep.* 197 and 199, the latter, *De fine saeculi*, being the size of a small treatise. Augustine refers in the *City of God* (XX, 5, 4) to this text, which dated to 420.

34. *Enarr. in Psalm.* 64, 4: this is the basis of the 'inchoative eschatology' mentioned by Marrou in his *Theologie de l'histoire*, p. 89. 'Work as if you were going to live forever, live as if you were going to die this very day': this was the maxim for living of Anne-Marie La Bonnardière, whom we had the sorrow of losing in the spring of 1998.

35. See the final page of the *Confessions* (XIII, 50–3) on the peace of the seventh day which has no night. Augustine accused himself (*City of God*, XX, 7, 1) for having been a 'millenarian' in the texts of his youth (for instance, sermon 259, 2) which made the distinction between the temporal repose of the seventh day and the timeless beatitude of the eighth day. But the limits of Augustine's 'millenarism' in that period have been shown: see G. Folliet, 'La typologie du sabbat chez saint Augustin', in *Revue des ét. aug.*, 2, 1956, pp. 371–90.

CHAPTER XXXII : Julian of Eclanum

1. There is sometimes hesitation about his name, whether Memorius, given to him by Augustine (see the address of *Ep.* 101), or Memor, to be read in Paulinus of Nola (*Carmen* 25, 1. 101, 212 and passim). But this name, Memorius, with its three short consecutive syllables, could find no place

in the elegiac distichs of Paulinus, who was moreover all too happy to play with the variations of Memor/*memor* (cf. *Carmen* 25, 1. 225, 240 and 241). It is true, however, that the name of Julian's father appears in the form Memor in the *Contra Iulianum*.

2. We have already seen (above, pp. 140–1) that this crowning piece was quite different in tone and inspiration. Its 'introduction' at least (*De musica*, VI, 1) dates to the years of his episcopacy, as H.-I. Marrou thought (*Saint Augustin et la fin de la culture antique*, p. 583).

3. Cf. F. Refoulé, 'Julien d'Éclane, théologien et philosophe', in *Recherches de sci. rel.*, 52, 1964, pp. 42–84 and 233–47 (for the sources of his philosophy); to read with the critical remarks of F.-J. Thonnard, 'L'aristotélisme de Julien d'Éclane et saint Augustin', in *Revue des ét. aug.*, 11, 1965, pp. 296–304, who notes that it is a matter of an 'eclectic aristotelianism', chiefly put to use for polemical ends.

4. One may however suspect that as regards sexuality, the Manichaean 'hearer' he had been had submitted to the demands of the sect, since no other birth arrived in the twelve years of certainly not abstinent co-habiting that followed the birth of Adeodatus. In any case, Augustine himself virtually made the admission two or three years after the break with his companion in his pamphlet against the sect: 'Was it not you who were in the habit of ordering us to observe, as far as possible, the time when the woman after her period is likely to conceive, and to abstain during that time from sleeping with her in order to avoid engaging a soul in the flesh?' (*De mor. manich.*, II, 65). That was to turn his companion, as he says a little further on, from a 'spouse' (*uxor*) into a 'courtesan' (*meretrix*). It is obvious that those years had weighed on him retrospectively.

5. At the end of winter 411–12, Augustine warned Honoratus against those – Pelagius and his followers – who, although *continenter viventes*, had ideas about the grace of Christ that he deemed heretical (*Ep.* 140, 83); Julian could have been among those Pelagians encountered by Honoratus.

6. Cf. C. Pietri, *Roma christiana*, vol. II, pp. 1230–2.

7. Cf. *Ep.* 200 (to Count Valerius), 1. On these movements of the letter-carriers, notably the priest Firmus, see Y.-M. Duval, 'Julien d'Éclane et Rufin d'Aquilée', pp. 246–7. But it is an unlikely theory that Firmus brought back to Italy a copy of the first book of the *De nuptiis*, already composed by Augustine, before the start of winter 418–19.

8. Cf. M.-F. Berrouard, 'Un tournant dans la vie de l'Église d'Afrique', pp. 46–70. There were many motives for this mission and reasons for Alypius' visits to the Court: cf. above, p. 260.

9. The *chartula* ('paper': the word used by Augustine) had this clumsy title: 'Passages taken from a writing by Augustine, together with, in opposition, several extracts from the books (in other words, from the *Ad Turbantium*)': *De nuptiis et conc.*, II, 2.

10. See Perler and Maier, *Les Voyages de saint Augustin*, p. 360.

11. In 421 (and more likely after 13 June, the date of the council which met in Carthage in that year), as 420 must be ruled out because the bishop of Thagaste had just returned home, and also because the delivery of the *Contra duas ep. pelag.* to Pope Boniface necessarily occurred before his death on 4 September 422; in any case, we know that in the spring of 422 Alypius was in Africa, taking part then with Augustine in the episcopal commission charged with the affair of Antoninus of Fussala: *Ep.* 20*, 12 (see above, p. 255).

12. Berrouard, 'Un tournant dans la vie de l'Église d'Afrique', p. 62.

13. On the known activities of Alypius in these years, cf. lastly O. Wermelinger, in *Augustinus-Lexikon*, vol. 1, 1994, col. 263–5.

14. The abundance and accuracy of quotations from Ambrose's works has been noted, and the theory advanced that Augustine may have been helped – if he did not have available a previously gathered collection of *excerpta* – by former colleagues of the bishop of Milan, perhaps by Paulinus of Milan: G. Madec, *Saint Ambroise et la philosophie*, Paris, Ét. aug., 1974, pp. 269–72, and *Introduction aux 'Revisions'*, p. 112.

15. *Ep.* 224, 2. The relative chronology of these post-*Retractations* texts has recently been clarified by A. Mutzenbecher, 'Der Nachtrag zu den Retraktationen mit Augustins letzten Werken', in *Revue des ét. aug.*, 30, 1984, pp. 60–83, especially pp. 77–81. The conclusion is that the order in which they are mentioned in an appendix to the *Retractations* (cf. *CCL*, 57, p. 143) is really the chronological order: the last text on which Augustine's copyists remained calamus poised is the seventh book, which was not completed – and thus not published – of the second reply to Julian. The chronology of Perler and Maier differed somewhat (*Les Voyages de saint Augustin*, pp. 475–7).

16. Julian of Eclanum's texts were the subject of a recent, but unfortunately incomplete, critical edition in the *Corpus Christianorum, series latina*, vol. 88, 1977: cf. Y.-M. Duval, 'Iulianus Aeclanensis restitutus. La premiere édition – incomplète – de l'oeuvre de Julian d'Éclane', in *Revue des ét. aug.*,

25, 1979, pp. 162–70. It is particularly regrettable that the first six books of the *Ad Florum* are missing from this edition, although Augustine reproduced them in his *Contra Iulianum opus imp.*, the critical edition of which is itself still incomplete (the first three books in *CSEL*, 85/1).

17. I am adopting the subtle analyses by G. de Broglie on Augustine's difficulties in penetrating his adversary's thinking to try to extract the best from it, and to emphasize what might be true and usable in the perspective of his own theological construction. To the obstinacy of his 'heterodox' opponents, Augustine replied by the intransigent reaffirmation of his position and its radicalization, avoiding giving even the appearance of any concession whatsoever: cf. G. de Broglie, in *Augustinus Magister*, vol. III, 1954, p. 323. See also the fair reflections by A. Mandouze on the bishop of Hippo's 'polemical alignment' in relation to Julian of Eclanum, which trapped him in the problems that it imposed on him: cf. Mandouze, *Saint Augustin*, p. 424.

18. Cf. *De Genesi ad litt.*, X, 32, and, on the problem of the holiness of the Virgin Mary, the note by G. De Plinval about the *De natura et gratia*, 42, in *BA*, 21, pp. 609–10.

19. *Contra Iulianum opus imp.*, VI, 12 and 20. P. Brown, *Augustine of Hippo*, p. 382, dismisses these few rapid words ('a charming strain of "primitivism"') and is heedless of the contradiction which, with Julian, results in making paradise before the Fall into a by no means unpleasant place, but very ordinarily 'human', with its limitations and troubles. Augustine enjoyed caricaturing this paradise according to Julian: if an artist painted a picture of it and wrote 'paradise' above it, one could only assume he was joking (*Contra Iulianum opus imp.*, III, 154).

20. It is Augustine's insistence on this text which made it the only scriptural text invoked in favour of the existence of original sin by the councils of Carthage (418), Orange (529) and lastly Trent (1546): the 4th canon of this last council would take up the text of Rom. 5.12 in the same terms as at Carthage in 418.

21. On the *eph'hô* and the meaning now attributed to it by exegetists, see above, p. 518, note 50 to Chapter XXVIII.

22. *Retract.*, II, 22, 1. See M.-F. Berrouard's article on this book in *Augustinus-Lexikon*, 1, 658–66.

23. *City of God*, XIV, 16. P. Brown rightly credits Augustine with the first non-physiological but psychosomatic analyses of the phenomena of impotence and frigidity: cf. *Le Renoncement à la chair. Virginité, célibat et continence dans le christianisme primitif*, Paris, 1995, pp. 499–500. (*The Body and Society: Men, Women and Sexual Renunciation in Early Christianity*, London, Faber, 1989.)

24. Cf. among others, *City of God*, XIV, 11 and 12, on a Garden of Eden both 'animal' and 'spiritual'. On Adam's 'animality' and 'sexuality', see the texts commentated by G. Bonner, in *Augustinus-Lexikon*, vol. 1, 1994, s. v. 'Adam', col. 73–4 and 77–8.

25. *C. Iulianum opus imp.*, I, 70 and II, 42; the theme is taken up again in almost the same terms in V, 16 and VI, 22. Let me stress here that Augustine's theological thinking was never linear or simplistic; thus he did not rule out that God might have created the first man without preserving him from concupiscence; on this hypothesis, creation would not have ceased to be good. The question was the subject of one of the most interesting debates of the great Augustinian congress of 1954; cf. the communications and replies of C. Boyer, J. Lebourlier and A. Trape, in *Augustinus Magister*, 1954, vol. II, pp. 737–44, 795–803; vol. III, pp. 301–16.

26. Augustine's notion of concupiscence is very comprehensive and includes numerous harmonics; cf. the article by F.-J. Thonnard, 'La notion de concupiscence en philosophie augustinienne', in *Recherches aug.*, 3, 1965, pp. 59–105, more particularly pp. 95–105 on concupiscence and original sin.

27. The inventory of quotations was made by A. Sage, who had benefited from A.-M. La Bonnardière's files: cf. A. Sage, 'Praeparatur voluntas a Domino', in *Revue des ét. aug.*, 10, 1964, pp. 1–20. There is a memorable sentence (p. 16): 'In St Augustine's eyes, *Prov.* 8, 35 possesses the double advantage of witnessing in favour of free will and in favour of grace.' And, to qualify the workings of grace, these two others (p. 16): 'Grace comes from God alone, for God alone, like the perfect workman, can penetrate the innermost machinery of the will to ensure that it works correctly. He does so in a wonderful way, *miris modis*, as He did in the Old Testament, regarding the widow of Sarepta, with Ahasuerus to Esther's prayer. Neither the widow of Sarepta nor Ahasuerus, under God's secret touch which probes loins and hearts, acted "like robots"!'

28. See the texts quoted and commentated by G. de Broglie in *Augustinus Magister*, vol. III, 1954, pp. 320–2, to illustrate both Augustine's awareness of the problem and his metaphysical inability to resolve it. On the same lines, Sage would say soon after that Augustine 'did not go more deeply into the question of reconciling grace and freedom: he was not equipped to do so' (in *Revue des ét. aug.*, 6, 1960, p. 39).

29. This assessment is taken from a text by Dom Odilon Rottmanner (quoted here in Fr. trans.: 'L'augustinisme. Étude d'histoire doctrinale', in *Mélanges de science religieuse*, 6, 1949, p. 44) which made its mark at the end of the nineteenth century by its fairly narrow presentation of Augustinianism, understood as 'the doctrine of unconditional predestination and special salvific will' ('L'augustinisme', p. 31).

30. *Ep.* 216 (letter from Valentinus to Augustine); on Florus' reactions, noted by Augustine in Hippo, cf. *De correptione et gratia*, 2. For details of the affair and its protagonists, cf. *Prosopographie chretienne du Bas-Empire. I. Afrique (303–533)*, s. v. Felix 58, p. 430; Florus 2, p. 478; Valentine 3, p. 1133.

31. First, the historical context: although persecutions had been over for a good century, Augustine first thought of the martyrs whom grace had supported in their worst ordeals (and who were the only ones in his time to be canonized); next, the polemical context: the debate with the Pelagians gave the bishop's words their keenest edge (here the two famous adverbs, which were both rare and impressive).

32. On this date and Cassian's activities in Marseille, cf. H.-I. Marrou, 'Jean Cassien à Marseille', in *Patristique et Humanisme. Mélanges*, pp. 363–72 (taken from *Revue du Moyen Âge latin*, 1, 1945, pp. 17–26.

33. Here I am keeping to this convenient title, although it did not appear before the sixteenth century, and is fairly arguable in that, even if they sometimes came across Pelagian positions, or drew near them, the Provençal monks made no claim to Pelagius.

34. Prosper diverged from Hilarius in detecting two groups among the Marseillais monks, one of which 'strayed very little from Pelagian paths' (*Ep.* 225, 4). This distinction is less apparent from reading his text than by comparison with that of Hilarius: cf. the additional note by J. Chéné in *BA*, 24, pp. 799–802, taking up one of his own studies which appeared in *Recherches de science relig.*, 43, 1955, pp. 321–41.

35. Prospect of Aquitaine would unfailingly defend Augustine in his *Liber contra collatorem* (a text directed against Jean Cassien and his 'XIIIth Conference') and in his *Pro Augustino responsiones*.

36. Cf. A. Solignac, 'Les excès de l'"*intellectus fidei*" dans la doctrine d'Augustin sur la grâce', in *Nouv. Revue théol.*, 110, 1988, pp. 825–49, especially pp. 835–9 on the limited dispensation of saving grace, complementing an article by A. Sage, 'La volonté salvifique universelle de Dieu dans la pensée de saint Augustin', in *Recherches aug.*, 3, 1965, pp. 107–31.

37. A. Sage, in *Revue des et. aug.*, 6, 1960, p. 37.

38. On this theme, read the evocative pages and excellent explanations of texts by P. Hombert, *Gloria gratiae*, pp. 330–5.

CHAPTER XXXIII : Death and the hereafter

1. His experience as a pastor, but also his meditations as a theologian, have been brilliantly analysed by E. Rebillard, *In hora mortis. Évolution de la pastorale chrétienne de la mort aux IVe et Ve siècles*, BEFAR, 283, Rome, 1994, especially pp. 34–45, 51–75, 78–92. E. Rebillard's work broadens the perspectives of another recent book, more closely centred on the evolution of Augustine's attitudes toward death: J.-M. Girard, *La Mort chez saint Augustin. Grandes lignes de l'évolution de sa pensée, telle qu'elle apparaît dans ses traités*, Fribourg, 1992. The title indicates that his preaching is not taken into account here.

2. *City of God*, XIII, 6. These Augustinian texts on 'passing over' have been commented by C. Carozzi, *Le Voyage de l'âme après la mort dans la littérature latine (V^e–XIII^{e}e siècle)*, Coll. École fr. de Rome, 189, Rome, 1994, pp. 14–15.

3. Cf. *De Genesi contra manich.*, I, 29, and II, 8, notably, and the commentaries by Girard, *La Mort chez saint Augustin*, pp. 34–58.

4. *De vera relig.*, 23. Cf. A.-M. La Bonnardière, *Biblia Augustiniana. A.T. Le livre de la Sagesse*, p. 38.

5. Cf. *De libero arb.*, III, 51–64 and G. Madec's additional note in *BA*, 6, pp. 578–80.

6. *Sermon* 172, 1 (dating to 420/24), quoted by E. Rebillard, from whom I have also borrowed parts of the commentary (*In hora mortis*, pp. 44–5).

7. *Tract. in Ioh. evang.*, 60, 2. See the substantial commentaries by E. Rebillard, *In hora mortis*, pp. 73–5.

8. *De libero arbitrio*, III, 23. With reference to these texts, see the commentaries by E. Zum Brunn in *Recherches aug.*, 6, 1969, pp. 47–9.

9. See above, pp. 167–8. Cf. lastly, on these practices of the Donatists and circumcellions: A. J. Droge and J. D. Tabor, *A Noble Death, Suicide and Martyrdom among Christians and Jews in Antiquity*, San Francisco, 1992, pp. 167–83.

10. On the fear of judgement day as it is analysed in Augustine's sermons, see the very fine pages by E. Rebillard, *In hora mortis*, pp. 145–67.

11. Cf. notably *sermon* 299, 8; 344, 4; *Enarr. in Psalm.* 68, 1, 3. These texts have the benefit of excellent analyses by E. Rebillard, *In hora mortis*, pp. 58–60.

12. They have been reviewed as milestones in a 'prehistory' of purgatory by J. Le Goff, *Naissance du purgatoire*, Paris, Gallimard, 'Bibliothèque des Histoires', 1981, pp. 64–8, and more recently by N. Gauthier, 'Les images de l'au-delà durant l'Antiquité chrétienne', in *Revue des ét. aug.*, 33, 1987, pp. 7–9.

13. This refusal is well perceived and commentated by Carozzi, *Le Voyage de l'âme*, p. 34, clearly showing how Julian of Toledo, at the end of the seventh century, used a good few Augustinian texts in his description of the hereafter: pp. 90–8.

14. Cf. the last page of a posthumous article by H.-I. Marrou, 'Une inscription chrétienne de Tipasa', p. 269.

15. J. Le Goff, *Naissance du purgatoire*, p. 74. Cf. also J. Delumeau, *Une histoire du Paradis*, Paris, Fayard, 1992, pp. 43–5.

16. *De Genesi contra manichaeos*, II, 30. This invalidates the remark by J. Ntedika, *L'Evolution de la doctrine du purgatoire chez saint Augustin*, Paris, Ét. aug., 1966, p. 67, according to whom, until 413, Augustine still placed the purificatory fire not in an intermediate period between death and resurrection, but at the moment of the Last Judgement.

17. *Enarr. in Psalm.* 37, 3, quoted by Le Goff, *Naissance du purgatoire*, p. 99, as one of the 'authorities' on medieval purgatory.

18. Cf. Le Goff, *Naissance du purgatoire*, p. 101, and the Augustinian texts on penitence, quoted and analysed by E. Rebillard, *In hora mortis*, pp. 157–67, notably.

19. Cf. *De natura et origine animae*, II, 8, where Augustine congratulates Vincentius Victor on his sound doctrine on personal judgement, to be precise, regarding the parable of the wicked rich man. He had had it from a Spanish priest, Petrus (cf. above, p. 361), which indicates that, early in the fifth century at least, belief regarding a personal judgement, without prejudice to the universal judgement but in most cases prefiguring it, was already well established, independently of Augustine.

20. *De natura et origine animae*, III, 12, for the good thief, in whose case he hesitated between a 'baptism of blood' and a 'baptism of desire': see the references in the note by A. C. De Veer, *BA*, 22, pp. 777–9. In the case of Dinocrates, Augustine was quite ready to make up a little story: the child might have been baptized, but later diverted from the faith by his father, for instance in a time of persecution: *De natura et origine animae*, I, 12; III, 12. In any case, the bishop warned against the non-canonical nature of this text.

21. Cf. S. Lancel, 'Une inscription martyrologique de Tipasa', in *Bulletin d'arch. alg.*, II, 1966–7, pp. 251–9 (= no. 178, in Y. Duval, *Loca sanctorum Africae*, I, pp. 377–80).

22. See notably P. Courcelle, 'Propos antichrétiens rapportés par saint Augustin', in *Recherches aug.*, I, 1958, pp. 149–86, especially, pp. 163–70.

23. See the *Vita Plotini*, 1, by Porphyry, quoted by H.-I. Marrou, 'Le dogme de la résurrection des corps et la théologie des valeurs humaines selon l'enseignement de saint Augustin', in *Patristique et Humanisme. Mélanges*, Paris, Le Seuil, 1976, p. 435 (text first published in *Revue des ét. aug.*, 12, 1966, pp. 112–36).

24. A study of the future of the metaphor of the body as 'the soul's prison' was made by P. Courcelle, 'Tradition platonicienne et traditions chrétiennes du corps-prison', in *Revue des ét. lat.*, 43, 1965, pp. 406–33.

25. Cf. M. R. Miles, art. 'Corpus', in *Augustinus-Lexikon*, 2, 1–2, 1996, col. 14, which dates this maturation of the Augustinian doctrine of the Incarnation to around 411–12.

26. Well observed by E. Rebillard, *In hora mortis*, p. 64.

27. Rebillard, *In hora mortis*, p. 66, nicely turns around the proposition of H.-I. Marrou, in the text reproduced in *Patristique et Humanisme*, p. 439, for whom reflection on the dogma of the resurrection 'leads the Christian thinker to a quite different anthropology from that of pagan philosophy'. In fact, the intellectual approach is without doubt the opposite.

28. Texts quoted by J.-M. Girard, *La Mort chez saint Augustin*, p. 71.

29. It is to be regretted that the problem was not tackled from this angle in the fine book by

C. Trottmann, *La Vision béatifique des disputes scolastiques à sa définition par Benoît XII* (BEFAR, 289), Rome, 1995, who considers the Augustinian texts (pp. 54–67), but from the mystical angle and not in the eschatological perspective.

CHAPTER XXXIV : Epilogue

1. Augustine is silent about those who were present on this occasion – at least three bishops were required for an ordination – and for an episcopal succession such as this, the provincial primate must have been present. He was probably still Aurelius of Macomades (cf. S. Lancel, in *Les Lettres de saint Augustin découvertes par J. Divjak*, pp. 280–1), before Alypius succeeded him shortly before Augustine's death.

2. I saw these vestiges being surveyed when I visited the site in 1964 in the company of Jean Lassus. Subsequent excavations completely exposed the monument (cf. *Bulletin d'arch. alg.*, IV, 1970, pp. 19–23, with figures). It is a pity that these traces were not clearly enough recognized to appear, as a good example of the ancient 'evidence of passage' from Christianity to Islam, in *Les Basiliques chrétiennes d'Afrique du Nord. I. Inventaire de l'Algérie*, Paris, Ét. aug., 1992.

3. The expression 'a writer's examination of his conscience', to describe the *Retractations*, is due to J. de Ghellinck, in *Nouv. Revue théol.*, 57, 1930, pp. 481–500. Early in the twentieth century, A. von Harnack had spoken of 'confessions of a writer' and G. Bardy had remembered these words when he himself called the *Retractations* the 'confessions of Augustine's old age' (in his edition of the text: *BA*, 12, p. 217). The most critical remarks about Augustine's change of aim were made by J. Burnaby, 'The "Retractationes" of Saint Augustine: Self-criticism or Apologia?' in *Augustinus Magister*, I, 1954, pp. 85–92, notably p. 91. For details, refer to the recent and balanced assessment by G. Madec, *Introduction aux 'Révisions'*, especially pp. 9–24 and 119–26.

4. On these realities in Augustine's time and in relation to himself, see the enlightening text by P. Petitmengin, art. 'Codex', in *Augustinus-Lexikon*, vol. 1, col. 1022–35. Augustine was mistaken about the total number of these 'books'! Some twenty more must be added: cf. A. Mandouze, *Saint Augustin*, p. 57: lastly, A. Mutzenbecher, in his introduction to the critical edition of the 'Révisions' in *CCL*, 57 (1984), p. XIII, and Madec, *Introduction aux 'Révisions'*, p. 21.

5. Augustine says less than we might wish about the organization of his secretariat's practices. Cf. above, pp. 214–17 and, to go further, B. Altaner, 'In der Studierstube des heiigen Augustinus. Beiträge zur Kenntnis seines schriftstellerischen Schaffens', in *Amt und Sendung. Beiträge zu seelsorglichen und religiosen Fragen*, Fribourg en Breisgau, 1950, pp. 416–24 (taken up again in *Kleine Patristische Schriften (Texte und Untersuchungen*, 83, Berlin, 1967).

6. Cf. Madec, *Introduction aux 'Révisions'*, p. 119, summarizing the conclusions drawn earlier by A. von Harnack and, more recently, by A. Mandouze in a university work (*Retractatio Retractationum*) which unfortunately has not been published.

7. Cf. G. Bardy, p. 61 of his general Introduction to *Révisions*, which in the middle of last century already clarified magnificently not only these texts, but also retrospectively the entire work and, in its breadth, made a fine overall study of the whole.

8. Notably Bardy in *BA*, 12, p. 175.

9. Cicero, however, preferred to say, in more 'Roman' fashion, the 'solemn' style: cf. A. Michel, *Les Rapports de la rhétorique et de la philosophie dans l'oeuvre de Cicéron*, Paris, 1960, p. 380. On the 'reception' of Ciceronian rhetoric in the *De doctrina christiana*, cf. P. Prestel, *Die Rezeption der ciceronischen Rhetorik durch Augustinus in 'De doctrina christiana'*, Frankfurt, 1992; A. Primmer, 'The Function of the *genera dicendi* in De doctrina christiana, 4', in *De doctrina christiana, a Classic of Western Culture*, Notre-Dame-London, 1995, pp. 68–86.

10. Cf. J. Fontaine, in *Aspects et Problèmes de la prose d'art latine au IIIe siècle*, Turin, 1968, p. 37; cf. H.-I. Marrou, *Saint Augustin et la fin de la culture antique*, pp. 519–20.

11. Cf. J.-C. Fredouille, *Tertullien et la conversion de la culture antique*, Paris, Ét. aug., 1972, pp. 143–78, especially pp. 171–8.

12. *Doctr. chr.*, IV, 40; that would have made a cretic, followed by a ditrochee, one of Augustine's favourite clausulae: cf. F. di Capua, 'Il ritmo prosaico in S. Agostino', in *Miscellanea Agostiniana*, II, Rome, 1931, p. 363 and pp. 374–5.

13. It has been noted that the years 420–21, assuredly busy ones, were not among the most overcrowded in the bishop's life: cf. above, p. 416 and O. Perler and J.-L. Maier, *Les Voyages de saint Augustin*, p. 363 and pp. 374–5.

14. Cf. Y. Duval, 'Flora était-elle africaine?' in *Revue des et. aug.*, 34, 1988, pp. 70–7. The author

rectifies the errors that were often made on the preliminary page of the *De cura pro mortuis gerenda*, 1; but it escaped her that, with his usual perspicacity, P. Courcelle had already well identified the persons in this story: cf. *Les 'Confessions' de saint Augustin dans la tradition littéraire*, p. 595.

15. See the texts collected and the analyses carried out by Y. Duval, *Auprès des saints, corps et âme*, Paris, Ét. aug., 1988, notably pp. 51–98; see also, by the same author, 'Sanctorum sepulcris sociari', in *Les Fonctions des saints dans le monde occidental (IIIᵉ–XIIIᵉ siècle)*, Coll. École fr. de Rome, 149, Rome, 1991, pp. 333–51.

16. See P.-A. Février, 'Tombes privilégiées en Maurétanie et en Numidie', in *L'inhumation privilégiée du IVᵉ au VIIIᵉ siècle en Occident*, Paris, De Boccard, 1986, pp. 13–23; lastly, S. Lancel, 'Modalités de l'inhumation privilégiée dans la nécropole de Sainte-Salsa à Tipasa (Algérie)', in *CRAI*, 1998, pp. 791–812.

17. P. Brown, *The Cult of the Saints. Its Rise and Function in Latin Christianity*, London, SCM Press, 1981.

18. Whatever Brown may think (*The Cult of the Saints*), seeing here a 'victory of the vulgar', and moreover rather rapidly lumping together Christian miracles and pre-Christian religious practices.

19. Cf. in this sense V. Saxer, 'Das Problem der Kultrezeption, illustriert am Beispiel des afrikanischen Reliquienskult zur Zeit des hl. Augustinus', in *Antikerezeption (. . .) Eine Aufsatzsammlung*, 1983 (1988), pp. 101–12.

20. Regarding the date, it is difficult to determine between two possibilities, 399 and the end of 404; see the note by G. Madec in *BA*, 11, 1, 1991, pp. 233–7.

21. *Ep.* 227, 'ad *senem* Alypium' (certain examples of the manuscript tradition have ad *sanctum* Alypium, but the *lectio difficilior* is to be preferred). The word *senex*, when not bluntly meaning old age, is the title of reverence borne by prelates who by seniority of ordination (thus also because of their age) acceded to the primacy in their province. Alypius, a bishop since 394/95, was thus, at a date unknown to us, successor as 'doyen' of Numidia to Aurelius of Macomades, whom we see still in this role at the time of the Antoninus of Fussala affair, in 421/22 (cf. above, p. 256).

22. It is not easy to be exact about the date; Perler and Maier, in *Les Voyages de saint Augustin*, pp. 367–8, propose 421, with some hesitation, but with good arguments drawn from what is known from other sources of the career of Bonifatius; this is also the dating used by O. Wermelinger in *Augustinus-Lexikon*, art. 'Alypius', vol. 1, col. 260, whereas R. A. Markus, *Augustinus-Lexicon*, art. 'Bonifatius comes Africae', col. 654–5, prefers 423, which is too late.

23. Modern historians are too ready to call him 'Count', a rather passe-partout title which is often wrongly used; but Darius was a *vir illustris* and the terms used about him by Augustine (*Ep.* 229, 1) indicate that he was a personage of some considerable consequence; his letter (*Ep.* 230) is elegant.

24. On their advance, the pages of C. Courtois, *Les Vandales et l'Afrique* (pp. 158–63) are still valid. Courtois assessed the whole of the troop at 180,000 people. The Vandals' passage through Altava (Ouled Mimoun, ex-Lamoricière) has been proved. Making public the treasure discovered at Cartennae (Ténès) J. Heurgon thought he could identify as a portrait of Galla Placidia the repoussé gold medallion (*Le Trésor de Ténès*, Paris, 1958, p. 69). However, for good reasons he resisted the temptation to date the burying of the treasure to the time of the Barbarians' passage through Ténès. Nevertheless, it could be that the coastal trail was one of their itineraries, parallel to that of the Chélif valley.

25. A well-deserved reputation, despite the soothing commentaries by Courtois, *Les Vandales et l'Afrique*, pp. 164–8.

26. *Vita Aug.*, XXIX, 5. Here we rediscover the inspiration of the miraculous cures of the *City of God*, XXII, 8, and it must be emphasized that Possidius, with Evodius, had been at the origin of the 'exploitation' of St Stephen's relics: the protomartyr's chapel at Calama had preceded the one at Hippo and the 'confirmed' miracles were noticeably more numerous there.

27. *Vita Aug.*, XXXI, 2. These are *Psalms* 6, 31, 37, 50, 101, 129 and 142. On the realities and the practical problems posed by Augustine's request on his deathbed, see the note by M. Pellegrino to *Vita Aug.*, XXXI, 2, p. 229 in his edition. A commentary on this penitential attitude is made by E. Rebillard, *In hora mortis*, pp. 213–14.

28. On the technical problems of publishing in late Antiquity, the pages by H.-I. Marrou are still relevant on 'La technique de l'édition à l'époque patristique', in *Vigiliae Christianae*, 1949, pp. 208–24 (taken up in *Patristique et Humanisme. Mélanges*, pp. 239–52).

29. The critical edition of this catalogue was made by A. Wilmart, 'Operum s. Augustini elenchus',

in *Miscellanea Agostiniana*, II, Rome, 1931, pp. 149–233. See the critical remarks by A. Mutzenbecher on a recent study relating to Possidius' text, in *Revue des ét. aug.*, 33, 1987, pp. 128–31.

30. *Elenchus*, X^3, 15 (Wilmart, p. 179): *Quaternio unus quem propria manu sanctus episcopus Augustinus initiavit*; perhaps it was the *De Genesi ad litteram liber imperfectus*; but in the *Retractations* the bishop clearly says that the beginning of this book had been dictated (*Retract.*, I, 18). According to a recent theory, it might have been the *Liber viginti unius sententiarum*: cf. F. Dolbeau, 'Un poème philosophique de l'Antiquité tardive: *De pulchritudine mundi*. Remarques sur le *Liber XXI sententiarum* (*CPR*, 373)', in *Revue des ét. aug.*, 42, 1996, p. 41.

31. The excavations at Hippo have revealed no trace of a massive fire such as the one that destroyed Carthage, for example, in 146 BC, nor any indications of a brutal destruction definitely attributable to a reasonably datable human action. But I said earlier (pp. 240–1) in what a state a long deterioration had left the ruins brought to light in the middle of the twentieth century. As for the fortifications which halted the Vandals, nothing has been found of them; but that comes as no surprise to archaeologists who are well aware that a town's walls are the prime source of new materials once they have been dismantled, and may disappear right down to the foundations. The best example in this respect is still that of Punic Carthage.

32. These trails have been followed and made use of with much plausibility and erudition by a good specialist in Augustinian *nach leben*: J.-P. Bouhot, 'La transmission d'Hippone à Rome des oeuvres de saint Augustin', in *Du copiste au collectionneur. Mélanges en l'honneur d'André Vernet*, to be published by Brepols. One cannot, however, agree with the author when he replaced Hippo in the orbit of the Empire after 442. How the transfer of the works was effected remains a complete mystery.

Principal chronological highlights

354	13 November: birth of Augustine at Thagaste (Souk-Ahras, in Algeria).
366–9	Studies with a *grammaticus*, at Madauros (Mdaourouch, Algeria).
369–70	Year of idleness at Thagaste.
370–3	Higher studies at Carthage; birth of Adeodatus (371/72); reading the *Hortensius*; entry into the Manichaean sect.
373–4	Teaching at Thagaste.
374–83	Teaching at Carthage; writing of the *De pulchro et apto*, a text that will not be preserved.
383–4	First year in Rome.
384–7	The years in Milan; Monica joins her son (385); reading the *Libri platonicorum* (spring 386); the scene in the garden and the conversion (August 386); retreat at Cassiciacum and writing of the first *Dialogues* (autumn 386); baptism at Milan (Easter 387).
387–8	Second year in Rome; death of Monica at Ostia (August 387); Augustine's second stay in Rome, with Alypius.
388–90	Return to Africa and retreat at Thagaste; death of Adeodatus and Nebridius.
391–5	Priesthood at Hippo (Hippo Regius, Annaba, in Algeria); Augustine as priest speaks at the council of Hippo (October 393); he is ordained bishop 'coadjutor' to Valerius (spring–summer 395).
396	Rereading St Paul, a decisive step in his elaboration of the theology of grace.
397	Participation in the councils of Carthage (June and August); preaching campaign during the summer; probable beginning of the composition of the *Confessions*.
400	Augustine goes to Constantine; first indirect contacts with the Donatist bishop Petilianus.
403	Council of Carthage (25 August): plan for a meeting with the Donatist Church, inspired by Augustine, who luckily escapes an ambush set for him.
407	*Dilige et quod vis fac*: first commentaries on the *First Epistle of John*; Augustine does a tour in the company of Maximinus of Siniti, a 'turned' Donatist bishop.
411	Augustine plays a decisive role at the conference between Donatists and Catholics.
411–12	Augustine has connections with the Roman aristocratic milieu (pagan and Christian) which the sack of Rome has brought to Africa; he begins the composition of the *City of God*; the start of the battle against Pelagianism and of his development of the doctrine of original sin.
413	Augustine cannot prevent the execution of his friend Flavius Marcellinus at Carthage.

416	The councils of Carthage and Milevis ratify by their condemnations Augustine's refutation of the arguments of Caelestius and Pelagius.
418	The council of Carthage (1 May) takes a doctrinal stand on original sin and the need to baptize infants; Augustine spends the summer in Caesarean Mauretania in company with Alypius and Possidius to deal with ecclesiastical matters; he meets the Donatist Emeritus at Caesarea (Cherchell). Winter 418–19: the beginning of a long duel with Julian of Eclanum, which will end only on Augustine's death.
420–1	In company with Alypius, Augustine visits Bonifatius, then on duty on the *limes* of Numidia.
422	Disciplinary procedures undertaken against Antoninus of Fussala send Augustine and Alypius on a journey into Hippo's hinterland.
426	Augustine has to settle the succession of Severus at Milevis (Mila, in Algeria); he deals with his own succession by designating the priest Eraclius to succeed him; he starts work on his *Retractations*.
430	Augustine dies on 28 August, in the third month of the Vandals' siege of Hippo.

Table of St Augustine's works in chronological order[a]

Explanation of the initials:

PL (or éd. bénédictine) *Patrologie latine*, Migne, Paris, 1861–2.

CSEL
Corpus Scriptorum Ecclesiasticorum Latinorum, Vienna, Academy of Vienna, from 1887.

CC
Corpus Christianorum, Brepols, Turnhout, from 1955.

BA
Bibliotheque augustinienne, Desclée de Brouwer, then Institut d'études augustiniennes (Paris), Latin text, translation and notes.

Title	Abbreviation	Date	Edition
– Contra Academicos	C. Acad.	386	PL 32, 905–58; CC 29, 3; BA 4, 1948, Éd. bénéd. Jolivet
– De beata vita	Beata vita	386	PL 32, 959–76; CC 29; BA 4/1, 1986, Éd. bénéd., Doignon
– De ordine	De ord.	386	PL 32, 977–1020; CC 29; BA 4, 1948, Éd. bénéd., Jolivet
– Soliloquia	Sol.	386–7	PL 32, 869–904; CSEL 89; BA 5, 1948, Éd. bénéd., Labriolle
– De immortalitate animae	De imm. an.	387	PL 32, 1021–34; CSEL 89; BA 5, 1948, Éd. bénéd., Labriolle
– De musica	De mus.	387–9	PL 32, 1081–194; BA 7, 1947, Éd. bénéd., Finaert Thonnard
– De moribus ecclesiae catholicae et de moribus Manichaeorum	De mor. eccl. cath. – De mor. manich.	388–9	PL 32, 1309–78; CSEL 90; BA 1, 1949, Éd. bénéd., Roland-Gosselin
– De quantitate animae	De quant. an.	388	PL 32, 1035–80; CSEL 89; BA 5, 1948, Éd. bénéd., Labriolle
– De libero arbitrio	De lib. arb.	388–I 391–5 II–III	PL 32, 1221–310; CC 29; BA 6, 1976, Madec
– De Genesi adversus Manichaeos	Gen. adv. Man.	388–9	PL 34, 173–220
– De diversis quaestionibus LXXXIII	De div. qu.	388–96	PL 40, 11–100; CC 44 A; BA 10, 1952, Éd. bénéd., Bardy Beckaert Boutet

[a] Some dates are difficult to fix; the reader should refer to my text, in which the chronology is often discussed.

Title	Abbreviation	Date	Edition
– De magistro	De mag.	389	PL 32, 1193–220; BA 6, 1976, Éd. bénéd., Madec
– De vera religione	De vera rel.	389–91	PL 34, 121–72; BA 8, 1982, Éd. bénéd., Pegon, mise à jour Madec
– De utilitate credendi	De util. cred.	391–2	PL 42, 65–92; BA 8, 1982, Éd. bénéd., Pegon, mise à jour Madec
– De duabus animabus contra Manichaeos	De duab. an.	391–2	PL 42, 93–112; BA 17, 1961, Éd. bénéd. + CSEL (Zycha), Jolivet Jourjon
– Contra Fortunatum disputatio	C. Fort.	392	PL 42, 111–30; CSEL 25, 1; BA 17, 1961, Éd. bénéd. + CSEL (Zycha), Jolivet Jourjon
– Enarrationes in Psalmos	Enarr. in Psalm.	392–420	PL 36–7; CSEL 38, 39, 40
– De Genesi ad litteram imperfectus liber	De Gen. ad lit. lib. imp.	393	PL 34, 219–46
– De fide et symbolo	De fide et symb.	393	PL 40, 181–96; CSEL 41; BA 9, 1975, Éd. bénéd., Rivière, mise à jour Madec Bouhot
– De sermone Domini in monte	De serm. dom. in monte	394	PL 34, 1229–308; CC 35
– Epistulae ad Romanos inchoata expositio	Ep. ad Rom. inch. exp.	394–5	PL 35, 2063–88; CSEL 84
– Expositio Epistulae ad Galatas	Exp. Galat.	394–5	PL 35, 2105–48
– De mendacio	De mend.	394–5	PL 40, 487–518; BA 2, 1948, Éd. bénéd., Combès
– De diversis quaestionibus ad Simplicianum	Ad Simpl.	396	PL 40, 101–48; BA 10, 1952, Éd. bénéd., Bardy Beckaert Boutet
– Contra epistulam quam vocant fundamenti	C. epist. fund.	396	PL 42, 173–206; BA 17, 1961, Éd. bénéd. + CSEL (Zycha), Jolivet Jourjon
– De agone christiano	De ag. christ.	396–7	PL 40; CSEL 41; BA 1, 1949, Roland-Gosselin
– De doctrina christiana	De doctr. christ.	396/397; 426/427	PL 34, 15–122; BA 11/2, 1997, CC., Moreau
– Confessiones	Conf.	397–400	PL 32, 659–868; CSEL 33; BA 13, 1993, Bibl. Teubneriana (Skutella), Solignac, Tréhorel Bouissou BA 14, 1992, Bibl. Teubneriana (Skutella), Solignac, Tréhorel Bouissou
– Contra Faustum	C. Faust.	397–8	PL 42, 207–518
– Contra Felicem	C. Felicem	398	PL 42, 519–52; BA 17, 1961, Éd. bénéd. + CSEL (Zycha), Jolivet Jourjon
– Contra Secundinum Manichaeum	C. Secund.	399	PL 42, 577–602; BA 17, 1961, Éd. bénéd. + CSEL (Zycha), Jolivet Jourjon
– De catechizandis rudibus	De catech. rud.	399–400	PL 40, 309–48; BA 11/1, 1991, CC, Madec

Title	Abbreviation	Date	Edition
– De Trinitate	De Trin.	399–419	PL 42, 819–1098; CC 50, 50 A; BA 15, 1991, Éd. bénéd., Mellet Camelot Hendrickx Madec BA 16, 1991, Éd. bénéd., Agaësse Moingt
– De natura boni	De nat. boni	399	PL 42, 551–72; CSEL 25, 2; BA 1, 1949, Éd. bénéd., Roland-Gosselin
– De consensu evangelistarum	De cons. evang.	400	PL 34, 1041–230; CSEL 43
– De baptismo contra Donatistas	De bapt.	400–1	PL 43, 107–244; CSEL 51; BA 29, 1964, CSEL (Petschenig), Bavaud Finaert
– De bono coniugali	De bono coniug.	401	PL 40, 371–96; CSEL 41; BA 2, 1948, Éd. bénéd., Combès
– De Genesi ad litteram	De Gen. ad litt.	401–14	PL 34, 245–486; CSEL 28, 1; BA 48, 1972, CSEL (Zycha), Agaësse Solignac BA 49, 1972, CSEL (Zycha), Agaësse Solignac
– Contra Cresconium grammaticum et donatistam	C. Cresc.	405–6	PL 43, 445–597; CSEL 52; BA 31, 1968, CSEL (Petschenig), Finaert De Veer
– Tractatus in Iohannis evangelium	Tract. in Iohan.	407–17	PL 35, 1379–976; CC 36; BA 71 (I–XVI), 1969, Éd. bénéd., Berrouard BA 72 (XVII–XXXIII), 1977, Éd. bénéd., Berrouard BA 73A (XXXIV–XLIII), 1988, CC + Éd. bénéd., Berrouard BA 73B (XLIV–LIV), 1989, CC + Éd. bénéd., Berrouard BA 74 (LV–LXXIX), 1993, CC + Éd. bénéd., Berrouard
– Tractatus in epistulam Iohannis ad Parthos	Tract. in ep. Iohan.	407–16	PL 35, 1977–2062
– Contra Adimantum	C. Adimant.	410	PL 42, 129–72; CSEL 25, 1; BA 17, 1961, Éd. bénéd. + CSEL (Zycha), Jolivet Jourjon
– De unico baptismo contra Petilianum	De unico bapt.	410	PL 43, 595–614; CSEL 53; BA 31, 1968, CSEL (Petschenig), Finaert De Veer
– De peccatorum meritis et remissione	De pecc. mer. et rem.	412	PL 44, 109–200
– Breviculus conlationis	Brev. conl.	412	PL 43; CSEL 53; CC 149A; BA 32, 1965, Finaert Lamirande
– Ad Donatistas post conlationem	Ad Donat. post. conl.	412	BA 32, 1965, CSEL (Petschenig), Finaert Lamirande
– De spiritu et littera	De sp. et litt.	412	PL 44, 201–46
– De fide et operibus	De fide et op.	413	PL 40, 197–230
– De natura et gratia	De nat. et gratia	413–15	PL 44, 247–90; BA 21, 1966, CSEL (Urba et Zycha), Plinval
– De civitate Dei	De civ. Dei	413–26	PL 41; CSEL 40, 1 et 2; BA 33–7, 1959–60, Bibl. Teubneriana (Dombart et Kalb) + PL + CC, Bardy Combès, révision Thonnard De Veer Folliet

Title	Abbreviation	Date	Edition
– De gratia Christi et de peccato originali	De gratia chr.	418	PL 44, 359–410; CSEL 42; BA 22, 1975, CSEL (Urba et Zycha), Chirat Plagnieux
– De nuptiis et concupiscentia	De nupt. et concup.	419–21	PL 44, 413–74; CSEL 42; BA 23, 1974, CSEL (Urba et Zycha), Thonnard Bleuzen De Veer
– De natura et origine animae	De nat. et orig. animae	419–21	PL 44, 475–548; CSEL 60; BA 22, 1975, CSEL (Urba et Zycha), Thonnard
– Contra mendacium	C. mend.	420	PL 40, 517–48; CSEL 41; BA 2, 1948, Éd. bénéd., Combès
– Contra duas epistulas pelagianorum	C. duas ep. pelag.	420–1	PL 44, 549–638; CSEL 60; BA 23, 1974, CSEL (Urba et Zycha), Thonnard Bleuzen De Veer
– Contra Gaudentium	C. Gaud.	419–20	PL 43; CSEL 53; BA 32, 1965 Finaert Lamirande
– Contra Iulianum	C. Iulianum	421	PL 44, 641–874
– Enchiridion ad Laurentum de fide spe et caritate	Ench.	421–3	PL 40, 231–90; CC 46
– De cura pro mortuis gerenda ad Paulinum episcopum	De cura	420–1	PL 40, 591–610, CSEL 41; BA 2, 1948, Éd. bénéd., Combès
– De gratia et libero arbitrio	De gratia et lib. arb.	426–7	PL 44, 881–912; BA 24, 1962, Éd. bénéd., Pintard Chéné
– De correptione et gratia	De corrept. et gratia	426–7	PL 44, 915–46; BA 24, 1962, Éd. bénéd., Pintard Chéné
– Retractationes	Retract.	426–7	PL 32, 583–656; BA 12, 1950, Éd. bénéd., Bardy
– De praedestinatione sanctorum	De praed. sanct.	428–9	PL 44, 959–92; BA 24, 1962, Chéné, Pintard
– De dono perseverantiae	De dono perseu.	428–9	PL 45, 993–1034; BA 24, 1962, Éd. bénéd., Chéné Pintard
– Contra Iulianum opus imperfectum	C. Iulianum op. imp.	429–430	PL 45, 1049–608; CSEL 85, 1
– Epistulae	Ep.	387–430	PL 33; CSEL 34, 44, 57, 58
– Epistulae Divjak	Ep.*	387–430	CSEL 88, 1981; BA 46 B, 1987
– Sermones	Serm.	392–430	PL 38, 39; CC 41
– Sermones Denis Guelf Morin			*Miscellanea Agostiniana* 1, Rome, 1931
– Sermones Dolbeau			*Vingt-Six Sermons au peuple d'Afrique*, Études aug., 1996

Bibliography

Augustinian bibliography is rich, even superabundant. The main French language bibliographical list, the *Bulletin augustinien*, regularly published by the *Revue des études augustiniennes*, records on average, giving brief analyses of them, some 400 annual publications, in all the main cultural languages, including Japanese, and comprising both short articles and much larger works: which means that no one can claim to dominate the whole of this output, even in the heart of the international community of specialists.

Given below are only those books and articles which have been used and quoted in the notes in this book, except where indicated. For the use of non-specialist readers who may wish to go further, I have indicated by an asterisk (*) the works of synthesis to which they can refer, either in addition or by way of comparison.

Attention is particularly drawn to the interest offered by an Augustinian lexicon, produced at Würzburg with the collaboration of an international editorial team: the *Augustinus-Lexikon*, ed. C. Mayer, published in Basel by Schwabe & Co. A. G. vol. 1 (*Aaron-Conversio*) came out in 1994, vol. 2, fasc. 1–2 (*Cor-Deus*) in 1996; the addition to this second volume will be published soon.

Lastly, it is impossible to over-emphasize, for Francophone readers, the wealth of perceptiveness, scrupulous attention to the texts, and often erudition, given in their introductions and additional notes by the Augustinian commentators of the volumes of the *Bibliothèque augustinienne* (abbreviated to *BA* here), who are too numerous to be named individually. Moreover, St Augustine's quite recent entry (late 1998) into the 'Bibliothèque de la Pléiade' (Paris, Gallimard), must be pointed out: the first volume – Saint Augustin, *Oeuvres*, I – comprising, as well as the *Confessions*, those of his works prior to his episcopacy which the compilers of this edition have considered to be most significant of Augustine's philosophical shifts pre-395.

Actes de la conférence de Carthage en 411, ed. S. Lancel, *Sources chrétiennes*, vol. 194, 195, 224 and 373, Paris, Éd. du Cerf, 1972–91.

Alfaric, P., *L'Évolution intellectuelle de saint Augustin*, Paris, 1918.

Archambault, P., 'Augustin et Camus', in *Recherches augustiniennes*, 6, 1969, pp. 195–221.

Arminjon, V., *Monique de Thagaste*, Montmélian, 1989.

Atkinson, J. E., 'Out of order: the Circumcellions and Codex Theodosianus, 16, 5, 52' in *Historia*, 41, 1992, pp. 488–99.

Banniard, M., *Genèse culturelle de l'Europe, V^e–VIIe siècle* (Coll. 'Points Histoire'), Paris, Le Seuil, 1989.

— *Viva Voce. Communication écrite et communication orale du IVe au IXe siècle en Occident latin*, Paris, Ét. aug., 1992.

*Bardy, G., *Saint Augustin, l'homme et l'oeuvre*, Paris, Desclée, 1940.

Barnes, T. D., 'Augustinus, Symmachus and Ambrose', in *Augustine. From Rhetor to Theologian*, Waterloo, Ontario, W. Laurier Univ. Press, 1992, pp. 7–13.

Beatrice, P. F., *Tradux peccati. Alle fonti della dottrina agostiniana del peccato originale*, Milan, 1978.

— 'Quosdam platonicorum libros. The Platonic readings of Augustine in Milan', in *Vigiliae Christianae*, 43, 1989, pp. 248–81.

Berrouard, M.-F., 'La date des "Tractatus I–LIV in Iohannis Evangelium" de saint Augustin', in *Recherches augustiniennes*, 7, 1971, pp. 105–68.

— 'L'exégèse augustinienne de Rom., 7, 7–25 entre 396 et 418, avec des remarques sur les deux périodes de la crise pélagienne', in *Recherches augustiniennes*, 16, 1981, pp. 101–95.

— 'Les lettres 6* et 19* de saint Augustin. Leur date et les renseignements qu'elles apportent sur l'évolution de la crise pélagienne', in *Revue des études aug.*, 27, 1981, pp. 264–77.

— 'L'activité littéraire de saint Augustin du 11 septembre au 1er décembre 419 d'après la lettre 23* à Possidius de Calama', in *Les Lettres de saint Augustin découvertes par Johannes Divjak*, Paris, Ét. aug., 1983, pp. 301–27.

— 'Un tournant dans la vie de l'Église d'Afrique: les deux missions d'Alypius en Italie à la lumière des lettres 10*, 15*, 16*, 22* et 23*A de saint Augustin', in *Revue des études aug.*, 31, 1985, pp. 46–70.

Blanchard-Lemée, M., 'La "maison de Bacchus" à Djemila. Architecture et décor d'une grande demeure provinciale à la fin de l'Antiquité' in *Bulletin archéologique du Comité des travaux historiques*, n. s. 17 B, 1981, pp. 131–43.

Bochet, I., ' "*La lettre tue, l'esprit vivifie*". L'exégèse augustinienne de II. Cor. 3, 6', in *Nouvelle Revue théologique*, 114, 1992, pp. 341–70.

— 'Le livre VIII des *Confessions*: récit de conversion et réflexion théologique', in *Nouvelle Revue théologique*, 118, 1996, pp. 363–84.

Bolgiani, F., *La conversione di S. Agostino e l'VIII libro delle Confessioni*, Turin, 1956.

*Bonner, G., *St Augustine of Hippo. Life and Controversies*, London, 1963 (reissued 1986).

— 'Augustine's Conception of Deification', in *Journal of Theological Studies*, 37, 1986, pp. 369–86.

— 'Augustinus (vita)', in *Augustinus-Lexikon*, vol. 1, 1994, col. 519–50.

Borgomeo, P., *L'Église de ce temps dans la prédication de saint Augustin*, Paris, Ét. aug., 1972.

Bouhot, J.-P., 'Une lettre d'Augustin d'Hippone à Cyrille d'Alexandrie (Ep. 4*)', in *Les lettres de saint Augustin découvertes par Johannes Divjak*, Paris, Ét. aug., 1983, pp. 47–154.

— 'Augustin predicateur d'après le *De doctrina christiana*', in *Augustin prédicateur (395–411). Actes du colloque int. de Chantilly (5–7 Sept. 1996)*, Paris, Ét. aug., 1998, pp. 49–61.

— 'La transmission d'Hippone à Rome des oeuvres de saint Augustin', in *Du copiste au collectionneur. Mélanges d'histoire des textes et des bibliothèques en l'honneur d'André Vernet*, Brepols, forthcoming.

Broglie, G. de, 'Pour une meilleure intelligence du *De correptione et gratia*', in *Augustinus Magister*, vol. III, Paris, Ét. aug., 1954, pp. 317–37.

Brown, P., 'Aspects of the Christianization of the Roman Aristocracy', in *Journal of Roman Studies*, 51, 1961, pp. 1–11.

— 'Pelagius and his supporters: aims and environment', in *Journal of Theological Studies*, 19, 1968, pp. 93–112.

— *Augustine of Hippo. A Biography*, London, Faber, 1967.

— 'St Augustine's Attitude to Religious Coercion', in *Religion and Society in the Age of Saint Augustine*, London, Faber, 1972, pp. 260–78.

— *The Cult of the Saints. Its Rise and Function in Latin Christianity*. London, SCM Press, 1981.

— *The Body and Society: Men, Women and Sexual Renunciation in Early Christianity*, London, Faber, 1989.

Caillet, J.-P.: cf. Gui, I.

Cambronne, P., 'Le vol des poires', in *Revue des études latines*, 71, 1993, pp. 220–38.

Carozzi, C., *Le Voyage de l'âme après la mort dans la littérature latine (V^e–XIIIe siècle)*, Coll. École française de Rome, 189, Rome, 1994.

Cecconi, G. A., 'Un evergete mancato. Piniano a Ippona', in *Athenaeum*, 66, 1988, pp. 371–89.

Chadwick, H., 'Augustine on pagans and Christians: reflections on religious and social change', in *History, Society and the Churches. Essays in Honour of Owen Chadwick*, Cambridge, Cambridge Univ. Press, 1985, pp. 17–18.

— *Augustine*, Oxford, Oxford Univ. Press, 1986.

— Donatism and the Confessions of Augustine', in *Philanthropia kai Eusebeia. Festschrift für A. Dihle*, Göttingen, 1993, pp. 23–35.

Chastagnol, A., 'Le sénateur Volusien et la conversion d'une famille de l'aristocratie romaine au Bas-Empire', in *Revue des études anciennes*, 58, 1956, pp. 240–53.

— *Les Fastes de la préfecture de Rome au Bas-Empire*, Paris, 1962.

— *L'album municipal de Timgad*, Bonn, 1978.

— 'Les jubilés impériaux de 260 à 387', in *Crise et Redressement dans les provinces européennes de l'Empire*, Strasbourg, 1983, pp. 11–25.

Chiesa, P., 'Un testo agiografico africano ad Aquileia: gli *Acta* di Gallonio e dei martiri di Timida Regia', in *Analecta Bollandiana*, 114, 1996, pp. 241–68.

Chomarat, J., 'Les "Confessions" de saint Augustin', in *Revue française de psychanalyse*, 52, 1988, pp. 153–74.

Concilia Africae (a. 345–a. 525), ed. C. Munier, *Corpus Christ., series latina (CCL)*, vol. 149, 1974.

Courcelle, P., 'Les premières "Confessions" de saint Augustin', in *Revue des études latines*, XXI–XXII, 1943–4, pp. 155–74.

— *Les Lettres grecques en Occident de Macrobe à Cassiodore*, Paris, De Boccard, 1948.

— 'Plotin et saint Ambroise', in *Revue de philologie*, 76, 1950, pp. 29–56.

— *Les 'Confessions' de saint Augustin dans la tradition littéraire. Antécédents et postérité*, Paris, Ét. aug., 1963.

— *Histoire littéraire des grandes invasions germaniques*, 3rd ed., Paris, Ét. aug., 1964.

— Recherches sur les 'Confessions' de saint Augustin, Paris, De Boccard, 1968.

Courtois, C., *Les Vandales et l'Afrique*, Paris, AMG, 1955.

Cracco Ruggini, L., *Il paganesimo romano tra religione e politica (384–394 d.C.)*, Rome, 1979.

Crespin, R., *Ministère et Sainteté. Pastorale du clergé et solution de la crise donatiste dans la vie et la doctrine de saint Augustin*, Paris, Ét. aug., 1965.

De Beer, F., 'Une tessère d'orthodoxie. Le "Libellus emendationis" de Leporius (vers 418–21)', in *Revue des études aug.*, 10, 1964, pp. 145–85.

Decret, F., *Aspects du manichéisme dans l'Afrique romaine*, Paris, Ét. aug., 1970.

— *Mani et la tradition manichéenne*, coll. 'Les maîtres spirituels', 40, Paris, Le Seuil, 1974.

— 'Augustin d'Hippone et l'esclavage', in *Dialogues d'histoire ancienne*, 11, 1985, pp. 675–85.

— 'Aspects de l'Église manichéenne. Remarques sur le manuscrit de Tébessa', in *Cassiciacum*, XL, 1989, pp. 123–51.

— 'L'utilisation des épîtres de Paul chez les manichéens d'Afrique', in *Sussidi patristici*, V, Rome, Augustinianum, 1989, pp. 29–83.

— 'Le traité d'Evodius "Contre les manichéens": un compendium à l'usage du parfait controversiste', in *Augustinianum*, 31, 2, 1991, pp. 387–409.

Delaroche, B., 'La date du *De peccatorum meritis et remissione*' in *Revue des études aug.*, 41, 1995, pp. 37–57.

Derycke, H., 'Le vol des poires, parabole du péché originel', in *Bulletin de littérature ecclésiastique*, 88, 3–4, 1987, pp. 337–48.

Desanges, J., and Lancel, S., 'L'apport des nouvelles lettres à la géographie historique de l'Afrique antique et de l'Église d'Afrique', in *Les lettres de saint Augustin decouvertes par Johannes Divjak*, Paris, Ét. aug., 1983, pp. 87–99.

De Veer, A. C., 'L'exploitation du schisme maximianiste par saint Augustin dans sa lutte contre le donatisme', in *Recherches augustiniennes*, 3, 1965, pp. 219–37.

— 'Une mesure de tolérance de l'empereur Honorius', in *Revue des études byzantines*, 24, 1966, pp. 189–95.

— 'Aux origines du *De natura et origine animae* de saint Augustin', in *Revue des études aug.*, 19, 1973, pp. 121–57.

Doignon, J., 'La prière liminaire des *Soliloquia* dans la ligne philosophique des *Dialogues* de Cassiciacum', in *Augustiniana Traiectina*, Paris, Ét. aug., 1987, pp. 85–105.

— '*Factus erectior (B. vita*, I, 4). Une étape dans l'évolution du jeune Augustin à Carthage', in *Vetera Christianorum*, 27, 1990, pp. 77–83.

— 'Oracles, prophéties, "on-dit" sur la chute de Rome. Les réactions de Jérôme et d'Augustin', in *Revue des études aug.*, 36, 1990, pp. 120–46.

Dolbeau, F., *Vingt-Six Sermons au peuple d'Afrique*, Paris, Ét. aug., 1996 (this volume comprises, with additions, the previously unpublished sermons of Augustine published by the author since 1991 in various journals).

— 'Un poème philosophique de l'Antiquité tardive: *De pulchritudine mundi*: Remarques sur le *Liber XXI Sententiarum (CPR*, 373)', in *Revue des études aug.*, 42, 1996, pp. 21–43.

— 'Le sermonnaire augustinien de Mayence (Mainz, Stadtbibliothek I 9): analyse et histoire', in *Revue bénédictine*, 106, 1–2, 1996, pp. 5–22.

Doucet, D., 'L'*ars Memoriae* dans les "Confessions"', in *Revue des études aug.*, 33, 1987, pp. 49–69.

— 'Recherche de Dieu, Incarnation et philosophie: *Sol.*, I, 2–6', in *Revue des études aug.*, 36, 1990, pp. 91–119.

Dulaey, M., *Le Rêve dans la vie et la pensée de saint Augustin*, Paris, Ét. aug., 1973.

Dunbabin, K., *The Mosaics of Roman North Africa. Studies in Iconography and Patronage*, Oxford, Clarendon Press, 1978.

Du Roy, O., *L'Intelligence de la foi en la Trinité selon saint Augustin. Genèse de sa théologie trinitaire jusqu'en 391*, Paris, Ét. aug., 1966.

Dutoit, E., *Tout saint Augustin* (texts collected and edited by Esther Bréguet), Fribourg, 1988.

Duval, N., *Les églises africaines à deux absides*, vols I and II (BEFAR, 218 and 218 bis), Paris, De Boccard, 1973.

— 'Hippo Regius', in *Reallexikon für Antike und Christentum*, XV, 1989, col. 442–66.
— 'Architecture et liturgie', in *Revue des études aug.*, 42, 1, 1996, pp. 121–7.
— cf. Gui, I.
Duval, Y.-M., 'L'éloge de Théodose dans la *Cité de Dieu* (V, 26, 1). Sa place, son sens et ses sources', in *Recherches augustiniennes*, 4, 1996, pp. 135–79.
— 'Julien d'Éclane et Rufin d'Aquilée. Du Concile di Rimini à la répression pélagienne. L'intervention impériale en matière religieuse', in *Revue des études aug.*, 24, 1978, pp. 243–71.
— 'La date du "De natura" de Pélage', in *Revue des études aug.*, 36, 1990, pp. 257–83.
Duval, Y., *Loca sanctorum Africae. Le culte des martyrs en Afrique du IVe au VIIe siècle*, vols I and II (Coll. École française de Rome, 58), Rome, 1982.
— *Auprès des saints, corps et âme. L'inhumation 'ad sanctos' dans la chrétienté d'Orient ed d'Occident du IIIe au VIIe siècle*, Paris, Ét. aug., 1988.
— 'Flora, était-elle africaine?' in *Revue des études aug.*, 34, 1988, pp. 70–7.
— '*Sanctorum sepulcris sociari*' in *Les fonctions des saints dans le monde occidental (IIIe–XIIIe siècle)* (Coll. École française de Rome, 149), Rome, 1991, pp. 333–51.

Ennabli, L., *Carthage. Une métropole chrétienne du IVe siècle à la fin du VIIe siècle*, Paris, CNRS, 1997.
Evans, R. F., *One and Holy: The Church in Latin Patristic Thought*, London, 1972.

Feldmann, E., *Der Einfluss des Hortensius und des Manichäismus auf das Denken des jungen Augustins von 373*, Münster, 1973.
— 'Confessiones' in *Augustinus-Lexikon*, vol. 1, 1994, col. 1134–93.
Ferrari, L. C., 'The Pear-Theft in Augustine's *Confessions*', in *Revue des études aug.*, 16, 1970, pp. 233–42.
— 'The Arboreal Polarisation in Augustine's *Confessions*', in *Revue des études aug.*, 25, 1979, pp. 35–46.
— 'Saint Augustine on the Road to Damascus', in *Augustinian Studies*, 13, 1982, pp. 151–70.
— '*Ecce audio vocem de vicina domo: Conf.*, 8, 12, 29', in *Augustiniana*, 33, 1983, pp. 232–45.
— 'Isaiah and the early Augustine', in *Mélanges T. J. Van Bavel*, vol. II, Louvain, 1990, pp. 739–56.
Février, P.-A., 'À propos du repas funéraire: culte et sociabilité', in *Cahiers archéologiques*, 26, 1977, pp. 29–45.
— 'Tombes privilégiées en Maurétanie et en Numidie', in *L'Inhumation privilégiée du IVe au VIIIe siècle en Occident*, Paris, De Boccard, 1986, pp. 13–23.
*Flasch, K., *Augustin. Einführung in sein Denken*, Stuttgart, 1980.
— *Logik des Schrekens. Augustinus von Hippo. Die Gnadenlehre von 397*, Mainz, 1990.
Folliet, G., 'La typologie du sabbat chez saint Augustin', in *Revue des études aug.*, 2, 1956, pp. 371–90.
— '"*Deificare in otio*": Aug., *Ep.* X, 2', in *Recherches augustiniennes*, 2, 1962, pp. 225–36.
— 'Le dossier de l'affaire Classicianus' (*Ep.* 250 et 1*), in *Les Lettres de saint Augustin découvertes par J. Divjak*, Paris, Ét. aug., 1983, pp. 129–46.
— 'La correspondance entre Augustin et Nebridius', in *L'opera letteraria di Agostino tra Cassiciacum e Milano. Agostino nelle terre di Ambrogio*, Palermo, 1987, pp. 191–215.
Fontaine, J., *Aspects et Problèmes de la prose d'art latine au IIIe siècle. La genèse des styles latins chrétiens*, Turin, Bottega d'Erasmo, 1968.
— *Naissance de la poésie dans l'Occident chrétien*, Paris, 1981.
— 'Une revolution littéraire dans l'Occident latin: les *Confessions* de saint Augustin', in *Bulletin de littérature ecclésiastique*, 88, 3–4, 1987, pp. 173–93.
— 'Genres et styles dans les *Confessions* de saint Augustin', in *L'Information littéraire*, 42, 1, 1990, pp. 13–20.
Fontanier, J., 'Sur le traité d'Augustin *De pulchro et apto*. Convenance, beauté et adaptation', in *Revue des sciences philos. et théolog.*, 73, 1989, pp. 413–21.
Fredouille, J.-C., *Tertullien et la conversion de la culture antique*, Paris, Ét. aug., 1972.
— 'Deux mauvais souvenirs d'Augustin', in *Philanthropia kai Eusebeia. Festschrift für A. Dihle*, Göttingen, 1993, pp. 74–9.
— 'Les *Confessions* d'Augustin, autobiographie au présent', in *L'invention de l'autobiographie d'Hésiode à saint Augustin*, Paris, Presses de l'ENS, 1993, pp. 167–78.
— 'Les sermons d'Augustin sur la chute de Rome', in *Augustin predicateur (395–411). Actes du colloque int. de Chantilly (5–7 Sept. 1996)*, Paris, Ét. aug., 1998, pp. 439–48.

Frend, W. H. C., *The Donatist Church. A Movement of Protest in Roman North Africa*, Oxford, 1952.
— 'The Family of Augustine. A Microcosm of Religious Change in North Africa', in *Atti del Congr. intern. su S. Agostino nel XVI centenario della sua conversione*, Rome, 1987, vol. I, pp. 135–51.

Gabillon, A., 'Romanianus, alias Cornelius. De nouveau sur le bienfaiteur et l'ami de saint Augustin', in *Revue des études aug.*, 24, 1978, pp. 58–70.
— 'Pour une datation de la lettre 243 d'Augustin à Laetus', in *Revue des ét. aug.*, 40, 1, 1994, pp. 127–42.
— 'Redatation de la lettre 109 de Severus de Milev', in *Augustin predicateur (395–411). Actes du Colloque int. de Chantilly (5–7 Sept. 1996)*, Paris, Ét. aug., 1998, pp. 431–7.
Gaudemet, J., *L'Église dans l'Empire romain (IVᵉ–Vᵉ siècle)*, Paris, Sirey, 1958.
Gauthier, N., 'Les images de l'au-delà durant l'Antiquité chrétienne', in *Revue des études aug.*, 33, 1987, pp. 3–22.
*Gilson, E., *Introduction à l'étude de saint Augustin*, Paris, Vrin, 1929.
Girard, J.-M., *La Mort chez saint Augustin. Grandes lignes de l'évolution de sa pensée, telle qu'elle apparaît dans ses traités*, Fribourg, 1992.
Gorman, M., 'Aurelius Augustinus: the Testimony of the oldest Manuscripts of Saint Augustine's Works', in *Journal of Theological Studies*, 35, 1984, pp. 475–80.
— 'The text of Saint Augustine's De Genesi ad litteram imperfectus liber', in *Recherches augustiniennes*, 20, 1985, pp. 65–86.
Greshake, G., *Gnade als konkrete Freiheit*, Mainz, 1972.
Gros, P., 'Le forum de la ville haute dans la Carthage romaine d'après les textes et l'archéologie', in *Comptes rendus de l'Acad. des inscriptions et belles-lettres*, 1982, pp. 636–58.
Gui, I., Duval, N. and Caillet, J.-P., *Basiliques chrétiennes d'Afrique du Nord. I. Inventaire de l'Algérie*, Paris, Ét. aug., 1992.
Guy, J.-C., *Unité et Structure logique de la 'Cité de Dieu' de saint Augustin*, Paris, Ét. aug., 1961.

Hadot, I., *Arts libéraux et philosophie dans la pensée antique*, Paris, Ét. aug., 1984.
Hadot, P., 'Platon et Plotin dans trois sermons de saint Ambroise', in *Revue des études latines*, 34, 1956, pp. 202–20.
— *Marius Victorinus. Recherches sur sa vie et ses oeuvres*, Paris, Ét. aug., 1971.
Hagendahl, H., *Augustine and the Latin Classics*, Göteborg, 1967.
Hamman, A., *La Vie quotidienne en Afrique du Nord au temps de saint Augustin*, Paris, Hachette, 1979.
Hanoune, R., 'Le paganisme philosophique de l'aristocratie municipale', in *L'Afrique dans l'Empire romain (Iᵉʳ siècle avant J.-C.–IVᵉ siècle après J.-C.)*, Coll. École française de Rome, 134, Paris–Rome 1990, pp. 63–75.
Henry, P., 'Plotin et l'Occident', in *Spicilegium sacrum Lovaniense*, XV, Louvain, 1934.
— *La Vision d'Ostie. Sa place dans la vie et l'oeuvre de saint Augustin*, Paris, Vrin, 1938.
Holte, R., *Béatitude et Sagesse. Saint Augustin et le problème de la fin de l'homme dans la philosophie ancienne*, Paris, Ét. aug., 1962.
Hombert, P.-M., *Gloria gratiae. Se glorifier en Dieu, principe et fin de la théologie augustinienne de la grâce*, Paris, Ét. aug., 1996.
Humbert, M., 'Enfants à louer ou à vendre: Augustin et l'autorité parentale (Ep. 10* et 24*)', in *Les Lettres de saint Augustin découvertes par Johannes Divjak*, Paris, Ét. aug., 1983, pp. 189–203.

Inglebert, H., *Les Romains chrétiens face à l'histoire de Rome*, Paris, Ét. aug., 1996.

Jacques, F., 'Le défenseur de cité d'après la lettre 22* de saint Augustin', in *Revue des études augustiniennes*, 32, 1986, pp. 56–73.

Kevane, E., 'Augustine's De Doctrina christiana: a Treatise on Christian Education', in *Recherches augustiniennes*, 4, 1966, pp. 97–133.
Knauer, N. G., *Psalmenzitate in Augustins Konfessionen*, Göttingen, 1955.
Kotula, T., 'Modicam terram habes, id est villam. Sur une notion de villa chez saint Augustin', in *L'Africa romana*, 5, Sassari, 1988, pp. 339–44.

Kriegbaum, B., *Kirche der Traditoren oder Kirche der Martyrer. Die Vorgeschichte des Donatismus*, Innsbruck-Vienna, 1986.

Kunzelman, A., 'Die Chronologie der Sermones des Hl. Augustinus', in *Miscellanea Agostiniana*, II, Rome, 1931, pp. 417–520.

La Bonnardière, A.-M., *Recherches de chronologie augustinienne*, Paris, Ét. aug., 1965.

— *Biblia Augustiniana. A. T.: le livre de la Sagesse*, Paris, Ét. aug., 1970.

— *Biblia Augustiniana. A. T.: le livre des Proverbes*, Paris, Ét. aug., 1975.

— 'Les *Enarrationes in Psalmos* prêchées par saint Augustin à Carthage en décembre 409', in *Recherches augustiniennes*, 11, 1976, pp. 52–90.

— ' "Aurelius Augustinus" ou "Aurelius, Augustinus"?' in *Revue bénédictine*, 91, 1981, pp. 213–37.

— 'Les deux vies. Marthe et Marie', in *Saint Augustin et la Bible*, Paris, Beauchesne, 1986, pp. 411–25.

— 'Aurelius episcopus' in *Augustinus-Lexikon*, vol. 1, 1994, col. 550–66.

Labrousse, M., 'Le baptême des hérétiques d'après Cyprien, Optat et Augustin: influences et divergences' in *Revue des études aug.*, 42, 1996, pp. 223–42.

Lamirande, E., 'Quand Monique, la mère d'Augustin, prend la parole', in *Signum pietatis. Festgabe für C. P. Mayer O.S.A. zum 60. Geburtstag*, Würzburg, 1989, pp. 3–19.

Lancel, S., 'Originalité de la province ecclésiastique de Byzacène', in *Cahiers de Tunisie*, 45–6, 1964, pp. 139–52.

— 'Les débuts du donatisme: la date du "Protocole de Cirta" et de l'élection épiscopale de Silvanus', in *Revue des études aug.*, 25, 1979, pp. 217–29.

— 'La fin et la survie de la latinité en Afrique du Nord', in *Revue des études latines*, 59, 1981, pp. 269–97.

— 'L'affaire d'Antonius de Fussala: pays, choses et gens de la Numidie d'Hippone saisis dans la durée d'une procédure d'enquête épiscopale', in *Les Lettres de saint Augustin découvertes par Johannes Divjak*, Paris, Ét. aug., 1983, pp. 267–85.

— 'Études sur la Numidie d'Hippone au temps de saint Augustin. Recherches de topographie ecclésiastique', in *Mélanges de l'École fr. de Rome, Antiquité*, 96, 2, 1984, pp. 1085–1113.

— 'Saint Augustin et la Maurétanie Césarienne; les années 418 et 419 à la lumière des nouvelles lettres récemment publiées', in *Revue des études aug.*, 30, 1984, pp. 48–59.

— 'Le sort des évêques et des communautés donatistes après la conférence de Carthage en 411', in *Internationales Symposion uber den Stand der Augustinus-Forschung*, Würzburg, 1989, pp. 149–67.

— 'Victor de Vita et la Carthage vandale', in *L'Africa romana*, VI, Sassari, 1989, pp. 649–61.

— *Tipasa de Maurétanie* (3rd ed. in coll. with M. Bouchenaki) Algiers, 1990.

— 'Évêchés et cités dans les provinces africaines', in *L'Afrique dans l'Empire romain (Ier siècle av. J.-C.–IVe siècle après J.-C.)*, Rome, 1990, pp. 273–90.

— 'Le recrutement de l'Église d'Afrique au début du Ve siècle: aspects qualitatifs et quantitatifs', in *De Tertullien aux Mozarabes. Mélanges offerts a Jacques Fontaine*, vol. I, Paris, Ét. aug., 1992, pp. 325–38.

— 'Africa, organisation ecclésiastique', in *Augustinus-Lexikon*, vol. 1, 1994, col. 206–16.

— 'Donatistae', in *Augustinus-Lexikon*, vol. 2, 1999.

— 'Modalités de l'inhumation privilégiée dans la nécropole de Sainte-Salsa à Tipasa (Algérie)', in *CRAI*, 1998, pp. 791–812.

Lassère, J.-M., *Ubique populus*, Paris, CNRS, 1977.

Law, V. A., 'St Augustine's *De grammatica*: Lost or Found?' in *Recherches aug.*, 19, 1984, pp. 155–83.

Lawless, G. P., 'Augustine's first monastery: Thagaste or Hippo?' in *Augustinianum*, 25, 1985, pp. 65–78.

— *Augustine of Hippo and His Monastic Rule*, Oxford, Clarendon Press, 1990.

Legewie, B., 'Die körperliche Konstitution und die Krankheiten Augustins', in *Miscellanea Agostiniana*, II, Rome, 1931, pp. 5–21.

Le Goff, J., *Naissance du purgatoire*, Paris, Gallimard, 1981.

Lejeune, P., *Le Pacte autobiographique*, Paris, Le Seuil, 1975.

*Lenain de Tillemont, S., *Mémoires pour servir à l'histoire ecclésiastique des six premiers siècles*: vol. XIII: *Vie de saint Augustin*, Paris, 1702.

Lepelley, C., *Les Cités de l'Afrique romaine au Bas-Empire*, vol. I, Paris, Ét. aug., 1979, vol. II, 1981.

— '*Juvenes* et circoncellions: les derniers sacrifices humains de l'Afrique antique', in *Antiquités africaines*, 15, 1980, pp. 261–71.

— 'Un aspect de la conversion d'Augustin: la rupture avec les ambitions sociales et politiques', in *Bulletin de littérature ecclesiastique*, 88, 3–4, 1987, pp. 229–46.

— 'Quelques parvenus de la culture de l'Afrique romaine tardive', in *Der Tertullien aux Mozarabes. Mélanges offerts à Jacques Fontaine*, vol. I. Paris, Ét. aug., 1992, pp. 583–94.

— 'Le musée des statues divines', in *Cahiers archéologiques*, 42, 1994, pp. 5–15.

— 'Circumcelliones', in *Augustinus-Lexikon*, vol. 1, 1994, col. 930–5.

Leveau, P., *Caesarea de Maurétanie, une ville romaine et ses campagnes*, Coll. École française de Rome, 70, Rome, 1984.

Lewis, G., 'Augustinisme et cartésianisme', in *Augustinus Magister*, vol. II, Paris, Ét. aug., 1954, pp. 1087–104.

Lim, R., 'Manichaeans and public disputation in Late Antiquity', in *Recherches augustiniennes*, 26, 1992, pp. 233–72.

Madec, G., 'Une lecture de *Confessions*, VII, 13–27', in *Revue des études aug.*, 16, 1970, pp. 79–137.

— *Saint Ambroise et la philosophie*, Paris, Ét. aug., 1974.

— 'Christus, scientia et sapientia nostra. Le principle de cohérence de la doctrine augustinienne', in *Recherches augustiniennes*, 10, 1975, pp. 77–85.

— 'L'historicité des *Dialogues* de Cassiciacum', in *Revue des études aug.*, 32, 1986, pp. 207–31.

— 'Le milieu milanis. Philosophie et christianisme', in *Bulletin de littérature ecclesiastique*, 88, 3–4, 1987, pp. 194–205.

— La Patrie et la Voie. Le Christ dans la pensée et la vie de saint Augustin, Paris, Desclée, 1989.

— 'Le néoplatonisme dans la conversion d'Augustin. État d'une question centénnaire (depuis Harnack et Boissier, 1883)', in *Internationales Symposion über den Stand der Augustinus-Forschung*, Würzburg, 1989, pp. 9–25.

— 'Le Christ des païens d'après le *De consensu evangelistarum* de saint Augustin', in *Recherches augustiniennes*, 26, 1992, pp. 3–67.

— 'Augustin prêtre', in *De Tertullien aux Mozarabes. Mélanges offerts à Jacques Fontaine*, vol. I, Paris, 1992, pp. 185–99.

— 'Saint Augustin et le maître intérieur', in *Connaissance des Pères de l'Eglise*, 48, Dec. 1992, pp. 16ff.

— 'Le neveu d'Augustin', in *Revue des études aug.*, 39, 1993, pp. 149–53.

— *Petites Études augustiniennes*, Paris, Ét. aug., 1994 (the book comprises some 20 studies which have appeared since 1975, plus a previously unpublished text).

— *Saint Augustin et la philosophie. Notes critiques*, Paris, Ét. aug., 1996.

— Introduction aux 'Révisions' et à la lecture de saint Augustin, Paris, Ét. aug., 1996.

— 'Deus', in *Augustinus-Lexikon*, vol. 2, fasc. 1–2 and 3–4, 1996–8.

— *Le Dieu d'Augustin*, Paris, Éd. du Cerf, 1998 (I was unable to read this work, which came out in autumn 1998).

Maier, J.-L., 'La date de la rétractation de Leporius et celle du "sermon 396" de saint Augustin', in *Revue des études aug.*, 11, 1965, pp. 39–42.

— see Perler, O.

— *Le Dossier du donatisme*, vol. I: *Des origines à la mort de Constance II (303–61)*, Berlin, 1987; vol. II: *De Julien l'Apostat à saint Jean Damascene (361–750)*, Berlin, 1989.

Mandouze, A., 'L'"extase d'Ostie". Possibilités et limites de la méthode des parallèles textuels', in *Augustinus Magister*, vol. I, Paris, Ét. augustiniennes, 1954, pp. 67–84.

— 'Saint Augustin et la religion romaine', in *Recherches augustiniennes*, 1, 1958, pp. 187–223.

— Saint Augustin. L'aventure de la raison et de la grâce, Paris, Ét. aug., 1968.

— 'Quelques principes de "linguistique augustinienne" dans le *De magistro*', in *Forma futuri. Studi in onore del cardinale Michele Pellegrino*, Turin, Bottega d'Erasmo, 1975, pp. 790–5.

— *Prosopographie chrétienne du Bas-Empire. I. Afrique (303–533)*, Paris, CNRS, 1982.

— 'Se/nous/le confesser? Question à saint Augustin', in *Individualisme et autobiographie en Occident*, Brussels, Éd. de l'université de Bruxelles, 1983, pp. 73–83.

— 'Le livre V des "Confessions" de saint Augustin', in *Le Confessioni di Agostino d'Ippona, libri III–V*, Palermo, 1984, pp. 39–55.

Marec, E., *Hippone-la-Royale, antique Hippo Regius*, 2nd ed. Algiers, 1956.

— *Monuments chrétiens d'Hippone, ville épiscopale de saint Augustin*, Paris, AMG, 1958.

Markus, R. A., *Saeculum. History and Society in the Theology of St Augustine*, Cambridge, 1970.

Marrou, H.-I., 'Un lieu dit "Cité de Dieu" ', in *Augustinus Magister*, vol. I, Paris, Ét. aug., 1954, pp. 101–10.

— 'La théologie de l'histoire', in *Augustinus Magister*, vol. III, Paris, Ét. aug., 1954, pp. 193–204.

*— (in coll. with A.-M. La Bonnardière), *Saint Augustin et l'augustinisme*, Coll. 'Les maîtres spirituels', Paris, Le Seuil, 1955.

— 'Civitas Dei, civitas terrena. Num tertium quid?' in *Studia patristica*, 2, 1957, pp. 342–50.

*— *Saint Augustin et la fin de la culture antique*, 4th ed., Paris, De Boccard, 1958.

— 'La basilique chrétienne d'Hippone d'après les résultats des dernières fouilles', in *Revue des études aug.*, 6, 1960, pp. 109–54 (resumed in *Patristique et Humanisme. Mélanges*, Paris, Le Seuil, 1976, pp. 183–231).

— 'Le dogme de la résurrection des corps et la théologie des valeurs humaines selon l'enseignement de saint Augustin', in *Revue des études aug.*, 12, 1966, pp. 112–36 (reprinted in *Patristique et Humanisme. Mélanges*, pp. 429–55).

— 'Les attaches orientales du pélagianisme', in *Comptes rendus de l'Acad. des inscriptions et belles-lettres (CRAI)*, 1968, pp. 459–72 (reprinted in *Patristique et Humanisme. Mélanges*, pp. 331–44).

— *Théologie de l'histoire*, Paris, Le Seuil, 1968.

— 'Une inscription chrétienne de Tipasa et le refrigerium', in *Antiquités africaines*, 14, 1979, pp. 261–9.

Martin, R., 'Apulée, Virgile, Augustin: reflexions nouvelles sur la structure des *Confessions*', in *Revue des études latines*, 68, 1990, pp. 136–50.

Martinetto, G., 'Les premières réactions antiaugustiniennes de Pélage', in *Revue des études aug.*, 17, 1971, pp. 83–117.

Mayer, C. P., *Die Zeichen in der geistigen Entwicklung und in der Theologie Augustins*, vol. I, Würzburg, Augustinus-Verlag, 1969, vol. II, 1974.

Meslin, M., *Les Ariens d'Occident (335–430)*, Paris, Le Seuil, 1967.

Modéran, Y., 'Gildon, les Maures et l'Afrique', in *Mélanges de l'École fr. de Rome, Antiquité*, 101, 2, 1989, pp. 821–72.

Monceaux, P., *Histoire littéraire de l'Afrique chrétienne*, vol. IV, Paris, 1912; vols VI and VII, Paris, 1922 (repr. Brussels, 1966).

— 'Un couvent de femmes à Hippone', in *Comptes rendus de l'Acad. des inscriptions et belles-lettres*, 1913, pp. 570–95.

— 'Saint Augustin et saint Antoine. Contribution à l'histoire du monachisme', in *Miscellanea Agostiniana*, II, Rome, 1931, pp. 61–89.

Moreau, M., 'Le dossier Marcellinus dans la correspondance de saint Augustin', in *Recherches augustiniennes*, 9, 1973, pp. 51–258.

— 'Qui était donc Publicola?' in *Revue des études aug.*, 28, 1982, pp. 225–38.

— 'Lecture du *De doctrina christiana*', in *Saint Augustin et la Bible*, Paris, Beauchesne, 1986, pp. 253–85.

Morel, J.-P., 'Recherches stratigraphiques a Hippone', in *Bulletin d'arch. alg.*, III, 1968, pp. 35–84.

Morizot, P., 'L'âge au mariage des jeunes romaines à Rome et en Afrique', in *Comptes rendus de l'Acad. des inscriptions et belles-lettres*, 1989, pp. 656–69.

Mourant, J. A., 'Ostia Reexamined: A Study in the Concept of Mystical Experience', in *Philosophy of Religion*, I, 1970, pp. 38–49.

Munier, C., 'La question des appels à Rome d'après la lettre 20* d'Augustin', in *Les Lettres de saint Augustin découvertes par J. Divjak*, Paris, Ét. aug., 1983, pp. 287–99.

Nauroy, G., 'Le fouet et le miel. Le combat d'Ambroise en 386 contre l'arianisme milanais', in *Recherches augustiniennes*, 23, 1988, pp. 4–86.

Ntedika, J., *L'Evolution de la doctrine du purgatoire chez saint Augustin*, Paris, Ét. aug., 1966.

O'Daly, G. J. P., 'Anima, animus', in *Augustinus-Lexikon*, vol. 1, 1994, col. 315–40; 'Civitate Dei (de)', in *Augustinus-Lexikon*, vol. 1, 1994, col. 969–1010.

Olivar, A., *La predicación cristiana antigua*, Barcelona, 1991.

O'Meara, J. J., 'The Historicity of the Early Dialogues of Saint Augustine', in *Vigiliae Christianae*, 5, 1951, pp. 150–78.

— *The Young Augustine: an introduction to the 'Confessions' of St Augustine*, London, Longman, 1980.

Palanque, J.-R., *Saint Ambroise et l'Empire romain*, Paris, De Boccard, 1933.

Paredi, A., 'Agostino ed i Milanesi', in *Agostino a Milano*, Palermo, Edizione Augustinus, 1988, pp. 57–62.

Paschoud, F., *Roma aeterna. Études sur le patriotisme romain à l'époque des Grandes Invasions*, Rome, Institut suisse de Rome, 1967.

Pelland, G., 'Augustin rencontre le livre de la *Genèse*', in *Lectio Augustini*, VII, Palermo, 1992, pp. 15–53.

Pellegrino, M., *Les Confessions de saint Augustin. Guide de lecture* (trans. from the Italian by H. Chirat), Paris, Éd. Alsatia, 1960.

Pépin, J., 'Saint Augustin et le symbolisme néoplatonicien de la vêture', in *Augustinus Magister*, vol. I, Paris, Ét. aug., 1954, pp. 293–306.
— *Ex platonicorum persona. Études sur les lectures philosophiques de saint Augustin*, Amsterdam, 1977.
*Perler, O., and Maier, J.-L., *Les Voyages de saint Augustin*, Paris, Ét. aug., 1969.
Picard, G.-C., *La Carthage de saint Augustin*, Paris, Fayard, 1965.
— *La Civilisation de l'Afrique romaine*, 2nd ed., Paris, Ét. aug., 1990.
Pierron, J.-P., 'La question du temoignage dans les *Confessions* de saint Augustin', in *Revue des études aug.*, 41, 1995, pp. 253–66.
Pietri, C., *Roma christiana. Recherches sur l'Église de Rome, son organisation, sa politique, son idéologie de Miltiade à Sixte III (311–440)*, vols I and II (BEFAR, 224), Rome, 1976.
— 'Le temps de la semaine à Rome et dans l'Italie chrétienne (IVe–VIe s.)', in *Le Temps chrétien de la fin de l'Antiquité au Moyen Âge (IIIe–XIIIe siècle)*, Paris, CNRS, 1984, pp. 63–97.
*Pincherle, A., *Vita di sant'Agostino*, Rome-Bari, Laterza, 1980.
Plinval, G. de, *Pélage, ses écrits, sa vie et sa réforme*, Lausanne, 1943.
Poque, S., *Le Langage symbolique dans la prédication de saint Augustin*, vol. I, Paris, Ét. aug., 1984.
— 'L'écho des événements de l'été 413 à Carthage dans la prédication de saint Augustin', in *Homo spiritalis. Festgabe für L. Verheijen*, Würzburg, 1987, pp. 391–9.
Puech, H.-C., *Le Manichéisme, son fondateur et sa doctrine*, Paris, Publications du musée Guimet, 1949.

Rebillard, E., *In hora mortis. Évolution de la pastorale chrétienne de la mort au IVe et Ve siècles*, BEFAR, 283, Rome, 1994.
Refoulé, F., 'Datation du premier concile de Carthage contre les pélagiens et du "Libellus fidei" de Rufin', in *Revue des études aug.*, 9, 1963, pp. 41–9.
— 'Julien d'Éclane théologien et philosophe', in *Recherches de science religieuse*, 52, 1964, pp. 48–84 and 233–47.
Rigobello, A., 'Lettura del IV libro delle Confessioni di Agostino d'Ippona', in *Le 'Confessioni' di Agostino d'Ippona*, libri III–V, Palermo, 1984, pp. 27–38.
Rougé, J., 'Escroquerie et brigandage en Afrique romaine au temps de saint Augustin', in *Les Lettres de saint Augustin découvertes par J. Divjak*, Paris, Ét. aug., 1983, pp. 177–88.

Sage, A., 'Praeparatur voluntas a Domino', in *Revue des études aug.*, 10, 1964, pp. 1–20.
— 'La volonté salvifique universelle de Dieu dans la pensée de saint Augustin', in *Recherches augustiniennes*, 3, 1965, pp. 107–31.
— 'Péché originel. Naissance d'un dogme', in *Revue des études aug.*, 13, 1967, pp. 211–48.
— 'Le péché originel dans la pensée de saint Augustin de 412 a 430, in *Revue des études aug.*, 15, 1969, pp. 75–112.
Salama, P., 'Vulnérabilité d'une capitale: Caesarea de Maurétanie', in *L'Africa romana*, 5, Sassari, 1988, pp. 253–69.
— 'La parabole des milliaires chez saint Augustin', in *L'Africa romana*, 6, Sassari, 1989, pp. 697–707.
Savon, H., *Ambroise de Milan (340–97)*, Paris, Desclée, 1997.
Schindler, A., *Wort und Analogie in Augustins Trinitätlehre*, Tübingen, 1965.
— 'Die Unterscheidung von Schisma und Häresie in Gesetzgebung und Polemik gegen den Donatismus (mit einer Bemerkung zur Datierung von Augustins Schrift Contra epistulam Parmeniani)' in *Pietas. Festschrift für B. Kötting*, Münster, 1980, pp. 228–36.
— 'Augustine and the History of the Roman Empire', in *Studia Patristica*, 32, Louvain, 1989, pp. 326–36.
Shanzer, D., 'Pears before Swine: Augustine, *Confessions* 2. 4. 9', in *Revue des études aug.*, 42, 1996, pp. 45–55.
Shaw, B. D., 'The Family in Late Antiquity: the Experience of Augustine', in *Past and Present*, 115, 1987, pp. 3–51.
Solignac, A., 'La condition de l'homme pécheur d'après saint Augustin', in *Nouvelle Revue théologique*, 88, 1956, pp. 359–87.
— 'Doxographies et manuels dans la formation philosophique de saint Augustin', in *Recherches augustiniennes*, 1, 1958, pp. 113–48.
— 'Exégèse et métaphysique. *Genèse*, I, 1–3 chez saint Augustin' in *In principio. Interprétations des premiers versets de la Genèse*, Paris, Ét. aug., 1973, pp. 153–71.
— 'Les excès de l'"intellectus fidei" dans la doctrine d'Augustin sur la grâce', in *Nouvelle Revue théologique*, 110, 1988, pp. 825–49.

Studer, B., 'Saint Augustin et la foi de Nicée', in *Recherches augustiniennes*, 19, 1984, pp. 133–54.

— 'Zum Aufbau von Augustins *De civitate Dei*', in *Mélanges T. J. Van Bavel*, vol. II, Louvain, 1990, pp. 937–51.

Swift, L. J., 'On the Oath of Pinianus', in *Atti del Congr. intern. su S. Agostino nel XVI centenario della sua conversione*, vol. I, Rome, 1987, pp. 371–9.

Tengström, E., *Donatisten und Katholiken. Soziale, wirtschaftliche und politische Aspekte einer nordafrikanischen Kirchenspaltung*, Göteborg, 1964.

TeSelle, E., 'Nature and Grace in Augustine's Exposition of Genesis I, 1–5', in *Recherches augustiniennes*, 5, 1968, pp. 95–137.

— '*Regio dissimilitudinis* in the Christian Tradition and its Context in Late Greek Philosophy', in *Augustinian Studies*, 6, 1975, pp. 153–79.

Teske, R. J., 'Augustine's Epistula X: Another Look at *deificare in otio*', in *Augustinianum*, 32, 1992, pp. 289–99.

Testard, M., *Saint Augustin et Cicéron*, Paris, Ét. aug., 1958.

Thonnard, F.-J., 'La prédestination augustinienne', in *Revue des études aug.*, 9, 1963, pp. 259–87, and 10, 1964, pp. 97–123.

— 'L'aristotélisme de Julien d'Éclane et saint Augustin', in *Revue des études aug.*, 11, 1965, pp. 296–304.

— 'La notion de concupiscence en philosophie augustinienne', in *Recherches augustiniennes*, 3, 1965, pp. 59–105.

Tilley, M. A., 'Dilatory Donatists or procrastinating Catholics: the trial at the Conference of Carthage', in *Church History*, 60, 1990, pp. 7–19.

Tilliette, J.-Y., 'Saint Augustin entre Moïse et Jean-Jacques? L'aveu dans les *Confessions*', in *L'Aveu. Antiquité, Moyen Âge*, Coll. École française de Rome, 88, Rome, 1986, pp. 147–68.

*Trapé, A., *Saint Augustin, l'homme, le pasteur, le mystique* (trans. from the Italian by V. Arminjon), Paris, Fayard, 1988.

Tresmontant, C., *Introduction à la theologie chrétienne*, Paris, Le Seuil, 1974.

Trottmann, C., *La Vision béatifique, des disputes scolastiques à sa définition par Benoît XII* (BEFAR, 289), Rome, 1995.

Trout, D. E., 'The dates of the ordination of Paulinus of Bordeaux and of his departure for Nola', in *Revue des études aug.*, 37, 1991, pp. 239–47.

Van Bavel, T. J., 'Woman as image of God in Augustine's *De Trinitate XII*', in *Signum pietatis. Festgabe für C. P. Mayer O.S.A. zum 60. Geburtstag*, Würzburg, 1989, pp. 267–88.

*Van der Meer, F., *Saint Augustin pasteur d'âmes*, vols I and II (trans. from the Dutch), Colmar-Paris, Ed. Alsatia, 1955.

Van Fleteren, F., 'Background and commentary on Augustine's *De vera religione*', in *Lectio Augustini*, X, Rome, 1994, pp. 33–49.

Verheijen, L. M., *Eloquentia pedisequa. Observations sur le style des 'Confessions' de saint Augustin*, Nijmegen, 1949.

— *La Règle de saint Augustin*, vols I and II, Paris, Ét. aug., 1967.

— 'Le *De doctrina christiana*, de saint Augustin. Un manuel d'herméneutique et d'expression chrétienne avec, en II, 19 (29)–42 (63), une "charte fondamentale pour une culture chrétienne"', in *Augustiniana*, 24, 1974, pp. 10–20.

— 'Spiritualité et vie monastique chez saint Augustin. L'utilisation monastique des Actes des apôtres 4, 31, 32–5 dans son oeuvre', in *Jean Chrysostome et Augustin. Actes du colloque de Chantilly 22–4 Sept. 1974*, Paris, Beauchesne, 1975, pp. 94–123.

Verwilghen, A., *Christologie et Spiritualité selon saint Augustin*, Paris, Beauchesne, 1985.

Wermelinger, O., *Rom und Pelagius. Die theologische Position der römischen Bischöfe im pelagianischen Streit in den Jahren 411–32*, Stuttgart, 1975.

— 'Alypius (V: Alpypius et Augustin entre 412 et 430)', in *Augustinus-Lexikon*, vol. 1, 1994, col. 256–65.

Wischmeyer, W., 'Zum Epitaph der Monica', in *Römische Quartalschrift*, 70, 1975, pp. 32–41.

Zum Brunn, E., 'Le dilemme de l'être et du néant chez saint Augustin. Des premiers dialogues aux *Confessions*', in *Recherches augustiniennes*, 6, 1969, pp. 3–102.

Complementary
bibliography in English

Brown, P., *The Making of Late Antiquity*, Cambridge (Mass.), Harvard Univ. Press, 1978.

Burnaby, J., *Amor Dei. A Study of the Religion of Saint Augustine*, Norwich, Canterbury Press, 1991.

Clark, M. T., *Augustine the Reader. Meditation, Self-Knowledge and the Ethics of Interpretation*, Cambridge (Mass.), Harvard Univ. Press, 1996.

MacCormack, S. G., *The Shadows of Poetry. Virgil in the Mind of Augustine*, Berkeley, Univ. of California Press, 1998.

Markus, R., *The End of Ancient Christianity*, Cambridge, Cambridge Univ. Press, 1992.

O'Donnell, J. J., *Augustine: Confessions*, 3 vols., Oxford, Clarendon Press, 1992.

Tilley, M., *Donatist Martyrs Stories: the Church in conflict in Roman North Africa*, Liverpool, Liverpool Univ. Press, 1996.

Wills, G., *Saint Augustine* (Penguin Lives), London, Weidenfeld & Nicolson; New York, Viking, 1999.

Index of names of people and places

Index of authors other than Augustine

Augustinian index

Subject index

The index covers the general development of Augustine's life, works and teaching. Accordingly, subheadings beneath main headings are arranged according to the number of the first page on which the subject is considered in order to reflect the chronological development of the topic. Occasionally, people and places are included where it was felt that they required a fuller treatment than is accorded to them in the index of people and places. Similarly, Augustine's works are listed where they have been mentioned in the course of the discussion, but references of citations will be found in the index of citations.

Where reference is made to the notes that appear at the end of chapters, the reference will be to page number and note letter, for example, 115n. a. Where reference is made to the additional notes, the reference will be to page number, chapter number and note number, for example, 508 XXIV n.18.